PRABHAT VIDYARTHI

ENGLISH-HINDI DICTIONARY

~·~

प्रभात विद्यार्थी

अंग्रेजी-हिंदी कोश

PRABHAT VIDYARTHI
ENGLISH-HINDI DICTIONARY

~~~·~~~

प्रभात विद्यार्थी
अंग्रेजी-हिंदी कोश

बदरीनाथ कपूर

~~~

PRABHAT VIDYARTHI ENGLISH-HINDI DICTIONARY
Ed. Dr. Badri Nath Kapoor
Published by Prabhat Prakashan Pvt. Ltd.
4/19 Asaf Ali Road, New Delhi-2
Edition • 2025

Price • ₹ 400.00 (Rupees Four Hundred only)
ISBN • 978-93-89982-80-0
e-mail • prabhatbooks@gmail.com
Website • www.prabhatbooks.com

प्रकाशक • **प्रभात प्रकाशन प्रा. लि.**
4/19 आसफ अली रोड,
नई दिल्ली–110002
संस्करण • 2025

मूल्य • चार सौ रुपए
मुद्रक • नरुला प्रिंटर्स, दिल्ली
अ.मा.पु.सं. • 978-93-89982-80-0

विद्यार्थियों से

कुछ वर्ष पहले 'प्रभात बृहत् अंग्रेजी-हिंदी कोश' तथा 'प्रभात व्यावहारिक अंग्रेजी-हिंदी कोश' प्रकाशित हुए थे, जिनका पाठकों ने अद्भुत स्वागत किया और अपनी जो प्रतिक्रियाएँ व्यक्त कीं वे संपादक और प्रकाशक दोनों के लिए उत्साहवर्धक रहीं। मुझे इस बात की विशेष प्रसन्नता हुई कि हिंदी में कोशों के प्रबुद्ध पाठकों की अभिवृद्धि हो रही है।

कुछ मित्रों का आग्रह था कि विद्यार्थियों के लिए इतना ही उपयोगी छोटा कोश भी तैयार हो, जिससे विद्यार्थियों में भाषा-ज्ञान बढ़े और भाषा-प्रेम भी। विद्यार्थियों के लिए कोश बनाना अधिक कठिन कार्य है। पहले तो प्रविष्टियों के रूप में उन्हीं शब्दों को ग्रहण किया जाना चाहिए जो उनकी पाठ्य-पुस्तकों में प्रयुक्त हों और दूसरे, उनके वही या उतने ही अर्थ लिये जाने चाहिए जिनका उनसे प्रयोजन हो। तीसरे, अर्थ-विवेचन में ऐसे सरल शब्दों का प्रयोग हो जिनका ज्ञान सामान्यत: विद्यार्थियों को रहता है। प्रस्तुत कोश का निर्माण करते समय इन बातों का ध्यान रखा गया है।

भाषिक-सामर्थ्य सफल जीवन-निर्वाह का मूल्य उपकरण है। इस उपकरण की प्राप्ति शब्दों के उपयुक्त अर्थों और प्रयोगों की सिद्धि से ही संभव है।

आशा है, बृहत् और व्यावहारिक संस्करणों की तरह यह कोश भी उपयोगी तथा संतोषप्रद सिद्ध होगा।

—बदरीनाथ कपूर

उच्चारण-तालिका

स्वर : Vowels

संकेत		मुख्य शब्द	
नागरी	अंतरराष्ट्रीय	अंग्रेज़ी	हिंदी
अ	ʌ	cut	कट् = क् + अ + ट्
अॅ	ə	about	अॅबाउट् = अॅ + ब् + आ + उ + ट्
अॆ	e	bed	बॆड् = ब् + अॆ + ड्
आ	ɑ:	father	फ़ादॅः = फ़् + आ + द् + अॅ + र्
ऑ	ɒ	pot	पॉट् = प् + ऑ + ट्
आः	ɔ:	caught	काःट् = क् + आः + ट्
इ	i	ship	शिप् = श् + इ + प्
ई	i:	sheep	शीप् = श् + ई + प्
उ	u	put	पुट् = प् + उ + ट्
ऊ	u:	boot	बूट् = ब् + ऊ + ट्
ए	e i	make	मेक् = म् + ए + क्
ऐ	æ	bad	बैड् = ब् + ऐ + ड्
ओ	ə u	note	नोट् = न् + ओ + ट्

Abbreviations

abbrev.	abbreviation	n.	noun
adj.	adjective	naut.	nautical
adv.	adverb	neg.	negative
conj.	conjunction	obs.	obsolete
esp.	especially	phr.	phrase
etc.	etcetera	plu.	plural
fem.	feminine	poet.	poetical
fig.	figurative	poss.	possessive
fml.	formal	p.p.	past participle
Fr.	French	pref.	prefix
Ger.	German	prep.	preposition
G.K.	Greek	pres.	present
infin.	infinitive	pron.	pronoun
infml.	informal	p.t.	past tense
interj.	interjection	refl.	reflexive
It.	Italian	sing.	singular
Lat.	Latin	suff.	suffix
lit.	literary	t.	tense
mas.	masculine	usu.	usually
med.	medical	v.	verb

A, a (ए) ***n.*** the first letter of the English alphabet, अंग्रेज़ी वर्णमाला का पहला वर्ण। **prefix** 1. without, not, विपरीतता-सूचक उपसर्ग; apolitical अराजनीतिक। 2. in the act of, क्रियोन्मुख; asleep, सोया हुआ। **article** 1. one, एक। 2. any, कोई। 3. per, प्रति, फ़ी।

aback (अॅबैक्) ***adv.*** behind, पीछे (की ओर)। □ **taken aback,** चकित, भौचक्का।

abacus (ऐब्अॅकॅस्) ***n.*** a frame with beads used for counting, गिनतारा।

abandon (अॅबैन्डॅन्) ***v.*** 1. to give up, त्याग देना। 2. to yield completely to an emotion, भावाभिभूत हो उठना, आवेश में आ जाना।

abandoned ***adj.*** 1. deserted, छोड़ा हुआ। 2. lacking restraint, असंयमी।

abase (अॅबेस्) ***v.*** 1. to humiliate, बेइज़्ज़त करना। 2. to degrade, अधोगति को प्राप्त होना।

abasement ***n.*** 1. humiliation, बेइज़्ज़ती, अपमान। 2. degradation, अधोगति।

abash (अॅबेश्) ***v.*** to embarrass or confound, लज्जित करना। □ **feel abashed,** मारे शर्म के गड़ जाना, पानी-पानी हो जाना।

abate (अॅबेट्) ***v.*** 1. to make or become less, घटाना या घटना, कम करना या होना। 2. to reduce, हलका करना या होना।

abatement ***n.*** कमी, घटाव; उपशमन।

abattoir (ऐब्अॅट्वाः) ***n.*** a slaughter-house, बूचड़ख़ाना।

abbey (ऐब्ई) ***n.*** a monastery, ईसाई मठ।

abbot (ऐब्अॅट्) ***n.*** the head of an abbey, ईसाई मठाध्यक्ष।

abbreviate (अॅब्रीविएट्) ***v.*** to shorten, संक्षिप्त करना।

abbreviation ***n.*** संक्षिप्तीकरण, संक्षेप या संक्षिप्त रूप।

ABC ***n.*** the elementary knowledge of a subject, किसी विषय का आरंभिक ज्ञान।

abdicate (ऐब्डिकेट्) ***v.*** to resign from a throne, गद्दी छोड़ना।

abdomen (ऐब्डॅमॅन्) ***n.*** the lower belly, उदर।

abduct (ऐब्डक्ट्) ***v.*** 1. to carry off by force, ज़बरदस्ती उठा ले जाना। 2. to kidnap, भगा ले जाना, अपहरण करना।

abduction ***n.*** भगा ले जाना, अपहरण।

abed (अॅबेड्) ***adv.*** in bed, शय्या पर, बिस्तर पर। ***adj.*** confined to bed, शय्याग्रस्त।

aberration (ऐब्अॅरैशॅन्) ***n.*** 1. deviation विपथन। 2. mental deviation, बुद्धिभ्रंश।

abet (अॅबेट्) ***v.*** to assist or encourage in committing an offence, दुष्प्रेरित करना।

abetment ***n.*** दुष्प्रेरण।

abeyance (अॅबेअॅन्स्) ***n.*** the state of being suspended for a period, आस्थगन। □ **in abeyance,** आस्थगित।

abhor (एब्हॉः) ***v.*** (abhorred, abhorring) to detest, घृणा करना।

abhorrence (ऐब्हॉर्अॅन्स्) ***n.*** घृणा।

abhorrent (ऐब्हॉर्अॅन्ट्) ***adj.*** घिनौना।

A

abide (ॲबाइड्) ***v.*** (abided or abode, abiding) 1. to dwell, वास करना, रहना। 2. to endure, सहन करना। □ **abide by**, अनुपालन करना।

ability (ॲबिल्इटी) ***n.*** 1. the capacity or power to do something, योग्यता, क्षमता, सामर्थ्य। 2. talent, प्रतिभा।

ab initio (ऐब्इनिशिओ) ***adv.*** from the beginning, आरंभ से।

abject (ऐब्जेक्ट्) ***adj.*** wretched, तुच्छ, अधम।

abjure (ऐब्ज्योः) ***v.*** to renounce under oath, शपथ लेकर त्याग करना।

ablaze (ॲब्लेज़्) ***adj.*** on fire, blazing, जलता या दहकता हुआ।

able (एबॅल्) ***adj.*** 1. capable, योग्य, क़ाबिल। 2. competent, सक्षम, समर्थ। 3. skilful, कुशल।

ablush (ॲब्लश्) ***adj.*** blushing, शर्माया हुआ।

ablution (ॲब्लूशॅन्) ***n.*** 1. washing oneself before performing a religious ceremony, (धार्मिक अनुष्ठान से पूर्व) नहाना-धोना। 2. an act of purifying, पवित्रीकरण।

ably (एब्ली) ***adv.*** with ability, योग्यतापूर्वक।

abnormal (ऐब्नॉर्मल) ***adj.*** 1. different from what is normal, अपसामान्य। 2. irregular अनियमित।

aboard (ॲबोड्) ***adv., prep.*** on or into a train, ship, plane etc., यान में, सवारी पर।

abode (ॲबोड्) ***n.*** a dwelling place, घर, निवास।

abolish (ॲबॉल्इश्) ***v.*** to put an end to, अंत कर देना, उन्मूलन कर देना।

abolition (ऐब्ॲलिश्ॲन्) ***n.*** समाप्ति, उन्मूलन।

abominable (ॲबॉम्इनम्बॅल्) ***adj.*** detestable, घृणित, घिनौना।

abomination ***n.*** घृणा।

aboriginal (ऐबऑरिजिनल) ***adj.*** inhabiting a country from the beginning, मूल, आदिम।

aborigines (ऐबऑरिजिनीज़) ***n.*** (plu.) first inhabitants of a country, आदिवासी, मूल निवासी।

abortion (एबॉर्शन) ***n.*** miscarriage, गर्भपात, भ्रूणहत्या।

abortive (एबॉर्टिव) ***adj.*** unsuccessful, निष्फल, अकारथ।

abound (ॲबाउन्ड्) ***v.*** to be plentiful, भरपूर होना, प्रचुर होना।

abounding ***adj.*** plentiful, भरा-पूरा, प्रचुर, भरपूर।

about (ॲबाउट्) ***adv.*** 1. all around, चारों तरफ़ / ओर। 2. near, आस-पास, यहीं कहीं। 3. nearly, लगभग। 4. absolutely, बिलकुल। 5. in the opposite direction, सामने। ***prep.*** 1. surrounding, के चारों ओर, के इधर-उधर। 2. here and there, somewhere near, के आस-पास, यहाँ-वहाँ। 3. approximately, के लगभग। 4. in connection with, के विषय में।

above (ॲबव्) ***adv.*** 1. higher up, overhead, ऊपर। 2. in heaven, स्वर्ग में। □ **over and above**, और अधिक। ***prep.*** 1. on the top of, to a higher place, के ऊपर, से ऊपर। 2. more than, in addition to, से अधिक। 3. beyond, से परे। □ **above all,** सबसे बढ़कर, सर्वोपरि; **above par**, अधिमूल्य पर। ***adj.*** preceding, previous, उपर्युक्त।

above-board ***adj.*** fair, honourable, ईमानदार, निश्छल, निष्कपट।

above-mentioned ***adj.*** mentioned above, उपरोक्त, उपर्युक्त।

abreast (ॲब्रेस्ट्) ***adv.*** side by side, on a level, साथ-साथ, कंधे से कंधा मिलाकर। ☐ **keep abreast of,** नई जानकारी, तथ्यों आदि से अपने को अवगत रखना।

abridge (ॲब्रिज्) ***v.*** to shorten, संक्षिप्त करना या बनाना।

abridgement, abridgment ***n.*** 1. an act of abridging, संक्षिप्तीकरण। 2. abridged version, संक्षिप्त रूप, संक्षेप।

abroad (ॲब्रॉड्) ***adv.*** away from one's own country, विदेश में, देश से बाहर।

abrogate (ऐब्रोगेट्) ***v.*** to cancel or repeal, निरस्त करना, रद्द करना।

abrupt (एब्रप्ट) ***adj.*** 1. sudden, आकस्मिक। 2. curt, रूखा। 3. steep, खड़ा।

abruptly ***adv.*** all of a sudden, suddenly, अचानक, सहसा।

abcess (ऐब्सिस्) ***n.*** a swelling with pus, (मवाद से भरा) फोड़ा।

abscond (ऐब्स्कॉन्ड्) ***v.*** to go away secretly to avoid arrest, भाग जाना, फ़रार हो जाना।

absconder ***n.*** one who absconds, भगोड़ा, फ़रार व्यक्ति।

absence (ऐब्सॅन्स्) ***n.*** 1. being away, अनुपस्थिति, गैरहाज़िरी। 2. period of being away from work, नागा, गैरहाज़िरी। 3. nonexistence, अभाव।

absent (ऐब्सेंट) ***adj.*** 1. not present, अनुपस्थित, गैरहाज़िर। 2. non-existent, अविद्यमान।

absentee (ऐब्सेंटी) ***n.*** a person who stays away from work, नागा करनेवाला, गैरहाज़िर।

absent-minded ***adj.*** inattentive, अन्यमनस्क, अनमना।

absolute (ऐब्सोल्यूट) ***adj.*** 1. complete, perfect, पूर्ण, परिपूर्ण। 2. despotic, निरंकुश। ***n.*** The Absolute, परम तत्त्व, परब्रह्म।

absolutely ***adv.*** 1. completely, पूर्ण रूप से, पूर्णतया, बिलकुल, नितांत। 2. unconditionally, बिना शर्त।

absolve (ऐब्ज़ॉल्व) ***v.*** to clear of blame or guilt, दोषमुक्त या पापमुक्त करना।

absorb (ऐब्सॉ:ब्) ***v.*** 1. to soak up, सोख लेना। 2. to suck up, चूस लेना। 3. to engross, तन्मय हो जाना, डूब जाना। 4. to make into a part of itself, आत्मसात् कर लेना, मिला लेना।

absorption (ऐब्सॉ:प्शॅन्) ***n.*** 1. the act of absorbing, सोख लेना, अवशोषण; आत्मसात्करण। 2. the state of mental concentration, तन्मयता, तल्लीनता।

abstain (ऐब्स्टेन्) ***v.*** to refrain from, बाज़ आना, परे रहना, परहेज़ करना।

abstract[1] (ऐब्स्ट्रैक्ट) ***adj.*** 1. not material, not concrete, अमूर्त। 2. theoretical rather than practical, सैद्धांतिक, अव्यावहारिक। ***n.*** a summary, सारांश, संक्षेप, सार।

abstract[2] ***v.*** 1. to take out or remove, हटा या अलग कर देना। 2. to make a written summary, सारांश तैयार करना।

abstruse (ऐब्स्ट्रूस) ***adj.*** difficult to understand, कठिन, गूढ़।

absurd (ऐब्स:ड्) ***adj.*** contrary to common sense, बेहूदा, बेतुका।

absurdity (ऐब्स:ड्इटी) ***n.*** 1. the state of being absurd, बेहूदापन, बेतुकापन। 2. a foolish statement, बेतुकी बात।

A

abundance (ॲबन्डॅन्स्) ***n.*** plenty, बहुतायत, प्रचुरता।

abundant (ॲबन्डॅन्ट्) ***adj.*** plentiful, बहुत अधिक, प्रचुर।

abuse[1] (अब्यूज़्) ***v.*** 1. to misuse, दुरुपयोग करना। 2. to maltreat, दुर्व्यवहार करना। 3. to vituperate, गाली देना, गाली-गलौज करना।

abuse[2] ***n.*** 1. misuse, दुरुपयोग। 2. maltreatment, दुर्व्यवहार। 3. abusive words, गाली, अपशब्द।

abusive (एब्यूसिव) ***adj.*** 1. dirty, अश्लील, गंदा। 2. insulting, अपमानजनक।

abutment (ॲबट्मॅन्ट्) ***n.*** a structure that supports a bridge or arch, पुल का खंभा, पीलपाया।

abysmal (ॲबिस्मॅल्) ***adj.*** very deep, बहुत गहरा, अथाह।

abyss (एबिस) ***n.*** a bottomless pit, अत्यंत गहरा गड्ढा, खाई।

academic (ऐक्ॲडेमिक) ***adj.*** 1. of an academy, अकादमिक। 2. scholarly, विद्वत्तापूर्ण।

academy (एकैडमी) ***n.*** an institution devoted to the study of arts and sciences, अकादमी, परिषद्।

accede (ऐक्सीड्) ***v.*** 1. to become monarch, गद्दी पर बैठना। 2. to take office, पदग्रहण करना। 3. to agree to, राज़ी हो जाना, मान लेना।

accelerate (ऐक्सेल्ॲरैट्) ***v.*** to increase the speed of, रफ़्तार या गति बढ़ाना।

acceleration (ऐक्सेल्ॲरैशॅन्) ***n.*** the increase of speed, गतिवर्धन।

accelerator ***n.*** a contrivance for increasing the speed of a motor engine, गतिवर्धक, एक्सेलरेटर।

accent[1] (ऐक्सेन्ट्) ***n.*** 1. stress on a syllable or word, किसी अक्षर या शब्द पर दिया जानेवाला बल, बलाघात। 2. a mark denoting stress, बलाघात का सूचक चिह्न। 3. characteristic manner of speech, उच्चारण का ढंग, लहजा। 4. emphasis, बल, ज़ोर।

accent[2] ***v.*** 1. to pronounce with a stress, बल देते हुए उच्चारण करना। 2. to emphasize, बल देना। 3. to mark with an accent, बलाघात का सूचक चिह्न लगाना।

accentuate (ऐक्सेन्चूएट्) ***v.*** to emphasize, ज़ोर देना।

accept (ऐक्सेप्ट्) ***v.*** 1. to take, receive or undertake, स्वीकार करना। 2. to take as true, to believe or admit, मान लेना, मानना। 3. to agree to pay, (हुंडी आदि) सकारना।

acceptable ***adj.*** worthy of acceptance, स्वीकार्य, ग्राह्य।

acceptance (ऐक्सैप्टेन्स) ***n.*** 1. the act of accepting, ग्रहण, स्वीकरण। 2. approval, स्वीकृति, मंजूरी।

access (ऐक्सेस) ***n.*** 1. approach, पहुँच। 2. reach, प्रवेश, पैठ।

accessible ***adj.*** 1. approachable, पहुँच के भीतर, अभिगम्य। 2. easy to get, सुलभ, सुगम।

accession (ऐक्सेशन) ***n.*** 1. enthronement, गद्दीनशीनी। 2. the act of coming to an office, पदारोहण, पदग्रहण। 3. addition, अधिमिलन, मिलना।

accessory (ऐक्सेसरी) ***adj.*** extra, additional, अतिरिक्त, आनुषंगिक। ***n.*** 1. a person who helps another in a crime, अपराध-सहायक, अपसहायक। 2. (plu.) things that are extra, but not essential, गौण वस्तुएँ, असेसरी।

accident (ऐक्सिडेन्ट) ***n.*** an

undesirable event, दुर्घटना। □ **by accident,** संयोगवश।

accidental ***adj.*** occurring by chance, संयोगजन्य, आकस्मिक।

acclaim (एक्लेम) ***v.*** 1. to greet with applause, करतलध्वनि करना। 2. to welcome with shouts, जय-जयकार करना। ***n.*** 1. applause, करतलध्वनि, तालियों की गड़गड़ाहट। 2. shout of welcome, जय-जयकार।

acclamation (ऐक्लेमेशन) ***n.*** applause, करतलध्वनि, जयघोष।

acclimatize (एक्लाइमेटाइज़) ***v.*** to get used to a new climate or surroundings, नई जलवायु या परिस्थितियों के अनुकूल (अपने को) ढालना या ढलना।

accommodate (एकॉमोडेट) ***v.*** 1. to make room for, जगह देना, गुंजाइश निकालना। 2. to take into one's house, टिकाना, ठहराना। 3. to bring to agreement, समझौता कर लेना।

accommodating ***adj.*** obliging, conciliatory, मुरव्वती।

accommodation (एकॉमोडेशन) ***n.*** lodging, टिकने-ठहरने का स्थान, वास-सुविधा।

accompaniment (एकम्पनिमेंट) ***n.*** secondary instrument, उपवाद्य, संगत।

accompany (एकम्पनी) ***v.*** 1. to go along with, to travel with, साथ देना, साथ जाना, साथ रहना। 2. to make supporting music for, संगत करना।

accomplice (एकंप्लिस) ***n.*** a partner in evil-doing, सह-अपराधी।

accomplish (एकंप्लिश) ***v.*** 1. to complete, पूरा करना। 2. to fulfil, निष्पन्न करना।

accomplished ***adj.*** 1. completed, पूरा किया हुआ, पूर्ण। 2. fulfilled, निष्पन्न, संपादित। 3. highly skilled, अत्यंत कुशल। 4. refined and civilized, सुसंस्कृत तथा सभ्य।

accomplishment (एकंप्लिशमेन्ट) ***n.*** something completely and successfully done, उपलब्धि, सिद्धि।

accord (एकॉर्ड) ***n.*** 1. agreement, harmony mutual understanding, मतैक्य, मेल, समझौता। 2. treaty, संधि। □ **of one's own accord,** अपनी इच्छा या मर्ज़ी से; **with one accord,** सबकी सहमति से। ***v.*** 1. to be in harmony, मेल होना। 2. to give or grant, देना, प्रदान करना; 3. to make conform or agree, दूसरे की बात मान लेना या तरज़ीह दे देना।

accordance (एकॉर्डेन्स) ***n.*** 1. agreement, संगति, मेल। 2. conformity, अनुरूपता। □ **in accordance with,** के अनुसार, के अनुरूप।

according ***adv.*** □ **according to,** (i) के अनुसार। (ii) के अनुरूप, तदनुसार।

accordingly ***adv.*** therefore, इसलिए, अतः।

accordion (एकॉर्डियन) ***n.*** a portable musical instrument consisting of keys and bellows, आरगन बाजा।

accost (एकॉस्ट) ***v.*** to approach a person in order to open conversation with, किसी के समीप जाकर बातचीत की पहल करना।

account (अॅकाउन्ट्) ***n.*** 1. a statement of money received and paid out,

A

हिसाब, लेखा। 2. a credit arrangement specially with a bank, खाता। 3. description, विवरण, वृत्तांत।

accountable ***adj.*** responsible, उत्तरदायी, जवाबदेह।

accountant (अॅकाउन्टॅन्ट्) ***n.*** an expert in accounts, लेखाकार, मुनीम।

account book ***n.*** a book for keeping accounts in, बही-खाता, लेखा-बही।

accredit (एक्रेडिट) ***v.*** to recognise officially, सरकारी मान्यता प्रदान करना।

accredited ***adj.*** officially recognised, सरकारी मान्यता-प्राप्त।

accretion (एक्रीशन) ***n.*** increase, वृद्धि।

accrue (एक्रू) ***v.*** to increase by regular growth, बढ़ना (जैसे ब्याज का)।

accumulate (एक्यूमुलेट) ***v.*** to amass or collect, संचय या संग्रह करना, ढेर लगाना।

accumulation (एक्यूमुलेशन) ***n.*** something accumulated, संचय, ढेर।

accuracy (ऐक्यूरेसी) ***n.*** 1. correctness, शुद्धता। 2. exactness, यथार्थता।

accurate (ऐक्यूरेट) ***adj.*** 1. correct, right, शुद्ध, सही। 2. exact, यथार्थ।

accursed (एकर्स्ड) ***adj.*** under a curse, damned, शापित।

accusation (एक्यूज़ेशन) ***n.*** a blame, दोषारोप, अभियोग।

accusative (एक्यूज़ेटिव) ***n.*** objective case, कर्मकारक। ***adj.*** of or related to the objective case, कर्मकारक-संबंधी।

accuse (एक्यूज़) ***v.*** 1. to put blame to, दोष लगाना, आरोप लगाना। 2. to charge with an offence, अभियोग लगाना।

accused ***n.*** a person charged with an offence, अभियुक्त, मुलज़िम।

accustom (एकस्टम) ***v.*** to make or become used to, अभ्यस्त होना या बनाना।

accustomed ***adj.*** 1. used to, आदी, अभ्यस्त, लती। 2. customary, रूढ़, प्रचलित।

ace (एस) ***n.*** 1. a playing card with one pip, इक्का। 2. one who excels in performance, प्रवीण या कुशल व्यक्ति। ☐ **play one's ace,** ब्रह्मास्त्र चलाना।

acetic (एसेटिक) ***adj.*** 1. sour, खट्टा। 2. pertaining to vinegar, सिरके का।

ache (एक) ***n.*** pain, पीड़ा, दर्द। ***v.*** to be painful, दर्द करना।

achieve (एचीव) ***v.*** 1. to attain or obtain, प्राप्त करना, पाना। 2. to accomplish, निष्पन्न करना, पूरा करना।

achievement ***v.*** success, सफलता।

acid (ऐसिड) ***n.*** a chemical substance having a sour taste, अम्ल, तेज़ाब। ***adj.*** 1. sour, खट्टा। 2. acidic, अम्लीय, तेज़ाबी।

acidity (एसिडिटी) ***n.*** 1. sourness, अम्लता। 2. an over-acid condition of the stomach, अम्लपित्त।

acid test ***n.*** a severe or decisive test, अग्नि-परीक्षा।

acknowledge (एक्नॉलिज) ***v.*** 1. to admit the validity or truth of, स्वीकार करना, कबूलना, मान लेना। 2. to report the receipt of, पावती देना, प्राप्ति स्वीकार करना। 3. to express thanks or gratitude for, आभार स्वीकार करना।

acknowledgement, acknowledgment ***n.*** 1. the act of acknowledging, स्वीकृति। 2. a receipt, पावती।

acorn (एकॉर्न) ***n.*** fruit of the oak tree, बंजुफल।

acoustics (अॅकूस्टिकस्) ***n.*** (plu.) the science of sound, ध्वनि-विज्ञान, ध्वानिकी।

acquaint (एक्वेन्ट) ***v.*** 1. to make informed, जानकारी देना या कराना, अवगत या विदित कराना। 2. to make familiar, परिचय करना, जान-पहचान करना।

acquaintance (एक्वेन्टेन्स) ***n.*** 1. the state of being acquainted with, जानकारी, परिचय। 2. a person whom one knows slightly, जान-पहचानवाला।

acquiesce (ऐक्विएस) ***v.*** to give silent or passive assent to, मौन स्वीकृति देना।

acquiescence (ऐक्विएसेन्स) ***n.*** tacit consent, मौन स्वीकृति।

acquire (एक्वाइर) ***v.*** 1. to earn, कमाना, अर्जित करना। 2. to obtain, प्राप्त या हस्तगत करना।

acquisition (अॅक्विज़ीशॅन्) ***n.*** the act of earning or obtaining, अर्जन, प्राप्ति।

acquisitive (अॅक्विज़िटिव्) ***adj.*** eager to possess, लालायित।

acquit (अॅक्विट्) ***v.*** to discharge, बरी करना, छोड़ देना।

acquittal ***n.*** discharge, रिहाई, छुटकारा।

acquitted ***adj.*** released, discharged, बरी, रिहा।

acre (एकर) ***n.*** a unit of area equal to 4840 sq. yards, एकड़।

acreage (एकॅरिज्) ***n.*** the total number of acres, एकड़ों में होनेवाला क्षेत्रफल।

acrid (ऐक्रिड) ***adj.*** 1. pungent, चरपरा। 2. bitter, कड़वा।

acrimonious (ऐक्रिमोनिअस) ***adj.*** bitterly angry, कटु, रूखा।

acrimony (ऐक्रिमनी) ***n.*** bitterness in speech, कटुता।

acrobat (ऐक्रोबैट) ***n.*** a person skilled in feats, नट, बाज़ीगर।

acrobatics (ऐक्रोबैटिक्स) ***n.*** feats of an acrobat, कलाबाज़ी, बाज़ीगरी।

acronym (ऐक्रोनिम) ***n.*** a word made up from the first letters of the name of something, परिवर्णी शब्द (जैसे—माकपा, भाजपा)।

across (एक्रॉस) ***adv.*** 1. from one side to another, आर-पार। 2. on the opposite side, उस पार। 3. crosswise, आड़े या तिरछे बल। ***prep.*** 1. from side to side of, के आर-पार। 2. on the opposite side of, के पार।

act (ऐक्ट) ***n.*** 1. something done, काम, कार्य। 2. a deed, कर्म। 3. an action, क्रिया, व्यापार। 4. statute or law, अधिनियम। 5. a major division of a play, नाटक का अंक। ***v.*** 1. to do, काम करना, करना-धरना। 2. to fulfil functions, कर्तव्य निभाना, काम पूरा करना। 3. to behave, व्यवहार या बरताव करना। 4. to perform a part in a play, अभिनय करना।

actable (ऐक्टेबल) ***adj.*** easy to act, अभिनेय।

acting ***n.*** a dramatic part, performing in plays, अभिनय। ***adj.*** serving temporarily, कार्यकारी।

action (ऐक्शन) ***n.*** 1. the act of doing something, कार्य, क्रिया। 2. an activity, क्रिया, क्रियाकलाप। 3. (legal) process or (judicial) proceeding, (कानूनी) काररवाई, (न्यायिक) अनुयोजन। 4. a legal suit, मुकदमा, वाद। 5. a way or manner of functioning, ढंग,

A

चेष्टा। 6. active operation against enemy, लड़ाई, संघर्ष। 7. a battle, लड़ाई। □ **take action**, काररवाई करना, (के) विरुद्ध कदम उठाना; **out of action**, ख़राब, बेकार।

actionable (ऐक्शनेबल) ***adj.*** affording ground for an action at law, वाद योग्य।

activate (ऐक्टिवेट) ***v.*** to make active, सक्रिय करना।

active (ऐक्टिव) ***adj.*** 1. energetic, सक्रिय, चुस्त, क्रियाशील। 2. agile, फुर्तीला। 3. (gram.) not passive, कर्तृवाचक; active voice, कर्तृवाच्य।

activist (ऐक्टिविस्ट) ***n.*** one who takes vigorous action to achieve an end, सक्रियतावादी।

activity (ऐक्टिविटी) ***n.*** 1. energetic action, सरगरमी, सक्रियता। 2. agility, फुर्ती, चुस्ती। 3. (plu.) instances of being active in any field, क्रियाकलाप, गतिविधियाँ।

actor (ऐक्टर) ***n.*** 1. a performer in a film etc., अभिनेता, पात्र। 2. one who performs an action, कर्ता।

actress (ऐक्ट्रिस्) ***n.*** a female actor, अभिनेत्री।

actual (ऐक्चुअल) ***adj.*** 1. real, वास्तविक, असल। 2. present, वर्तमान।

actually ***adv.*** in fact, वास्तव में, सचमुच।

actuate (ऐक्चुएट) ***v.*** to cause to act, प्रेरित करना, प्रवृत्त करना।

acumen (एक्यूमन) ***n.*** mental acuteness, बुद्धि की प्रखरता।

acupuncture (ऐक्युपंक्चर) ***n.*** the science of pricking with needles for the purpose of treating various bodily disorders or diseases, एकूपंचर, सुंई-चिकित्सा।

acute (एक्यूट) ***adj.*** 1. pointed, नुकीला। 2. sharp, पैना, तीक्ष्ण। 3. keen-witted, कुशाग्र-बुद्धि। 4. intense, प्रचंड। 5. less than 90^0, न्यून (कोण)।

acuteness (एक्यूटनिस) ***n.*** intensity, sharpness, प्रचंडता, उत्कटता, तीव्रता।

ad (ऐड) ***n.*** an advertisement, विज्ञापन।

adage (ऐडिज) ***n.*** a proverb, कहावत।

Adam (ऐडम) ***n.*** the firstman, आदम, आदिमानव।

adamant (ऐडेमेन्ट) ***adj.*** 1.stubborn, हठी। 2. firm, दृढ़, कठोर।

Adam's apple ***n.*** the visible projection at front of the neck, टेंटुआ।

adapt (एडैप्ट) ***v.*** 1. to make or become suitable for a new situation, अनुकूल बनना या बनाना। 2. to alter so as to make fit, रूपांतरित करना।

adaptable (एडैप्टेबल) ***adj.*** 1. able to be adapted, अनुकूलनीय, रूपांतरणीय। 2. able to adapt himself to new conditions, अनुकूलन-क्षम।

adaptation (एडैप्टेशन) ***n.*** an alteration or adjustment, रूपांतर, समायोजन।

add (ऐड) ***v.*** 1. to get a total, जोड़ निकालना या लगाना, योग करना, जोड़ना। 2. to include, शामिल करना। □ **add up**, जोड़ निकालना, जोड़ना; **add up to**, जोड़ प्राप्त होना या निकलना।

addendum (एडेन्डम) ***n.*** (plu. addenda) supplement, परिशिष्ट।

addict[1] (एडिक्ट) ***v.*** to devote or habituate oneself to, आदी बनना, अभ्यस्त हो जाना।

addict[2] ***n.*** one who is addicted to drugs etc., व्यसनी, नशेड़ी।

addiction (एडिक्शन) ***n.*** a bad habbit, लत, व्यसन, नशेबाज़ी।

addition (एडिशन) ***n.*** 1. the act of adding, जोड़, योग। 2. something that is added, वृद्धि, बढ़त, बढ़ोतरी। □ **in addition**, साथ में।

additional ***adj.*** extra, अतिरिक्त।

addle (एडेल) ***v.*** to become rotten, सड़-गल जाना, सड़ना-गलना।

address[1] (एड्रैस) ***v.*** 1. to speak to, संबोधित करना। 2. to make with a destination or location, पता लिखना।

address[2] ***n.*** 1. a formal spoken or written communication, अभिभाषण। 2. the indication of destination or location, पता, सरनामा।

addressee (ऐड्रेसी) ***n.*** a person to whom a letter or packet is sent, प्राप्तकर्ता, पानेवाला।

adept (एडैप्ट) ***adj.*** highly skilled, अत्यंत दक्ष, निपुण।

adeptly ***adv.*** skilfully, कुशलता से, दक्षतापूर्वक।

adequate (ऐडिक्विट) ***adj.*** 1. sufficient, पर्याप्त। 2. satis-factory, संतोषजनक।

adhere (एडहिअर) ***v.*** 1. to stick or hold fast, चिपक/सट जाना। 2. to be faithful to, निष्ठावान् (बने) रहना। 3. to follow closely, अनुसरण/पालन करना।

adherence (एडहिअरेन्स) ***n.*** 1. fidelity, निष्ठा। 2. observance, पालन, अनुसरण।

adherent ***adj.*** sticking, साथ लगा या चिपका हुआ, संसक्त, संलग्न। ***n.*** a supporter, पक्षधर, समर्थक।

adhesion (एडहीज़्हन) ***n.*** 1. the act of adhering or the state of being adhered, चिपकाव, संलग्नता। 2. support, पक्षधरता, हिमायत।

adhesive (एडहीसिव) ***adj.*** sticky, चिपकनेवाला, चिपचिपा। ***n.*** an adhesive substance, चिपकने या चिपकानेवाला पदार्थ।

ad hoc (ऐड हॉक) ***adj.*** for a specific case, purpose or situation, तदर्थ। (लैटिन)

ad hoc committee ***n.*** a committee for a specific purpose, तदर्थ समिति।

adieu (एड्यू) ***interj. & n.*** goodbye, विदा।

adipose (ऐडिपोस) ***adj.*** 1. fatty, मोटा, स्थूलकाय, स्थूल। 2. of fat, स्निग्ध।

adjacent (एजेसेन्ट) ***adj.*** 1. lying near, समीपवर्ती। 2. adjoining, संलग्न।

adjectival (ऐड्जिक्टाइवल) ***adj.*** pertaining to an adjective, विशेषण-संबंधी।

adjective (ऐड्जिक्टिव) ***n.*** a word that modifies a noun, विशेषण।

adjoining (एजॉइनिंग) ***adj.*** adjacent, near, संलग्न।

adjourn (एजर्न) ***v.*** to postpone, स्थगित होना या करना।

adjournment ***n.*** postponement, स्थगन।

adjudge (एजज) ***v.*** to decide judicially, निर्णय करना।

adjunct (ऐजंक्ट) ***n.*** a subordinate thing, गौण वस्तु या बात।

adjust (एजस्ट) ***v.*** 1. to change so as to match or fit, समायोजित करना, ठीक करना। 2. to arrange, व्यवस्थित करना। 3. to adapt (oneself) to new circumstances, अभ्यस्त बनना या बनाना।

adjustable (एजस्टेबल) ***adj.*** able to

A

be adjusted, समायोज्य, समायोजनीय।

adjustment ***n.*** the process of adjusting or the state of being adjusted, समायोजन।

administer (ऐडमिनिस्टर) ***v.*** 1. to manage the affairs of, प्रशासन करना या चलाना, प्रशासित या निर्देशित करना। 2. to provide or give, देना। ☐ **administer a dose**, ख़ुराक देना या पिलाना; **administer an oath**, शपथ दिलाना।

administration (ऐडमिनिस्ट्रेशन) ***n.*** 1. the act of administering, प्रबंध, व्यवस्था, प्रशासन। 2. an administering group, प्रशासक-वर्ग।

administrative (ऐडमिनिस्ट्रेटिव) ***adj.*** pertaining to the administration, प्रशासन-संबंधी, प्रशासनिक।

administrator (ऐडमिनिस्ट्रेटर) ***n.*** one who administers, प्रशासक।

admirable (ऐडमिरेबल) ***adj.*** 1. deserving admiration, प्रशंसनीय। 2. excellent, उत्कृष्ट।

admiral (ऐडमिरल) ***n.*** the commander-in-chief of a navy, नौसेनाध्यक्ष।

admiralty (ऐडमिरल्टी) ***n.*** office of an admiral, नौसेना विभाग।

admiration (ऐडमिरेशन) ***n.*** 1. respect, आदर। 2. praise, प्रशंसा।

admire (एडमाइर) ***v.*** 1. to think highly of, to respect, आदर करना। 2. to praise, प्रशंसा करना।

admissible (ऐडमिसिबल) ***adj.*** worthy of being accepted, स्वीकार्य।

admission (ऐडमिशन) ***n.*** 1. the act of admitting, प्रवेश। 2. the right to enter, प्रवेशाधिकार। 3. some-thing confessed, स्वीकृति।

admission fee ***n.*** a fee paid to enter a place, प्रवेश-शुल्क।

admit (ऐडमिट) ***v.*** 1. to permit to enter, अंदर आने देना। 2. to accept into an institution, भर्ती या दाख़िल करना। 3. to accept for the purpose of consideration, ग्रहण करना। 4. to confess, स्वीकार कर लेना, मान लेना।

admonish (ऐडमॉनिश) ***v.*** 1. to re prove, डाँटना-फटकारना, झिड़कना। 2. to warn, चेतावनी देना।

admonition (ऐडमॉनिशन) ***n.*** 1. rebuke, झिड़की, डाँट-फटकार। 2. a warning (against fault), चेतावनी।

adolescence (ऐडोलेसेन्स) ***n.*** the period between childhood and adulthood, किशोरावस्था।

adolescent (ऐडोलेसेन्ट) ***adj.*** 1. between childhood and adulthood, किशोर या किशोरी। 2. of adolescence, किशोरावस्था-संबंधी, किशोर-सुलभ।

adopt (एडॉप्ट) ***v.*** 1. to take as one's child, गोद लेना। 2. to take as one's own, अपना लेना।

adoption (एडॉप्शन) ***n.*** 1. the act of adopting or taking as one's own, अपनाना, अंगीकरण, ग्रहण। 2. the action of adopting a child, दत्तक ग्रहण।

adorable (एडोरेबल) ***adj.*** very respected and lovable, पूजनीय, श्रद्धेय।

adoration (ऐडोरेशन) ***n.*** worship, पूजा, उपासना, आराधना।

adore (एडोर) ***v.*** to worship as divine, पूजा करना, आराधना करना।

adorn (एडोर्न) ***v.*** 1. to decorate with ornaments, अलंकृत करना।

2. to decorate, सजाना-सँवारना।

adrenal (एड्रीनल) ***n.*** a gland on top of the kidneys, अधिवृक्क ग्रंथि।

adrift (एड्रिफ़्ट) ***adj.*** drifting, बहता हुआ। ***adv.*** without purpose, बिना मतलब।

adroit (एड्राइट) ***adj.*** dexterous, पटु, दक्ष।

adulation (ऐजुलेशन) ***n.*** excessive praise, ख़ुशामद, चापलूसी।

adult (ऐडल्ट्) ***n.*** a full grown person, वयस्क, बालिग। ***adj.*** mature प्रौढ़।

adulterate (एडल्टरेट) ***v.*** to make inferior by adding another substance, खोट मिलाना, मिलावट करना।

adulteration (एडल्टरेशन) ***n.*** the act of adulterating, मिलावट करना, अपमिश्रण।

adulterer (एडल्टरर) ***n.*** a man guilty of adultery, व्यभिचारी, परस्त्रीगामी।

adultery (एडल्टरी) ***n.*** sexual intercourse between a married person and someone outside the marriage, व्यभिचार।

adulthood (एडल्टहुड) ***n.*** the state of being adult, वयस्कता, प्रौढ़ता।

advance (एडवान्स) ***v.*** 1. to bring forward or onward, आगे बढ़ाना, सामने रखना। 2. to move or come forward, आगे आना, आगे बढ़ना। 3. to develop, विकसित होना। 4. to increase, बढ़ोतरी होना, उन्नति होना। ***n.*** 1. the act of moving or going forward, बढ़ाव, आगे बढ़ना। 2. progress, प्रगति, उन्नति। 3. payment of money before legally due, अग्रिम, पेशगी। 4. (plu.) efforts for winning someone or attempts to establish a friendly relationship, छेड़खानी। □ **in advance**, अग्रिम रूप से, पहले ही। ***adj.*** prior, पूर्व, अग्रिम।

advanced ***adj.*** 1. highly developed, उच्च, उन्नत, विकसित। 2. progressive, प्रगतिशील, उन्नतिशील।

advancement (एडवान्समेन्ट) ***n.*** 1. the action of advancing, बढ़ाव, बढ़ावा। 2. progress, प्रगति, उन्नति, विकास।

advantage (एड्वान्टिज) ***n.*** 1. profit, फ़ायदा, नफ़ा, लाभ। 2. a favourable condition, लाभप्रद स्थिति। 3. benefit, हित, लाभ।

advantageous (एडवान्टेजस) ***adj.*** beneficial, लाभदायक।

advent (ऐडवेन्ट) ***n.*** a coming or arrival, आगमन, आना, शुभागमन।

adventure (एडवैन्चर) ***n.*** 1. a risky undertaking, साहसिक कार्य, जोखिम-भरा कार्य। 2. a risk, जोखिम, साहस।

adventurer ***n.*** 1. one who takes risky ventures, जोखिम-भरे काम करनेवाला, साहसकर्मी। 2. one who seeks wealth or position by unscrupulous means, तिकड़मी, चालबाज़।

adventuresome (ऐडवैन्चरसंम) ***adj.*** adventurous, bold, साहसी, दिलेर।

adverb (ऐडवर्ब) ***n.*** a word used to modify a verb, क्रियाविशेषण।

adverbial (ऐडवर्बिअल) ***adj.*** like or used as an adverb, क्रिया-विशेषी, क्रियाविशेषणात्मक।

adversary (ऐडवर्सरी) ***n.*** an opponent, विरोधी।

adverse (ऐडवर्स) ***adj.*** 1. opposite, hostile, उलटा, प्रतिकूल। 2. harmful, हानिकर।

adversity (ऐडवर्सिटी) ***n.*** 1. bad fortune, misfortune, दुर्भाग्य, बदक़िस्मती। 2. something

A

unfortunate, trouble, विपत्ति, मुसीबत।

advertise (ऐडवर्टाइज़) ***v.*** 1. to make known by announcement in a paper or journal, विज्ञापित करना, विज्ञापन करना या देना। 2. to issue a public notice, विज्ञापित करना, सूचना निकालना।

advertisement (ऐडवर्टिज़मेन्ट) ***n.*** the act of advertising or something advertised, विज्ञापन।

advertising ***n.*** the business of preparing and distributing advertisements, विज्ञापन-व्यवसाय।

advice (एडवाइस) ***n.*** an opinion सलाह, परामर्श।

advisable (एडवाइज़ेबल) ***adj.*** proper, appropriate, उचित, उपयुक्त।

advise (एडवाइज़) ***v.*** to give advice to, सलाह देना, परामर्श देना।

advised ***adj.*** deliberate, considered, विचारित, सुविचारित; ill-advised, कुमंत्रित।

adviser, advisor (एडवाइज़र) ***n.*** one who gives advice, परामर्शदाता, सलाहकार।

advisory (ऐडवाइज़री) ***adj.*** giving advice, परामर्शदात्री; advisory committee, सलाहकार समिति।

advocate (ऐडवोकेट) ***n.*** 1. a person who pleads on behalf of another, एडवोकेट, अधिवक्ता, वकील। 2. public supporter of a proposal, पक्ष-समर्थक, पैरोकार। ***v.*** to uphold or recommend publicly, पक्ष-समर्थन करना, पैरवी करना।

adz, adze (ऐड्ज़) ***n.*** a kind of axe for trimming wood, बसूला।

aegis (ईजिस) ***n.*** protection, संरक्षण। □ **under the aegis of,** संरक्षण में।

aerate (एअरेट) ***v.*** to charge (a liquid) with a gas, गैसयुक्त करना।

aerial (एरिअल) ***adj.*** of or like air, वायवीय, हवाई। ***n.*** an antenna, एरियल, तड़ित्-चालक।

aerie (एअरी) ***n.*** the nest built on a high place, ऊँचे स्थान पर बना/बनाया हुआ घोंसला।

aerodrome (एअरोड्रोम) ***n.*** a landing area smaller than an airport, छोटा हवाई अड्डा।

aerogram (एअरोग्राम) ***n.*** an air-mail letter, हवाई-पत्र।

aeronaut (एअरोनॉट) ***n.*** the pilot of an aircraft, विमानचालक, वैमानिक।

aeronautics (एअरोनॉटिक्स) ***n.*** the science of operation of aircrafts, विमान-विद्या।

aeroplane (एअरोप्लेन) ***n.*** an airplane, वायुयान, विमान।

aesthete (एस्थीट) ***n.*** one who appreciates artistic beauty, सौंदर्यप्रेमी, सौंदर्यवादी।

aesthetic (एस्थेटिक) ***adj.*** 1. of or pertaining to aesthetics, सौंदर्यशास्त्र-संबंधी। 2. artistic, कलात्मक, सौंदर्यपरक।

aesthetics ***n.*** the study of beauty, सौंदर्यशास्त्र।

afar (एफ़ार) ***adv.*** far away, (बहुत) दूर।

affability (ऐफ़ेबिलिटी) ***n.*** 1. the quality of being affable, सुशीलता। 2. the quality of being friendly बंधु-भावना।

affable (ऐफ़ेबल) ***adj.*** 1. polite and gentle, सुशील। 2. showing friendliness, मिलनसार, बंधुप्रेमी।

affair (अफ़ेयर) ***n.*** 1. something that has been done or to be done, काम, बात, मामला, प्रसंग। 2. an event or happening, घटना।

3. a temporary romantic or sexual relationship, प्रेम-संबंध, प्रेम-प्रपंच। 4. (plu.) business of any kind, काम-काज, कार्यकलाप।

affect (एफ़ैक्ट) ***v.*** 1. to produce an effect on, प्रभावित करना, छाप छोड़ना। 2. to pretend or feign, बनना, ढोंग रचना, दिखावा करना।

affectation (ऐफ़ेक्टेशन) ***n.*** artificial or unnatural behaviour, दिखावा, ढोंग, बनावट।

affected ***adj.*** 1. assumed to impress others, ढोंगी, ढकोसलेबाज़। 2. pretended, कृत्रिम, बनावटी। 3. deeply moved, अभिभूत, प्रभावित। 4. afflicted, आक्रांत, ग्रस्त।

affection (एफ़ैक्शन) ***n.*** kind feeling, स्नेह, अनुराग।

affectionate (एफ़ैक्शनिट) ***adj.*** showing affection, loving, स्नेही या स्नेहपूर्ण।

affiance (एफ़ाइएन्स) ***v.*** to betroth, मँगनी करना।

affianced ***adj.*** betrothed, मँगेतर।

affidavit (ऐफ़िडेविट) ***n.*** a written statement on oath हलफ़नामा।

affiliate (एफ़िलिएट) ***v.*** 1. to connect, संबद्ध करना। 2. to adopt as a member or branch, सदस्य बनाना, शाखा बनाना, सहबद्ध करना।

affiliated ***adj.*** related, connected, सहबद्ध, संबद्ध।

affinity (एफ़िनिटी) ***n.*** relationship, संबंध, रिश्ता, रिश्तेदारी।

affirm (एफ़र्म) ***v.*** 1. to declare to be true, सच बतलाना। 2. to confirm, दृढ़तापूर्वक कहना।

affirmation (एफ़र्मेशन) ***n.*** assertion, confirmation, अभिपुष्टि।

affirmative (एफ़र्मेटिव) ***adj.*** positive, सकारात्मक।

affix (एफ़िक्स) ***v.*** 1. to stick on, चिपका देना, लगा देना। 2. to add in writing, लिखना।

afflict (एफ़्लिक्ट) ***v.*** 1. to cause pain or sorrow to, दुख या कष्ट देना। 2. to torment, यातना देना, सताना।

afflicted ***adj.*** 1. distressed, oppressed, दुखी, संतप्त, पीड़ित। 2. grievously troubled with sickness, व्याधिग्रस्त।

affliction (एफ़्लिक्शन) ***n.*** 1. pain, पीड़ा, दर्द, व्यथा, वेदना। 2. trouble, distress, झंझट, विपत्ति। 3. a disease, बीमारी, रोग।

affluence (ऐफ़्लुएन्स) ***n.*** 1. abundance, प्रचुरता। 2. wealth, दौलत। 3. prosperity, समृद्धि।

affluent (ऐफ़्लुएन्ट) ***adj.*** 1. plentiful, abundant, प्रचुर। 2. wealthy, धनी। 3. prosperous, समृद्ध।

afford (एफ़ोर्ड) ***v.*** 1. to have the financial means for, धन जुटा पाना, खरीद पाना, ले सकना। 2. to be able to spare or give up, दे पाना, छोड़ सकना। 3. to bear, सह सकना। 4. to provide, उपलब्ध कराना। 5. to be in a position to do something, कर पाना, करने में समर्थ होना।

affray (एफ़्रे) ***n.*** a riot, दंगा, दंगा-फ़साद, बलवा। 2. a noisy quarrel, हंगामा, शोर-शराबा।

affront (एफ़्रंट) ***v.*** 1. to insult, अपमान करना। 2. to confront, डटकर सामना करना। ***n.*** insult, अपमान।

afield (एफ़ील्ड) ***adj. & adv.*** 1. away from home, घर से दूर। 2. astray, आवारा।

A

afloat (एफ़्लोट) ***adj.*** 1. floating, तैरता हुआ।

afoot (एफ़ुट) ***adv.*** 1. on foot, पैदल, चलकर। 2. in progress, चालू, जारी, अग्रसर।

aforesaid (एफ़ोर्सेड) ***adj.*** said before, पूर्वकथित।

afraid (एफ़्रेड) ***adj.*** 1. frightened, डरा हुआ, भयभीत। 2. somewhat regretful, कुछ-कुछ खिन्न।

afresh (एफ़्रेश) ***adj.*** anew, again, फिर से, नए सिरे से।

African (ऐफ़्रिकन) ***adj.*** of or pertaining to Africa, अफ़्रीका-संबंधी, अफ़्रीकी।

afro (एफ़्रो) ***adj.*** = African.

aft (आफ़्ट) ***adv.*** towards the stern, पिछले हिस्से में।

after (आफ़्टर) ***prep.*** 1. following in time, के बाद, के उपरांत; 2. following in space, के बाद; ***adv.*** 1. behind, पीछे। 2. afterwards, बाद में।

after all ***adv.*** 1. when everything is considered, अंत में, अंततोगत्वा, आख़िरकार। 2. inspite of expectations, efforts etc, फिर, जो हो।

aftereffect ***n.*** an effect that follows the main effect, पश्चप्रभाव।

aftermath (आफ़्टरमैथ) ***n.*** the result of an occurrence considered collectively, बाद का असर, परिणाम।

afternoon (आफ़्टरनून) ***n.*** The time from noon to evening तीसरा पहर।

afterthought (आफ़्टरथॉट) ***n.*** an idea that occurs to one after the opportunity to deliver it has passed, बाद में ध्यान में आनेवाली बात।

afterward, afterwards ***adv.*** after an earlier event पीछे, बाद में।

again (एगेन) ***adv.*** once more, anew, दुबारा, पुनः। □ **again and again**, बार-बार।

against (एगेन्स्ट) ***prep.*** 1. contrary to, के विरुद्ध। 2. in opposition or resistance to, के विरोध में।

agate (ऐगेट) ***n.*** a kind of precious stone, गोमेद।

age (एज) ***n.*** 1. the period of time during which someone or something exists, उम्र, वय। 2. a life time, जीवनकाल, आयु। 3. one of the periods of life, जीवन की कोई विशेष अवधि। **for ages,** युगों से; **of age**, वयस्क। ***v.*** (aged, ageing or aging) to grow older, उम्र बढ़ना या ढलना।

aged (एजिड) ***adj.*** 1. of the age of..., की उम्रवाला, वर्षीय। 2. old, वृद्ध, बूढ़ा।

ageing ***adj.*** growing and looking older, बढ़ती उम्रवाला।

ageless (एजलिस) ***adj.*** 1. apparently never growing old, चिर युवा। 2. timeless, चिर नूतन।

agency (एजेन्सी) ***n.*** the business or office of an agent, एजेंसी, अभिकरण।

agenda (एजेन्डा) ***n.*** a list of items to be attended to at a meeting, कार्यसूची, एजंडा।

agent (एजेन्ट) ***n.*** 1. one who acts, कर्ता। 2. one who acts for another, अभिकर्ता, एजेंट, प्रतिनिधि। 3. (Chem.) something that produces a change, कारक।

age-old (एज-ओल्ड) ***adj.*** ancient, प्राचीन, पुरातन।

agglomerate (एग्लोमरेट) ***v.*** to collect in a mass, ढेर लगाना, जमा या संग्रह करना।

agglomeration (एग्लोमरेशन) ***n.*** a mass, ढेर, पुंज।

agglutinate (एग्लूटिनेट) ***v.*** to stick together, चिपकना या चिपकाना, जुड़ना या जोड़ना।

aggravate (एग्रेवेट) ***v.*** 1. to make worse or more serious, उत्तेजित या प्रकुपित करना, छेड़ना। 2. to provoke, चिढ़ाना।

aggravation (ऐग्रेवेशन) ***n.*** provocation, प्रकोप।

aggregate[1] (ऐग्रिगेट) ***adj.*** total, कुल। ***n.*** a total, जोड़, योग। ***v.*** to add up to, जोड़नां, योग करना।

aggregation (ऐग्रिगेशन) ***n.*** 1. a total, योग, जोड़। 2. a collection, संग्रह, संकलन।

aggression (एग्रेशन) ***n.*** an unprovoked attack, आक्रमण।

aggressive (एग्रेसिव) ***adj.*** 1. prone to attack, आक्रामक। 2. quarrelsome, झगड़ालू।

aggressor (एग्रेसर) ***n.*** one who attacks, आक्रामक।

aggrieve (एग्रीव) ***v.*** to torment, सताना।

aggrieved ***adj.*** 1. tormented, सताया हुआ। 2. bereaved, शोकसंतप्त।

aghast (एगास्ट) ***adj.*** 1. amazed, भौचक्का।

agile (एजाइल) ***adj.*** quick in work, nimble, चुस्त, फुर्तीला।

agility (एजिलिटी) ***n.*** 1. nimbleness, चुस्ती, फुर्तीलापन।

agitate (ऐजिटेट) ***v.*** 1. to stir violenty, ज़ोर से हिलाना, विक्षुब्ध करना। 2. to fight for a cause, आंदोलन या संघर्ष करना।

agitation (ऐजिटेशन) ***n.*** the public unrest in support of some demand, आंदोलन।

agitator ***n.*** one who takes part in an agitation, आंदोलनकारी।

agnostic (ऐग्नॉस्टिक) ***n.*** one who believes that the God is unknowable, अज्ञेयवादी।

ago (एगो) ***adv.*** in the past, पहले। ☐ **long ago**, बहुत पहले।

agog (एगॉग) ***adj.*** 1. eager, उत्सुक। 2. curious, जिज्ञासु।

agonise (ऐगोनाइज़) ***v.*** to cause agony, यातना देना।

agony (ऐगोनी) ***n.*** extreme mental or physical suffering, घोर व्यथा, उत्कट वेदना।

agrarian (एग्रेरिअन) ***adj.*** 1. pertaining to agriculture, कृषि-संबंधी। 2. pertaining to land, भूमि-संबंधी।

agree (एग्री) ***v.*** 1. to grant consent, सहमत होना। 2. to be suitable or beneficial, अनुकूल होना।

agreeable (एग्रीएबल) ***adj.*** 1. willing to consent, राज़ी, सहमत। 2. pleasing, pleasant, सुखद, रुचिकर।

agreement (एग्रीमेन्ट) ***n.*** 1. mutual understanding, करार, समझौता। 2. legal contract binding on the signatories, अनुबंध। 3. concord, मेल, समझौता। 4. conformity, अनुरूपता।

agricultural (ऐग्रिकल्चरल) ***adj.*** pertaining to the agriculture, कृषि-संबंधी।

agriculturist (ऐग्रिकल्चरिस्ट) ***n.*** 1. a farmer, किसान, खेतिहर, कृषक। 2. an expert in agricultural science, कृषिविज्ञानी।

aground (एग्राउन्ड) ***adv.*** on the shore, किनारे।

ah (आ) ***interj.*** expressing surprise,

regret, admiration etc., अरे, ओफ़्, वाह।

aha (आहा) ***interj.*** expressing jubilation, triumph etc., अहा, वाह!

ahead (एहेड) ***adv.*** forward or onward, आगे। ☐ **ahead of**, से पहले; **get ahead**, आगे निकल जाना।

aid (एड) ***v.*** to help, to assist, सहायता करना, मदद करना। ***n.*** assistance, सहायता, मदद।

aided ***adj.*** receiving help, सहायता-प्राप्त।

aide-de-camp (एड-डि-कैम्प) ***n.*** an officer who assists a General in military duties, सहायक सैनिक-अधिकारी।

AIDS (एड्स) ***abbrev*** of Acquired Immune Deficiency Syndrome, एड्स।

ailing (एलिंग) ***adj.*** ill, बीमार।

ailment (एलमेन्ट) ***n.*** a mild or slight illness, छोटी-मोटी बीमारी, तकलीफ़।

aim (एम) ***v.*** 1. to direct towards target to be struck, निशाना साधना, लक्ष्य साधना। 2. to direct one's efforts or purpose, लक्ष्य बनाना। 3. to try, प्रयत्नशील होना, चेष्टा करना। ***n.*** 1. the act of aiming, लक्ष्य-साधन। 2. something aimed, लक्ष्य, निशाना। 3. intention, purpose, लक्ष्य, ध्येय, उद्देश्य।

aimless (एमलिस) ***adj.*** without a purpose, उद्देश्यहीन।

aimlessly ***adv.*** purposelessly, निरुद्देश्य, निष्प्रयोजन।

air (एअर) ***n.*** 1. the gaseous substance surrounding the earth, हवा, वायु। 2. (plu.) affectation, बनावट, दिखावा, बनावटी रंग-ढंग। ☐ **by air**, विमान द्वारा; **in the air,** (i) उड़ता हुआ; (ii) चर्चित; (iii) undecided, अनिश्चित; **in the open air**, खुले में; **on the air**, जो प्रसारित हो रहा हो; **put on airs**, नखरा दिखाना।

airbase ***n.*** airfield, हवाई अड्डा।

airborne ***adj.*** transported by an airplane, विमान-वाहित।

air-conditioned ***adj.*** having kept the air to the specific temperature in a room etc., वातानुकूलित।

air-conditioner ***n.*** an apparatus for keeping a room to the spe-cific temperature, एयरकंडिशनर।

aircraft ***n.*** an aeroplane, हवाई जहाज़, विमान।

Air Force ***n.*** armed forces that attack through airplanes, वायुसेना।

air-hostess ***n.*** a stewardess on airliner, विमान-परिचारिका, व्योमबाला।

airing ***n.*** exposing to air, हवा दिखाना, हवा में रखना।

airlift ***n.*** transport of supplies by aircraft, वायु-परिवहन।

airline ***n.*** service of passenger aircraft, वायुसेवा।

airmail ***n.*** the mail carried by aircraft, हवाई डाक।

airport ***n.*** an airfield, हवाई अड्डा।

air raid ***n.*** an attack by aircraft, हवाई हमला।

airsickness (एअरसिक्निस) ***n.*** nausea resulting from flight in an aircraft, आकाशी बीमारी।

airtight ***adj.*** not allowing air to pass in or out, हवाबंद।

air-to-air ***adj.*** fired from one aircraft at another aircraft, हवाई, आकाशीय।

airway ***n.*** an airline, वायुसेवा।

airworthy (एअरवर्दी) ***adj.*** fit to fly, उड़ने योग्य या उड़ाने योग्य।

[illegible] well-ventilated, हवादार।

aisle (आइल) ***n.*** passage गलियारा।

ajar (एजार) ***adv. & adj.*** partly open, कुछ-कुछ खुला।

akimbo (एकिम्बो) ***adv.*** with hands on hips, कूल्हों पर हाथ रखे हुए।

akin (एकिन) ***adj.*** 1. from the same family, सजातीय। 2. similar, समान, सदृश।

alabaster (ऐलेबैस्टर) ***n.*** a variety of gypsum, सेलखड़ी।

alacrity (एलैक्रिटी) ***n.*** 1. briskness, फुर्तीलापन। 2. readiness, तत्परता।

alarm (एलार्म) ***n.*** 1. fear, भय। 2. a warning signal, ख़तरे की घंटी। 3. a warning of danger, ख़तरा। ***v.*** 1. to frighten, डरा देना, भयभीत कर देना। 2. to warn by alarm, ख़तरे की घंटी बजाना।

alarm clock ***n.*** a clock which can be set to ring a bell at a certain time, अलार्म घड़ी।

alarmed ***adj.*** frightened, भयभीत।

alarming (एलार्मिंग) ***adj.*** frightening, भयप्रद, भयावह।

alarmist (एलार्मिस्ट) ***n.*** one who needlessly alarms others, वह जो दूसरों को भयभीत करता रहता हो, अफ़वाहें फैलानेवाला।

alas (एलास) ***interj.*** used to express regret or anxiety, हाय! अफ़सोस! ओफ़!

album (ऐल्बम) ***n.*** a book for collecting photographs, stamps etc., अलबम।

albumen (ऐल्ब्यूमिन) ***n.*** the white of an egg, अंडे की सफ़ेदी।

alchemist (ऐल्केमिस्ट) ***n.*** an expert in alchemy, कीमियागर, रसायनशास्त्री।

alchemy (ऐल्केमी) ***n.*** the science of converting base metals into gold, कीमियागिरी, रसायन-विद्या।

alcohol (ऐल्कोहॉल) ***n.*** an intoxicating liquid present in whiskey, wine etc., अलकोहल।

alcove (ऐल्कोव) ***n.*** 1. a recess in a wall, आला। 2. a grove, कुंज।

alderman (ऐल्डरमैन) ***n.*** a member of the municipal body, नगरपालिका का सदस्य।

ale (एल) ***n.*** a type of beer, जौ की शराब।

alert (एलर्ट) ***adj.*** attentive, watchful, सचेत, सावधान, सतर्क। ***v.*** 1. to make alert, सचेत करना, सतर्क करना। 2. to warn of a danger, ख़तरे से सावधान करना।

alertness (एलर्टनिस) ***adj.*** vigilance, watchfulness, सतर्कता, सावधानी।

Alexander (एलेग्ज़ेन्डर) ***n.*** सिकंदर।

algebra (ऐल्जेब्रा) ***n.*** a branch of mathematics in which symbols represent quantities, बीजगणित।

algorithm (ऐल्गोरिथम) ***n.*** the process of calculating something, परिकलन-प्रक्रिया।

alias (एलिएस) ***n.*** an assumed name, उपनाम।

alibi (ऐलिबाइ) ***n.*** (plu. alibis) a plea that accused was elsewhere when the crime was committed, अन्यत्रस्थिति।

alien (एलिएन) ***adj.*** foreign, विदेशीय। ***n.*** a resident of foreign country, विदेशी।

alienate (ऐलिअनेट) ***v.*** 1. to cause to become unfriendly or hostile, वैरी या

शत्रु बना लेना। 2. to transfer property to the ownership of another, स्वामित्व बदलना।

alienation (एलिअनेशन) ***n.*** 1. estrangement, मनमुटाव, विरोध। 2. transfer of ownership, स्वामित्व-परिवर्तन।

alight (एलाइट) ***v.*** to get down or descend, उतरना, नीचे उतरना। ***adj.*** 1. on fire, flaming, जलता हुआ। 2. lit up, lighted up, प्रज्वलित। 3. shining, चमकता हुआ।

alignment (एलाइनमेन्ट) ***n.*** the state of being arranged in a straight line, सीध में होना, सीध। ☐ **out of alignment**, ऊँचा-नीचा, ऊबड़-खाबड़।

alike (एलाइक) ***adj.*** similar, समान, सदृश। ***adv.*** in the same way, उसी तरह।

alimony (ऐलिमोनी) ***n.*** the allowance paid by a husband to his wife after a legal separation, ख़र्चा, तलाक-भत्ता।

alive (एलाइव) ***adj.*** 1. having life, living, जीवित। 2. full of life, सजीव, जीवंत।

alkali (ऐल्केलाइ) ***n.*** (plu. alkalis, alkalies) any of the class of substances that form chemical salts when combined with acids and turn litmus blue, क्षार, अल्कली।

alkaline (ऐल्केलाइन) ***adj.*** having the nature of an alkali, क्षारीय, खारा।

all (ऑल) ***adj.*** 1. the whole amount or number of, सब, कुल, सभी। 2. the whole of, पूरा, सारा, संपूर्ण, अखिल। ***pron.*** each and everyone, सब-कुछ, सब कोई।

allay (एले) ***v.*** 1. to calm, शांत करना। 2. to relieve, राहत पहुँचाना।

allegation (ऐलिगेशन) ***n.*** accusation, blame, आरोप, दोषारोप।

allege (एलैज) ***v.*** to accuse, आरोप लगाना, दोषारोपण करना।

allegiance (एलीजेन्स) ***n.*** loyalty, निष्ठा।

allegorical (ऐलिगॉरिकल) ***adj.*** pertaining to allegory, रूपक-संबंधी, लाक्षणिक।

allegory (ऐलिगोरी) ***n.*** a literary device in which objects symbolize some deeper underlying meaning, रूपक।

allergic (एलर्जिक) ***adj.*** 1. suffering from allergy, अलर्जी-पीड़ित। 2. having strong dislike, नापसंद करनेवाला, घृणा करनेवाला।

allergy (ऐलर्जी) ***n.*** bodily reaction from particular things, अलर्जी।

alleviate (एलीविएट) ***v.*** to make less severe, कम करना, राहत पहुँचाना।

alleviation (एलीविएशन) ***n.*** the act of alleviating, प्रशमन, राहत, कमी।

alley (ऐली) ***n.*** a (narrow) street, गली।

alliance (एलाइएन्स) ***n.*** 1. a group or association of countries, राष्ट्रों का गठबंधन, मैत्री। 2. union by marriage, विवाह-संबंध।

allied (एलाइड) ***adj.*** 1. related, संबद्ध, सहबद्ध। 2. united, संयुक्त। 3. similar, समान।

allies (एलाइज़) ***n.*** (plu.) nations united by a treaty, मित्रराष्ट्र।

alligator (ऐलिगेटर) ***n.*** a reptile resembling the crocodile, घड़ियाल।

alliteration (एलिटरेशन) ***n.*** the repetition of the same sound at the beginning of several words in succession, अनुप्रास।

allocate (ऐलोकेट) ***v.*** to set apart for a purpose, किसी विशिष्ट प्रयोजन के लिए अलग रखना या निकालना, विनिधान करना।

allocation (ऐलोकेशन) ***n.*** act of allocating, विनिधान।

allopathy (एलोपैथी) ***n.*** a medical science of treating disease, एलोपैथी।

allot (एलॉट) ***v.*** to divide and give as a share, हिस्सा लगाना और देना, आवंटित करना।

allotment (एलॉटमेन्ट) ***n.*** act of allotting, आवंटन।

all-out (ऑल-आउट) ***adj. & adv.*** with all effort, पूरी शक्ति से।

allow (एलाउ) ***v.*** 1. to permit, अनुमति देना। 2. to allow as a discount, to grant or concede, छूट देना। 3. to admit or concede, मान लेना, स्वीकार करना।

allowance (एलाउएन्स) ***n.*** 1. money provided regularly for special purpose to a worker, भत्ता। 2. a price discount, छूट, कमीशन।

allowed (एलाउड) ***adj.*** permitted, अनुमति-प्राप्त।

alloy (ऐलॉइ) ***n.*** a mixture of two or more different metals, मिश्रधातु। ***v.*** to combine two or more metals, मिश्रधातु बनाना।

all-powerful (ऑल-पावरफ़ुल) ***adj.*** having the absolute power, सर्वशक्तिमान।

all right (ऑल राइट) ***adv.*** 1. satisfactorily, संतोषजनक रूप में। 2. very well, बहुत ठीक। ***adj.*** satisfactory, संतोषजनक।

all-round (ऑल राउन्ड) ***adj.*** having ability in many things, सर्वतोमुखी। ***adv.*** in every way, हर दृष्टि से।

all-rounder ***n.*** having ability in many things esp. in various sports, बहुमुखी योग्यतावाला व्यक्ति।

all-time (ऑल टाइम) ***adj.*** greatest, महान।

all told (ऑल टोल्ड) ***adv.*** with everything considered, अच्छी तरह सोच-विचार कर।

allude to (एल्यूड टू) ***v. prep.*** to make an indirect reference to, इशारा करना।

allure (एल्यूर) ***v.*** 1. to entice, ललचाना, प्रलोभन देना। 2. to attract, लुभाना।

allurement (एल्यूरमेन्ट) ***n.*** 1. enticement, प्रलोभन, चारा। 2. fascination, सम्मोहन।

alluring ***adj.*** 1. attractive, आकर्षक, लुभावना। 2. enticing, मोहक।

allusion (एल्यूज़्हन) ***n.*** an indirect reference, इशारा, संकेत।

allusive (एल्यूसिव) ***adj.*** containing an allusion, सांकेतिक।

alluvial (एल्यूविअल) ***adj.*** made of soil put down by floods, कछारी, जलोढ़।

ally[1] (ऐलाइ) ***n.*** 1. one who helps another, मित्र, सहयोगी। 2. a friendly nation, मित्रराष्ट्र।

ally[2] ***v.*** to join or unite, जोड़ना या जुड़ना।

alma mater (ऐल्मा मेटर) ***n.*** one's college or school, मातृ-विद्यालय, मातृ-संस्था।

almanac (ऐल्मेनैक) ***n.*** a kind of calendar, पंचांग या जंत्री।

almighty (ऑलमाइटी) ***adj.*** all-powerful, सर्वशक्तिमान, महाबली।

A

almirah (आल्मिरा) ***n.*** a cupboard, अलमारी।

almond (आमन्ड) ***n.*** a nut with a soft shell, बादाम। ***adj.*** containing almonds, बादाम से बना हुआ, बादामी।

almost (ऑल्मोस्ट) ***adv.*** very nearly, लगभग, करीब-करीब, प्रायः।

alms (आम्ज़) ***n.*** (plu.) money or goods given to the poor in charity, भिक्षा, भीख।

almsbox ***n.*** a box for receiving money for charity, दानपात्र।

aloft (एलॉफ़्ट) ***adv.*** in or into a high place, ऊँचे, आकाश में, शिखर पर।

alone (अॅलोन) ***adj.*** solitary, अकेला। ***adv.*** 1. only, सिर्फ़, केवल। 2. solely, अकेले।

along (एलॉन्ग) ***adv.*** in a line with, साथ-साथ। ***prep.*** beside and in the same direction, के समानांतर। ☐ **all along**, हर समय, सदा; **along with**, के साथ-साथ; **get along**, आगे बढ़ना।

alongside ***adv.*** beside, बगल में।

aloof (एलूफ़) ***adv.*** at a distance, दूरी पर, अलग-थलग।

aloud (एलाउड) ***adv.*** loudly, ऊँचे स्वर में, ज़ोर से।

alphabet (ऐल्फ़ेबेट) ***n.*** 1. a set of letters used in any language, वर्णमाला। 2. elementary knowledge, प्रारंभिक ज्ञान।

alpine (ऐल्पाइन) ***adj.*** of the alps, ऐल्प्स पहाड़-संबंधी।

already (ऑलरेडी) ***adv.*** before, previously, पहले, पहले ही, पहले से ही।

also (ऑल्सो) ***adv.*** in addition, besides, too, भी।

also-ran ***n.*** one who is defeated in a competition, परास्त प्रतियोगी।

altar (ऑल्टर) ***n.*** a raised structure upon which sacrifices may be offered, वेदी, वेदिका।

alter (ऑल्टर) ***v.*** to change or become different, फेरबदल करना या होना, परिवर्तन करना या होना।

alterable (ऑल्टरेबल) ***adj.*** that can be altered, जिसमें परिवर्तन किया जा सके, परिवर्त्य।

alteration ***n.*** an act of altering, परिवर्तन, फेरबदल, रद्दोबदल।

altercate (ऑल्टर्केट) ***v.*** to quarrel fiercely, झगड़ना, लड़ना-झगड़ना।

altercation ***n.*** a fierce quarrel, झगड़ा, कहासुनी।

alternate (ऑल्टर्नेट) ***adj.*** happening or following in turns, बारी-बारी से होनेवाला, एक छोड़कर दूसरा, एकांतर। ***v.*** to occur in successive turns, बारी-बारी से होना।

alternately ***adj.*** by turns, बारी-बारी से, एक-एक छोड़कर।

alternative (आल्टर्नेटिव) ***n.*** the choice between two or more things, विकल्प।

although (ऑल्दो) ***conj.*** though, हालाँकि।

altitude (ऐल्टिट्यूड) ***n.*** the height above the sea level, उच्चता, ऊँचाई।

alto (ऐल्टो) ***n.*** a high male singing voice, मरदानी टीप, उच्चतम पुरुष-स्वर।

altogether (ऑल्टूगैदर) ***adv.*** entirely, पूर्ण रूप से, पूर्णतया।

altruism (ऐल्ट्रूइज़म) ***n.*** consideration of the good of the others before one's own, परोपकार की भावना।

aluminium (ऐल्यूमिनियम) ***n.*** a white metal, अल्यूमिनियम।

always (आल्वेज) ***adv.*** at all times, सदा, हर समय।

am (ऐम) ***v.*** first person singular present tense of be, हूँ।

a.m. (ए. एम.) abbreviation of ***ante meridiem***, दोपहर से पहले, पूर्वाह्न में।

amalgamate (एमैल्गेमेट) ***v.*** 1. to mix, मिश्रित करना, मिलाना। 2. to combine into one, एकीकृत करना, समामेलित करना।

amalgamation (एमैल्गेमेशन) ***n.*** 1. mixture, मिश्रण। 2. act of combining into one, एकीकरण, समामेलन।

amass (एमैस) ***v.*** to heap up, ढेर लगाना।

amateur (ऐमेच्योर) ***n.*** one who does something as a pastime rather than as a profession, शौकिया खिलाड़ी, शौक़ीन।

amaze (एमेज़) ***v.*** to astonish, चकित करना, विस्मित करना।

amazement (एमेज़मेन्ट) ***n.*** astonishment, आश्चर्य, विस्मय।

amazing ***adj.*** causing astonishment, आश्चर्यजनक, विस्मयजनक।

amazon (ऐमेज़न) ***n.*** 1. a female warrior, वीरांगना। 2. very strong athletic woman, मर्दानी औरत।

ambassador (एम्बैसेडर) ***n.*** country's permanent representative, राजदूत।

amber (ऐम्बर) ***n.*** a yellow or brownish yellow resin, राल, अंबर।

ambidextrous (ऐम्बिडेक्स्ट्रस) ***adj.*** able to use either hand equally well, सव्यसाची।

ambiguity (ऐम्बिग्यूइटी) ***n.*** the state of being ambiguous, द्वयर्थकता; संदिग्धता।

ambiguous (ऐम्बिग्युअस) ***adj.*** 1. having two meanings, द्वयर्थक। 2. doubtful, संदिग्ध, अस्पष्ट।

ambit (ऐम्बिट) ***n.*** 1. circumference, परिधि, घेरा। 2. extent, विस्तार।

ambition (ऐम्बिशन) ***n.*** the strong desire to gain something or achieve something, उच्चाकांक्षा, महत्त्वाकांक्षा।

ambitious (ऐम्बिशस) ***adj.*** eager for success, उच्चाकांक्षी, महत्त्वाकांक्षी।

amble (ऐम्बल) ***v.*** to walk at an easy pace, चहलक़दमी करना। ***n.*** a slow easy pace, चहलक़दमी।

ambrosia (ऐम्ब्रोज़िया) ***n.*** the food of the gods, अमृत।

ambulance (ऐम्ब्यूलेन्स) ***n.*** a vehicle for carrying sick, injured or dead persons, रोगी-वाहन, रोगी-गाड़ी।

ambush (ऐम्बुश) ***n.*** 1. the act of lying in wait to attack by surprise, घात। 2. the place where such attackers hide, आड़।

ameliorate (एमीलिओरेट) ***v.*** to improve, सुधरना या सुधारना।

amelioration ***n.*** improvement, सुधार।

amen (आमैन) ***interj.*** so be it, तथास्तु, आमीन!

amenable (ॲमीनेबल) ***adj.*** 1. responsible, उत्तरदायी। 2. responsive, अनुकूल आचरण करनेवाला।

amend (एमेन्ड) ***v.*** 1. to correct or improve, सुधारना, संशोधन करना। 2. to alter, बदलना, परिवर्तन करना।

amendment (एमेन्डमेन्ट) ***n.*** 1. a formal alteration of a law, संशोधन। 2. correction, सुधार।

amends ***n.*** (plu.) compensation, क्षतिपूर्ति, हरजाना। ☐ **make amends,**

A

क्षतिपूर्ति करना।

amenity (एमेनिटी) ***n.*** 1. a thing or condition which makes life pleasant, सुविधा। 2. pleasantness, मनोहरता, रमणीयता, चारुता। 3. (plu. amenities) social courtesies, सामाजिक शिष्टाचार।

American (अमेरिकन) ***adj.*** of America, अमरीकी।

amiability ***n.*** the quality of being amiable, मिलनसारी, भलमनसाहत।

amiable (एमिएबल) ***adj.*** 1. of a pleasant nature, friendly, मिलनसार, भला। 2. friendly, मैत्रीपूर्ण, सौहार्दपूर्ण।

amicability (एमिकेबिलिटी) ***n.*** the quality of being amicable, मैत्री, मैत्री-भावना।

amicable (ऐमिकेबल) ***adj.*** friendly, मैत्रीपूर्ण, मिलनसार।

amid (एमिड) **amidst** (एमिड्स्ट) ***prep.*** in the middle of, के बीच, के दरमियान, के दौरान।

amiss (एमिस) ***adj.*** 1. out of order, unsatisfactory, ख़राब, असंतोषजनक। 2. wrong, ग़लत।

amity (एमिटी) ***n.*** friendship, मित्रता।

ammunition (ऐम्यूनिशन) ***n.*** 1. explosive materials, गोला-बारूद। 2. a means of offence or defence, हथियार।

amnesty (एम्नेस्टी) ***n.*** a general pardon for political offences, सामूहिक क्षमादान।

amoeba (अमीबा) ***n.*** (***plu.*** amoebae, amoebas) an unicellular organism, अमीबा।

amoebic ***adj.*** pertaining to or caused by amoeba, अमीबा-संबंधी।

among (अमंग) ***prep.*** 1. in the middle of, surrounded by, के बीच। 2. in association with, के साथ। 3. in the group or number of, में से एक।

amorous (ऐमोरस) ***adj.*** showing sexual love, कामुकतापूर्ण, कामुक।

amorphous (एमॉर्फ़स) ***adj.*** without definite form or shape, आकारहीन।

amount (एमाउन्ट) ***n.*** 1. the total quantity or number, रक़म, राशि, जमा। 2. total, योग, योगफल, कुल जमा।

amphibian (ऐम्फ़िबिअन) ***n.*** an amphibious creature, उभयचर जीव, जलथलचर जंतु।

amphibious (ऐम्फ़िबिअस) ***adj.*** able to live in water and land, उभयचर।

amphitheatre (ऐम्फ़िथीएटर) ***n.*** a round structure having tiers of seats, सोपान-मंडप।

ample (ऐम्पल) ***adj.*** quite enough, प्रचुर, यथेष्ट।

amplification (ऐम्प्लिफ़िकेशन) ***n.*** the act of amplifying, प्रवर्धन।

amplifier (ऐम्प्लिफ़ाइअर) ***n.*** a device that increases the loudness of sounds, एम्प्लिफ़ायर, प्रवर्धक।

amplify (ऐम्प्लिफ़ाइ) ***v.*** to increase the strength of, तीव्र या तेज़ करना, प्रवर्धित करना।

amplitude (ऐम्प्लिट्यूड) ***n.*** 1. breadth, चौड़ाई। 2. abundance, प्रचुरता, अधिकता।

amply (ऐम्प्ली) ***adv.*** abundantly, प्रचुर मात्रा में।

amputate (ऐम्प्यूटेट) ***v.*** to cut off by surgery, अंगोच्छेदन करना।

amputation (ऐम्प्यूटेशन) ***n.*** an act of amputating, अंगोच्छेदन।

amuck (एमक) ***adv.*** madly, पागलों

की तरह।

amulet (ऐम्युलिट) ***n.*** a charm, तावीज़, कवच।

amuse (एम्यूज़) ***v.*** 1. to entertain, मनोरंजन करना, मन बहलाना। 2. to cause to laugh, हँसाना।

amusement (अम्यूज़मेन्ट) ***n.*** pastime, recreation, मनोरंजन, मन-बहलाव।

amusing ***adj.*** entertaining, विनोदपूर्ण, मन बहलानेवाला।

an (ऐन) ***article.*** form of a used before vowel sounds.

anaemia (अनीमिया) ***n.*** lack of red corpuscles in blood, रक्ताल्पता, रक्तक्षीणता।

anaemic (अनीमिक) ***adj.*** 1. suffering from anaemia, रक्ताल्प। 2. feeble, अशक्त, दुर्बल।

anaesthesia (ऐनिस्थीज़िया) ***n.*** 1. loss of sensation, संवेदनाहरण। 2. insensibility to pain, असंवेदनशीलता, संवेदनहीनता।

anagram (ऐनाग्रैम) ***n.*** a word formed by reordering the letters of another word, वर्ण-विपर्यय।

analogous (एनैलोगस) ***adj.*** alike in certain ways, मिलता-जुलता, समान।

analogy (एनैलॉजी) ***n.*** correspondence in some respects between things otherwise dissimilar, तुल्यता, सादृश्य, समानता।

analyse, analyze (ऐनेलाइज़) ***v.*** to make an analysis of, विश्लेषण करना।

analysis (अनैलिसिस) ***n.*** a detailed description of the parts or elements of something, विश्लेषण।

analyst (ऐनेलिस्ट) ***n.*** one skilled in analysis of chemical substances, विश्लेषण-विशेषज्ञ, विश्लेषक।

analytic (ऐनेलिटिक) ***adj.*** of or pertaining to analysis, विश्लेषणात्मक, वैश्लेषिक।

ananas (ऐनानैस) ***n.*** pineapple plant or fruit, अनन्नास।

anarchic (ऐनार्किक) ***adj.*** pertaining to anarchy, अराजक।

anarchism (ऐनार्किज़म) ***n.*** lawlessness, अराजकतावाद।

anarchist ***n.*** one whe believes in anarchism, अराजकतावादी।

anarchy (ऐनार्की) ***n.*** 1. absence of any law or authority, अराजकता। 2. political disorder, राजनीतिक अस्थिरता।

anathema (एनैथेमा) ***n.*** a curse of the church, गिरजे का अभिशाप।

anatomical (ऐनैटॉमिकल) ***adj.*** pertaining to anatomy, शरीर-विज्ञान-संबंधी, शरीर-रचना-संबंधी।

anatomy (एनैटॉमी) ***n.*** 1. science dealing with bodily structures, शरीर-विज्ञान। 2. dissection, चीर-फाड़।

ancestor (ऐन्सेस्टर) ***n.*** any person from whom one is descended, पितर, पूर्वज।

ancestral (ऐन्सेस्ट्रल) ***adj.*** inherited from ancestors, पैतृक।

ancestry (ऐन्सेस्ट्री) ***n.*** a line of ancestors, वंश-परंपरा।

anchor (ऐंकर) ***n.*** a device to keep the vessel in place, लंगर। ***v.*** to lower the anchor, लंगर डालना।

ancient (एन्शेन्ट) ***adj.*** very old, पुराना, प्राचीन, पुरातन। ***n.* the ancients**, पुराने लोग।

ancillary (ऐन्सिलेरी) ***adj.*** subordinate, सहायक, गौण।

and (ऐन्ड) ***conj.*** together with or along with, और, तथा, एवम्।

anecdote (ऐनिक्डोट) ***n.*** a short entertaining account, क़िस्सा, चुटकुला।

anew (एन्यू) ***adv.*** afresh, again, नए सिरे से, फिर से।

angel (एन्जेल) ***n.*** a messenger of God, देवदूत, फ़रिश्ता।

anger (ऐंगर) ***n.*** wrath, क्रोध, गुस्सा।

angina (ऐन्जाइना) ***n.*** choking of the throat, कंठशूल।

angina pectoris (ऐन्जाइना पेक्टोरिस) ***n.*** a sharp pain in the chest with feeling of suffocation, हृत्शूल।

angle (ऐन्गल) ***v.*** to fish with a hook and line, काँटे या बंसी से मछलियाँ पकड़ना। ***n.*** 1. the shape made by two straight lines meeting in a point, कोण। 2. a point of view, दृष्टिकोण।

angler (ऐन्गलर) ***n.*** one who fishes with hook and line, काँटे या बंसी से मछलियाँ पकड़नेवाला।

Anglican (ऐंग्लिकन) ***adj.*** of the Church of England, इंग्लैंड के चर्च से संबद्ध।

Anglicism (ऐंग्लिसिज़म) ***n.*** a phrase or idiom, peculiar to the English language, अंग्रेज़ी मुहावरा या प्रयोग।

anglicize (ऐंग्लिसाइज़) ***v.*** to make English in form or character, अंग्रेज़ीकरण करना।

Anglo (ऐंग्लो) ***adj.*** 1. of English, आंग्ल, अंग्रेज़ी। 2. of England, ब्रितानवी, अंग्रेज़ी।

Anglophobia (ऐंग्लोफ़ोबिआ) ***n.*** an excessive hatred of English people, customs etc. आंग्लद्वेष।

angry (ऐन्ग्री) ***adj.*** feeling, showing or resulting from anger, क्रुद्ध, क्रोधी या क्रोधजनित।

anguish (ऐंग्विश) ***n.*** a severe physical or mental pain, व्यथा, वेदना, यंत्रणा।

angular (ऐंग्युलर) ***adj.*** 1. of or pertaining to the angle, कोणीय। 2. lean and thin, पतला-दुबला।

animal (ऐनिमल) ***n.*** 1. a living creature, जीव, जंतु, प्राणी। 2. a four-footed animal, पशु, जानवर।

animate (ऐनिमेट) ***v.*** 1. to give life to, जान डालना, जीवंत बनाना। 2. to encourage or inspire, प्रेरणा देना। ***adj.*** having life, lively, जीवंत, सजीव।

animosity (ऐनिमॉसिटी) ***n.*** bitter enmity or hatred, वैर, विद्वेष।

ankle (ऐंकल) ***n.*** the joint between the foot and leg, टखना।

anklet (ऐंक्लिट) ***n.*** an ornament worn round the ankle, पायल, पाज़ेब।

annals (ऐनैल्ज़) ***n.*** (plu.) a chronological record of the events of successive years, इतिवृत्त, वार्षिक वृत्तांत।

annex (ऐनैक्स) ***v.*** to add or join to a larger thing, अनुबद्ध करना, जोड़ना। ***n.*** a small building attached to a larger one, उपभवन।

annexation (अनेक्सेशन) ***n.*** 1. the act of annexing, जोड़ना, मिलाना। 2. something annexed, जोड़ी या मिलाई हुई वस्तु।

annihilate (एनिहिलेट) ***v.*** to destroy completely, ध्वस्त करना, ढा देना।

annihilation (ऐनिहिलेशन) ***n.*** an act of annihilating, विध्वंस, विनाश।

anniversary (ऐनिवर्सरी) ***n.*** the yearly return of the date of an event and the celebration of it, जयंती, वर्षगाँठ।

A

Anno Domini (एनो डोमिनाइ) ***adv.*** in a specified year of the Christian era,... ईसवी सन् में।

annotate (एनोटेट) ***v.*** to furnish with notes, टिप्पणियाँ लिखना, टीका करना।

annotation (एनोटेशन) ***n.*** 1. an act of annotating, टिप्पणीकरण, टिप्पण। 2. something annotated, टिप्पणी, टीका।

announce (एनाउन्स) ***v.*** to declare publicly, घोषणा करना, उद्घोषणा करना।

announcement (एनाउन्समेन्ट) ***n.*** the act of announcing or something announced, घोषणा, उद्घोषणा।

announcer (एनाउन्सर) ***n.*** one who announces something, उद्घोषक, घोषक।

annoy (एनॉइ) ***v.*** 1. to make angry, खिजाना, चिढ़ाना। 2. to vex, तंग करना, परेशान करना।

annoyance (एनॉइअन्स) ***n.*** an act of annoying or being annoyed, चिढ़, खीज, परेशानी।

annual (ऐन्युअल) ***adj.*** yearly, वार्षिक, सालाना।

annually ***adv.*** each year, प्रति वर्ष, हर साल।

annuity (एनूइटी) ***n.*** an amount of money paid annually, वार्षिक वृत्ति, वार्षिकी।

annul (एनल) ***v.*** to cancel, रद करना।

anoint (एनॉइन्ट) ***v.*** to apply oil or ointment, तेल या मलहम लगाना।

anomalous (एनॉमेलस) ***adj.*** abnormal, असामान्य, अनियमित।

anomaly (ऐनोमेली) ***n.*** inconsistency, अनियमितता, विसंगति।

anonymous (एनॉनिमस) ***adj.*** whose name is not known, अनाम, अज्ञात।

another (ऐनदर) ***adj.*** different, दूसरा।

answer (आन्सर) ***n.*** a reply, उत्तर, जवाब। ***v.*** to reply to, उत्तर देना, जवाब देना।

answerable (आन्सरेबल) ***adj.*** responsible, उत्तरदायी, जवाबदेह।

ant (ऐन्ट) ***n.*** a small insect, चींटी।

antagonism (ऐन्टेगोनिज़्म) ***n.*** active opposition, वैर-विरोध।

antagonist (ऐन्टेगोनिस्ट) ***n.*** an opponent, adversary, विरोधी, वैरी।

antagonize (ऐन्टेगोनाइज़) ***v.*** to arouse antagonism in, वैरी बना लेना।

antarctic (ऐन्टार्कटिक) ***adj.*** pertaining to the regions surrounding the South Pole, दक्षिण ध्रुव-संबंधी।

antecedent (ऐन्टिसीडेन्ट) ***adj.*** preceding, पूर्ववर्ती। ***n.*** 1. an event prior to another, पूर्ववर्ती घटना, पूर्ववृत्त। 2. the word, phrase or clause to which a pronoun refers, पूर्वपद। 3. (plu.) one's ancestors, पूर्वज।

antechamber (ऐन्टिचेम्बर) ***n.*** a smaller room leading into a larger room, उपकक्ष।

antedate (ऐन्टिडेट) ***v.*** to give a date earlier than the actual date, पहले की तारीख डालना।

antediluvian (ऐन्टिडिल्युविअन) ***adj.*** of the era before the Biblical Flood, प्रलयपूर्व।

antelope (ऐन्टिलोप) ***n.*** a deer like animal, एक तरह का हिरन।

antemeridian (ऐन्टिमेरिडिअन) ***adv. & adj.*** (abbreviated form a.m.) before noon, दोपहर से पहले, पूर्वाह्न में।

antenna (ऐन्टेना) ***n.*** an aerial, ऐंटीना।

anterior (ऐन्टीरिअर) ***adj.*** prior in time, पूर्ववर्ती।

anteroom (ऐन्टिरूम) ***n.*** an

A

antechamber, उपकक्ष।

anthem (ऐन्थेम) ***n.*** 1. a devotional song, भजन। 2. a national anthem, राष्ट्रगीत।

anthill (ऐन्टहिल) ***n.*** a mound of earth formed by ants, बाँबी।

anthology (ऐन्थॉलोजी) ***n.*** a collection of literary pieces, संग्रह, संकलन।

anthropology (ऐन्थ्रोपॉलोजी) ***n.*** the study of mankind, नृविज्ञान, मानव–विज्ञान।

anti (ऐन्टी) ***prefix.*** opposed to, against, प्रतिरोधी, विरोधी। ***n.*** a person who opposes a certain rule or policy, विरोधी, प्रतिरोधी।

antiaircraft (ऐन्टिएअरक्राफ़्ट) ***adj.*** used against aircrafts, विमानभेदी।

antibiotic (ऐन्टिबॉइओटिक) ***n.*** a medicine that treats diseases by destroying microorganisms, प्रतिजीवाणु।

antibody (ऐन्टिबॉडी) ***n.*** a protein in the blood which destroys bacteria, प्रतिपिंड, एन्टीबॉडी।

anticipate (ऐन्टिसिपेट) ***v.*** 1. to foresee, अनुमान लगाना। 2. to regard as likely, expect, आशा या प्रतीक्षा करना।

anticipation ***n.*** 1. expectation, प्रत्याशा, पूर्वापेक्षा। 2. foreknowledge, पूर्वानुमान।

anticipatory (ऐन्टिसिपेटरी) ***adj.*** 1. showing anticipation, पूर्वानुमानिक। 2. occurring in advance, पूर्वापेक्षित, प्रत्याशित।

anticlimax (ऐन्टिक्लाइमैक्स) ***n.*** concluding in disappointing contrast to a previous climax, उत्कर्ष के बाद होनेवाला अपकर्ष।

antics (ऐन्टिक्स) ***n.*** (plu) buffoonery and posturing, भँड़ैती।

antidote (ऐन्टिडोट) ***n.*** 1. a medicine that counteracts a poison, विषहर।

antimony (ऐन्टिमनी) ***n.*** a metallic element, ऐन्टिमनी।

antipathy (ऐन्टिपैथी) ***n.*** a strong dislike, विरुचि, विरक्ति।

antiquarian (ऐन्टिक्वेरिॲन) ***adj.*** pertaining to antiquity, पुरातात्त्विक। ***n.*** an antiquary, पुरावेत्ता।

antiquary (ऐन्टिक्वेरी) ***n.*** a person who collects or studies antiquities, पुरावेत्ता, पुराविद्।

antiquated (ऐन्टिक्वेटिड) ***adj.*** out of date, old-fashioned, पुरातन।

antique (ऐन्टीक) ***adj.*** ancient, प्राचीन, पुरातन, पुराकालीन। ***n.*** an antique object, प्राचीन दुर्लभ वस्तु।

antiquity (ऐन्टिक्विटी) ***n.*** 1. an ancient time, पुराकाल। 2. the quality of being ancient, पुरातनता। 3. ancient monuments, पुरावशेष।

antiseptic (ऐन्टिसैप्टिक) ***adj.*** hostile to bacteria, रोगाणु-विरोधी।

antisocial (ऐन्टिसोशल) ***adj.*** against the welfare of the society, समाज-विरोधी।

antithesis (ऐन्टिथीसिस) ***n.*** direct contrast, वैषम्य, विरोध।

antler (ऐन्टलर) ***n.*** a branched horn of a deer, हिरन के सींग की शाखा, शृंग शाखा।

antonym (ऐन्टॉनिम) ***n.*** a word whose meaning is opposite to another word, विपर्याय, विलोम शब्द।

anus (एनस) ***n.*** the opening at the lower end of the alimentary canal, गुदा, मलद्वार।

anvil (ऐन्विल) ***n.*** an iron block of an

ironsmith, निहाई। □ **on the anvil**, विचाराधीन, परीक्षाधीन।

anxiety (ऐंग्ज़ाइटी) ***n.*** worry, चिंता, दुश्चिंता।

anxious (ऐंक्शस) ***adj.*** 1. worried, चिंतित। 2. eager, आतुर, उत्सुक।

any (एनी) ***adj & pron.*** no matter which one, कोई। ***adv.*** in some degree, कुछ।

anybody (एनिबॉडी) ***n. & pron.*** any person, कोई व्यक्ति, कोई भी।

anyhow (एनिहाउ) ***adv.*** 1. in any way, किसी तरह, किसी भी तरह। 2 . in any case, हर हालत में।

anyone (एनिवन) ***pron.*** = anybody.

anyplace (एनिप्लेस) ***adv.*** = anywhere.

anything (एनिथिंग) ***n.*** any object, कोई वस्तु।

anytime (एनिटाइम) ***adv.*** at any time, कभी भी, चाहे जब।

anyway (एनिवे) ***adv.*** 1. in any way, किसी तरह। 2. in any case, हर हालत में।

anywhere (एनिवेअर) ***adv.*** to any place, in any place, कहीं भी।

A one (ए वन) ***adj.*** first rate, सर्वोत्तम।

aorta (एओर्टा) ***n.*** the great artery, महाधमनी।

apace (एपेस) ***adv.*** swiftly, तेज़ी से।

apart (एपार्ट) ***adv.*** 1. at a distance, (से) दूर। 2. away from one another, एक-दूसरे से दूर। 3. to one side, aside, अलग, एक तरफ़। 4. separately, से अलग। 5. in or into pieces, अलग-अलग। □ **apart from**, के अलावा, के अतिरिक्त।

apartheid (एपार्टहेड) ***n.*** a policy of racial segregation, रंगभेद।

apartment (एपार्टमेंट) ***n.*** a suit of rooms for a family, परिवार-कक्ष, परिकक्ष।

apathetic (ऐपेथेटिक) ***adj.*** indifferent, lacking interest, उदासीन।

apathy (ऐपेथी) ***n.*** indifference, lack of interest, उदासीनता।

ape (एप) ***n.*** a tailless chimpanzee, gorilla or gibbon, पुच्छविहीन बनमानुस। ***v.*** to imitate or mimic, नकल करना या उतारना।

aperture (ऐपर्चर) ***n.*** an opening or hole, सुराख़, छेद।

apex (एपेक्स) ***n.*** a peak, चोटी।

apiary (एपिअरी) ***n.*** a place for raising bees for honey, मधुमक्खी-वाटिका।

apiece (एपीस) ***adv.*** for, to or from each one, एक-एक के विचार से।

apish (एपिश) ***adj.*** 1. like an ape, बनमानुस या वानर का-सा, वानरी। 2. imitative, नकलची। 3. silly, मूर्ख।

aplomb (एप्लॉम) ***n.*** self-confidence, आत्मविश्वास।

apocalypse (एपॉकेलिप्स) ***n.*** a prophetic revelation, पैगंबर या देवदूत द्वारा रहस्योद्घाटन।

Apollo (अपोलो) ***n.*** the sun god, सूर्यदेव।

apologetic (एपॉलोजेटिक) ***adj.*** making excuses, क्षमासूचक।

apologize (एपॉलोजाइज़) ***v.*** to make an apology, माफ़ी माँगना, क्षमा माँगना।

apology (एपॉलोजी) ***n.*** a statement or expression of regret, क्षमा, माफ़ी।

apoplexy (ऐपोप्लेक्सी) ***n.*** sudden loss of consciousness, मूर्च्छा, मिर्गी।

apostasy (एपॉस्टेसी) ***n.*** 1. abandonment of one's religion, party or principle, धर्मत्याग, दल त्याग,

सिद्धांत का त्याग।

apostle, Apostle (अपॉसल) ***n.*** any of the disciples sent out by Christ to teach the gospel, येशु का कोई धर्मप्रचारक शिष्य।

apostrophe (एपॉस्ट्रॉफ़ी) ***n.*** the sign used to indicate the possessive case, संबंधकारक का सूचक चिह्न ('), लोपक।

apotheosis (एपॉथिओसिस) ***n.*** an act of attributing of divinity to a human being, मनुष्य में देवत्व का आरोपण, देवत्वीकरण।

appal, appall (एपैल) ***v.*** 1. to dismay, हताश कर देना। 2. to horrify, दहला देना।

appalling ***adj.*** shocking, दहला देनेवाला। 2. unpleasant, अप्रिय।

apparatus (ऐपेरेटस) ***n.*** an equipment or instrument, उपकरण।

apparel (एपैरल) ***n.*** clothing or garments, पोशाक, पहनावा।

apparent (एपैरेन्ट) ***adj.*** 1. evident, स्पष्ट, प्रत्यक्ष, प्रकट। 2. not real, ऊपरी, दिखावटी।

apparently ***adv.*** 1. clearly, स्पष्टत:। 2. outwardly, बाहर से, ऊपर-ऊपर से।

apparition (एपैरिशन) ***n.*** a ghost, प्रेत, भूत।

appeal (एपील) ***v.*** 1. to make an earnest request, निवेदन करना, अपील करना। 2. to be attractive or interesting, आकृष्ट या आकर्षित करना। 3. to carry to a higher court अपील करना। ***n.*** 1. an earnest request, अपील, निवेदन। 2. attraction, आकर्षण, खिंचाव।

appealing ***adj.*** attractive, आकर्षक।

appear (अपिअर) ***v.*** 1. to come into view, सामने आना, प्रकट होना, दिखाई पड़ना। 2. to seem, प्रतीत होना, जान् पड़ना, लगना। 3. to sit (in an examination, परीक्षा में) बैठना।

appearance (अपिअरैन्स) ***n.*** 1. an act of appearing, आविर्भाव, प्रकटीकरण। 2. presence, उपस्थिति, हाज़िरी, पेशी। 3. outward aspect of anything, बाह्य रूप, शक्ल।

appease (एपीज़) ***v.*** 1. to pacify, समझा-बुझाकर शांत करना, प्रशमित करना। 2. to placate by granting demands, तुष्टीकरण करना।

appeasement (एपीज़मेन्ट) ***n.*** 1. the act of pacifying or appeasing, प्रशमन। 2. the act of placating, तुष्टीकरण।

appellant (एपेलैन्ट) ***n.*** one who makes an appeal, अपीलकर्ता।

appellate (एपेलेट) ***adj.*** 1. pertaining to appeal, अपील-संबंधी।2. having authority to hear appeals, जिसे अपील सुनने का अधिकार हो।

append (एपैन्ड) ***v.*** 1. to attach, संलग्न या नत्थी करना, टाँकना। 2. to add at the end, अंत में जोड़ना।

appendage (एपैन्डिज) ***n.*** something attached to a larger entity, संलग्न वस्तु।

appendicitis (एपैन्डिसाइटिस) ***n.*** inflamation of the appendix, उपांत्र-शोथ।

appendix (एपैन्डिक्स) ***n.*** 1. a tube like outgrowth near the large intestine, उपांत्र। 2. a supplement, परिशिष्ट।

appertain (ऐपर्टेन) ***v.*** to belong संबद्ध होना।

appetite (ऐपिटाइट) ***n.*** a desire for food, भूख, क्षुधा।

appetizer (ऐपिटाइज़र) ***n.*** anything

that stimulates the appetite, क्षुधावर्धक पदार्थ।

applaud (एप्लॉड) ***v.*** to express approval of something by clapping one's hands, तालियाँ बजाकर हर्ष या प्रसन्नता व्यक्त करना।

applause (एप्लॉज) ***n.*** 1. hand-clapping, करतलध्वनि, तालियाँ। 2. approval loudly expressed, वाहवाह, वाहवाही।

apple (ऐपल) ***n.*** a tree and its fruit, सेब।

appliance (एप्लाइएन्स) ***n.*** a domestic instrument or device, घरेलू उपकरण।

applicable (ऐप्लिकेबल) ***adj.*** appropriate, उपयुक्त।

applicant (ऐप्लिकेन्ट) ***n.*** one who applies, आवेदक, प्रार्थी।

application (ऐप्लिकेशन) ***n.*** 1. the act of applying, आवेदन। 2. a letter for applying something, आवेदन-पत्र। 3. the putting of anything to use, प्रयोग, अनुप्रयोग। 4. diligence, लगन, अध्यवसाय।

applied (ऐप्लाइड) ***adj.*** 1. put to practical use, अनुप्रयुक्त। 2. practical, व्यावहारिक, प्रायोगिक।

apply (ऐप्लाई) ***v.*** 1. to put one thing into contact with another, लगाना, सटाना, टाँकना। 2. to bring into use, इस्तेमाल करना। 3. to make a formal request, आवेदन-पत्र भेजना।

appoint (एपॉइन्ट) ***v.*** 1. to nominate, नियुक्त करना, रखना। 2. to fix, नियत करना।

appointed ***adj.*** 1. fixed, नियत, निश्चित। 2. nominated, नियुक्त।

appointment (एपॉइन्टमेन्ट) ***n.*** 1. the act of appointing, नियुक्ति। 2. an arrangement for meeting at a given time at a particular place, ठहराव, अप्वाइन्टमेंट।

apposite (ऐपॉज़िट) ***adj.*** suitable उपयुक्त।

apposition (ऐपॉजिशन) ***n.*** an explanatory word or phrase that follows a word of same grammatical construction, समानाधिकरण।

appraise (एप्रेज़) ***v.*** to fix a price for, दाम निश्चित करना, दाम लगाना।

appreciable (एप्रीशेबल) ***adj.*** sufficient to be easily noticed or measured, बुद्धि-ग्राह्य, स्पष्ट या आँकने योग्य।

appreciate (एप्रीशिएट) ***v.*** 1. to esteem highly, to praise, प्रशंसा या कद्र करना। 2. to understand, समझना। 3. to rise in value, दाम बढ़ना।

appreciation (एप्रीशिएशन) ***n.*** 1. the ability to perceive qualities, merits etc, गुणग्राहकता। 2. understanding, समझ, बोध। 3. increase or rise in value, मूल्यवृद्धि।

apprehend (ऐप्रिहेन्ड) ***v.*** 1. to arrest, गिरफ़्तार कर लेना। 2. to understand, समझना। 3. to fear, डरना, भयभीत होना।

apprehension (ऐप्रिहेन्शन) ***n.*** 1. the act of arresting, गिरफ़्तारी। 2. anxiety, आशंका। 3. understanding, समझ, बोध।

apprehensive ***adj.*** fearful, भयभीत।

apprentice (एप्रेन्टिस) ***n.*** a person who is working under another person in order to learn a trade or craft, काम सीखनेवाला व्यक्ति, शिक्षु। ***v.*** to work as an apprentice, काम सीखना।

A

apprenticeship (एप्रेन्टिसशिप) ***n.*** 1. the status of an apprentice, शिक्षुता। 2. the time during which one works as an apprentice, शिक्षुता-काल।

apprise (एप्राइज़) ***v.*** to inform, जानकारी कराना/देना।

approach (एप्रोच) ***v.*** to come near to, पास जाना, पहुँचना। ***n.*** 1. the act of approaching, पहुँच। 2. means of access, पहुँच, पैठ।

approachable (एप्रोचेबल) ***adj.*** 1. that can be approached, जिस तक पहुँचा जा सके, सुगम्य। 2. friendly, मिलनसार, मैत्रीपूर्ण।

approbation (एप्रोबेशन) ***n.*** approval, अनुमोदन, स्वीकृति।

appropriate (एप्रोप्रिएट) ***adj.*** specially suitable, proper, समुचित।

appropriation (एप्रोप्रिएशन) ***n.*** 1. money set aside for a special purpose, विनियोग। 2. the act of using, उपयोग।

approval (एप्रूवल) ***n.*** the act of approving, अनुमोदन, मंज़ूरी, स्वीकृति।

approve (एप्रूव) ***v.*** 1. to consider as good, ठीक समझना, स्वीकृति देना, पसंद कर लेना। 2. to confirm authoritatively, अनुमोदित करना, स्वीकृति देना, मंज़ूरी देना।

approver (एप्रूवर) ***n.*** a person who confesses offence and who turns state's evidence, इक़बाली गवाह।

approximate (एप्रॉक्सिमेट) ***adj.*** nearly accurate, लगभग, क़रीब-क़रीब। ***v.*** to come close to, लगभग होना, क़रीब होना।

approximately ***adv.*** nearly, लगभग।

apricot (ऐप्रिकॉट) ***n.*** a tree and its fruit, ख़ुबानी।

April (एप्रिल) ***n.*** the fourth month of the year, अप्रैल।

April fool ***n.*** a victim of jokes on 1st April, एप्रिल फ़ूल।

apron (एप्रन) ***n.*** a garment worn in front of the body to protect the clothing, अग्रवस्त्र, एप्रन।

apt (ऐप्ट) ***adj.*** appropriate, उपयुक्त।

aptitude (ऐप्टिट्यूड) ***n.*** a natural tendency or inclination, रुझान, अभिवृत्ति।

aptly ***adv.*** ably, योग्यतापूर्वक।

aqua (ऐक्वा) ***n.*** water, पानी, जल।

aquarium (एक्वेरिअम) ***n.*** an artificial pond for keeping fish and other water animals and plants, जलजीवशाला।

Aquarius (एक्वेरिअस) ***n.*** a sign of the zodiac, कुंभ राशि।

aquatic (एक्वैटिक) ***adj.*** living in the water, जल में होने या रहनेवाला, जलीय।

aquatics (एक्वैटिक्स) ***n.*** (plu.) aquatic sports, पानी के खेल, जल-क्रीड़ाएँ।

aqueduct (ऐक्विडक्ट) ***n.*** an artificial channel, कृत्रिम जलमार्ग, नाली, मोरी।

aqueous (एक्विअस) ***adj.*** of water, watery, जलीय।

aquiline (ऐक्विलाइन) ***adj.*** curved like an eagle's beak, गरुड़ की चोंच की तरह टेढ़ा, गरुड़ीय।

Arab (ऐरब) ***n.*** a native of Arabia, अरबवासी।

arabesque (ऐरेबेस्क) ***n.*** an ornamental design of interwoven flowers and leaves, बेल-बूटों का काम, गुलकारी।

Arabia (एरेबिआ) ***n.*** a peninsula between the Red sea and the Persian Gulf, अरब।

Arabian (एरेबिअन) ***adj.*** 1. of Arabia,

अरब-संबंधी। 2. of Arabs, अरबों का।

Arabic (ऐरेबिक) ***adj.*** of the Arabs or their language, अरबी।

arable (ऐरेबल) ***adj.*** fit for tillage, जोतने-बोने लायक।

arbiter (आर्बिटर) ***n.*** an arbitrator, मध्यस्थ, पंच।

arbitrary (आर्बिट्रेरी) ***adj.*** 1. based on one's whims, मनमाना, यादृच्छिक। 2. despotic, स्वेच्छाचारी, निरंकुश।

arbitrate (आर्बिट्रेट) ***v.*** to mediate, मध्यस्थता करना।

arbitration (आर्बिट्रेशन) ***n.*** 1. the act of arbitrating, मध्यस्थता। 2. the verdict of arbitrators, पंच-निर्णय।

arbitrator (आर्बिट्रेटर) ***n.*** one who arbitrates, मध्यस्थ, पंच।

arboreal (आर्बोरिअल) ***adj.*** 1. of or pertaining to trees, वृक्ष-संबंधी, वृक्षीय। 2. living in trees, वृक्षों पर रहनेवाला।

arbour, arbor (आर्बर) ***n.*** 1. a shaded retreat, bower, लतामंडप, कुंज। 2. a hut made of leaves, पर्णशाला, पर्णकुटी।

arc (आर्क) ***n.*** a curved line or object, चाप।

arcade (आर्केड) ***n.*** a covered passage, आच्छादित मार्ग, ढकी गली।

arcane (आर्केन) ***adj.*** secret, mysterious, गुप्त, रहस्यमय।

arch (आर्च) ***n.*** 1. any structure shaped like a curve, तोरण, मेहराब। 2. an arc, चाप। ***v.*** to build an arch over, मेहराब बनाना, तोरण बनाना। ***adj.*** 1. chief, मुख्य, प्रधान। 2. wicked, दुष्ट, धूर्त।

archaeological (आर्किऑलोजिकल) of archaeology, पुरातत्त्व-संबंधी, पुरातात्त्विक।

archaeologist (आर्किऑलोजिस्ट) ***n.*** an expert in archaeology, पुरातत्त्ववेत्ता।

archaeology (आर्किऑलोजी) ***n.*** the scientific study of cultural remains of the remote past, पुरातत्त्व।

archaic (आर्केइक) ***adj.*** 1. belonging to the ancient times, आर्ष, पुराकालीन।

archbishop (आर्चबिशप) ***n.*** a chief bishop of a diocese, आर्चबिशप।

arch enemy ***n.*** the chief enemy, घोर शत्रु।

archer (आर्चर) ***n.*** one who shoots with bow and arrow, धनुर्धारी।

archery (आर्चरी) ***n.*** an art of shooting with bows and arrows, धनुर्विद्या।

archipelago (आर्किपेलगो) ***n.*** a group of island, द्वीपसमूह, द्वीपपुंज।

architect (आर्किटेक्ट) ***n.*** an expert in designing the buildings, वास्तुकार, वास्तुविद्।

architectural (आर्किटेक्चरल) ***adj.*** of or related to architecture, वास्तु-संबंधी।

architecture (आर्किटेक्चर) ***n.*** the art or science of designing buildings, वास्तुविद्या।

archives (आर्काइव्ज़) ***n.*** (pl.) a place where historical documents are kept and preserved, अभिलेखागार, पुरालेखागार।

Arctic (आर्कटिक) ***adj.*** pertaining to the North Pole, उत्तरध्रुवीय।

ardent (आर्डेन्ट) ***adj.*** enthusiastic, उत्साही।

ardour (आर्डर) ***n.*** 1. enthusiasm, उत्साह, उमंग। 2. passion, लगन।

arduous (आर्डुअस) ***adj.*** difficult, कठिन, मुश्किल।

are (आर) ***v.*** plural present tense

A

A

of be, हैं।

area (एरिआ) ***n.*** 1. total space, क्षेत्रफल। 2. a particular extent of surface, क्षेत्र, भूभाग। 3. the field of an activity, कार्यक्षेत्र, कर्मक्षेत्र।

arena (एरीना) ***n.*** 1. a raised platform where people wrestle, अखाड़ा, मल्लभूमि। 2. a battlefield, युद्धभूमि।

argue (आर्ग्यू) ***v.*** 1. to give a reason, तर्क या दलील देना। 2. to debate, तर्क-वितर्क करना।

argument (आर्ग्युमेन्ट) ***n.*** 1. a statement for or against a proposition, तर्क, दलील, युक्ति। 2. a quarrel, झगड़ा, विवाद।

arid (ऐरिड) ***adj.*** dry, सूखा।

Aries (एअरीज़) ***n.*** a sign of the zodiac, मेष राशि।

aright (एराइट) ***adv.*** rightly, ठीक, ठीक से।

arise (एराइज़) ***v.*** (arose, arisen) 1. to get up, जागना, उठना। 2. to come into being, अस्तित्व में आना।

aristocracy (ऐरिस्टॉक्रेसी) ***n.*** 1. rich classes, कुलीन वर्ग, अभिजात वर्ग। 2. the government by such a class, कुलीन तंत्र, अभिजात तंत्र।

aristocrat (ऐरिस्टॉक्रेट) ***n.*** a member of an upper class, अभिजात, कुलीन।

aristocratic ***adj.*** 1. pertaining to the aristocracy, अभिजातीय, कुलीन। 2. refined, सुसंस्कृत, शिष्ट।

arithmetic (ऐरिथ्मेटिक) ***n.*** the science of numbers, अंकगणित, हिसाब।

arm[1] (आर्म) ***n.*** 1. either of the two upper limbs of a human body from the shoulder to the hand, बाँह, भुजा। 2. forelimb of a vertebrate animal, अगली टाँग, बाँह। 3. a sleeve, कमीज़, कुरते आदि की बाँह।

arm[2] ***n.*** a weapon, शस्त्र, हथियार। ***v.*** 1. to supply arms, शस्त्रों की पूर्ति करना। 2. to equip with arms, शस्त्र-सज्जित करना।

armada (आर्माडा) ***n.*** a fleet of warships, युद्धपोतों का बेड़ा।

armament (आर्ममेन्ट) ***n.*** 1. the process of arming or equipping for the war, शस्त्रीकरण, शस्त्रसज्जा, हथियारबंदी।

armature (आर्मेचर) ***n.*** the revolving part of an electric motor wound with coils, आर्मेचर।

armchair (आर्मचेअर) ***n.*** a chair with supports for arms, बाँहदार कुर्सी।

armed (आर्म्ड) ***adj.*** having an arm or arms, सशस्त्र।

armistice (आर्मिस्टिस) ***n.*** truce, युद्धविराम, विराम-संधि।

armlet (आर्मलिट) ***n.*** an ornament worn around the upper arm, बाजूबंद।

armour, armor (आर्मर) ***n.*** a protective covering for the body worn by medieval warriors, कवच, बख़्तर।

armoured, armored (आर्मर्ड) ***adj.*** equipped or covered with armour, बख़्तरबंद।

armoury, armory (आर्मरी) ***n.*** a store house for weapons, शस्त्रागार।

armpit (आर्मपिट) ***n.*** the hollow under the arm below the shoulder, काँख, बगल।

arms (आर्म्स) ***n.*** weapons collectively, अस्त्र-शस्त्र, आयुध, हथियार।

arms race ***n.*** the competition

A

among nations in accumulating arms, शस्त्रों की होड़।

army (आर्मी) ***n.*** 1. organised body of soldiers, सेना, फौज़। 2. any large body of people, सेना, फौज़।

aroma (एरोमा) ***n.*** fragrance, सुगंध।

aromatic (ऐरोमेटिक) ***adj.*** fragrant, सुगंधित।

arose (एरोज़) ***v.*** p. t. of arise.

around (एराउन्ड) ***adv.*** 1. on all sides, चारों ओर। 2. in all directions, चारों दिशाओं में। 3. nearby, आसपास। 4. nearly, about, लगभग। ***prep.*** 1. on all sides of, के चारों तरफ़। 2. in all directions, सभी दिशाओं में।

arouse (एराउज़) ***v.*** 1. to awaken, जगाना या जागना। 2. to stir up, उद्वेलित करना।

arrange (एरेन्ज) ***v.*** 1. to put into a proper order, व्यवस्थित करना। 2. to make preparations in advance, तैयारी करना।

arrangement (एरेन्जमेन्ट) ***n.*** 1. the act of arranging or being arranged, व्यवस्था, प्रबंध। 2. a preparation, तैयारी, आयोजन।

arrant (ऐरेन्ट) ***adj.*** out and out, पूरा, पक्का।

array (एरे) ***v.*** 1. to put in order, व्यवस्थित करना, क्रम से रखना। 2. to marshal troops, व्यूह-रचना करना। 3. to adorn, सजाना। ***n.*** 1. arrangement, व्यवस्था, आयोजन। 2. an ordered force or army, व्यूह-रचना।

arrears (एरिअर्ज़) ***n.*** (plu.) overdue debts, बकाया, बाकी, शेष।

arrest (अरेस्ट) ***v.*** 1. to take into custody by the police, गिरफ़्तार करना। 2. to stop or check, रोकना। ***n.*** the act of arresting, गिरफ़्तारी।

arrival (एराइवल) ***n.*** 1. act of arriving, आगमन, पहुँच। 2. a thing person who arrives, आगंतुक, आवक।

arrive (एराइव) ***v.*** to reach, to come, पहुँचना, आना।

arrogance (ऐरोगेन्स) ***n.*** haughtiness, अक्खड़पन, घमंड।

arrogant (ऐरोगेन्ट) ***adj.*** haughty, अक्खड़, घमंडी।

arrow (ऐरो) ***n.*** a pointed shaft to be shot from a bow, तीर, बाण।

arsenal (आर्सनल) ***n.*** a place for making or storing weapons and other munitions, शस्त्रागार।

arsenic (आर्सनिक) ***n.*** a kind of very poisonous chemical element, संखिया।

arson (आर्सन) ***n.*** the intentional act of setting fire to property, आगज़नी।

arsonist (आर्सनिस्ट) ***n.*** a person guilty of arson, आग लगानेवाला।

art (आर्ट) ***n.*** 1. the activity of creating beautiful or artistic things, कला। 2. skill, knack, कौशल। 3. cunning, चालाकी।

arterial (आर्टिरिअल) ***adj.*** pertaining to an artery, धमनी-संबंधी।

artery (आर्टरी) ***n.*** any of the tubes carrying blood from the heart to all parts of the body, धमनी, नस।

artful (आर्टफ़ुल) ***adj.*** crafty, धूर्त।

arthritls (आर्थ्राइटिस) ***n.*** a disease of the joints, गठिया, जोड़ों का दर्द।

article (आर्टिकल) ***n.*** 1. a particular thing, item, वस्तु, चीज़। 2. a piece of writing, लेख, रचना। 3. a separate clause in an agreement, अनुबंध की धारा, अनुच्छेद, उपपद। 4. a class of words, the words a, an and the, प्रविशेषण।

articulate (आर्टिक्यूलेट) ***v.*** to pronounce, उच्चारण करना। ***adj.*** distinct, सुस्पष्ट।

artifice (आर्टिफ़िस) 1. deception, चालाकी। 2. a device, युक्ति।

artificial (आर्टिफ़िशल) ***adj.*** 1. not natural, कृत्रिम, मनुष्य-निर्मित। 2. imitated, नकली।

artillery (आर्टिलरी) ***n.*** 1. large guns and cannons, तोपों का समूह। 2. troops armed with cannons, तोपख़ाना।

artisan (आर्टिज़न) ***n.*** a craftsman, शिल्पी।

artist (आर्टिस्ट) ***n.*** one who practises or works in one of the Fine Arts, कलाकार। 2. an expert in painting, चित्रकार। 3. a professional entertainer, कलाकार, अदाकार।

artistic (आर्टिस्टिक) ***adj.*** showing skill and good taste, कलापूर्ण, कलात्मक।

artless (आर्टलिस) ***adj.*** lacking artfulness, भोला-भाला, सीधा, सीधा-सादा।

arts (आर्ट्स) ***n.*** (plu.) imaginative and creative branches of knowledge other than scientific, कलाएँ।

as (ऐज़) ***conj.*** 1. while, जैसे ही। 2. in the way that, like, की तरह। 3. because, क्योंकि। 4. equally, के समान, के बराबर। 5. for example, उदाहरण के लिए। ***adv.*** 1. not differently from, उसी तरह। 2. as before, पहले ही की तरह।

ascend (एसेन्ड) ***v.*** 1. to go up, ऊपर उठना। 2. to climb up, चढ़ना।

ascendancy, ascendency (एसेन्डेन्सी) ***n.*** controlling power, प्रभुत्व, आधिपत्य।

ascendant, ascendent (एसेन्डेन्ट) ***adj.*** rising, आरोही, उदीयमान।

ascent (एसेन्ट) ***n.*** 1. act of ascending, आरोहण। 2. advancement, उन्नति। 3. slope leading upward, चढ़ाई।

ascertain (ऐसर्टेन) ***v.*** to find out, पता लगना।

ascetic (ऐसेटिक) ***n.*** a religious person who practises rigid self-denial, संन्यासी, तपस्वी।

ascribe (एस्क्राइब) ***v.*** to attribute to, का कारण बताना, का श्रेय देना, के नाम से जोड़ना।

aseptic (एसेप्टिक) ***adj.*** free from bacteria, रोगाणुरहित।

ash (ऐश) ***n.*** the grey powder that remains after something has burned, राख, भस्म।

ashamed (एशेम्ड) ***adj.*** feeling or showing shame, लज्जित, शर्मिंदा।

ashes (ऐशिज़) ***n.*** (plu.) human remains after cremation, अस्थियाँ।

ashore (एशोर) ***adv.*** on the shore, किनारे।

ashtray (ऐशट्रे) ***n.*** a small receptacle for tobacco ashes, राखदानी।

Asian (एशिअन) ***adj.*** of Asia or its people, एशियाई। ***n.*** a native of Asia, एशियावासी।

aside (एसाइड) ***adv.*** 1. to one side, एक तरफ़, किनारे, दूर। 2. apart, अलग, पृथक्।

asinine (ऐसिनाइन) ***adj.*** 1. like an ass, गधे जैसा। 2. stupid, मूर्ख।

ask (आस्क) ***v.*** 1. to put a question to, प्रश्न करना। 2. to enquire, पूछना। 3. to make a request, कहना, निवेदन

astronaut (एस्ट्रोनॉट) ***n.*** a crew member of the spaceship, अंतरिक्ष-यात्री।

astronomer (एस्ट्रॉनोमर) ***n.*** an expert in astronomy, खगोलज्ञ, खगोलवेत्ता।

astronomy (एस्ट्रॉनोमी) ***n.*** the science dealing with the movements of stars, खगोल विज्ञान।

astute (एस्ट्यूट) ***adj.*** shrewd, होशियार।

asunder (एसन्डर) ***adv.*** 1. apart, अलग-अलग। 2. into pieces, टुकड़े-टुकड़े।

asylum (एसाइलम) ***n.*** 1. a place of refuge, शरणस्थान। 2. refuge, protection, शरण, पनाह, संरक्षण।

at (ऐट) ***prep.*** में, पर, के ऊपर।

atheism (एथिइज़्म) ***n.*** the disbelief in the existence of a God, अनीश्वरवाद।

atheist (एथिइस्ट) ***n.*** one who does not believe in the existence of a God, अनीश्वरवादी।

athlete (ऐथ्लीट्) ***n.*** one who is skilled in athletics, एथलीट, व्यायामी।

athletic (ऐथ्लेटिक) ***adj.*** 1. of athletics, खेलकूद या व्यायाम-संबंधी। 2. muscular in built, हृष्ट-पुष्ट।

athletics (ऐथ्लेटिक्स) ***n.*** physical exercises and sports, व्यायाम और खेलकूद।

at-home ***n.*** a reception for visitors, प्रीतिगोष्ठी।

atlas (ऐटलस) ***n.*** a book of maps, मानचित्रावली, एटलस।

atmosphere (ऐट्मॉस्फ़िअर) ***n.*** 1. the gaseous mass surrounding the earth, पर्यावरण। 2. a feeling or psychological environment, वातावरण।

atmospheric (ऐट्मॉस्फेरिक) ***adj.*** of or pertaining to the atmosphere, पर्यावरण-संबंधी।

atom (ऐटम) ***n.*** 1. a smallest particle of an element, परमाणु। 2. a very small quantity of a thing, अणु, कण।

atomic (एटॉमिक) ***adj.*** of or pertaining to an atom, परमाणविक, परमाणु-संबंधी।

at once ***adv.*** immediately, तुरंत, तत्काल।

atone (एटोन) ***v.*** 1. to make amends, प्रायश्चित्त करना। 2. to repay, क्षतिपूर्ति करना।

atop (एटॉप) ***adj.& adv.*** at or on the top, ऊपर, ऊपरी। ***prep.*** on the top of, के ऊपर।

atrocious (एट्रोशस) 1. extremely wicked, दुष्ट या दुष्टतापूर्ण। 2. brutal, नृशंस, निर्मम। 3. very bad or disgusting, बुरा, कोफ़्त-भरा।

atrocity (एट्रॉसिटी) ***n.*** 1. a wicked act, दुष्टता। 2. brutality, बर्बरता, नृशंसता। 3. tyranny, अत्याचार।

attach (एटैच) ***v.*** 1. to join, fasten or fix, जुड़ना या जोड़ना। 2. to seize or to be seized by the legal authority, जब्त करना या होना। 3. to attribute or to be attributed, आरोपित होना या करना।

attache (एटैशे) ***n.*** an officer attached with an ambassador, राजदूत-सहायक।

attached (एटैच्ड) ***adj.*** 1. fastened on, लगा, सटा या बँधा हुआ। 2. bound by affection, अनुरक्त, आसक्त।

attachment (एटैच्मेंट) ***n.*** 1. affection, आसक्ति, लगाव। 2. legal seizure of property, कुर्की।

attack (एटैक) ***v.*** to act violently against, आक्रमण करना, भर्त्सना करना। ***n.*** 1. an act of violence, आक्रमण। 2. a sudden on- set of illness, दौरा।

A

attain (एटेन) ***v.*** to succeed in getting (something, कुछ) प्राप्त करना, पाना।

attainable (एटेनेबल) ***adj.*** that can be attained, प्राप्य।

attainment (एटेनमेन्ट) ***n.*** achievement, सफलता, उपलब्धि।

attempt (एटेम्ट) ***v.*** to try, प्रयास करना। ***n.*** an effort, प्रयास।

attend (एटेन्ड) ***v.*** 1. to pay attention, ध्यान देना। 2. to look after, देख-रेख करना, टहल करना। 3. to be present at, उपस्थित होना।

attendance (एटेन्डेन्स) ***n.*** the act of being present, उपस्थिति, हाज़िरी।

attendant (एटेन्डेन्ट) ***n.*** a person who is employed to look after, परिचारक, सेवक।

attention (एटेन्शन) ***n.*** 1. applying one's mind to something, ध्यान। 2. care, consideration, ध्यान, देख-रेख। 3. a soldier's erect motionless posture of readiness, सावधान होने की अवस्था, अवधान। 4. (plu.) act of courtesy, शिष्टाचार, आदर-सम्मान।

attentive (एटेन्टिव) ***adj.*** 1. listening attentively, सावधान। 2. paying attention, watchful, सतर्क, चौकस। 3. showing courtesy to someone, शिष्टता दिखलानेवाला।

attest (अटेस्ट) ***v.*** to certify by signing as a witness, अनुप्रमाणित/तसदीक करना।

attestation (एटेस्टेशन) ***n.*** verification of someone's signature, अनुप्रमाणन, तसदीक।

attic (ऐटिक) ***n.*** the space or room directly below the roof, परछत्ती, मियानी।

attire (एटाइर) ***n.*** clothes, पोशाक, कपड़े।

attitude (ऐटिट्यूड) ***n.*** mental disposition, रुख, अभिवृत्ति, मानसिकता।

attorney (एटोर्नी) ***n.*** a properly qualified legal agent, न्यायवादी, अटॉर्नी।

attract (एट्रैक्ट) ***v.*** 1. to cause to draw near, खींचना, आकृष्ट करना। 2. to allure, मुग्ध करना, लुभा लेना।

attraction (एट्रैक्शन) ***n.*** 1. the act of attracting, आकर्षण, खिंचाव। 2. anything that attracts attention, आकर्षक पदार्थ या व्यक्ति।

attractive (एट्रैक्टिव) ***adj.*** pleasing in appearance or effect, आकर्षक, लुभावना।

attribute (एट्रिब्यूट) ***v.*** to ascribe, (का) कारण बताना, (के) नाम से जोड़ना, (को) श्रेय देना। ***n.*** a characteristic quality, लक्षण, विशेषता, गुण।

attributive (एट्रिब्यूटिव) ***n.*** an adjective विशेषण।

attrition (एट्रिशन) ***n.*** the act of wearing away or the state of being worn away, छीजना, घर्षण, रगड़, घिसाई।

attune (एट्यून) ***v.*** 1. to bring into musical accord, सुर मिलाना। 2. to adapt or adjust, अनुकूल करना, समंजित करना।

auction (ऑक्शन) ***n.*** a public sale of goods to the highest bidder, नीलाम। ***v.*** to sell by auction, नीलाम करना।

auctioneer (ऑक्शनिअर) ***n.*** one who conducts an auction, नीलामकर्ता।

audacious (ऑडेशस) ***adj.*** bold or daring, दुस्साहसी, दबंग।

audacity (ऑडैसिटी) ***n.*** the quality of being audacious, दुस्साहस।

audible (ऑडिबल) ***adj.*** capable of

being heard, कर्णगोचर, श्रव्य।

audience (ऑडिएन्स) ***n.*** a gathering of listeners or spectators, श्रोतागण, दर्शकगण।

audio (ऑडिओ) ***adj.*** of or relating to sound or hearing, श्रव्य।

audit (ऑडिट) ***n.*** official examination of accounts, लेखा-परीक्षण। ***v.*** to examine acounts officially, लेखा-परीक्षण करना।

audition (ऑडिशन) ***n.*** a trial to test the ability of a performer, अदाकारी परीक्षण।

auditor (ऑडिटर) ***n.*** a qualified person whose business is to check account or account books, लेखा-परीक्षक।

auditorium (ऑडिटोरिअम) ***n.*** a public hall or theatre in which the audience sits, प्रेक्षागृह, प्रेक्षागार।

auger (ऑगर) ***n.*** a tool for boring holes in wood, बरमा, गिरमिट।

augment (ऑगमेन्ट) ***v.*** to increase, वृद्धि करना या होना।

augur (ऑगर) ***v.*** to serve as an omen of, शकुन होना।

augury (ऑग्यूरी) ***n.*** prediction, भविष्य-कथन, भविष्यवाणी।

August (ऑगस्ट) ***n.*** the eighth month of the year, अगस्त।

august ***adj.*** imposing, majestic, भव्य, राजसी।

aunt (ऑन्ट) ***n.*** the sister of one's father or mother, बुआ, मौसी, आन्टी।

aura (औरा) ***n.*** a faintly shining shadow that surrounds the human body, प्रभा-मंडल।

aurora (औरोरा) ***n.*** bands of many coloured light seen at night in polar regions, ध्रुव ज्योति।

auspice (ऑस्पिस) ***n.*** (plu.) patronage, संरक्षण। ☐ **under the auspices of**, किसी के संरक्षण या तत्त्वावधान में।

auspicious (ऑस्पिशस) ***adj.*** of good omen, शुभ,मंगलकारक।

Aussie (ऑसी) ***n.*** an Australian, आस्ट्रेलियावासी।

austere (ऑस्टिअर) ***adj.*** 1. very simple, plain, सीधा-सादा, सादा, सादगी-भरा। 2. stern, कठोर।

austerity (ऑस्टेरिटी) ***n.*** 1. the state of being austere, सादगी, आडंबरहीनता; संयम। 2. severity, कठोरता।

authentic (ऑथेन्टिक) ***adj.*** genuine, real, वास्तविक, प्रामाणिक।

authenticate (ऑथेन्टिकेट) ***v.*** to prove something to the true, प्रामाणिकता सिद्ध करना।

author (ऑथर) ***n.*** a writer, लेखक।

authoritarian (ऑथॉरिटेरिअन) ***adj.*** despotic, निरंकुश।

authoritative (ऑथॉरिटेटिव) ***adj.*** official, आधिकारिक।

authority (ऑथॉरिटी) ***n.*** the person (or group) having right or power, प्राधिकारी, सत्ताधारी।

authorize (ऑथोराइज़) ***v.*** to give authority to, प्राधिकृत करना।

autobiography (ऑटोबाइयोग्राफ़ी) ***n.*** life of a person written by himself, आत्मकथा।

autocracy (ऑटोक्रेसी) ***n.*** 1. government by a single absolute ruler, तानाशाही, निरंकुश शासन।

autocrat (ऑटोक्रैट) ***n.*** an absolute ruler, तानाशाह, निरंकुश शासक।

autocratic (ऑटोक्रैटिक) ***adj.*** of or like

A

an autocrat, निरंकुश, तानाशाही।

autograph (ऑटोग्राफ़) ***n.*** a person's own signature, स्वहस्ताक्षर।

automatic (ऑटोमैटिक) ***adj.*** operating by itself, स्वचालित।

automobile (ऑटोमोबील) ***n.*** a motor vehicle, a car, कार, मोटरकार, मोटरगाड़ी।

autonomous (ऑटोनॉमस) ***adj.*** self-governing, स्वायत्त।

autonomy (ऑटोनॉमी) ***n.*** right of self-government, स्वायत्तता।

autopsy (ऑटोप्सी) ***n.***शव-परीक्षा, शव-परीक्षण।

autumn (ऑटम) ***n.*** the season between summer and winter, शरद् ऋतु, शरत्काल।

auxiliary (ऑग्ज़िल्यरी) ***adj.*** helping, supporting, सहायक; auxiliary verb, सहायक क्रिया।

avail (अवेल) ***v.*** to be of use, उपयोगी होना, काम आना।

available (अवेलेबल) ***adj.*** easy to get, at hand, उपलब्ध, सुलभ।

avalanche (ऐवेलान्श) ***n.*** a large mass of snow sliding down a mountain side, हिमस्खलन।

avarice (ऐवेरिस) ***n.*** excessive greed for wealth, धनलोलुपता।

avaricious (ऐवेरिशस) ***adj.*** greedy for wealth, धनलोलुप, लोभी।

avenge (एवेन्ज) ***v.*** to take revenge, बदला लेना। ***n.*** revenge, बदला।

avenue (ऐवेन्यू) ***n.*** a wide street, चौड़ा रास्ता।

average (ऐवरिज) ***n.*** normal amount, level, degree or quality, औसत। ***adj.*** of normal standard, औसत दर्जे का।

averse (एवर्स) ***adj.*** disinclined, विमुख।

aversion (एवर्ज़न) ***n.*** dislike, नफ़रत।

avert (एवर्ट) ***v.*** 1. to turn away, फेर लेना, घुमा लेना, मोड़ लेना। 2. to prevent from happening, रोकना, बचाना।

aviation (एविएशन) ***n.*** the art or science of flying aircraft, विमान चलाना।

aviator (एविएटर) ***n.*** a pilot of an aircraft, विमानचालक।

avocation (ऐवोकेशन) ***n.*** minor occupation, उपव्यवसाय, शगल।

avoid (एवॉइड) ***v.*** to keep away from, दूर रहना, बाज़ आना।

avoidable (एवॉइडेबल) ***adj.*** that can be avoided, परिहार्य।

avow (एवाउ) ***v.*** 1. to assert, दृढ़तापूर्वक कहना। 2. to confess, स्वीकार करना।

await (एवेट) ***v.*** to wait for, प्रतीक्षा करना।

awake (एवेक) ***v.*** (awoke / awaked, awaking) to wake, जागना या जगाना।

awaken (एवेकन) ***v.*** to awake, जागना या जगाना।

awakening ***n.*** the state of being awaken, जागृति।

award (एवार्ड) ***v.*** to give as a reward, पुरस्कार देना, इनाम देना। ***n.*** 1. something given as a reward, पुरस्कार, इनाम। 2. a court's decision, न्यायालय का निर्णय।

aware (एवेअर) ***adj.*** 1. having knowledge, अवगत। 2. having good understanding, समझदार।

awareness ***n.*** the state of being aware, जानकारी, ज्ञान।

away (एवे) ***adv.*** to another place, at a distance, दूर, परे।

awe (औ) ***n.*** a feeling of respect mixed with fear or wonder, दबदबा, रोब, संभ्रम, विस्मय। ***v.*** to fill with awe, दबदबे में आना, संभ्रमित हो जाना।

awesome (औसम) ***adj.*** causing feelings of awe, विस्मयकारी।

awful (ऑफुल) ***adj.*** terrible, shocking, भयावह, भयंकर।

awkward (ऑकवर्ड) ***adj.*** clumsy, भद्दा, बेढंगा।

awl (ऑल) ***n.*** a tool for making holes, सुआ।

awning (ऑनिंग) ***n.*** a covering (of canvas), सायबान, तिरपाल।

ax, axe (ऐक्स) ***n.*** a tool for cutting down trees, कुल्हाड़ी, कुठार।

axiom (ऐक्सिअम) ***n.*** maxim, सूक्ति।

axis (ऐक्सिस) ***n.*** a shaft or the (imaginary) straight line around which a body rotates, धुरी, अक्ष।

axle (ऐक्सल) ***n.*** a spindle on or with which a wheel revolves, धुरा, कीली।

azure (ऐज़्योर) ***adj.*** sky-blue, आसमानी।

B, b (बी) ***n.*** the second letter of the English alphabet, अंग्रेज़ी वर्णमाला का दूसरा वर्ण।

babble (बैबल) ***v.*** to utter meaningless sounds, बड़बड़ करना, बड़बड़ाना।

baboon (बैबून) ***n.*** a large African doglike monkey, अफ़्रीकी बंदर।

baby (बेबी) ***n.*** an infant, दूधपीता छोटा बच्चा, शिशु।

babysitter (बेबीसिटर) ***n.*** a person who takes care of babies, शिशु-सेवक।

bachelor (बैचलर) ***n.*** 1. an unmarried man, कुमार, कुँआरा लड़का। 2. the holder of a bachelor's degree, स्नातक।

bacillus (बैसिलस) ***n.*** (plu. bacilli) a rod like bacteria, दंडाणु।

back (बैक) ***n.*** 1. the part of the body from neck to hip, पीठ। 2. the part behind the front, पिछवाड़ा। ***v.*** 1. to move backward, पीछे हटना या हटाना, पीछे ले जाना या जाना। 2. to support, समर्थन करना, सहारा देना।

backbite ***v.*** to speak ill of others in their absence, चुगली खाना।

backbone ***n.*** the spine, रीढ़।

backdated ***adj.*** marked with previous date, पूर्व दिनांकित।

backdoor ***adj.*** secret, गुप्त।

backdrop ***n.*** a painted curtain hung at the back of the stage, पिछला परदा।

background ***n.*** 1. the back surface of a scene or picture, पृष्ठभूमि। 2. conditions and events forming a setting or influencing something, पृष्ठभूमि।

backing ***n.*** support, समर्थन।

backward (बैकवर्ड) ***adj.*** retarded in progress, पिछड़ा।

bacon (बेकन) ***n.*** salted or smoked meat of a pig, सुअर का भुना तथा नमकीन गोश्त।

bacteria (बैक्टीरिआ) ***n.*** plu. of bacterium, जीवाणु।

bad (बैड) ***adj.*** (worse, worst) 1. not good, बुरा, बद। 2. spoiled, बिगड़ा हुआ।

badge (बैज) ***n.*** an emblem worn to indicate rank, membership etc., बिल्ला, बैज।

badger (बैजर) ***n.*** a mammal who lives in holes, बिज्जू।

badly (बैडली) ***adv.*** in a bad manner, बुरी तरह।

badminton (बैडमिन्टन) ***n.*** a game played with shuttlecocks and rackets, बैडमिंटन।

bad-tempered (बैड-टेम्पर्ड) ***adj.*** showing bad temper, चिड़चिड़ा।

baffle (बैफ़ल) ***v.*** to puzzle, क्षुब्ध कर देना।

bag (बैग) ***n.*** 1. a flexible container, थैला, झोला। 2. a small box, पेटी। 3. a sack, बोरा, बोरी। 4. a purse, बटुआ, बैग। 5. a pouch in an animal's body, थैली।

baggage (बैगिज) ***n.*** luggage, असबाब, सामान।

bagpipe (बैगपाइप) ***n.*** a musical wind instrument, मशकबीन।

bail (बेल) ***v.*** to set free from custody on security for reappearance, ज़मानत मंजूर करना। ***n.*** 1. money or property pledged as security to get an arrested person released temporarily, ज़मानत। 2. one who provides bail, ज़मानतदार।

bailable (बेलेबल) ***adj.*** that can be released on bail, ज़मानत पर छूटने लायक।

bailiff (बेलिफ़) ***n.*** 1. an official who executes writs and arrests, बेलिफ़। 2. a steward, कारिंदा।

bait (बेट) ***n.*** 1. food used or animal placed to attract prey, चारा। 2. an enticement, प्रलोभन।

bake (बेक) ***v.*** 1. to cook in an oven, बेक करना, सेकना। 2. to be cooked in an oven, सिकना। 3. to cause to become hard by heating, पकाना। 4. to become hard by heat, पकना।

baker (बेकर) ***n.*** one who makes (or sells) bread, नानबाई, बेकर।

bakery (बेकरी) ***n.*** a place where bread is baked or sold, बेकरी।

balance (बैलेन्स) ***n.*** 1. the scales, तराज़ू। 2. any appara-tus for measuring weight, काँटा, तुलायंत्र, बैलंस। 3. a state of equilibrium, संतुलन, बराबरी। 4. a weight tending to produce equilibrium, पासंग। 5. an amount or anything that is left over, बाकी, शेष। ☐ **lose one's balance**, लड़खड़ा जाना, डगमगा जाना। ***v.*** to bring into equilibrium, संतुलित करना।

balance sheet ***n.*** a written statement of assets and liabilities, तुलनपत्र, पक्का चिट्ठा।

balcony (बैल्कनी) ***n.*** 1. an enclosed platform projecting outside an upper story of a building, छज्जा, बरामदा। 2. the seats upstairs in a theatre, बालकनी।

bald (बाल्ड) ***adj.*** 1. having no hair on the scalp, गंजा। 2. without vegetation, जो हरा-भरा न हो।

bale (बेल) ***n.*** a large bundle, गाँठ, गट्ठर, गट्ठा। ***v.*** to make into a bale, गाँठ या गट्ठर बाँधना।

baleful ***adj.*** harmful, हानिकर।

bale out ***v.*** to make a parachute jump from an aircraft, हवाई छतरी से उतरना या कूदना।

balk, baulk (बॉक) ***n.*** 1. a beam, शहतीर, धरन। 2. a ridge between furrows, मेंड़। 3. an obstacle or hindrance, बाधा, रुकावट।

ball[1] (बॉल) ***n.*** 1. a spherical body, पिंड, गोला। 2. such a body used in games, गेंद, बॉल। ☐ **set the ball rolling,** श्रीगणेश करना, शुरुआत करना।

ball[2] ***n.*** a formal gathering for social dancing, सामूहिक नृत्य के लिए इकट्ठे होनेवाले लोग।

ballad (बैलेड) ***n.*** a narrative poem, गाथा-गीत।

ballast (बैलास्ट) ***n.*** any heavy material used to stabilize a vessel, बोझ, धड़ा।

ball bearing (बॉल बेअरिंग) ***n.*** a bearing with moving balls, बाल बेयरिंग।

ballerina (बैलेरीना) ***n.*** a female ballet dancer, बैले की नर्तकी।

ballet (बैले) ***n.*** 1. a dance by a group of dancers, बैले। 2. a company of ballet dancers, बैले-दल, नर्तक-मंडली।

B

ballistic (बेलिस्टिक) ***adj.*** pertaining to ballistics, प्रक्षेपण-संबंधी, प्राक्षेपिक।

ballistics (बेलिस्टिक्स) ***n.*** the study of the functioning of firearms and flight characteristics of projectiles, प्रक्षेपण विज्ञान।

balloon (बेलून) ***n.*** a flexible bag which can float in the air when inflated with gas, गुब्बारा।

ballot (बैलट) ***n.*** 1. a slip used to cast a vote, मतपत्र। 2. the act of voting, मतदान। ***v.*** to vote by ballot, मतदान करना।

ballot-box ***n.*** a box in which the voters put their ballots, मतपेटी।

ballroom (बॉलरूम) ***n.*** a large room for dancing, नृत्यकक्ष।

ballyhoo (बैलीहू) ***n.*** uproar, शोरगुल, हो-हल्ला, शोर।

balm (बाम) ***n.*** a medicinal ointment, बाम, मलहम।

bamboo (बैम्बू) ***n.*** a tall plant with jointed stems, बाँस; bamboo curtain, चिक।

ban (बैन) ***v.*** to forbid officially, रोक लगाना, निषेध या मनाही करना, प्रतिबंधित करना। ***n.*** an order banning something, रोक, प्रतिबंध।

banal (बेनैल) ***adj.*** common place, साधारण, मामूली।

banana (बनाना) ***n.*** a plant and its fruit, केला।

band[1] (बैन्ड) ***n.*** 1. a flexible strip used to encircle and bind together, पेटी, बंद, पट्टी। 2. a range of wave lengths, बैंड। ***v.*** to bind with a band, पेटी लगाना, बंद से कसना, पट्टी बाँधना।

band[2] ***n.*** 1. a group of persons having common interest, मंडली, टोली, जत्था। 2. a group, समूह, दल, झुंड। 3. a group of musicians, गाने-बजानेवालों का दल, बैंड।

bandage (बैन्डिज) ***n.*** a strip of cloth used to protect a wound, पट्टी। ***v.*** to bind up with a bandage, पट्टी करना / बाँधना।

bandit (बैन्डिट) ***n.*** a robber, लुटेरा, बटमार।

banditry (बैन्डिटरी) ***n.*** the activity of a bandit, a bandit's work, लुटेरापन, बटमारी।

bandmaster (बैन्डमास्टर) ***n.*** the leader of a band of musicians, बैंडमास्टर।

bandy (बैन्डि) ***v.*** to exchange, आदान-प्रदान करना, देना-लेना।

bandy legged ***adj.*** having croocked legs, टेढ़ी-मेढ़ी टाँगोंवाला।

baneful (बेनफ़ुल) ***adj.*** 1. poisonous, विषैला, विषाक्त, ज़हरीला। 2. destructive, विनाशक।

bang (बैंग) ***v.*** 1. to make a violent noise, like an explosion, धमाका करना। 2. to strike or shut noisily, आघात या आवाज़ करना। ***n.*** 1. a sudden explosive noise, धमाका। 2. a hard knock, आघात, प्रहार। □ **go with a bang,** खुशियाँ मनाना, विजय मनाना। ***adv.*** with a bang, ज़ोर-शोर से।

bangle (बैंगल) ***n.*** a bracelet or anklet, चूड़ी, कड़ा या कंगन।

banian (बैनिअन) ***n.*** a fig tree, बरगद।

banish (बैनिश) ***v.*** to expel from the country, to exile, देश से निर्वासित करना, देश-निकाला देना।

banister, bannister (बैनिस्टर) ***n.*** the handrail with supporting railings, सीढ़ी का जंगला, रेलिंग।

banjo (बैन्जो) ***n.*** a guiter like instrument, बैंजो।

bank[1] (बैंक) ***n.*** 1. an institution performing financial transactions, बैंक। 2. the building in which such an institution is located, बैंक। 3. a place of reserve supply, पूर्तिकेंद्र, बैंक। 4. a pool in a game of chance, बाज़ी का रुपया। ***v.*** 1. to deposit money in a bank, बैंक में रुपया जमा करना। 2. to transact business with a bank, बैंक से लेन-देन करना। 3. to operate a bank, बैंक चलाना। ☐ **bank upon/on,** भरोसा करना।

bank[2] ***n.*** 1. a piled up mass, ढेर, अंबार। 2. a steep natural slope, ढाल। 3. a slope at the side of a river, किनारा, तट।

banker (बैंकर) ***n.*** one who is authorised to perform financial transactions, महाजन, बैंकर।

banking ***n.*** the business of a bank or a banker, महाजनी, बैंक व्यवसाय।

bankrupt (बैंकरप्ट) ***n.*** insolvent, दिवालिया।

banner (बैनर) ***n.*** 1. a flag, झंडा, पताका। 2. a piece of cloth with a slogan, motto etc., बैनर। 3. a headline of a newspaper, मुख्य शीर्षक।

banquet (बैंक्विट) ***n.*** a ceremonial dinner, भोज, ज्योनार, दावत, पार्टी।

banter (बैन्टर) ***n.*** humorous jesting, हँसी-मज़ाक, हास-परिहास। ***v.*** to tease gently, to talk jocularly, हँसी-मज़ाक करना, दिल्लगी करना।

banyan (बैनिअन) ***n.*** = banian.

baptise, baptize (बैप्टाइज़) ***v.*** 1. to perform the rites of baptism, to sprinkle water on, बपतिस्मा देना, अभिसिंचित करना। 2. to give a christian name, ईसाई धर्मानुसार नामकरण करना। 3. to initiate, दीक्षित करना।

baptism (बैप्टिज़म) ***n.*** the Christian ceremony to accept someone as a member of Church through the symbolic application of water, बपतिस्मा, ईसाई-दीक्षा।

baptist (बैप्टिस्ट) ***n.*** one who baptizes, बपतिस्मा-दाता।

bar[1] (बार) ***n.*** 1. a long piece of metal, wood etc., छड़, डंडा। 2. a rectangular block of any substance, टिकिया, पिंडी, चक्की। 3. anything that prevents or obstructs, रोक, बाधा, अड़चन। 4. a counter or place where drinks are served, मदिरा-पटल या मधुशाला। 5. a counter where things are sold, काउंटर, पटल। 6. the wooden barrier in court at which the prisoner stands, कटघरा। 7. a band, पट्टी, धारी। 8. the legal profession, वकालत, वकील का पेशा। 9. the members of the legal profession, वकील-समुदाय।

bar[2] ***v.*** 1. to close or fasten with a bar, अर्गला से (दरवाज़ा आदि) बंद करना। 2. to block, रास्ता रोकना, बाधा डालना, अड़चन खड़ी करना। 3. to prohibit, प्रतिबंधित करना, वर्जित करना। 4. to exclude, अलग करना।

barb (बार्ब) ***n.*** 1. a hook, काँटा। 2. a cutting or wounding remark, ताना, आक्षेप।

barbarian (बार्बैरिअन) ***adj.*** uncivilized, savage, असभ्य, बर्बर।

barbaric (बार्बैरिक) ***adj.*** of or like barbarians, बर्बरतापूर्ण, नृशंस।

B

barbarity (बार्बैरिटी) ***n.*** savage cruelty, बर्बरता, नृशंसता।

barbarous (बार्बेरस) ***adj.*** 1. uncivilized, uncultured, असभ्य, अशिष्ट। 2. brutal, cruel, बर्बर, नृशंस, निर्दय। 3. inhuman, अमानवीय।

barbed (बार्ब्ड) ***adj.*** having barbs, काँटेदार, कँटीला।

barber (बार्बर) ***n.*** one who cuts hair and shaves, नाई, नाऊ, हज्जाम।

bard (बार्ड) ***n.*** a poet or singer of formerly times, चारण, भाट।

bare (बेअर) ***adj.*** 1. without clothing, unclothed, naked, नंगा, निर्वस्त्र। 2. without covering, uncovered, नंगा, अनावृत। 3. unadorned, अनलंकृत, सादा। ***v.*** to make naked, नंगा करना, अनावृत करना।

barebacked ***adj.*** without a saddle, बिना काठी का।

barefaced ***adj.*** shameless, निर्लज्ज, बेशर्म, बेहया।

barehanded ***adj.*** without a weapon or tool, खाली हाथ, निहत्था।

bareheaded ***adj.*** without a cap, नंगे सिर।

barely ***adv.*** hardly, मुश्किल से, नाम मात्र के लिए, मात्र।

bargain (बार्गेन) ***n.*** 1. an agreement about transaction, सौदा। 2. an agreement, समझौता, क़रार। ***v.*** to negotiate the terms of a sale, सौदा करना।

bargaining ***n.*** negotiation of the terms of a bargain, सौदेबाज़ी, मोल-तोल, मोल-भाव।

barge (बार्ज) ***n.*** a large boat for transporting freight, बोझ ढोनेवाली नाव। ***v.*** 1. to transport by barge, नाव से माल की ढुलाई करना। 2. to move clumsily, भद्दी तरह चलना।

bark[1] (बार्क) ***n.*** the harsh sound made by a dog, भौं-भौं, भौंक। ***v.*** to make such a sound, भौंकना, भौं-भौं करना।

bark[2] ***n.*** the outer layer of the stem of a tree, छाल। ***v.*** to remove the bark from the tree, छाल उतारना।

barley (बार्ली) ***n.*** 1. a plant bearing grain used as food, जौ। 2. barley grains, जौ, यव; ~ water, जौ का पानी।

barman (बारमैन) ***n.*** a man who serves alcoholic drinks, bartender, मधुवितरक, साक़ी। [Fem. barmaid, साक़ी।]

barn (बार्न) ***n.*** 1. a building for storing grain, खत्ता, बखार। 2. a place for housing livestock, बाड़ा, तबेला।

barometer (बेरॉमिटर) ***n.*** an instrument which registers changes in the atmosphere, वायुदाबमापी।

baron (बैरन) ***n.*** the lowest rank title in the British peerage, सामंत, बैरन।

barrack (बैरक) ***v.*** 1. to house in barracks, बैरकों में रहना या रखना। 2. to jeer, उपहास करना, फबती कसना, खिल्ली उड़ाना।

barracks ***n.*** (often plu.) a building or group of buildings for soldiers to live in, बैरक, सेनावास।

barrage (बैराज़) ***n.*** 1. a dam, बाँध। 2. a heavy bombardment, गोलों की बौछार। 3. a rapid outpouring, बौछार।

barrel (बैरल) ***n.*** 1. a large wooden cylindrical container, बैरल, ढोल,

पीपा। 2. the amount this contains, बैरल। 3. a tubelike part of a gun, बैरल, नाल।

barren (बैरन) ***adj.*** 1. infertile, अनुपजाऊ, अनुर्वर। 2. not producing offspring, बाँझ, बंध्या।

barricade (बैरिकेड) ***n.*** a temporary fence or wall to block a passage, रोक, आड़।

barrier (बैरिअर) ***n.*** a fence, wall or anything that obstructs the movement, रोक, आड़।

barring (बारिंग) ***prep.*** excluding, को छोड़कर, के सिवा।

barrister (बैरिस्टर) ***n.*** one who pleads cases in superior courts, बैरिस्टर।

barter (बार्टर) ***v.*** 1. to trade by exchanging some goods for other goods, अदला-बदली करना, विनिमय करना। 2. to exchange, बदल लेना। ***n.*** trading by exchange, अदला-बदली, विनियम।

bascule bridge (बैस्क्यूल ब्रिज) ***n.*** a bridge hinged at the bank to allow ships to pass under it, उत्तोलन सेतु, उठौआ पुल।

base (बेस) ***n.*** 1. the bottom, तल, पेंदा। 2. the foundation or basis, आधार, नींव, बुनियाद। 3. the main ingredient, मूलाधार, बेस, मूलांश। 4. the starting point, आरंभ-बिंदु। 5. a centre of operations or source of supply, अड्डा। ***v.*** 1. to make a base or foundation for, नींव रखना, बुनियाद डालना, आधार बनाना। 2. to put on a base, आधारित करना। 3. to establish, स्थापित करना। ***adj.*** 1. low-minded, कमीना, नीच। 2. of inferior value, worthless, निकृष्ट, घटिया। 3. counterfeit, जाली।

baseball (बेसबॉल) ***n.*** a game played with a bat and ball by two opposing teams, बेसबॉल।

baseless (बेसलिस) ***adj.*** having no basis or foundation, आधारहीन, निराधार।

basement (बेसमेन्ट) ***n.*** the underground floor, तहख़ाना, तलघर।

bashful (बैशफ़ुल) ***adj.*** 1. shy, शर्मीला, लजालू। 2. timid, संकोची, झेंपू।

bashfulness (बैशफ़ुलनिस) ***n.*** 1. shyness, शर्म, लाज। 2. timidness, संकोच, झेंप।

basic (बेसिक) ***adj.*** 1. forming a base, बुनियादी, आधारिक। 2. fundamental, मूल, आधारभूत, मौलिक। 3. elementary, प्राथमिक, प्रारंभिक।

basically (बेसिकली) ***adv.*** 1. at basis, आधार रूप में। 2. fundamentally, मूलतः।

basin (बेसिन) ***n.*** 1. a round open shallow dish, चिलमची। 2. the amount a basin holds, चिलमची-भर सामान। 3. a washbasin, वाशबेसिन। 4. a sunken place where water collects, ताल, जलकुंड।

basis (बेसिस) ***n.*** 1. the base or foundation, आधार, नींव, बुनियाद। 2. a main principle, मूल सिद्धांत। 3. the main part, मुख्य आधार, मूलाधार।

bask (बास्क) ***v.*** to lie in or be exposed to pleasant warmth of the sun, धूप में लेटना, धूप सेंकना, धूप-स्नान करना।

basket (बास्किट) ***n.*** an interwoven wicker container, टोकरी, डलिया, पिटारी।

B

basketball ***n.*** 1. a game played between two teams in which points are scored by throwing a ball into the basket of the opposite party, बास्केटबॉल। 2. the ball used in this game, बास्केटबॉल।

bastard (बैस्टर्ड) ***n.*** a child born out of wedlock, an illegitimate child, दोगला, वर्णसंकर। ***adj.*** illegitimate, जारज, दोगला, हरामी।

bastion (बैस्टिअन) ***n.*** 1. a fortified place, गढ़। 2. a stronghold, केंद्र, गढ़; a bastion of democracy, प्रजातंत्र का गढ़।

bat[1] (बैट) ***n.*** a wooden stick or club used in the game of cricket, baseball etc., बल्ला, बैट। ***v.*** 1. to strike with a bat, बल्ले से प्रहार करना। 2. to take a turn at batting, बल्लेबाज़ी करना।

bat[2] ***n.*** a mouse like flying mammal, चमगादड़।

batch (बैच) ***n.*** 1. a group of similar persons, जत्था, टोली, वर्ग। 2. a set of similar things, बैच, वर्ग।

bath (बाथ) ***n.*** 1. the act of washing the body in water, स्नान, नहाना। 2. a bathroom, स्नानागार, ग़ुसलख़ाना।

bathe (बेद) ***v.*** 1. to take a bath, स्नान करना, नहाना। 2. to immerse, गोता या डुबकी लगाना।

bathing suit ***n.*** a garment worn for bathing, नहाने की पोशाक।

bathos (बेथॉस) ***n.*** decline from the sublime to the trivial, anticlimax, अपकर्ष, गिरावट।

bathroom ***n.*** a room for taking a bath, स्नानघर, ग़ुसलख़ाना।

baton (बैटन) ***n.*** 1. a staff serving as a symbol of office, (अधिकारी का) डंडा, बेंत। 2. a stick used by the conductor in leading an orchestra, बैंडमास्टर की छड़ी।

battalion (बटैल्यन) ***n.*** 1. a large army unit, बटालियन, पलटन, वाहिनी। 2. a large organised body of people, सेना, फौज।

batten (बैटन) ***n.*** a strip of wood for fastening or holding something in place, पट्टी, तख़्ती। ***v.*** to fasten with battens, पट्टियाँ लगाना।

battery (बैटरी) ***n.*** a device for generating electric current, बैटरी।

batting (बैटिंग) ***n.*** the act of striking a ball with the bat, बल्लेबाज़ी।

battle (बैटल) ***n.*** 1. a combat between two armed forces, युद्ध, लड़ाई। 2. a hard struggle, संघर्ष, लड़ाई। ***v.*** 1. to fight against, युद्ध करना, लड़ना। 2. to struggle, संघर्ष करना।

battlefield ***n.*** a field where a battle was fought, युद्धक्षेत्र, लड़ाई का मैदान।

battlement ***n.*** a wall with holes for shooting purposes, परकोटा।

bauxite (बॉक्साइट) ***n.*** the ore of aluminium, बाक्साइट।

bawl (बौल) ***v.*** to shout, to cry loudly, चीखना, चिल्लाना।

bay[1] (बे) ***n.*** a part of the sea partly enclosed by land, खाड़ी।

bay[2] ***n.*** a deep bark or howl, भौंक, भौं-भौं, हुआँ-हुआँ। □ **at bay,** दूर। ***v.*** to bark at, भौंकना।

bay leaf ***n.*** aromatic leaves of a bay tree, तेजपत्ता, तेजपात।

bayonet (बेअनिट) ***n.*** a long knife for stabbing attached to the muzzle of a rifle, संगीन। ***v.*** to stab with a bayonet, संगीन भोंक देना।

be (बी) ***v.*** 1. to exist, to live, होना। 2. to take place, होना, घटना। 3. to become, होना, बनना। ☐ **Let it be.** छेड़छाड़ की जरूरत नहीं; **would be,** भावी।

beach (बीच) ***n.*** the sea-shore, समुद्रतट। ***v.*** to bring ashore, किनारे (पर) लाना।

beacon (बीकन) ***n.*** a light used as a signal, संकेतदीप।

bead (बीड) ***n.*** 1. a pierced small ball for threading, मनका, गुरिया, दाना। 2. a drop, बूँद, जलकण। 3. (plu.) a rosary, जपमाला।

beagle (बीगल) ***n.*** a small dog used for hunting, छोटा शिकारी कुत्ता, बीगल।

beak (बीक) ***n.*** a bird's bill, चोंच।

beaker (बीकर) ***n.*** a container with a lip for pouring liquids, बीकर, जीभदार प्याला।

beam (बीम) ***n.*** 1. a ray, किरण, रश्मि। 2. a long piece of wood used to support the roof, शहतीर, धरन। 3. a bright look or smile, हँसी, मुस्कान। ***v.*** 1. to shine, चमकना। 2. to smile, मुस्करा देना।

beaming ***adj.*** shining, giving off light, चमकीला, चमकता हुआ।

bean (बीन) ***n.*** a long seed vessel like that of a pea, फली।

bear[1] (बेअर) ***n.*** a wild mammal with thick fur and strong claws, भालू, रीछ। ☐ **the Great Bear,** सप्तर्षि मंडल।

bear[2] ***v.*** (bore, borne) 1. to hold up, धारण करना। 2. to carry, वहन करना। 3. to accept or assume the responsibility of, स्वीकार करना, ग्रहण करना। 4. to give birth to, जन्म देना। 5. to produce, उत्पन्न करना, फलना-फूलना। 6. to tolerate, बरदाश्त करना, सहना।

bearable (बेअरेबल) ***adj.*** tolerable, endurable, सहने योग्य, सह्य।

beard (बिअर्ड) ***n.*** hair growing on a man's chin and cheeks, दाढ़ी।

bearded (बिअर्डिड) ***adj.*** having a beard, दाढ़ीवाला, दढ़ियल।

bearer (बेअरर) ***n.*** one who carries, something, वाहक, धारक।

bearing (बेअरिंग) ***n.*** manner of conducting oneself, आचरण, व्यवहार।

beast (बीस्ट) ***n.*** 1. any four-footed animal, पशु। 2. a brutal person, निर्दय व्यक्ति, पशु, वहशी।

beastly ***adj.*** of or like a beast, पाशविक, जानवरों-सा।

beat (बीट) ***v.*** (beat, beaten, beating) 1. to strike repeatedly, मारना, पीटना। 2. to defeat, हराना। 3. to throb, धड़कना, धकधक करना, स्पंदन करना। 5. to batter, फेंटना। ***n.*** 1. a blow or stroke, आघात, चोट। 2. the sound made by a stroke or blow, आघात या चोट की आवाज़। 3. a throb, धड़कन। 4. a rhythmic stress, ताल। 5. a regular round or habitual route, गश्त। 6. an act of driving out a game, हाँका।

beating ***n.*** 1. the punishment by blows, प्रहार, आघात, मार। 2. a defeat, हार, पराजय। 3. throbbing, धड़कन।

beatitude (बिऐटिट्यूड) ***n.*** supreme happiness, परमानंद।

beau (बो) ***n.*** 1. a fop, छैला, बाँका। 2. a young girl's boy-friend, प्रेमी, यार।

B

beauteous (ब्युटिअस) ***adj.*** beautiful, सुंदर।

beautician (ब्युटिशन) ***n.*** a person who is skilled in cosmetic treatment, ब्युटिशियन, सौंदर्य-विशेषज्ञा, श्रृंगारवेत्ता।

beautification (ब्युटिफ़िकेशन) ***n.*** an act of beautifying, सुंदरीकरण, श्रृंगारीकरण, सजावटीकरण।

beautiful (ब्युटिफ़ुल) ***adj.*** 1. full of beauty, सुंदर, ख़ूबसूरत। 2. very satisfactory, अत्यंत संतोषजनक, बहुत बढ़िया।

beautify (ब्युटिफ़ाइ) ***v.*** to make beautiful, सुंदर बनाना, सजाना।

beauty (ब्युटी) ***n.*** 1. the quality of being beautiful, सुंदरता। 2. a beautiful thing or person, सुंदर वस्तु या व्यक्ति।

beauty parlour ***n.*** an establishment for giving beautifying treatments to hair, face, body etc., ब्यूटी पार्लर, सौंदर्यशाला, श्रृंगारगृह।

beauty queen ***n.*** a woman who has won a beauty contest, सुंदरियों की रानी, महासुंदरी, रूपरानी।

beaver (बीवर) ***n.*** a rodent that lives both on land and in water, ऊदबिलाव।

becalm (बिकाम) ***v.*** to make calm, शांत करना।

because (बिकॉज़) ***conj.*** for the reason that, क्योंकि, इसलिए कि। □ **because of,** के परिणामस्वरूप।

beck (बेक) ***n.*** 1. a small hill stream, पहाड़ी नाला। 2. a beckoning gesture, इशारा, इंगित, संकेत। □ **at someone's beck and call,** किसी के इशारों पर चलना, हुकुम बजाना।

beckon (बेकन) ***v.*** to signal, इशारा करना, इंगित करना।

become (बिकम) ***v.*** 1. to come to be, हो जाना, बन जाना। 2. to suit, जँचना, फबना।

becoming ***adj.*** suitable, appropriate, उपयुक्त, भला, सुहावना।

bed (बेड) ***n.*** 1. a piece of furniture for sleeping, चारपाई, खाट। 2. a piece of ground prepared for plants, क्यारी। 3. a bottom of the sea, river etc., समुद्र, नदी आदि का तल। 4. a layer, परत। □ **a bed of roses,** फूलों की सेज; **take to one's bed,** खाट पर पड़ जाना। ***v.*** to furnish with bed, चारपाई लगाना।

bedbug ***n.*** a bloodsucking insect infesting beds, खटमल।

bedcover ***n.*** a cover on a bed, पलंगपोश, चादर।

bedding ***n.*** the sheets, covers etc. put on a bed, बिछौना, बिस्तर।

bedeck (बिडेक) ***v.*** to adorn, सजाना।

bedevil (बिडैविल) ***v.*** 1. to harass, परेशान करना। 2. to worry, चिंता करना।

bedridden (बेडरिडन) ***adj.*** confined to bed, शय्याग्रस्त, रुग्ण।

bedroom ***n.*** a room for sleeping in, शयनकक्ष, सोने का कमरा।

bedsore (बेडसोर) ***n.*** a sore occurring during long confinement to bed, शय्याव्रण।

bedspread (बेडस्प्रेड) ***n.*** a bed-covering, पलंगपोश, चादर।

bedstead (बेडस्टेड) ***n.*** the frame supporting a bed, चारपाई, चौकी आदि।

bedtime ***n.*** a time for going to bed, सोने का समय, शयनकाल।

bee (बी) ***n.*** 1. an insect that

produces honey, मधुमक्खी। 2. a black bee, भौंरा, भ्रमर। 3. a gathering for work or competition, कार्य-गोष्ठी, प्रतियोगिता-गोष्ठी; spelling bee, वर्तनी-प्रतियोगिता। ☐ **a bee in one's bonnet,** दिमाग़ में घूमती रहनेवाली बात।

beef (बीफ़) ***n.*** the meat (of a cow or ox), गोमांस।

beehive (बीहाइव) ***n.*** a hive, मधुमक्खियों का छत्ता।

beekeeping (बीकीपिंग) ***n.*** raising of bees, मधुमक्खी-पालन।

beeline (बीलाइन) ***n.*** a direct line between two points, सरल रेखा, सीधी रेखा।

been (बीन, बिन) ***v.*** p.p. of be.

beep (बीप) ***n.*** a short high-pitched sound made by electronic equipment, इलेक्ट्रॉनिक ध्वनि-संकेत, पीं-पीं।

beer (बिअर) ***n.*** a drink made from barley, बीयर, यविरा।

beet (बीट) ***n.*** a plant with a dark-red root used as a vegetable, चुकंदर।

beetle[1] (बीटल) ***n.*** a heavy mallet for striking pegs, हथौड़ा।

beetle[2] ***n.*** an insect with a hard covering, भौंरा, भ्रमर।

befall (बिफ़ॉल) ***v.*** to happen, to happen to, घटित होना।

befit (बिफ़िट) ***v.*** to be suitable to, फबना।

befitting ***adj.*** suitable, उपयुक्त।

befool (बिफ़ूल) ***v.*** to make a fool (of someone किसी को) मूर्ख बनाना।

before (बिफ़ोर) ***adv.*** 1. in the past, previously, पहले, पूर्व में, पहले भी, आगे भी। 2. ahead, in advance, पहले। 3. in front, सामने, आगे। ***prep.*** 1. prior to, के पहले। 2. in front of, के सामने, के आगे। 3. in the presence of, की उपस्थिति में, के सम्मुख।

Before Christ ***adv.*** before the birth of Christ, ईसा-पूर्व।

beforehand ***adv.*** in advance, पहले से।

befriend (बिफ़्रेंड) ***v.*** to act as a friend to, मित्रवत् व्यवहार करना, दोस्ती निभाना।

beg (बेग) ***v.*** 1. to ask humbly for anything, माँगना, याचना करना। 2. to request humbly, विनती करना।

began (बिगैन) ***v.*** p.t. of begin,

beget (बिगेट) ***v.*** (begot, begotten, begetting) 1. to give birth to, जन्म देना। 2. to produce, उत्पन्न करना।

beggar (बेगर) ***n.*** 1. one who solicits alms for living, भिखारी, भिखमंगा, भिक्षुक।

begin (बिगिन) ***v.*** (began, begun, beginning) to commence, to start, आरंभ करना/होना, शुरू करना/होना।

beginner (बिगिनर) ***n.*** a novice, नौसिखुआ।

beginning ***n.*** 1. commenc-ement, start, प्रारंभ। 2. a source, स्रोत।

begone (बिगॉन) ***interj.*** go away, परे हटो, दूर हो जाओ, भागो यहाँ से!

begot (बिगॉट) ***v.*** p.t. & p.p. of beget.

begrudge (बिग्रज) ***v.*** 1. to grudge, ईर्ष्या करना। 2. grumble, कुढ़ना।

beguile (बिगाइल) ***v.*** 1. to deceive or cheat, धोखा देना, छलना। 2. to amuse or divert, मन बहलाना, ध्यान बँटाना। 3. to coax, फुसलाना।

begun (बिगन) ***v.*** p.p. of begin.

behalf (बिहाफ़) ***n.*** interest, benefit, हित। ☐ **in behalf of,** के हित में; **on**

B

behalf of, की तरफ़ से, का प्रतिनिधि बनकर।

behave (बिहेव) ***v.*** to act, व्यवहार/बरताव करना।

behaviour, behavior (बिहेव्यर) ***n.*** a way of bahaving, व्यवहार, बरताव।

behead (बिहेड) ***v.*** to cut off the head, सिर काट देना, सिर उड़ा देना।

beheld (बिहेल्ड) ***v.*** p.t. & p.p. of behold.

behest (बिहेस्ट) ***n.*** an order or command, आदेश; at the behest of, के आदेशानुसार।

behind (बिहाइन्ड) ***adv.*** at the back, पीछे। ***prep.*** in the rear of, के पीछे।

behold (बिहोल्ड) ***v.*** to see, to observe, देखना, गौर करना, ध्यान देना।

being (बीइंग) ***n.*** 1. existence, अस्तित्व, अस्तित्व ग्रहण करना। 2. something that exists and has life, जीवधारी, प्राणी।

belabour (बिलेबर) ***v.*** to beat soundly, अच्छी तरह मारना, धुनाई करना।

belated (बिलेटिड) ***adj.*** arriving late, tardy, देर से आनेवाला, देर से पहुँचनेवाला, मंदगति।

belch (बेल्च) ***v.*** to expel gas from the stomach through the mouth, डकार लेना।

beleaguered (बिलीगर्ड) ***adj.*** harassed, परेशान, तंग।

belfry (बेलफ़्री) ***n.*** a bell-tower, घंटा-घर।

belie (बिलाइ) ***v.*** to give a false idea of, to misrepresent, झुठला देना, भ्रमित करना।

belief (बिलीफ़) ***n.*** 1. trust, confidence, विश्वास, भरोसा, यक़ीन। 2. opinion, धारणा, राय।

believable (बिलीवेबल) ***adj.*** that can be believed, विश्वसनीय, विश्वासयोग्य।

believe (बिलीव) ***v.*** 1. to have trust or confidence in. विश्वास करना। 2. to accept as truthful, सच मानना, सही समझना, मान लेना। 3. to have religious faith, निष्ठा या श्रद्धा होना। 4. to hold as an opinion, धारणा होना।

belittle (बिलिटल) ***v.*** to make seem less important, दर्जा घटाना, महत्त्व या मान कम करके आँकना।

bell (बेल) ***n.*** 1. an object made of metal which rings when struck, घंटा, घंटी, घड़ियाल। 2. the sound made by bell, घंटा या घंटी की आवाज़। ***v.*** to hang or provide with a bell on, घंटा लगाना, घंटी बाँधना।

belladonna (बेलाडोना) ***n.*** a poisonous plant, धतूरा, बेलाडोना।

belle (बेल) ***n.*** a beautiful woman, सुंदरी, रूपसी।

bellicose (बेलिकोस) ***adj.*** warlike, लड़ाकू।

belligerent (बिलिजरेन्ट) ***adj.*** aggressively hostile, युद्धप्रिय, युद्धोन्मुखी।

bell-metal ***n.*** an alloy used in bells, काँसा।

bellow (बेलो) ***v.*** to roar in the manner of a bull, बैल की तरह हुँकारना। ***n.*** the loud deep sound of a bull, बैल की हुँकार।

bellows (बेलोज़) ***n.*** (singular or plural) a device for supplying a strong blast of air, भाथी, धौंकनी।

belly (बेली) ***n.*** the stomach, पेट, उदर।

belong (बिलॉन्ग) ***v.*** to be an inhabitant or native of, ···का होना।

belongings (बिलॉन्गिंग्ज़) ***n.*** personal possessions, संपत्ति, जायदाद।

beloved (बिलव्ड) ***adj.*** dearly loved, परम प्रिय। ***n.*** one who is beloved, प्रियतम या प्रिया।

below (बिलो) ***adv.*** in or to a lower place or level, beneath, नीचे, तले। ***prep.*** 1. lower in position than, के नीचे, के तले। 2. lower in amount than, से कम।

belt (बेल्ट) ***n.*** 1. a band worn around the waist, पेटी। 2. a strap used to transfer motion from one wheel to another, पट्टा। 3. a specific region, कटिबंध, क्षेत्र। ☐ **under one's belt,** किसीके अधिकार में।

belvedere (बेल्वेडिअर) ***n.*** a high turret, बुर्ज।

bemoan (बिमोन) ***v.*** to lament, रोना-कलपना, विलाप करना।

bench (बेन्च) ***n.*** 1. a long seat for two or more persons, बेंच। 2. the judge's seat in court, न्यायपीठ, पीठ। 3. the court, न्यायालय। 4. judges as a group, न्यायाधीशों का समूह।

bend (बेन्ड) ***v.*** (bent, bending) 1. to make curved, मोड़ना, टेढ़ा कर देना। 2. to become curved, मुड़ना, टेढ़ा हो जाना। 3. to turn or deflect, मुड़ना, प्रवृत्त होना। 4. to turn downward, झुकाना। 5. to yield, झुकना। 6. to concentrate, संकेंद्रित करना। 7. to coerce or subdue, दबाना। 8. to change, बदलना। ***n.*** a curve or turn, मोड़, घुमाव।

beneath (बिनीथ) ***adv.*** below, नीचे। ***prep.*** below, के नीचे, के तले।

benediction (बेनिडिक्शन) ***n.*** a solemn blessing, आशीर्वचन, आशीर्वाद।

benefactor (बेनिफ़ैक्टर) ***n.*** 1. one who gives money for a good cause, दाता, दानी। 2. a person who does good, उपकारकर्ता।

beneficence (बिनेफ़िसेन्स) ***n.*** an act of kindness, उपकार, हित, भलाई।

beneficial (बेनिफ़िशल) ***adj.*** helpful, हितकर।

beneficiary (बेनिफ़िशिअरी) ***n.*** a person who gets benefits under a will, जिसके नाम वसीयत हो।

benefit (बेनिफ़िट) ***n.*** 1. financial gain, profit, लाभ, फ़ायदा। 2. good, भलाई, उपकार। 3. an advantage, सुविधा, लाभ। ***v.*** 1. to do good to, उपकार करना, सहायता करना। 2. to profit from, लाभान्वित होना।

benevolence (बेनेवोलेन्स) ***n.*** 1. inclination to do good, परोपकार, हित-कामना। 2. generosity, उदारता।

benign (बिनाइन) ***adj.*** 1. generous, उदार, दयालु, सौम्य। 2. mild and gentle in its effects, हलका, हितकर।

bent (बेन्ट) ***adj.*** not straight, crooked, टेढ़ा, तिरछा। ***n.*** 1. a twist or turn, मोड़, घुमाव। 2. a natural liking, रुझान, झुकाव, नति। ☐ **bent on,** तुला हुआ, सन्नद्ध, तत्पर।

benumbed (बिनम्ड) ***adj.*** deprived of feeling, सुन्न।

bequeath (बिक्वीथ) ***v.*** to leave as a legacy, वसीयत कर देना।

bequest (बिक्वेस्ट) ***n.*** a legacy, वसीयत।

bereave (बिरीव) ***v.*** 1. to deprive of, वंचित करना। 2. to snatch away, छीन लेना, उठा लेना। 3. to inflict the loss of a relative by death, शोकसंतप्त करना, शोकार्त बनाना।

B

bereaved ***adj.*** whose relative has died, शोकसंतप्त, शोकार्त, शोकाकुल।

bereavement ***n.*** 1. the loss of a relative or friend through death, वियोग, विच्छेद। 2. the state of being bereaved, शोक, गम।

bereft (बिरेफ्ट) ***adj.*** deprived, वंचित; bereft of reason, सनकी।

beriberi (बेरीबेरी) ***n.*** a disease caused by deficiency of certain vitamins, बेरी-बेरी।

berry (बेरी) ***n.*** a small round juicy fruit with seeds, रसभरी।

berserk (बर्सर्क) ***adj.*** mad with violent anger, क्रोधाभिभूत।

berth (बर्थ) ***n.*** a sleeping place in a train, ship etc., बर्थ, शायिका।

beryl (बेरिल) ***n.*** a precious stone of green colour, हरे रंग का रत्न, लहसुनिया, वैदूर्य।

beseech (बिसीच) ***v.*** (besought, beseeching) to entreat, चिरौरी या अनुनय-विनय करना।

beset (बिसेट) ***v.*** 1. to attack from all sides, चौतरफ़ा आक्रमण करना। 2. to imbed, जड़ना।

beside (बिसाइड) ***prep.*** 1. by the side of, के बगल में, के पास। 2. compared with, की तुलना में। 3. having nothing to do with, से भिन्न, से अलग।

besides (बिसाइड्स) ***prep.*** in addition to, के अतिरिक्त। ***adv.*** also, more, in addition, अतिरिक्त रूप से, साथ में।

besiege (बिसीज) ***v.*** to lay siege to, घेर लेना।

besiegement ***n.*** an act of besieging, घेरबंदी।

besotted (बिसॉटिड) ***adj.*** infatuated, मुग्ध।

bespatter (बिस्पेटर) ***v.*** to spatter, गंदा करना।

bespeak (बिस्पीक) ***v.*** to speak for in advance, पहले से कह रखना।

best (बेस्ट) ***adj.*** of excellent quality, उत्तम, श्रेष्ठ। ***adv.*** 1. in the best way, भली-भाँति, अच्छी तरह। 2. most, अत्यधिक।

bestir (बिस्टर) ***v.*** to become active, सक्रिय होना।

bestow (बिस्टो) ***v.*** to give, to grant, देना, प्रदान करना।

bestowal (बिस्टोअल) ***n.*** an act of bestowing, देना, प्रदान।

bestride (बिस्ट्राइड) ***v.*** (bestrode, bestridden, bestriding) to sit with legs apart, दोनों टाँगें फैलाकर बैठना।

bet (बेट) ***n.*** an agreement to risk money on the result of something uncertain, दाँव, बाज़ी, शर्त। ***v.*** to make a bet, शर्त लगाना।

betel (बीटल) ***n.*** a leaf of a plant used for chewing, पान, पान का पत्ता।

betelnut (बीटलनट) ***n.*** the areca nut, सुपारी।

bethink (बिथिन्क) ***v.*** to think, सोचना, सोच-विचार करना।

betide (बिटाइड) ***v.*** to happen, घटित होना।

betray (बिट्रे) ***v.*** 1. to be unfaithful to, विश्वासघात करना, 2. to deceive, दग़ा देना, धोखा देना।

betrayal (बिट्रेअल) ***n.*** an act of treachery, विश्वासघात, दग़ा।

betrayer (बिट्रेअर) ***n.*** one who betrays, विश्वासघाती, दग़ाबाज़।

betroth (बिट्रॉथ) ***v.*** to promise to

marry, विवाह करने का वचन देना।
betrothal (बिट्रॉथल) ***n.*** engagement for marriage, मँगनी, सगाई।
better (बेटर) ***adj.*** (compar. of good) 1. higher in quality, बेहतर। 2. more useful, अधिक उपयोगी, अपेक्षाकृत अच्छा। 3. improved in health, पहले से अच्छा या ठीक, स्वस्थ। ***adv.*** 1. in a more excellent manner, अधिक अच्छी तरह। 2. to a better degree, अधिक, बहुत।
betterment ***n.*** an improvement, सुधार, बेहतरी।
between (बिट्वीन) ***prep.*** 1. in the middle, के बीच, में।
beverage (बेवरिज) ***n.*** a drink, पेय।
bevy (बेवी) ***n.*** a large group, समूह, झुंड।
bewail (बिवेल) ***v.*** to mourn for, विलाप करना, रोना-कलपना।
beware (बिवेअर) ***v.*** to be careful, सावधान रहना या होना, बचकर रहना।
bewilder (बिविल्डर) ***v.*** to perplex or confuse, विचलित कर या चौंका देना।
bewilderment ***n.*** perplexity, संभ्रम, घबराहट, हैरानगी।
bewitch (बिविच) ***v.*** 1. to influence by witchcraft, जादू कर देना। 2. to charm, मुग्ध कर लेना।
beyond (बियॉन्ड) ***prep.*** 1. outside the territory of, के बाहर, से दूर। 2. on the farther side of, के पार, से परे, के आगे। 3. in addition to, besides, के अतिरिक्त।
biannual (बाइऐन्युअल) ***adj.*** coming, appearing twice a year, अर्धवार्षिक, छमाही।
bias (बाइअस) ***n.*** a prejudice, पूर्वाग्रह। 2. an inclination, झुकाव। ***v.*** to incline to one side, पक्षपात करना।
biased ***adj.*** prejudiced, पूर्वाग्रह से युक्त, पक्षपातपूर्ण, इकतरफ़ा।
bib (बिब) ***n.*** a cloth covering put under a baby's chin, बिब।
Biblical (बिब्लिकल) ***adj.*** of or pertaining to the Bible, बाइबिल-संबंधी, बाइबिली।
bibliography (बिब्लिऑग्रफ़ी) ***n.*** a particular list of books, ग्रंथसूची।
bicameral (बाइकैमरल) ***adv.*** having two legislative chambers, द्विसदनी।
bicentenary (बाइसेन्टिनेरी) ***n.*** a 200th anniversary or its celebration, bicentennial, द्विशती समारोह, द्विशतवार्षिकी।
bicentennial (बाइसेन्टेनिअल) ***n.*** a bicentenary, द्विशती समारोह।
biceps (बाइसेप्स) ***n.*** the large muscle on the front of the upper arm, दोसिरी पेशी।
bicker (बिकर) ***v.*** to wrangle, झिकझिक करना। ***n.*** a wrangle, झिकझिक।
bicycle (बाइसिकल) ***n.*** a two-wheeled vehicle propelled by pedalling, साइकिल, बाइसिकल।
bid[1] (बिड) ***n.*** 1. an offer of price for something, बोली, डाक। 2. attempt, प्रयत्न। ***v.*** (bid, bidding) to make a bid, बोली बोलना, देना या लगाना।
bid[2] ***v.*** (bid/bade, bidden, bidding) 1. to command, आदेश देना, हुकुम देना। 2. to tell, बतलाना। 3. to say (goodbye, welcome etc.,) कहना। 4. to ask to come, बुलाना।
bidding ***n.*** 1. offers of prices at an auction, बोली। 2. an offer of number of hands in the bridge, हाथ।
biennial (बाइएनिअल) ***adj.*** 1. living or lasting for two years, द्विवर्षीय।

B

2. happening every second year, द्विवार्षिक।

bier (बिअर) ***n.*** a portable stand on which a dead body is placed, अरथी।

bifocal (बाइफ़ोकल) ***adj.*** having two different focal lengths (ऐसा चश्मा) जिसमें दूर और पास के दोनों लेंस हों, बाइफ़ोकल, दुफ़ोकसी।

bifurcate (बाइफ़र्केट) ***v.*** 1. to divide into two parts, दो हिस्से करना। 2. to separate into two branches, दो शाखाओं में बाँटना, द्विशाखित करना।

bifurcation (बाइफ़र्केशन) ***n.*** an act of bifurcating, विभाजन; द्विशाखन।

big (बिग) ***adj.*** 1. of great size, number, quantity etc., बड़ा। 2. grown-up, बड़ा। 3. of great importance, महत्त्वपूर्ण, महान। 4. generous, magnanimous, उदार, विशाल हृदय।

bigamist (बिगेमिस्ट) ***n.*** one who commits bigamy, द्विपत्नीक या द्विपतिका।

bigamy (बिगेमी) ***n.*** the criminal offence of marrying one person while still legally married to another, द्विविवाह।

bigot (बिगॉट) ***n.*** a narrow-minded intolerant person in matters of religion, race or politics, कट्टरपंथी, धर्मांध।

bigotry (बिगॉट्री) ***n.*** the state of being a bigot, कट्टरता, धर्मांधता।

bigwig (बिगविग) ***n.*** an important person, बड़ा आदमी, बड़ी तोप।

bike (बाइक) ***n.*** a bicycle, साइकिल। ***v.*** to cycle, साइकिल चलाना।

bikini (बिकिनी) ***n.*** a woman's two-piece bathing suit, बिकनी।

bilateral (बाइलेटरल) ***adj.*** relating to two sides, parties, द्विपक्षीय, दुतरफ़ा।

bile (बाइल) ***n.*** a digestive fluid secreted by the liver, पित्त।

bilingual (बाइलिंग्वल) ***adj.*** 1. able to speak two languages, द्विभाषी। 2. written in two languages, द्विभाषिक।

bilious (बिलिअस) ***adj.*** suffering from the disorder of the bile, पित्तदोष से पीड़ित।

bill[1] (बिल) ***n.*** 1. a statement of costs for goods or charges for services, बिल, प्राप्यक, उधार पुर्ज़ा। 2. a draft of a law presented for approval to a legislative body, विधेयक, बिल। ***v.*** to prepare a statement of costs or charges, बिल बनाना।

bill[2] ***n.*** the beak of a bird, चोंच। ***v.*** 1. to touch beaks together, चोंच से चोंच मिलाना। 2. to caress, प्यार करना, चूमना-चाटना।

billet (बिलेट) ***n.*** 1. an order to provide boarding and lodging for soldiers, बिलेट, सैनिक को टिकाने का आदेश। 2. accommodation of this kind, टिकान। 3. target, निशाना।

billet-doux (बिले-डू) ***n.*** a love-letter, प्रेमपत्र।

billiards (बिल्यर्ड्स) ***n.*** a game played on the table with balls and cues, बिलियर्ड।

billion (बिल्यन) ***adj. & n.*** 1. a thousand million (U.S.), एक अरब। 2. a million millions (U.K.), दस खरब।

billionaire (बिल्यनेअर) ***n.*** a very rich person, अरबपति, धनाढ्य व्यक्ति।

billow (बिलो) ***n.*** a large swelling sea-wave, ऊँची लहर, हिलोर। ***v.*** to roll in billows, हिलोरें लेना, लहराना।

bimonthly (बाइमंथली) ***adj.*** 1. happening, coming or occurring every two months, द्विमासिक। 2. twice a month, biweekly, अर्धमासिक, पाक्षिक।

bin (बिन) ***n.*** a container, पात्र, आधान, डिब्बा; a dustbin, कूड़ेदान।

bind (बाइन्ड) ***v.*** (bound, binding) 1. to fasten or tie, बाँधना। 2. to bandage, पट्टी बाँधना। 3. to hold or restrain, बाँध देना, बंधन में लाना, जकड़ना। 4. to fasten the pages of a book into a cover, जिल्द बाँधना, जिल्दबंदी करना। 5. to place under an obligation, बाध्य करना, मजबूर करना।

binder (बाइन्डर) ***n.*** a bookbinder, दफ़्तरी, जिल्दसाज़।

binding ***n.*** 1. the act of fastening the pages of a book, जिल्दबंदी। 2. a book cover, जिल्द। 3. the order or rule which must be obeyed, बंधन।

binoculars (बाइनॉक्युलर्ज़) ***n.*** (plu.) an instrument for both eyes for seeing distant objects, दूरबीन, द्विनेत्री।

biochemistry (बाइओकेमिस्ट्री) ***n.*** the chemistry of living organisms, जीव-रसायन।

biographer (बाइओग्रैफ़र) ***n.*** one who writes a biography, जीवनी-लेखक।

biography (बाइओग्रैफ़ी) ***n.*** a written account of an individual's life, जीवनी, जीवनचरित।

biological (बाइओलॉजिकल) ***adj.*** of or pertaining to biology, जीव-विज्ञान-संबंधी।

biologist (बाइओलॉजिस्ट) ***n.*** an expert in biology, जीवविज्ञानी।

biology (बाइऑलोजी) ***n.*** the scientific study of the life and structure of living things, जीवविज्ञान, जैविकी।

bioplasm (बाइओप्लाज़्म) ***n.*** a living matter, जीवद्रव्य।

biopsy (बाइऑप्सी) ***n.*** an examination of tissue cut from a living body, प्राणी के काटे हुए ऊतक का परीक्षण, ऊतक-परीक्षण।

bioscope (बाइओस्कोप) ***n.*** an early kind of cinematograph, बाइस्कोप, सिनेमा।

biotic (बाइऑटिक) ***adj.*** of or pertaining to living things, जैव, जीव-संबंधी।

bipartite (बाइपार्टाइट) ***adv.*** divided into two parts, द्विभागीय।

biped (बाइपेड) ***adj. & n.*** having two feet, द्विपाद।

bipolar (बाइपोलर) ***adj.*** having two poles, द्विध्रुवी।

bird (बर्ड) ***n.*** a feathered animal with two wings and two legs, पक्षी, पंछी।

birdie (बर्डी) ***n.*** a little bird, पक्षीशावक।

birth (बर्थ) ***n.*** 1. the fact of being born, जन्म, पैदाइश। 2. a beginning, उद्भव, उत्पत्ति।

birth control ***n.*** voluntary control of the number of children conceived esp. by use of contraception, संतति-नियमन, संतति-निरोध।

birthday ***n.*** the day of anniversary of a person's birth, जन्मदिन।

birthmark ***n.*** a mark present on the body dating from birth, पैदाइशी निशान, जन्मचिह्न।

B

birthplace ***n.*** the place where someone is born, जन्मभूमि।

birthrate ***n.*** proportion of births to the population of the country, जन्मदर।

birthright ***n.*** a right to which a person is entitled by birth, जन्मसिद्ध अधिकार, पैदाइशी हक।

biscuit (बिस्किट) ***n.*** a small cake, बिस्कुट।

bisect (बाइसेक्ट) ***v.*** to divide into two equal parts, दो बराबर हिस्से लगाना, समद्विभाजित करना।

bisector (बाइसेक्टर) ***n.*** a line which bisects, समद्विभाजक रेखा, अर्धक रेखा।

bisexual (बाइसेक्सुअल) ***adj.*** having both type of sexual organs, उभयलिंगी, द्विलिंगी।

bishop (बिशप) ***n.*** a head of a diocese, धर्माचार्य, बिशप।

bison (बाइसन) ***n.*** a wild buffalo or ox, जंगली भैंसा, अरना।

bit[1] (बिट) ***n.*** 1. a small piece of something, टुकड़ा। 2. a piece bitten off, a morsel, कौर, ग्रास। 3. a short time, अल्प समय। 4. a small coin, छोटा सिक्का।

bit[2] a cutting point of an electric drill, बरमे का सिरा।

bitch (बिच) ***n.*** a female dog or wolf, कुतिया या मादा भेड़िया। 2. a spiteful woman, घृणित औरत, छिनाल।

bite (बाइट) ***v.*** (bit, bitten, biting) 1. to cut with the teeth, दाँतों से काट लेना, काटना। 2. to sting, डंक मारना, दंश मारना। ***n.*** 1. an act of biting, दाँत काटना, दंशन। 2. a wound made by this, दंतक्षत, दंश का घाव। 3. a mouthful cut, कौर। 4. food to eat, खाद्य-पदार्थ। □ **bite the dust,** धूल चाटना।

biting ***adj.*** 1. piercingly cold, अत्यधिक ठंडा, ग़ज़ब का ठंडा; biting cold, कड़ाके की ठंड। 2. sharp, तेज़, तीखा।

bitten (बिटन) ***v.*** p.p. of bite.

bitter (बिटर) ***adj.*** 1. sharp in taste, कड़वा, कटु। 2. causing sorrow, दुखद।

bitterness (बिटरनिस) ***n.*** the quality of being bitter, कड़वाहट, कटुता।

bitumen (बिटूमिन) ***n.*** asphalt, डामर, बिटुमन।

biweekly (बाइवीकली) ***adj.*** fortnightly, पाक्षिक।

bizarre (बिज़ार) ***adj.*** peculiar, odd, बेतुका, ऊटपटांग।

blab (ब्लैब) ***v.*** to let out a secret, भेद खोल देना।

black (ब्लैक) ***adj.*** 1. of the very darkest colour, काला, स्याह, साँवला। 2. without light, अंधकारपूर्ण, काला। 3. having dark skin, काला। 4. gloomy, निराशाजनक, अवसादपूर्ण। ***n.*** 1. black colour, काला रंग। 2. the black thing, काली वस्तु। 3. a person of a dark-skinned race, हब्शी। ***v.*** to make black, काला करना।

black art ***n.*** black magic.

black berry ***n.*** the bramble and its fruit, झड़बेरी।

blackboard ***n.*** a board for writing on with chalk, ब्लैकबोर्ड, श्यामपट्ट।

blacken (ब्लैकन) ***v.*** 1. to make or become black, काला होना या करना। 2. to defame, बदनाम होना या करना।

blackfaced (ब्लैकफ़ेस्ड) ***n.*** defamed, बदनाम, कुख्यात।

blackish (ब्लैकिश) ***adj.*** somewhat black, कुछ-कुछ काला, काला-सा।

black leg ***n.*** a person who works while his mates are on strike, विद्रोहकर्मी, काला कर्मचारी।

blacklist ***n.*** a list of dishonest or disapproved persons, काली सूची।

black magic ***n.*** witchcraft, जादू-टोना।

blackmail ***n.*** extortion by the threat of revealing a discreditable or criminal secret, भयादोहन। ***v.*** to obtain money from someone by blackmail, भयादोहन करना।

black market ***n.*** the illegal buying and selling of goods, काला बाज़ार।

blackout ***n.*** the extinguishing of all lights, घुप्प अँधेरा, अंधाकुप्प।

blacksheep ***n.*** a worthless member of the family, कुलकलंक, कुलद्रोही।

blacksmith ***n.*** a worker in iron, लुहार, लोहार।

bladder (ब्लैडर) ***n.*** 1. any membranous sac found in most animals capable of inflation to receive and contain liquids or gases, थैली, ब्लैडर। 2. a bag which can be filled with air or liquid, थैली, ब्लैडर।

blade (ब्लेड) ***n.*** 1. the flat edged cutting part (of a knife, sword etc., चाकू, छुरे, तलवार आदि का) फल, पत्ती। 2. razor-blade, (हजामत बनाने का) ब्लेड।

blame (ब्लेम) ***v.*** to hold responsible for something bad, दोष लगाना या मढ़ना। ***n.*** a fault, दोष।

blameworthy (ब्लेमवर्दी) ***adj.*** deserving blame, निंदनीय, सदोष।

blandish (ब्लैन्डिश) ***v.*** to coax by flattery, फुसलाना, चापलूसी करना।

blandishment ***n.*** a flattering speech, चापलूसी, ख़ुशामद।

blank (ब्लैंक) ***adj.*** 1. bearing no writing or marking, कोरा, खाली, निरंक। 2. empty, vacant, खाली, रिक्त। 3. not completed or filled in, जो भरा न गया हो। 4. expressing nothing, भावशून्य। ***n.*** 1. an empty space, रिक्त स्थान, खाली जगह। 2. a space to be filled in on a document, खाली जगह।

blanket (ब्लैंकिट) ***n.*** a thick woollen covering, कंबल।

blank verse (ब्लैंक वर्स) ***n.*** a verse without rhyme, अतुकांत छंद।

blare (ब्लेअर) ***v.*** to make a harsh loud sound, फटी आवाज़ में बोलना या बजना।

blasphemous (ब्लैसफ़ेमस) ***adj.*** full of blasphemy, निंदापूर्ण।

blasphemy (ब्लैसफ़ेमी) ***n.*** disrespectful talk about God or something sacred, ईशनिंदा, धर्मनिंदा।

blast (ब्लास्ट) ***n.*** 1. a strong gust of wind, हवा का झोंका। 2. ignition of an explosive charge, धमाका, विस्फोट। 3. a riotous party, शोर-शराबेवाली पार्टी। ☐ **at full blast,** पूरी शक्ति से। ***v.*** 1. to blow up, उड़ा देना। 2. to destroy, नष्ट कर देना।

blast furnace ***n.*** a furnace in which combustion is intensified by a blast of air, धमन-भट्ठी।

blatant (ब्लेटैन्ट) ***adj.*** glaringly obvious, बिलकुल स्पष्ट।

blaze (ब्लेज़) ***n.*** 1. a brightly burning fire, लपट, धधक। 2. a bright light, चमक, दीप्ति। ☐ **like blazes,** तेज़ी से, आँधी की तरह। ***v.*** 1. to burn brightly, लपलपाना, धधकना। 2. to shine brightly, चमचमाना, चमक उठना।

blazer (ब्लेज़र) ***n.*** a sports jacket

B

of a team, दल के खिलाड़ियों की जाकेट या कोट।

blazing ***adj.*** 1. burning fiercely, धधकता हुआ। 2. dazzling, प्रदीप्त।

bleach (ब्लीच) ***v.*** to make or become colourless, विरंजित होना या करना।

bleak (ब्लीक) ***adj.*** 1. harsh, कठोर, रूखा। 2. discouraging, gloomy, निराशाजनक, अंधकारपूर्ण।

bleary (ब्लिअरी) ***adj.*** dim, धुँधला।

bleat (ब्लीट) ***n.*** the cry of a goat, sheep, etc., मेंमें। ***v.*** 1. to make this cry, मेंमें करना, मिमियाना। 2. to speak foolishly, मूर्खतापूर्वक बातें करना।

bleed (ब्लीड) ***v.*** to lose blood, ख़ून बहना।

bleeding ***n.*** flow of the blood, ख़ून बहना, रक्तस्राव।

bleep (ब्लीप) ***n.*** a high-pitched repeated sound as a signal, खटखट, संकेत-ध्वनि, ब्लीप। ***v.*** to make this sound, संकेत-ध्वनि करना।

blemish (ब्लेमिश) ***n.*** a defect, flaw or deficiency, ऐब, दोष, कमी, त्रुटि।

blend (ब्लेन्ड) ***v.*** to mix or mingle, मिल जाना या मिलाना। ***n.*** a mixture of different sorts, मिश्रण।

bless (ब्लेस) ***v.*** to invoke divine favour on, आशीर्वाद देना।

blessed (ब्लेसिड) ***adj.*** 1. benedicted, आशीर्वादप्राप्त। 2. sacred, holy, पवित्र, पावन।

blessing ***n.*** 1. an act of asking or receiving God's favour, आशीर्वाद। 2. a gift from God, वरदान। ☐ **a blessing in disguise,** छिपा वरदान।

blind (ब्लाइन्ड) ***adj.*** 1. without sight, अंधा, नेत्रहीन, सूर। 2. not based on reason, अविचारित, विवेकशून्य। ***n.*** a blind person, अंधा व्यक्ति, सूरदास।

blind alley ***n.*** an alley that is closed at one end, बंद गली।

blindfold ***v.*** to cover the eyes with a bandage, आँखों पर पट्टी बाँधना। ***n.*** a piece of cloth used to block one's sight, आँखों पर बाँधी जानेवाली पट्टी, अंधौटी।

blindly ***adv.*** 1. thoughtlessly, बिना विचारे। 2. gropingly, टटोलते हुए।

blindness (ब्लाइंडनिस) ***n.*** the state of being blind, अंधापन, अंधता।

blink (ब्लिंक) ***v.*** 1, to close and open one's eyes rapidly, आँखें झपकना। 2. to flash on and off, झपझप करना, झपझपाना।

blip (ब्लिप) ***n.*** a very short sound as if produced by a machine, हलकी ध्वनि, खट।

bliss (ब्लिस) ***n.*** complete and perfect happiness, आनंद, परमानंद।

blissful (ब्लिसफ़ुल्) ***adj.*** full of bliss, आनंदमय, परम सुखी, अत्यंत सुखद।

blister (ब्लिस्टर) ***n.*** a thin watery swelling under the skin, छाला, फफोला।

blistering ***adj.*** 1. hot, तप्त, गरम। 2. strong, उग्र, प्रचंड, घोर।

blithe (ब्लाइथ) ***adj.*** joyful, ख़ुश, प्रसन्न।

blitz (ब्लिट्स) ***n.*** 1. a sudden or swift attack, धावा। ***v.*** to attack suddenly, धावा बोल देना।

blizzard (ब्लिज़र्ड) ***n.*** a snow-storm, बर्फ़ीला तूफ़ान।

bloated (ब्लोटिड) ***adj.*** swollen, फूला हुआ।

blob (ब्लॉब) ***n.*** 1. zero, शून्य, सिफ़र। 2. a drop of liquid, बूँद। 3. a stain, धब्बा।

bloc (ब्लॉक) ***n.*** a group of persons, nations etc., गुट। □ **en bloc**, एक साथ, सब-के-सब।

block (ब्लॉक) ***n.*** 1. a piece of wood, गुटका, कुंदा। 2. a lump of rock, शिलाखंड। 3. a piece of land, भूखंड, खंड। 4. a wooden plate for printing, ठप्पा, ब्लॉक। 5. a mould, ढाँचा। 6. a row of separate buildings, ब्लॉक, प्रखंड। 7. a large section of seats, shares etc., प्रखंड। 8. an obstruction, बाधा। 9. a person's head, सिर। ***v.*** 1. to prevent or obstruct, बाधा डालना, रोकना। 2. to stop or impede, अवरुद्ध करना, बंद करना। 3. to shape or form with a block, साँचे में ढालना, ठप्पे से बनाना।

blockade (ब्लॉकेड) ***n.*** the complete closure of a place by the forces, नाकेबंदी। ***v.*** to set up a blockade of, नाकेबंदी करना।

blockage (ब्लॉकेज) ***n.*** the state of being blocked or something that blocks, अवरोध, बाधा।

blockhead (ब्लॉकहेड) ***n.*** a stupid person, मूढ़ व्यक्ति।

blond (ब्लॉन्ड) ***adj.*** having a pink and white skin and yellowish brown hair, गौर वर्ण तथा सुनहरे बालोंवाला / वाली।

blonde (ब्लॉन्ड) ***n.*** a blond girl, सुनहरे बालोंवाली गोरी लड़की।

blood (ब्लड) ***n.*** 1. the red liquid in the bodies of animals, ख़ून, रक्त। 2. life, जीवन। 3. bloodshed, रक्तपात, ख़ून-ख़राबा। 4. a murder, हत्या।

blood bank ***n.*** a place where blood is stored, रक्त-केंद्र।

blood bath ***n.*** a massacre, नरसंहार, क़त्लेआम।

blood brother ***n.*** a real brother, सगा भाई।

blood donor ***n.*** one who donates his blood, रक्तदाता।

blood group ***n.*** a group of persons having blood with same properties, रक्त वर्ग।

bloodhound (ब्लडहाउन्ड) ***n.*** a hound with a keen sense of smell, एक तरह का शिकारी कुत्ता, भेदिया कुत्ता।

bloodless (ब्लडलिस) ***adj.*** without bloodshed, रक्तविहीन।

blood poisoning ***n.*** poisoning of the blood, रक्त-विषाक्तता।

blood pressure ***n.*** the pressure of the blood within the arteries, रक्तचाप।

blood-red ***adj.*** red as blood, ख़ून की तरह लाल, ख़ूनी।

bloodshed (ब्लडशेड) ***n.*** the killing or wounding of people, मारकाट, रक्तपात।

bloodstain (ब्लडस्टेन) ***n.*** a mark made by blood, ख़ून का दाग़।

bloodsucker (ब्लडसकर) ***n.*** one who sucks blood, ख़ून चूसनेवाला।

bloodthirsty (ब्लडथर्स्टी) ***adj.*** eager for bloodshed, ख़ून का प्यासा, रक्तपिपासु।

blood transfusion ***n.*** transfusion of blood from one person to another, एक व्यक्ति का रक्त दूसरे व्यक्ति को चढ़ाया जाना।

blood vessel ***n.*** a vessel through which blood circulates, रक्तवाहिका।

bloody (ब्लडी) ***adj.*** 1. bleeding, जिसमें से रक्त बह रहा हो। 2. stained with blood, रक्तरंजित। 3. causing or marked by bloodshed, ख़ूनी। 4. damned, कम्बख़्त।

B

bloom (ब्लूम) ***n.*** 1. a flower, फूल, पुष्प। 2. prime of life, यौवन। ***v.*** 1. to bear flower, फूलना, खिलना। 2. to flourish, पनपना, समृद्ध होना।

blossom (ब्लॉसम) ***n.*** 1. a flower of a fruit tree, फूल, पुष्प। 2. a mass of such flowers, मंजरी। ***v.*** 1. to bloom, फूलना, खिलना, फलना। 2. to flourish, पनपना, फलना-फूलना।

blot (ब्लॉट) ***n.*** 1. a spot or stain, दाग़, धब्बा। 2. a moral disgrace, कलंक, लांछन।

blotting paper ***n.*** an absorbent paper for drying ink writing, सोख़्ता।

blouse (ब्लाउज़) ***n.*** a loose shirtlike garment worn by women, ब्लाउज़, कुरती।

blow[1] (ब्लो) ***v.*** (blew, blown, blowing) 1. (of the wind) to move or flow, बहना, चलना। 2. to move by the current of air, बहना, उड़ना। 3. to send out strong current of air from the lungs, फूँकना, फूँक मारना। 4. to give out a current of air as from a pair of bellows, धौंकनी से हवा देना, धौंकना। 5. to sound or cause to sound by expelling a current of air, बजाना, फूँकना। 6. to pant, हाँफना। 7. to cause to explode, विस्फोट करना। □ **blow one's own trumpet,** अपने मुँह मियाँ मिट्ठू बनना; **blow out,** (i) फूँक मारकर बुझाना; (ii) फट जाना; **blow over,** थम जाना, टल जाना, निकल जाना, शांत हो जाना; **blow up,** (i) फट उठना; (ii) फुलाना; (iii) बड़ा बनाना; (iv) गरम हो जाना, क्रुद्ध होना; (v) आना, आ धमकना। (vi) धमाके से फट या उड़ जाना अथवा उड़ा देना।

blow[2] ***n.*** 1. a hard or violent stroke, आघात, प्रहार, वार। 2. a push, धक्का। 3. a shock, आघात, धक्का, झटका।

blower (ब्लोअर) ***n.*** an apparatus for blowing, धौंकनी।

blowpipe (ब्लोपाइप) ***n.*** a pipe used for blowing, धौंकनी।

blubber (ब्लबर) ***n.*** whale fat, व्हेल मछली की चरबी। ***v.*** to weep noisily, ज़ोर-ज़ोर से रोना।

blue (ब्लू) ***adj.*** of the colour of the sky, नीला, आसमानी। 2. dirty, obscene, गंदा, अश्लील। ***n.*** 1. blue colour, नीला रंग। 2. the blue; the clear sky, नीला आकाश। □ **a bolt from the blue,** सहसा होनेवाला वज्रपात। ***v.*** to make blue, नीला करना, नीले रंग में रंगना।

blueblack (ब्लूब्लैक) ***adj.*** very dark blue, कालापन लिये नीला, गहरा नीला।

blueblood (ब्लूब्लड) ***n.*** a noble, कुलीन व्यक्ति।

bluebook (ब्लूबुक) ***n.*** an official printed report, सरकारी दस्तावेज़।

bluejacket (ब्लूजैकिट) ***n.*** a sailor in the navy, नौसैनिक।

bluemoon (ब्लूमून) ***n.*** a very long time, दीर्घकाल। □ **once in a bluemoon,** यदा-कदा, कभी-कभार।

blueprint (ब्लूप्रिन्ट) ***n.*** 1. a blue photographic print of building plans, नीला नक्शा। 2. a programme of action, कार्य-योजना।

blue ribbon ***n.*** the first prize, प्रथम पुरस्कार।

blue-stocking ***n.*** a well-read woman, प्रबुद्ध / सुशिक्षित महिला।

bluff (ब्लफ़) ***v.*** to deceive by making a bold pretence, झाँसा देना, धुप्पल देना। ***n.*** the act of bluffing, झाँसा, धुप्पल।

blunder (ब्लन्डर) ***n.*** a stupid mistake, मूर्खता-भरी भूल। ***v.*** to make such a mistake, मूर्खता-भरी भूल करना, भारी भूल करना।

blunt (ब्लन्ट) ***adj.*** 1. not sharp, भोथरा, कुंद। 2. dull, मंदबुद्धि। 3. bold in speech, outspoken, मुँहफट। 4. curt, रूखा।

bluntly ***adv.*** 1. outspokenly, साफ़-साफ़, मुँह पर। 2. curtly, रुखाई से।

blur (ब्लर) ***v.*** 1. to smear or stain, गंदा कर देना, दाग़ लगा देना। 2. to dim, धुँधला कर देना। ***n.*** 1. a smear or stain, दाग़, धब्बा या लेप। 2. dimness, धुँधलापन।

blurt (ब्लर्ट) ***v.*** to utter abruptly and without thought, बिना सोचे-समझे सहसा बक देना।

blush (ब्लश) ***v.*** 1. to become suddenly red in face from shame or modesty, लाज से भर उठना या शर्म से गड़ जाना। 2. to feel ashamed, शर्मिंदा होना, लज्जित होना।

blushing ***adj.*** becoming red in the face, लाज-भरा।

bluster (ब्लस्टर) ***v.*** to blow in violent gusts, (हवा या पानी के) थपेड़े चलना या उठना।

boa (बोआ) ***n.*** a large non-poisonous snake that coils around its prey, अजगर।

boar (बोर) ***n.*** a male wild pig, बनैला सुअर।

board (बोर्ड) ***n.*** 1. a flat piece of wood, तख़्ता, पटरा, पट। 2. a thick stiff paper used for book covers, बोर्ड, दफ़्ती। 3. food served daily to paying guests, भोजन। 4. a committee or group of officials, परिषद्, बोर्ड, मंडल। 5. the side of the ship, जहाज़ का किनारा। ***v.*** 1. to cover with boards, तख़्ते जड़ना। 2. to provide with food and lodging for a charge, ठहरने और भोजन की सशुल्क व्यवस्था करना। 3. to receive food and lodging for a charge, शुल्क देकर कहीं ठहरना और भोजन पाना। 4. to go aboard, सवार होना, गाड़ी, जहाज़ आदि पर चढ़ना।

boarder (बोर्डर) ***n.*** 1. one who pays for both meals and lodging at another's house, सशुल्क अतिथि। 2. a student living in a boarding house, छात्रावासी।

boarding house ***n.*** 1. a house that provides meals and lodging for a charge, सशुल्क आहारगृह। 2. such place for outdoor students, छात्रावास।

boast (बोस्ट) ***n.*** an expression of self-praise, शेख़ी, डींग। ***v.*** to talk proudly, शेख़ी हाँकना, डींग मारना।

boastful ***adj.*** tending to boast, शेख़ी-भरा।

boat (बोट) ***n.*** a small open sailing vessel, नाव, नौका, किश्ती।

boating ***n.*** going out in a boat for pleasure, नौकाविहार।

boatman (बोटमैन) ***n.*** one who rows or hires out small boats, मल्लाह, माँझी।

bob (बॉब) ***v.*** to cut hair short so that it hangs loosely on shoulders, (औरतों के) बाल इस प्रकार काटना कि वे कंधों पर झूलते रहें। ***n.*** the style of bobbed hair, बॉब, लटकते बाल।

bobbin (बॉबिन) ***n.*** a spool or reel for thread, फिरकी, अटेरन या परेता।

B

bobtailed (बॉबटेल्ड) ***adj.*** having a docked tail, दुमकटा।

bode (बोड) ***v.*** to be an omen of, (का) लक्षण या शकुन होना।

bodice (बॉडिस) ***n.*** the fitted upper part of a woman's dress, कुरती, चोली।

bodily (बॉडिली) ***adj.*** of or pertaining to the body, शरीरी, दैहिक। ***adv.*** as a whole, सब मिलाकर।

body (बॉडी) ***n.*** 1. the physical structure of a man or animal, शरीर, देह। 2. the main or central part of a vehicle, ship etc., framework, ढाँचा। 3. a corpse or carcass, शव, जानवर की लाश। 4. the main part of the body, धड़। 5. a person, व्यक्ति।

bodyguard (बॉडीगार्ड) ***n.*** a personal guard, अंगरक्षक।

bog (बॉग) ***n.*** marsh, दलदल, कीचड़।

bogus (बोगस) ***adj.*** fake, counterfeit, नकली, जाली, बोगस।

boil[1] (बॉइल) ***n.*** a painful pus-filled swelling under skin, फोड़ा।

boil[2] ***v.*** 1. to heat to boiling point, उबालना, खौलाना। 2. to bubble up when heated, उबलना, खौलना, उबाल खाना। 3. to cook or be cooked by boiling, उबालना या उबलना। 4. to be greatly excited, आवेश में आना।

boiler (बॉइलर) ***n.*** a plant or tank in which steam is made, बॉयलर, वाष्पित्र।

boisterous (बॉइस्टेरस) ***adj.*** 1. rough and stormy, हुड़दंगी, ऊधमी। 2. violent, प्रचंड, उग्र।

bold (बोल्ड) ***adj.*** fearless and courageous, दिलेर, साहसी।

bole (बोल) ***n.*** stem of a tree, तना।

bolster (बोल्स्टर) ***n.*** a large pillow, बड़ा तकिया, मसनद। ***v.*** 1. to give support to, सहारा देना। 2. to encourage, उत्साहित करना।

bolt (बोल्ट) ***n.*** 1. a metal bar for fastening a door, सिटकिनी, चटखनी। 2. a screw for fastening things together, बोल्ट। ***v.*** 1. to fasten with a bolt, सिटकिनी लगाना, बोल्ट कसना। 2. to gulp down, भकोसना, गटकना।

bomb (बॉम) ***n.*** an explosive container used as weapon, बम। ***v.*** to attack or destroy with bombs, बम मारना या गिराना, बमबारी करना।

bombard (बॉम्बार्ड) ***v.*** to attack with bombs, बमबारी करना।

bombastic (बॉम्बैस्टिक) ***adj.*** full of high sounding words, शब्दाडंबरपूर्ण।

bomber (बॉमर) ***n.*** an aircraft that drops bombs, बमवर्षक विमान।

bombshell (बॉमशेल) ***n.*** 1. a bomb, बम। 2. a shocking surprise, अनहोनी घटना।

bona fide (बोनाफ़ाइडि) ***adj.*** 1. genuine, सच्चा, सही, प्रामाणिक। 2. done in good faith, सद्भावपूर्ण, सदाशयपूर्ण, निष्कपट।

bonanza (बोनैन्ज़ा) ***n.*** a windfall, अप्रत्याशित लाभ।

bond (बॉन्ड) ***n.*** 1. something that binds together, बाँधनेवाली चीज़ या बात, बंद। 2. a binding agreement, अनुबंध, अनुबंध-पत्र। 3. a certificate of debt, बॉन्ड, बंधपत्र। 4. something that unites people, बंधन। 5. writing paper of high quality, लिखने का बढ़िया काग़ज़, बॉन्ड पेपर। 6. money deposited as a guarantee, मुचलका। ***v.*** 1. to tie or unite, बाँधना, बाँधकर

B

रखना। 2. to stick together, जोड़ना।

bondage (बॉन्डिज) ***n.*** slavery, दासता, गुलामी।

bonded (बॉन्डिड) ***adj.*** tied, united, बँधा हुआ, बद्ध; bonded labour, बँधुआ मज़दूर।

bone (बोन) ***n.*** one of the hard parts of the body, हड्डी, अस्थि। □ **bone of contention,** झगड़े की जड़।

bonfire (बॉनफ़ाइअर) ***n.*** a large outdoor fire, अलाव।

bonnet (बॉनिट) ***n.*** 1. a hat with strings, तस्मेदार टोपी। 2. a metal lid over the front of the car, बॉनिट।

bonny (बॉनी) ***adj.*** goodlooking, सुदर्शन, सलोना।

bonus (बोनस) ***n.*** a share of the profit given to the workers or shareholders, लाभांश।

bony (बोनी) ***adj.*** very thin, बहुत दुबला।

book (बुक) ***n.*** a collection of written, printed or blank sheets of paper bound together, पुस्तक, किताब। ***v.*** to reserve, आरक्षित करना।

booking ***n.*** an act of entering in the schedule, सूची में लिखा जाना, बुक करना।

bookish (बुकिश) ***adj.*** fond of books, fond of reading, पुस्तकप्रेमी।

book-keeping (बुककीपिंग) ***n.*** the systematic recording of business transactions, बही-लेखन।

booklet (बुकलिट) ***n.*** a small book, पुस्तिका।

bookseller (बुकसेलर) ***n.*** one who sells books, पुस्तक-विक्रेता।

bookstall (बुकस्टॉल) ***n.*** a stall for books, बुकस्टॉल।

bookworm (बुकवर्म) ***n.*** a person who is very fond of reading books, किताबी कीड़ा।

boom (बूम) ***v.*** 1. to make a deep resonant sound, गरज उठना, दनदनाना। 2. to flourish swiftly, तेज़ी से पनपना, समृद्ध होना। ***n.*** 1. a booming sound, गरज, दनदनाहट। 2. a sudden increase, तेज़ी, बढ़ती, बढ़ोतरी, समृद्धि। 3. a period of growth, गरम बाज़ारी, समृद्धिकाल।

boon (बून) ***n.*** a blessing, वरदान, वर।

boor (बूर) ***n.*** a rude or ill-mannered person, उजड्ड व्यक्ति, अशिष्ट व्यक्ति।

boost (बूस्ट) ***v.*** to promote, उन्नत करना, बढ़ावा देना, ***n.*** an upward thrust, बढ़ावा।

boot (बूट) ***n.*** a shoe, जूता, बूट।

booth (बूथ) ***n.*** a small enclosed compartment, बूथ, मंडप, कोष्ठ।

booty (बूटी) ***n.*** 1. loot taken from the enemy, लूटा हुआ माल, लूट। 2. stolen goods, चोरी का माल।

border (बॉर्डर) ***n.*** 1. an edge, किनारा। 2. a boundary, सीमा। 3. the part near the boundary, सीमांत, किनारा, तट।

bore (बोर) ***v.*** to make a hole by drilling, बोर करना, परिवेधन करना, बेधना। ***n.*** a hole made by drilling, छेद।

boredom (बोर्डम) ***n.*** the condition of being bored, उकताहट, ऊब।

born (बॉर्न) ***adj.*** brought into existence by birth, पैदा, उत्पन्न, जात।

borne (बोर्न) ***v.*** p.p. of bear.

borough (बरो) ***n.*** a town or a division of a large town, नगर या महानगर का भाग।

borrow (बॉरो) ***v.*** to receive

temporarily on loan, माँगना, उधार लेना।

bosom (बूज़म) ***n.*** a (woman's) breast, chest, छाती, वक्षस्थल।

boss (बॉस) ***n.*** an employer, नियोजक।

botanical (बॉटैनिकल) ***adj.*** 1. of botany, वनस्पति-विज्ञान संबंधी। 2. of plants and trees, वानस्पतिक।

botanical garden ***n.*** वानस्पतिक उद्यान।

botanist (बॉटनिस्ट) ***n.*** an expert in botany, वनस्पति-विज्ञानी।

botany (बॉटनी) ***n.*** the scientific study of plants and trees, वनस्पति-विज्ञान।

botch (बॉच) ***v.*** to spoil, ख़राब कर देना, बिगाड़ देना। ***n.*** a spoiled work, रद्दी काम।

both (बोथ) ***pron. adj.*** the two, दोनों।

bother (बॉदर) ***v.*** to annoy or pester, तंग करना, परेशान करना।

bothersome ***adj.*** troublesome, कष्टकारक।

bottle (बॉटल) ***n.*** a glass container with a narrow neck, बोतल, शीशी।

bottom (बॉटम) ***n.*** 1. the lowest part of anything, तल, पेंदा। 2. the ground under a stretch of water, नदी, समुद्र आदि का तल। 3. the buttocks, चूतड़।

bough (बॉउ) ***n.*** a large branch of a tree, टहनी, शाखा, डाल।

boulder (बोल्डर) ***n.*** a large rounded mass of stone, शिलाखंड, प्रस्तरखंड।

bounce (बाउन्स) ***v.*** 1. to spring back from a collision, (गेंद का या गेंद की तरह) टकराकर लौटना, उछाल लेना, उछलना। 2. (of a cheque) to be returned by a bank, बैंक से चेक का वापस आना। ***n.*** 1. a spring or rebound, उछाल। 2. a leap or jump, छलाँग।

bouncing ***adj.*** healthy and active, स्वस्थ और सक्रिय, हृष्ट-पुष्ट।

bound[1] (बाउन्ड) ***adj.*** heading toward, (की ओर या को) जानेवाला।

bound[2] ***v.*** to limit, घेरना।

boundary (बाउन्डरी) ***n.*** 1. a border, सीमा, हद। 2. hit to the boundary, बाउंड्री, चौका।

boundless (बाउन्डलिस) ***adj.*** without limits, सीमाहीन, निस्सीम।

bountiful (बाउन्टिफ़ुल) ***adj.*** 1. giving generously, उदार। 2. plentiful, अत्यधिक।

bounty (बाउन्टी) ***n.*** 1. generosity, उदारता, दानशीलता। 2. a generous gift, उपहार। 3. money given by a government as a reward, राजकीय सहायता, आनुतोषिक।

bouquet (बुके) ***n.*** a bunch or cluster of flowers, गुलदस्ता।

bourgeois (बूर्ज्वा) ***n.*** a member of the middle class, मध्यमवर्गीय व्यक्ति।

bout (बाउट) ***n.*** a boxing contest, मुक्केबाज़ों की लड़ाई।

boutique (बूटीक) ***n.*** a small shop for fashionable clothes etc., बुटीक।

bovine (बोवाइन) ***adj.*** of or pertaining to an ox or cow, गोजातीय।

bow[1] (बो) ***n.*** a device for shooting arrows, धनुष, कमान।

bow[2] ***v.*** 1. to make a bow, नमन करना, सिर झुकाना। 2. to bend, झुकना या झुकाना। 3. to submit, झुक जाना, मान जाना।

bowels (बॉवल्स) ***n.*** (plu.) an intestine, आँत, अँतड़ी।

bower (बॉवर) ***n.*** a leafy recess or shelter, कुंज, लतामंडप।

bowl[1] (बोल) ***n.*** 1. a rounded hollow container, कटोरा, कटोरदान। 2. the contents of a bowl, कटोरा-भर सामान।

B

bowl[2] ***n.*** a ball in certain games, गेंद। ***v.*** 1. to throw a ball towards a batsman, गेंदबाज़ी करना। 2. to put out a batsman by bowling the balls, बोल्ड कर देना।

bowler (बोलर) ***n.*** a person who bowls regularly in the game of cricket, गेंदबाज़।

bowman (बोमैन) ***n.*** an archer, तीरंदाज़।

box[1] (बॉक्स) ***n.*** 1. a rectangular container with a lid, संदूक, बक्सा, पेटी। 2. a separate seating compartment in a theatre, कक्ष। 3. an enclosed stand where a witness gives evidence, कटघरा।

box[2] ***n.*** 1. a slap on the ears, थप्पड़। 2. a blow with a fist, मुक्का। ***v.*** 1. to slap, थप्पड़ या मुक्का मारना। 2. to fight with the fists, मुक्केबाज़ी करना।

boxer (बॉक्सर) ***n.*** a person who fights with his fists, मुक्केबाज़।

boxing ***n.*** the sport and art of fighting with the fists, मुक्केबाज़ी, बॉक्सिंग।

boy (बॉइ) ***n.*** a male child, लड़का, बालक।

boycott (बॉइकॉट) ***v.*** to refuse to accept, use or attend,बायकाट/बहिष्कार करना। ***n.*** an act of boycotting, बायकाट, बहिष्कार।

boyfriend (बॉइफ्रेन्ड) ***n.*** a male companion of a young lady, यार, प्रेमी, प्रेमपात्र।

boyhood (बॉइहुड) ***n.*** the period of being a boy, बचपन, बाल्यावस्था, लड़कपन।

brace (ब्रेस) ***n.*** 1. something used for supporting, stiffening or fastening, टेक या पट्टी। 2. a pair, जोड़ा। 3. a mark }or {, बंधनी। 4. (plu.) suspenders for trousers, गेलिस। ***v.*** 1. to support or render firm, टेक लगाना, दृढ़ बनाना, मज़बूत करना। 2. to put or set firmly, दृढ़ता से स्थापित करना।

bracelet (ब्रेसलिट) ***n.*** an ornament for the wrist, कंगन, कड़ा।

bracket (ब्रैकिट) ***n.*** 1. a support, टेक। 2. a piece of metal or wood fixed in wall to support something, ब्रैकिट। 3. either of the marks used in pairs for enclosing a piece of information, (), {}, [ ], ब्रैकिट, कोष्ठक। ***v.*** to enclose in brackets, कोष्ठक लगाना।

brag (ब्रैग) ***n.*** a boast, शेख़ी, डींग। ***v.*** to boast, शेख़ी हाँकना, डींग मारना।

braggart (ब्रैगर्ट) ***n.*** one who brags a lot, शेख़ीख़ोर।

braid (ब्रेड) ***v.*** to twist or intertwine together, गूँथना। ***n.*** a plait of hair, लट या चोटी।

brain (ब्रेन) ***n.*** 1. a mind, मस्तिष्क, दिमाग़। 2. intelligence, बुद्धि।

brainless (ब्रेनलिस) ***adj.*** stupid, मूर्ख।

brake (ब्रेक) ***n.*** 1. a device for slowing or stopping motion, ब्रेक। 2. a restraint, नियंत्रण।

bran (ब्रैन) ***n.*** the husk of grain, चोकर, भूसी।

branch (ब्रान्च) ***n.*** 1. any woody extension growing from the trunk or main stem, टहनी, डाल, शाखा। 2. a part or division of a larger system, शाखा। 3. a separately located unit of a firm, शाखा। ***v.*** to spread out branches, शाखाएँ फूटना या निकलना; शाखाएँ फैलाना।

brand (ब्रैन्ड) ***n.*** a trademark or

B

distinctive name of a product, छाप, ब्रैंड। *v.* 1. to mark, to mark with a brand, चिह्नित करना, छाप डालना। 2. to stigmatize, कलंक लगाना।

brandish (ब्रैन्डिश) *v.* to wave (a sword) menacingly, चमकाना, भाँजना।

brandy (ब्रैन्डी) *n.* a strong alcoholic drink, ब्रांडी।

brass (ब्रास) *n.* 1. an alloy of copper and zinc, पीतल। 2. impudence, उद्धतता।

brassiere (ब्रेसिअर) *n.* a woman's under-garment, चोली, ब्रा।

brat (ब्रैट) *n.* a spoiled child, बिगड़ैल बच्चा।

bravado (ब्रेवाडो) *n.* the (often unnecessery) showing of courage, (दिखावे की) दिलेरी या बहादुरी।

brave (ब्रेव) *adj.* 1. powerful and courageous, वीर, बहादुर।

brawl (ब्रॉल) *n.* a noisy quarrel, लड़ाई-झगड़ा। *v.* to quarrel, लड़ाई-झगड़ा करना।

brawny (ब्रॉनी) *adj.* strong and muscular, हट्टा-कट्टा।

bray (ब्रे) *n.* a cry of a donkey, रेंक। *v.* to make such cry, रेंकना।

brazen (ब्रेजन) *adj.* 1. made of brass, पीतल का। 2. impudent, उद्धत।

brazier (ब्रेज़िअर) *n.* a metal container to hold burning coals, अँगीठी। 2. a brass worker, कसेरा।

breach (ब्रीच) a violation, उल्लंघन, अतिक्रमण। *v.* to make a breach in, दरार डालना।

bread (ब्रेड) *n.* a food made of flour, रोटी।

breadth (ब्रेड्थ) *n.* width, चौड़ाई।

break (ब्रेक) *v.* (broke, broken, breaking) 1. to fall or cause to fall into pieces, टूटना या तोड़ना, 2. to open the surface of, तोड़ना, खोलना। 3. to transgress, उल्लंघन करना, भंग करना। 4. to force a way, बलात् घुस जाना।

breakage (ब्रेकिज) *n.* the things broken, टूट-फूट।

breakdown (ब्रेकडाउन) *n.* a collapse, निपात।

breakfast (ब्रेकफ़ास्ट) *n.* the first meal of the day, नाश्ता।

break-in (ब्रेक-इन) *n.* a forcible entry, घुसपैठ।

breakneck (ब्रेकनेक) *adj.* dangerously fast, तीव्र।

breast (ब्रेस्ट) *n.* the front part of a woman's body, छाती, सीना। *v.* to boldly meet or confront, डटकर सामना करना।

breath (ब्रेथ) *n.* the air taken into and let out of the lungs, साँस, श्वास।

breathe (ब्रीद) *v.* 1. to inhale, साँस लेना। 2. to exhale, साँस छोड़ना। 3. to utter quietly, फुसफुस करना।

bred (ब्रेड) *v.* p.t. & p.p. of breed.

breech (ब्रीच) *n.* 1. the buttocks, चूतड़। 2. the rear of gun-barrel, नालपृष्ठ।

breed (ब्रीड) *v.* (bred, breeding) 1. to produce offspring, प्रजनन करना। 2. to rear, पालन-पोषण करना। *n.* a variety of animals with special features, नस्ल, प्रजाति।

breeding *n.* 1. the production of young from animals, प्रजनन। 2. good manners and behaviour, कुल-शील, आचरण-व्यवहार। 4. education, शिक्षा, शिक्षण।

breeze (ब्रीज़) *n.* a light, gentle wind, समीर।

brethren (ब्रेदरन) ***n.*** (plu. of brother), भाई-बंधु।

brevity (ब्रेविटी) ***n.*** briefness, संक्षिप्तता।

brew (ब्रू) ***v.*** 1. to make beer, tea etc., तैयार करना, बनाना। 2. to develop, विकसित होना, उद्‌भूत होना, खड़ा होना। ***n.*** the drink brewed, बनाया या तैयार किया हुआ पेय।

brewery (ब्रूअरी) ***n.*** a place or factory where brewing is carried on, मद्य-निर्माणशाला।

bribe (ब्राइब) ***n.*** something given to a person to influence his judgement, घूस, रिश्वत। ***v.*** to give a bribe to, रिश्वत/घूस देना।

bribery (ब्राइबरी) ***n.*** the practice of offering or accepting bribe, घूसख़ोरी, रिश्वतखोरी।

brick (ब्रिक) ***n.*** 1. a rectangular block of baked clay used as construction material, ईंट। 2. such block of any other substance, ईंट।

brickwork (ब्रिकवर्क) ***n.*** the act of bricklaying, चुनाई, ईंटों का काम।

bridal (ब्राइडल) ***adj.*** of wedding, विवाह-संबंधी।

bride (ब्राइड) ***n.*** a newly married woman, नववधू, दुल्हन।

bridegroom (ब्राइडग्रूम) ***n.*** a man who has just been married or is about to be married, दुल्हा, वर।

bridesmaid (ब्राइड्ज़मेड) ***n.*** a young girl attending the bride, सहबाली, वधू-सखी।

bridge (ब्रिज) ***n.*** 1. a structure built over a river, highway etc., to provide a way across, पुल, सेतु, ब्रिज। 2. something that connects other parts, सेतु। 3. a card game, ब्रिज। ***v.*** 1. to build a bridge over, पुल बाँधना। 2. to get across, पार करना या उतरना।

bridle (ब्राइडल) ***n.*** the part of a horse's harness that goes on its head, लगाम। ***v.*** 1. to put a bridle on, लगाम डालना। 2. to restrain, नियंत्रित करना।

brief (ब्रीफ़) ***adj.*** short in length or duration, छोटा, अल्पकालिक। ***n.*** 1. a short or condensed statement, सार, सारकथन, संक्षेप। 2. (plu.) underwear, जाँघिया।

briefcase (ब्रीफ़केस) ***n.*** a small portable flat case for carrying documents, ब्रीफ़केस।

briefly ***adv.*** in short, संक्षेप में।

brigade (ब्रिगेड) ***n.*** a unit of army, वाहिनी, ब्रिगेड।

brigadier (ब्रिगेडिअर) ***n.*** a military officer commanding a brigade, ब्रिगेडियर।

bright (ब्राइट) ***adj.*** 1. full of light, shining, चमकदार। 2. cheerful, प्रसन्न, प्रफुल्ल। 3. quickwitted, तीव्रबुद्धि, चतुर। 4. clear, vivid, स्पष्ट, चटक, तेज़।

brighten (ब्राइटन) ***v.*** to make or become bright, चमका देना या चमक उठना।

brilliance (ब्रिल्यन्स) ***n.*** the quality of being brilliant, चमकीलापन।

brilliant (ब्रिल्यन्ट) ***adj.*** 1. very bright, चटक, चटकीला। 2. very clever, होशियार, चतुर। 3. having or showing great skill, पटु, प्रवीण। 4. talented, प्रतिभासंपन्न। 5. fine, शानदार, वैभवपूर्ण।

brim (ब्रिम) ***n.*** the top edge of cup, bowl etc., किनारा, लब, मुँह।

brimful, brimfull (ब्रिम्फ़ुल) ***adj.*** full to the brim, मुँह तक भरा हुआ।

B

brine (ब्राइन) ***n.*** water saturated with salt, खारा पानी।

bring (ब्रिंग) ***v.*** (brought, bringing) 1. to cause to come with oneself by carrying or leading, लाना, ले आना। 2. to produce, निकालना, प्रस्तुत करना।

brink (ब्रिंक) ***n.*** the edge of a steep descent, कगार, किनारा।

brinkmanship (ब्रिंकमैनशिप) ***n.*** extreme courage, अति साहस।

brisk (ब्रिस्क) ***adj.*** 1. moving or acting quickly, फुर्तीला, तेज़। 2. lively, सजीव, जीवंत, जानदार।

bristle (ब्रिसल) ***n.*** 1. a short stiff hair, छोटा कड़ा बाल, शूक। 2. a hair, wire, etc. in a brush, ब्रुश का बाल।

British (ब्रिटिश) ***adj.*** 1. of Great Britain, ग्रेट ब्रिटेन का, ब्रितानवी। 2. of Britishers, अंग्रेज़ों का, अंग्रेज़ी।

brittle (ब्रिटल) ***adj.*** fragile, जल्दी टूटनेवाला, भंगुर, भुरभुरा।

broach (ब्रोच) ***v.*** 1. to pierce छेदना। 2. to introduce (as a subject) बात चलाना।

broad (ब्रॉड) ***adj.*** wide, चौड़ा।

broadcast (ब्रॉडकास्ट) ***v.*** to transmit by radio or television, प्रसारित करना। ***n.*** 1. transmission of a radio or television, प्रसारण।

broaden (ब्रॉडन) ***v.*** to make or become broad, चौड़ा होना या करना।

broadly (ब्रॉडली) ***adv.*** generally, सामान्यत:।

broadminded (ब्रॉडमाइन्डिड) ***adj.*** open-minded, उदार।

brocade (ब्रोकेड) ***n.*** a heavy silk fabric woven with gold or silver threads, ज़री।

brochure (ब्रोशुअर) ***n.*** a booklet containing information about some event, स्मारिका, विवरणिका।

broil[1] (ब्रॉइल) ***n.*** a noisy quarrel, झगड़ा।

broil[2] ***v.*** to cook, पकाना, भूनना।

broken (ब्रोकन) ***v. adj.*** separated into pieces, टूटा, टूटा-फूटा।

broker (ब्रोकर) ***n.*** an agent who gets commission on purchases, sales or contracts done for another, दलाल।

brokerage (ब्रोकरिज) ***n.*** 1. the business or work of a broker, दलाली। 2. the commission of a broker, दलाली, कमीशन।

bronchial tube ***n.*** either of the two branches connecting the windpipe, श्वासनली।

bronchitis (ब्रॉन्काइटिस) ***n.*** inflammation of the membrane of the bronchial tube, श्वासनली में होनेवाली सूजन।

bronze (ब्रॉन्ज़) ***n.*** an alloy of copper and tin, काँसा।

bronze age ***n.*** the time when tools were made of bronze, कांस्य युग।

brood (ब्रूड) ***v.*** 1. to sit on eggs to hatch them, अंडे सेना। 2. to think or worry anxiously, चिंतामग्न होना या रहना, व्याकुल होना।

brook (ब्रुक) ***n.*** a small stream, छोटी नदी, नाला।

broom (ब्रूम) ***n.*** a large sweeping brush, डंडेदार बड़ा झाड़ू।

broth (ब्रॉथ) ***n.*** a mixed soup, सूप, रसा, शोरबा।

brothel (ब्रॉथल) ***n.*** a house of prostitutes, वेश्यालय, चकला।

brother (ब्रदर) ***n.*** a male relative with the same parents, भाई, भ्राता, बंधु।

brotherhood (ब्रदरहुड) ***n.*** 1. the relationship of brothers, भ्रातृभाव, बंधुत्व। 2. fellowship, भाईचारा।

brother-in-law ***n.*** the brother of one's wife, साला।

brotherly ***adj.*** of or like brother, भ्रातृवत्, भाई का-सा।

brow (ब्राउ) ***n.*** 1. an eyebrow, भौंह, भृकुटी। 2. the forehead, माथा।

browbeat (ब्राउबीट) ***v.*** to intimidate, धमकी देना।

brown (ब्राउन) ***adj.*** of a colour between orange and black, भूरा। ***n.*** brown colour, भूरा रंग।

brownie (ब्राउनी) ***n.*** a good natured fairy, भली परी।

browze (ब्राउज़) ***v.*** 1. to graze, चरना। 2. to read for pleasure, मन बहलाने के लिए पढ़ना।

bruise (ब्रूज़) ***n.*** an injury in which the skin is not broken, रगड़, खरोंच। ***v.*** to cause bruises, रगड़ खाना, छिल जाना।

brunette (ब्रूनेट) ***n.*** a woman with a dark complexion, साँवली औरत।

brunt (ब्रन्ट) ***n.*** the heaviest stress, ज़ोरदार दबाव।

brush (ब्रश) ***n.*** a device consisting of bristles of hair, wire, nylon etc. with a handle, ब्रश, ब्रुश।

brutal (ब्रूटल) ***adj.*** very cruel, merciless, नृशंस, निर्दय, निर्मम।

brutality (ब्रूटैलिटी) ***n.*** the quality or state of being brutal, नृशंसता, निर्दयता।

brute (ब्रूट) ***adj.*** cruel, क्रूर, नृशंस।

bubble (बबल) ***n.*** a hollow ball of liquid containing air or gas, बुलबुला, बुल्ला। ***v.*** to rise in bubble, बुलबुले उठना।

buck (बक) ***n.*** 1. a male animal, नर। 2. a well dressed person, बाँका, छैला।

bucket (बकिट) ***n.*** a container with a handle, डोल, बाल्टी।

buckle (बकल) ***n.*** a device for fastening a belt, strap etc., बकसुआ, बकल। ***v.*** to fasten with a buckle, बकसुआ लगाना।

buckram (बकरम) ***n.*** a stiffen cotton cloth used for lining garments, बकरम।

buckskin (बकस्किन) ***n.*** the leather made from deer skin, मृगचर्म।

bud (बड) ***n.*** a knob containing undeveloped flower, leave etc., कली।

Buddhism (बूडिज़म) ***n.*** the religion of the Buddhists, बौद्ध धर्म।

Buddhist (बूडिस्ट) ***n.*** a follower of the Buddhism, बौद्ध।

budding (बडिंग) ***adj.*** beginning to develop, उदीयमान, होनहार।

buddy (बडी) ***n.*** a friend, मित्र, यार।

budge (बज) ***v.*** to move a little, सरकना, खिसकना, हिलना।

budget (बजिट) ***n.*** an estimate of income and expenditure, बजट।

buff (बफ़) ***n.*** leather, चमड़ा। ***v.*** to polish with something soft, मुलायम वस्तु (कपड़े, रुई आदि) से पालिश करना।

buffalo (बफ़ैलो) ***n.*** a cow-like mammal, भैंस।

buffer (बफ़र) ***n.*** a device that lessens the effect of an impact, बफ़र।

buffet[1] (बुफ़े) ***n.*** the food placed on the table which guests serve themselves, मेज़ पर लगाया हुआ भोजन जिसे अतिथि स्वतः परोसते हैं, बुफ़े।

buffet[2] (बफ़िट) ***n.*** a blow (struck with the hand), आघात, थप्पड़।

B

buffoon (बफून) ***n.*** a clown, जोकर, विदूषक, मसख़रा।

bug (बग) ***n.*** a blood-sucking insect, खटमल।

bugbear (बगबेअर) ***n.*** anything which inspires fear, जूजू, हौआ।

bugle (ब्यूगल) ***n.*** a small trumpet, बिगुल। ***v.*** to sound a bugle, बिगुल बजाना।

bugler (ब्यूगलर) ***n.*** one who sounds a bugle, बिगुल बजानेवाला।

build (बिल्ड) ***v.*** (built, building) to construct or erect, बनाना, निर्मित करना।

builder (बिल्डर) ***n.*** one who builds, निर्माता।

building (बिल्डिन्ग) ***n.*** a house or edifice, भवन, इमारत।

bulb (बल्ब) ***n.*** 1. an underground rounded stem of some plants, कंद। 2. an electric lamp, बल्ब।

bulbous (बल्बस) ***adj.*** shaped like a bulb, कंद-जैसा।

bulge (बल्ज) ***n.*** a protruding part, swelling, उभार, फुलाव,. सूजन। ***v.*** to swell or cause to swell out, उभरना या उभारना, फूलना या फुलाना।

bulk (बल्क) ***n.*** 1. great size, magnitude or mass, आकार या विस्तार की अधिकता, ढेर, राशि, अंबार। 2. the greater part, अधिकांश। 3. the majority, बहुसंख्या, बहुमत। □ **in bulk,** in huge quantity, बड़ी मात्रा में।

bulky (बल्की) ***adj.*** having great size or mass, भारी-भरकम।

bull (बुल) ***n.*** an uncastrated ox, साँड़।

bulldozer (बुलडोज़र) ***n.*** a heavy machine used for pushing heavy objects, levelling earth etc., बुलडोज़र।

bullet (बुलिट) ***n.*** a metal projectile fired from a rifle or revolver, गोली।

bulletin (बुलेटिन) ***n.*** 1. a statement on a matter of public interest, विज्ञप्ति, बुलेटिन। 2. a journal, पत्रिका।

bulletproof (बुलिटप्रूफ़) ***adj.*** that can protect from bullets, गोलीसह, बुलेटप्रूफ़, अभेद्य।

bullion (बुल्यन) ***n.*** gold or silver (in bulk or bars), सोना या चाँदी; ~ market, सर्राफ़ा।

bullock (बुलॉक) ***n.*** a bull after castration, बैल।

bullock-cart ***n.*** a carriage driven by a bull, बैलगाड़ी।

bull's eye (बुल्ज़ आई) ***n.*** the centre of a target, लक्ष्य, निशाना।

bully (बुली) ***n.*** one who persecutes the weak, दुर्बलों को तंग करनेवाला या डराने-धमकानेवाला।

bulwark (बुलवर्क) ***n.*** a rampart, परकोटा।

bump (बम्प) ***v.*** to strike or collide with, टकराना, भिड़ जाना। ***n.*** 1. a sudden forceful blow or shock, सहसा लगनेवाला आघात या धक्का। 2. a raised round swelling, गुमड़ा।

bumper[1] (बम्पर) ***n.*** a horizontal bar attached to the front or back of a vehicle, बंपर।

bumper[2] ***adj.*** plentiful, प्रचुर, भरपूर; ~ crop, भरपूर फसल।

bun (बन) ***n.*** 1. a small sweetened bread roll, बन।

bunch (बन्च) ***n.*** a cluster or group of things, गुच्छा।

bundle (बन्डल) ***n.*** a number of things wrapped and bound together, बंडल, गठरी।

bungalow (बंगलो) ***n.*** a single story building with open space, बँगला।

bungle (बंगल) ***v.*** to spoil, ख़राब कर देना।

bunk (बंक) ***n.*** a built-in seat for sleeping, सोने के लिए दीवार में लगा हुआ पटरा, शायिका।

bunker (बंकर) ***n.*** a strongly built underground shelter, बंकर, तहख़ाना।

buoy (बूई) ***n.*** a floating but fixed object in a sea as a warning of danger, ख़तरे का चिह्न या निशान।

buoyant (बॉइएन्ट) ***adj.*** 1. able to float, तरणक्षम। 2. cheerful, उत्फुल्ल, प्रफुल्ल।

burble (बर्बल) ***v.*** 1. to flow with a bubbling sound, (झरने का) झरझर शब्द करना। 2. to babble, बुदबुदाना।

burden (बर्डन) ***n.*** 1. a heavy load, भार, बोझ। 2. something difficult to endure, दायित्व।

burdensome (बर्डनसम) ***adj.*** heavy to bear, बोझिल, भारी।

bureau (ब्यूरो) ***n.*** an office or department, कार्यालय या विभाग।

bureaucracy (ब्यूरोक्रेसी) ***n.*** body of officials, अधिकारी-वर्ग, नौकरशाही।

bureaucrat (ब्यूरोक्रेट) ***n.*** a member of the bureaucracy, नौकरशाह।

burette (ब्यूरेट) ***n.*** a glass tube with marks, मापन-नलिका, मापनली।

burgeon (बर्जन) ***v.*** 1. to sprout, कोंपलें फूटना, प्रस्फुटित होना। 2. to flourish, पनपना।

burglar (बर्गलर) ***n.*** a house breaker, सेंधमार।

burglary (बर्गलरी) ***n.*** the act of breaking into the house in order to steal, सेंधमारी।

burial (बेरिअल) ***n.*** the act of burying, दफ़नाना, दफ़न; **~ ground,** क़ब्रिस्तान।

burlesque (बर्लेस्क) ***n.*** a ludicrous imitation, भोंडी नकल।

burly (बर्ली) ***adj.*** heavy and strong, हट्टा-कट्टा।

burn (बर्न) ***v.*** (burned / burnt, burning) 1. to undergo combustion, जलना, जल उठना। 2. to cause to undergo combustion, जलाना। 3. to be destroyed or damaged by fire, जल या झुलस जाना। 4. to destroy or damage by fire, जला देना, फूँक देना। 5. to use as fuel, जलाना। 6. to emit or light by means of fire, जलाना। ***n.*** an injury produced by fire or heat, जलने से होनेवाला घाव या पड़नेवाला फफोला।

burning (बर्निंग) ***adj.*** 1. very hot, जलता हुआ। 2. intense, प्रचंड, तीव्र। 3. having very great importance, ज्वलंत।

burrow (बरो) ***n.*** a hole dug by an animal, बिल, माँद, गड्ढा।

bursar (बर्सर) ***n.*** treasurer, ख़जांची।

bursary (बर्सरी) ***n.*** scholarship, छात्रवृत्ति, वज़ीफ़ा।

burst (बर्स्ट) ***v.*** (burst. bursting) 1. to break suddenly and loudly from internal pressure, फट जाना। 2. to emerge suddenly, सहसा प्रकट होना। 3. to give sudden expression, फट पड़ना।

bury (बेरी) ***v.*** to place in a grave, दफ़नाना।

bus (बस) ***n.*** a large passenger-carrying motor vehicle, बस।

bush (बुश) ***n.*** a shrub, झाड़ी।

business (बिज़निस) ***n.*** one's usual occupation, employment or trade, व्यवसाय, व्यापार।

businessman (बिज़निसमैन) ***n.*** a

B

man engaged in business, व्यापारी, व्यवसायी।

bust (बस्ट) ***n.*** a piece of sculpture representing the head, shoulders and upper chest of a human body, आवक्ष प्रतिमा।

bustle (बसल) ***v.*** to hurry with a great show of activity, चहल-पहल होना, धूमधाम होना। ***n.*** excited activity, धूमधाम, चहल-पहल।

busy (बिज़ी) ***adj.*** working, not free, engaged, कार्यरत, व्यस्त। ***v.*** to keep busy, व्यस्त रहना या रखना।

but (बट) ***conj.*** on the contrary, मगर, परंतु, पर।

butcher (बूचर) ***n.*** 1. one who slaughters animals, बूचड़, कसाई। ***v.*** 1. to slaughter animals, जानवर काटना, हलाल करना। 2. to kill a human being, हत्या करना।

butler (बटलर) ***n.*** the chief male servant of a house, मुख्य परिचर या सेवक, ख़ानसामाँ।

butt (बट) ***n.*** 1. the thicker end of a gun or rifle, कुंदा। 2. the last unsmoked end of a cigarette, सिगरेट का बचा हुआ टुकड़ा, टोटा।

butter (बटर) ***n.*** the fat made from milk, curd or cream by churning, मक्खन। ***v.*** 1. to spread with butter, मक्खन लगाना। 2. to flatter, ख़ुशामद करना।

butterfly (बटरफ़्लाइ) ***n.*** an insect with colourful wings, तितली।

buttermilk (बटरमिल्क) ***n.*** the liquid that remains after the fat has been removed, लस्सी, मट्ठा।

buttock (बटक) ***n.*** either of the two fleshy parts at the back of hips, चूतड़।

button (बटन) ***n.*** a disc or knob of plastic, steel, wood etc. attached to a garment, बटन, बुताम।

buttress (बटरिस) ***n.*** a brick construction built to support a wall, पुश्ता, टेक।

buy (बाइ) ***v.*** (bought, buying) to purchase, खरीदना।

buyer (बाइअर) ***n.*** one who buys something, ख़रीदार।

buzz (बज़) ***n.*** the sound of a bee, भिनभिन, गुनगुन। ***v.*** to make a buzz, भिनभिन करना, गुनगुन करना।

buzzer (बज़र) ***n.*** a bell which produces buzzing sound, घंटी।

by (बाइ) ***adv.*** near, पास, पास ही।

bye ***interj.*** goodbye, बाइ-बाइ।

bygone (बाइगॉन) ***adj.*** gone by, बीता हुआ, गत।

bylaw (बाइलॉ) ***n.*** a rule concerning internal organization, उपविधि।

bypass (बाइपास) ***n.*** 1. an alternative or secondary road that passed to one side of a congested area, बाइपास, उपमार्ग, गौण मार्ग। 2. a surgically created alternative passage between two blood vessels, बाइपास सर्जरी।

by-product (बाइप्रॉडक्ट) ***n.*** something formed in addition 0to the main product, उप-उत्पाद।

byword (बाइवर्ड) ***n.*** a proverb, कथन, उक्ति, कहावत।

C, c (सी) the third letter of the English alphabet, अंग्रेज़ी वर्णमाला का तीसरा वर्ण।

cab (कैब) ***n.*** a taxi, टैक्सी।

cabbage (कैबिज) ***n.*** a vegetable plant with green leaves, बंदगोभी, पत्तागोभी।

cabin (कैबिन) ***n.*** a small room, कक्ष।

cabinet (कैबिनिट) ***n.*** 1. a cupboard, खानेदार आलमारी। 2. the outer case of a television, टेलीविज़न रखने की आलमारी, कैबनिट। 3. the body of ministers of a state or country, मंत्रिमंडल।

cable (केबल) ***n.*** 1. a strong thick rope or chain, मोटा रस्सा या जंजीर। 2. a wire for carrying electricity or telegraphic messages, तार। 3. a cablegram, समुद्री तार।

cackle (कैकल) ***n.*** 1. a clucking noise of hen, मुर्गी की कुड़कुड़। 2. a silly laugh, हेंहें। ***v.*** 1. to give a cackle, कुड़कुड़ करना। 2. to laugh in a silly manner, हेंहें या हीही करना।

cactus (कैक्टस) ***n.*** any leafless spiny plant, कैक्टस, नागफनी।

cadence (केडेन्स) ***n.*** the rise and fall of the voice, आवाज़ का उतार-चढ़ाव, आरोह-अवरोह।

cadet (केडेट) ***n.*** 1. a student who is undergoing military training, छात्र-सैनिक, कैडिट। 2. a younger brother, छोटा भाई, अनुज।

cadre (काडर) ***n.*** 1. an inner group of trained personnel, संवर्ग, काडर। 2. an organisation, संघठन।

cafe (कैफ़े) ***n.*** a small restaurant, लघु जलपानगृह।

cafeteria (कैफ़िटिरिआ) ***n.*** a self-service restaurant, कैफ़िटेरिया।

cage (केज) ***n.*** a framework in which birds or animals are kept, पिंजरा।

cajole (कैजोल) ***v.*** to coax, फुसलाना।

cake (केक) ***n.*** a baked sweet bread-like food, केक।

calamitous (केलैमिटस) ***adj.*** disastrous, अनर्थकारी।

calamity (केलैमिटी) ***n.*** 1. a disaster, संकट, विपत्ति। 2. great distress, भारी मुसीबत। 3. misfortune, दुर्भाग्य।

calcareous (कैल्केरिअस) ***adj.*** of or containing calcium, कैल्शियमयुक्त, चूनेदार।

calcium (कैल्सिअम) ***n.*** a chemical element, एक रासायनिक तत्त्व, कैल्शियम।

calculate (कैलक्युलेट) ***v.*** 1. to compute mathematically, गिनना। 2. to estimate, कूतना, हिसाब लगाना।

calculation (कैलक्युलेशन) ***n.*** the act or process of calculating, गणना, हिसाब, परिकलन।

calculator (कैलक्युलेटर) ***n.*** a machine that performs calculations, कैलकूलेटर।

calculus (कैलक्युलस) ***n.*** a branch of mathematics, कलन।

calendar (कैलेन्डर) ***n.*** a table showing dates and days of the 12 months of a year, कैलेन्डर, पंचांग।

calf[1] (काफ़) ***n.*** 1. the young one of cattle, बछड़ा, पाड़ा। 2. the hide of a calf, calf skin, बछड़े का चमड़ा।

C

calf[2] ***n.*** the fleshy part of the human leg between the knee and ankle, पिंडली।

calibre, caliber (कैलिबर) ***n.*** 1. the diameter, bullet, etc., व्यास। 2. ability, योग्यता, क्षमता।

calico (कैलिको) ***n.*** a printed cotton fabric, एक प्रकार का छींटदार कपड़ा, छींट।

caliper (कैलिपर) ***n.***(usu.plu.) an instrument used to measure dimensions, कैलिपर, परकार।

caliph (कैलिफ़) ***n.*** a Muslim religious leader in some Muslim countries, ख़लीफ़ा।

call (कॉल) ***v.*** 1. to cry or utter loudly, आवाज़ देना, पुकारना। 2. to ask or order to come, बुलाना। 3. to make a visit, मिलने के लिए जाना। 4. to telephone, फ़ोन करना।

callbell ***n.*** a bell for calling, बुलाने की घंटी।

caller (कॉलर) ***n.*** a person who makes a brief visit, अभ्यागत, मुलाक़ाती।

call girl ***n.*** a prostitute, कॉलगर्ल।

calligraphy (कैलिग्रफ़ी) ***n.*** (the art of) fine handwriting, सुलेखन, सुंदर लिखाई।

callous (कैलस) ***adj.*** 1. (of skin) hardened and thickened, कड़ा, सख़्त। 2. insensitive, संवेदनहीन।

callow (कैलो) ***adj.*** 1. immature, अपरिपक्व, अप्रौढ़। 2. inexperienced, अनुभवहीन।

callus (कैलस) ***n.*** an area of thick hardened skin, घट्ठा।

calm (काम) ***adj.*** still, quiet, शांत। ***n.*** 1. stillness, शांति। 2. an absence of disturbance, peace, शांति। 3. serenity, सौम्यता, गंभीरता। ***v.*** to make or become calm, शांत हो जाना या शांत करना।

calorie (कैलोरी) ***n.*** 1. a unit for measuring the quantity of heat, कैलोरी, ऊष्मांक। 2. a unit for measuring the energy value of food, कैलोरी।

calumnious (कैलम्निअस) ***adj.*** slanderous, निंदात्मक, बदनामी-भरा।

calumny (कैलम्नी) ***n.*** slander, निंदा, बुराई, बदनामी।

calve (काव) ***v.*** to give birth to a calf, मादा चौपाए का ब्याना।

cambric (कैम्ब्रिक) ***n.*** a fine cotton cloth, एक तरह का बढ़िया सूती कपड़ा, कैम्ब्रिक।

camel (कैमल) ***n.*** a long-necked animal, ऊँट।

cameo (कैमिओ) ***n.*** a gem with a design cut in raised relief, उभारदार रत्न।

camera (कैमेरा) ***n.*** an apparatus for taking photographs, कैमरा।

camouflage (कैमॉफ़्लाज़) ***n.*** a method or means of concealment that creates the effect of being part of the natural surroundings, ढक-तोपकर छिपाने का काम, छद्मावरण। ***v.*** to conceal in this way, छिपाना, ढकना-तोपना, छद्मावरण करना।

camp (कैम्प) ***n.*** a temporary shelter in tents, huts, cabins etc., शिविर, पड़ाव।

campaign (कैम्पेन) ***n.*** a series of military operations, अभियान। ***v.*** to start or conduct a campaign, अभियान चलाना।

campfire (कैम्पफ़ाइर) ***n.*** an outdoor

fire in camp used for warmth, अलाव।

camphor (कैम्फ़र) ***n.*** a strong smelling white substance, कपूर, कर्पूर।

campus (कैम्पस) ***n.*** the grounds of a university, परिसर, कैंपस।

can[1] (कैन) ***aux. v.*** (p.t. & p.p. could) to be able, सकना।

can[2] ***n.*** 1. a metal container for liquids, पीपा, कनस्तर।

canal (कनैल) ***n.*** 1. an artificial waterway for navigation or irrigation, नहर। 2. a duct or tube, नली, नलिका।

cancel (कैन्सल) to cross out by drawing a line through, काट देना, रद करना।

cancellation (कैन्सलेशन) ***n.*** the act of cancelling, रद करना, निरसन।

Cancer (कैन्सर) ***n.*** a sign of the zodiac, the Crab, कर्क राशि।

cancer ***n.*** a malignant tumour, कैंसर।

candescent (कैन्डेसेन्ट) ***adj.*** glowing, प्रज्वलित, जगमग।

candid (कैन्डिड) ***adj.*** straightforward, frank, स्पष्टवादी, ख़रा।

candidate (कैन्डिडेट) ***n.*** 1. one who is seeking a post or prize, प्रत्याशी, उम्मीदवार। 2. someone taking an examination, परीक्षार्थी।

candidly ***adv.*** in a candid manner, निष्कपट भाव से, सरलता से।

candle (कैन्डल) ***n.*** a wax stick with a wick, मोमबत्ती।

candy (कैन्डी) ***n.*** any item of confectionery, मिठाई। ***v.*** to cook or coat with sugar, चाशनी में पकाना, पागना।

cane (केन) ***n.*** 1. sugarcane, गन्ना। 2. a jointed pithy or hollow stem of the bamboo carried when walking, बेंत। ***v.*** to beat with a cane, बेंत लगाना।

canine (केनाइन) ***adj.*** of or pertaining to dogs, कुत्तों का, कुत्तों से संबद्ध।

canister (कैनिस्टर) ***n.*** a metal container, कनस्तर।

canker (कैंकर) ***n.*** a sore, व्रण, नासूर।

cankerous (कैंकरस) ***adj.*** evil, बुरा, विनाशकारी।

canned (कैन्ड) ***adj.*** preserved and sealed in an airtight jar, डिब्बाबंद।

cannibal (कैनिबल) ***n.*** a person who eats human flesh, नरभक्षी।

cannon (कैनन) ***n.*** any heavy gun, तोप। ***v.*** to collide forcefully with, टकरा या भिड़ जाना।

cannonade (कैननेड) ***n.*** a continuous heavy firing by guns, गोलाबारी।

canny (कैनी) ***adj.*** shrewd in worldly affairs, सयाना, धूर्त।

canoe (कैनू) ***n.*** a small boat propelled by paddles, छोटी नाव जिसे पैरों से चलाते हैं।

canon (कैनन) ***n.*** 1. a general rule, नियम, सिद्धांत। 2. a set of sacred writings, धर्मग्रंथ। 3. a priest, पादरी, पुरोहित। 4. criterion or standard, कसौटी या मानक।

canopy (कैनोपी) ***n.*** a cloth covering fixed above a seat or carried over an important person, छतरी, छत्र।

cant (कैन्ट) ***n.*** insincere talk, बुराई, निंदा।

canteen (कैन्टीन) ***n.*** 1. a restaurant attached to a factory or office, कैन्टीन, जलपानगृह। 2. a store, भंडार।

C

canter (कैन्टर) ***n.*** a gait slower than the gallop but faster than the trot, दुलकी और सरपट के बीच की चाल।

canto (कैन्टो) ***n.*** a division of a long poem, महाकाव्य का खंड, सर्ग, कांड, स्कंध।

cantonment (कैन्टॉनमेन्ट) ***n.*** a group of (temporary) buildings for housing troops, छावनी, कैंट।

canvas (कैन्वेस) ***n.*** a closely woven fabric for tents, sails and shoes, कैन्वस, किरमिच।

canvass (कैन्वेस) ***v.*** to go through in order to solicit votes, orders, subscriptions etc., कन्वैसिंग करना।

canvasser (कैन्वेसर) ***n.*** one who convasses, प्रचारक।

canyon (कैन्यन) ***n.*** a deep narrow valley with a river flowing through, नदी-घांटी।

cap (कैप) ***n.*** 1. a close-fitting head-covering, टोपी। 2. a caplike cover, ढक्कन। ***v.*** to put a cap on, टोपी या ढक्कन लगाना।

capability (केपेबिलिटी) ***n.*** the quality of being capable, क्षमता, सामर्थ्य, शक्ति।

capable (केपेबल) ***adj.*** having ability or capacity, सक्षम, समर्थ।

capacious (केपेशस) ***adj.*** spacious, खुला, लंबा-चौड़ा।

capacity (केपैसिटी) ***n.*** the ability to hold or contain, धारिता, क्षमता।

cap-a-pie (कैप-ऐ-पी) ***adv.*** from head to foot, सिर से पैर तक।

cape (केप) ***n.*** the part of land projecting into a sea, अंतरीप।

capillary (कैपिलैरी) ***n.*** any of the tiny blood vessels that connect the arteries and veins, केशिका।

capital (कैपिटल) ***adj.*** 1. most important, principal, प्रधान, महत्त्वपूर्ण। 2. excellent, उत्कृष्ट, उत्तम। 3. involving the death penalty, मृत्युदंड-संबंधी। 4. fatal, घातक। 5. pertaining to capital, पूँजी-संबंधी। ***n.*** 1. a city that is the official seat of government, राजधानी। 2. a capital letter, बड़ा अक्षर। 3. wealth or property that is invested to produce more wealth, पूँजी, राशि।

capital goods ***n.*** (plu.) goods used in the production of commodities, पूँजीगत माल।

capitalism (कैपिटलिज़म) ***n.*** an economic system based on the private ownership of wealth, पूँजीवाद।

capitalist (कैपिटलिस्ट) ***n.*** owning or controlling a large amount of wealth, पूँजीपति।

capitalistic (कैपिटलिस्टिक) ***adj.*** of capitalism or capitalist, पूँजीवादी।

capitation (कैपिटेशन) ***n.*** a tax fixed at an equal sum per person, प्रतिव्यक्ति कर।

capitulate (कैपिच्युलेट) ***v.*** to surrender, आत्मसमर्पण कर देना।

caprice (कैप्रीस) ***n.*** a whim, सनक।

capricious (कैप्रिशस) ***adj.*** whimsical, सनकी।

Capricorn (कैप्रिकॉर्न) ***n.*** a sign of the zodiac, मकर राशि।

capstan (कैप्स्टन) ***n.*** a thick revolving post used to pull in a rope for raising a ship's anchor, ढोल चर्खी, हवीत।

capsule (कैप्स्यूल) ***n.*** 1. a small

soluble container enclosing a dose of an oral medicine, कैप्सूल, संपुटिका। 2. a case, संपुटिका, खोल।

captain (कैप्टिन) ***n.*** a leader of a team, कप्तान, नायक। ***v.*** to act as a captain of, कप्तानी करना।

captaincy (कैप्टेन्सी) ***n.*** the state of being a captain, कप्तानी, नायकत्व।

caption (कैप्शन) ***n.*** a heading or title, शीर्षक।

captivate (कैप्टिवेट) ***v.*** to fascinate, मोहित कर लेना।

captive (कैप्टिव) ***n.*** taken as a prisoner, बंदी। ***adj.*** who is enslaved by strong emotion, (से) अभिभूत, वशीभूत।

captivity (कैप्टिविटी) ***n.*** the state of being held captive, बंधनावस्था, बंधन।

captor (कैप्टर) ***n.*** one who captures a person or animal, बंदीकर्ता।

capture (कैप्चर) ***v.*** to take captive, बंदी बना लेना। ***n.*** the act of capturing, गिरफ़्तारी।

car (कार) ***n.*** an automobile, कार, यान।

carat (कैरेट) ***n.*** 1. a unit of weight equal to 200 milligrams, कैरट। 2. = karat.

caravan (कैरेवैन) ***n.*** a company of travellers journeying together, काफ़िला, कारवाँ।

carbine (कार्बाइन) ***n.*** an automatic rifle with a short barrel, कारबीन।

carbohydrate (कार्बोहाइड्रेट) ***n.*** a chemical compound containing carbon, hydrogen and oxygen such as sugars, starches etc., कारबोहाइड्रेट।

carbon (कार्बन) ***n.*** pure charcoal, कार्बन।

carbuncle (कार्बन्कल) ***n.*** a large painful abscess, बड़ा फोड़ा।

carburettor (कार्बुरेटर) ***n.*** a device for mixing fuel and air in oil engines, कार्बुरेटर।

carcass (कार्केस) ***n.*** a dead body of an animal, लाश, शव।

card[1] (कार्ड) ***n.*** 1. a small flat piece of cardboard, कार्ड, पत्रक। 2. a playing card, ताश का पत्ता।

card[2] ***v.*** to comb wool, धुनकना, धुनना।

cardamom (कार्डमम) ***n.*** a plant and its seeds, इलायची।

cardboard (कार्डबोर्ड) ***n.*** a stiff pasteboard, कार्डबोर्ड, गत्ता।

cardiac (कार्डिएक) ***adj.*** of or pertaining to the heart, हृदय-संबंधी; ~ failure, दिल का दौरा।

cardigan (कार्डिगन) ***n.*** a sweater with sleeves, opening down the front, आगे से खुला स्वेटर, कार्डीगन।

cardinal (कार्डिनल) ***n.*** an official ranking just below the pope, कार्डिनल।

cardiology (कार्डिऑलोजी) ***n.*** the study of the diseases and functioning of the heart, हृद्विज्ञान।

care (केअर) ***n.*** 1. caution, सावधानी। 2. serious attention, ध्यान, देखभाल। 3. worry, anxiety, चिंता। ***v.*** to look after, देखभाल करना।

career (कैरिअर) ***n.*** a chosen pursuit, जीविका, पेशा।

carefree (केअरफ़्री) ***adj.*** free from worry, निश्चिंत, बेफ़िक्र।

careful (केअरफुल) ***adj.*** cautious, सावधान, सतर्क।

careless (केअरलिस) ***adj.*** inattentive, असावधान।

C

caress (केरैस) ***v.*** 1. to touch lovingly, लाड़ करना, दुलार करना।

caret (कैरिट) ***n.*** a proof-reading mark (^) to show omission, काकपद, लोपचिह्न।

cargo (कार्गो) ***n.*** the freight carried by a ship, plane or vehicle, माल।

caricature (कैरिकेचर) ***n.*** a pictorial representation for comic effect, व्यंग्यचित्र।

caries (केअरीज़) ***n.*** decay of a bone, अस्थिक्षय।

carmine (कार्माइन) ***adj.*** having deep red colour, किरमिजी।

carnage (कार्निज) ***n.*** massive slaughter, नरसंहार।

carnal (कार्नल) ***adj.*** 1. bodily, शारीरिक। 2. sexual, यौन-संबंधी।

carnation (कार्नेशन) ***n.*** a plant and its flower, कार्नेशन। ***adj.*** pink, गुलाबी।

carnival (कार्निवल) ***n.*** a fete, आनंद-मेला।

carnivorous (कार्निवोरस) ***adj.*** feeding on flesh, मांसाहारी।

carol (कैरल) ***n.*** 1. a joyful song, आनंदगीत। 2. a hymn, भजन।

carouse (कैराउज़) ***v.*** to drink excessively, ख़ूब मदिरापान करना।

carp (कार्प) ***v.*** to find fault, मीन-मेख या दोष निकालना।

carpenter (कारपैन्टर) ***n.*** one who makes and repairs wooden furniture, बढ़ई।

carpentry (कारपैन्ट्री) ***n.*** the art or work of a carpenter, बढ़ईगीरी।

carpet (कार्पिट) ***n.*** a woollen covering for a floor, कालीन, गलीचा।

carriage (कैरिज) ***n.*** 1. a four-wheeled vehicle, चौपहिया गाड़ी, यान, वाहन। 2. the posture of the body, ठवन, मुद्रा।

carrier (कैरिअर) ***n.*** 1. a person who carries goods, कुली, वाहक। 2. a vehicle that carries goods, माल ढोनेवाली गाड़ी, छकड़ा। 3. an extra seat on a cycle, कैरियर।

carrot (कैरट) ***n.*** a plant and its root, गाजर।

carry (कैरी) ***v.*** 1. to take something from one place to another, उठाकर ले जाना, ढोना। 2. to move in a certain way, आचरण करना। 3. to be pregnant, गर्भवती होना।

cart (कार्ट) ***n.*** a two-wheeled vehicle used for carrying loads, छकड़ा, ठेला।

cartage (कार्टिज) ***n.*** the act of transporting by cart, ढुलाई।

cartel (कार्टेल) ***n.*** an association of business organisations, उद्योग-संघटन।

cartilage (कार्टिलिज) ***n.*** an elastic tissue found round the joints, कार्टिलेज, कुरकुरी, उपास्थि।

carton (कार्टन) ***n.*** 1. a cardboard box , गत्ते का डिब्बा, कार्टन।

cartoon (कार्टून) ***n.*** a satirical drawing or caricature, व्यंग्यचित्र, कार्टून।

cartoonist (कार्टूनिस्ट) ***n.*** an artist who draws cartoons, व्यंग्यचित्रकार।

cartridge (कार्ट्रिज) ***n.*** a metal case containing explosive and a bullet for a rifle etc., कारतूस।

carve (कार्व) ***v.*** to inscribe, नक़्क़ाशी करना, तराशना।

cascade (कैस्केड) ***n.*** a waterfall, झरना।

case[1] (केस) ***n.*** 1. a specific

instance, उदाहरण। 2. an occurrence of disease or injury, बीमारी की घटना, हादसा। 3. a person attended by a doctor, solicitor etc., मुवक्किल। 4. a problem or matter, समस्या, विषय, मामला। 5. a law suit, मुकदमा, वाद। 6. something being investigated by police, मामला। 7. the form of a noun or pronoun that shows its relation to another word, कारक।

case[2] ***n.*** a container or suitcase, बक्सा, बक्स, पेटी।

cash (कैश) ***n.*** readily available money, नक़दी, रोकड़। ***v.*** to exchange (a cheque etc.,) for cash, भुनाना।

cashew (कैशू) ***n.*** a tree and its nut, काजू।

cashier (कैशिअर) ***n.*** an official in a bank or office responsible for handling cash, ख़ज़ांची।

cashmemo (कैशमेमो) ***n.*** a memo for goods delivered against cash, नक़दी पुर्ज़ा।

casing (केसिंग) ***n.*** a protective case or cover, आवरण, खोल।

casino (कैसीनो) ***n.*** a public building for gambling, जुआघर।

cask (कास्क) ***n.*** a barrel, पीपा।

casket (कैस्किट) ***n.*** 1. a small box or chest, संदूकची, मंजूषा। 2. a coffin, शवपेटिका, ताबूत।

cassette (कैसेट) ***n.*** a small container for magnetic tape, कैसेट।

cassock (कैसक) ***n.*** a long garment worn by certain clergymen, लबादा।

cast (कास्ट) ***v.*** 1. to throw, फेंकना। 2. to give (one's vote), देना, डालना। 3. to turn or direct, मोड़ना, डालना। 4. to form by moulding, साँचे में ढालना। ***n.*** 1. an act of throwing, प्रक्षेपण। 2. something moulded, ढलवाँ पदार्थ। 3. a mould, साँचा। 4. a group of actors assigned roles, पात्र-सूची।

caste (कास्ट) ***n.*** any of the major hereditary classes into which Hindu Society is divided, जाति, वर्ण।

caste system ***n.*** the hereditary division of Hindu Society based on class differences, जाति-प्रथा, वर्ण-व्यवस्था।

castigate (कैस्टिगेट) ***v.*** to chastise severely, डाँटना-फटकारना।

casting (कास्टिंग) ***n.*** an object that has been cast, साँचे में ढली वस्तु।

cast iron ***n.*** a hard but easily breakable type of iron, कांति लोहा, ढलवाँ लोहा।

castle (कैसल) ***n.*** a fortified building or group of buildings, क़िला, दुर्ग।

castrate (कैस्ट्रेट) ***v.*** to remove the testicles, बधिया करना।

casual (कैजुअल) ***adj.*** 1. happening by accident, आकस्मिक। 2. informal, अनौपचारिक।

casualty (केजुअल्टी) ***n.*** a person who is killed or wounded in an accident or war, हत या आहत, मृत या घायल व्यक्ति।

cat (कैट) ***n.*** a small domesticated animal which catches rats, बिल्ली।

catalogue, catalog (कैटैलॉग) ***n.*** a list, सूची।

catapult (कैटैपुल्ट) ***n.*** an apparatus for hurling missiles, गुलेल।

cataract (कैटैरैक्ट) ***n.*** 1. a large waterfall, बहुत बड़ा जलप्रपात। 2. partial or total opacity of the lens of the eye, मोतियाबिंद।

C

catarrh (कैटार) *n.* inflammation of a nose accompanied by a watery discharge, जुकाम।

catastrophe (कैटैस्ट्रॉफ़ी) *n.* a sudden disaster, विपत्ति।

catch (कैच) *v.* (caught, catching) to capture, पकड़ लेना, पकड़ना। 2. to hold a flying object, लपक लेना, पकड़ लेना। 3. to reach in time to board, (समय पर पहुँचकर गाड़ी या बस) पकड़ना। 4. to become infested with, पकड़ लेना, ग्रस्त होना। *n.* 1. the act of catching, पकड़ने की क्रिया या भाव। 2. something caught, पकड़ी हुई वस्तु।

catching *adj.* 1. attractive, आकर्षक। 2. contagious, संक्रामक, छुतहा।

catchment area (कैचमेन्ट एरिआ) *n.* the area from which a river gets its water, जलग्रहण-क्षेत्र।

catchy (कैची) *adj.* 1. easily remembered, सहज-स्मरणीय। 2. deceptive, छलपूर्ण।

categorical (कैटेगॉरिकल) *adj.* 1. unconditional, without conditions, बिना शर्त का, सुनिश्चित, सुस्पष्ट। 2. positive, सकारात्मक।

category (कैटेगरी) *n.* a class or group, श्रेणी, वर्ग।

cater (केटर) *v.* to provide and serve food and drink, खान-पान का प्रबंध करना।

caterer (केटरर) *n.* a person who supplies food and drink at parties, भोज-प्रबंधक।

caterpillar (कैटरपिलर) *n.* a larva of a moth, सूँडी, इल्ली।

cathedral (कैथीड्रल) *n.* the principal church of a diocese, धर्मप्रांत का मुख्य गिरजाघर, कथेड्रिल।

catholic (कैथलिक) *adj.* 1. universal, विश्वीय, सामान्य। 2. broad-minded, उदारमना, सहिष्णु।

Catholic *n.* a member of the Roman Catholic Church, कैथोलिक ईसाई। *adj.* of Catholics, कैथोलिक।

catling (कैटलिंग) *n.* a young one of a cat, बिल्ली का बच्चा, बिलौटा।

cat's eye *n.* a gem reflecting light, लहसुनिया।

cattle (कैटल) *n.* (plu.) large four-footed horned mammals, पशु, मवेशी, ढोर; ~ pound काँजी हाउस।

catwalk (कैटवाक) *n.* a narrow walk along a bridge, पुल के किनारे का सँकरा रास्ता।

caucus (कॉकस) *n.* a clique, गुट।

cauldron (कॉलड्रन) *n.* a large open metal pot, कड़ाहा, हंडा।

cauliflower (कॉलिफ़्लाउअर) *n.* a cabbage like plant, फूलगोभी।

causal (कॉज़ल) *adj.* implying cause, कारणात्मक।

cause (कॉज़) *n.* 1. a thing or person which produces an effect, कारण। 2. a reason, कारण। *v.* to be the cause of, कारण होना या बनना।

causeway (कॉज़वे) *n.* a paved way, पक्का रास्ता।

caustic (कॉस्टिक) *adj.* 1. able to burn, corrode or dissolve, क्षारक, कास्टिक। 2. bitter, कटु, कड़वा, अप्रिय।

caution (कॉशन) *n.* 1. something intended or serving as a warning, चेतावनी। 2. alertness, सावधानी। *v.* to warn to be careful, सावधान करना।

cautious (कॉशस) *adj.* showing or having caution, सावधान, सतर्क।

cavalcade (कैवलकेड) *n.* a

procession of horsemen, घुड़सवारों का जुलूस।

cavalier (कैवेलिअर) ***n.*** a horseman, अश्वारोही। ***adj.*** haughtly, घमंडी।

cavalry (कैवेलरी) ***n.*** an army of horsemen, अश्वारोही सेना, घुड़सवार सेना।

cave (केव) ***n.*** a deep natural hollow place, गुफा, कंदरा। ***v.*** 1. to collapse, ध्वस्त हो जाना। 2. to yield, झुक जाना।

caveman (केवमैन) ***n.*** one who lives in a cave, गुफावासी।

cavern (कैवर्न) ***n.*** a large cave, गहरी गुफा।

cavity (कैविटी) ***n.*** a hollow or hole, छिद्र, गड्ढा।

cease (सीस) ***v.*** 1. to come to an end, ख़त्म होना, रुक जाना। 2. to bring to an end, ख़त्म करना, रोक देना।

cease-fire ***n.*** a suspension of active hostilities, युद्धविराम।

ceaseless (सीसलिस) ***adj.*** unending, continuous, endless, निरंतर।

cedar (सीडर) ***n.*** a tall evergreen tree, देवदार।

ceiling (सीलिंग) ***n.*** 1. the undersurface of the top of a room, छत, भीतरी छत। 2. an upper limit, उच्चतम सीमा।

celebrate (सैलिब्रेट) ***v.*** 1. to observe (a day or event), (दिन या त्योहार) मनाना। 2. to perform (a religious ceremony), (उत्सव) मनाना।

celebrated ***adj.*** famous, well-known, प्रसिद्ध, विख्यात।

celebration (सैलिब्रेशन) ***n.*** an occasion of celebrating, समारोह, उत्सव, मेला।

celebrity (सिलेब्रिटी) ***n.*** 1. a famous person, प्रसिद्ध यशस्वी व्यक्ति। 2. fame, प्रसिद्धि, यश।

celestial (सिलेस्ट्यल) ***adj.*** of heaven, दिव्य, स्वर्गीय।

celibacy (सेलिबेसी) ***n.*** the state of being celibate, कुँआरापन, ब्रह्मचर्य।

celibate (सेलिबिट) ***adj.*** unmarried, कुँआरा, ब्रह्मचारी।

cell (सैल) ***n.*** 1. a narrow small room, कोठरी। 2. a very small division of living matter able to act independently, कोशिका, कोशाणु। 3. a device for producing electric current by chemical action, सेल।

cellar (सैलर) ***n.*** a basement, तहख़ाना।

cellophane (सैलोफ़ेन) ***n.*** a thin transparent material used as a moisture-proof wrapping, सेलोफेन, अमरी।

cellular (सैल्युलर) ***adj.*** made of cells, कोशिकीय।

cement (सिमेन्ट) ***n.*** a building material of powdered rocks, clay, limestone etc., सीमेंट। ***v.*** 1. to cover or coat with cement, सीमेंट से पक्का करना, सीमेंट करना। 2. to bind with or as if with cement, जोड़ना, बाँध देना, पक्का या दृढ़ करना।

cemetery (सेमिटेरी) ***n.*** a graveyard, क़ब्रिस्तान।

censor (सेन्सर) ***n.*** an official who examines news, films, private letters etc. with the power to remove anything harmful, सेंसरकर्ता। ***v.*** to examine (newspapers, books, films etc.) with the intention of removing anything offensive, सेंसर करना।

C

censorious (सेन्सोरिअस) ***adj.*** severely critical, घोर आलोचनात्मक, छिद्रान्वेषी।

censorship (सेन्सरशिप) ***n.*** 1. the act or process of censoring, सेंसर-व्यवस्था। 2. the office of the censor, सेंसरकर्ता का पद।

censure (सेन्शर) ***n.*** strong criticism, कड़ी आलोचना, फटकार।

censure motion ***n.*** a motion for condemnation, निंदा-प्रस्ताव।

census (सेन्सस) ***n.*** a periodic count of population (of a country), जनगणना।

cent (सेन्ट) ***n.*** one 100th of a dollar, सेन्ट (सिक्का)। □ **per cent,** प्रतिशत, फ़ीसदी।

centaur (सेन्टोर) ***n.*** a monster said to be half man and half horse, अश्वमानव।

centenarian (सेन्टिनेरिअन) ***n.*** a person who is one hundred years old or older, शतजीवी।

centenary (सेन्टिनेरी) ***n.*** a 100th anniversary or celebration, शतवार्षिकी, शताब्दी-समारोह।

centimetre (सेन्टिमीटर) ***n.*** one 100th of a metre, सेंटीमीटर।

central (सेन्ट्रल) ***adj.*** pertaining to or in the centre, केंद्रीय। 2. principal, essential, मुख्य, प्रमुख, महत्त्वपूर्ण।

centralize (सेन्ट्रलाइज़) ***v.*** to bring under a central authority, केंद्रीकरण करना।

centre, center (सेन्टर) ***n.*** 1. a middle point of a circle, केंद्र। 2. the middle part, मध्यभाग, केंद्र। 3. a place of concentrated activity, केंद्र। ***v.*** 1. to place in or at the centre, केंद्र में रखना। 2. to gather at a centre, केंद्रित होना।

centrifugal (सेन्ट्रिफ़्युगल) ***adj.*** moving away from the centre or axis, अपकेंद्री।

century (सेन्चरी) ***n.*** 1. a period of 100 years, शताब्दी, शती, सदी। 2. a score of 100 runs, शतक।

ceramic (सिरैमिक) ***adj.*** of pottery, मिट्टी (चीनी मिट्टी) के बर्तनों से संबद्ध।

ceramics ***n.*** (plu.) 1. things made of clay, (चीनी) मिट्टी के बर्तन। 2. the art of making pottery, (चीनी) मिट्टी के बर्तन बनाने की कला।

cereal (सिअरिअल) ***n.*** foodgrain, अनाज, अन्न। ***adj.*** made of grains, अनाजी।

cerebral (सेरिब्रल) ***adj.*** of the brain, मस्तिष्कीय।

ceremonial (सेरिमोनिअल) ***adj.*** of or characterized by ceremony, रस्मी, रिवाजी।

ceremony (सेरिमनी) ***n.*** 1. a formal act or set of acts prescribed by ritual, custom etc., अनुष्ठान, संस्कार, समारोह। 2. a conventionally polite social act, औपचारिकता।

certain (सर्टन) ***adj.*** 1. definite, निश्चित। 2. inevitable, अनिवार्य। 3. particular, विशेष।

certainty (सर्टन्टी) ***n.*** 1. the state of being certain, निश्चय, निश्चितता। 2. an established fact, सच्चाई।

certificate (सर्टिफ़िकिट) ***n.*** an official written or printed statement giving certain facts, प्रमाणपत्र, प्रमाणक।

certify (सर्टिफ़ाइ) ***v.*** to confirm as true or genuine, प्रमाणित करना।

cessation (सेसेशन) ***n.*** ceasing, end, अंत, समाप्ति।

cesspool (सेसपूल) ***n.*** a covered pit or hole for receiving waste or sewage, मलकुंड।

chaff (चैफ़) ***n.*** 1. the husk of grains, भूसी। 2. the fodder, चारा।

chagrin (शैग्रिन) ***n.*** a feeling of embarrassment, झुँझलाहट, चिढ़।

chain (चेन) ***n.*** 1. a series of metal links, लड़ी, ज़ंजीर, चेन, सिकड़ी। 2. a connected series or sequence, शृंखला, सिलसिला, लड़ी। ***v.*** to bind or tie with a chain, ज़ंजीर से बाँधना या जकड़ना।

chair (चेअर) ***n.*** 1. a movable seat, कुर्सी। 2. a seat of office, authority or dignity, आसन, पीठ। ***v.*** to preside over as chairman of, अध्यक्षता करना, सभापतित्व करना।

chairman (चेअरमैन) ***n.*** one who presides over a meeting, सभापति, अध्यक्ष।

chalk (चाक) ***n.*** a piece of white limestone, used for writing or drawing, खड़िया, चाक।

challenge (चैलिन्ज) ***n.*** 1. a call or invitation to try one's strength or skill against another, ललकार, चुनौती, आह्वान। 2. a difficult or demanding work, चुनौती-भरा काम, चुनौती।

chamber (चेम्बर) ***n.*** 1. a room or hall, सदन। 2. an office of a vakil, judge, doctor etc., कक्ष, चेंबर, प्रकोष्ठ। 3. a legislative assembly, विधानभवन, सभाभवन। 4. an enclosed space, cavity, गड्ढा, विवर, छेद।

chameleon (कैमीलिअन) ***n.*** a lizard, गिरगिट।

champagne (शैम्पेन) ***n.*** a white French wine, शैम्पेन।

champion (चैम्पिअन) ***n.*** 1. a winner in a contest, विजेता। 2. a player or team who has defeated all others in a competition, सर्वजेता, चैंपियन।

championship (चैम्पिअनशिप) ***n.*** a competition held to find the champion, प्रतियोगिता, खेल-प्रतियोगिता।

chance (चान्स) ***n.*** 1. an opportunity, अवसर, मौका। 2. likelihood, probability, संयोग, दैवयोग। 3. luck, भाग्य। ***v.*** to happen by chance, का संयोग होना।

chancellor (चान्सलर) ***n.*** 1. the head of a university, कुलाधिपति। 2. a minister, मंत्री।

chandelier (शैन्डिलिअर) ***n.*** an ornamental holder for lights, झाड़, फ़ानूस।

change (चेन्ज) ***v.*** to make different, बदल देना, परिवर्तित करना। ***n.*** the act or fact of changing or being changed, बदलाव, परिवर्तन।

changeable (चेन्जेबल) ***adj.*** able to change or be changed, परिवर्तनीय।

channel (चैनल) ***n.*** 1. a stretch of water connecting two seas, जलधारा, चैनल। 2. a course into which something can be directed or moved, माध्यम, साधन। 3. a band of radio frequencies reserved for a particular station, चैनेल।

chant (चान्ट) ***n.*** a song, गीत। ***v.*** to sing, गाना।

chaos (केऑस) ***n.*** total disorder or confusion, उथल-पुथल, गड़बड़ी।

chaotic (केऑटिक) ***adj.*** in the state of complete disorder or confusion, गड़बड़, उथल-पुथल-भरा।

chapel (चैपल) ***n.*** a small church, छोटा गिरजा।

C

chaplain (चैपलिन) ***n.*** a clergyman, पुरोहित, पादरी।

chaplet (चैपलिट) ***n.*** 1. a wreath, हार, पुष्पमाला। 2. a short rosary, सुमिरनी, माला।

chapter (चैप्टर) ***n.*** a main division of a book, अध्याय, प्रकरण, पाठ।

char (चार) ***v.*** to become or make black by burning, जलकर कोयला हो जाना, कोयला कर देना।

character (कैरक्टर) ***n.*** the combination of the qualities of a person, चरित्र, व्यक्तित्व।

characteristic (कैरक्टरिस्टिक) ***n.*** a distinguishing quality, चरित्रगत विशेषता।

characterize (कैरक्टराइज़) ***v.*** to describe or portray the character of, चरित्र-चित्रण करना।

characterless ***adj.*** having no character, चरित्रहीन।

charcoal (चार्कोल) ***n.*** 1. a black substance used as fuel made by burning wood in absence of air, लड़की या कोयला।

charge (चार्ज) ***v.*** 1. to entrust with a duty, responsibility etc., भार सौंपना। 2. to command, आदेश देना। 3. to accuse, अभियोग लगाना, दोषारोपण करना। 4. to set as a price, दाम लगाना। 5. to demand or recover, माँगना, वसूल करना। 6. to attack violently, चढ़ाई करना, टूट पड़ना, चढ़ जाना। 7. to fill or load a gun, container, etc., भरना, युक्त करना। 8. to give an electric charge to, आवेशित करना, चार्ज करना। ***n.*** 1. the price asked or paid for goods or services, मूल्य, दाम, मज़दूरी देना/लेना। 2. responsibility, कार्यभार, पदभार, दायित्व। 3. a command, आदेश। 4. accusation, आरोप, दोषारोप।

chargeable (चार्जेबल) ***adj.*** liable to be charged, वसूलने योग्य।

charger (चार्जर) ***n.*** 1. a military horse, सैनिक का घोड़ा। 2. an apparatus for charging batteries, चार्जर।

chariot (चैरिअट) ***n.*** a horse-drawn two-wheeled carriage used in ancient times, रथ।

charioteer (चैरिअटिअर) ***n.*** the driver of a chariot, सारथी, रथी।

charitable (चैरिटेबल) ***adj.*** 1. of or for charity, दातव्य, धर्मार्थ, ख़ैराती। 2. generous, उदार, परोपकारी, दानशील।

charity (चैरिटी) ***n.*** 1. the giving of food, money etc. to those in need, दान, भिक्षा, ख़ैरात। 2. a kindly attitude to other people, उदारता, परोपकार। 3. love of one's fellow men, brotherly love, बंधुप्रेम, भ्रातृप्रेम।

charm (चार्म) ***n.*** 1. the power of attracting, आकर्षण, लुभावनापन। 2. ability to please or win one, मुग्ध करनेवाला गुण, सम्मोहन, मोहिनी। ***v.*** to bewitch, अभिभूत करना, मोह लेना।

charming (चार्मिंग) ***adj.*** attractive and delightful, मनोहर, चित्ताकर्षक।

chart (चार्ट) ***n.*** 1. a map, नक़्शा। 2. a sheet of paper with information in the form of graphs and tables, चार्ट।

charter (चार्टर) ***n.*** a document from a government to establish an institution and defining its rights and privileges, अधिकार-पत्र, घोषणा-पत्र। ***v.*** to hire an aircraft, vehicle or ship, गाड़ी, जहाज़ आदि भाड़े पर लेना, चार्टर करना।

chartered (चार्टर्ड) ***adj.*** hired by contract, भाड़े पर।

chary (चैरी) ***adj.*** cautious, सावधान।

chase (चेस) ***v.*** to pursue or follow, पीछा करना, पीछे जाना। ***n.*** the act of chasing, pursuit, पीछा।

chasm (कैज़्म) ***n.*** a deep crack in earth or rock, खाई, दरार।

chassis (शैसी) ***n.*** 1. a steel frame of a vehicle, ढाँचा, चेसिज़। 2. the framework of a radio or television, ढाँचा, चेसिस।

chaste (चेस्ट) ***adj.*** pure, पवित्र, पावन, विशुद्ध।

chasten (चेसन) ***v.*** 1. to discipline, अनुशासित करना। 2. to punish, दंडित करना, सज़ा देना।

chastise (चैस्टाइज) ***v.*** to punish severely by beating, पिटाई करना, मारना-पीटना।

chastity (चैस्टिटी) ***n.*** purity, विशुद्धता, पवित्रता।

chat (चैट) ***v.*** to talk in a friendly or informal manner, बात करना, गपशप करना। ***n.*** a friendly or informal conversation, बातचीत, गपशप।

chatter (चैटर) ***v.*** to talk rapidly and incessantly, बकबक करना। ***n.*** an informal unimportant conversation, बकबक, गपशप।

chauffeur (शोफ़र) ***n.*** a person who is hired to drive an automobile, भाड़े का चालक, शोफ़र।

chauvinism (शोविनिज़म) ***n.*** exaggerated patriotism, उग्र राष्ट्रवाद।

cheap (चीप) ***adj.*** 1. low in price, inexpensive, सस्ता। 2. worth relatively little, महत्त्वहीन, निकम्मा।

cheaply (चीपली) ***adv.*** at a low price, सस्ते में।

cheat (चीट) ***v.*** to deceive or swindle, छलना, धोखा देना। ***n.*** 1. one who cheats, धोखेबाज़, ठग। 2. deception, धोखा, ठगी।

check (चेक) ***v.*** 1. to pause or cause to pause abruptly, रुकना या रोकना। 2. to restrain or control, नियंत्रित करना। 3. to examine, जाँच-पड़ताल करना। 4. to place an opponent's king in check, शह देना। ***n.*** 1. a pause, stoppage, रुकना, विराम। 2. anything that stops, अवरोध, अवरोधक तत्त्व। 3. restraint or control, नियंत्रण। 4. an examination to ensure the correctness of, जाँच, परीक्षण।

checkmate (चेकमेट) ***n.*** a position (in chess) in which an opponent's king is under attack and unable to escape, शहमात।

checkpost (चेकपोस्ट) ***n.*** a place for official inspection, जाँच-चौकी।

checkup (चेकअप) ***n.*** a medical examination, डॉक्टरी जाँच, चेकअप।

cheek (चीक) ***n.*** either side of the face below the eye, गाल, कपोल।

cheer (चिअर) ***n.*** 1. a sort of encouragement or congratulations, वाहवाह, शाबाशी। 2. a sort of applause, करतलध्वनि। 3. happiness, joy, प्रसन्नता, ख़ुशी।

cheerful (चिअरफ़ुल) ***adj.*** 1. in good spirits, प्रसन्नचित्त, प्रफुल्लित।

cheerless (चिअरलिस) ***adj.*** gloomy, उदास, खिन्न।

cheese (चीज़) ***n.*** a preparation of milk, पनीर।

cheetah (चीटा) ***n.*** an Indian leopard, चीता।

chef (शेफ़) ***n.*** a chief cook in a

C

restaurant, प्रमुख रसोइया या बावर्ची।

chemical (केमिकल) ***n.*** a substance produced by or used in a chemical process, रसायन, रासायनिक पदार्थ।

chemist (केमिस्ट) ***n.*** 1. a scientist skilled in chemistry, रसायनविज्ञानी, रसायनज्ञ। 2. a pharmacist, औषध-विक्रेता।

chemistry (केमिस्ट्री) ***n.*** the scientific study of the composition of the substances and their elements, रसायनविज्ञान।

cheque (चेक) ***n.*** a written order to a bank to pay an amount from one's account, चेक।

chequered (चेकर्ड) ***adj.*** 1. having a pattern of squares, चारख़ानेदार। 2. fluctuating, उतार-चढ़ाव भरा।

cherish (चेरिश) ***v.*** to keep in one's heart, दिल में बनाए रखना, सँजोए रखना, पाल रखना।

cheroot (शेरूट) ***n.*** a cigar with both ends open, चुरुट।

cherry (चेरी) ***n.*** 1. a small deep red round fruit with a stone, चेरी। 2. a tree producing this fruit, चेरी का वृक्ष। 3. deep red colour, गहरा लाल रंग।

chess (चेस) ***n.*** a game played on a chessboard, शतरंज।

chessboard (चेसबोर्ड) ***n.*** a board with sixty-four squares for playing chess, बिसात, शतरंजी।

chessman (चेसमैन) ***n.*** one of the pieces used in playing chess, मोहरा, गोटी।

chest (चेस्ट) ***n.*** 1. the upper front part of the human body, छाती, सीना। 2. a box used for storage of valuable objects, संदूक, पेटी; ~ of drawers, ख़ानेदार या दराजोंवाला बक्सा या अलमारी।

chevalier (शेवलिअर) ***n.*** a knight, वीरपुरुष।

chew (च्यू) ***v.*** to grind with the teeth, चबाना।

chic (शिक) ***adj.*** stylish, सजीला।

chick (चिक) ***n.*** 1. a young chicken, चूज़ा। 2. a girl, युवती, लड़की।

chicken (चिकन) ***n.*** 1. the domestic fowl, मुर्गा या मुर्गी। 2. its flesh, मुर्गे का गोश्त।

Chickenpox ***n.*** a disease caught especially by children, causing fever and spots on the skin, चेचक, छोटी माता।

chide (चाइड) ***v.*** to reprimand, to scold, डाँटना-डपटना, झिड़कना, बिगड़ना।

chief (चीफ़) ***n.*** a leader, नेता, मुखिया, सरदार। ***adj.*** highest in rank or authority, सर्वोच्च, मुख्य।

chiefly (चीफ़ली) ***adv.*** mainly, मुख्यत:, मुख्य रूप से।

chieftain (चीफ़्टन) ***n.*** the leader of tribe, सरदार।

chiffon (शिफ़ॉन) ***n.*** a soft, transparent fabric of silk, शिफ़ॉन।

child (चाइल्ड) ***n.*** a boy or girl between birth and puberty, शिशु।

childhood (चाइल्डहुड) ***n.*** the state or period of being a child, बचपन, शैशव।

childish (चाइल्डिश) ***adj.*** 1. of or like a child, बालकों-जैसा। 2. immature in behaviour, नादान, बचकाना।

childlike (चाइल्डलाइक) ***adj.*** like or befitting a child, बालोचित, बालसुलभ।

chill (चिल) ***n.*** severe coldness, ठंड।

chilli, chili (चिली) ***n.*** a pod of red pepper, लाल मिर्च; ~ sauce चिल्ली सॉस।

chimney (चिम्नी) ***n.*** a vertical passage carrying off smoke from a fire or furnace, चिमनी, धुआँकश।

chimpanzee (चिम्पैन्ज़ी) ***n.*** a gorrilla, बनमानुस, चिम्पैंज़ी।

chin (चिन) ***n.*** the central lower portion of the lower jaw, ठुड्डी, चिबुक।

china (चाइना) ***n.*** porcelain or ceramic ware, चीनी मिट्टी के बर्तन।

chink (चिंक) ***n.*** a narrow opening or crack, दरार, दरज।

chip (चिप) ***n.*** 1. a small piece broken or cut off, टुकड़ा, चिप्पड़। 2. a minute component with electrical characteristics, चिप।

chirp (चर्प) ***n.*** the short sharp sound made by small birds, चींचीं, चेंचें। ***v.*** to make this sound, चींचीं/चेंचें करना।

chisel (चिज़ल) ***n.*** a tool for cutting a solid material, छेनी, टाँकी। ***v.*** to cut or shape with a chisel, छेनी से काटना या तराशना।

chit (चिट) ***n.*** a short written note, पुर्ज़ा, पर्ची।

chitchat (चिटचैट) ***n.*** gossip, small talk, बतकही, बातचीत।

chivalrous (शिवैलरस) ***adj.*** having the qualities of a knight, शूर तथा दयालु, वीर।

chivalry (शिवैलरी) ***n.*** the qualities of a knight, शूरता तथा दयालुता, वीरता।

chlorine (क्लोरीन) ***n.*** a gaseous element, क्लोरीन।

chloroform (क्लोरोफ़ॉर्म) ***n.*** a strong liquid that causes unconsciousness, क्लोरोफ़ॉर्म।

chlorophyl, chlorophyll (क्लोरोफ़िल) ***n.*** the green coloured substance found in stems and leaves, क्लोरोफ़िल।

chocolate (चॉकलिट) ***n.*** 1. a powder of cacao seeds, चाकलेट। 2. dark brown colour, कत्थई या चाकलेटी रंग।

choice (चॉइस) ***n.*** 1. the act of choosing, चयन, चुनाव। 2. a thing or person chosen, चुना हुआ व्यक्ति या वस्तु। 3. an alternative, विकल्प। ***adj.*** of the best quality, बढ़िया, श्रेष्ठ।

choir (क्वाइर) ***n.*** a group of singers, गायक-मंडली।

choke (चोक) ***v.*** 1. to feel difficulty in breathing, दम घुटना। 2. to cause to stop breathing by pressing the windpipe, गला दबाना।

cholera (कॉलेरा) ***n.*** a fatal epidemic, हैज़ा, कॉलरा।

choose (चूज़) ***v.*** 1. to pick out, चुनना, चुनाव करना। 2. to prefer, पसंद करना।

choosey, choosy (चूज़ी) ***adj.*** hard to please, नकचढ़ा।

chop (चॉप) ***v.*** to cut by striking with a knife or axe, टुकड़े-टुकड़े करना, कीमा बनाना, कुतरना। ***n.*** a small piece of meat, मांस का टुकड़ा।

chorus (कोरस) ***n.*** a group of singers or dancers, गायक / नर्तक दल।

chosen (चोज़न) ***adj.*** select, चुनिंदा, चयनित।

chow mein (चौमेन) ***n.*** a preparation of noodles with the bits of meat and vegetables, चौमेन, नूडल्स।

Christ (क्राइस्ट) ***n.*** Jesus, येशु, ईसा, ईसा मसीह।

christen (क्रिसन) ***v..*** 1. to give a name, नामकरण करना, नाम देना। 2. to baptize, बपतिस्मा देना।

Christian (क्रिस्चन) ***n.*** one who believes in Christianity, ईसाई।

Christianity (क्रिस्चिऐनिटी) ***n.*** the Christian religion, ईसाई धर्म।

Christmas (क्रिसमस) ***n.*** the day celebrated as the anniversary of the birth of Jesus, बड़ा दिन, ख्रीस्त जयंती, येशु-जन्मोत्सव।

chronic (क्रॉनिक) ***adj.*** of long duration, चिरकालिक, पुराना।

chronicle (क्रॉनिकल) ***n.*** a record of historic events, इतिवृत्त, इतिहास।

chronological (क्रॉनोलॉजिकल) ***adj.*** arranged in order of time of occurrence, कालक्रमिक।

chronology (क्रॉनोलॉजी) ***n.*** the arrangement of dates and sequences of events, कालानुक्रम, कालक्रम।

chrysanthemum (क्रिसैन्थेमम) ***n.*** a garden plant and its flower, गुलदाउदी।

chuck (चक) ***v.*** 1. to throw out or discard, फेंक देना। 2. to forsake, छोड़ देना। 3. to tap, थपथपाना।

chuckle (चकल) ***n.*** a quiet laugh, मंद मुस्कान।

chum (चम) ***n.*** a close friend, पक्का यार, घनिष्ठ मित्र, बेली।

chummy (चमी) ***adj.*** very friendly, घनिष्ठ, पक्का।

chunk (चंक) ***n.*** a thick mass or piece, ढेला।

church, Church (चर्च) ***n.*** 1. a building for Christian worship, गिरजा, कलीसिया, चर्च। 2. the collective body of all Christians, ईसाई समुदाय।

churchyard ***n.*** the grounds round a church used as a graveyard, चर्च का क़ब्रिस्तान।

churn (चर्न) ***v.*** to shake or agitate milk, cream or curd to make butter, मथना, बिलोना।

cicatrix (सिकैट्रिक्स) ***n.*** a scar, व्रणचिह्न।

C.I.D. (सी.आई.डी.) ***abbr.*** Criminal Investigation Department, सी.आई. डी.।

cigar (सिगार) ***n.*** a roll of tobacco leaves for smoking, सिगार।

cigarette (सिगरेट) ***n.*** a roll of finely cut tobacco enclosed in paper for smoking, सिगरेट।

cinchona (सिन्कोना) ***n.*** a tree whose bark yields quinine, सिंकोना वृक्ष जिसकी छाल से कुनैन बनाई जाती है।

cinder (सिन्डर) ***n.*** a half-burned substance, अधजला पदार्थ।

cinema (सिनिमा) ***n.*** a motion picture theatre, सिनेमा।

cinnamon (सिनैमन) ***n.*** a bark used as a spice, दालचीनी।

cipher (साइफ़र) ***n.*** 1. a symbol 0, शून्य, सिफ़र, ज़ीरो। 2. nonentity, नगण्य व्यक्ति/वस्तु।

circle (सर्कल) ***n.*** 1. a perfectly round plane figure, वृत्त, सर्कल, दायरा। 2. something formed or arranged in the shape of a circle, घेरा, मंडल। 3. a group of persons having or sharing a common interest or activity, मंडल, मंडली। ***v.*** 1. to move in a circle, चक्कर लगाना, परिक्रमा करना। 2. to enclose in a circle, घेरना।

circuit (सर्किट) ***n.*** 1. a circular course or route, चक्कर, परिधि।

2. the area enclosed within such a route, क्षेत्र, मंडल।

circuitous (सर्क्यूइटस) ***adj.*** round about, घुमावदार, चक्करदार।

circular (सर्क्युलर) ***adj.*** shaped like a circle, वृत्ताकार, गोल।

circulate (सर्क्युलेट) ***v.*** 1. to move or flow through a circuit or system, घूमना, संचरित होना या संचरण करना। 2. to move around, चक्कर लगाना। 3. to spread or distribute widely, वितरित करना।

circulation (सर्क्युलेशन) ***n.*** 1. the movement of blood through bodily vessels, रक्तसंचार, परिसंचरण। 2. the number of copies of a newspaper sold or distributed, प्रसार, पाठक संख्या।

circumcise (सर्कमसाइज़) ***n.*** to remove the foreskin of male sex organ, खतना करना, सुन्नत करना, मुसलमानी करना।

circumcision (सर्कमसिज़न) ***n.*** the act of circumcising or the state of being circumcised, सुन्नत, ख़तना।

circumference (सर्कमफ़रेंस) ***n.*** the boundary line of a circle, परिधि।

circumlocution (सर्कमलोक्यूशन) ***n.*** use of many words where a few would do, शब्दाडंबर, शब्दजाल।

circumscribe (सर्कमस्क्राइब) ***v.*** to mark the limits of, सीमाबद्ध करना।

circumspection (सर्कमस्पेक्शन) ***n.*** alertness, सतर्कता, चौकसी।

circumstances (सर्कमस्टैन्सिज़) ***n.*** (plu.) the conditions or facts connected with an event or person and having bearing on it, परिस्थितियाँ।

circumvent (सर्कमवेन्ट) ***v.*** 1. to evade, टाल जाना, बच निकलना। 2. to outwit, चकमा देना।

circus (सर्कस) ***n.*** a travelling company of trained animals, acrobats, clowns etc., सर्कस।

cistern (सिस्टर्न) ***n.*** a water tank, पानी की टंकी, हौज़।

citadel (सिटैडल) ***n.*** a fort, दुर्ग, क़िला।

citation (साइटेशन) ***n.*** 1. an act of citing or something cited, उद्धरण, हवाला। 2. a formal statement of the achievements of a person receiving an academic honour, प्रशस्ति, प्रशस्ति-पत्र।

cite (साइट) ***v.*** 1. to quote as an example, उद्धरण देना, हवाला देना। 2. to mention as a proof, प्रमाण देना। 3. to commend for meritorious action, प्रशंसा करना।

citizen (सिटिज़न) ***n.*** a person who has full rights in a country, नागरिक।

citizenship (सिटिज़नशिप) ***n.*** the rights of a citizen, नागरिकता।

city (सिटी) ***n.*** a big town, नगर, शहर।

civic (सिविक) ***adj.*** of citizen, नागरिक-संबंधी।

civics (सिविक्स) ***n.*** the science dealing with government and the citizens, नागरिकशास्त्र।

civil (सिविल) ***adj.*** 1. of a citizen, नागरिक-संबंधी, सिविल, नागर। 2. polite, शिष्ट, सविनय; civil disobedience, सविनय अवज्ञा।

civilian (सिविल्यन) ***n.*** a person not serving in the armed forces, असैनिक व्यक्ति, सामान्य नागरिक।

civility (सिविलिटी) ***n.*** an act of courtesy, शिष्टाचार।

C

civilization (सिविलिज़ेशन) ***n.*** the advanced stage of human social development, सभ्यता।

civilize (सिविलाइज़) ***v.*** to bring out of savagery to a highly developed stage, सभ्य बनाना।

civil war ***n.*** a war between the groups or factions of the citizens of the same country, गृहयुद्ध।

claim (क्लेम) ***v.*** to demand as one's due or right, दावा करना। ***n.*** a demand for something as due or right, दावा।

claimant (क्लेमेन्ट) ***n.*** one who makes a claim, दावेदार।

clamorous (क्लैमरस) ***adj.*** causing clamour, कोलाहलपूर्ण।

clamour, clamor (क्लैमर) ***n.*** an outcry, शोर, कोलाहल। ***v.*** to make a loud protest or demand, ज़ोरदार ढंग से आपत्ति या माँग करना।

clamp (क्लैम्प) ***n.*** a mechanical device for holding two or more things together, क्लैम्प, शिकंजा। ***v.*** to fasten or grip with a clamp, शिकंजे में कसना।

clan (क्लैन) ***n.*** a group of families with common surname, वंश, कुल।

clandestine (क्लैन्डेस्टिन) ***adj.*** secret and concealed, गुप्त, चोरी-छिपे किया जानेवाला।

clang (क्लैन्ग) ***n.*** a loud, singing, metallic sound, घनघन, टनटन।

clap (क्लैप) ***v.*** to strike the palms of the hands together, ताली बजाना। ***n.*** the act or sound of clapping, ताली।

claret (क्लैरिट) ***n.*** red wine, लाल मदिरा।

clarification (क्लैरिफ़िकेशन) ***n.*** the act of clarifying, स्पष्टीकरण, सफ़ाई।

clarify (क्लैरिफ़ाइ) ***v.*** 1. to make clear to understand, स्पष्ट करना, सफाई देना। 2. to make pure, विशुद्ध करना, साफ़ करना।

clarinet (क्लैरिनेट) ***n.*** a wind instrument, शहनाई।

clarion (क्लैरिअन) ***n.*** a trumpet, तुरही।

clarity (क्लैरिटी) ***n.*** clearness, स्पष्टता।

clash (क्लैश) ***v.*** to collide or strike together with a loud harsh sound, टकरा जाना, भिड़ जाना, लड़ जाना। ***n.*** 1. a collision, भिड़ंत, टक्कर। 2. conflict, संघर्ष, विरोध।

clasp (क्लैस्प) ***n.*** 1. a device for fastening or joining a belt, बकसुआ, बकलस। 2. an embrace, आलिंगन। ***v.*** 1. to fasten or join with a clasp, बकसुआ लगाना। 2. to embrace, आलिंगन करना।

class (क्लास) ***n.*** 1. a division of people or things sharing a common characteristic, वर्ग, श्रेणी। 2. the people of a similar social or economic position, वर्ग, जाति। 3. the group of students who are taught together, कक्षा, जमात, दर्जा। 4. kind, sort, किस्म, प्रकार।

classic (क्लैसिक) ***adj.*** of the highest class or rank, उच्च कोटि का, उच्च श्रेणी का। 2. pertaining to ancient Sanskrit, Greek or Roman literature or art, शास्त्रीय।

classical (क्लैसिकल) ***adj.*** influenced by the art, literature or culture of ancient times, शास्त्रीय।

classification (क्लैसिफ़िकेशन) ***n.*** the act of classifying or state of being classified, वर्गीकरण।

classify (क्लैसिफ़ाइ) ***v.*** to arrange in classes, वर्गीकृत करना, वर्गीकरण करना।

classless (क्लासलिस) ***adj.*** socially not divided into classes, वर्गहीन।

classmate (क्लासमेट) ***n.*** a member of the same class, सहपाठी।

classroom ***n.*** any of the rooms in which classes are conducted in a school or college, कक्षा।

clatter (क्लैटर) ***n.*** 1. a rattling noise, खड़खड़।

clause (क्लॉज़) ***n.*** 1. a part of a compound or complex sentence, उपवाक्य। 2. a separate article or provision of a document, धारा, दफा।

claw (क्लॉ) ***n.*** 1. a sharp curved nail on the toe of an animal or bird, खाँग, काँटा। 2. the foot of a bird or animal with such nails, पंजा।

clay (क्ले) ***n.*** a soft earth used in making bricks, pottery etc., मिट्टी।

clean (क्लीन) ***adj.*** 1. free from dirt, स्वच्छ, साफ़। 2. free from impurities, शुद्ध, विशुद्ध। 3. direct, सीधे। ***v.*** to make clean, साफ़ करना, सफ़ाई करना।

cleanliness (क्लीन्लिनिस) ***n.*** habitual cleanness, सफ़ाई।

cleanse (क्लीन्ज़) ***v.*** to make clean and pure, साफ़ करना, शुद्ध करना।

clear (क्लिअर) ***adj.*** 1. free from anything that dims, transparent, पारदर्शक, साफ़। 2. free from obstruction or impediment, open, साफ़, खुला, सफा। 3. easily perceptible, distinct, साफ़, स्पष्ट, प्रांजल। 4. free from blemish, निष्कलंक, बेदाग। ***v.*** 1. to make or become clear, साफ़ होना या करना। 2. to rid of obstructions or impediments, बाधाएँ हटाना, रास्ता साफ़ करना। 3. to free from a charge of guilt, दोषमुक्त करना, बरी करना।

clearance (क्लिअरेन्स) ***n.*** 1. the act of clearing, साफ़ करना, सफ़ाई, निकासी। 2. the permission to leave, जाने की अनुमति, छुट्टी।

cleavage (क्लीविज) ***n.*** a break caused by splitting, दरार, फटन।

cleave (क्लीव) ***v.*** to cling, चिपकना, लगा रहना।

cleft (क्लेफ़्ट) ***n.*** a split or opening, दरार।

clemency (क्लेमेन्सी) ***n.*** mercy, दया।

clench (क्लेन्च) ***v.*** to grip or hold tightly, कसकर पकड़ना, भींच लेना।

clergy (क्लर्जी) ***n.*** the body of people ordained for religious service, पुरोहित-वर्ग, याजकवर्ग।

cleric (क्लेरिक) ***n.*** a clergyman, पादरी, याजक।

clerical (क्लेरिकल) ***adj.*** 1. of or pertaining to the clerks, लिपिक-संबंधी, लिपिकीय। 2. of a clergyman, याजक-संबंधी, याजकीय।

clerk (क्लर्क) ***n.*** a person employed to do work in an office, लिपिक, क्लर्क।

clever (क्लेवर) ***adj.*** quick at learning and understanding, चतुर, होशियार, बुद्धिमान, समझदार।

cleverness (क्लेवरनिस) ***n.*** the quality of being clever, चतुराई।

click (क्लिक) ***n.*** a brief short sound, खट। ***v.*** to make a brief short sound, खट से बोलना।

client (क्लाइएन्ट) ***n.*** a customer, ग्राहक, मुअक्किल।

clientele (क्लाइएन्टील) ***n.*** clients collectively, ग्राहक-वृंद।

cliff (क्लिफ़) ***n.*** a steep rock, खड़ी चट्टान।

climactic (क्लाइमैक्टिक) ***adj.*** of or having a climax, चरम, पराकाष्ठापूर्ण।

climate (क्लाइमिट) ***n.*** the prevailing weather conditions of an area, जलवायु, हवा-पानी।

climatic (क्लाइमैटिक) ***adj.*** of climate, जलवायु-संबंधी।

climax (क्लाइमैक्स) ***n.*** the event or point marked by greatest intensity or effect in a series, चरमबिंदु, पराकाष्ठा।

climb (क्लाइम) ***v.*** 1. to go up or higher, (ऊपर) चढ़ना, ऊँचे जाना। 2. to mount, सवार होना। 3. to grow up or upward, ऊपर की ओर बढ़ना।

clinch (क्लिन्च) ***v.*** 1. to fasten securely (with a nail or bolt, कील या रिपिट) जड़ देना। 2. to settle decisively or conclusively, निपटा देना, पक्का। ***n.*** 1. the act, process or result of clinching, जड़ना, जड़ाई, निपटारा। 2. an embrace, आलिंगन।

cling (क्लिंग) ***v.*** (clung, clinging) 1. to hold fast or adhere closely, चिपक या लिपट जाना, पकड़े रहना। 2. to remain emotionally attached, जुड़े रहना, चिपके रहना।

clinic (क्लिनिक) ***n.*** a private hospital or nursing home, निदानगृह।

clinical (क्लिनिकल) ***adj.*** of or relating to the observation and treatment of patients, निदान-संबंधी, नैदानिक।

clink (क्लिंक) ***v.*** to make or produce a sharp ringing sound, झनझन करना।

clip[1] (क्लिप) ***n.*** a device for gripping or holding things tightly, क्लिप।

clip[2] ***v.*** 1. to cut with scissors, कैंची से काट देना। 2. to make shorter by cutting, कुतर देना।

clique (क्लीक) ***n.*** a small group of people, गुट।

cloak (क्लोक) ***n.*** 1. a sleeveless outer garment, लबादा। 2. something that covers or conceals, आवरण, आड़।

cloakroom ***n.*** a room in which luggage can be deposited, यात्री-सामान-घर।

clock (क्लॉक) ***n.*** a timepiece, घड़ी।

clock tower ***n.*** a tower with a clock, घंटाघर।

clockwise (क्लॉकवाइज़) ***adj.*** & ***adv.*** in the direction in which the hands of a clock rotate, दक्षिणावर्त।

clod (क्लॉड) ***n.*** 1. a lump of clay, मिट्टी का ढेला। 2. a foolish person, मंदबुद्धि व्यक्ति। 3. a knot, गाँठ।

cloister (कलॉइस्टर) ***n.*** a monastery, विहार, मठ।

clone (क्लोन) ***n.*** an exact copy of someone or something else, क्लोन।

close[1] (क्लोस) ***adj.*** 1. near in space or time, पास का, नज़दीक। 2. near in relationship. रिश्ते में नज़दीक, नज़दीकी। 3. affectionate, घनिष्ठ, अंतरंग। 4. near alike, लगभग समान।

close[2] (क्लोज़) ***v.*** 1. to shut or become shut, बंद होना या करना। 2. to end, finish, ख़त्म होना या करना, समाप्त होना या करना।

closefisted (क्लोसफिस्टिड) ***adj.*** miserly, stingy, कंजूस।

close shave ***n.*** a narrow escape, बाल-बाल बचाव।

closet (क्लोज़िट) ***n.*** a small cupboard, छोटी अलमारी।

close-up (क्लोस-अप) ***n.*** a photograph taken at close range, क्लोज़-अप, नज़दीकी चित्र।

closure (क्लोज़र) ***n.*** the act of closing or the state of being closed, बंदी, समाप्ति, समापन।

clot (क्लॉट) ***n.*** a thick lump formed from liquid, थक्का।

cloth (क्लॉथ) ***n.*** fabric woven, knitted or felted, कपड़ा, वस्त्र।

clothe (क्लोद) ***v.*** 1. to put clothes on, कपड़े पहनना या पहनाना।

clothes (क्लोद्ज़) ***n.*** (plu.) articles of dress, पहनने के कपड़े, पोशाक।

cloud (क्लॉउड) ***n.*** 1. a mass watery vapour visible in the sky, बादल, मेघ। 2. a similar mass in the air as smoke cloud, (धुएँ का) बादल। 1. to cover with clouds, बादल छाना। 2. to darken, धुँधला कर देना। 3. to become gloomy, विषादमग्न होना।

cloudy (क्लॉउडी) ***adj.*** covered with clouds, मेघाच्छन्न, बादलों से भरा।

clove (क्लोव) ***n.*** a tree and its flower bud, लौंग और उसका पेड़।

clown (क्लॉउन) ***n.*** a comic entertainer, विदूषक, जोकर, मसख़रा।

club (क्लब) ***n.*** 1. a heavy stick used as a weapon, लट्ठ, लाठी। 2. a stick used to drive a ball in golf, क्लब, डंडा। 3. a playing card marked with a black figure shaped like a cloverleaf, चिड़ी का पत्ता। 4. an organisation or association of people with common aims or interest, क्लब। ***v.*** 1. to strike with a club, डंडे या क्लब से प्रहार करना। 2. to unite or combine for a common purpose, मिलाना, मिल जाना, इकट्ठा हो जाना।

clue (क्लू) ***n.*** any information that guides or directs in the solution of a problem, अता-पता, संकेत।

clump (क्लम्प) ***n.*** a lump, ढेला, लोंदा।

clumsy (क्लम्ज़ी) ***adj.*** 1. awkward, भद्दा, बेढंगा, फूहड़, भोंड़ा। 2. lacking physical coordination or grace, बेडौल, अनगढ़।

cluster (क्लस्टर) ***n.*** 1. a number of things occurring, growing or fastened close together, गुच्छा।

clutch (क्लच) ***v.*** to hold or grasp firmly, कसकर पकड़ना या जकड़ना। ***n.*** 1. a tight grasp, पकड़, चंगुल। 2. device for engaging and disengaging certain working parts in machinery, क्लच।

coach (कोच) ***n.*** 1. a large, closed, four-wheeled horse-drawn carriage, टमटम। 2. a railroad car, रेल का डिब्बा। 3. a motor coach, बस। 4. a tutor, शिक्षक, प्रशिक्षक। ***v.*** to train, प्रशिक्षित करना, प्रशिक्षण देना।

coachman (कोचमैन) ***n.*** a driver of a horse-drawn carriage, कोचवान।

coagulate (कोऐग्युलेट) ***v.*** to change from liquid to a mass or to form a semi-solid mass, जमना या जमाना, थक्का बनना या बना देना।

coal (कोल) ***n.*** 1. a hard black mineral used as fuel, कोयला। 2. an ember, अंगार, अंगारा।

coalesce (कोअलेस) ***v.*** to combine or unite, एकजुट होना, इकट्ठा हो जाना।

coalition (कोअलिशन) ***n.*** an alliance between parties, गठबंधन।

C

coalmine (कोलमाइन) ***n.*** a mine containting coal, कोयले की खान।

coaltar (कोलटार) ***n.*** a black sticky liquid produced from heating coal, अलकतरा।

coarse (कोर्स) ***adj.*** 1. not fine, rough, खुरदरा। 2. rough in manner, रूखा, फूहड़, अशिष्ट। 3. of low quality, inferior, मोटा। 4. vulgar, अश्लील।

coast (कोस्ट) ***n.*** the seashore, समुद्रतट।

coastline (कोस्टलाइन) ***n.*** the outline of a coast, तटरेखा।

coat (कोट) ***n.*** 1. an outer garment, कोट। 2. a covering layer, ऊपरी परत, तह। ***v.*** to cover with a layer, लेप करना, परत चढ़ाना।

coax (कोक्स) ***v.*** to try to persuade by pleading or flattery, फुसलाना, ख़ुशामद करना।

cobbler (कॉब्लर) ***n.*** 1. one who mends shoes, जूते गाँठनेवाला, मोची।

cobra (कोब्रा) ***n.*** a poisonous snake having a flattened hood, फनवाला ज़हरीला साँप, फनधर, कोबरा।

cobweb (कॉबवेब) ***n.*** a fine web spun by a spider, मकड़ी का जाल, जाला।

cocaine (कोकेन) ***n.*** an addictive drug, कोकीन।

cock (कॉक) ***n.*** 1. a male domestic fowl, मुर्गा। 2. a tap, टोंटी। 3. the hammer in a gun, बंदूक का घोड़ा या कुत्ता।

cock-and-bull story ***n.*** a foolish story, बेवकूफ़ी की बात, मनगढ़ंत कहानी।

cockpit (कॉकपिट) ***n.*** a pilot's compartment in an aircraft, वायुयान का चालक-कक्ष।

cockroach (कॉकरोच) ***n.*** a household large black insect, तिलचट्टा।

cocktail (कॉक्टेल) ***n.*** a mixed alcoholic drink, मिश्रित मादक पेय, कॉकटेल।

cocoa (कोको) ***n.*** a powder made from cacoa seeds, कोको।

coconut (कोकोनट) ***n.*** a large hardshelled nut of a palm tree, नारियल, खोपड़ा।

cocoon (कोकून) ***n.*** pupa's silky case, कोया।

cod (कॉड) ***n.*** a large food fish, एक तरह की बड़ी मछली, कॉड।

coddle (कॉडल) ***v.*** 1. to boil just below the boiling point, हलकी आँच पर पकाना या उबालना। 2. to treat indulgently to pamper, दुलार करना, लाड़-प्यार करना।

code (कोड) ***n.*** 1. a collection of laws or rules, संहिता, विधान। 2. a system of signals used in transmitting messages, संकेत भाषा, गूढ़लिपि। ***v.*** to convert into a code, संकेत भाषा में बदलना।

codify (कोडिफ़ाइ) ***v.*** to arrange rules or laws into a system or code, संहिताबद्ध करना।

co-education (को-एजुकेशन) ***n.*** education of boys and girls at the same institution, सहशिक्षा।

coefficient (कोइफ़िशेन्ट) ***n.*** a multiplier, गुणांक।

coerce (कोअर्स) ***v.*** to compel or force to act against one's wishes, ज़ोर-ज़बरदस्ती करना।

coercion (कोअर्शन) ***n.*** the act of coercing, ज़ोर-ज़बरदस्ती।

coexist (कोइग्ज़िस्ट) ***v.*** to exist

together at the same time and in peace, साथ-साथ जीना।

coexistence (कोइग्ज़िस्टेन्स) ***n.*** the state of existing together at the same time and in peace, सह-अस्तित्व।

coffee (कॉफ़ी) ***n.*** 1. the seeds of a coffee tree, कहवा वृक्ष के बीज। 2. a drink prepared from the above seeds, कॉफ़ी, कहवा।

coffer (कॉफ़र) ***n.*** a strong box for keeping money and valuables, तिजोरी, पेटी।

coffin (कॉफ़िन) ***n.*** a box in which a dead body is buried, ताबूत, शवपेटी।

cog (कॉग) ***n.*** one of the teeth on the rim of a gearwheel, दाँता।

cogent (कोजेन्ट) ***adj.*** convincing, विश्वासोत्पादक, विश्वासदायी।

cognate (कॉग्नेट) ***adj.*** having the same origin or source, सजातीय।

cognition (कॉग्निशन) ***n.*** 1. knowledge, ज्ञान। 2. the mental faculty by which knowlegde is acquired, मनःशक्ति।

cognizable (कॉग्निज़ेबल) ***adj.*** capable of being taken cognizance of, संज्ञेय।

cognizance (कॉग्निज़ेन्स) ***n.*** 1. knowledge, ज्ञान। 2. the legal right to deal with a matter, संज्ञान।

cohabit (कोहैबिट) ***v.*** to live together as husband and wife, सहवास करना।

cohere (कोहिअर) ***v.*** to stick together, जुड़े रहना।

coherence (कोहिअरेन्स) ***n.*** consistency, संगति, सुसंगति।

cohesion (कोहीज़न) ***n.*** the act or state of cohering, संगति, सामंजस्य।

cohesive (कोहीसिव) ***adj.*** tending to stick together, संगत, सामंजस्यपूर्ण।

coil (कॉइल) ***v.*** to wind or twist into rings, कुंडल या लच्छा बनाना। ***n.*** something coiled, कुंडल, लच्छा।

coin (कॉइन) ***n.*** a piece of metal used as money, सिक्का। ***v.*** 1. to make coins, सिक्के ढालना। 2. to invent a word or phrase, शब्द या पद गढ़ना।

coincide (कोइन्साइड) ***v.*** 1. to occur at the same time, एक साथ होना या घटना। 2. to agree, समान या एक जैसा होना, मेल खाना।

coincidence (कोइन्सिडेन्स) ***n.*** 1. the fact, condition or state of coinciding, संयोग, दैवयोग। 2. correspondence in the events, अनुरूपता, समानता।

coincident (कोइन्सिडेन्ट) ***adj.*** corresponding, अनुरूप, समान।

colander (कॉलेन्डर) ***n.*** a bowl-shaped perforated pan, छलनी।

cold (कोल्ड) ***adj.*** 1. of a rather low temperature, ठंडा, सर्द। 2. lacking in affection or enthusiasm, ठंडा, रूखा, स्नेहहीन। ***n.*** 1. lack of heat or warmth, ठंड, सर्दी। 2. an infectious illness causing sneezing etc., जुकाम, नज़ला, सर्दी।

cold-blooded (कोल्डब्लडिड) ***adj.*** ruthless, निर्मम, नृशंस।

cold storage (कोल्ड स्टोरिज) ***n.*** storage in a cool place, शीतागार, कोल्ड-स्टोरेज।

colic (कौलिक) ***n.*** severe abdominal pain, उदरशूल।

collaborate (कोलैबोरेट) ***v.*** to work

C

together or jointly, मिलकर काम करना, एक दूसरे से सहयोग करना।

collapse (कोलैप्स) ***v.*** 1. to fall down suddenly, भर्रा जाना, ध्वस्त हो जाना। 2. to fail completely, पूरी तरह विफल हो जाना। ***n.*** 1. a breakdown, पतन, निपात। 2. destruction, ध्वंस, विनाश। 3. failure, विफलता।

collapsible (कोलैप्सिबल) ***adj.*** foldable, मोड़ने या भाँजने योग्य; सिमटवाँ।

collar (कॉलर) ***n.*** the part of a garment that encircles the neck, कॉलर।

collateral (कोलैटरल) ***adj.*** 1. situated or running side by side, समपार्श्विक। 2. serving to support, सहायक।

colleague (कॉलीग) ***n.*** a fellow worker, सहकर्मी, सहयोगी, सांथी।

collect (कलेक्ट) ***v.*** 1. to gather together or be gathered together, इकट्ठा करना या होना। 2. to accumulate, संग्रह करना।

collection (कलैक्शन) ***n.*** 1. the act or process of collecting, संचयन। 2. something collected, संचय, संग्रह।

collective (कलैक्टिव) ***adj.*** done by or involving all the members of a group, सामूहिक।

collector (क्लेक्टर) ***n.*** 1. one who collects, संग्रहकर्ता, संचयक। 2. one who collects debts, rents etc, समाहर्ता। 3. the head of a district administration, जिलाधिकारी, कलक्टर।

college (कॉलिज) ***n.*** an institution of higher education, महाविद्यालय, कॉलेज।

collegian (कलीजिअन) ***n.*** a college student, महाविद्यालय का छात्र।

collide (कोलाइड) ***v.*** to strike together with a violent impact, टकराना।

colliery (कॉलिअरी) ***n.*** a coal mine, कोयले की खान।

collision (कोलिज़न) ***n.*** 1. the act of striking violently against each other, टक्कर। 2. conflict, संघर्ष, टकराव।

colloquial (कलोक्विअल) ***adj.*** pertaining to conversation, बोल-चाल का।

collusion (कल्यूज़न) ***n.*** conspiracy, साँठ-गाँठ।

colon (कोलन) ***n.*** 1. the lower part of large intestine, बृहदांत्र। 2. the punctuation mark (:), अपूर्ण विराम।

colonel (कर्नल) ***n.*** an army officer next below a brigadier, कर्नल।

colonial (कॉलोनिअल) ***adj.*** of or pertaining to a colony, उपनिवेशीय। ***n.*** a inhabitant of a colony, उपनिवेशी।

colonialist (कॉलोनिअलिस्ट) ***n.*** one who controls a foreign territory, उपनिवेशवादी।

colonize (कॉलोनाइज़) ***v.*** to establish a colony in, उपनिवेश बसाना, नई बस्ती बसाना।

colonizer (कॉलोनाइज़र) ***n.*** one who establishes a colony, नई बस्ती बसानेवाला।

colony (कॉलोनी) ***n.*** 1. a territory occupied by a foreign settler, उपनिवेश। 2. a particular new area for living purposes, नई बस्ती, कॉलोनी।

colossal (कलॉसल) ***adj.*** enormous, विशाल।

colour, color (कलर) ***n.*** 1. an attribute of things that results from light, रंग, वर्ण। 2. a dye or paint, रंग द्रव, रोगन। 3. a skin complexion of a person, रंग, वर्ण, रंगत। *v.* 1. to apply or impart colour to, रँगना, रँग देना। 2. to influence, प्रभावित करना।

colour blind *adj.* unable to see differences in colours, वर्णांध।

coloured *adj.* having colour, रंगीन।

colourful (कलरफ़ुल) *adj.* full of colour, रंगीन। 2. vivid or rich in character, रंग-बिरंगा, रंगारंग।

colt (कोल्ट) *n.* 1. a young male horse, बछेरा। 2. a young and inexperienced player, युवा तथा अनुभवहीन खिलाड़ी।

column (कॉलम) *n.* 1. a round pillar of a building, गोल खंभा, स्तंभ। 2. a single row of types on a newspaper, स्तंभ। 3. a regular feature of a newspaper, स्तंभ।

columnist (कॉलम्निस्ट) *n.* a journalist who writes a regular feature in a newspaper, स्तंभलेखक, स्तंभकार।

coma (कोमा) *n.* a state of prolonged unconsciousness, मूर्च्छा, बेहोशी।

comb (कोम) *n.* a toothed device for arranging hair, कंघी। *v.* 1. to arrange hair with a comb, कंघी करना। 2. to card, धुनना।

combat (कॉम्बैट) *n.* fighting, लड़ाई। *v.* to fight against, लड़ना, युद्ध करना।

combatant (कॉम्बैटेन्ट) *n.* a person engaged in a fight, लड़ाकू, योद्धा।

comber (कोमर) *n.* a person who combs, धुनिया।

combination (कॉम्बिनेशन) *n.* 1. the act of combining or the state of being combined, संयोजन, मिश्रण। 2. an alliance of people or parties, गठबंधन, मेल, सम्मिलन। 3. the result or product of combining, संयोजन।

combine (कम्बाइन) *v.* 1. to make or become united, संगठित करना या होना। 2. to mix or get mixed, मिश्रित करना या होना।

combustible (कम्बस्टिबल) *adj.* capable of burning easily, ज्वलनशील, दाह्य।

combustion (कम्बस्चन) *n.* the process of burning, दहन, ज्वलन।

come (कम) *v.* (came, come, coming) 1. to move toward the speaker or a place or point, आना। 2. to reach or arrive, पहुँचना। 3. to occur or happen, घटित होना। 4. to be descended, उत्पन्न होना।

comedian (कॉमीडिअन) *n.* a humorous entertainer or actor, विदूषक।

comedy (कॉमिडी) *n.* a drama written to amuse, a play which ends happily, सुखांत नाटक, कॉमिडी।

comely (कमली) *adj.* good-looking, मनोहर, चारु, मनोरम।

comet (कॉमिट) *n.* a heavenly body with a tail, पुच्छल तारा, धूमकेतु।

comfort (कम्फ़र्ट) *n.* 1. a condition of ease or well-being, सुख, सुख-सुविधा। 2. relief of suffering or grief, आराम, चैन, शांति। *v.* to give comfort to, आराम देना, सुख देना, सांत्वना देना।

comfortable (कम्फ़र्टेबल) *adj.* giving or providing comfort, आराम देनेवाला।

comic (कॉमिक) *adj.* funny, विनोदपूर्ण, मज़ेदार। *n.* (plu.) a book of comic strips, मनोरंजक चित्र पुस्तक।

coming (कमिंग) *adj.* next, approaching, आगामी, भावी।

C

comma (कॉमा) ***n.*** the punctuation mark (,) indicating a slight pause, अल्पविराम, कॉमा।

command (कमान्ड) ***n.*** 1. an authoritative order, समादेश, आदेश, कमान। 2. ability to control, नियंत्रण-क्षमता, प्रभुत्व। ***v.*** 1. to give a command, समादेश या आदेश देना। 2. to have authority over, प्रभुत्व या नियंत्रण होना।

commander (कमान्डर) ***n.*** a commanding officer, कमांडर, सेनानायक।

commander-in-chief ***n.*** the supreme commander, प्रधान सेनापति।

commanding (कमान्डिंग) ***adj.*** dominating, रोबदार, प्रभावशाली।

commandment (कमान्डमेंट) ***n.*** 1. a command, आदेश। 2. any of the ten commandments, नियम।

commando (कमान्डो) ***n.*** a militaryman trained to make raids, छापामार सैनिक, कमांडो।

commemorate (कमेमरेट) ***v.*** to honour the memory of, पुण्यस्मरण करना, जयंती मनाना।

commemoration (कमेमरेशन) ***n.*** a commemorating ceremony, जयंती।

commence (कमेन्स) ***v.*** to begin or start, प्रारंभ होना या करना।

commencement (कमेन्समेन्ट) ***n.*** a beginning, प्रारंभ, शुरुआत।

commend (कमेन्ड) ***v.*** 1. to praise, प्रशंसा करना। 2. to recommend, सिफ़ारिश करना।

commensurate (कमेन्शुरिट) ***adj.*** proportionate, आनुपातिक।

comment (कॉमेन्ट) ***n.*** 1. an expression of critical observation, टीका, टीका-टिप्पणी। 2. a statement of opinion, विचार, मत, राय। ***v.*** 1. to express an opinion, मत प्रकट करना, राय देना। 2. to write notes explaining or criticizing a text, टीका करना।

commentary (कॉमन्टरी) ***n.*** 1. an explanatory treatise, भाष्य, टीका। 2. a description, विवरण; running commentary, आँखों-देखा हाल।

commentator (कॉमन्टेटर) ***n.*** 1. one who writes a commentary, टीकाकार, भाष्यकार। 2. one who gives a running commentary, वर्णनकर्ता, प्रसारणकर्ता।

commerce (कॉमर्स) ***n.*** the buying and selling of goods, वाणिज्य, व्यापार।

commercial (कमर्शल) ***adj.*** of or engaged in commerce, वाणिज्यिक, वाणिज्य-संबंधी। ***n.*** a broadcast advertisement, रेडियो विज्ञापन, दूरदर्शन का विज्ञापन।

commiserate (कमिज़रेट) ***v.*** to express sympathy or pity for, सहानुभूति दिखलाना, दया करना।

commission (कमिशन) ***n.*** 1. authorization to carry out a task, अधिकार-प्रदान। 2. the authority so granted, प्रदत्त अधिकार। 3. the task so entrusted, सौंपा हुआ कार्य, कार्यभार। 4. a body of persons entrusted with some specific function, कमीशन, आयोग। 5. an agent's remuneration, आढ़त, कमीशन, दलाली। ***v.*** to grant a commission to, कमीशन देना, अधिकार देना या सौंपना।

commissionary (कमिशनरी) ***n.*** the area under a commissioner, मंडल।

commissioner (कमिशनर) ***n.*** 1. a member of a commission, आयोग का सदस्य। 2. the head of a commissionary, आयुक्त, मंडलायुक्त, कमिश्नर।

commit (कमिट) ***v.*** 1. to do, to perform, करना। 2. to entrust, सौंपना, सुपुर्द करना। 3. to bind with an obligation, प्रतिबद्ध होना। 4. to give a pledge, वचन देना, वादा करना।

commitment (कमिटमेन्ट) ***n.*** 1. the state of being obligated or bound, प्रतिबद्धता। 2. a pledge, वचन, वादा।

committee (कमिटी) ***n.*** a body of persons elected or appointed, समिति, कमेटी।

commode (कमोड) ***n.*** a pot mounted in a chair with a cover, कमोड।

commodious (कमोडिअस) ***adj.*** spacious, खुला, विस्तृत।

commodity (कमॉडिटी) ***n.*** something of use or profit, वस्तु, चीज़, शै।

common (कॉमन) ***adj.*** 1. ordinary, सामान्य, साधारण, मामूली। 2. shared by two or more persons or things, साँझा। 3. average, सामान्य।

commoner (कॉमनर) ***n.*** a common man, साधारण व्यक्ति।

commonly (कॉमनली) ***adv.*** generally, सामान्यतः, आम तौर पर।

commonplace (कॉमनप्लेस) ***adj.*** ordinary, मामूली, सामान्य।

common sense (कॉमनसेन्स) ***n.*** sound practical sense, सहज बुद्धि।

Commonwealth, the ***n.*** the British Commonwealth of Nations, राष्ट्रकुल।

commotion (कमोशन) ***n.*** 1. a confused noise, शोरगुल, हो-हल्ला, अशांति। 2. upheaval, disturbance, उथल-पुथल, उपद्रव।

communal (कम्यूनल) ***adj.*** 1. pertaining to a community, समुदाय-संबंधी, सामुदायिक। 2. of a religious community, सांप्रदायिक।

communalism (कम्यूनलिज़म) ***n.*** the idea to favour one's own or particular community, संप्रदायवाद, सांप्रदायिकता।

communalist (कम्यूनलिस्ट) ***n.*** a communal-minded person, संप्रदायवादी, फ़िरक़ापरस्त।

commune (कॉम्यून) ***n.*** a group of families living together and having common interest, समुदाय, कम्यून।

communicable (कम्यूनिकेबल) ***adj.*** that can be communicated, संचारी, सूचनीय।

communicate (कम्यूनिकेट) ***v.*** to give by way of information, संसूचित करना।

communication (कम्यूनिकेशन) ***n.*** the act of communicating, संसूचन, संचार।

communion (कम्यून्यन) ***n.*** 1. an exchange of thoughts and feelings, विचारों का आदान-प्रदान। 2. social dealings between people, सहभागिता, भाईचारा। 3. a spiritual union, आध्यात्मिक मिलन।

communique (कम्यूनिके) ***n.*** an official communication, विज्ञप्ति।

communism (कॉम्यूनिज़म) ***n.*** a political doctrine of classless society, साम्यवाद।

communist (कॉम्यूनिस्ट) ***n.*** a supporter of communism, साम्यवादी।

community (कम्यूनिटी) ***n.*** the people living in one locality, समुदाय।

C

community centre ***n.*** a place for social activities, सामुदायिक केंद्र।

commutation (कॉम्युटेशन) ***n.*** 1. a substitution or exchange, प्रतिस्थापन, अदला-बदली, परिवर्तन। 2. the reductions (in severity), न्यूनीकरण; commutation of sentence, दंडादेश का न्यूनीकरण।

commute (कम्यूट) ***v.*** 1. to travel daily or regularly a long distance between one's home and work, नियमित यात्रा करना, दैनिक यात्रा करना। 2. to change or make (a punishment) less severe, न्यूनीकृत करना।

compact[1] (कॉम्पैक्ट) ***n.*** a contract or agreement, क़रार, समझौता।

compact[2] (कम्पैक्ट) ***adj.*** 1. solid, सघन, ठोस। 2. concise, संक्षिप्त, संहत, छोटा।

companion (कम्पैनियन) ***n.*** an associate, साथी, सखा, संगी।

companionship ***n.*** the relationship between the companions, संग-साथ।

company (कम्पनी) ***n.*** 1. a group of people, संगति, संगत। 2. a firm, bussines organization, व्यापारिक, संस्था, कंपनी। 3. a subdivision of a military battalion, कंपनी।

comparable (कॉम्पेरेबल) ***adj.*** similar, समान, तुल्य।

comparative (कम्पैरेटिव) ***adj.*** based on comparison or estimated by comparison, तुलनात्मक।

comparatively ***adv.*** relatively, अपेक्षाकृत, अपेक्षया।

compare (कम्पेअर) ***v.*** to mark the similarities and differences between one thing or person with another, तुलना करना।

comparison (कम्पैरिसन) ***n.*** 1. the act of comparing, तुलना। 2. likeness, समानता।

compartment (कम्पार्टमेन्ट) ***n.*** 1. any separate section (of a building), खंड, प्रखंड। 2. a railway compartment, रेलगाड़ी का डिब्बा।

compass (कम्पस) ***n.*** a device with a needle that points the north direction, दिक्सूचक, क़ुतुबनुमा।

compassion (कम्पैशन) ***n.*** the deep feeling of sharing the suffering of another, करुणा, संवेदना।

compassionate (कम्पैशनेट) ***adj.*** having or showing compassion, संवेदनशील, दयालु।

compatible (कम्पैटिबल) ***adj.*** consistent, संगत।

compatriot (कम्पेट्रिअट) ***n.*** a fellow countryman, देशवासी, देशबंधु, हमवतन।

compel (कम्पेल) ***v.*** 1. to force, ज़बरदस्ती करना, बलात् कराना। 2. to make someone to have it or do it, बाध्य करना।

compelling ***adj.*** that compels, प्रबल, ज़बरदस्त।

compendium (कम्पेन्डिअम) ***n.*** a short complete summary, सार, सारसंग्रह, संक्षेप।

compensate (कॉम्पेन्सेट) ***v.*** to make a suitable payment in return for loss or injury, क्षतिपूर्ति करना, हरजाना देना या भरना।

compensation (कॉम्पेन्सेशन) ***n.*** the act of compensating, क्षतिपूर्ति, मुआवज़ा।

compete (कम्पीट) ***v.*** to strive or contend with another, स्पर्धा करना।

competence (कॉम्पिटेन्स) *n.* the quality or state of being competent, क्षमता।

competent (कॉम्पिटेन्ट) *adj.* well or fully qualified, सक्षम।

competition (कॉम्पिटिशन) *n.* a contest, प्रतियोगिता।

competitive (कम्पेटिटिव) *adj.* involving rivalry, प्रतिस्पर्धात्मक, स्पर्धात्मक।

competitor (कम्पेटिटर) *n.* one who competes with others, प्रतियोगी, प्रतिस्पर्धी।

compilation (कॉम्पिलेशन) *n.* the act of compiling or something compiled, संकलन, संग्रह।

compile (कम्पाइल) *v.* to write or produce by collecting from various sources, संकलन करना, संग्रह करना।

complacence (कम्प्लेसेन्स) *n.* the state or quality of being complacent, आत्मसंतुष्टि, आत्मतुष्टि।

complain (कम्प्लेन) *v.* 1. to express feeling of pain, कष्ट बतलाना, शिकायत करना। 2. to protest that something is wrong, शिकायत करना।

complainant (कम्प्लेनेन्ट) *n.* a person who makes a formal accusation, शिकायत करनेवाला।

complaint (कम्प्लेन्ट) *n.* 1. an expression of grief, dissatisfaction or pain, शिकायत। 2. a disease or illness, रोग, बीमारी, शिकायत। 3. a formal accusation or charge, परिवाद।

complement (कॉम्प्लिमेन्ट) *n.* something that completes or makes up a whole, पूरक। *v.* to add as a complement to, पूरक जोड़ना या लगाना।

complementary (कॉम्प्लिमेन्टरी) *adj.* forming a complement, पूरक।

complete (कम्प्लीट) *adj.* 1. having all its normal or necessary parts, संपूर्ण, सर्वांगपूर्ण। 2. finished, समाप्त, ख़त्म, पूर्ण। 3. perfect, पूर्ण, पक्का। *v.* 1. to make whole or complete, पूरा करना, तैयार करना।

completely *adv.* fully, पूरी तरह से, पूर्णतया।

completion (कम्प्लीशन) *n.* 1. the act of making complete, पूर्ण करना, पूरा करना। 2. end, समाप्ति।

complex (कम्प्लेक्स) *adj.* 1. complicated, intricate, पेचीदा, जटिल। 2. difficult to understand, दुर्बोध, दुरूह। 3. made up of inter-connected parts, बहुभागी, जटिल। *n.* 1. a whole made up of many parts, बहुभागी रचना, संकुल। 2. a set of buildings, भवन-समूह। 3. a group of emotional unconscious feelings which influence a person's behaviour, मनोग्रंथि।

complexion (कम्प्लेक्शन) *n.* the colour and general appearance of the skin esp. of the face, रूप, रंग, रंगत।

complexity (कम्प्लेक्सिटी) *n.* intricacy, जटिलता, पेचीदापन।

compliance (कम्प्लाइएन्स) *n.* the acting in accordance with a desire, request, condition etc, अनुपालन, पालन।

complicate (कॉम्प्लिकेट) *v.* 1. to make complex, जटिल या पेचीदा बना देना। 2. to make difficult to understand, दुरूह या दुर्बोध बना देना।

complicated *adj.* = complex.

C

complicity (कम्प्लिसिटी) ***n.*** the state or fact of being an accomplice in a criminal act, साँठ-गाँठ, मिलीभगत।

compliment (कॉम्प्लिमेन्ट) ***n.*** 1. an expression of regard, अभिवादन। 2. an expression of praise, बधाई। 3. (plu.) greetings, शुभकामनाएँ। ***v.*** 1. to express regard for, अभिवादन करना। 2. to express praise for, to congratulate, बधाई देना।

comply (कम्प्लाइ) ***v.*** to act in accordance with rules, wishes etc., अनुपालन करना।

component (कम्पोनेन्ट) ***n.*** a constituent part, घटक।

compose (कम्पोज़) ***v.*** to make up or constitute, बनाना, रचना।

composed (कम्पोज़्ड) ***adj.*** calm and tranquil, शांत, प्रकृतिस्थ।

composer (कम्पोज़र) ***n.*** a person who writes music, स्वर लिपिकार, संगीतकार।

composite (कॉम्पोज़िट) ***adj.*** made up of many parts or materials, सामासिक।

composition (कॉम्पज़िशन) ***n.*** 1. the act of composing, संयोजन, संरचना, गठन। 2. something composed, संयोजित पदार्थ, संरचना, कृति। 3. constitution, make-up, बनावट, संरचना, गठन। 4. a short essay, कंपोज़िशन, निबंध।

compositor (कम्पोज़िटर) ***n.*** a typesetter, कंपोज़िटर।

compost (कॉम्पोस्ट) ***n.*** a mixture of decaying organic matter used as fertilizer, (हरी) खाद।

composure (कम्पोज़र) ***n.*** the complete control over one's feelings, calmness, धैर्य, गंभीरता।

compound (कॉम्पाउन्ड) ***adj.*** 1. made up of several parts, संयोजित। 2. made up of many ingredients, यौगिक, सम्मिश्र। ***n.*** 1. a combination of two or more parts, संयोजन। 2. a combination of two or more ingredients, यौगिक, मिश्रण। 3. a combination of two or more words, समस्तपद, समास, समासपद। ***v.*** to combine or mix, मिश्रित करना, यौगिक बनाना। ***n.*** 1. a courtyard, आँगन। 2. a group of buildings set off and enclosed by a barrier, अहाता।

compounder (कॉम्पाउन्डर) ***n.*** one who compounds, सम्मिश्रक, कंपाउंडर।

comprehend (कॉम्प्रिहेन्ड) ***v.*** to understand thoroughly, अच्छी तरह समझना।

comprehensible (कॉम्प्रिहेन्सिबल) ***adj.*** that can be easily understood, बोधगम्य।

comprehension (कॉम्प्रिहेन्शन) ***n.*** the act or capacity of understanding, समझ, समझदारी।

comprehensive (कॉम्प्रिहेन्सिव) ***adj.*** including much, broad, व्यापक, विशद।

compress (कम्प्रेस) ***v.*** to squeeze or press together, दबाना।

compression (कम्प्रेशन) ***n.*** the act of compressing, संपीड़न।

comprise (कम्प्राइज) ***v.*** 1. to consist of, मिलकर बना होना। 2. to include, समाविष्ट होना या करना।

compromise (कॉम्प्रोमाइज़) ***n.*** a settlement of a dispute, समझौता। ***v.*** to settle a dispute, समझौता करना, समझौता कर लेना।

compulsion (कम्पल्शन) ***n.*** the state of being compelled, बाध्यता, विवशता।

compulsory (कम्पल्सरी) ***adj.*** compelling, essential, अनिवार्य।

compunction (कम्पंक्शन) ***n.*** remorse, पश्चात्ताप।

compute (कम्प्यूट) ***v.*** to reckon mathematically, संगणना करना, हिसाब लगाना।

computer (कम्प्यूटर) ***n.*** a machine for making calculations and storing and analyzing information, कंप्यूटर।

comrade (कॉम्रेड) ***n.*** a friend or companion, मित्र, संगी, साथी।

concave (कॉन्केव) ***adj.*** curved like an inner surface of a ball, अवतल।

conceal (कन्सील) ***v.*** to hide, छिपाना।

concealment (कन्सीलमेन्ट) ***n.*** the act of concealing, छिपाना, गोपन।

concede (कन्सीड) ***v.*** to admit that something is true, मान लेना, स्वीकार कर लेना।

conceit (कन्सीट) ***n.*** pride, अहंकार, घमंड।

conceivable (कन्सीवेबल) ***adj.*** capable of being understood or imagined, कल्पनीय।

conceive (कन्सीव) ***v.*** 1. to think or imagine, सोचना, कल्पना करना। 2. to form in mind, दिमाग में आना, सूझना। 3. to become pregnant, गर्भधारण करना।

concentrate (कॉन्सेन्ट्रेट) ***v.*** to direct or draw all one's thoughts or attention on something, केंद्रित करना, संकेंद्रित करना।

concentrated (कॉन्सेन्ट्रेटिड) ***adj.*** 1. not diluted, गाढ़ा, सांद्र। 2. intense, तीव्र।

concentration (कॉन्सेन्ट्रेशन) ***n.*** the act of concentrating, संकेंद्रण, एकाग्रता।

concept (कॉन्सेप्ट) ***n.*** general idea, thought, धारणा, संकल्पना।

conception (कन्सेप्शन) ***n.*** 1. something conceived, संकल्पना, धारणा। 2. the state of an ovum being fertilized by a sperm in a womb, गर्भधारण।

concern (कन्सर्न) ***v.*** 1. to relate to, से संबद्ध होना, से जुड़ा होना। 2. to be of importance or interest to, के लिए रुचि या महत्त्व का विषय होना। 3.to cause anxiety, चिंता उत्पन्न करना। ***n.*** 1. something of interest or importance, महत्त्व या रुचि की बात, सरोकार, वास्ता। 2. earnest regard, ध्यान, ख़्याल। 3. anxiety, चिंता। 4. a business establishment, दुकान, फ़र्म, संस्था।

concerned (कन्सर्न्ड) ***adj.*** 1. worried, troubled, चिंतित, परेशान। 2. having or showing concern, वास्ता रखनेवाला।

concert (कॉन्सर्ट) ***n.*** a musical performance, संगीत का कार्यक्रम, संगीत गोष्ठी।

concerted (कन्सर्टिड) ***adj.*** arranged by mutual agreement, सबकी सहमति से होनेवाला, साँझा।

concession (कन्सेशन) ***n.*** the act of conceding or something conceded, रियायत, छूट।

concessional (कन्सेशनल) ***adj.*** of concession, रियायती।

conch (कॉन्च) ***n.*** a spiral shell, घोंघा, शंख।

conciliate (कन्सिलिएट) ***v.*** to reconcile, सुलह कराना, संराधन करना।

C

conciliation (कन्सिलिएशन) ***n.*** the act of conciliating, संराधन।

concise (कन्साइस) ***adj.*** brief and to the point, संक्षिप्त।

conclave (कॉन्क्लेव) ***n.*** a private or secret meeting, गुप्त बैठक।

conclude (कन्क्लूड) ***v.*** to bring or come to an end, समाप्त करना या होना।

conclusion (कन्क्लूज़न) ***n.*** 1. an end, अंत, समाप्ति। 2. decision, निर्णय। 3. result, निष्कर्ष, परिणाम।

conclusive (कन्क्लूसिव) ***adj.*** decisive, निर्णयात्मक, निश्चायक।

concoct (कन्कॉक्ट) ***v.*** to invent or contrive, गढ़ना।

concord (कॉन्कॉर्ड) ***n.*** 1. agreement, करार, समझौता। 2. harmony, मेल, समरसता, सामंजस्य।

concourse (कॉन्कोर्स) ***n.*** a crowd or gathering, भीड़, जनसमुदाय।

concrete (कॉन्क्रीट) ***adj.*** 1. existing in reality, मूर्त, यथार्थ। 2. specific, विशिष्ट। 3. solid, ठोस, पक्का। 4. definite, निश्चित। 5. made of concrete, कंक्रीट का बना। ***n.*** a mixture of cement with sand, gravel and water, कंक्रीट।

concur (कन्कर) ***v.*** to have the same opinion, सहमत होना, एकमत होना।

concurrence (कन्करेन्स) ***n.*** agreement, करार, सहमति, समझौता।

concurrent (कन्करेन्ट) ***adj.*** happening at the same time, समकालिक, समकालीन।

concussion (कन्कशन) ***n.*** a violent shock, झटका, हिचकोला।

condemn (कन्डेम) ***v.*** 1. to denounce, भला-बुरा कहना, कोसना, निंदा करना। 2. to convict, दोषी ठहराना।

condemnation (कॉन्डेम्नेशन) ***n.*** the act of condemning, बुरा-भला, बुराई, निंदा।

condemned (कन्डेम्ड) ***adj.*** pronounced guilty, अपराधी।

condensation (कन्डेन्सेशन) ***n.*** an act of condensing, संघनन, गाढ़ा करने का कार्य।

condense (कन्डेन्स) ***v.*** 1. to increase the density of, गाढ़ा करना, संघनित करना। 2. to form a liquid from vapour, भाप से द्रव बनाना। 3. to abridge, संक्षिप्त करना।

condenser (कन्डेन्सर) ***n.*** a device for storing electricity, कन्डेन्सर।

condiment (कॉन्डिमेन्ट) ***n.*** 1. seasoning, छौंक। 2. spice, मसाला।

condition (कन्डिशन) ***n.*** 1. a particular state of being or existence, अवस्था, स्थिति, दशा। 2. a prerequisite, शर्त।

conditional (कन्डिशनल) ***adj.*** containing or expressing a condition, सशर्त, सप्रतिबंध।

condole (कन्डोल) ***v.*** to express sorrow or sympathy with someone in grief, अफ़सोस करना, मातमपुर्सी करना।

condolence (कन्डोलेन्स) ***n.*** an expression of sorrow or sympathy, अफ़सोस, शोक, मातमपुर्सी।

condone (कन्डोन) ***v.*** to forgive, माफ़ करना।

conducive (कॉन्ड्यूसिव) ***adj.*** likely to contribute, प्रेरक, सहायक।

conduct[1] (कन्डक्ट) ***v.*** 1. to behave, आचरण करना। 2. to direct the course of, संचालन करना। 3. to lead or guide, पथ-प्रदर्शन करना।

conduct[2] (कॉन्डक्ट) ***n.*** the way one acts, behaviour, आचरण, चाल-चलन, रंग-ढंग।

conduction (कन्डक्शन) ***n.*** transmission of electricity, heat, water etc., चालन, संवहन।

conductor (कन्डक्टर) ***n.*** a substance that conducts electricity, heat etc., चालक, चालन-सक्षम। 2. the person in charge of a bus, tram etc. and who collects payments from passengers, कंडक्टर।

conduit (कॉन्ड्युट) ***n.*** 1. a pipe for conveying liquids, पाइप, नल।

cone (कोन) ***n.*** a solid object with a round base that narrows to a point at the top, कोन, शंकु।

confection (कन्फ़ेक्शन) ***n.*** a sweet preparation, मिठाई, पाक।

confectioner (कन्फ़ेक्शनर) ***n.*** one who makes or sells confections, मिठाई बनाने या बेचनेवाला, हलवाई।

confederation (कन्फ़ेडरेशन) ***n.*** a union of states, राज्यसंघ, महासंघ।

confer (कन्फ़र) ***v.*** 1. to bestow (an honour), प्रदान करना, प्रदत्त करना। 2. to hold a discussion or conference, सलाह या परामर्श करना।

conference (कॉन्फ़रेंस) ***n.*** a meeting for exchange of ideas, कॉन्फ्रेंस, सम्मेलन।

confess (कन्फ़ेस) ***v.*** to acknowledge or admit one's fault, sin or weakness, ग़लती, पाप या कमज़ोरी मान लेना।

confession (कन्फ़ेशन) ***n.*** the act of confessing, ग़लती या अपराध स्वीकार करना।

confidant (कॉन्फ़िडैन्ट) ***n.*** a person to whom one tells one's secrets, विश्वासपात्र, विश्वासभाजन।

confide (कन्फ़ाइड) ***v.*** to tell a secret to a person one trusts, विश्वासभाजन समझकर किसी को कोई रहस्यपूर्ण या निजी बात बतलाना।

confidence (कॉन्फ़िडेन्स) ***n.*** full trust, पूर्ण विश्वास, भरोसा, यकीन।

confident (कॉन्फ़िडेन्ट) ***adj.*** having confidence, भरोसा करनेवाला, विश्वस्त।

confidential (कॉन्फ़िडेन्शल) ***adj.*** to be kept secret, गोपनीय।

configuration (कन्फ़िग्युरेशन) ***n.*** the arrangement of the parts of something, रचना, बनावट, आकृति।

confine (कन्फ़ाइन) ***v.*** 1. to imprison, क़ैद या बंद रखना। 2. to restrict or keep within certain limits, सीमित करना या रखना।

confinement (कन्फ़ाइनमेन्ट) ***n.*** the act of confining or the state of being confined, क़ैद।

confirm (कन्फ़र्म) ***v.*** 1. to verify or ratify, पुष्टि करना। 2. to give approval to, अनुमोदन करना।

confirmation (कॉन्फ़र्मेशन) ***n.*** the act of confirming, पुष्टि, अनुमोदन।

confirmed (कन्फ़र्म्ड) ***adj.*** firmly settled in a particular way of life, पक्का।

confiscate (कॉन्फ़िस्केट) ***v.*** to seize by authority, क़ुर्क़ करना, ज़ब्त करना।

confiscation (कॉन्फ़िस्केशन) ***n.*** seizure of private property, क़ुर्क़ी, ज़ब्ती।

conflagration (कॉन्फ़्लेग्रेशन) ***n.*** a wide-spread and destructive fire, अग्निकांड।

conflict (कॉन्फ़्लिक्ट) ***n.*** 1. disagreement between people with different ideas or beliefs, विरोध। 2. a struggle or clash, संघर्ष।

C

3. a fight, लड़ाई, द्वंद्व। *v.* to be in opposition or disagreement, विरोध होना, वैषम्य होना।

conflicting (कन्फ़्लिक्टिंग) *adj.* opposing, परस्पर-विरोधी, द्वंद्वात्मक।

confluence (कॉन्फ़्लुएन्स) *n.* 1. the place or point where two rivers meet, संगम। 2. a concourse, समागम।

conform (कन्फ़ॉर्म) *v.* 1. to make or become similar, समान या अनुरूप होना अथवा करना। 2. to adapt, अनुकूल बनना या बनाना।

conformity (कन्फ़ॉर्मिटी) *n.* 1. similarity in form or character, अनुरूपता। 2. action or behaviour in agreement to the established rules, नियमानुवर्तन, अनुपालन।

confound (कन्फ़ाउन्ड) *v.* to confuse and surprise, भ्रमित और हैरान होना या करना, दुविधा में पड़ना या डाल देना।

confront (कन्फ़्रन्ट) *v.* 1. to come or bring face to face with, आमना-सामना होना या करना। 2. to face boldly, डटकर सामना करना, लोहा लेना।

confrontation (कॉन्फ़्रन्टेशन) *n.* 1. the act of confronting, सामना, आमना-सामना। 2. a fight, battle or war, भिड़ंत, टक्कर, युद्ध। 3. a serious dispute, उग्र विवाद।

confuse (कन्फ़्यूज़) *v.* to cause to be mistaken, भ्रम में डाल देना।

confused (कन्फ़्यूज़्ड) *adj.* perplexed, confounded, भ्रमित, क्षुब्ध, घबराया हुआ।

confusion (कन्फ़्यूज़न) *n.* the act of confusing or the condition of being confused, भ्रम, विभ्रम।

congenial (कन्जीनिअयल) *adj.* 1. friendly, मैत्रीपूर्ण, सौहार्दपूर्ण। 2. agreeable, सुखद, अनुकूल, प्रीतिकर।

congenital (कन्जेनिटल) *adj.* 1. existing since someone's birth, जन्मजात। 2. being such as if by nature, सहज।

congest (कन्जेस्ट) *v.* to overfill, ठसाठस भर देना या भर जाना।

congested (कन्जेस्टिड) *adj.* overcrowded, खचाखच भरा, घना।

congestion (कन्जेस्चन) *n.* 1. a congested condition, भीड़-भाड़। 2. excessive accumulation, जमाव, संकुलता।

conglomerate (कंग्लॉमैरेट) *v.* to collect into a mass, पिंड का रूप धारण करना।

conglomeration (कंग्लॉमैरेशन) *n.* a mass, पिंड।

congratulate (कन्ग्रैच्युलेट) *v.* to express pleasure at another's good fortune, बधाई देना, मुबारकबाद देना।

congratulations (कन्ग्रैच्युलेशन्स) *n.* (plu.) an expression of joy on someone's good fortune, बधाई, मुबारक, मुबारकबाद।

congregate (कॉन्ग्रिगेट) *v.* 1. to gather together, इकट्ठा होना, जुटना। 2. to cause to gather together, इकट्ठा करना, जुटाना।

congregation (कॉन्ग्रिगेशन) *n.* a group of people gathered together to take part in religious worship, समागम।

congress (कॉन्ग्रेस) *n.* a formal meeting or assembly of representatives, कांग्रेस, सम्मेलन।

congruence (कॉन्ग्रूएन्स) *n.* the state of being congruent, समरूपता; संगति।

congruent (कॉन्ग्रूएन्ट) *adj.* 1. having the same shape and size as another, समरूप। 2. corresponding, अनुकूल, संगत।

conical (कॉनिकल) ***adj.*** shaped like a cone, शंकु के आकार का, शंक्वाकार।

conjectural (कन्जेक्चरल) ***adj.*** based on conjecture, अटकल-पच्चू।

conjecture (कन्जेक्चर) ***v.*** to guess, अनुमान करना, अटकल लगाना। ***n.*** a guess, अनुमान, अटकल।

conjoin (कन्जॉइन) ***v.*** to join, जुड़ना या जोड़ना, मिलना या मिलाना।

conjugal (कॉन्जुगल) ***adj.*** of the marriage, वैवाहिक।

conjugate (कॉन्जुगेट) ***v.*** to give the various forms of a verb that show number, person, tense etc., क्रिया का रूप-साधन करना, क्रिया-रूप बनाना।

conjugation (कॉन्जुगेशन) ***n.*** the act or state of being conjugated, क्रिया का रूप-साधन।

conjunction (कन्जंक्शन) ***n.*** 1. the act or state of being conjoined, मिलन, युति, सहमिलन, संयोजन; conjunctions of stars, नक्षत्रों की युति। 2. in grammar, a word that joins other words, phrases, clauses etc., योजक।

conjuncture (कन्जंक्चर) ***n.*** crisis, संकट।

conjuration (कॉन्जुरेशन) ***n.*** 1. trickery, चालाकी। 2. sorcery, हाथ की सफ़ाई, जादू। 3. submission, निवेदन।

conjure (कॉन्ज्योर) ***v.*** to do clever tricks, हाथ की सफ़ाई दिखाना, जादू के खेल दिखाना।

connect (कनेक्ट) ***v.*** to join, जोड़ना, मिलाना, संबद्ध करना।

connected ***adj.*** related, संबद्ध, संबंधित।

connection (कनेक्शन) ***n.*** 1. the act of connecting or the state of being connected, संबंध। 2. a person connected by family or marriage, रिश्ता, नाता। 3. a link, जोड़, शृंखला। 4. the relation of a word to its context, संबंध। 5. a transfer from one train, plane etc. to another, मेल। 6. (plu.) people with whom one is associated, ऐसे लोग जिनसे संबंध हो।

connivance (कनाइवेन्स) ***n.*** passive consent for some wrong, मिलीभगत।

connive (कनाइव) ***v.*** to work together secretly for some wrong, मिलीभगत होना।

connoisseur (कॉनिशर) ***n.*** an expert of fine arts, पारखी।

connotation (कॉनोटेशन) ***n.*** the implied meaning, संकेतार्थ, विवक्षा।

connote (कनोट) ***v.*** to suggest in addition to literal meaning, संकेत करना, लक्षित करना।

conquer (कॉन्कर) ***v.*** 1. to defeat in war, to win, जीत लेना, हरा देना। 2. to overcome, काबू में कर लेना, पराभूत कर देना।

conqueror (कॉन्करर) ***n.*** one who conquers, विजेता, विजयी।

conquest (कॉन्क्वेस्ट) ***n.*** the act of conquering, विजय, जीत।

conscience (कॉन्शन्स) ***n.*** an inner sense of what is right and wrong, अंतश्चेतना।

conscientious (कॉन्शिएन्शस) ***adj.*** 1. honest, ईमानदार। 2. careful, सावधान।

conscious (कॉन्शस) ***adj.*** awake, सजग, सचेत।

consciousness (कॉन्शसनिस) ***n.*** awareness, चेतनता, सजगता।

C

conscription (कंस्क्रिप्शन) ***n.*** the practice of forcing people by law to serve in armed forces, फौज में ज़बरन भरती।

consecrate (कॉन्सिक्रेट) ***v.*** to make or declare holy, पवित्र करना या बनाना, संस्कारित करना।

consecration (कॉन्सिक्रेशन) ***n.*** the act of consecrating, पवित्रीकरण।

consecutive (कन्सेक्युटिव) ***adj.*** following, क्रमिक, क्रमवार।

consensus (कन्सेन्सस) ***n.*** general agreement, collective opinion, आम राय।

consent (कन्सेन्ट) ***v.*** to give permission, अनुमति देना, सहमत होना। ***n.*** permission, agreement, अनुमति, सहमति, स्वीकृति, मंज़ूरी।

consequence (कॉन्सिक्वेंस) ***n.*** as an effect or result, परिणाम, फल, नतीजा। 2. importance, महत्त्व।

consequent (कॉन्सिक्वेन्ट) ***adj.*** following, परिणामात्मक।

conservative (कन्सर्वेटिव) ***adj.*** & ***n.*** favouring the established order of the society, रूढ़िवादी, अनुदारवादी।

conservator (कन्सर्वेटर) ***n.*** one who preserves forests, वनपाल।

conserve (कन्सर्व) ***v.*** to protect and preserve, संरक्षण करना, सुरक्षित करना या रखना। ***n.*** a fruit jam, जैम, मुरब्बा।

consider (कन्सिडर) ***v.*** 1. to think about, सोच-विचार करना। 2. to make allowances for, लिहाज़ करना।

considerable (कन्सिडरेबल) ***adj.*** 1. fit to be considered, important, महत्त्वपूर्ण। 2. fairly large or great, अच्छा-ख़ासा, लंबा-चौड़ा।

considerate (कन्सिडरिट) ***adj.*** having regard for the feelings of others, मुरव्वती, लिहाज़ी, विचारवान।

consideration (कन्सिडरेशन) ***n.*** 1. deliberation, careful thought, सोच-विचार। 2. the state of being considerate, मुरव्वत, लिहाज़।

consign (कन्साइन) ***v.*** to entrust, सौंपना, सुपुर्द करना।

consignee (कॉन्साइनी) ***n.*** a person to whom goods are consigned, प्रेषिती।

consignment (कन्साइनमेन्ट) ***n.*** 1. the act of consigning, भेजने की क्रिया, प्रेषण। 2. something consigned, प्रेषित माल।

consigner (कन्साइनर) ***n.*** one who consigns (goods) to another, प्रेषक।

consist (कन्सिस्ट) ***v.*** to be made up or composed of, बना होना, गठित होना।

consistency (कन्सिस्टेन्सी) ***n.*** the state of being consistent, uniformity, एकरूपता, स्थिरता।

consistent (कन्सिस्टेन्ट) ***adj.*** 1. unchanging, अपरिवर्तनशील, एकरूप। 2. having agreement among things or parts, संगत।

consolation (कॉन्सोलेशन) ***n.*** the act of consoling or the state of being consoled, सांत्वना।

console (कन्सोल) ***v.*** to comfort or solace, सांत्वना देना।

consolidate (कन्सॉलिडेट) ***v.*** to become or cause to become strong, दृढ़ीभूत होना या करना, जमना या जमाना।

consolidated (कन्सॉलिडेटिड) ***adj.*** combined, समेकित।

consonant (कॉन्सनेन्ट) ***n.*** a letter other than a vowel, व्यंजन।

consort[1] (कन्सोर्ट) ***n.*** a husband or wife, पति या पत्नी, जीवनसंगी।

consort[2] (कन्सॉर्ट) ***v.*** 1. to keep company, साथ रहना, साथ देना। 2. to be in agreement, सहमति होना, मतैक्य होना।

consortium (कन्सॉर्टियम) an international body or association, अंतर्राष्ट्रीय निकाय या संघटन।

conspicuous (कंस्पिक्युअस) ***adj.*** 1. obvious, सुस्पष्ट। 2. remarkable, उल्लेखनीय, महत्त्वपूर्ण। 3. attracting attention, ध्यानाकर्षक।

conspiracy (कंस्पिरेसी) ***n.*** an illegal plot, षड्यंत्र, कुचक्र।

conspirator (कंस्पिरेटर) ***n.*** one who takes part in a conspiracy, षड्यंत्रकारी।

conspire (कंस्पाइर) ***v.*** 1. to plan together secretly for some unlawful purpose, षड्यंत्र रचना।

constable (कॉन्स्टेबल) ***n.*** a policeman of a lower rank, सिपाही।

constabulary (कॉन्स्टेब्युलरी) ***n.*** an armed police force, पुलिस-बल।

constant (कॉन्स्टेंट) ***adj.*** 1. fixed, unchanging, एकरूप, अचल। 2. happening all the time, continuous, अनवरत, सतत।

constellation (कॉन्स्टेलेशन) 1. a group of stars with a fixed shape, नक्षत्र।

consternation (कॉन्स्टर्नेशन) ***n.*** dismay, निराशा।

constipation (कॉन्स्टिपेशन) ***n.*** difficulty in emptying the bowels, क़ब्ज़, क़ब्ज़ियत।

constituency (कंस्टिचूएन्सी) 1. a body of voters, मतदाता-वर्ग। 2. an area and its residents represented by an elected legislator, चुनाव-क्षेत्र, निर्वाचन-क्षेत्र।

constituent (कंस्टिचूएन्ट) ***n.*** a constituent part, घटक, अवयव, पुरज़ा।

Constituent Assembly ***n.*** संविधान-सभा।

constitute (कॉन्स्टिट्यूट) ***v.*** to form or make up, बनना या बनाना, गठित होना या करना।

constitution (कॉन्स्टिट्यूशन) ***n.*** the body of principles according to which the country is governed, संविधान, विधान।

constitutional ***adj.*** of or related to the constitution, संवैधानिक।

constrain (कन्स्ट्रेन) ***v.*** 1. to force, विवश करना। 2. to bind, to restrain, रोकना, नियंत्रित करना।

constraint (कन्स्ट्रेन्ट) ***n.*** 1. compulsion, विवशता, मजबूरी। 2. restraint, नियंत्रण। 3. embarrassment, परेशानी।

construct (कन्स्ट्रक्ट) ***v.*** to build, बनाना, रचना।

construction (कन्स्ट्रक्शन) ***n.*** 1. the act of constructing, निर्माण। 2. a building, भवन, इमारत।

constructive (कन्स्ट्रक्टिव) ***adj.*** serving a useful purpose, offering helpful suggestions, रचनात्मक।

construe (कन्स्ट्रू) ***v.*** 1. to give the sense or meaning, अर्थ देना। 2. to interpret, निर्वचन करना।

consul (कॉन्सल) ***n.*** an officer appointed to live in a foreign city to look after the interest of his country, वाणिज्यदूत, कौंसल।

consulate (कॉन्सुलिट) ***n.*** the office of

C

a consul, वाणिज्यदूतावास, कौंसल वास।

consult (कन्सल्ट) ***v.*** 1. to seek advice, परामर्श लेना। 2. to confer, विचार-विमर्श करना।

consultant (कन्सल्टेन्ट) ***n.*** a person who gives professional advice, परामर्शदाता।

consultation (कॉन्सल्टेशन) ***n.*** the act of consulting, परामर्श, सलाह।

consume (कन्स्यूम) ***v.*** 1. to use up, उपभोग करना। 2. to destroy, नष्ट कर देना। 3. to spend wastefully, बहा देना, फूँक डालना।

consumer (कन्स्यूमर) ***n.*** a person who buys goods or uses services, उपभोक्ता।

consummate (कॉन्समेट) ***v.*** to make complete or perfect, पूर्ण करना, पक्का करना, निष्पन्न करना। ***adj.*** 1. complete, पूर्ण। 2. skilled, पूर्ण रूप से कुशल, कुशलता-प्राप्त।

consumption (कन्सम्प्शन) ***n.*** the act of consuming, using up anything, उपभोग।

contact (कॉन्टैक्ट) ***n.*** 1. the condition of touching of objects or surfaces, स्पर्श, संस्पर्श। 2. a relationship, संबंध। 3. the state of being in touch or association, संपर्क। 4. an acquaintance, परिचित व्यक्ति। ***v.*** to get in touch with, संपर्क स्थापित करना।

contact lens ***n.*** a very thin lens worn in contact with the eyeball, कंटैक्ट लेन्स।

contagious (कन्टेजस) ***adj.*** infectious, संक्रामक, छुतहा।

contain (कन्टेन) ***v.*** 1. to restrain, नियंत्रण में रखना। 2. to include or comprise, अंतर्विष्ट होना, समावेशित होना।

contained (कन्टेन्ड) ***adj.*** 1. controlled, नियंत्रित। 2. calm, शांत।

container (कन्टेनर) ***n.*** 1. a box, barrel or bottle etc., designed to contain a substance, पात्र, आधान। 2. a large box used for transporting goods, कंटेनर, बक्सा।

contaminate (कन्टैमिनेट) ***v.*** to pollute, प्रदूषित हो जाना, बिगड़ जाना।

contamination (कन्टैमिनेशन) ***n.*** pollution, प्रदूषण।

contemplate (कॉन्टेम्प्लेट) ***v.*** 1. to think deeply about, चिंतन करना।

contemplation (कॉन्टेम्प्लेशन) ***n.*** the act of contemplating, चिंतन, ध्यान।

contemplative (कॉन्टेम्प्लेटिव) ***adj.*** thoughful, विचारशील।

contemporary (कन्टेम्परेरी) ***adj.*** belonging to the same time or period, समकालीन, समकालिक।

contempt (कन्टेम्प्ट) ***n.*** feeling of scorn or disrespect, घृणा, तिरस्कार।

contemptible (कन्टेम्प्टिबल) ***adj.*** despicable, घृणित, निंदनीय।

contemptuous (कन्टेम्चुअस) ***adj.*** showing contempt, तिरस्कारपूर्ण।

contend (कन्टेन्ड) ***v.*** 1. to strive for, प्रयत्न करना। 2. to contest, मुकाबला करना, लड़ना। 3. to assert, हक जतलाना।

contender (कन्टेन्डर) ***n.*** a rival, प्रतियोगी, प्रतिस्पर्धी।

content[1] (कन्टेन्ट) ***adj.*** contented, संतुष्ट, संतोषी। ***n.*** satisfaction, संतोष। □ **one's heart's content** as much as one desires, जी भर, छककर।

content[2] (कॉन्टेन्ट) ***n.*** (often plu.) 1. the amount of a substance contained in something, विषय-वस्तु। 2. the subject matter of a book, अंतर्वस्तु, विषय-सामग्री। 3. the list of chapter headings of a book, विषय-सूची।

contented (कन्टेन्टिड) ***adj.*** satisfied, संतुष्ट।

contention (कन्टेन्शन) ***n.*** 1. a dispute, झगड़ा, विवाद।

contentment (कन्टेन्टमेन्ट) ***n.*** satisfaction, संतोष, संतुष्टि।

contest (कन्टेस्ट) ***n.*** a competition, प्रतियोगिता। ***v.*** 1. to compete for, स्पर्धा करना। 2. challenge, चुनौती देना।

contestant (कन्टेस्टेन्ट) ***n.*** a competitor, प्रतिस्पर्धी, प्रतियोगी।

context (कॉन्टेक्स्ट) ***n.*** the parts which immediately precede any particular passage, संदर्भ, प्रसंग।

contiguity (कॉन्टिग्युइटी) ***n.*** the state of being contiguous, संलग्नता, समीपस्थता।

contiguous (कॉन्टिग्युअस) ***adj.*** adjoining, संलग्न, समीपस्थ।

continent (कॉन्टिनेन्ट) ***n.*** any one of the seven principal land masses of the earth, महाद्वीप।

continental (कॉन्टिनेन्टल) ***adj.*** of the continent, यूरोपीय।

contingency (कन्टिन्जेन्सी) ***n.*** an unforeseen event, अप्रत्याशित घटना, आकस्मिक घटना।

contingent (कन्टिन्जेन्ट) ***adj.*** 1. happening by chance, आकस्मिक। 2. possible, संभावित।

continual (कन्टिन्युअल) ***adj.*** 1. occurring frequently, सतत, लगातार होनेवाला।

continue (कन्टिन्यू) ***v.*** 1. to go on without stopping, जारी रहना। 2. to do something without ceasing, जारी रखना, आगे बढ़ाना।

continuity (कॉन्टिन्यूइटी) ***n.*** the condition or quality of being continuous, निरंतरता, अविच्छिन्नता।

continuous (कन्टिन्यूअस) ***adj.*** continuing without interruption, unbroken, अविच्छिन्न, सतत।

contort (कन्टॉर्ट) ***v.*** to twist or force out of shape, शक्ल बिगाड़ देना, मरोड़ देना।

contortion (कन्टॉर्शन) ***n.*** twisted position, विकृति, विरूपता।

contour (कॉन्टूर) ***n.*** the outline of a figure, बाह्याकृति, रूपरेखा।

contraband (कॉन्ट्रबैन्ड) ***adj.*** prohibited by law, निषिद्ध, वर्जित।

contraceptive (कॉन्ट्रसेप्टिव) ***adj.*** preventing conception, गर्भनिरोधक, गर्भनिरोधी।

contract (कॉन्ट्रैक्ट) ***n.*** a business agreement, क़रार, अनुबंध, ठेका, संविदा। ***v.*** 1. to enter into a contract, क़रार करना, ठेका करना, अनुबंध करना। 2. to catch (an illness, बीमारी) पकड़ना।

contraction (कन्ट्रैक्शन) ***n.*** the act of becoming shorter, संकुचन।

contractor (कन्ट्रैक्टर) ***n.*** one who contracts to supply anything or perform any service, ठेकेदार।

contradict (कॉन्ट्रडिक्ट) ***v.*** 1. to declare untrue, खंडन करना। 2. to be inconsistent with, विपरीत या उलटा होना।

contradiction (कॉन्ट्रडिक्शन) ***n.*** the act of contradicting, खंडन, विरोध।

contradictory (कॉन्ट्रडिक्टरी) ***adj.*** that contradicts, खंडनात्मक, प्रतिकूल।

contrary (कॉन्ट्रेरी) ***adj.*** opposite, प्रतिकूल।

contrast[1] (कन्ट्रास्ट) ***v.*** 1. to compare

C

two things so that differences are made clear, वैषम्य दिखलाना, भेद दिखलाना।

contrast[2] (कॉन्ट्रास्ट) ***n.*** a difference or unlikeliness, अंतर।

contravene (कॉन्ट्रवीन) ***v.*** 1. to transgress, उल्लंघन करना। 2. to contradict, खंडन करना, प्रतिवाद करना।

contravention (कॉन्ट्रवेन्शन) ***n.*** the act of contravening, उल्लंघन, खंडन।

contribute (कन्ट्रिब्यूट) ***v.*** 1. to give in common with others, अंशदान करना, चंदा देना। 2. to participate in, योग देना, सहयोग करना।

contribution (कॉन्ट्रिब्यूशन) ***n.*** the act of contributing or something contributed, अंशदान, सहयोग।

contributor (कन्ट्रिबयूटर) ***n.*** one who contributes, अंशदाता, सहयोगकर्ता।

contributory (कन्ट्रिब्यूटरी) ***adj.*** contributing to some purpose or fund, अंशदायी, योगदायी।

contrivance (कन्ट्राइवेन्स) ***n.*** scheme, योजना।

contrive (कन्ट्राइव) ***v.*** 1. to plan or devise, योजना बनाना, उपाय करना। 2. to make or fabricate, रचना, बनाना।

control (कन्ट्रोल) ***v.*** to exercise power or authority, नियंत्रण करना, नियंत्रण में रखना। ***n.*** the power to check or restraint, नियंत्रण, अंकुश।

controllable (कन्ट्रोलेबल) ***adj.*** that can be controlled, नियंत्रणीय।

controller (कन्ट्रोलर) ***n.*** a person who controls, नियंत्रक।

controversial (कॉन्ट्रोवर्शल) ***adj.*** disputable, विवाद्य, विवादास्पद, झगड़े का।

controversy (कॉन्ट्रोवर्सी) ***n.*** a disputed question, विवाद, झगड़े का विषय।

convalesce (कॉन्वैलेस) ***v.*** to recover from illness or injury, स्वास्थ्य-लाभ करना।

convalescence (कॉन्वैलेसेन्स) ***n.*** gradual recovery of health after illness or injury, स्वास्थ्य-लाभ।

convene (कन्वीन) ***v.*** to call to meet or gather, बुलाना, आहूत करना।

convener, convenor (कन्वीनर) ***n.*** one who convenes a meeting, संयोजक।

convenience (कन्वीनिएन्स) ***n.*** 1. personal comfort, सुविधा, सहूलियत। 2. material advantage, लाभ।

convenient (कन्वीनिएन्ट) ***adj.*** suited to one's needs or comfort, सुविधाजनक, आरामदेह।

convent (कॉन्वेन्ट) ***n.*** an establishment of nuns, ईसाई साध्वियों का संघ, कॉन्वेन्ट।

convention (कन्वेन्शन) ***n.*** 1. a formal agreement, अभिसमय, समझौता, संधि। 2. a formal assembly, सम्मेलन, जुलसा, सभा। 3. an accepted practice, प्रथा, परिपाटी, रीति।

conventional (कन्वेन्शनल) ***adj.*** traditional, प्रथागत, परंपरागत, पारंपरिक।

converge (कन्वर्ज) ***v.*** to come together towards a common point, एक बिंदु पर आकर मिलना।

convergent (कन्वर्जेन्ट) ***adj.*** tending towards a point, केंद्राभिमुखी, अभिसारी।

conversant (कन्वर्सेन्ट) ***adj.*** familiar, परिचित।

conversation (कॉन्वर्सेशन) ***n.*** oral exchange of ideas, बात-चीत, वार्तालाप।

C

converse (कन्वर्स) ***v.*** to talk informally, बातचीत करना, वार्तालाप करना। ***adj.*** opposite, contrary, विरुद्ध, उलटा।

conversion (कन्वर्ज़न) ***n.*** change of religion, धर्म-परिवर्तन।

convert (कन्वर्ट) ***v.*** 1. to change or transform, बदल देना या बदल जाना। 2. to change into another form or from one use to another, रूपांतर करना।

convertible (कन्वर्टिबल) ***adj.*** that can be converted, परिवर्तनीय।

convex (कॉन्वेक्स) ***adj.*** curved outward like the surface of a ball as seen from the outside, उत्तल।

convey (कन्वे) ***v.*** 1. to transport, ढोना, ढुलाई करना। 2. to transmit or communicate, संप्रेषण करना, भेजना।

conveyance (कन्वेअन्स) ***n.*** 1. the act of conveying, ढुलाई, संप्रेषण। 2. a vehicle, गाड़ी, यान।

convict (कन्विक्ट) ***v.*** to find guilty, दोषी ठहराना। ***n.*** a convicted person, दोषी।

conviction (कन्विक्शन) ***n.*** 1. the act of convicting or the state of being convicted, दोषसिद्धि। 2. a firm or strong belief, धारणा।

convince (कन्विन्स) ***v.*** to cause to believe, विश्वास दिलाना।

convivial (कन्विविअल) ***adj.*** 1. jovial, खुशमिज़ाज। 2. sociable, मिलनसार।

convocation (कॉन्वोकेशन) ***n.*** a meeting convened by the university for conferring degrees, दीक्षांत समारोह।

convoy[1] (कन्वॉइ) ***v.*** to escort for protection, रक्षार्थ किसी के साथ जाना।

convoy[2] (कॉन्वॉइ) ***n.*** a group of vehicles, ships or people travelling together and generally protected by an armed escort, काफ़िला।

convulse (कन्वल्स) ***v.*** to disturb violently, उथल-पुथल मचाना।

convulsion (कन्वल्शन) ***n.*** a violent upheaval, उथल-पुथल, हलचल, खलबली।

convulsive (कन्वल्सिव) ***adj.*** causing convulsions, मरोड़ पैदा करनेवाला; उथल-पुथल, गड़बड़ पैदा करनेवाला।

coo (कू) ***n.*** a soft murmuring sound as of a dove, कूजन, गुटरगूँ, टुटरूँटूँ।

cook (कुक) ***v.*** to prepare food by using heat, पकाना, सेकना, सिझाना। ***n.*** one whose job is cooking, रसोइया।

cooker (कुकर) ***n.*** an apparatus or pot for cooking food, कूकर।

cookery (कुकरी) ***n.*** the art or practice of cooking food, पाकविद्या, पाककला।

cookware (कुकवेअर) ***n.*** utensils used in cooking, रसोई के बर्तन।

cool (कूल) ***adj.*** 1. moderately cold, ठंडा, शीतल। 2. calm, unexcited, शांत, अनुद्विग्न, संयमित। ***n.*** 1. coolness, ठंडक, शीतलता। 2. calmness, शांति, सौम्यता। ***v.*** 1. to make cool, ठंडा करना। 2. to become cool, ठंडा होना। 3. to make or become calm, शांत होना या करना।

cooler (कूलर) an apparatus for keeping rooms cool, कूलर, शीतक।

cool-headed ***adj.*** not easily excited, शांत-प्रकृति, ठंडे स्वभाववाला।

coolie (कूली) ***n.*** a hired labourer, कुली, मज़दूर।

coop (कूप) ***n.*** a poultry cage, दरबा।

co-operate (को-ऑपरेट) ***v.*** to help

C

one another in a common aim, एक-दूसरे का सहयोग करना।

co-operation (को-ऑपरेशन) ***n.*** the act of co-operating, सहयोग, सहकार।

co-operative (को-ऑपरेटिव) ***adj.*** of co-operation, सहकारी। ***n.*** a firm organized on a co-operative basis, सहकारी संस्था।

co-opt (को-ऑप्ट) ***v.*** to appoint as a fellow member, सहयोजित करना।

co-option (को-ऑप्शन) ***n.*** the act of co-opting, सहयोजन।

co-ordinate[1] (को-ऑर्डिनिट) ***adj.*** equal in status, degree or importance, समान, तुल्य, समकक्ष।

co-ordinate[2] (को-ऑर्डिनेट) ***v.*** to work together, साथ-साथ काम करना, मिलकर काम करना।

co-ordination (को-ऑर्डिनेशन) ***n.*** the act of co-ordinating, समन्वयन।

co-owner (को-ओनर) ***n.*** one who possesses some property jointly with someone else, सहस्वामी।

co-partner (को-पार्टनर) ***n.*** a partner, भागीदार।

cope (कोप) ***v.*** to deal successfully (with), पार पाना।

copier (कॉपिअर) ***n.*** a machine that makes copies, प्रतिलिपित्र।

copious (कोपिअस) ***adj.*** plentiful, प्रचुर।

copiousness (कोपिअसनिस) ***n.*** the quality or state of being copious, प्रचुरता।

copper (कॉपर) ***n.*** 1. a reddish-brown metal, ताँबा, ताम्र। 2. a coin or object made of copper, ताँबे का सिक्का या बर्तन। ***adj.*** reddish brown, ताँबे के रंग का।

copula (कॉप्यूला) ***n.*** a verb which links a subject and predicate of a sentence, योजन-क्रिया, संयोजन क्रिया।

copulate (कॉप्यूलेट) ***v.*** to engage in sexual intercourse, मैथुन करना।

copulation (कॉप्यूलेशन) ***n.*** the act of copulating, मैथुन।

copy (कॉपी) ***n.*** 1. a reproduction or imitation of something original, प्रतिलिपि, नकल, कापी। 2. an exercise book, कापी। 3. a manuscript, पांडुलिपि। 4. a single example of a book, magazine etc. कापी, प्रति। ***v.*** 1. to make a copy of, प्रतिलिपि करना, नकल करना। 2. to imitate, नकल उतारना, अनुकरण करना।

copyist (कॉपीइस्ट) ***n.*** one whose job is to prepare the copies of documents etc., नकलनवीस, प्रतिलिपिकार।

copyright (कॉपीराइट) ***n.*** the sole legal right for a certain term of years to an author, composer etc. to print, publish, sell etc. copies of his original work, कापीराइट, स्वामिस्व।

coquet (कोकेट) ***v.*** to flirt, चोचले करना, नखरे दिखाना।

coquetry (कोकिट्री) ***n.*** flirtatious behaviour, चोचलेबाज़ी, नखरा-तिल्ला।

coral (कोरल) ***n.*** a stony substance of red, pink or white colour often used for jewellery, मूँगा, प्रवाल।

cord (कॉर्ड) ***n.*** 1. a long thin flexible material of twisted fibre or strands, डोरी, रज्जु, रस्सी। 2. a raised line on the surface of a cloth, धारी। 3. cloth with raised lines, डोरिया। 4. a wire, तार।

cordial (कॉर्डिअल) ***adj.*** hearty, warm, हार्दिक, सौहार्दपूर्ण।

cordless (कॉर्डलिस) ***adj.*** needing no electric cord, बेतार।

cordon (कॉर्डन) ***n.*** a line of persons or soldiers etc. stationed around an area to enclose it, घेरा।

core (कोर) ***n.*** 1. the central part of some fruits, गूदा, गिरी, मग़ज़। 2. the central part of something, मध्यभाग। 3. the most important part of something, महत्त्वपूर्ण अंश।

cork (कॉर्क) ***n.*** a bottle stopper, काग, कॉर्क, डाट। ***v.*** to close with a cork, कॉर्क से बंद करना, डाट लगाना।

corn (कॉर्न) ***n.*** a seed or fruit of various cereal plants, गल्ला, अनाज, अन्न।

cornea (कॉर्निआ) ***n.*** a membrane that covers the lens of the eye, चक्षुपटल, कार्निया।

corner (कॉर्नर) ***n.*** the area or position where two walls, sides, lines etc. meet, कोना, मोड़, नुक्कड़।

cornerstone (कार्नरस्टोन) ***n.*** a vital foundation, आधारशिला।

cornet (कॉर्नेट) ***n.*** a brass musical instrument of the trumpet family, तुरही।

cornice (कॉर्निस) ***n.*** an ornamental moulding at the top of the wall of a room, कार्निस, कंगनी।

corollary (करॉलरी) ***n.*** a proposition that logically results from another proposition, उपप्रमेय।

corona (करोना) ***n.*** a small circle of light around a luminous body, प्रभामंडल।

coronary (कॉरोनरी) ***adj.*** pertaining to the heart or the two arteries that supply blood to the heart, हृदय-संबंधी, रक्तवाहिनी-संबंधी।

coronation (कॉरोनेशन) ***n.*** the act or ceremony of crowning a king or queen, राज्याभिषेक।

coronet (कॉरोनेट) ***n.*** 1. a small crown worn by a prince or a nobleman, छोटा मुकुट। 2. a band of jewels worn on the head, शृंगार पट्टी।

corporal (कॉर्पोरल) ***adj.*** of or related to the body, शारीरिक।

corporate (कॉर्पोरेट) ***adj.*** 1. of a corporation, निगम-संबंधी, निगमित। 2. united, संघटित। 3. formed into a legal body, विधिक निकाय के रूप में होनेवाला।

corporation (कॉर्पोरेशन) ***n.*** 1. a body of persons legally authorised to act as a single person, निगम, कॉरपोरेशन। 2. a group of persons elected to govern a town, नगरपालिका, नगर निगम।

corporeal (कॉर्पोरिअल) ***adj.*** bodily, शारीरिक।

corps (कोर) ***n.*** 1. a specialized branch of the armed forces, कोर। 2. an organised body of persons under a common di-rection, कोर, संघ।

corpse (कॉर्प्स) ***n.*** a dead (human) body, लाश।

corpulence (कॉर्प्युलेन्स) ***n.*** fatness, मुटापा।

corpulent (कॉर्प्युलेन्ट) ***adj.*** very fat, मोटा।

corpus (कॉर्पस) ***n.*** (plu. corpora) all the writings of a particular

C

subject or of a particular person, समग्र साहित्य।

corpuscle (कॉर्पसल) ***n.*** a cell capable of movement in the blood, रक्त-कणिका।

correct (करेक्ट) ***v.*** 1. to remove mistakes or errors from, शुद्ध करना, संशोधन करना। 2. to set right, सही करना।

correction (करेक्शन) ***n.*** 1. the act of correcting, संशोधन। 2. improvement, सुधार।

correctly (करेक्टली) ***adv.*** rightly, accurately, सही ढंग से, ठीक-ठीक।

correlate (कॉरिलेट) ***v.*** to show or establish how two things are related to each other, परस्पर संबंध स्थापित करना या दिखाना।

correlation (कॉरिलेशन) ***n.*** mutual relationship, पारस्परिक संबंध, सह-संबंध।

correspond (कॉरिस्पॉन्ड) ***v.*** 1. to be similar, समरूप होना। 2. to agree, अनुरूप होना। 3. to hold correspondence, पत्रव्यवहार करना, पत्राचार करना।

correspondence (कॉरिस्पॉन्डेन्स) ***n.*** 1. similarity, समरूपता। 2. conformity, अनुरूपता। 3. the act, fact or process of exchanging letters, पत्र-व्यवहार, पत्राचार।

correspondent (कॉरिस्पॉन्डेन्ट) ***n.*** a reporter of a newspaper, संवाददाता। ***adj.*** 1. similar, समरूप। 2. analogous, अनुरूप।

corresponding (कॉरिस्पॉन्डिंग) ***adj.*** similar, समरूप, तत्समान।

corridor (कॉरिडॉर) ***n.*** a narrow passageway or strip of land, गलियारा।

corroborate (करॉबरेट) ***v.*** to confirm, संपुष्टि करना।

corroboration (करॉबरेशन) ***n.*** the act of corroborating, संपुष्टि।

corrode (करोड) ***v.*** to wear away, छीजना, क्षीण होना, क्षय होना।

corrosion (करोज़न) ***n.*** 1. the act or process of corroding, क्षय, विनाश। 2. rust, जंग, मोरचा।

corrosive (करोसिव) ***adj.*** 1. tending to corrode, छीजनेवाला, संक्षारक। 2. destroying, विनाशक।

corrugate (कॉरुगेट) ***v.*** to make wave-like folds, लहरिया डालना, नालीदार बनाना।

corrugated (कॉरुगेटिड) ***adj.*** having wavelike folds, नालीदार, लहरियादार।

corrupt (करप्ट) ***adj.*** 1. dishonest, बेईमान। 2. open to bribe, घूसख़ोर, रिश्वतख़ोर। ***v.*** 1. to cause to become dishonest, बेईमान बनाना। 2. to persuade to accept bribes, घूस देना। 3. to spoil, भ्रष्ट या विकृत करना।

corruption (करप्शन) ***n.*** 1. the act of corrupting or the state of being corrupted, भ्रष्टाचार। 2. dishonesty, बेईमानी। 3. bribery, घूसख़ोरी।

cortex (कॉर्टिक्स) ***n.*** the outer layer, छाल या झिल्ली।

co-signatory (को-सिग्नेटरी) ***n.*** a person signing jointly with another or others, सह-हस्ताक्षरकर्ता।

cosmetic (कॉज़्मेटिक) ***n.*** any substance (such as a powder or cream) used to apply on face and hair to improve the appearance, सौंदर्य-सामग्री, प्रसाधन। ***adj.*** that improves the appearance, सौंदर्य-वर्धक।

C

cosmic (कॉज़्मिक) ***adj.*** of or pertaining to the cosmos, ब्रह्मांडीय।

cosmology (कॉज़्मॉलोजी) ***n.*** the philosophy relating to the universe, ब्रह्मांड-दर्शन।

cosmonaut (कॉज़्मोनॉट) ***n.*** an astronaut, अंतरिक्ष-यात्री।

cosmopolitan (कॉज़्मोपॉलिटन) ***adj.*** 1. common to the whole world or of whole world, सर्वदेशीय। 2. composed of people from all parts of the world, सर्वदेशीय; cosmopolitan city, विश्वनगर। ***n.*** one who is free of national prejudices, राष्ट्रीय पूर्वाग्रह से मुक्त, विश्व-मानव, विश्वबंधु।

cosmos (कॉज़्मोस) ***n.*** the whole universe, ब्रह्मांड।

co-sponsor (को-स्पॉन्सर) ***n.*** one who sponsors with another or others, सह-प्रायोजक।

cost (कॉस्ट) ***n.*** 1. the amount paid at the time of purchasing something, दाम, क़ीमत, मूल्य। 2. the expenses, खर्च, व्यय। 3. a loss, sacrifice or penalty, (चुकाया जानेवाला) मूल्य, क़ीमत। 4. outlay, लागत मूल्य। 5. (plu.) the expenses of litigation, वाद-व्यय। ***v.*** 1. to pay as a price, दाम देना या चुकाना। 2. to require an effort or loss, क़ीमत चुकाना।

co-star (को-स्टार) ***n.*** an actor or actress performing with another of equal importence, सह-अभिनेता या सह-अभिनेत्री।

costly (कॉस्टली) ***adj.*** of high price, expensive, महँगा, क़ीमती।

costume (कॉस्ट्यूम) ***n.*** a set of clothes belonging to a particular group, place or period, परिधान, वेशभूषा।

cosy (कोज़ी) ***adj.*** 1. warm, हार्दिक। 2. friendly, मैत्रीपूर्ण।

cot (कॉट) ***n.*** a bed, चारपाई, खाट।

coterie (कोटरी) ***n.*** a group of friends, मित्र-मंडली, यार-दोस्त।

cottage (कॉटिज) ***n.*** a small house, कुटिया, झोंपड़ी।

cotton (कॉटन) ***n.*** 1. fibre gathered from plants, रुई, कपास। 2. the cloth made from cotton fibre, सूती कपड़ा।

couch (कॉउच) ***n.*** a long piece of furniture used for sitting or reclining, सोफ़ा, कोच।

cough (कॅफ़) ***v.*** 1. to expel air from the lungs suddenly with noise, खाँसना। 2. to expel something in this way, खखारना।

could (कुड) ***v.*** p.t. of can.

council (काउन्सल) ***n.*** any legislative or advisory body, कौंसिल, परिषद्।

councillor (काउन्सलर) ***n.*** a member of a council, पारिषद, पार्षद।

counsel (काउन्सल) ***v.*** to advise, सलाह देना, परामर्श देना। ***n.*** 1. advice, सलाह, राय, परामर्श। 2. a legal advisor, विधिक परामर्शदाता, कानूनी सलाहकार।

counsellor (काउन्सलर) ***n.*** an advisor, सलाहकार, परामर्शदाता।

count[1] (काउन्ट) ***v.*** 1. to recite numerals in order, गिनना, गिनती करना। 2. to find the total of, जोड़ लगाना या करना, जोड़ना। ***n.*** the act of counting, गणना, गिनती।

count[2] ***n.*** a nobleman, सामंत।

countable (काउन्टेबल) ***adj.*** that can be counted, गिनने योग्य।

C

countdown (काउन्टडाउन) ***n.*** a count in reverse order, उलटी गिनती।

countenance (काउन्टेनन्स) ***n.*** the appearance of the face, चेहरा।

counter[1] (काउन्टर) ***n.*** 1. a table or flat surface on which money is counted, business transacted or food served, काउन्टर, पटल। 2. any piece used for keeping a count in games, टोकन, काउन्टर।

counter ***v.*** to move or act in opposition to, विरोध करना, प्रतिरोध करना। ***n.*** one that is counter, प्रतिरोधी।

counteract (काउन्टरऐक्ट) ***v.*** to lessen or prevent the effect of, प्रतिकार करना, बेअसर करना।

counterattack (काउन्टरअटैक) ***n.*** an attack made to repel the attack, प्रत्याक्रमण, जवाबी हमला। ***v.*** to make a counterattack, प्रत्याक्रमण करना, जवाबी हमला करना।

counterbalance (काउन्टरबैलेन्स) ***n.*** anything that balances another, प्रति-संतुलन, धड़ा।

counterfeit (काउन्टरफ़ीट) ***adj.*** fake, जाली, नकली, खोटा।

counterfoil (काउन्टरफ़ॉइल) ***n.*** a part of a receipt, cheque, money order etc., kept by the sender as a record, प्रतिपर्ण।

countermand (काउन्टरमैन्ड) ***v.*** to revoke, रद्द करना।

counterpart (काउन्टरपार्ट) ***n.*** one who or that serves the same purpose as another, प्रतिरूप, प्रतिस्थानी।

countersign (काउन्टरसाइन) ***v.*** to sign an already signed document, प्रतिहस्ताक्षर करना।

counterweight (काउन्टरवेट) ***n.*** a weight used as a counterbalance, पासंग।

countess (काउन्टिस) ***n.*** the wife of a count, सामंत की पत्नी।

counting (काउन्टिंग) ***n.*** the act of finding the total of, गिनती, गणन, गणना।

countless (काउन्टलिस) ***adj.*** too many to be counted, innumerable, अगणित, असंख्य।

country (कन्ट्री) ***n.*** 1. a territory distinguished by its people, culture, geography or government, देश, मुल्क। 2. its people, देशवासी। 3. rural area, देहात।

countryside (कन्ट्रिसाइड) ***n.*** a rural region, देहात।

county (काउन्टी) ***n.*** a district of a state, जनपद, जिला, क्षेत्र।

coup d'etat (कू-ड-एटा) ***n.*** the sudden act of overthrowing the government by force, तख़्ता-पलट, राज्य-विप्लव। (फ्रांसीसी)

coupe (कूपे) ***n.*** a closed two-seated compartment, दो सीटों/बर्थोंवाला डिब्बा।

couple (कपल) ***n.*** 1. two items of the same kind, जोड़ा, जोड़ी। 2. husband and wife, पति-पत्नी, वर-वधू, दंपति, जोड़ा।

couplet (कप्लिट) ***n.*** two successive lines of verse, दोहा, द्विपदी।

coupon (कूपन) ***n.*** a ticket or token that entitles the holder to receive something, कूपन।

courage (करिज) ***n.*** bravery, साहस, दिलेरी।

courageous (करेजस) ***adj.*** showing courage, साहसी, दिलेर।

courier (कूरिअर) ***n.*** one who carries correspondence, संदेशवाहक, कूरियर।

course (कोर्स) ***n.*** 1. path, मार्ग, रास्ता, पथ। 2. the continuous or habitual process or succession of events, क्रम, सिलसिला, ढर्रा। 3. a body of prescribed studies, पाठ्यक्रम। 4. duration, अवधि।

court (कोर्ट) ***n.*** 1. a sovereign's establishment with councillors, attendants etc., दरबार। 2. a law court where justice is administered, न्यायालय, अदालत, कचहरी, कोर्ट।

courteous (कर्टिअस) ***adj.*** polite and considerate, विनम्र, शिष्ट।

courtesan (कोर्टिज़न) ***n.*** a prostitute, नगरवधू, गणिका।

courtesy (कर्टिसी) ***n.*** polite behaviour, शिष्टता, भद्रता, शिष्टाचार।

courtier (कोर्टिअर) ***n.*** a noble of the king's court, दरबारी।

court martial ***n.*** a military court, सैनिक न्यायालय, फ़ौजी अदालत।

courtship (कोर्टशिप) ***n.*** the act of wooing, प्रेमाचार।

courtyard (कोर्टयार्ड) ***n.*** a space enclosed by walls, आँगन, चौक।

cousin (कज़न) ***n.*** the child of one's uncle or aunt, चचेरा (ममेरा, फुफेरा या मौसेरा) भाई अथवा चचेरी (ममेरी, फुफेरी या मौसेरी) बहन।

covenant (कवेनैन्ट) ***n.*** 1. a contract, समझौता।

cover (कवर) ***v.*** 1. to place or spread something over in order to conceal or protect, आच्छादित करना, ढकना, तोपना। 2. to hide or conceal, छिपाना। 3. to protect by insurance, बीमा करा लेना, बीमे द्वारा सुरक्षित होना। 4. to cover a distance, (दूरी) तय करना। 5. to report news about के बारे में समाचार देना। ***n.*** 1. anything that covers, आवरण, आच्छादन, ढक्कन, कवर। 2. something that conceals or disguises, आड़, ओट, आश्रय। 3. a wrapper of a book, कवर, रैपर।

coverage (कवरिज) ***n.*** 1. the extent of covering, व्याप्ति, विस्तार। 2. the area covered, व्याप्ति-क्षेत्र, क्षेत्र। 3. reporting of an event, घटना-विवरण।

covet (कविट) ***v.*** to desire eagerly to possess (something that belongs to others), लालायित होना, ललचाना।

covetous (कविटस) ***adj.*** greedy and jealous, लालची, लोलुप।

covetousness (कविटसनिस) ***n.*** greed, jealousy, लालच, लोलुपता।

cow (काउ) ***n.*** a famous domesticated cattle, गाय, गौ। ***v.*** to intimidate, धमकी देना, आतंकित करना।

coward (काउअर्ड) ***n.*** a person without courage, कायर या डरपोक आदमी।

cowbell (काउबेल) ***n.*** a bell hung around a cow's neck, गाय के गले में बाँधी जानेवाली घंटी।

cowboy (काउबॉइ) ***n.*** a cowherd, चरवाहा।

cowherd (काउहर्ड) ***n.*** a cowboy, चरवाहा।

cowhide (काउहाइड) ***n.*** the skin of a cow, गाय की खाल, गोचर्म।

co-worker (को-वर्कर) ***n.*** one who works with another, a fellow worker, सहकर्मी।

cowrie, cowry (काउरी) ***n.*** a small sea shell, कौड़ी।

C

coy (कॉइ) ***adj.*** modest and shy, लजालू, लाज भरा, लजीला।

cozy (कोज़ी) ***adj.*** warm and comfortable, सुखद, आरामदेह।

crab (क्रैब) ***n.*** 1. an edible shellfish with ten legs, केकड़ा, कर्कट। 2. the sign of the zodiac, कर्क (राशि)।

crabby (क्रैबी) ***adj.*** bad-tempered, चिड़चिड़ा, तुनुकमिज़ाज।

crack (क्रैक) ***v.*** 1. to break without complete separation of parts, चिटकना, चटकना, तड़क जाना। 2. to cause to break without complete separation of parts, चिटकाना, चटकाना। 3. to break into or force open, तोड़ना, तोड़ देना। 4. to break or cause to break with a sharp sound, फटना या फोड़ना। 5. to strike, आघात करना, प्रहार करना। 6. to tell (a joke, मज़ाक़) करना। ***n.*** 1. a line or mark where something seems to be broken, चटक, चिटक, तड़क। 2. a sudden sharp noise, धमाका। 3. a sharp blow, तीव्र आघात या प्रहार।

crackbrained (क्रैकब्रेन्ड) ***adj.*** crazy, सनकी।

crackdown (क्रैकडाउन) ***n.*** a raid, छापा।

cracker (क्रैकर) ***n.*** a firecracker, पटाखा।

crackle (क्रैकल) ***v.*** to make series of slight cracking sounds, चिटचिट करना, चटचट करना।

cradle (क्रेडल) ***n.*** 1. an infant's bed on rockers, पालना, झूला। 2. a supporting framework, आधार, ठाठ, ढड्ढा। ***v.*** 1. to place in a cradle, पालने में डालना। 2. to swing, झुलाना।

craft (क्राफ़्ट) ***n.*** 1. skill or ability in handwork or the arts, कारीगरी, शिल्प, हस्तशिल्प। 2. an aircraft, ship or other vessel, जहाज़, नाव।

craftiness (क्राफ़्टिनिस) ***n.*** the state or quality of being crafty, चालाकी, धूर्तता।

craftsman (क्राफ़्ट्समैन) ***n.*** a skilled worker, कुशल कारीगर, शिल्पी, शिल्पकार।

craftsmanship ***n.*** artistic skill, कारीगरी, कला, शिल्पकला।

crafty (क्राफ़्टी) ***adj.*** cunning, चालाक, धूर्त।

crag (क्रैग) ***n.*** a steep rock, खड़ी चट्टान।

cram (क्रैम) ***v.*** to stuff, ठूँसना।

cramp (क्रैम्प) ***n.*** 1. contraction of muscles, ऐंठन। 2. a sharp pain in the abdomen, मरोड़। 3. a clamp, क्लैंप, शिकंजा। ***v.*** 1. to hold with a cramp, शिकंजे में पकड़ना या कसना। 2. to prevent, रोकना।

cramped (क्रैम्प्ड) ***adj.*** 1. restricted, जकड़ा हुआ। 2. narrow, तंग, सँकरा। 3. (of handwriting) small and irregular, छोटी और टेढ़ी-मेढ़ी (लिखावट)।

crane (क्रेन) ***n.*** 1. a bird with long legs, neck and bill, सारस। 2. a device for lifting and moving heavy objects, क्रेन। ***v.*** to lift by a crane, क्रेन से उठाना।

cranium (क्रेनिअम) ***n.*** the skull, खोपड़ी, कपाल।

crank (क्रैंक) ***n.*** 1. a handle of a machine or engine, हत्था। 2. a crazy person, सनकी व्यक्ति, झक्की व्यक्ति। ***v.*** to start an engine by pulling a crank, इंजन, मोटर आदि चालू करना।

cranky (क्रैंकी) ***adj.*** ill-tempered, चिड़चिड़ा।

crash (क्रैश) ***v.*** 1. to collide, fall or break noisily, धमाके के साथ टूटना, टकराना या गिरना। 2. to enter forcefully, घुस जाना। ***n.*** 1. a sudden loud noise, धमाका, शोर। 2. a collision, टक्कर, भिड़ंत।

crate (क्रेट) ***n.*** a wooden case for holding bottles, क्रेट, पेटी।

crater (क्रेटर) ***n.*** 1. a bowl-shaped cavity, कटोरेनुमा गड्ढा। 2. a volcano mouth,ज्वालामुखी का मुँह।

crave (क्रेव) ***v.*** to have an intense desire for, तीव्र लालसा होना।

craving (क्रेविंग) ***n.*** a longing, लालसा।

crawl (क्रॉल) ***v.*** to move on hands or knees or on the belly, रेंगना, सरकना।

crayon (क्रेऑन) ***n.*** a pencil of coloured chalk, रंगीन खड़िया।

craze (क्रेज़) ***n.*** a wild enthusiasm, ललक, सनक।

crazy (क्रेज़ी) ***adj.*** 1. insane, पागल, बावला, सनकी, झक्की। 2. over-enthusiastic, अति-उत्साही।

creak (क्रीक) ***v.*** to make the sound as of an unoiled hinge, चरचराना। ***n.*** a harsh noise, चरमराहट।

cream (क्रीम) ***n.*** 1. the fatty part of the milk, क्रीम, मलाई। 2. a cream like cosmetic substance, क्रीम। 3. the best part of anything, चुनिंदा भाग। 4. a yellowish white colour, क्रीम कलर। ***v.*** to take off cream from, मलाई उतारना।

creamy (क्रीमी) ***adj.*** full of cream, क्रीमयुक्त, मलाईवाला।

crease (क्रीज़) ***n.*** 1. a line made by folding or pressing, क्रीज़, तह। 2. the line near the wicket that marks the positions for the bowler or batsman, क्रीज़। ***v.*** to make a line or lines by folding or pressing, क्रीज़ करना।

create (क्रिएट) ***v.*** 1. to bring into existence, बनाना, निर्माण करना। 2. to produce, पैदा करना।

creation (क्रिएशन) ***n.*** 1. the act of creating, निर्माण, सर्जन, सृष्टि, रचना। 2. any or all created things, रचना, सृष्टि। 3. the world and all things in it, सृष्टि, संसार।

creative (क्रिएटिव) ***adj.*** 1. characterized by originality, रचनात्मक, सृजनात्मक। 2. having the ability to create, having or showing imagination, सृजनशील, रचनात्मक।

creator (क्रिएटर) ***n.*** 1. one who creates, रचयिता, रचनाकार। 2. the Creator, स्रष्टा, ईश्वर, ब्रह्मा।

creature (क्रीचर) ***n.*** 1. a living being, जीव, जंतु, प्राणी। 2. a human being, मनुष्य, मानव।

creche (क्रेश) ***n.*** a day nursery for very young children while their mothers work, शिशुसदन, क्रच।

credence (क्रीडेन्स) ***n.*** belief, विश्वास।

credentials (क्रिडेन्शल्स) ***n.*** the letters of introduction, recommendation or authority, प्रत्यय-पत्र।

credible (क्रेडिबल) ***adj.*** reliable, विश्वसनीय।

credit (क्रेडिट) ***n.*** 1. belief, trust, विश्वास। 2. reputation, प्रसिद्धि। 3. reputation for financial integrity, साख। 4. loan, उधार। ***v.*** 1. to believe, to trust, विश्वास करना। 2. to give credit to, श्रेय देना।

C

creditable (क्रेडिटेबल) ***adj.*** deserving praise, स्तुत्य, प्रशंसनीय।

creditor (क्रेडिटर) ***n.*** one to whom money is owed, लेनदार, महाजन।

credulous (क्रेड्यूलस) ***adj.*** ready to believe something on little evidence, कान का कच्चा, भोला।

creed (क्रीड) ***n.*** a system of beliefs or principles, मत, पंथ, संप्रदाय।

creek (क्रीक) ***n.*** a small stream, छोटी नदी, नाला।

creep (क्रीप) ***v.*** 1. to crawl along the ground, रेंगना। 2. to move slowly, धीरे-धीरे चलना, खिसकना।

creeper (क्रीपर) ***n.*** a creeping plant, लता, बेल।

cremate (क्रीमेट) ***v.*** to burn a dead body, शव को जलाना।

cremation (क्रिमेशन) ***n.*** the act of cremating, दाह-संस्कार।

crepe (क्रेप) ***n.*** a kind of fabric, क्रेप।

crescent (क्रेसेन्ट) ***n.*** the curved shape of the moon in the first (or last) quarter चंद्रकला, नवचंद्र।

crest (क्रेस्ट) ***n.*** a tuft on the head of a bird or animal, चोटी, कलगी। 2. something like this worn on top of helmets, कलगी। 3. the top of a mountain, hill etc., चोटी, शिखर।

crestfallen (क्रेस्टफ़ालन) ***adj.*** disappointed, निराश।

crevice (क्रेविस) ***n.*** a narrow crack, पतली दरार।

crew (क्रू) ***n.*** 1. a group of people working in an aircraft or ship, कर्मीदल, क्रू। 2. a group of people working together, दल, समूह।

crib (क्रिब) ***n.*** a pot for fodder, नाँद।

crick (क्रिक) ***n.*** a painful stiffening in the neck or back, साल, अकड़न, ऐंठन।

cricket[1] (क्रिकिट) ***n.*** a game played between two teams of eleven players each with bats and ball, क्रिकेट, गेंद-बल्ला।

cricket[2] ***n.*** an insect that makes a shrill chirping sound, झींगुर।

crime (क्राइम) ***n.*** an act committed or omitted in violation of the law, अपराध, जुर्म।

criminal (क्रिमिनल) ***adj.*** of or related to crime, आपराधिक, अपराधपूर्ण। ***n.*** a person who is guilty of crime, अपराधी, मुजरिम।

crimson (क्रिमज़न) ***adj.*** deep red, किरमिजी।

cringe (क्रिन्ज) ***v.*** to behave in a timid way, सकुचाते हुए कुछ कहना या करना।

crinkle (क्रिंकल) ***v.*** to be full of wrinkles or creases, झुरियों या सिलवटों से भरा होना।

cripple (क्रिपल) ***n.*** a lame, पंगु।

crisis (क्राइसिस) ***n.*** 1. a crucial situation, संकट। 2. a critical or decisive time, नाजुक स्थिति, संकट की घड़ी।

crisp (क्रिस्प) ***adj.*** dry and brittle, कुरकुरा, ख़स्ता।

criterion (क्राइटिअरिअन) ***n.*** a standard, कसौटी।

critic (क्रिटिक) ***n.*** 1. one who criticizes, आलोचक। 2. a reviewer, समीक्षक।

critical (क्रिटिकल) ***adj.*** 1. of or pertaining to criticism, आलोचना-संबंधी, आलोचनात्मक। 2. requiring careful judgment or evaluation, समीक्षात्मक। 3. of the nature of crisis, संकटपूर्ण, नाजुक।

criticism (क्रिटिसिज़म) ***n.*** 1. the act of finding faults, नुक्ताचीनी। 2. the evaluation or analysis of a work of art or literature, समीक्षा।

criticize (क्रिटिसाइज़) ***v.*** 1. to find fault with, आलोचना करना। 2. to evaluate critically, समीक्षा करना।

croak (क्रोक) ***v.*** to make frog-like sound, टर्र-टर्र करना, टरटराना।

crochet (क्रोशे) ***n.*** a kind of fancy work done with a hooked needle, क्रोशिए का काम, कसीदा।

crockery (क्रॉकरी) ***n.*** household articles as plates, cups etc., क्रॉकरी, प्लेटें-प्याले।

crocodile (क्रॉकोडाइल) ***n.*** a large reptile with a thick skin and huge jaws that lives on land and in rivers, मगरमच्छ, मगर।

crocodile tears ***n.*** insincere sorrow, नकली आँसू, झूठा खेद-प्रकाश।

crone (क्रोन) ***n.*** a bent old woman, कुबड़ी बुढ़िया, कुब्जा।

crony (क्रोनी) ***n.*** an old companion, पुराना मित्र।

crook (क्रुक) ***n.*** 1. a hooked stick, मुड़े हुए सिरेवाली छड़ी। 2. a person given to fraudulent practices, जालसाज़, ठग।

crooked (क्रुकिड) ***adj.*** 1. having bends or curves, वक्र, घुमावदार। 2. deceitful, धोखेबाज़।

crop (क्रॉप) ***n.*** agricultural produce, yield, फ़सल, पैदावार। ***v.*** to cultivate, खेती करना।

cross (क्रॉस) ***n.*** 1. a symbol consisting of two intersecting lines, क्रॉस, काटा। 2. a wooden structure used as a means of execution in ancient times, क्रॉस, सलीब, सूली। 3. an object shaped like this used as a Christian emblem, क्रॉस। 4. a hybrid plant or animal, संकर पशु या पौधा। ***v.*** 1. to go or extend across, पार करना, पार जाना। 2. to intersect, रेखाओं आदि का एक दूसरी को काटना। 3. to draw a line across, आर-पार रेखा खींचना। 4. to breed by hybridizing, to crossbreed, संकर जाति बनाना। 5. to oppose, विरोध करना।

crossbred (क्रॉसब्रेड) ***adj.*** produced by mixing breeds, संकर, दोगला।

cross-examination (क्रॉस-इग्ज़ैमिनेशन) ***n.*** the act or process of cross-examining, प्रतिपरीक्षा, जिरह, बहस।

cross-eyed (क्रॉस-आइड) ***adj.*** having eyes turn toward the nose, भेंगा।

crossing (क्रॉसिंग) ***n.*** 1. a place where streets, roads etc. cross, चौराहा। 2. the place where road, river etc. be crossed, पारण पथ।

cross-reference (क्रॉस-रेफ़रेन्स) ***n.*** the act of referring from one part of a book to another, प्रतिसंदर्भ, प्रत्यभिदेश।

crossroads (क्रॉसरोड्ज़) ***n.*** a place where too roads intersect, चौमुहानी, चौराहा, क्रॉसिंग। ☐ **at the crossroads,** in a suspense, दुविधा में।

crosswise (क्रॉसवाइज़) ***adv.*** across, खड़े और बेड़े।

crossword (क्रॉसवर्ड) ***n.*** a puzzle in which words are inserted according to clues, वर्ग-पहेली।

crotchety (क्रॉचेटी) ***adj.*** bad-tempered, बदमिज़ाज।

C

crouch (क्राउच) ***v.*** to bend low with the limbs pulled up close together, दुबक या सिकुड़कर बैठना।

crow[1] (क्रो) ***n.*** a large black bird, कौआ, काग।

crow[2] ***v.*** (crowed/crew, crowing) 1. to utter a shrill cry as a cock, बाँग देना। 2. to speak proudly, शेख़ी बघारना।

crowbar (क्रोबार) ***n.*** an iron bar used as a lever, सब्बल, रंभा।

crowd (क्राउड) ***n.*** a large number of people gathered together, भीड़। ***v.*** to gather together in large numbers, भीड़ लगाना।

crown (क्राउन) ***n.*** 1. an ornamental cap worn by a king or queen, राजमुकुट, ताज। 2. the top part of something, शिखर। ***v.*** to put a crown on one's head, ताज पहनना या पहनाना।

crown prince ***n.*** the male heir to a throne, युवराज, टिकैत।

crucial (क्रूशल) ***adj.*** 1. critical, नाज़ुक। 2. decisive, निर्णायक।

crucible (क्रूसिबल) ***n.*** a pot used for melting metals at high temperature, घरिया, कुठाली।

crucifix (क्रूसिफ़िक्स) ***n.*** a model of a cross with a figure of Christ upon it, क्रूसीफ़िक्स, क्रॉस।

crucifixion (क्रूसिफ़िक्शन) ***n.*** the act of crucifying, सलीब या सूली पर चढ़ाने की क्रिया या भाव।

crude (क्रूड) ***adj.*** 1. in an unrefined or natural state, raw, अशोधित, कच्चा। 2. rough, रूखा। 3. vulgar, अशिष्ट।

cruel (क्रूअल) ***adj.*** 1. causing pain or suffering, क्रूर। 2. merciless, निर्दय।

cruelty (क्रूअल्टी) ***n.*** 1. the quality of being cruel, क्रूरता, निर्दयता। 2. a cruel act, जुल्म, अत्याचार।

cruise (क्रूज़) ***v.*** to sail for pleasure, समुद्र-विहार करना। ***n.*** a cruising voyage, समुद्र-विहार।

cruiser (क्रूज़र) ***n.*** a medium size fast warship, तीव्रगामी युद्धपोत।

crumb (क्रम्ब) ***n.*** a fragment, टुकड़ा, कण।

crumble (क्रम्बल) ***v.*** 1. to break into small parts, टुकड़े-टुकड़े होना, चूर-चूर होना। 2. to disintegrate, विघटित होना या करना।

crunch (क्रन्च) ***v.*** to bite or chew with a crushing sound, कचर-कचर करते हुए खाना।

crusade (क्रूसेड) ***n.*** 1. a military expedition by Christians to recover their holy lands from Muslims, धर्मयुद्ध। 2. any organised movement against an abuse, संगठित आंदोलन।

crusader (क्रूसेडर) ***n.*** one who takes part in a crusade, धर्मयोद्धा; आंदोलनकर्ता।

crush (क्रश) ***v.*** 1. to press with great force so as to break, injure or destroy, रौंदना, कुचलना, मसलना। 2. to break into powder by pressure, पीसना, रगड़ना। 3. to subdue or defeat, कुचल डालना, रौंद डालना।

crusher (क्रशर) ***n.*** a crushing device, कोल्हू।

crushing (क्रशिंग) ***adj.*** destroying, विनाशकारी।

crust (क्रस्ट) ***n.*** 1. a hard outer covering of a bread, पपड़ी। 2. a hard surface, परत, छिलका। ***v.*** to

C

become covered with a crust, पपड़ियाना।

crusty (क्रसटी) ***adj.*** 1. covered with a crust, पपड़ीदार। 2. bad-mannered, बदमिज़ाज।

crutch (क्रच) ***n.*** 1. a support used as an aid by a lame person, बैसाखी। 2. something that supports, सहारा, संबल।

crux (क्रुक्स) ***n.*** a vital point, मुख्य बिंदु, मर्म।

cry (क्राइ) ***v.*** 1. to shout, चिल्लाना, चीख़ना। 2. to weep, रोना। ***n.*** 1. a shout, a loud call, चीख़, पुकार, गुहार, चिल्लाहट। 2. an act of wailing, रोना, रोना-धोना।

cryptic (क्रिप्टिक) ***adj.*** 1. hidden, गुप्त, प्रच्छन्न। 2. mysterious, रहस्यमय।

crystal (क्रिस्टल) ***n.*** 1. a clear transparent colourless mineral, बिल्लौर, स्फटिक। 2. one of the pieces into which certain substances solidify, रवा।

crystal clear ***adj.*** obvious, सुस्पष्ट, स्फटिक की भाँति साफ़।

crystallize (क्रिस्टेलाइज़) ***v.*** to form or cause to form crystals, रवेदार बनना या बनाना, रवे बनना या बनाना।

cub (कब) ***n.*** a young of a lion, bear, fox etc., पशु-शावक, जानवर का बच्चा।

cube (क्यूब) ***n.*** 1. a solid body with six equal sides, क्यूब, छहपहला पिंड, घन। 2. the product that results when the same number is used three times as a factor, घनफल ($4^3 = 4 \times 4 \times 4 = 64$).

cubic (क्यूबिक) ***adj.*** 1. having the shape of a cube, घनाकार। 2. having three dimensions, त्रिविमीय। 3. of the third power or degree, त्रिघाती।

cubicle (क्यूबिकल) ***n.*** small room, कोठरी।

cuckoo (कुकू) ***n.*** 1. a bird with a call that is like its name, कोयल। 2. the call of this bird, कू, कूक।

cucumber (क्यूकम्बर) ***n.*** a plant and its fruit used as a salad, ककड़ी, खीरा।

cud (कड) ***n.*** the food that cattle bring back from the first stomach for chewing, जुगाली।

cuddle (कडल) ***v.*** to hug tenderly, प्यार से गले लगाना।

cudgel (कजल) ***n.*** a thick stick, सोंटा, लाठी।

cue[1] (क्यू) ***n.*** a hint, संकेत।

cue[2] ***n.*** a rod used in playing billiards, बिलियर्ड खेलने का डंडा।

cuff[1] (कफ़) ***n.*** a band or fold at the bottom of a sleeve, कफ़।

cuff[2] ***n.*** a slap, थप्पड़, तमाचा। ***v.*** to slap, थप्पड़ मारना।

cuisine (क्विज़ीन) ***n.*** 1. the style of cooking, पाक शैली। 2. a cooked food, व्यंजन।

cull (कल) ***v.*** 1. to pick or select, चुनना, छाँटना। 2. to gather, इकट्ठा करना।

culminate (कल्मिनेट) ***v.*** to reach highest and last point of development, ऊँचाई या शिखर पर पहुँचना।

culmination (कल्मिनेशन) ***n.*** the peak, शिखर।

culpable (कल्पेबल) ***adj.*** blameworthy, responsible for wrong, दोषी, आपराधिक।

culprit (कल्प्रिट) ***n.*** 1. one who has

C

committed a crime or offence, अपराधी। 2. an accused person, अभियुक्त।

cult (कल्ट) ***n.*** a system of religious worship, संप्रदाय, पंथ।

cultivate (कल्टिवेट) ***v.*** 1. to prepare land and raise crop, खेती करना, खेती-बारी करना। 2. to develop, विकसित करना।

cultivation (कल्टिवेशन) ***n.*** the act of cultivating, कृषि, खेती-बारी।

cultivator (कल्टिवेटर) ***n.*** one who cultivates, खेतिहर, किसान।

cultural (कल्चरल) ***adj.*** of or related to the culture, सांस्कृतिक।

culture (कल्चर) ***n.*** 1. the customs, institutions and beliefs of a particular society, संस्कृति। 2. development of mind or body, विकास, संवर्धन। 3. the practice of growing bacteria for scientific analysis or study, जीवाणु-संवर्धन, जीवाणु-संस्कार। ***v.*** to grow bacteria for scientific analysis or study, जीवाणुओं का संवर्धन करना, जीवाणुओं का संस्कार करना।

cultured (कल्चर्ड) ***adj.*** educated and refined, सुसंस्कृत।

culvert (कल्वर्ट) ***n.*** a bridge over a drain, पुलिया।

cumbersome (कम्बरसम) ***adj.*** weighty and clumsy, भारी-भरकम और बेढब।

cummin (कमिन) ***n.*** a plant and its aromatic seed, जीरा।

cumulative (क्यूम्यूलेटिव) ***adj.*** 1. increasing by successive addition, बढ़ता और जुड़ता चलनेवाला, संचयमान। 2. amassed, aggregate, पुंजीभूत, एकत्र।

cuneiform (क्यूनीफ़ॉर्म) ***n.*** wedge-shaped letters used in old writings of the Babylonians, Assyrians etc., कीलाक्षर, फन्नी लिपि।

cunning (कनिंग) ***adj.*** crafty, धूर्त, मक्कार।

cup (कप) ***n.*** 1. a small container with a handle used for drinking, कप, प्याला, चषक। 2. the amount it holds, प्याला-भर वस्तु, प्याला। 3. an ornamental cuplike vessel given to a prize-winner, कप।

cupboard (कबर्ड) ***n.*** a set of shelves enclosed by doors, आलमारी।

cupful (कपफ़ुल) ***n.*** the contents of a cup, प्याला-भर वस्तु।

Cupid (क्यूपिड) ***n.*** the God of love, कामदेव।

cupidity (क्यूपिडिटी) ***n.*** greed, लोभ, लालच, लिप्सा।

curable (क्यूरेबल) ***adj.*** capable of being cured, चिकित्स्य, साध्य।

curative (क्यूरेटिव) ***adj.*** tending to cure, आरोग्यकर।

curator (क्यूरेटर) ***n.*** a person incharge of a museum, संग्रहालयाध्यक्ष।

curb (कर्ब) ***n.*** a restraint or check, नियंत्रण, रोक। ***v.*** to apply curb to, to restrain, नियंत्रित करना, लगाम लगाना।

curd (कर्ड) ***n.*** a substance formed from coagulation of milk, दही।

curdle (कर्डल) ***v.*** to become curd or turn into curd, दही जमना या जमाना।

cure (क्यूर) ***v.*** 1. to restore to health, निरोग या चंगा कर देना। 2. to preserve (fish, meat etc.), परिरक्षित करना। ***n.*** 1. the act of curing or state of being cured, रोगमुक्ति, स्वास्थ्य-प्राप्ति। 2. a remedy, उपचार, चिकित्सा। 3. preservation, परिरक्षण।

C

curfew (कर्फ़्यू) ***n.*** an official order to remain indoor within certain hours, कर्फ़्यू।

curio (क्यूरिओ) ***n.*** a rare or unusual object of art, कोई अलभ्य या असाधारण कलाकृति।

curiosity (क्यूरिऑसिटी) ***n.*** inquisitiveness, जिज्ञासा, कौतूहल।

curious (क्यूरिअस) ***adj.*** eager to know or learn, जिज्ञासु।

curl (कर्ल) ***v.*** to grow into ringlets, छल्लेदार बनना, घुँघराला बनना। ***n.*** a curve of hair, घुँघराले या छल्लेदार बाल।

curly (कर्ली) ***adj.*** having curls, घुँघराला।

currency (करेन्सी) ***n.*** the money current in a country, मुद्रा।

current (करेन्ट) ***adj.*** in general circulation or use, प्रचलित, चालू; current account, चालू खाता। ***n.*** 1. natural flow of water or air, धारा, प्रवाह। 2. the flow of electricity, विद्युत्प्रवाह, करेंट।

currently (करेन्टली) ***adv.*** now-a-days, आजकल, इन दिनों।

curricular (करिक्युलर) ***adj.*** of curriculam, पाठ्यक्रम-संबंधी।

curriculum (करिक्युलम) ***n.*** a course of study, पाठ्यक्रम, पाठ्यचर्या।

curry[1] (करी) ***n.*** 1. spicy seasoning, बघार, छौंक। 2. a dish flavoured with this, शोरबा, सालन, कढ़ी।

curry[2] ***v.*** to rub down (horse), खरहरा करना।

curse (कर्स) ***n.*** an appeal to a super natural power to bring harm to a person or thing, अभिशाप, शाप। ***v.*** to invoke a super natural power to bring harm to someone or something, शाप देना, कोसना।

cursed (कर्सिड) ***adj.*** under a curse, शापित।

cursive (कर्सिव) ***adj. & n.*** (a writing) in which the letters are joined together, घसीट (लिखाई)।

cursory (कर्सरी) ***adj.*** hasty and quick, hurried, सरसरी।

curt (कर्ट) ***adj.*** 1. rudely, blunt, (व्यक्ति) अक्खड़ या रूखा; (उत्तर) मुँहतोड़। 2. brief, संक्षिप्त।

curtail (कर्टेल) ***v.*** to cut short, काटना-छाँटना, कम कर या घटा देना।

curtailment (कर्टेलमेन्ट) ***n.*** the act of curtailing, काट-छाँट, कमी, घटाव।

curtain (कर्टन) ***n.*** 1. a cover for a window or door, पर्दा। 2. a screen, पर्दा, आड़। ***v.*** 1. to provide with curtains, पर्दे लगाना। 2. to conceal, छिपाना, पर्दा डालना।

curvature (कर्वेचर) ***n.*** the condition of being curved, गोलाई, वक्रता।

curve (कर्व) ***n.*** a continuously bending line, वक्र-रेखा। ***v.*** to bend so as to form a curve, वक्र होना या करना।

cushion (कुशन) ***n.*** a pillow to sit, rest or lie on, गद्दी, कुशन।

cuspid (कस्पिड) ***n.*** a canine tooth, नुकीला दाँत।

custard (कस्टर्ड) ***n.*** a sweet (frozen) dish, कस्टर्ड, फिरनी।

custodian (कस्टोडिअन) ***n.*** a keeper or caretaker, अभिरक्षक, रखवाला।

custody (कस्टडी) ***n.*** 1. guardianship, अभिरक्षा। 2. imprisonment, हिरासत, क़ैद।

custom (कस्टम) ***n.*** 1. a long continued practice, प्रथा, रिवाज।

C

2. (plu.) a tax on imported goods, सीमा-शुल्क। 3. (plu.) the government department dealing with customs, सीमा-शुल्क विभाग।

customary (कस्टमरी) ***adj.*** 1. established by custom, रूढ़िगत। 2. usual, सामान्य।

customer (कस्टमर) ***n.*** 1. one who buys goods or services from a shop etc., ग्राहक। 2. a person one has to deal with, ग्राहक।

cut (कट) ***v.*** (cut, cutting) 1. to divide into pieces, काटना, चीरना। 2. to bite, काटना, काट खाना। 3. to shorten or trim, काटना-छाँटना। 4. to harvest, कटाई करना। 5. to divide the pack of cards, (पत्ते या गड्डी) काटना। ***n.*** 1. a wound made by a sharp-edged instrument, घाव, कट। 2. a piece of meat, मांस की बोटी या टुकड़ा। 3. a style of cutting, काटने की शैली, काट। 4. a reduction, कटौती, घटाव, कमी।

cutaneous (क्युटेनिअस) ***adj.*** relating to the skin, त्वचीय।

cute (क्यूट) ***adj.*** very attractive or beautiful, अत्यंत आकर्षक या अति सुंदर।

cutlass (कटलस) ***n.*** a short curved sword, खुखरी, दराँती।

cutler (कटलर) ***n.*** a person who makes or sells cutlery, चाकू, छुरियाँ, काँटे, चम्मच आदि बनाने या बेचनेवाला।

cutlery (कटलरी) ***n.*** 1. cutting instruments, काटने के उपकरण।

cutlet (कटलिट) ***n.*** a fried dish of meat or potatoes, मीट चाप, आलूचाप।

cutout (कटआउट) ***n.*** something cut out or intended to be cut out, तराशी हुई वस्तु।

cutter (कटर) ***n.*** 1. one who cuts, काटनेवाला। 2. that which cuts, काटने का उपकरण। 3. a small boat, एक प्रकार की छोटी नाव।

cutthroat (कटथ्रोट) ***adj.*** fierce, प्रचंड।

cutting (कटिंग) ***n.*** 1. the act of cutting, कटाई; hair-cutting, बाल-कटाई। 2. a shoot cut from a plant for grafting, कलम। 3. a piece or news item cut out from a newspaper, कतरन। ***adj.*** hurtful, चुटीला।

cycle (साइकल) ***n.*** 1. a periodically repeated sequence of events, चक्र। 2. a short form of bicycle, साइकिल। ***v.*** to travel by or ride a cycle, साइकिल चलाना।

cyclic (साइक्लिक) ***adj.*** recurring or revolving in cycles, चक्रीय।

cyclist (साइक्लिस्ट) ***n.*** one who rides a bicycle or motorcycle, साइकिल-सवार, मोटर-साइकिल-सवार।

cyclone (साइक्लोन) ***n.*** a violent rotating windstorm, चक्रवात।

cyclonic (साइक्लॉनिक) ***adj.*** of or relating to a cyclone, चक्रवात-संबंधी, तूफ़ानी।

cylinder (सिलिन्डर) ***n.*** a solid or hollow roller-shaped object, बेलन, सिलेंडर।

cylinderical (सिलिन्ड्रिकल) ***adj.*** shaped like a cylinder, बेलनाकार।

cymbal (सिम्बल) ***n.*** a pair of brass plates that are struck together in a musical performance, झाँझ, मंजीरा।

cynic (सिनिक) ***n.*** one who believes people's motives are bad, नकचढ़ा।

cynicism (सिनिसिज़म) ***n.*** the theory that pleads that everyone acts

selfishly, दोषदर्शिता, स्वार्थवाद।

cynosure (साइनोज़्युअर) ***n.*** a centre of admiration or attraction, आकर्षण-केंद्र।

cypher (साइफ़र) ***n.*** 1. the figure of zero, सिफ़र, शून्य। 2. secret writing, गूढ़लेख।

cyst (सिस्ट) ***n.*** a semisolid bodily sac, रसौली, गट्ठा।

Czar (ज़ार) ***n.*** a title of former emperors of Russia, पुराने रूसी सम्राटों की पदवी, ज़ार।

Czech (चेक) ***n.*** 1. a native of Czechoslovakia, चेकोस्लोवाकिया का वासी। 2. the language of Czechoslovakia, चेकोस्लोवाकिया की भाषा।

D, d (डी) ***n.*** the fourth letter of the English alphabet, अंग्रेज़ी वर्णमाला का चौथा वर्ण।

dab (डैब) ***v.*** 1. to pat, थपथपाना। 2. to apply, पोतना, लगाना।

dabble (डैबल) ***v.*** to splash in or out of water playfully, जल-क्रीड़ा करना।

dacoit (डैकॉइट) ***n.*** one who commits dacoity, डाकू।

dacoity (डैकॉइटी) ***n.*** robbery with violence committed by a gang, डकैती।

dad (डैड) ***n.*** father, पिता, बाप।

daddy (डैडी) ***n.*** father, पिता, बाप।

daffodil (डैफ़डिल) ***n.*** a garden plant and its flower, डैफ़ोडिल, नरगिस।

dagger (डैगर) ***n.*** a short two-edged weapon, कटार।

dahlia (डेलिया) ***n.*** a garden plant and its flower, डहलिया।

daily (डेली) ***adj.*** happening everyday, दैनिक। ***n.*** a daily newspaper, दैनिक समाचारपत्र, दैनिक।

dainty (डेन्टी) ***adj.*** 1. elegant, सुंदर। 2. delicious, स्वादिष्ट।

dairy (डेअरी) ***n.*** a farm or building where milk and milk products are produced, दुग्धशाला, दुग्ध उद्योग।

dais (डेइस) ***n.*** a raised platform in a lecture hall, मंच।

daisy (डेज़ी) ***n.*** a garden plant and its flower, डेज़ी।

dale (डेल) ***n.*** a valley, घाटी, उपत्यका।

dalliance (डैलिएन्स) ***n.*** the act of dallying, खिलवाड़, छेड़छाड़; समय की बरबादी।

dally (डैली) ***v.*** 1. to flirt playfully, छेड़छाड़ करना। 2. to lose time, समय बरबाद करना।

dam[1] (डैम) ***n.*** a wall or barrier built (across a river) to control the flow of water, बाँध, डैम।

dam[2] ***n.*** a female parent of a four-footed animal, मादा चौपाया।

damage (डैमिज) ***n.*** loss, injury or harm, क्षति, हानि, नुक़सान। ***v.*** to cause damage to, नुक़सान पहुँचाना।

damaged (डैमिज्ड) ***adj.*** impaired, broken or injured, क्षतिग्रस्त, कटा-फटा।

dame (डेम) ***n.*** a lady, महिला।

damn (डैम) ***v.*** to condemn, भर्त्सना करना।

damnation (डैम्नेशन) ***n.*** condemnation, लानत-मलामत।

damned (डैम्ड) ***adj.*** accursed, अभिशप्त, शापित।

damp (डैम्प) ***adj.*** slightly wet, moist. नम, सीलन-भरा।

dampen (डैम्पन) ***v.*** to make or become damp, नम करना या होना।

dampness (डैम्पनिस) ***n.*** the state of being damp, नमी, आर्द्रता।

damp-proof (डैम्प-प्रूफ़) ***n.*** a substance that resists dampness, सीलनरोधी पदार्थ।

damsel (डैम्ज़ल) ***n.*** a girl, युवती, किशोरी।

dance (डान्स) ***v.*** to move the feet and body rhythmically, नाचना, नृत्य करना। ***n.*** a set of rhythmic steps and motions, नाच, नृत्य।

dandle (डैन्डल) ***v.*** to move a small

child up and down in one's arms or on one's knees. छोटे बच्चे को बाँहों में या घुटनों पर उछालना।

dandruff (डैन्ड्रफ़) ***n.*** small particles of dead skin shed from the scalp, रूसी।

dandy (डैन्डी) ***n.*** a fop, छैला, बाँका।

danger (डेन्जर) ***n.*** peril, संकट, ख़तरा।

dangerous (डेन्जरस) ***adj.*** causing danger, alarming, ख़तरनाक, भयंकर।

dangle (डैंगल) ***v.*** 1. to swing, झुलाना।

dapper (डैपर) ***adj.*** neat and smart, बना-ठना।

dare (डेअर) ***v.*** 1. to be courageous, हौसला होना। 2. to challenge, ललकारना, चुनौती देना।

daredevil (डेअरडेविल) ***n.*** a person who is recklessly bold, दुस्साहसी।

daring (डेअरिंग) ***adj.*** bold, निर्भीक। ***n.*** boldness, निर्भीकता।

dark (डार्क) ***adj.*** 1. lacking light, अंधकारपूर्ण। 2. not fair, काला, साँवला। ***n.*** absence of light, अँधेरा, अंधकार।

Dark Ages ***n.*** unenlightened period in our history, अंधकार युग।

darken (डार्कन) ***v.*** 1. to become dark, काला होना। 2. to make dark, काला करना।

dark horse ***n.*** a competitor about whom little is known before the contest but who wins it, छिपा रुस्तम।

darkroom (डार्करूम) ***n.*** a closed room, बंद कमरा।

darling (डार्लिंग) ***adj.*** beloved, प्यारा, प्रिय। ***n.*** a dearly loved person, प्रिय/प्रिया।

darn (डार्न) ***v.*** to mend by weaving thread across a hole, रफ़ू करना।

dart (डार्ट) ***n.*** 1. a small pointed arrowlike missile, शर, छोटा नुकीला तीर।

dash (डैश) ***v.*** 1. to hurl or throw violently, फेंक देना। 2. to rush, तेज़ी से आगे बढ़ना या दौड़ पड़ना। 3. to knock against, टकरा जाना, भिड़ जाना। ***n.*** 1. a short rapid run, दौड़। 2. anything used in a small quantity to give flavour, पुट। 3. vigour, उत्साह, जोश। 4. a violent stroke or blow, तीव्र आघात, टक्कर। 5. the sound of splashing, छपछप। 6. the punctuation mark (—) रेखिका, डैश।

dashing (डैशिंग) ***adj.*** spirited, bold, जोशीला, दिलेर।

data (डेटा) ***n.*** 1. basic facts, आधार-सामग्री, डाटा। 2. numerical information, आँकड़ा।

date[1] (डेट) ***n.*** a specified or precise day of the month, तारीख़, दिनांक, तिथि। ***v.*** to mark with a date, तारीख़ डालना।

date[2] ***n.*** the fruit of the date palm, ख़जूर।

dated (डेटिड) ***adj.*** 1. marked with a date, दिनांकित। 2. old fashioned, पुराना।

dating (डेटिंग) ***n.*** 1. assessment of a date, तिथि-निर्धारण। 2. social engagements with the opposite sex on appointment, पर-स्त्री या पर-पुरुष से निर्धारित तिथि को होनेवाला मिलन।

dative (डेटिव) ***adj.*** belonging to the indirect object of the verb, संप्रदानकारक-संबंधी।

datum (डेटम) ***n.*** singular of data,

daughter (डॉटर) ***n.*** a female child, बेटी।

daughter-in-law (डॉटर-इन-लॉ) ***n.*** son's wife, बहू।

D

daunt (डॉन्ट) ***v.*** 1. to intimidate, डाँटना, फटकारना, दहलाना। 2. to discourage, हतोत्साहित करना।

dauntless (डॉन्टलिस) ***adj.*** fearless, निडर।

dawdle (डॉडल) ***v.*** to waste (time, समय) बरबाद करना।

dawn (डॉन) ***n.*** daybreak, भोर, प्रभात, उषा-काल। ***v.*** to begin to grow light in the morning, भोर होना।

day (डे) ***n.*** 1. the time during which the sun is above the horizon, दिन। 2. the time for one rotation of Earth, a period of twenty four hours, दिवस, दिन।

daybook (डेबुक) ***n.*** a journal in which daily transactions are recorded, रोज़नामचा।

daybreak (डेब्रेक) ***n.*** dawn, भोर।

daydream (डेड्रीम) ***n.*** idle or pleasant thought, दिवास्वप्न।

daylight (डेलाइट) ***n.*** the light of day, सूर्य की रोशनी।

daze (डेज़) ***v.*** 1. to stun, चौंका देना। 2. to dazzle, चौंधिया देना।

dazzle (डैज़ल) ***v.*** to overpower with intense light, चौंधिया देना। ***n.*** a dazzling light, चकाचौंध।

dead (डेड) ***adj.*** 1. no longer alive, मृत, मरा हुआ। 2. lifeless, निर्जीव, निष्प्राण। 3. no longer active, निष्क्रिय। 4. inanimate, जड़। 5. no longer in use, अप्रचलित, पुराना।

deaden (डेडन) ***v.*** to make or become less intense, धीमा करना या होना।

dead end (डेड एन्ड) ***n.*** a blind alley, बंद गली।

deadline (डेडलाइन) ***n.*** a time-limit, अंतिम समय-सीमा।

deadlock (डेडलॉक) ***n.*** a complete standstill, जिच, गतिरोध।

dead loss ***n.*** complete loss, पूर्ण क्षति।

deadly (डेडली) ***adj.*** causing death, जानलेवा।

deaf (डेफ़) ***adj.*** unable to hear, बधिर।

deafen (डेफ़न) ***v.*** to make deaf, बहरा बना देना।

deaf-mute (डेफ़-म्यूट) ***n.*** mute as well as deaf, गूँगा-बहरा, मूक-बधिर।

deal (डील) ***v.*** 1. to distribute, बाँटना। 2. to treat, व्यवहार करना। □ **deal in,** व्यापार करना। ***n.*** transaction, सौदा, लेन-देन।

dealer (डीलर) ***n.*** one who buys and sells goods, व्यापारी, व्यवसायी।

dealings (डीलिंग्स) ***n.*** trade relations, लेन-देन।

dealt (डेल्ट) ***v.*** p.t. of deal.

dean (डीन) ***n.*** the head of a faculty, संकायाध्यक्ष।

dear (डिअर) ***adj.*** 1. much loved, प्रिय, प्यारा। 2. esteemed, आदरणीय। 3. costly, महँगा। 4. precious, बहुमूल्य। ***n.*** a darling, प्रिया या प्रियतम।

dearness allowance ***n.*** allowance paid to meet a rise in the cost of living, महँगाई भत्ता।

dearth (डर्थ) ***n.*** paucity, कमी, अभाव।

death (डेथ) ***n.*** 1. the act of dying, the end of life, मौत, मृत्यु। 2. termination, extinction, अंत, समाप्ति।

death-bed (डेथ-बेड) ***n.*** the bed on which a person dies or is dying, मृत्युशय्या।

death-blow (डेथ-ब्लो) ***n.*** a blow that causes death, जानलेवा आघात।

death certificate ***n.*** a certificate showing the time and cause of a person's death, मृत्यु-प्रमाणक।

deathless (डेथलिस) ***adj.*** immortal, अमर।

debacle (डिबाकल) ***n.*** 1. a sudden downfall or ruin, आकस्मिक पतन या विनाश। 2. a rout or collapse, घोर या शर्मनाक पराजय।

debar (डिबार) ***v.*** 1. to bar from entrance, प्रवेश न करने देना, रोकना। 2. to exclude, निकाल देना या वंचित रखना।

debase (डिबेस) ***v.*** 1. to lower in quality or value, महत्त्व गिरा या कम कर देना। 2. to adulterate, मिलावट करना।

debased (डिबेस्ड) ***adj.*** low, पतित, भ्रष्ट।

debatable (डिबेटेबल) ***adj.*** arguable, open to dispute, विवादास्पद, विवादग्रस्त।

debate (डिबेट) ***n.*** a formal discussion, बहस, वाद-विवाद, विचार-विमर्श। ***v.*** to discuss or deliberate upon, बहस करना, वाद-विवाद करना।

debater (डिबेटर) ***n.*** a person skilled in argument, वाद-विवाद में कुशल।

debauch (डिबॉच) ***v.*** to corrupt morally, पथभ्रष्ट करना; असंयमी बना देना।

debenture (डिबेन्चर) ***n.*** an interest-bearing bond, ऋणपत्र।

debilitate (डिबिलिटेट) ***v.*** to weaken, कमज़ोर करना।

debility (डिबिलिटी) ***n.*** weakness, कमज़ोरी।

debit (डेबिट) ***n.*** an item of debt नाम डाली मद। ***v.*** to enter a debit in an account, नामे डालना।

debris (डेब्री) ***n.*** ruins, मलबा, खंडहर।

debt (डैट) ***n.*** 1. something owed, कर्ज़, ऋण, उधार। 2. the state of owing something, देनदारी।

debtor (डैटर) ***n.*** one who is indebted to another, ऋणी, कर्ज़दार।

debut (डेब्यू) ***n.*** one's first appearance as a performer, मंच पर होनेवाली पहली उपस्थिति।

decade (डेकेड) ***n.*** a period of ten years, दशक।

decadence (डेकेडेन्स) ***n.*** decline, deterioration, गिरावट।

decagon (डेकागन) ***n.*** a geometrical figure with ten sides, दशभुज।

decamp (डिकैम्प) ***v.*** to go away secretly, खिसक जाना।

decant (डिकैन्ट) ***v.*** to pour a liquid, wine etc. from one container to another without disturbing any sediment, निथारना।

decapitate (डिकैपिटेट) ***v.*** to behead, सिर उड़ा देना।

decay (डिके) ***v.*** 1. to rot, सड़ जाना, सड़-गल जाना। 2. to lose strength, health etc., क्षय होना, क्षीण हो जाना। 3. to fall, पतन होना। ***n.*** 1. rot, सड़न, सड़ाव। 2. fall, क्षय, ह्रास, पतन।

decease (डिसीस) ***n.*** death, निधन, मृत्यु।

deceased (डिसीस्ड) ***adj.*** dead, मृत, मृतक।

deceit (डिसीट) ***n.*** 1. fraud, धोख़ा, कपट। 2. a trick, चाल, चालाकी।

deceive (डिसीव) ***v.*** 1. to cause a person to believe something that is false, धोख़ा देना। 2. to mislead, बहकाना।

December (डिसेम्बर) ***n.*** the twelfth month of the year, दिसंबर।

decency (डीसेंसी) ***n.*** the quality of being decent, शालीनता।

decent (डीसेन्ट) ***adj.*** 1. conforming to the standards of propriety,

D

उपयुंक्त, उचित, शालीन, मर्यादापूर्ण, शिष्ट। 2. generous, उदार।

decentralize (डीसेन्ट्रलाइज़) *v.* to distribute the central power to smaller units, विकेंद्रीकरण करना।

decentralized (डीसेन्ट्रलाइज़्ड) *adj.* that has been decentralized, विकेंद्रित।

deception (डिसेप्शन) *n.* the act of deceiving, धोखा।

deceptive (डिसेप्टिव) *adj.* misleading, भ्रामक।

decide (डिसाइड) *v.* to make a decision, निश्चय या फ़ैसला करना।

deciding (डिसाइडिंग) *adj.* that decides, निर्णायक।

decimal (डेसिमल) *adj.* relating to or using powers of ten, दशमिक, दशमलव। *n.* a decimal fraction, दशमलव भिन्न।

decimal system *n.* a system of weights, measures etc. having a base of ten and each unit ten times that immediately below it, दशमलव पद्धति, दशमिक पद्धति।

decipher (डिसाइफ़र) *v.* to make out the meaning of something obscure or illegible, अस्पष्ट या दुरूह लेख का अर्थ लगाना।

decision (डिसिज़न) *n.* the act of deciding or something decided, निर्णय, फ़ैसला।

decisive (डिसाइसिव) *adj.* conclusive निर्णायक।

deck[1] (डेक) *n.* any of the platforms built into a vessel, डेक।

deck[2] *v.* 1. to dress up, वस्त्र धारण करना। 2. to decorate, सजना या सजाना, सँवरना या सँवारना।

declaim (डिक्लेम) *v.* to speak loudly and with rhetorical effect, ज़ोरदार भाषण करना।

declamatory (डिक्लैमेटरी) *adj.* loud and rhetorical, ज़ोरदार।

declaration (डेक्लरेशन) *n.* the act of declaring or something declared, घोषणा।

declaratory (डिक्लैरेटरी) *adj.* pertaining to declaration, घोषणापरक।

declare (डिक्लेअर) *v.* to announce, घोषणा करना।

declared (डिक्लेअर्ड) *adj.* announced, घोषित।

declension (डिक्लेन्शन) *n.* 1. the systematic inflection of nouns, pronouns, adjectives etc., व्याकरण में, रूपसाधन। 2. a decline, अवनति, क्षय, पतन।

declinable (डिक्लाइनेबल) *adj.* 1. capable of declension, विकारी। 2. tending to decline, जिसका क्षय या ह्रास हो।

decline (डिक्लाइन) *v.* 1. to refuse to do or accept, अस्वीकार करना, इन्कार करना। 2. to slope downward, झुकना, ढलना। 3. to deteriorate gradually, क्रमशः ह्रास होना, क्षय होना, उतार पर होना। 4. to decrease, घटना, कम होना। *n.* 1. the process or result of declining, ह्रास, क्षय, अवनति, गिरावट, पतन। 2. a downward slope, ढाल, उतार।

decompose (डीकम्पोज़) *v.* to rot, गलना, सड़ना।

decomposition (डीकॉम्पज़िशन) *n.* decay, सड़ाव, सड़न।

decontrol (डीकन्ट्रोल) *v.* to release from control, विनियंत्रित कर देना।

n. the act of decontrolling, विनियंत्रण।

decorate (डैकरेट) *v.* 1. to furnish with something attractive, सजाना। 2. to confer a medal or honour on, पदक या सम्मान प्रदान करना।

decoration (डैकरेशन) *n.* 1. the act of decorating, सजावट।

decorator (डैकरेटर) *n.* one who is expert in furnishings etc., डेकोरेटर, सजावटवाला।

decorous (डैकरस) *adj.* decent, शालीन।

decorum (डिकोरम) *n.* propriety, शालीनता।

decoy (डीकॉइ) *n.* 1. a snare, फंदा, जाल। 2. a trained or artificial animal used to entice game, शिकार को लुभाकर फँसाने के लिए सधाया हुआ या कृत्रिम जानवर।

decrease (डिक्रीस) *v.* 1. to make shorter, smaller or less, छोटा करना, कम करना, घटाना। 2. to become shorter, smaller or less, छोटा या कम होना, घटना। *n.* a reduction, कमी, घटती, घटाव।

decree (डिक्री) *n.* an order having the force of law, अधिदेश, फ़रमान।

decrepit (डिक्रेपिट) *adj.* weakened by old age or illness, जर्जर, जीर्ण।

decry (डिक्राइ) *v.* to speak ill of, बुराई या बदनामी करना।

dedicate (डेडिकेट) *v.* to devote, समर्पित करना।

dedicated (डेडिकेटिड) *adj.* devoted, समर्पित, एकनिष्ठ।

dedication (डेडिकेशन) *n.* 1. the act of dedicating or something dedicated, समर्पण; भेंट। 2. the whole-hearted devotion, समर्पण-भावना, निष्ठा।

deduce (डिड्यूस) *v.* to draw a conclusion, निष्कर्ष निकालना।

deduct (डिडक्ट) *v.* to subtract, घटाना, कम करना।

deduction (डिडक्शन) *n.* 1. the act of deducting or something deducted, कटौती, काटी जानेवाली रक़म। 2. a logical conclusion reached by reasoning, तर्कसंगत निष्कर्ष, निगमन।

deductive (डिडक्टिव) *adj.* pertaining to a logical conclusion, निगमनात्मक, युक्तियुक्त।

deed (डीड) *n.* 1. an act or feat, क्रिया, कार्य, करतब, कर्म। 2. a notable achievement, कारनामा, महत्त्वपूर्ण उपलब्धि। 3. a legal contract, विलेख, पट्टा, दस्तावेज़।

deem (डीम) *v.* to consider, सोचना, विचार करना।

deep (डीप) *adj.* 1. extending far down from a surface, गहरा, अगाध। 2. extreme, intense, तीव्र, उत्कट, गंभीर। 3. low in pitch, resonant, मंद, मध्यम। 4. heart-felt, हार्दिक, हृदयस्पर्शी। 5. difficult to understand, गूढ़, गहन। 6. dark in shade, गहरा।

deeply (डीपली) *adj.* at a great depth, गहराई से।

deepness (डीपनिस) *n.* the quality or state of being deep, गहराई।

deer (डिअर) *n.* a hoofed and swift-footed animal, हिरन।

deerskin (डिअरस्किन) *n.* the skin of a deer, मृगछाला।

deface (डिफ़ेस) *v.* to spoil the appearance, विरूपित करना।

D

defalcation (डीफ़ैल्केशन) ***n.*** slander, ग़बन।

defamation (डेफ़मेशन) ***n.*** the act of defaming or the state or fact of being defamed, मानहानि।

defame (डिफ़ेम) ***v.*** to attack the good name or reputation of, बदनामी करना।

default (डिफ़ॉल्ट) ***n.*** a failure to act or fulfil an obligation or legal requirement, दोष, चूक।

defaulter (डिफ़ॉल्टर) ***n.*** one who commits a default, चूक करनेवाला, दोषी।

defeat (डिफ़ीट) ***v.*** to win victory over, to beat, पराजित करना, परास्त करना, हराना। ***n.*** loss of battle or same, पराजय, हार।

defecate (डेफ़िकेट) ***v.*** to empty the bowels of waste matter, मल त्यागना, शौच करना, हगना।

defect (डीफ़ेक्ट) ***n.*** a blemish, त्रुटि, दोष। ***v.*** to desert one's party and join another, दल-बदल करना।

defection (डिफ़ेक्शन) ***n.*** the act of defecting, दल-बदल।

defective (डिफ़ेक्टिव) ***adj.*** having a defect, त्रुटिपूर्ण, दोषपूर्ण।

defence, defense (डिफ़ेन्स) ***n.*** 1. resistance against danger or attack, बचाव, रक्षा, सुरक्षा। 2. protection of a country against an opponent, रक्षा, प्रतिरक्षा। 3. taking measures against the prosecutor's complaint, प्रतिवाद। 4. the proceedings by a defendant for defending himself in a law-suit, प्रतिवाद। 5. one or more lawyers who defend someone in a court, बचाव-पक्ष। 6. the defending players in the team, प्रतिरक्षा।

defenceless (डिफ़ेन्सलिस) ***adj.*** unable to defend himself, अरक्षित, असहाय।

defend (डिफ़ेन्ड) ***v.*** 1. to protect from attack, harm or danger, रक्षा या बचाव करना, सुरक्षा करना। 2. to try to preserve a title etc. in sports, रक्षा करना। 3. to uphold by argument in a law-suit, प्रतिवाद करना।

defendant (डिफ़ेन्डेन्ट) ***n.*** a person sued in a court of law, प्रतिवादी।

defender (डिफ़ेन्डर) ***n.*** one who defends, प्रतिरक्षक।

defensive (डिफ़ेन्सिव) ***adj.*** intended for defence, रक्षात्मक, प्रतिरक्षात्मक।

defer (डिफ़र) ***v.*** to postpone, आस्थगित करना।

deference (डेफ़रेन्स) ***n.*** respect, regard, मान, सम्मान, आदर।

defiance (डिफ़ाइएन्स) ***n.*** the act of defying, अवज्ञा, उल्लंघन।

defiant (डिफ़ाइएन्ट) ***adj.*** 1. opposing or challenging, प्रतिरोध करनेवाला, चुनौती देनेवाला। 2. openly disobeying, खुल्लम-खुल्ला अवज्ञा करनेवाला।

deficiency (डिफ़िशन्सी) ***n.*** want, lack, अभाव, कमी।

deficient (डिफ़िशन्ट) ***adj.*** insufficient, wanting, अपूर्ण, त्रुटिपूर्ण।

deficit (डेफ़िसिट) ***n.*** 1. shortage, कमी। 2. the excess of liabilities over assets, घाटा।

defile (डिफ़ाइल) ***v.*** 1. make filthy, गंदा कर देना। 2. to corrupt, भ्रष्ट कर देना।

define (डिफ़ाइन) ***v.*** 1. to give the

definition of, परिभाषित करना। 2. to limit, सीमित करना।

definite (डेफ़िनिट) ***adj.*** having exact or distinct limits, निश्चित, नियत।

definition (डेफ़िनिशन) ***n.*** the statement about the meaning of a word or term, परिभाषा।

deflate (डिफ़्लेट) ***v.*** 1. to let the air or gas release from, हवा निकाल देना। 2. to reduce inflated prices, मुद्रास्फीति कम करना।

deflation (डिफ़्लेशन) ***n.*** the act of reducing the amount of money in circulation, अवस्फीति।

deflect (डिफ़्लेक्ट) ***v.*** 1. to turn aside, मुड़ जाना, मुड़ना। 2. to cause to turn aside, मोड़ देना। 3. to go astray, पथभ्रष्ट या पथच्युत होना।

deflection (डिफ़्लेक्शन) ***n.*** the act of going astray, विपथन, पथच्युति, विचलन।

defoliate (डीफ़ोलिएट) ***v.*** to strip off leaves, पत्रविहीन या पत्ररहित करना।

deforest (डीफ़ॉरिस्ट) ***v.*** to cut down forests, वनों को नष्ट करना।

deform (डिफ़ॉर्म) ***v.*** to spoil the form of, विरूपित करना।

deformation (डिफ़ॉर्मेशन) ***n.*** the act of deforming or the state of being deformed, विरूपण, विकृति।

deformity (डिफ़ॉर्मिटी) ***n.*** 1. the condition of being deformed, विरूपता, विकृति। 2. a deformed part of the body, विकृत अंग।

defraud (डिफ्रॉड) ***v.*** to take away by fraud, ठग लेना, झँस लेना।

defray (डिफ्रे) ***v.*** to meet or pay out, भुगतान करना, चुकाना।

defrost (डिफ्रॉस्ट) ***v.*** to make free from ice, बर्फ़ गलाकर हटाना।

deft (डेफ़्ट) ***adj.*** skillful, कुशल, दक्ष।

deftness (डेफ़्टनिस) ***n.*** the quality of being deft, कुशलता, दक्षता।

defunct (डिफ़ंक्ट) ***adj.*** 1. no longer functioning, no longer in existence or use, निष्क्रिय। 2. without life, lifeless, dead, निष्प्राण, निर्जीव, मृत।

defuse (डिफ़्यूज़) ***v.*** 1. to remove the fuse of (a bomb etc.), फ्यूज़ हटा देना (ताकि बम फटे नहीं)। 2. to make calm, शांत करना।

defy (डिफ़ाइ) ***v.*** 1. to refuse to obey, अवज्ञा करना, कहना मानने से इन्कार करना। 2. to challenge, चुनौती देना, ललकारना। 3. to resist successfully, सफलतापूर्वक प्रतिरोध करना।

degenerate (डिजेनरेट) ***v.*** to deteriorate, गिरावट आना, अपभ्रष्ट होना।

degeneration (डिजेनरेशन) ***n.*** the process of degenerating or the state of being degenerated, अपकर्ष, गिरावट।

degradation (डेग्रडेशन) ***n.*** the state of being degraded, पदावनति, अवनति, अधोगति।

degrade (डिग्रेड) ***v.*** 1. to reduce to a lower rank or position, पदावनत करना, दर्जा घटा देना। 2. to debase, अधोगति को प्राप्त होना। 3. to corrupt, भ्रष्ट होना या करना।

degree (डिग्री) ***n.*** 1. one of a series of steps or stages, क्रम, सोपान, कोटि, दर्जा। 2. an academic title or official rank, डिग्री, पदवी, उपाधि। 3. a unit of measurement, डिग्री, अंश, इकाई। 4. relative extent, आपेक्षिक सीमा।

dehydration (डीहाइड्रेशन) ***n.*** the act of dehydrating or the state of being dehydrated, निर्जलीकरण।

deify (डीइफ़ाइ) ***v.*** 1. to treat as a god, ईश्वर या देवता के रूप में स्वीकार करना। 2. to worship, पूजा करना।

deity (डीइटी) ***n.*** a god or goddess, देवता या देवी।

deject (डिजेक्ट) ***v.*** to dishearten, हतोत्साहित करना, दिल तोड़ देना।

dejected (डिजेक्टिड) ***adj.*** depressed, downhearted, उदास, निराश।

delay (डिले) ***v.*** to make or be late, देर करना या होना, विलंब करना या होना। ***n.*** the act of delaying or the state of being delayed, देरी, विलंब।

delegate (डेलिगेट) ***n.*** a representative, प्रतिनिधि, नुमाइंदा। ***v.*** to give or transfer powers or duties to another as representative, प्रतिनिधि बनाना, प्रतिनिधि बनाकर अपने अधिकार आदि उसे सौंपना।

delegation (डेलिगेशन) ***n.*** a body of delegates, प्रतिनिधिमंडल, शिष्टमंडल।

delete (डिलीट) ***v.*** to strike out or omit something written or printed, काट, निकाल या हटा देना।

deletion (डिलीशन) ***n.*** the act of deleting something written or printed, काट या निकाल देने की क्रिया या भाव।

deliberate[1] (डिलिबरेट) ***adj.*** 1. fully considered, सुविचारित। 2. intentional, सोद्देश्य। 3. careful, सतर्कतापूर्ण।

deliberate[2] (डिलिबरेट) ***v.*** 1. to think over, सोचना-विचारना। 2. to discuss carefully, अच्छी तरह विचार-विमर्श करना।

deliberation (डिलिबरेशन) ***n.*** careful consideration, चिंतन-मनन, सोच-विचार।

delicacy (डेलिकेसी) ***n.*** 1. delicateness, कोमलता, नज़ाकत। 2. refinement of feeling, सुशीलता, शालीनता। 3. a rare or costly dish, बढ़िया व्यंजन या मिठाई।

delicate (डेलिकेट) ***adj.*** 1. tender, कोमल, नाज़ुक। 2. fragile or frail, नाज़ुक, कमज़ोर। 3. delicious, savoury, स्वादिष्ट, सुस्वादु, मज़ेदार। 4. elegant, fine, उत्कृष्ट, उत्तम।

delicious (डिलिशस) ***adj.*** 1. palatable, tasty, savoury, स्वादिष्ट, मज़ेदार। 2. delightful, आनंददायक।

delight (डिलाइट) ***v.*** 1. to take great pleasure in, आनंद या मज़ा लेना, ख़ुश होना। 2. to please greatly, ख़ुश कर देना, मज़ा देना। ***n.*** great pleasure, आनंद, ख़ुशी, मज़ा।

delightful (डिलाइटफ़ुल) ***adj.*** giving delight, आनंदप्रद।

delineate (डिलिनिएट) ***v.*** to portray by drawing or de-scription, चित्रित करना।

delineation (डिलिनिएशन) ***n.*** the act of delineating or something delineated, चित्रण।

delinquency (डिलिंक्वेन्सी) ***n.*** a psychological tendency to commit offences against the law, अपराधवृत्ति।

delinquent (डिलिंक्वेन्ट) ***n.*** a person guilty of an offence or misdeed, अपराधी।

delirious (डिलिरिअस) ***adj.*** 1. affected with delirium, उन्मादग्रस्त। 2. wildly excited, उन्मत्त।

delirium (डिलिरिअम) ***n.*** a state of mental disorder due to shock or injury, उन्माद, विक्षिप्तता।

deliver (डिलिवर) ***v.*** 1. to hand over, सौंपना, प्रदान करना, देना। 2. to throw or hurl, फेंकना, डालना। 3. to utter (a speech, भाषण) करना या देना। 4. to give (a blow) देना, लगाना, मारना। 5. to rescue, बचाना। 6. to set free, उद्धार/मुक्त करना।

delivery (डिलिवरी) ***n.*** 1. the act of delivering, वितरण, सुपुर्दगी। 2. the act or manner of delivering (a speech, भाषण) देने की कला। 3. the act or manner of delivering (a ball, गेंद) फेंकने का ढंग या शैली। 4. a rescuing or being rescued, मुक्ति, मोक्ष।

dell (डेल) ***n.*** a small valley, छोटी घाटी।

delta (डेल्टा) ***n.*** a triangular track of land at the mouth of a river, मुहाना।

delude (डिल्यूड) ***v.*** to deceive, धोख़ा देना।

deluge (डेल्यूज) ***n.*** 1. a great flood, जलप्रलय। 2. a heavy downpour of water, घोर वर्षा। ***v.*** 1. to cause flood, बाढ़ लाना। 2. to arrive in a large number, बड़ी मात्रा में आना या उपस्थित होना। 3. to submerge, डूब जाना या डुबा देना।

delusion (डिल्यूज़न) ***n.*** a mistaken idea, भ्रम।

deluxe, de luxe (डिलक्स) ***adj.*** superior in quality, उच्चकोटि का।

delve (डेल्व) ***v.*** to search, खोज करना।

demand (डिमान्ड) ***v.*** 1. to ask for, माँगना, कहना। 2. to need or require, आवश्यकता होना, ज़रूरत होना, चाहना। ***n.*** 1. the act of demanding or something demanded, माँग। 2. something that requires special effort or sacrifice, तक़ाज़ा, माँग।

demarcate (डिमार्केट) ***v.*** to determine and mark the boundaries of, सीमांकन करना, हदबंदी करना।

demarcation (डिमार्केशन) ***n.*** the act of demarcating, सीमांकन, हदबंदी।

demean (डिमीन) ***v.*** to debase in dignity or stature, मान घटाना।

demeanour, demeanor (डिमीनर) ***n.*** 1. behaviour, व्यवहार, बरताव। 2. deportment, रवैया, तौर-तरीक़ा।

demented (डिमेन्टिड) ***adj.*** 1. crazy, ख़ब्ती। 2. insane, पागल, विक्षिप्त।

dementia (डिमेन्शिआ) ***n.*** mental deterioration, उन्मत्तता, विक्षिप्तता।

demerit (डीमेरिट) ***n.*** a bad point of character, अवगुण, बुराई।

demise (डिमाइज़) ***n.*** death, मृत्यु, मौत।

democracy (डिमॉक्रसी) ***n.*** a system of government run by the elected representatives of the people, जनतंत्र, लोकतंत्र।

democrat (डेमोक्रैट) ***n.*** an advocate of democracy, लोकतंत्रवादी, जनतंत्रवादी।

democratic (डेमोक्रैटिक) ***adj.*** of or pertaining to democracy, जनतांत्रिक।

demolish (डिमॉलिश) ***v.*** 1. to tear down completely, ढा/गिरा देना, तोड़ देना। 2. to destroy, नष्ट या उन्मूलित कर देना।

demolition (डेमोलिशन) ***n.*** the act of demolishing or the state of being demolished, ध्वंस, विध्वंस।

demon (डीमन) ***n.*** 1. a devil, राक्षस, दानव, दैत्य। 2. a cruel person, नृशंस व्यक्ति।

demonstrate (डेमन्स्ट्रेट) ***v.*** 1. to display something, प्रदर्शित या निदर्शित करना। 2. to take part in a demonstration, प्रदर्शन करना।

demonstration (डेमन्स्ट्रेशन) ***n.*** 1. a gathering of agitators to express their strong feelings publicly against authorities, (सार्वजनिक) प्रदर्शन। 2. an experiment showing how something works, प्रदर्शन।

demonstrative (डिमॉन्स्ट्रेटिव) ***adj.*** pertaining to demonstrations, प्रदर्शनात्मक।

demoralize (डिमॉरैलाइज़) ***v.*** to corrupt, भ्रष्ट करना।

demote (डिमोट) ***v.*** to lower in rank, पदावनत करना, दर्जा घटाना।

demotion (डिमोशन) ***n.*** the act of demoting or the state of being demoted, पदावनति।

demure (डिम्यूर) ***adj.*** quiet and serious, धीर-गंभीर, शालीन।

den (डेन) ***n.*** 1. a lair of a wild animal, माँद, खोह। 2. a place used as a hideout, चोरों आदि के छिपने की गुफा।

dengue (डेन्गे) ***n.*** a fever causing acute pain, डेंगू ज्वर।

denial (डिनाइअल) ***n.*** 1. the act of denying or the state of being denied, इन्कार, नकार। 2. a refusal, अस्वीकृति। 3. a statement denying something, खंडन।

denim (डेनिम) ***n.*** a kind of cotton fabric, एक तरह का सूती कपड़ा।

denomination (डिनॉमिनेशन) ***n.*** a particular religious body, पंथ, संप्रदाय।

denounce (डिनाउन्स) ***v.*** to condemn or censure, बुराई करना।

dense (डेन्स) ***adj.*** thick, घना, सघन।

density (डेन्सिटी) ***n.*** the measure of the compactness of a substance, सघनता, घनत्व।

dent (डेन्ट) ***n.*** a mark made by pressure or a blow, गड्ढा, छेद।

dental (डेन्टल) ***adj.*** of or related to the teeth, दाँत-संबंधी, दंत्य।

dentist (डेन्टिस्ट) ***n.*** a doctor who treats the teeth and gums, दंत-चिकित्सक।

denture (डेन्चर) ***n.*** a set of artificial teeth, नकली बत्तीसी।

denude (डिन्यूड) ***v.*** to make naked, नंगा करना।

denunciation (डिनन्सिएशन) ***n.*** the act of denouncing, निंदा, बुराई।

deny (डिनाइ) ***v.*** to refuse to accept, अस्वीकार करना।

depart (डिपार्ट) ***v.*** 1. to go away, to leave, चल देना, जाना। 2. to start, रवाना होना, चल पड़ना। 3. to deviate, मार्ग से हट-बढ़ जाना। 4. to die, मर जाना।

departed (डिपार्टिड) ***adj.*** dead, दिवंगत, मृत।

department (डिपार्टमेन्ट) ***n.*** a separate division or branch, विभाग, शाखा।

departure (डिपार्चर) ***n.*** the act of departing, a starting out, प्रस्थान, रवानगी।

depend (डिपेन्ड) ***v.*** 1. to rely on, निर्भर होना। 2. to place trust on, भरोसा करना।

dependable (डिपेन्डेबल) ***adj.*** trustworthy, विश्वसनीय, भरोसे का।

dependence (डिपेन्डेन्स) ***n.*** 1. the state of being dependent, निर्भरता, अवलंबन। 2. reliance, भरोसा, सहारा, आश्रय।

dependent (डिपेन्डेन्ट) ***adj.*** depending, आश्रित, पराश्रित।

depict (डिपिक्ट) ***v.*** 1. to show or represent in a picture, चित्रित करना, चित्रांकन करना। 2. to describe, वर्णन करना।

D

depiction (डिपिक्शन) ***n.*** the act of depicting or something depicted, चित्रण, सजीव वर्णन।

deplorable (डिप्लोरेबल) ***adj.*** regrettable, pitiable, खेदजनक, शोचनीय।

deplore (डिप्लोर) ***v.*** to express strong disapproval of, निंदा करना, कोसना।

deploy (डिप्लॉइ) ***v.*** to spread out (troops) (सेना को) चारों ओर फैलाना।

depopulate (डीपॉपुलेट) ***v.*** to be or cause to be reduced in population, जनसंख्या कम होना या कम करना।

deport (डिपोर्ट) ***v.*** 1. to expel by law, निर्वासित करना। 2. to behave, आचरण/व्यवहार करना।

deportation (डिपोर्टेशन) ***n.*** act of expelling, निर्वासन, देश-निकाला।

deportment (डिपोर्टमेन्ट) ***n.*** 1. behaviour, व्यवहार। 2. demeanour, रवैया, तौर-तरीक़ा।

depose (डिपोज़) ***v.*** to remove from the throne, गद्दी से उतार देना।

deposit (डिपॉज़िट) ***v.*** to store or entrust for safe-keeping, जमा करना, धरोहर रखना, ज़मानत रखना। ***n.*** 1. the act of depositing or something deposited, जमा, निक्षेप। 2. the money or valuables so entrusted, धरोहर, अमानत, जमा।

deposition (डेपोज़िशन) ***n.*** the act of deposing or being deposed from throne, power or post, पदच्युति।

depositor (डिपॉजिटर) ***n.*** one who deposits, जमाकर्ता।

depot (डीपो) ***n.*** 1. a place where goods are stored or deposited, डिपो। 2. a bus station, बस डिपो, बस अड्डा।

deprave (डिप्रेव) ***v.*** to make morally bad, चरित्रभ्रष्ट करना।

depraved (डिप्रेव्ड) ***adj.*** 1. corrupt, अधम, भ्रष्ट। 2. wicked, दुष्ट, दुराचारी, पापी।

deprecate (डेप्रिकेट) ***v.*** to protest against, विरोध या आपत्ति करना।

depreciate (डिप्रीशिएट) ***v.*** to make or become lower in value, मूल्य (या महत्त्व) गिरना या गिराना, मुद्रा का अवमूल्यन होना या करना।

depreciation (डिप्रीशिएशन) ***n.*** the act of depreciating or the state of being depreciated, मूल्यह्रास, ह्रास।

depress (डिप्रेस) ***v.*** 1. to press down, दबाना। 2. to lower in spirits, हतोत्साहित होना या करना।

depression (डिप्रेशन) ***n.*** 1. a mental condition of sadness or gloom, अवसाद। 2. the period when the demand of goods is diminished, मंदी।

deprivation (डेप्रिवेशन) ***n.*** 1. a deprival, वंचन। 2. be-reavement, दुखद वियोग।

deprive (डिप्राइव) ***v.*** to dispossess, वंचित करना।

deprived (डिप्राइव्ड) ***adj.*** dispossessed, वंचित।

depth (डेप्थ) ***n.*** 1. deepness, गहराई। 2. profundity, विदग्धता। 3. intensity (of colour, रंग का) गहरापन, तेज़ी।

deputation (डेपुटेशन) ***n.*** a delegation, प्रतिनिधिमंडल, शिष्टमंडल।

depute (डिप्यूट) ***v.*** 1. to appoint as an agent, प्रतिनिधि नियुक्त करना, प्रतिनियुक्त करना। 2. to assign (a task or authority) to a deputy, (कार्य, भार) सौंपना।

D

deputy (डेप्यूटी) ***n.*** a person appointed to act on behalf of another, डिप्टी (साहब)। ***prefix*** assistant, उप।

derange (डीरेन्ज) ***v.*** to put out of order, अव्यवस्थित कर देना, अस्त-व्यस्त कर देना।

deride (डिराइड) ***v.*** to ridicule, हँसी उड़ाना, उपहास करना।

derision (डिरिज़न) ***n.*** ridicule, उपहास, हँसी।

derivation (डेरिवेशन) ***n.*** a source to which a word or thing is traced, व्युत्पत्ति।

derivative (डेरिवेटिव) ***adj.*** derived from a source, व्युत्पन्न।

derive (डिराइव) ***v.*** 1. to obtain from a source. (से) प्राप्त होना या करना। 2. to be produced or descended from, (से) व्युत्पन्न या उत्पन्न होना।

derogatory (डिरॉगेटरी) ***adj.*** disparaging, अपमानसूचक।

descend (डिसेन्ड) ***v.*** 1. to come or go down, नीचे आना, नीचे उतरना। 2. to slope or incline downward, ढलना। 3. to be derived from ancestors, to pass by inheritance, विरासत में मिलना। 4. to make a sudden attack, चढ़ जाना। 5. to stoop (to meanness, कमीनेपन पर) उतर आना।

descendant, descendent (डिसेन्डेन्ट) ***n.*** one descended from an ancestor, वंशज, वंशधर।

descent (डिसेन्ट) ***n.*** 1. the act of descending, उतार, अवरोह। 2. slope, ढाल, ढलान। 3. family origins, कुल, वंश। 4. ancestry, वंश-परंपरा, पीढ़ी। 5. a sudden attack, धावा। 6. a decline, उतार, पतन, अवनति।

describe (डिस्क्राइब) ***v.*** to give description of, वर्णन करना।

description (डिस्क्रिप्शन) ***n.*** the act of describing, वर्णन।

descriptive (डिस्क्रिप्टिव) ***adj.*** full of description, giving a description, वर्णनात्मक।

desecrate (डेसिक्रेट) ***v.*** to abuse the sacredness of, अपवित्र करना।

desecration (डेसिक्रेशन) ***n.*** the act of desecrating, अपवित्रीकरण।

desert[1] (डेज़र्ट) ***n.*** a barren and sand-covered region, रेगिस्तान, मरुस्थल। ***adj.*** uninhabited, वीरान, निर्जन।

desert[2] (डिज़र्ट) ***v.*** 1. to forsake or abandon, परित्याग करना। 2. to run away from (one's work) or leave (one's service) (काम या नौकरी) छोड़ भागना।

deserter (डिज़र्टर) ***n.*** one who deserts, छोड़ भागनेवाला, भगोड़ा।

desertion (डिज़र्शन) ***n.*** 1. the act of deserting, परित्याग। 2. running away from, पलायन।

deserve (डिज़र्व) ***v.*** to be worthy of, अधिकारी/पात्र होना।

deservedly (डिज़र्विडली) ***adv.*** as is right or fair, उचित रूप से, न्यायतः।

deserving (डिज़र्विंग) ***adj.*** worthy or help or support, सुपात्र, भाजन।

design (डिज़ाइन) ***v.*** 1. to prepare a sketch or drawing, डिज़ाइन बनाना, ख़ाका खींचना या बनाना, रूपरेखा तैयार करना। 2. to work out a plan, योजना बनाना। ***n.*** 1. a sketch or drawing, डिज़ाइन, ख़ाका, रूपरेखा। 2. an artistic or decorative work, डिज़ाइन, अभिकल्प, रूपांकन। 3. an intention, इरादा, इच्छा, योजना।

designate (डेज़िग्नेट) *v.* to appoint to a position, मनोनीत करना, नियुक्त करना।

designer (डिज़ाइनर) *n.* a person who designs, डिज़ाइनर।

desirable (डिज़ाइरेबल) *adj.* 1. worth desiring, वांछनीय, मनचाहा, अभीष्ट। 2. advisable, स्पृहणीय, अच्छा, उचित, मुनासिब।

desire (डिज़ाइर) *n.* a wish, craving, इच्छा, चाह। *v.* to wish, इच्छा करना, चाहना।

desirous (डिज़ाइरस) *adj.* wishing, desiring, इच्छुक।

desist (डिज़िस्ट) *v.* 1. to discontinue or to cease doing (किसी काम से) बाज़ आना।

desk (डेस्क) *n.* a piece of furniture with a flat top for writing, डेस्क।

desolate (डेसोलिट) *adj.* 1. deserted, निर्जन, उजाड़। 2. lonely, एकाकी। 3. dismal, अंधकारमय। *v.* to devastate, उजाड़ देना, नष्ट कर देना।

desolation (डेसोलेशन) *n.* the condition of being devastated, ध्वंस, विनाश।

despair (डिस्पेअर) *n.* utter lack or loss of hope, निराशा। *v.* to lose all hope, निराश होना, उम्मीद छोड़ बैठना।

desperate (डेस्परिट) *adj.* 1. utterly hopeless, अत्यंत निराशमय। 2. violent because of despair, बौखलाया हुआ, निराशोन्मत्त। 3. serious, गंभीर।

desperation (डेस्परेशन) *n.* 1. the condition of being desperate, घोर निराशा। 2. recklessness arising from despair, निराशाजन्य व्यग्रता, उद्विग्नता, दुस्साहस।

despicable (डेस्पिकेबल) *adj.* deserving contempt, contemptible, निंदनीय, घृणित।

despise (डिस्पाइज़) *v.* 1. to regard with contempt, घृणित या जघन्य समझना, घृणा करना। 2. to feel disrespect for, अपमान करना।

despite (डिस्पाइट) *prep.* in spite of, के बावजूद, के होने पर भी।

despoil (डिस्पॉइल) *v.* to rob or plunder, लूट लेना।

despondent (डिस्पॉन्डेन्ट) *adj.* dejected, उदास, खिन्न, निराश।

despot (डेस्पॉट) *n.* an oppressive ruler, निरंकुश शासक।

despotic (डिस्पॉटिक) *adj.* having unrestricted power, स्वेच्छाचारी, अत्याचारपूर्ण।

dessert (डिज़र्ट) *n.* a sweet dish served as the last course of a meal, भोजन के अंत में परोसा जानेवाला मधुर व्यंजन।

destination (डेस्टिनेशन) *n.* the place to which a person or something is going, मंज़िल, गंतव्य।

destiny (डेस्टिनी) *n.* 1. fate, fortune, भाग्य, क़िस्मत। 2. that which must or had to happen, होनी।

destitute (डेस्टिट्यूट) *adj.* 1. totally impoverished, अकिंचन, निर्धन, दरिद्र। 2. without refuge or shelter, बेसहारा, असहाय।

destroy (डिस्ट्रॉइ) *v.* 1. to spoil or ruin completely, नष्ट कर देना, तबाह या बरबाद करना। 2. to demolish, ढा देना, विध्वस्त कर देना। 3. to kill, मार डालना। 4. to put out of existence, मटियामेट कर देना।

destroyer (डिस्ट्रॉइअर) *n.* 1. one who destroys, विनाशक,

D

विध्वंसक। 2. a warship, एक प्रकार का युद्धपोत।

destruction (डिस्ट्रक्शन) ***n.*** the act of destroying or something destroyed, ruin, विनाश, ध्वंस।

destructive (डिस्ट्रक्टिव) ***adj.*** causing destruction, विनाशकारी, विध्वंसक।

detach (डिटैच) ***v.*** to disconnect, अलग कर देना।

detachment (डिटैचमेन्ट) ***n.*** the act of detaching or the state of being detached, अलगाव, पार्थक्य, बिलगाव।

detail (डिटेल) ***n.*** 1. a small point or fact, बात, तथ्य। 2. such small points or facts considered together, ब्योरा, तफ़सील, विवरण।

detailed (डिटेल्ड) ***adj.*** giving all facts available, पूरे ब्योरे सहित, ब्योरेवार।

detain (डिटेन) ***v.*** 1. to keep from proceeding, रोक लेना, रोक रखना, जाने न देना। 2. to arrest, गिरफ्तार करना।

detect (डिटेक्ट) ***v.*** 1. to find out, पता लगाना। 2. to notice, भाँप या जान लेना। 3. to discover or reveal a crime or criminal, अपराधी को पकड़ लेना, अपराध को पहचान लेना।

detective (डिटेक्टिव) ***n.*** one who is expert in investigating crimes, जासूस, गुप्तचर।

detention (डिटेन्शन) ***n.*** 1. the action of detaining or the state of being kept in custody, नज़रबंदी। 2. a prison, कारावास।

detenu (डेटनू) ***n.*** a person detained in a prison, कारारुद्ध, नज़रबंद।

deter (डिटर) ***v.*** (deterred, deterring) 1. to prevent from doing, रोकना, मना करना। 2. to discourage, हतोत्साहित करना।

detergent (डिटर्जेन्ट) ***n.*** a synthetic substance for cleansing, डिटर्जेन्ट, धोने या साफ़ करनेवाला द्रव्य, साबुन आदि, स्वच्छक पदार्थ। ***adj.*** having a cleansing effect, स्वच्छ करनेवाला, स्वच्छक।

deteriorate (डिटिरिअरेट) ***v.*** 1. to become worse, बिगड़ना, विकृत होना, ख़राब होना। 2. to wear away, क्षय होना, छीजना।

deterioration (डिटिरिअरेशन) ***n.*** the process of growing worse, the condition of being deteriorated, ह्रास, अपकर्ष, क्षय।

determination (डिटर्मिनेशन) ***n.*** formal intention, पक्का इरादा, संकल्प।

determine (डिटर्मिन) ***v.*** (determined, determining) 1. to decide, निश्चय करना। 2. to be a decisive factor, निर्धारक होना।

determined (डिटर्मिन्ड) ***adj.*** showing determination, firm, कृतसंकल्प।

deterrent (डिटरेन्ट) ***adj.*** that deters, रोकनेवाला, रोक-थाम करनेवाला।

detest (डिटेस्ट) ***v.*** to dislike intensely, बहुत अधिक घृणा करना।

dethrone (डीथ्रोन) ***v.*** 1. to remove from a throne, सिंहासन या गद्दी से उतार देना। 2. to remove from power, अपदस्थ करना।

detonate (डेटोनेट) ***v.*** to explode, विस्फोट होना/करना।

detonation (डेटोनेशन) ***n.*** a loud explosion, ज़ोरदार धमाका, विस्फोट।

detonator (डेटोनेटर) ***n.*** a device to set off an explosion from a distance, विस्फोटक, डेटोनेटर।

detractor (डिट्रैक्टर) ***n.*** one who says bad things about someone or something, निंदक, आलोचक।

detrain (डिट्रेन) ***v.*** to get off a railway train, रेलगाड़ी से उतरना या उतारना।

detrimental (डेट्रिमेन्टल) ***adj.*** harmful, अहितकर, हानिकर।

devaluation (डीवैल्युएशन) ***n.*** the act of reducing the exchange value of money, अवमूल्यन।

devalue (डीवैल्यू) ***v.*** to reduce the value of one's currency in relation to other currencies, अवमूल्यन करना।

devastate (डेवस्टेट) ***v.*** to ruin, उजाड़ देना, विनष्ट, कर देना।

devastation (डेवस्टेशन) ***n.*** the act of devastating or the state of being devastated, विनाश, बरबादी।

develop (डिवेलप) ***v.*** 1. to become or grow larger, complete or more complex, विकसित होना, पनपना। 2. to cause to grow larger, विकसित करना। 3. to expand or elaborate, विस्तृत या विस्तीर्ण करना, फैलाना, बढ़ाना। 4. to make economically developed, आर्थिक दृष्टि से विकसित करना। 5. (in photography, to) appear or cause to appear on a film or paper, डेवलप करना, फोटो-प्लेट या फ़िल्म धोना।

developed (डिवेलप्ड) ***adj.*** grown larger, complete or complex, विकसित।

developing ***adj.*** progressing economically, विकासशील।

development (डिवेलपमेन्ट) ***n.*** 1. the act or process of developing or the state of being developed, विकास। 2. a happening, घटना। 3. (plu.) things that have developed, गतिविधियाँ, घटनाक्रम।

deviate (डीविएट) ***v.*** to move away from an accepted, course, पथभ्रष्ट हो जाना, विपथित होना।

deviation (डीविएशन) ***n.*** an act or instance of deviating, मार्गच्युति।

device (डिवाइस) ***n.*** 1. an instrument or machine, उपकरण या मशीन। 2. an arrangement or plan, योजना, व्यवस्था। 3. a trick, युक्ति, तिकड़म, चाल।

devil (डेविल) ***n.*** 1. an evil spirit, दुष्टात्मा, शैतान। 2. a wicked or mischievous person, दुष्ट व्यक्ति।

devious (डीविअस) ***adj.*** 1. deviating from the right course, विपथित, पथभ्रष्ट। 2. not straightforward, कुटिल, अनाचारी। 3. underhand, कपटपूर्ण।

devise (डिवाइज़) ***v.*** 1. to plan, सोचना, योजना बनाना। 2. to invent, आविष्कार करना।

devoid (डिवॉइड) ***adj.*** completely lacking, विहीन या रहित।

devolve (डिवॉल्व) ***v.*** to pass on to a successor or deputy, उत्तराधिकारी या सहायक को सौंपना।

devote (डिवोट) ***v.*** 1. to dedicate, समर्पित करना। 2. to give or apply entirely, अर्पित करना, लगा देना।

devoted (डिवोटिड) ***adj.*** 1. loyal, निष्ठावान्। 2. fond of, शौक़ीन।

devotee (डेवोटी) ***n.*** a devoted person, भक्त, श्रद्धालु।

devotion (डिवोशन) ***n.*** 1. great loyalty, श्रद्धा, निष्ठा। 2. religious observance or worship, भक्ति, पूजा। 3. great love, zeal, अनुराग, लगन।

devotional (डिवोशनल) ***adj.*** of or related to devotion, भक्तिपूर्ण।

devour (डिवॉउर) ***v.*** to eat up greedily, ठूँसना।

devout (डिवॉउट) ***adj.*** **& *n.*** seriously

D

concerned with religion, श्रद्धालु, भक्त।

dew (ड्यू) ***n.*** water droplets that condense on cool surfaces during the night, ओस, शबनम।

dexterity (डेक्स्टेरिटी) ***n.*** skill, दक्षता।

dexterous, dextrous (डेक्स्ट्रस) ***adj.*** skillful, दक्ष।

diabetes (डाइअबीटीज़) ***n.*** a disease in which there is excessive sugar in the blood, मधुमेह।

diabetic (डाइअबेटिक) ***n.*** a person suffering from diabetes, मधुमेह का रोगी।

diabolic (डाइअबॉलिक) ***adj.*** of or coming from the devil, राक्षसी, पैशाचिक।

diagnose (डाइअग्नोज़) ***v.*** to identify a disease from its signs and symptoms, (रोग का) निदान करना।

diagnosis (डाइअग्नोसिस) ***n.*** identification of a disease, निदान।

diagonal (डाइएगनल) ***n.*** a straight line joining two opposite corners of a square, विकर्ण। ***adj.*** oblique, slanting, तिरछा, विकर्णी।

diagram (डाइअग्रैम) ***n.*** 1. a figure or plan drawn to explain an idea, आरेख। ***v.*** to depict by a diagram, आरेख बनाना, आरेखित करना।

dial (डाइअल) ***n.*** a movable disc of a telephone with finger holes over a circle of numbers, डायल। ***v.*** to make a telephone call, डायल करना।

dialect (डाइअलेक्ट) ***n.*** a variety of a language spoken in a particular area, बोली, विभाषा।

dialogue (डाइअलॉग) ***n.*** 1. a conversation, वार्तालाप।

dialysis (डाइऐलिसिस) ***n.*** an act of purifying the blood of the body, रक्त-शोधन, डायलसिस।

diameter (डाइऐमिटर) ***n.*** a straight line passing from side to side of a circle through the centre, व्यास।

diamond (डाइमन्ड) ***n.*** 1. a very hard precious stone, हीरा। 2. a playing card marked with such a figure or figures, ईंट का पत्ता।

diamond jubilee ***n.*** the sixtieth anniversary, हीरक जयंती।

diaphragm (डाइअफ़्रैम) ***n.*** a muscular membrane that separates the organ of the chest from those of the abdomen, मध्यपट।

diarrhoea, diarrhea (डाइअरिआ) ***n.*** abnormally frequent bowel movement, अतिसार, दस्त लगना।

diary (डाइअरी) ***n.*** 1. a daily record of the events in a person's life, डायरी, दैनिकी। 2. a book used for such a record, डायरी, दैनंदिनी।

dibble (डिबल) ***n.*** a pointed instrument used to make holes in the soil, सब्बल, कुदाली, खुरपी। ***v.*** to prepare soil with a dibble, सब्बल से ज़मीन तैयार करना, खुरपी से खुदाई करना।

dice (डाइस) ***n.*** (actually plu. of die) 1. one of small cube marked on each side with one to six dots, पाँसा। 2. a game of chance which is played with these, पाँसे का खेल, पाँसा।

dictaphone (डिक्टफ़ोन) ***n.*** a machine into which one can dictate, श्रुतलेख-यंत्र।

dictate (डिक्टेट) ***v.*** 1. to say or read aloud for someone else or others to write down, बोलकर लिखाना,

डिक्टेशन देना। 2. to give order to, आज्ञा देना।

dictation (डिक्टेशन) ***n.*** 1. act of dictating or something dictated, श्रुतलेख, इमला। 2. a command or order, आज्ञा, आदेश।

dictator (डिक्टेटर) ***n.*** a ruler who has absolute power or unrestricted authority, अधिनायक, तानाशाह।

diction (डिक्शन) ***n.*** 1. vocabulary, शब्दावली। 2. a manner of pronunciation, लहजा, उच्चारण-ढंग।

dictionary (डिक्शनरी) ***n.*** a book containing alphabetical list of words with their pronunciations, meanings, usages etc., कोश, शब्दकोश।

didactic (डाइडैक्टिक) ***adj.*** instructive, शिक्षाप्रद।

die[1] (डाइ) ***v.*** to cease living, मरना, मर जाना।

die[2] ***n.*** (plu. dice) a cube marked with dots used in the game of chance, पाँसा।

die[3] ***n.*** an engraved device that shapes materials by stamping, punching etc., डाई, ठप्पा, साँचा।

diehard (डाइहार्ड) ***n.*** a person who resists change to the end, हठधर्मी।

diesel (डीज़ल) ***n.*** an engine in which hot air sets fire to heavy oil, डीज़ल इंजन। ***v.*** a kind of heavy oil used in diesel engines, डीज़ल ऑयल।

diet (डाइअट) ***n.*** food usually taken by a person, family or group, आहार, ख़ुराक।

differ (डिफ़र) ***v.*** 1. to be unlike or distinguishable, भिन्न या अलग होना। 2. to disagree in opinion, मतभेद होना, राय न मिलना।

difference (डिफ़रेन्स) ***n.*** 1. the quality or state of being different or unlike, भिन्नता, विभिन्नता। 2. degree or amount of unlikeness, अंतर, फ़र्क। 3. the remainder left after subtraction, बाकी, शेष। 4. disagreement in opinion, मदभेद।

different (डिफ़रेन्ट) ***adj.*** 1. unlike in quality, nature, form etc., अलग भिन्न, विभिन्न। 2. another, अन्य, दूसरा, और।

differential (डिफ़रेन्शल) ***adj.*** of showing or constituting a difference, विभेदक।

differentiate (डिफ़रेन्शिएट) ***v.*** to distinguish or discriminate, अंतर या भेद करना।

difficult (डिफ़िक्ल्ट) ***adj.*** 1. hard to do or manage, कठिन, मुश्किल। 2. hard to understand, दुर्बोध, दुरूह। 3. hard to please, विकट, टेढ़ा।

difficulty (डिफ़िकल्टी) ***n.*** 1. a thing hard to do or overcome, कठिनाई, मुश्किल। 2. a problem or trouble, समस्या, झंझट या परेशानी।

diffident (डिफ़िडेन्ट) ***adj.*** lacking self-confidence, आत्मविश्वासहीन।

diffuse (डिफ़्यूज़) ***v.*** to spread or cause to spread in all directions, प्रसार करना।

diffusion (डिफ़्यूज़न) ***n.*** the act of diffusing, प्रसार।

dig (डिग) ***v.*** 1. to turn up soil with a spade, खोदना। 2. to make an excavation by digging, खुदाई करना।

digest[1] (डाइजेस्ट) ***v.*** 1. to absorb

D

(food, खाना) पचना या पचाना। 2. to comprehend, अच्छी तरह समझना।

digest[2] ***n.*** 1. a short account of a book, subject or other written material, संक्षेप, सार, सारसंग्रह। 2. a compilation or collection, संग्रह।

digestion (डाइजेस्चन) ***n.*** the power of digesting food, पाचन-शक्ति, हाज़मा।

digit (डिजिट) ***n.*** 1. any numeral from 0 to 9, अंक। 2. a finger or toe, उँगली, अँगूठा।

digital (डिजिटल) ***adj.*** of or relating to digits, अंक-संबंधी, अंकीय।

dignified (डिग्निफ़ाइड) ***adj.*** having, showing or expressing dignity, गौरवपूर्ण।

dignitary (डिग्निटरी) ***n.*** a person holding high office, उच्चपदस्थ।

dignity (डिग्निटी) ***n.*** honour, prestige, महत्ता, प्रतिष्ठा, सम्मान।

digress (डाइग्रेस) ***v.*** 1. to depart from the basic topic, point or subject, भटक जाना।

dike (डाइक) ***n.*** a ditch from land, खाई।

dilapidated (डिलैपिडेटिड) ***adj.*** in the state of disrepair, जर्जर, ख़स्ता।

dilapidation (डिलैपिडेशन) ***n.*** the state of being dilapidated, जर्जरता।

dilation (डाइलेशन) ***n.*** expansion, विस्तार, फैलाव।

dilatory (डिलेटरी) ***adj.*** causing delay or wasting time, विलंबकारी।

dilemma (डिलेमा) ***n.*** a situation that requires a choice between two equally unpleasant or undesirable alternatives, धर्मसंकट, दुविधा।

diligence (डिलिजेन्स) ***n.*** perseverance, अध्यवसाय।

diligent (डिलिजेन्ट) ***adj.*** persevering, अध्यवसायी।

dilly-dally (डिली-डैली) ***v.*** 1. to waste time, व्यर्थ समय नष्ट करना। 2. to vacillate, डाँवाँडोल/अस्थिर होना।

dilute (डाइल्यूट) ***v.*** to reduce in strength by addition of water or thinner, पतला करना, तनुकृत करना।

dilution (डाइल्यूशन) ***n.*** the act of diluting, पतला करना।

diluvial (डाइल्यूविअल) ***adj.*** of or connected with a deluge, प्रलय-संबंधी, प्रलयकारी।

dim (डिम) ***adj.*** faint, मंद, हलका।

dimension (डाइमेन्शन) ***n.*** a measurement in any one direction, आयाम।

dimensional (डाइमेन्शनल) ***adj.*** of or pertaining to a dimension, आयामी।

diminish (डिमिनिश) ***v.*** 1. to become less or smaller, घट जाना, कम हो जाना। 2. to make less or smaller, कम करना, घटा देना।

diminutive (डिमिन्युटिव) ***adj.*** very small, छोटा, ठिगना।

dimple (डिम्पल) ***n.*** a small hollow or dent on the cheeks or chin, गाल या ठोड़ी पर का गड्ढा।

din (डिन) ***n.*** loud, confused and prolonged noise, शोर, शोरगुल, हो-हल्ला, शोर-शराबा।

dine (डाइन) ***v.*** to eat dinner, भोजन करना।

diner (डाइनर) ***n.*** one who dines, भोज़न करनेवाला।

dinghy (डिंगी) ***n.*** a small boat, डोंगी।

dingy (डिन्जी) ***adj.*** 1. dirty, गंदा, मैला-कुचैला। 2. discoloured, बदरंग।

dinner (डिनर) ***n.*** 1. a meal taken

in the evening or night, रात का खाना। 2. a formal evening banquet, दावत, रात्रिभोज।

dinosaur (डाइनोसॉर) ***n.*** an extinct large-sized reptile, पुराने ज़माने का एक रेंगनेवाला विशाल जंतु, डाइनासोर।

diocese (डाइओसीज़) ***n.*** the district under the jurisdiction of a bishop, धर्मप्रांत।

dip (डिप) ***v.*** 1. to put or lower quickly or briefly into water or other liquid, पानी या घोल में डुबोकर निकालना। 2. to plunge into water and emerge quickly, डुबकी / गोता लगाना। ***n.*** a plunge, डुबकी, गोता।

diphtheria (डिफ़्थीरिआ) ***n.*** an infectious disease of the throat, कंठरोग।

diphthong (डिफ़्थॉन्ग) ***n.*** a compound vowel sound, द्विस्वर, संधि स्वर।

diploma (डिप्लोमा) ***n.*** a certificate conferring a qualification who has completed a course of study, उपाधि-पत्र, डिप्लोमा, सनद।

diplomacy (डिप्लोमेसी) ***n.*** 1. the skill or practice of conducting international relations, कूटनीति। 2. tact, व्यवहार-कुशलता, चतुराई।

diplomat (डिप्लोमैट) ***n.*** an official engaged in diplomacy, कूटनीतिज्ञ।

dire (डाइअर) ***adj.*** 1. dreadful, भीषण, भयानक। 2. urgent, अत्यावश्यक, ज़रूरी।

direct (डाइरेक्ट) ***v.*** 1. to manage or conduct the affairs of, संचालन करना, संचालित करना। 2. to give direction to, निर्देशन करना। 3. to aim, निशाना साधना। 4. to cause to have a specified direction, उन्मुख करना, मोड़ना, घुमाना। 5. to address (a letter etc.) पते पर भेजना। 6. to address (remarks etc.) (किसी को लक्षित करके) कहना। ***adj.*** 1. not curved, जो टेढ़ा-मेढ़ा या वक्र न हो, सीधा। 2. straightforward, सीधा, ईमानदार, भोला-भाला, निष्कपट। 3. total, पूरा। 4. in direct contact, without intervening agency, सीधा, प्रत्यक्ष। 5. main, मुख्य। 6. in an unbroken line of descent, सीधा। ***adv.*** directly, सीधे।

direction (डाइरेक्शन) ***n.*** 1. the act, process or function of directing or instructing, निर्देशन। 2. a command. आदेश, निर्देश। 3. the side or place towards which a person or thing moves, दिशा, तरफ़, सीध। 4. a line of action or a course, दिशा।

directive (डाइरेक्टिव) ***n.*** an instruction or order, निर्देश।

directly (डाइरेक्टली) ***adv.*** 1. in a direct manner, सीधे। 2. without delay, सीधे, तुरंत, अभी।

director (डाइरेक्टर) ***n.*** a person who supervises any institution or some kind of performance, निदेशक, निर्देशक, संचालक।

directorate (डाइरेक्टरिट) ***n.*** the office of a director, निदेशालय।

directory (डाइरेक्टरी) ***n.*** a book listing names, addresses, telephone numbers of the members of an institution, association or telephone users. निदेशिका।

dirge (डर्ज) ***n.*** 1. a chant of lamentation for the dead, विलाप। 2. a mournful song, शोक-गीत।

dirt (डर्ट) ***n.*** unclean substance, earth filth or soil, मिट्टी, गर्द, धूल, गर्द़ग़ुबार।

D

dirty (डर्टी) ***adj.*** 1. full of dirt, धूल-भरा, गंदा। 2. unclean, मैला-कुचैला। 3. obscene, अश्लील, गंदा।

disability (डिसेबिलिटी) ***n.*** the state or condition of being disabled, अशक्तता, असमर्थता।

disabled (डिसेबल्ड) ***adj.*** physically unfit, अशक्त, असमर्थ।

disabuse (डिसब्यूज़) ***v.*** to set right, to disillusion, सही करना, भ्रम दूर करना।

disadvantage (डिसैडवान्टिज) ***n.*** 1. an unfavourable condition or circumstance, प्रतिकूल स्थिति या परिस्थिति। 2. inconvenience, असुविधा, परेशानी।

disadvantageous (डिसैडवान्टेजस) ***adj.*** causing disadvantage, असुविधापूर्ण; हानिकर।

disaffected (डिसफ़ेक्टिड) ***adj.*** discontended, असंतुष्ट।

disaffection (डिसफ़ेक्शन) ***n.*** absence of affection, असंतोष।

disagree (डिसग्री) ***v.*** to differ, असहमत होना।

disagreeable (डिसग्रीएबल) ***adj.*** distasteful, अरुचिकर।

disagreement (डिसग्रीमेन्ट) ***n.*** lack of agreement, असहमति, मतभेद, असंगति।

disallow (डिसलाउ) ***v.*** to refuse to allow, अनुमति न देना।

disappear (डिसपिअर) ***v.*** to vanish, ग़ायब, अदृश्य या ओझल हो जाना।

disappearance (डिसपिअरेन्स) ***n.*** the state of being vanished, अदृश्यता, अंतर्धान।

disappoint (डिसपॉइन्ट) ***v.*** to fail to satisfy hope or expectation of, निराश कर देना।

disappointment (डिसपॉइन्टमेन्ट) ***n.*** the condition of being disappointed, निराशा।

disapprove (डिसप्रूव) ***v.*** to have an unfavourable opinion, नापसंद करना, अस्वीकृत करना।

disarm (डिसार्म) ***v.*** to deprive of weapons, निरस्त्र/निहत्था करना।

disarmament (डिसार्ममेन्ट) ***n.*** the act of disarming or the state of being disarmed, निरस्त्रीकरण।

disarrange (डिसरेन्ज) ***v.*** to put into disorder or confusion, अव्यवस्थित कर देना।

disarray (डिसरे) ***v.*** to throw into disorder or confusion, गड़बड़ा देना, अस्त-व्यस्त कर देना।

disaster (डिज़ास्टर) ***n.*** 1. great destruction, विनाश। 2. misfortune, दुर्भाग्य।

disastrous (डिज़ास्टरस) ***adj.*** causing disaster विनाशकारी।

disavowal (डिसवाउअल) ***n.*** the act of disavowing, इन्कार, अस्वीकृति।

disband (डिस्बैन्ड) ***v.*** to break up, विघटित होना या कर देना।

disbelief (डिस्बिलीफ़) ***n.*** lack of faith, अविश्वास।

disburden (डिस्बर्डन) ***v.*** to relieve of a burden, भारमुक्त करना।

disburse (डिस्बर्स) ***v.*** to pay out, भुगतान करना।

disbursement (डिस्बर्समेंट) ***n.*** the act of disbursing or the state of being disbursed, भुगतान।

disc (डिस्क) ***n.*** 1. a flat circular plate, तश्तरी। 2. something resembling this, मंडल, डिस्क। 3. a phonograph record, तवा, रिकॉर्ड।

4. any approximately circular flat structure in the body, डिस्क, चक्रिका।

discard (डिस्कार्ड) ***v.*** to reject, or throw away, त्याग/फेंक देना।

discern (डिसर्न) ***v.*** 1. to perceive with the eye or mind, देखना, समझना। 2. to distinguish, विभेद/अंतर करना।

discerning ***adj.*** having insight, सूझ-बूझवाला।

discernment (डिसर्नमेन्ट) ***n.*** the act of discerning, सूझ-बूझ।

discharge (डिस्चार्ज) ***v.*** 1. to emit, निकालना, फेंकना, निक्षिप्त करना, निस्सारण करना। 2. to relieve, भारमुक्त करना। 3. to dismiss from employment, बर्ख़ास्त करना। 4. to relieve (a prisoner) from charges or custody, बरी करना। 5. to fire चलाना, दागना या दगना। 6. to fulfil or execute, निर्वाह करना, पालन करना। ***n.*** 1. a dismissal or release from an office or job, बर्ख़ास्तगी। 2. execution, निर्वहन, पालन; discharge of duty, कर्तव्य-पालन। 3. the act of firing or some thing fired, दागने की क्रिया या दागी जानेवाली वस्तु। 4. a release, उन्मोचन, बरी होना।

disciple (डिसाइपल) ***n.*** 1. a follower of a teacher, शिष्य, चेला। 2. a follower or active adherent, अनुयायी।

disciplinary (डिसिप्लिनरी) ***adj.*** of or for discipline, अनुशासनिक।

discipline (डिसिप्लिन) ***n.*** systematic training for the improve-ment of physical powers, self control, character building, obedience etc., अनुशासन। ***v.*** to enforce discipline, अनुशासन का पालन कराना।

disclaim (डिस्क्लेम) ***v.*** to disown, त्यागना।

disclose (डिस्क्लोज़) ***v.*** to make known, प्रकट करना।

disclosure (डिस्क्लोज़र) ***n.*** the act of disclosing, प्रकटीकरण, रहस्योद्घाटन।

disco (डिस्को) ***n.*** a nightclub where amplified recorded music is played for dancing, डिस्को क्लब।

discomfiture (डिस्कम्फ़िचर) ***n.*** uneasiness, बेचैनी।

discomfort (डिस्कम्फ़र्ट) ***n.*** the condition of being uncomfortable, कष्ट, तकलीफ़।

disconcert (डिस्कन्सर्ट) ***v.*** to upset, विचलित करना।

disconnect (डिस्कनेक्ट) ***v.*** to break the connection between, वियोजित कर देना।

disconnection (डिस्कनेक्शन) ***n.*** the act of disconnecting or the state of being disconnected, वियोजन, काटना।

discontent (डिस्कन्टेन्ट) ***n.*** dissatisfaction, असंतोष। ***v.*** to make discontented, असंतुष्ट करना।

discontinue (डिस्कन्टिन्यू) ***v.*** 1. to give up, to abandon, छोड़ देना, त्याग देना। 2. to put a stop to, रोक या बंद कर देना।

discord (डिस्कॉर्ड) ***n.*** 1. lack of accord, agreement or harmony, कलह, झगड़ा। 2. dissension, मतभेद।

discordant (डिस्कॉर्डेन्ट) ***adj.*** harsh in sound, कर्कश, बेसुरा।

discount[1] (डिस्काउन्ट) ***n.*** any deduction from the full amount of a price or debt, बट्टा, छूट, कमीशन।

discount[2] ***v.*** to leave out of count, गिनती में न लाना।

discourage (डिस्करिज) ***v.*** to deprive of courage, to dispirit, निरुत्साहित करना।

D

discourse (डिस्कोर्स) ***n.*** 1. a learned talk or speech, प्रवचन, उपदेश, व्याख्यान। 2. an essay, निबंध। ***v.*** to utter a discourse, प्रवचन करना, व्याख्यान देना।

discourteous (डिस्कर्टिअस) rude, अशिष्ट, बदतमीज़।

discover (डिस्कवर) ***v.*** 1. to bring to light, प्रकाश में लाना। 2. to find out, खोज निकालना। 3. to realize, अनुभूत/महसूस करना।

discovery (डिस्कवरी) ***n.*** 1. the act of discovering, आविष्कार, खोज। 2. something discovered, आविष्कृत वस्तु, आविष्कार।

discredit (डिस्क्रेडिट) ***v.*** to damage the good reputation of, बदनाम करना। ***n.*** disrepute, ill-repute, बदनामी।

discreet (डिस्क्रीट) ***adj.*** 1. prudent, विवेकशील।

discrepancy (डिस्क्रेपेन्सी) ***n.*** any error or variation between facts, figures etc., विसंगति।

discretion (डिस्क्रीशन) ***n.*** the power to decide, विवेक। 2. the quality of being discreet, विवेकशीलता।

discretionary (डिस्क्रीशनरी) ***adj.*** pertaining to or left to discretion, विवेकाधीन।

discriminate (डिस्क्रिमिनेट) ***v.*** 1. to make a clear distinction, अंतर/भेद करना। 2. to treat differently, भेदभाव करना।

discrimination (डिस्क्रिमिनेशन) ***n.*** 1. the power to see fine distinctions, विवेक, सूझ-बूझ। 2. unfair treatment of a person, group or minority, भेदभाव, पक्षपात, तरफ़दारी।

discus (डिस्कस) ***n.*** a plate used in throwing in competitions, डिस्क।

discuss (डिस्कस) ***v.*** 1. to speak together about, विचार-विमर्श करना। 2. to treat, विवेचन करना।

discussion (डिस्कशन) ***n.*** the act of discussing, विचार-विमर्श, परिचर्चा।

disdain (डिस्डेन) ***n.*** contempt, तिरस्कार, निंदा। ***v.*** to regard with disdain, तिरस्कार करना।

disease (डिज़ीज़) ***n.*** ailment, बीमारी, रोग।

disembark (डिसेम्बार्क) ***v.*** to land or cause to land from a ship, train, aircraft etc., उतरना या उतारना।

disenchant (डिसेन्चैन्ट) ***v.*** to disillusion, भ्रम दूर करना।

disengage (डिसेन्गेज) ***v.*** to detach, अलग होना या करना।

disentangle (डिसेन्टैंगल) ***v.*** to free or become free from entanglement, बंधन से छूटना या छुड़ाना।

disfavour (डिस्फ़ेवर) ***n.*** the condition of being disliked or disapproved of, अवकृपा, अननुग्रह, घृणा, नफ़रत। ☐ **fall into disfavour**, कृपापात्र न रहना।

disfigure (डिसफ़िगर) ***v.*** to spoil the figure or shape of, शक्ल बिगाड़ देना।

disfranchise (डिस्फ़्रैन्चाइज़) ***v.*** to deprive of the right to vote, मताधिकार से वंचित करना।

disgrace (डिस्ग्रेस) ***n.*** loss of respect or reputation, अपमान, अवमान। ***v.*** to humiliate, अपमानित/अवमानित करना।

disgraceful (डिस्ग्रेसफुल) ***adj.*** bringing disgrace, अपयशकर।

disgruntled (डिसग्रन्टल्ड) ***adj.*** dissatisfied, discontented, असंतुष्ट।

disguise (डिस्गाइज़) ***v.*** 1. to conceal by false show, छिपाना। 2. to conceal one's true identity by changing the usual appearance etc., भेष बदलना, स्वाँग रचना। ***n.*** a mask, costume or manner that dis-guises, छद्‌मवेश।

disgust (डिस्गस्ट) ***n.*** a feeling of annoyance or repugnance, खीझ, झल्लाहट। ***v.*** to make feel annoyed or offended, खीझ पैदा करना, खिझा देना।

disgusted (डिस्गस्टिड) ***adj.*** feeling disgust, खीझा हुआ, कुपित।

dish (डिश) ***n.*** an open shallow container, plate, तश्तरी, प्लेट, रिकाबी।

disharmony (डिसहार्मनी) ***n.*** lack of harmony, समरसता का अभाव, असामंजस्य की स्थिति।

dishearten (डिसहार्टन) ***v.*** to cause to lose confidence, विश्वास डिगा देना।

dishevelled (डिशेवल्ड) ***adj.*** disarrayed, untidy, अस्त-व्यस्त।

dishonest (डिसऑनिस्ट) ***adj.*** not honest, बेईमान, खोटा।

dishonesty (डिसऑनिस्टी) ***n.*** the state or quality of being dishonest, बेईमानी।

dishonour, dishonor (डिसऑनर) ***n.*** loss of honour, अनादर, बेइज़्ज़ती। ***v.*** 1. to treat with disrespect, अनादर करना, बेइज़्ज़त करना। 2. to refuse to pay the amount of a cheque etc., चेक आदि का अनादरण करना, अनादृत करना।

dishonoured (डिसऑनर्ड) ***adj.*** not honoured, अनादृत।

dishy (डिशी) ***adj.*** charming, आकर्षक।

disillusion (डिसिल्यूज़न) ***v.*** to deprive of illusion, भ्रम दूर करना, मोहभंग करना। ***n.*** the state of being disillusioned, भ्रम-निवारण, मोहभंग।

disincline (डिसिन्क्लाइन) ***v.*** to make or be reluctant, अनिच्छुक होना या बना देना।

disinfect (डिसिन्फ़ेक्ट) ***v.*** to cleanse by destroying bacteria by chemical means, रोगाणुओं का विनाश करना, विसंक्रामित करना।

disinfectant (डिसिन्फ़ेक्टेन्ट) ***n.*** a substance that destroys bacteria, विसंक्रामक पदार्थ, रोगाणुनाशी पदार्थ।

disinherit (डिसिनहेरिट) ***v.*** to deprive or prevent from inheriting, उत्तराधिकार से वंचित करना, उत्तराधिकारी न मानना।

disintegrate (डिसिन्टिग्रेट) ***v.*** to break into small parts, विघटित होना।

disintegration (डिसिन्टिग्रेशन) ***n.*** the act of disintegrating or the state of being disintegrated, विघटन।

disinterested (डिसिन्टरेस्टिड) ***adj.*** not interested, uninterested, रुचि न रखनेवाला।

disjoin (डिस्जॉइन) ***v.*** to separate, अलग-अलग करना, तोड़ना।

disjointed (डिस्जॉइन्टिड) ***adj.*** 1. separated at the joints, जोड़ से खुला हुआ। 2. disconnected, असंबद्ध, क्रमरहित।

dislike (डिस्लाइक) ***v.*** to regard with distaste or aversion, नापसंद करना, घृणा करना, नफ़रत करना। ***n.*** the feeling of not liking something, नापसंदगी, घृणा, नफ़रत।

dislocate (डिस्लोकेट) ***v.*** to displace from its normal position (esp. a bone from its joint, हड्डी का जोड़ से) उतर जाना, विस्थापित हो जाना।

dislocation (डिस्लोकेशन) ***n.*** the state of being dislocated, विस्थापन।

dislodge (डिस्लॉज) ***v.*** to force out of

established position, हटाना, खदेड़ना।

disloyal (डिस्लॉइअल) ***adj.*** not loyal or faithful, बेवफ़ा, ग़द्दार।

disloyalty (डिस्लॉइअल्टी) ***n.*** the state of being disloyal, बेवफ़ाई, गद्दारी।

dismal (डिज़्मल) ***adj.*** 1. causing sadness, निराशाजनक। 2. causing gloom, विषादमय।

dismantle (डिस्मैन्टल) ***v.*** 1. to disassemble, खोल देना, पुर्ज़े-पुर्ज़े अलग कर देना। 2. to demolish, ढा देना। 3. to take away fittings or furnishings from, साज-सज्जा उखाड़ लेना।

dismay (डिस्मे) ***n.*** the strong feeling of fear, hopelessness or apprehension, निराशा, भय, आशंका।

dismember (डिस्मेम्बर) ***v.*** to remove, cut or pull the limbs of, अपंग या विकलांग कर देना, अंग-भंग करना।

dismiss (डिस्मिस) ***v.*** 1. to remove from a position, office or employment, पदच्युत करना, बर्ख़ास्त कर देना, निकाल देना। 2. to reject, ख़ारिज कर देना, अस्वीकृत कर देना। 3. to get out (the batting side cheaply, टीम को सस्ते में) आउट कर देना।

dismissal (डिस्मिसल) ***n.*** the act of dismissing or the state of being dismissed, पदच्युति, बर्ख़ास्तगी।

dismount (डिस्मॉउन्ट) ***v.*** to get down (from a horse, घोड़े पर से) उतरना, उतर जाना।

disobedience (डिसोबीडिएन्स) ***n.*** the act of disobeying, अवज्ञा।

disobey (डिसोबे) ***v.*** to refuse to obey, अवज्ञा करना।

disorder (डिसॉर्डर) ***n.*** 1. a lack of order, अव्यवस्था, कुप्रबंध, गड़बड़ी। 2. disturbance, उपद्रव, दंगा, शांतिभंग। 3. an ailment, विकार, रोग।

disown (डिसोन) ***v.*** to refuse to acknowledge as one's own, अपनाने से इन्कार कर देना।

disparage (डिस्पैरिज) ***v.*** to speak contemptuously of, निंदा या बुराई करना।

disparate (डिस्पैरिट) ***adj.*** dissimilar, तरह-तरह के, अलग-अलग प्रकार के।

disparity (डिस्पैरिटी) ***n.*** inequality, असमानता, विषमता।

dispassionate (डिस्पैशनिट) ***adj.*** 1. free from passion, आवेगहीन, आवेशहीन। 2. calm, शांत, गंभीर।

dispatch (डिस्पैच) ***v.*** to send to a destination, भेजना, प्रेषित करना।

dispatcher (डिस्पैचर) ***n.*** one whose duty is to dispatch letters etc., प्रेषणकर्मी।

dispel (डिस्पेल) ***v.*** to drive away, दूर करना, भगाना।

dispensable (डिस्पेन्सेबल) ***adj.*** 1. that can be dispelled, जिसे दूर किया या भगाया जा सके। 2. not essential, जो अपरिहार्य न हो, परिहार्य, अनावश्यक।

dispensary (डिस्पेन्सरी) ***n.*** a place where medicines and medical aid are dispensed, औषधालय, दवाघर, डिस्पेन्सरी।

dispense (डिस्पेन्स) ***v.*** 1. to prepare and give out (me-dicines), (दवा आदि) तैयार करके देना, बाँटना, वितरित करना। 2. to carry out, to administer, प्रबंध करना, विधान करना, संचालन करना। 3. to deal out in portions, थोड़ा-थोड़ा करके निपटाना।

disperse (डिस्पर्स) ***v.*** 1. to scatter,

बिखेरना। 2. to end, ख़त्म/समाप्त होना।

dispirited (डिस्पिरिटिड) ***adj.*** dicouraged, disheartened, नाउम्मीद, हताश।

displace (डिस्प्लेस) ***v.*** 1. to remove from the usual place or position, विस्थापित करना, अपनी जगह से हटा देना। 2. to oust, हटा देना, निकाल देना।

displaced person ***n.*** a refugee, शरणार्थी।

display (डिस्प्ले) ***v.*** to exhibit, to show, दिखाना, प्रदर्शित करना; ***n.*** 1. the act of displaying, प्रदर्शन, दिखावा,। 2. something displayed, प्रदर्शित वस्तु।

displease (डिस्प्लीज़) ***v.*** to cause displeasure, नाराज़/नाख़ुश करना।

displeasure (डिस्प्लेज़र) ***n.*** annoyance, नाराज़गी, रोष।

disposable (डिस्पोज़ेबल) ***adj.*** that can be thrown away after being used once, एक बार काम में लाने के बाद फेंक दिए जाने योग्य।

disposal (डिस्पोज़ल) ***n.*** 1. the act of disposing or the state of being disposed, निपटारा, निपटान। 2. arrangement, व्यवस्था। 3. sale, बिक्री, विक्रय। 4. the act of transferring ownership by sale or gift, हस्तांतरण, सुपुर्दगी। 5. the act of throwing out, फेंकना, परित्याग। 6. the power to use something, उपभोग का अधिकार। □ **at one's disposal,** उपलब्ध, हर तरह की सेवा के लिए हाज़िर।

dispose (डिस्पोज़) ***v.*** 1. to arrange or place in a particular order, व्यवस्थित करना। 2. to incline, प्रवृत्त होना। 3. to give, sell or transfer, देना, सौंपना या बेचना। 4. to throw out, फेंक या निकाल देना। 5. to arrange or settle (matters), निपटाना, निपटारा करना। □ **dispose of,** निकाल डालना, पिंड छुड़ाना।

disposition (डिस्पोज़िशन) ***n.*** 1. temperament, स्वभाव, प्रकृति। 2. inclination, प्रवृत्ति।

dispossess (डिसपोज़ेस) ***v.*** 1. to put out of possession, बेदख़ल करना।

dispossession (डिस्पोज़ेशन) ***n.*** the act of dispossessing or the state of being dispossessed, बेदख़ली।

disproportionate (डिस्प्रपोर्शनिट) ***adj.*** unequal, असमान।

disprove (डिस्प्रूव) ***v.*** to prove to be false, खंडन करना, मिथ्या सिद्ध करना।

disputable (डिस्प्यूटेबल) ***adj.*** questionable, विवादास्पद, विवाद्य।

dispute (डिस्प्यूट) ***n.*** quarrel, विवाद, झगड़ा। ***v.*** 1. to argue or debate, विवाद/झगड़ा करना। 2. to question the truth or validity of, विरोध करना।

disputed (डिस्प्यूटिड) ***adj.*** about which there is a dispute, विवादित।

disqualification (डिस्क्वालिफ़िकेशन) ***n.*** the act of disqualifying or the state of being disqualified, अपात्रता।

disqualify (डिसक़्वालिफ़ाइ) ***v.*** to declare or make unfit to do something, अयोग्य/अपात्र ठहराना।

disquiet (डिसक़्वाइअट) ***n.*** anxiety, विकलता, बेचैनी।

disregard (डिसरिगार्ड) ***n.*** lack of regard, आदर का अभाव, उपेक्षा। ***v.*** to neglect, उपेक्षा/अवहेलना करना।

disreputable (डिसरेप्युटेबल) ***adj.*** having a bad name, बदनाम, कुख्यात।

disrepute (डिसरिप्यूट) ***n.*** loss or lack of reputation, बदनामी, कुख्याति।

D

disrespect (डिसरिस्पेक्ट) *n.* 1. lack of respect, निरादर। 2. contempt, तिरस्कार।

disrupt (डिसरप्ट) *v.* to throw into disorder, अस्त-व्यस्त कर देना।

disruption (डिसरप्शन) *n.* the act of disrupting or the state of being disrupted, अव्यवस्था।

disruptive (डिसरप्टिव) *adj.* causing disruption, अस्त-व्यस्त करनेवाला।

dissatisfaction (डिस्सैटिस्फ़ैक्शन) *n.* lack of satisfaction, असंतोष।

dissect (डिसेक्ट) *v.* 1. to cut open, चीरा देना। 2. to examine critically, आलोचना करना।

dissection (डिसेक्शन) *n.* the act of dissecting, चीर-फाड़, शल्यक्रिया।

dissemble (डिसेम्बल) *v.* to conceal (one's character, felling, intention etc., अपने चरित्र, भावनाओं, इरादों आदि को) छिपाना, गुप्त रखना।

dissemination (डिसेमिनेशन) *n.* the act of disseminating, प्रसार, फैलाव।

dissension (डिसेन्शन) *n.* strife or discord leading to division or into factions, मतभेद, फूट, मनमुटाव, झगड़ा।

dissent (डिसेन्ट) *n.* 1. a difference of opinion, मतभेद। 2. refusal, इन्कार।

dissertation (डिसर्टेशन) *n.* 1. a written thesis, शोध-निबंध, प्रबंध। 2. a formal discourse, व्याख्यान।

disservice (डिस्सर्विस) *n.* a harmful action, अपकार, कुसेवा।

dissidence (डिसिडेन्स) *n.* dissent, असहमति।

dissident (डिसिडेन्ट) *adj.* 1. disagreeing, असहमत। 2. opposite, विरोधी।

dissimilar (डिसिमिलर) *adj.* unlike, असमान, विषम।

dissimilarity (डिसिमिलैरिटी) *n.* lack of similarity, असमानता, विषमता।

dissipate (डिसिपेट) *v.* 1. to dispel, छितराना, तितर-बितर करना। 2. to squander away, अपव्यय करना, उड़ाना।

dissociate (डिसोशिएट) *v.* to separate from union with someone else, संबंध/मेल-जोल न रखना।

dissolute (डिसल्यूट) *adj.* debauched, दुराचारी, लंपट।

dissolution (डिसोल्यूशन) *n.* the breaking up of any constitutional body, विघटन, भंग।

dissolve (डिज़ॉल्व) *v.* 1. to make or become liquid, घुल जाना या घुला देना। 2. to cause to end or break up, विघटित होना/करना।

dissuade (डिस्वेड) *v.* to advise to refrain, मना करना, रोकना।

distance (डिस्टेन्स) *n.* 1. the space between the two points, दूरी, फ़ासला। 2. coldness in personal relationship, अलगाव, दूरी।

distant (डिस्टेन्ट) *adj.* 1. far off, far away, दूरवर्ती, दूरस्थित। 2. not closely related, जिससे निकट संबंध न हो, दूर का।

distaste (डिस्टेस्ट) *n.* dislike, नफ़रत।

distasteful (डिस्टेस्टफुल) *adj.* causing distaste, अरुचिकर।

distemper (डिस्टेम्पर) *n.* a water soluble paint, डिस्टेम्पर।

distend (डिस्टेन्ड) *v.* 1. to expand or cause to expand, फैलना या फैलाना। 2. to swell or cause to swell, फूलना या फुलाना।

distil (डिस्टिल) *v.* to treat by distillation, चुआना, आसवित करना।

distillation (डिस्टिलेशन) ***n.*** a process of evaporating a liquid and condensing its vapour, आसवन।

distillery (डिस्टिलरी) ***n.*** a place where distilling is done, मद्य-निर्माणशाला, कलवरिया।

distinct (डिस्टिंक्ट) ***adj.*** 1. easily perceived, सुस्पष्ट। 2. different in kind, अलग तरह का, विशिष्ट।

distinction (डिस्टिंक्शन) ***n.*** 1. a distinguishing factor or characteristic, विशिष्टता, वैशिष्ट्य। 2. a mark of honour, उपाधि, सम्मान।

distinctive (डिस्टिंक्टिव) ***adj.*** characteristic, विशिष्ट, प्रभेदक।

distinguish (डिस्टिंग्विश) ***v.*** 1. to draw distinction, भेद दरशाना, विशिष्टता दिखलाना या लाना। 2. to recognise as different, पहचान होना।

distinguished (डिस्टिंग्विश्ड) eminent, प्रमुख, विशिष्ट।

distort (डिस्टॉर्ट) ***v.*** to twist, तोड़-मरोड़कर पेश करना, झूठा बयान देना।

distortion (डिस्टॉर्शन) ***n.*** deformity, विकृति।

distract (डिस्ट्रैक्ट) ***v.*** to draw away the attention of, to divert, ध्यान बँटा देना, ध्यान हटाना।

distraction (डिस्ट्रैक्शन) ***n.*** 1. mental upset, उन्माद, विक्षिप्तता।

distraught (डिस्ट्रॉट) ***adj.*** agitated, विक्षुब्ध।

distress (डिस्ट्रेस) ***n.*** 1. mental or physical pain, वेदना, व्यथा। 2. a trouble or hardship, विपत्ति, परेशानी; ***v.*** to cause distress to, दुख देना, सताना।

distressing (डिस्ट्रेसिंग) ***adj.*** causing distress, दुखप्रद, कष्टप्रद।

distribute (डिस्ट्रिब्यूट) ***v.*** to divide among several or many, वितरण करना, बाँट देना।

distribution (डिस्ट्रिब्यूशन) ***n.*** the act of distributing, वितरण, बाँट।

distributor (डिस्ट्रिब्यूटर) ***n.*** one who distributes, वितरक, वितरणकर्ता।

district (डिस्ट्रिक्ट) ***n.*** 1. a division of a state, ज़िला, जनपद। 2. a region, प्रदेश।

distrust (डिस्ट्रस्ट) ***n.*** lack of trust, अविश्वास। ***v.*** to lack confidence in, अविश्वास करना।

distrustful (डिस्ट्रस्टफ़ुल) ***adj.*** having or showing distrust, अविश्वासी, संशयी।

disturb (डिस्टर्ब) ***v.*** 1. to trouble emotionally or mentally, छेड़ना, छेड़छाड़ करना। 2. to distrub the peace of, शांति भंग करना, दंगा करना।

disturbance (डिस्टर्बेन्स) ***n.*** 1. a commotion or tumult, उपद्रव। 2. a troubled state or provocation, अशांति, उत्तेजना।

disturbed (डिस्टर्ब्ड) ***adj.*** 1. agitated, worried, विक्षुब्ध, अशांत। 2. riotridden, उपद्रवग्रस्त, दंगाग्रस्त।

disuse (डिस्यूज़) ***v.*** to cease to use, उपयोग या प्रयोग बंद कर देना।

ditch (डिच) ***n.*** a narrow channel dug in the earth, खाई, खंदक।

dive (डाइव) ***v.*** 1. to plunge head first into water, गोता लगाना, डुबकी लगाना। 2. to plunge sharply downward, सहसा नीचे आना या उतरना। ***n.*** 1. an act of diving, गोता, डुबकी। 2. a sharp downward movement, निम्नगति।

diver (डाइवर) ***n.*** 1. one who is

D

expert in diving, गोताख़ोर। 2. a person who works underwater, पनडुब्बा।

diverge (डाइवर्ज) ***v.*** to go aside from a path, मार्गभ्रष्ट होना, पथभ्रष्ट होना।

divergent (डाइवर्जेन्ट) ***adj.*** of different kinds, नानाविध।

diverse (डाइवर्स) ***adj.*** of different kinds, नानाविध।

diversification (डाइवर्सिफ़िकेशन) the act of diversifying, विविधीकरण।

diversify (डाइवर्सिफ़ाइ) ***v.*** to make different or various in form or quality, विभिन्नता/विविधता लाना।

diversion (डाइवर्शन) ***n.*** 1. the act of diverting from a specified course, पथांतरण, दिशा-परिवर्तन। 2. a pastime, ध्यान बँटानेवाली बात या आमोद-प्रमोद,। 3. an alternative road used by traffic when a main route is closed, पथांतर, सहपथ।

diversionary (डाइवर्शनरी) ***adj.*** 1. causing diversion, पथांतरण या विषयांतरण करनेवाला।

diversity (डाइवर्सिटी) ***n.*** 1. difference, विभिन्नता, भिन्नता। 2. variety, विविधता।

divert (डाइवर्ट) ***v.*** 1. to cause to turn from one direction to another, दिशा बदल देना, मोड़/घुमा देना। 2. to amuse or entertain, जी बहलाना, मनोरंजन करना। 3. to distract, ध्यान बँटाना।

divest (डाइवेस्ट) ***v.*** 1. to strip विवस्त्र करना। 2. to dispossess, वंचित करना।

divide (डिवाइड) ***v.*** 1. to separate or become separated into parts, विभक्त होना या करना, बँटना या बाँटना। 2. to find how many times one number contains another, भाग देना, तक़सीम करना। □ **divide and rule,** फूट डालो और राज्य करो।

dividend (डिविडेन्ड) ***n.*** 1. a number that is to be divided, भाज्य। 2. share of profit, लाभांश।

divider (डिवाइडर) ***n.*** anything that divides, विभाजक।

dividers (डिवाइडर्स) ***n.*** a device used for measuring lines or dividing them, परकार।

divination (डिविनेशन) ***n.*** prediction, भविष्यवाणी।

divine (डिवाइन) ***adj.*** 1. of or related to a deity or God, ईश्वरीय, दैवी। 2. superhuman, godlike, दिव्य, अतिमानवीय।

Divinity (डिविनिटी) ***n.*** God, ईश्वर।

divisible (डिविज़िबल) ***adj.*** capable of being divided usually with no remainder, विभाज्य, भाज्य।

division (डिविज़न) ***n.*** 1. the act of dividing or the state of being divided, विभाजन। 2. a major unit of an organization, विभाग। 3. a self-contained military unit, डिवीज़न, विभाग। 4. disagreement, disunion, मतभेद, विभेद, अनबन, फूट। 5. the operation of determining how many times one quantity is contained in another, भाग, तक़सीम।

divisional (डिविज़नल) ***adj.*** of or pertaining to a division, प्रभागीय, विभागीय।

divisive (डिवाइसिव) ***adj.*** disruptive, बाँटनेवाला, फूट डालनेवाला।

divisor (डिवाइज़र) ***n.*** the quantity by which dividend is to be divided, हर, भाजक।

divorce (डिवोर्स) ***n.*** 1. a legal

dissolution or termination of marriage, तलाक़। 2. a complete separation, पूर्ण विच्छेद।

divorcee (डिवोर्सी) ***n.*** a person who has been divorced, वह जिसे तलाक़ मिला हो, तलाक़शुदा आदमी/औरत।

divulge (डिवल्ज) ***v.*** to reveal or disclose, रहस्योद्घाटन करना, भंडा फोड़ना।

dizziness (डिज़िनिस) ***n.*** the state of being dizzy, चक्कर आना।

dizzy (डिज़ी) ***adj.*** giddy, जिसका सिर चकरा रहा हो।

do (डू) ***v.*** to act, carry out, perform or execute, करना, पालन करना, निर्वाह करना।

docile (डोसाइल) ***adj.*** 1. easily taught, जिसे सरलता से सिखाया-पढ़ाया जा सके, शिक्षणीय। 2. humble, विनयी, विनम्र।

dock[1] (डॉक) ***n.*** a place where ships are loaded and unloaded, बंदरगाह, घाट, पत्तन, गोदी। ***v.*** 1. to bring or come into dock, बंदरगाह में आना या लाना। 2. to join together in space, आकाश में इकट्ठे होना या मिलना।

dock[2] ***n.*** an enclosure in a court where defendant stands, कटघरा।

dock[3] ***v.*** to cut short (an animal's tail, किसी पशु की दुम) काट देना।

dockyard (डॉकयार्ड) ***n.*** shipyard, गोदीबाड़ा।

doctor (डॉक्टर) ***n.*** 1. a medical practitioner, डॉक्टर, चिकित्सक, वैद्य, हकीम। 2. a person who holds the highest academic degree, डॉक्टर।

doctorate (डॉक्टरिट) ***n.*** the highest academic degree in any field of knowledge, डॉक्टरेट, डॉक्टर की उपाधि।

doctrine (डॉक्ट्रिन) ***n.*** a principle or belief, सिद्धांत, मत।

document (डॉक्युमेन्ट) ***n.*** a paper that provides information, proof or evidence, दस्तावेज़।

documentary (डाक्युमेन्टरी) ***adj.*** consisting of documents, दस्तावेज़ी। ***n.*** a film about an actual event presenting the facts with little or no fiction, वृत्तचित्र।

dodge (डॉज) ***v.*** to cheat, चकमा देना, झाँसा देना, धोख़ा देना। ***n.*** a trick, चकमा, झाँसा।

doe (डो) ***n.*** the female of the deer, hare, rabbit etc., मादा हिरन, मादा खरगोश।

doer (डूअर) ***n.*** one who does something, कर्ता, करनेवाला।

does (डज़) ***v.*** third person singular present tense of do, करता / करती है।

dog (डॉग) ***n.*** 1. a common four-legged flesh-eating animal, कुत्ता। 2. a worthless or despicable man, क्षुद्र व्यक्ति, नीच व्यक्ति। 3. a mechanical device for gripping things, कुत्ता, काँटा।

dogged (डॉगिड) ***adj.*** obstinate, हठी, ज़िद्दी।

dogma (डॉग्मा) ***n.*** a principle, सिद्धांत।

doings (डूइंग्स) ***n.*** (plu.) actions, deeds, काम-धाम, क्रिया-व्यापार, करनी।

doldrums (डोलड्रम्ज़) ***n.*** a region of light winds along the equator, शांत कटिबंध।

dole (डोल) ***n.*** an allowance to the unemployed, बेकारी भत्ता।

doleful (डोलफ़ुल) ***adj.*** 1. sad, उदास। 2. mournful, विषादमय।

doll (डॉल) ***n.*** 1. a toy representing

D

a human figure, गुड्डा/गुड़िया। a pretty girl, सुंदर लड़की, गुड़िया।

dollar (डॉलर) ***n.*** a standard unit of money in some countries, डॉलर।

dolorous (डोलरस) ***adj.*** mournful, विषादपूर्ण, शोकमय।

dolphin (डॉल्फ़िन) ***n.*** a sea animal with a beaklike snout, सूँस।

domain (डोमेन) ***n.*** 1. an area for particular activity, क्षेत्र, कार्यक्षेत्र। 2. a province, प्रांत।

dome (डोम) ***n.*** a hemispheric roof, गुंबद।

domestic (डोमेस्टिक) ***adj.*** 1. pertaining to the home/household, घरेलू, पारिवारिक। 2. of one's own country, देशी।

domesticate (डोमेस्टिकेट) ***v.*** to make tame, पालतू बनाना।

domicile (डोमिसाइल) ***n.*** 1. a residence, निवास-स्थान, घर, निवास। 2. a permanent residence, स्थायी निवास।

dominance (डॉमिनेन्स) ***n.*** the state or quality of being dominant, प्रभुत्व, प्रधानता।

dominant (डॉमिनेन्ट) ***adj.*** most influential, हावी, प्रभावी।

dominate (डॉमिनेट) ***v.*** to be dominant in position/authority, प्रभावी या प्रभावशाली होना।

domineer (डॉमिनिअर) ***v.*** to behave in a forceful way, धौंस जमाना, रोब दिखाना।

domineering (डॉमिनिअरिंग) ***adj.*** behaving forcefully, हुक्म चलानेवाला, रोब या धौंस दिखानेवाला।

dominion (डोमिनियन) ***n.*** 1. the area under a ruler or government, डोमिनियन, शासित क्षेत्र। 2. a self-governing nation of the British Commonwealth, ब्रिटिश राष्ट्रमंडल का स्वशासी राष्ट्र।

don (डॉन) ***n.*** 1. a nobleman, कुलीन व्यक्ति। 2. a person of consequence, महत्त्वपूर्ण व्यक्ति।

donate (डोनेट) ***v.*** to bestow, दान करना, प्रदान करना, देना।

donation (डोनेशन) ***n.*** 1. the act of donating or something donated, दान। 2. a contribution, चंदा।

done (डन) ***adj.*** completed, finished, किया हुआ, कृत।

donkey (डन्की) ***n.*** 1. an ass, गधा। 2. a stupid person, मूर्ख व्यक्ति।

donor (डोनर) ***n.*** a person who donates something, दानी, दाता।

doom (डूम) ***n.*** an inescapable fate, दुर्भाग्य।

Doomsday (डूम्ज़डे) ***n.*** the day of the Last Judgement, क़यामत/प्रलय का दिन।

door (डोर) ***n.*** a hinged, sliding or movable panels used to open or close an entrance, द्वार, दरवाज़ा।

doorkeeper (डोरकीपर) ***n.*** one who guards an entrance, द्वाररक्षक, द्वारपाल।

doorstep (डोरस्टेप) ***n.*** a step leading to a door, बाहरी या मुख्य द्वार के पहलेवाली सीढ़ी।

doorway (डोरवे) ***n.*** an entrance way, द्वार-पथ।

dormant (डॉर्मेन्ट) ***adj.*** in the state of being sleepy or inactive, सुप्त, अक्रिय, प्रसुप्त।

dormitory (डॉर्मिटरी) ***n.*** a large room with many beds, शयनागार।

dose (डोज़) ***n.*** the amount or size of a medicine taken or given at a time, ख़ुराक, मात्रा।

dot (डॉट) ***n.*** a point, बिंदी, बिंदु।

dotage (डोटिज) ***n.*** the feebleness of mind caused by old age, बुढ़भस।

dote (डोट) ***v.*** to show great fondness, मुग्ध या लट्टू हो जाना।

doting (डोटिंग) ***adj.*** showing great fondness, लट्टू, मुग्ध।

double (डबल) ***adj.*** twice as much or as many as, दूना, दुगना। ***adv.*** twice over, दुगनी मात्रा में। ***n.*** 1. something increased two-fold, दुगनी मात्रा, दूना परिमाण, दुहरा आकार। 2. a hotel room for two persons, दो व्यक्तियों के रहने के लिए होटल का कमरा, डबल रूम। ***v.*** 1. to make or become twice as much or twice as many, दुगना करना या होना। 2. to make or become two-fold, दुहरा करना या होना।

double-dealing (डबल-डीलिंग) ***n.*** treachery, deceit, धोखाधड़ी।

double-minded (डबल-माइन्डिड) ***adj.*** in a fix, दुविधाग्रस्त, दुचित्ता।

doubt (डॉउट) ***n.*** 1. a lack of certainty, अनिश्चय। 2. a lack of conviction, संदेह। ***v.*** 1. to feel uncertain, अनिश्चय की स्थिति में होना। 2. to distrust, अविश्वास/संदेह करना।

doubtful (डॉउटफुल्) ***adj.*** 1. uncertain, अनिश्चित। 2. causing or showing doubt, संदेहपूर्ण, संदिग्ध।

doubtless (डॉउटलिस) ***adj.*** with no doubt or uncertainty, निश्चित, पक्का।

dough (डो) ***n.*** 1. flour mixed with water, गुँधा आटा या गुँधे आटे की लोई। 2. money, रुपया-पैसा, धन।

dove (डव) ***n.*** a kind of bird, पेंडुकी, फ़ाख्ता।

dowager (डॉवेजर) ***n.*** a rich widow, धनी विधवा।

down (डाउन) ***adv.*** 1. from a higher to a lower place of position, नीचे। 2. downwards, नीचे की ओर। 3. towards south, दक्षिण की ओर। 4. from an important part of the city to one supposed to be of less importance, कम महत्त्व के स्थान की ओर। 5. to or towards a point away from speaker, वक्ता से दूरी पर। ***prep.*** 1. in a lower or descending position, नीचे की ओर। 2. in the direction of current, प्रवाह या बहाव की ओर। ***n.*** 1. downward movement, निम्न गति। 2. a descent, उतराई, उतार। ***adj.*** 1. directed downward, निम्नगामी, अधोगामी। 2. lying on the ground, भूस्थित। 3. being at a low level, निम्न स्तर पर होनेवाला। 4. behind an opponent, प्रतियोगी से पिछड़ा हुआ। 5. finished, समाप्त, ख़त्म।

downcast (डाउनकास्ट) ***adj.*** dejected, उदास, खिन्न, हताश।

downfall (डाउनफ़ॉल) ***n.*** a sudden fall, पतन, गिरावट, पराभव।

downhill (डाउनहिल) ***adv.*** down the slope of a hill, ढाल या उतार की ओर। ***adj.*** sloping, ढालवाँ।

downpour (डाउनपोर) ***n.*** a heavy continuous fall of rain, घनघोर/मूसलाधार वर्षा।

downright (डाउनराइट) ***adj.*** 1. frank, खरा, ईमानदार। 2. blunt, स्पष्टवादी, मुँहफट। 3. complete, पूर्ण। ***adv.*** thoroughly, पूरी तरह से।

downstairs (डाउनस्टेअर्ज़) ***adv.*** on

D

the lower floor, निचले तल्ले पर।

downstream (डाउनस्ट्रीम) ***adv.*** towards the lower part of the stream, बहाव की ओर।

downtown (डाउनटाउन्) ***n.*** the central part or main commercial area of the city, नगर का मध्य भाग या व्यापार-केंद्र।

downtrodden (डाउनट्रॉडन) ***adj.*** 1. trodden down, कुचला/रौंदा हुआ। 2. oppressed, subjugated, पददलित, सताया हुआ।

downwards (डाउनवर्ड्स) ***adv.*** from higher to lower place or condition, नीचे की ओर।

dowry (डाउरी) ***n.*** the money and property given to a girl by her parents at the time of her marriage, दहेज।

doyen (डॉयेन) ***n.*** the senior member of a group, नायक, सरदार।

doze (डोज़) ***v.*** to sleep lightly and intermittently, ऊँघना। ***n.*** a short light sleep, झपकी, ऊँघ।

dozen (डज़न) ***n.*** a set of twelve, दर्जन। ***adj.*** twelve, दर्जन-भर।

drab (ड्रैब) ***adj.*** 1. of a light greyish brown colour, बादामी या हलका भूरा। 2. dull, नीरस।

draconian (ड्रेकोनिअन) ***adj.*** harsh, कठोर, निर्मम।

draft (ड्राफ़्ट) ***n.*** 1. a rough or preliminary sketch of anything written, नक्शा, प्रारूप। 2. a preliminary outline of a speech, book, letter etc., मसौदा, ख़ाका, प्रारूप। 3. a written note for the payment of money by a bank, ड्राफ़्ट। ***v.*** to prepare a draft or outline, मसौदा/प्रारूप तैयार करना।

draftsman (ड्राफ़्ट्समैन) ***n.*** one who draws sketches or plans, प्रारूपकार, नक्शानवीस।

drag (ड्रैग) ***v.*** 1. to pull or draw along by force, खींच ले जाना। 2. to cause to trail on ground, घसीट कर ले जाना।

dragnet (ड्रैगनेट) ***n.*** a net to catch fish, मत्स्यजाल।

dragon (ड्रैगन) ***n.*** a huge mythical reptile breathing fire, आग उगलनेवाला पौराणिक अजगर।

drain (ड्रेन) ***n.*** 1. a pipe or channel for carrying away waste water, नाली। 2. something that exhausts one's resources, energy etc., शक्ति या स्रोतों के क्षय का मार्ग। ***v.*** to draw or flow off water by means of pipes or channels, जल निकालना या बहाना, प्रवाहित करना।

drainage (ड्रेनिज) ***n.*** system of drains, नाली-व्यवस्था।

dram (ड्रैम) ***n.*** one sixteenth of an ounce, औंस का सोलहवाँ भाग, ड्राम।

drama (ड्रामा) ***n.*** 1. a stage show, नाटक, ड्रामा। 2. such a piece of literature, नाटक। 3. a situation that is highly emotional and conflicting, नाटकबाज़ी।

dramatic (ड्रमैटिक) ***adj.*** of or related to a drama, thrilling or sensational, नाटकीय।

dramatics (ड्रमैटिक्स) ***n.*** the art of acting or producing plays, नाट्यकला।

dramatist (ड्रामेटिस्ट) ***n.*** a playwright, नाटककार।

dramatize, dramatise (ड्रामेटाइज़) ***v.*** to render a story, fiction etc., into a play, नाट्य रूप देना।

drape (ड्रेप) ***v.*** to cover with cloth, पर्दा लगाना या लटकाना।

draper (ड्रेपर) ***n.*** a dealer in fabrics, कपड़े का व्यापारी, बज़ाज़।

drastic (ड्रैस्टिक) ***adj.*** severe or radical, कठोर, प्रचंड।

draught (ड्राफ़्ट) ***n.*** 1. the amount drunk in one swallow, घूँट। 2. a dose of medicine, दवा की ख़ुराक। 3. (plu.) the game of checkers, चेकर खेल।

draw (ड्रॉ) ***v.*** 1. to pull, खींचना, घसीटना या तानना। 2. to take out, निकालना। 3. to attract or entice, आकृष्ट करना, लुभाना।

drawback (ड्रॉबैक) ***n.*** defect or deficiency, कमी, दोष, त्रुटि।

drawee (ड्रॉई) ***n.*** a person on whom an order or a bill of exchange is drawn, आदेशिती, अदाकर्ता।

drawer (ड्राअर) ***n.*** 1. a person who draws a cheque, आदेशक, चेक काटनेवाला। 2. a sliding box-like container in a table or chest, ड्राअर, ख़ाना। 3. (plu.) underpants, जाँघिया।

drawing (ड्राइंग) ***n.*** 1. the art of drawing with lines आरेखन। 2. a representation of lines, रेखाचित्र, आरेख।

drawing room ***n.*** a room for visitors, बैठक, ड्राइंग रूम।

drawl (ड्रॉअल) ***v.*** to speak slowly with drawn-out vowel sounds, धीरे-धीरे या लटक-लटककर बोलना।

dread (ड्रेड) ***n.*** great fear, अत्यधिक भय, आतंक।

dreadful (ड्रेडफ़ुल) ***adj.*** causing dread, भयावह, भीषण।

dream (ड्रीम) ***n.*** 1. an event experienced during sleep, सपना, स्वप्न। 2. something imagined, कल्पना, कपोल-कल्पना। ***v.*** 1. to experience a dream, स्वप्न देखना। 2. to indulge in day-dreams, दिवास्वप्न देखना, ख़्याली पुलाव पकाना।

dreamland, dreamworld ***n.*** an imaginary land, स्वप्नलोक।

dreamy (ड्रीमी) ***adj.*** lost in imaginations, विचारमग्न।

dreary (ड्रिअरी) ***adj.*** dull, उबाऊ।

dredge (ड्रेज) ***n.*** an appartus that digs up and removes mud, silt, fish, shellfish etc., from the river or seabed, नदी या समुद्र-तल से मिट्टी, कीचड़, सीप, मछली आदि निकालनेवाला यंत्र, ड्रेजर।

drench (ड्रेन्च) ***v.*** to make thoroughly wet, तर-ब-तर कर देना, भिगोना।

dress (ड्रेस) ***n.*** 1. clothing esp., outer clothing, पोशाक, परिधान। 2. formal clothes, वर्दी। ***v.*** 1. to put on clothes, कपड़े पहनना या पहनाना। 2. to clean and prepare (meat or bird) for cooking, साफ़ करना। 3. to prepare (land) for sowing, (ज़मीन) तैयार करना। 4. to tan, (चमड़ा) सिझाना।

dressing (ड्रेसिंग) ***n.*** 1. the act or action of a person who dresses, वस्त्रधारण, कपड़े पहनने का कार्य। 2. material used to cover a wound, मरहम-पट्टी।

dribble (ड्रिबल) ***v.*** 1. to trickle, बूँद-बूँद कर टपकना या टपकाना। 2. to move (a ball) with repeated light kicks or bounces, बार-बार हलका प्रहार करते या उछालते हुए (गेंद को) लेकर आगे बढ़ना, ड्रिबल करना। ***n.*** the act of dribbling a ball, ड्रिबलिंग, ड्रिबल।

D

dried (ड्राइड) pt. of dry. ***adj.*** preserved by drying, सुखाया हुआ, सूखा।

drift (ड्रिफ़्ट) ***v.*** 1. to be carried along by a current, बहा या उड़ा ले जाना। 2. to carry along by a current, बहना, उड़ना, बह या उड़ जाना। 3. to move aimlessly, इधर-उधर व्यर्थ घूमना।

drill[1] (ड्रिल) ***n.*** 1. a pointed implement that bores holes in solid materials, बरमा, ड्रिल। 2. strict training in military exercises, कवायद, ड्रिल 3. repetition of exercises as a means of training, अभ्यास, मशक। ***v.*** 1. to bore with a drill, बेधना, बेधन करना। 2. to train or be trained by repetition, बार-बार अभ्यास करना या कराना, प्रशिक्षण प्राप्त करना या कराना।

drill[2] ***n.*** a machine for planting seeds in rows, पंक्तियों में बीज बोने का एक यंत्र, ड्रिल मशीन।

drink (ड्रिंक) ***v.*** 1. to swallow (liquid), पान करना, पीना, घूँटना। 2. to take alcoholic beverages, मद्यपान करना। ***n.*** 1. anything used for drinking, पेय। 2. alcoholic liquor, मदिरा, शराब।

drinking water ***n.*** water for drinking, पीने का पानी।

drip (ड्रिप) ***v.*** to fall in drops, चूना या चुआना, टपकना या टपकाना। ***n.*** 1. a small drop of liquid, बूँद। 2. the intravenous drop by drop administration of a medicinal liquid, ड्रिप।

drive (ड्राइव) ***v.*** 1. to urge onwards by force, हाँकना, आगे बढ़ाना। 2. to operate and control (a vehicle, horse etc.), चलाना, ड्राइव करना। 3. to take someone in a vehicle, गाड़ी में बैठाकर (अपने साथ) ले जाना। 4. to force to penetrate, ठोंकना, धँसाना। ***n.*** 1. an excursion or journey in a vehicle, गाड़ी की यात्रा, गाड़ी की सैर। 2. a road for vehicles, सड़क। 3. driving of game, हाँका। 4. a well-planned effort, सुनियोजित प्रयास। 5. a forceful hit, ज़ोरदार आघात या प्रहार। 6. a strong motivating tendency, जोश, उत्साह।

drive-in (ड्राइव-इन) ***adj.*** (a place) people can use while sitting in their cars, (वह स्थान) जहाँ कार में बैठे-बैठे सिनेमा या नाट्यशाला के कार्यक्रम देखे जा सकते हों, ड्राइव-इन।

driver (ड्राइवर) ***n.*** a person who drives a vehicle, ड्राइवर, चालक।

drizzle (ड्रिज़ल) ***n.*** very light rain, झींसी, बूँदाबाँदी, फुहार। ***v.*** to rain lightly, झींसी पड़ना, बूँदा-बाँदी होना।

drone (ड्रोन) ***n.*** 1. a male honey-bee, नर-मधुमक्खी। 2. an idler, निठल्ला व्यक्ति, पराश्रयी। ***v.*** to hum, भिनभिन करना।

droop (ड्रूप) ***v.*** to incline downwards, झुकना, लटकना।

drop (ड्रॉप) ***n.*** 1. a small quantity of liquid in a spherical mass, बूँद। 2. a small round sweet, छोटी गोलाकार मिठाई। 3. a sudden decrease or fall, गिरावट, कमी। 4. unloading of (troops) by parachute, पैराशूट से नीचे उतरना। ***v.*** 1. to fall, गिरना। 2. to allow to fall, गिराना। 3. to decrease in amount or value, कम होना, गिरना, घटना। 4. to set down, उतरना।

dropout (ड्रॉपआउट) ***n.*** a student who leaves the classes and examinations (prematurely, समय

से पहले) स्कूल छोड़ देनेवाला छात्र।

dropper (ड्रॉपर) ***n.*** a device for administering liquid in drops, ड्रापर।

droppings (ड्रॉपिंग्स) ***n.*** 1. the dung of birds, बीठ। 2. the dung of certain animals, विष्ठा, मल, लीद।

drop-scene (ड्रॉपसीन) ***n.*** the dropping of the curtain at the end of a play enacted at the stage, पटाक्षेप।

dropsy (ड्रॉप्सी) ***n.*** a disease with watery fluid accumulating in the body, जलोदर।

drought (ड्राउट) ***n.*** a long period of little or no rain, सूखा, अनावृष्टि।

drown (ड्राउन) ***v.*** 1. to die or kill by immersion in liquid, डूब जाना या डुबो देना। 2. to drench thoroughly, अच्छी तरह तर करना, डुबो देना।

drowse (ड्राउज़) ***v.*** to fall into a light slumber, ऊँघना, झपकी आना। ***n.*** an act of drowsing, ऊँघ, झपकी।

drowsy (ड्राउज़ी) ***adj.*** sleepy, उनींदा।

drub (ड्रब) ***v.*** 1. to thrash, पिटाई करना, मारना-पीटना।

drudge (ड्रज) ***n.*** a person who does unpleasant and laborious work, उबाऊ काम करनेवाला। ***v.*** to do the work of a drudge, उबाऊ काम करना।

drudgery (ड्रजरी) ***n.*** unpleasant or laborious work, उबाऊ काम।

drug (ड्रग) ***n.*** 1. a substance used as medicine, दवा, ओषधि। 2. a medicine that produces numbness and stupor, नशीली दवा।

drug addict (ड्रग एडिक्ट) ***n.*** a person who is habituated to take narcotic drug, नशेड़ी।

drum (ड्रम) ***n.*** a musical instrument played by hands or sticks, ढोल, नगाड़ा, मृदंग। ***v.*** to beat a drum, ढोल बजाना।

drummer (ड्रमर) ***n.*** a person who plays a drum, ढोल बजानेवाला।

drum stick (ड्रम स्टिक) ***n.*** a stick for beating a drum, चोब, कमाची।

drunk (ड्रंक) ***v.*** p.p. of drink. ***adj.*** intoxicated, नशे में चूर या धुत्त।

drunkard (ड्रंकर्ड) ***n.*** a drunk, शराबी, पियक्कड़, मदिरा-सेवी।

dry (ड्राइ) ***adj.*** 1. free from liquid or moisture, सूखा, शुष्क। 2. without water, जलहीन, निर्जल। 3. having little or no rain fall, सूखा। 4. not in or under water, सूखा। 5. without oil, रूखा, सूखा। 6. uninteresting, नीरस, शुष्क। 7. not yielding milk, दूध न देनेवाली (गाय)। 8. prohibiting the sale of alcoholic liquor, नशाबंद। 9. lacking warmth, सहानुभूतिहीन, भाव-शून्य। ***v.*** to make or become dry, सूख जाना या सुखा देना।

dry-clean (ड्राइक्लीन) ***n.*** the process of cleaning by a solvent not by water, सूखी धुलाई।

dryer (ड्राइअर) ***n.*** an instrument or device used for drying, सुखानेवाला उपकरण।

dry farming ***n.*** a method of farming without or little water, बिरानी खेती, सूखी खेती।

dual (ड्यूअल) ***adj.*** relating to or denoting two, द्वैत।

dualism (ड्यूअलिज़म) ***n.*** recognition of two different or independent principles, द्वैतवाद।

D

dubious (ड्यूबिअस) ***adj.*** doubtful, संदिग्ध, संशयात्मक।

duck[1] (डक) ***n.*** 1. a waterbird with a flat bill and webbed feet, बत्तख। 2. zero score in a cricket, अंडा, शून्य।

duck[2] ***v.*** to submerge briefly in water, गोता या डुबकी लगाना।

duct (डक्ट) ***n.*** 1. a tube or channel, नाली, पाईप। 2. a bodily passage for conveying secretions or excretions, नस, वाहिनी।

due (ड्यू) ***adj.*** 1. payable, देय। 2. owed as a debt or obligation, देय, शोध्य। 3. proper, उचित। 4. scheduled to arrive, प्रत्याशित, अपेक्षित।

duel (ड्यूअल) ***n.*** a combat between two persons, द्वंद्वयुद्ध।

dues (ड्यूज़) ***n.*** official charges or fees, चंदा, फ़ीस, कर आदि।

duet (ड्यूट) ***n.*** a piece of music performed by two persons, दुगाना।

duffer (डफ़र) ***n.*** a foolish fellow, मूढ़।

duke (ड्यूक) ***n.*** (in Britain) a noble man of high rank, ड्यूक।

dulcet (डल्सिट) ***adj.*** sounding sweet, श्रुतिमधुर।

dull (डल) ***adj.*** 1. slow in understanding, मंदबुद्धि। 2. lacking sharpness, not acute, भोथरा, कुंठ। 3. not bright, हलका, मंद, निस्तेज। 4. not clear, धुँधला, अंधकारमय। 5. listless, स्फूर्तिहीन। 6. not loud, मंद। 7. not brisk, मंदा। 8. not interesting, अरोचक। ***v.*** to make or become dull, मंद होना या करना, हलका होना या करना।

duly (ड्यूली) ***adv.*** 1. properly, बाक़ायदा, विधिवत्। 2. at the proper time, यथासमय।

dumb (डम) ***adj.*** 1. mute, गूँगा। 2. speechless or silent, मूक। 3. stupid, मूर्ख।

dumb-bell (डम्बेल) ***n.*** a heavy bar with a disc at either end for lifting, डंबल।

dumbfound (डमफॉउन्ड) ***v.*** to confuse, भ्रमित करना।

dummy (डमी) ***n.*** 1. an imitation of an object, प्रतिकृति, डमी। 2. a model of human figure used to display clothes, डमी। 3. a person who appears to act for others or does nothing, डमी। ***adj.*** sham, नकली।

dump (डम्प) ***v.*** 1. to drop or unload (something) in a heap carelessly, ढेर या अंबार लगा देना। 2. to place (something) in larger quantities, (बाज़ार को किसी चीज़ से) पाट देना। ***n.*** 1. a heap of waste matter, कूड़े का ढेर, घूरा। 2. something heaped up, ढेर, ढेरी।

dunce (डन्स) ***n.*** a bad learner, जड़मति।

dune (ड्यून) ***n.*** a sandhill, बालू का टीला।

dung (डंग) ***n.*** 1. animal excrement, गोबर, लीद, विष्ठा, मल। 2. manure, खाद।

dungeon (डन्जन) ***n.*** a dark underground prison, ज़मीन के नीचे बना कैदख़ाना।

dupe (ड्यूप) ***n.*** a fool, मूर्ख व्यक्ति। ***v.*** to make a dupe of, मूर्ख बनाना।

duplex (ड्यूप्लेक्स) ***adj.*** double, दुहरा या दुगुना।

duplicate (डूप्लिकेट) ***n.*** something that corresponds exactly to something else, प्रतिलिपि। ***v.*** to

make an identical copy of, प्रतिलिपि तैयार करना।

duplicator (डूप्लिकेटर) ***n.*** a machine for making identical copies, डुप्लिकेटर।

duplicity (डूप्लिसिटी) ***n.*** deception, deceitfulness, धोखाधड़ी, ठगी।

durable (ड्युरेबल) ***adj.*** 1. long lasting, स्थायी। 2. able to withstand wear and tear, strong, टिकाऊ, मज़बूत, पाएदार।

duration (ड्युरेशन) ***n.*** the length of time during which something exists or continues, अवधि, मियाद।

duress (ड्युरेस) ***n.*** 1. coercion, उत्पीड़न। 2. imprisonment, कारावास, क़ैद।

during (ड्यूरिंग) ***prep.*** through the whole course of, के दौरान।

dusk (डस्क) ***n.*** the darker part of twilight, झुटपुटा, गोधूलि वेला, साँझ। ***adj.*** dim, धुँधला।

dusky (डस्की) ***adj.*** 1. dim, धुँधला। 2. dark, अँधियारा।

dust (डस्ट) ***n.*** 1. finely powdered earth, dirt, धूल, मिट्टी, गर्द। 2. a cloud of this, गर्द-ग़ुबार। 3. any powdery material, बुकनी, चूरा। ***v.*** to clean the dust by wiping or sweeping, धूल झाड़ना, बुहारना, झाड़ू देना।

dustbin (डस्टबिन) ***n.*** a container for trash or rubbish, कूड़ेदान।

duster (डस्टर) ***n.*** a cloth for dusting furniture, windows doors etc., झाड़न।

dutiful (ड्यूटिफ़ुल) ***adj.*** doing one's duty, कर्तव्यशील, कर्तव्यपरायण।

duty (ड्यूटी) ***n.*** 1. a moral or legal obligation, ड्यूटी, कर्तव्य, फ़र्ज। 2. a function or work, काम, कार्य। 3. a tax charged by government, कर, शुल्क।

duty free ***adj.*** (a thing) not liable to tax, कर-मुक्त, शुल्क-मुक्त।

dwarf (ड्वार्फ़) ***n.*** an abnormally undersized person, बौना।

dwell (ड्वेल) ***v.*** to live/reside, रहना, बसना, वास करना।

dwelling (ड्वेलिंग) ***n.*** a place to live in, residence, वास, निवास, निवास-स्थान।

dwindle (ड्विन्डल) ***v.*** to become less in size, number or intensity, घटना, कम होना, छीजना।

dye (डाइ) ***n.*** 1. a colouring substance, रंग, रंगद्रव्य, रंजक। 2. a colour produced by dyeing, चढ़ा हुआ रंग। ***v.*** to colour with a dye, रंग में रँगना, रँगना।

dying (डाइंग) ***adj.*** 1. about to die, at death's door, जो मर रहा हो, मरणोन्मुख, मरणासन्न। 2. relating to the moment of death, मरते समय का।

dynamic (डाइनैमिक) ***adj.*** 1. relating to force or power causing movement, गति-संबंधी, गतिक। 2. energetic, गतिशील, कर्मठ।

dynamics (डाइनैमिक्स) ***n.*** the science that deals with matter in motion, गति-विज्ञान।

dynamism (डाइनेमिज़्म) ***n.*** the quality of being dynamic, गतिशीलता।

dynamite (डाइनेमाइट) ***n.*** 1. a powerful explosive, डाइनामाइट। 2. great vitality, प्रभूत शक्ति।

dynamo (डाइनमो) ***n.*** a machine

D

which turns mechanical energy into electrical energy, डायनमो।

dynastic (डाइनैस्टिक) ***adj.*** of or related to a dynasty, राजवंशीय।

dynasty (डाइनेस्टी) ***n.*** a line or sequence of hereditary rulers, राजवंश।

dysentery (डिसेन्टरी) ***n.*** a disease of the bowels causing severe diarrhoea पेचिश, मरोड़, आँव।

dyspepsia (डिस्पेप्सिआ) ***n.*** indigestion, अपच, बदहज़मी।

E, e (ई) the fifth letter of the English alphabet, अंग्रेज़ी वर्णमाला का पाँचवाँ वर्ण।

each (ईच) ***adj. pron.*** every one of two or more considered individually, हर, हर एक, प्रत्येक।

eager (ईगर) ***adj.*** full of intense desire, उत्सुक।

eagerness (ईगरनिस) ***n.*** a state or condition of being eager, उत्सुकता।

eagle (ईगल) ***n.*** any of various large birds of prey with a hooked bill, गरुड़, गिद्ध, चील, बाज़ या ऐसी ही किसी जाति का पक्षी।

eagle-eyed (ईगल-आइड) ***adj.*** having keen eyesight, तीक्ष्ण दृष्टि।

ear[1] (इअर) ***n.*** 1. the organ of hearing, कान, कर्ण। 2. the visual outer part of this organ, कान।

ear[2] ***n.*** the seed bearing spike of corn, wheat, barley etc., (गेहूँ या जौ की) बाल।

earache (इअरेक) ***n.*** an ache in the ear, कान का दर्द।

early (अर्ली) ***adv.*** 1. before the usual time, पहले, जल्दी। 2. near the beginning of a course of events, आरंभ में, आरंभिक काल में। 3. occurring in the near future, जल्दी ही। 4. far back in time, बहुत पहले।

earmark (इअरमार्क) ***v.*** to set aside for a specific purpose, किसी निश्चित प्रयोजन के लिए (धन या रक़म) अलग रखना या निर्धारित करना।

earn (अर्न) ***v.*** to receive as return for services rendered or work done, कमाना।

earnest (अर्निस्ट) ***adj.*** 1. serious in mind or intention, गंभीर, संजीदा, तत्पर। 2. of good intentions, हार्दिक, आंतरिक, सच्चा।

earring (इअररिंग) ***n.*** an ornament worn on the earlobe, कर्णफूल, कान का आभूषण।

earth (अर्थ) ***n.*** 1. our planet, पृथ्वी। 2. the world in which we live, संसार, जगत्। 3. the living beings of this world, जीव-जगत्, प्राणी-जगत्।

earthenware (अर्थनवेअर) ***n.*** pottery made of baked clay, मिट्टी के बर्तन।

earthly (अर्थली) ***adj.*** 1. of this world, worldly, सांसारिक, भौतिक।

earthquake (अर्थक्वेक) ***n.*** a violent movement in the crust of the earth, भूकंप।

earthworm (अर्थवर्म) ***n.*** a long worm that burrows into the soil, केंचुआ।

earthy (अर्थी) ***adj.*** 1. made of earth, मिट्टी का बना। 2. worldly, सांसारिक।

ease (ईज़) ***n.*** 1. relief from pain or worry, आराम, राहत। 2. rest, leisure or relaxation, आराम, विश्राम, चैन।

easel (ईज़ल) ***n.*** a wooden frame to support a blackboard or an artist's canvas or picture, ब्लैकबोर्ड अथवा चित्रफ़लक को खड़ा करने का चौखटा, चित्रफ़लक-आधार।

easily (ईज़िली) ***adv.*** without difficulty, सरलतापूर्वक।

East (ईस्ट) ***n.*** the eastern part of the world, पूरब, पूर्व।

east (ईस्ट) ***n.*** the point or direction of horizon where the sun rises, पूर्व

E

दिशा। ***adj.*** 1. facing east, पूर्वोन्मुखी। 2. coming from east, पूर्वी।

Easter (ईस्टर) ***n.*** the Christian festival commemorating Christ's resurrection, ईस्टर, ईस्टर का त्योहार।

eastern (ईस्टर्न) ***adj.*** of the east, पूर्वी, प्राच्य।

easy (ईज़ी) ***adj.*** not difficult, सरल, सुगम, आसान।

easygoing (ईज़ीगोइंग) ***adj.*** living without worry or concern, निश्चिंत।

eat (ईट) ***v.*** 1. to take in and swallow, खाना, पेट में डालना, उदरस्थ करना। 2. to have a meal, भोजन करना, खाना खाना।

eatable (ईटबल) ***adj.*** edible, खाद्य।

eaves (ईव्स) ***n.*** the edge of a roof that projects beyond the wall, छज्जा।

ebb (एब) ***v.*** 1. to flow back or recede (said of a tide), भाटा आना। 2. to decline, ह्रास होना। ***n.*** 1. the period of a tide between high tide and a succeeding low tide, भाटा, उतार। 2. a period or condition of decline, अवनति या ह्रास।

ebonite (एबनाइट) ***n.*** black hard rubber, एक प्रकार का काला कड़ा रबर।

ebony (एबनी) ***n.*** 1. a tree and its hard black wood, आबनूस का वृक्ष या उसकी लकड़ी। 2. a black colour, काला रंग। ***adj.*** black as ebony, आबनूसी।

ebullient (इबुल्यन्ट) ***adj.*** showing or feeling ebullience, मस्त, उत्साहपूर्ण, जोशीला।

eccentric (इक्सेन्ट्रिक) ***adj.*** 1. situated away from the centre, उत्केंद्रक, उत्केंद्री। 2. whimsical, सनकी, ख़ब्ती।

ecclesiastic (एक्लीज़िऐस्टिक) ***adj.*** of or pertaining to a church, गिरजा-संबंधी, क्लीसियाई।

echo (एको) ***n.*** the reflection of sound, प्रतिध्वनि, गूँज। ***v.*** to repeat or be repeated by an echo, प्रतिध्वनित होना या करना, गूँज पैदा करना या होना।

eclipse (इक्लिप्स) ***n.*** the partial or complete blocking of the light of the sun or the moon by another body, ग्रहण।

economic (ईकनॉमिक) ***adj.*** 1. of economics, अर्थशास्त्रीय। 2. of or related to finance, आर्थिक।

economical (ईकनॉमिकल) ***adj.*** 1. not wasteful, avoiding waste, thrifty, कमख़र्चीला। 2. economic, आर्थिक।

economics (ईकनॉमिक्स) ***n.*** the science dealing with production, consumption, exchange and distribution of goods and services, अर्थशास्त्र, अर्थविज्ञान।

economist (इकॉनमिस्ट) ***n.*** an expert in economics, अर्थशास्त्री, अर्थविज्ञानी।

economize (इकॉनमाइज़) ***v.*** to save (money, time etc.) instead of being wasteful, किफ़ायत करना, बचत करना, बचाना।

economy (इकॉनमी) ***n.*** a system for the management and development of resources, अर्थव्यवस्था।

ecstasy (एक्स्टसी) ***n.*** feeling of extreme rapture, हर्षातिरेक, हर्षोन्माद।

ecstatic (एक्स्टैटिक) ***adj.*** causing ecstasy, हर्षोन्मादक।

eczema (एक्ज़िमा) ***n.*** a skin disease marked by itching and sores, दाद, खाज, पामा, एक्ज़िमा।

eddy (एडी) ***n.*** 1. a swirling patch

E

of water, भँवर। 2. a swirling patch of air, बवंडर।

Eden (ईडन) ***n.*** the place or home of Adam and Eve, स्वर्ग, अदन।

edge (एज) ***n.*** 1. the cutting or sharpened side of a blade, knife etc., धार, कोर। 2. a border, किनारा, छोर। 3. an advantage, लाभ, फ़ायदा। ***v.*** 1. to form the border of, किनारा बनाना। 2. to sharpen the edge, धार तेज़ करना, धार बनाना, सान लगाना। 3. to advance gradually, धीरे-धीरे आगे बढ़ना।

edible (एडिबल) ***adj.*** fit to be eaten, खाद्य।

edict (ईडिक्ट) ***n.*** 1. a decree, राजादेश, राजाज्ञा। 2. a proclamation, घोषणा।

edifice (एडिफ़िस) ***n.*** an imposing building, भव्य भवन।

edify (एडिफ़ाइ) ***v.*** 1. to improve spiritually, सुधार करना। 2. to teach good thoughts, शिक्षा देना, सन्मार्ग पर लाना।

edit (एडिट) ***v.*** to correct and prepare for printing or publication, संपादित करना।

edition (एडिशन) ***n.*** the entire number of copies of a book, newspaper etc., printed at one time, संस्करण।

editor (एडिटर) ***n.*** a person who edits a newspaper, magazine, etc., संपादक।

editorial (एडिटोरियल) ***n.*** an article written by the editor, संपादकीय, अग्रलेख।

educate (एजुकेट) ***v.*** to impart knowledge and develop skills, शिक्षित करना।

educated (एजुकेटिड) ***adj.*** having received education, शिक्षित, पढ़ा-लिखा।

education (एजुकेशन) ***n.*** 1. the act or process of imparting knowledge and developing skill, शिक्षा, शिक्षण। 2. the knowledge or skill obtained, शिक्षा।

educational (एजुकेशनल) ***adj.*** of or pertaining to education, शैक्षिक।

educationist (एजुकेशनिस्ट) ***n.*** a person expert in the science of education, शिक्षाशास्त्री।

educative (एजुकेटिव) ***adj.*** instructive, शिक्षाप्रद, ज्ञानप्रद।

eel (ईल) ***n.*** a snakelike freshwater fish, सर्पमीन, ईल मछली।

eerie (ईरी) ***adj.*** causing fear, डरावना, भयानक।

efface (इफ़ेस) ***v.*** to rub out, रगड़कर मिटा देना।

effect (इफ़ेक्ट) ***n.*** 1. a result, परिणाम, फल। 2. influence, प्रभाव, असर, छाप। ***v.*** to accomplish, निष्पन्न करना, पूरा करना।

effective (इफ़ेक्टिव) ***adj.*** powerful in its effect, प्रभावपूर्ण, उपयोगी।

effeminate (इफ़ेमिनिट) ***adj.*** (a person) having womanly characteristics, unmanly, स्त्रैण, जनाना।

effervesce (एफ़र्वेस) ***v.*** to give off bubbles, बुलबुले छोड़ना।

efficacious (एफ़िकेशस) ***adj.*** producing desired result, अमोघ, अचूक।

efficacy (एफ़िकेसी) ***n.*** the state of being efficacious, प्रभावोत्पादकता।

efficiency (इफ़िशिअन्सी) ***n.*** the quality or state of being efficient, दक्षता।

E

efficient (इफ़िशन्ट) ***adj.*** competent, capable, दक्ष, दक्षतापूर्ण।

effigy (एफ़िजी) ***n.*** a crude figure of a (hated or despised) person, पुतला।

effluent (एफ़्लुएन्ट) ***adj.*** flowing out, बाहर बहता हुआ।

effort (एफ़र्ट) ***n.*** an attempt, चेष्टा, प्रयत्न।

effortless (एफ़र्टलिस) ***adj.*** needing no effort, बिना यत्न के होनेवाला, सहज।

effrontery (इफ़्रन्टरी) ***n.*** shamelessness, निर्लज्जता, ढिठाई।

effulgence (इफ़ल्जेन्स) ***n.*** brightness, lustre, चमक, दीप्ति।

effulgent (इफ़ल्जेन्ट) ***adv.*** shining brilliantly, दीप्त, चमकदार।

effusion (इफ़्यूज़न) ***n.*** 1. a pouring forth, स्राव, बहाव, प्रवाह। 2. an unrestrained pouring, उद्गार, भड़ास।

e.g. (abbreviation of exempli gratia) ***adv.*** for example, उदाहरणार्थ, उदाहरण के लिए।

egg (एग) ***n.*** 1. the oval or round body laid by the females of domestic fowls, birds, reptiles, insects etc., अंडा। 2. its contents, अंडे के अंदर का तत्त्व।

ego (ईगो) ***n.*** the self-esteem bordering on conceit, अहं।

egoism (ईगोइज़्म) concern for one's own welfare and interests, स्वार्थपरता।

egregious (इग्रीजस) ***adj.*** conspicuously bad, बहुत बुरा, हानिकर।

egress (ईग्रेस) ***n.*** the act of going out, बाहर जाना, निर्गमन, रवानगी।

eh (ए) ***interj.*** an exclamation of surprise, confirmation or inquiry, ओह! (विस्मयादि बोधक)

eight (एट) ***adj. & n.*** a cardinal number equal to one more than seven, आठ।

eighteen (एटीन) ***adj. & n.*** one more than seventeen, अठारह।

eightfold (एटफ़ोल्ड) ***adj.*** 1. having eight folds, अठपहला। 2. by eight times as much, आठगुना।

eighties (एटीज़) ***n.*** the years from 80 to 89, अस्सी से नवासी वर्षों के बीच का काल।

eighty (एटी) ***adj. & n.*** a cardinal number equal to 8 × 10, अस्सी।

either (आइदर/ईदर) ***pron.*** one or the other, यह या वह। ***adj.*** one or the other of two, दो में से कोई।

either-or (आइदर/ईदर-ऑर) ***adj.*** alternative, यह या वह।

ejaculate (इजेक्यूलेट) ***v.*** to utter abruptly, सहसा बोल उठना।

eject (इजेक्ट) ***v.*** 1. to throw out with force, बाहर फेंक देना। 2. to expel, निकाल बाहर करना।

eke (ईक) ***v.*** to increase or prolong, बढ़ाना, खींच ले चलना।

elaborate[1] (इलैबरिट) ***adj.*** marked by detail, detailed, विस्तृत, लंबा-चौड़ा।

elaborate[2] (इलैबरेट) ***v.*** to add more detail to, विस्तार देना, विस्तृत बनाना।

elaboration (इलैबरेशन) ***n.*** 1. the act of elaborating, विस्तृतीकरण। 2. something elaborated, विस्तार, विस्तारित रूप।

elapse (इलैप्स) ***v.*** to pass गुज़र जाना, बीत जाना।

elastic (इलैस्टिक) ***adj.*** flexible, लचीला।

elasticity (इलैस्टिसिटी) ***n.*** the quality or state of being elastic, लचीलापन।

elate (इलेट) ***v.*** to fill with joy, ख़ुशी से भर उठना या भर देना।

elation (इलेशन) ***n.*** the act of elating or the state of being elated, उल्लास, ख़ुशी।

elbow (एल्बो) ***n.*** the joint between the forearm and upper arm, कोहनी।

elder (एल्डर) ***adj.*** comparative form of old, अपेक्षाकृत बड़ा, ज्येष्ठ।

eldest (एल्डिस्ट) ***adj.*** first-born, ज्येष्ठ।

El Dorado (एल डराडो) ***n.*** an imaginary city of great riches, स्वर्ण नगरी।

elect (इलेक्ट) ***v.*** 1. to choose, चुनना, पसंद करना। 2. to select by vote as for office or membership, चुनना, निर्वाचित करना। ***adj.*** elected, निर्वाचित।

election (इलेक्शन) ***n.*** the act or process of electing, निर्वाचन, चुनाव।

electioneering (इलेक्शनिअरिंग) ***n.*** the work done for a candidate or political party in an election, चुनाव-अभियान।

electorate (इलेक्टरिट) ***n.*** all the people living in the country who have the voting rights, निर्वाचकगण।

electric (इलेक्ट्रिक) ***adj.*** produced, powered or operated by electricity, बिजली का, विद्युत्-संबंधी।

electrical (इलेक्ट्रिकल) ***adj.*** 1. electric, विद्युत्-संबंधी। 2. very exciting, उत्तेजनापूर्ण।

electrician (इलेक्ट्रिशन) ***n.*** one who installs, maintains or repairs the electrical devices, बिजली मिस्त्री।

electricity (इलेक्ट्रिसिटी) ***n.*** electric current, बिजली, विद्युत्।

electrification (इलेक्ट्रिफ़िकेशन) ***n.*** the act of electrifying, विद्युतीकरण।

electrify (इलेक्ट्रिफ़ाइ) ***v.*** 1. to equip for the use of electric power, विद्युतीकरण करना, बिजली लगाना। 2. to startle or shock, चौंका देना।

electrocute (इलेक्ट्रक्यूट) ***v.*** to kill with electricity, बिजली से मरना।

electrolyte (इलेक्ट्रलाइट) ***n.*** a solution which can be separated into its chemical parts by passing electricity through it, इलेक्ट्रोलाइट।

electron (इलेक्ट्रॉन) ***n.*** a particle of an atom with a negative electric charge, इलेक्ट्रान।

electronic (इलेक्ट्रॉनिक) ***adj.*** of or pertaining to electrons, इलेक्ट्रानिक, इलेक्ट्रानीय।

electronics (इलेक्ट्रॉनिक्स) ***n.*** (usu. singular) the science and technology of electronic devices and systems, इलेक्ट्रानिक्स।

electroplate (इलेक्ट्रोप्लेट) ***v.*** to coat with a thin surface of metal by electricity, बिजली से मुलम्मा करना, कलई करना।

elegance (एलिगेन्स) ***n.*** 1. beauty, सौंदर्य। 2. refinement, परिष्कृत व्यवहार। 3. grace, भव्यता।

elegant एलिगेन्ट) ***adj.*** 1. refined and graceful, चारु, सुंदर। 2. tasteful in dress, style or manners, रमणीक, सुरुचिपूर्ण, सुसुष्ठु।

elegy (एलिजि) ***n.*** a mournful poem or song, शोकगीत, मर्सिया।

element (एलिमेन्ट) ***n.*** 1. any of the 105 known substances of which other things are made up, तत्त्व। 2. a fundamental or essential

E

part of a whole, घटक, अवयव। 3. the heating part of a piece of electrical apparatus, एलिमेंट। 4. (plu.) a group, वर्ग, तत्त्व। 5. (plu.) the basic principles, मूल सिद्धांत।

elementary (एलिमेन्टरी) ***adj.*** 1. introductory, प्राथमिक, प्रारंभिक। 2. fundamental, मूलभूत, मौलिक, बुनियादी।

elephant (एलिफ़ैन्ट) ***n.*** a large animal with a trunk, हाथी।

elevate (एलिवेट) ***v.*** 1. to raise or lift up, ऊपर/ऊँचा उठाना। 2. to elate, उत्साहित करना।

elevation (एलिवेशन) ***n.*** 1. the act of elevating or the state of being elevated, उत्थान, उन्नयन। 2. the altitude of a place, the height above sea-level, उत्सेध। 3. a piece of rising ground, ऊँची जगह, टीला, पहाड़ी। 4. an elevated position, उत्कर्ष, पदोन्नति। 5. a drawing of a flat upright side of a building, भवन के सामनेवाले भाग का आरेख, खड़ा नक़्शा।

elevator (एलिवेटर) ***n.*** a machine or apparatus for transporting people or goods from one floor of a building to another, एलिवेटर, लिफ़्ट।

eleven (इलेवन) ***adj.*** **&** ***n.*** 1. one more than ten, ग्यारह। 2. a team consisting of eleven players, एकादश।

elf (एल्फ़) ***n.*** a small fairy, छोटी-सी परी।

elicit (इलिसिट) ***v.*** to search out, ढूँढ़/खोज निकालना।

eligibility (एलिजिबिलिटी) ***n.*** the state or quality of being eligible, पात्रता।

eligible (एलिजिबल) ***adj.*** 1. fit or qualified to be chosen, पात्र, अधिकारी। 2. regarded as suitable or desirable, उपयुक्त।

eliminate (इलिमिनेट) ***v.*** 1. to leave out, हटा देना, निरस्त कर देना। 2. to kill, मार डालना।

elimination (इलिमिनेशन) ***n.*** the act of eliminating or the state of being eliminated, निरसन, बहिष्कार, समाप्ति।

elite (एलीट) ***n.*** the superior, rich or more powerful members of a social group, अभिजात वर्ग।

elixir (इलिक्सिर) ***n.*** 1. an imaginary liquid which can change other metals into gold, धातुओं को सोने में बदल देनेवाला कल्पित रसायन। 2. a medicine believed to cure all ills, panacea, रामबाण ओषधि।

ellipse (इलिप्स) ***n.*** a flat egg-shaped figure, अंडाकार आकृति।

elocution (एलोक्यूशन) ***n.*** the art of public speaking, भाषण-कला।

elongate (इलॉन्गेट) ***v.*** to make longer, बढ़ाना, लंबा करना।

elope (इलोप) ***v.*** to run away secretly with a lover, प्रेमी के साथ निकल भागना, सहपलायन करना।

eloquence (एलोक्वेन्स) ***n.*** the act of speaking fluently, भाषणपटुता।

eloquent (एलोक्वेन्ट) ***adj.*** speaking fluently and powerfully, धाराप्रवाह बोलनेवाला, वाग्मी।

else (एल्स) ***adj.*** other, अन्य, दूसरा।

elsewhere (एल्सव्हेअर) ***adv.*** somewhere else, at another place, कहीं और, अन्यत्र।

elucidate (इल्यूसिडेट) ***v.*** to make clear, स्पष्ट करना।

elucidation (इल्यूसिडेशन) ***n.*** the act of elucidating, स्पष्टीकरण।

elude (इल्यूड) ***v.*** 1. to avoid, बचा या कतरा जाना। 2. to escape from the memory of, याद न आना, न सूझना।

elusion (इल्यूज़न) ***n.*** 1. the act of eluding, बचाव। 2. illusion, भ्रम, धोखा।

elusive (इल्यूसिव) ***adj.*** 1. difficult to catch, पकड़ में न आनेवाला। 2. illusory, भ्रामक, भ्रांतिजनक।

emaciate (इमेशिएट) ***v.*** to become or make feeble, दुबला होना/कर देना।

emaciation (इमेशिएशन) ***n.*** the state of being emaciated, दुबलापन।

emanate (एमनेट) ***v.*** to come forth from, निकलना, उद्भूत होना।

emancipate (इमैन्सिपेट) ***v.*** to free from bondage or slavery, मुक्त/उद्धार करना।

emancipation (इमैन्सिपेशन) ***n.*** the act of emancipating or the state of being emancipated, मुक्ति, उद्धार।

emasculate (इमैस्क्युलेट) ***v.*** to castrate, बधिया करना।

embalm (एम्बाम) ***v.*** to preserve (a dead body) by using chemicals, spices etc., रसायनों या मसालों के लेप से शव को सुरक्षित रखना।

embankment (एम्बैंकमेन्ट) ***n.*** a wall or long mound of earth which is built to keep a river from overflowing its banks, तटबंध।

embargo (एम्बार्गो) ***n.*** 1. an official order restricting some kind of economic activity, रोक, प्रतिबंध। 2. an official order forbidding ships to enter or leave a port, घाटबंदी।

embark (एम्बार्क) ***v.*** 1. to board (a ship or aircraft, जहाज़ पर) चढ़ना, लदना। 2. to begin, आरंभ करना।

embarrass (एम्बैरस) ***v.*** to cause to feel ill at ease or awkward, विचलित/व्याकुल कर देना।

embarrassment (एम्बैरसमेन्ट) ***n.*** the state of being embarrassed, व्याकुलता, उलझन।

embassy (एम्बसी) ***n.*** 1. the official headquarters of an ambassador, राजदूतावास। 2. an ambassador and his staff, राजदूत और उसके कर्मचारीगण।

embellish (एम्बेलिश) ***v.*** to adorn, सजाना, सुसज्जित करना।

embellishment (एम्बेलिशमेन्ट) ***n.*** the act of embellishing or the state of being embellished, शृंगार।

ember (एम्बर) ***n.*** a red hot piece of live coal, अंगारा, अंगार।

embezzle (एम्बेज़ल) ***v.*** to take and use (money or property) in violation of a trust, ग़बन करना।

embezzlement (एम्बेज़लमेन्ट) ***n.*** misappropriation of money or property in violation of a trust, ग़बन।

embitter (एम्बिटर) ***v.*** to make bitter, कड़वा कर या बना देना।

embitterment (एम्बिटरमेन्ट) ***n.*** bitter feelings, कड़वाहट।

emblem (एम्ब्लम) ***n.*** a symbol, प्रतीक।

embody (एम्बॉडी) ***v.*** 1. to give concrete form to, मूर्त रूप देना। 2. to include, सन्निविष्ट करना।

emboss (एम्बॉस) ***v.*** to print or decorate with a raised design, उभारदार अक्षर या चित्र बनाना।

embrace (एम्ब्रेस) ***v.*** 1. to hug, गले से लगाना। 2. to adopt or accept, अंगीकार करना, अपनाना। ***n.*** the act of embracing, आलिंगन; अंगीकरण।

E

embroider (एम्ब्रॉइडर) ***v.*** to ornament with needle work, कसीदा काढ़ना, कढ़ाई करना।

embroidery (एम्ब्रॉइडरी) ***n.*** the act or process of embroidering, decorative needle work, कसीदा, कढ़ाई।

embroil (एम्ब्रॉइल) ***v.*** to entangle, झगड़े में घसीटना, उलझाना।

embryo (एम्ब्रिओ) ***n.*** an organism or animal in its earliest stages of development esp. before birth or hatching, भ्रूण।

emerald (एमेरल्ड) ***n.*** a green transparent precious stone, मरकत, पन्ना।

emerge (इमर्ज) ***v.*** to appear, प्रकट होना। 2. to become obvious, प्रकाश में आना।

emergence (इमर्जेन्स) ***n.*** the act or process of emerging, आविर्भाव।

emergency (इमर्जेन्सी) ***n.*** an unexpected condition or dangerous happening needing prompt action, आपात्-स्थिति, आपात्काल।

emeritus (इमेरिटस) ***adj.*** retired but retaining an honorary title, सेवानिवृत्त परंतु उपाधि-विभूषित, सम्माननीय।

emetic (इमेटिक) ***n.*** medicine that induces vomiting, वमनकारी ओषधि।

emigrant (एमिग्रेन्ट) ***n.*** a person who emigrates, दूसरे देश में जा बसनेवाला, उत्प्रवासी।

emigrate (एमिग्रेट) ***v.*** to leave one's country and go to settle in another, परदेश-गमन करना।

emigration (एमिग्रेशन) ***n.*** the act of emigrating or the state of being emigrated, उत्प्रवास, परदेश-गमन।

eminence (एमिनेन्स) ***n.*** 1. the state of being distinguished and outstanding, उत्कृष्टता, श्रेष्ठता। 2. fame, ख्याति।

eminent (एमिनेन्ट) ***adj.*** 1. distinguished and outstanding, उत्कृष्ट, श्रेष्ठ। 2. famous, ख्यातिलब्ध।

emissary (एमिसरी) ***n.*** a messenger, दूत।

emit (इमिट) ***v.*** 1. to send out or discharge, बाहर फेंकना, निकालना। 2. to utter, मुँह से निकालना, कहना या बोलना। 3. to issue, जारी करना।

emolument (इमॉल्युमेन्ट) ***n.*** 1. a salary, वेतन। 2. (plu.) the profit arising from an office, परिलब्धियाँ।

emotion (इमोशन) ***n.*** 1. a strong mental feeling as of joy, sorrow, hate or fear, भावावेश, भावावेग। 2. sentiment, भाव, मनोभाव, भावना। 3. excitement, उत्तेजना।

emotional (इमोशनल) ***adj.*** characterized by strong emotion, भावुकतापूर्ण।

emperor (एम्परर) ***n.*** one who rules over an empire, सम्राट, शहंशाह।

emphasis (एम्फ़ेसिस) ***n.*** stress or force, बल, ज़ोर।

emphasize (एम्फ़ेसाइज़) ***v.*** to stress, ज़ोर देना, बल देना।

emphatic (एम्फ़ैटिक) ***adj.*** expressed or performed with emphasis, ज़ोरदार, सशक्त।

empire (एम्पाइर) ***n.*** a group of countries ruled by an emperor, साम्राज्य।

empirical (एम्पिरिकल) ***adj.*** based on observation, अनुभवजन्य।

employ (एम्प्लॉय) ***v.*** give work to, काम पर लगाना, नियोजित करना।

employee (एम्प्लॉई) ***n.*** a person who is employed by another, कर्मचारी।

employer (एम्प्लॉयर) ***n.*** one who employs, नियोजक।

employment (एम्प्लॉयमेन्ट) ***n.*** 1. the act of employing or the state of being employed, नियोजन। 2. work done as an occupation, व्यापार, धंधा।

emporium (एम्पोरिअम) ***n.*** a large store, बड़ी दुकान या स्टोर।

empower (एम्पावर) ***v.*** to give power, अधिकृत करना।

empress (एम्प्रिस) ***n.*** a female emperor, सम्राज्ञी।

empty (एम्प्टी) ***adj.*** containing nothing ख़ाली, रिक्त। 2. vacant, ख़ाली।

empty-headed ***adj.*** lacking good sense or intelligence, बुद्धू।

emulate (एम्युलेट) ***v.*** to attempt to equal or excel by imitation, स्पर्धा/होड़ करना।

emulsion (इमल्शन) ***n.*** a creamy mixture of liquids, इमल्शन, तैलोद।

enable (इनेबल) ***v.*** 1. to render able, समर्थ/योग्य बनाना। 2. to make possible, संभव बनाना।

enact (इनैक्ट) ***v.*** 1. to make into an act, क़ानून बनाना। 2. to act or perform, अभिनय करना।

enactment (इनैक्टमेन्ट) ***n.*** the law, क़ानून, अधिनियम।

enamel (इनैमल) ***n.*** 1. a kind of paint, एक तरह का पेंट, इनैमल। 2. the hard outer covering of teeth, इनैमल, दंतवल्क।

enamoured (इनैमर्ड) ***adj.*** captivated, मुग्ध, आसक्त।

en bloc (एन् ब्लॉक) ***adv.*** all together, सामूहिक रूप से। (फ्रांसीसी)

encamp (एन्कैम्प) ***v.*** to lodge in a camp, खेमे में रहना।

encash (एन्कैश) ***v.*** to exchange (a cheque or draft) for cash, भुनाना।

enchant (एन्चैन्ट) ***v.*** to bewitch, मंत्रमुग्ध कर लेना।

encircle (एन्सर्कल) ***v.*** to surround, घेरना।

enclosure (एन्क्लोज़र) ***n.*** 1. an enclosed space or area, घिरा हुआ भू-भाग, बाड़ा। 2. a wall or fence, दीवार या बाड़। 3. something enclosed with a letter, पत्र के साथ नत्थी की हुई वस्तु, संलग्न-पत्र।

encompass (एन्कम्पस) ***v.*** to enclose within a circle, घेर लेना।

encounter (एन्कॉउन्टर) ***n.*** 1. a sudden or unexpected meeting, मुलाक़ात, भेंट, सामना। 2. a battle or hostile meeting, मुठभेड़, सामना।

encourage (एन्करिज) ***v.*** to give courage to, प्रोत्साहित करना।

encouragement (एन्करिजमेन्ट) ***n.*** the act of encouraging, प्रोत्साहन।

encroach (एन्क्रोच) ***v.*** to trespass, अधिक्रमण करना, दबा लेना।

encroachment (एन्क्रोचमेन्ट) ***n.*** the act of encroaching, अतिक्रमण।

encumber (एन्कम्बर) ***v.*** to burden, बोझ से लाद देना।

encumberance (एन्कम्बरेन्स) ***n.*** a burden or obligation, बोझ, भार।

encyclopedia (एंन्साइक्लोपीडिआ) ***n.*** a book for general knowledge, विश्वकोश, ज्ञानकोश।

end (एन्ड) ***n.*** 1. the extreme limit of something, a tip, सिरा, किनारा।

E

2. the extreme extent or degree of something, अंत, समाप्ति, 3. a purpose or goal, ध्येय, प्रयोजन, उद्देश्य। 4. a result or outcome, फल, परिणाम, नतीजा। 5. death, मृत्यु, मौत।

endanger (इन्डेन्जर) ***v.*** to put in danger, संकट / ख़तरे में डालना।

endear (इन्डिअर) ***v.*** to cause to be loved, प्रिय बन जाना।

endeavour, endeavor (इन्डेवर) ***v.*** to try or attempt, प्रयास / प्रयत्न करना। ***n.*** an attempt or effort, प्रयत्न, प्रयास।

endemic (इन्डेमिक) ***adj.*** prevalent in a particular place or locality, किसी स्थान या बस्ती में व्याप्त।

endorse (इन्डोर्स) ***v.*** 1. to write one's signature on the back of a cheque etc., पृष्ठांकन करना, पृष्ठांकित करना। 2. to support or express approval, समर्थन करना।

endorsement (इन्डोर्समेन्ट) ***n.*** the act of endorsing, पृष्ठांकन; समर्थन।

endow (इन्डाउ) ***v.*** to provide with income, आय का प्रबंध कर देना, साधन जुटा देना।

endowment (इन्डाउमेन्ट) ***n.*** 1. the act of endowing, आय का प्रबंध। 2. the endowed income, दान, धर्मादा, निधि।

endurance (इन्ड्यूरेन्स) ***n.*** the power of enduring, सहनशक्ति, धैर्य।

endure (इन्ड्यूर) ***v.*** to bear patiently, झेलना, बर्दाश्त करना।

enema (एनिमा) ***n.*** the insertion of a liquid into the rectum for cleansing the stomach, अनीमा, वस्तिकर्म।

enemy (एनिमि) ***n.*** a hostile opponent, वैरी, शत्रु, दुश्मन।

energetic (एनर्जेटिक) ***adj.*** full of energy, ऊर्जस्वी, उत्साही।

energy (एनर्जी) ***n.*** 1. the capacity or force of a body or system to do work, ऊर्जा, शक्ति। 2. vigour, तेज, ऊर्जस्विता।

enervate (एनर्वेट) ***v.*** to weaken, दुर्बल कर देना।

enforce (इन्फ़ोर्स) ***v.*** to compel obedience to, बाध्य या मजबूर करना।

enforcement (इन्फ़ोर्समेन्ट) ***n.*** 1. the action or process of enforcing, लागू करना, 2. compulsion, बाध्यता, मजबूरी।

enfranchise (इन्फ़्रैन्चाइज़) ***v.*** to endow with the right to vote, मताधिकार प्रदान करना।

engage (इन्गेज) ***v.*** 1. to take into one's employment, नियुक्त करना, काम पर लगाना। 2. to get reserved (a room, कमरा) आरक्षित कराना।

engaged (इन्गेज्ड) ***adj.*** 1. pledged to ,be married, betrothed, जिसकी सगाई या मंगनी हो गई हो, वाग्दत्त या वाग्दत्ता। 2. reserved or occupied, आरक्षित, लगा हुआ।

engagement (इन्गेजमेन्ट) ***n.*** 1. an agreement to marry, मंगनी, सगाई। 2. a contract, करार।

engender (इन्जेन्डर) ***v.*** to cause to be born, जन्म देना, पैदा करना।

engine (एन्जिन) ***n.*** 1. a railway locomotive, इंजन। 2. a fire engine, आग बुझानेवाली मोटर। 3. a machine designed to convert energy into mechanical work, मोटर।

engineer (एन्जिनिअर) ***n.*** a person versed in design, construction or machines, इंजीनियर, अभियंता। ***v.*** to plan, construct or manage as an engineer, इंजीनियर का काम करना, रचना, बनाना या चलाना।

E

engineering (एन्जिनिअरिंग) ***n.*** the application of scientific principles to practical purposes of public utility, अभियांत्रिकी, इंजीनियरी।

English (इंग्लिश) ***n.*** the language of the people of England, America etc., अंग्रेज़ी, इंग्लिश। ***adj.*** of England or its people, अंग्रेज़ी, ब्रितानवी।

engrave (इन्ग्रेव) ***v.*** to carve or etch, उकेरना, नक़्क़ाशी करना।

engraving ***n.*** the art of a person who engraves, नक़्क़ाशी।

engross (इन्ग्रॉस) ***v.*** to fill completely the time and attention of, मग्न/तल्लीन हो जाना।

engrossing ***adj.*** interesting, absorbing, रोचक, मज़ेदार।

engulf (इन्गल्फ़) ***v.*** to swallow up, निगल जाना।

enhance (इन्हान्स) ***v.*** to increase, बढ़ाना, वृद्धि करना।

enigma (इनिग्मा) something very difficult to understand, पेचीदी बात, पहेली।

enigmatic (एनिग्मैटिक) ***adj.*** intricate, पेचीदा।

enjoin (इन्जॉइन) ***v.*** 1. to command, आदेश देना। 2. to prohibit, मना/निषेध करना।

enjoy (इन्जॉइ) ***v.*** to relish, आनंद लेना, मज़ा लेना।

enjoyment (इन्जॉइमेन्ट) ***n.*** the act of enjoying, आनंद, मज़ा।

enlarge (इन्लार्ज) ***v.*** 1. to make larger, बड़ा करना, बढ़ाना। 2. to become larger, बड़ा होना, बढ़ना।

enlighten (इन्लाइटन) ***v.*** 1. inform, जानकारी देना। 2. to give spritual revelation to, प्रबोधन करना।

enlightened (इन्लाइटन्ड) ***adj.*** having true understanding, प्रबुद्ध, ज्ञानी।

enlightenment (इन्लाइटनमेन्ट) ***n.*** the act of enligthening or the state of being enlightened, आत्मज्ञान।

enlist (इन्लिस्ट) ***v.*** 1. to enter on a list, सूची में डालना। 2. to enroll, भर्ती करना।

enmity (एन्मिटी) ***n.*** deep seated hatred or hostility, वैर, शत्रुता, दुश्मनी।

enormity (इनॉर्मिटी) ***n.*** the quality of being enormous, विशालता।

enormous (इनॉर्मस) ***adj.*** huge, विशाल।

enough (इनफ़) ***adj.*** sufficient, ample, यथेष्ट, पर्याप्त।

enplane (इन्प्लेन) ***v.*** to board an air-plane, विमान पर चढ़ना।

enrage (इन्रेज) ***v.*** to infuriate, क्रुद्ध करना।

enrich (इन्रिच) ***v.*** 1. to make rich, समृद्ध बना देना। 2. to improve in quality, flavour etc., बढ़िया बना देना, संवर्धन करना।

enriched (इन्रिच्ड) ***adv.*** made rich, संवर्धित।

enrol, enroll (इन्रोल) ***v.*** 1. to note in a roll or list, रजिस्टर या सूची में चढ़ाना, नाम लिखना। 2. to admit as a member, भर्ती करना, सदस्य बनाना।

enrolment (इन्रोलमेन्ट) ***n.*** the act of enrolling or the state of being enrolled, नाम-लिखाई, नामांकन, भर्ती।

en route (एन् रूट) ***adv.*** on the way, along the way, रास्ते में, मार्ग में। (फ्रांसीसी)

enshrine (इन्श्राइन) ***v.*** to hold as sacred, पवित्र समझकर सँजोना।

ensign (एन्साइन) ***n.*** 1. a flag, झंडा। 2. a symbol, प्रतीक।

E

enslave (एन्स्लेव) ***v.*** to make a slave of, दास/ग़ुलाम बनाना।

ensnare (एन्स्नेअर) ***v.*** to trap in a snare, जाल में फँसाना।

ensuing (एन्स्यूइंग) ***adj.*** next, आगामी।

ensure (एन्श्योर) ***v.*** to make sure, सुनिश्चित कर या बना देना।

entail (एन्टेल) ***v.*** to have as a necessary consequence, साथ लगा होना।

entangle (एन्टैंगल) ***v.*** to complicate, फँसा/उलझा देना।

enter (एन्टर) ***v.*** 1. to go into, प्रवेश करना, अंदर जाना, प्रविष्ट होना। 2. to record, लिखना।

enterprise (एन्टर्प्राइज़) ***n.*** 1. an undertaking, साहसिक कार्य, उद्यम। 2. business, व्यापार।

enterprising ***adj.*** having or showing enterprise, साहसिक, जोखिमी।

entertain (एन्टर्टेन) ***v.*** to amuse, मनोरंजन करना, दिल बहलाना।

entertainment (एन्टर्टेनमेन्ट) ***n.*** 1. the act of entertaining or the state of being entertained, मनोरंजन, दिल-बहलाव। 2. amusement, मनोरंजन-संबंधी क्रियाकलाप।

enthral, enthrall (इन्थ्रॉल) ***v.*** to hold spellbound, मंत्रमुग्ध / अभिभूत कर लेना।

enthrone (एन्थ्रोन) ***v.*** to place on a throne, सिंहासन पर बैठाना।

enthusiasm (इन्थ्यूज़िऐज़म) great or fervent interest, उमंग, जोश, उत्साह।

enthusiastic (इन्थ्यूज़िऐस्टिक) ***adj.*** full of enthusiasm, उत्साही, उत्साहपूर्ण।

entice (इन्टाइस) ***v.*** to lure, लुभा लेना।

enticing ***adj.*** attractive, आकर्षक, लुभावना।

entire (एन्टाइर) ***adj.*** whole, complete, संपूर्ण, समग्र।

entitle (एन्टाइटल) ***v.*** 1. to give a title or name to, उपाधि, शीर्षक या नाम देना। 2. to give a right, अधिकार देना, हक़दार बनाना।

entitled (एन्टाइटल्ड) ***adj.*** having a title to, हक़दार, अधिकारी, पात्र।

entity (एन्टिटी) ***n.*** the fact of existence, अस्तित्व, सत्ता।

entrance (एन्ट्रेन्स) ***n.*** 1. the act of entering, प्रवेश। 2. the door or passage of entry, प्रवेश-द्वार, प्रवेश-मार्ग। 3. the permission or right to enter, प्रवेशाधिकार।

entreat (एन्ट्रीट) ***v.*** to ask earnestly, चिरौरी/मिन्नत करना।

entreaty (एन्ट्रीटी) ***n.*** an earnest request, चिरौरी, मिन्नत।

entrepreneur (आन्ट्रप्रनर) ***n.*** a person who undertakes the risk of business, उद्योगी, उद्यमी।

entrust (एन्ट्रस्ट) ***v.*** to place in someone's care or charge सौंपना।

entry (एन्ट्री) ***n.*** 1. the act of entering, प्रवेश, दाख़िला। 2. the right of entering, प्रवेशाधिकार। 3. a means of entrance, प्रवेश-द्वार या प्रवेश-पथ। 4. the writing down of an item in a record, इंदराज। 5. an item thus entered, प्रविष्टि, मद।

enumerate (इन्यूमरेट) ***v.*** to count one by one, गिनती करना, गिनना।

enunciate (इनन्सिएट) ***v.*** to pronounce, उच्चारण करना।

envelop (एन्वेलप) ***v.*** to cover or wrap up completely, ढक या लपेट लेना, परिवेष्टन करना।

envelope (एन्वलोप) ***n.*** a flat paper container, लिफ़ाफ़ा।

enviable (एन्विएबल) ***adj.*** 1. to

be envied, ईर्ष्या करने योग्य, ईर्ष्य। 2. desirable, वांछनीय।

envious (एन्विअस) ***adj.*** jealous, ईर्ष्यालु।

environment (इन्वाइरनमेन्ट) ***n.*** external conditions or surroundings, वातावरण, पर्यावरण।

envisage (एन्विज़िज) ***v.*** to form a picture in the mind, प्रतीत होना।

envoy (एन्वॉइ) ***n.*** a diplomatic representative of a government, राजदूत।

envy (एन्वी) ***n.*** 1. the desire to have something possessed by another, ईर्ष्या। 2. an object of envy, ईर्ष्या की वस्तु या व्यक्ति। ***v.*** to feel envy toward or because of, ईर्ष्या करना।

enzyme (एन्ज़ाइम) ***n.*** a protein formed in living cells, एन्ज़ाइम।

ephemeral (इफ़ेमरल) ***adj.*** transitory, क्षणिक।

epic (एपिक) ***n.*** a heroic poem, वीरकाव्य।

epidemic (एपिडेमिक) ***n.*** an outbreak of a disease affecting many persons simultaneously in a particular region, महामारी। ***adj.*** attacking or affecting many persons simultaneously, संक्रामक।

epiglottis (एपिग्लॉटिस) ***n.*** a flap that prevents food from entering the windpipe during swallowing, गले की घंटी, कौआ।

epigram (एपिग्रैम) ***n.*** a concise and witty remark, चुटकुला।

epigraph (एपिग्राफ़) ***n.*** an inscription on a monument, शिलालेख।

epilepsy (एपिलेप्सी) ***n.*** a disorder of the nervous system marked by periodic loss of consciousness, मिर्गी।

epilogue, epilog (एपिलॉग) ***n.*** a short poem or speech to the audience at the end of a play, अंतवचन, उपसंहार।

episode (एपिसोड) ***n.*** 1. an event, घटना। 2. one part of a serial, धारावाहिक का एक आख्यान।

epistle (इपिसल) ***n.*** a letter, पत्र।

epitaph (एपिटाफ़) ***n.*** an inscription on a tomb in memory of a dead person, समाधि-लेख।

epithet (एपिथेट) ***n.*** 1. a descriptive word added to a person's name, उपनाम। 2. a title, उपाधि।

epitome (इपिटमी) ***n.*** 1. a brief summary, उपसंहार। 2. a typical example, अनोखा उदाहरण।

epoch (ईपॉक) ***n.*** a unit of geological time, युग, कल्प।

epoch-making (ईपॉक-मेकिंग) marking the beginning of a new epoch, युगांतरकारी।

equal (ईक्वल) ***adj.*** having the same size, value or amount as another, समान, सम, बराबर। ***v.*** to be equal to, समान होना, बराबर होना।

equalitarian (इक्वॉलिटेरिअन) ***n.*** a person holding the belief that all men should have equal political and social rights, समतावादी। ***adj.*** pertaining to this belief, समतावादी।

equality (इक्वॉलिटी) ***n.*** the state of being equal, समता, समानता।

equalize (ईक्वलाइज़) ***v.*** to make equal, बराबर करना।

equanimity (ईक्वनिमिटी) ***n.*** calmness of mind or temper, शांति, धीरज।

E

equanimous (इक्वैनिमस) tranquil, शांत, शांतचित्त।

equate (इक्वेट) ***v.*** to treat or regard as equal, बराबरी का दर्जा देना।

equation (इक्वेशन) ***n.*** a mathematical statement that two expressions are equal, तुल्यता, बराबरी, समीकरण।

equator (इक्वेटर) ***n.*** an imaginary line that divides the earth's surface into the Northern Hemisphere and the Southern Hemisphere, भूमध्य रेखा, विषुवत् रेखा।

equatorial (इक्वेटोरिअल) ***adj.*** of an equator, भूमध्य रेखा-विषयक।

equestrian (इक्वेस्ट्रिअन) ***adj.*** of or pertaining to a horse or horse riding, घोड़े या घुड़सवारी-संबंधी।

equidistant (ईक्विडिस्टेन्ट) ***adj.*** at an equal distance, समदूरस्थ, समदूरवर्ती।

equilateral (ईक्विलेटरल) ***adj.*** having all sides equal, समभुज, समपार्श्व।

equilibrium (ईक्विलिब्रिअम) ***n.*** a state of equality, or balance between opposite forces, साम्य, साम्यावस्था, संतुलन।

equine (ईक्विन) ***adj.*** of or pertaining to a horse, अश्वीय।

equinox (ईक्विनॉक्स) ***n.*** either of the two times during a year when the length of day and night are equal, विषुव।

equip (इक्विप) ***v.*** to furnish with, सज्जित/सुसज्जित करना।

equipment (इक्विपमेन्ट) ***n.*** the things with which one is equipped, साज़-सामान।

equipped (इक्विप्ड) ***adj.*** furnished with, सज्जित, सन्नद्ध।

equitable (एक्विटेबल) ***adj.*** 1. just and fair, न्यायसंगत। 2. impartial, निष्पक्ष।

equity (एक्विटी) ***n.*** 1. fairness, impartiality, न्यायसंगति, निष्पक्षता।

equivalent (इक्विवेलेन्ट) ***adj.*** equal, समान, बराबर।

equivocal (इक्विवोकल) ***adj.*** 1. having two or more meanings, द्व्यर्थक, अनेकार्थक। 2. vague, ambiguous, अस्पष्ट, भ्रामक।

era (ईरा) ***n.*** a period of history, युग, कल्प।

eradicate (इरैडिकेट) ***v.*** to uproot, जड़ से उखाड़ देना, उन्मूलित करना।

eradication (इरैडिकेशन) ***n.*** the act of eradicating, उन्मूलन।

erase (इरेज़) ***v.*** to wipe out, मिटा देना।

eraser (इरेज़र) ***n.*** a thing that removes marks, stains etc., स्याही के दाग़ या निशान मिटानेवाला रबर।

erect (इरेक्ट) ***v.*** 1. to raise to an upright position, खड़ा करना। 2. to build, बनाना, निर्मित करना। 3. to set up, स्थापित करना।

erection (इरेक्शन) ***n.*** the act of erecting or something erected, निर्माण।

erode (इरोड) ***v.*** to wear away or destroy gradually, क्षीण या नष्ट होना।

erosion (इरोज़न) ***n.*** the wearing away of rocks etc., अपरदन, क्षरण।

erotic (इरॉटिक) ***adj.*** tending to arouse sexual desire, कामोत्तेजक।

err (अर) ***v.*** to make an error, भूल/ग़लती करना।

errand (एरन्ड) ***n.*** a short trip taken to perform a specific task, छोटी-मोटी यात्रा।

errant (एरन्ट) ***adj.*** wandering aimlessly, घुमक्कड़।

erratic (इरैटिक) ***adj.*** 1. irregular, अनियत। 2. deviating from the customary course, पथभ्रष्ट।

erratum (इरेटम) ***n.*** an error in printing or writing, अशुद्धि, ग़लती।

erroneous (एरोनिअस) ***adj.*** containing or based on error, ग़लत, अशुद्ध, भ्रामक।

error (एरर) ***n.*** 1. a mistake, ग़लती, भूल, अशुद्धि। 2. a wrong act, ग़लत काम, ग़लती।

erstwhile (अर्स्टव्हाइल) ***adj.*** former, भूतपूर्व। ***adv.*** long ago, बहुत पहले।

erudite (एरुडाइट) ***adj.*** 1. very learned, ज्ञानी, विद्वान। 2. scholarly, विद्वत्तापूर्ण।

erudition (एरुडिशन) ***n.*** extensive learning, ज्ञान।

erupt (इरप्ट) ***v.*** 1. to explode, विस्फोट होना। 2. to burst forth suddenly, भड़ास निकालना, आग उगलना।

eruption (इरप्शन) ***n.*** a bursting forth (of a lava from a volcano), विस्फोट।

escalate (एस्कलेट) ***v.*** 1. to increase or intensify, तीव्र/तेज़ करना, बढ़ाना।

escalation (एस्कलेशन) ***n.*** 1. the act of escalating, तीव्रीकरण, तेज़ी लाना।

escalator (एस्कलेटर) ***n.*** a moving staircase, चलसोपान।

escape (इस्केप) ***v.*** 1. to get away or break out, बच निकलना, निकल भागना, पलायन करना। 2. to succeed in avoiding, बच जाना, जान बचाना। 3. to leak, रिसना। ***n.*** 1. the act of escaping or the state of having escaped, बचाव, रक्षा, निस्तार। 2. a means of escaping, बचाव का रास्ता। 3. a leakage, रिसाव, निस्सरण।

eschew (इस्च्यू) ***v.*** to avoid, बचना, बाज़ आना, परहेज़ करना।

escort (एस्कॉर्ट) ***n.*** a guard, रखवाला, रक्षक। ***v.*** to accompany as an escort, रक्षार्थ साथ जाना।

Eskimo (एस्किमो) ***n.*** 1. a member of a group of people living in Greenland, Alaska, Siberia etc., एस्किमो। 2. the language of Eskimos, एस्किमो भाषा।

esoteric (एसोटेरिक) ***adj.*** private, confidential, गोपनीय।

espionage (एस्पिअनाज़) ***n.*** the act of spying, जासूसी।

esplanade (एस्प्लेनेड) ***n.*** a long open level stretch of ground for walking along a shore, समुद्र का खुला समतल तट।

espousal (इस्पाउज़ल) ***n.*** a betrothal, मँगनी, सगाई।

espouse (इस्पाउज़) ***v.*** to take as a spouse, जीवन-साथी बनाना, ब्याह करना।

espy (इस्पाइ) ***v.*** 1. to catch sight of, झलक पाना। 2. to detect, भाँप लेना, ढूँढ़ निकालना।

Esquire, Esq. (एस्क्वाइर) ***n.*** a title of courtesy placed after a man's name, महोदय (नाम के बाद प्रयुक्त)।

essay (एसे) ***n.*** a short literary composition, निबंध, लेख।

essence (एसेन्स) ***n.*** 1. the intrinsic properties of a thing, सत, सार, तत्त्व। 2. a concentrated extract of substance, अर्क। 3. a liquid perfume, इत्र।

essential (इसेन्शल) ***adj.*** absolutely necessary, अपरिहार्य, अनिवार्य।

establish (एस्टैब्लिश) ***v.*** to make permanent in a certain place, स्थापित करना।

E

establishment (एस्टैब्लिशमेन्ट) ***n.*** 1. the act of establishing, स्थापन, स्थापना। 2. a business firm or public institution, प्रतिष्ठान, संस्थान। 3. the staff of a business firm or institution, कार्यकर्ता वर्ग।

estate (एस्टेट) ***n.*** a large piece of landed property, भू-संपदा, जागीर, रियासत।

estate duty ***n.*** a duty levied on property after the owner's death, संपदा-कर।

esteem (एस्टीम) ***n.*** high regard, respect, आदर, सम्मान।

estimate[1] (एस्टिमेट) ***n.*** a preliminary or rough calculation of value, अनुमान, अंदाज़।

estimate[2] ***v.*** 1. to calculate roughly, अनुमान करना या लगाना। 2. to evaluate, मूल्यांकन करना। 3. to form an opinion about, राय बनाना।

estrange (इस्ट्रेन्ज़) ***v.*** to alienate the affection of, संबंध बिगाड़ लेना, अनबन पैदा कर लेना।

estuary (एस्चुअरी) ***n.*** the wide mouth of a river where the tides meet the current, ज्वार-मुहाना, नदीमुख।

et cetera (एट सेटरा) ***adv.*** and other unspecified things, इत्यादि, वग़ैरह।

etch (एच) ***v.*** to cut or engrave (a picture or design) on a plate, उत्कीर्ण करना।

etching (एचिंग) ***n.*** the art or process of preparing etched metal plates, उत्कीर्णन।

eternal (इटर्नल) ***adj.*** 1. without beginning or end, अनादि, चिरंतन, शाश्वत, सनातन। 2. lasting for ever, अमर।

eternity (इटर्निटी) ***n.*** 1. the state of being eternal, अनंतता, सनातनता, चिरंतनता, अमरत्व। 2. a very long time, अनंत काल।

ether (ईथर) ***n.*** 1. the upper regions beyond the clouds, आकाश, व्योम। 2. the medium supposed to fill all space, ईथर।

ethereal (इथीरिअल) ***adj.*** 1. extremely delicate, सुकुमार। 2. almost as light as air, वायवीय।

ethic (एथिक) ***n.*** a principle of good conduct, नीति, आचार।

ethical (एथिकल) ***adj.*** 1. of or relating to ethics, नीतिशास्त्र-संबंधी। 2. of ethic, नैतिक।

ethics (एथिक्स) ***n.*** (plu.) the study of moral principles, नीतिशास्त्र, आचारशास्त्र।

ethnic (एथ्निक) ***adj.*** of or belonging to a particular group having racial, religious and linguistic traits in common, प्रजातीय, जातीय।

ethos (ईथॉस) ***n.*** (plu.) the characteristic attitudes and habits of a racial group, जातीय गुण या स्वभाव, जातीय विशेषताएँ या संस्कार।

etiquette (एटिकेट) ***n.*** the rules of correct behaviour, शिष्टाचार।

etymological (एटिमलॉजिकल) ***adj.*** of or pertaining to the etymology, व्युत्पत्तीय।

etymology (एटिमॉलोजी) ***n.*** 1. the study of the sources and development of words, व्युत्पत्ति-विज्ञान। 2. an account of this, व्युत्पत्ति, व्युत्पत्तिक विवरण।

Eucharist (यूकरिस्ट) ***n.*** the Christian ceremony in which bread and wine are consecrated and consumed, महाप्रसाद।

eulogize, eulogise (यूलजाइज़) ***v.*** to praise highly in speech or writing, गुणगान करना।

eulogy (यूलॉजी) ***n.*** a speech or a piece of writing in praise of someone, गुणगान, स्तुति, प्रशस्ति।

eunuch (यूनक) ***n.*** 1. a castrated man, हिजड़ा। 2. an ineffective man, बेदम व्यक्ति।

euphonic (यूफ़ॉनिक) ***adj.*** having a pleasant sound, श्रुतिमधुर।

Eurasia (यूरेशिआ) ***n.*** Europe and Asia, युरेशिया।

eureka (यूरेका) ***interj.*** 1. an exclamation for discovering something, मिल गया! 2. an exclamation of triumph, पा लिया! जीत लिया!

Europe (यूरोप) ***n.*** the continent west of Asia, युरोप।

euthanasia (यूथनेज़्या) ***n.*** the act of killing a person painlessly for reasons of mercy, सुखमृत्यु।

evacuate (इवैक्युएट) ***v.*** 1. to discharge waste matter from the bowels, मलत्याग करना, हगना। 2. to make empty, (किसी भू-भाग को) ख़ाली कर देना।

evade (इवेड) ***v.*** 1. to avoid or escape by cleverness, to dodge, कतराकर निकल जाना। 2. to avoid (paying taxes, करों का) अपवंचन करना।

evaluate (इवैल्युएट) ***v.*** to assess or ascertain the value of something, मूल्यांकन करना।

evaluation (इवैल्युएशन) ***n.*** the act of evaluating, मूल्यांकन।

evaluator (इवैल्युएटर) ***n.*** one who evaluates, मूल्यांकनकर्ता।

evangelical (ईवैन्जेलिकल) ***adj.*** of or according to the gospels, सुसमाचार-संबंधी।

evangelize, evangelise (इवैन्ज-लाइज़) ***v.*** 1. to preach the Christian gospel, सुसमाचार का प्रचार करना। 2. to win over to Christianity, ईसाई बना लेना।

evaporate (इवैपरेट) ***v.*** 1. to convert into a vapour, भाप बना देना। 2. to vanish, अंतर्धान या ग़ायब हो जाना।

evaporation (अवैपरेशन) ***n.*** the process of evaporating, वाष्पण, वाष्पीकरण।

evasion (इवेज़न) ***n.*** the act of evading, बचाव, परिहार; evasion of tax, करापवंचन।

evasive (इवेसिव) ***adj.*** 1. seeking to evade, कतरा जानेवाला। 2. not straight forward, बहानेबाज़ या कुटिल।

eve (ईव) ***n.*** the evening or day preceding an event, पूर्वसंध्या।

Eve (ईव) ***n.*** the first woman, हौआ।

even (ईवन) ***adj.*** 1. flat, चपटा, सपाट। 2. level, समतल, चौरस। 3. without variation, एक-सा, एकरूप। 4. calm, शांत। 5. equally balanced, समान। 6. identical or exact, the very same, वही। 7. (of a number) exactly divisible by 2, सम, जूस। 8. uniform, regular, नियमित। ***adv.*** 1. indeed, भी। 2. at the very time, तब भी।

evening (ईवनिंग) ***n.*** late afternoon and early night, शाम, संध्या, सांझ, सायंकाल।

evening star ***n.*** Venus, शुक्र तारा, सांध्य तारा।

E

evenness (ईवननिस) ***n.*** the state of being even, समता, बराबरी।

event (इवेन्ट) ***n.*** 1. any significant occurrence, घटना, बात। 2. an item, मद, विषय।

eventually (इवेन्चुअली) ***adv.*** finally, as a result, अंततः, परिणामतः।

ever (एवर) ***adv.*** 1. at all times, सदा, सर्वदा। 2. at any time, कभी।

evergreen (एवरग्रीन) ***adj.*** having green leaves throughout the year, सदाबहार।

everlasting (एवरलास्टिंग) ***adj.*** 1. lasting for ever, शाश्वत। 2. lasting for a long time, चिरस्थायी।

every (एवरी) ***adj.*** each without exception, हर, प्रत्येक, हर एक।

everybody (एवरीबॉडी) ***pron.*** every person, हर कोई।

everyday (एवरीडे) ***adj.*** daily, प्रतिदिन का, दैनिक।

everything (एवरीथिंग) ***pron.*** all things, सब-कुछ।

everywhere (एवरीवेअर) ***adv.*** in every place, हर जगह।

evict (इविक्ट) ***v.*** to expel (a tenant) by legal process, बेदख़ल करना, निकाल बाहर करना।

eviction (इविक्शन) ***n.*** the act of evicting or the state of being evicted, बेदख़ली, निष्कासन।

evidence (एविडेन्स) ***n.*** 1. something presented before the court of law to prove or disprove a point in issue, साक्ष्य, गवाही। 2. something that serves to indicate, संकेत, लक्षण।

evident (एविडेन्ट) ***adj.*** easily recognized, obvious, प्रकट, प्रत्यक्ष।

evil (ईवल) ***adj.*** 1. morally bad, बुरा, दूषित, ख़राब; the evil eye, बुरी नज़र। 2. harmful, हानिकर। ***n.*** 1. something that is morally bad, बुराई। 2. something that causes trouble, बला, मुसीबत, परेशानी।

evil-doer (ईवल-डूअर) ***n.*** a person who does evil, बुरा काम करनेवाला।

evince (इविन्स) ***v.*** to show or manifest, दिखलाना, प्रदर्शित करना।

evoke (इवोक) ***v.*** to call or summon up, बुलाना, आह्वान करना।

evolution (इवल्यूशन) ***n.*** process of growth development, विकास।

evolve (इवॉल्व) ***v.*** 1. to develop, विकसित होना। 2. to cause to develop, विकसित करना।

exacerbate (इग्ज़ैसरबेट) ***v.*** 1. to increase the severity of, तेज़ या तीव्र कर देना, बढ़ा देना। 2. to make worse, बिगाड़ देना।

exact (इग्ज़ैक्ट) ***adj.*** fully accurate, precise, यथातथ्य, यथार्थ, सटीक। ***v.*** 1. to obtain by threat, force or authority, छीनना या वसूल करना। 2. to press, दबाव डालना, सख़्ती बरतना।

exacting (इग्ज़ैक्टिंग) ***adj.*** 1. requiring great care and effort, श्रमसाध्य। 2. making rigorous demands, भारी दबाव डालनेवाला।

exactly (इग्ज़ैक्टली) ***adv.*** accurately, precisely, यथार्थ रूप से, यथार्थतः।

exaggerate (इग्ज़ैजरेट) ***v.*** to overstate, अतिरंजित करना।

exaggeration (इग्ज़ैजरेशन) ***n.*** the act of exaggerating, अतिरंजन।

exalt (इग्ज़ाल्ट) ***v.*** 1. to elevate, ऊपर उठाना, उन्नत करना। 2. to raise in position or rank, पदोन्नत करना, तरक्की देना। 3. to glorify, यशोगान करना।

E

exam (इग्ज़ैम) ***n.*** an examination, परीक्षा।

examination (इग्ज़ैमिनेशन) ***n.*** the act or process of examining, परीक्षण, जाँच।

examine (इग्ज़ैमिन) ***v.*** 1. to test knowledge or skills by written or oral questions, परीक्षा करना, परीक्षा लेना, इम्तहान लेना। 2. to interrogate formally in order to get information, पूछताछ करना।

examinee (इग्ज़ैमिनी) ***n.*** a candidate for examination, परीक्षार्थी।

examiner (इग्ज़ैमिनर) ***n.*** one who examines, परीक्षक।

example (इग्ज़ैम्पल) ***n.*** 1. something selected to show the nature or the character of the rest, उदाहरण, दृष्टांत। 2. a model, pattern, नमूना, प्रतिमान।

exasperate (इग्ज़ैस्परेट) ***v.*** 1. to enrage, क्रुद्ध करना। 2. to infuriate, उत्तेजित करना।

excavate (एक्सकवेट) ***v.*** to dig out, खुदाई/खनन करना।

excavation (एक्सकवेशन) ***n.*** the act of excavating, खुदाई, खनन, उत्खनन।

excavator (एक्सकवेटर) ***n.*** a person who excavates, खुदाई करनेवाला, खनक।

exceed (इक्सीड) ***v.*** 1. to be more or greater than, बढ़ जाना, अधिक हो जाना। 2. to go beyond (the limit, सीमा से) आगे बढ़ जाना, बढ़त लेना।

exceedingly (इक्सीडिंगली) ***adv.*** to a great degree, अत्यधिक, अत्यंत।

excel (इक्सेल) ***v.*** to be superior to, (किसी से) बढ़-चढ़ जाना, आगे निकल जाना।

excellence (एक्सलेन्स) ***n.*** 1. superiority, श्रेष्ठता। 2. very great merit, अच्छाई।

Excellency (एक्सलेन्सी) ***n.*** a title of honour used to address or refer to high-ranking officials, महामहिम।

excellent (एक्सलेन्ट) ***adj.*** extremely or exceptionally good, अत्यंत उत्कृष्ट।

except (इक्सेप्ट) ***prep.*** other than, apart from, के सिवा, के अतिरिक्त, के अलावा, को छोड़कर।

exception (इक्सेप्शन) ***n.*** anything not in conformity with a general rule, principle, class etc., अपवाद।

exceptional (इक्सेप्शनल) ***adj.*** 1. forming an exception, अपवादस्वरूप। 2. extraordinary, outstanding, असाधारण, विशेष।

exceptionally (इक्सेप्शनली) ***adv.*** in an exceptional way, अपवाद रूप में।

excerpt (एक्सर्प्ट) ***n.*** 1. a passage quoted from a book, उद्धरण। 2. extract, सार, सारांश।

excess (इक्सेस) ***n.*** 1. over-abundance, बहुतायत, प्रचुरता। 2. too much, अति, पराकाष्ठा। 3. overdoing, high-handedness, ज़्यादती।

excessive (इक्सेसिव) ***adj.*** too much, बहुत अधिक, अत्यधिक।

exchange (इक्सचेन्ज) ***v.*** to give and receive reciprocally, अदला-बदली करना, विनिमय करना। ***n.*** the act of exchanging, अदला-बदली, विनिमय।

exchequer (एक्सचेकर) ***n.*** a treasury, कोषागार, खज़ाना।

excise[1] (एक्साइज़) ***n.*** a tax on the production of certain goods within the country, उत्पादन-शुल्क, आबकारी।

excise[2] (इक्साइज़) ***v.*** to remove (a part of the body) surgically, काटकर अलग कर देना, निकाल देना।

excision (इक्सिज़न) ***n.*** the act of

E

excising, काटकर अलग कर देना।

excite (इक्साइट) ***v.*** to provoke, उत्तेजित करना, उकसाना।

excitement (इक्साइटमेन्ट) ***n.*** the state of being excited, उत्तेजना, कुतूहल।

exciting (इक्साइटिंग) ***adj.*** causing excitement, कुतूहलजनक या उत्तेजनापूर्ण।

exclaim (इक्स्क्लेम) ***v.*** to cry out excitedly in surprise, delight, pain or horror, चीख़ पड़ना।

exclamation (एक्स्क्लेमेशन) ***n.*** 1. the act of exclaiming, चीख़, चिल्लाहट। 2. an exclamatory word or phrase, विस्मयादिबोधक शब्द।

exclamation mark ***n.*** the punctuation mark (!) used after exclamatory words, विस्मयादिबोधक या विस्मयबोधक चिह्न (!)।

exclude (इक्स्क्लूड) ***v.*** to keep or leave out, निकाल देना, अलग कर देना।

exclusion (इक्स्क्लूज़न) ***n.*** the act or an instance of excluding, बहिष्कार, वर्जन।

exclusive (इक्स्क्लूसिव) ***adj.*** 1. excluding all others, अनन्य। 2. not divided or shared by, एकाकी, निजी।

excommunicate (एक्स्कम्यूनिकेट) ***v.*** to exclude (as a punishment) from participation in church or society, बहिष्कृत करना।

excommunication (एक्स्कम्यूनिकेशन) the act of excommunicating, धर्म-बहिष्कार, जाति-बहिष्कार।

excrement (एक्स्क्रिमेन्ट) ***n.*** excreta, faeces, मल, विष्ठा, बीठ, गोबर।

excreta (एक्स्क्रीटा) ***n.*** (plu.) waste matter discharged from the body, faeces, मल, विष्ठा, गूह, बीठ, गोबर।

excrete (एक्स्क्रीट) ***v.*** to discharge waste matter from the body, हगना, पाख़ाना करना, गोबर या लीद करना।

excretion (एक्स्क्रीशन) ***n.*** the act of excreting, उत्सर्जन, मलोत्सर्ग, मलत्याग।

exculpate (एक्स्कल्पेट) ***v.*** to clear of guilt or blame, निर्दोष या निरपराध घोषित करना।

excursion (इक्स्कर्शन) ***n.*** a pleasure trip, सैर, सैर-सपाटा।

excusable (इक्स्क्यूज़ेबल) ***adj.*** that can be excused, क्षम्य।

excuse (इक्स्क्यूज़) ***v.*** to forgive or pardon, क्षमा कर देना, माफ़ कर देना। ***n.*** a pretext, बहाना।

execute (एक्सिक्यूट) ***v.*** 1. to carry out, पालन/अनुपालन करना। 2. to put into effect, कार्यान्वित करना। 3. to put to death in pursuance of a sentence, फाँसी देना, मृत्युदंड देना।

execution (एक्सिक्यूशन) ***n.*** 1. the act or process of execution, अनुपालन, निष्पादन, कार्यान्वयन। 2. an act of executing a condemned person, फाँसी।

executioner (एक्सिक्यूशनर) ***n.*** one who executes a condemned person, फाँसी देनेवाला, जल्लाद।

executive (इग्ज़ेक्यूटिव) ***n.*** 1. an ad-ministrative official, कार्यकारी अधिकारी। 2. the branch of the government which is entrusted with the enforcement of laws, कार्यपालिका। 3. an executive committee, प्रबंध-समिति, कार्यकारिणी समिति। ***adj.*** having the function of executing, कार्यकारी।

executor (इग्ज़ेक्यूटर) ***n.*** one who

executes or carries out, निष्पादक, संपादनकर्ता, कर्ता।

exemplary (इग्ज़ेम्प्लरी) ***adj.*** serving as a model or example, अनुकरणीय, आदर्श।

exemplify (इग्ज़ेम्प्लिफ़ाइ) ***v.*** to illustrate by example, उदाहरण प्रस्तुत करना, उदाहरण या मिसाल देना।

exempt (इग्ज़ेम्प्ट) ***v.*** to free from a rule, duty or obligation which binds others, छूट देना, विमुक्त रखना, माफ़ी देना। ***adj.*** free from a rule, duty or obligation, छूट-प्राप्त, विमुक्त।

exemption (इग्ज़ेम्प्शन) ***n.*** the act of exemption or the freedom from liability, obligation or rule, छूट, विमुक्ति, माफ़ी।

exercise (एक्सर्साइज़) ***n.*** 1. active use or operation, प्रयोग, इस्तेमाल। 2. physical activity to develop fitness, व्यायाम, अभ्यास, कसरत। 3. a lesson or task designed to develop skill or understanding, अभ्यास। 4. (plu.) a series of movements, operations or acts related to a public ceremony, अभ्यास। ***v.*** 1. to put into action, प्रयोग या इस्तेमाल करना। 2. to use habitually, उपयोग में लाना, काम लेना। 3. to take exercise, व्यायाम करना।

exercise book ***n.*** a student's book for writing in, अभ्यास-पुस्तिका।

exert (इग्ज़र्ट) ***v.*** to make an effort, प्रयास/प्रयत्न करना।

exertion (इग्ज़र्शन) ***n.*** 1. a great effort, उद्यम, प्रयास, प्रयत्न। 2. fatigue or exhaustion, थकान, थकावट।

exhale (एक्सहेल) ***v.*** to breathe out, साँस छोड़ना।

exhaust (इग्ज़ॉस्ट) ***v.*** 1. to tire out completely, थककर चूर हो जाना। 2. to be used up, प्रयोग में आ जाना, समाप्त हो जाना।

exhaustion (इग्ज़ॉस्चन) ***n.*** fatigue, थकान, थकावट, श्रांति।

exhaustive (इग्ज़ॉस्टिव) ***adj.*** comprehensive, विस्तृत, व्यापक।

exhibit (इग्ज़िबिट) ***v.*** 1. to display to the public, प्रदर्शित करना।

exhibition (एक्सिबिशन) ***n.*** 1. the act or fact of exhibiting or the state of being exhibited, प्रदर्शन, दिखावा। 2. a public display of objects, प्रदर्शनी, नुमाइश।

exhilarate (इग्ज़िलरेट) ***v.*** 1. to make happy or cheerful, आनंदित/आह्लादित करना। 2. to make lively, जीवंत बनाना।

exhort (इग्ज़ॉर्ट) ***v.*** to encourage, उत्साहित करना। 2. to advise earnestly, शिक्षा/नसीहत देना।

exhume (इग्ज़्यूम) ***v.*** to dig up a corpse from a grave, क़ब्र खोदकर लाश निकालना।

exigency (एक्सिजेन्सी) ***n.*** a pressing requirement, अत्यावश्यकता।

exile (एग्ज़ाइल) ***n.*** 1. the official expulsion of a person from his native land, देश-निकाला, निर्वासन। 2. an exiled person, देश से निकाला हुआ व्यक्ति। ***v.*** to send (a person) into exile, देश-निकाला देना, निर्वासित करना।

exist (इग्ज़िस्ट) ***v.*** 1. to be, विद्यमान होना, अस्तित्व में होना। 2. to occur, घटित होना। 3. to live, जीवित होना।

existence (इग्ज़िस्टेन्स) ***n.*** 1. the fact or state of existing, अस्तित्व, सत्ता।

E

2. presence, विद्यमानता, उपस्थिति।

existent (इग्ज़िस्टेन्ट) ***adj.*** existing now, विद्यमान, वर्तमान।

exit (एग्ज़िट) ***n.*** 1. a way out, बाहर जाने का रास्ता। 2. an act or instance of going out, प्रस्थान, निर्गमन, बाहर जाना, रवानगी।

exodus (एक्सोडस) ***n.*** a going out or leaving by a large number of people, सामूहिक प्रस्थान।

ex-officio (एक्स-ऑफ़िशिओ) ***adj. & adv.*** by virtue of one's office or position, पदेन।

exonerate (इग्ज़ॉनरेट) ***v.*** to free from blame, दोषमुक्त करना।

exorbitant (इग्ज़ॉर्बिटेन्ट) ***adj.*** excessive, अत्यधिक, अतिशय।

exorcize, exorcise (एक्सॉर्साइज़) ***v.*** to drive out an evil spirit by prayer, झाड़-फूँक करना, ओझाई करना, जादू-टोना करना।

exotic (इग्ज़ॉटिक) ***adj.*** 1. foreign, विजातीय, विदेशी। 2. unusual, असाधारण।

expand (इक्स्पैन्ड) ***v.*** 1. to spread out, फैलाना या फैलना। 2. to extend, विस्तृत करना या होना।

expandable (इक्स्पैन्डेबल) ***adj.*** that can be expanded, विस्तार्य।

expanse (इक्स्पैन्स) ***n.*** 1. a large open area, खुला मैदान, विस्तृत भूभाग। 2. expansion, प्रसार, फैलाव।

expansion (इक्स्पैन्शन) ***n.*** the state of being expanded, विस्तार, फैलाव, व्याप्ति।

ex parte (एक्स पार्टी) ***adj.*** one-sided, एकपक्षीय।

expatiate (एक्स्पेशिएट) ***v.*** to elaborate, सविस्तार वर्णन करना।

expatiation (एक्स्पेशिएशन) ***n.*** the act of expatiating or the state of being expatiated, विस्तृत वर्णन।

expatriate (एक्स्पेट्रिएट) ***v.*** to exile, देशनिकाला देना, निर्वासित कर देना।

expect (इक्स्पेक्ट) ***v.*** 1. to wait, प्रतीक्षा करना। 2. to anticipate, प्रत्याशा/आशा करना।

expectant (इक्स्पेक्टेन्ट) ***adj.*** 1. expecting, प्रतीक्षा करनेवाला, आशावान। 2. pregnant, गर्भवती।

expectation (एक्स्पेक्टेशन) ***n.*** 1. the act or condition of expecting, प्रतीक्षा। 2. hope, आशा, उम्मीद।

expectorant (एक्स्पेक्टोरेन्ट) ***adj.*** increasing discharge of phlegm from the lungs, कफ़-निस्सारक।

expediency (इक्स्पीडिएन्सी) ***n.*** appropriateness, उपयुक्तता, समीचीनता।

expedient (इक्स्पीडिएन्ट) ***adj.*** suitable, fit, appropriate, उपयुक्त, समीचीन।

expedite (एक्स्पिडाइट) ***v.*** to speed the progress of, (कार्य में) तेज़ी लाना, शीघ्रता लाना।

expedition (एक्स्पिडिशन) ***n.*** a journey undertaken with definite purpose, अभियान।

expeditious (एक्स्पिडिशस) ***adj.*** acting speedily, तेज़, चुस्त, फुर्तीला।

expel (इक्स्पेल) ***v.*** to drive out with force, निष्कासित कर देना।

expend (इक्स्पेन्ड) ***v.*** to spend, व्यय करना, ख़र्च करना।

expenditure (इक्स्पेन्डिचर) ***n.*** the amount of money expended, व्यय, ख़र्च।

expense (इक्स्पेन्स) ***n.*** expenditure, व्यय, ख़र्च।

expensive (इक्स्पेन्सिव) ***adj.*** costly, high-priced, महँगा।

E

experience (इक्स्पीरिअन्स) ***n.*** practical knowledge gained from direct personal participation or observation, अनुभव। ***v.*** to have experience of, अनुभव होना।

experienced (इक्स्पीरिअन्स्ट) ***adj.*** having had much experience, अनुभवी।

experiment (इक्स्पेरिमेन्ट) ***n.*** any test or action undertaken to discover something unknown, प्रयोग। ***v.*** to conduct an experiment, प्रयोग करना।

experimental (इक्स्पेरिमेन्टल) ***adj.*** relating to experiment, प्रयोगात्मक।

expert (एक्स्पर्ट) ***n.*** a person who has made special study of a particular subject, विशेषज्ञ। ***adj.*** skillful, दक्ष।

expertise (एक्स्पर्टीज़) ***n.*** expert knowledge or skill, विशेष ज्ञान या दक्षता।

expiate (एक्स्पिएट) ***v.*** to atone for, प्रायश्चित करना।

expire (इक्स्पाइर) ***v.*** 1. to die, मर जाना। 2. to end, समाप्त हो जाना।

expiry (इक्स्पाइरी) ***n.*** 1. termination, अंत। 2. death, मृत्यु।

explain (इक्स्पलेन) ***v.*** 1. to make clear, स्पष्ट करना। 2. to give the meaning or interpretation of, व्याख्या करना।

explanation (एक्स्प्लनेशन) ***n.*** 1. meaning or interpretation, व्याख्या। 2. clarification, स्पष्टीकरण।

explanatory (इक्स्प्लैनटरी) ***adj.*** intended to explain, व्याख्यात्मक।

explicit (इक्स्प्लिसिट) ***adj.*** 1. clearly stated, सुस्पष्ट। 2. outspoken, स्पष्टवादी।

explode (इक्स्प्लोड) ***v.*** to burst with a loud noise, फटना, विस्फोट होना।

exploit[1] (एक्स्प्लॉइट) ***n.*** a notable act or heroic deed, पराक्रम, शौर्य, कारनामा।

exploit[2] ***v.*** 1. to utilize fully, पूर्ण उपयोग करना। 2. to make selfish use, स्वार्थ साधना। 3. to use unethically or unfairly for one's own profit, शोषण करना।

exploitation (एक्स्प्लॉइटेशन) ***n.*** 1. an act of exploiting, समुपयोजन। 2. unethical utilization for selfish purposes, शोषण।

exploration (एक्स्प्लरेशन) ***n.*** the act of exploring, अन्वेषण, गवेषणा।

exploratory (एक्स्प्लोरेटरी) ***adj.*** of, in or for exploration, गवेषणात्मक, अन्वेषणात्मक।

explore (इक्स्प्लोर) ***v.*** 1. to investigate systematically, अन्वेषण करना। 2. to travel through a country for the purpose of discovery, पर्यवेक्षण करना, ढूँढ़ना।

explorer (इक्स्प्लोरर) ***n.*** a person who explores, अन्वेषक।

explosion (इक्स्प्लोज़न) ***n.*** 1. the loud noise accom-panying such an act, विस्फोट, धमाका। 2. a sudden increase or outbreak, फट पड़ना, भड़क उठना।

explosive (इक्स्प्लोसिव) ***adj.*** tending to explode, विस्फोटक। ***n.*** a substance that can explode, विस्फोटक पदार्थ।

expo (एक्स्पो) ***n.*** a large public exhibition, महाप्रदर्शनी।

exponent (इक्स्पोनेन्ट) ***n.*** one who interprets, explains or advocates, व्याख्याता, प्रतिपादक।

export (एक्स्पोर्ट) ***v.*** to send abroad for sale or trade, निर्यात करना। ***n.***

E

goods exported abroad, निर्यात।

exporter (एक्स्पोर्टर) ***n.*** a person, company or country that exports goods to the foreign country, निर्यातक, निर्यातकर्ता।

expose (इक्स्पोज़) ***v.*** 1. to lay bare or uncover, खुला रखना, खुला छोड़ देना, खोल देना। 2. to subject to the action of light, धूप या रोशनी दिखाना। 3. to make known, or reveal, रहस्य खोलना।

exposition (एक्स्पोज़िशन) ***n.*** the act of expounding, प्रतिपादन।

exposure (इक्स्पोज़र) ***n.*** 1. the act of exposing, खुले में रखना। 2. the exposing of a photographic film or plate to the light, रोशनी दिखाने का कार्य, उद्‌भासन। 3. first appearance before the public, प्रथम प्रस्तुति। 4. disclosure of someone's secrets, भंडाफोड़, पर्दाफ़ाश।

expound (इक्स्पॉउन्ड) ***v.*** to explain, प्रतिपादन करना।

express (इक्स्प्रेस) ***v.*** 1. to put into words, अभिव्यक्त करना। 2. to make known, प्रकट करना। ***adj.*** 1. clearly stated, अभिव्यक्त, सुस्पष्ट। 2. sent by rapid transportation, आशु, द्रुतगामी। ***n.*** an express train or bus, द्रुतगामी रेलगाड़ी या बस, शीघ्रगामी सवारी।

expression (इक्स्प्रेशन) ***n.*** 1. the act of expressing or the state of being expressed, अभिव्यक्ति। 2. a manner of expression, ढंग, शैली। 3. a look on a person's face that conveys meaning, चेहरे की रंगत, भावभंगी, मुखाकृति।

expressionless (इक्स्प्रेशनलिस) ***adj.*** without expression, भावशून्य।

expressive (इक्स्प्रेसिव) ***adj.*** of or characterized by expression, भावपूर्ण, भाव-भरा।

expulsion (इक्स्पल्शन) ***n.*** 1. the act of expelling or the state of being expelled, निष्कासन, बेदख़ली।

expunge (इक्स्पन्ज) ***v.*** to strike out or delete, निकाल या हटा देना।

expurgate (एक्स्पर्गेट) ***v.*** to remove obscene or objectionable matter from, अश्लील या आपत्तिजनक अंश निकाल देना, परिष्कार करना।

exquisite (एक्स्क्विज़िट) ***adj.*** 1. very finely made or done, उत्कृष्ट, उत्तम। 2. very beautiful, अतिसुंदर। 3. refined, परिष्कृत।

extempore (एक्स्टेम्परि) ***adj.*** not prepared in advance, आशु। ***adv.*** without preparation, बिना तैयारी के, सहसा।

extend (इक्स्टेन्ड) ***v.*** 1. to spread, stretch or enlarge to greater length, area or scope, फैलना या फैलाना, तनना या तानना, विस्तृत होना या करना, बढ़ना या बढ़ाना। 2. to continue, आगे बढ़ाना या चलाना, जारी रखना।

extendable (इक्स्टेन्डेबल) ***adj.*** that can be extended, बढ़ाए जाने योग्य।

extension (इक्स्टेन्शन) ***n.*** 1. the act of extending or the state of being extended, विस्तार, फैलाव। 2. an added part, बढ़ाया हुआ अंश। 3. an extra period, बढ़ाई हुई अवधि।

extensive (इक्स्टेन्सिव) ***adj.*** 1. large in area, विस्तृत। 2. far-reaching, व्यापक।

extent (इक्स्टेन्ट) ***n.*** 1. the range over which something extends, विस्तार, फैलाव, प्रसार। 2. the scope, कार्यक्षेत्र। 3. an area, क्षेत्र। 4. the boundary, सीमा, हद।

extenuate (इक्स्टेन्युएट) ***v.*** to lessen the seriousness of, (सज़ा) हलकी या कम करना।

exterior (इक्स्टीरिअर) ***adj.*** external, out-of-door, outer, बाहरी, बाह्य।

exterminate (इक्स्टर्मिनेट) ***v.*** to kill or destroy completely, मटियामेट कर देना, न रहने देना।

external (इक्स्टर्नल) ***adj.*** of outside, बाहरी, बाह्य।

extinct (इक्स्टिंक्ट) ***adj.*** 1. extinguished, बुझा हुआ। 2. no longer existing in living form, लुप्त, विलुप्त, समाप्त।

extinction (इक्स्टिंक्शन) ***n.*** 1. the act of extinguishing, बुझाने की क्रिया या भाव, निर्वापन। 2. the state of being extinct, लोप, विलोप, विनाश।

extinguish (इक्स्टिंग्विश) ***v.*** 1. to put out बुझाना। 2. to destroy or put to an end, विनष्ट कर देना, न रहने देना।

extirpate (एक्स्टर्पेट) ***v.*** to uproot, उन्मूलन करना।

extol (इक्स्टोल) ***v.*** to praise enthusiastically or lavishly, गुणगान करना।

extort (इक्स्टॉर्ट) ***v.*** to obtain by force or intimidation, ऐंठ या छीन लेना, नोच-खसोट लेना।

extortion (इक्स्टॉर्शन) ***n.*** 1. the act of extorting or the state of being extorted, छीन-झपट।2. something extorted, छीन-झपटकर प्राप्त की हुई वस्तु।

extra (एक्स्ट्रा) ***adj.*** additional, अतिरिक्त। ***adv.*** more than usually, especially, अतिरिक्त रूप से, विशेष रूप से। ***n.*** 1. an extra person or thing, अतिरिक्त व्यक्ति या वस्तु। 2. an actor hired to play a minor role, अतिरिक्त पात्र। 3. in cricket, a run not made by a hit, अतिरिक्त रन।

extract (इक्स्ट्रैक्ट) ***v.*** 1. to draw or pull out forcibly, उखाड़ना, खींचकर निकाल देना। 2. to extort, ज़बरदस्ती वसूलना। 3. to obtain by distilling or pressing, (रस) निकालना, (अर्क) खींचना या उतारना, (सार या सत) निकालना, कर्षण करना। 4. to obtain or derive, प्राप्त करना। ***n.*** 1. something obtained by extracting, रस, अर्क, सत। 2. a passage that has been extracted, उद्धरण। 3. gist, निचोड़, निष्कर्ष।

extraction (इक्स्ट्रैक्शन) ***n.*** 1. the act of extracting, कर्षण, निकालना; उद्धरण। 2. something extracted, रस, अर्क, सत। 3. descent, lineage, वंश, नस्ल।

extracurricular (एक्स्ट्राकुरिक्युलर) outside the curriculum, पाठ्येतर।

extradite (एक्स्ट्रडाइट) ***v.*** to hand over a fugitive criminal to the country where the crime was committed, प्रत्यर्पण करना।

extradition (एक्स्ट्रडिशन) ***n.*** the act of extraditing, प्रत्यर्पण।

extramarital (एक्स्ट्रामैरिटल) ***adj.*** occurring outside marriage, विवाहेतर।

extraneous (इक्स्ट्रेनिअस) ***adj.*** 1. foreign, विदेशी। 2. irrelvent, अप्रासंगिक।

extraordinary (इक्स्ट्रॉर्डिनरी) ***adj.*** not ordinary or usual, असाधारण, विशेष।

extraterritorial (एक्स्ट्राटेरिटोरिअल) ***adj.*** outside territorial boundaries of a state, अराज्यक्षेत्रीय, राज्यक्षेत्रातीत।

extravagance (इक्स्ट्रैवेगेन्स) ***n.*** the quality or state of being extravagant, फ़ज़ूलख़र्ची, अपव्यय।

E

extravagant (इक्स्ट्रैवेगेन्ट) ***adj.*** wasteful or lavish in the spending of money, अपव्ययी, फ़जूलख़र्च।

extravaganza (इक्स्ट्रैवेगैन्ज़ा) ***n.*** a very grand and costly show or entertainment, भव्य प्रदर्शन या मनोरंजन।

extreme (इक्स्ट्रीम) ***adj.*** going beyond the usual limits, अत्यंत अत्यधिक। ***n.*** 1. the extreme condition, चरम अवस्था, पराकाष्ठा। 2. the farthest point or limit, चरम बिंदु या चरम सीमा।

extremely (इक्स्ट्रीमली) ***adj.*** very, अत्यधिक।

extremism (इक्स्ट्रीमिज़म) ***n.*** the quality or state of going to extremes, उग्रवाद, चरमपंथ।

extremist (इक्स्ट्रीमिस्ट) ***n. & adj.*** pretaining to extremism, उग्रवादी, चरमपंथी।

extremity (इक्स्ट्रेमिटी) the highest degree, चरम सीमा, पराकाष्ठा।

extricate (एक्स्ट्रिकेट) ***v.*** 1. to set free, छोड़ देना। 2. to disentangle, छुड़ाना।

extrinsic (एक्सट्रिन्सिक) ***adj.*** originating from outside, बाहरी, बाह्य।

extrovert (एक्स्ट्रोवर्ट) ***n.*** a person concerned more with other people than himself, बहिर्मुखी।

exuberance (इग्जूबरेन्स) ***n.*** liveliness, जीवंतता, उल्लास।

exuberant (इग्जूबरेन्ट) ***adj.*** 1. lively, high-spirited, cheerful, जीवंत, उल्लसित। 2. prosperous, समृद्ध, संपन्न।

exude (इग्ज़्यूड) ***v.*** to ooze or pass in drops, रिसना, चूना।

exult (इग्ज़ल्ट) ***v.*** to rejoice greatly, आनंद मनाना, ख़ुशी मनाना।

exultant (इग्ज़ल्टेन्ट) ***adj.*** jubilant, उल्लसित, आह्लादित, प्रसन्न।

exultation (इग्ज़ल्टेशन) ***n.*** jubilation, उल्लास, आह्लाद।

eye (आइ) ***n.*** 1. an organ of sight, आँख, नेत्र, नयन। 2. the power of seeing, देखने की शक्ति, दृष्टि, नज़र। 3. a look or gaze, दृष्टि, नज़र। 4. a thing or hole like an eye, आँख, छेद।

eyeball ***n.*** the ball-shaped portion of the eye within the lids, आँख की पुतली।

eyebrow ***n.*** the hair covering the bony ridge over the eye, भौंह, भृकुटी।

eyeglasses ***n.*** (plu.) glasses, spectacles, चश्मा, ऐनक।

eyelash ***n.*** a fringe of hair that grows from the edge of eyelids, बरौनी।

eyelet (आइलिट) ***n.*** a small metal ring with a hole, छल्ला, अक्षिका।

eyelid ***n.*** the movable cover of the eye, पलक।

eye-opener ***n.*** something startling or shocking, आँखें खोल देनेवाली बात या घटना।

eyesight ***n.*** the ability or power of seeing, दृष्टि, नज़र।

eyesore ***n.*** an ugly sight, आँख का काँटा।

eyewitness ***n.*** a person who saw an accident or crime and can bear witness to the fact, प्रत्यक्षदर्शी।

eyrie (आइअरी) ***n.*** the nest of a flesh-eating bird, गिद्ध आदि का ऊँचा घोंसला।

F, f (एफ़) ***n.*** the sixth letter of the English alphabet, अंग्रेज़ी वर्णमाला का छठा वर्ण।

fable (फ़ेबल) ***n.*** a story that teaches a lesson, कथा।

fabric (फ़ैब्रिक) ***n.*** 1. any woven, knitted or felted cloth, कपड़ा, वस्त्र। 2. the structure, ढाँचा।

fabricate (फ़ैब्रिकेट) ***v.*** 1. to weave, बुनना। 2. to manufacture or construct, निर्माण करना, बनाना। 3. to make, build or invent, गढ़ना, रचना। 4. to forge (a document), जाल रचना, जाली बनाना।

fabulous (फ़ैब्यूलस) ***adj.*** 1. fictitious or legendary, काल्पनिक या पौराणिक। 2. excellent, उत्तम, उत्कृष्ट।

facade (फैसाड) ***n.*** the front of the building, मकान का सामना।

face (फ़ेस) ***n.*** 1. the front of the head from the forehead to the chin, मुँह, मुखड़ा। 2. the main side of something, सामना, अग्रभाग।

facet (फ़ैसिट) ***n.*** any of the many flat sides of a jewel, पहलू, फ़लक।

facial (फ़ेशल) ***adj.*** of or concerning the face, मुख-संबंधी, मुखीय। ***n.*** a beauty treatment of the face, सौंदर्योपचार।

facile (फ़ेसाइल) ***adj.*** easy, सरल, सुगम।

facilitate (फ़ेसिलिटेट) ***v.*** to make easier, सरल बना देना।

facilitation (फ़ेसिलिटेशन) ***n.*** the act of facilitating, सरलीकरण।

facility (फ़ेसिलिटी) ***n.*** 1. the quality of being easy, सरलता, सहजता। 2. ease in doing something or resulting from skill or aptitude, दक्षता, कौशल। 3. convenience, सुविधा।

facsimile (फैक्सिमिली) ***n.*** an exact copy, नक़ल।

fact (फ़ैक्ट) ***n.*** something known to be true or accepted as true, तथ्य, वास्तविकता।

faction (फ़ैक्शन) ***n.*** a small group within a larger group, गुट, पक्ष।

factionalism (फैक्शनलिज़म) ***n.*** the strife or dissension between the factions, गुटबंदी।

factitious (फ़ैक्टिशस) ***adj.*** not genuine, artificial, कृत्रिम, बनावटी।

factor (फ़ैक्टर) ***n.*** 1. an agent, घटक, कारक, उपादान। 2. one of two or more quantities which form product when multiplied together, गुणनखंड।

factory (फ़ैक्टरी) ***n.***a building where goods are made, कारख़ाना।

factual (फ़ैक्चुअल) ***adj.*** based on facts, तथ्यपूर्ण, तथ्यात्मक।

faculty (फ़ैकल्टी) ***n.*** 1. ability to do or perform, क्षमता, कार्यक्षमता। 2. a special attitude or power, शक्ति। 3. a department of a university, संकाय।

fad (फ़ैड) ***n.*** a craze, सनक, धुन।

faddish (फ़ैडिश) ***adj.*** crazy, सनकी, धुनी।

fade (फ़ेड) ***v.*** to lose colour, freshness or strength, कुम्हलाना, मुरझाना।

faeces (फ़ीसीज़) ***n.*** (plu.) the solid waste material passed from the bowels, गूह, मल।

F

fag (फ़ैग) ***n.*** an unpleasant work, उबाऊ काम।

fag-end (फ़ैग-एन्ड) ***n.*** the last and least useful part of something, बचा-खुचा अंश।

fagged (फ़ैग्ड) ***adj.*** very tired, बहुत अधिक थका हुआ।

fahrenheit (फ़ैरनहाइट) a scale of temperature, फारेनहाइट।

fail (फ़ेल) ***v.*** 1. to be unsuccessful, अनुत्तीर्ण/फ़ेल होना। 2. to disappoint, निराश करना। 3. to leave or neglect, चूक जाना, छोड़ देना या उपेक्षा कर जाना, विफल रहना।

failing (फ़ेलिंग) ***n.*** a weak point, कमज़ोरी, दुर्बलता।

failure (फ़ेल्यर) ***n.*** the act or fact of failing, विफलता।

faint (फ़ेन्ट) ***adj.*** 1. dim, indistinct, मंद, हलका, धुँधला। 2. weak, feeble, क्षीण, कमज़ोर। ***n.*** an abrupt loss of consciousness, मूर्च्छा, बेहोशी। ***v.*** to lose consciousness, मूर्च्छित, बेहोश होना।

faint-hearted (फ़ेन्ट-हार्टिड) ***adj.*** timid, डरपोक।

fair[1] (फ़ेअर)***n.*** 1. a festival, उत्सव, समारोह। 2. a periodical gathering of buyers and sellers at a particular place and time for trade, मेला, पैंठ। 3. an exhibition, प्रदर्शनी।

fair[2] ***adj.*** 1. beautiful, attractive, सुंदर, आकर्षक; 2. fine, अच्छा, बढ़िया। 3. just, निष्पक्ष, न्यायपूर्ण।

fairly (फ़ेअर्ली) ***adv.*** 1. in a fair manner, उचित रीति से, ईमानदारी से। 2. equitably, निष्पक्षतापूर्वक। 3. moderately, साधारणतः।

fair-minded (फ़ेअर-माइन्डिड) ***adj.*** just and impartial, न्यायी और निष्पक्ष।

fairness (फ़ेअरनिस) ***n.*** the quality or state of being fair, गोरापन; सौंदर्य; औचित्य; निष्पक्षता; ईमानदारी।

fair play (फ़ेअर प्ले) ***n.*** fairness in dealing, खरा व्यवहार।

fair sex, the (फ़ेअर-सेक्स) ***n.*** women collectively, स्त्री समुदाय, स्त्री जाति।

fairy (फेअरी) ***n.*** an elf, अप्सरा, परी।

fairyland ***n.*** the land of fairies, परीलोक।

fairy tale ***n.*** 1. a story about fairies, परीकथा। 2. a fictitious story, कल्पित कथा, गप।

faith (फ़ेथ) ***n.*** 1. strong belief, आस्था, निष्ठा। 2. belief in God or religion, विश्वास, निष्ठा। 3. a religion or a system of religious beliefs, धर्म, धर्मतंत्र।

faithful (फ़ेथफ़ुल) ***adj.*** reliable, निष्ठावान, वफ़ादार।

faithfully (फ़ेथफ़ुली) ***adv.*** in a faithful manner, वफ़ादारी से, ईमानदारी से।

faithless (फ़ेथलिस) ***adj.*** having no faith in religion or God, नास्तिक।

fake (फ़ेक) ***adj.*** not genuine but made to deceive others, नक़ली, जाली।

falcon (फ़ैल्कन) ***n.*** a bird of prey with a curved beak, बाज़ पक्षी।

fall (फ़ॉल) ***v.*** 1. to come down from an erect position, गिर पड़ना, गिर जाना, ढह जाना। 2. to be killed or severely wounded in battles, युद्ध में काम आ जाना या घायल हो जाना। 3. to become lower in level, नीचे आना, गिरना, उतरना। 4. to come or happen, आना, होना। ***n.*** 1. a decrease in degree, price, quantity etc., कमी, गिरावट। 2. the defeat of a city or country, नगर या राज्य का पतन। 3. the season when leaves fall, पतझड़। 4. a waterfall, झरना, प्रपात।

fallacious (फ़लेशस) ***adj.*** misleading, भ्रांतिजनक।

fallacy (फ़ैलसी) ***n.*** a mistaken belief, भ्रांत धारणा।

fallible (फ़ैलिबल) ***adj.*** liable to make mistakes, भूल करनेवाला।

fallow (फ़ैलो) ***adj.*** (the land) ploughed but left unseeded in order to restore its fertility, परती (ज़मीन)।

false (फ़ॉल्स) ***adj.*** 1. lying, झूठा। 2. contrary to truth, मिथ्या, असत्य, झूठा। 3. artificial, नक़ली, कृत्रिम, दिखावटी। 4. fake, जाली, खोटा। 5. deceptive, भ्रांत, भ्रामक।

falsehood (फ़ॉल्सहुड) ***n.*** 1. the telling of an untrue statement, झूठ।

falsely (फ़ॉल्सली) ***adv.*** in a false manner, झूठमूठ।

falsify (फ़ॉल्सिफ़ाइ) ***v.*** to state falsely, ग़लतबयानी करना, झूठ कहना।

falter (फ़ॉल्टर) ***v.*** 1. to stumble, लड़खड़ाना। 2. to stammer, हकलाना।

fame (फ़ेम) ***n.*** reputation, प्रसिद्धि, ख्याति।

familiar (फ़मिलिअर) ***adj.*** well known, सुपरिचित।

familiarity (फ़मिलिऐरिटी) ***n.*** substantial acquaintance, सुपरिचय।

family (फ़ैमिली) ***n.*** 1. parents and their children, परिवार। 2. a group descended from a common ancestor, कुल, कुटुंब। 3. a group of related things, वर्ग या समूह।

family planning ***n.*** birth control, परिवार-नियोजन, संतति-निग्रह।

family tree ***n.*** a genealogical diagram of a family, वंशवृक्ष, शजरा।

famine (फ़ैमिन) ***n.*** an acute shortage of food in a region, अकाल।

famish (फ़ैमिश) ***v.*** 1. to starve, भूखों मरना।

famous (फ़ेमस) ***n.*** well known, प्रसिद्ध, विख्यात।

fan[1] (फ़ैन) ***n.*** 1. a hand-held implement for creating cool breeze, पंखी, पंखा। 2. an electrical device for creating cool air, बिजली का पंखा, पंखा। 3. an apparatus for winnowing grain, पंखा। ***v.*** 1. to move or agitate a current of air upon, पंखा झलना, हवा करना, पंखा चलाना। 2. to separate grain from chaff, (अनाज) फटकना, (भूसी) उड़ाना।

fan[2] ***n.*** an admirer प्रशंसक।

fanatic (फ़नैटिक) ***adj.*** irrationally zealous, कट्टर, धर्मांध।

fanaticism (फ़नैटिसिज़म) irrational zeal, कट्टरता, धर्मांधता।

fancy (फ़ैन्सी) ***n.*** 1. playful imagination, कल्पना, उड़ान। 2. an unreasonable desire for something, वहम। ***adj.*** of superior grade, बढ़िया क़िस्म का।

fanfare (फ़ैनफ़ेअर) ***n.*** a loud blast of trumpets, शहनाई का स्वर, मंगलध्वनि।

fang (फ़ैंग) ***n.*** a long sharp tooth of a dog or wolf, कुत्ते या भेड़िए का लंबा नुकीला दाँत।

fantastic (फ़ैन्टैस्टिक) ***adj.*** 1. imaginary, काल्पनिक। 2. illusory, भ्रामक। 3. unrealistic, बेतुका। 4. excellent, बहुत बढ़िया।

fantasy (फ़ैन्टेसी) ***n.*** 1. a product of

F

imagination, कल्पित रचना। 2. illusion, भ्रम, भ्रांति।

far (फ़ार) ***adv.*** 1. at a great distance, दूर, परे। 2. very much, बहुत अधिक।

farce (फ़ार्स) ***n.*** 1. a funny play, हास्यप्रधान नाटक। 2. something absurd, ढोंग, तमाशा।

farcical (फ़ार्सिकल) ***adj.*** absurd, बेतुका, भोंडा।

fare[1] (फ़ेअर) ***n.*** the amount of money paid for transportation, किराया, भाड़ा।

fare[2] ***v.*** to turn out, घटित होना, गुज़रना।

farewell (फ़ेअरवेल) ***interj.*** goodbye, अलविदा, नमस्कार। ***n.*** a leave-taking, विदा, विदाई।

farfetched (फ़ारफ़ेच्ड) ***adj.*** not related, दूर का, असंबद्ध।

farm (फ़ार्म) ***n.*** a piece of land on which crops or animals are raised, खेत, कृषिक्षेत्र।

farmer (फ़ार्मर)***n.*** a person who earns his living by farming, किसान।

far-off (फ़ार-ऑफ़) ***adj.*** remote, दूरवर्ती।

far-reaching (फ़ार-रीचिंग) ***adj.*** 1. having a wide range, अतिव्यापक। 2. having a wide effect, अत्यंत प्रभावपूर्ण।

farsighted (फ़ारसाइटिड) ***adj.*** foreseeing, दूरदर्शी।

farther (फ़ार्दर) ***adv.*** more remote, अपेक्षाकृत दूर, और आगे। ***adj.*** remote, दूरस्थित।

farthermost (फ़ार्दरमोस्ट) ***adj.*** most remote, दूरस्थित।

farthest (फ़ार्दिस्ट) ***adj.*** most distant, अत्यधिक दूर, दूरतम।

fascinate (फ़ैसिनेट) ***v.*** to charm greatly, मुग्ध कर लेना।

fascinating (फ़ैसिनेटिंग) ***adj.*** having great charm or attraction, लुभावना।

fascination (फ़ैसिनेशन) ***n.*** 1. charm, सौंदर्य। 2. the quality of fascinating, आकर्षण, सम्मोहन।

fascism (फ़ैसिज़म) ***n.*** a system of dictatorial government characterized by one party government, फासिस्टवाद।

fascist (फ़ैसिस्ट) ***n.*** one who believes in fascism, फासिस्टवादी।

fashion (फ़ैशन) ***n.*** the current or prevailing style, फ़ैशन।

fashionable (फ़ैशनेबल) ***adj.*** following the current style or fashion, फ़ैशन-परस्त।

fast[1] (फ़ास्ट) ***adj.*** 1. swift, rapid, तेज़, द्रुतगामी, शीघ्रगामी। 2. firm, दृढ़, अटल। 3. firmly fastened, कसकर बँधा हुआ। 4. devoted, पक्का, घनिष्ठ। 5. deep, गहरा; fast colour, गहरा रंग। ***adv.*** 1. quickly, speedily, तेज़ी से, जल्दी-जल्दी, फ़ुर्ती से। 2. firmly, दृढ़तापूर्वक, मज़बूती से। 3. deeply, गहराई से।

fast[2] ***v.*** to go without food, उपवास करना, फ़ाका करना, अनशन करना। ***n.*** the act of fasting, उपवास, फ़ाका, लंघन।

fasten (फ़ासन) ***v.*** to tie or join together, बाँधना, जकड़ना।

fast food ***n.*** a food that can be prepared and served very quickly, तुरंता, फ़ास्ट फ़ूड।

fastidious (फ़ैस्टिडिअस) ***adj.*** very difficult to please, तुनुकमिज़ाज, नकचढ़ा।

fat (फ़ैट) ***adj.*** 1. fleshy, plumb or thick, स्थूल, मोटा, मांसल। 2. oily, greasy, चिकना, चर्बीयुक्त। ***n.*** 1.

an organic compound occurring in animal and plant tissue, चर्बी, वसा। 2. solidified animal or vegetable oil, वनस्पति तेल।

fatal (फ़ेटल) ***adj.*** deadly, जानलेवा, घातक।

fate (फ़ेट) ***n.*** 1. the supernatural power that supposed to be controlling all events, नियति। 2. a person's destiny, भाग्य।

fateful (फ़ेटफ़ुल) ***adj.*** decisively important, निर्णायक।

father (फ़ादर) ***n.*** 1. a male parent, पिता, जन्मदाता। 2. an originator, जनक, प्रवर्तक। 3. a title used for a priest, फ़ादर, स्वामी।

fatherhood (फ़ादरहुड) ***n.*** the state of being a father, पितृत्व, जनकत्व।

father-in-law (फ़ादर-इन-लॉ) ***n.*** the father of one's wife (or husband), श्वसुर, ससुर।

fatherland (फ़ादरलैन्ड) ***n.*** one's native country, पितृदेश, जन्मभूमि।

fatherly (फ़ादर्ली) ***adj.*** like a father, पितृवत्।

fathom (फ़ैदम) ***n.*** a measure of 6 feet used in stating the depth of water, जल की गहराई नापने का छह फ़ुट का एक नाप। ***v.*** 1. to measure the depth. of, गहराई नापना। 2. to get the bottom of, थाह पाना।

fatigue (फ़टीग) ***n.*** physical or mental exhaustion, थकावट, थकान।

fatty (फ़ैटी) ***adj.*** fat, मोटा, स्थूल।

fault (फ़ॉल्ट) ***n.*** an error, त्रुटि, ग़लती।

faulty (फ़ॉल्टी) ***adj.*** ·defective, दोषपूर्ण।

fauna (फ़ॉना) ***n.*** the animals of a specified region or time, किसी विशिष्ट क्षेत्र या काल के जीवजंतु।

favour, favor (फ़ेवर) ***n.*** 1. a friendly attitude, अनुकंपा, कृपादृष्टि। 2. an act of kindness, a kind act, अनुग्रह। ***v.*** 1. to regard with favour, अनुग्रह करना। 2. to be favourable, अनुकूल होना।

favourable, favorable (फ़ेवरेबल) ***adj.*** 1. helpful, अनुकूल, सहायक। 2. advantageous, लाभप्रद, फ़ायदेमंद।

favourite, favorite (फ़ेवरिट) ***adj.*** liked above others, प्रिय।

favouritism, favoritism (फ़ेवरि-टिज़्म) ***n.*** partiality, पक्षपात, तरफ़दारी।

fawn[1] (फ़ॉन) ***n.*** a young deer मृगशावक।

fawn[2] ***v.*** to try to gain favour of someone, किसी का अनुग्रह प्राप्त करना।

fear (फ़िअर) ***n.*** 1. a feeling of anxiety and agitation caused by the presence or nearness of evil, danger, pain etc., भय। 2. danger, ख़तरा।

fearful (फ़िअरफ़ुल) ***adj.*** 1. causing fear, डरावना, भयानक।

fearless (फ़िअरलिस) ***adj.*** feeling no fear, निर्भय, निडर।

fearsome (फ़िअरसम) ***adj.*** causing fear, डरावना।

feasibility (फ़ीजिबिलिटी) ***n.*** the state or quality of being feasible, व्यावहारिकता।

feasible (फ़ीज़िबल) ***adj.*** practical, व्यावहारिक।

feast (फ़ीस्ट) ***n.*** a large, rich and elaborate meal, भोज, प्रीतिभोज।

feat (फ़ीट) ***n.*** a remarkable deed, कमाल, करतब।

feather (फ़ेदर) ***n.*** any of the

F

structures that grow from a bird's skin with a fringe of fine strands on each side, पंख, पर।

featherweight (फ़ेदरवेट) ***n.*** a boxer weighing between 54 to 57 kilograms, ५४ से ५७ किलोग्राम तक वज़नवाला मुक्केबाज़।

feature (फ़ीचर) ***n.*** 1. a distinctive or prominent characteristic, लक्षण, विशिष्टता। 2. a prominent article in a newspaper or periodical, पत्र-पत्रिका का विशिष्ट लेख।

feature film ***n.*** a long film, फ़ीचर फ़िल्म।

February (फ़ेब्रुअरी) ***n.*** the second month of the year, फ़रवरी महीना।

fecund (फ़ीकन्ड) ***adj.*** fruitful, फलदायक।

federal (फ़ेडरल) ***adj.*** of or formed into a federation, संघीय, संघबद्ध।

federation (फ़ेडरेशन) ***n.*** a union of several states, राज्यों का संघ।

fed up (फ़ेड अप) ***adj.*** annoyed and bored, ऊबा हुआ, तंग, परेशान।

fee (फ़ी) ***n.*** a payment, or remuneration asked or given for professional services, शुल्क, फ़ीस।

feeble (फ़ीबल) ***adj.*** lacking strength, कमज़ोर, दुर्बल।

feed (फ़ीड) ***v.*** 1. to give food to, भोजन कराना, खिलाना। 2. to supply, पूर्ति करना, देना। ***n.*** food for animals, चारा, सानी।

feedback (फ़ीडबैक) ***n.*** 1. the return of a part of the output to the input, पुनर्निवेश, प्रतिसंभरण। 2. an information in response to a request, प्रतिसूचना।

feeder (फ़ीडर) ***n.*** 1. a child's feeding bottle, बच्चे की दूध पीने की शीशी या बोतल। 2. a power line from a generating station to a distribution network, प्रदाय, फीडर।

feel (फ़ील) ***v.*** 1. to touch, छूना, स्पर्श करना। 2. to appear to be to the senses, लगना, प्रतीत होना।

feeling (फ़ीलिंग) ***n.*** 1. the mental or physical awareness, अनुभूति, संवेदना। 2. emotion or sentiment, भावना।

feet (फ़ीट) ***n.*** plu. of foot.

feign (फ़ेन) ***v.*** to pretend, बहाना करना या बनाना।

feint (फ़ेन्ट) ***n.*** a feigned attack to attract someone's attention, शत्रु का ध्यान हटाने के लिए किया जानेवाला झूठ-मूठ का आक्रमण या प्रहार। ***v.*** to make a feint, झूठ-मूठ का आक्रमण या प्रहार करना।

felicitate (फ़ेलिसिटेट) ***v.*** to congratulate, बधाई/मुबारकबाद देना।

felicitation (फ़ेलिसिटेशन) ***n.*** congratulation, बधाई, मुबारकबाद।

felicitous (फ़ेलिसिटस) ***adj.*** 1. apt, उपयुक्त। 2. happy, प्रसन्न।

felicity (फ़ेलिसिटी) ***n.*** 1. aptness, उपयुक्तता। 2. happiness, प्रसन्नता।

feline (फ़ीलाइन) ***adj.*** catlike, बिल्लियों का-सा।

fell (फ़ेल) ***v.*** to knock down, गिरा देना।

fellow (फ़ेलो) ***n.*** 1. a man or boy, आदमी या लड़का। 2. a boyfriend, यार। 3. one who is associated with another, जोड़ीदार; 4. a partner, सहभागी, साथी। 5. a member of a learned society, किसी विद्वद् समाज का सदस्य।

fellow feeling ***n.*** 1. mutual understanding, मित्रभाव। 2. sympathy, सहानुभूति।

fellowship (फ़ेलोशिप) ***n.*** 1. friendly association, दोस्ताना, मैत्री, यारी। 2. brotherhood, भाई-चारा। 3. a group of people with same interest, बिरादरी, संस्था, संघ। 4. the position of a graduate, स्नातकत्व। 5. membership (of an institution, संस्था की) सदस्यता। 6. scholarship, अध्येतावृत्ति।

felon (फ़ेलन) ***n.*** a criminal, (घोर) अपराधी।

felony (फ़ेलनी) ***n.*** a major crime, महापराध।

felt (फ़ेल्ट) ***n.*** a matted fabric of wool., जमाया हुआ ऊनी कपड़ा।

female (फ़ीमेल) ***adj.*** 1. of or characteristic of the sex that can bear offspring or fruit, मादा। 2. of or characteristic of a woman, मादा, स्त्रीसुलभ, नारीसुलभ। ***n.*** a female animal or plant, स्त्री, मादा पशु या मादा पौधा।

feminine (फ़ेमिनिन) ***adj.*** 1. of or belonging to the female sex, मादा। 2. having characteristics of a woman, स्त्रियोचित।

feminism (फ़ेमिनिज़म) ***n.*** a doctrine that advocates equal rights for women, नारीवाद।

femoral (फ़ेमोरल) ***adj.*** pertaining to femur, ऊर्वस्थि-संबंधी।

femur (फ़ीमर) ***n.*** (plu. femora, femurs) the thigh bone, जाँघ की हड्डी, ऊर्वस्थि।

fen (फ़ेन) ***n.*** swampy land, दलदल।

fence (फ़ेन्स) ***n.*** a barrier of wooden posts, wires etc. to mark a boundary, घेरा, बाड़। ***v.*** to surround with a fence, बाड़ लगाना, घेरा बनाना।

fencing (फ़ेन्सिंग) ***n.*** 1. the art or sport of fighting with foils, पटेबाज़ी, भोथरी तलवारों से लड़ी जानेवाली लड़ाई। 2. material for fencing, बाड़।

fend (फ़ेन्ड) ***v.*** □ **fend for oneself,** अपनी ज़रूरतें खुद पूरी करना, अपने लिए स्वयं सामान जुटाना; **fend off,** दूर करना, हटाना।

fermentation (फ़र्मेन्टेशन) ***n.*** the act or process of fermenting, ख़मीरीकरण।

ferocious (फ़रोशस) ***adj.*** fierce, बर्बर, विकराल।

ferocity (फ़रॉसिटी) ***n.*** the quality or state of being ferocious, बर्बरता, विकरालता।

ferrous (फ़ेरस) ***n.*** containing iron, लौहयुक्त।

ferry (फ़ेरी) ***v.*** 1. to transport by boat, नाव से ले जाना, पार उतारना। 2. to go by ferry, नाव से पार जाना। ***n.*** a boat, नाव।

fertile (फ़र्टाइल) ***adj.*** producing abundantly, उपजाऊ, उर्वर।

fertility (फ़र्टिलिटी) ***n.*** the quality or state of being fertile, उर्वरता।

fertilization (फ़र्टिलाइज़ेशन) ***n.*** the act of fertilization, उर्वरीकरण।

fertilize (फ़र्टिलाइज़) ***v.*** to make fertile, उपजाऊ/उर्वर बनाना।

fertilizer (फ़र्टिलाइज़र) ***n.*** chemical manure, रासायनिक खाद, उर्वरक।

fervent (फ़र्वेन्ट) ***adj.*** passionate, भावपूर्ण, उत्साहपूर्ण।

fervour, fervor (फ़र्वर) ***n.*** zeal, जोश।

fester (फ़ेस्टर) ***v.*** 1. to form pus, मवाद पड़ना। 2. to decay, सड़ने लगना।

festival (फ़ेस्टिवल) ***n.*** 1. a day or time of religious celebration

F

or feasting, त्योहार, पर्व। 2. any occasion for celebration, मेला, आनंद-मेला। 3. an organized series of music, drama, films etc. given periodically, समारोह।

festive (फ़ेस्टिव) ***adj.*** 1. of a festival, उत्सव-संबंधी। 2. merry, joyous, आनंदमय।

festivity (फ़ेस्टिविटी) ***n.*** 1. festival, उत्सव। 2. mirth, gaity, आनंद, आनंदमंगल।

festoon (फ़ेस्टून) ***n.*** a decorative chain of leaves, flowers etc., बंदनवार, झालर, तोरण।

fetch (फ़ेच) ***v.*** 1. to bring, ले आना, लेकर आना। 2. to get, पाना।

fete (फ़ेट) ***n.*** a gala entertainment held outdoor, आनंद-मेला, फेट।

fetish (फ़ेटिश) ***n.*** any object believed by primitive people to have magical power. वह वस्तु जिसे चमत्कारिक समझकर प्राचीन लोग पूजते थे।

fetter (फ़ेटर) ***n.*** 1. (usually plu.) a chain or shackle for the feet, बेड़ी। 2. restraint, बाधा, रुकावट, बंधन। ***v.*** 1. to bind with fetters, बेड़ियाँ पहनाना। 2. to hold in check, बंधन में रखना।

feud (फ़्यूड) ***n.*** a prolonged quarrel, पुराना झगड़ा, कलह, वैर।

feudal (फ़्यूडल) ***adj.*** of or having to do with feudalism, सामंती।

feudalism (फ़्यूडलिज़म) ***n.*** economic, social and political organization of medieval Europe, सामंतवाद।

fever (फ़ीवर) ***n.*** 1. abnormally high body temperature, ताप। 2. a disease characterized by this, बुख़ार, ज्वर। 3. craze, ललक। 4. excitement, आवेश।

few (फ़्यू) ***adj. & pron.*** a small number, not many, कुछ।

fiance (फ़ीआन्से) ***n.*** the man to whom a woman is to be married, मँगेतर।

fiancee (फ़ीआन्से) ***n.*** the woman to whom a man is engaged to be married, मँगेतर।

fiasco (फ़िऐस्को) ***n.*** a complete failure, पूर्ण विफलता, सत्यानाश। (इतालवी)

fibre, fiber (फ़ाइबर) ***n.*** 1. a threadlike structure that combines with others to form a tissue, रेशा, तंतु। 2. the texture of something, बुनावट। 3. strength of character, चरित्रबल।

fickle (फ़िकल) ***adj.*** inconstant, अस्थिर।

fiction (फ़िक्शन) ***n.*** 1. any literary work portraying imaginary characters and events, गल्प, कथा, कहानी या उपन्यास। 2. the category of literature with imaginary characters and events, कथा-साहित्य।

fictitious (फ़िक्टिशस) ***adj.*** not real or genuine, बनावटी।

fiddle (फ़िडल) ***n.*** a violin, वायलिन। ***v.*** to play a violin, वायलिन बजाना।

fiddler (फ़िडलर) ***n.*** a violinist, वायलिन-वादक।

fidelity (फ़ाइडेलिटी) ***n.*** faithfulness, निष्ठा, वफ़ादारी।

fidgety (फ़िजिटी) ***adj.*** nervous or restless, अधीर, चुलबुला।

field (फ़ील्ड) ***n.*** 1. a wide open space, मैदान, क्षेत्र। 2. a piece of land devoted to a particular crop, खेत। 3. an area containing specified natural product, क्षेत्र; a coal field, कोयला-क्षेत्र। 4. a battle field, रणक्षेत्र। 5. a playground, खेल का मैदान। 6. an area of human activity, कार्यक्षेत्र। 7. a subject or sphere of knowledge, विषय, क्षेत्र। ***v.*** 1. to put (a team) into a field, (दल को) मैदान में उतारना। 2. to catch and return the ball in cricket etc., क्षेत्र-रक्षण करना।

fielding (फ़ील्डिंग) ***n.*** in cricket, taking the field, क्षेत्ररक्षण।

field marshal ***n.*** an army officer of the highest rank, फ़ील्ड मार्शल।

field work ***n.*** the work done or observations made in the field, क्षेत्रकार्य।

fiend (फ़ीन्ड) ***n.*** 1. an evil spirit, भूत, पिशाच। 2. a cruel person, क्रूर व्यक्ति।

fiendish (फ़ीन्डिश) ***adj.*** 1. devilish, पैशाचिक। 2. cruel, क्रूर।

fierce (फ़िअर्स) ***adj.*** 1. extremely violent, भयानक, भयंकर। 2. unpleasantly strong, प्रचंड, घोर, विकराल।

fierceness (फ़िअर्सनिस) ***adj.*** quality or state of being fierce, भयंकरता, प्रचंडता।

fiery (फ़ाइअरी) ***adj.*** 1. of or like fire, जलता हुआ। 2. exhibiting intense emotion, जोशीला। 3. easily provoked, गुस्सैल।

fifteen (फ़िफ़्टीन) ***adj. & n.*** five more than ten, पंद्रह।

fifth (फ़िफ़्थ) ***adj.*** next after fourth, पाँचवाँ।

fifth column (फ़िफ़्थ कॉलम) ***n.*** a secret body working for the enemy within a country, देशद्रोहियों का गुप्त संघटन।

fifty (फ़िफ़्टी) ***adj. & n.*** ten more than forty, पचास।

fifty-fifty ***adj.*** shared in two equal portions, आधा-आधा। ***adv.*** equally, बराबर-बराबर।

fig (फ़िग) ***n.*** a tree and its fruit, अंजीर।

fight (फ़ाइट) ***n.*** 1. a battle, लड़ाई, युद्ध। 2. a struggle, संघर्ष। ***v.*** 1. to take part in a battle, लड़ाई करना, युद्ध करना, लड़ना। 2. to struggle, संघर्ष करना। 3. to quarrel, झगड़ा करना, बहस या तर्क-वितर्क करना। 4. to wrestle, कुश्ती लड़ना।

fighter (फ़ाइटर) ***n.*** 1. one who fights योद्धा। 2. a wrestler, पहलवान। 3. a combat aircraft, लड़ाकू विमान।

fighting (फ़ाइटिंग) ***adj.*** engaged in a battle, युद्धरत, लड़ाकू।

figment (फ़िग्मेन्ट) ***n.*** something imagined, कल्पना।

figurative (फ़िग्युरेटिव) ***adj.*** not literal, metaphorical, लाक्षणिक।

figure (फ़िगर) ***n.*** 1. a symbol representing number, अंक। 2. an amount represented in numbers, अंकों में लिखी संख्या या राशि। 3. a diagram, outline or design, आरेख, रेखाचित्र। 4. bodily shape, काठी, आकृति, रूप।

figurehead (फ़िगरहेड) ***n.*** a person at the head of an organization but no actual authority, नाममात्र का प्रधान।

figure of speech ***n.*** a word or phrase having dramatic effects, अलंकार, लाक्षणिक प्रयोग।

F

filament (फ़िलामेन्ट) ***n.*** 1. a threadlike structure, तंतु। 2. a fine wire in a electric bulb which gives light when electrically heated, फ़िलामेंट, तंतु।

file[1] (फ़ाइल) ***n.*** 1. a holder for keeping papers, फ़ाइल, पंजी। 2. a collection of papers kept in a file, फ़ाइल में रखे कागज़-पत्र, मिसिल। ***v.*** to place in a file, फ़ाइल में रखना, नत्थी करना।

file[2] ***n.*** a tool for smoothing or shaping things, रेती। ***v.*** to smooth, shape or remove with a file, रेतना।

filial (फ़िलिअल) ***adj.*** relating to a son or daughter, संतान-संबंधी।

filibuster (फ़िलिबस्टर) ***n.*** obstructionist tactics, अड़ंगेबाज़ी।

filigree (फ़िलिग्री) ***n.*** ornamental lace-like work of twisted gold or silver wire, ज़रदोजी का काम।

filings (फ़ाइलिंग्स) ***n.*** plu. small pieces removed by a file, चूरा।

fill (फ़िल) ***v.*** 1. to make full or supply with material, भर देना, भरना। 2. to become full, भर जाना, भर आना। 3. to appoint, नियुक्त करना। 4. to occupy, (पद) ग्रहण करना।

fillet (फ़िलिट) ***n.*** a band or ribbon worn around the head, सिर पर बाँधी जानेवाली पट्टी या रिबन।

filling (फ़िलिंग) ***n.*** something used to fill a space or cavity, भरी जानेवाली वस्तु, भरान।

film (फ़िल्म) ***n.*** 1. a thin skin or membrane, झिल्ली। 2. a thin flexible strip of cellulose used to make negatives and trans-parencies, फ़िल्म। 3. a motion picture, चलचित्र, सिने-फ़िल्म। ***v.*** to make a motion picture, फ़िल्म बनाना।

film star ***n.*** an actor or actress in films, फ़िल्म-अभिनेता या फ़िल्म-अभिनेत्री।

filter (फ़िल्टर) ***n.*** a device or porous substance through which a liquid or gas is passed in order to remove impurities, फ़िल्टर, निथारनेवाला उपकरण। ***v.*** 1. to pass through a filter, निथरना। 2. to cause to pass through a filter, निथारना।

filth (फ़िल्थ) ***n.*** 1. foul or dirty matter, गंदगी, कूड़ा-कर्कट, कूड़ा-कचरा। 2. obscenity, अश्लीलता, गंदगी।

filthy (फ़िल्दी) ***adj.*** 1. dirty, गंदा, मैला। 2. obscene, अश्लील, गंदा।

filtration (फ़िल्ट्रेशन) ***n.*** the act of fil-tering, निथारने की क्रिया या भाव।

fin (फ़िन) ***n.*** 1. a thin flat swimming and balancing projection of a fish, पंख। 2. something resembling a fin, पंख।

final (फ़ाइनल) ***adj.*** 1. coming at the end, अंतिम। 2. ultimate, conclusive, निर्णायक, चरम।

finale (फ़िनालि) ***n.*** the last section of any activity, समापन-किस्त।

finalize (फ़ाइनलाइज़) ***v.*** to put into final form, अंतिम रूप देना।

finally (फ़ाइनली) ***adv.*** at last, अंत में, आख़िरकार।

finance (फ़ाइनैन्स) ***n.*** 1. the management of public money, वित्त-व्यवस्था। 2. (plu.) the money and the other resoures, funds, धन, निधि, वित्त। ***v.*** to provide the money for, धन उपलब्ध करना या कराना।

finance commission ***n.*** वित्त आयोग।

finance minister ***n.*** वित्तमंत्री, अर्थमंत्री।

financial (फ़ाइनैन्शल) ***adj.*** of finance, आर्थिक, वित्तीय।

financier (फ़ाइनैन्सिअर) ***n.*** one who is engaged in financing parties or businesses, वित्तपोषक।

find (फ़ाइन्ड) ***v.*** (found, finding) 1. to come upon by accident, मिलना, पड़ा पाना। 2. to come upon after a search, खोज निकालना, ढूँढ़ निकालना। 3. to attain, प्राप्त करना, पाना। 4. to become aware of, पता लगना, पता चलना। 5. to arrive at conclusion, decide, निष्कर्ष निकालना, निश्चय करना। ***n.*** 1. a discovery, खोज, ईज़ाद। 2. something found, प्राप्त वस्तु।

finding (फ़ाइन्डिंग) ***n.*** (plu.) the conclusions reached by judicial inquiry, निष्कर्ष, जाँच-परिणाम।

fine[1] (फ़ाइन) ***adj.*** 1. of high or superior quality, उत्तम, बढ़िया। 2. of great merit, उच्च कोटि का, श्रेष्ठ। 3. beautiful, charming, सुंदर, चारु, ललित। 4. pleasant, सुहावना; 5. most enjoyable, मज़ेदार। 6. consisting of small particles, बारीक, महीन। 7. precise or subtle, सूक्ष्म।

fine[2] ***n.*** a pecuniary punishment for an offence, अर्थदंड, जुर्माना। ***v.*** to punish by a fine, जुर्माना लगाना।

fine arts ***n.*** (plu.) the arts appealing to the sense of beauty, ललित कलाएँ।

fineness (फ़ाइननिस) ***n.*** the quality of being fine, उत्तमता, बढ़ियापन।

finesse (फ़िनेस) ***n.*** skill, कौशल।

finger (फ़िंगर) ***n.*** any of the five parts of the hand, उँगली।

fingerprint (फ़िंगरप्रिन्ट) ***n.*** the impression of a finger, उँगलियों की छाप।

finish (फ़िनिश) ***v.*** 1. to bring to an end, पूरा करना। 2. to use up, उपयोग करना। 3. to overthrow or kill, ख़त्म कर देना, मार डालना। ***n.*** 1. the final part or last stage of something, अंत, समाप्ति। 2. the appearance of having been properly finished with paint, polish etc., फिनिश, चमक।

finishing (फ़िनिशिंग) ***n.*** 1. the surface texture or appearance (of cloth, wood etc.,) चमक, सज्जा। 2. (plu.) the fixtures for lighting, plumbing etc., of a building, भवन की परिसज्जा।

finite (फ़ाइनाइट) ***adj.*** having an end or limit, ससीम, सीमित।

finite verb ***n.*** a verb form having limits of person, number and tense, समापिका क्रिया।

fiord (फ़्योर्ड) ***n.*** a long narrow inlet of the sea between steep cliffs, खड़ी चट्टानों के बीच का सँकरा समुद्री मार्ग।

fir (फ़र) ***n.*** 1. an evergreen tree of a pine family, देवदार। 2. the wood of a fir tree, देवदार की लकड़ी।

fire (फ़ाइअर) ***n.*** 1. the condition or process of burning, आग, अग्नि। 2. a heap of burning material, आग, आग की ढेरी। 3. destruction by fire, आग से होनेवाला विनाश या हानि। 4. the firing of guns, बंदूकों का चलना, बंदूकबाज़ी। ***v.*** 1. to discharge (a fire arm, बंदूक, तोप आदि) चलाना, दागना। 2. to dismiss from employment, बर्ख़ास्त कर देना। 3. to kindle, जलाना।

firearm (फ़ाइअरआर्म) ***n.*** a weapon capable of firing a missile, आग्नेयास्त्र।

firebrand (फ़ाइअरब्रैन्ड) ***n.*** 1. a piece of burning wood, जलती हुई लकड़ी।

F

2. a person who stirs up trouble, आग लगानेवाला, फ़साद खड़ा करनेवाला।

firebrigade (फ़ाइअरब्रिगेड) ***n.*** a party of fire extinguishers, अग्निशामक दल।

fire extinguisher ***n.*** a portable apparatus containing chemicals that can be sprayed on fire to extinguish it, अग्निशामक।

firefly (फ़ाइअरफ़्लाइ) ***n.*** a winged beetle that gives off a flashing light, जुगनूँ।

fireplace (फ़ाइअरप्लेस) ***n.*** a place for fire, अग्निस्थल, अँगीठी, चूल्हा।

fireproof (फ़ाइअरप्रूफ़) ***adj.*** capable of with standing fire, अग्निसह, फ़ायरप्रूफ़।

fire station ***n.*** a place where fire engines are kept, अग्निशमन-केंद्र, दमकल-स्टेशन।

firewood (फ़ाइअरवुड) ***n.*** wood used as feul, जलाने की लकड़ी, जलावन।

fireworks (फ़ाइअरवर्क्स) ***n.*** (plu.) 1. explosives used to produce light and noise for entertainment, आतिशबाज़ी। 2. a display of fireworks, आतिशबाज़ी।

firing (फ़ाइअरिंग) ***n.*** the shooting of firearms, गोलीबारी, अग्निवर्षा।

firm[1] (फ़र्म) ***n.*** a commercial establishment, फ़र्म, व्यावसायिक प्रतिष्ठान।

firm[2] ***adj.*** 1. not yielding easily to pressure, कड़ा, मज़बूत, सख़्त। 2. fixed or stable, स्थिर, अटल, स्थायी। 3. constant, unchanging, resolute, दृढ़, पक्का, अपरिवर्तनशील। 4. fixed, स्थिर, स्थापित।

firmament (फ़र्मामेन्ट) ***n.*** the sky, आकाश।

firmly (फ़र्मली) ***adv.*** in a firm way, दृढ़तापूर्वक, मज़बूती से।

first (फ़र्स्ट) ***adj.*** 1. coming before all others in a series, पहला, प्रथम, प्राथमिक। 2. foremost in importance or quality, सबसे बढ़कर होनेवाला। ***adv.*** 1. before all others, पहले। 2. for the first time, पहले-पहल, पहली बार।

first aid ***n.*** emergency treatment given to injured or sick persons before regular treament can be obtained, प्राथमिक चिकित्सा।

first class ***n.*** the first, highest or best category, प्रथम श्रेणी।

first floor ***n.*** the floor above the ground floor, दूसरी मंजिल।

firsthand (फ़र्स्टहैन्ड) ***adj.*** obtained directly, सीधे प्राप्त होनेवाला; firsthand knowledge, प्रत्यक्ष ज्ञान।

firstly (फ़र्स्टली) ***adv.*** in the first place, सबसे पहले, प्रथमतः।

first person ***n.*** the form of a pronoun which refers to the speaker or speakers, उत्तम पुरुष।

first-rate (फ़र्स्ट-रेट) ***adj.*** of the highest class or rank, प्रथम श्रेणी का, उच्च कोटि का।

firth (फ़र्थ) ***n.*** a narrow inlet of the sea, पतली या तंग खाड़ी।

fiscal (फ़िस्कल) ***adj.*** having to do with (public) finances, (राज) वित्तीय, राजकोषीय।

fish (फ़िश) ***n.*** 1. an acquatic animal having fins and gills, मछली। 2. its flesh as food, मछली का मांस, मछली। 3. a sign of the Zodiac, Pisces, मीन। ***v.*** to catch or try to catch fish, मछलियाँ पकड़ना, मछलियाँ मारना।

fisherman (फ़िशरमैन) ***n.*** a person who fishes for sport or for a living, मछुआ।

fishery (फ़िशरी) ***n.*** 1. a place where fishes are caught, मछलीगाह, मत्स्यक्षेत्र। 2. the industry of catching, packing and selling fish, मछली-उद्योग।

fishing (फ़िशिंग) ***n.*** the catching of fish for sport or for a living, मछली पकड़ने का काम या धंधा।

fishing rod ***n.*** a rod for catching fish, मछली पकड़ने की छड़ी या डंडा।

fission (फ़िशन) ***n.*** 1. the act or process of splitting into parts, विखंडन। 2. a nuclear reaction in which an atomic nucleus splits into fragments, नाभिकीय विखंडन।

fissure (फ़िशर) ***n.*** a deep crack in rock or earth, दरार।

fist (फ़िस्ट) ***n.*** the hand when tightly closed with the fingers bent against the palm, मुट्ठी, मुक्का।

fit[1] (फ़िट) ***adj.*** 1. suited for a given circumstance, purpose, or demand, उपयुक्त। 2. of right size and shape, appropriate, उपयुक्त, सही, फ़िट। 3. physically sound, स्वस्थ, सही; ठीक। ***v.*** 1. to be suitable (for), उपयुक्त होना। 2. to make suitable, उपयुक्त बनाना।

fit[2] ***n.*** 1. a brief but a cute spell of an illness, दौरा। 2. a period of loss of consciousness with convulsions, मूर्च्छा, बेहोशी। 3. a sudden violent feeling, आवेश।

fitful (फ़िट्फुल) ***adj.*** 1. restless, अशांत। 2. irregular, अनियमित। 3. uncertain, अनिश्चित।

fitness (फ़िटनिस) ***n.*** 1. the quality or state of being fit, उपयुक्तता। 2. physical soundness, पूर्ण स्वस्थता।

fitter (फ़िटर) ***n.*** a mechanic who fits together the parts of a machinery, मिस्त्री।

fitting (फ़िटिंग) ***adj.*** suitable, उपयुक्त।

five (फ़ाइव) ***adj. & n.*** one more than four, पाँच।

five year plan ***n.*** programmes for five years for the development of a country, पंचवर्षीय योजना।

fix (फ़िक्स) ***v.*** 1. to place, fasten or attach firmly, जड़ना, जमाना, बैठाना। 2. to direct steadily, लगाना। 3. to arrange, set or establish, 4. to influence wrongly, मिला लेना, ठीक कर लेना; ***n.*** a difficult or awkward situation, झंझट, परेशानी।

fixed (फ़िक्स्ड) ***adj.*** 1. fastened, जड़ा या बैठा हुआ। 2. settled, नियत, निर्धारित।

fixture (फ़िक्स्चर) ***n.*** 1. anything fixed, जड़ी हुई वस्तु, या पक्की की हुई बात। 2. a match or contest taking place on an agreed date, निर्धारित समय पर होनेवाला मैच या खेल-प्रतियोगिता।

fizz (फ़िज़) ***v.*** to make hissing sound, बुदबुदाना।

flabbergast (फ़्लैबरगैस्ट) ***v.*** to astound, चकित/स्तब्ध कर देना।

flabby (फ़्लैबी) ***adj.*** having too soft flesh, थुलथुल।

flaccid (फ़्लैक्सिड) ***adj.*** 1. feeble, कमज़ोर। 2. flabby, थुलथुल।

flag[1] (फ़्लैग) ***n.*** 1. a piece of cloth with a pattern or picture attached to a staff, झंडा, पताका। 2. a small paper device resembling a flag, झंडी।

flag[2] ***v.*** 1. to droop, कुम्हला जाना। 2. to decline in vigour, कमज़ोर हो जाना।

flagellate (फ़्लैजलेट) ***v.*** to whip, कोड़े लगाना।

F

flag-hoisting (फ़्लैग-होइस्टिंग) ***n.*** the hoisting of a flag, झंडा फहराने की क्रिया या भाव।

flagon (फ़्लैगन) ***n.*** a wine cantainer with a handle and narrow neck, सुराही की तरह का मदिरा-पात्र।

flagrant (फ़्लेग्रेन्ट) ***adj.*** 1. bad, notorious, बुरा, कुख्यात। 2. shameless, लज्जाजनक।

flail (फ़्लेल) ***n.*** a hand tool for threshing grain, मूसल।

flair (फ़्लेअर) ***n.*** 1. a natural aptitude, सहज प्रवृत्ति। 2. keenness, सूझ, कुशाग्रबुद्धि।

flake (फ़्लेक) ***n.*** a light leaf-like small piece of somethng, पपड़ी, कचरी। ***v.*** to form into flakes, पपड़ी बनाना।

flamboyance (फ्लैम्बॉइएन्स) ***n.*** the quality or state of being flamboyant, भड़कीलापन, चटकपन, शब्दाडंबर।

flamboyant (फ्लैम्बॉइएन्ट) ***adj.*** 1. of florid decoration, भड़कीला। 2. brilliant in form or colour, चटकदार। 3. bombastic, शब्दा-डंबरपूर्ण।

flame (फ़्लेम) ***n.*** 1. a flickering tongue of light rising from a fire, लौ, लपट। 2. a strong passion of love, प्यार का जोश, आग।

flamingo (फ्लेमिंगो) ***n.*** a long-legged water-bird with a broad beak curved downward, मराल।

flammable (फ़्लैमेबल) ***adj.*** inflammable, ज्वलनशील।

flange (फ़्लैन्ज़) ***n.*** a protruding edge, उभरा हुआ किनारा, उभारदार किनारा।

flank (फ़्लैंक) ***n.*** 1. the side of an animal between the ribs and hip, पहलू, पक्ष, बगल, बाज़ू। 2. the side of a body of troops, पक्ष, पहलू। ***v.*** 1. to be at the side of, एक तरफ़ होना। 2. to attack the side, सेना के किसी पहलू या पक्ष पर आक्रमण करना। 3. to surround, घेर लेना।

flannel (फ़्लैनल) ***n.*** 1. a kind of soft woollen cloth, फ़लालेन। 2. a type of cotton cloth that looks like flannel, फ़लालेन की तरह का सूती कपड़ा।

flap (फ़्लैप) ***v.*** 1. to move up and down (as wings, पंख) फड़फड़ाना। 2. to flutteer, लहराना। ***n.*** 1. the sound of flapping, फड़फड़ाहट। 2. a light blow with a flat thing, पंखी आदि से किया जानेवाला हलका प्रहार।

flare (फ़्लेअर) ***v.*** to burn with a bright wavering light, झलझलाना। ***n.*** 1. a flaring light, झलझलाहट। 2. a bright light, तेज़ रोशनी।

flash (फ़्लैश) ***v.*** 1. to send out a sudden brief blaze or light, कौंध उठना, कौंध जाना। 2. to be brilliant, चमक उठना। ***n.*** 1. a sudden, brief and intense light, कौंध, चमक। 2. a sudden brief play or appearance, झलक। 3. an instant, क्षण।

flashback (फ़्लैशबैक) ***n.*** the interruption of a story or narrative to show or tell about an incident from the past, पूर्वप्रसंग-चर्चा।

flashy (फ़्लैशी) ***adj.*** 1. showy, दिखावटी। 2. gaudy, भड़कीला।

flask (फ़्लास्क) ***n.*** a small container with a narrow neck and cover, फ़्लास्क।

flat[1] (फ़्लैट) ***adj.*** 1. level, horizontal, समतल, क्षैतिज। 2. having smooth surface, चौरस, सपाट। 3. having little depth or thickness, छिछला, पतला। 4. fixed, निश्चित।

F

flat² ***n.*** a set of rooms for a family on one floor of a building, फ़्लैट।

flatten (फ़्लैटन) ***v.*** to make or become flat, समतल होना या करना।

flatter (फ़्लैटर) ***v.*** to praise insincerely or excessively, ख़ुशामद करना।

flattery (फ़्लैटरी) ***n.*** excessive praise, ख़ुशामद, चापलूसी।

flatulence (फ़्लैट्युलेन्स) ***n.*** gas in the stomach, वात, वायु-विकार।

flaunt (फ़्लॉन्ट) ***v.*** to display proudly, दिखावा करना।

flavour, flavor (फ़्लेवर) ***n.*** 1. taste perceived in food or drink in the mouth, स्वाद, मज़ा। 2. anything added to a food to give a particular taste, पुट, गमक। ***v.*** to give flavour to, पुट देना।

flaw (फ़्लॉ) ***n.*** a blemish or defect, दोष, त्रुटि, कमी।

flawless (फ़्लॉलिस) ***adj.*** having no flaw, निर्दोष।

flax (फ़्लैक्स) ***n.*** fibers of a particular plant, सन का रेशा।

flaxen (फ़्लैक्सन) ***adj.*** of or made of flax, सन का बना हुआ।

flay (फ़्ले) ***v.*** to strip off the skin or hide by whipping, कोड़े मार-मारकर ख़ाल उधेड़ लेना।

flea (फ़्ली) ***n.*** a blood-sucking insect, पिस्सू।

fledgling (फ़्लेजलिंग) ***n.*** 1. a young bird, पक्षीशावक। 2. an inexperienced person, नौसिखिया।

flee (फ़्ली) ***v.*** to run away, भाग खड़े होना, फ़रार हो जाना।

fleece (फ़्लीस) ***n.*** the coat of wool that covers the body of a sheep, भेड़ की ऊन। ***v.*** 1. to shear the fleece from a sheep, ऊन कतरना। 2. to swindle, rob or cheat, ठगना, मूँड़ लेना, लूट लेना।

fleet¹ (फ़्लीट) ***n.*** the group of warships, जहाज़ी बेड़ा।

fleet² ***adj.*** moving swiftly, द्रुतगति।

fleeting (फ़्लीटिंग) ***adj.*** transient, क्षणिक, अनित्य।

flesh (फ़्लेश) ***n.*** 1. the soft substance of the body, मांस। 2. meat, गोश्त, मांस। 3. the pulpy part of vegetables and fruit, गूदा। 4. the body (opposed to the mind or soul, मन या आत्मा से भिन्न) शरीर, देह।

fleshy (फ़्लेशी) ***adj.*** 1. of flesh, मांसल। 2. pulpy, गूदेदार।

flex (फ़्लेक्स) ***v.*** 1. to bend, मोड़ना। 2. to be bent, मुड़ना।

flexibility (फ़्लेक्सिबिलिटी) ***n.*** the quality of being flexible, नम्यता, लचीलापन।

flexible (फ़्लेक्सिबल) ***adj.*** 1. not stiff or rigid, लचीला। 2. capable of modification, नमनीय, लचीला।

flick (फ़्लिक) ***n.*** a light blow with a whip, कोड़े का हलका प्रहार, हलका आघात। ***v.*** to strike with a flick, हलका आघात करना, झटका देना।

flicker (फ़्लिकर) ***v.*** 1. to burn unsteadily, लुपलुपाना, टिमटिमाना। 2. to flutter, फड़फड़ाना। ***n.*** the act of flickering, लुपलुप, टिमटिमाहट; फड़फड़ाहट।

flight¹ (फ़्लाइट) ***n.*** 1. the act of flying, उड़ान। 2. a journey made by air, हवाई यात्रा। 3. a scheduled airline trip, नियत हवाई सेवा। 4. a series of stairs, सोपान, ज़ीना।

F

flight[2] ***n.*** the act of fleeting or running away, पलायन।

flimsy (फ़्लिम्ज़ी) ***adj.*** 1. thin, झीना। 2. ineffectual, निष्प्रभावी।

flinch (फ़्लिन्च) ***v.*** to shrink from one's duty, कर्तव्यविमुख होना।

fling (फ़्लिंग) ***v.*** 1. to throw forcefully or violently, प्रक्षेपण करना, फेंकना, चलाना। 2. to move suddenly or forcefully, एकाएक या तेज़ी से आगे बढ़ना। ***n.*** 1. the act of flinging, क्षेपण। 2. a sarcastic or taunting remark, छींटा, व्यंग्य।

flint (फ़्लिन्ट) ***n.*** a kind of hard stone that sparks when struck with steel, चकमक।

flip (फ़्लिप) ***v.*** 1. to toss, उछालना। 2. to turn with a quick motion, झटके से हिलाना। 3. to flick, उँगली द्वारा हलका आघात करना।

flippancy (फ़्लिपेन्सी) ***n.*** impertinence, उद्धतता, छिछोरापन।

flippant (फ़्लिपेन्ट) ***adj.*** impertinent, उद्धत।

flirt (फ़्लर्ट) ***v.*** to behave amorously without serious intentions, छेड़छाड़ करना। ***n.*** one who toys amorously, छिछोरा या छिछोरी।

flirtation (फ़्लर्टेशन) ***n.*** the act of flirting, छेड़छाड़, छिछोरापन।

flit (फ़्लिट) ***v.*** 1. to fly or move lightly or quickly, फुदकना। 2. to move house, घर बदल लेना।

float (फ़्लोट) ***v.*** 1. to rest or drift on the surface of water without sinking, बहना, तैरना। 2. to cause to move on the surface, बहा ले जाना। 3. to fly, उड़ना, उड़ान भरना। 4. to issue (bonds etc.), जारी करना।

floating (फ़्लोटिंग) ***adj.*** drifting in water, तैरता या बहता हुआ।

flock (फ़्लॉक) ***n.*** 1. a group (of animals or birds, पशु-पक्षियों का) झुंड, गल्ला। 2. a large group of people, झुंड, भीड़। ***v.*** to gather in a large number, झुंड बनाना, भीड़ लगाना।

floe (फ़्लो) ***n.*** a mass of floating ice, तैरता बरफ़ का पहाड़।

flog (फ़्लॉग) ***v.*** to beat with a whip, कोड़े लगाना।

flogging (फ़्लॉगिंग) ***n.*** punishment by beating with a whip, कोड़ों की मार।

flood (फ़्लड) ***n.*** 1. an overflowing of water over a place that is usually dry, बाढ़, सैलाब। 2. the great outpouring or flow, बाढ़, भरमार। ***v.*** 1. to cover or submerge with a flood, बाढ़ आना। 2. to fill or overwhelm like a flood, प्लावित होना, भर जाना।

floodlight (फ़्लडलाइट) ***n.*** an electric lamp etc., that produces intense bright light, तीव्र प्रकाश देनेवाली बत्ती।

floodtide (फ़्लडटाइड) ***n.*** an incoming tide, ज्वार।

floor (फ़्लोर) ***n.*** 1. the surface of the room, फ़र्श। 2. the gound surface, earth, भूतल, ज़मीन। 3. the bottom of the sea, cave etc., तल। 4. a legislative chamber where legislators occupy their seats, विधान-भवन। 5. a story of a building, मंज़िल, खंड। ***v.*** 1. to put a floor in a building, फ़र्श डालना, बनाना या बिछाना। 2. to knockdown, गिरा देना, पटक देना।

flooring (फ़्लोरिंग) ***n.*** material used for making floors, फ़र्श बनाने की सामग्री।

flop (फ़्लॉप) ***v.*** 1. to bend loosely,

झुक या लटक जाना। 2. to fall down clumsily, धड़ाम से गिर जाना। ***n.*** 1. the act or noise of flopping, धड़ाम, धम शब्द। 2. a complete failure, वह कार्यक्रम, फ़िल्म, पुस्तक आदि जो बुरी तरह पिट गई हो।

floppy disc ***n.*** a magnetic disc used in a computer for storing information, चुंबकीय चक्रिका, फ़्लापी।

flora (फ़्लोरा) ***n.*** all the plants of a particular place or time, किसी विशिष्ट स्थान या काल के सभी पेड़-पौधे।

floral (फ़्लोरल) ***adj.*** of flowers, फूलों का।

floral tribute ***n.*** a bunch of flowers given as a tribute, श्रद्धा-सुमन।

florid (फ़्लोरिड) ***adj.*** 1. flowery, बेल-बूटोंवाला। 2. ornamented, भड़कीला। 3. rosy, गुलाबी।

florist (फ़्लोरिस्ट) ***n.*** a person who grows or sells flowers or flower plants, पुष्पोत्पादक, फूलवाला।

flotation (फ़्लोटेशन) ***n.*** the act of floating (bonds, बॉण्ड) निकालना, प्रवर्तन।

flotila (फ़्लॉटिला) ***n.*** a small fleet, छोटा बेड़ा।

flounce[1] (फ़्लाउन्स) ***n.*** an ornamental piece of cloth sewn to a skirt etc., स्कर्ट आदि में शोभा के लिए लगाया जानेवाला कपड़े का टुकड़ा, झालर, फीता आदि।

flounce[2] ***v.*** to go or move with agitated movements, आवेश में आकर या हड़बड़ाते हुए निकल पड़ना या चल देना। ***n.*** the act of flouncing, हड़बड़ाहट, हड़बड़ी।

flounder (फ़्लाउन्डर) ***v.*** 1. to struggle awkwardly to move in mud or snow, दलदल या बर्फ़ में चलने के लिए संघर्ष करना। 2. to make mistakes, भूलें करना।

flour (फ़्लाउर) ***n.*** a fine powder obtained by grinding grain, आटा, मैदा, बेसन आदि।

flourish (फ़्लरिश) ***v.*** to thrive or prosper, फूलना-फलना।

flout (फ़्लाउट) ***v.*** 1. to disobey, अवज्ञा करना। 2. to show contempt for, निरादर / उपहास करना।

flow (फ़्लो) ***v.*** 1. to move as water, बहना। 2. to hand down loosely, लटकना, लहराना। 3. to be plentiful, प्रचुर होना। ***n.*** a stream, current, धारा।

flower (फ़्लावर) ***n.*** a part of the plant having brightly coloured leaves or petals, फूल, पुष्प। ***v.*** 1. to bloom, खिलना, फूलना, फूल लगना। 2. to prosper, समृद्ध होना।

flowerpot (फ़्लावरपॉट) ***n.*** a pot in which plants may be grown, गमला।

flower show ***n.*** an exhibition of flowering plants, पुष्प-प्रदर्शनी।

flowery (फ़्लावरी) ***adj.*** 1. abounding in flowers, फूलों से लदा हुआ। 2. figurative, आलंकारिक।

flowing (फ़्लोइंग) ***adj.*** 1. moving as a fluid, बहता हुआ। 2. continuous, सतत, निरंतर।

flu (फ़्लू) ***n.*** influenza, फ़्लू, इन्फ़्लूएन्जा।

fluctuate (फ़्लक्चूएट) ***v.*** 1. to move up and down, उतरना-चढ़ना, उतार-चढ़ाव होना। 2. to be irregular, घटते-बढ़ते रहना। 3. to cause to fluctuate, घटाना-बढ़ाना, परिवर्तन करना।

fluctuation (फ़्लक्चूएशन) ***n.*** the moving up and down, घट-बढ़, उतार-चढ़ाव।

F

flue (फ़्लू) ***n.*** a pipe or tube to carry off smoke, gas etc., धुआँकश, चिमनी।

fluency (फ़्लूएन्सी) ***n.*** the state of being fluent, प्रवाहशीलता।

fluent (फ़्लूएन्ट) ***adj.*** 1. speaking smoothly and readily, धाराप्रवाह बोलनेवाला। 2. smoothly and naturally flowing, धाराप्रवाह, प्रवाहशील।

fluffy (फ़्लफ़ी) ***adj.*** covered with fluff, रोएँदार।

fluid (फ़्लूइड) ***n.*** a substance that flows easily, तरल पदार्थ, द्रव। ***adj.*** 1. able to flow, तरल, प्रवाहशील। 2. unstable, अस्थिर।

fluke (फ़्लूक) ***n.*** good luck, सौभाग्य।

flurry (फ़्लरी) ***n.*** 1. a sudden brief gust of wind or rain, हवा या बारिश का झोंका। 2. a sudden wish to do something, झोंक।

flush (फ़्लश) ***v.*** 1. to clean with a sudden flow of water, पानी बहाकर साफ़ कर देना। 2. to blush, झेंप जाना, शरमा जाना। ***n.*** 1. rapid flow, तेज़ बहाव। 2. a blush, लाली या लाज। 3. excitement caused by emotion, उत्तेजना, भावावेश, आवेश। 4. the redness of the skin, लाली, सुर्ख़ी। ***adj.*** 1. blushing, लाज-भरा, आरक्त, लाल। 2. plentiful, प्रचुर। 3. prosperous, समृद्ध।

fluster (फ़्लस्टर) ***v.*** to confuse, क्षुब्ध कर देना। ***n.*** confusion, क्षोभ, घबराहट।

flute (फ़्लूट) ***n.*** a wind instrument with finger holes, बाँसुरी।

flutist (फ़्लूटिस्ट) ***n.*** one who plays the flute, बाँसुरीवादक।

flutter (फ़्लटर) ***v.*** 1. to move or fly with a quick flapping (of wings, पर) फड़फड़ाना। 2. to vibrate rapidly or erratically, ज़ोर-ज़ोर से या अनियमित रूप से धड़कना।

fly[1] (फ़्लाइ) ***v.*** 1. to move through the air, उड़ना। 2. to cause to move through air, उड़ाना। 3. to direct or control the flight (of an aircraft, हवाई जहाज़) उड़ाना, चलाना। 4. to travel in an aircraft, वायुयान में यात्रा करना। 5. to cross by means of flying, पार करना, लाँघ जाना। 6. to flee, भाग जाना।

fly[2] ***n.*** a small insect with two wings, मक्खी, मक्षिका।

flying (फ़्लाइंग) ***adj.*** able to fly or that flies, उड़नेवाला या उड़ता हुआ; flying dish, उड़न तश्तरी। ***n.*** 1. the act of flying, उड़ना, उड्डयन। 2. a journey by an aircraft, हवाई जहाज़ का सफ़र।

flying colours ***n.*** (plu.) 1. flags shown as sign of victory, विजय की सूचक पताकाएँ। 2. victory, विजय, सफलता।

flying squad ***n.*** a small group of police ready for quick action at the time of a mishap, उड़ाका दल, उड़न-दस्ता।

flying visit ***n.*** a very short visit, क्षणिक भेंट।

flyover (फ़्लाइओवर) ***n.*** a bridge over a crossing, फ़्लाइओवर, उपरिसेतु।

flypast (फ़्लाइपास्ट) ***n.*** a ceremonial flight of aircraft over a given area, फ्लाइपास्ट, विमानों की सामूहिक उड़ान।

foal (फ़ोल) ***n.*** the young of a horse, बछेड़ा।

foam (फ़ोम) ***n.*** 1. a mass of small bubbles formed on a liquid, झाग, फेन। 2. spongy rubber, फ़ोम।

focal (फ़ोकल) ***adj.*** 1. of focus, फ़ोकस-संबंधी। 2. central, केंद्रीय।

focus (फ़ोकस) ***n.*** 1. the point at

which rays come together or from which they diverge, फ़ोकस। 2. any centre of activity, केंद्र। *v.* 1. to adjust the focal distance in order to produce a clear image, फ़ोकस को ठीक करना। 2. to concentrate, केंद्रित करना।

fodder (फ़ॉडर) ***n.*** food for cattle, चारा।

foe (फ़ो) ***n.*** an enemy, दुश्मन, शत्रु।

foetus (फ़ीटस) ***n.*** the unborn young in the womb, भ्रूण।

fog (फ़ॉग) ***n.*** 1. a cloudlike mass of water vapour at or just above the earth's surface, कोहरा, कुहासा, धुंध। 2. confusion or bewilderment, भ्रम, भ्रांति।

foggy (फ़ॉगी) ***adj.*** 1. full of fog, covered with fog, कुहासे से भरा। 2. dim, धुँधला, अस्पष्ट।

foible (फ़ॉइबल) ***n.*** weakness in character, चारित्रिक दुर्बलता।

foil[1] (फ़ॉइल) ***n.*** a thin leaf of metal, पन्नी। ***v.*** to cover with foil, पन्नी लगाना।

foil[2] ***v.*** to frustrate or thwart, विफल कर देना, विफल बना देना।

foil[3] ***n.*** a blunt sword, भोथरी तलवार।

foist (फ़ॉइस्ट) ***v.*** to impose with trick, गले मढ़ देना।

fold[1] (फ़ोल्ड) ***v.*** 1. to bend or press (cloth, paper etc.) so that one part lies on another, तह लगाना। 2. to bring from extended to closed position, मोड़ना, 3. to clasp in arms, बाँहों में भींच लेना।

fold[2] ***n.*** an enclosure for sheep, भेड़ों का बाड़ा।

folder (फ़ोल्डर) ***n.*** 1. a folded sheet of cardboard used as a holder for papers, फ़ोल्डर। 2. a folded leaflet, कई तहोंवाला विज्ञापन या सूचनापत्र, फ़ोल्डर।

folding (फ़ोल्डिंग) ***adj.*** having two or more parts that can be folded one against another, फ़ोल्डिंग, टुटवाँ, मुड़वाँ।

foliage (फ़ोलिइज) ***n.*** the leaves of a plant or tree, पौधे या वृक्ष के पत्ते।

folio (फ़ोलिओ) ***n.*** 1. the two opposite pages of a ledger, पन्ना। 2. page number of a printed book, (पुस्तक के) पृष्ठ की संख्या।

folk (फ़ोक) ***n.*** people in general, लोग, जन, लोक; ~ lore, लोक कथा।

follow (फ़ॉलो) ***v.*** 1. to come after, to go after, पीछे आना। 2. to become a follower, अनुयायी या शिष्य बन जाना। 3. to go along, अनुसरण करना। 4. to pursue, पीछा करना। 5. to result from or come after as a logical consequence, परिणाम के रूप में घटित होना। 6. to obey or comply, अनुसरण/पालन करना।

follower (फ़ॉलोअर) ***n.*** 1. a disciple, अनुयायी। 2. a servant or attendant, सेवक।

following (फ़ॉलोइंग) ***n.*** 1. a group of disciples or adherents, अनुयायियों का वर्ग। 2. a group of servants, सेवक वृंद। ***adj.*** 1. that follows, आगामी, अगला। 2. to be mentioned immediately, निम्न-लिखित।

follow-on (फ़ॉलो-ऑन) ***n.*** an immediate second innings forced on a team, (क्रिकेट के खेल में) फ़ालो-ऑन।

folly (फ़ॉली) ***n.*** a foolish act, मूर्खता।

foment (फ़ोमेन्ट) ***v.*** 1. to treat with heat and moisture, सेंकना। 2. to stir up, आंदोलित करना।

F

fond (फ़ॉन्ड) ***adj.*** 1. kind and loving, स्नेही, प्यारा। 2. foolishly affectionate, आसक्त, मुग्ध। □ **fond of,** शौक़ीन, प्रेमी, चाव-भरा।

fondle (फ़ॉन्डल) ***v.*** to love or caress, लाड़-प्यार या दुलार करना।

font[1] (फ़ॉन्ट) ***n.*** a basin in a church for holding holy water for baptism, चर्च में अभिषेक के लिए पवित्र जल रखने का पात्र, जलपात्र।

font[2] ***n.*** a complete set of printing types of one style and size, एक ही मोटाई और आकार के टाईपों का समूह, फॉन्ट।

food (फ़ूड) ***n.*** 1. something solid for eating, अन्न, खाद्य पदार्थ, भोजन। 2. a diet, आहार, ख़ुराक।

foodgrains (फ़ूडग्रेन्स) ***n.*** (plu.) seeds of wheat, rice etc., खाद्यान्न।

food poisoning ***n.*** poisoning caused by eating something poisonous or contaminated, खाद्यान्न-विषाक्तता।

food processor ***n.*** a kitchen appliance for cutting, shredding or grinding food, फ़ूड प्रोसेसर।

foodstuff (फ़ूडस्टफ़) ***n.*** a substance that can be used as food, खाद्य पदार्थ, खाद्यान्न।

fool (फ़ूल) ***n.*** 1. a person who lacks understanding or judgment, मूर्ख व्यक्ति। 2. a jester or clown, मसख़रा, जोकर। ***v.*** to make a fool of, मूर्ख/उल्लू बनाना।

foolhardy (फ़ूलहार्डी) ***adj.*** foolishly bold, उजड्ड।

foolish (फ़ूलिश) ***adj.*** 1. unwise, मूर्ख। 2. ridiculous, silly, मूर्खतापूर्ण।

foolishness (फ़ूलिशनिस) ***n.*** the state or quality of being foolish, मूर्खता, बेवक़ूफ़ी।

foolproof (फ़ूलप्रूफ़) ***adj.*** easy, सरल।

foolscap (फ़ूल्ज़कैप) ***n.*** a size of printing paper approximately 13×16 inches, छपाई के कागज़ का एक साइज़, फुलस्केप।

foot (फ़ुट) ***n.*** (plu. feet) 1. the lower part of a leg, पैर, पाँव। 2. the lower end of a table etc., पाया, पैर। 3. the lower end of a bed or grave, पयताना। 4. the lower part or bottom of something, निचला हिस्सा, तल। 5. a unit of length equal to 12 inches, फ़ुट। 6. a metrical unit or division of verse, पाद, चरण। ***v.*** to walk (not ride), पैदल चलना।

football (फ़ुटबॉल) ***n.*** 1. an inflated leather ball, फ़ुटबाल। 2. a game played between two teams with a football, फ़ुटबाल का खेल।

footboard (फ़ुटबोर्ड) ***n.*** a board or platform for the feet, पायदान।

foothold (फ़ुटहोल्ड) ***n.*** 1. a place for a foot, पायदान। 2. a secure position, सुरक्षित स्थिति।

footing (फ़ुटिंग) ***n.*** 1. a foothold, पायदान। 2. position in the society, सामाजिक स्थिति; 3. foundation, आधार।

footlights (फ़ुटलाइट्स) ***n.*** (plu.) a row of lights along the front of the stage floor, फ़ुटलाइट्स, पाददीप, पादबत्ती।

footnote (फ़ुटनोट) ***n.*** a note printed at the bottom of a page, पादटिप्पणी।

footpath (फ़ुटपाथ) ***n.*** a path for the pedestrians, पटरी, पगडंडी।

footprint (फ़ुटप्रिन्ट) ***n.*** the mark of a foot, पदचिह्न।

footstep (फ़ुटस्टेप) ***n.*** a step taken in walking, पग, कदम, डग।

footwear (फ़ुटविअर) ***n.*** shoes and boots, जूता, चप्पल आदि।

fop (फ़ॉप) ***n.*** a dandy, छैला, बाँका।

for (फ़ॉर) ***prep.*** 1. to serve as, के लिए, के वास्ते। 2. in place of, की जगह, के बदले में। 3. in favour of or on the side of, की ओर से, की तरफ़ से। 4. with the aim or purpose of, के उद्‌देश्य से।

forage (फ़ॉरिज) ***n.*** fodder, चारा, रातब।

foray (फ़ॉरे) ***n.*** a sudden raid, धावा, छापा।

forbear[1] (फ़ॉर्बेअर) ***v.*** to endure or tolerate, सहना, बर्दाश्त करना।

forbearance (फ़ॉर्बेअरेन्स) ***n.*** tolerance, सहनशीलता, सहिष्णुता।

forbearing (फ़ार्बेअरिंग) ***adj.*** tolerant, patient, सहिष्णु, धैर्यवान।

forbid (फ़ॉर्बिड) ***v.*** to prohibit, वर्जित/मना करना।

forbiddance (फ़ॉर्बिडेन्स) ***n.*** prohibition, वर्जन, मनाही।

forbidding (फ़ॉर्बिडिंग) ***adj.*** threatening, भयानक, डरावना, धमकी देनेवाला।

force (फ़ोर्स) ***n.*** 1. power, strength, बल, शक्ति। 2. exertion of such power, violence, बलप्रयोग, जबरी। 3. moral strength, मनोबल। 4. the intensity of power, आवेग, प्रचंडता। 5. a person or thing having uncontrollable power, शक्ति-स्रोत। 6. a body of troops or police, सेना, फौज़। 7. a body of persons organised for a certain purpose, शक्ति। □ **in force,** जारी, लागू, प्रवृत्त। ***v.*** 1. to compel to perform an action, मजबूर करना, विवश करना। 2. to use force in order to do something, बलप्रयोग करना, दबाव डालना।

forced (फ़ोर्स्ड) ***adj.*** done or brought about by force, जबरी, बलात्।

forceful (फ़ोर्सफ़ुल) ***adj.*** full of force, प्रबल।

forceps (फ़ॉर्सेप्स) ***n.*** a surgeons pincers, शल्य चिकित्सक की चिमटी, सँड़सी।

forcible (फ़ोर्सिबल) ***adj.*** 1. done by force, जबरी। 2. forceful, सशक्त, प्रबल।

ford (फ़ोर्ड) ***n.*** a shallow place where a river may be crossed on foot, horseback or car, छिछला पाट। ***v.*** to cross at a ford, छिछले पाट से पार करना।

fore (फ़ोर) ***adv.*** in, at or toward the front, आगे, सामने।

forearm[1] (फ़ोरआर्म) ***n.*** the part of the arm from ellbow to wrist, कोहनी और कलाई के बीच का हिस्सा, अग्रबाहु।

forearm[2] ***v.*** to arm oneself beforehand, पहले से हथियारबंद हो जाना।

forebode (फ़ोरबोड) ***v.*** 1. to give a hint, लक्षण बताना, सूचक होना। 2. to have a premonition of, पहले से जान पड़ना, लगना।

forecast (फ़ोरकास्ट) ***v.*** to predict in advance, भविष्यवाणी करना।

foreclose (फ़ोरक्लोज़) ***v.*** to bar, रोकना, अवरुद्ध करना।

forefather (फ़ोरफ़ादर) ***n.*** an ancestor, पूर्वज।

forefinger (फ़ोरफ़िंगर) ***n.*** the index finger, तर्जनी (उँगली)।

forefront (फ़ोरफ़्रन्ट) ***n.*** the foremost part of something, सामने का भाग, सामना।

F

forego (फ़ोरगो) ***v.*** (forewent, foregone, foregoing) to give up or relinquish, त्याग देना।

foregone (फ़ोरगॉन) ***adj.*** 1. previously determined, पूर्वनिर्धारित, पूर्वनिश्चित। 2. inevitable, अनिवार्य।

forehead (फ़ोरहेड) ***n.*** the part of the face above the eyes, माथा, ललाट।

foreign (फ़ॉरिन) ***adj.*** situated outside one's own country, विदेशी।

foreigner (फ़ॉरिनर) ***n.*** a person from a foreign country, विदेशी।

foreknowledge (फ़ोरनॉलिज) ***n.*** knowledge about something before it happens or occurs, पूर्वज्ञान।

forelock (फ़ोरलॉक) ***n.*** a lock of hair just falling over a person's forehead, लट, अलक।

foreman (फ़ोरमैन) ***n.*** a skilled man incharge of a group of workers in a factory, कर्मचारियों के किसी समूह का प्रमुख, फ़ोरमैन।

foremost (फ़ोरमोस्ट) ***adj.*** most important, सर्वाधिक महत्त्वपूर्ण। 2. first in rank, सर्वप्रमुख।

forenoon (फ़ोरनून) ***n.*** the period between sunrise and noon, पूर्वाह्न।

forensic (फ़ोरेन्सिक) ***adj.*** of or used in courts of law, न्यायालय-संबंधी।

forerunner (फ़ोररनर) ***n.*** a herald, अग्रदूत।

foresee (फ़ोरसी) ***v.*** to see or know beforehand, पूर्वाभास होना।

foreshadow (फ़ोरशैडो) ***v.*** 1. to suggest before hand, पूर्वाभास होना। 2. to be a sign or warning of something going to be happened, पूर्वसंकेत होना।

foresight (फ़ोरसाइट) ***n.*** 1. the ability to see what will probably happen, दूरदृष्टि। 2. the thoughtful regard or provision for the future, दूरदर्शिता, सूझ-बूझ।

foresighted (फ़ोरसाइटिड) ***adj.*** having foresight, दूरदर्शी, समझदार।

forest (फ़ॉरेस्ट) ***n.*** a large track of land covered with trees and bushes, जंगल, वन।

forestall (फ़ोरस्टॉल) ***v.*** to prevent or hinder by doing something before hand, पेशबंदी करना।

forestation (फ़ॉरेस्टेशन) ***n.*** the planting of forests, वनरोपण।

forester (फ़ॉरेस्टर) ***n.*** a person incharge of a forest, वनाधिकारी, वनरक्षक। 2. one who lives in a forest, वनवासी।

foretell (फ़ोरटेल) ***v.*** to prophesy, भविष्यवाणी करना।

forethought (फ़ोरथॉट) ***n.*** a thinking or planning beforehand, पूर्वविचार, पूर्वचिंतन।

forever (फ़ॉरेवर) ***adv.*** 1. for all time, सदा के लिए। 2. evermore, सदा, हमेशा।

forewarn (फ़ोरवार्न) ***v.*** to warn in advance, पहले से सावधान करना।

foreword (फ़ोरवर्ड) ***n.*** an introductory note in a book, भूमिका, प्रस्तावना।

forfeit (फ़ॉरफ़िट) ***n.*** a penalty, जुर्माना। ***v.*** 1. to lose by fault, दंड भरना। 2. to confiscate, ज़ब्त करना।

forfeiture (फ़ॉरफिचर) ***n.*** the action of forfeiting ज़ब्ती।

forge[1] (फ़ोर्ज) ***v.*** to move forward gradually धीरे-धीरे आगे बढ़ना।

forge[2] ***n.*** 1. a furnace, भट्ठी (लुहार की)। 2. smithy, लुहारख़ाना, लुहार की

दुकान। *v.* 1. to give form by heating and hammering, (धातु को) तपा तथा पीटकर गढ़ना। 2. to commit forgery, जालसाज़ी करना।

forged (फ़ोर्ज्ड) *adj.* made by forgery, जाली।

forgery (फ़ोर्जरी) *n.* the act of imitating fraudulently, जालसाज़ी।

forget (फ़ॉर्गेट) *v.* to fail to remember, भूल जाना।

forgetful (फ़ॉर्गेटफ़ुल) *adj.* having the habit of forgetting, भुलक्कड।

forgivable (फ़ॉर्गिवेबल) *adj.* that can be forgiven, क्षम्य, क्षमायोग्य।

forgive (फ़ॉर्गिव) *v.* to excuse for a fault or offence, क्षमा/माफ़ कर देना।

forgiveness (फ़ॉर्गिवनिस) *n.* the act of forgiving or the state of being forgiven, क्षमा, माफ़ी।

forgo (फ़ॉरगो) *v.* to give up, छोड़/त्याग देना।

fork (फ़ॉर्क) *n.* 1. a pronged instrument with handle used in eating, काँटा, फ़ोर्क। 2. a branch, शाखा। *v.* 1. to raise with a fork, काँटे से उठाना। 2. to divide into branches, शाखाओं में विभक्त करना।

forlorn (फ़ॉरलॉर्न) *adj.* 1. without hope, निराश। 2. deserted, त्यक्त।

form (फ़ॉर्म) *n.* 1. outward appearance, आकृति, सूरत-शक्ल। 2. structure, ढाँचा। 3. an established way of acting or behaving, रीति। 4. shape, रूप। 5. a document with blanks that are to be filled, प्रपत्र। *v.* 1. to shape or become shaped, रूपायित करना या होना। 2. to develop, विकसित करना। 3. to constitute, बनाना। 4. to draw up, खींचना, बनाना।

formal (फ़ॉर्मल) *adj.* according to the accepted rules, औपचारिक।

formality (फ़ॉर्मैलिटी) *n.* 1. formal or conventional act, रस्म, रिवाज। 2. compliance with established rules, औपचारिकता।

formalize (फ़ॉर्मेलाइज़) *v.* to give a definite shape, रूपायित करना।

format (फ़ॉर्मैट) *n.* general make-up, सामान्य आकार-प्रकार।

formation (फ़ॉर्मेशन) *n.* 1. the style or way in which something is formed, रचना, रचना-प्रकार, बनावट। 2. the act of forming, रचना, रूपायन, निर्माण।

former (फ़ॉर्मर) *adj.* 1. of an earlier time, प्राचीन, पहलेवाला। 2. mentioned before another, पूर्ववर्ती।

formerly (फ़ॉर्मरली) *adv.* in former times, in the past, पुराने ज़माने में, पहले।

formidable (फ़ॉर्मिडेबल) *adj.* difficult to surmount, दुर्जेय, अभेद्य, विकट।

formula (फ़ॉर्म्युला) *n.* 1. a set form of words or symbols, सूत्र, फ़ार्मूला। 2. a rule or principle, नियम या सिद्धांत।

formulate (फ़ॉर्म्युलेट) *v.* 1. to reduce to a formula, सूत्रबद्ध करना। 2. to devise, तैयार करना, बनाना।

formulation (फ़ॉर्म्युलेशन) *n.* 1. the act of formulating, सूत्रीकरण। 2. the act of putting into words, निरूपण।

forsake (फ़ॉर्सेक) *v.* to renounce, परित्याग करना।

fort (फ़ोर्ट) *n.* a fortified place, गढ़, क़िला।

forte[1] (फ़ॉर्टे) *n.* something in which

F

a person excels, वह काम जिसमें व्यक्ति बहुत अधिक प्रवीण हो।

forte[2] ***adv.*** loudly, ऊँचे स्वर में।

forth (फ़ोर्थ) ***adv.*** 1. forward, आगे। 2. in future, भविष्य में। 3. away, दूर, परे। ☐ **and so forth,** and so on, इत्यादि-इत्यादि, वगैरह-वगैरह।

forthcoming (फ़ोर्थकमिंग) ***adj.*** about to appear, आनेवाला, आगामी।

forthwith (फ़ोर्थविद) ***adv.*** at once, immediately, तुरंत, फ़ौरन।

fortification (फ़ॉर्टिफ़िकेशन) ***n.*** the act of fortifying, क़िलेबंदी।

fortify (फ़ॉर्टिफ़ाइ) ***v.*** to strengthen (a position) militarily, मोर्चेबंदी करना, क़िलेबंदी करना।

fortitude (फ़ार्टिट्यूड) ***n.*** endurance, सहनशक्ति।

fortnight (फ़ोर्टनाइट) ***n.*** a period of two weeks, पखवाड़ा।

fortnightly (फ़ोर्टनाइटली) ***n.*** a fortnightly publication, पाक्षिक पत्रिका।

fortress (फ़ोर्ट्रिस) ***n.*** a castle, क़िला।

fortuitous (फ़ॉर्ट्युइटस) ***adj.*** happening by chance, आकस्मिक।

fortunate (फ़ॉर्चनिट) ***adj.*** lucky, भाग्यशाली, भाग्यवान।

fortunately ***adv.*** luckily, सौभाग्यवश।

fortune (फ़ॉर्चून) ***n.*** 1. the supposed power that governs the events of one's life, नियति, तक़दीर। 2. good or bad luck, सौभाग्य या दुर्भाग्य। 3. prosperity, समृद्धि।

fortune-teller (फ़ॉर्चूनटेलर)***n.*** one who predicts future events in others' lives, ज्योतिषी।

forty (फ़ॉर्टी) ***adj. & n.*** four times ten, चालीस।

forum (फ़ोरम) ***n.*** 1. a public place, सभा-स्थल। 2. a place for open discussion, मंच, माध्यम।

forward (फ़ॉर्वर्ड) ***adj.*** 1. located or situated in the front, अग्रवर्ती, अगला। 2. going or moving toward the front, अग्रगामी। 3. ready, तैयार। ***n.*** an attacking player in a front position, फ़ारवर्ड। ***adv.*** 1. toward the front, आगे। 2. in the view, सम्मुख, सामने। ***v.*** 1. to advance, आगे बढ़ाना। 2. to send, भेजना।

forwardness (फ़ॉर्वर्डनिस) ***n.*** 1. the state of being forward, प्रगतिशीलता। 2. boldness, धृष्टता।

fossil (फ़ॉसिल) ***n.*** 1. the remains of organism preserved in rocks, जीवाश्म। 2. an old-fashioned person, दकियानूस व्यक्ति। 3. an outdated idea, पुराना विचार।

foster (फ़ॉस्टर) ***v.*** 1. to nourish, पालना-पोसना, पालन-पोषण करना। 2. to promote, बढ़ावा देना। 3. to cherish, सँजोए रखना।

foul (फ़ाउल) ***adj.*** 1. very dirty, बहुत गंदा, मलिन। 2. having an offensive smell or taste, बदबूदार, दुर्गंधित। 3. bad, abominable, ख़राब, बुरा, घृणित। 4. obscene, अश्लील। 5. unfair, अनुचित, नियमविरुद्ध। ***n.*** unfair play, ग़लत खेल, नियमोल्लंघन।

found (फ़ाउन्ड) ***v.*** 1. to establish, स्थापित करना। 2. to establish the foundation of, नींव रखना। 3. to base, आधारित करना, जमाना। 4. to cast, ढालना।

foundation (फ़ाउन्डेशन) ***n.*** 1. the basis on which a thing stands, आधार, नींव, बुनियाद। 2. (plu.) the base, नींव, बुनियाद।

founder[1] (फ़ाउन्डर) *n.* a person who establishes an institution, association etc., संस्थापक, प्रवर्तक।

founder[2] *n.* a person who makes metal castings, ढलाई करनेवाला।

foundry (फ़ाउन्ड्री) *n.* a place where metals are cast and moulded, ढलाई-घर।

fount (फ़ाउन्ट) *n.* 1. a spring of water, सोता। 2. a source, स्रोत। 3. a complete set of type of one size and shape, फ़ॉन्ट।

fountain (फ़ाउन्टिन) *n.* 1. a spring, सोता। 2. an artificial structure from which water spouts or flows, फुहारा। 3. a source, स्रोत।

fountainhead (फ़ाउन्टिनहेड) *n.* an original source, मूल स्रोत।

fountain pen *n.* a pen containing reservoir of ink, फ़ॉउन्टेनपेन।

four (फ़ोर) *adj. & n.* 1. one more than three, चार। 2. group of four persons or things, चार व्यक्तियों या वस्तुओं का समूह, चतुष्ट्य। 3. a playing card marked with four pips, चौका, चौआ। 4. a shot that brings four runs, चौका।

fourfold (फ़ोरफ़ोल्ड) *adj.* four times as many or as much, चौगुना।

fourfooted (फ़ोरफ़ुटिड) *adj.* having four feet, चार पैरोंवाला।

fourteen (फ़ोर्टीन) *adj. & n.* four more than ten, चौदह।

fourth estate (फ़ोर्थ एस्टेट) *n.* the press, पत्र-पत्रिकाओं की दुनिया, समाचार-जगत्।

fowl (फ़ाउल) *n.* 1. a domestic cock or hen, मुर्गा या मुर्गी। 2. its flesh, मुर्गे या मुर्गी का गोश्त। 3. a bird, पक्षी।

fowler (फ़ाउलर) *n.* a person who shoots or traps wild birds, चिड़ीमार, बहेलिया।

fox (फ़ॉक्स) *n.* 1. a mammal related to the dogs and wolves, लोमड़/लोमड़ी। 2. the fur of a fox, लोमड़ी की फ़र। 3. a crafty person, धूर्त व्यक्ति। *v.* to deceive, धोखा देना।

foxy (फ़ॉक्सी) *adj.* crafty, धूर्त।

fracas (फ़्रैकास) *n.* a noisy quarrel, फ़साद।

fraction (फ़्रैक्शन) *n.* 1. a division or part of a whole number, भिन्न। 2. a small part of something, टुकड़ा, अंश।

fractional (फ़्रैक्शनल) *adj.* 1. pertaining to a fraction, भिन्न-संबंधी, भिन्नात्मक। 2. insufficient, अपर्याप्त, बहुत थोड़ा।

fractious (फ़्रैक्शस) *adj.* bad-tempered, बदमिज़ाज।

fracture (फ़्रैक्चर) *n.* a crack or break in a bone, हड्डी का टूटना। *v.* to break, (हड्डी) टूट जाना।

fragile (फ़्रैजाइल) *adj.* 1. easily broken, भंगुर। 2. delicate, नाज़ुक।

fragment[1] (फ़्रैगमेन्ट) *n.* a part broken off, टुकड़ा, चिप्पड़, खंड।

fragment[2] *v.* to break or cause to break into fragments, टुकड़े-टुकड़े होना/करना।

fragmentation (फ़्रैगमेन्टेशन) *n.* the act of separating into fragments, विखंडन।

fragrance (फ़्रेग्रेन्स) *n.* a sweet or pleasant smell, सुगंध, ख़ुशबू।

fragrant (फ़्रेग्रेन्ट) *adj.* having sweet or pleasant smell, सुगंधित, ख़ुशबूदार।

frail (फ़्रेल) *adj.* 1. fragile, भंगुर। 2. weak, दुर्बल।

F

frame (फ़्रेम) ***v.*** 1. to construct or build, निर्माण करना, बनाना। 2. to design or draw up, अंकित या चित्रित करना। 3. to arrange, व्यवस्थित करना। 4. to express, अभिव्यक्त करना। 5. to surround with a frame, चौखटा लगाना। 6. to fabricate evidence against, आरोप गढ़ना। ***n.*** 1. something composed of parts fitted and joined together, structure, ढाँचा, फ़्रेम। 2. a structural support, ढाँचा, चौखटा। 3. the general structure of anything, ढाँचा, रूपरेखा। 4. the human skeleton, अस्थि-पंजर।

franc (फ़्रैंक) ***n.*** the standard coin of France, Belgium, Switzerland etc., फ्रांस, बेल्जियम, स्विट्ज़रलैंड आदि की मुद्रा।

franchise (फ़्रैन्चाइज़) ***n.*** the right to vote in an election, मताधिकार। ***v.*** to grant a franchise to, मताधिकार देना।

frank[1] (फ़्रैंक) ***adj.*** 1. straightforward, स्पष्टवादी, खरा। 2. sincere, सच्चा, निष्कपट।

frank[2] ***v.*** 1. to send (mail) free of postage, बिना टिकट के (डाक) भेजना। 2. to allow to pass free of charge, बिना शुल्क लिये आने-जाने देना। ***n.*** 1. the right to send mail free, निःशुल्क पत्र भेजने का अधिकार। 2. a letter sent free, निःशुल्क भेजा जानेवाला पत्र।

frankly (फ़्रैंकली) ***adv.*** 1. in a frank manner, स्पष्ट रूप से। 2. honestly, ईमानदारी/सचाई से।

frankness (फ़्रैंकनिस) ***n.*** the quality of being frank, स्पष्टवादिता, निश्छलता।

frantic (फ़्रैन्टिक) ***adj.*** 1. wildly excited, अत्यंत उत्तेजित, आपे से बाहर। 2. greatly upset, अत्यंत विक्षुब्ध, परेशान। 3. mad, पागल।

fraternal (फ़्रेटर्नल) ***adj.*** of a brother or brothers, भ्रात्रीय, बिरादराना।

fraternity (फ़्रेटर्निटी) ***n.*** 1. a society of people with common interest, बिरादरी। 2. fraternalism, भाई-चारा।

fraternize (फ़्रैटर्नाइज़) ***v.*** to have friendly relations, भाई-चारा होना।

fraud (फ़्रॉड) ***n.*** 1. a deliberate deception, कपट, धोखाधड़ी। 2. a person who deceives, धूर्त व्यक्ति, ठग।

fraudulent (फ़्रॉडूलेन्ट) ***adj.*** deceitful, कपटी या कपटपूर्ण, धूर्त या धूर्ततापूर्ण।

fraught (फ़्रॉट) ***adj.*** full of, से भरपूर, भरा हुआ।

fray[1] (फ़्रे) ***n.*** 1. a fight or scuffle, लड़ाई, मार-पीट। 2. a heated dispute, झगड़ा, संघर्ष।

fray[2] ***v.*** to become worn so that there are loose threads at the edge, (घिसने के कारण) फुसले निकल आना, तार-तार हो जाना या कर देना।

frayed (फ़्रेड) ***adj.*** worn, tattered, घिसा-फटा, तार-तार।

freak (फ़्रीक) ***n.*** 1. an unusal happening, असामान्य घटना। 2. an unusual person, सनकी।

freckle (फ़्रेकल) ***n.*** a light brown spot on the skin, चकत्ता, ददोरा।

free (फ़्री) ***adj.*** 1. at liberty, मुक्त, बंधनमुक्त। 2. unrestricted, अबाध। 3. politically independent, स्वतंत्र, आज़ाद। 4. exempt, मुक्त। 5. without, रहित, विहीन। 6. not costing anything, मुफ़्त, निःशुल्क। 7. not fixed, loose, ढीला, खुला। 8. open to all, खुला। ***v.*** to make free, मुक्त करना।

freedom (फ़्रीडम) ***n.*** the condition of

being free, independence, स्वतंत्रता, आज़ादी।

freedom fighter ***n.*** a person who fights to obtain independence, स्वतंत्रता-सेनानी।

freehold (फ़्रीहोल्ड) ***n.*** absolute ownership of building or land for an unlimited time, मालिकाना हक।

freelance (फ़्रीलैन्स) ***n.*** a self-employed person, स्वतंत्र लेखक, कलाकार या पत्रकार।

freeship (फ़्रीशिप) ***n.*** exemption from the payment of fee, फ़ीस माफ़ी।

freestyle (फ़्रीस्टाइल) ***adj.*** without any style, शैलीमुक्त, फ़्रीस्टाइल (कुश्ती)।

free trade ***n.*** trade with little government control, मुक्त व्यापार।

free verse ***n.*** unrhymed verse, अतुकांत या छंदमुक्त पद्य।

freewheel (फ़्रीह्वील) ***n.*** a part of the cycle which permits the wheel to rotate freely, फ़्रीह्वील।

freeze (फ़्रीज़) ***v.*** 1. to become solid due to low temperature, जमना। 2. to become ice, बर्फ़ हो जाना। 3. to become hard or stiff from cold, ठंड से जकड़ जाना। 4. to make cold or cover with ice, ठंडा करना। 5. to preserve food by subjection to extreme cold, प्रशीतित करना, संरक्षित रखना। 6. to make or become rigid, कड़ा हो जाना या कर देना।

freezer (फ़्रीजर) ***n.*** a compartment for storing perishable goods by freezing them, फ़्रीज़र, प्रशीतक।

freezing point ***n.*** the temperature at which a liquid freezes, हिमांक।

freight (फ़्रेट) ***n.*** the charge of carrying goods by a truck, ship or train, भाड़ा, माल-भाड़ा।

freighter (फ़्रेटर) ***n.*** a ship carrying mainly goods, मालपोत।

French (फ़्रेन्च) ***adj.*** pertaining to France or its people, फ़्रांस या फ़्रांसीसियों से संबद्ध। ***n.*** 1. the language of France, फ़्रांसीसी भाषा। 2. **the French,** फ़्रांसीसी लोग।

French leave ***n.*** an unauthorised leave, बिना सूचना दिए लिया जानेवाला अवकाश, नागा।

frenetic (फ़्रेनेटिक) ***adj.*** frantic, उन्मत्त।

frenzy (फ़्रेन्ज़ी) ***n.*** craze, सनक।

frequency (फ़्रीक्वेन्सी) ***n.*** frequent occurrence, आवृत्ति।

frequent[1] (फ़्रीक्वेन्ट) ***adj.*** appearing or happening often, प्रायिक।

frequent[2] ***v.*** to visit often, बराबर आते-जाते रहना।

frequently ***adv.*** often, बहुधा।

fresco (फ़्रेस्को) ***n.*** a picture painted on a wall, भित्तिचित्र।

fresh (फ़्रेश) ***adj.*** 1. recently produced or made, ताज़ा। 2. lately arrived, new, नया, नवीन। 3. not used, कोरा। 4. lively, सक्रिय, जीवंत। 5. (of air) refreshing or pure, ताज़ा। 6. inexperienced, अनुभवहीन।

freshen (फ़्रेशन) ***v.*** to become or make fresh, ताज़ा होना/करना।

fresher (फ़्रेशर) ***n.*** a first-year student at university or college, नवछात्र।

freshness (फ़्रेशनिस) ***n.*** the quality of being fresh, ताज़ापन, ताज़गी, नवीनता।

fret (फ़्रेट) ***v.*** 1. to gnaw or wear away by gnawing, खा डालना या खाया जाना। 2. to irritate or be irritated, खीझ उठना या खिझा देना।

fretful (फ़्रेटफ़ुल) ***adj.*** tending to fret, चिड़चिड़ा।

F

friable (फ़्राइएबल) ***adj.*** easily broken into powder, भुरभुरा।

friar (फ़्राइअर) ***n.*** a Christian mendicant, ईसाई भिक्षु।

friction (फ़्रिक्शन) ***n.*** 1. the act of rubbing one thing against another, घर्षण, रगड़। 2. a clash or conflict, संघर्ष, द्वंद्व।

Friday (फ़्राइडे) ***n.*** the sixth day of the week, शुक्रवार, जुम्मा।

friend (फ़्रेन्ड) ***n.*** 1. an intimate associate, दोस्त, मित्र। 2. a sympathizer, हितैषी।

friendly ***adj.*** befitting a friend, मैत्रीपूर्ण, दोस्ताना।

friendship (फ़्रेन्डशिप) ***n.*** relationship between friends, मैत्री, दोस्ती।

frigate (फ़्रिगेट) ***n.*** a small fast-sailing warship, तीव्रगति से चलनेवाला छोटा युद्धपोत।

fright (फ़्राइट) ***n.*** 1. sudden intense fear, डर, भय। 2. something alarming, भयावह या डरावनी।

frighten (फ़्राइटन) ***v.*** to make suddenly afraid, डरा/दहला देना।

frightened (फ़्राइटन्ड) ***adj.*** in a state of fear, भयभीत।

frightful (फ़्राइट्फुल) ***adj.*** causing fright, डरावना, भयानक।

frigid (फ़्रिजिड) ***adj.*** 1. very cold, बहुत अधिक ठंडा। 2. cold in manner, रूखा। 3. lacking in warmth, उत्साहविहीन।

frill (फ़्रिल) ***n.*** a fringe, झालर।

fringe (फ़्रिन्ज) ***n.*** an ornamental edge of hanging threads, झालर। ***v.*** to decorate with frills, झालर लगाना।

frisk (फ़्रिस्क) ***v.*** to move about briskly and playfully, उछलना-कूदना, फुदकना या थिरकना।

fritter (फ़्रिटर) ***v.*** to waste, नष्ट/बरबाद करना।

frivolity (फ़्रिवॉलिटी) ***n.*** 1. the quality of being frivolous, ओछापन, छिछोरापन। 2. frivolous behaviour, ओछा व्यवहार।

frivolous (फ़्रिवलस) ***adj.*** 1. trivial, insignificant, तुच्छ, टुच्चा, बेकार। 2. not sensible, silly, मूर्खतापूर्ण। 3. not with serious attention, ओछा, क्षुद्र।

frizzle (फ़्रिज़ल) ***v.*** 1. to cook in a hot fat, तलना, भूनना। 2. to be cooked with a sizzling noise, छनना, छाना जाना।

frizzy (फ़्रिज़ी) ***adj.*** tightly curled, घुँघराला।

frock (फ़्रॉक) ***n.*** 1. a woman's or girl's dress, फ़्राक। 2. a monk's robe, चोला, लबादा।

frog (फ़्रॉग) ***n.*** a tailless jumping amphibian animal, मेंढक।

frolic (फ़्रॉलिक) ***n.*** gaiety, merriment, entertainment, अठखेली, उछल-कूद। ***v.*** to engage in merrymaking, अठखेलियाँ करना।

frolicsome (फ़्रॉलिकसम) ***adj.*** playful, lively, खिलवाड़ी, उछल-कूद में मस्त।

from (फ़्रॉम) ***prep.*** 1. beginning at, since, से। 2. beginning at, after, से। 3. with a person, place, or thing as the source or instrument, से। 4. distant in regard to, से। 5. with regard to, से। 6. because of, से। 7. considering, की दृष्टि से, के विचार से।

frond (फ़्रॉन्ड) ***n.*** the divided leaf like that of a fern, palm tree etc., फ़र्न या पामवृक्ष का (द्विभाजित) पत्ता।

front (फ़्रन्ट) ***n.*** 1. the most

important part of something facing forwards, outwards or upwards, सामने का हिस्सा, आगा। 2. an area where major fighting is taking place, लड़ाई का मुख्य मैदान। 3. the foremost line of an army, हरावल। 4. combined effort against opposing forces, मोर्चा। 5. the manner and appearance of a person, ढंग, बरताव, व्यवहार, रुख़। 6. outward appearance, बाह्य रूप। 7. an area or scene of a particular activity, क्रियाक्षेत्र, कार्यक्षेत्र। 8. the land bordering a lake, river, street etc., झील, नदी, सड़क आदि से सटा भूभाग। ***adj.*** in or facing the front or being at the front, सामनेवाला, आगेवाला, अग्र। ***v.*** 1. to have the front toward, सामने होना। 2. to confront or oppose, सामना करना, मुक़ाबला करना।

frontage (फ़्रन्टिज) ***n.*** the front part of a building, सामना।

frontal (फ़्रन्टल) ***adj.*** of, at or to the front, सामनेवाला, अग्र।

frontier (फ़्रन्टिअर) ***n.*** an international border, सीमांत, सरहद।

frontispiece (फ़्रन्टिसपीस) ***n.*** a picture on the lefthand page oppsite the title page, पुस्तक के आरंभ में मुख्य पृष्ठ के सामनेवाला चित्र, मुख्यचित्र।

frost (फ़्रॉस्ट) ***n.*** white powder like coating of frozen vapour, पाला, तुषार। ***v.*** 1. to become covered with frost, पाला पड़ना। 2. to damage or kill (plants etc.) with frost, पाला मार जाना।

frostbite (फ़्रॉस्टबाइट) ***n.*** the injury caused by excessive cold, शीतक्षत, तुषारदंशन।

froth (फ़्रॉथ) ***n.*** 1. foam, झाग, फेन। 2. a worthless thing, असार वस्तु।

frown (फ़्राउन) ***v.*** to wrinkle one's brows in anger, भौंहें/त्योरी चढ़ाना। ***n.*** a frowning look, त्योरी, तेवर।

frozen (फ़्रोज़न) ***adj.*** turned into ice, बर्फ़ के रूप में जमा या जमाया हुआ।

frugal (फ़्रूगल) ***adj.*** practising economy, किफ़ायतशिआर।

frugality (फ़्रूगैलिटी) ***n.*** thrift, किफ़ायतशिआरी।

fruit (फ़्रूट) ***n.*** 1. the ripened, fleshy and edible seed-bearing part of a plant, फल। 2. offspring, संतान। 3. result, परिणाम, फल। 4. reward, पुरस्कार। ***v.*** to bear fruit, फलना।

fruitcake (फ़्रूटकेक) ***n.*** a cake containing nuts, raisins etc., मेवेवाला केक।

fruitful (फ़्रूटफुल) ***adj.*** 1. producing fruit, फलनेवाला। 2. producing result, लाभदायक।

fruition (फ़्रूइशन) ***n.*** 1. attainment or fulfilment, सिद्धि, उपलब्धि। 2. the condition of bearing fruit, फलन।

frustrate (फ़्रस्ट्रेट) ***v.*** 1. to prevent from accomplishing a purpose, नाकाम कर देना। 2. to prevent the accomplishment of, कुंठाग्रस्त कर देना।

frustration (फ़्रस्ट्रेशन) ***n.*** the state of feeling frustrated, हताशा, कुंठा।

fry[1] (फ़्राइ) ***v.*** to cook in hot fat or oil, तलना, भूनना।

fry[2] ***n.*** (plu.) the young of fish, frogs etc., मछली, मेंढक आदि के बच्चे।

frying pan ***n.*** a pan for frying purposes, कड़ाही, फ़्राइपेन।

fuddle (फ़डल) ***v.*** to cause to be intoxicated, मदहोश कर देना।

F

fudge (फ़ज) ***v.*** to put together clumsily, गड्ड-मड्ड/घाल-मेल करना।

fuel (फ़्यूअल) ***n.*** 1. any thing used to produce heat, ईंधन, जलावन। 2. that which increases emotion etc., उत्तेजनाप्रद काम या बात। ***v.*** to provide with fuel, ईंधन डालना।

fugitive (फ़्यूजिटिव) ***n.*** a person who has fled from captivity, oppression etc., भगोड़ा।

fuhrer, fuehrer (फ़्यूरर) ***n.*** 1. a title of Hitler, हिटलर की उपाधि, फ़्यूहरर। 2. a despot, निरंकुश शासक।

fulcrum (फ़ल्क्रम) ***n.*** the point on which a lever turns, टेक, आधार।

fulfil (फुलफ़िल) ***v.*** 1. to carry out or complete, पूरा करना, निर्वाह करना। 2. to satisfy, संतुष्ट करना।

fulfilment/fulfillment (फ़ुल-फ़िलमेन्ट) ***n.*** 1. an act of fulfilling, पूर्ति। 2. the state of being fulfilled, पूर्णता। 3. compliance, पालन, निर्वाह। 4. satisfaction, संतुष्टि।

full (फ़ुल) ***adj.*** 1. having or containing as much as possible, भरा हुआ, परिपूर्ण। 2. complete, पूर्ण, पूरा। 3. fed to satisfaction, तृप्त, अघाया हुआ। 4. born of the same parents, real, सगा। ***adv.*** entirely, completely, पूर्ण रूप से, पूर्णतः।

fullback (फ़ुलबैक) ***n.*** a defensive back-field player, फ़ुलबैक, रक्षक खिलाड़ी।

full-blooded (फ़ुलब्लडिड) ***adj.*** 1. of unmixed ancestry, कुलीन। 2. vigorous, ज़ोरदार।

full-blown (फ़ुल-ब्लोन) ***adj.*** 1. in full blossom, पूरा खिला हुआ, पुष्पित। 2. fully developed, पूर्ण विकसित।

full-grown (फ़ुल-ग्रोन) ***adj.*** fully mature, प्रौढ़।

fullness, fulness (फ़ुलनिस) ***n.*** the state or quality of being full, पूर्णता।

full stop ***n.*** a punctuation mark at the end of a sentence, पूर्णविराम।

full-time (फ़ुल-टाइम) ***adj.*** working whole day, पूर्णकालिक।

fully (फ़ुली) ***adv.*** 1. totally, completely, पूरी तरह से। 2. abundantly, अधिकता से।

fulminate (फ़ुल्मिनेट) ***v.*** to denounce severely, भर्त्सना करना।

fulsome (फ़ुलसम) ***adj.*** 1. excessive, अतिशय। 2. insincere, कपट-पूर्ण, कुटिल।

fumble (फ़म्बल) ***v.*** to handle clumsily, गड़बड़ा देना।

fume (फ़्यूम) ***n.*** 1. strong-smelling smoke or gas, धुआँ या भाप। 2. strong smelling or pungent odour, भभक। ***v.*** 1. to emit smoke, धुआँ छोड़ना। 2. to rage, क्रुद्ध होना।

fumigate (फ़्यूमिगेट) ***v.*** to disinfect by applying smoke to, धुआँ दिखाकर कीटमुक्त करना।

fun (फ़न) ***n.*** 1. enjoyment, amusement, मज़ा, आनंद। 2. a source of enjoyment, खेल, तमाशा।

function (फ़ंक्शन) ***n.*** 1. work, कृत्य, कार्य। 2. duty, कर्तव्य, ज़िम्मेदारी। 3. particular purpose or activity of a thing, प्रकार्य। 4. a social or official ceremony, समारोह।

functional (फ़ंक्शनल) ***adj.*** of or concerning a function, कार्य-संबंधी।

fund (फ़न्ड) ***n.*** a reserve of money set aside for specific purpose,

निधि, कोष। *v.* 1. to furnish money, धन सुलभ कराना, धन देना। 2. to invest in fund, किसी निधि में (ब्याज के लिए) जमा करना।

fundamental (फ़न्डामेन्टल) ***adj.*** serving as foundation, basic, बुनियादी, मूलभूत। 2. very important, अत्यावश्यक।

fundamentalist (फ़न्डामेन्टलिस्ट) ***n.*** one who believes in tradition, रूढ़िवादी।

funeral (फ़्यूनरल) ***n.*** 1. a ceremony at which a dead person is buried or cremated, दफ़न, दाहकर्म। 2. a procession accompanying a body to the cremation ground or grave, शवयात्रा, जनाज़ा।

funereal (फ़्यूनिअरिअल) ***adj.*** suitable for a funeral, अंत्येष्टि-संबंधी।

fun-fair (फ़न-फ़ेअर) ***n.*** a fair with amusement, मेला, मेला-तमाशा।

fungus (फ़ंगस) ***n.*** a division of plants having no leaves, flowers, stems, roots etc., फफूँद, कुकरमुत्ता।

funicular (फ़्यूनिक्युलर) ***n.*** a cable railway with ascending and descending cars counterbalancing each other, रज्जुरेल।

funnel (फ़नल) ***n.*** 1. a wide-mouthed utensil for pouring liquids into a narrow-necked vessel, कीप, छुच्छी। 2. a metal chimney or smokestack, चिमनी, धुआँकश।

funny (फ़नी) ***adj.*** causing laughter, हास्यजनक, हास्यप्रद।

fur (फ़र) ***n.*** the thick coat of soft hair of some mammals, फ़र।

furious (फ़्यूरिअस) ***adj.*** 1. full of anger, आगबबूला। 2. fierce, घोर।

furl (फ़र्ल) ***v.*** to roll up, लपेटना।

furlong (फ़रलॉन्ग) ***n.*** a unit of length equal to 220 yards or about 201 metres, फलांग।

furlough (फ़र्लो) ***n.*** a leave of absence from duty, छुट्टी।

furnace (फ़र्नेस) ***n.*** an enclosed chamber for producing heat, भट्ठी।

furnish (फ़र्निश) ***v.*** 1. to equip with furniture, फ़र्नीचर लगाना। 2. to supply, पूर्ति करना।

furnishings (फ़र्निशिंग्स) ***n.*** (plu.) articles of furniture for the interior of a building, घर का साज़-सामान, सज्जा-सामग्री।

furniture (फ़र्निचर) ***n.*** movable articles (such as chairs, tables etc.) for a room, house or office, फ़र्नीचर।

furore, furor (फ़्यूरोर) ***n.*** an uproar, होहल्ला, हंगामा।

furrow (फ़रो) ***n.*** a long cut by a plough, कूँड़, सीता। ***v.*** to make furrows in, कूँड़ बनाना, खाँचा डालना।

further (फ़र्दर) ***adj.*** 1. more, additional, अधिक, अतिरिक्त। 2. more distant in space, time etc., अपर, अगला, परला। ***adv.*** 1. in addition, और। 2. at a greater distance, और आगे, दूर। ***v.*** to help the progress of, आगे बढ़ाना।

furthermore (फ़र्दरमोर) ***adv.*** in addition, इसके अलावा।

furtive (फ़र्टिव) ***adj.*** stealthy, secretive, चोरी-छिपे किया जानेवाला, गुप्त।

fury (फ़्यूरी) ***n.*** violent rage, रोष, आवेश, उन्माद।

F

fuse[1] (फ़्यूज़) ***v.*** 1. to melt or be melted, गलना या गलाना। 2. amalgamate or be amal-gamated, मिलाना या मिलाया जाना।

fuse[2] ***n.*** an electric circuit that melts when the current becomes too strong, फ़्यूज़, फ़्यूज़ तार।

fuselage (फ़्यूज़िलिज) ***n.*** the main body of an aircraft, वायुयान का ढाँचा।

fusillade (फ़्यूसिलेड) ***n.*** 1. a rapid and continuous discharge of firearms, तेज़, गोली वर्षा। 2. a rapid outburst, विस्फोट, प्रस्फोट।

fusion (फ़्यूज़न) ***n.*** the act of fusing i.e. melting and blending together, गलन, संलयन।

fuss (फ़स) ***n.*** unnecessary commotion, हो-हल्ला, उपद्रव। ***v.*** to make a fuss, होहल्ला मचाना।

fusty (फ़स्टी) ***adj.*** 1. smelling of dampness, जिसमें से सीलन की गंध आ रही हो। 2. old-fashioned, दकियानूसी, पुराना।

futile (फ़्यूटाइल) ***adj.*** producing no result, useless, निष्फल, निरर्थक।

futility (फ़्यूटिलिटी) ***n.*** the quality of being futile, निष्फलता, निरर्थकता।

future (फ़्यूचर) ***n.*** the time yet to come, भविष्यत्काल, आनेवाला समय।

fuzz (फ़ज़) ***n.*** a mass of soft light hair, रोएँ, रोम।

fuzzy (फ़ज़ी) ***adj.*** 1. covered with fuzz, रोएँदार। 2. unclear, अस्पष्ट।

G

G, g (जी) ***n.*** the seventh letter of the English alphabet, अंग्रेज़ी वर्णमाला का सातवाँ वर्ण।

gab (गैब) ***v.*** 1. to talk idly, बकबक करना। 2. to gossip, गपशप करना।

gabble (गैबल) ***v.*** to speak or talk rapidly and indistinctly, बकबक करना, बड़बड़ाना।

gadfly (गैडफ़्लाइ) ***n.*** a fly that sucks blood of the animals, डांस।

gadget (गैजिट) ***n.*** a small mechanical appliance, कोई छोटा-मोटा उपकरण या औज़ार।

gag (गैग) ***n.*** something forced into or put over the mouth, मुँह में ठूँसी जानेवाली कोई चीज़ या बाँधी जानेवाली पट्टी। ***v.*** 1. to retch, मिचली होना। 2. to tell jokes, मज़ाक सुनाना, चुटकुले सुनाना।

gaiety (गेअटी) ***n.*** joyful activity, आनंद-मंगल, रंगरली।

gain (गेन) ***v.*** 1. to get, प्राप्त करना। 2. to earn, कमाना, अर्जित करना। 3. to make profit, लाभ प्राप्त करना। 4. to make progress, प्रगति करना। ***n.*** 1. something gained, लाभ, मुनाफ़ा। 2. increase, वृद्धि, बढ़ोतरी।

gainful (गेनफ़ुल) ***adj.*** profitable, लाभप्रद।

gainsay (गेनसे) ***v.*** to deny or contradict, खंडन करना।

gait (गेट) ***n.*** a way of walking or running, चाल।

gala (गाला) ***n.*** a festive occasion or celebration, समारोह, उत्सव, मेला।

galaxy (गैलेक्सी) ***n.*** 1. the Milky Way, आकाशगंगा। 2. a group of distinguished persons, विशिष्ट व्यक्तियों का समूह।

gale (गेल) ***n.*** a very strong wind, अंधड़।

gall[1] (गॉल) ***n.*** 1. liverbile, पित्त। 2. the gallbladder, पित्ताशय। 3. bitterness, कड़वाहट।

gall[2] ***n.*** a skin sore, छिल जाने से या रगड़ से होनेवाला घाव। ***v.*** 1. to rub and make sore, इस प्रकार रगड़ खाना कि घाव हो जाए। 2. to irritate, चिढ़ाना, खिझाना।

gallant (गैलेन्ट) ***adj.*** 1. brave, वीर। 2. stately, majestic, राजसी। 3. noble, कुलीन, संभ्रांत।

gallantry (गैलेन्ट्री) ***n.*** bravery, courage, वीरता, शौर्य।

gall-bladder (गॉल-ब्लैडर) ***n.*** a sac attached to the liver in which bile secreted by the liver is stored, पित्ताशय।

gallery (गैलरी) 1. a balcony or verandah used for showing works of art, गैलरी, दीर्घा। 2. the balcony of a theatre, बालकोनी, दीर्घा। 3. the seats in such a section, दीर्घा की सीटें।

galley (गैली) ***n.*** (plu. galleys) a long tray used for holding types, blocks etc., (प्रेस की) गैली।

Gallic (गैलिक) ***adj.*** French, फ्रांसीसी।

gallon (गैलन) ***n.*** a measure of liquids equal to 4½ litres, गैलन।

gallop (गैलप) ***n.*** swiftest pace of a horse, घोड़े की तेज़ से तेज़ चाल, चौकड़ी। ***v.*** to cause to gallop, (घोड़े का) चौकड़ियाँ भरना।

G

gallows (गैलोज़) ***n.*** the wooden structure on which criminals are hanged, फाँसी का फंदा।

gallstone (गॉलस्टोन) ***n.*** a small hard mass formed in the gallbladder, पथरी।

galore (गेलोर) ***adv.*** in abundance, ख़ूब, ढेरों।

galvanize (गैल्वेनाइज़) ***v.*** to cover with a zinc coating, क़लई चढ़ाना।

gambit (गैम्बिट) ***n.*** a subtle move, गहरी चाल।

gamble (गैम्बल) ***v.*** 1. to play a game of chance to win money, जूआ खेलना। 2. to risk, जोख़िम उठाना। ***n.*** 1. a game of chance to win money, जूआ। 2. a risky act, जोख़िम का काम।

gambler (गैम्बलर) ***n.*** one who gambles, जुआरी।

gambling (गैम्ब्लिंग) ***n.*** any sport in which money is risked, जूआ।

gambol (गैम्बल) ***v.*** to leap or jump playfully, उछल-कूद मचाना। ***n.*** the act of gambolling, उछल-कूद।

game (गेम) ***n.*** 1. an amusement or diversion, pastime, खेल, क्रीड़ा। 2. any competitive activity, हार-जीत का खेल। 3. a single contest between opposing players, बाज़ी। 4. hunting of wild animals or birds, आखेट, शिकार। 5. a prey, शिकार।

gamesmanship (गेम्ज़मैनशिप) ***n.*** the skill in defeating others by dubious means, छलविद्या।

gamesome (गेमसम) ***adj.*** frolicsome, खिलवाड़ी।

gammon[1] (गैमन) ***n.*** nonsense, अंडबंड।

gammon[2] ***n.*** a cured or smoked ham, सुअर के पुट्ठे का मसालेदार या भूना हुआ मांस।

gamut (गैमट) ***n.*** 1. the whole range of notes, सरगम, सप्तक। 2. a complete range, संपूर्ण क्षेत्र।

gang (गैंग) ***n.*** 1. a group of people who work together, गिरोह, जत्था। 2. a group of criminals or hoodlums, अपराधियों या गुंडों की टोली या गिरोह। ***v.*** to form into a gang, गिरोह बनाना।

gangrene (गैंग्रीन) ***n.*** death of body tissues, गैंग्रीन, गलन।

gangster (गैंग्स्टर) ***n.*** a member of a group of criminals, लुटेरा, डाकू, गुंडा।

gangway (गैंगवे) ***n.*** a passage between rows of seats, बीच का रास्ता, गली।

gaol (जेल) ***n.*** a jail, जेल, कारागार, बंदीगृह।

gap (गैप) ***n.*** an empty space, ख़ाली जगह, अंतराल, रिक्ति।

gape (गेप) ***v.*** 1. to open the mouth wide, मुँह फाड़ना। 2. to stare in wonder, मुँह बा देना, हक्का-बक्का हो जाना।

garage (गैराज) ***n.*** 1. a building for housing cars, गैराज। 2. a place where cars are repaired and serviced, कारों की मरम्मत का स्थान, कार-घर।

garb (गार्ब) ***n.*** clothing, dress, पहनावा, पोशाक।

garbage (गार्बिज) ***n.*** 1. rubbish, कूड़ा, कूड़ा-करकट। 2. trash, गंदगी, अश्लील साहित्य।

garden (गार्डन) ***n.*** a plot of land used for growing flowers, vegetables, fruit etc, बाग़, बग़ीचा, उद्यान। *v.* to work in a garden, बाग़वानी करना।

gardener (गार्डनर) *n.* one who takes care of a garden, माली, बाग़वान।

gardening (गार्डनिंग) *n.* the act of growing flowers, vegetables or fruit in a garden, बाग़वानी।

gargle (गार्गल) *v.* to rinse the throat by breathing air from the lungs, गरारे करना।

gargoyle (गार्गॉइल) *n.* a roof spout carved to represent a grotesque creature, एक तरह का परनाला जिसका मुँह किसी जानवर के आकार का होता है।

garish (गैरिश) *adj.* gaudy, भड़कीला, शोख़।

garland (गार्लेन्ड) *n.* a wreath of flowers, फूलों का हार। *v.* to adorn or decorate with a garland or garlands, फूलों की माला पहनाना या फूल-मालाओं से सजाना।

garlic (गार्लिक) *n.* a bulb with a pungent taste, लहसुन।

garment (गार्मेन्ट) *n.* an article of clothing, सिला-सिलाया कपड़ा।

garner (गार्नर) *v.* to collect or amass, संग्रह करना।

garnet (गार्निट) *n.* a mineral used as a gemstone, गार्नेट।

garnish (गार्निश) *v.* to adorn, सजाना।

garret (गैरिट) *n.* an upper storey, अटारी।

garrison (गैरिसन) *n.* the troops stationed in a fortress, दुर्ग सेना।

garrotte (गैरोट) *v.* to strangle, गला घोटना।

garrulous (गैरुलस) *adj.* talkative, बातूनी, वाचाल।

garter (गार्टर) *n.* an elastic band to hold up a sock, गेटिस, मोज़ाबंद।

gas (गैस) *n.* any air like substance, गैस।

gaseous (गैशस) *adj.* of or pertaining to gas, गैसीय।

gash (गैश) *n.* a long deep cut, कटने से होनेवाला गहरा घाव। *v.* to make a long deep cut, घाव करना।

gasify (गैसिफ़ाइ) *v.* to convert into gas, गैस में बदल देना।

gasket (गैस्किट) *n.* a ring of rubber, गैसकिट।

gasoline (गैसलीन) *n.* a liquid derived from crude petroleum, पेट्रोल।

gasp (गैस्प) *v.* 1. to make violent attempts at breathing, हाँफना। 2. to utter breathlessly, हाँफते हुए बोलना।

gastric (गैस्ट्रिक) *adj.* of or concerning the stomach, जठरीय।

gastritis (गैस्ट्राइटिस) *n.* acute or chronic inflammation of stomach, आमाशय-शोथ।

gate (गेट) *n.* 1. a structure that blocks an entrance or passage, द्वार, फाटक, कपाट। 2. the total attendance, दर्शकगण। 3. the total admission receipts, प्राप्त प्रवेश-शुल्क।

gatekeeper (गेटकीपर) *n.* one who attends and guards the gate, द्वारपाल।

gatepass (गेटपास) *n.* a free ticket, पास, निःशुल्क प्रवेशपत्र।

gateway (गेटवे) *n.* a means of entry or access, मार्ग, रास्ता।

gather (गैदर) *v.* 1. to bring or come together, इकट्ठा करना। 2. to accumulate or collect, संग्रह करना,

G

जुटाना। 3. to pick, (फूल) चुनना। 4. to harvest, लुनाई करना, लुनना। 5. to increase or cause to increase gradually, धीरे-धीरे बढ़ना या बढ़ाना। 6. to conclude, निष्कर्ष निकालना। ***n.*** the act of gathering, संग्रहण।

gathering (गैदरिंग) ***n.*** an assembly of people, सभा, जनसमूह।

gaudiness (गॉडिनिस) ***n.*** the quality or state of being gaudy, भड़कीलापन।

gaudy (गॉडी) ***adj.*** showy, भड़कीला।

gauge (गेज) ***n.*** 1. a scale of measurement, पैमाना। 2. a means of estimating or evaluating, मानदंड, कसौटी। 3. the distance between the two rails or wheels, गेज। 4. thickness or diameter of a sheet or wire, गेज। ***v.*** 1. to measure precisely, ठीक-ठीक नापना या नाप लेना। 2. to estimate, अंदाज़ लगाना।

gaunt (गॉन्ट) ***adj.*** thin and bony, मरियल।

gauze (गॉज़) ***n.*** 1. a thin transparent fabric of open texture, जाली। 2. fine wire mesh, लोहे की जाली।

gay (गे) ***adj.*** 1. cheerful, प्रसन्न, प्रफुल्ल। 2. bright-coloured, चमकीला। 3. attractive, आकर्षक। 4. licentious, लंपट, विषयी। ***n.*** a homosexual, समलिंगकामी।

gaze (गेज़) ***v.*** to look long and fixedly, टकटकी लगाना। ***n.*** a long steady look, टकटकी।

gazette (गज़ेट) ***n.*** an official journal, राजपत्र, गज़ट।

gazetted (गज़ेटिड) ***adj.*** published in the gazette, गज़ट में छपा हुआ, राजपत्रित।

gazetteer (गैज़िटिअर) ***n.*** a dictionary of geographical places, भूगोलकोश, गजेटियर।

gear (गिअर) ***n.*** 1. equipment, apparatus, साज़-सामान, उपस्कर। 2. tools, औज़ार। 3. a toothed wheel that regulates motion, गियर। 4. clothes, वस्त्र, परिधान। ***v.*** to provide with or connect by gears, गियर लगाना, गियर में करना।

gearbox (गिअरबॉक्स) ***n.*** a small box enclosing the gears of a car, गियरबॉक्स।

geese (गीस) ***n.*** plu. of goose.

geisha (गीशा) ***n.*** a trained Japanese dancing girl, जापानी नर्तकी।

gelatin, gelatine (जेलेटिन) ***n.*** a colourless brittle protein formed by boiling the bones, hoofs etc, जेलटीन।

gem (जेम) ***n.*** 1. a precious stone, हीरा, रत्न। 2. one that is valued highly, हीरा (आदमी)।

Gemini (जेमिनी) ***n.*** a sign of the Zodiac, मिथुन (राशि)।

gemstone (जेमस्टोन) ***n.*** a jewel, रत्न।

gender (जेन्डर) ***n.*** any of two or more categories into which nouns are divided, लिंग।

gene (जीन) ***n.*** unit of heredity characteristics transmitted from parents to offspring, जीन।

genealogy (जीनिऑलोजी) ***n.*** 1. the study of ancestry, वंशविद्या। 2. a table of ancestry, वंशवृक्ष, वंशावली।

genera (जेनिरा) ***n.*** = genus.

general (जेनरल) ***adj.*** 1. applicable to every member of a group, सार्विक, सामान्य, साधारण। 2. widespread or involving various kinds, आम, सामान्य, व्यापक। 3. prevalent, प्रचलित। 4. highest in rank, महा; General Manager, महाप्रबंधक। ***n.*** an officer of the high rank in army, जनरल।

general assembly ***n.*** a legislative body, विधान सभा।

general election ***n.*** an election on national level, आम चुनाव।

generality (जेनरैलिटी) ***n.*** 1. the condition or quality of being genaral, सार्विकता, सामान्यता। 2. a general state-ment, आम बात, सामान्य बात।

generalize (जेनरलाइज़) ***v.*** to form general conclusion or to express in general terms, साधारणीकरण करना, सामान्यीकरण करना।

generalship (जेनरलशिप) ***n.*** 1. the rank or office of a general, जनरल या सेनापति का पद। 2. skill in conducting the war, युद्धसंचालन-क्षमता, युद्ध-कौशल।

generate (जेनरेट) ***v.*** 1. to create or produce, उत्पन्न करना, पैदा करना।

generation (जेनरेशन) ***n.*** 1. the act of generating, उत्पत्ति, उत्पादन, जनन। 2. a group of contemporaneous individuals, पीढ़ी, पुश्त।

generation gap ***n.*** the years separating the people of different generations, दो पीढ़ियों का अंतर।

generator (जेनरेटर) ***n.*** a device for converting mechanical energy into electricity, जेनरेटर, विद्युत्प्रजनक।

generic (जिनेरिक) ***adj.*** of, including or indicating a whole class or group, सामान्य, प्रजातीय, जातीय।

generosity (जेनरॉसिटी) ***n.*** the quality of being generous, उदारता, दानशीलता।

generous (जेनरस) ***adj.*** 1. ready to give freely, उदार, दानी। 2. given freely, उदारतापूर्ण। 3. full or plentiful, प्रचुर।

genesis (जेनिसिस) ***n.*** a beginning or origin, आरंभ, शुरुआत।

genetic (जेनेटिक) ***adj.*** 1. of or pertaining to genetics, जनन-विज्ञान-संबंधी, जननिक। 2. of or relating to genes, जीन-संबंधी। 3. inherited, आनुवंशिक, पैतृक, विरासत में प्राप्त।

geneticist (जेनेटिसिस्ट) ***n.*** an expert in genetics, जनन-विज्ञानी, जनन-विज्ञानवेत्ता।

genetics (जेनेटिक्स) ***n.*** 1. the study of hereditary transmission and variations, जनन-विज्ञान। 2. heredity, आनुवंशिकता।

genial (जीनियल) ***adj.*** 1. warm in manners, cordial, kind, मिलनसार, मैत्रीपूर्ण। 2. cheerful, हँसमुख, प्रफुल्ल।

geniality (जीनिऐलिटी) ***n.*** the quality or state of being genial, मिलनसारी, मैत्री-भावना; प्रफुल्लता।

genital (जेनिटल) ***adv.*** of the genitalia, जननेंद्रिय-संबंधी।

genitals (जेनिटल्ज़) ***n.*** (plu.) the external sex organs, जननेंद्रियाँ, जननांग।

genitive (जेनिटिव) ***n.*** possessive case, संबंधकारक, षष्ठी विभक्ति। ***adj.*** of possessive case, संबंधकारकीय।

genius (जीनिअस) ***n.*** 1. brilliant mental ability, प्रतिभा। 2. outstanding creative power, सर्जनात्मक शक्ति। 3. a person having exceptional mental ability, प्रतिभासंपन्न व्यक्ति। 4. a peculiar, distinctive or

G

identifying character (of language, भाषा का) स्वभाव, प्रकृति।

genocide (जेनोसाइड) ***n.*** the planned killing of a racial or ethnic people, जाति-संहार, जन-संहार।

gent (जेन्ट) ***n.*** a man, व्यक्ति, आदमी।

genteel (जेन्टील) ***adj.*** 1. well-bred, भद्र, कुलीन। 2. fashionable, बना-ठना, फैशनेबुल। 3. trying to seem polite, affectedly polite, ऊपर से भला बना हुआ, खोटा।

gentility (जेन्टिलिटी) ***n.*** the quality or state of being genteel, भद्रता, कुलीनता।

gentle (जेन्टल) ***adj.*** 1. moderate, mild, मंद, हलका। 2. of kind nature, सौम्य, भला, दयालु। 3. of good family, भद्र, कुलीन।

gentleman (जेन्टलमैन) ***n.*** a man of noble birth, a well-bred man, भद्र व्यक्ति, सज्जन, ख़ानदानी व्यक्ति।

gentlemanly (जेन्टलमैनली) ***adj.*** of or like a gentleman, सज्जनोचित, भद्र।

gentleness (जेन्टलनिस) ***n.*** the quality or state of being gentle, कुलीनता, भद्रता।

gentry (जेन्ट्री) ***n.*** 1. people of good family, भद्र लोग। 2. people, लोग।

genuine (जेन्युइन) ***adj.*** 1. real, खरा, वास्तविक। 2. authentic, प्रामाणिक। 3. sincere and frank, सच्चा, ईमानदार।

genuinely ***adv.*** in a genuine manner, ईमानदारी से, शुद्ध हृदय से।

genus (जीनस) ***n.*** (plu. genera) a category or class with common characteristics, श्रेणी, वर्ग।

geocentric (जिओसेन्ट्रिक) ***adj.*** having the earth as centre, भूकेंद्रिक।

geographer (जिऑग्रफ़र) ***n.*** an expert in geography, भूगोलविज्ञानी, भूगोलज्ञ।

geography (जिऑग्रफ़ी) ***n.*** the study of earth and its features, भूगोल।

geologist (जिऑलोजिस्ट) ***n.*** an expert in geology, भूविज्ञानी।

geology (जिऑलोजी) ***n.*** the scientific study of the origin, structure and history of the earth, भूविज्ञान।

geometry (जिऑमिट्री) ***n.*** the branch of mathematics dealing with the properties, measurement and relationships of points, lines, angles etc, ज्यामिति, रेखागणित।

geophysics (जिओफ़िज़िक्स) ***n.*** the branch of physics dealing with the physical properties of the earth, भूभौतिकी।

georgette (जॉर्जेट) ***n.*** a kind of silk fabric, जार्जेट।

geriatrics (जेरिऐट्रिक्स) ***n.*** the branch of medicine dealing with the diseases of old age, जरा-चिकित्सा, वृद्ध-परिचर्या।

germ (जर्म) ***n.*** 1. a living cell from which a new organism may develop, जीवाणु। 2. a bud, अंकुर।

German (जर्मन) ***adj.*** of Germany, जर्मनी-संबंधी, जर्मन। ***n.*** a native of Germany, जर्मनीवासी।

germane (जर्मेन) ***adj.*** 1. related, संबद्ध। 2. relevant, संगत।

germicidal (जर्मिसाइडल) ***adj.*** that kills germs, जीवाणुनाशक।

germicide (जर्मिसाइड) ***n.*** a substance that kills germs, जीवाणुनाशक पदार्थ।

germinal (जर्मिनल) ***adj.*** 1. of or pertaining to germs, जीवाणु-संबंधी। 2. in the earliest stage of development, आरंभिक।

G

germinate (जर्मिनेट) ***v.*** 1. to sprout, उगना, अंकुरित होना। 2. to cause to sprout, उगाना, अंकुरित करना।

germination (जर्मिनेशन) ***n.*** the act of germinating, अंकुरण।

gerund (जीरन्ड) ***n.*** a verbal noun, क्रियार्थक संज्ञा।

gestation (जेस्टेशन) ***n.*** 1. the state of being pregnant, गर्भावस्था। 2. the period of pregnancy, गर्भकाल, गर्भावधि।

gesticulate (जेस्टिक्यूलेट) ***v.*** to make gestures while speaking, बोलते समय हाथों की मुद्रा से हाव-भाव अभिव्यक्त करना।

gesticulation (जेस्टिक्यूलेशन) ***n.*** gestures made with hands while speaking, हस्तमुद्राएँ, हाव-भाव।

gesture (जेस्चर) ***n.*** 1. an expressive movement of any part of the body, इशारा, इंगित, संकेत। 2. an act or expression made to convey one's intentions, मुद्रा, हाव-भाव। ***v.*** to make a gesture, इशारा या संकेत करना।

get (गेट) ***v.*** 1. to obtain or receive, प्राप्त करना, पाना, मिलना। 2. to fetch, लाना, ले आना। 3. to earn, अर्जित करना। 4. to catch or contract, ग्रस्त या मुबतला होना, (बीमारी) लगना, पकड़ना। 5. to have, पास होना। 6. to move in a particular direction, जाना।

get-up (गेट-अप) ***n.*** 1. a costume, पोशाक। 2. outward decoration, बाह्य सज्जा।

geyser (गीज़र) ***n.*** 1. a hot water spring, गर्म पानी का सोता, उष्णोत्स। 2. a water heater, पानी गरम करने का बिजली का उपकरण, गीज़र।

ghastly (गास्टली) ***adj.*** 1. dreadful, terrifying, भयानक, भयावह, बीभत्स। 2. very bad or unpleasant, घिनौना। 3. deathly pale, पीला, मुर्दे-जैसा।

ghat (घाट) ***n.*** 1. a flight of steps down to a river, घाट। 2. a bathing or landing place on the bank of a river, घाट। 3. a mountain pass, घाट, दर्रा।

ghee (घी) ***n.*** clarified butter, घी।

ghost (गोस्ट) ***n.*** 1. the spirit of a dead person that haunts living beings, मृतात्मा, भूत, प्रेत। 2. a false image produced by an optical system, छाया, आकृति। ***v.*** to haunt, पीछा करना।

ghoul (गूल) ***n.*** an evil demon, पिशाच।

giant (जाइअन्ट) ***n.*** a mythical figure of very great height and size, दैत्य, दानव। ***adj.*** 1. of unusual size, दैत्याकार, दीर्घकाय। 2. of exceptional ability or reputation, अत्यधिक गुणी या कीर्तिशाली।

gibber (जिबर) ***v.*** to speak rapidly and unintelligibly, बड़बड़ या बकबक करना।

gibbon (गिबन) ***n.*** an ape, लंगूर।

gibe (जाइब) ***v.*** to jeer or taunt, फ़ब्ती या ताना कसना। ***n.*** a jeering remark, फ़ब्ती, ताना।

giddiness (गिडिनिस) ***n.*** the feeling that everything is spinning around, चक्कर, घुमटा, घुमरी, सिर चकराना।

giddy (गिडी) ***adj.*** 1. feeling giddiness, जिसे चक्कर आ रहा हो। 2. causing giddiness, जिससे चक्कर आता हो, चक्कर लानेवाला। 3. frivolous, चंचल।

G

gift (गिफ़्ट) ***n.*** 1. something given or received as a present, उपहार, तोहफ़ा; gift tax, उपहार-कर। 2. a natural ability, प्रतिभा।

gifted (गिफ़्टिड) ***adj.*** having natural ability or talent, गुणी, मेघावी, प्रतिभासंपन्न।

gigantic (जाइगैन्टिक) ***adj.*** 1. huge, enormous, विशाल, दीर्घकाय, विराट। 2. giant-like, दैत्यकार, दैत्यों-जैसा।

giggle (गिगल) ***v.*** to laugh foolishly, हीही/हेंहें करना। ***n.*** such a laugh, हीही, हेंहें।

gild (गिल्ड) ***v.*** 1. to cover with a thin layer of gold, सोने का पानी या पत्तर चढ़ाना, मुलम्मा करना। 2. to give an attractive appearance to, सजाना-सँवारना।

gill (गिल) ***n.*** the respiratory organ of a fish, मछली का गलफड़ा।

gilt (गिल्ट) ***v.*** p.t. of gild. ***n.*** 1. a substance used for gilding, मुलम्मा। 2. a thin layer of gold, सोने की परत। ***adj.*** 1. gilded, जिसपर सोने की परत चढ़ी हो या सोने का मुलम्मा हुआ हो। 2. gold-coloured, सुनहरा।

gilt-edged (गिल्ट-एज्ड) ***adj.*** (of securities) considered to be of highest quality or to be very safe, सर्वोत्तम या सुरक्षित।

gimlet (गिम्लिट) ***n.*** a small boring tool, बरमा।

gimmick (गिमिक) ***n.*** 1. a gadget, छोटा उपकरण। 2. any trick or mannerism designed to attract extra attention, interest or publicity, ध्यान आकर्षित करने की चाल, कौतुक, ऊटक-नाटक।

gin (जिन) ***n.*** an alcoholic drink distilled from malted berry, maize etc., जिन, मदिरा।

ginger (जिन्जर) ***n.*** 1. the pungent root of a tropical plant, अदरक, आदी। 2. this plant, अदरक का पौधा। 3. liveliness, vigour, जीवंतता, स्फूर्ति, जोश। ***v.*** to make more lively, स्फूर्त बनाना, जोश दिलाना, जान डालना।

gingerly ***adv.*** 1. cautiously, सावधानी से, सतर्कतापूर्वक। 2. reluctantly, अनिच्छापूर्वक। 3. timidly, डरते-डरते, संकोचपूर्वक।

gingivitis (जिन्जिवाइटिस) ***n.*** inflamation of the gums, मसूड़ों की सूजन।

gipsy (जिप्सी) ***n.*** 1. a member of a nomadic people, बंजारा, जिप्सी, ख़ानाबदोश। 2. their language, बंजारों की भाषा, जिप्सी भाषा।

giraffe (जिराफ़) ***n.*** an African mammal with a long neck, जिराफ़।

gird (गर्ड) ***v.*** 1. to fasten with a belt, पेटी बाँधना। 2. to attach with a belt, पेटी में लगाना।

girder (गर्डर) ***n.*** a strong horizontal iron beam गर्डर।

girdle (गर्डल) ***n.*** a belt or band worn around the waist, कटिबंध, कमरबंद, मेखला। ***v.*** to encircle with a belt or band, पेटी बाँधना, घेरना।

girl (गर्ल) ***n.*** a female child or young unmarried woman, लड़की, किशोरी, कन्या, बालिका।

girlhood (गर्लहुड) ***n.*** the state of being a girl, लड़कपन, किशोरावस्था।

girlish (गर्लिश) ***adj.*** like a girl, लड़की-जैसा, कन्यासुलभ।

girth (गर्थ) ***n.*** 1. circumference, घेरा, परिधि। 2. a strap encircling a horse's belly holding the saddle in place, घोड़े की काठी कसने की पेटी, कसन।

gist (जिस्ट) ***n.*** the general sense or central idea of anything, सार, निष्कर्ष, निचोड़, भावार्थ।

give (गिव) ***v.*** 1. to present voluntarily (something) to another, देना, प्रदान करना। 2. to convey, पहुँचाना। 3. to entrust, सौंपना, हवाले करना। 4. to make or perform, देना, लगाना; to give a kick, ठोकर लगाना; to give a scolding, डाँट देना। 5. to provide, पेश करना, प्रस्तुत करना। 6. to yield or relinquish, झुक जाना या छोड़ देना।

gizzard (गिज़र्ड) ***n.*** the second stomach of a bird, चिड़िया का पेडू, पेषणी।

glacial (ग्लेशल) ***adj.*** 1. of or relating to a glacier, हिमनदी से संबद्ध। 2. of ice, बर्फ़ीला।

glacier (ग्लेशर) ***n.*** a large mass of slowly moving ice, हिमनद।

glad (ग्लैड) ***adj.*** feeling joy or pleasure, happy, ख़ुश, प्रसन्न।

gladden (ग्लैडन) ***v.*** to make glad, प्रसन्न/ख़ुश करना।

glade (ग्लेड) ***n.*** an open space in a forest, वनक्षेत्र में खुली जगह।

glair (ग्लेअर) ***n.*** white of egg, अंडे की सफ़ेदी।

glamorize (ग्लैमराइज़) ***v.*** to make glamorous, सजीला या आकर्षक रूप देना, मोहक/लुभावना बना देना।

glamour, glamor (ग्लैमर) ***n.*** 1. alluring beauty, लावण्य, लुभावनापन, सजीलापन। 2. brightness, चमक, दीप्ति।

glance (ग्लान्स) ***v.*** 1. to look briefly or hastily, एक झलक या सरसरी निगाह से देखना। 2. to strike a surface and be deflected, सरकते हुए निकल जाना, ग्लांस हो जाना। 3. to glitter, चमकना। ***n.*** 1. a brief or hasty look, एक झलक, सरसरी निगाह। 2. lustre, glitter, चमक।

gland (ग्लैन्ड) ***n.*** a cell or organ that secretes a particular substance for the body, ग्रंथि।

glandular (ग्लैन्ड्यूलर) ***adj.*** of gland, ग्रंथि-संबंधी, ग्रंथिल।

glare (ग्लेअर) ***v.*** 1. to shine intensely, चमचमाना, चकाचौंध उत्पन्न करना। 2. to stare angrily, घूरना। ***n.*** 1. an intense light, चमचमाहट, चकाचौंध, तेज़ रोशनी। 2. an angry stare, कोपदृष्टि, घूराघूरी।

glass (ग्लास) ***n.*** 1. a hard, brittle and transparent substance, शीशा, काँच। 2. a mirror, शीशा, दर्पण। 3. a tumbler, गिलास। 4. (plu.) eye glasses, चश्मा, ऐनक।

glasshouse (ग्लासहाउस) ***n.*** the house made of glass, काँच-घर।

glassware (ग्लासवेअर) ***n.*** utensils/objects made of glass, शीशे के बर्तन।

glassy (ग्लासी) ***adj.*** 1. resembling glass, काँच-सा। 2. expressionless, भावशून्य।

glaucoma (ग्लॉकोमा) ***n.*** a disease of the eyes causing complete or partial loss of vision, ग्लूकोमा।

glaze (ग्लेज़) ***n.*** a thin smooth shiny coating (on pottery), पतली, चमकीली तथा चिकनी परत, ग्लेज़। ***v.*** 1. to apply glaze to, चमकीला तथा चिकना बनाना। 2. to furnish with glass, शीशा लगाना। 3. to become glassy, चिकना तथा चमकीला होना।

glazier (ग्लेज़िअर) ***n.*** one who cuts and fits window glasses, शीशा जड़नेवाला।

gleam (ग्लीम) ***n.*** 1. a beam or ray,

किरण। 2. a brief or dim indication, हलका-सा संकेत। *v.* to send out gleams, चमकना।

glean (ग्लीन) *v.* 1. to pick up grain left behind by harvesters, खेतों में गिरे-पड़े दाने चुनना, सिल्ला चुनना। 2. to collect bit by bit, कण-कण जोड़ना, एकत्र करना।

glee (ग्ली) *n.* joy, merriment, आनंद, उल्लास।

glen (ग्लेन) *n.* a narrow valley, सँकरी घाटी।

glib (ग्लिब) *adj.* smooth tongued, fast-talking, बोलने में कुशल, वाचाल, वाक्पटु, वाग्विदग्ध।

glide (ग्लाइड) *v.* 1. to move or pass smoothly and easily, बहना, सरकना। 2. to fly in a glider, ग्लाइडर में उड़ना। 3. to fly a glider, ग्लाइडर उड़ाना। *n.* a gliding movement, बहने या सरकने की क्रिया या भाव।

glider (ग्लाइडर) *n.* a light engineless aircraft, इंजनविहीन विमान, ग्लाइडर।

glimmer (ग्लिमर) *v.* to give off a dim or unsteady light, झिलमिलाना, टिमटिमाना। *n.* 1. a dim or unsteady light, झिलमिल, टिमटिमाहट। 2. a faint indication, झलक, आभास।

glimpse (ग्लिम्प्स) *n.* 1. a brief or incomplete view, झलक, झाँकी, आभास। *v.* 1. to catch a glimpse of, झलक पाना या मिलना।

glint (ग्लिन्ट) *v.* to send out a brief flash of light, झिलमिलाना, चमकना। *n.* a brief flash of light, झिलमिल, चमक।

glisten (ग्लिसन) *v.* to reflect with brightness, झलझल करना, जगमगाना। *n.* a glistening shine, झलझल, जगमगाहट।

glitter (ग्लिटर) *v.* to sparkle, चमकना, चमचमाना। *n.* 1. a sparkling light or brightness, चमक-दमक। 2. showy attractiveness, तड़क-भड़क।

global (ग्लोबल) *adj.* worldwide, विश्वव्यापी, सार्वभौम।

globe (ग्लोब) *n.* 1. a spherical object with a map of earth on it, ग्लोब, गोलक। 2. the world, विश्व, संसार।

globe-trotter (ग्लोब-ट्राटर) *n.* one who travels widely, विश्व-भर में घूमनेवाला।

globular (ग्लोब्युलर) *adj.* shaped like a globe, गोलाकार।

globule (ग्लोब्यूल) *n.* a small rounded mass, गोली।

gloom (ग्लूम) *n.* 1. darkness, अंधकार। 2. a feeling of dejection, विषाद।

glorification (ग्लोरिफ़िकेशन) *n.* 1. the act of glorifying, गुणगान, स्तुति।

glorify (ग्लोरिफ़ाइ) *v.* 1. to praise highly, ख़ूब प्रशंसा करना, बड़ाई करना। 2. to extol, गुणगान करना।

glorious (ग्लोरिअस) *adj.* 1. having glory, गौरवपूर्ण, शानदार। 2. illustrious, यशस्वी। 3. delightful, आनंददायक।

glory (ग्लोरी) *n.* 1. renown and honour won by great deeds, यश, गौरव, महिमा।

gloss (ग्लॉस) *n.* 1. the shine on a smooth surface, चमक। 2. a superficially attractive appearance, तड़क-भड़क, चमक-दमक। *v.* to make glossy, चमकदार बनाना, चमक लाना। □ **gloss over,** अनदेखी करना।

glossary (ग्लॉसरी) *n.* an alphabetical list of words, शब्दावली।

glossy (ग्लॉसी) ***adj.*** having a smooth and shining surface, shiny, चमकदार, चमकीला।

glottal (ग्लॉटल) ***adj.*** of glottis, कंठद्वार-संबंधी, स्वरयंत्र-मुख-संबंधी।

glove (ग्लव) ***n.*** a protective covering for the palm and fingers, दस्ताना।

glow (ग्लो) ***v.*** 1. to shine. 2. to be very cheerful and enthusiastic, खिल उठना। ***n.*** 1. a light emitted by a heated body, चमक। 2. flush, लाली, सुर्ख़ी। 3. cheerfulness, प्रफुल्लता।

glower (ग्लोअर) ***v.*** to look angrily, आँखें तरेरना, घूरना, आँखें दिखाना।

glowing (ग्लोइंग) ***adj.*** 1. in a glow, चमकता हुआ। 2. enthusiastic, उत्साहपूर्ण, उत्साहप्रद।

glowworm (ग्लोवर्म) ***n.*** a kind of beetle, female of which emits greenish light, जुगनूँ।

glucose (ग्लूकोस) ***n.*** grape sugar, ग्लूकोस, द्राक्षा-शर्करा।

glue (ग्लू) ***n.*** 1. an adhesive prepared by boiling animal bones, horns etc., सरेस। 2. any sticky substance, गोंद। ***v.*** 1. to fasten with glue, गोंद से चिपकाना। 2. to be constantly associated with, (किसी के साथ) लगे या चिपके रहना।

glum (ग्लम) ***adj.*** sad and gloomy, उदास और दुखी, निराश, हताश।

glut (ग्लट) ***v.*** 1. to eat excessively, भकोसना, ठूँसना। 2. to feed fully, to gratify to excess, अघा देना, तृप्त कर देना, छका देना। 3. to fill or supply excessively, ठूँस देना, भर देना, पाट देना। ***n.*** an excessive supply, अधिक मात्रा में उपलब्धता, भरमार।

glutinous (ग्लूटिनस) ***adj.*** sticky, चिपचिपा।

glutton (ग्लटन) ***n.*** a person who overeats habitually, भुक्खड़, पेटू।

glycerine, glycerin (ग्लिसरिन) ***n.*** a sticky fluid obtained from fats and oils, ग्लिसरीन।

gnarl (नार्ल) ***n.*** a knot in tree-trunk or wood, पेड़ या लकड़ी में होनेवाली गाँठ।

gnash (नैश्) ***v.*** to grind (one's teeth) in rage, गुस्से में (दाँत) पीसना।

gnat (नैट) ***n.*** a mosquito, मच्छर।

gnaw (नॉ) ***v.*** 1. to bite persistently at something hard, कुतरना। 2. to cause persistent pain or distress, सताना, यंत्रणा देना।

gnawing (नॉइंग) ***adj.*** causing pain or distress, कष्टदायक, दुखदायक।

gnome (नोम) ***n.*** a dwarfish person, बौना।

gnomic (नोमिक) ***adj.*** aphoristic, सूत्रात्मक।

go (गो) ***v.*** 1. to proceed, जाना, प्रस्थान करना, रवाना होना, आगे बढ़ना। 2. to engage in a specified activity, रहना; They went hungry. वे भूखे रहे। 3. to be functioning, काम करना या देना, चलना; That clock does not go. वह घड़ी चलती नहीं। 4. to become, बनना, होना; to go crazy, सनकी बनना, सनक जाना। 5. to fail, विफल होना, बेकाम हो जाना। 6. to be used or spent, up, व्यय होना, समाप्त होना। 7. to disappear, लुप्त होना। 8. to be abolished, नष्ट होना, उन्मूलन होना। ☐ **go about,** (i) व्यस्त रहना, (ii) सामना या मुकाबला करना, (iii) प्रचलित होना; **go along with,** सहमत होना; **go at,** आक्रमण करना; **go by,** (i) बीतना, (ii) मार्गनिर्देशन होना; (iii)

हार जाना; **go for,** (i) प्राप्त करने के लिए प्रयास करना, (ii) तरजीह देना, वरीयता देना, **go in for,** प्रयत्न करना; **go into,** जाँच करना, पूछ-ताछ करना; **go off,** (i) घटित होना, (ii) (गोली) चलना या छूटना, (बम) फटना, **go on,** (i) बने रहना, चले चलना, चलाए चलना, (ii) घटित होना, (iii) सवार होना, सवारी करना, (iv) तर्क करना, हुज्जत करना; **go round,** (i) पूरा पड़ना, (ii) पूरा घेरना; (iii) फैलना; **go out,** (i) बाहर जाना, (ii) बुझना; **go over,** सूक्ष्मतापूर्वक अध्ययन करना; **go through,** (i) गुज़रना, अनुभव करना, (ii) अच्छी तरह जाँचना-पड़तालना, (iii) पढ़ना, पढ़ जाना; **go under,** (i) डूब जाना, (ii) विफल होना; **go with,** (i) साथ देना, (ii) मिलना-जुलना; **go without,** (से) वंचित होना। ***n.*** (plu. goes) 1. a try or venture, चेष्टा, प्रयास, प्रयत्न। 2. a turn, बारी। 3. energy, vitality, शक्ति, स्फूर्ति।

goad (गोड) ***n.*** 1. a sharp pointed stick for driving animals, अंकुश। 2. stimulus, प्रोत्साहन, प्रेरणा। ***v.*** 1. to drive forward with a goad, छड़ी से हाँकना। 2. to provoke or incite, उकसाना, प्रेरित करना।

goal (गोल) ***n.*** 1. an objective or aim, उद्‌देश्य, लक्ष्य, ध्येय। 2. the structure or area into which the ball must pass to score a point, गोल। 3. a point scored in this way, गोल।

goalkeeper (गोलकीपर) ***n.*** the player who defends the goal, गोलकीपर, गोली।

goat (गोट) ***n.*** 1. a domesticated mammal related to the sheep, बकरी। 2. a lecherous man, लंपट या कामुक व्यक्ति।

gobble (गॉबल) ***v.*** to eat quickly and greedily, भकोसना, हड़पना, निगलना।

goblin (गॉब्लिन) ***n.*** an evil and mischievous spirit, दुष्टात्मा, प्रेत।

god (गॉड) ***n.*** 1. the creator, operator and destroyer of the universe, ईश्वर, परमात्मा, प्रभु, ख़ुदा। 2. deity, देवता। 3. a person that is excessively admired, पूज्य व्यक्ति।

goddess (गॉडिस) ***n.*** a female god, देवी।

godfather (गॉडफ़ादर) ***n.*** 1. a male godparent, धर्मपिता।

godfearing (गॉडफ़िअरिंग) ***adj.*** pious, धर्मशील, धर्मभीरु, साधु-प्रकृति।

godforsaken (गॉडफ़ॉर्सेकन) ***adj.*** 1. wicked, दुष्ट। 2. desolate, वीरान, उजाड़।

godlike (गॉडलाइक) ***adj.*** like god, देवतुल्य।

godly (गॉडली) ***adj.*** sincerely religious, धर्मपरायण, धार्मिक, पवित्र।

godmother (गॉडमदर) ***n.*** a female godparent, धर्ममाता।

godown (गोडाउन) ***n.*** a warehouse, भंडार-गृह, गोदाम।

godsend (गॉडसेन्ड) ***n.*** an unexpected piece of good fortune, ईश्वरीय वरदान, सौभाग्य।

goggle (गॉगल) ***v.*** to stare with wide open eyes, आँखें फाड़कर देखना, घूरना।

goggles (गॉगल्ज़) ***n.*** (plu.) tinted eyeglasses worn as a protection against dust or glare, धूप का चश्मा।

goitre, goiter (गॉइटर) ***n.*** enlargement of thyroid gland of neck, घेंघा, गलगंड।

gold (गोल्ड) ***n.*** 1. a yellow metal of very high value, सोना, स्वर्ण। 2. a coin made of gold, स्वर्णमुद्रा।

3. wealth, धन-दौलत, संपत्ति। ***adj.*** made of gold, सोने का (बना हुआ)।

golden (गोल्डन) ***adj.*** 1. made of gold, सोने का बना हुआ, सुनहरा। 2. like gold, सोने-जैसा, सुनहरा।

golden age ***n.*** the period of highest prosperity and happiness, स्वर्णकाल।

golden anniversary ***n.*** the celebration of the fiftieth year of foundation, marriage etc. स्वर्ण जयंती।

golden jubilee ***n.*** = golden anniversary.

goldfield (गोल्डफ़ील्ड) ***n.*** an area in which gold is found, स्वर्णक्षेत्र।

goldfish (गोल्डफ़िश) ***n.*** a small orange coloured fish, सोन मछली।

goldleaf ***n.*** a leaf of gold, सोने का पत्तर।

gold-plated (गोल्ड-प्लेटिड) ***adj.*** plated with gold, जिसपर सोने का मुलम्मा चढ़ाया हुआ हो।

goldsmith (गोल्डस्मिथ) ***n.*** one who prepares or sells articles of gold, सुनार।

golf (गोल्फ़) ***n.*** a game played with a stick and ball on an open course, गोल्फ़। ***v.*** to play golf, गोल्फ़ खेलना।

golf club ***n.*** a club used in golf, गोल्फ़ खेलने की छड़ी।

golf course ***n.*** the area of land on which golf is played, गोल्फ़ का मैदान।

golfer (गोल्फ़र) ***n.*** one who plays golf, गोल्फ़ का खिलाड़ी।

golf-links ***n.*** = golf course.

gonad (गोनैड) ***n.*** the reproductive gland, जनन-ग्रंथि (अंडकोश या डिंब ग्रंथि)।

gong (गॉन्ग) ***n.*** a metal disc that resounds when struck, घंटा।

gonorrhoea (गॉनरीआ) ***n.*** an infectious venereal disease, सूज़ाक।

good (गुड) ***adj.*** 1. having desirable qualities, अच्छा, उत्तम। 2. morally excellent, virtuous, kind, well-behaved, सच्चरित्र, भला, नेक। 3. proper, right, उचित, ठीक। □ **a good deal,** अच्छी ख़ासी मात्रा; **as good as,** (i) बराबर, (ii) के लगभग; **for good,** सदा के लिए; **make good,** (i) पूरा करना, (ii) क्षति-पूर्ति करना, (iii) सफल होना। ***adv.*** entirely, पूर्णतः। ***n.*** 1. goodness, अच्छाई, भलाई। 2. profit, लाभ, फ़ायदा। 3. a good thing, अच्छी वस्तु।

goodby, goodbye (गुडबाइ) ***interj.*** farewell, अलविदा, विदा।

good-for-nothing (गुड-फ़ॉर-नथिंग) ***adj.*** worthless, बेकार, रद्दी। ***n.*** a worthless person, निकम्मा आदमी।

Good Friday ***n.*** the Friday before Easter, गुडफ़ाइडे, ईस्टर के पहले का शुक्रवार।

goodness (गुडनिस) ***n.*** 1. the quality of being good, अच्छाई। 2. kindness, दयालुता। 3. virtuousness, सदाचार, सद्गुण। 4. welfare, कल्याण, भलाई। ***interj.*** a euphemistic word for god, परमात्मा (मंगलभाषित)।

good offices ***n.*** (plu.) influence deriving from one's position, व्यक्तिगत प्रभाव।

goods (गुड्स) ***n.*** (plu.) 1. articles of trade, सामग्री, माल। 2. personal belongings, व्यक्तिगत सामान।

goodwill (गुडविल) ***n.*** 1. a friendly

feeling, benevolence, सद्भावना। 2. value of reputation and popularity of a business firm, गुडविल, सुनाम, साख।

goody (गुडी) ***n.*** 1. something good or attractive, कोई अच्छी या आकर्षक वस्तु। 2. a person of good character, सच्चरित्र व्यक्ति।

goof (गूफ़) ***n.*** 1. a stupid person, मूर्ख व्यक्ति। 2. a mistake, भूल, त्रुटि। ***v.*** 1. to kill time, समय बरबाद करना। 2. to blunder, भूल करना।

googly (गूग्ली) ***n.*** an off-break ball bowled with leg-break action, गुगली।

goose (गूस) ***n.*** (plu. geese) 1. a bird of a duck family, हंस। 2. a stupid fellow, मूर्ख व्यक्ति।

gore[1] (गोर) ***v.*** to stab or pierce with a horn or tusk, सींग घुसेड़ देना, दाँत चुभो देना। ***n.*** thickened blood shed from a wound, ख़ून का थक्का।

gore[2] ***n.*** a triangular piece of cloth, कपड़े का तिकोना टुकड़ा, कली।

gorge (गॉर्ज) ***n.*** 1. a narrow valley with steep walls, सँकरी गहरी घाटी। ***v.*** 1. to eat greedily, भकोसना। 2. to stuff, ठूस देना या लेना।

gorgeous (गॉर्जस) ***adj.*** 1. dazzlingly brilliant, अत्यंत चमकीला, भड़कीला। 2. magnificent, भव्य, शानदार।

gorget (गॉर्जिट) ***n.*** 1. a necklace, गले का हार। 2. a patch of colour on bird's neck, कंठी।

gorilla (गोरिला) ***n.*** a large African ape, गुरिल्ला, बनमानुस।

gorse (गॉर्स) ***n.*** a shrub with yellow flower, पीले फूलोंवाला एक पौधा।

gory (गोरी) ***adj.*** 1. bloodstained, ख़ून से लथपथ, रक्तरंजित। 2. involving bloodshed, हिंसापूर्ण, मार-काट से भरा।

gosling (गॉज़लिन्ग) ***n.*** a young goose, हंस का बच्चा, हंसशावक।

gospel (गॉस्पल) ***n.*** the teachings of Christ, येशु का उपदेश, सुसमाचार, शुभ संदेश।

gossamer (गॉसमर) ***n.*** a cobweb, मकड़जाल।

gossip (गॉसिप) ***n.*** 1. trivial talk especially about other people's affairs, गपशप, बतकही। 2. one who is fond of gossiping, गप्पी, गपोड़संख। ***v.*** to engage in gossip, गपशप करना, गप लड़ाना।

got (गॉट) ***v.*** p.t. & p.p. of get.

Goth (गॉथ) ***n.*** a member of a Germanic tribe that invaded the Roman Empire from the third to fifth centuries, गाथ जाति।

Gothic (गॉथिक) ***adj.*** 1. of the Goths or their language, गाथों का या उनकी भाषा से संबद्ध। 2. of an architectural style prevalent in Western Europe in the 12th-16th centuries, गाथिक। 3. of or relating to Middle Ages. मध्ययुगीन। 4. full of sensational horrors, भयानक, भयावह।

gotten (गॉटन) ***v.*** p.p. of get.

gouge (गाउज) ***n.*** a chisel with curved blade, रुखानी। ***v.*** to cut out with a gouge, रुखानी से खाँचा बनाना।

gourd (गॉर्ड) ***n.*** 1. a plant and its fleshy fruit, लौकी, कद्दू। 2. the dried hollowed out shell of a gourd, तूँबी।

gourmand (गुअरमन्ड) ***n.*** 1. a person who eats too much, भोजनभट्ट, पेटू। 2. who takes delight in eating, चटोरा।

gout (गाउट) ***n.*** painful swelling of the joints, गठिया, जोड़ों का दर्द, जोड़ों की सूजन।

govern (गवर्न) ***v.*** 1. to rule, शासन या राज्य करना। 2. to control and guide, नियंत्रित तथा निर्देशित करना, परिचालन करना। 3. to regulate, नियमित करना। 4. to determine, विनिश्चित करना।

governess (गवर्निस) ***n.*** a woman engaged to educate and train the children of a private household, गृह-शिक्षिका।

government (गवर्नमेन्ट) ***n.*** 1. the act or process of governing, शासन। 2. the group or organization governing a country, सरकार, शासन।

governor (गवर्नर) ***n.*** 1. one who governs the province or state, राज्यपाल, गवर्नर। 2. a device that automatically controls the speed or functioning of a machine, गति-नियंत्रक, गवर्नर।

gown (गाउन) ***n.*** a loose flowing garment, गाउन, लबादा, चोगा।

grab (ग्रैब) ***v.*** 1. to attempt to seize or arrest, पकड़ना, गिरफ़्तार करना, दबोचना। 2. to snatch, छीनना, झपटना, ज़बरदस्ती हथिया लेना। ***n.*** 1. the act of grabbing, छीना-झपटी, छीन-झपट, झपट्टा। 2. a device for gripping things, पकड़।

grabble (ग्रैबल) ***v.*** to grope about, टटोलना, टोहना।

grace (ग्रेस) ***n.*** 1. elegance in movement, शोभा, लालित्य। 2. charm, beauty, सौंदर्य, सुंदरता, चारुता। 3. elegance in manner, शालीनता। 4. favour, goodwill, अनुग्रह, कृपादृष्टि। 5. temporary respite, रियायत, छूट; grace period, मोहलत, छूट की अवधि। 6. a virtue or gift granted by God, ईश्वरीय वरदान, प्रसाद। 7. a short prayer at meal-time, भोजन के समय की जानेवाली ईश-वंदना। ***v.*** 1. to do favour, अनुग्रह करना। 2. to embellish, सजाना, अलंकृत करना, शोभा बढ़ाना।

grace marks ***n.*** extra marks given as a favour, अनुग्रहांक।

gracious (ग्रेशस) ***adj.*** kind and pleasant in manner, दयालु, कृपालु।

gradation (ग्रेडेशन) ***n.*** 1. a series of gradual progression, सोपानक्रम, अनुक्रम। 2. a degree or mark in such a progression, चिह्न, स्तर। 3. the act of arranging in grades, श्रेणीकरण।

grade (ग्रेड) ***n.*** 1. a degree or stage in a process, श्रेणी, स्तर। 2. a class of people or things of the same category, वर्ग, जमात। 3. a standard of quality, गुणवत्ता का मानक। 4. a mark showing the quality of a student's work, ग्रेड। 5. slope, ढाल। ***v.*** 1. to arrange in grades, श्रेणीकरण करना। 2. to give an academic grade (to the student, विद्यार्थी को) श्रेणी प्रदान करना। 3. to level, समतल करना।

gradient (ग्रेडिएन्ट) ***n.*** 1. a slope, ढाल। 2. a degree of slope, ढाल का मान।

gradual (ग्रैजुअल) ***adj.*** taking place by degrees, क्रमिक, आनुक्रमिक।

gradually (ग्रैजुअली) ***adv.*** 1. in a gradual way, क्रमशः। 2. slowly, धीरे-धीरे।

graduate[1] (ग्रैजुएट) ***v.*** 1. to obtain a

G

university degree, स्नातक की उपाधि प्राप्त करना। 2. to classify, वर्गीकृत करना, श्रेणीबद्ध करना। 3. to mark with units of measurement, अंशांकित करना।

graduate[2] ***n.*** one who has obtained a university degree, स्नातक।

graffito (ग्रैफ़ीटो) ***n.*** (plu. graffiti) an inscription or drawing on a wall, भित्तिलेख, भित्तिचित्र। (इटैलियन)

graft (ग्राफ़्ट) ***n.*** 1. a detached shoot from one plant attached with a growing plant by insertion, क़लम, पैबंद। 2. a piece of tissue transplanted surgically to replace damaged tissue, ऊतक प्रतिरोपण। 3. bribe, रिश्वत, घूस। ***v.*** 1. क़लम लगाना, पैबंद लगाना। 2. ऊतक-प्रतिरोपण करना। 3. रिश्वत लेना।

grain (ग्रेन) ***n.*** 1. a small hard seed or fruit of wheat, rice etc., दाना, कण। 2. the seeds of such plants collectively, अन्न, अनाज, गल्ला। 3. the plants themselves, गेहूँ, धान आदि के पौधे। 4. a small hard particle, कण, ज़र्रा। 5. a tiny quantity, कण, टुकड़ा। 6. texture, बुनावट, तंतुरचना। 7. temperament, स्वभाव, प्रकृति। ***v.*** to form grains, दानेदार बनाना।

gram[1] (ग्राम, ग्रैम) ***n.*** one-thousandth part of a kilogram, ग्राम (तौल)।

gram[2] ***n.*** a plant and its seeds, चना; gram flour, बेसन।

grammar (ग्रैमर) ***n.*** rules of correct usage of a language, व्याकरण।

grammatical (ग्रमैटिकल) ***adj.*** 1. of or related to grammar, व्याकरण-संबंधी, व्याकरणिक। 2. regarded as correct, सही या शुद्ध (रूप या प्रयोग)।

gramophone (ग्रैमफ़ोन) ***n.*** a phonograph, ग्रामोफ़ोन।

granary (ग्रेनरी) ***n.*** 1. a storehouse for grain, धान्यागार, कोठार।

grand (ग्रैन्ड) ***adj.*** 1. splendid, imposing, भव्य, शानदार, वैभवपूर्ण। 2. distinguished, प्रतिष्ठित, विशिष्ट। 3. including everything, समग्र, कुल।

granddaughter ***n.*** the daughter of one's son or daughter, पोती, नतिनी।

grandeur (ग्रैन्जर) ***n.*** 1. splendour, grandness, वैभव, प्रताप, गौरव, शान। 2. greatness, महत्ता, महिमा।

grandfather ***n.*** the father of one's father or mother, दादा, नाना।

grandiloquence (ग्रैन्डिलक्वेन्स) ***n.*** bombastic or pompous eloquence, शब्दजाल, शब्दाडंबर।

grandiose (ग्रैन्डिओस) ***adj.*** majestic, वैभवपूर्ण, भव्य।

grandmother ***n.*** the mother of one's father or mother, दादी, नानी।

grandson ***n.*** the son of one's son or daughter, पोता, नाती।

granite (ग्रैनाइट) ***n.*** a hard grey stone widely used for building, ग्रेनाइट।

grant (ग्रान्ट) ***v.*** 1. to give or bestow, प्रदान करना। 2. to permit or allow, अनुमति देना। 3. to give as a grant, अनुदान देना। 4. to agree or consent to, मानना, स्वीकार करना। ☐ **take for granted,** सत्य मान लेना। ***n.*** 1. the act of granting, देने की क्रिया या भाव, प्रदान। 2. something granted spl, money given by the government as help, अनुदान।

grantee (ग्रान्टी) ***n.*** one who gets

a grant, अनुदान पानेवाला, अनुदानग्राही।

granular (ग्रैन्यूलर) ***adj.*** 1. composed of grains or granules, दानेदार, रवेदार। 2. rough, ख़ुरदरा।

granulate (ग्रैन्यूलेट) ***v.*** 1. to form into grains or granules, दानेदार बनाना, रवेदार बनाना। 2. to make rough, ख़ुदरा बनाना।

granule (ग्रैन्यूल) ***n.*** a small grain or particle, कण, कणिका, कनी, दाना।

grape (ग्रेप) ***n.*** a juicy edible berry borne in clusters on vines, अंगूर।

grapefruit (ग्रेपफ्रूट) ***n.*** a kind of large yellow citrus fruit, चकोतरा।

grapevine (ग्रेपवाइन) ***n.*** 1. a vine on which grapes grow, अंगूर की लता। 2. a means of spreading an information unofficially, अनधिकारिक रूप से सूचना फैलाने का तरीका।

graph (ग्राफ़) ***n.*** a drawing used to show relationship between two sets of numbers, ग्राफ़, आलेख। ***v.*** to represent by a graph, ग्राफ़ बनाना, आलेख बनाना।

-graph ***suffix*** an apparatus that writes or records, आलेखी।

graphic (ग्रैफ़िक) ***adj.*** 1. written or printed, लिखा या छपा हुआ। 2. drawn or engraved, खींचा या नक़्क़ाशी किया हुआ। 3. giving a vivid description, सजीव, जीवंत। 4. of or pertaining to graphi, ग्राफ़-संबंधी, ग्राफ़ीय, आलेखीय।

graphite (ग्रैफ़ाइट) ***n.*** the soft black form of carbon, ग्रैफ़ाइट।

grapnel (ग्रैप्नेल) ***n.*** a small anchor, छोटा लंगर।

grapple (ग्रैपल) ***v.*** 1. to struggle, भिड़ना, जूझना, द्वंद्व करना। 2. to seize firmly, दबोच लेना, जकड़ लेना। 3. to wrestle, कुश्ती लड़ना। ***n.*** 1. hand-to-hand fight, भिड़ंत, द्वंद्व।

grasp (ग्रास्प) ***v.*** 1. to seize and hold firmly with the hands, दबोच लेना, धर-दबोचना। 2. to comprehend, बुद्धि में आना, समझ में आना। ***n.*** 1. hold or grip, पकड़, चंगुल। 2. possession, क़ब्ज़ा। 3. understanding, समझ।

grasping (ग्रास्पिंग) ***adj.*** greedy, लोभी।

grass (ग्रास) ***n.*** 1. any of numerous plants with narrow leaves and jointed stems that are eaten by animals, घास। 2. a ground covered with such plants, घास का मैदान। 3. an informer, मुख़बिर। 4. marijuana, एक नशीला पदार्थ। ***v.*** 1. to cover with grass, घास उगाना। 2. to be covered with grass, घास उगना, घास से आच्छादित होना।

grasshopper (ग्रासहॉपर) ***n.*** an insect with long hind legs adapted for jumping, टिड्डा।

grassland (ग्रासलैन्ड) ***n.*** land reserved for natural grass pasture, घास का मैदान।

grassroots (ग्रासरूट्स) ***n.*** (plu.) 1. ordinary people, जन-साधारण। 2. the essentials, मूल तत्त्व।

grate (ग्रेट) ***v.*** 1. to reduce to small threads by rubbing against jagged surface, कद्दूकस करना। 2. to make a harsh noise by rubbing, रगड़ से आवाज़ होना या करना, किरकिराना। 3. to annoy, चिढ़ाना, क्रुद्ध करना। ***n.*** a framework that keeps fuel in a fireplace, अँगीठी की जाली।

grateful (ग्रेटफ़ुल) ***adj.*** 1. feeling or

G

showing gratitude, कृतज्ञ, एहसानमंद।

gratify (ग्रैटिफ़ाइ) ***v.*** 1. to please, प्रसन्न करना, ख़ुश करना। 2. to satisfy, संतुष्ट करना। 3. to give pleasure to, आनंदित करना।

grating (ग्रेटिंग) ***n.*** a framework of spaced parallel or crossed bars serving as a cover, जाली।

gratis (ग्रेटिस) ***adj.*** free of charge, नि:शुल्क।

gratitude (ग्रैटिट्यूड) ***n.*** a feeling of thankfulness, कृतज्ञता, आभार।

gratuitous (ग्रेट्यूइटस) ***adj.*** 1. given or done without payment, मुफ़्त में दिया या किया जानेवाला, नि:शुल्क। 2. unjustified, अनुचित, अवांछित।

gratuity (ग्रेच्यूइटी) ***n.*** a gift or reward for services rendered, उपदान, आनुतोषिक।

grave[1] (ग्रेव) ***n.*** a hole dug for the burial of a corpse, क़ब्र।

grave[2] ***adj.*** 1. extremely serious, अत्यंत गंभीर, विकट, संगीन। 2. causing great anxiety or alarm, चिंताजनक। 3. important, महत्त्वपूर्ण। 4. dull, जो खिला न हो, मंद, बुझा हुआ, उदास।

grave[3] ***v.*** to engrave, नक़्क़ाशी करना।

gravel (ग्रैवल) ***n.*** rock fragments or pebbles, बजरी, रोड़ी। ***v.*** to cover with gravel, बजरी डालना या बिछाना।

graver (ग्रेवर) ***n.*** one who engraves, उत्कीर्णक, नक़्क़ाश।

gravestone (ग्रेवस्टोन) ***n.*** a stone put up over a grave, समाधि-शिला, समाधि-प्रस्तर।

graveyard (ग्रेवयार्ड) ***n.*** a burial ground, क़ब्रिस्तान।

gravitate (ग्रैविटेट) ***v.*** to be drawn toward, आकृष्ट होना, खिंचना।

gravitation (ग्रैविटेशन) ***n.*** the force of gravity, गुरुत्वाकर्षण, गुरुत्व।

gravity (ग्रैविटी) ***n.*** 1. the attractive central gravitational force exerted by a celestial body, गुरुत्वाकर्षण, गुरुत्व। 2. seriousness, गंभीरता।

gravy (ग्रेवी) ***n.*** 1. the juice that comes out from meat during cooking, यख़नी, शोरबा, रसा।

graze[1] (ग्रेज़) ***v.*** 1. to feed on grass, चरना, घास चरना। 2. to cause to feed on grass, चराना, घास चराना।

graze[2] ***v.*** to touch or scrape gently (in passing, चलते समय) छू जाना या रगड़ खा जाना।

grease (ग्रीस) ***n.*** 1. animal fat, चर्बी। 2. any semi-solid oily substance used as a lubricant, ग्रीस। ***v.*** to lubricate with grease, ग्रीस देना, चिकनाना।

great (ग्रेट) ***adj.*** 1. of extemely large size, बड़ा, बृहत्, दीर्घकाय, विशाल। 2. outstanding, remarkable, भव्य, उल्लेखनीय, शानदार, विशिष्ट, उत्कृष्ट। 3. very good, first-rate, उच्चकोटि का, महान, श्रेष्ठ। 4. indicating further step in genealogical relationship, और ऊपर की पीढ़ी का, पर—; great grandfather, परदादा; great grandmother, परदादी।

great-hearted (ग्रेट-हार्टिड) ***adj.*** generous, उदार, विशालहृदय।

Grecian (ग्रीशन) ***adj.*** Greek, यूनानी। ***n.*** a native of Greece, यूनानवासी।

greed (ग्रीड) ***n.*** an excessive desire for food or wealth, लोभ, लालच, लालसा।

Greek (ग्रीक) ***n.*** 1. an inhabitant of Greece, यूनानवासी। 2. the language of the Greeks, यूनानी भाषा।

green (ग्रीन) ***n.*** 1. the colour of growing grass, हरा रंग। 2. a grassy lawn, हरा मैदान। 3. greenery, हरियाली। 4. (plu.) green vegetables, हरी सब्जियाँ, साग-भाजी। ***adj.*** 1. of the colour green, हरा, हरित। 2. covered with green growth, हरा-भरा। 3. fresh, ताज़ा। 4. not ripe, कच्चा, अपरिपक्व, हरा। 5. lacking experience, अनुभवहीन। ***v.*** to make or become green, हरा होना या बनाना।

greenhouse (ग्रीनहाउस) ***n.*** a building made of glass for raising plants, शीशे की बनी पौधशाला, काँचघर।

greenroom (ग्रीनरूम) ***n.*** a room for actors and actresses near the stage, सज्जागृह, नेपथ्यशाला।

greet (ग्रीट) ***v.*** 1. to address in a friendly and respectful way, अभिवादन करना। 2. to welcome, स्वागत करना। 3. to receive with a certain reaction, मिलने पर कोई प्रतिक्रिया करना।

greeting (ग्रीटिंग) ***n.*** 1. a form of words or gestures used to greet a person, अभिवादन। 2. (plu.) good wishes, शुभ-कामनाएँ, बधाई।

greeting card ***n.*** a card sent as a greeting, ग्रीटिंग कार्ड, बधाई-पत्र, शुभकामना-पत्र।

gregarious (ग्रिगेरिअस) ***adj.*** 1. living in groups, झुंड में रहनेवाला। 2. seeking and enjoying the company of others, मिलनसार, समाजशील।

gremlin (ग्रेम्लिन) ***n.*** an imaginary wicked spirit, दुष्टात्मा, प्रेत।

grenade (ग्रिनेड) ***n.*** a small bomb designed to be thrown by hand, हथगोला।

grey (ग्रे) ***adj.*** 1. of the colour like black mixed with white, स्लेटी, धूसर, मटमैला। 2. having grey hair, पके हुए या सफ़ेद बालोंवाला। 3. pale, पीला। 4. sad, उदास।

greyhound (ग्रेहाउन्ड) ***n.*** a long-legged swift running hunting dog, ग्रेहाउन्ड।

grid (ग्रिड) ***n.*** 1. a grating, जाली। 2. a network of electric and power cables etc., ग्रिड।

gridiron (ग्रिडआइरन) ***n.*** a framework of straight iron bars for cooking or broiling, जाली।

grief (ग्रीफ़) ***n.*** great sorrow, घोर दुख, संताप, शोक।

grievance (ग्रीवैन्स) ***n.*** 1. a cause of complaint, कष्टकर बात, तकलीफ़ देनेवाली बात। 2. a complaint, शिकायत।

grieve (ग्रीव) ***v.*** 1. to cause grief to, दुख देना, संतप्त करना। 2. to feel grief, दुखी होना, संतप्त होना।

grievous (ग्रीवस) ***adj.*** 1. causing grief, दुखदायक। 2. grave, serious, गंभीर, घोर, दारुण।

grill (ग्रिल) ***n.*** 1. a cooking utensil made of parallel bars, जाली। 2. the food cooked or broiled on a grill, जाली पर भूना या सेंका हुआ पदार्थ। ***v.*** 1. to cook on a grill, जाली पर भूनना या सेंकना। 2. to question closely and relentlessly, कड़ी पूछताछ करना।

grille (ग्रिल) ***n.*** a framework of metal bars, ग्रिल, जाली, जालीदार जंगला।

grim (ग्रिम) 1. severe, stern, कठोर, कड़ा, सख़्त। 2. merciless, क्रूर, निर्दय, निष्ठुर। 3. terrible, भयंकर, डरावना। 4. gloomy, विषादमय।

grimace (ग्रिमेस) ***n.*** a contortion of

the face expressing pain, disgust or contempt, मुँह बिचकाने की क्रिया या भाव, विरक्ति या घृणा का भाव। *v.* to make a grimace, मुँह बिचकाना।

grimly (ग्रिम्ली) ***adv.*** mercilessly, क्रूरतापूर्वक, कड़ाई या सख़्ती से।

grimy (ग्राइमी) ***adj.*** dirty, गंदा, मैला-कुचैला।

grin (ग्रिन) ***v.*** to smile broadly, दाँत निपोरना। ***n.*** the act of grinning, दाँत निपोरने की क्रिया या भाव, भद्दी हँसी, खीसें निपोरना।

grind (ग्राइन्ड) ***v.*** (ground, grinding) 1. to crush into fine particles, पीसना, दलना। 2. to be crushed into fine particles, पिसना, दला जाना। 3. to rub together (as teeth, दाँत) रगड़ना, पीसना, किटकिटाना। 4. to sharpen with friction, सान चढ़ाना या सान पर चढ़ना, घिसना। 5. to turn by a handle, हैंडल घुमाना। ***n.*** 1. the act of grinding, पिसाई, दलाई, रगड़ाई, सान चढ़ाई। 2. dull or strenuous work, कोई उबाऊ या मेहनत का काम।

grinder (ग्राइन्डर) ***n.*** 1. one who grinds, पीसने या दलनेवाला, सान धरनेवाला। 2. an electric apparatus that grinds, ग्राइन्डर, पीसने की मशीन, चक्की। 3. a large back tooth that grinds food, चौभड़, दाढ़।

grindstone (ग्राइन्डस्टोन) ***n.*** 1. a thick revolving disk used for sharpening, सान। 2. a millstone, चक्की का पाट।

grip (ग्रिप) ***n.*** 1. a tight hold, पकड़। 2. the power of holding, पकड़, नियंत्रण। 3. the understanding, समझ, बोध। 4. mastery, command, अधिकार, वर्चस्व। 5. a handle, मूठ, दस्ता। 6. a suitcase, सूटकेस। ***v.*** 1. to take a firm hold on, कसकर पकड़ना, नियंत्रण में करना। 2. to hold the interest or attention of, आकृष्ट या मंत्रमुग्ध करना।

gripe (ग्राइप) ***v.*** 1. to cause or suffer sharp pain in the bowels, पेट दर्द करना या होना। 2. to complain, शिकायत करना। 3. to irritate, चिढ़ाना।

gripes (ग्राइप्स) ***n.*** (plu.) sharp repeated pains in the bowels, पेट में रह-रहकर होनेवाला दर्द, उदरशूल, मरोड़, ऐंठन।

grisly (ग्रिज़्ली) ***adj.*** 1. horrifying, भयानक, भयावह। 2. disgusting, घिनौना, बीभत्स।

grist (ग्रिस्ट) ***n.*** grain to be ground, पीसा जानेवाला अन्न।

grit (ग्रिट) ***n.*** 1. small particles of stone, रोड़ी, बजरी। 2. courage, साहस, जीवट। 3. endurance, धैर्य, सहिष्णुता। 4. resolution, दृढ़ निश्चय। ***v.*** 1. to cover with grit, रोड़ी या बजरी डालना या फैलाना। 2. to keep (the teeth) tightly together, (पीड़ा आदि के समय दाँतों को) दबाना।

grizzle[1] (ग्रिज़ल) ***v.*** to cry quietly and continually, रींरीं करना। ***n.*** the act of grizzling, रींरीं।

grizzle[2] ***v.*** to make or become grey, धूसर होना या बनाना। ***n.*** 1. grey colour, धूसर या स्लेटी रंग। 2. grey hair, धूसर बाल, पके बाल।

groan (ग्रोन) ***v.*** to utter a deep prolonged sound expressive of pain or annoyance, कराहना, आह भरना। ***n.*** sound expressive of pain or annoyance, कराह, आह, ओफ़।

grocer (ग्रोसर) ***n.*** a dealer in household supplies, बनिया, परचूनिया, पंसारी।

G

grocery (ग्रोसरी) ***n.*** 1. the shop of a grocer, बनिए, पंसारी या किराने की दुकान। 2. the business of a grocer, बनिए का व्यवसाय। 3. (plu. groceries) the goods sold by a grocer, किराना।

grog (ग्रॉग) ***n.*** an alcoholic liquor mixed with water, पानी मिली शराब।

groggy (ग्रॉगी) ***adj.*** 1. weak because of illness, बीमारी के कारण कमज़ोर, शिथिल। 2. unsteady, shaky, अस्थिर, लड़खड़ाता हुआ।

groin (ग्रोइन) ***n.*** 1. the area where the thigh meets the trunk, ऊरुमूल। 2. a curved edge where two intersecting vaults meet, चापांतर।

groom (ग्रूम) ***n.*** 1. a person employed to look after horses, साईस। 2. a bridegroom, दुल्हा, वर। ***v.*** 1. to clean and rub down horses, घोड़ों को खरहरा करना। 2. to clean and brush, सफ़ाई करना, रगड़ना-पोंछना। 3. to make trim, बनाव-श्रृंगार करना। 4. to prepare and train for a particular task or job, तैयार करना, प्रशिक्षित करना।

groove (ग्रूव) ***n.*** 1. a long narrow furrow or channel, खाँचा, नाली। 2. a spiral cut, चूड़ी। 3. a routine, बँधा क्रम, नियत क्रम, नित्यकर्म। ***v.*** to make grooves in, खाँचे बनाना।

grooved (ग्रूव्ड) ***adj.*** having grooves, खाँचेदार, चूड़ीदार।

grope (ग्रोप) ***v.*** to search about uncertainly in dark, टटोलना, टोहना।

gross (ग्रॉस) ***adj.*** 1. heavily built, fat, भारी-भरकम, स्थूल, मोटा। 2. thick, dense, सघन। 3. excessive, terrible, अत्यधिक, प्रचंड। 4. total, entire, कुल, समग्र, सकल। 5. vulgar, अशिष्ट, असभ्य। 6. coarse, rough, घटिया, रद्दी। 7. obscene, अश्लील, गंदा। ***n.*** 1. the entire body, whole, समग्रता। 2. a group of 144 items, गुर्स, बारह दर्जन। ***v.*** to earn as total revenue prior to deducting expenses, taxes etc., कुल आय होना, कुल आमदनी होना।

grotesque (ग्रोटेस्क) ***adj.*** odd and ludicrous, ऊलजलूल, भोंडा, बेतुका, अनगढ़। ***n.*** 1. a person of grotesque appearance, भोंड़ा व्यक्ति। 2. a comically distorted figure, हास्यास्पद विकृत आकृति, भोंडा या विरूपित चित्र। 3. distortion, विकृति, भोंडापन।

grotto (ग्रॉटो) ***n.*** a picturesque cave, चित्रात्मक गुफ़ा।

ground[1] (ग्राउन्ड) ***n.*** 1. solid surface of the earth, भूतल, धरातल, 2. soil, earth, ज़मीन, भूमि। 3. a piece of land, भूक्षेत्र, ज़मीन का टुकड़ा, ज़मीन। 4. land surrounding a building, अहाता, हाता। 5. the bottom of the sea, समुद्र-तल। 6. first covering of the paint, पेंट की पहली परत। 7. basis for an argument, कारण, आधार। 8. background, पृष्ठभूमि। 9. (plu.) sediment at the bottom of a liquid esp. coffee, (कॉफ़ी के प्याले में) जमा होनेवाली तलछट। ***v.*** 1. to place on the ground, ज़मीन पर रखना या उतारना। 2. to strike against the ground, ज़मीन से टकराना। 3. to instruct in fundamentals, किसी विषय की मूल बातें समझाना। 4. to provide a basis for, आधार प्रस्तुत करना, आधारित करना। 5. to prevent from flying or confine to the ground, उड़ने न देना, उड़ान भरने से रोकना। 6. to connect to a ground, ज़मीन से जोड़ना।

ground[2] ***v.*** p.t. & p.p. of grind,

G

ground floor *n.* the floor at a ground level, भूखंड, पहली मंज़िल।

grounding (ग्राउन्डिंग) *n.* 1. a base, आधार, पीठिका। 2. basic training, मूलभूत प्रशिक्षण।

groundnut (ग्राउन्डनट) *n.* a plant and its underground nut, मूँगफली, चिनिया बादाम।

ground water *n.* water beneath the earth's surface, भूतल के नीचे का जल, भूजल।

groundwork (ग्राउन्डवर्क) *n.* preliminary work, आधारिक कार्य, प्रारंभिक कार्य।

group (ग्रूप) *n.* number of persons or objects considered as a collective unit, ग्रुप, समूह, दल, वर्ग। *v.* 1. to form a group, ग्रुप या दल बनाना। 2. to place in groups, वर्गीकरण करना, वर्गों या समूहों में बाँटना।

grouse[1] (ग्राउस) *n.* (plu. grouse) a chicken like bird with feathered feet, तीतर।

grouse[2] *v.* 1. to grumble in discontent, झीखना, भुनभुनाना। 2. to complain, शिकायत करना। *n.* 1. the act of grousing, झीख, भुनभुनाहट। 2. a complaint, शिकायत।

grout (ग्राउट) *n.* a thin mortar used to fill joints between tiles, सीमेंट का घोल।

grove (ग्रोव) *n.* 1. a group of trees, वृक्षावली, वृक्ष-समूह। 2. a small wooded area, कुंज।

grovel (ग्रॉवल) *v.* 1. to crawl on the ground, रेंगते हुए चलना। 2. to bow down, झुक जाना। 3. to abase oneself, अपने को गिराना।

grow (ग्रो) *v.* (grew, grown, growing) 1. to increase in size, बढ़ना, विकसित होना। 2. to increase in number or amount, बढ़ना, फैलना। 3. to cultivate, उगाना, उपजाना, पैदा करना। 4. to thrive or flourish, पनपना, बढ़ना। 5. to become, होना, हो जाना, होते चलना; to grow old, बूढ़ा हो जाना। □ **grow into,** (i) हो या बन जाना; (ii) अभ्यस्त हो जाना, आदी हो जाना; **grow on,** धीरे-धीरे स्वीकार्य या लोकप्रिय होते चलना।

growl (ग्राउल) *v.* to make a low threatening sound गुर्राना। *n.* a growling sound, गुर्राहट, बड़बड़ाहट।

growth (ग्रोथ) *n.* 1. the act or process of growing, विकास, वृद्धि। 2. something grown, उगी, बढ़ी या विकसित वस्तु। 3. the cultivation of produce, उपज, पैदावार। 4. an increase, बढ़ती, वृद्धि। 5. an abnormal formation due to unhealthy growth, बढ़ा हुआ अंग, अपवृद्धि।

grub[1] (ग्रब) *n.* 1. a worm-like larva of certain insects, सूँडी। 2. food, भोज्य पदार्थ।

grub[2] *v.* 1. to turn over the soil, ज़मीन खोदना। 2. to dig up by the roots, जड़ से खोदना। 3. to toil arduously, कठोर परिश्रम करना।

grudge (ग्रज) *v.* 1. to allow or give unwillingly, अनिच्छा से देना या करना, देते या करते हुए आनाकानी करना। 2. to feel envious of (someone's success), ईर्ष्या करना। *n.* feeling of envy, डाह, जलन।

gruel (ग्रूअल) *n.* a thin porridge made by boiling crushed grain in milk or water, दलिया, लपसी।

grueling, gruelling (ग्रूअलिंग)

adj. very hard and tiring, exhausting, थका डालनेवाला, पस्त कर देनेवाला। *n.* a tiring work, थका देनेवाला काम।

gruesome (ग्रूसम) *adj.* horrifying, disgusting, भयावह, बीभत्स।

gruff (ग्रफ़) *adj.* rough and unfriendly, रूखा, ओछा।

grumble (ग्रम्बल) *v.* 1. to express discontent, असंतोष व्यक्त करना, शिकवा करना। 2. to mutter angrily, बुड़बुड़ करना, कुलबुलाना। 3. to grouse or complain, झीखना, शिकायत करना। 4. to rumble, गड़गड़ाना। *n.* 1. an act of grumbling, असंतोष, शिकवा। 2. a complaint, शिकायत। 3. rumbling sound, गड़गड़ाहट।

grumpy (ग्रम्पी) *adj.* bad-tempered, तुनुकमिज़ाज, चिड़चिड़ा।

grunt (ग्रन्ट) *v.* 1. to utter a low guttural sound, घुरघुराना। 2. to speak with such a sound, घुरघुराते हुए बोलना। *n.* a grunting sound, घुरघुर, घुरघुराहट।

guano (ग्वानो) *n.* the dung of seabirds used as fertilizer, ग्वानो।

guarantee (गैरन्टी) *n.* 1. a formal assurance that a thing is of a specified quality and durability, गारंटी। 2. an agreement to be responsible for the fulfilment of someone else's obligations in the event of default, ज़मानत। 3. anything held as security for something, ज़मानत के रूप में रखी हुई वस्तु, प्रतिभूति। 4. a guarantor, ज़मानतदार, गारंटीकर्ता। *v.* 1. to give a guarantee, गारंटी देना। 2. to be a guarantee for, to furnish security for, ज़मानत देना। 3. to state with certainty, विश्वासपूर्वक कहना। 4. to promise, वचन देना, ज़िम्मा लेना।

guard (गार्ड) *v.* 1. to watch over, पहरा देना, निगरानी करना। 2. to protect or defend, रक्षा करना। 3. to keep in check, नियंत्रण में रखना, संभालना। 4. to take precautions, सतर्कता बरतना, सावधानी बरतना। *n.* 1. one who protects, रक्षक, रखवाला। 2. a sentry or armed escort, सिपाही या सशस्त्र मार्गरक्षक। 3. an official in charge of a railway train, गार्ड। 4. watchful care, vigilance, निगरानी, पहरा, देख-रेख। 5. safety, रक्षा, बचाव। 6. a defensive attitude, सुरक्षात्मक दृष्टिकोण।

guarded (गार्डिड) *adj.* 1. cautious, careful, सतर्क या सतर्कतापूर्ण। 2. discreet, विवेकपूर्ण, समझदारी-भरा।

guardian (गार्डिअन) *n.* 1. one who guards, रक्षक। 2. a person who is legally responsible for the safety and maintenance of a minor or lady, अभिभावक। 3. one who looks after and protects someone's property, संरक्षक, परिरक्षक। *adj.* protecting, रक्षा करनेवाला।

guava (ग्वावा) *n.* a tree and its fruit, अमरूद।

gubernatorial (गबर्नेटोरिअल) *adj.* pertaining to a governor, राज्यपाल-संबंधी।

gudgeon (गजन) *n.* 1. a small fish, एक प्रकार की छोटी मछली। 2. a person who is easily cheated, भोला।

guerrilla, guerilla (गरिला) *n.* a member of an armed band that uses harassing tactics against the regular army, छापामार; guerrilla war, छापामार युद्ध।

G

guess (गेस) ***v.*** 1. to form an estimate based on insufficient information, अंदाज़ करना, अनुमान लगाना। 2. to suppose, मान लेना, समझना। 3. to form an opinion, राय बनाना। ***n.*** an estimate, अंदाज़, अनुमान।

guest (गेस्ट) ***n.*** 1. a person who receives hospitality at the home of another, अतिथि, मेहमान, अभ्यागत। 2. a person staying at a hotel, होटल में ठहरनेवाला व्यक्ति, मेहमान।

guest house (गेस्ट-हॉउस) ***n.*** a private boarding house offering accommodation, अतिथिगृह, अतिथिशाला।

guest room (गेस्ट-रूम) ***n.*** a room reserved for guests, अतिथि-कक्ष।

guffaw (गफ़ॉ) ***n.*** a coarse and boisterous laugh, a hearty laugh, ठहाका। ***v.*** to give a guffaw, ठहाका लगाना।

guidance (गाइडेन्स) ***n.*** 1. the act of guiding or the state of being guided, मार्गदर्शन। 2. counselling, परामर्श।

guide (गाइड) ***n.*** 1. one who shows the way, मार्गदर्शक। 2. one who leads others, नेता, अगुआ। 3. one who leads a tour, गाइड। 4. a handbook of information about a place or subject, संदर्शिका, मार्गदर्शिका। ***v.*** 1. to act as guide to, मार्गदर्शन करना, रास्ता दिखलाना। 2. to supervise, निर्देशित करना।

guild (गिल्ड) ***n.*** 1. an association of merchants, craftsmen etc., संघ। 2. an organisation or club, संघटन, क्लब।

guile (गाइल) ***n.*** craftiness, छल, धूर्तता।

guileless (गाइललिस) ***adj.*** straightforward, निश्छल, ईमानदार।

guillotine (गिलटीन) ***n.*** 1. a machine for beheading criminals, एक मशीन जिससे अपराधियों का सिर काटा जाता था। 2. a cutting machine, कटाई मशीन।

guilt (गिल्ट) ***n.*** 1. the fact or feeling of having done wrong, दोषभावना, दोषभार। 2. the responsibility for a criminal offence, अपराधिता। 3. an offence or crime, दोष, अपराध, पाप।

guilty (गिल्टी) ***adj.*** responsible for an offence or crime, दोषी, अपराधी।

guinea (गिनी) ***n.*** an old British gold coin, गिन्नी।

guinea pig ***n.*** a small rodent, बिसचूहिया की जाति का एक जीव, गिनी-पिग।

guise (गाइज़) ***n.*** 1. outward appearance, बाह्य रूप। 2. clothing, dress, वेशभूषा, वेश। 3. false appearance, छद्मरूप, छद्मावरण।

guitar (गिटार) ***n.*** a stringed musical instrument, गिटार।

gulch (गल्च) ***n.*** a ravine, खड्ड।

gulf (गल्फ़) ***n.*** 1. a large area of sea partially enclosed by land, खाड़ी, गल्फ़। 2. a deep wide hole, गहरा गड्ढा, खाई। 3. a wide difference or gap, विषमता, खाई।

gull[1] (गल) ***n.*** a webbed feet large seabird with long wings, मुर्गाबी, गल।

gull[2] ***n.*** a person who is easily befooled, घोंचू, भोला-भाला। ***v.*** to befool, मूर्ख बनाना।

gullet (गलिट) ***n.*** 1. the passage by which food goes from the mouth to the stomach, कंठनाल। 2. the throat, कंठ, गला।

gullible (गलिबल) ***adj.*** easily befooled or cheated, भोला-भाला।

gully (गली) ***n.*** 1. a channel cut by heavy rainwater, बरसाती नाला। 2. a fielding position between slip and point in cricket, गली।

gulp (गल्प) ***v.*** 1. to eat or drink hastily or greedily, निगलना, भकोसना, गटकना। 2. to breathe quickly, जल्दी-जल्दी साँस लेना, हाँफना। ***n.*** 1. the act of gulping, निगलने की क्रिया या भाव। 2. a large mouthful, बड़ा कौर।

gum[1] (गम) ***n.*** the fleshy tissue that covers the jaw bones, मसूड़ा।

gum[2] ***n.*** a water-soluble sticky substance that comes out of certain trees, गोंद। ***v.*** to stick with gum, गोंद से चिपकाना।

gummy (गमी) ***adj.*** covered with gum, sticky, चिपचिपा, गोंदीला।

gumption (गम्पशन) ***n.*** common sense, समझ, सहजबुद्धि।

gun (गन) ***n.*** 1. a weapon that sends bullets from a metal tube, बंदूक या तोप। 2. a device which forces out and spreads a substance by pressure, पिचकारी। ***v.*** to shoot with a gun, गोली मारना, तोप से उड़ाना।

gunman (गनमैन) ***n.*** an armed person, बंदूकधारी।

gunnery (गनरी) ***n.*** 1. the science of constructing and operating large guns or cannons, तोप विद्या। 2. the guns collectively, तोपख़ाना। 3. the firing of the guns, गोलाबारी।

gunny (गनी) ***n.*** a coarse fabric made of jute, टाट।

gunpowder (गनपाउडर) ***n.*** an explosive powder, बारूद।

gunsmith (गनस्मिथ) ***n.*** one who makes or repairs firearms, बंदूकें बनानेवाला या बंदूकों की मरम्मत करनेवाला।

gurgle (गर्गल) ***v.*** to make low sounds, गरगर या गड़गड़ शब्द करना। ***n.*** the sound of gurgling, गरगर, गड़गड़।

gush (गश) ***v.*** 1. to flow or pour out suddenly and in large quantity, फूट या बह निकलना। 2. to utter or admire in a sentimental manner, भावुकतापूर्वक कुछ कहना या बड़ाई करना। ***n.*** 1. a sudden and violent flow, सहसा होनेवाला तेज़ बहाव, धार। 2. act of admiring in a sentimental manner, भावुकतापूर्ण प्रशंसा। 3. show of emotion, आवेश।

gust (गस्ट) ***n.*** 1. a sudden strong rush of wind, rain or smoke, झोंका। 2. an outburst of emotion, झोंक, भावावेग। ***v.*** to blow in gusts, झोंके आना या चलना।

gusto (गस्टो) ***n.*** 1. zeal, उत्साह, जोश। 2. vigorous enjoyment, मौज-मस्ती, चाव, आनंद।

gut (गट) ***n.*** 1. food pipe, आहार-नली। 2. (plu.) the intestines, अँतड़ी, आँतें। 3. a cord made from animal intestines, ताँत। 4. (plu.) courage, will-power, साहस। 5. (plu.) value; force. महत्त्व; शक्ति। 6. (plu.) inner parts or contents of something, भीतरी पुर्ज़े या विषयवस्तु। ***adj.*** 1. fundamental, मूलभूत। 2. instinctive, सहज, नैसर्गिक। ***v.*** 1. to remove the guts from, अँतड़ियाँ निकाल देना। 2. to destroy the internal parts or the contents of, खोखला कर देना, सब-कुछ निकाल या नष्ट कर देना।

G

gutter (गटर) ***n.*** 1. a channel at the side of a street for draining off water, नाली, नाला, गंदा नाला। 2. poverty-stricken environment, दरिद्रताजन्य स्थिति।

guttural (गटरल) ***adj.*** 1. of or relating to the throat, कंठ-संबंधी, कंठ्य; guttural sound, कंठध्वनि।

guttural-labial (गटरल-लेबिअल) ***adj.*** pertaining to the throat as well as lips, कंठ्योष्ठ्य।

guttural-palatal (गटरल-पैलेटल) ***adj.*** pertaining to the throat and palate (the roof of the mouth), कंठ्यतालव्य।

guy[1] (गाइ) ***n.*** a rope, chain or cable used for steadying or guiding, कोई चीज़ स्थिर रखने या कहीं लाने-ले जाने के लिए प्रयुक्त रस्सा।

guy[2] ***n.*** 1. a man, व्यक्ति, आदमी। 2. a person in odd clothes, फूहड़ व्यक्ति।

guzzle (गज़ल) ***v.*** to eat or drink greedily, भकोसना, गटकना।

gym (जिम) ***n.*** a gymnasium, जिमख़ाना।

gymkhana (जिमकाना) ***n.*** the place for sports events, जिमख़ाना।

gymnasium (जिम्नेज़ियम) ***n.*** a room or hall equipped for teaching or practising gymnastics, व्यायामशाला।

gymnast (जिम्नैस्ट) ***n.*** an expert in physical exercises, व्यायाम-विशेषज्ञ, व्यायाम-कुशल, जिमनास्ट, व्यायामी।

gymnastics (जिम्नैस्टिक्स) ***n.*** 1. (plu.) athletic exercises, जिमनास्टिक्स, व्यायाम।

gynaecology (गाइनिकॉलोजी) ***n.*** study of the female reproductive system and its diseases, स्त्रीरोग-विज्ञान।

gynephobia (जाइनिफ़ोबिआ) ***n.*** abnormal fear of women, स्त्रीभीति, नारीभय।

gypsum (जिप्सम) ***n.*** a white mineral, एक प्रकार का सफ़ेद रंग का खनिज, जिप्सम।

gypsy (जिप्सी) ***n.*** a member of a nomadic tribe, जिप्सी, ख़ानाबदोश।

gyrate (जाइरेट) ***v.*** to revolve, घूमना, चक्कर खाना।

H, h (एच) ***n.*** the eighth letter of the English alphabet, अंग्रेज़ी वर्णमाला का आठवाँ वर्ण।

ha (हा) ***interj.*** an exclamation of surprise, ओह, वाह!

habeas corpus (हेबिअस कॉर्पस) ***n.*** a writ issued to bring a person before a court to prevent his unlawful detention, बंदी प्रत्यक्षीकरण।

habit (हैबिट) ***n.*** 1. usual behaviour or tendency, आदत, बान, अभ्यास। 2. the customary dress of a particular occupation, किसी पेशे के लोगों का पहनावा।

habitable (हैबिटेबल) ***adj.*** suitable to live in, रहने लायक, निवास-योग्य।

habitant (हैबिटेन्ट) ***n.*** an inhabitant, वासी।

habitat (हैबिटैट) ***n.*** the natural home or locality of a plant or animal, प्राकृतिक वास।

habitation (हैबिटेशन) ***n.*** a dwelling place, निवास, निवास-स्थान।

habitual (हैबिचुअल) ***adj.*** 1. done regularly and repeatedly, अभ्यासजनित, आभ्यासिक। 2. usual, regular, सामान्य, नियमित। 3. doing something as a habit, आदी, अभ्यस्त।

habituate (हैबिचुएट) ***v.*** to accustom by repetition or exposure, आदी हो जाना, आदत पड़ जाना।

hack[1] (हैक) ***v.*** to cut or chop roughly, काटना, चीरना। ***n.*** 1. a cut from a blow or kick, कटाव, चीरा, आघात। 2. an agricultural instrument, फावड़ा, गैंती।

hack[2] ***n.*** 1. a worn-out horse, बूढ़ा घोड़ा, सामान्य घोड़ा। 2. one who is hired to do routine writing, भाड़े का लेखक। 3. a taxi, टैक्सी। ***adj.*** 1. hired, भाड़े का, किराए का। 2. hackneyed, घिसा-पिटा, साधारण, मामूली। ***v.*** to ride on horseback, घुड़सवारी करना।

hacking cough ***n.*** a cough in short dry bursts, खोंखों, सूखी खाँसी।

hackney (हैक्नी) ***n.*** 1. a horse for ordinary riding, सवारी का साधारण घोड़ा। 2. a taxi or coach for hire, टैक्सी।

hackneyed (हैक्नीड) ***adj.*** commonplace, trite, साधारण, घिसा-पिटा।

hacksaw (हैकसॉ) ***n.*** a saw used for cutting metal, धातु काटने की आरी।

had (हैड) ***v.*** p.t. & p.p. of have.

haematology (हीमेटॉलोजी) ***n.*** the branch of medical science dealing with diseases of the blood, रक्त-रोग विज्ञान।

haemoglobin (हीमोग्लोबिन) ***n.*** a red colouring matter in the blood, हीमोग्लोबिन।

haemophilia (हीमोफ़िलिआ) ***n.*** a hereditary human disease which causes severe bleeding from even a slight injury, अधिक रक्तस्राव का रोग, हीमोफिलिया।

haemorrhage (हेमरिज) ***n.*** flow of blood form ruptured blood vessels, रक्तस्राव।

H

haft (हैफ़्ट) ***n.*** the handle of a knife, axe etc., मूठ, दस्ता, हैंडल।

haggard (हैगर्ड) ***adj.*** 1. looking exhausted, थका-हारा। 2. careworn, चिंताग्रस्त।

haggle (हैगल) ***v.*** to argue in an attempt to bargain, मोल-भाव करना। ***n.*** the act of haggling, मोल-भाव; हुज्जत।

haiku (हाइकू) ***n.*** a type of Japanese poems in 17 syllables, १७ अक्षरोंवाली जापानी कविता, हाइकू।

hail[1] (हेल) ***n.*** 1. the frozen rain drops falling in a shower, ओलों की बौछार। 2. something coming in great numbers, बाढ़, बौछार। ***v.*** to fall as hail, ओले पड़ना।

hail[2] ***v.*** 1. to salute or greet, अभिवादन करना, स्वागत करना। 2. to recognize or acknowledge, मानना, स्वीकार करना, अपनाना, मान्यता देना। 3. to signal or call to, बुलाने या ठहरने के लिए संकेत करना, आवाज़ लगाना। □ **hail from,** मूल निवासी होना, से आना।

hailstone (हेलस्टोन) ***n.*** a small ball of hail, ओला।

hair (हेअर) ***n.*** 1. a fine threadlike growth from the skin, बाल, रोआँ, रोम। 2. a covering of such growth, बाल, केशराशि, केश।

hairbreadth (हेअरब्रेड्थ) ***n.*** a minute distance, बाल बराबर दूरी।

haircut (हेअरकट) ***n.*** 1. a shortening of the hair by cutting, केश कर्तन, हजामत। 2. the style in which one's hair is cut in, बाल काटने का ढंग।

hairdo (हेअरडू) ***n.*** 1. the act or process of setting and arranging the hair, बाल सँवारने का काम, कंघी-चोटी। 2. a hair style, बाल सँवारने का ढंग, केश-विन्यास।

hairdresser (हेअरड्रेसर) ***n.*** a person who shapes the hair into a style by cutting, setting and colouring, केशकर्मी।

hairless (हेअरलिस) ***adj.*** with no hair, बिन बालों का, केशविहीन, गंजा।

hairline (हेअरलाइन) ***n.*** 1. a very thin line, अति सूक्ष्म रेखा, बाल बराबर पतली रेखा। 2. a very narrow crack, बहुत बारीक दरार।

hairpin (हेअरपिन) ***n.*** a pin for keeping hair in position on the head, हेअरपिन, क्लिप।

hair-raising (हेअररेज़िंग) ***adj.*** causing one's hair stand, horrifying, रोमांचक।

hairy (हेअरी) ***adj.*** 1. full of hair, covered with hair, बालों से भरा, बालोंवाला। 2. like hair, बाल-जैसा। 3. causing fear, dangerous, भयानक, ख़तरनाक।

hale (हेल) ***adj.*** sound in health, healthy, स्वस्थ, चंगा।

half (हाफ़) ***n.*** (plu. halves) 1. either of the two equal parts into which something is divided, आधा भाग, आधा। 2. either of the two time periods that make up a game, आधा समय। ***adj.*** 1. being half in amount or quantity, आधा, अर्ध। 2. incomplete, अपूर्ण। 3. partial, आंशिक।

halfback (हाफ़बैक) ***n.*** one of the two players in the game of hocky or football whose position is between the forwards and the backs, हाफ़बैक।

H

half-baked (हाफ़बेक्ड) ***adj.*** partly baked, अधपका।

half-breed (हाफ़ब्रीड) ***n.*** a person having parents of different ethnic races, वर्णसंकर, दोगला।

half-hearted (हाफ़हार्टिड) ***adj.*** lacking interest or enthusiasm, बेमन से काम करनेवाला या बेमन से किया जानेवाला।

half-mast (हाफ़मास्ट) ***n.*** the position of a flag lowered halfway down the staff as a sign of mourning, आधा झुका झंडा।

half-time (हाफ़-टाइम) ***n.*** the intermission between halves, आधा समय, मध्यांतर।

halftone (हाफ़टोन) ***n.*** an illustration or block in which light and dark shades are reproduced by means of small and large dots, हाफ़टोन, बिंदुचित्र।

halfwit (हाफ़विट) ***n.*** a foolish person, मूर्ख व्यक्ति।

halitosis (हैलिटोसिस) ***n.*** bad breath, श्वास की गंध, मुँह की बदबू।

hall (हॉल) ***n.*** a large room, बड़ा कमरा, हाल, विशाल कक्ष।

hallmark (हॉलमार्क) ***n.*** 1. a mark placed on an article of genuineness or high quality, प्रामाणिकता या श्रेष्ठतासूचक चिह्न, निशानी। 2. a distinguished characteristic, महत्त्वपूर्ण विशेषता।

hallo (हैलो) ***interj.*** = hello.

hallucination (हेल्यूसिनेशन) ***n.*** 1. an illusion of seeing, hearing or experiencing something that does not really exist, भ्रम, मतिभ्रम, विभ्रम। 2. the thing seen, heard or experienced in this way, भ्रांति, विभ्रांति।

halo (हेलो) ***n.*** (plu. halos, haloes) 1. a disk of light surrounding the head of a holy person, प्रभामंडल। 2. a bright circle of light around a luminous body, प्रकाशचक्र।

halt (हॉल्ट) ***v.*** 1. to cease moving, to stop, रुकना, ठहरना। 2. to bring to a halt, रोकना। 3. to falter, लड़खड़ाना, लंगड़ाना। ***n.*** 1. the act of halting, विराम। 2. stopping place, पड़ाव। 3. a small railway station or bus-stop, छोटा रेलवे स्टेशन या बस-स्टाप।

halve (हाव) ***v.*** 1. to divide into halves, दो हिस्से करना। 2. to reduce by half, आधा हो जाना।

ham (हैम) ***n.*** 1. the upper part of the hind leg of a pig, सुअर की रान। 2. the back of the thigh and buttock, पुट्ठा। 3. a performer who overacts, अस्वाभाविक अभिनय या ओवर एक्टिंग करनेवाला अभिनेता। ***v.*** to overact, अस्वाभाविक अभिनय करना, ओवर-एक्टिंग करना।

hamlet (हैम्लिट) ***n.*** a small village, छोटा गाँव, पुरवा।

hammer (हैमर) ***n.*** 1. a hand tool with a heavy head for driving nails, breaking things etc., हथौड़ा, हथौड़ी। 2. something shaped like this, हथौड़ी। ***v.*** to strike with a hammer, हथौड़ी से ठोंका या पीटा जाना।

hammock (हैमक) ***n.*** a hanging bed of netting suspended between two supports, दो खूँटियों से बँधा जालीदार झूला।

hamper[1] (हैम्पर) ***v.*** to hinder or impede, बाधा पहुँचाना, अवरुद्ध करना।

H

hamper[2] ***n.*** a large basket with a cover, पिटारा।

hamstring (हैम्स्ट्रिंग) ***n.*** a cordlike tendon at the back of the leg, घुटने के पीछे की नस, घुटनस। ***v.*** 1. to cut the hamstring, घुटनस काट देना। 2. to cripple or impede the efficiency (of, को) पंगु कर देना।

hand (हैन्ड) ***n.*** 1. the end part of the arm below the wrist, हाथ। 2. active help, सक्रिय सहायता। 3. a workman, कार्यकर्ता। 4. workmanship, कारीगरी, कौशल। 5. handwriting, लिखावट। 6. side or direction, तरफ़, ओर। 7. the cards held by or dealt to a player, बाज़ी। 8. a unit of four inches used in measuring a horse's height, घोड़े की ऊँचाई नापने का चार अंगुल का नाप, मुट्ठी। 9. the indicator on a dial, सुई। 10. applause, करतलध्वनि, साधुवाद। □ **at hand,** पास ही; **from hand to mouth,** जिसका गुज़ारा बड़ी मुश्किल से हो रहा हो; **get the upper hand of,** नियंत्रण में लाना; **lay hands on,** क़ब्ज़ा करना; **lend a hand,** सहायता करना; **off hand,** एकाएक; **on hand,** उपलब्ध; **show one's hand,** इरादा जतलाना; **wash one's hands of,** संबंध तोड़ लेना, नाता न रखना; **win hands down,** सरलता से जीत लेना। ***v.*** 1. to give, देना। 2. to help, सहायता करना।

handbag (हैन्डबैग) ***n.*** a bag for holding small personal articles, हैंडबैग।

handball (हैन्डबॉल) ***n.*** a game played with a ball, हैंडबाल।

handbill (हैन्डबिल) ***n.*** a printed notice distributed by hand, हैंडबिल, पर्चा, इश्तहार।

handbook (हैन्डबुक) ***n.*** a small book that provides useful information, पुस्तिका।

handcuff (हैन्डकफ़) ***n.*** one of a pair of metal rings that can be locked around the prisoner's wrist, हथकड़ी। ***v.*** to put handcuffs on, हथकड़ी पहनाना।

handful (हैन्डफुल) ***n.*** 1. the quantity that can be held in the hand, मुट्ठी-भर। 2. a small number of people or things, गिनती के लोग या वस्तुएँ।

handicap (हैन्डिकैप) ***n.*** 1. a disadvantage, कठिनाई, बाधा, असुविधा, अड़ंगा। 2. a competition in which disadvantages are imposed, सप्रतिबंध प्रतियोगिता। 3. a defect, disability or deficiency, दोष, अक्षमता या कमी। ***v.*** 1. to impose handicap(s) on, बाधा(एँ) खड़ी करना। 2. to hinder, रोकना।

handicapped (हैन्डिकैप्ड) ***adj.*** physically or mentally disabled, असमर्थ, पंगु, विकलांग।

handicraft (हैन्डिक्राफ़्ट) ***n.*** 1. the skill with the hands, हस्तकौशल। 2. a craft or occupation requiring such skill, हस्तशिल्प, हस्तकला, दस्तकारी।

handkerchief (हैंग्कर्चिफ़) ***n.*** a small square of cloth for wiping the nose, mouth etc., रूमाल।

handle (हैन्डल) ***n.*** a part of an object that is held or manipulated with the hand, मूठ, हत्था, हैंडल। ***v.*** 1. to touch, feel or move with the hands, हाथ से छूना, उठाना-रखना या हटाना-बढ़ाना। 2. to operate, परिचालन करना, चलाना। 3. to manage, प्रबंध करना। 4. to treat, बरताव करना। 5. to deal in, व्यापार करना।

H

handmade (हैन्डमेड) ***adj.*** made by hand, हस्तनिर्मित।

handout (हैन्डआॅउट) ***n.*** 1. anything given to a beggar or poor, भिक्षा, दान। 2. a leaflet, पर्चा, इश्तहार।

handshake (हैन्डशेक) ***n.*** the act of grasping each other's right hand when two people meet or leave each other, हथमिलाव।

handsome (हैन्सम) ***adj.*** 1. beautiful, good-looking, सुंदर, चारु, ख़ूबसूरत। 2. ample, plentiful, समुचित, प्रचुर।

handwriting (हैन्डराइटिंग) ***n.*** 1. the writing by hand, लिखावट, हस्तलेख, हस्तलिपि। 2. the style of writing peculiar to each person, लिखावट, लेखन-शैली।

handy (हैन्डी) ***adj.*** 1. easy to use or handle, सहज, सुगम, उपयोगी। 2. manually adroit, दक्ष, प्रवीण, पटु। 3. near, समीपस्थ।

hang (हैंग) ***v.*** (hung, hanging) 1. to fasten from above with no support from below, लटकाना, टाँगना। 2. to be fastened in this way, लटकना, टँगना। 3. to droop, लटकना, झुकना। 4. (p.p. & p.t. hanged) to execute by suspending by the neck from a noose, फाँसी पर टाँगना या लटकाना। □ **hang about,** आसपास आवारा फिरना; **hang around,** आवारा फिरना, मँडराना; **hang back,** हिचकना; **hang on,** (i) कसकर पकड़े रहना; (ii) भरोसे पर रहना, भरोसा करना; (iii) जुटे या जमे रहना; (iv) थोड़ी प्रतीक्षा करना। ***n.*** 1. the way in which something hangs, लटके होने की अवस्था या भाव, लटकन। 2. the particular meaning, कोई विशिष्ट अर्थ। 3. the proper method of doing something, ढंग, ढब, पद्धति।

hangar (हैंगर) ***n.*** a shed where aircrafts are kept or repaired, विमान-घर।

hanger (हैंगर) ***n.*** a device for hanging a garment on, हैंगर।

hanging (हैंगिंग) ***n.*** an execution by hanging, फाँसी।

hangings (हैंगिंग्स) ***n.*** (plu.) curtains etc. hung on walls, doors, windows etc., परदे तथा लटकाई जानेवाली अन्य चीज़ें।

hangover (हैंगओवर) ***n.*** unpleasant aftereffects resulting from drinking too much alcohol, शराब की ख़ुमारी।

hank (हैंक) ***n.*** a coil of thread or wool, अट्टी, लच्छी।

hanker (हैंकर) ***v.*** to have a longing, लालायित होना, आतुर होना, ललक जगना।

hanky-panky (हैंकी-पैंकी) ***n.*** 1. mischievous behaviour, बेतुका व्यवहार, छेड़छाड़। 2. deceit, धोखा, छल।

haphazard (हैपहैज़र्ड) ***adv.*** characterized by lack of order or plan, गड्डमड्ड, ऊटपटांग, विशृंखलित।

hapless (हैपलिस) ***adj.*** unfortunate, अभागा।

happen (हैपन) ***v.*** 1. to take place, घटित होना। 2. to take place by chance, संयोग से होना।

happening (हैपनिंग) ***n.*** an event, घटना।

happy (हैपी) ***adj.*** 1. feeling pleasure or joy, ख़ुश, प्रसन्न, सुखी। 2. pleasing, सुखद। 3. characterized by good fortune, शुभ।

H

happy-go-lucky (हैपी-गो-लकी) ***adj.*** easy-going, carefree, बेफ़िक्र, मनमौजी।

harangue (हैरैंग) ***n.*** a bombastic and lengthy speech, लंबा-चौड़ा भाषण। ***v.*** to make a harangue (to), लंबा भाषण देना।

harass (हैरस) ***v.*** 1. to annoy or irritate continually, बराबर तंग करना, परेशान कर डालना। 2. to irritate (an enemy) by repeated raids, (शत्रु पर) बार-बार आक्रमण कर उसे परेशान कर डालना।

harassment (हैरसमेन्ट) ***n.*** an act of harassing or the state of being harassed, परेशानी, व्यथा, तवालत।

harbinger (हार्बिन्जर) ***n.*** one who or that announces the approach of another, अग्रदूत।

harbour, harbor (हार्बर) ***n.*** 1. a place of shelter for ships, बंदरगाह। 2. a place of shelter, शरणस्थल। ***v.*** 1. to give shelter to, शरण देना। 2. to protect, रक्षा करना। 3. to hold a thought or feeling about, (किसी के प्रति कोई बात) मन में रखना, धारणा बनाना।

hard (हार्ड) ***adj.*** 1. resistant to pressure, firm, कड़ा, कठोर, सख़्त। 2. difficult to cut or break, जिसे सरलता से काटा या तोड़ा न जा सके, कड़ा। 3. difficult to do or understand, दुष्कर, दुरूह। 4. intense, severe, तीव्र, उग्र, प्रचंड। 5. energetic, परिश्रमी। 6. unjust, cruel, कठोर, निर्मम, नृशंस। 7. real, वास्तविक; hard facts, वास्तविक तथ्य। 8. strongly alcoholic, तेज़ (शराब)। 9. (of water) containing mineral salts, खनिज तत्त्वों से युक्त (जल)। 10. (currency) money which cannot be exchanged freely, दुर्लभ (मुद्रा)। ***adv.*** 1. with great effort, मुश्किल से। 2. heavily, ज़ोर से। 3. severely, कठोरता से।

hardbitten (हार्डबिटन) ***adj.*** stubborn, दृढ़, हठी।

harden (हार्डन) ***v.*** 1. to become hard, कठोर या कड़ा हो जाना। 2. to cause to become hard, कड़ा या कठोर बनाना।

hardheaded (हार्डहेडिड) ***adj.*** practical, realistic, व्यवहारशील, दुनियादार।

hardhearted (हार्डहार्टिड) ***adj.*** unsympathetic, cold, निर्दय, कठोर।

hard luck (हार्ड लक) ***n.*** bad luck, दुर्भाग्य, बदक़िस्मती।

hardly (हार्डली) ***adv.*** 1. with difficulty, मुश्किल से, कठिनाई से। 2. almost not, not at all, बिल्कुल नहीं। 3. not really, वस्तुत: नहीं। 4. in a hard manner, सख़्ती से।

hardness (हार्डनिस) ***n.*** the quality of being hard, कड़ापन, कठोरता; कड़ाई, सख़्ती।

hardship (हार्डशिप) ***n.*** 1. that which is hard to bear, suffering, कठिनाई, विपत्ति। 2. lack of necessities, अभाव, तंगी।

hardware (हार्डवेअर) ***n.*** 1. metal goods, tools and utensils, धातु के बर्तन तथा उपकरण। 2. the mechanical and electronic parts of a computer, हार्डवेअर।

hardwood (हार्डवुड) ***n.*** tough timber, मज़बूत लकड़ी, कठोर लकड़ी।

hardy (हार्डी) ***adj.*** strong and rugged, तगड़ा, मज़बूत, सशक्त।

hare (हेअर) ***n.*** a rabbit-like mammal with long ears, खरगोश।

harebrained (हेअरब्रेन्ड) ***adj.*** 1. wild and foolish, उतावला, अव्यावहारिक।

harelipped (हेअरलिप्ड) ***adj.*** having split upper lip, कटावदार होंठवाला।

harem (हैरम) ***n.*** 1. part of a house in which (Muslim) women live, हरम, अंतःपुर, रनिवास। 2. the women who live in this, हरम में रहनेवाली औरतें (बेगमें, रखैलें, नौकरानियाँ आदि)।

hark (हार्क) ***v.*** to listen carefully, ध्यान से सुनना। ☐ **hark back,** पिछली बात या विषय पर लौटना, गड़े मुर्दे उखाड़ना।

harlequin (हार्लिक्विन) ***n.*** a clownlike character in pantomime, मसखरा, विदूषक। ***adj.*** dressed in multi-coloured clothing, जो विदूषकों की तरह रंग-बिरंगे कपड़े पहने हो।

harlot (हार्लट) ***n.*** a prostitute, वेश्या, रंडी।

harm (हार्म) ***n.*** an injury or damage, नुकसान, हानि, क्षति, चोट। ***v.*** to cause harm to, हानि या क्षति करना, चोट पहुँचाना।

harmonic (हार्मोनिक) ***adj.*** having a harmonious sound, समस्वरित, समरस।

harmonium (हार्मोनिअम) ***n.*** a musical instrument, with metal reeds, हारमोनियम।

harmony (हार्मनी) ***n.*** 1. the combination of musical sounds pleasing to the ears, समस्वरता, श्रुतिमाधुर्य। 2. pleasing and peaceful relationship, मधुर संबंध, समरसता। 3. agreement, accord, संगति, ताल-मेल। 4. peacefulness, शांति।

harness (हार्निस) ***n.*** 1. the straps and fittings of a horse, घोड़े का साज़। 2. a strap, पट्टी, फीता। ***v.*** 1. to put a harness on, (घोड़े पर) साज़ डालना या पहनाना। 2. to control, नियंत्रित करना।

harp (हार्प) ***n.*** a musical instrument with long strings, हार्प नामक बाजा। ***v.*** to play a harp, हार्प बजाना।

harpoon (हार्पून) ***n.*** a spear with a long rope used as a missile, भाला, हार्पून। ***v.*** to hunt with a harpoon, हार्पून से शिकार करना।

harrier (हैरिअर) ***n.*** 1. one who harries, धावे पर धावा बोलनेवाला, बार-बार तंग या परेशान करनेवाला। 2. a kind of falcon, बाज़ पक्षी।

harrow (हैरो) ***n.*** a farm implement with teeth or disks for breaking up soil, जोते हुए खेत में मिट्टी के ढेले तोड़ने का दाँतेदार उपकरण, हैरो। ***v.*** 1. to break up soil with a harrow, हैरो चलाना, पाटा फेरना। 2. to torment, यातना देना, सताना।

harry (हैरी) ***v.*** 1. to trouble continually, परेशान किए रहना, निरंतर तंग करना। 2. to attack repeatedly, बार-बार आक्रमण करना।

harsh (हार्श) ***adj.*** 1. unpleasant to the sense of hearing, कर्णकटु, कटु, कड़वा। 2. severe, stern, उग्र, कड़ा। 3. cruel, निर्दय, क्रूर, क्रूरतापूर्ण।

hartal (हरटाल) ***n.*** closing of shops and stopping of work as a sign of dissatisfaction, हड़ताल।

harvest (हार्विस्ट) ***n.*** 1. the act of gathering crops, फ़सल की कटाई, लुनाई। 2. the season when this is done, फ़सल काटने का समय या ऋतु, कटनी। 3. a gathered crop, उपज, पैदावार, फ़सल। 4. the product of any action, परिणाम, फल। ***v.*** 1. to gather crop, फ़सल की कटाई करना; फ़सल इकट्ठी करना। 2. to acquire, प्राप्त करना, पाना।

H

harvest moon *n.* the full moon in autumn, शरच्चंद्र, शरद् पूर्णिमा।

has (हैज़) *v.* third person singular, present tense of have, रखता है, (के) पास है।

hash (हैश) *n.* 1. a dish of chopped meat, क़ीमा। 2. a mess or mixed-up affair, घाल-मेल, गड्डमड्ड। *v.* 1. to mince or chop up, क़ीमा करना। 2. to mess up, घाल-मेल करना, गड्डमड्ड करना।

hashish (हैशिश) *n.* a narcotic extract prepared from the dried flowers of hemp, चरस, हशिश।

hasp (हैस्प) *n.* a metal fastener for a door, box etc., कुंडी।

hassle (हैसल) *n.* 1. an argument or quarrel, तर्क या विवाद। 2. something troublesome or annoying, कठिन कार्य, मुश्किल काम, परेशानी। *v.* 1. to argue or quarrel, तर्क या विवाद करना। 2. to bother or harass, परेशान करना।

haste (हेस्ट) *n.* 1. quickness, hurry, शीघ्रता, जल्दी। 2. rashness, जल्दबाज़ी, हड़बड़ी। 3. swiftness, तेज़ी, तेज़ रफ़्तार।

hasten (हेसन) *v.* 1. to move swiftly, तेज़ी से आगे बढ़ना, जल्दी करना। 2. to cause to move swifty, तेज़ी से आगे बढ़ाना।

hat (हैट) *n.* a covering for the head, हैट।

hatch[1] (हैच) *n.* an opening, द्वार या मार्ग।

hatch[2] *v.* 1. to produce young ones from the egg, अंडे सेना। 2. to emerge from an egg, अंडे से निकलना। 3. to make up a plan in secret, चोरी-छिपे योजना बनाना, खिचड़ी पकाना। *n.* 1. the act of hatching, अंडे सेने का कार्य। 2. that which is hatched, अंडे से निकला हुआ जीव।

hatchery (हैचरी) *n.* a place where eggs are hatched, अंडे सेने का स्थान।

hatchet (हैचिट) *n.* a short-handled axe, कुल्हाड़ी। □ **bury the hatchet,** विवाद को दूर कर मेल करना।

hatching (हैचिंग) *n.* the drawing of closely spaced parallel lines, समानांतर रेखांकन।

hate (हेट) *v.* 1. to dislike intensely, घृणा करना, नफ़रत करना। 2. to have a great dislike (of), नफ़रत होना। 3. to be reluctant, अनिच्छुक होना, पसंद न होना। *n.* 1. intense dislike, hatred, घृणा, नफ़रत। 2. the thing hated or an object of hatred, नापसंद वस्तु या काम।

hatred (हेट्रिड) *n.* 1. hate, घृणा, नफ़रत। 2. animosity, द्वेष, वैर, विद्वेष।

hat trick *n.* three successes in a row, लगातार तीन सफलताएँ।

haughty (हॉटी) ***adj.*** 1. arrogant, अक्खड़, हेकड़, उद्धत। 2. disdainfully proud, scornful, अहंकारी।

haul (हॉल) *v.* 1. to pull or drag, धकेलना या घसीटना। 2. to cart, गाड़ी से (माल) ढोना, ढुलाई करना। 3. to force to appear, उपस्थिति के लिए बाध्य करना। *n.* 1. the act of hauling, धकेलने या घसीटने की क्रिया, 2. the distance over which something is hauled, (माल) ढोने की दूरी। 3. the amount of something gained, प्राप्त राशि, पाया या लूटा हुआ माल, लूट।

haunch (हॉन्च) *n.* the hip and upper thigh, नितंब, चूतड़, पुट्ठा।

haunt (हॉन्ट) *v.* 1. to visit or appear frequently to (as a ghost or spirit, प्रेत या आत्मा के रूप में (कहीं)जाते रहना,

लगना, दिखाई देते रहना। 2. to persecute by frequent visitations, बराबर आ धमकना, जा-जाकर तंग करना। 3. to linger in the mind of, दिमाग़ पर छाया रहना, कचोटते रहना।

haunted (हॉन्टिड) ***adj.*** frequented by a ghost or spirit, भुतहा।

have (हैव) ***v.*** (had, having) 1. to own or possess, होना, पास होना, रखना, रहना। 2. to possess as a characteristic quality, युक्त होना, धारण करना। 3. to experience, अनुभव होना या करना। 4. to be experiencing, अनुभूत होना, लगना, प्रभावित होना। 5. to receive or accept, लेना, प्राप्त करना, स्वीकार करना। 6. to cause a thing to be done, कराना। 7. used as an auxiliary with a past participle to form perfect tenses, इसका प्रयोग सहायक क्रिया के रूप में पूर्ण वर्तमान, पूर्ण भूत तथा पूर्ण भविष्यत् काल बनाने के लिए होता है।

haven (हेवन) ***n.*** 1. a place of safety, शरणस्थल, सुरक्षित स्थल। 2. a port, बंदरगाह।

haversack (हैवरसैक) ***n.*** a bag worn over the shoulder, झोला, थैला।

haves (हैव्ज़) ***n.*** (plu.) rich people, अमीर लोग।

havoc (हैवक) ***n.*** 1. widespread destruction, विनाश, तबाही, बर्बादी। 2. widespread confusion or disorder, अव्यवस्था, अशांति।

hawk[1] (हॉक) ***n.*** 1. a bird of prey, बाज़ पक्षी। 2. a hostile or a violent person, आक्रामक व्यक्ति, उग्रवादी।

hawk[2] ***v.*** to sell goods in the streets, घर-घर सामान बेचने के लिए जाना, फेरी लगाना।

hawk-eyed (हॉक-आइड) ***adj.*** having very keen eyesight, तीक्ष्ण दृष्टि।

hay (हे) ***n.*** grass or other herbage cut and dried for fodder, सूखी घास, भूसा।

haywire (हेवाइर) ***adj.*** 1. not functioning properly, जो ठीक से काम न कर रहा हो। 2. out of control, अनियंत्रित।

hazard (हैज़र्ड) ***n.*** 1. an obstacle, बाधा, रुकावट। 2. a risk or danger, जोखिम, ख़तरा। ***v.*** 1. to run the risk of, जोखिम उठाना, ख़तरा मोल लेना। 2. to expose to risk, ख़तरे में डालना।

hazardous (हैज़र्डस) ***adj.*** involving risk, dangerous, जोखिम-भरा, ख़तरनाक।

haze (हेज़) ***n.*** 1. thin mist, धुंध। 2. slightly mental confusion, हलकी भ्रांति, उलझन। ***v.*** 1. to become hazy, धुँधला हो जाना। 2. to make hazy, धुँधला कर देना। 3. to harass, परेशान करना।

hazel (हेज़ल) ***n.*** 1. a small tree bearing edible nuts, पिंघल वृक्ष। 2. yellowish brown colour, पीलापन लिये भूरा रंग। ***adj.*** yellowish brown, पीलापन लिये भूरे रंग का।

he (ही) ***pronoun.*** 1. third person singular pronoun used to refer a male or unspecified person, वह (पुरुष या व्यक्ति)। 2. a male animal, नर; he-goat, बकरा।

head (हेड) ***n.*** 1. the upper part of the body consisting of skull and brain, सिर। 2. the part of a bed where one rests one's head, सिरहाना। 3. the upper and higher end of something, अग्रभाग, शीर्ष। 4. the brain or mind, मस्तिष्क, मन।

H

5. the intellect or mental ability, बुद्धि। 6. the side of a coin with a person's head, बुत, चेहरा। 7. each individual in the group, व्यक्ति। 8. a single animal within a herd, पशु, रास। 9. the top part of a blister or boil, फोड़े का मुँह। 10. rounded upper part or top of something, गोल सिरा, सिर। 11. a leader or ruler, नेता, शासक। 12. the upper end of a stretch of water, उद्‌गम, दहाना। 13. an item, मद। ***adj.*** chief, मुख्य। ***v.*** 1. to be at the head of, सबसे आगे होना, अगुआई करना। 2. to be at the top of, सबसे ऊपर होना, शिखर पर होना। 3. to move in a certain direction, किसी दिशा में अग्रसर होना।

headache (हेडिक) ***n.*** 1. a pain of the head, सिरदर्द। 2. a problem or difficulty, समस्या, झमेला, सिरदर्द।

headgear (हेडगिअर) ***n.*** a covering for the head, सिर पर पहनने की टोपी, पगड़ी या टोप।

heading (हेडिंग) ***n.*** a word or words written as a title at the top of an article or poem, शीर्षक, हेडिंग।

headland (हेडलैन्ड) ***n.*** the highland jutting out into the sea, शीर्ष भूमि, अंतरीप।

headlight (हेडलाइट) ***n.*** a headlamp, हेडलाइट, हेडलैंप।

headline (हेडलाइन) ***n.*** a boldly printed heading at the top of the front page in a newspaper, मुख्य शीर्षक, सुर्ख़ी, मुख्य समाचार।

headlong (हेडलॉन्ग) ***adv.*** 1. headfirst, सिर के बल। 2. hastily, जल्दबाज़ी में।

headmaster (हेडमास्टर) ***n.*** the principal master of a school, प्रधानाचार्य, प्रधानाध्यापक। [Fem. headmistress, प्रधानाचार्या, प्रधानाध्यापिका]

head office (हेड ऑफ़िस) ***n.*** the principal office, प्रधान कार्यालय।

head-on (हेड-ऑन) ***adj.*** facing forward, सामने का।

headphone (हेडफ़ोन) ***n.*** an apparatus with receivers held over the ears, हेडफ़ोन।

headquarters (हेडक्वार्टर्ज़) ***n.*** (plu.) central office of an organisation, मुख्यालय।

headstrong (हेडस्ट्रॉन्ग) ***adj.*** obstinate, हठी, जिद्दी।

headway (हेडवे) ***n.*** progress, प्रगति।

heady (हेडी) ***adj.*** 1. rash, जल्दबाज़, उतावला। 2. intoxicating, नशीला। 3. violent, प्रचंड।

heal (हील) ***v.*** to return to health, स्वस्थ हो जाना।

health (हेल्थ) ***n.*** the overall condition of being free from illness, स्वास्थ्य, सेहत।

healthy (हेल्दी) ***adj.*** possessing good health, स्वस्थ, सेहतमंद, नीरोग।

heap (हीप) ***n.*** 1. a pile or mass of things, ढेर, अंबार। 2. (plu.) a great amount, lots, ढेरों। ***v.*** 1. to pile up, ढेर लगाना। 2. to be piled up, ढेर लगना। 3. to load with large quantities, लाद देना।

hear (हिअर) ***v.*** 1. to perceive by the ears, सुनना, कान में पड़ना। 2. to learn by hearing, सुनने में आना। 3. to listen with attention, ध्यान देना, सुनना। 4. to listen and try (a case

in a court) सुनवाई करना, सुनना। □ **Hear! Hear!** बहुत अच्छे! वाह वाह!

heard (हर्ड) ***v.*** p.t. & p.p. of hear.

hearing (हिअरिंग) ***n.*** 1. the ability or capacity to hear, श्रवण-शक्ति।2. a session for listening to arguments, सुनवाई, पेशी।

hearing aid ***n.*** a device worn by a partially deaf person to improve hearing, श्रवण-यंत्र।

hearsay (हिअरसे) ***n.*** information heard from another which may not be true, सुनी-सुनाई बात, अफ़वाह, उड़ती ख़बर।

hearse (हर्स) ***n.*** a vehicle for carrying the dead body to cemetery, शववाहन, शवयान।

heart (हार्ट) ***n.*** 1. the organ inside the chest that pumps blood into the arteries, हृदय, दिल। 2. something in a shape like the shape of this organ, दिल। 3. courage, साहस, हिम्मत, जीवट। 4. enthusiasm, उत्साह, जोश। 5. a beloved person, प्रिया या प्रियतम। 6. the vital part, मर्मस्थल, केंद्र, मध्य भाग। 7. any of a suit of playing cards marked with a red heart-shaped symbol, पान का पत्ता।

heartache (हार्टेक) ***n.*** deep sorrow, anguish, घोर व्यथा, मनोव्यथा।

heart attack ***n.*** partial failure of the pumping action of the heart, दिल का दौरा।

heart-beat (हार्ट-बीट) ***n.*** the beating of the heart, दिल की धड़कन, धकधक।

heart-burning (हार्ट-बर्निंग) ***n.*** 1. jealousy, ईर्ष्या। 2. concealed bitterness, जलन।

hearten (हार्टन) ***v.*** to encourage and cheer, दिल बढ़ाना, बढ़ावा देना।

heart failure ***n.*** the stopping of the movement of the heart, हृदयगति का रुकना।

hearth (हार्थ) ***n.*** 1. the floor of a fireplace, चूल्हा जलाने की जगह। 2. the home, घर।

heartily (हार्टिली) ***adv.*** 1. in a hearty way, ख़ुशी-ख़ुशी। 2. very, ख़ूब, अत्यधिक।

heartless (हार्टलिस) ***adj.*** 1. without compassion, हृदयहीन। 2. cruel, क्रूर, नृशंस।

hearty (हार्टी) ***adj.*** 1. cordial, affectionate, हार्दिक। 2. cheery, jovial, प्रसन्नचित्त। 3. healthy and vigorous, स्वस्थ तथा उत्साही। 4. large, ज़्यादा; a hearty meal, छककर किया जानेवाला भोजन।

heat (हीट) ***n.*** 1. the energy associated with the motion of atoms or molecules, ताप, उष्णता, उष्मा। 2. The condition or quality of being hot, hotness, ताप, गर्मी। 3. sexual excitement (in female mammals, मादा पशुओं का) गर्म होना, गर्मी में आना। 4. excitement, जोश, उत्तेजना। 5. a single division in a competition, प्रतियोगिता का एक भाग। ***v.*** 1. to make or become hot, गर्म होना या करना, तपना या तपाना। 2. to excite or become excited, उत्तेजित करना या उत्तेजना में आना।

heated (हीटिड) ***adj.*** angry, क्रुद्ध।

heater (हीटर) ***n.*** a device providing heat, हीटर, तापक।

heath (हीथ) ***n.*** an uncultivated tract of land covered with shrubs, झाड़ियों से भरा भूखंड।

H

heatstroke (हीटस्ट्रोक) ***n.*** an illness caused by exposure to sun, लू का लगना, तापाघात।

heave (हीव) ***v.*** 1. to raise or pull (with great effort, ज़ोर लगाकर) उठाना या खींचना। 2. to throw, फेंकना। 3. to rise and fall regularly, (लहरों का) उठना और गिरना। 4. to breathe, साँस लेना; to heave a sigh, आह भरना। 5. to vomit, कै करना। ***n.*** the act of heaving, उठाने, खींचने, फेंकने या साँस लेने की क्रिया।

heaven (हेवन) ***n.*** 1. the abode of God, स्वर्ग, जन्नत, बहिश्त। 2. a place of intense pleasure, स्वर्ग, जन्नत। 3. (plu. the heavens) sky, आकाश।

heavy (हेवि) ***adj.*** 1. having great weight, भारी, वजनी, बोझिल। 2. indigestible, भारी, गरिष्ठ। 3. large in number or volume, अत्यधिक, बड़ा, भारी। 4. intense, severe, violent or forceful, तीव्र, प्रचंड, ज़ोरदार। 5. unhappy, sad, उदास, खिन्न, दुखी। 6. dull, नीरस।

heavy-hearted (हेवि-हार्टिड) ***adj.*** melancholy, उदास, दुखी।

heavyweight (हेविवेट) ***n.*** a boxer weighting more than 81 kilograms, हैवीवेट मुक्केबाज़। ***adj.*** having great influence, प्रभावशाली।

Hebrew (हीब्रू) ***n.*** 1. a member of a Semitic people, हिब्रू। 2. the Semitic language esp. the language of Israelis, हिब्रू या इब्रानी भाषा। ***adj.*** of the Hebrews, हिब्रू लोगों से संबद्ध।

heckle (हेकल) ***v.*** to harass (a speaker) with questions, abuses or taunts, टोका-टाकी करना, चिढ़ाना-खिझाना।

hectic (हेक्टिक) ***adj.*** full of activities and exciting, चहल-पहल भरा, अति व्यस्त।

hecto- (हेक्टो) ***prefix.*** one hundred, सौ, शत।

hector (हेक्टर) ***v.*** to bully, डराना-धमकाना।

hedge (हेज) ***n.*** 1. a closely planted line of bushes or shrubs forming a boundary, बाड़। 2. protection, सुरक्षा। ***v.*** 1. to surround with a hedge, बाड़ लगाना। 2. to protect, सुरक्षित करना। 3. to speak ambiguously, गोल-मोल बात कहना।

hedgehog (हेजहॉग) ***n.*** a small wild animal with stiff spines on the back, साही।

hedonism (हीडनिज़्म) ***n.*** the doctrine that only that which is pleasurable is good, भोगवाद, सुखवाद।

heed (हीड) ***n.*** careful attention, ध्यान, सावधानी। ***v.*** to pay attention to, ध्यान देना, सावधानी बरतना।

heel[1] (हील) ***n.*** 1. the rounded back part of the foot, एड़ी। 2. the part of shoe or sock that covers this part, एड़ी।

heel[2] ***n.*** a tilt to one side, एक ओर झुकाव, उलार। ***v.*** 1. to tilt to one side, एक ओर झुकना, उलरना। 2. to cause to tilt to one side, एक ओर झुकाना, उलारना।

hefty (हेफ़्टी) ***adj.*** 1. heavy, weighty, भारी, भारी-भरकम। 2. strong and powerful, हृष्ट-पुष्ट, तगड़ा।

heifer (हेफ़र) ***n.*** young cow, जवान बछिया, कलोर।

height (हाइट) ***n.*** 1. the distance from the base to the top of something, ऊँचाई। 2. the distance above ground or sea level, ऊँचाई। 3. the condition of being relatively tall, लंबाई। 4. the highest degree of something, पराकाष्ठा, चरम सीमा।

heinous (हेनस) ***adj.*** very wicked or abominable, बहुत बुरा या घृणित, घोर, जघन्य।

heir (ऐअर) ***n.*** one who is legally entitled to inherit the property of another, उत्तराधिकारी, वारिस।

heiress (ऐअरिस) ***n.*** a female heir उत्तराधिकारिणी।

heirloom (ऐअरलूम) ***n.*** a valuable object that has been handed down to a family for several generations, पुश्तैनी चीज़।

helical (हेलिकल) ***adj.*** shaped like a helix, कुंडलाकार, कुंडलीदार।

helicopter (हेलिकॉप्टर) ***n.*** a kind of small aircraft which can land in a small place, हेलिकॉप्टर।

helipad (हेलिपैड) ***n.*** heliport.

heliport (हेलिपोर्ट) ***n.*** an airport of helicopters, हेलिकॉप्टरों का अड्डा, हेलिपोर्ट।

helix (हीलिक्स) ***n.*** (plu. helices) a spiral form or object, कुंडली या कुंडलाकार पदार्थ।

hell (हेल) ***n.*** 1. the place of the dead wicked persons, नरक, दोज़ख़, जहन्नुम। 2. something that causes trouble, दुख देनेवाली बात या वस्तु। ***interj.*** used to express anger, dismay or impatience, ओफ़।

hello (हेलो) ***interj.*** used to greet someone, हैलो!

helm (हेल्म) ***n.*** 1. a steering device of a ship, पतवार। 2. control, नियंत्रण।

helmet (हेल्मिट) ***n.*** a covering to protect the head, शिरस्त्राण, हेल्मिट।

helmsman (हेल्म्ज़मैन) ***n.*** (plu. helmsmen) one who steers, पतवारिया, कर्णधार।

help (हेल्प) ***v.*** 1. to assist or aid, सहायता करना, सहयोग देना। 2. to work jointly with, योग देना, योगदान करना। 3. to prevent or avoid, रोकना, दूर करना, बचाना। 4. to encourage, बढ़ावा देना। ***n.*** 1. aid, assistance, सहायता, सहयोग। 2. a person or a thing that helps, सहायक वस्तु या व्यक्ति, सहारा। 3. a part-time servant, अंशकालिक सेवक।

helpless (हेल्पलिस) ***adj.*** unable to act without help, लाचार, असहाय, विवश।

helpline (हेल्पलाइन) ***n.*** a telephone service providing useful help, सेवा केंद्र।

helter-skelter (हेल्टर-स्केल्टर) ***adv.*** in disordered hurry, हड़बड़ी में, हड़बड़ाते हुए। ***adj.*** disorderly, अस्त-व्यस्त, अव्यवस्थित। ***n.*** confusion, विभ्रम, हड़बड़ाहट।

hem (हेम) ***n.*** a smooth folded edge of a garment, किनारा। ***v.*** to turn and sew down the edge of, किनारा सीना या बनाना।

hematology = haematology.

hemi- (हेमि) ***prefix*** half, अर्ध।

hemisphere (हेमिस्फ़िअर) ***n.*** 1. half a sphere, अर्धवृत्त। 2. either of the halves into which the earth is divided, गोलार्ध।

hemoglobin = haemoglobin.

hemorrhage = haemorrhage.

hemp (हेम्प) ***n*** 1. an Indian plant that yields a coarse fiber, सन। 2. a narcotic drug, गाँजा।

H

hen (हेन) ***n.*** 1. the female of the domestic fowl, मुर्गी। 2. any female bird, मादा पक्षी।

hence (हेन्स) ***adv.*** 1. for this reason, अतः, इसलिए। 2. from this time or place, यहाँ से, अब से।

henchman (हेन्चमैन) ***n.*** a loyal supporter who obeys without question, जी हुजूर।

henna (हेना) ***n.*** 1. a plant, मेहंदी का पौधा। 2. its leaves used as a dye, मेहंदी की पत्ती।

henpecked (हेनपेक्ड) ***adj.*** under wife's control, जोरू का गुलाम, पत्नीभक्त।

hepatitis (हेपेटाइटिस) ***n.*** inflammation of the liver, यकृत-शोथ, जिगर की सूजन।

heptagon (हेप्टगॉन) ***n.*** a seven-sided figure, सप्तभुज।

her (हर) ***pron.*** objective case of she, उसको। ***adj.*** of or belonging to she, उसका।

herald (हेरल्ड) ***n.*** 1. a harbinger, अग्रदूत। 2. one that gives an indication of what is to follow, पूर्वसूचक, आगमनसूचक। ***v.*** to proclaim the approach of, आगमन की सूचना देना।

herb (हर्ब) ***n.*** a soft-stemmed plant used in medicine or as seasoning, जड़ी, बूटी, जड़ी-बूटी।

herbivore (हर्बिवोर) ***n.*** a herbivorous animal, शाकाहारी प्राणी।

herculean (हरक्यूलीअन) ***adj.*** 1. as strong as Hercules, (हर्कुलिस की तरह) बलशाली। 2. needing great effort, जिसे पूरा करने के लिए अत्यधिक बल की आवश्यकता हो; herculean effort, भागीरथ प्रयास।

herd (हर्ड) ***n.*** a large number of animals, पशुओं का झुंड। ***v.*** 1. to group together, झुंड बनाना। 2. to look after or drive animals in a herd, पशुओं के झुंड की देख-भाल करना या उसे हाँकना।

here (हिअर) ***adv.*** 1. at (or in) this place, यहाँ, इस स्थान में (पर), इस जगह। 2. at this time, अब, यहाँ। 3. at this point, यहाँ।

hereafter (हिअराफ़्टर) ***adv.*** from now on, अब से, आइंदा, आगे से।

hereby (हिअरबाई) ***adv.*** 1. by this means, इसके द्वारा, एतद्द्वारा। 2. as a result of this, इसके फलस्वरूप।

hereditary (हेरिडिटरी) ***adj.*** inherited, passing down by inheritance, पुश्तैनी, आनुवंशिक।

heredity (हेरिडिटी) ***n.*** 1. transmission from parents to offspring of characteristics, आनुवंशिकता। 2. the characteristics inherited in this way, आनुवंशिक गुण या लक्षण।

herein (हिअरिन) ***adv.*** in this, इसमें।

heritage (हेरिटिज) ***n.*** 1. property that is or can be inherited, विरासत, दाय। 2. values or traditions passed down from preceding generations, कुल-परंपरा।

hermaphrodite (हर्मैफ़्रडाइट) ***n.*** a creature having both male and female sex-organs, उभयलिंगी।

hermetic (हर्मेटिक) ***adj.*** very tightly closed, airtight, हवाबंद, एअरटाईट।

hermit (हर्मिट) ***n.*** a holy person who lives alone, तपस्वी, साधु, संन्यासी, एकांतवासी।

hero (हीरो) ***n.*** 1. a man celebrated for his noble or brave deeds,

वीर, हीरो। 2. the principal male character in a literary work, नायक, हीरो।

heroine (हेरोइन) ***n.*** fam. of hero, वीरांगना, नायिका, हिरोइन।

heron (हेरन) ***n.*** a wading bird with long neck and legs, बगुला।

herpes (हर्पीज़) ***n.*** a skin disease, त्वचा का एक रोग, विसर्पिका, हर्पीज़।

herring (हेरिंग) ***n.*** a fish used for food, हिलसा मछली।

hers (हर्ज़) ***pron.*** of or belonging to her, उस स्त्री का, उसका।

hertz (हर्ट्ज़) ***n.*** a unit of frequency, हर्ट्ज़।

hesitant (हेज़िटेन्ट) ***adj.*** tending to hesitate, hesitating, हिचकनेवाला, संकोची।

hesitate (हेज़िटेट) ***v.*** 1. to be slow to act or decide, हिचकना, संकोच होना। 2. to be reluctant, अनिच्छुक होना।

hessian (हेसिअन) ***n.*** a fabric made of hemp, टाट।

hetero- (हेटरो) ***prefix.*** different or opposite, विरोधी, इतर।

heterodoxy (हेटरोडॉक्सी) ***n.*** the state of being heterodox, रूढ़ि-विरोध, परंपरा-भंग।

heterogeneous (हेटरोजीनिअस) ***adj.*** not homogeneous, विषम, विषमजातीय।

heterosexual (हेटरोसेक्सुअल) ***adj. & n.*** (a person) characterized by attraction to the opposite sex, जिसमें भिन्नलिंगी प्राणी के प्रति आकर्षण हो, विषमलिंगकामी।

hew (ह्यू) ***v.*** 1. to cut with an axe, कुल्हाड़ी से काटना या चीरना। 2. to cut and shape, तराशना।

hexagon (हेक्सगॉन) ***n.*** a geometric figure with six sides, षड्भुज।

heyday (हेडे) ***n.*** the period of greatest success or prosperity, सुख-समृद्धि का समय, बहार, स्वर्णकाल।

hiatus (हाइएटस) ***n.*** (plu. hiatus, hiatuses) a gap or interruption in a sequence, अंतराल, छूट, लुप्त पद या अंश, विलुप्त कड़ी।

hibernate (हाइबर्नेट) ***v.*** to spend the winter in a dormant state, जाड़ा भर सोकर बिताना, शीतशयन करना।

hiccup (हिकप) ***n.*** a movement in the chest which stops breath with a cough-like sound, हिचकी। ***v.*** to have the hiccups, हिचकी आना।

hide[1] (हाइड) ***n.*** the skin of an animal, खाल, चर्म।

hide[2] ***v.*** (hid, hidden, hiding) 1. to put or keep out of sight, छिपाना, छिपा रखना। 2. to place oneself so as to be unseen, छिप जाना। ***n.*** a place of hiding, छिपने की जगह, ओट, आड़।

hide-and-seek (हाइड-एन-सीक) ***n.*** a children's game in which someone tries to find out his or her hidden playmates, आँख-मिचौनी।

hideous (हिडिअस) ***adj.*** 1. very ugly, कुरूप। 2. repulsive, घिनौना। 3. terrible, भयंकर।

hiding (हाइडिंग) ***n.*** the state of being hidden, छिपे होने का भाव।

hierarchy (हाइरार्की) ***n.*** 1. an arrangement of body of persons in a graded series, पदानुक्रम, श्रेणीबद्धता। 2. a group of ruling priests, शासक पुरोहित-वर्ग।

hieroglyph (हाइरोग्लिफ़) ***n.*** a picture-like sign representing sound, word

H

or idea, चित्रलिपि का कोई चिह्न, चित्रलेख।

hieroglyphics (हाइरोग्लिफ़िक्स) ***n.*** (plu.) the set of hieroglyphs, चित्रलिपि।

hi-fi (हाइ-फ़ाइ) ***n.*** high fidelity, हू-ब-हू ध्वनि उत्पन्न करने का गुण। ***adj.*** reproducing sound with high fidelity, हू-ब-हू ध्वनि उत्पन्न करनेवाला, हाइ-फाइ।

high (हाइ) ***adj.*** 1. extending far upward, tall, उच्च, ऊँचा। 2. ranking above others, उच्च। 3. showing goodness, महान, उच्च। 4. greater than what is normal, तीव्र, तेज़, अधिक। 5. costly, महँगा। 6. piercing in sound, कर्णकटु।

highbrow (हाइब्रो) ***n.*** a cultured and intellectual person, सभ्य तथा बुद्धिमान व्यक्ति।

high-handed (हाइ-हैन्डिड) ***adj.*** arrogant, उद्धत, उद्दंड, स्वेच्छाचारी।

highland (हाइलैन्ड) ***n.*** elevated land, उच्च भूमि, पर्वतीय प्रदेश। ***adj.*** of high lands, पर्वतीय प्रदेश-संबंधी।

highlight (हाइलाइट) ***n.*** an outstanding feature, विशिष्टता। ***v.*** to emphasize, ज़ोर देना।

highlights (हाइलाइट्स) ***n.*** (plu.) most important or outstanding features of an occurrence, झलकियाँ।

Highness (हाइनिस) ***n.*** a title of honour for royalty, राजघराने के लोगों की उपाधि।

high-rise (हाइ-राइज़) ***n.*** a multi-storied building, अट्टालिका, ऊँची इमारत। ***adj.*** very tall, बहुत ऊँचा।

high-strung (हाइस्ट्रंग) ***adj.*** extremely sensitive, अतिसंवेदनशील, तुनकमिज़ाज।

high tide ***n.*** the highest level of the tide, ज्वार।

highway (हाइवे) ***n.*** a main public road, राजमार्ग, जनपथ।

highwayman (हाइवेमैन) ***n.*** one who robs passing travellers, राहज़न, बटमार, लुटेरा।

hijack (हाइजैक) ***v.*** to seize forcibly, अपहरण करना। ***n.*** an act of hijacking, अपहरण।

hike (हाइक) ***v.*** 1. to go for a long walk, पैदल लंबी यात्रा करना, पदयात्रा करना। 2. to raise, ऊँचा करना, बढ़ाना। ***n.*** 1. a long walk, पैदल लंबी यात्रा, पदयात्रा। 2. a rise in prices, मूल्यवृद्धि।

hilarious (हिलेरिअस) ***adj.*** noisily merry, हर्ष-भरा, उल्लासपूर्ण। 2. funny, हास्यपूर्ण। 3. cheerful, प्रसन्नचित्त।

hill (हिल) ***n.*** 1. a raised part of the earth's surface, पहाड़ी। 2. a heap, ढेर।

hillock (हिलॉक) ***n.*** a small hill, टीला।

hilt (हिल्ट) ***n.*** the handle of a tool or sword, हत्था, मूठ।

him (हिम) ***pron.*** the objective case of he, उसे, उसको।

himself (हिमसेल्फ़) ***pron.*** the reflexive form of he, (वह) स्वयं या अपने आप।

hind[1] (हाइन्ड) ***n.*** a female deer, हिरनी।

hind[2] ***adj.*** at the back or rear, पिछला।

hinder (हिन्डर) ***v.*** 1. to get in the way, बाधक होना। 2. to keep back or prevent, रुकावट डालना, रोकना, अड़ंगा लगाना।

Hindi (हिन्डी) ***n.*** India's national language, हिंदी।

hindrance (हिन्ड्रेन्स) ***n.*** the act of hindering or the thing that hinders, बाधा, रुकावट।

hindsight (हाइन्डसाइट) ***n.*** an understanding about an event after it has occurred, बाद में सूझनेवाली अक़्ल की बात, पश्चदृष्टि।

Hindu (हिन्डू) ***n.*** a believer in Hinduism, हिंदू।

Hinduism (हिन्डुइज़म) ***n.*** 1. The Hindu religion, हिंदू धर्म। 2. the Hindu philosophy, हिंदू दर्शन।

hinge (हिन्ज) ***n.*** a device or joint on which a door, lid etc. turns, swings or hangs, क़ब्ज़ा। ***v.*** 1. to equip with a hinge, क़ब्ज़ा जड़ना या लगाना। 2. to turn or swing on a hinge, क़ब्ज़े पर घूमना। 3. to depend on, आश्रित या निर्भर होना।

hint (हिन्ट) ***n.*** 1. a slight or indirect suggestion, परोक्ष संकेत, इशारा। 2. a small piece of practical information, छोटी-मोटी सलाह, उपयोगी सलाह। ***v.*** to give a hint, इशारा करना।

hinterland (हिन्टरलैन्ड) ***n.*** an area remote from urban region, दूर-देहात।

hip[1] (हिप) ***n.*** The fleshy part of either side of human body above the legs, कूल्हा, नितंब।

hip[2] ***interj.*** hip, hip, hooray! हिप-हिप हुर्रे! वाह! वाह!

hippie (हिपी) ***n.*** a young person who rejects conventional ideas and takes drugs for pleasure, हिप्पी।

hippopotamus (हिपोपॉटेमस) ***n.*** a large African quadruped, दरियाई घोड़ा।

hire (हाइर) ***v.*** to get the use of something on payment, किराए पर लेना, भाड़े पर लेना। ***n.*** 1. the act of hiring, किराए पर देना। 2. payment for this, किराया, भाड़ा।

hire-purchase (हाइर-पर्चेज़) ***n.*** a system of payment in instalments after receiving the goods, किराया-ख़रीद, भाड़ा-क्रय।

hirsute (हर्सूट) ***adj.*** hairy, बालोंवाला, रोएँदार।

his (हिज़) ***adj.*** belonging to him, उसका (with general meaning, अपना)। ***pron.*** that (or those) belonging to him, उसका।

hiss (हिस) ***n.*** 1. a hissing sound, सीसी, सिसकारी, फुफकार। 2. a whistle, सीटी। ***v.*** 1. to make a hiss, सिसकारी भरना, फुफकारना। 2. to show disapproval by hissing, सीसी करते हुए अरुचि या असहमति प्रकट करना।

historian (हिस्टोरिअन) ***n.*** an expert in history, इतिहासवेत्ता, इतिहासज्ञ।

historic (हिस्टॉरिक) ***adj.*** having importance in history, ऐतिहासिक महत्त्व का।

history (हिस्टरी) ***n.*** 1. a chronological record of events, इतिहास, तवारीख़। 2. a long narrative, इतिवृत्त।

histrionic (हिस्ट्रिऑनिक) ***adj.*** 1. of theatre or acting, रंगमंच या अभिनय-संबंधी। 2. dramatic, नाटकीय।

histrionics (हिस्ट्रिऑनिक्स) ***n.*** 1. the art of acting, अभिनय-कला।

hit (हिट) ***v.*** (hit, hitting) 1. to give a blow, to strike, आघात या प्रहार करना, मारना। 2. to affect adversely, बुरी तरह प्रभावित करना, बुरा प्रभाव डालना। 3. to reach, पहुँचना। ***n.*** 1. a blow or strike, आघात, प्रहार, मार। 2. a shot that hits the target, निशाना।

H

3. a successful performance, सफल प्रदर्शन, सफल कार्यक्रम।

hitch (हिच) ***v.*** 1. to move (a thing) with a slight jerk (किसी वस्तु को) झटके से उठाना। 2. to fasten, बाँध देना, साथ लगा देना, अटकाना। 3. to be fastened, बँध जाना, जुड़ जाना, अटक या फँस जाना। ☐ **get hitched,** विवाह हो जाना, बँध जाना। ***n.*** 1. a slight jerk, झटका। 2. a loop or hook, फंदा या हुक। 3. a difficulty, कठिनाई, अड़चन, विघ्न।

hitchhike (हिच-हाइक) ***v.*** to travel by getting free rides in other people's vehicles, मुफ़्त यात्रा करना, अनुरोध-यात्रा करना।

hither (हिदर) ***adv.*** toward this place, इधर।

hitherto (हिदरटू) ***adv.*** until this time, अब तक।

hive (हाइव) ***n.*** 1. a structure or container for bees to live in, छत्ता या मधुपेटी। 2. the bees living in this, छत्ते या मधुपेटी में रहनेवाली मधुमक्खियाँ। 3. a crowded place, भीड़-भाड़वाली जगह। ***v.*** 1. to live in a hive, छत्ते या मधुपेटी में रहना। 2. to live together, साथ-साथ रहना। 3. to gather, संग्रह करना।

ho (हो) ***interj.*** an exclamation of triumph or scorn, हो-हो, अहो।

hoard (होर्ड) ***n.*** a store of something valuable, संचय, जमा। ***v.*** to accumulate a hoard, संचय/जमा करना।

hoarding (होर्डिंग) ***n.*** 1. the act or practice of accumulating, संचयन, संचयवृत्ति, जमाख़ोरी। 2. a fence around a building being constructed, टट्टी, घेरा। 3. a large board on which advertisements are attached or stuck, विज्ञापन-पट्ट, होर्डिंग।

hoarse (होर्स) ***adj.*** harsh-sounding, कर्कश या फटी-फटी आवाज़वाला।

hoary (होरी) ***adj.*** 1. (of hair) grey or white, सफ़ेद, धवल। 2. (of a person) having grey hair, सफ़ेद बालोंवाला, बूढ़ा। 3. very old, ancient, प्राचीन, पुराना।

hoax (होक्स) ***n.*** a joke or plot to deceive, झाँसा, जुल, झाँसा-पट्टी, चकमा। ***v.*** to deceive by a hoax, झाँसा देना, धोखा देना।

hob[1] (हॉब) ***n.*** a flat metal plate for heating purposes, तवा।

hob[2] ***n.*** = hobgoblin.

hobble (हॉबल) ***v.*** 1. to limp, लँगड़ाते हुए चलना, लँगड़ाना। 2. to fasten together the legs (of a horse or donkey to limit its movement), छाँदना। ***n.*** 1. a clumsy walk, भद्दी चाल। 2. a device for hobbling an animal, छाँदा।

hobby (हॉबी) ***n.*** an occupation or activity carried on for pleasure, शौक़, शुग़ल, रुचि।

hobgoblin (हॉबगॉब्लिन) ***n.*** 1. a goblin which plays tricks on people, दुष्टात्मा। 2. a bugbear, हौआ, जूजू।

hobnob (हॉबनॉब) ***v.*** to drink and chat together in a friendly way, हमप्याला और हमनिवाला होना, हिल-मिलकर रहना, यारी निभाना।

hock (हॉक) ***n.*** the joint in the hind leg of an animal, पिछली टाँग का घुटना।

hockey (हॉकी) ***n.*** 1. a game played with a ball and curved sticks, हॉकी का खेल। 2. a stick used in this game, हॉकी।

hocuspocus (होकसपोकस) ***n.*** a trickery, झाँसा, चाल, तिकड़म।

hoe (हो) ***n.*** a tool for breaking up surface soil, कुदाल। ***v.*** to use a hoe, कुदाल चलाना।

hog (हॉग) ***n.*** 1. a castrated domestic pig, सुअर। 2. a greedy or gluttonous person, लोभी या पेटू व्यक्ति। ***v.*** to take more than one's fair share, अपने हिस्से से ज़्यादा लेना, लोभी या पेटू होना।

hoist (हॉइस्ट) ***v.*** 1. to raise or lift, ऊपर उठाना, चढ़ाना। 2. to raise (the flag, झंडा) फहराना।

hold (होल्ड) ***v.*** (held, holding) 1. to take and keep in one's hands, थामना, पकड़ना, उठाना, धारण करना। 2. to bear the weight of, संभालना। 3. to put in a particular position or maintain, विशेष स्थिति में रखना, बनाए रखना। 4. to possess, contain, or control, धारण करना, नियंत्रण करना। 5. to stop or detain in custody, रोकना, रोके रखना, क़ब्ज़े में रखना। 6. to occupy, ग्रहण करना। 7. to cause to take place, मनाना, आयोजित करना। 8. to believe or assert, मानना, दावा करना। 9. to give verdict, फ़ैसला देना। □ **hold on,** (i) जारी रहना; (ii) प्रतीक्षा करना, कुछ देर के लिए रुकना; **hold out,** (i) चलना; (ii) प्रस्तावित करना; (iii) प्रतिरोध करना, डटे रहना; **hold out for,** (अपनी माँग पर) अडिग रहना; **hold with,** सहमत होना। ***n.*** 1. the act of holding, पकड़, नियंत्रण, संभाल। 2. the means of holding, पकड़ने का साधन। 3. controlling influence, दबदबा, प्रभाव। 4. the part below deck where goods are stored, जलयान का तहख़ाना।

holdall (होल्डॉल) ***n.*** a portable case or bag, होल्डाल, बिस्तरबंद।

holder (होल्डर) ***n.*** one who holds, पकड़ने या थामनेवाला, धारण करनेवाला, धारक।

holding (होल्डिंग) ***n.*** 1. land rented or leased from another, जोत। 2. legally owned property, जायदाद।

hold-up (होल्ड-अप) ***n.*** 1. delay, विलंब। 2. interruption, व्यवधान। 3. armed robbery, डाका, राहज़नी।

hole (होल) ***n.*** 1. a cavity, छेद, सुराख़, छिद्र। 2. an animal's burrow, बिल, विवर या माँद। 3. a fault or defect, दोष। 4. a bad situation, विषम परिस्थिति। ***v.*** to make hole in, छेद करना, छेदना।

holiday (हॉलिडे) ***n.*** a day of rest, छुट्टी का दिन, अवकाश-दिवस, छुट्टी। ***v.*** to have a period of holiday, छुट्टियाँ मनाना।

hollow (हॉलो) ***adj.*** 1. having an empty space inside, खोखला, पोला। 2. sunken, पिचका हुआ। 3. empty, worthless, ख़ाली, तुच्छ, थोथा। ***n.*** 1. a hole, छेद, छिद्र। 2. a sunken place, पिचक। ***v.*** to make hollow, खोखला बनाना, खोखला कर देना।

holocaust (हॉलोकॉस्ट) ***n.*** complete destruction (of the people) by fire, सर्वदाह, जनदाह, सर्वनाश, अग्निकांड।

holster (होल्स्टर) ***n.*** a leather case for a pistol, पिस्तौल का चमड़े का खोल।

holy (होली) ***adj.*** 1. sacred, पवित्र, पावन। 2. devoted to the service of god, धर्मी।

homage (हॉमिज) ***n.*** honour or respect shown publicly, सार्वजनिक सम्मान, सम्मान-प्रदर्शन, श्रद्धांजलि।

home (होम) ***n.*** 1. a dwelling place, घर, मकान, निवास। 2. one's

H

native land, जन्मभूमि। 3. the native habitat, मूल निवास या उद्‌गम स्थल। 4. (in some games) a place which a player must aim to reach, गोल। 5. an institution where people are cared for, भवन, गृह, आवास; a children's home, बालभवन, बालगृह। ***adj.*** 1. connected or related with one's home or country, घरेलू। 2. of native land, देशीय। ***adv.*** 1. to or at one's home or family, घर में, परिवार में। 2. on target, to the right place, निशाने पर, ठीक जगह पर। ***v.*** to go home, घर लौटना।

home guard ***n.*** a local guard, होमगार्ड, गृहरक्षक।

homeland (होमलैन्ड) ***n.*** one's native land, स्वदेश।

homely (होमली) ***adj.*** 1. simple or plain, सीधा-सादा। 2. not good looking, सामान्य शक्ल-सूरत का।

homeopath (होमिओपैथ) ***n.*** an expert in homeopathy, होमियोपैथ।

homeopathy (होमिओपेथी) ***n.*** a system of medical treatment, होमियोपैथी।

home rule ***n.*** self-government, स्वशासन।

home science ***n.*** the science dealing with the management of home, गृहविज्ञान।

homesick (होमसिक) ***adj.*** longing for home, जिसे घर की याद सता रही हो, गृहासक्त।

home truth ***n.*** a true but unpleasant fact, कटुसत्य, मर्मोक्ति।

homework (होमवर्क) ***n.*** 1. work to be done at home, गृहकार्य, घर का काम। 2. work of a preparatory nature, प्राथमिक कार्य।

homicide (होमिसाइड) ***n.*** 1. murder, मानव-वध, नरहत्या। 2. a murderer, हत्यारा।

homily (होमिली) ***n.*** a moralizing lecture, उपदेश, सीख।

homoeopath ***n.*** = homeopath.

homoeopathy ***n.*** = homeopathy.

homogeneous (हॉमोजीनिअस) ***adj.*** 1. of the same kind, समजातीय। 2. uniform, एकरूप, एकरस, समांगी।

homologous (हॉमोलोगस) ***adj.*** corresponding, समजात, समजातीय।

homophone (हॉमोफ़ोन) ***n.*** a word with the same sound as another, समध्वनिक शब्द।

homosexual (हॉमोसेक्सुअल) ***adj.*** one who is sexually attracted to the members of the same sex, समलिंगकामी, होमोसेक्सुअल।

hone (होन) ***n.*** a stone used to sharpen cutting tools, सान। ***v.*** to sharpen on a hone, सान पर चढ़ाना।

honest (ऑनिस्ट) ***adj.*** 1. truthful, upright, सच्चा, ईमानदार, निष्कपट। 2. true, genuine, सच्चा, भला। 3. earned by fair methods, ईमानदारी से कमाया हुआ।

honesty (ऑनिस्टी) ***n.*** 1. the state or quality of being honest, ईमानदारी। 2. sincerity, सच्चाई।

honey (हनी) ***n.*** 1. a sweet syrupy substance made by bees, शहद, मधु। 2. darling, प्रिय।

honeybee (हनीबी) ***n.*** a bee that makes honey, मधुमक्खी।

honeycomb (हनीकोम) ***n.*** a wax structure made by honeybees to hold honey, शहद का छत्ता।

honeydew (हनीड्यू) ***n.*** a sweet fluid

excreted by some insects, मधुरस।

honeymoon (हनीमून) ***n.*** the period spent together by a newly-married couple, नवदंपती की विहार-वेला, अभिसारकाल।

honk (हॉन्क) ***n.*** 1. the harsh cry of a goose, काँ-काँ। 2. the sound of a car horn, पों-पों। ***v.*** to make a honk, काँ-काँ करना, पों-पों करना।

honorarium (ऑनरेरिअम) ***n.*** a voluntary payment made for services on which no fee is legally obtainable, मानदेय।

honorary (ऑनरेरी) ***adj.*** 1. given as an honour, मानद, सम्मानार्थ। 2. unpaid, अवैतनिक।

honour, honor (ऑनर) ***n.*** 1. great respect, मान, सम्मान, समादर। 2. public regard, glory, प्रतिष्ठा, गौरव, यश। 3. personal integrity, सत्यनिष्ठा, वैयक्तिक चरित्र, मर्यादा। 4. a privilege, विशेषाधिकार। ***v.*** 1. to respect greatly, आदर करना। 2. to confer an honour on, सम्मान देना, सम्मानित करना। 3. to accept and pay when due, सकारना।

hood (हुड) ***n.*** 1. a loose covering for the head and neck, एक तरह की टोपी। 2. a cover over an automobile engine, कार के इंजन का ढक्कन, हुड।

hoodlum (हुडलम) ***n.*** a gangster, गुंडा।

hoodwink (हुडविंक) ***v.*** to deceive, धोखा देना।

hoof (हूफ़) ***n.*** the horny part of the foot of some mammals, खुर, टाप, सुम।

hook (हुक) ***n.*** 1. a curved device for holding or catching something, हुक, टेढ़ा काँटा। 2. a bend in a stream, नदी का घुमाव या मोड़। 3. a blow delivered with a bent arm, हुक। ☐ **by hook or by crook,** चाहे जैसे भी, येन-केन-प्रकारेण। ***v.*** 1. to get hold of or catch with a hook, हुक से लटकाना या पकड़ना। 2. to hit or pull (the ball, गेंद को) मारना, हुक करना।

hookah (हुका) ***n.*** a smoking pipe with a water-pot, हुक्का।

hook-up (हुक-अप) ***n.*** a connection, संयोजन, विशेषत: एक ही कार्यक्रम प्रसारित करनेवाले सभी केंद्रों का; on the national hook-up, देश के सभी केंद्रों पर।

hookworm (हुकवर्म) ***n.*** a worm with hooked mouth parts that infest the intestines, अंकुशकृमि।

hooligan (हुलिगन) ***n.*** a hoodlum, गुंडा।

hoop (हूप) ***n.*** a circular band, छल्ला, वलय।

hooray (हुरे) ***interj.*** = hurray.

hoot (हूट) ***n.*** 1. the cry of an owl, उल्लू की आवाज़, घूघू। 2. a sound of a horn or whistle, भोंभों। 3. a cry expressing scorn or jeer, हो-हो। ***v.*** 1. to make a hoot, घूघू करना। 2. to sound a horn, भोंभों करना। 3. to make a jeering or contemptuous cry, हो-हो करना, हूट करना।

hooter (हूटर) ***n.*** a whistle or horn, सीटी, भोंपू।

hop (हॉप) ***v.*** 1. to jump, कूदना, फुदकना। 2. to jump on one foot, उछलना। 3. to cross by hopping, कूदकर लाँघना। 4. to take a trip by air, हवाई यात्रा या दौरा करना। ***n.*** 1. the act of hopping, कूद, उछल-कूद। 2. a dance, एक प्रकार का नृत्य। 3. a trip, दौरा।

H

hope (होप) ***v.*** 1. to wish for something expected, आशा करना, उम्मीद करना। 2. to feel fairly confident, आशावान होना, आशान्वित होना। ***n.*** 1. a desire for certain events to happen, आशा, उम्मीद। 2. some-thing that is desired, चाही हुई वस्तु, अभिप्रेत वस्तु, चाह। 3. anything that is cause for hope, आशा की किरण।

hopper (हॉपर) ***n.*** 1. a hopping insect, टिड्डा। 2. a container with opening in which materials are held ready for dispensing, एक प्रकार का आधान, हॉपर।

horde (होर्ड) ***n.*** a throng, झुंड, दल, भीड़।

horizon (हराइज़न) ***n.*** 1. the apparent line at which the earth and sky seem to meet, क्षितिज। 2. the limit of one's knowledge or experience, ज्ञान की सीमा, अनुभव की परिधि।

horizontal (हॉरिज़ॉन्टल) ***adj.*** 1. parallel to the horizon or ground, क्षैतिज, पट। 2. relating to the people of same status, समस्तरीय।

hormone (हॉर्मोन) ***n.*** a substance produced by living cells within the body that stimulates other cells and organs, हारमोन।

horn (हॉर्न) ***n.*** 1. a hard pointed outgrowth found in a pair on the heads of certain animals, सींग। 2. a wind instrument made of horn, सिंही, तुरही। 3. a device that produces a sound in a car for giving signals, भोंपू, हार्न।

hornet (हॉर्निट) ***n.*** an insect of the wasp family, बर्र, भिड़, ततैया।

horny (हॉर्नी) ***adj.*** 1. hard and tough, कठोर। 2. sexually excited, कामोत्तेजित।

horoscope (हॉरस्कोप) ***n.*** the diagram showing the position of stars at the time of someone's birth, जन्मपत्री, जन्मकुंडली।

horrible (हॉरिबल) ***adj.*** 1. causing horror, भयावह, भयानक। 2. very ugly or unpleasant, अत्यंत कुरूप, बीभत्स।

horrid (हॉरिड) ***adj.*** very unpleasant, अरुचिकर, घृणित।

horrify (हॉरिफ़ाइ) ***v.*** to fill with horror, दहला देना।

horror (हॉरर) ***n.*** 1. a feeling of disgust and fear, त्रास, दहशत, आतंक। 2. that which rouses the feeling of disgust and fear, वह जो दहशत या आतंक फैलाए, त्रासदायक।

horrorstruck (हॉररस्ट्रक) ***adj.*** horrified, भयविह्वल, आतंकित।

horse (हॉर्स) ***n.*** 1. a four legged mammal used for riding and drawing vehicles, घोड़ा, अश्व। 2. a frame with four legs, चार पैरोंवाला ढाँचा।

horsefly (हॉर्सफ़्लाइ) ***n.*** an insect which stings horses, कुकुरमाछी, घुड़मक्खी।

horseman (हॉर्समैन) ***n.*** a rider on horseback, अश्वारोही।

horsepower (हॉर्सपॉवर) ***n.*** a unit for measuring the power equal to 746 watts, अश्वशक्ति।

horse-racing (हॉर्स-रेसिंग) ***n.*** the practice of racing horses, घुड़दौड़।

horse sense ***n.*** common sense, सामान्य बुद्धि।

horseshoe (हॉर्सशू) ***n.*** a U-shaped

strip of metal fitted to a horse's hoof, नाल।

horticulture (हॉर्टिकल्चर) ***n.*** the science or art of cultivating fruits, vegetables, flowers etc. in the garden, बाग़वानी, उद्यान-विद्या, उद्यान-कृषि।

hose (होज़) ***n.*** 1. (plu. hose) socks, मोज़ा, जुराब। 2. (plu. hoses) a tube or pipe, ट्यूब, पाइप। ***v.*** to use a hose for washing or watering, पाइप से धोना या पानी देना।

hosiery (होज़री) ***n.*** socks, underclothes etc., मोज़े, कच्छे, बनियानें आदि, होज़री।

hospitable (हॉस्पिटेबल) ***adj.*** cordial to guests, अतिथिसेवी, ख़ातिर करनेवाला।

hospital (हॉस्पिटल) ***n.*** a place where medical aid is provided, अस्पताल, चिकित्सालय।

hospitality (हॉस्पिटैलिटी) ***n.*** cordial reception of guests, अतिथि-सत्कार, आवभगत, ख़ातिरदारी।

hospitalize (हॉस्पिटलाइज़) ***v.*** to put or admit (a patient) into a hospital, (रोगी को) अस्पताल में भर्ती करवाना या भर्ती कर लेना।

host[1] (होस्ट) ***n.*** one who entertains guests, मेज़बान, आतिथेय।

host[2] ***n.*** a large number of things or people, समूह।

hostage (हॉस्टिज) ***n.*** a person abducted or held as security by an enemy, शत्रु द्वारा अपहृत या बंधक बनाया हुआ व्यक्ति, बंधक।

hostel (हॉस्टल) ***n.*** a lodging for travellers, students etc., होस्टल।

hostess (होस्टिस) ***n.*** a female host, अतिथि-सेविका।

hostile (हॉस्टाइल) ***adj.*** 1. of or pertaining to an enemy, विरोधी, शत्रुपक्षीय। 2. feeling or showing enmity, पक्षद्रोही, शत्रुतापूर्ण, वैरमूलक। 3. contrary, प्रतिकूल।

hostility (हॉस्टिलिटी) ***n.*** the state of being hostile, शत्रुता, पक्षद्रोह, संघर्ष।

hot (हॉट) ***adj.*** 1. having or possessing great heat, गर्म, उष्ण, उत्तप्त। 2. pungent or spicy, तेज़, मसालेदार। 3. sexually excited or exciting, गर्म। 4. excitable, गर्ममिज़ाज। 5. fresh or very recent, ताज़ा। 6. very popular or very interesting, अत्यंत लोकप्रिय या रोचक। ☐ **in hot water,** दुख या कष्ट में; **sell like hot cakes,** ख़ूब माँग होना, हाथोहाथ बिकना।

hotbed (हॉटबेड) ***n.*** a place or environment conducive to the growth of something evil, बुराइयों के पनपने के लिए अनुकूल स्थान, उद्गम स्थल, विशेषत: बुराइयों का अड्डा।

hotchpotch (हॉचपॉच) ***n.*** a medley or mixture, घाल-मेल, खिचड़ी।

hot dog (हॉट डॉग) ***n.*** a kind of breadroll, हॉटडॉग।

hotel (होटेल) ***n.*** a lodging house which provides meals on payment, होटल।

hotfoot (हॉटफ़ुट) ***adv.*** in eager haste, जल्दी-जल्दी, उतावली से।

hotheaded (हॉटहेडिड) ***adj.*** rash, उतावला, जल्दबाज़।

hotline (हॉटलाइन) ***n.*** a direct telephone line for emergency communications, हाटलाइन।

hotplate ***n.*** a stove, (गैस या बिजली का) चूल्हा।

H

hot spring ***n.*** a spring of hot water, गर्म पानी का सोता।

hound (हाउन्ड) ***n.*** a dog used in hunting, शिकारी कुत्ता। ***v.*** 1. to pursue relentlessly, किसी काम के पीछे लग जाना। 2. to harass, परेशान करना।

hour (ऑवर) ***n.*** 1. a twenty-fourth part of a day, a period of sixty minutes, घंटा। 2. a specified or customary time, निश्चित समय, बँधा समय। 3. the present time, यही समय, प्रस्तुत समय।

hour hand ***n.*** the small pointer on a watch or clock, घंटे की सुई।

houri (हूरी) ***n.*** a beautiful young woman of the Muslim paradise, जन्नत की हूर।

hourly (ऑवर्ली) ***adj.*** 1. occurring or happening every hour, हर घंटे पर होनेवाला। 2. by the hour as unit, घंटेवार। ***adv.*** 1. at every hour, हर घंटे। 2. frequently, प्रायः, अक्सर।

house (हाउस) ***n.*** 1. a building used as dwelling, घर, मकान, आवास। 2. the people living in the house, घर में रहनेवाले लोग, सारा घर। 3. a building used for a particular purpose, भवन। 4. a commercial firm, प्रतिष्ठान। 5. the audience or patrons, उपस्थित दर्शकों या शुभचिंतकों का समूह। 6. one of the 12 parts in which the celestial sphere is divided in astrology, घर, ख़ाना। □ **on the house,** मुफ़्त। ***adj.*** of or for the people of a particular firm, किसी प्रतिष्ठान के लोगों के लिए होनेवाला। ***v.*** 1. to provide residential quarters for, रहने के लिए आवास सुलभ कराना। 2. to provide space for storing, जगह निकालना या देना।

house arrest ***n.*** detention in one's own house, नज़रबंदी।

houseboat (हाउसबोट) ***n.*** a boat used as a dwelling, बजड़ा, नौका-गृह, शिकारा।

housebreaking (हाउसब्रेकिंग) ***n.*** burglary, सेंधमारी।

housefly (हाउसफ़्लाइ) ***n.*** a most common fly found in the houses, मक्खी।

household (हाउसहोल्ड) ***n.*** 1. a home and its affairs, गृहस्थी, घर-बार। 2. all the members of a family living in a house, घर के सभी लोग, सारा घर। ***adj.*** of or related to house, घर-गृहस्थी का, घरेलू।

housekeeping (हाउसकीपिंग) ***n.*** the management of household affairs, गृह-प्रबंध।

houseless (हाउसलिस) ***adj.*** without house, बेघर, निर्गृह।

housemaid (हाउसमेड) ***n.*** a woman servant who does housework, नौकरानी।

housewife (हाउसवाइफ़) ***n.*** a married woman managing a household, गृह-स्वामिनी, गृहिणी।

housing (हाउज़िंग) ***n.*** 1. the act of providing accommodation, आवास उपलब्ध कराना। 2. a dwelling, गृह।

hove (होव) ***v.*** p.t. & p.p. of heave.

hovel (हॉवल) ***n.*** a small and miserable dwelling place, छोटा-मोटा घर, मामूली झोंपड़ी, झुग्गी।

hover (हॉवर) ***v.*** to remain suspended in the air above one spot, आकाश में मँडराना।

how (हाउ) ***adv. & conj.*** 1. in what way? कैसे? 2. in what condition?

H

कैसे? 3. to what degree, कितना?

however (हाउएवर) ***adv.*** 1. by whatever means, चाहे जैसे भी। 2. to whatever degree, चाहे जितना भी। ***conj.*** 1. nevertheless, तो भी। 2. in any way, कैसे भी।

howitzer (हाउइट्सर) ***n.*** a small cannon, छोटी तोप।

howl (हाउल) ***v.*** to utter a long cry, चीख़ना, रोना, विलाप करना। ***n.*** a long loud cry, चीख़, चिल्लाहट।

howler (हाउलर) ***n.*** a stupid and ridiculous blunder, बड़ी भारी ग़लती, हास्यास्पद भूल।

hub (हब) ***n.*** 1. the central part of a wheel, हब, चक्रनाभि, नाभि। 2. a centre of activity or interest, केंद्रस्थल, केंद्रबिंदु।

hubbub (हबब) ***n.*** a loud confused noise of voices, शोरगुल, शोर-शराबा।

hubris (ह्यूब्रिस) ***n.*** arrogance, घमंड, दर्प।

huddle (हडल) ***v.*** 1. to crowd together, जमघट लगाना, भीड़ लगाना। 2. to pile up, ढेर लगाना। ***n.*** a confused mass, जमघट या ढेर।

hue (ह्यू) ***n.*** 1. a colour, रंग। 2. a shade, रंगत।

hue and cry ***n.*** a public clamour of alarm or protest, शोरगुल, चीख़-पुकार, हो-हल्ला।

huff (हफ़) ***n.*** a fit or burst of anger, झुंझलाहट, झल्लाहट, रोष। ***v.*** 1. to breathe rapidly and with effort, साँस फूलने लगना। 2. to bully, डराना-धमकाना।

hug (हग) ***v.*** 1. to embrace tightly, छाती से कसकर लगाना, बाँहों में भर लेना। 2. to keep close to, चिपके रहना। ***n.*** an affectionate embrace, आलिंगन, गलबाँही।

huge (ह्यूज) ***adj.*** extremely large, बहुत बड़ा, विशाल।

hulk (हल्क) ***n.*** 1. an old unworthy ship, पुराना तथा बेकार जलयान। 2. a heavy person or thing, भारी-भरकम व्यक्ति या वस्तु। 3. an awkward person or thing, भोंडा व्यक्ति या वस्तु।

hull[1] (हल) ***n.*** the main body of a ship, जलयान का ढाँचा।

hull[2] ***n.*** the outer covering of fruit, beans etc., फलों, फलियों आदि का छिलका। ***v.*** to remove the hull from, छिलका उतारना।

hullabaloo (हलबलू) ***n.*** an uproar, शोरगुल, कोलाहल।

hum (हम) ***v.*** 1. to make a low sound as bees do, भिनभिन करना, भिनभिनाना, गुनगुनाना। 2. to sing without opening the lips, गुनगुनाना। 3. to be in a state of activity, फुर्ती दिखाना। ***n.*** a humming sound, भिनभिन, गुनगुनाहट।

human (ह्यूमन) ***adj.*** 1. of or concerning a person or persons, मानवीय, मानुषिक, इन्सानी। 2. having the qualities of the people, मनुष्योचित, मानवोचित। ***n.*** a human being, मनुष्य, मानव, इन्सान।

humane (ह्यूमेन) ***adj.*** 1. having what are considered best qualities of mankind, having feelings proper to a man, मानवीय, मानवोचित। 2. compassionate, सहृदय, उदार।

humanitarian (ह्यूमेनिटेरिअन) ***n.*** a person devoted to the promotion of human welfare, लोकोपकारी, मानवतावादी। ***adj.*** concerning human

H

welfare, लोकोपकारी, मानवतावादी।

humanities (ह्यूमेनिटीज़) ***n.*** (plu.) the arts, साहित्य, इतिहास, दर्शन आदि विषयों का समाहार, मानविकी।

humanity (ह्यूमेनिटी) ***n.*** 1. the human race, मानव जाति। 2. the quality or state of being humane, मानवता। 3. kindheartedness, दयालुता।

humble (हम्बल) ***adj.*** 1. not self-assertive, modest, विनम्र, विनीत। 2. low in condition, सामान्य-सा, साधारण-सा। 3. of low social rank, दीन, दीन-हीन। ***v.*** 1. to lower in pride, नीचा दिखाना, हेकड़ी भुला देना। 2. to degrade, अवनत करना, महत्त्व गिरा देना। 3. to defeat, परास्त कर देना।

humbug (हम्बग) ***n.*** 1. something made or done to deceive, छल, धोखा। 2. one who cheats or deceives, धूर्त, कपटी।

humdrum (हमड्रम) ***adj.*** dull, नीरस, बेमज़ा।

humid (ह्यूमिड) ***adj.*** containing water vapour, आर्द्र, नम।

humidity (ह्यूमिडिटी) ***n.*** the amount of moisture in the air, आर्द्रता, नमी।

humiliate (ह्यूमिलिएट) ***v.*** to lower the pride or dignity of, नीचा दिखाना, अपमानित करना।

humility (ह्यूमिलिटी) ***n.*** the quality or condition of being humble, शालीनता, विनयशीलता, विनम्रता, दीनता।

humour, humor (ह्यूमर) ***n.*** 1. the quality of being amusing, विनोद। 2. the ability to perceive or enjoy what is funny, हँसोड़पन, विनोदशीलता। 3. a state of mind, चित्तवृत्ति, स्वभाव, मनोवृत्ति। ***v.*** to keep (a person) contended by doing as he or she wishes, संतुष्ट करना, का मन रखना।

hump (हम्प) ***n.*** 1. the fleshy mass on the back of a camel, कूबड़। 2. a rounded projecting part, उभार। ***v.*** 1. to bend, झुकाना। 2. to carry on the back, पीठ पर लादकर ले चलना।

humpback (हम्पबैक) ***adj & n.*** (a person) with a hump on his back, कुबड़ा।

humus (ह्यूमस) ***n.*** rich soil made of decomposed animal or vegetable matter, खाद मिली मिट्टी।

hunch[1] (हन्च) ***n.*** an intuitive feeling, अंतर्ज्ञान या अटकल।

hunch[2] ***n.*** hump, कूबड़। ***v.*** to bend, झुकाना।

hunchback (हन्चबैक) ***n.*** a person with a hunch on his back, कुबड़ा।

hundred (हन्ड्रिड) ***adj. & n.*** ten times ten, सौ; hundred per cent, शतप्रतिशत।

hung (हन्ग) ***v.*** p.t. & p.p. of hang.

hunger (हन्गर) ***n.*** 1. a strong desire for food, भूख। 2. a strong desire for something, भूख, लालसा। ***v.*** 1. to have a desire for food, भूख लगना, भूख होना। 2. to have a strong desire, लालसा होना।

hunger strike ***n.*** a refusal to eat as a sign of protest, भूखहड़ताल, अनशन।

hungry (हन्ग्री) ***adj.*** 1. feeling hunger, wanting or needing food, भूखा। 2. having a strong desire for, लालायित, उत्कंठित, उत्सुक।

hunt (हन्ट) ***v.*** 1. to chase (wild animals) for food or sport, शिकार करना, शिकार खेलना। 2. to search carefully, खोज करना, अनुसंधान करना। ***n.*** the act of hunting, शिकार करने की क्रिया या भाव।

hunter (हन्टर) ***n.*** 1. one who hunts, शिकारी। [fem. huntress] 2. a dog (or other animal) used for hunting, शिकारी कुत्ता।

hunting expedition ***n.*** an expedition or outing for the purpose of hunting, आखेट-यात्रा।

hurdle (हर्डल) ***n.*** 1. a portable framelike barrier to be jumped over in obstacle races, फाँद, बाधा। 2. an obstacle or difficulty, रुकावट, बाधा। ***v.*** to leap over a hurdle, बाधा फाँदना।

hurl (हर्ल) ***v.*** to throw forcefully, झटके या ज़ोर से फेंकना। ***n.*** the act of hurling, प्रक्षेपण।

hurly-burly (हर्ली-बर्ली) ***n.*** an uproar, शोर-शराबा, शोरगुल।

hurrah (हुरा) ***interj.*** = hurray.

hurray (हुरे) ***interj.*** an exclamation of joy or triumph, वाह! वाह!!, ख़ूब! ***v.*** to shout hurray, वाह-वाह करना।

hurricane (हरिकेन) ***n.*** a violent cyclone with heavy rains, तूफ़ान।

hurried (हरिड) ***adj.*** done in haste, जल्दी में किया जानेवाला, जल्दबाज़ी-भरा।

hurry (हरी) ***v.*** (hurried, hurrying) 1. to move with haste, जल्दी करना। 2. to cause to move with speed, जल्दी मचाना। ***n.*** haste, जल्दी; जल्दबाज़ी।

hurt (हर्ट) ***v.*** (hurt, hurting) 1. to cause injury or damage to, चोट या क्षति पहुँचाना। 2. to distress, यातना देना। 3. to feel pain, दर्द होना। ***n.*** 1. something that hurts, चोट, आघात। 2. mental suffering, व्यथा। 3. harm, हानि।

husband (हज़्बेन्ड) ***n.*** a man to whom a woman is married, पति, शौहर। ***v.*** to manage economically, किफ़ायत से प्रबंध करना।

husbandry (हज़्बेन्ड्री) ***n.*** 1. farming, खेती-बारी। 2. economy, अर्थ-व्यवस्था।

hush (हश) ***v.*** 1. to make silent, चुप कराना, शांत करना। 2. to become silent, चुप हो जाना। □ **hush up,** दबा या छिपा देना। ***n.*** silence, चुप्पी, निस्तब्धता, शांति।

hush money ***n.*** money paid to prevent someone from telling the truth, मुँह-भराई, रिश्वत।

husk (हस्क) ***n.*** the dry outer covering of certain seeds, भूसी, छिलका। ***v.*** to take the husks off, भूसी या छिलका उतारना।

husky (हस्की) ***adj.*** hoarse, फटी-फटी या भर्राई आवाज़वाला।

hustle (हसल) ***v.*** 1. to push roughly, धक्का देना, धकियाना। 2. to move hurriedly, तेज़ी से आगे बढ़ना। 3. to make money by wrong means, ग़लत ढंग से धन कमाना। ***n.*** 1. busy activity, व्यस्ततापूर्ण क्रिया या व्यापार; जल्दबाज़ी। 2. hustle and bustle, धक्कम-धक्का।

hut (हट) ***n.*** a small and make-shift dwelling, झोंपड़ी, कुटिया, मढ़ी।

hybrid (हाइब्रिड) ***adj. & n.*** (the offspring) of two animals or plants of different race, संकर, दोगला।

hybridize (हाइब्रिडाइज़) ***v.*** to crossbreed, संकरण करना, संकर उत्पत्ति करना।

hydrant (हाइड्रन्ट) ***n.*** an upright pipe with a nozzle for public use, बंबा।

hydraulic (हाइड्रॉलिक) ***adj.*** operated by a liquid, द्रवचालित।

hydrocarbon (हाइड्रोकार्बन) ***n.*** a

H

compound that contains carbon and hydrogen, हाइड्रोकार्बन।

hydroelectric (हाइड्रोइलेक्ट्रिक) ***adj.*** concerning electricity produced by water, जल-विद्युत संबंधी।

hydrogen (हाइड्रोजन) ***n.*** a highly flammable gaseous element, हाइड्रोजन, उद्‌जन; hydrogen bomb, हाइड्रोजन बम।

hydrolysis (हाइड्रॉलिसिस) ***n.*** decomposition of a compound by reaction with water, जल-अपघटन।

hydrometre (हाइड्रॉमिटर) ***n.*** an-instrument for measuring the gravity of liquids, हाइड्रोमीटर।

hydrophobia (हाइड्रफ़ोबिआ) ***n.*** fear of water, जलभीति। 2. rabies, पागल कुत्ते के काटने से होनेवाला रोग।

hydroplane (हाइड्रोप्लेन) ***n.*** a light fast motorboat, यंत्रचालित नौका।

hydrotherapy (हाइड्रोथेरपी) ***n.*** the use of water in the treatment of diseases, जल-चिकित्सा।

hydrous (हाइड्रस) ***adj.*** containing water, जलीय, जलयुक्त।

hyena (हाईना) ***n.*** an animal of wolf family, लकड़बग्घा।

hygiene (हाइजीन) ***n.*** the science of health and its maintenance, स्वास्थ्य-विज्ञान।

hygienic (हाइजीनिक) ***adj.*** 1. of hygiene, स्वास्थ्य-विज्ञान-संबंधी। 2. promoting health, स्वास्थ्यवर्धक। 3. sanitary, स्वच्छ, स्वच्छता-संबंधी।

hymen (हाइमन) ***n.*** a membrane closing the external opening of the vagina, योनिच्छद।

hymn (हिम) ***n.*** a song of praise to god, ईश्वर-स्तुति, स्तोत्र।

hyperacidity (हाइपरएसिडिटी) ***n.*** excessive acidity, अतिअम्लता।

hyperbole (हाइपरबोली) ***n.*** an exaggerated statement, अतिशयोक्ति।

hypersensitive (हाइपरसेन्सिटिव) ***adj.*** excessively sensitive, अति-संवेदनशील।

hypertension (हाइपरटेन्शन) ***n.*** 1. abnormally high blood pressure, असामान्य रूप से उच्च रक्तचाप, अतिरक्तचाप। 2. a state of high emotional tension, अत्यधिक मानसिक तनाव।

hyphen (हाइफन) ***n.*** a punctuation mark used to join two words together, योजिका, हाइफ़न।

hypnosis (हिप्नोसिस) ***n.*** an induced sleep like condition, सम्मोहन, सम्मोह।

hypnotism (हिप्नॉटिज़्म) ***n.*** the act of inducing hypnosis, सम्मोहन क्रिया।

hypocrisy (हिपॉक्रिसी) ***n.*** the professing of virtue or goodness that one does not possess, पाखंड, ढोंग, मिथ्याचार।

hypodermic (हाइपोडर्मिक) ***adj.*** injected beneath the skin, अधस्त्वचीय। ***n.*** a hypodermic injection or needle, सुई।

hypotension (हाइपोटेन्शन) ***n.*** abnormally low blood pressure, असामान्य रूप से निम्न रक्तचाप, क्षीण रक्तचाप।

hypotenuse (हाइपॉटिन्यूज़) ***n.*** the side of a right angled triangle opposite the right angle, समकोण त्रिभुज का कर्ण।

hypothecate (हाइपॉथिकेट) ***v.*** to

mortgage, बंधक रखना, रेहन रखना।

hypothesis (हाइपॉथिसिस) ***n.*** (plu. hypotheses) 1. supposition, अनुमान। 2. an explanation or assumption tentatively accepted to explain certain facts, किसी तथ्य को समझाने के लिए मान ली जानेवाली बात, प्राक्कल्पना।

hypothetical (हाइपथेटिकल) ***adj.*** of or based on a hypothesis, अनुमान पर आधारित, प्राक्कल्पित या प्राक्काल्पनिक।

hysteria (हिस्टिरिआ) ***n.*** 1. a nervous disorder of women, मूर्च्छा, उन्माद।

I, i (आई) ***n.*** the ninth letter of the English alphabet, अंग्रेज़ी वर्णमाला का नौवाँ वर्ण। ***pron.*** the person who is the speaker or writer, मैं।

ibex (आइबेक्स) ***n.*** a mountain goat, पहाड़ी बकरी।

ibid (आइबिड) ***adv.*** in the same book, उसी पुस्तक में, वहीं।

ice (आइस) ***n.*** water in frozen state, बर्फ़। □ **break the ice,** बात छेड़ना; **cut no ice,** कुछ भी प्रभाव न डाल पाना; **on thin ice,** अत्यंत नाजुक स्थिति में। ***v.*** 1. to freeze, जमाना, ठंडा करना। 2. to decorate with icing, बर्फ़ के कणों से सजाना।

ice age ***n.*** the glacial epoch, हिमयुग।

ice bag ***n.*** a bag filled with ice used to make parts of the body cool, बर्फ़ की थैली।

iceberg (आइसबर्ग) ***n.*** a large piece of ice floating in the sea, हिमशैल, आइसबर्ग।

icebox (आइसबॉक्स) ***n.*** a box in which ice is put to preserve food, आइसबॉक्स।

icecap (आइसकैप) ***n.*** a large ice sheet covering the top of a mountain, पहाड़ की चोटी पर जमी हुई बर्फ़ की परत।

ice-cream (आइसक्रीम) ***n.*** a frozen food consisting of milk, sugar etc., आइसक्रीम, मलाई की बर्फ़।

ice-skating (आइस-स्केटिंग) ***n.*** the art of skating on the ice, हिमसरण, आइस-स्केटिंग।

icing (आइसिंग) ***n.*** a mixture of butter, sugar, etc. used on cakes, आइसिंग, सजावटी मसाला।

icon (आइकॉन) ***n.*** a sacred image, प्रतिमा, मूर्ति।

iconoclast (आइकॉनोक्लैस्ट) ***n.*** one who attacks traditional beliefs and institutions, रूढ़िभंजक, मूर्तिभंजक।

icy (आइसी) ***adj.*** (icier, iciest) 1. as cold as ice, बर्फ़-सा ठंडा। 2. covered with ice, हिमाच्छादित।

ID Card ***n.*** an identity card, परिचय-पत्र।

idea (आइडीआ) ***n.*** 1. a thought or opinion, mental impression, विचार, मत या बात। 2. a plan, योजना। 3. a guess, अनुमान। 4. a suggestion, सुझाव। 5. a purpose, प्रयोजन।

ideal (आइडीअल) ***adj.*** 1. perfect or standard, आदर्श, मानक। 2. imaginary, काल्पनिक। ***n.*** 1. a person, thing or idea that is regarded as model of perfection, आदर्श। 2. a goal, ध्येय।

idealism (आइडीअलिज़म) ***n.*** the system of living according to one's ideals, आदर्शवाद।

idealize (आइडीअलाइज़) ***v.*** to regard or represent as ideal, आदर्श रूप में प्रस्तुत करना या मानना, आदर्शीकरण करना।

identical (आइडेन्टिकल) ***adj.*** 1. being the same, वही। 2. exactly alike, वैसा ही।

identification (आइडेन्टिफ़िकेशन) ***n.*** 1. the act of identifying or the state of being identified, पहचान, शिनाख़्त। 2. proof of identity, पहचान का प्रमाण। 3. making identical, तदात्मीकरण, तद्रूपीकरण।

identify (आइडेन्टिफ़ाइ) *v.* 1. to determine the identity of, पहचानना, शिनाख़्त करना। 2. to cause to be identical, तदात्मीकरण करना। 3. to consider to be identical, अभिन्न समझना, एक मान लेना।

identity (आइडेन्टिटी) *n.* 1. the quality of being the same, समरूपता, अनन्यता। 2. the set of characteristics by which a person is known, पहचान, अभिज्ञान। 3. the condition of being the same, तादात्म्य, अभेद।

ideogram (आइडिओग्रैम) *n.* a symbol representing an idea, प्रतीक, भावचित्र।

ideological (आइडिओलॉजिकल) *adj.* of or based on an ideology, वैचारिक, सैद्धांतिक, मतवादी।

ideology (आइडिऑलोजी) *n.* a body of ideas that form the basis of a theory, विचारधारा, मतवाद।

idiom (इडिअम) *n.* 1. a phrase having a special meaning different from the meanings of the individual words, मुहावरा। 2. a specific character of a given language, मुहावरेदारी। 3. the language used by a people or group, बोली।

idiosyncrasy (इडिओसिन्क्रेसी) *n.* 1. peculiar attitude or behaviour, विचित्र प्रवृत्ति या व्यवहार, प्रकृति, वैशिष्ट्य। 2. eccentricity, सनक, पागलपन।

idiot (इडिअट) *n.* a person of weak intellect, stupid person, मंदबुद्धि या मूढ़ व्यक्ति।

idle (आइडल) *adj.* 1. not working, unemployed, बेकार, बेरोज़गार। 2. inactive, lazy, अक्रिय, सुस्त, आलसी। 3. worthless, व्यर्थ का, बेकार का। *v.* 1. to pass time without working, व्यर्थ समय गँवाना। 2. (of an engine) to run slowly in neutral gear, खाली चलना।

idol (आइडल) *n.* 1. an image used as object of worship, मूर्ति, प्रतिमा, देवप्रतिमा, देवमूर्ति। 2. an object of adoration or admiration, आराध्य/श्रद्धास्पद वस्तु या व्यक्ति।

idolater (आइडॉलेटर) *n.* one who worships idols, मूर्तिपूजक, बुतपरस्त।

idolize (आइडलाइज़) *v.* 1. to worship as an idol, पूजा/आराधना करना। 2. to regard with blind devotion, अंधभक्त होना।

i.e. (आइ.ई.) ***abbrev.*** that is to say, अर्थात्।

if (इफ़) ***conj.*** 1. in the event, on condition that, यदि, अगर। 2. even though, भले ही। 3. that, कि। *n.* a condition, शर्त; ifs and buts, अगर-मगर।

igloo (इग्लू) *n.* a house built of blocks of ice, हिमकुटी।

igneous (इग्निअस) *adj.* 1. of or relating to the fire, अग्नि-संबंधी। 2. formed by volcanic action, लावे का बना, ज्वालामुखी से निकला हुआ।

ignite (इग्नाइट) *v.* 1. to set fire to, जलाना, सुलगाना। 2. to catch fire, जलना।

ignoble (इग्नोबल) *adj.* 1. not noble, अकुलीन, साधारण, हेय।

Ignominious (इग्नॉमिनिअस) *adj.* 1. characterized by dishonour, नीच, पतित, नाम को बट्टा लगानेवाला। 2. despicable, जघन्य। 3. humiliating, अपमानकारी।

ignominy (इग्नॉमिनी) *n.* dishonour, humiliation, बदनामी, अपयश, कलंक।

I

ignorant (इग्नरेन्ट) ***adj.*** 1. wanting in knowledge, अनभिज्ञ, अज्ञ, अनाड़ी, अनजान, नासमझ। 2. without education or knowledge, अशिक्षित, अनजान।

ignore (इग्नोर) ***v.*** 1. to take no notice of, अनदेखी करना। 2. to disregard, उपेक्षा करना।

iguana (इग्वाना) ***n.*** a large lizard, गोह।

ill (इल) ***adj.*** (worse, worst) 1. unwell, sick, अस्वस्थ, बीमार, रुग्ण। 2. not good, ख़राब, बुरा। 3. harmful, hostile, unfriendly, अहितकर, वैरपूर्ण, अमैत्रीपूर्ण। ***adv.*** 1. in an ill manner, ख़राब ढंग से, बुरी तरह। 2. with difficulty, कठिनाई से। ***n.*** 1. evil, बुराई। 2. harm or injury, हानि, क्षति। 3. an ailment, बीमारी, रोग।

I'll (आइल) ***Short form.*** I will, I shall......, मैं ...... ऊँगा।

ill-advised (इल-ऐड्वाइज़्ड) ***adj.*** done without wise counsel or careful deliberation, कुमंत्रित, अविचारित, अविचारपूर्ण।

illegal (इलीगल) ***adj.*** prohibited by law, not legal, अवैध, गैरक़ानूनी।

illegible (इलेजिबल) ***adj.*** not legible, अस्पष्ट, अपाठ्य।

illegitimate (इलिजिटिमेट) ***adj.*** 1. not allowed by the rules, अवैध, गैरक़ानूनी। 2. born of parents not married to each other, दोगला, जारज।

ill-fame (इल-फ़ेम) ***n.*** disrepute, बदनामी, अपयश।

ill-fated (इल-फेटिड) ***adj.*** unfortunate, unlucky, अभागा, क़िस्मत का मारा।

ill-gotten (इल-गॉटन) ***adj.*** obtained by dishonest or unlawful means, अनुचित या अवैध रूप से प्राप्त।

illicit (इलिसिट) ***adj.*** unlawful, अवैध, गैरक़ानूनी।

illiteracy (इलिटरेसी) ***n.*** the state of being illiterate, निरक्षरता, अशिक्षा।

illiterate (इलिटरिट) ***adj.*** not literate, बेपढ़ा-लिखा, अनपढ़, निरक्षर। ***n.*** an illiterate person, निरक्षर व्यक्ति।

ill-mannered (इल-मैनर्ड) ***adj.*** having bad manners, उजड्ड, अशिष्ट, बदतमीज़।

illness (इलनिस) ***n.*** the state of being ill, sickness, बीमारी, रोग।

illogical (इलॉजिकल) ***adj.*** not logical, असंगत, तर्कविरुद्ध।

ill-treat (इल-ट्रीट) ***v.*** to treat badly, बुरा बरताव करना, बुरा व्यवहार करना।

illuminate (इल्यूमिनेट) ***v.*** 1. to light up, रोशन करना, प्रदीप्त करना। 2. to decorate with lights, जगमग कर देना, बत्तियों से सजाना। 3. to make understandable, प्रकाश डालना, व्याख्या करना।

illusion (इल्यूज़न) ***n.*** 1. a false perception or belief, भ्रम, भ्रांति। 2. something a person wrongly supposes to exist, माया।

illustrate (इलस्ट्रेट) ***v.*** 1. to provide with pictures and diagrams, सचित्र करना या बनाना, चित्रों से युक्त करना। 2. to explain or clarify, व्याख्या करना, उदाहरण देकर समझाना।

illustration (इलस्ट्रेशन) ***n.*** that which illustrates, उदाहरण, दृष्टांत।

illustrious (इलस्ट्रिअस) ***adj.*** renowned, famous, प्रसिद्ध, यशस्वी।

ill-will (इल-विल) ***n.*** unfriendly feeling, दुर्भाव, वैमनस्य।

image (इमिज) ***n.*** 1. a picture or appearance, चित्र, आकृति। 2. a sculptured picture, प्रतिमा, मूर्ति। 3. a mental picture, बिंब, मानसिक चित्र। 4. something very like another in appearance, प्रतिरूप, प्रतिच्छाया, प्रतिबिंब। 5. a personification, मानवीकृत रूप। 6. a vivid description, विशद विवरण।

imagery (इमिजरी) ***n.*** 1. images, प्रतिमाएँ, मूर्तियाँ। 2. figure of speech conveying poetic images, बिंब-चित्रण, बिंब-विधान।

imaginary (इमैजिनरी) ***adj.*** existing only in imagination, काल्पनिक, मनगढ़ंत।

imagination (इमैजिनेशन) ***n.*** 1. the ability to imagine, कल्पना-शक्ति। 2. something imagined, कल्पना। 3. creativity, सृजनशीलता, सूझ-बूझ।

imaginative (इमैजिनेटिव) ***adj.*** having or showing imagination, कल्पनाशील, कल्पनात्मक, सूझ-बूझ भरा।

imagine (इमैजिन) ***v.*** 1. to form a mental image of, मन में चित्र बनाना। 2. to think, सोचना, विचार करना। 3. to suppose, मान लेना, कल्पना करना।

imbalance (इम्बैलेन्स) ***n.*** lack of balance, असंतुलन।

imbecile (इम्बेसाइल) ***n.*** a stupid person, मूढ़ व्यक्ति।

imbed (इम्बेड) ***v.*** to embed, जड़ना।

imbibe (इम्बाइब) ***v.*** 1. to drink, पीना। 2. to absorb into mind, आत्मसात्/हृदयंगम करना।

imbroglio (इम्ब्रोल्यो) ***n.*** a confused or difficult situation, उलझन, कठिनाई, परेशानी।

imitate (इमिटेट) ***v.*** to copy the appearance, action, sounds (of someone, किसी की) नक़ल उतारना, नक़ल करना, अनुकरण करना।

imitation (इमिटेशन) ***n.*** 1. the act of imitating, नक़ल, अनुकरण। 2. an artificial likeness, रूपाभास।

imitative (इमिटेटिव) ***adj.*** 1. not original, नक़ली। 2. showing resemblance, अनुकरणात्मक, अनुकारी।

immaculate (इमैक्युलेट) ***adj.*** 1. without blemish, spotless, निर्दोष, बेदाग़। 2. pure, विशुद्ध, निर्मल, खरा। 3. free from moral blemish, सच्चरित्र, निष्कलंक।

immaterial (इमैटिरिअल) ***adj.*** 1. not consisting of matter, अभौतिक। 2. having no body or form, विदेह, अरूप। 3. that does not matter, अनावश्यक।

immature (इमैच्योर) ***adj.*** 1. not mature or ripe, अप्रौढ़, अपरिपक्व। 2. childish, बचकाना।

immeasurable (इमैज़रेबल) ***adj.*** not measurable, जिसकी नाप-जोख न हो सके,

immediate (इमीडिएट) ***adj.*** 1. occuring without delay, instant, तात्कालिक, फ़ौरी, अविलंब। 2. nearby, सन्निकट, आसन्न। 3. coming next or very soon, आगामी।

immemorial (इमेमोरिअल) ***adj.*** extending back beyond memory, tradition or recorded history, अतिप्राचीन, स्मरणातीत।

immense (इमेन्स) ***adj.*** very large, असीम, विशाल।

immensity (इमेन्सिटी) ***n.*** the state of being immense, असीमता, विशालता।

immerse (इमर्स) ***v.*** 1. to plunge into a liquid, डुबकी लगाना, गोता लगाना। 2. to engross, निमग्न होना, तल्लीन होना।

I

immersion (इमर्शन) ***n.*** the act of immersing or the state of being immersed, निमज्जन, अवगाहन।

immigrant (इमिग्रेन्ट) ***adj.*** immigrating, आप्रवासी। ***n.*** a person who has immigrated, आप्रवासी।

immigrate (इमिग्रेट) ***v.*** to come into a country from abroad in order to settle there, विदेश से आकर बसना, आप्रवास करना।

imminence (इमिनेन्स) ***n.*** the quality or state of being imminent, आसन्नता।

imminent (इमिनेन्ट) ***adj.*** about to occur, आसन्न, जो शीघ्र ही होने को हो।

immobile (इमोबाइल) ***adj.*** not moving, immovable, अचल, स्थिर।

immobilize (इमोबिलाइज़) ***v.*** to make immobilized, अचल कर देना, स्थिर बना देना।

immoderate (इमॉडरिट) ***adj.*** 1. not moderate, without restraint, अमर्यादित, असंयमित। 2. excessive, अत्यधिक।

immolate (इमोलेट) ***v.*** to offer as a sacrifice, बलि देना।

immolation (इमोलेशन) ***n.*** the act of immolating or the state of being immolated, बलि, क़ुरबानी।

immoral (इमॉरल) ***adj.*** 1. contrary to the moral principles, नीतिविरुद्ध, अनीतिपूर्ण। 2. morally wrong, अनैतिक, अनुचित।

immorality (इमरैलिटी) ***n.*** 1. the state or quality of being immoral, अनैतिकता, अनीति। 2. immoral behaviour, अनैतिक आचरण, दुराचार।

immortal (इमॉर्टल) ***adj.*** 1. living for ever, शाश्वत, अमर, सनातन। 2. having lasting fame, चिरस्मरणीय।

immortality (इमॉर्टैलिटी) ***n.*** 1. endless existence, अमरता, सनातनता। 2. lasting fame, चिरख्याति।

immortalize (इमॉर्टलाइज़) ***v.*** 1. to make immortal, अमर कर या बना देना। 2. to give lasting fame to, स्मृति को अमिट बना देना।

immovable (इमूवेबल) ***adj.*** that cannot be moved, अचल, स्थावर।

immune (इम्यून) ***adj.*** 1. exempt (from a tax, duty or penalty, कर, शुल्क, दंड आदि से) उन्मुक्त, रहित। 2. protected against infection, (छूत से) निरापद, प्रतिरक्षित।

immunity (इम्यूनिटी) ***n.*** 1. exemption, उन्मुक्ति, छूट। 2. protection against infection, निरापदता, बचाव, प्रतिरक्षा।

immunize (इम्यूनाइज़) ***v.*** to make immune, निरापद बनाना, प्रतिरक्षित करना।

immutable (इम्यूटेबल) ***adj.*** never changing, अपरिवर्तनीय, अपरिवर्तशील, निर्विकार।

impact (इम्पैक्ट) ***n.*** 1. a shock, धक्का, आघात। 2. a collision, टक्कर।

impair (इम्पेअर) ***v.*** 1. to damage, बिगाड़ देना, ख़राब कर देना। 2. to diminish the quality, value or strength of a thing, ह्रास करना, क्षति पहुँचाना।

impairment (इम्पेअरमेन्ट) ***n.*** 1. damage, क्षति, हानि। 2. deterioration, ह्रास।

impart (इम्पार्ट) ***v.*** 1. to give or bestow, देना, प्रदान करना। 2. to reveal or disclose, प्रकट करना, बतलाना।

impartial (इम्पार्शल) ***adj.*** not partial, तटस्थ, निष्पक्ष, पक्षपातविहीन।

impassable (इम्पासेबल) ***adj.*** which

I

cannot be travelled over or crossed, दुर्गम।

impasse (इम्पास) ***n.*** a deadlock, गतिरोध।

impassioned (इम्पैशन्ड) ***adv.*** 1. filled with passion, भावपूर्ण, भावाभिभूत। 2. fiery, जोश-भरा, आवेशपूर्ण।

impassive (इम्पैसिव) ***adj.*** not feeling or showing emotion, calm, स्थिरचित्त, शांतचित्त।

impatient (इम्पेशन्ट) ***adj.*** 1. feeling or showing a lack of patience, अधीर, बेचैन। 2. intolerant, असहिष्णु।

impeach (इम्पीच) ***v.*** to charge a public official with misconduct before a proper tribunal, महाभियोग लगाना, अभियोग लगाना।

impeachment (इम्पीचमेन्ट) ***n.*** the act of impeaching or the state of being impeached, महाभियोग, अभियोजन।

impeccable (इम्पेकेबल) ***adj.*** faultless, निर्दोष, त्रुटिहीन, निष्कलंक।

impede (इम्पीड) ***v.*** to obstruct or hinder, अड़ंगा लगाना, बाधा डालना।

impediment (इम्पेडिमेन्ट) ***n.*** 1. an obstruction or hinderance, अड़ंगा, बाधा। 2. a defect, दोष, त्रुटि।

impel (इम्पेल) ***v.*** 1. to urge or incite, प्रेरित या उत्तेजित करना। 2. to force, ज़ोर डालना, विवश करना। 3. to drive forward, आगे बढ़ाना, चलाना।

impenetrable (इम्पेनिट्रेबल) ***adj.*** 1. that cannot be penetrated, अभेद्य, दुर्भेद्य। 2. impassable, दुर्गम, अगम।

imperative (इम्पेरेटिव) ***adj.*** 1. expres sing a command, आज्ञासूचक, विध्यर्थक, आदेशात्मक। 2. essential or urgent, अत्यावश्यक, अनिवार्य, लाज़िमी। ***n.*** the imperative mood, आज्ञासूचक क्रियाभाव।

imperceptible (इम्पर्सेप्टिबल) ***adj.*** 1. not perceptible, अगोचर, अवगम्य। 2. subtle, सूक्ष्म।

imperfect (इम्पर्फ़ेक्ट) ***adj.*** 1. not perfect, अपूर्ण। 2. not complete, अधूरा। 3. defective, सदोष, त्रुटिपूर्ण। ***n.*** imperfect tense, अपूर्णकाल।

imperfection (इम्पर्फ़ेक्शन) ***n.*** 1. the quality or condition of being imperfect, अपूर्णता, अधूरापन। 2. a fault or blemish, दोष, त्रुटि, कमी।

imperial (इम्पीरिअल) ***adj.*** 1. of an empire, साम्राज्य-संबंधी। 2. of an emperor or empress, सम्राट-संबंधी, सम्राज्ञी-संबंधी। 3. royal or majestic, राजसी।

imperialistic (इम्पीरिअलिस्टिक) ***adj.*** of imperialism or imperialist, साम्राज्यवादी।

imperil (इम्पेरिल) ***v.*** to endanger, ख़तरे में डालना, संकट में फँसाना।

imperious (इम्पीरिअस) ***adj.*** 1. overbearing, घमंडी। 2. pressing, आवश्यक। 3. commanding, रोबीला।

imperishable (इम्पेरिशेबल) ***adj.*** not perishable, अविनाशी, अनश्वर।

impermeable (इम्पर्मिएबल) ***adj.*** not permeable, अभेद्य, अपारगम्य।

impersonal (इम्पर्सनल) ***adj.*** not referring to or intended for any particular person, अवैयक्तिक, निर्वैयक्तिक।

impersonate (इम्पर्सनेट) ***v.*** to pretend to be another, पररूप धारण करना, स्वाँग रचना, छद्म रूप धारण करना।

impertinent (इम्पर्टिनेन्ट) ***adj.*** impudent, rude, ढीठ, उद्धत, धृष्ट, बेरुख़ा।

I

imperturbable (इम्पर्टर्बेबल) ***adj.*** not easily disturbed or excited, गंभीर, शांत।

impervious (इम्पर्विअस) ***adj.*** 1. not able to be penetrated, अभेद्य। 2. not affected or influenced by, अप्रभाव्य।

impetuous (इम्पेचुअस) ***adj.*** 1. acting too hastily, rash, उतावला, जल्दबाज़। 2. violent, प्रचंड, घोर।

impetus (इम्पिटस) ***n.*** 1. driving force, चालन-शक्ति, गतिबल, शक्ति। 2. encouragement, बढ़ावा, प्रोत्साहन।

impinge (इम्पिन्ज) ***v.*** 1. to collide or strike, टकराना या टक्कर लगाना। 2. to have an effect on, प्रभावित करना। 3. to encroach, अतिक्रमण करना।

impious (इम्पिअस) ***adj.*** 1. not pious, अपवित्र, अपावन। 2. lacking reverence for God, नास्तिक, अनास्थावान।

implant (इम्प्लान्ट) ***v.*** 1. to fix or insert in the mind, मन में बैठाना या धँसाना। 2. to insert surgically, शल्यकर्म द्वारा लगाना, बैठाना या रोपना।

implausible (इम्प्लॉज़िबल) ***adj.*** not plausible, अयुक्तियुक्त या अविश्वसनीय।

implement[1] (इम्प्लिमेन्ट) ***n.*** a tool or instrument, उपकरण, औज़ार।

implement[2] ***v.*** to put into practice, अमल में लाना, कार्यान्वित करना।

implementation (इम्प्लिमेन्टेशन) ***n.*** the act of implementing or the state of being implemented, कार्यान्वयन।

implicate (इम्प्लिकेट) ***v.*** 1. to involve or entangle, उलझाना, सानना, फँसाना। 2. to imply, विवक्षित करना।

implication (इम्प्लिकेशन) ***n.*** 1. an act of implicating, उलझाव, सनाव, फँसाव। 2. a suggestion not expressed but understood, hidden meaning, विवक्षा, निहितार्थ।

implicit (इम्प्लिसिट) ***adj.*** 1. not expressed but understood, विवक्षित, निहित, अंतर्निहित। 2. absolute, पूर्ण, समग्र।

implode (इम्प्लोड) ***v.*** to burst inward, भीतर-भीतर फूटना, अंत:विस्फोट होना।

implore (इम्प्लोर) ***v.*** to ask or beg earnestly, विनती/चिरौरी करना।

imply (इम्प्लाइ) ***v.*** 1. to express without stating directly, विवक्षित करना। 2. to mean, अर्थ देना। 3. to include, अंतर्निहित होना।

impolite (इम्पोलाइट) ***adj.*** not polite, अशिष्ट, अविनीत, अभद्र।

imponderable (इम्पॉन्डरेबल) ***adj.*** 1. that cannot be estimated or calculated, जिसे आँका या कूता न जा सके, अमित। 2. very light, हलका।

import (इम्पोर्ट) ***v.*** 1. to bring in from a foreign country, आयात करना। 2. to mean or signify, अर्थ होना, संकेत करना। ***n.*** 1. something imported, आयात। 2. meaning, significance, अर्थ, अभिप्राय, आशय। 3. importance, महत्त्व।

importance (इम्पॉर्टेन्स) ***n.*** the state or quality of being important, महत्त्व।

important (इम्पॉर्टेन्ट) ***adj.*** 1. of great consequence, महत्त्वपूर्ण। 2. noteworthy, उल्लेखनीय। 3. having great authority or influence, प्रभावशाली।

importer (इम्पोर्टर) ***n.*** one who imports goods from other countries, आयातकर्ता।

I

importunate (इम्पॉर्चुनिट) ***adj.*** unreasonably persistent, ज़िद पकड़ लेनेवाला, दुराग्रही।

importune (इम्पॉर्चून) ***v.*** to make persistent requests, बार-बार विनती/आग्रह करना।

impose (इम्पोज़) ***v.*** 1. to levy, लगाना, अधिरोपित करना। 2. to take unfair advantage, अनुचित लाभ उठाना। 3. to arrange pages in proper order at the time of printing, इंपोज़ करना।

imposing (इम्पोज़िन्ग) ***adj.*** grand, impressive, शानदार, भव्य, प्रभावपूर्ण।

imposition (इम्पोज़िशन) ***n.*** 1. the act of imposing, अधिरोपण। 2. something imposed, लगाया या अधिरोपित किया हुआ कर, विचार आदि। 3. burden, बोझ, भार।

impossible (इम्पॉसिबल) ***adj.*** 1. not possible, असंभव। 2. difficult, कठिन।

impostor (इम्पॉस्टर) ***n.*** a person who deceives others under an assumed identity, छद्मवेशी, कपटी, ढोंगी, झूठा दावेदार।

impotence (इम्पोटेन्स) ***n.*** 1. lack of ability to cohabit or procreate, नपुंसकता, नामर्दी। 2. weakness, कमज़ोरी, अशक्तता।

impotent (इम्पोटेन्ट) ***adj.*** 1. incapable of sexual intercourse or unable to procreate, नपुंसक, नामर्द। 2. powerless, अशक्त, शक्तिहीन, असहाय।

impound (इम्पॉउन्ड) ***v.*** 1. to enclose into a pound, बाड़े (या कांजी हाउस) में बंद करना। 2. to seize, ज़ब्त करना, कुर्क़ करना।

impoverish (इम्पॉवरिश) ***v.*** 1. to make poor, दरिद्र बना देना, कंगाल कर देना। 2. to deprive of natural strength, बेदम कर देना, निष्प्राण कर देना।

impracticability (इम्प्रैक्टिकेबिलिटी) ***n.*** the quality of being impracticable, अव्यवहार्यता, अव्यावहारिकता।

impracticable (इम्प्रैक्टिकेबल) ***adj.*** impractical, अव्यवहार्य, अव्यावहारिक।

impractical (इम्प्रैक्टिकल) ***adj.*** not practical, अव्यवहार्य, अव्यावहारिक, अव्यवहारशील।

impregnable (इम्प्रेग्नेबल) ***adj.*** unconquerable, अजेय, अभेद्य।

impregnate (इम्प्रेग्नेट) ***v.*** 1. to make pregnant, गर्भाधान करना, गर्भवती बनाना। 2. to fill or infuse, भरना, पूरित करना, अंतर्वेशित करना।

impress (इम्प्रेस) ***v.*** 1. to mark or stamp with pressure, छापना या ठप्पा लगाना। 2. to produce a favourable effect or influence on, प्रभावित करना। 3. to fix firmly in the mind, अच्छी तरह मन में बैठाना।

impression (इम्प्रेशन) ***n.*** 1. a mark left by pressure, छाप, ठप्पा। 2. an effect or influence produced on the mind, छाप, प्रभाव। 3. an uncertain idea or belief, धारणा। 4. a reprint of a book, संस्करण।

impressionable (इम्प्रेशनेबल) ***adj.*** easily influenced, जिसे सरलतापूर्वक प्रभावित किया जा सके, प्रभाव्य।

impressive (इम्प्रेसिव) ***adj.*** 1. making a strong impression, प्रभावपूर्ण, प्रभावोत्पादक। 2. arousing admiration and approval, मुग्धकारी, चित्ताकर्षक।

imprint[1] (इम्प्रिन्ट) ***v.*** to produce a mark or pattern on a surface, छाप या ठप्पा लगाना।

I

imprint² ***n.*** 1. a mark or pattern produced by printing, छाप। 2. the name of the printer (or publisher) as it appears on the book, मुद्रक (या प्रकाशक) का पुस्तक में छपा नाम, छाप।

imprison (इम्प्रिज़न) ***v.*** to put in prison, कारावास में रखना, क़ैद करना।

imprisonment (इम्प्रिज़नमेन्ट) ***n.*** the act of imprisoning or the state of being imprisoned, कारावास, क़ैद।

improbable (इम्प्रॉबेबल) ***adj.*** not probable, असंभाव्य।

impromptu (इम्प्रॉम्प्टू) ***adj. & adv.*** without preparation, बिना तैयारी का/के।

improper (इम्प्रॉपर) ***adj.*** 1. not proper, अनुचित। 2. unsuitable or not consistent, अनुपयुक्त, असंगत। 3. indecent, अशोभनीय, भद्दा। 4. not correct, अशुद्ध, ग़लत।

impropriety (इम्प्रॉप्राइटी) ***n.*** 1. the quality or state of being improper, अनौचित्य, अनुपयुक्तता, असंगति। 2. an improper act or behaviour, अशोभनीय व्यवहार।

improve (इम्प्रूव) ***v.*** 1. to become better, अच्छा होना, सुधरना। 2. to make better, सुधारना, उन्नत करना या बनाना।

improvement (इम्प्रूवमेन्ट) ***n.*** the act of improving or the state of being improved, सुधार, उन्नति।

improvident (इम्प्रॉविडेन्ट) ***adj.*** 1. wanting in foresight, अदूरदर्शी। 2. thriftless, unthrifty, अपव्ययी।

improvisation (इम्प्रॉविज़ेशन) ***n.*** the act of improvising, आशु कविता करना; कामचलाऊ व्यवस्था।

improvise (इम्प्रोवाइज़) ***v.*** 1. to recite without preparation, आशु कविता करना। 2. to make or provide from available materials, (जो प्रस्तुत हो उससे) काम चला लेना।

imprudence (इम्प्रूडेन्स) ***n.*** 1. rashness, उतावलापन। 2. thoughtlessness, अविवेक।

imprudent (इम्प्रूडेन्ट) ***adj.*** 1. rash, उतावला। 2. thoughtless, अविवेकी।

impugn (इम्प्यून) ***v.*** to raise doubt about, संदेह प्रकट करना, शंका करना।

impulse (इम्पल्स) ***n.*** 1. sudden force, आवेग। 2. an impelling wish to do something, मन की मौज, उमंग, सनक।

impunity (इम्प्यूनिटी) ***n.*** exemption from punishment or penalty, दंड से मुक्ति या छुटकारा, छूट।

impure (इम्प्योर) ***adj.*** 1. not pure, अशुद्ध, मिलावटी। 2. immoral, अनैतिक।

impurity (इम्प्योरिटी) ***n.*** the state or quality of being impure, अशुद्धता, मिलावट।

impute (इम्प्यूट) ***v.*** 1. to lay the responsibility of, जवाबदेह ठहराना। 2. to ascribe or blame, आरोप लगाना, दोषारोप करना। 3. to attribute, आरोपित करना।

in (इन) ***prep.*** 1. within the limits or boundaries, में, के अंदर। 2. toward the inside of, के अंदर। 3. used to indicate a condition or state, में; in anger, ग़ुस्से में। 4. of method or means of expression, में; in Hindi, हिंदी में। 5. with reference to, के विचार से, में। ***adv.*** to or toward the inside, भीतर, अंदर। ***adj.*** 1. internal, भीतरी। 2. extremely

I

fashionable, फ़ैशनदार। 3. incoming, आगामी। 4. having power, सत्ताधारी।

inability (इनेबिलिटी) ***n.*** lack of ability, अयोग्यता, असमर्थता।

in absentia (इन ऐब्सेन्शिआ) ***adv.*** in absence, अनुपस्थिति में, ग़ैरहाज़िरी में।

inaccessible (इनैक्सेसिबल) ***adj.*** not accessible, अगम्य।

inaccurate (इनैक्युरेट) ***adj.*** not accurate, incorrect, अशुद्ध, ग़लत।

inaction (इनैक्शन) ***n.*** 1. lack of action, निष्क्रियता। 2. doing nothing, निठल्लापन।

inactive (इनैक्टिव) ***adj.*** not active, निष्क्रिय, अक्रिय, निठल्ला।

inadequate (इनैडिक्विट) ***adj.*** not adequate, अपर्याप्त, अयथेष्ट, नाकाफ़ी।

inadmissible (इनैडमिसिबल) ***adj.*** not admissible, not allowable, अस्वीकार्य, अग्राह्य।

inadvertent (इनैडवर्टेन्ट) ***adj.*** 1. unintentional, अनभिप्रेत। 2. careless, असावधान।

inadvisable (इनैडवाइज़ेबल) ***adj.*** not advisable, अनुचित।

inalienable (इनेल्यनेबल) ***adj.*** that cannot be given up or taken away, जो दिया या लिया न जा सके, अदेय, अहरणीय।

inane (इनेन) ***adv.*** lacking sense, नासमझ, मूर्ख।

inanimate (इनैनिमिट) ***adj.*** not animate, निर्जीव, अचेतन, जड़।

inappropriate (इनप्रोप्रिइट) ***adj.*** unsuitable, अनुपयुक्त।

inasmuch as ***conj.*** bacause, क्योंकि।

inattentive (इनटेन्टिव) ***adj.*** not paying attention, असावधान, बेख़बर, लापरवाह।

inaudible (इनॉडिबल) ***adj.*** incapable of being heard, जो सुनाई न पड़े, अश्रव्य।

inaugural (इनॉग्युरल) ***adj.*** of or related to an inauguration, उद्घाटन-संबंधी।

inaugurate (इनॉग्युरेट) ***v.*** to open formally, उद्घाटन करना, आरंभ करना।

inauguration (इनॉग्युरेशन) ***n.*** the act of inaugurating, उद्घाटन, आरंभ।

inborn (इनबॉर्न) ***adj.*** existing from birth, जन्मजात, नैसर्गिक।

inbred (इनब्रेड) ***adj.*** 1. inborn, जन्मजात, नैसर्गिक। 2. bred from closely related people or animals, एक ही नस्ल के नर-मादा से उत्पन्न, अंत:प्रजात।

incalculable (इन्कैल्क्यूलेबल) ***adj.*** 1. that cannot be calculated, गणनातीत। 2. unpredictable, अनिश्चित, अपूर्वकथनीय।

in camera (इन कैमेरा) ***adv.*** in closed room, बंद कमरे में।

incandescent (इन्कैन्डेसेन्ट) ***adj.*** glowing or shining brilliantly, दीप्त, प्रकाशमान।

incantation (इन्कैन्टेशन) ***n.*** the chanting of magical words to produce a magic effect, मंत्रपाठ, झाड़-फूँक।

incapable (इन्कैपेबल) ***adj.*** not capable, असमर्थ, अक्षम, अयोग्य।

incapacitate (इन्कपैसिटेट) ***v.*** to make feeble, अशक्त या असमर्थ कर देना।

incarcerate (इन्कासैरेट) ***v.*** to confine or jail, कारागार में रखना।

incarnate¹ (इन्कार्निट) ***adj.*** in human form, मनुष्यरूपधारी।

incarnate² (इन्कार्नेट) ***v.*** to take bodily form, मनुष्य शरीर धारण करना, अवतार लेना।

I

incarnation (इन्कार्नेशन) ***n.*** 1. the act of incarnating or the state of being incarnated, देहधारण, मानव शरीर में अवतरण। 2. embodiment of a god, अवतार।

incendiary (इन्सेन्डिअरी) ***adj.*** 1. causing or producing fire, आग उत्पन्न करने या लगानेवाला। 2. inflammatory, भड़कानेवाला। ***n.*** 1. an incendiary bomb, अग्निबम। 2. an arsonist, आग लगानेवाला व्यक्ति।

incense[1] (इन्सेन्स) ***n.*** 1. an aromatic substance that produces sweet smell when burning, ऐसा पदार्थ जिसके जलने से सुगंध निकलती हो। 2. its smoke, (धूप आदि का) धुआँ।

incense[2] ***v.*** 1. to make fragrant with incense, धूनी देना। 2. to cause to be angry, क्रुद्ध करना।

incentive (इन्सेन्टिव) ***n.*** something that incites or encourages to an action, प्रोत्साहन, प्रोत्साहन देनेवाली वस्तु या बात।

inception (इन्सेप्शन) ***n.*** the commencement, प्रारंभ, शुरुआत, सूत्रपात, श्रीगणेश।

incessant (इन्सेसेन्ट) ***adj.*** never ending or ceasing, unceasing, सतत, अविरल।

incest (इन्सेस्ट) ***n.*** illegal sexual intercourse between nearly related persons, निषिद्ध संभोग, अगम्यागमन।

inch (इन्च) ***n.*** 1. the twelfth part of a foot, इंच, स्वल्प मात्रा। ***v.*** to move very slowly, बहुत धीरे चलना।

incharge (इन्चार्ज) ***n.*** one having the charge, इंचार्ज, प्रभारी।

incidence (इन्सिडेन्स) ***n.*** 1. the act or fact of falling upon, आपात, आपतन। 2. a burden, भार।

incident (इन्सिडेन्ट) ***n.*** an event, घटना, प्रसंग। ***adj.*** falling on surface, आपतित।

incidental (इन्सिडेन्टल) ***adj.*** 1. occurring by chance, आकस्मिक। 2. secondary, minor, गौण। 3. accompanying something else, आनुषंगिक।

incinerate (इन्सिनरेट) ***v.*** to burn to ashes, जलाकर राख कर डालना, फूँक डालना।

incise (इन्साइज़) ***v.*** to carve or engrave, नक़्क़ाशी करना, उत्कीर्ण करना, कटाई करना।

incision (इन्सिज़न) ***n.*** 1. the act of incising, नक़्क़ाशी, उत्कीर्णन, कटाई। 2. a cut made into an organ, चीरा।

incisor (इन्साइज़र) ***n.*** any of the sharp-edged eight teeth for cutting at the front of the mouth, सामने का काटनेवाला कोई नुकीला दाँत, कृंतक।

incite (इन्साइट) ***v.*** to provoke to action, उत्तेजित करना, उकसाना, भड़काना।

incitement (इन्साइटमेन्ट) ***n.*** 1. the act of inciting, उत्तेजन, उद्दीपन, उकसाव। 2. something that incites, उकसानेवाली बात, उत्तेजना।

incivility (इन्सिविलिटी) ***n.*** rudeness, बदतमीज़ी, अशिष्टता।

inclement (इन्क्लेमेन्ट) ***adj.*** stormy, तूफ़ानी (मौसम)।

inclination (इन्क्लिनेशन) ***n.*** 1. an act of inclining, झुकाव, नति। 2. a tendency, प्रवृत्ति, रुझान। 3. a liking, रुचि।

incline (इन्क्लाइन) ***v.*** 1. to slant, bend or bow, झुकना या झुकाना।

2. to slope, ढालुआँ होना या करना। 3. to have a particular disposition, प्रवृत्ति होना। 4. to have a liking, रुचि होना। ***n.*** a slope, ढाल।

include (इन्क्लूड) ***v.*** to have as part of a whole, शामिल करना, समाविष्ट करना।

including ***prep.*** having something or somebody as a part, (इस) के सहित, (इस) को लेकर, (इस) के समेत।

inclusion (इन्क्लूज़न) ***n.*** 1. the act of including or the state of being included, समावेशन, अंतर्गत करना, समावेश। 2. something included, समावेश, समाविष्ट वस्तु।

inclusive (इन्क्लूसिव) ***adj.*** including, (के) सहित।

incognito (इन्कॉग्नीटो) ***adv. & adj.*** with one's identity disguised or concealed, छद्म रूप से, भेस बदलकर।

incoherence (इन्कोहिअरेन्स) ***n.*** = incohesion.

incoherent (इन्कोहिअरेन्ट) ***adj.*** 1. not coherent, असंगत। 2. lacking connection or order, असंबद्ध या अव्यवस्थित।

incohesion (इन्कोहीज़न) ***n.*** the state of being incoherent, असंगति; असंबद्धता।

incombustible (इन्कम्बस्टिबल) ***adj.*** incapable of burning, जिसे जलाया न जा सके, अदाह्य।

income (इन्कम) ***n.*** money earned, आय, आमदनी।

income tax ***n.*** a tax levied on income, आयकर।

incomparable (इन्कॉम्पेरेबल) ***adj.*** incapable of being compared, अनुपम, बेजोड़।

incompatible (इन्कम्पैटिबल) ***adj.*** not compatible, बेमेल, असंगत।

incompetent (इन्कॉम्पिटेन्ट) ***adj.*** not competent, अयोग्य, अक्षम।

incomplete (इन्कम्प्लीट) ***adj.*** not complete, अधूरा, अपूर्ण।

incomprehensible (इन्कॉम्प्रिहेन्सिबल) ***adj.*** incapable of being comprehended, अबोधगम्य, समझ में न आनेवाला।

inconceivable (इन्कन्सीवेबल) ***adj.*** 1. that cannot be conceived, अचिंत्य। 2. unable to be imagined, अकल्पनीय।

inconclusive (इन्कन्क्लूसिव) ***adj.*** not final or decisive, अनिश्चायक, अनिर्णीत।

incongruous (इन्कॉन्ग्रूअस) ***adj.*** 1. not congruent, बेमेल, विसंगत। 2. not harmonious, बेडौल।

inconsequential (इन्कॉन्सिक्वेन्शल) ***adj.*** unimportant, अमहत्त्वपूर्ण, महत्त्वहीन।

inconsiderable (इन्कन्सिडरेबल) ***adj.*** unimportant, नगण्य, महत्त्वहीन।

inconsiderate (इन्कन्सिडरिट) ***adj.*** not considerate, बेमुरौवत, बेलिहाज़।

inconsistent (इन्कन्सिस्टेन्ट) ***adv.*** not consistent, असंगत, बेमेल, विसंगत।

inconsolable (इन्कन्सोलेबल) ***adj.*** that cannot be consoled, जिसे सांत्वना न दी जा सके, शोकविह्वल।

inconspicuous (इन्कॉन्स्पिक्युअस) ***adj.*** not conspicuous, अस्पष्ट, धुँधला।

incontestable (इन्कन्टेस्टेबल) ***adj.*** unquestionable, indisputable, असंदिग्ध, निर्विवाद, अकाट्य।

incontinent (इन्कॉन्टिनेन्ट) ***adj.*** incapable of controlling the

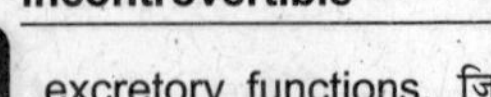

excretory functions, जिसका टट्टी-पेशाब पर नियंत्रण न हो।

incontrovertible (इन्कॉन्ट्रोवर्टिबल) ***adj.*** indisputable, अविवाद्य, निर्विवाद।

inconvenience (इन्कन्वीन्यन्स) ***n.*** lack of convenience, असुविधा, कष्ट। ***v.*** to cause inconvenience, असुविधा उत्पन्न करना, कष्ट देना।

inconvenient (इन्कन्वीन्यन्ट) ***adj.*** not convenient, असुविधापूर्ण, असुविधाजनक।

incorporate (इन्कॉर्पोरेट) ***v.*** 1. to combine or unite with something else so as to form one body, मिला देना, निगमित करना। 2. to form into a corporation, निगम बनाना।

incorporation (इन्कॉर्पोरेशन) ***n.*** the act of incorporating or the state of being incorporated, निगमीकरण; सम्मिलन, समावेशन।

incorrect (इन्करेकट) ***adj.*** not correct, ग़लत, अशुद्ध, मिथ्या।

incorrigible (इन्कॉरिजिबल) ***adj.*** that cannot be improved or reformed, असाध्य, असुधार्य।

incorruptible (इन्करप्टिबल) ***adj.*** 1. that cannot be corrupted or bribed, जिसे भ्रष्ट न किया जा सके, रिश्वत न लेनेवाला, सच्चरित्र। 2. not liable to decay, नाशविहीन, शाश्वत, सनातन।

increase (इन्क्रीस) ***v.*** 1. to become larger or greater, बढ़ना, वृद्धि होना। 2. to make larger or greater, बढ़ाना, वृद्धि करना। ***n.*** 1. the act of increasing or the state of being increased, बढ़ती, वृद्धि। 2. the amount by which something increases, बढ़ोतरी, वृद्धि।

increasing (इन्क्रीसिंग) ***adj.*** progressing, enlarging, वर्धमान।

incredible (इन्क्रेडिबल) ***adj.*** 1. not credible, अविश्वसनीय। 2. hard to believe, surprising, आश्चर्यजनक, अद्भुत।

increment (इन्क्रिमेन्ट) ***n.*** an increase, बढ़ती, बढ़ोतरी।

incriminate (इन्क्रिमिनेट) ***v.*** to involve in a crime, अपराध में फँसाना।

incubation (इन्क्युबेशन) ***n.*** the act of incubating, अंडे सेने की क्रिया या भाव, सेनाई।

incubator (इन्क्युबेटर) ***n.*** an apparatus for hatching eggs, अंडे सेने की मशीन।

inculcate (इन्कल्केट) ***v.*** to instill, मन में बैठाना।

incumbent (इन्कम्बेन्ट) ***adj.*** holding an office, पदधारी, पदधारक। ***n.*** the holder of an office, पदधारी।

incur (इन्कर) ***v.*** to bring upon oneself, मिलना, उठाना, ओढ़ना, उपगत करना।

incurable (इन्क्यूरेबल) ***adj.*** that cannot be cured, असाध्य, अचिकित्स्य।

incursion (इन्कर्शन) ***n.*** 1. a sudden attack, धावा, चढ़ाई। 2. a raid, छापा।

indebted (इन्डेटिड) ***adj.*** 1. owing money, ऋणी, कर्ज़दार। 2. grateful, आभारी, कृतज्ञ।

indecency (इन्डीसेन्सी) ***n.*** the quality or state of being indecent, अशोभनीयता, अभद्रता, अश्लीलता।

indecent (इन्डीसेन्ट) ***adj.*** not decent, अभद्र, अशोभनीय, अश्लील, लज्जाजनक।

indecision (इन्डिसिज़न) ***n.*** 1. inability to make a decision, निश्चयहीनता, अनिश्चय। 2. hesitation, हिचक, असमंजस।

I

indecisive (इन्डिसाइसिव) ***adj.*** not decisive, अनिश्चित, ढुलमुल।

indeclinable (इन्डिक्लाइनेबल) ***adj.*** not declinable, अविकारी। ***n.*** an indeclinable word, अव्यय।

indeed (इन्डीड) ***adv.*** really, सचमुच, निश्चय ही।

indefatigable (इन्डिफ़ैटिगेबल) ***adj.*** tireless, न थकनेवाला, अथक।

indefensible (इन्डिफ़ेन्सिबल) ***adj.*** 1. that cannot be defended, अरक्षणीय। 2. unable to be justified, जिसे उचित न ठहराया जा सके, असमर्थनीय।

indefinable (इन्डिफ़ाइनेबल) ***adj.*** 1. that cannot be defined, अपरिभाष्य। 2. indescribable, अवर्णनीय, वर्णनातीत।

indefinite (इन्डेफ़िनिट) ***adj.*** not definite or fixed, अनिश्चित, अस्पष्ट।

indefinitely ***adv.*** 1. in an indefinite way, अनिश्चिततापूर्वक, अस्पष्ट रूप से। 2. for indefinite time, अनिश्चित काल के लिए।

indelible (इन्डेलिबल) ***adj.*** that cannot be removed or washed way, न मिटनेवाला, अमिट, स्थायी, पक्का (दाग़ या धब्बा)।

indemnify (इन्डेम्निफ़ाइ) ***v.*** 1. to insure against loss or damage, क्षतिपूर्ति की गारंटी देना। 2. to compensate, क्षतिपूर्ति करना।

indemnity (इन्डेम्निटी) ***n.*** 1. protection against loss or damage, क्षतिपूर्ति की गारंटी। 2. compensation, क्षतिपूर्ति।

indent (इन्डेन्ट) ***v.*** 1. to set back the first line of a paragraph further from the margin, हाशिया छोड़कर नए पैरे की पहली पंक्ति आरंभ करना। 2. to notch the edge of, दाँता निकालना, दाँतेदार बनाना। 3. to send an order of goods, माँगपत्र या आदेशपत्र भेजना। ***n.*** 1. a notch, दाँता। 2. a written order of goods, आदेशपत्र, माँगपत्र।

indenture (इन्डेन्चर) ***n.*** a written deed or contract, अनुबंध-पत्र। ***v.*** to bind by indenture, अनुबंधित करना।

independence (इन्डिपेन्डेन्स) ***n.*** the state of being independent, स्वतंत्रता, आज़ादी।

independent (इन्डिपेन्डेन्ट) ***adj.*** 1. not dependent, अनाश्रित, स्वाधीन। 2. politically autonomous, स्वतंत्र, आज़ाद, स्वाधीन। 3. self-reliant or self-sufficient, आत्मनिर्भर, स्वावलंबी। 4. not committed to any one political party, स्वतंत्र, निर्दलीय।

indescribable (इन्डिस्क्राइबेबल) ***adj.*** beyond description, वर्णनातीत, अवर्णनीय।

indestructible (इन्डिस्ट्रक्टिबल) ***adj.*** that cannot be destroyed, अविनाशी, अनश्वर।

indeterminate (इन्डिटर्मिनिट) ***adj.*** 1. not determined, अनिश्चित, अनिर्णीत। 2. vague, अस्पष्ट, अनिर्दिष्ट।

index (इन्डेक्स) ***n.*** (plu. indices, indexes) 1. an alphabetized list of names, subjects etc. given at the end of a book, अनुक्रमणिका। 2. a symbol or indication, संकेत, चिह्न। 3. a list, catalogue or table of contents, सूची, तालिका। ***v.*** 1. to prepare an index, अनुक्रमणिका या तालिका तैयार करना, सूचीबद्ध करना। 2. to enter in an index, अनुक्रमणिका में जोड़ना या बढ़ाना, सूची में जोड़ना।

index finger ***n.*** the forefinger, तर्जनी (उँगली)।

index number ***n.*** a number used to

I

measure change in prices, wages etc. सूचकांक।

Indian (इन्डिअन) ***adj.*** of India or Indians, भारतीय, हिंदोस्तानी। ***n.*** a native of India, भारतीय, भारतवासी, हिंदोस्तानी।

indicate (इन्डिकेट) ***v.*** 1. to point out, संकेत करना, इंगित करना, बतलाना। 2. to be a sign of, प्रतीक या संकेत होना। 3. to state briefly, संक्षेप में उल्लेख करना।

indication (इन्डिकेशन) ***n.*** something that indicates, संकेत, चिह्न, लक्षण।

indicator (इन्डिकेटर) ***n.*** 1. anything that indicates, सूचक। 2. a pointing needle, सुई।

indict (इन्डाइट) ***v.*** to accuse formally for some offence, औपचारिक रूप से अभियोग लगाना, अभ्यारोप लगाना।

indictment (इन्डाइटमेन्ट) ***n.*** an act of indicting, अभ्यारोपण।

indifference (इन्डिफ़रेन्स) ***n.*** 1. disinterestedness, उदासीनता। 2. lack of concern, विमुखता, विरति।

indifferent (इन्डिफ़रेन्ट) ***adj.*** 1. disinterested, उदासीन, विमुख, विरत। 2. average, सामान्य कोटि का, साधारण।

indigenous (इन्डिजनस) ***adj.*** born or living naturally in an area, देशी, स्वदेशी।

indigestible (इन्डिजेस्टिबल) ***adj.*** that cannot be disgested, हज़म न होनेवाला, अपाच्य।

indigestion (इन्डिजेस्चन) ***n.*** the inability to digest food, अपच, बदहज़मी।

indignant (इन्डिग्नेन्ट) ***adj.*** feeling or showing indignation, क्रुद्ध, रुष्ट, रोषपूर्ण।

indignation (इन्डिग्नेशन) ***n.*** feeling of anger (against something wrong), क्रोध, रोष।

indignity (इन्डिग्निटी) ***n.*** 1. something that injures the dignity, अपमानसूचक कार्य, बात या व्यवहार।

indigo (इन्डिगो) ***n.*** a deep blue dye, नील।

indirect (इन्डिरेक्ट) ***adj.*** 1. not direct, अप्रत्यक्ष, परोक्ष। 2. secondary, गौण। 3. circumlocutory, घुमाव-फिराववाला।

indirectly ***adv.*** in an indirect manner, अप्रत्यक्ष रूप से, परोक्ष रूप से।

indiscernible (इन्डिसर्निबल) ***adj.*** that cannot be discerned, अज्ञेय, अगोचर।

indiscreet (इन्डिस्क्रीट) ***adj.*** lacking discretion, not wise, अविवेकी, असावधान।

indiscriminate (इन्डिस्क्रिमिनिट) ***adj.*** 1. lacking in discrimination, विवेकहीन। 2. not choosing carefully, सावधानी से चयन न करनेवाला, भेदभाव-भरा।

indiscriminately ***adv.*** in an indiscriminate manner, अविवेकपूर्वक, बेतहाशा।

indispensable (इन्डिस्पेन्सेबल) ***adv.*** not dispensable, अपरिहार्य, अनिवार्य।

indisposed (इन्डिस्पोज़्ड) ***adj.*** slightly or mildly ill, कुछ-कुछ अस्वस्थ।

indisposition (इन्डिस्पोज़िशन) ***n.*** 1. the state of being indisposed, किंचित् अस्वस्थता। 2. unwillingness, अनिच्छा।

indisputable (इन्डिस्प्यूटेबल) ***adj.*** that cannot be disputed, अविवाद्य, निर्विवाद।

indistinguishable (इन्डिस्टिंग्विशेबल) ***adj.*** not distinguishable, अविभेद्य।

individual (इन्डिविजुअल) ***adj.***

1. pertaining to a single person, वैयक्तिक, व्यक्तिगत। 2. single or separate, एकल या अलग। *n.* a single person, व्यक्ति।

individuality (इन्डिविजुऐलिटी) character and qualities which make someone different from all others, पृथक् अस्तित्व, विशिष्टता, व्यक्तित्व।

indivisible (इन्डिविज़िबल) *adj.* not divisible, अविभाज्य।

indoctrinate (इन्डॉक्ट्रिनेट) *v.* to fill (one's mind) with particular ideas, सिखाना-पढ़ाना, दिमाग़ में भरना।

indolent (इन्डोलेन्ट) *adj.* idle, lazy, सुस्त, काहिल, आलसी।

indomitable (इन्डॉमिटेबल) *adj.* stubbornly persistent, दबंग, अदम्य, दुर्दमनीय।

indoor (इन्डोर) *adj.* situated or carried on inside the building, भीतरी।

indoors (इन्डोर्स) *adv.* in or into a house or building, घर या भवन में या के अंदर।

induce (इन्ड्यूस) *v.* 1. to persuade, राज़ी करना, मनाना। 2. to entice, प्रलोभन देना। 3. to influence or inspire, प्रभावित करना, उत्प्रेरित करना। 4. to infer by induction, अनुमान करना, नतीजा निकालना।

induced (इन्ड्यूस्ड) *adj.* inspired, उत्प्रेरित।

induct (इन्डक्ट) *v.* 1. to bring in or introduce, सामने लाना, परिचय देना या कराना। 2. to install, पदासीन करना। 3. to enroll, भर्ती करना।

induction (इन्डक्शन) *n.* 1. the act of inducting or the state of being inducted, पद पर बैठाना, पदारोहण। 2. an introduction, परिचय, भूमिका। 3. a logical reasoning or a general conclusion, आगमन।

indulge (इन्डल्ज) *v.* 1. to yield to the whims or desires, इच्छापूर्ति में लगना, प्रवृत्त होना, लिप्त होना, बह जाना। 2. to gratify, तृप्त करना, मज़ा लेना।

indulgent (इन्डल्जेन्ट) *adj.* 1. inclined to indulge, रसिया, मनमौजी, प्रवृत्त, लिप्त। 2. kind or lenient, कृपालु, उदार।

Indus (इन्डस) *n.* a river now flowing in Pakistan, सिंधु नदी।

industrial (इन्डस्ट्रिअल) *adj.* 1. pertaining to or used in industry, उद्योग-संबंधी, औद्योगिक। 2. having highly developed industries, औद्योगिक।

industrialist (इन्डस्ट्रिअलिस्ट) *n.* an owner of an industry, उद्योगपति।

industrious (इन्डस्ट्रिअस) *adj.* hard-working, परिश्रमी, उद्योगी, उद्यमी, मेहनती।

industry (इन्डस्ट्री) *n.* 1. a unit of manufacture or trade, उद्योग। 2. the state or quality of being industrious, परिश्रमशीलता।

inebriate (इनीब्रिएट) *v.* to intoxicate, मत्त कर देना, नशे में चूर करना।

inedible (इनेडिबल) *adj.* not edible, न खाने योग्य, अखाद्य।

ineffective (इनिफ़ेक्टिव) *adj.* not effective, अप्रभावी, बेअसर।

inefficacious (इनेफ़िकेशस) *adj.* not efficacious, बेअसर।

inefficiency (इनिफ़िशन्सी) *n.* the state or quality of being inefficient, अकुशलता, अदक्षता।

inefficient (इनिफ़िशन्ट) *adj.* not efficient, अकुशल, अदक्ष।

I

inelastic (इनिलैस्टिक) ***adj.*** not elastic, बेलोच, अनम्य।

inelegant (इनेलिगेन्ट) ***adj.*** not elegant, अनुत्कृष्ट, भद्दा, भोंडा।

ineligibility (इनेलिजिबिलिटी) ***n.*** the state or quality of being ineligible, अपात्रता, अयोग्यता।

ineligible (इनेलिजिबल) ***adj.*** not entitled to be chosen, अपात्र, अयोग्य।

inept (इनेप्ट) ***adj.*** 1. not ept, unsuitable. अनुपयुक्त। 2. lacking skill, अकुशल।

ineptitude (इनेप्टिट्यूड) ***n.*** lack of eptitude, अनुपयुक्तता, अकुशलता, असंगति।

inequality (इनिक्वैलिटी) ***n.*** 1. the state or quality of being unequal, असमता। 2. disparity, विषमता।

inequitable (इनेक्विटेबल) ***adj.*** not equitable, अनुचित, अन्यायपूर्ण।

inert (इनर्ट) ***adj.*** 1. not moving, अचल, जड़। 2. not active, अक्रिय, आलसी।

inertia (इनर्शिआ) ***n.*** 1. the tendency of a matter to remain at rest, जड़ता। 2. disinclination to move or act, निश्चेष्टता, अक्रियता। 3. laziness, आलस्य।

inescapable (इनिस्केपेबल) ***adj.*** that cannot be escaped, अपरिहार्य, अनिवार्य।

inevitable (इनेविटेबल) ***adj.*** certain to happen, अनिवार्य।

inexcusable (इनिक्सक्यूज़ेबल) ***adj.*** unpardonable, अक्षम्य।

inexhaustible (इनिग्ज़ॉस्टिबल) ***adj.*** 1. that cannot be exhausted, अक्षय, असमाप्य। 2. limitless, अमित, असीम।

inexpensive (इनिक्स्पेन्सिव) ***adj.*** not expensive, सस्ता, कम दाम का।

inexperienced (इनिक्स्पीरिएन्स्ड) ***adj.*** not experienced, अनुभवहीन, नातजुर्बेकार।

inexplicable (इनेक्सप्लिकेबल) ***adj.*** that cannot be explained, अव्याख्येय।

inexpressible (इनिक्स्प्रेसिबल) ***adj.*** that cannot be expressed, अवर्णनीय।

inextricable (इनेक्सट्रिकेबल) ***adj.*** 1. intricate, पेचीदा। 2. complex, जटिल।

infallibility (इन्फ़ैलिबिलिटी) ***n.*** the quality or state of being infallible, अमोघता।

infallible (इन्फ़ैलिबल) ***adj.*** 1. never wrong, ग़लती न करनेवाला। 2. never failing, अमोघ, अचूक।

infamous (इन्फ़ेमस) ***adj.*** having a very bad reputation, बदनाम, कुख्यात।

infancy (इन्फ़ेन्सी) ***n.*** early childhood, बाल्यावस्था, शैशव, बचपन।

infant (इन्फ़ेन्ट) ***adj.*** a child in the earliest period of its life, बच्चा, शिशु, बाल।

infanticide (इन्फ़ैन्टिसाइड) ***n.*** 1. the act of killing an infant, बालहत्या, शिशुहत्या। 2. one who kills an infant, बाल-हत्यारा।

infantry (इन्फेन्ट्री) ***n.*** foot soldiers collectively, पैदल सेना।

infatuated (इन्फ़ैचुएटिड) ***adj.*** completely carried away by foolish love or attraction, मोहित, आसक्त, प्रेमांध।

infect (इन्फ़ेक्ट) ***v.*** to contaminate with bacteria, कीटाणुग्रस्त होना।

infection (इन्फ़ेक्शन) ***n.*** the act of infecting or the state of being infected, संक्रमण; an infectious

disease, छूत की बीमारी, संक्रामक रोग।

infectious (इन्फ़ेक्शस) ***adj.*** causing infection, संक्रामक, छुतहा।

infer (इन्फ़र) ***v.*** 1. to conclude by reasoning or implication, अनुमान करना। 2. to conclude from evidence, निष्कर्ष निकालना।

inference (इन्फ़रेन्स) ***n.*** conclusion from known facts, अनुमान या निष्कर्ष।

inferior (इन्फ़ीरिअर) ***adj.*** 1. lower in quality or importance, घटिया, निकृष्ट। 2. lower in order, अवर, छोटा। 3. subordinate, अधीनस्थ, निचला, छोटा।

inferiority (इन्फ़ीरिऑरिटी) ***n.*** the quality or state of being inferior, घटियापन, निकृष्टता; अवरता।

inferiority complex ***n.*** a strong and persistent feeling of inferiority, हीनभावना, हीनत्व।

infernal (इन्फ़र्नल) ***adj.*** 1. of or pertaining to hell, नरक-संबंधी। 2. abominable, detestable, घृणित, जुगुप्सित, नारकीय।

infertile (इन्फ़र्टाइल) ***adj.*** 1. not fertile, अनुर्वर। 2. unproductive. अनुपजाऊ।

infest (इन्फ़ेस्ट) ***v.*** to swarm in or about (said of germs, क़ीटाणुओं का) आक्रमण करना, (कीड़े) पड़ जाना, (कीड़ों से) ग्रस्त होना।

infidel (इन्फ़िडल) ***n.*** one who does not believe in religion, नास्तिक, काफ़िर।

infidelity (इन्फ़िडेलिटी) ***n.*** 1. lack of religious faith, नास्तिकता। 2. lack of loyalty, अनिष्ठा, बेवफ़ाई।

infighting (इन्फ़ाइटिंग) ***n.*** fighting between the close members of a party, group or organization, अंतर्कलह।

infiltrate (इन्फ़िल्ट्रेट) ***v.*** to enter quietly and unlawfully for disruptive purposes, घुसपैठ करना।

infinite (इन्फ़िनिट) ***adj.*** 1. having no limits, असीम, अंतहीन, अपरिमित। 2. very great or immense, विशाल, बहुत बड़ा।

infinitesimal (इन्फ़िनिटेसिमल) ***adj.*** very small, अत्यंत लघु, अत्यल्प।

infinity (इन्फिनिटी) ***n.*** 1. the state or quality of being infinite, असीमता, अनंतता। 2. very large amount of space or time, अनंत अवकाश या काल।

infirm (इन्फ़र्म) ***adj.*** 1. not firm, अदृढ़, बेदम। 2. weak, कमज़ोर, अशक्त।

infirmity (इन्फ़र्मिटी) ***n.*** the quality of being infirm, अदृढ़ता, अशक्तता, कमज़ोरी।

inflame (इन्फ़्लेम) ***v.*** 1. to set on fire, जलाना। 2. to make angry, ग़ुस्सा दिलाना, क्रुद्ध करना।

inflammable (इन्फ़्लैमेबल) ***adj.*** 1. flammable, ज्वलनशील। 2. easily excited, आसानी से भड़कनेवाला, ग़ुस्सैल, क्रोधी।

inflammation (इन्फ़्लैमेशन) ***n.*** the state of being swollen, सूजन, शोथ।

inflammatory (इन्फ़्लैमेटरी) ***adj.*** likely to arouse strong feelings of hatred or violence, भड़कानेवाला, उत्तेजनात्मक।

inflate (इन्फ़्लेट) ***v.*** 1. to fill with air, हवा भरना, फुलाना। 2. to swell up, फूल जाना।

inflation (इन्फ़्लेशन) ***n.*** general increase of price and fall in the purchasing value of money, मुद्रास्फीति।

inflect (इन्फ़्लेक्ट) ***v.*** 1. to change the ending or form of a word, रूपांतरण

I

करना, विकार लाना, विकारी बनाना। 2. to change the pitch or the tone of voice, सुर बदलना।

inflexible (इन्फ़्लेक्सिबल) ***adj.*** 1. not flexible, अनम्य। 2. unalterable, अपरिवर्तनीय, कठोर।

inflict (इन्फ़्लिक्ट) ***v.*** to cause or carry out by aggressive action, (पीड़ा या चोट) पहुँचाना, (प्रहार) करना।

inflorescence (इन्फ़्लोरेसेन्स) ***n.*** 1. act of flowering, पुष्पण। 2. the arrangement of flower on a stem, टहनी पर फूलों की सजावट, पुष्पावली, पुष्प-समूह।

inflow (इन्फ़्लो) ***n.*** the act of flowing in, अंदर की ओर होनेवाला प्रवाह, अंतर्प्रवाह।

influence (इन्फ़्लुएन्स) ***n.*** 1. the power to produce an effect on others, प्रभाव, असर। 2. one exercising such power, प्रभावशाली व्यक्ति। ***v.*** to have an influence on, प्रभाव डालना, असर डालना।

influential (इन्फ़्लुएन्शल) ***adj.*** having great influence, प्रभावशाली, प्रभावपूर्ण।

influenza (इन्फ़्लुएन्ज़ा) ***n.*** an acute infectious disease causing fever and muscular pain, इन्फ़्लुएन्ज़ा, फ़्लू।

influx (इन्फ़्लक्स) ***n.*** a continual coming in of persons or things, अंतर्प्रवाह, बाढ़।

inform (इन्फ़ॉर्म) ***v.*** to give information or knowledge of something, सूचित करना, सूचना देना, बतलाना।

informal (इन्फ़ॉर्मल) ***adj.*** not formal, अनौपचारिक।

information (इन्फ़र्मेशन) ***n.*** 1. something told, सूचना, इत्तला। 2. the knowledge acquired in any manner, जानकारी।

informative (इन्फ़ॉर्मेटिव) ***adj.*** 1. giving or providing information, सूचना देनेवाला। 2. educative, शिक्षाप्रद, ज्ञानप्रद।

informed (इन्फ़ॉर्म्ड) ***adj.*** having much information or knowledge, जानकार।

informer (इन्फ़ॉर्मर) ***n.*** one who informs to the police against others, मुखबिर।

infrared (इन्फ़्रारेड) ***adj.*** of those invisible rays just beyond the red of the visible spectrum, अवरक्त।

infrastructure (इन्फ़्रास्ट्रक्चर) ***n.*** subordinate parts that form the basis of an enterprise, आधार-तंत्र, आधारभूत ढाँचा।

infringe (इन्फ़्रिन्ज) ***v.*** 1. to violate, उल्लंघन या अतिलंघन करना। 2. to trespass, अतिक्रमण करना।

infringement (इन्फ़्रिन्जमेन्ट) ***n.*** the act of infringing or the state of being infringed, उल्लंघन, अतिलंघन, अतिक्रमण।

infuriate (इन्फ़्यूरिएट) ***v.*** to make furious, गुस्सा दिलाना, भड़काना।

infuse (इनफ़्यूज) ***v.*** 1. to pour in, उँड़ेलना। 2. to instil, भरना। 3. to inspire, प्रेरित करना, अनुप्राणित करना।

infusion (इन्फ़्यूज़न) ***n.*** the act of infusing or the state of being infused, उँड़ेलने या भरने की क्रिया या भाव, अनुप्राणन।

ingenious (इन्जीन्यस) ***adj.*** 1. having genius, clever, प्रतिभाशाली, मेधावी। 2. cleverly contrived, प्रतिभाजन्य, कौशलपूर्ण।

ingenuity (इन्जेन्यूइटी) ***n.*** the quality of being ingenious, प्रतिभा, कौशल।

ingenuous (इन्जेन्युअस) ***adj.***

straigthforward, सरल, सच्चा, निष्कपट।

ingest (इन्जेस्ट) ***v.*** to take in by swallowing, खाना, निगलना।

inglorious (इन्लोरिअस) ***adj.*** 1. not glorious, जो गौरवपूर्ण न हो, अयशस्कर। 2. shameful, लज्जास्पद, लज्जाजनक।

ingot (इन्गॉट) ***n.*** a brick-shaped mass of metal, धातु आदि की सिल्ली, ईंट।

ingratiate (इन्ग्रेशिएट) ***v.*** to bring oneself into the favour of another, किसी का कृपाभाजन बन जाना।

ingratitude (इन्ग्रैटिट्यूड) ***n.*** ungratefulness, अकृतज्ञता।

ingredient (इन्ग्रीडिएन्ट) ***n.*** something that is a component part of any combination or mixture, अवयव, अंश, संघटक।

ingress (इन्ग्रेस) ***n.*** 1. going in, अंतर्प्रवेश। 2. an entrance, द्वार।

inhabit (इन्हैबिट) ***v.*** to live in, निवास करना, रहना, बसना।

inhabitable (इन्हैबिटेबल) ***adj.*** habitable, रहने-योग्य, रहने-लायक।

inhabitant (इन्हैबिटेन्ट) ***n.*** a permanent resident, बाशिंदा, निवासी।

inhale (इन्हेल) ***v.*** 1. to breathe in, साँस लेना, कश लेना।

inherent (इन्हेरेन्ट) ***adj.*** 1. existing in someone or something as a natural quality, अंतर्निहित। 2. innate, जन्मजात, सहज।

inherit (इन्हेरिट) ***v.*** 1. to receive from one's parents, माता-पिता से प्राप्त करना।2. to get (property) as a heir, उत्तराधिकारी के रूप में प्राप्त करना।

inheritance (इन्हेरिटेन्स) ***n.*** the act of inheriting or something inherited, उत्तराधिकार, विरासत।

inherited (इन्हेरिटिड) ***adj.*** received from ancestors, पूर्वजों से मिला हुआ, वंशागत।

inhibit (इन्हिबिट) ***v.*** to check or prohibit, रोकना, मना करना।

inhibition (इन्हिबिशन) ***n.*** the act of inhibiting or the state of being inhibited, prevention, रोक, वर्जन, मनाही।

inhospitable (इन्हॉस्पिटेबल) ***adj.*** not hospitable, असत्कारी, आवभगत न करनेवाला।

inhuman (इन्ह्यूमन) ***adj.*** 1. lacking human qualities, अमानवीय, अमानुषिक। 2. cruel, क्रूर या क्रूरतापूर्ण।

inimical (इनिमिकल) ***adj.*** 1. harmful or unfriendly, अहितकर या अमैत्रीपूर्ण। 2. hostile, शत्रुतापूर्ण, विद्वेषपूर्ण, विद्वेषी।

inimitable (इनिमिटेबल) ***adj.*** 1. that cannot be imitated, जिसका अनुकरण न हो सके, अननुकरणीय। 2. unique, अनुपम, अद्वितीय।

iniquity (इनिक्विटी) ***n.*** 1. injustice, अन्याय। 2. wickedness, दुष्टता।

initial (इनिशल) ***adj.*** 1. pertaining to or occurring in the beginning, आरंभिक, प्राथमिक। 2. first, प्रथम। ***n.*** the first letter of a name or word, आद्यक्षर।

initially (इनिशली) ***adv.*** at first, शुरू में।

initials (इनिशल्स) ***n.*** (plu.) the initial letters of an individul's name and surname, आद्यक्षर।

initiate (इनिशिएट) ***v.*** 1. to start or originate, आरंभ करना, सूत्रपात करना, पहल करना। 2. to admit into an association, प्रविष्ट करना। 3. to give instructions or informations to a new person, निदेश देना, दीक्षा देना, परिचय कराना।

I

initiation (इनिशिएशन) ***n.*** 1. the act of initiating, सूत्रपात, श्रीगणेश। 2. the ceremony of initiating, दीक्षा।

initiative (इनिशिएटिव) ***n.*** 1. the first step or action, पहल। 2. the ability to take lead, अगुआई।

inject (इन्जेक्ट) ***v.*** 1. to force into the body by a syringe, सुई लगाना, इंजेक्शन लगाना। 2. to introduce a new life or element into, जान फूँकना, नवीनता लाना।

injection (इन्जेक्शन) 1. the act of injecting, सुई लगाना। 2. the liquid or medicine that is injected, सुई, इंजेक्शन।

injunction (इन्जंक्शन) ***n.*** 1. a court order requiring a person to refrain from doing a certain action, निषेधाज्ञा, व्यादेश, इंजंक्शन। 2. an order, आदेश।

injure (इन्जर) ***v.*** 1. to cause harm or damage, आघात या चोट करना, हानि या क्षति पहुँचाना। 2. to commit an injustice, अन्याय करना।

injurious (इन्जूरिअस) ***adj.*** causing damage, हानिप्रद, क्षतिकारक।

injury (इन्जरी) ***n.*** (plu. injuries) 1. a wound or harm done, घाव, चोट। 2. damage done, क्षति, हानि। 3. injustice, अन्याय।

injustice (इन्जस्टिस) ***n.*** lack of justice or an unjust action, अन्याय।

ink (इन्क) ***n.*** a coloured liquid used in writing, स्याही, मसी।

inkling (इन्कलिंग) ***n.*** 1. a hint, संकेत, इशारा, इंगित। 2. a vague idea, आभास, धारणा।

inlaid (इन्लेड) ***v.*** p.t. & p.p. of inlay.

inland (इन्लैन्ड) ***adj.*** of or located in the interior part of a country, अंतर्देशीय। ***adv.*** toward the interior of a country, देश के अंदरूनी भाग में, अंतर्देश में। ***n.*** the interior of a country, देश का अंदरूनी भाग, अंतर्देश।

inlay (इन्ले) ***v.*** (inlaid, inlaying) to insert layers of fine materials in the surface of an object to form a design, जड़ना, जड़ाई करना।

inlet (इन्लेट) ***n.*** a way in, अंदर जाने का मार्ग, अंतर्मार्ग।

inmate (इन्मेट) ***n.*** 1. a resident in a building, घर में रहनेवाला, गृहवासी। 2. one who is confined in a hospital, prison etc., अस्पताल या कारा में रहनेवाला, अंतेवासी।

in memoriam (इन मैमोरिअम) ***prep.*** in memory of, की स्मृति में।

inmost (इन्मोस्ट) ***adj.*** most inward, सबसे भीतरवाला।

inn (इन) ***n.*** a tavern, सराय।

innate (इनेट) ***adj.*** 1. inborn, जन्मजात। 2. natural, प्रकृत, सहज।

inner (इनर) ***adj.*** 1. interior, भीतरी, अंतर्वर्ती, अंदरूनी। 2. of the spirit or mind, आत्मिक या मानसिक।

innings (इनिन्ग़्ज़) ***n.*** a turn for batting in the game of cricket, पारी, पाली।

innocence (इनोसेन्स) ***n.*** the quality or state of being innocent, निरीहता, निर्दोषता, निष्पापता, भोलापन।

innocent (इनोसेन्ट) ***adj.*** 1. sinless, guiltless, बेगुनाह, निष्पाप, निरपराध। 2. simple or harmless, निरीह या अहानिकर।

innocuous (इनॉक्युअस) ***adj.*** harmless, अहानिकर।

innovate (इनोवेट) ***v.*** 1. to introduce a new process, नया ढंग निकालना, नई राह निकालना। 2. to give a new

I

shape, नवीनता लाना, नया रूप देना।

innovation (इनोवेशन) ***n.*** 1. the act of innovating, नवीनीकरण, नवप्रवर्तन। 2. new form or shape, नया रूप, नवरूप।

innumerable (इन्यूमरेबल) ***adj.*** too many to be counted, अनगिनत, असंख्य, बेशुमार।

inoculate (इनॉक्युलेट) ***v.*** to introduce the virus of a disease into the body in order to immunize, सुई लगाना, टीका लगाना।

inoculation (इनॉक्युलेशन) ***n.*** the act of inoculating, सुई, टीका।

inoffensive (इनॉफ़ेन्सिव) ***adj.*** not offensive, आघात या हानि न पहुँचानेवाला।

inoperative (इनॉपरेटिव) ***adv.*** not working, not functioning, अक्रिय, बंद, निष्क्रिय।

inopportune (इनॉपर्ट्यून) ***adj.*** not opportune, असामयिक, बेमौक़े का।

inordinate (इनॉर्डिनिट) ***adj.*** exceeding reasonable limits, अत्यधिक, अमर्यादित या अनुचित।

inorganic (इनॉर्गैनिक) ***adj.*** not organic, अजैव, जड़।

inpatient (इन्पेशन्ट) ***n.*** a patient staying in a hospital while undergoing treatment, अंतरंग रोगी।

input (इन्पुट) ***v.*** (input/inputted, inputting) to put in or into, निवेश।

inquest (इन्क्वेस्ट) ***n.*** 1. an investigation, जाँच। 2. a judicial inquiry for somebody's death, किसी की मृत्यु के कारणों की न्यायिक जाँच।

inquire (इन्क़्वाइर) ***v.*** 1. to ask about, पूछ-ताछ करना। 2. to investigate, जाँच करना, पता लगाना।

inquiry (इन्क़्वाइरी) ***n.*** an act of inquiring, पूछ-ताछ, जाँच, जाँच-पड़ताल।

inquisition (इन्क़्विज़िशन) ***n.*** an official investigation, आधिकारिक जाँच।

inquisitive (इन्क़्विज़िटिव) ***adj.*** 1. eager to learn, जिज्ञासु। 2. unduly curious, व्यग्र।

inroad (इन्रोड) ***n.*** intrusion, घुसपैठ।

insane (इन्सेन) ***adj.*** 1. not sane, अविवेकी। 2. mad, पागल। 3. very foolish, मूर्खतापूर्ण।

insanitary (इन्सैनिटरी) ***adj.*** 1. unhealthy, अस्वास्थ्यकर। 2. filthy, मलिन।

insanity (इन्सैनिटी) ***n.*** the quality or state of being insane, पागलपन; मूर्खता।

insatiable (इन्सेशिएबल) ***adj.*** that cannot be satiated, जिसे तृप्त न किया जा सके, अतृप्य।

inscribe (इन्स्क्राइब) ***v.*** 1. to engrave, उत्कीर्ण करना। 2. to write or print, लिखना या छापना। 3. to dedicate, समर्पित करना।

inscription (इन्स्क्रिप्शन) ***n.*** words or names engraved on a monument, coin etc., उत्कीर्ण लेख, अंकन, खुदे अक्षर।

insect (इन्सेक्ट) ***n.*** a tiny creature with wings and six legs, कीट, कीड़ा।

insecticide (इन्सेक्टिसाइड) ***n.*** a substance for killing insects, कीटनाशक पदार्थ।

insectivorous (इन्सेक्टिवोरस) ***adj.*** feeding on insects, कीटभक्षी।

insecure (इन्सिक्योर) ***adj.*** 1. not secure, unsafe, अरक्षित, असुरक्षित। 2. shaky, अस्थिर; दुर्बल।

inseminate (इन्सेमिनेट) ***v.*** to introduce semen into, शुक्रस्थापन

I

करना, बीजारोपण करना, गर्भाधान करना।

insemination (इन्सेमिनेशन) ***n.*** the act of inseminating, शुक्रस्थापन, गर्भाधान।

insensibility (इन्सेन्सिबिलिटी) ***n.*** the state or quality of being insensible, संवेदनशून्यता; बेहोशी; उदासीनता।

insensible (इन्सेन्सिबल) ***adj.*** 1. lacking sensation, संवेदनशून्य। 2. having lost sensation, unconscious, मूर्छित, बेहोश।

insensitive (इन्सेन्सिटिव) ***adj.*** not sensitive, संवेदनशून्य, असंवेदनशील।

inseparable (इन्सैपरेबल) ***adj.*** that cannot be separated, अविच्छेद्य।

insert (इन्सर्ट) ***v.*** to put or place in, डालना, जोड़ना या बैठाना, अंत:स्थापित करना।

insertion (इन्सर्शन) ***n.*** the act of inserting or something inserted, जोड़ने या बैठाने की क्रिया अथवा जोड़ी या बैठाई जानेवाली वस्तु।

inset (इन्सेट) ***v.*** (inset, insetting) to set or place in, जड़ना, लगानां। ***n.*** something inserted, जड़ी, जमाई या लगाई हुई वस्तु।

inside (इन्साइड) ***n.*** the inner side or part, भीतरी भाग। ***adv.*** in the interior, भीतर, अंदर, अंदर की तरफ़। ***prep.*** within, के अंदर। ***adj.*** lying on or in the inside, भीतरी, अंदरूनी।

insider (इन्साइडर) ***n.*** an influential member of the group, अंतरंग व्यक्ति, भीतर के हाल से परिचित व्यक्ति।

insidious (इन्सिडिअस) ***adj.*** 1. working or spreading in a stealthy and harmful manner, प्रच्छन्न रूप से सक्रिय या घातक। 2. treacherous, कपटी या कपटपूर्ण।

insight (इन्साइट) ***n.*** the capacity to perceive the true nature of something, अंतर्दृष्टि।

insignia (इन्सिग्निआ) ***n.*** 1. a distinguished sign of authority or office, अधिचिह्न, पदचिह्न। 2. an identifying badge, तगमा।

insignificant (इन्सिग्निफ़िकेन्ट) ***adj.*** having no significance, नगण्य, तुच्छ, महत्त्वहीन, निरर्थक।

insinuate (इन्सिन्यूएट) ***v.*** 1. to push in by subtle and artful means, छल या चालाकी से अंदर घुसाना। 2. to hint indirectly esp. something malicious, परोक्ष रूप से (किसी ग़लत काम के लिए) इशारा करना, इंगित करना। 3. to infuse into the mind, दिमाग़ में भर या बैठा देना।

insipid (इन्सिपिड) ***adj.*** 1. tasteless, फीका, बेस्वाद। 2. lacking in interest, नीरस, अरुचिकर। 3. lacking in liveliness or excitement, कुतूहलरहित, उत्तेजनाविहीन, निर्जीव।

insist (इन्सिस्ट) ***v.*** 1. to be firm in one's demand, अपनी माँग पर अडिग रहना, डटे रहना। 2. to demand persistently, आग्रह करना, हठ करना।

insistence (इन्सिस्टेन्स) ***n.*** the act of insisting, आग्रह, हठ।

in situ (इन सिटू) ***adv.*** in its original place, अपने मूल स्थान में/पर।

in so far as ***conj. & adv.*** to the extent that, जहाँ तक कि।

insolence (इन्सोलेन्स) ***n.*** impertinence, धृष्टता, गुस्ताख़ी।

insolent (इन्सोलेन्ट) ***adj.*** impertinent, धृष्ट, गुस्ताख़।

insoluble (इन्सॉल्युबल) ***adj.*** 1. not soluble, न घुलनेवाला, अविलेय। 2. that cannot be solved, जिसका समाधान या निपटारा न हो सके।

insolvent (इन्सॉल्वेन्ट) ***adj.*** bankrupt, दिवालिया। ***n.*** an insolvent person, दिवालिया व्यक्ति।

insomnia (इन्सॉम्निआ) ***n.*** chronic inability to sleep, नींद न आने का रोग, अनिद्रा।

in so much as ***adv.*** to such an extent, यहाँ तक कि।

inspect (इन्स्पेक्ट) ***v.*** 1. to examine carefully, ग़ौर से देखना, जाँच करना। 2. to examine officially, निरीक्षण करना, मुआयना करना।

inspection (इन्स्पेक्शन) ***n.*** the act of inspecting, निरीक्षण, मुआयना।

inspector (इन्स्पेक्टर) ***n.*** an officer who inspects, निरीक्षक, इन्स्पेक्टर।

inspiration (इन्स्पिरेशन) ***n.*** 1. the act of inhaling, साँस लेना, श्वसन। 2. an urge to creative thought or action, प्रेरणा। 3. a brilliant idea, सूझ।

inspire (इन्स्पाइर) ***v.*** 1. to inhale, साँस लेना। 2. to stimulate to creativity or action, प्रेरित करना, प्रेरणा देना।

inspiring (इन्स्पाइरिंग) ***adj.*** giving inspiration, प्रेरक, प्रेरणादायी।

instability (इन्स्टेबिलिटी) ***n.*** unstableness, अस्थिरता, अस्थायित्व।

install (इन्स्टॉल) ***v.*** 1. to get in official position with ceremony, पदासीन करना, पदारूढ़ करना। 2. to set in position for use, स्थापित करना, प्रतिष्ठित करना, लगाना।

installation (इन्स्टॉलेशन) ***n.*** 1. the act of installing or something being installed, प्रतिष्ठापन, (मशीन, यंत्र आदि का) लगाना। 2. a plant installed, लगाया हुआ संयंत्र।

instalment (इन्स्टॉलमेन्ट) ***n.*** 1. one of several successive payments of a debt, किस्त। 2. a portion of anything issued at intervals, खेप, किस्त, कड़ी।

instance (इन्स्टेन्स) ***n.*** 1. a case or example, उदाहरण। 2. a request or suggestion, प्रार्थना या सुझाव; at the instance of his wife, अपनी पत्नी के आग्रह पर। 3. an occasion, अवसर, मौक़ा; in the first instance, सर्वप्रथम, प्रथमतः। ***v.*** to cite, उदाहरण देना, उद्धृत करना।

instant (इन्स्टेन्ट) ***n.*** a moment, क्षण, पल। ***adj.*** 1. urgent, अत्यावश्यक। 2. without delay, तात्कालिक, अविलंब, तुरंत। 3. of the current month, इसी महीने का।

instantaneous (इन्स्टेन्टेनिअस) ***adj.*** happening at once, तात्कालिक, तात्क्षणिक।

instead (इन्स्टेड) ***adv.*** as an alternative, बदले में। ☐ **instead of,** के बजाए, के स्थान पर।

instigate (इन्स्टिगेट) ***v.*** 1. to goad or incite, उकसाना, भड़काना, दुष्प्रेरित करना, शह देना। 2. to make something begin or happen, चलाना या बनाना।

instigation (इन्स्टिगेशन) ***n.*** the act of instigating, दुष्प्रेरण, उकसावा, भड़कावा।

instil (इन्स्टिल) ***v.*** to put (ideas in someone's mind) gradually, धीरे-धीरे (किसी के मन में) भरना या डालना, सिखाना।

instinct (इन्स्टिंक्ट) ***n.*** 1. an inborn or natural tendency, नैसर्गिक प्रवृत्ति, सहजवृत्ति, मूलवृत्ति। 2. a natural ability, प्रतिभा।

instinctive (इन्स्टिंक्टिव) ***adj.*** prompted by instinct, नैसर्गिक, सहज।

I

institute (इन्स्टिट्यूट) ***v.*** to found, प्रवर्तित करना, संस्थापित करना। ***n.*** an organization promoting educational, social and other activities, संस्थान।

institution (इन्स्टिट्यूशन) ***n.*** 1. the act of instituting or the state of being instituted, संस्थापन। 2. an institute, संस्था। 3. its building, संस्था-भवन, संस्थान। 4. an established practice or law, रिवाज़, प्रथा। 5. a person of remarkable activities, संस्था।

institutional (इन्स्टिट्यूशनल) ***adj.*** of or pertaining to the institution, संस्थानिक, संस्थागत।

instruct (इन्स्ट्रक्ट) ***v.*** 1. to teach or educate, सिखाना, शिक्षित करना। 2. to direct, निदेश करना, अनुदेश देना। 3. to inform, सूचना देना।

instruction (इन्स्ट्रक्शन) ***n.*** 1. the act of instructing, शिक्षण, शिक्षा, सीख। 2. (plu.) directions, निदेश, अनुदेश।

instructive (इन्स्ट्रक्टिव) ***adj.*** giving knowledge, शिक्षाप्रद।

instructor (इन्स्ट्रक्टर) ***n.*** one who instructs, teacher, अनुदेशक, शिक्षक।

instrument (इन्स्ट्रुमेन्ट) ***n.*** 1. a mechanical implement, औज़ार, उपकरण। 2. a device for producing music, वाद्य। 3. a thing by means of which something is done, साधन, माध्यम। 4. a formal legal document, दस्तावेज़, लिखत।

instrumental (इन्स्ट्रुमेन्टल) ***adj.*** 1. serving as an instrument or agency, माध्यम, सहायक। 2. of or performed with an instrument, वाद्य; instrumental music, वाद्य संगीत।

insubordinate (इन्सबॉर्डिनिट) ***adj.*** disobedient, अवज्ञाकारी या अवज्ञापूर्ण।

insubodination (इन्सबॉर्डिनेशन) ***n.*** disobedience, अवज्ञा।

insufferable (इन्सफ़रेबल) ***adj.*** intolerable, असह्य।

insufficiency (इन्सफ़िशन्सी) ***n.*** lack of sufficiency, कमी, अभाव, अपर्याप्तता।

insufficient (इन्सफ़िशन्ट) ***adj.*** not sufficient, inadequate, कम, थोड़ा, अपर्याप्त।

insular (इन्सुलर) ***adj.*** 1. of an island, द्वीपीय। 2. narrow-minded, संकीर्ण विचारों-वाला।

insulate (इन्सुलेट) ***v.*** 1. to cover with non-conducting material in order to prevent leakage of electricity, heat, sound etc., विद्युत-रोधी/ताप-रोधी बनाना। 2. to detach, अलग करना, विद्युत-रोध या ताप-रोध करना।

insulator (इन्सुलेट) ***n.*** a device for detaching electric wire, इन्सुलेटर, विसंवाहक।

insulin (इन्सुलिन) ***n.*** a harmone that controls the absorption of sugar by the body, इन्सुलिन।

insult (इन्सल्ट) ***v.*** to hurt the feelings or pride of a person by act or word, अपमानित करना, अपमान करना। ***n.*** an insulting remark or action, अपमान, अनादर।

insulting (इन्सल्टिंग) ***adj.*** intending to hurt someone's pride or feelings, अनादरपूर्ण, अपमानजनक, अपमानकारक।

insurable (इन्शुअरेबल) ***adj.*** that can be insured, जिसका बीमा हो सके।

insurance (इन्शुअरेन्स) ***n.*** a system of protection against risk, harm or damage, इन्शोरेन्स, बीमा।

insure (इन्शुअर) ***v.*** 1. to issue or obtain insurance on or for, बीमा करना या कराना। 2. to make sure, पक्का करना, निश्चित कर लेना।

insurgence (इन्सर्जेन्स) ***n.*** uprising, विद्रोह, बग़ावत।

insurgent (इन्सर्जेन्ट) ***adj.*** rising in revolt, rebellious, विद्रोही, बाग़ी।

insurmountable (इन्सर्माउन्टेबल) ***adj.*** that cannot be surmounted, अजेय, विकट।

insurrection (इन्सरेक्शन) ***n.*** revolt, rebellion, विद्रोह, बग़ावत, विप्लव।

intact (इन्टैक्ट) ***adj.*** 1. unimpaired or whole, साबुत, अक्षत, सही-सलामत। 2. complete, पूर्ण, पूरा।

intake (इन्टेक) ***n.*** 1. the act of taking in, ग्रहण या अंतर्भुक्त करने की क्रिया या भाव, ग्राह्यता। 2. the amount taken in, ग्रहण की जानेवाली वस्तु या उसकी मात्रा, ग्रहणक्षमता।

integer (इन्टिजर) ***n.*** a whole number, पूर्ण संख्या, पूर्णांक।

integral (इन्टिग्रल) ***adj.*** 1. complete, whole, पूर्ण, समग्र, समाकल। 2. of integer, पूर्णसंख्या-संबंधी, पूर्णसांख्यिक।

integrate (इन्टिग्रेट) ***v.*** 1. to unify, एकीकृत या समन्वित करना। 2. to unite, एक होना या करना।

integration (इन्टिग्रेशन) ***n.*** the act of integrating or the state of being integrated, एकीकरण, समन्वयन।

integrity (इन्टेग्रिटी) ***n.*** 1. strict personal honesty, ईमानदारी, निष्ठा। 2. unity, एकता। 3. entirety, समग्रता।

intellect (इन्टिलेक्ट) ***n.*** the ability of the mind to think, reason and learn, प्रज्ञा, बुद्धि।

intellectual (इन्टिलेक्चुअल) ***adj.*** 1. of or relating to the intellect, बुद्धिगत, बौद्धिक। 2. rational, बुद्धिसंगत। 3. having superior intelligence, मनीषी, प्रबुद्ध, विद्वान। ***n.*** an intellectual person, बुद्धिजीवी।

intelligence (इन्टेलिजेन्स) ***n.*** 1. the capacity of learning and applying knowledge, बुद्धिमत्ता, मेधा। 2. secret information, गुप्त सूचना, आसूचना।

intelligent (इन्टेलिजेन्ट) ***adj.*** having intelligence, बुद्धिमान, प्रज्ञावान, मेधावी।

intelligentsia (इन्टेलिजेन्ट्सिआ) ***n.*** the intelligent people of a society or nation, बुद्धिजीवी वर्ग, प्रबुद्ध लोग।

intelligible (इन्टेलिजिबल) ***adj.*** that can be understood, बुद्धिग्राह्य, सुबोध।

intemperance (इन्टेम्परेन्स) ***n.*** lack of temperance, असंयम।

intend (इन्टेन्ड) ***v.*** 1. to wish, plan or propose, चाहना, इरादा रखना, मन में होना, योजना होना। 2. to be used for a special purpose, निमित्त होना। 3. to mean, अभिप्राय होना।

intense (इन्टेन्स) ***adj.*** 1. existing in high degree, very great or severe, तीव्र, तेज़, प्रचंड। 2. deeply felt, गहरा, गंभीर, अत्यधिक।

intensify (इन्टेन्सिफ़ाइ) ***v.*** to make or become more intense, तीव्र करना या बढ़ाना, तीव्र होना या बढ़ना।

intensity (इन्टेन्सिटी) ***n.*** the quality of being intense, तेज़ी, तीव्रता, ज़ोर, प्रबलता।

intensive (इन्टेन्सिव) ***adj.*** 1. expressing or showing intensity, तीव्र। 2. giving force or emphasis, ज़ोरदार। 3. concentrated, सघन।

intent (इन्टेन्ट) ***n.*** 1. aim or purpose, उद्देश्य या प्रयोजन। 2. intention, इरादा।

I

adj. 1. having the specified firm attention, determined, कटिबद्ध, तत्पर। 2. engrossed, लीन, निमग्न।

intention (इन्टेन्शन) ***n.*** 1. a plan or design to achieve something, आशय, इरादा, परिकल्पना, धारणा। 2. an aim or purpose, उद्देश्य, प्रयोजन। 3. meaning, अर्थ, अभिप्राय।

intentional (इन्टेन्शनल) ***adj.*** done purposely, साशय, साभिप्राय।

inter[1] (इन्टर) ***v.*** to bury, गाड़ना, दफ़नाना, दफ़न करना।

inter[2] ***prefix.*** 1. between, among, अंतर, मध्य, बीच। 2. together, साथ-साथ, मिलकर।

interact (इन्टर्‌ऐक्ट) ***v.*** 1. to have an effect on each other, एक दूसरे को प्रभावित करना। 2. to act reciprocally, परस्परता दिखाना, दोनों ओर से सक्रिय रहना।

interaction (इन्टर्‌ऐक्शन) ***n.*** reciprocal action, पारस्परिक क्रिया या व्यवहार, अन्योन्यक्रिया।

inter alia (इन्टर एलिआ) ***adv.*** among other things, अन्य बातों के साथ।

interbreeding (इन्टब्रीडिंग) ***n.*** a crossbreed, संकरण।

intercaste (इन्टर्कास्ट) ***adj.*** between the castes, अंतर्जातीय।

intercept (इन्टर्सेप्ट) ***v.*** to take, seize or stop in the way, बीच में रोकना, बीच में पकड़ लेना, अंतर्रोधन करना।

interchange (इन्टर्चेन्ज) ***v.*** 1. to exchange, विनिमय करना। 2. to put each of two things in the place of the other, अदल-बदल करना। ***n.*** exchange, विनिमय।

inter-city (इन्टर्सिटी) ***adj.*** operating between the two cities, अंतर्नगरी।

intercommunication (इन्टर्कम्यूनिकेशन) ***n.*** communication with each other, अंत:संचार।

interconnection (इन्टर्कनेक्शन) ***n.*** 1. the act of interconnecting, अंत:संबंधन। 2. the state of being interconnected, अंत:संबंध।

intercontinental (इन्टर्कॉन्टिनेन्टल) ***adj.*** between or among continents, अंतर्महाद्वीपीय।

intercourse (इन्टर्कोर्स) ***n.*** 1. sexual intercourse, मैथुन, सहवास। 2. the dealings between the people, countries etc., पारस्परिक व्यवहार।

interdepartmental (इन्टर्डीपार्टमेन्टल) ***adj.*** relating to different departments, अंतर्विभागीय।

interdependent (इन्टर्डिपेन्डेन्ट) ***adj.*** mutually dependent, अन्योन्याश्रित, परस्पर-निर्भर।

interest (इन्ट्रिस्ट) ***n.*** 1. a feeling of curiosity about something, रुचि, अभिरुचि, दिलचस्पी, कौतूहल। 2. something that arouses such feeling, रस। 3. importance, महत्त्व। 4. a right or legal share in something, हित। 5. money paid for the use of money, ब्याज, सूद।

interesting (इन्ट्रिस्टिन्ग) ***adj.*** arousing interest, रोचक, दिलचस्प।

interface (इन्टर्फ़ेस) ***n.*** a point where two systems/processes interact, मिलन-बिंदु।

interfere (इन्टर्फ़िअर) ***v.*** 1. to intervene in the affairs of others, हस्तक्षेप करना, दख़ल देना। 2. to obstruct, बाधा पहुँचाना।

interference (इन्टर्फ़िअरेन्स) ***n.*** the act of interfering, हस्तक्षेप, दख़ल, बाधा।

interim (इन्टेरिम) ***adj.*** temporary, अस्थायी, अंतरिम, अंत:कालीन।

interior (इन्टीरिअर) ***adj.*** of or located nearer the centre, अंदरूनी, भीतरी, आभ्यंतर। ***n.*** the inner part, भीतरी भाग।

interjection (इन्टर्जेक्शन) ***n.*** a word that expresses some abrupt emotion and having no grammatical connection, exclamation, विस्मयादिबोधक।

interlace (इन्टर्लेस) ***v.*** to weave together, गूँथना।

interlink (इन्टर्लिंक) ***v.*** to link together, जोड़ या मिला देना, शृंखलित करना।

interlock (इन्टर्लॉक) ***v.*** 1. to lock together, एक साथ जोड़ या बाँध देना। 2. to connect so as to work together, अंत:पाशित करना।

interlocutor (इन्टर्लॉक्यूटर) ***n.*** a person taking part in a conversation, वार्तालाप करनेवाला, वार्तालापी।

interlope (इन्टर्लोप) ***v.*** to meddle in others' affairs, दख़ल देना, हस्तक्षेप करना।

interlude (इन्टर्ल्यूड) ***n.*** 1. an intervening period of time between the acts of a play, मध्यांतर, अंतराल। 2. something performed during this, मध्यांतर का कार्यक्रम।

intermediary (इन्टर्मीडिअरी) ***adj.*** 1. acting as a mediator, मध्यस्थता करनेवाला। 2. intermediate, बिचला, माध्यमिक।

intermediate (इन्टर्मीडिएट) ***adj.*** coming or lying in between two things in time, place or order, मध्यवर्ती, माध्यमिक।

interment (इन्टर्मेन्ट) ***n.*** burial, दफ़न।

intermission (इन्टर्मिशन) ***n.*** an interlude, अंतराल, मध्यांतर।

intermittent (इन्टर्मिटेन्ट) ***adj.*** not continuous, occurring at intervals, रुक-रुककर होनेवाला, आंतरायिक।

intern (इन्टर्न) ***n.*** a doctor serving as assistant and undergoing practical training, प्रशिक्षणाधीन चिकित्सक। ***v.*** to detain in wartime, युद्धकाल में बंदी बनाना।

internal (इन्टर्नल) ***adj.*** 1. inward, interior, आंतरिक, अंदरूनी, भीतरी। 2. of domestic affairs of a country, देशी, राष्ट्रीय, घरेलू।

international (इन्टर्नेशनल) ***adj.*** of or concerning two or more nations, अंतर्राष्ट्रीय।

internee (इन्टर्नी) ***n.*** a person interned during war, नज़रबंद।

internet (इन्टर्नेट) ***n.* the Internet**, the international computer network, अंतर्राष्ट्रीय कंप्यूटर-तंत्र, इंटरनेट।

internment (इन्टर्नमेन्ट) ***n.*** the act of interning or the state of being interned, नज़रबंदी।

Interpol (इन्टर्पोल) ***n.*** International Criminal Police Commission, अंतर्राष्ट्रीय पुलिस, अंतर्पोल।

interpolate (इन्टर्पोलेट) ***v.*** 1. to change a text by adding new or false material, क्षेपक मिलाना, प्रक्षिप्त करना। 2. to insert, अंतर्वेशन करना, सन्निवेश करना।

interpose (इन्टर्पोज़) ***v.*** 1. to interject, बीच में फेंकना, विशेषत: बीच में बोलना। 2. to intervene, दख़ल देना, हस्तक्षेप करना।

interpret (इन्टर्प्रिट) ***v.*** 1. to explain the meaning of, व्याख्या करना। 2. to act as interpreter, दुभाषिए का काम करना, समझाना।

I

interrelate (इन्टररिलेट) ***v.*** to relate to each other, एक दूसरे से संबंध स्थापित होना या करना।

interrelation (इन्टररिलेशन) ***n.*** mutual relationship, पारस्परिक संबंध।

interrogate (इन्टेरोगेट) ***v.*** to question formally, पूछ-ताछ करना, प्रश्न करना।

interrogation (इन्टेरोगेशन) ***n.*** the act of interrogating or the state of being interrogated, पूछ-ताछ, प्रश्न पूछना।

interrogator (इन्टेरॉगेटर) ***n.*** one who interrogates, पूछ-ताछ करनेवाला, प्रश्नकर्ता।

interrupt (इन्टरप्ट) ***v.*** 1. to break the continuity, क्रमभंग करना, विच्छिन्न करना, व्यवधान डालना। 2. to break the flow of the speech, टोकना, टोकाटाकी करना।

interruption (इन्टरप्शन) ***n.*** the act of interrupting or the state of being interrupted, क्रमभंग, व्यवधान; टोकाटाकी, बाधा।

intersect (इन्टर्सेक्ट) ***v.*** to cross each other (as lines or roads) एक दूसरे को काटना।

intersection (इन्टर्सेक्शन) ***n.*** 1. the act of intersecting, परस्पर काटना। 2. a place where lines or roads intersect, चौराहा।

interstate (इन्टर्स्टेट) ***adj.*** of or existing between two or more states, अंतर्राज्यीय।

interval (इन्टर्वल) ***n.*** a period of time between the recurrence of two events, अंतराल।

intervene (इन्टर्वीन) ***v.*** 1. to occur between two events, things or points, बीच में आना। 2. to come between and hinder, बीच में आकर बाधा पहुँचाना, हस्तक्षेप करना।

intervention (इन्टर्वेन्शन) ***n.*** the act of interfering, हस्तक्षेप, दख़ल, छेड़छाड़।

interview (इन्टर्व्यू) ***n.*** a formal meeting with a person in order to obtain his views or ascertain personal qualities, साक्षात्कार, भेंट, इंटरव्यू। ***v.*** to hold an interview with, साक्षात्कार लेना, इंटरव्यू लेना।

interviewer (इन्टर्व्यूअर) ***n.*** one who holds an interview, भेंटकर्ता।

interweave (इन्टर्वीव) ***v.*** (interwove, interwoven, interweaving) to weave together, गूँथना, गुंफन करना।

intestate (इन्टेस्टेट) ***adj.*** without leaving a will, जिसने वसीयत न की हो, बेवसीयती।

intestine (इन्टेस्टाइन) ***n.*** the lower portion of the alimentary canal extending from the outlet of the stomach to the anus, आँत, अँतड़ी, आंत्र।

intimacy (इन्टिमेसी) ***n.*** the quality of being intimate, आत्मीयता, घनिष्ठता।

intimate (इन्टिमेट) ***adj.*** 1. very close, familiar, आत्मीय, अंतरंग, घनिष्ठ, सुपरिचित। 2. private and personal, निजी, वैयक्तिक। ***v.*** to make known, अवगत करना, सूचना देना, प्रज्ञापित करना।

intimation (इन्टिमेशन) ***n.*** 1. a formal notification, सूचना, प्रज्ञापन। 2. something intimated, सूचित की हुई बात।

intimidate (इन्टिमिडेट) ***v.*** to subdue by threats, धमकाना, डराना।

intimidation (इन्टिमिडेशन) ***n.*** threat, धमकी।

into (इन्टु) ***prep.*** 1. to the inside of, के अंदर, के भीतर, में। 2. to the

I

condition or form of, में। 3. times, गुणित करने पर।

intolerable (इन्टॉलरेबल) ***adj.*** that cannot be tolerated, असह्य, असहनीय।

intolerance (इन्टॉलरेन्स) ***n.*** lack of tolerance, असहिष्णुता, असहनशीलता।

intone (इन्टोन) ***v.*** to recite in a singing or chanting voice, स्वर या लय से पढ़ना।

in toto (इन टोटो) ***adv.*** completely, पूर्णतः।

intoxicant (इन्टॉक्सिकेन्ट) ***n.*** something that intoxicates, नशीली वस्तु, मादक पदार्थ।

intoxicate (इन्टॉक्सिकेट) ***v.*** 1. to make drunk, नशे में लाना, बेसुध कर देना। 2. to excite or stimulate beyond control, उन्मत्त कर देना।

intoxication (इन्टॉक्सिकेशन) ***n.*** 1. the act of intoxicating or the state of being intoxicated, नशा, मद, मत्तता। 2. great excitement, उन्माद, उतावलापन।

intra (इन्ट्रा) ***prefix.*** within, भीतरी।

intractable (इन्ट्रैक्टेबल) ***adj.*** 1. difficult to control, अनियंत्रणीय। 2. incurable, असाध्य। 3. stubborn, अड़ियल, हठी।

intramural (इन्ट्राम्युरल) ***adj.*** occurring or carried on within an institution, अंतःसंस्थानिक, संस्थागत।

intransigent (इन्ट्रैन्सिजेन्ट) ***adj.*** stubborn, uncompromising, हठी, दुराग्राही।

intransitive (इन्ट्रैन्सिटिव) ***adj.*** not having a direct object, अकर्मक।

intrepid (इन्ट्रेपिड) ***adj.*** 1. fearless, निडर, निर्भीक, निर्भय। 2. courageous, साहसी, दिलेर।

intrepidity (इन्ट्रेपिडिटी) ***n.*** the state or quality of being intrepid, निर्भीकता, निर्भयता, साहस, दिलेरी।

intricacy (इन्ट्रिकेसी) ***n.*** the state or quality of being intricate, complexity, जटिलता, पेचीदापन, पेचीदगी।

intricate (इन्ट्रिकेट) ***adj.*** very complicated, पेचीदा, जटिल।

intrigue (इन्ट्रीग) ***n.*** 1. an underhand plot, षड्यंत्र, कुचक्र। 2. a secret love affair, गुप्त प्रेम-संबंध, प्रेम-प्रपंच। ***v.*** to plot, षड्यंत्र करना, कुचक्र रचना।

intrinsic (इन्ट्रिन्सिक) ***adj.*** 1. located within, भीतरी। 2. essential, मूलभूत, तात्त्विक। 3. inherent, अंतर्निहित।

introduce (इन्ट्रड्यूस) ***v.*** 1. to present formally, पेश करना, प्रस्तुत करना। 2. to make (a person) known by name to others, परिचय कराना। 3. to conduct in, प्रविष्ट करना, डालना, घुसाना। 4. to bring into use, प्रयोग में लाना। 5. to offer first time for sale, (नई चीज़) बिक्री के लिए उपलब्ध करना। 6. to start, आरंभ करना।

introduction (इन्ट्रडक्शन) ***n.*** 1. the act of introducing or the state of being introduced, प्रस्तुति। 2. the action of making known personally, परिचय। 3. the preliminary section of a book, भूमिका, प्रस्तावना।

introductory (इन्ट्रडक्टरी) ***adj.*** serving to introduce, परिचायक।

introspection (इन्ट्रोस्पेक्शन) ***n.*** self-examination, आत्मविश्लेषण, आत्मनिरीक्षण।

introversion (इन्ट्रोवर्शन) ***n.*** the state or quality of being an introvert, अंतर्मुखता।

I

introvert (इन्ट्रोवर्ट) ***n.*** a person whose thoughts are directed inward, अंतर्मुखी।

intrude (इन्ट्रूड) ***v.*** 1. to enter without being invited or wanted, घुसना, बलात् प्रवेश करना। 2. to enter illegally, घुसपैठ करना।

intrusion (इन्ट्रूज़न) ***n.*** the act of intruding, बलात् प्रवेश, घुसपैठ।

intuition (इन्ट्यूशन) ***n.*** the power of knowing or understanding something immediately without conscious reasoning, अंतर्ज्ञान, अंतःस्फुरण, सहजज्ञान।

inundate (इनन्डेट) ***v.*** 1. to cover with or as with a flood, प्लावित करना। 2. to flood, बाढ़ लाना, पाट देना।

inundation (इनन्डेशन) ***n.*** 1. the act of inundating, प्लावन। 2. the state of being flooded, बाढ़, भरमार।

invade (इन्वेड) ***v.*** 1. to enter by force in order to conquer, चढ़ाई करना, धावा बोलना, आक्रमण करना। 2. to crowd into, चढ़ आना या चढ़ जाना, घुस आना या घुस जाना।

invalid (इन्वैलिड) ***adj.*** 1. infirm, disabled, अशक्त, दुर्बल। 2. not valid, अमान्य।

invalidate (इन्वैलिडेट) ***v.*** to make invalid, अमान्य करना।

invalidity (इन्वैलिडिटी) ***n.*** 1. lack of validity, अमान्यता। 2. disable-ness, weakness, अशक्तता, निर्बलता।

invaluable (इन्वैल्युएबल) ***adj.*** extremely valuable, बहुमूल्य, अमूल्य।

invariable (इन्वेरिएबल) ***adj.*** not subject to change, अपरिवर्तनशील, नित्य।

invariably (इन्वेरिएब्ली) ***adv.*** constantly, सदा, हमेशा।

invasion (इन्वेज़न) ***n.*** the act of invading or the state of being invaded, आक्रमण।

invent (इन्वेन्ट) ***v.*** 1. to devise for the first time, आविष्कार करना। 2. to fabricate, बनाना, गढ़ लेना।

invention (इन्वेन्शन) ***n.*** 1. the act of inventing, आविष्करण। 2. something invented, आविष्कार।

inventor (इन्वेन्टर) ***n.*** one who invents, आविष्कारक।

inventory (इन्वेन्टरी) ***n.*** a detailed list of goods, property etc., विस्तृत सूची, तालिका।

inverse (इन्वर्स) ***adj.*** 1. inverted, reversed, उलटा, औंधा। 2. directly opposite, उलटा, प्रतिलोम।

inversion (इन्वर्शन) ***n.*** the act of inverting or the state of being inverted, उलटा करना, उलटा क्रम या रूप, उलटाव।

invert (इन्वर्ट) ***v.*** to change upside down, उलटा देना, पलट देना।

invertebrate (इन्वर्टिब्रिट) ***adj.*** without backbone, not vertebrate, रीढ़विहीन, अकशेरुकी; डाँवाँडोल, अस्थिर। ***n.*** an invertebrate animal, अकशेरुकी प्राणी।

invertible (इन्वर्टिबल) ***adj.*** that can be inverted, जिसे उलटा किया जा सके।

invest (इन्वेस्ट) ***v.*** 1. to put money to buy securities, property etc., for future benefit, धन (या रुपया) लगाना, विनिधान करना, निवेश करना। 2. to endow with power or authority, अधिकार देना।

investigate (इन्वेस्टिगेट) ***v.*** to enquire carefully and in detail, अन्वेषण करना, अनुसंधान करना, खोज करना।

investigation (इन्वेस्टिगेशन) ***n.***

the act of investigating, अन्वेषण, अनुसंधान, खोज।

investiture (इन्वेस्टिचर) ***n.*** a formal investing with an office, authority etc., पदारोहण-समारोह, अलंकरण-वितरण-समारोह।

investment (इन्वेस्टमेन्ट) ***n.*** the act of investing, विनिधान, निवेश।

invigilate (इन्विजिलेट) ***v.*** 1. to be alert, चौकस रहना। 2. to watch carefully, चौकसी करना, निगरानी करना, निरीक्षण करना।

invigilator (इन्विजिलेटर) ***n.*** one who invigilates, निरीक्षक।

invigorate (इन्विगरेट) ***v.*** to give vigour, बलशाली बनाना, अनुप्राणित करना।

invigoration (इन्विगरेशन) ***n.*** the act of invigorating, बलवर्धन।

invincible (इन्विन्सिबल) ***adj.*** that cannot be conquered, अजेय, दुर्भेद्य।

inviolable (इन्वाइअलेबल) ***adj.*** not to be violated, अनुल्लंघनीय।

invisibility (इन्विज़िबिलिटी) ***n.*** the state or condition of being invisible, अदृश्यता।

invisible (इन्विज़िबल) ***adj.*** not visible, अदृश्य, अप्रकट, ग़ायब।

invitation (इन्विटेशन) ***n.*** 1. the act of inviting, आमंत्रण, न्योता। 2. a written or printed request for one's presence, निमंत्रण।

invite (इन्वाइट) ***v.*** 1. to request the presence or participation of, निमंत्रित करना, न्योता देना, दावत देना। 2. to ask for, आमंत्रित करना। 3. to attract or lure, आकृष्ट करना, लुभाना, प्रलोभन देना। ***n.*** an invitation, निमंत्रण।

invocation (इन्वोकेशन) ***n.*** 1. an act of invoking, आवाहन, आह्वान, पुकार। 2. a prayer used in invoking, प्रार्थना, विनय।

invoice (ईन्वॉइस) ***n.*** detailed list of goods sent with prices and charges, बीजक। ***v.*** to make an invoice, बीजक बनाना।

invoke (इन्वोक) ***v.*** 1. to call upon (God) for help in prayer, (देवता का) आह्वान करना। 2. to implore, प्रार्थना करना, चिरौरी करना।

involuntary (इन्वॉलन्टरी) ***adj.*** 1. not performed willingly, अस्वैच्छिक, अनैच्छिक। 2. not subject to control, नियंत्रणविहीन।

involve (इन्वॉल्व) ***v.*** 1. to coil up, लपेटना। 2. to make intricate, उलझाना, पेचीदा बना देना। 3. to contain or include as a part, अंतर्ग्रस्त होना, शामिल होना।

involvement (इन्वाल्वमेन्ट) ***n.*** entanglement, उलझन, उलझाव, ग्रस्तता।

invulnerability (इन्वल्नरेबिलिटी) ***n.*** the state of being invulnerable, अभेद्यता, दुर्भेद्यता।

invulnerable (इन्वल्नरेबल) ***adj.*** not vulnerable, अभेद्य, दुर्भेद्य।

inward (इन्वर्ड) ***adj.*** 1. placed within, भीतरी, अंदरूनी। 2. going toward inside, आवक। 3. in the mind or spirit, आंतरिक, अंतर्मुखी।

iodine (आइअडीन) ***n.*** a chemical element, एक रासायनिक तत्त्व, आयोडीन।

ion (आइअन) ***n.*** an atom having an electric charge, आयन।

ionosphere (आइऑनस्फ़िअर) ***n.*** an ionized region of the upper atmosphere, आयनमंडल।

iota (आइओटा) ***n.*** the smallest possible amount, कण, ज़र्रा।

I

ipso facto (इप्सो फ़ैक्टो) ***adv.*** by that very fact, स्वयंमेव ही, इसी से, इसी आधार पर।

irascible (इरैसिबल) ***adj.*** easily angered, irritable, चिड़चिड़ा, गर्ममिज़ाज।

irate (आइरेट) ***adj.*** angry, wrathful, क्रुद्ध, क्रोधी।

ire (आइर) ***n.*** anger, wrath, क्रोध, ग़ुस्सा।

iris (आइरिस) ***n.*** (plu. irises, irides) 1. a rainbow, इंद्रधनुष। 2. a membrane surrounding the pupil of the eye, आँख की पुतली। 3. a plant with sword shaped leaves, आइरिस नामक पौधा।

irk (अर्क) ***v.*** 1. to irritate, to annoy, ग़ुस्सा दिलाना, चिढ़ाना। 2. to make weary or bored, थका डालना, ऊबा देना।

irksome (अर्कसम) ***adj.*** 1. causing annoyance, चिढ़ानेवाला। 2. tiresome, boring, annoying, थकानेवाला, ऊबानेवाला, परेशान करनेवाला।

iron (आइरन) ***n.*** 1. a very common and useful metal, लोहा। 2. (plu.) fetters, बेड़ियाँ। ***v.*** to smooth clothes with an iron, इस्त्री करना, लोहा करना।

iron horse ***n.*** a locomotive, रेल का इंजन।

ironic (आइरॉनिक) ***adj.*** = ironical.

ironical (आइरॉनिकल) ***adj.*** using or expressing irony, व्यंग्यात्मक, व्यंग्यपूर्ण।

irony (आइरनी) ***n.*** 1. speech intended to convey a contrary signification, व्यंग्य। 2. the incongruity between what might be expected and what actually occurs, विडंबना या अदृष्ट विधान।

irradiate (इरेडिएट) ***v.*** 1. to make bright, चमकाना, प्रकाशित करना। 2. to become bright, चमकना, चमकने लगना। 3. to expose to radiation, एक्सरे किरणों से उपचार करना।

irrational (इरैशनल) ***adj.*** 1. not rational, अविवेकपूर्ण, अयुक्तियुक्त। 2. illogical or absurd, बेतुका, हास्यास्पद।

irrecoverable (इरिकवरेबल) ***adj.*** 1. that cannot be recovered, जो वसूल न हो सके। 2. irretrievable, जिसे वापस न लिया जा सके।

irredeemable (इरिडीमेबल) ***adj.*** 1. not redeemable, जिसका उद्धार न किया जा सके। 2. that cannot be recovered, जिसे पुनः प्राप्त न किया जा सके।

irrefutable (इरिफ़्यूटेबल) ***adj.*** that cannot be refuted or disproved, अकाट्य।

irregular (इरेग्युलर) ***adj.*** 1. not regular, contrary to the rule or practice, अनियमित। 2. not straight, uniform or symmetrical, असम, विषम, असामान्य।

irregularity (इरेग्युलैरिटी) ***n.*** 1. the quality or state of being irregular, अनियमितता, विषमता।

irrelevant (इरेलिवेन्ट) ***adj.*** not relevant, विसंगत, अप्रासंगिक।

irremediable (इरिमीडिएबल) ***adj.*** incurable, असाध्य, असुधार्य।

irrepressible (इरिप्रेसिबल) ***adj.*** that cannot be repressed, अदमनीय, अदम्य।

irresistible (इरिज़िस्टिबल) ***adj.*** 1. too strong or compelling to be resisted, जिसे रोका न जा सके, अप्रतिरोध्य। 2. extremely tempting, अत्यधिक लुभावना।

irrespective of (इरिस्पेक्टिव ऑफ़) ***prep.*** regardless of, का विचार किए

I

बिना, को ध्यान में रखे बिना।

irresponsible (इरिस्पॉन्सिबल) ***adj.*** not responsible, ग़ैरज़िम्मेदार या ग़ैरज़िम्मेदाराना, अनुत्तरदायी या अनुत्तरदायित्वपूर्ण।

irreversible (इरिवर्सिबल) ***adj.*** that cannot be reversed, जिसे उलटा या बदला न जा सके, अपरिवर्त्य।

irrevocable (इरेवोकेबल) ***adj.*** that cannot be revoked, जिसे रद्द न किया जा सके, जिसे वापस न लिया जा सके, अपरिवर्तनीय, अप्रतिसंहरणीय।

irrigate (इरिगेट) ***v.*** to supply land with water by means of streams, pipes etc., सींचना, सिंचाई करना।

irrigation (इरिगेशन) ***n.*** the act of irrigating or the state of being irrigated, सिंचाई, सिंचन।

irritable (इरिटेबल) ***adj.*** 1. easily annoyed, चिड़चिड़ा। 2. ill-tempered, बदमिज़ाज। 3. abnormally sensitive, अतिसंवेदनशील। 4. responsive to stimuli, उत्तेजनशील।

irritate (इरिटेट) ***v.*** 1. to make angry or impatient, उत्तेजित करना, क्षुब्ध करना, चिढ़ाना। 2. to cause itching, ख़ारिश होना।

irritation (इरिटेशन) ***n.*** the act of irritating or the fact of being irritated, चिढ़; क्षोभ; ख़ारिश।

irrupt (इरप्ट) ***v.*** to enter forcibly, घुस आना या पड़ना।

is (इज़) ***v.*** third person singular, present tense of be, है।

island (आइलैन्ड) ***n.*** a piece of land surrounded by sea, द्वीप, टापू।

islet (आइलिट) ***n.*** a small island, छोटा टापू, उपद्वीप।

ism (इज़म) ***n.*** any doctrine, वाद, मत, सिद्धांत।

isobar (आइसोबार) ***n.*** a line on a weather map connecting places or points of equal atmospheric pressure, समदाब रेखा।

isolate (आइसोलेट) ***v.*** to separate from a group or whole, एकाकी, अलग या अलहदा कर देना।

isolation (आइसोलेशन) ***n.*** the act of isolating or the state of being isolated, अलगाव, एकाकीपन, निस्संगता, तन्हाई।

isometric (आइसोमेट्रिक) ***adj.*** of equal measure, सममितीय।

isosceles (आइसॉसेलीज़) ***adj.*** having two equal sides, समद्विबाहु।

issue (इशू) ***n.*** 1. the act of outflowing or passing out, निर्गम, निकास, बहाव। 2. something produced, published or offered, उत्पादित, प्रकाशित या प्रस्तावित वस्तु। 3. all the copies of a newspaper or magazine printed on a certain date, अंक, संस्करण। 4. an offspring, संतति। 5. the point or topic in question, विवाद विषय, विवाद्यक। ***v.*** 1. to flow out, बाहर आना, निकलना। 2. to send out, बाहर करना, निकालना। 3. to publish, प्रकाशित करना। 4. to give or distribute, देना, वितरण करना। 5. to circulate, जारी करना।

isthmus (इस्थमस) ***n.*** a narrow strip of land connecting two larger masses of land, थलडमरूमध्य।

it (इट) ***pronoun.*** the thing named or in question, यह, वह।

italics (इटैलिक्स) ***n.*** slanting printed letters, तिरछे अक्षर।

itch (इच) ***n.*** 1. a desire to scratch,

I

खुजली। 2. a craving, साध, इच्छा, खुजली। *v.* 1. to have an itch, खुजली होना। 2. to have a desire to do or to get something, कुछ पाने या करने की इच्छा होना, (हाथ में) खुजली होना।

item (आइटम) ***n.*** 1. a single article in a list or number of things, मद। 2. an entry in an account, मद। 3. a bit of news or information, विषय।

iterate (इटरेट) ***v.*** to repeat, दुहराना, बार-बार कहना, पुनर्कथन करना।

itinerant (इटिनरेन्ट) ***adj.*** travelling from place to place, घूमने या दौरा करनेवाला, भ्रमणशील।

itinerary (इटिनरेरी) ***n.*** a list of places to be visited on a trip, दौरे का कार्यक्रम, यात्राक्रम।

itself (इटसेल्फ़) ***pronoun.*** a reflexive form of it, स्वयं।

ivory (आइवरी) ***n.*** the hard white substance forming the tusks of elephants, हाथी दाँत।

J

J

J, j (जे) ***n.*** the tenth letter of the English alphabet, अंग्रेज़ी वर्णमाला का दसवाँ वर्ण।

jabber (जैबर) ***v.*** 1. to speak (or talk) rapidly, unintelligibly or incoherently, बड़बड़ करना, बकबक करना।

jack, Jack (जैक) ***n.*** 1. a portable mechanical device for raising the axle of a car, truck etc., जैक। 2. a fellow or person, आदमी, व्यक्ति। 3. a playing card ranking below a queen, ग़ुलाम, गुल्ला। 4. a sailor, नाविक। ***v.*** to raise or lift with a jack, जैक से ऊपर उठाना या ऊँचा करना।

jackal (जैकॉल) ***n.*** a mammal related to the dog family, गीदड़, सियार।

jackass (जैकैस) ***n.*** 1. a male donkey, गधा। 2. a foolish person, मूर्ख व्यक्ति।

jacket (जैकिट) ***n.*** 1. a sleeveless short coat, जैकेट, वास्कट। 2. an outer covering or wrapper, कवर।

jackknife (जैकनाइफ़) ***n.*** a large pocket knife, (खटकेदार) बड़ा जेबी चाकू।

jackpot (जैकपॉट) ***n.*** the top prize or accumulated stake that may be won in gambling, जैक पॉट, बड़ा पुरस्कार, दाँव पर लगी राशि।

jade[1] (जेड) ***n.*** 1. a semiprecious green stone used in jewellery, हरे रंग का एक प्रकार का रत्न, संगयशब। 2. the green colour of jade, उक्त रत्न का रंग।

jade[2] ***n.*** 1. an old overworked horse, बूढ़ा मरियल घोड़ा। 2. a disreputable woman, कुलटा, बदचलन स्त्री।

jagged (जैगिड) ***adj.*** rough, ख़ुरदरा।

jaguar (जैग्वार) ***n.*** a leopard like wild cat found in the jungles of America, अमरीका के जंगलों में पाया जानेवाला चीता, तेंदुआ।

jail (जेल) ***n.*** a public prison for convicted persons, जेल, बंदीगृह, कारागार, कारावास। ***v.*** to put in jail, जेल में डाल देना।

jailer, jailor (जेलर) ***n.*** the keeper of a jail, जेलर, काराधिकारी, कारापाल।

Jainism (जैनिज़्म) ***n.*** one of the Indian religions, जैन धर्म।

jalap (जैलप) ***n.*** a purgative drug, जुलाब।

jam[1] (जैम) ***v.*** 1. to fill to excess, ठूँसना या ठूँसा जाना। 2. to block, अवरुद्ध कर देना या हो जाना। 3. to crowd or pack, भीड़ लगा देना, जाम कर देना, ठसाठस हो जाना। 4. to lock in an unworkable position, (मशीन का) न चल पाना, जकड़ जाना। ***n.*** 1. the act of jamming or the condition of being jammed, जाम कर देना या हो जाना। 2. congestion, भीड़-भाड़।

jam[2] ***n.*** a sweet substance made by boiling fruit with sugar, जैम, मुरब्बा।

jamboree (जैम्बोरी) ***n.*** 1. a large gathering of scouts, स्काउटों का जमावड़ा। 2. a large party or celebration, पार्टी, समारोह, मेला।

jampacked (जैमपैक्ड) ***adj.*** packed to the capacity, ठसाठस, खचाखच, पूरा भरा हुआ।

J

jangle (जैन्गल) ***n.*** a harsh metallic sound, झनझन, झनझनाहट, खनखन, खनखनाहट। ***v.*** to make a harsh metallic sound, झनझनाना, खनखनाना।

January (जैन्युअरी) ***n.*** the first month of the year, जनवरी।

jape (जेप) ***n.*** a joke or quip, मज़ाक, दिल्लगी, परिहास। ***v.*** to joke or quip, मज़ाक करना, दिल्लगी या परिहास करना।

jar[1] (जार) ***n.*** a wide-mouthed cylindrical container, जग, सुराही, मर्तबान, कलश आदि।

jar[2] ***v.*** 1. to make a harsh discordant sound, कर्कश या कर्णकटु ध्वनि करना। 2. to have a disturbing or painful effect, विक्षुब्ध हो उठना। 3. to shake from impact, हिल उठना, हिचकोले खाना। 4. to clash, भिड़ जाना।

jargon (जार्गन) ***n.*** a specialized language of a group or profession, बोली, वर्ग-विशेष या व्यवसाय-विशेष की शब्दावली।

jasmine (जैस्मिन) ***n.*** a shrub with small fragrant flowers, चमेली।

jasper (जैस्पर) ***n.*** a quartz used as a gemstone, एक प्रकार का रत्न, जैस्पर।

jaundice (जॉन्डिस) ***n.*** a disease in which skin, eyes, urine etc., become yellowish, पीलिया, कमल रोग, कामला।

jaundiced (जॉन्डिस्ड) ***adj.*** 1. affected with jaundice, पीलिया रोग से ग्रस्त। 2. affected by jealousy or malice, द्वेषपूर्ण, ईर्ष्यापूर्ण।

jaunt (जॉन्ट) ***n.*** a short pleasurable trip, सैर, सैर-सपाटा।

jaunty (जॉन्टी) ***adj.*** 1. carefree, निश्चिंत। 2. self-confident, आत्मतुष्ट। 3. smart, stylish, चुस्त-दुरुस्त।

javelin (जैवलिन) ***n.*** a light spear, बरछा, भाला।

jaw (जॉ) ***n.*** either of the two bony structures of the mouth holding the teeth, जबड़ा, हनु।

jay (जे) ***n.*** a brightly coloured bird with a crest related to the crow, नीलकंठ पक्षी।

jazz (जैज़) ***n.*** a kind of music marked by strong but flexible rhythm, जैज़ या जाज़ संगीत।

jealous (जेलस) ***adj.*** 1. envious, grudging, ईर्ष्यालु, जलनेवाला। 2. taking watchful care, चौकन्ना, चौकस, सतर्क।

jealousy (जेलसी) ***n.*** the state or quality of being jealous, ईर्ष्या, डाह, जलन।

jeans (जीन्ज़) ***n.*** (plu.) trousers made of jean, ज़ीन की पतलून।

jeep (जीप) ***n.*** a four-wheeled vehicle, जीप।

jeer (जिअर) ***v.*** 1. to laugh scornfully, तिरस्कार या कुटिलतापूर्वक हँसना। 2. to speak derisively, उपहास करना, खिल्ली उड़ाना, फबती कसना। ***n.*** 1. a cry of derision, कुटिल हँसी। 2. a remark of derision, फबती, खिल्ली।

jelly (जेली) ***n.*** fruit juice set with gelatine, जेली।

jenny (जेनी) ***n.*** a female donkey, गधी।

jeopardise (जेपर्डाइज़) ***v.*** to imperil or endanger, ख़तरे में डालना, फँसा देना।

jeopardy (जेपर्डी) ***n.*** danger, risk of loss or injury, ख़तरा; जोखिम।

jerk (जर्क) ***n.*** 1. an abrupt movement, झटका। 2. a sudden push, pull or throw, धक्का, हिचकोला।

v. to push, pull or throw with a jerk, झटकना, झटका देना।

jerkin (जर्किन) *n.* a sleeveless jacket, जरकिन, फतुई, मिरजई।

jerky (जर्की) *adj.* characterized by jerks, झटके खाता या देता हुआ।

jersey[1] (जर्सी) *n.* a light knitted woollen garment worn to cover the upper part of the body, जर्सी, बंडी, स्वेटर, जैकेट।

Jersey[2] *n.* a breed of dairy cattle, जर्सी गाय।

jest (जेस्ट) *n.* joke, मज़ाक, परिहास, दिल्लगी। *v.* to joke, मज़ाक करना, परिहास करना।

jester (जेस्टर) *n.* one who jests, विदूषक, मसखरा, दिल्लगीबाज़।

Jesus (जीज़स) *n.* Jesus Christ, founder of Christianity, येशु, ईसा मसीह।

jet[1] (जेट) *n.* 1. a hard black mineral used for jewellery, एक प्रकार का काला कड़ा खनिज पदार्थ जिसका उपयोग जड़ाऊ गहनों में होता है, संगमूसा, कृष्णाश्म। 2. deep black colour, गहरा काला रंग।

jet[2] *n.* 1. a stream of gas, liquid etc., forced out of a small opening, धारा, प्रधारा। 2. an opening from which this comes, धारा-छिद्र। 3. a jet-propelled aircraft, जेट विमान। *v.* 1. to issue or cause to issue in a jet, धारा छोड़ना। 2. to travel by jet aircraft, जेट विमान से यात्रा करना।

jetblack (जेटब्लैक) *adj.* deep black, काला स्याह।

jettison (जेटिसन) *v.* 1. to throw overboard, जहाज़ पर से फेंकना। 2. to abandon, त्याग देना, छोड़ देना, तिलांजलि दे देना।

jetty (जेटी) *n.* a structure extending into the body of water to protect a harbour, घाट, जेट्टी।

Jew (जू) *n.* an adherent of Judaism, यहूदी।

jewel (जूअल) *n.* 1. a precious stone, रत्न, मणि। 2. a person or thing highly valued or admired, मूल्यवान वस्तु या व्यक्ति, नगीना।

jeweller, jeweler (जूअलर) *n.* one who deals in jewellery, जौहरी।

jewellery, jewelry (जूअलरी) *n.* gems and ornaments, रत्न तथा आभूषण।

jib (जिब) *n.* a triangular sail stretching forward from the mast, जहाज़ का तिकोना पाल। *v.* to refuse to go forward, अड़ जाना।

jiffy (जिफ़ी) *n.* a moment, क्षण।

jiggle (जिगल) *v.* 1. to move up and down or to and fro, झूलना। 2. to cause to move to and fro, झुलाना। *n.* a jiggling motion, झूलने या झुलाने की क्रिया या भाव।

jigsaw (जिगसॉ) *n.* a mechanical saw used to cut curves, एक प्रकार की आरी।

jihad (जिहाद) *n.* a Muslim holy war against non-Muslims, जिहाद।

jilt (जिल्ट) *v.* to cast aside (a lover, अपने प्रेमी को) छोड़ देना।

jingle (जिन्गल) *v.* to make or cause to make a ringing metallic sound, खनकना या खनखनाना, झनझनाना। *n.* 1. a jingling sound, खनक, खनखन, झनझन, झनझनाहट। 2. a catchy tune used in advertising, ग्राहकों का ध्यान आकृष्ट करनेवाली मोहक धुन।

J

jink (जिन्क) ***v.*** to move suddenly in order to dodge, (वार) बचा जाना।

jinks (जिंक्स) ***n.*** boisterous play or fun, धूम-धड़क्का, हुड़दंग।

jitter (जिटर) ***v.*** to feel nervous, घबराने लगना, घबरा जाना या उठना। ***n.*** **the jitters,** (plu.) extreme nervousness, बेहद घबराहट।

job (जॉब) ***n.*** 1. a specific piece of work or task, जॉब, फुटकर काम, कार्य, मज़दूरी। 2. a duty, कर्तव्य। 3. a responsibility, उत्तरदायित्व। 4. a position of employment, नौकरी। ***v.*** to do jobs, फुटकर काम करना।

jobber (जॉबर) ***n.*** a piece worker, फुटकर काम करनेवाला।

jockey (जॉकी) ***n.*** one who rides horses in races as a profession, घुड़दौड़ में घोड़े की सवारी करनेवाला, जाकी।

jocular (जॉक्युलर) ***adj.*** humorous, विनोदपूर्ण, परिहासपूर्ण।

jocularity (जॉक्युलैरिटी) ***n.*** humour, विनोद, परिहास, मसख़री।

jog (जॉग) ***v.*** 1. to run slowly for physical exercise, धीरे-धीरे दौड़ना, जॉगिंग करना। 2. to shake or push slightly, धीरे से हिलाना, धक्का या झटका देना। 3. to remind, याद दिलाना, स्मरण कराना। ***n.*** 1. an act of jogging, धीरे-धीरे लगाई जानेवाली दौड़, हलकी दौड़। 2. a slight push or nudge, हलका धक्का, झटका, झकोरा। 3. a reminder, स्मरण करानेवाली बात।

joggle (जॉगल) ***v.*** to shake slightly, झटका देना। ***n.*** a slight shake, झटका।

join (जॉइन) ***v.*** 1. to bring together, to connect, मिलाना, जोड़ना, संयोजित करना। 2. to put or bring into close association or relationship, जोड़ना, मिलाना, संबंध स्थापित करना। 3. to participate, सम्मिलित होना, शामिल होना। 4. to become a part or member of, सदस्य बनना, भर्ती होना। 5. to begin work, कार्यारंभ करना, नौकरी शुरू करना, कार्यभार ग्रहण करना। 6. to come into the company to unite with, मिल जाना, एक हो जाना, साथ देना।

joint (जॉइन्ट) ***n.*** 1. a place or point at which two or more things are joined, जोड़, गाँठ। 2. a marijuana cigarette, मारजुआना सिगरेट। ***adj.*** shared by two or more, संयुक्त, सम्मिलित। ***v.*** 1. to provide with a joint or joints, जोड़ बैठाना या लगाना। 2. to divide into joints, जोड़ों को अलग-अलग करना।

joist (जॉइस्ट) ***n.*** any of the parallel horizontal beams set from wall to wall to support the ceiling or floor, कड़ी, धरन।

joke (जोक) ***n.*** something said or done to cause laughter, मज़ाक, दिल्लगी, हँसी, चुटकुला। ***v.*** 1. to tell jokes, मज़ाक सुनाना। 2. to make jokes, मज़ाक करना।

joker (जोकर) ***n.*** 1. a person who jokes, मज़ाकिया, दिल्लगीबाज़। 2. a person in a circus who behaves in a funny way, जोकर। 3. an extra playing card in a pack, जोकर।

jollity (जॉलिटी) ***n.*** the condition of being jolly, ख़ुशमिज़ाजी, प्रफुल्लता, प्रफुल्ल स्वभाव।

jolly (जॉली) ***adj.*** 1. cheerful, merry, ख़ुशदिल, ख़ुशमिज़ाज, हँसमुख। 2. delightful, आनंददायक, मजेदार। ***adv.*** very, अत्यधिक।

jolt (जोल्ट) ***n.*** 1. a sudden jerk,

हिचकोला, झटका। 2. an emotional shock, धक्का, आघात। *v.* 1. to shake violently with a sudden jerk or blow, हिचकोले खाना या लगना, झटका देना या लगाना। 2. to move in a bumpy or jerky fashion, झूमते हुए चलना। 3. to surprise or shock, विस्मित या भौंचक्का कर देना।

jostle (जॉसल) *v.* 1. to bump or push roughly, धक्कम-धक्का करना, धकियाना। 2. to make one's way by pushing others, धकापेल करना, धक्का देकर रास्ता निकालना। *n.* the act of jostling, धकापेल, धक्कम-धक्का।

jot[1] (जॉट) *n.* a very small amount, नगण्य राशि, लेश, लेशमात्र, ज़रा सी वस्तु।

jot[2] *v.* to write down briefly, टाँकना, नोट कर लेना, टिप्पणी लिखना।

jottings (जॉटिंग्स) *n.* (plu.) jotted notes, टिप्पणियाँ, टाँकी हुई बातें।

joule (जूल) *n.* a unit of energy, ऊर्जा की इकाई, जूल।

journal (जर्नल) *n.* 1. a daily record of news, occurrences or observations, रोजनामचा, दैनंदिनी, दैनिकी। 2. a specialized periodical, जरनल, किसी विशिष्ट विषय से संबद्ध पत्रिका।

journalism (जर्नलिज़्म) *n.* the act of collecting, writing, editing, publishing or broadcasting news-items, पत्रकारिता, अख़बारनवीसी।

journalist (जर्नलिस्ट) *n.* one who is employed in writing for a newspaper, periodical or on television or radio, पत्रकार, अख़बारनवीस।

journey (जर्नी) *n.* a trip from one place to another, यात्रा, सफ़र।

journeyman (जर्नीमैन) *n.* one who works for an employer, नियोजित व्यक्ति, कमेरा।

jovial (जोविअल) *adj.* marked by good humour, विनोदप्रिय, हँसमुख, ख़ुशमिज़ाज।

joviality (जोविऐलिटी) *n.* the quality of being jovial, विनोदप्रियता, ख़ुशमिज़ाजी।

jowl (जाउल) *n.* the lower jaw, निचला जबड़ा।

joy (जॉइ) *n.* 1. a deep feeling of pleasure or happiness, delight, आनंद, हर्ष, प्रसन्नता। 2. something that causes delight, आनंद देनेवाली बात या वस्तु।

joyful (जॉइफ़ुल) *adj.* full of joy, ख़ुशी-भरा, आनंद-भरा, प्रसन्नता-भरा, उत्फुल्ल।

joyous (जॉइअस) *adj.* = joyful.

jubilant (जूबिलेन्ट) *adj.* feeling great joy, आनंदविभोर, अतिप्रसन्न।

jubilation (जूबिलेशन) *n.* rejoicing, आनंद-मंगल, आनंद-उल्लास, हर्षोल्लास।

jubilee (जूबिली) *n.* a special anniversary, जयंती, जुबली।

judder (जडर) *v.* to shake or vibrate, थरथराना। *n.* a juddering motion, थरथराहट।

judge (जज) *n.* 1. one who hears cases in the court of law, न्यायाधीश, जज। 2. a connoisseur, पारखी, विशेषज्ञ। *v.* 1. to pass judgement on, न्याय करना, फैसला करना। 2. to decide after enquiry, जाँच के बाद निर्णय करना। 3. to decide the result or winner in a competetion, प्रतियोगिता का विजेता या परिणाम घोषित करना।

judgement, judgment (जजमेन्ट) *n.* 1. the verdict pronounced by a judge or arbiter,

J

निर्णय, फैसला। 2. the ability to judge prudently, न्याय-क्षमता, निर्णय-क्षमता। 3. a rough estimation or guess, अनुमान।

Judgment Day (जजमेन्ट डे) ***n.*** the occasion of the last judgment by God at the end of the world, क़यामत का दिन।

judicial (जुडिशल) ***adj.*** 1. of law courts, न्यायालयिक। 2. of a judge or judgment, न्यायाधीश या उसके निर्णय से संबद्ध, न्यायिक।

judicially (जुडिशली) ***adv.*** legally, न्यायिक दृष्टि से, विधितः, न्यायतः।

judiciary (जुडिशरी) ***n.*** 1. the judicial branch of the government, न्याय-तंत्र, न्याय-विभाग, न्यायपालिका। 2. the judges collectively, न्यायाधीश-वर्ग।

judicious (जुडिशस) ***adj.*** 1. well-judged, विवेकसम्मत, न्यायपूर्ण। 2. judging wisely, विवेकपूर्ण, विवेकशील।

judo (जूडो) ***n.*** a Japanese form of combat, जूडो।

jug (जग) ***n.*** a rounded vessel for holding liquids, जग।

Juggernaut (जगरनॉट) ***n.*** 1. the huge-wheeled vehicle of Lord Krishna, जगन्नाथ का रथ। 2. any terrible force that crushes anything in the path, अत्यंत विध्वंसक शक्ति, महाशक्ति।

juggle (जगल) ***v.*** 1. to throw and catch a number of objects turn by turn so that most are in the air all the time, (बाज़ीगर का) अनेक गोलों या वस्तुओं को बराबर उछालते तथा लपकते चलना, मदारी का खेल करना। 2. to manipulate in order to deceive, धोखा देने के लिए गड़बड़ या हेराफेरी करना।

juggler (जगलर) ***n.*** one who performs juggling tricks, बाज़ीगर, ऐंद्रजालिक।

jugglery (जगलरी) ***n.*** 1. the profession of a juggler, बाज़ीगरी। 2. a trick, बाज़ीगर का खेल, इंद्रजाल, तमाशा।

jugular (जग्युलर) ***adj.*** of or relating to the throat, कंठ्य।

juice (जूस) ***n.*** 1. the fluid contained in fruits or vegetables, रस। 2. the fluid content of meat, रसा, मांस का रसा।

juicer (जूसर) ***n.*** a machine for extracting juice from fruits and vegetables, जूस निकालने का यंत्र, जूसर।

juicy (जूसी) ***adj.*** 1. full of juice, रसदार, रस से भरा, रसमय, रसीला। 2. interesting, रोचक, मज़ेदार, रसीला।

July (जुलाइ) ***n.*** the seventh month of the year, जुलाई।

jumble (जम्बल) ***v.*** to mix in a disordered or confused way, गड्ड-मड्ड करना, घाल-मेल कर देना। ***n.*** a disordered mass, गड्डमड्ड, घाल-मेल।

jumbo (जम्बो) ***n.*** something very large of its kind, बड़े डील-डौलवाला, दीर्घाकार, बृहत्।

jump (जम्प) ***v.*** 1. to spring off the ground, उछलना। 2. to leap over, कूदना, कूद जाना, छलाँग लगाना। 3. to move or proceed hastily, उछल पड़ना। 4. to pass or skip over, लाँघ जाना, कुछ छोड़ कर आगे बढ़ना। ***n.*** 1. an act of jumping, छलाँग, कूद; उछाल। 2. a space jumped or to be jumped, छलाँग से लाँघा जानेवाला क्षेत्र, छलाँगा हुआ क्षेत्र। 3. a descent by parachute from an aircraft, हवाई जहाज़ से पैराशूट द्वारा लगाई जानेवाली छलाँग। 4. a sudden change or abrupt transition, सहसा परिवर्तन। 5. a step or degree, पग, क़दम।

jumper[1] (जम्पर) ***n.*** one who jumps, छलाँगें लगानेवाला, छलाँगें भरनेवाला, कूदनेवाला।

jumper[2] ***n.*** 1. a sleeveless dress worn over a blouse, एक प्रकार की बिना बाँह की कुर्ती। 2. a blouse, ब्लाऊज, जंपर।

jumpy (जम्पी) ***adj.*** nervous, घबराया हुआ, उद्विग्न।

junction (जंक्शन) ***n.*** 1. a place where two things meet, संगम, मिलन-स्थल। 2. a place where two or more lines or routes cross each other, जंक्शन।

juncture (जंक्चर) ***n.*** 1. the act of joining, योजन। 2. the state of being joined, संधि। 3. a joint, जोड़। 4. a point, समयबिंदु; at this juncture, इस घड़ी।

June (जून) ***n.*** the sixth month of the year, जून।

jungle (जन्गल) ***n.*** 1. a forest area, जंगल। 2. any dense thicket or growth, झाड़-झंखाड़, जंगल। 3. a place of ruthless struggle, वह मैदान जहाँ विकट संघर्ष हो।

junior (जूनिअर) ***adj.*** 1. younger in years, छोटा, कनिष्ठ। 2. lower in rank, subordinate, अवर। 3. for younger persons, युवकों का, नई पीढ़ी का, बाल; junior library, बाल पुस्तकालय। ***n.*** a person who is younger to another, कनिष्ठ।

junk (जन्क) ***n.*** 1. discarded material (collectively) कबाड़, टूटा-फूटा सामान। 2. trash, rubbish, बेकार वस्तु, कूड़ा, कूड़ा-करकट। ***v.*** to discard as junk, रद्दी या कूड़ा समझकर फेंक देना।

junket (जन्किट) ***n.*** 1. a dessert, एक प्रकार का मीठा व्यंजन। 2. a pleasure trip, सैर। 3. a feast, भोज।

junkyard (जन्कयार्ड) ***n.*** a market place for secondhand things, गुदड़ी बाज़ार, कबाड़खाना।

junta (जन्टा) ***n.*** a group of persons who rule the country after a coup d'etat, क्रांतिकारी-सत्ता-परिषद्, शासक गुट, जुंटा।

Jupiter (जूपिटर) ***n.*** the fifth planet from the Sun, बृहस्पति (ग्रह)।

jurisdiction (जूरिस्डिक्शन) ***n.*** 1. the limits within which an authority may operate, अधिकार-क्षेत्र। 2. official power exercised within a particular sphere of activity, क्षेत्राधिकार, अधिकारिता।

jurisprudence (जूरिस्प्रूडेन्स) ***n.*** the science of law, विधिविज्ञान, विधिशास्त्र।

jurist (जूरिस्ट) ***n.*** one skilled in the law, विधिविज्ञानवेत्ता, विधिवेत्ता, विधिशास्त्री।

jury (जूरी) ***n.*** (plu. juries) a body of people constituted to give a verdict, जूरी, निर्णायक-मंडल।

just (जस्ट) ***adj.*** 1. honest and impartial, ईमानदार और निष्पक्ष, भला। 2. legally right, न्यायशील। 3. properly due, deserved, संगत, न्यायोचित, सही। 4. exact, सही, यथार्थ। ***adv.*** 1. exactly, ठीक-ठीक, बिल्कुल, पूरा-पूरा। 2. at that instant, तभी। 3. quite recently, अभी हाल में, अभी-अभी। 4. immediately, तुरंत, जल्दी

J

ही। 5. merely, सिर्फ़। 6. certainly, निश्चय ही।

justice (जस्टिस) ***n.*** 1. upholding of what is just, just treatment, fairness, न्याय, इंसाफ, न्यायशीलता। 2. legal proceedings, क़ानूनी कार्रवाई, विधिक कार्य-विवरण। 3. a judge, न्यायाधीश, न्यायमूर्ति।

justifiable (जस्टिफ़िएबल) ***adj.*** that can be justified, न्यायोचित।

justification (जस्टिफ़िकेशन) ***n.*** 1. the act of justifying, औचित्य-प्रतिपादन। 2. the reason provided to prove to be just, न्यायसंगत तर्क। 3. righteousness, औचित्य।

justify (जस्टिफ़ाइ) ***v.*** 1. to prove to be just, न्यायोचित ठहराना, सफ़ाई देना, न्यायसंगत सिद्ध करना। 2. to declare to be free from guilt or blame, निर्दोष सिद्ध करना।

jut (जट) ***v.*** to extend outwards, to protrude, बाहर की ओर निकला या बढ़ा होना।

jute (जूट) ***n.*** a plant or its fiber used in making sacks, जूट, पटसन।

juvenile (जुविनाइल) ***adj.*** 1. youthful, बाल, तरुण, किशोर। 2. childish, बचकाना। 3. immature, अपरिपक्व। 4. for young people, युवकों के उपयोग का। ***n.*** a young per-son i.e. not yet an adult, बालक, बच्चा।

juvenile delinquency ***n.*** illegal behaviour or act by a young offender, बाल-अपराध।

juxtapose (जक्स्टापोज़) ***v.*** to place side by side, एक दूसरे के निकट, पास-पास या सटाकर रखना।

juxtaposition (जकस्टापज़िशन) ***n.*** the condition of being juxtaposed, सन्निकटता।

K

K, k (के) ***n.*** the eleventh letter of the English alphabet, अंग्रेज़ी वर्णमाला का ग्यारहवाँ वर्ण।

Kaiser (काइज़र) ***n.*** the title of German emperors, जर्मनी के सम्राटों की उपाधि, काइज़र।

kaleidoscope (कैलाइडस्कोप) ***n.*** a small tube in which mirrors reflect the coloured fragments of glass contained in it, सैरबीन, बहुरूपदर्शी।

kangaroo (कैन्गारू) ***n.*** an Australian animal with strong hind legs used for leaping, कंगारू।

karat (कैरट) ***n.*** a measure of the purity of gold, कैरट।

karate (कराटे) ***n.*** a Japanese system of unarmed combat, कराटे।

kedge (केज) ***n.*** a small anchor, छोटा लंगर।

keel (कील) ***n.*** the base structure of a ship, जलयान की तली, नौतल। ***v.*** 1. to capsize, उलट जाना। 2. to collapse, ढह या बिलट जाना।

keen (कीन) ***adj.*** 1. having a sharp edge or point, तीक्ष्ण, पैना, तेज़, नुकीला। 2. eager, उत्सुक, लालायित। 3. intellectually acute, कुशाग्र, प्रखर, तेज़।

keep (कीप) ***v.*** (kept, keeping) 1. to retain possession of, पास रखे रहना। 2. to store, (जमा) रखना, बचा रखना। 3. to take in one's charge, अपने अधिकार या नियंत्रण में लेना। 4. to fulfil or observe, पालन करना। 5. to provide with the necessities of life, भरण-पोषण करना। 6. to continue, चलता रहना या रखना। 7. to celebrate, मनाना। 8. to support financially in return for sexual favours, to keep a woman, औरत रखना। 9. to associate with, सहकार रखना; to keep bad company, ग़लत व्यक्तियों से दोस्ती रखना। ***n.*** 1. charge, care, निगरानी, देख-रेख। 2. a means of support, जीविका। 3. a strongly fortified structure in a castle, क़िले का अत्यंत सुरक्षित भाग।

keeper (कीपर) ***n.*** a person in charge of something, रखवाला, रक्षक।

keeping (कीपिंग) ***n.*** charge or care, देख-रेख, निगरानी, हिफ़ाज़त।

keg (केग) ***n.*** a small barrel, पीपा।

kennel (केनल) ***n.*** 1. a shelter for a dog, कुत्ते के रहने की जगह, कुत्ते की कोठरी। 2. an establishment where dogs are bred, trained etc., कुत्ता-घर, कुकुर-प्रतिष्ठान।

kept (केप्ट) ***v.*** p.t. and p.p. of keep.

kerchief (कर्चिफ़) ***n.*** a square scarf as a head covering, सिर पर बाँधने का बड़ा रूमाल, स्कार्फ़।

kernel (कर्नल) ***n.*** 1. the edible part of a nut, गिरी, गरी। 2. the central part, core, सार भाग, सार। 3. a grain, दाना।

kerosene (केरॉसिन) ***n.*** an oil distilled from petroleum, किरासन, मिट्टी का तेल।

ketchup (केचप) ***n.*** a sauce made from tomatoes, टमाटर की सॉस।

kettle (केटल) ***n.*** a metal pot with a handle for boiling water, केतली।

kettledrum (केटलड्रम) ***n.*** a large drum, नक़्क़ारा, ताशा।

K

key (की) ***n.*** (plu. keys) 1. a metallic implement that operates the lock's mechanism, ताली, चाबी, कुंजी। 2. any means of entry, possession or a desired end, कुंजी। 3. any of the sets of levers operating a piano, typewriter, computer etc., कुंजी। 4. a button or lever on a musical instrument, कुंजी। 5. a set of answers to a test or problem, कुंजी। 6. pitch, सुर, तान। ***adj.*** of great importance, अत्यंत महत्त्वपूर्ण, मूल, आधारभूत।

keyboard (कीबोर्ड) ***n.*** the set of keys on a piano, typewriter, computer etc., कुंजीपटल।

keynote (कीनोट) ***n.*** the central idea or principle (in a speech, भाषण में) केंद्रीय विचार या सिद्धांत।

key-ring (की-रिंग) ***n.*** a ring on which keys are kept, वह छल्ला जिसमें चाबियाँ पिरोते हैं।

keyword (कीवर्ड) ***n.*** a word that serves as a key to a cipher, मूल शब्द।

khaki (काकी) ***adj.*** dull brownish yellow, ख़ाकी। ***n. khakis*** (plu.), khaki uniform used in the army, ख़ाकी वर्दी।

kick (किक) ***v.*** 1. to strike with a foot, ठोकर लगाना, ठोकर मारना, किक लगाना। 2. to recoil or strike in recoiling when fired, धक्का लगना। 3. to object or protest, आपत्ति या विरोध करना, ठुकरा देना। ***n.*** 1. a blow with the foot, ठोकर, किक, पादप्रहार। 2. the recoil of a gun, बंदूक को चलाने से लगनेवाला धक्का। 3. an objection or protest, आपत्ति, विरोध। 4. a pleasurable effect, thrill, गुदगुदी, पुलक, सिहरन।

kickback (किकबैक) ***n.*** 1. a reaction or repercussion, प्रतिक्रिया। 2. a part of income paid illegally to a person for his help in making profit, रिश्वत।

kid[1] (किड) ***n.*** 1. a young goat, बकरी का बच्चा, मेमना। 2. the leather made from the hide of a kid, मेमने का चमड़ा। 3. a child, बच्चा, बालक। ***v.*** to give birth to a young goat, बकरी का बयाना।

kid[2] ***v.*** 1. to tease, तंग या परेशान करना। 2. to deceive, धोखा देना, ठगना।

kidnap (किडनैप) ***v.*** to carry off and detain (a person, usually for ransom, प्रायः धन ऐंठने के लिए व्यक्ति का) अपहरण करना, बलात् हरण करना।

kidnapper (किडनैपर) ***n.*** one who kidnaps, अपहरणकर्ता, अपहर्ता।

kidney (किडनी) ***n.*** either of two bean-shaped organs which filter wastes as urine from the blood, गुर्दा, वृक्क।

kidney bean ***n.*** kidney-shaped seeds of certain plants, मोथा, मोठ।

kid skin (किड स्किन) ***n.*** the leather made from the skin of a young goat, मेमने का चमड़ा।

kill (किल) ***v.*** 1. to put to death, मार डालना, वध या हत्या कर डालना। 2. to put an end to, to destroy or finish, ख़त्म कर डालना। 3. to make (time) pass quickly, (समय) नष्ट करना। ***n.*** 1. the act of killing, हत्या, वध। 2. an animal killed during a hunt, मारा हुआ शिकार।

killing (किलिंग) ***adj.*** fatal, घातक, प्राणघातक। ***n.*** 1. murder, हत्या, वध। 2. a sudden large profit, सहसा होनेवाला अत्यधिक लाभ।

killjoy (किलजॉइ) ***n.*** a person who destroys other people's pleasure, दूसरों के रंग में भंग डालनेवाला, दूसरों का आनंद बिगाड़नेवाला।

kiln (किल्न) ***n.*** an oven, भट्टी, भट्ठा।

kilo (किलो) ***n.*** kilogram, किलोग्राम, किलो।

kimono (किमोनो) ***n.*** a wide sleeved Japanese robe, किमोनो, जापानी पहनावा।

kin (किन) ***adj.*** related, सगोत्र। ***n.*** (singular or plural) a relative or relatives, रिश्तेदार, कुटुंबी, स्वजन।

kind[1] (काइन्ड) ***adj.*** 1. showing sympathy, goodwill or generosity, उदार, भला, दयालु। 2. kind-hearted, सहृदय, रहमदिल।

kind[2] ***n.*** 1. a class or category having characteristics in common, वर्ग, जाति। 2. a type or sort, प्रकार, क़िस्म। □ **in kind,** माल के रूप में, जिन्स के रूप में।

kindergarten (किन्डर्गार्टन) ***n.*** a school for children, शिशुशाला, शिशु-निकेतन, किन्डरगार्टन।

kindle (किन्डल) ***v.*** 1. to start (a fire), जलाना। 2. to become kindled, जलना। 3. to glow or cause to glow, चमकना या चमकाना, जगमगाना। 4. to stimulate or excite, उद्दीप्त करना, उत्तेजित करना।

kindly (काइन्डली) ***adj.*** kind in manner, दयालु, कृपालु, भला। ***adv.*** in a kind manner, कृपापूर्वक।

kindred (किन्ड्रिड) ***adj.*** 1. related, सगोत्र। 2. of similar kind, वैसा ही, उसी प्रकार का। ***n.*** (singular or plural) a person's relative or relatives, नातेदार, रिश्तेदार, कुटुंबी।

kinetic (काइनेटिक) ***adj.*** of or produced by movement, गतिक, गत्यात्मक, गतिज।

king (किन्ग) ***n.*** 1. the male ruler of a country, राजा। 2. a playing card bearing the picture of a king, शाह, बादशाह। 3. the main piece in the game of chess, शाह, बादशाह, राजा।

kingdom (किन्गडम) ***n.*** a country ruled by a king (or queen), रियासत, बादशाहत, राज्य।

kingfisher (किन्गफ़िशर) ***n.*** a fish-eating large-billed bird, कौड़िल्ला।

kingpin (किन्गपिन) ***n.*** the most important and indispensable person (or thing) in a group, मुख्य व्यक्ति (या वस्तु), प्रधान व्यक्ति (या वस्तु)।

kink (किन्क) ***n.*** 1. a tight curl, घुमाव, ऐंठन, बल। 2. a slight flaw, छोटा-मोटा दोष या त्रुटि। 3. a peculiar characteristic, चारित्रिक विचित्रता। ***v.*** to form a kink or kinks, बल डालना, ऐंठ देना।

kinky (किन्की) ***adj.*** 1. full of kinks, घुमावदार, जिसमें बल या घुमाव हों, घुँघराला। 2. eccentric, perverted, उन्मादपूर्ण, अप्राकृतिक।

kinsman (किन्ज़मैन) ***n.*** a relative, रिश्तेदार।

kiosk (किऑस्क) ***n.*** a light structure used as a newsstand, refreshment booth etc., स्टाल, गुमटी, कीऑस्क।

kirk (कर्क) ***n.*** a Church, गिरजा।

kiss (किस) ***n.*** a touch with the lips as a sign of affection, चुंबन, चुम्मा, बोसा। ***v.*** to touch with the lips, चूमना, चुंबन लेना, बोसा लेना।

kit (किट) ***n.*** 1. a set of tools, उपकरण-समूह, किट। 2. a set of parts sold together, किट। 3. the clothing and

K

personal equipment of a soldier or traveller, सैनिक या यात्री का सामान।

kitchen (किचिन) ***n.*** a room or place of cooking, रसोई, रसोई-घर।

kitchenette (किचनेट) ***n.*** a small kitchen, छोटी रसोई, छोटा रसोई-घर।

kitchen garden (किचन गार्डन) ***n.*** a garden near kitchen where vegetables are grown, किचन गार्डन।

kitchenware (किचनवेअर) ***n.*** the utensils used in the kitchen, रसोई बनाने के बर्तन, खाना बनाने के बर्तन।

kite (काइट) ***n.*** 1. a light frame structure with thin paper flown at the end of a long string, पतंग, गुड्डी। 2. a bird with a long forked tail usually preying on small birds, चील।

kith and kin ***n.*** (plu.) one's friends and relations, मित्र तथा संबंधी, स्वजन।

kitten (किटन) ***n.*** the young of a cat, बिल्ली का बच्चा, बिलौटा।

kitty (किटी) ***n.*** a pool or fund of money, जमा साँझा धन।

kiwi (कीवी) ***n.*** a flightless New Zealand bird without a tail, कीवी।

kleptomania (क्लेप्टोमेनिआ) ***n.*** an uncontrollable impulse to steal, चोरी करने की लत, चौर्योन्माद।

knack (नैक) ***n.*** the ability or skill to do something gracefully, हुनर, कौशल, दक्षता।

knapsack (नैपसैक) ***n.*** a bag for carrying supplies and equipment strapped on the back, पीठ पर कसा जानेवाला थैला, पीठ-थैला।

knave (नेव) ***n.*** 1. a rogue, शठ, दुर्जन, धूर्त, बदमाश। 2. a Jack, गुलाम, गुल्ला।

knead (नीड) ***v.*** 1. to mix and press (moist flour or clay) into a uniform mass, गूँधना, सानना। 2. to massage, मालिश करना, मसाज करना।

knee (नी) ***n.*** 1. the joint or region between the thigh and the lower part of the human leg, घुटना। 2. the part of the garment covering this part, घुटना। ***v.*** to hit or push with the knee, घुटने से आघात करना या धकेलना।

kneecap (नीकैप) ***n.*** a flat triangular bone covering the front of the knee, चपनी।

kneel (नील) ***v.*** (kneeled/knelt, kneeling) to rest on bent knees, घुटनों के बल झुकना।

knell (नेल) ***n.*** a stroke or toll of a bell for a death or funeral, किसी के मरने पर अथवा उसकी अरथी ले जाते समय बजाया जानेवाला घंटा।

knew (न्यू) ***v.*** p.t. of know.

knicknack (निकनैक) ***n.*** a small ornamental article, कोई छोटी-मोटी सजावटी वस्तु।

knife (नाइफ़) ***n.*** (plu. knives) 1. a household cutting instrument with a blade fitted into a handle, चाकू, छुरी, छुरा। 2. the cutting blade of a machine, मशीन की छुरी। ***v.*** to stab, चाकू भोकना।

knight (नाइट) ***n.*** 1. an armed soldier of noble birth, शूरवीर, नाईट। 2. the holder of a rank conferred by a sovereign, सम्राट द्वारा प्रदत्त नाईट की उपाधि। 3. a chess piece with the head of a horse, घोड़ा। ***v.*** to confer a knighthood on, नाईट की उपाधि से विभूषित करना।

knighthood (नाइटहुड) ***n.*** the rank of a knight, नाईट की उपाधि।

knit (निट) ***v.*** (knit/knitted, knitting) 1. to make a fabric or garment with threads and needles, बुनना, बुनावट डालना, बुनाई करना। 2. to join together closely, जोड़ना।

knitwear (निटविअर) ***n.*** knitted garment, बुना हुआ पहनावा (स्वेटर, शाल, मोजा आदि)।

knob (नॉब) ***n.*** 1. a rounded projection or protuberance, गुमटा। 2. a rounded handle, मूठ, घुंडी या बटन, नाब। 3. a rounded hill, गोलाकार पहाड़ी।

knock (नॉक) ***v.*** 1. to strike with a sharp blow, ज़ोरदार आघात करना, प्रहार करना, मारना, पीटना। 2. to strike (a door) with a series of blows, (दरवाज़ा) खटखटाना, दस्तक देना। 3. to make by hitting or striking, ठोकना, गढ़ना। 4. to criticize severely, कड़ी आलोचना करना। 5. to collide, टकराना, भिड़ जाना। 6. to make a pounding noise, (मशीन का) घटर-घटर आवाज़ करना।

knock-kneed (नॉकनीड) ***adj.*** whose knees touch each other while walking, जिसके चलते समय घुटने लड़ते या टकराते हों।

knockout (नॉकआउट) ***n.*** 1. a blow that causes unconsciousness, मूर्च्छा लाने वाला आघात, मूर्च्छित कर देनेवाला प्रहार। 2. a competition in which competitors are eliminated progressively, वह प्रतियोगिता जिसमें हारनेवाले प्रतियोगी क्रमशः बाहर होते चलते हैं, नाकआउट प्रतियोगिता।

knoll (नोल) ***n.*** a mound, टीला।

knot (नॉट) ***n.*** 1. a fastening for-med by two threads (or cords) or by two ends of a thread (or cord), जोड़, गाँठ, ग्रंथि। 2. a tangle, उलझन, कठिनाई या समस्या। 3. the enlargement of a gland, ग्रंथि-शोथ, गाँठ। 4. a tie or bond, बंधन। ***v.*** 1. to tie or fasten with a knot, गाँठ डालना या लगाना। 2. to make entangled, उलझाना। 3. to become entangled, उलझ जाना।

knotty (नॉटी) ***adj.*** 1. full of knots, गाँठोंवाला, गाँठदार। 2. intricate, पेचीला, पेचीदा, जटिल।

know (नो) ***v.*** (knew, known, knowing) 1. to be familiar or acquainted with, विदित होना, परिचय होना, जानना, पहचानना। 2. to have a grasp of, जानना, ज्ञान होना। 3. to understand, समझना। 4. to be able to distinguish or discriminate, अंतर कर सकना, अंतर पहचानना।

know-how (नोहाउ) ***n.*** practical knowledge or skill of how to do a particular thing, व्यावहारिक ज्ञान या कौशल, जानकारी।

knowing (नोइंग) ***adj.*** 1. having knowledge or understanding, जानकार, जाननेवाला। 2. clever, होशियार, चालाक़। ***n.*** information, सूचना, जानकारी।

knowingly (नोइंगली) ***adv.*** wilfully, deliberately, जानकर, जान-बूझकर।

knowledge (नॉलिज) ***n.*** 1. the state or fact of knowing, जानकारी, ज्ञान। 2. specific information about a subject, जानकारी, ज्ञान। 3. acquaintance, परिचय।

knowledgeable (नॉलिजेबल) ***adj.*** 1. well-informed, जानकार। 2. experienced, अनुभवी। 3. intelligent, समझदार, बुद्धिमान।

known (नोन) ***v.*** p.p. of know. ***adj.*** perceived, realized or understood, जाना हुआ, ज्ञात।

knuckle (नकल) ***n.*** a joint of a finger, अंगुली की गाँठ, अंगुली का जोड़। ***v.*** to press with knuckles, अंगुलियों की गाँठों से दबाना।

Koran (कोरान) ***n.*** the sacred book of Islam, कुरान, मुसलमानों का प्रसिद्ध धर्मग्रंथ।

Krishna (क्रिश्न) ***n.*** a Hindu deity, भगवान कृष्ण।

kudos (क्यूडॉस) ***n.*** (functioning as singular) honour and glory, प्रतिष्ठा तथा वैभव, मान-सम्मान।

kukri (कुकरी) ***n.*** a large knife with a curve, खुखड़ी।

kung fu (कन्ग फ़ू) ***n.*** Chinese martial art, कराटे की तरह की चीनी युद्ध-विद्या।

L

L, l (एल) ***n.*** 1. the twelfth letter of the English alphabet, अंग्रेज़ी वर्णमाला का बारहवाँ वर्ण।

lab (लैब) ***n.*** a laboratory, प्रयोगशाला।

label (लेबल) ***n.*** 1. a piece of paper, cloth etc., attached to an object showing name, nature, use, destination etc., नामचिप्पी, नामपत्र, लेबिल। 2. a name given to someone or something, दिया हुआ नाम, प्रदत्त नाम। ***v.*** (labelled/labeled, labelling/labeling) 1. to attach or fasten a label, लेबिल लगाना, लेबिल चिपकाना। 2. to identify or call, नाम देना या धरना, बतलाना, कहना।

labial (लेबिअल) ***adj.*** 1. related to the lips, ओष्ठ-संबंधी। 2. formed with the lips, होंठों से उच्चरित, ओष्ठ्य।

labium (लेबिअम) ***n.*** a lip, होंठ, ओष्ठ।

laboratory (लैबॉरेटरी) ***n.*** a room or building equipped for conducting scientific experiments or manufacturing chemicals, medicines etc., प्रयोगशाला, लैब।

laborious (लबोरिअस) ***adj.*** 1. requiring much hard work, श्रमसाध्य। 2. given to hard work, परिश्रमी, मेहनती।

labour, labor (लेबर) ***n.*** 1. work, श्रम, परिश्रम, मेहनत। 2. work for wages, मज़दूरी। 3. a wage earner, मज़दूर, श्रमिक। 4. the physical efforts of childbirth, प्रसव; labour pains प्रसव-पीड़ा। ***v.*** 1. to work hard, कठोर श्रम करना। 2. to strive hard, घोर प्रयास करना। 3. to proceed slowly, मंद गति से आगे बढ़ना।

laboured, labored (लेबर्ड) ***adj.*** forced, strained, ज़बरदस्ती का, प्रयासपूर्ण, कठिन।

labour union ***n.*** the union of labourers, मज़दूर संघ।

labyrinth (लैबिरिन्थ) ***n.*** a place constructed of intricate pathways, भूलभुलैया।

labyrinthine (लैबिरिन्थाइन) ***n.*** complicated, intricate, भूलभुलैया-जैसा, जटिल, पेचीदा, उलझन-भरा।

lac[1] (लैक) ***n.*** a resinous substance secreted by some insects, लाख, लाक्षा।

lac[2] ***n.*** the number 100000, लाख।

lace (लेस) ***n.*** 1. a strip of decorative weblike fabric, लेस, बार्डर। 2. an ornamental braid, फीता। 3. a boot-lace, तस्मा। ***v.*** 1. to equip with the lace, लेस लगाना। 2. to fasten with a lace or laces, तस्मा या फीता बाँधना। 3. to add a dash of liquor to (a beverage, किसी पेय पदार्थ में) शराब का पुट देना।

lacerate (लैसरेट) ***v.*** 1. to tear (the flesh), खरोंच डालना। 2. to hurt the feelings, आघात पहुँचाना, दिल दुखाना।

laceration (लैसरेशन) ***n.*** 1. the act of lacerating, खरोंचने का कार्य, खरोंचना। 2. the marks of being lacerated, खरोंच।

lachrymal (लैक्रिमल) ***adj.*** of or relating to the tears, आँसुओं का, अश्रु-संबंधी।

lack (लैक) ***n.*** absence of something

L

required, अभाव, कमी। ***v.*** to be short of, कमी होना, अभाव होना।

lackey (लैकी) ***n.*** 1. a servile follower, अनुचर, सेवक। 2. a flatterer, ख़ुशामदी।

lacklustre, lackluster (लैकलस्टर) ***adj.*** lacking brilliance, lusterless, जिसमें चमक न हो, बुझा हुआ, निस्तेज।

laconic (लकॉनिक) ***adj.*** brief, to the point, अतिसंक्षिप्त, नपा-तुला, दो-हरफ़ी।

lacquer (लैकर) ***n.*** a resinous substance used as a glossy varnish, रोग़न, वार्निश। ***v.*** to varnish with the lacquer, रोग़न करना।

lactate (लैक्टेट) ***v.*** to secrete or produce milk, दूध देना।

lactation (लैक्टेशन) ***n.*** the act of secreting or producing milk, दूध देना।

lactic (लैक्टिक) ***adj.*** of milk, दुग्ध-संबंधी।

lactometer, lactometre (लैक्टॉ-मीटर) ***n.*** a device for determining milk contents, दुग्धमापी (यंत्र)।

lactose (लैक्टोस) ***n.*** the sugar present in the milk, दुग्धशर्करा।

lacuna (लक्यूना) ***n.*** (plu. lacunae, lacunas) 1. a gap, ख़ाली जगह, रिक्ति। 2. anything missing, बीच की लुप्त कड़ी, कमी।

lacy (लेसी) ***adj.*** like lace, लेस या फीते के जैसा।

lad (लैड) ***n.*** a boy, बालक, लड़का।

ladder (लैडर) ***n.*** 1. a device for climbing up and down, सीढ़ी, सोपान। 2. a series of stages or levels, सोपान, सीढ़ी।

laden (लेडन) ***adj.*** 1. loaded, लदा हुआ, चढ़ाया हुआ। 2. burdened, भाराक्रांत, लदा-फदा।

ladle (लेडल) ***n.*** a long-handled spoon for transferring or serving liquids, कलछी, कलछुल। ***v.*** to transfer or serve with a ladle, कलछी से देना, निकालना या परोसना।

lady (लेडी) ***n.*** 1. a woman of good social position and good manners, भद्र महिला। 2. a woman, स्त्री, औरत।

ladybird (लेडीबर्ड) ***n.*** a small reddish brown beetle, सोनपंखी।

lady's finger (लेडीज़ फिंगर) ***n.*** a finger-shaped vegetable, भिंडी।

lag (लैग) ***v.*** to fall behind, to go too slowly, पीछे रह जाना, पिछड़ जाना। ***n.*** 1. the act or condition of lagging, पिछड़ना, पिछड़ जाना। 2. a delay, देरी, विलंब।

laggard (लैगर्ड) ***adj. & n.*** one who lags behind, पिछड़ा हुआ व्यक्ति, फिसड्डी, मंदबुद्धि।

lagoon (लैगून) ***n.*** a shallow body of water separated from the sea by coral reefs or sand bars, कच्छ, समुद्री ताल, लैगून।

laid (लेड) ***v.*** p.t. & p.p. of lay.

lain (लेन) ***v.*** p.p. of lie.

lair (लेअर) ***n.*** 1. the hiding place of a wild animal, माँद। 2. a place of hiding, छिपने का स्थान।

laissez-faire (लेसे-फ़ेअर) ***n.*** the policy of non-interference, हस्तक्षेप न करने की नीति, अहस्तक्षेप-नीति।

lake (लेक) ***n.*** a large body of water entirely surrounded by land, झील, लेक, सरोवर।

lama (लामा) ***n.*** the Buddhist monk of Tibet, लामा।

lamb (लैम्ब) ***n.*** 1. the young of a sheep, मेमना। 2. the flesh of a lamb,

मेमने का मांस। 3. a meek or innocent person, भोला-भाला या निरीह व्यक्ति।

lambast (लैम्बेस्ट) ***v.*** to reprimand severely, ख़ूब डाँटना-डपटना, झाड़ना।

lame (लेम) ***adj.*** 1. crippled in the legs or feet, लँगड़ा, अपंग। 2. weak, कमज़ोर, अशक्त। 3. unconvincing, आश्वस्त न करनेवाला। ***v.*** to make lame, लँगड़ा कर देना।

lament (लेमेन्ट) ***v.*** to mourn or express deep sorrow, विलाप करना, रोना-कलपना। ***n.*** 1. an expression of sorrow, विलाप, रुदन, क्रंदन। 2. a song or poem in which death is lamented, शोक-गीत, अलानी। (पंजाबी)

lamentable (लैमन्टेबल) ***adj.*** 1. mournful, मातमी, शोकपूर्ण। 2. distressing, दुःखद। 3. deplorable, हेय, घटिया, तुच्छ।

laminate (लैमिनेट) ***v.*** 1. to form into thin layers, पतली परत के रूप में बनाना। 2. to divide into thin layers, पतली परतों में विभाजित करना। 3. to make by bounding together two or more sheets, दो या अधिक परतों को जोड़ना, लैमिनेट करना।

laminated (लैमिनेटिड) ***adj.*** bounded together or composed of many layers, जिसपर परत जमाई गई हो, परतबंद, परतदार।

lamp (लैम्प) ***n.*** a device for producing light, दीया, दीपक, चिराग़, लैंप।

lamppost (लैम्पोस्ट) ***n.*** a post supporting a street light, सड़क पर लगी बत्ती का खंभा।

lance (लान्स) ***n.*** a weapon with a long shaft and a pointed metal head, भाला, बरछा, बल्लम। ***v.*** 1. to pierce with a lance, बल्लम या बरछे से छेद देना। 2. to cut open a boil or wound, चीरा देना।

lancer (लान्सर) ***n.*** a cavalryman armed with a lance, बल्लमबरदार, लांसर।

lancet (लान्सिट) ***n.*** a surgeon's double-edged knife, शल्यचिकित्सक का दुधारी चाकू, दुधारी छुरी।

land (लैन्ड) ***n.*** 1. the solid part of the surface of the earth, भूमि, धरती, ज़मीन। 2. a nation or country, देश, राष्ट्र। 3. a piece of land owned or sold as property, भूखंड। ***v.*** 1. to put or arrive on land after travelling by water or air, उतरना या उतारना। 2. to alight after a jump or fall, कूदकर ज़मीन पर आना या उतरना। 3. to obtain, प्राप्त करना, पाना। 4. to arrive at or bring to a certain place, position or stage, किसी जगह पहुँचना या पहुँचाना। 5. to deliver a blow, आघात करना।

landed (लैन्डिड) ***adj.*** 1. owning land, जिसके पास ज़मीन हो, ज़मींदार। 2. consisting of or including land, ज़मीन सहित; a landed estate, भू-संपत्ति, ज़मीन-जायदाद।

landfill (लैन्डफ़िल) ***n.*** a low land filled with rubbish, भराऊ ज़मीन, भरती की ज़मीन।

landholder (लैन्डहोल्डर) ***n.*** one who holds or occupies a land, ज़मींदार या काश्तकार।

landing (लैन्डिंग) ***n.*** 1. the act of coming to land, अवतरण, उतरना। 2. the act of bringing something to land, उतारना। 3. landing place, घाट या अड्डा।

L

landlocked (लैन्डलॉक्ड) ***adj.*** completely surrounded by land, जिसके चारों ओर भूमि हो, भूमि से घिरा हुआ।

landlord (लैन्डलॉर्ड) ***n.*** 1. one who owns and leases property, ज़मींदार, भूस्वामी। 2. one who runs a lodging house, होटल का मालिक।

landmark (लैन्डमार्क) ***n.*** 1. a fixed marker indicating a boundary line, सीमाचिह्न। 2. a prominent feature of a landscape, भूचिह्न। 3. a turning point in one's life or history, जीवन का एक मोड़, युगांतरकारी घटना।

landscape (लैन्डस्केप) ***n.*** a scenery, painting or photograph depicting a rural scene, प्राकृतिक दृश्य, परिदृश्य।

landslide (लैन्डस्लाइड) ***n.*** 1. the slide of a mass of rock down a slope, भू-स्खलन। 2. an overwhelming victory (in an election निर्वाचन में) भारी बहुमत से होनेवाली विजय, भारी जीत।

lane (लेन) ***n.*** 1. a street or narrow road, गली। 2. a section of track, लेन, गली।

language (लैंग्विज) ***n.*** 1. the use of words as a system of conveying information i.e. the means of communication, भाषा, ज़बान। 2. a particular style of wording, भाषा-शैली। 3. the means of communication between creatures other than man, बोली, भाषा।

languid (लैंग्विड) ***adj.*** 1. lacking energy or vigour, बेजान, निढाल, बेदम। 2. sluggish, सुस्त। 3. slow, मंद।

languish (लैंग्विश) ***v.*** 1. to lose energy or vigour, बेदम हो जाना, जान निकल जाना। 2. to become depressed, हतोत्साहित हो जाना, मुरझा या सूख जाना।

langur (लैन्गुअर) ***n.*** an ape, लंगूर।

lanky (लैन्की) ***adj.*** ungracefully lean and tall, बहुत ही दुबला-पतला और लंबा, लंबू।

lantern (लैन्टर्न) ***n.*** a transparent case for holding and protecting a candle or oil wick flame, लालटेन।

lap[1] (लैप) ***v.*** 1. to take up (liquid) with the tongue, लपलप पीना, लपलपाना। 2. to make a gentle splashing sound, तट से टकराकर लहरों का ध्वनि करना। ***n.*** 1. an act of lapping, लपलप पीना। 2. the sound made when drinking with the tongue, जीभ से पीते समय होनेवाली लपलप ध्वनि। 3. the sound of small waves on a beach, तट से टकराने पर होनेवाली लहरों की ध्वनि।

lap[2] ***n.*** 1. the flat area formed by the front part of the legs above the knees of a seated person, गोद। 2. the part of a dress that covers the lap, आँचल, पल्ला, दामन।

lapel (लपेल) ***n.*** either of the two flaps of a coat below the collar, लैपल, लौट।

lapse (लैप्स) ***n.*** 1. a minor slip or error, भूल, चूक, त्रुटि, च्युति। 2. elapsing of time, समय का व्यवधान, काल का अंतराल। 3. the termination of a right through neglect or disuse, व्यपगति; लापरवाही अथवा प्रयोगाभाव के कारण अधिकार का छिन जाना। ***v.*** 1. to cease to exist, अस्तित्व में न रहना। 2. to become invalid as through the passage of time, समय बीत जाने के कारण व्यपगत हो जाना। 3. to fail to maintain one's position or standard, चूक कर बैठना, त्रुटि या च्युति हो जाना।

lapsed (लैप्स्ड) ***adj.*** 1. fallen into error, जिससे त्रुटि हुई हो। 2. in disuse, व्यपगत, रद, समाप्त।

larceny (लार्सनी) ***n.*** theft, चोरी।

lard (लार्ड) ***n.*** fat obtained from pig meat, सुअर की चर्बी, शूकर-वसा। ***v.*** 1. to smear with lard (before cooking the meat, मांस को पकाने से पहले) चर्बी का लेप करना। 2. to enrich (a speech or writing) with additions, to embellish, (भाषण या लेख को) कुछ जोड़-जाड़ कर सजाना।

larder (लार्डर) ***n.*** a room for storing food, खाद्य-सामग्री रखने की कोठरी।

large (लार्ज) ***adj.*** 1. big, बड़ा, भारी-भरकम। 2. spacious, खुला, विस्तृत, लंबा-चौड़ा। 3. comprehensive, व्यापक। 4. liberal, generous, उदार।

largely (लार्जली) ***adv.*** mainly, मुख्य रूप से, मुख्यत:।

largess, largesse (लार्जेस) ***n.*** money or gifts generously given, उदार दान, बख़्शीश।

lark[1] (लार्क) ***n.*** a variety of small birds of which the skylark is one, लार्क, भरत।

lark[2] ***n.*** 1. a joke or prank, मज़ाक, मस्खरी। 2. a playful adventurous action, छेड़छाड़, अठखेली।

larva (लार्वा) ***n.*** (plu. larvae) the worm-like form of a newly-hatched insect, इल्ली।

laryngitis (लैरिन्जाइटिस) ***n.*** inflammation of the larynx, गले की सूजन, कंठशोथ।

larynx (लैरिंक्स) ***n.*** (plu. larynges, larynxes) the cavity in the throat containing vocal cords, कंठ, स्वरयंत्र।

lascivious (लैसिविअस) ***adj.*** lustful, कामुक, कामुकतापूर्ण।

laser (लेज़र) ***n.*** any of several devices that generates highly concentrated beam of light, लेज़र।

lash[1] (लैश) ***n.*** 1. a blow with a whip, कोड़े का आघात, कोड़े की मार, साँट। 2. the strip of a whip, कोड़ा। 3. an eyelash, बरौनी। ***v.*** 1. to strike with a whip, कोड़े लगाना। 2. to strike against with force, प्रहार करना। 3. to attack verbally, भर्त्सना करना। 4. to move or wave rapidly, तेज़ी से हिलाना या लहराना।

lash[2] ***v.*** to bind with a rope, रस्सी से बाँधना, जकड़ना, कस देना।

lass (लैस) ***n.*** a girl, लड़की, बच्ची, कन्या।

lassitude (लैसिट्यूड) ***n.*** weariness of body or mind, tiredness, थकान, थकावट।

lasso (लैसो) ***n.*** (plu. lassos, lassoes) a long rope with a running noose at one end for catching horses and cattle. गरगो, फंदेदार रस्सी। ***v.*** to catch with a lasso, गरगो से बाँधना।

last[1] (लास्ट) ***adj.*** 1. coming at the end, अंतिम, आख़िरी, पिछला। 2. most recent, पिछला, गत। ***adv.*** 1. finally, अंत में। 2. recently, अभी हाल में। ***n.*** 1. one occurring at the end, वह जो अंत में हो, अंतिम वस्तु, व्यक्ति आदि। 2. the end, अंत, समाप्ति। ***v.*** 1. to continue, चलता रहना, जारी रहना, बना रहना।2. to be enough, चलना, पूरा पड़ना।

last[2] ***n.*** the mould on which a shoemaker shapes the shoes, कलबूत।

L

lasting (लास्टिंग) ***adj.*** continuing or remaining for a long time, चिरस्थायी।

lastly (लास्टली) ***adv.*** finally, अंत में, सबसे पीछे, सबके बाद।

latch (लैच) ***n.*** 1. a bar for fastening a door or window, सिटकनी। 2. a lock, ताला। ***v.*** to fasten with a latch, सिटकनी लगाकर बंद करना।

late (लेट) ***adj.*** 1. arriving after the appointed or usual time, विलंब से आनेवाला, देरी करनेवाला, विलंबित। 2. occurring, flowering or ripening late in the season, मौसम के अंत में होनेवाला। 3. being or occurring toward the end, अंत में होनेवाला। 4. recent, अभी हाल का, ताज़ा; latest news, ताज़ा ख़बर। 5. no longer alive, गत, दिवंगत। ***adv.*** 1. after the appointed or usual time, देर से, विलंब से। 2. toward the end of the day, month or year, दिन, महीने या वर्ष की समाप्ति पर। □ **of late,** हाल ही में।

lately (लेटली) ***adv.*** recently, अभी हाल में।

latent (लेटेन्ट) ***adj.*** 1. dormant, प्रसुप्त। 2. existing but not active or visible, अप्रकट, निहित।

lateral (लैटरल) ***adj.*** on, of or toward the side, पार्श्व का, पार्श्विक।

latest (लेटेस्ट) ***adj.*** recent, ताज़ा, अभी हाल का, अंतिम; at the latest by 5 O'clock, अधिक से अधिक पाँच बजे तक।

latex (लेटेक्स) ***n.*** a milky sap of certain plants, वानस्पतिक दुग्ध।

lathe (लेद) ***n.*** a machine for holding and turning a piece of wood, metal etc., against a tool that will shape it, खराद (मशीन)। ***v.*** to turn on a lathe, खरादना।

lather (लैदर) ***n.*** foam produced in water by soap, झाग, फेन। ***v.*** 1. to form a lather, झाग उत्पन्न करना। 2. to apply lather to, झाग से मलना या रगड़ना।

lathery (लैदरी) ***adj.*** full of lather, झाग से भरा, झागदार।

Latin America (लैटिन अमेरिका) ***n.*** Central and Southern America where Spanish or Portuguese is the main language, लैटिन अमरीका, लातीनी अमरीका।

latitude (लैटिट्यूड) ***n.*** 1. angular distance north or south of the equator, अक्षांश। 2. freedom from restrictions, छूट, स्वच्छंदता। 3. scope, विस्तार, व्याप्ति।

latrine (लैट्रीन) ***n.*** a toilet especially one in a camp or barracks, शौचघर, टट्टी, पाख़ाना।

latter (लैटर) ***adj.*** 1. coming after someone or something, being the second of the two things or persons mentioned, बादवाला, पिछला, परवर्ती। 2. nearer to the end, आख़िरी।

latterly (लैटरली) ***adv.*** of late, बाद में, अभी हाल में।

lattice (लैटिस) ***n.*** a framework of interwoven bars or laths, जाली।

laud (लॉड) ***v.*** to praise, प्रशंसा करना, स्तुति करना। ***n.*** praise, स्तुति।

laudable (लॉडेबल) ***adj.*** that can be lauded, praiseworthy, प्रशंसनीय, प्रशंसा के योग्य।

laugh (लाफ़) ***v.*** 1. to produce inarticulate sounds expressive of pleasure, joy or derision, हँसना। 2. to ridicule, उपहास करना, हँसी उड़ाना। ***n.*** 1. the sound or act of laughing,

हँसी। 2. an amusing incident, हँसी की बात।

laughable (लाफ़ेबल) ***adj.*** ridiculous, हँसने योग्य, हास्यास्पद।

laughing-stock (लाफ़िन्ग-स्टॉक) ***n.*** an object of scornful laughter, वह जिसकी हँसी उड़ाई जाए, हँसी का पात्र।

laughter (लाफ़्टर) ***n.*** 1. the sound of laughing, कहकहा, ठहाका। 2. the act of laughing, हँसी।

launch (लॉन्च) ***v.*** 1. to set afloat, पानी में उतारना, जलावतरण करना। 2. to start off, to set in motion, प्रारंभ करना, प्रवर्तन करना, चलाना। 3. to hurl, fire or project, प्रक्षेपण करना। ***n.*** 1. the act of launching, जलावतरण। 2. a motor-driven boat usually a pleasure boat, विहार-नौका, लांच।

launcher (लॉन्चर) ***n.*** a device for launching a rocket, satellite etc., प्रक्षेपण-यंत्र।

launder (लॉन्डर) ***v.*** 1. to wash and iron (clothes कपड़े) धोना तथा उनपर इस्त्री करना। 2. to make illegally earned money legal, नंबर दो की रक़म को नंबर एक बनाना।

laundry (लॉन्ड्री) ***n.*** 1. a place where clothes are washed and ironed, धोबीख़ाना, धुलाई-घर, लांड्री। 2. the clothes for washing and ironing, धुलाई के कपड़े।

laureate (लॉरिइट) ***adj.*** distinguished, honoured, प्रतिष्ठित, सम्मानित।

laurel (लॉरल) ***n.*** 1. a tree with aromatic leaves, लारेल वृक्ष। 2. (plu.) honour, distinction, सम्मान, प्रतिष्ठा।

lava (लावा) ***n.*** molten that comes out of the volcanoes, ज्वालामुखी से फूटनेवाला लावा।

lavatory (लैवेटरी) ***n.*** (plu. lavatories) a room equipped with toilet facilities, शौचालय, शौचगृह।

lavender (लैवेन्डर) ***n.*** 1. a shrub with fragrant light purple flowers, लैवंडर नामक पौधा और उसके फूल। 2. light purple, हलका बैंगनी रंग।

lavish (लैविश) ***adj.*** 1. generous, मुक्तहस्त, उदार। 2. wasteful, extravagant, फ़िज़ूलख़र्च, अपव्ययी, खर्चीला। 3. prolific, abundant, प्रचुर, अधिक।

lavishness (लैविशनिस) ***n.*** the state or quality of being lavish, extravagance, मुक्तहस्तता, खुला ख़र्च करना, अपव्यय करना।

law (लॉ) ***n.*** 1. a rule, नियम, सिद्धांत। 2. a rule established by a legislature or parliament, क़ानून, विधि। 3. a body of such rules, संहिता, विधान।

law-abiding (लॉ-अबाइडिंग) ***adj.*** observing/obeying the law, विधिपालक।

law-court (लॉ-कोर्ट) ***n.*** the court of law, न्यायालय, कचहरी।

lawful (लॉफ़ुल) ***adj.*** sanctioned by law, legal, विधिसम्मत, क़ानूनी।

lawlessness (लॉलिसनिस) ***n.*** the state of being without law, अराजकता, अंधेर।

lawn[1] (लॉन) ***n.*** a piece of ground cultivated with grass and mowed regularly, घास का मैदान, लॉन।

lawn[2] ***n.*** a kind of cotton fabric, एक तरह की मलमल।

lawn-mower (लॉन-मोअर) ***n.*** a person or machine that cuts grass, घास काटनेवाला, घसियारा या घास काटने की मशीन।

L

lawyer (लॉयर) ***n.*** one who gives legal advice, वकील, विधिवेत्ता, क़ानूनदाँ।

lax (लैक्स) ***adj.*** 1. loose, not strict, कड़ाई न करनेवाला, ढीला, नरम, शिथिल। 2. negligent, लापरवाह।

laxative (लैक्सेटिव) ***adj.*** helping or stimulating the bowels to move, रेचक, दस्तावर।

laxity (लैक्सिटी) ***n.*** 1. looseness, शिथिलता, ढिलाई। 2. negligence, लापरवाही, असावधानी। 3. remission, छूट।

lay[1] (ले) ***v.*** (laid, laying) 1. to place or put down, रखना, रख देना। 2. to spread, बिछाना, बिछा देना। 3. to knock down, पटक या गिरा देना। 4. to impose or assign, आरोपित करना, लगाना। 5. to produce (eggs, अंडे) देना, पैदा करना। 6. to present or submit, प्रस्तुत करना, पेश करना। 7. to bet, बाज़ी लगाना। 8. to prepare or formulate, बनाना। 9. to cause to settle, स्थिर होने देना। 10. to place in proper position, सही ढंग से रखना। 11. to place along or under a surface, ज़मीन पर रखना, बैठाना या बिछाना।

lay[2] ***v.*** p.t. of lie.

lay[3] ***adj.*** 1. of or belonging to the common people, सामान्य लोगों से संबद्ध, साधारण। 2. not professional, जो पेशेवर न हो, अव्यावसायिक।

layabout (लेअबाउट) ***n.*** a lazy person, सुस्त आदमी।

layer (लेअर) ***n.*** 1. a single thickness, coating or sheet of material laid over a surface, परत, तह, लेअर। 2. a hen that lays eggs, अंडे देनेवाली मुर्गी। ***adj.*** consisting of layers, परतोंवाला, परतीला। ***v.*** to arrange in layers, परतें लगाना, परत पर परत लगाना, रखना या बिछाना।

layman (लेमैन) ***n.*** (plu. laymen) a person who is not a clergyman, आम आदमी।

layout (लेआउट) ***n.*** 1. the act of laying out, व्यवस्थित करने का काम। 2. something laid out, व्यवस्थित की हुई वस्तु। 3. the arrangement of written matter, advertisements etc., on a page, आयोजन, व्यवस्था, फैलाव, ले-आउट। 4. a map or site plan, नक़्शा।

lazily (लेज़िली) ***adj.*** in a sluggish manner, धीरे-धीरे, मंद गति से, सुस्ती से।

lazy (लेज़ी) ***adj.*** 1. reluctant to work, doing little work, आलसी, सुस्त, कामचोर। 2. moving in a sluggish manner, धीरे-धीरे चलनेवाला, मंथर, मंद।

leach (लीच) ***v.*** to remove or to be removed from a substance by a percolating liquid, साफ़ होना या करना, धुल जाना या धो देना।

lead[1] (लीड) ***v.*** (led, leading) 1. to show the way, रास्ता दिखाना। 2. to guide or conduct, मार्गप्रदर्शन करना, अगुआई करना या संचालन करना। 3. to influence, प्रभावित करना। 4. to induce, प्रेरित करना। 5. to live, pass or spend, व्यतीत करना, बिताना। 6. to play principal part, मुख्य भूमिका निभाना। 7. to excel, आगे बढ़ या निकल जाना। 8. to make the initial play (as in a card game, ताश के खेल में) बाज़ी शुरू करना, पहल करना। ***n.*** 1. the position in advance of others, अग्रता। 2. the margin by which someone is ahead, बढ़त। 3. leadership, अगुआई, नेतागिरी। 4. first move, पहल।

5. the principal role in a drama or film, मुख्य भूमिका, प्रधान पात्र। 6. a wire or cable for making an electrical connection, बिजली का तार। 7. a strap, पट्टा।

lead[2] (लेड) ***n.*** 1. bluish-white highly malleable metal, सीसा। 2. in printing, a thin stick of above metal used for spacing between the lines, लेड, सीसे की पत्ती।

leader (लीडर) ***n.*** 1. one who leads, अगुआ, मार्गप्रदर्शक। 2. the head of a group, नेता, सरदार। 3. main editorial article (in a newspapaer, समाचारपत्र का) अग्रलेख।

leadership (लीडरशिप) ***n.*** the state or position of a leader, नेतृत्व, नेतागिरी, अगुआई।

leading question (लीडिंग क्वेस्चन) ***n.*** a question in which the answer is implicit, ऐसा प्रश्न जिसमें उत्तर निहित हो, अर्थगर्भित प्रश्न।

leaf (लीफ़) ***n.*** (plu. leaves) 1. the green blade like part of a plant or tree, पत्ता। 2. the page of a book, पन्ना। 3. a very thin sheet of a metal, वरक़। 4. a movable piece of wood inserted into a table, मेज़ के साथ जुड़ी पटरी।

leaflet (लीफ़लिट) ***n.*** a pamphlet, इश्तहार, पर्चा, पैम्फ़लेट।

league (लीग) ***n.*** 1. a group or association of persons or nations, संघटन, समुदाय या राष्ट्रकुल। 2. a group of sporting clubs that compete against each other for a championship, संघ, लीग; league match, लीग मैच। 3. a class or category, वर्ग, जाति।

leak (लीक) ***v.*** 1. to escape through a hole or crack (said of fluid, gas etc., द्रव, गैस आदि का) रिसना, चूना, टपकना, क्षरित होना। 2. to disclose or to be disclosed, (रहस्य) प्रकट करना या होना, खोलना या खुलना। ***n.*** 1. a hole or crack from which fluid or gas escapes, छेद या दरार जिसमें से द्रव या गैस रिसती हो। 2. the fluid or gas that has leaked out, रिसा हुआ द्रव या गैस।

leakage (लीकिज) ***n.*** 1. the act of leaking, रिसाव, क्षरण। 2. something that has leaked, रिसा हुआ पदार्थ, क्षरित पदार्थ। 3. disclosing of a secret, रहस्य का प्रकटन, रहस्योद्घाटन।

lean (लीन) ***v.*** (leant, leaning) 1. to incline, झुकना। 2. to have a leaning, झुकाव होना, नति होना, झुकना। 3. to rely for support, मदद या सहारा चाहना। ***n.*** 1. the state or condition of inclining, झुकाव। 2. tendency, झुकाव, नति। ***adj.*** 1. neither fat nor fleshy, पतला-दुबला, कृशकाय। 2. meagre, inadequate, अल्प, अपर्याप्त। 3. unimportant, महत्त्वहीन।

leaning (लीनिंग) ***n.*** a tendency, प्रवृत्ति।

leant (लेन्ट) ***v.*** p.t. & p.p. of lean.

leap (लीप) ***v.*** (leapt/leaped, leaping) 1. to jump off the ground, उछलना, कूदना, छलाँग लगाना। 2. to jump over, कूद जाना, छलाँग लगाना, उछलकर पार करना। 3. to cause to jump over, कुदाना। 4. to move abruptly and impulsively, कूदने लगना। ***n.*** 1. the act of jumping, कूदना, उछलना। 2. a jump, छलाँग।

leapfrog (लीपफ्रॉग) ***n.*** a children's

L

game in which one player bends over and the next leaps over him, मेंढक-कुदान।

leap year (लीप यिअर) ***n.*** a year occurring every four years with an extra day, लीप इयर, अधिवर्ष।

learn (लर्न) ***v.*** (learned/learnt, learning) 1. to acquire knowledge of, ज्ञान अर्जित करना, सीखना। 2. to gain mastery through study or experience, सीखना।3. to become aware by information, जानकारी प्राप्त करना।

learned (लर्निड) ***adj.*** 1. scholarly, erudite, विद्वान या विद्वत्तापूर्ण, पंडित या पांडित्यपूर्ण। 2. well-read, सुविज्ञ।

learning (लर्निंग) ***n.*** 1. acquiring knowledge, विद्या-प्राप्ति, विद्यार्जन। 2. the knowledge obtained by study, ज्ञान, विद्या। 3. scholarship, विद्वत्ता, पांडित्य।

lease (लीस) ***n.*** a contract by which the owner of a land or building grants occupation to another person for specific period in exchange of rent, लीज, पट्टा। ***v.*** 1. to grant by lease, पट्टे पर देना। 2. to hold under lease, पट्टे पर लेना।

leasehold (लीसहोल्ड) ***n.*** the land or building held under a lease, पट्टे पर ली हुई ज़मीन या इमारत।

leaseholder (लीसहोल्डर) ***n.*** a person having a land or property in possession by means of a lease, पट्टेदार।

leash (लीश) ***n.*** a strap or chain used to control a dog or other animal, कुत्ते आदि के गले की रस्सी या पट्टा। ***v.*** to secure or control by a leash, रस्सी या पट्टे से बाँधकर रखना।

least (लीस्ट) ***adj.*** 1. smallest, अदना, छोटे-से-छोटा, कम-से-कम। 2. lowest in rank, पद में सबसे छोटा। 3. of very little importance, महत्त्वहीन। ***adv.*** in a smallest degree, कम-से-कम मात्रा या परिमाण में। ***n.*** smallest quantity, अल्प मात्रा या परिमाण।

leather (लेदर) ***n.*** the tanned hide of an animal, चमड़ा, चर्म। ***adj.*** made of leather, चमड़े का।

leathery (लेदरी) ***adj.*** as tough as leather, चीमड़।

leave[1] (लीव) ***v.*** (left, leaving) 1. to go away from, to depart, चल या निकल पड़ना, चले जाना। 2. to part from, बिदा लेना। 3. to abandon, छोड़ देना। 4. to allow to remain or stay without interference, छोड़ देना, रहने देना, छेड़छाड़ न करना। 5. to bequeath, पीछे या विरासत में छोड़ना। 6. to entrust, सौंपना।

leave[2] ***n.*** 1. the permission to be absent from duty or work, छुट्टी, अवकाश। 2. the duration of such absence, छुट्टी। 3. permission, अनुमति।

leaven (लेवन) ***n.*** 1. yeast, ख़मीर। 2. influence that causes change, परिवर्तनकारी प्रभाव। ***v.*** 1. to raise by leaven, ख़मीर उठाना। 2. to transform, परिवर्तित करना।

lecher (लेचर) ***n.*** a lewd man, व्यभिचारी व्यक्ति, कामासक्त, लंपट।

lechery (लेचरी) ***n.*** lewdness, व्यभिचार, कामुकता, कामासक्ति, लंपटता।

lecture (लेक्चर) ***n.*** 1. a talk before an audience, भाषण, व्याख्यान। 2. reprimand, डाँट-डपट, झिड़की। ***v.*** 1. to give a lecture, भाषण देना, व्याख्या

देना। 2. to reprimand or admonish, झिड़कना, डाँटना-डपटना।

lecturer (लेक्चरर) ***n.*** one who delivers lectures to his students at college or university, व्याख्याता, प्रवक्ता।

led (लेड) ***v.*** p.t. & p.p. of lead.

ledger (लेजर) ***n.*** a book used by a businessman for recording transactions, खाता।

lee (ली) ***n.*** a shelter, आश्रय, ओट, आड़।

leech (लीच) ***n.*** 1. a small bloodsucking finger-sized animal living in water, जोंक, जलोका। 2. one who preys on others, दूसरों का ख़ून चूसनेवाला, जोंक।

leer (लिअर) ***n.*** a malicious look, बुरी नज़र, कुदृष्टि। ***v.*** to look maliciously, बुरी नज़र से देखना।

leeward (लीवर्ड) ***adv.*** toward the lee, आश्रय की ओर, अनुवात।

left[1] (लेफ़्ट) ***v.*** p.t. & p.p. of leave.

left[2] ***adj.*** 1. of or on the same side of the body as the heart, बायाँ। 2. belonging to the left parties, वाम। ***n.*** 1. left hand, बायाँ हाथ। 2. left direction, बाईं तरफ़।

leftist (लेफ़्टिस्ट) ***n.*** a supporter of the left, वामपंथी। ***adj.*** of or concerning leftism, वामपंथी।

left-over (लेफ़्ट-ओवर) ***adj.*** remaining unused or uneaten, बचा या छोड़ा हुआ, जूठा।

leg (लेग) ***n.*** 1. a limb of an animal used for locomotion or support, टाँग। 2. the part of garment that covers the leg, पाँयचा। 3. one of the four supporting parts of a chair, table etc., पाया। 4. a stage of a journey or course, चरण, हिस्सा।

legacy (लेगेसी) ***n.*** money or property left by someone or bequeathed to someone by will, विरासत, पैतृक संपत्ति।

legal (लीगल) ***adj.*** 1. of or relating to law, विधिक, कानूनी। 2. permitted by law, विधिसम्मत, वैध।

legality (लीगैलिटी) ***n.*** the state of being legal, वैधता।

legalization (लीगलाइज़ेशन) ***n.*** an act of legalizing, वैधीकरण।

legalize (लीगलाइज़) ***v.*** to make legal, वैध करना या बनाना, कानूनी रूप देना।

legate (लिगेट) ***n.*** an envoy or emissary, प्रतिनिधि, दूत।

legatee (लिगेटी) ***n.*** one who receives a legacy, वारिस, उत्तराधिकारी।

legation (लिगेशन) ***n.*** 1. a diplomatic envoy, दूत। 2. his official residence, दूतावास। 3. a delegation, प्रतिनिधि मंडल।

legend (लेजन्ड) ***n.*** 1. any popular story handed down from the past, पौराणिक कथा। 2. a person often spoken of, चर्चित व्यक्तित्व।

legendary (लेजन्डरी) ***adj.*** 1. described in legends, जिसका उल्लेख आख्यानों में हुआ हो, पौराणिक। 2. famous, प्रसिद्ध, कीर्तिशाली।

legible (लेजिबल) ***adj.*** capable of being read, सुवाच्य, सुपाठ्य।

legislate (लेजिस्लेट) ***v.*** to make laws, कानून बनाना।

legislation (लेजिस्लेशन) ***n.*** 1. the act of law making, कानून बनाने का काम, विधि-निर्माण, विधायन। 2. the laws themselves, विधान।

legislative (लेजिस्लेटिव) ***adj.*** of or

L

relating to legislation, विधान-संबंधी, विधायी।

legislator (लेजिस्लेटर) ***n.*** a member of a legislative assembly, विधायक।

legislature (लेजिस्लेचर) ***n.*** a legislative assembly, विधान-सभा।

legitimacy (लिजिटिमेसी) ***n.*** the state of being legitimate, वैधता।

legitimate (लिजिटिमिट) ***adj.*** 1. in accordance with law, विधिसम्मत, वैध। 2. logical, तर्कसंगत, युक्तियुक्त। 3. born in wedlock, औरस।

legitimatize / legitimize (लिजिटिमटाइज़/लिजिटिमाइज़) ***v.*** to make legitimate, वैध बनाना।

legume (लेग्यूम) ***n.*** any plant that bears pods, ऐसा पौधा जिसमें फलियाँ लगती हों, शिंब पादप।

leisure (लेज़र) ***n.*** 1. free time, ख़ाली समय, फ़ुर्सत। 2. freedom from work, अवकाश।

leisurely ***adv.*** without hurry, धीरे-धीरे।

lemon (लेमन) ***n.*** 1. an egg-shaped fruit with acid juice, नीबू। 2. the tree that bears it, नीबू का झाड़। 3. its pale yellow colour, पीला रंग।

lemonade (लेमनेड) ***n.*** a drink made from lemon juice, sugar etc., शिकंजवी, नीबू का शर्बत।

lemur (लीमर) ***n.*** a monkey-like animal, लीमूर।

lend (लेन्ड) ***v.*** (lent, lending) 1. to permit the use of something temporarily, मँगनी देना। 2. to provide at interest, उधार देना। 3. to be of use, उपयोगी होना।

lender (लेन्डर) ***n.*** one who lends money, ब्याजिया, उधारदाता।

length (लेंग्थ) ***n.*** 1. measurement from end to end, लंबाई। 2. distance, दूरी। 3. extent, विस्तार। □ **at length,** (i) विस्तार से, (ii) बहुत देर बाद, आख़िरकार।

lengthen (लेंग्थन) ***v.*** to become or make longer, लंबा होना या करना।

lengthy (लेंग्थी) ***adj.*** of great extent, विस्तृत, लंबा-चौड़ा।

lenience, leniency (लीनिएन्स, लीनिएन्सी) ***n.*** mildness, रियायत, नर्मी, लिहाज़।

lenient (लीनिएन्ट) ***adj.*** mild, kind, रियायत करनेवाला, नर्मी बरतनेवाला, लिहाज़ करनेवाला।

lens (लेन्ज़) ***n.*** a piece of glass used in glasses for the eyes, cameras etc., लेन्स।

lentil (लेन्टिल) ***n.*** a kind of bean plant and its seeds, मसूर; green lentil, मूँग।

Leo (लीओ) ***n.*** the fifth sign of the Zodiac, सिंह राशि।

leopard (लेपर्ड) ***n.*** a wild animal of the cat family, तेंदुआ।

leper (लेपर) ***n.*** a person afflicted with leprosy, कोढ़ी।

leprosy (लेप्रॉसी) ***n.*** an infectious disease which causes destruction of tissues, कोढ़।

lesbian (लेज़्बिअन) ***n.*** a female homosexual, समलिंगकामी स्त्री।

lesion (लीज़न) ***n.*** a wound, घाव।

less (लेस) ***adj.*** 1. smaller, अपेक्षाकृत कम या थोड़ा। 2. lower in importance or rank, हीन, घटिया, कमज़ोर। ***prep.*** minus, कम कर के, घटाकर। ***suffix.*** not having, -विहीन, -रहित।

lessee (लेसी) ***n.*** a tenant holding a lease, पट्टेदार, पट्टाधारी।

lessen (लेसन) ***v.*** to make or become less, कम होना या करना, घटना या घटाना।

lesser (लेसर) ***adj.*** less in size or importance, छोटा, हलका, घटिया।

lesson (लेसन) ***n.*** 1. a thing to be learned by a pupil, पाठ, सबक। 2. an example or experience by which one can learn, सीख, शिक्षा। 3. a reprimand or punishment, डाँट या दंड।

lessor (लेसर) ***n.*** one who grants a lease of property, पट्टाकर्ता।

lest (लेस्ट) ***conj.*** so as to prevent the possibility that, कहीं ऐसा न हो कि, कि कहीं।

let (लेट) ***v.*** (let, letting) 1. to rent, किराए पर देना या चढ़ाना। 2. to lease, पट्टे पर देना, लीज़ पर देना। 3. to allow, अनुमति या इजाज़त देना। 4. to do, करना। 5. used as an auxiliary verb, इच्छासूचक सहायक क्रिया। ***suffix.*** used to form nouns meaning smaller or minor, एक अल्पार्थक प्रत्यय; booklet, गुटका।

letdown (लेटडाउन) ***n.*** 1. disappointment, निराशा। 2. a decline or decrease, कमी, घटी।

lethal (लीथल) ***adj.*** fatal, घातक, प्राणहर।

lethargic (लिथार्जिक) ***adj.*** sluggish, आलसी, सुस्त, ढीला, बेदम।

lethargy (लेथर्जी) ***n.*** sluggishness, आलस्य, सुस्ती, ढिलाई।

letter (लेटर) ***n.*** 1. a written or printed communication, पत्र, चिट्ठी। 2. a written symbol representing a speech sound, वर्ण, अक्षर।

letterbox (लेटरबॉक्स) ***n.*** a private box into which letters are delivered, पत्र-पेटी।

lettered (लेटर्ड) ***adj.*** educated, शिक्षित।

lettering (लेटरिंग) ***n.*** 1. the act or method of writing letters, लिखावट, वर्णलेखन,. अक्षरांकन। 2. such written letters, वर्णलेख, अक्षरलेख, लिखावट।

letterpad (लेटरपैड) ***n.*** a number of sheets of writing paper glued together at one end, पत्राली, लेटरपैड।

letterpress (लेटरप्रेस) ***n.*** the process of printing from types and blocks, वर्णमुद्रण।

lettuce (लेटिस) ***n.*** a garden plant with broad edible leaves, सलाद।

level (लेवल) ***n.*** 1. surface, सतह, तल। 2. a flat horizontal surface, समतल भूमि। 3. standard, स्तर। 4. an instrument for ascertaining whether a surface is horizontal or not, गुनिया। ***v.*** 1. to make or become level, समतल होना या करना। 2. to equalize, बराबर करना। 3. to knock down, ढहा देना, गिरा देना। 4. to aim, निशाना साधना। ***adj.*** 1. having a flat smooth surface, समतल। 2. equal, समान, एक-सा। 3. of the same position or rank, समान स्तरवाला, समपदीय। ☐ **do one's level best,** भरसक प्रयास करना।

lever (लीवर) ***n.*** a mechanical device to lift something, लीवर, उत्तोलक। ***v.*** to lift with a lever, लीवर से उठाना।

leverage (लीवरिज) ***n.*** 1. the action or power of a lever, लीवर का कार्य या क्षमता। 2. influence, प्रभाव।

levy (लेवी) ***v.*** 1. to impose a tax or punishment, कर या दंड लगाना। 2. to

L

conscript, भर्ती करना। *n.* 1. an act of levying, कर या दंड लगाना/थोपना। 2. the payment levied, लगाया हुआ कर। 3. conscripted soldiers, भर्ती किए हुए सैनिक।

lewd (ल्यूड) *adj.* 1. lustful, कामुक, लंपट, अश्लील।

lexicographer (लेक्सिकॉग्रफ़र) *n.* a compiler of a dictionary, कोशकार।

lexicography (लेक्सिकॉग्रफ़ी) *n.* the compiling or editing dictionary, शब्दकोश-रचना, शब्दकोश-निर्माण।

lexicon (लेक्सिकॉन) *n.* a dictionary, शब्दकोश।

liability (लाइएबिलिटी) *n.* 1. the state of being liable, देयता, देनदारी, दायित्व।

liable (लाइएबल) *adj.* responsible, उत्तरदायी, जवाबदेह, ज़िम्मेदार।

liaison (लीएज़न) *n.* 1. an illicit sexual relationship, अवैध यौनसंबंध। 2. a link between two separate parts of an army, संपर्क।

liaison officer an officer who acts as a go-between, संपर्क अधिकारी।

liar (लाइअर) *n.* one who tells lies, झूठा व्यक्ति, मिथ्याभाषी।

libation (लाइबेशन) *n.* an act of pouring a liquid as a sacrifice, तर्पण।

libel (लाइबल) *n.* a written statement defaming one, अपमानलेख, मानहानि। *v.* (libeled/libelled, libeling/libelling) to make a libellous statement, अपमानलेख लिखना।

libellous (लाइबेलस) *adj.* being or containing a libel, मानहानिकारक।

liberal (लिबरल) *adj.* generous, उदार, उदारहृदय, उदारतापूर्ण।

liberality (लिबरैलिटी) *n.* 1. generosity, उदारता, विशाल-हृदयता।

liberalization (लिबरलाइज़ेशन) *n.* the act of liberalizing, उदारीकरण।

liberate (लिबरेट) *v.* to set free, स्वतंत्र कर देना, मुक्त कर देना।

liberation (लिबरेशन) *n.* setting free or being set free, स्वतंत्रता, आज़ादी।

libertine (लिबर्टीन) *n.* a sexually promiscuous person, व्यभिचारी, परस्त्रीगामी।

liberty (लिबर्टी) *n.* 1. freedom, स्वतंत्रता, स्वाधीनता, स्वच्छंदता।

libidinous (लिबिडिनस) *adj.* full of lust, lustful, कामातुर, विषयासक्त, कामी।

libido (लिबिडो) *n.* 1. the life force, जीवनी शक्ति। 2. sexual urge, कामोत्तेजना, कामावेग।

libra (लाइब्रा) *n.* the sign of the Zodiac, the Scales, तुला (राशि)।

librarian (लाइब्रेरिअन) *n.* a person in charge of a library, ग्रंथालयाध्यक्ष, पुस्तकालयाध्यक्ष।

library (लाइब्रेरी) *n.* 1. a room or building where books are kept for reading or borrowing, पुस्तकालय, लाइब्रेरी, ग्रंथालय। 2. a collection of records, संग्रह।

lice (लाइस) *n.* plu. of louse.

licence, license (लाइसेन्स) *n.* 1. an official order to do or own something, लाइसेंस, अनुज्ञप्ति। 2. permission, अनुमति। 3. freedom of action, स्वतंत्रता, स्वच्छंदता। *v.* to give licence to, लाइसेंस देना।

licenced, licensed (लाइसेन्स्ड) *adj.* having official permission, लाइसेंस-प्राप्त।

licensee (लाइसेन्सी) *n.* a person who holds a licence, लाइसेंसदार, अनुज्ञप्तिधारी।

lichen (लाइकन) ***n.*** a plant that grows on rocks, पहाड़ों पर होनेवाला एक जंगली पौधा, चरीला, शैवाक।

lick (लिक) ***v.*** 1. to pass the tongue over, जीभ से चाटना, जीभ फेरना। 2. to thrash, पीटना, पिटाई करना। 3. to defeat, हरा देना। ***n.*** the act of licking, चाटने की क्रिया या भाव, चटाई।

lid (लिड) ***n.*** 1. a cover of a pot or box, ढक्कन, ढकना। 2. an eyelid, पलक।

lie[1] (लाइ) ***v.*** (lay, lain, lying) 1. to be in a flat resting position, लेटना। 2. to remain in a flat position on a surface, पड़ा होना, पड़ा रहना। 3. to be situated, स्थित होना। 4. to be found, मिलना, प्राप्त होना।

lie[2] ***n.*** 1. an untrue statement, झूठ। 2. an imposture, धोखा। ***v.*** (lied, lying) to tell a lie, झूठ बोलना।

lien (लिअन) ***n.*** the right to keep possession of something belonging to a debtor until his debt has been paid, बंधक, रेहन। ☐ **a lien on a post,** पद पर वापस आने का अधिकार, पुनर्ग्रहणाधिकार।

lieu (ल्यू) ***n.***; ☐ **in lieu of,** in stead of, के बदले में।

lieutenant (लेफ़्टिनेन्ट) ***n.*** 1. deputy, उप-; lieutenant governor, उपराज्यपाल। 2. a military officer, सैनिक अधिकारी।

life (लाइफ़) ***n.*** 1. active force, vitality, जीवनी शक्ति। 2. period between birth and death, जीवन, ज़िंदगी, जीवनकाल। 3. living organisms collectively, प्राणी, जीव-जंतु। 4. liveliness, चहल-पहल। 5. a particular way of existence, जीने का ढंग, जीवन। 6. a biography, जीवनी।

life belt ***n.*** a life preserver worn as a belt, रक्षा-पेटी, रक्षा-चक्र।

lifeboat (लाइफ़बोट) ***n.*** a small boat carried on a large ship to rescue the ship passengers, रक्षा-नौका।

lifebuoy (लाइफ़बॉइ) ***n.*** a device to save from drowning a person afloat, रक्षा-बोया।

lifelong (लाइफ़लॉन्ग) ***adj.*** continuing for a lifetime, जीवन-भर साथ देने या रहनेवाला, आजीवन।

lifesentence (लाइफ़सेन्टेन्स) ***n.*** an order of imprisonment for whole life, उम्रक़ैद, आजीवन कारावास।

lifesize (लाइफ़साइज़) ***adj.*** representing actual size, आदमक़द।

lifespan (लाइफ़स्पैन) ***n.*** the span of life, जीवनकाल, उम्र।

lift (लिफ़्ट) ***v.*** 1. to rise or cause to rise upward, उठना या उठाना, ऊपर चढ़ना या चढ़ाना। 2. to raise, ऊँचा करना, उन्नत करना। 3. to bring to an end, to abolish, उठा देना, ख़त्म करना। 4. to steal, उड़ा देना, चुरा लेना। 5. to transport goods or persons, ले जाना। ***n.*** 1. the act of lifting or an upward movement, उठाने की क्रिया या भाव, उठाई, उठाव। 2. a free ride in a car offered to a pedestrian, राह चलते को सवारी देने की क्रिया, लिफ्ट। 3. an elevator, लिफ़्ट। 4. a feeling of increased strength, rising of spirits, उत्साहवर्धन।

ligament (लिगमेन्ट) ***n.*** a band of tough fibrous tissue, स्नायु।

light[1] (लाइट) ***n.*** 1. the natural force that makes sight possible, रोशनी, प्रकाश। 2. daylight, उजाला, दिन की रोशनी। 3. that which emits light, प्रकाश-यंत्र, बैटरी, लालटेन आदि। 4. brightness, चमक, रोशनी। 5. knowledge, understanding, ज्ञान, जानकारी। ***adj.*** 1. full of light, प्रकाशमान, उजाले से भरा। 2. not deep in colour, हलका। ***v.*** (lighted/lit, lighting) 1. to begin to burn, जलना, सुलगना। 2. to set burning, जलाना, सुलगाना। 3. to brighten, चमक उठना।

light² ***adv.*** 1. of little weight, हलका। 2. of less than the correct weight or value, हलका, घटिया। 3. soft or mild, नरम, मुलायम। 4. not serious, गंभीरताविहीन, हलका-फुलका, महत्त्वहीन। 5. free from worries or troubles, बेफ़िक्र, निश्चिंत। 6. entertaining, मनोरंजक। 7. gay, प्रफुल्ल। 8. loose in morals, चरित्रभ्रष्ट। ***adv.*** with little baggage, बिना अधिक सामान के, हलके-फुलके सामान के साथ।

lighten¹ (लाइटन) ***v.*** 1. to brighten, जगमगाना, दीप्त होना/करना। 2. to shed light on, प्रकाशित/स्पष्ट करना।

lighten² ***v.*** 1. to make or become lighter in weight, हलका होना/करना। 2. to relieve or be relieved of worry, चिंता, भार आदि से मुक्त होना/करना, राहत मिलना या देना।

lighter (लाइटर) ***n.*** a device for lighting cigarettes, stoves etc., लाइटर।

light-fingered (लाइट-फ़िंगर्ड) ***adj.*** having the habit of stealing small thing, उचक्का, चाइयाँ, गिरहकट, हथलपक।

light-hearted (लाइट-हार्टिड) ***adj.*** gay, प्रफुल्ल, ख़ुश, ख़ुशदिल।

lighthouse (लाइटहाउस) ***n.*** a tower equipped with a powerful flashing light, प्रकाशगृह।

lightning (लाइटनिंग) ***n.*** the flash of light in the sky, बिजली, कौंध। ***adj.*** very quick, तीव्रगामी, फुर्तीला।

lightweight (लाइटवेट) ***adj.*** 1. (a boxer) weighing between 126 to 135 pounds, (मुक्केबाज़) जिसका वज़न १२६ से १३५ पौंड हो। 2. of little importance, महत्त्वहीन।

light-year (लाइट-यिअर) ***n.*** the distance light travels in one year, प्रकाश-वर्ष।

lignite (लिग्नाइट) ***n.*** brown coal, भूरा कोयला।

likable, likeable (लाइकेबल) ***adj.*** pleasant, सुहावना, प्रिय।

like (लाइक) ***v.*** 1. to find pleasant or satisfactory, पसंद होना/करना। 2. to wish for, इच्छा होना, चाहना। ***adj.*** 1. similar, समान। 2. characteristic of, उसी तरह का, वैसा। ***n.*** 1. something of equal value, समान वस्तु। 2. something of the same kind, वैसी ही वस्तु। 3. liking, पसंद। ***prep.*** in the manner of, की तरह, के समान। ***conj.*** 1. in the same way, वैसे ही, मानो। 2. as if, जैसा कि। ***suffix.*** of the same form, की तरह का।

likelihood (लाइकलिहुड) ***n.*** probability, संभाव्यता।

likely (लाइकली) ***adj.*** 1. expected to occur, संभाव्य, संभावित। 2. promising, होनहार। 3. suitable, उपयुक्त। ***adv.*** probably, संभवतः।

likeness (लाइकनिस) ***n.*** 1. resemblance, समानता, साम्य, सादृश्य। 2. a copy or portrait, प्रतिरूप, प्रतिकृति।

likewise (लाइकवाइज़) ***adv.*** 1. similarly, वैसे ही, उसी तरह। 2. as well, also, और।

liking (लाइकिंग) ***n.*** pleasure or taste, पसंद, रुचि।

lilac (लाइलक) ***n.*** purple colour, जामुनी रंग।

lilliputian (लिलिप्यूशिअन) ***adj.*** very small, बौने क़द का, बौना, बहुत छोटा।

lily (लिली) ***n.*** a garden plant with large white or reddish flowers, लिली, कुमुदिनी।

limb (लिम्ब) ***n.*** 1. a projecting part of an animal body, अवयव, अंग। 2. a large branch of tree, डाली, शाखा।

lime (लाइम) ***n.*** 1. calcium oxide, चूना। 2. birdlime, लासा।

limelight (लाइमलाइट) ***n.*** 1. brilliant light, चमकीली रोशनी। 2. great publicity, अत्यधिक प्रचार, बहुत प्रसिद्ध होना।

limestone (लाइमस्टोन) ***n.*** a kind of rock from which lime is obtained, चूना पत्थर।

limit (लिमिट) ***n.*** 1. boundary, सीमा, हद। 2. the greatest amount or number allowed, परिसीमा। ***v.*** to keep below or at a certain point or amount, सीमित करना या रखना, सीमा निर्धारित करना।

limitation (लिमिटेशन) ***n.*** 1. the act of limiting or the state of being limited, परिसीमन। 2. limit, सीमा। 3. weakness, कमज़ोरी, कमी।

limited (लिमिटिड) ***adj.*** 1. having a limit or limits, सीमित, सीमाबद्ध, ससीम। 2. limiting the liability of each shareholder, लिमिटिड, परिसीमित।

limp[1] (लिम्प) ***v.*** to walk lamely, लँगड़ाते हुए चलना, लँगड़ाना। ***n.*** an irregular gait, लंगड़ चाल।

limp[2] ***adj.*** 1. lacking strength or energy, अशक्त, निर्जीव, निस्तेज। 2. not stiff, लचीला।

limpid (लिम्पिड) ***adj.*** clear or transparent, साफ़-सुथरा, पारदर्शक।

line (लाइन) ***n.*** 1. a thin contiuous mark, रेखा, लकीर, लीक, लाईन। 2. a row of people or things, queue, पंक्ति, लाईन। 3. a path or track, पथ, रास्ता। 4. a boundary, border or limit, सीमारेखा। 5. an outline, रूपरेखा। 6. a foot (poetry), चरण। 7. lineage, वंशक्रम, वंश-परंपरा। 8. a system of travelling or transport, यात्रा-पद्धति, यातायात-पद्धति। 9. an official policy, सरकारी नीति। 10. a course of action, कार्य-योजना। 11. a business or profession, व्यापार, धंधा, पेशा। 12. a piece of cord, रस्सी, डोरी। 13. a wire or cable, तार। 14. a brief letter, संक्षिप्त पत्र। ***v.*** 1. to draw lines on, रेखा खींचना। 2. to arrange in a line, to form rows along, पंक्ति बनाना।

lineage (लिनिइज) ***n.*** the line of one's ancestors, ancestry, वंशानुक्रम, वंश-परंपरा।

linear (लिनिअर) ***adj.*** 1. of a line, रेखीय, रैखिक। 2. arranged in a line, रेखाकार।

lineman (लाइनमैन) ***n.*** one who installs or repairs telephones or electric power lines, लाईनमैन।

linen (लिनिन) ***n.*** cloth made of flax, लिनन।

liner (लाइनर) ***n.*** a ship or airplane travelling on a regular route, किसी मार्ग पर नियमित रूप से चलनेवाला जहाज़, लाइनर।

linger (लिन्गर) ***v.*** to delay, देर लगाना।

lingerie (लैन्ज़री) ***n.*** undergarments

L

for women, स्त्रियों के अंदर के कपड़े।

lingua franca (लिंग्वा फ़्रैंका) ***n.*** a language used between peoples whose native languages are different, संपर्क भाषा।

linguist (लिंग्विस्ट) ***n.*** a specialist in linguistics, भाषाविद्, भाषाविज्ञानी।

linguistics (लिंग्विस्टिक्स) ***n.*** the scientific study of a particular language or dialect, भाषाविज्ञान, भाषिकी।

liniment (लिनिमेन्ट) ***n.*** a liquid medicine rubbed on the skin, लेप।

lining (लाइनिंग) ***n.*** the material used as the inner surface of a garment, अस्तर।

link (लिन्क) ***n.*** 1. a ring of a chain, कड़ी। 2. a connecting part or thing, कड़ी। 3. connection, संबंध। ***v.*** to join or to be joined, जोड़ना या जुड़ना, मिलाना या मिलना।

linkage (लिन्किज) ***n.*** the act of linking or state of being linked, जुड़े होने की अवस्था या भाव, जुड़ाव, संयोजन।

linoleum (लिनोलियम) ***n.*** a kind of floor covering, लिनोलियम।

linseed (लिन्सीड) ***n.*** the seed of flax, तीसी, अलसी।

lint (लिन्ट) ***n.*** a soft material for dressing wounds, फाहा।

lintel (लिन्टल) ***n.*** the horizontal beam of concrete, लिंटल।

lion (लाइअन) ***n.*** 1. a large carnivorous animal of cat family, शेर, सिंह, शेर-बबर। [fem. lioness, शेरनी, सिंहनी] 2. a man of great strength or courage, सिंहपुरुष, शेर।

lionize (लाइअनाइज़) ***v.*** to treat as a celebrity, अत्यधिक महत्त्व देना या भव्य स्वागत करना।

lip (लिप) ***n.*** 1. one of the two edges of the mouth, होंठ, ओष्ठ। 2. the edge (of a cup), (प्याले आदि का) ऊपर का किनारा।

lip-service (लिप-सर्विस) ***n.*** insincere show of sympathy or respect, झूठी सहानुभूति या आदर।

lipstick (लिपस्टिक) ***n.*** a stick for colouring the lips, लिपस्टिक।

liquefy (लिक्विफ़ाइ) ***v.*** to make or become liquid, द्रव बनाना या बनना।

liquid (लिक्विड) ***n.*** a substance other than solid or gas, तरल पदार्थ, द्रव। ***adj.*** 1. in the form of a liquid, द्रव, तरल। 2. readily converted into cash, नक़दी।

liquidate (लिक्विडेट) ***v.*** 1. to pay or settle, चुकता करना। 2. to close down, बंद या ख़त्म करना। 3. to kill, मार डालना।

liquidation (लिक्विडेशन) ***n.*** the act of liquidating, चुकता, बंद या ख़त्म करना, समापन।

liquidator (लिक्विडेटर) ***n.*** one who is authorised to close down someone's business, समापन अधिकारी, समापक।

liquidity (लिक्विडिटी) ***n.*** the state of being liquid, द्रवता।

liquor (लिकर) ***n.*** 1. an alcoholic drink, मदिरा। 2. a liquid substance, तरल पदार्थ, द्रव पदार्थ।

lisp (लिस्प) ***n.*** a speech defect, स् को थ् बोलने का दोष, थथलाहट।

list[1] (लिस्ट) ***n.*** a series of names, things, figures, सूची, तालिका। ***v.*** 1. to make a list of, सूची बनाना। 2. to enter in a list, सूची में डालना।

list[2] ***n.*** tilt, उलार, झुकाव, नति। ***v.*** to

lean over to one side, एक ओर झुकना, उलार होना।

listen (लिसन) ***v.*** to give attention in hearing, ध्यान से सुनना, ध्यान देना।

listener (लिसनर) ***n.*** one who listens (esp. to the radio) श्रोता, सुननेवाला।

listless (लिस्टलिस) ***adj.*** lacking energy, बेजान, निर्जीव।

litchi (लीची) ***n.*** a tree and its fruit, लीची।

liter (लीटर) ***n.*** = litre.

literacy (लिटरेसी) ***n.*** the ability to read and write, लिख और पढ़ सकने की क्षमता, साक्षरता।

literal (लिटरल) ***adj.*** 1. exact, यथातथ्य। 2. giving one word for each word, शाब्दिक। 3. of or expressed by letters, अभिधेय।

literary (लिटरेरी) ***adj.*** 1. of literature, साहित्य-संबंधी, साहित्यिक। 2. found in literature, साहित्य में होनेवाला, साहित्यिक।

literate (लिटरिट) ***adj. & n.*** 1. able to read and write, साक्षर। 2. well educated, सुशिक्षित।

literature (लिटरिचर) ***n.*** 1. imaginative and creative writing, साहित्य। 2. body of such writings, साहित्य, वाङ्मय।

lithograph (लिथोग्राफ़) ***n.*** print made by lithography, अश्ममुद्र, शिलामुद्र। ***v.*** to print by litho-graphy, अश्ममुद्रण करना।

lithography (लिथॉग्रफ़ी) ***n.*** the way or process of printing from a piece of stone, अश्ममुद्रण, शिलामुद्रण।

litigant (लिटिगेन्ट) ***n.*** one who is engaged in a law-suit, मुक़दमा लड़नेवाला।

litigate (लिटिगेट) ***v.*** to engage in legal proceedings, मुक़दमा लड़ना।

litigation (लिटिगेशन) ***n.*** action in law, मुक़दमेबाज़ी।

litmus paper (लिटमस पेपर) ***n.*** a paper used in chemical tests to find out if substance is acid or alkali, लिटमस पेपर।

litre, liter (लीटर) ***n.*** a metric unit to measure liquids, लीटर।

litter (लिटर) ***n.*** 1. worthless material, trash, rubbish, कूड़ा-कचरा, कूड़ा-कर्कट। 2. a couch for carrying a person, पालकी, डाँडी। 3. young animals produced at one birth, एक ब्यान के बच्चे, एक बार में होनेवाले बच्चे। ***v.*** to scatter, छितराना, फैलाना।

little (लिटल) ***adj.*** (less/lesser, least) 1. short in size, छोटा। 2. young, नन्हा, छोटा। 3. brief, छोटा, अल्प, संक्षिप्त। 4. trivial, तुच्छ। ***adv.*** 1. not much, थोड़ी मात्रा में। 2. not at all, बिल्कुल नहीं। 3. rarely, कदाचित ही। ***n.*** only a small amount, कुछ ही।

littleness (लिटलनिस) ***n.*** the state of being little, छोटापन, लघुता, तुच्छता।

little people ***n.*** (plu.) fairies, परियाँ।

livable, liveable (लिवेबल) ***adj.*** suitable to live in, रहने योग्य।

live (लिव) ***v.*** 1. to have life, जीना, जीवित रहना/होना। 2. to continue to be alive, रहना, जीवन बिताना। 3. to reside/ dwell, रहना। 4. to pass, गुज़ारना, व्यतीत करना। 5. to conduct one's life in a certain way, बसर करना, निर्वाह करना। ***adj.*** 1. alive, सजीव, ज़िंदा। 2. glowing, burning or carrying an electric current, गर्म, ज़िंदा, (तार) जिसमें बिजली हो।

3. of current interest, ज्वलंत, जीवंत।

livelihood (लाइवलीहुड) ***n.*** a means of living, जीविका, रोज़ी।

lively (लाइवली) ***adj.*** 1. full of life, सजीव, जानदार। 2. cheerful, प्रफुल्ल, हँसता-खेलता।

liver (लिवर) ***n.*** 1. a large gland in the abdomen secreting bile, जिगर, यकृत। 2. liver of an animal used as food, कलेजी (गोश्त)।

liveried (लिवरीड) ***adj.*** wearing a uniform, वर्दीधारी।

livery (लिवरी) ***n.*** a uniform worn by a servant, नौकर की वर्दी।

livestock (लाइवस्टॉक) ***n.*** domestic animals raised for home use or profit, पालतू जीव—गाय, भैंस, बकरी आदि, पशुधन।

livid (लिविड) ***adj.*** 1. bluish gray, नीला, नीलाभ। 2. furiously angry, आगबबूला।

living (लिविंग) ***adj.*** 1. alive, जीवित, जीता-जागता। 2. in active use, सजीव, जीवंत। 3. real, वास्तविक। ***n.*** 1. livelihood, जीविका। 2. a manner or style of living, जीवनयापन का ढंग, ढर्रा।

living room ***n.*** a room for general use, बैठने-उठने का कमरा, बैठक।

lizard (लिज़र्ड) ***n.*** a reptile with a long tail, छिपकली, गिरगिट आदि की जाति का जीव।

llama (लामा) ***n.*** a deer like animal kept as a beast of burden, लामा।

load (लोड) ***n.*** 1. a supported weight, भार, वजन। 2. material transported by a vehicle, person or animal, बोझा, बोझ, लादी। 3. a heavy responsibility, भार, दायित्व। 4. a large amount or quantity, बड़ी राशि। 5. the amount of electricity supplied, लोड, बिजली के ख़र्च की मात्रा, बिजली की खपत। ***v.*** 1. to put a load in or on, लादना, लाद देना। 2. to charge with ammunition, (बंदूक) भरना। 3. to insert into, भरना, डालना।

loaded (लोडिड) ***adj.*** 1. full, भरा हुआ। 2. drunk, नशे में चूर।

loadstone (लोडस्टोन) ***n.*** = lodestone.

loaf[1] (लोफ़) ***n.*** (plu. loaves) a mass of bread baked in one piece, पावरोटी।

loaf[2] ***v.*** to spend time idly, समय बर्बाद करना, आवारागर्दी करना।

loafer (लोफ़र) ***n.*** one who loafs, आवारागर्द।

loam (लोम) ***n.*** rich soil, दुम्मट।

loamy (लोमी) ***adj.*** fertile and productive, दुम्मटी।

loan (लोन) ***n.*** 1. some of money lent, क़र्ज़, ऋण, उधार। 2. anything lent for temporary use, उधार, मँगनी। ***v.*** to lend, उधार देना।

loath (लोथ) ***adj.*** unwilling, अनिच्छुक।

loathe (लोद) ***v.*** to abhor, घृणा/नफ़रत करना।

loathing (लोदिंग) ***n.*** extreme dislike, घिन।

loathsome (लोदसम) ***adj.*** repulsive, घिनौना।

lob (लॉब) ***v.*** (lobbed, lobbing) to hit in high arc, उछालना, फेंकना, लॉब करना।

lobby (लॉबी) ***n.*** a waiting room in a hotel etc., प्रकोष्ठ, लॉबी, सभाकक्ष। ***v.*** to seek to influence or support one's cause, मत का समर्थन करने के लिए प्रभाव डालना।

lobe (लोब) ***n.*** the lower soft part of the ear, ललरी।

lobster (लॉब्स्टर) ***n.*** a large shellfish, महाचिंगट, झींगा।

local (लोकल) ***adj.*** 1. of a particular place, स्थानीय। 2. limited to a part of body, क्षेत्रीय या सीमित।

locality (लोकैलिटी) ***n.*** a particular place or area, क्षेत्र, इलाका, हलका।

localize (लोकलाइज़) ***v.*** to restrict to or be restricted to a particular area, स्थानीय बना देना या बन जाना।

locate (लोकेट) ***v.*** 1. to find (by searching), (स्थान का) पता लगाना। 2. to become established, स्थित होना।

located (लोकेटिड) ***adj.*** situated, स्थित।

location (लोकेशन) ***n.*** 1. a place where something is located, जगह। 2. the act of locating, पता लगाना।

loci (लोकाइ) ***n.*** (maths.) plu. of locus, बिंदुपथ।

lock[1] (लॉक) ***n.*** a strand or curl of hair, लट।

lock[2] ***n.*** 1. a device used to secure a door, lid etc., ताला। 2. a section of a canal closed off with gates, बाँध। 3. a hold in wrestling, दाँव, पेंच। ***v.*** 1. to fasten with a lock, ताला लगाना। 2. to safeguard by putting behind a lock, ताले में रखना। 3. to put in a jail, कारागार में रखना, बंद करना। 4. to become blocked, रुक जाना, जाम हो जाना।

locker (लॉकर) ***n.*** a small cupboard that can be locked, तालेदार आलमारी या डिब्बा, लॉकर।

locket (लॉकिट) ***n.*** a small ornamental piece worn on a chain around the neck, लटकन, लॉकेट।

lockout (लॉकआउट) ***n.*** the closing down of a factory by the employer, तालाबंदी।

lock-up (लॉक-अप) ***n.*** a jail, कारागार, हवालात, बंदीगृह।

locomotion (लोकोमोशन) ***n.*** the act or ability to move from place to place, चलने की क्रिया या क्षमता, चलना, गतिक्षमता।

locomotive (लोकोमोटिव) ***adj.*** able to move, चल, गतिक्षम। ***n.*** a railway engine, रेलवे इंजन।

locus (लोकस) ***n.*** 1. a point, बिंदु, नुक़्ता। 2. a place, स्थान, स्थल।

locus standi (लोकस स्टैन्डी) ***n.*** (law), standing place, आधिकारिक स्थिति, अधिकारिता।

locust (लोकस्ट) ***n.*** a grasshopper which flies in groups, टिड्डा, टिड्डी।

lodestar (लोडस्टार) ***n.*** the North Star, ध्रुव तारा।

lodestone (लोडस्टोन) ***n.*** a piece of iron having magnetic properties, चुंबक पत्थर।

lodge (लॉज) ***n.*** 1. a place usually given on rent for temporary stay, बसेरा, लॉज। 2. a place for some activity, भवन या होटल। ***v.*** 1. to stay or provide accommodation, ठहरना या ठहराना। 2. to register (a protest, शिकायत) दर्ज करना, दाख़िल करना।

lodging (लॉजिन्ग) ***n.*** a temporary residence, बसेरा, आवास।

loft (लॉफ़्ट) ***n.*** 1. an attic, अटारी। 2. a gallery, दीर्घा।

loftiness (लॉफ़्टीनिस) ***n.*** the state of being lofty, ऊँचाई, ऊँचान; महानता, महत्ता।

lofty (लॉफ़्टी) ***adj.*** 1. tall, ऊँचा, उच्च।

L

2. noble, ऊँचा, उदात्त। 3. important or eminent, महत्त्वपूर्ण। 4. haughty, अहंकारी, दंभी, घमंडी।

log (लॉग) ***n.*** 1. a section of a trunk, लट्ठा। 2. a written record, लिखित विवरण।

logarithm (लॉगरिथम) ***n.*** (maths.), लघुगणक।

logbook (लॉगबुक) ***n.*** a record book, रोज़नामचा।

loggerhead (लॉगरहेड) ☐ **at loggerheads**, (आपस में) लड़ते हुए।

logic (लॉजिक) ***n.*** 1. the science of reasoning, तर्कशास्त्र। 2. an argument, तर्क। 3. a way of reasoning, तर्क-पद्धति, तर्कशीलता।

logical (लॉजिकल) ***adj.*** 1. according to the rules of logic, तर्कशास्त्रीय। 2. reasonable, sensible, तर्कसंगत।

logistics (लॉजिस्टिक्स) ***n.*** the science of the movement and maintenance of military forces, सेना-संचालन, सेना-व्यवस्था।

logo (लोगो) ***n.*** a special sign used by a company for publicity, लोगो, प्रतीक।

loin (लॉइन) ***n.*** the part between the ribs and hipbone, कमर।

loincloth (लॉइनक्लॉथ) ***n.*** a piece of cloth worn round the loins, लुंगी।

loiter (लॉइटर) ***v.*** to move about aimlessly, मटरगश्ती करना।

lollipop (लॉलिपॉप) ***n.*** a candy on a small stick, लॉलीपॉप।

lone (लोन) ***adj.*** solitary, अकेला, एकाकी।

lonely (लोनली) ***adj.*** 1. without companion, अकेला, तन्हा। 2. isolated, एकांत।

lonesome (लोनसम) ***adj.*** lonely,

long[1] (लॉन्ग) ***adj.*** 1. having great length, लंबा। 2. having a certain length or duration, निश्चित लंबाई या अवधिवाला। ***n.*** 1. a long time, लंबा समय। 2. a long vowel or syllable, दीर्घ स्वर या अक्षर। ***adv.*** for a certain period, निश्चित अवधि के लिए।

long[2] ***v.*** to wish earnestly, बहुत चाहना।

longcloth ***n.*** a kind of cotton cloth, लट्ठा, गाढ़ा, लंकलाट।

longevity (लॉन्जेविटी) ***n.*** 1. long life, दीर्घ आयु। 2. length of life, जीवनकाल।

long face ***n.*** उतरा हुआ चेहरा।

longhand (लॉन्गहैन्ड) ***n.*** ordinary writing, सामान्य लिपि।

longing (लॉन्गिंग) ***n.*** a persistent or intense desire, लालसा, साध।

longitude (लॉन्जिट्यूड) ***n.*** the distance east or west from the meridian, देशांतर, रेखांश।

long-range ***adj.*** capable of covering long distance, दूर तक मार करनेवाला, लंबी मारवाला।

long-sighted (लॉन्ग-साइटिड) ***adj.*** having foresight, दूरदर्शी।

long-standing (लॉन्ग-स्टैन्डिंग) ***adj.*** having existed for a long time, बहुत दिनों का, पुराना।

long-term (लॉन्ग-टर्म) ***adj.*** of or for a long period, दीर्घावधिक, दीर्घकालीन, दीर्घकालिक।

loo (लू) ***n.*** a toilet, lavatory, शौचालय।

loofa, loofah (लूफ़ा) ***n.*** a dried gourd used as a sponge, तुरई का झाँवा।

look (लुक) ***v.*** 1. to use the eyes to see, देखना, दृष्टिपात करना। 2. to search,

ढूँढ़ना, (इधर-उधर) देखना। 3. to appear, दिखाई पड़ना, दिखना। 4. to seem to be, भासित होना, लगना, प्रतीत होना। 5. to consider, ध्यान देना। ***n.*** 1. a gaze or glance, दृष्टि। 2. (plu.) physical appearance, शक्ल, स्वरूप, चेहरा-मोहरा, शक्ल-सूरत।

lookout (लुकआउट) ***n.*** 1. the act of keeping watch, निगरानी, देख-भाल। 2. worry or concern, ध्यान, चिंता। 3. a view, दृष्टिकोण।

loom[1] (लूम) ***n.*** an apparatus for weaving cloth, करघा।

loom[2] ***v.*** to come into view with threatening aspect, आँखों के आगे मँडराना।

loop (लूप) ***n.*** 1. a thread etc., that is folded over and joined at the end, फंदा। 2. any round or oval shaped thing, छल्ला, लूप। ***v.*** 1. to form into a loop, छल्ला/फंदा बनाना। 2. to fasten with a loop, लूप लगाना।

loophole (लूपहोल) ***n.*** a means of evasion, निकल भागने या बच निकलने का रास्ता।

loop line ***n.*** a railway branch line which leaves the main line and rejoins it after a short distance, लूप लाइन।

loose (लूस) ***adj.*** 1. not tight, ढीला, ढीला-ढाला। 2. not packed, खुला, फुटकर। 3. not strict or exact, असंयत, शिथिल, ढीला-ढाला। 4. not organized strictly, असंगठित। 5. immoral, व्यभिचारी, चरित्रहीन। ***v.*** to unfasten or untie, ढीला करना, खोलना।

loose motion (लूज़ मोशन) ***n.*** diarrhoea, दस्त।

loose-tongued (लूज़-टंग्ड) ***adj.*** speaking too freely, बकवादी।

loot (लूट) ***n.*** goods stolen or taken from the enemy, लूट, लूट का माल। ***v.*** to steal or plunder, लूट लेना, लूटना।

lope (लोप) ***v.*** to take long strides, छलाँगें लगाना।

lop-eared (लॉप-ईअर्ड) ***adj.*** having drooping ears, लटकते हुए कानोंवाला।

lopsided (लॉपसाइडिड) ***adj.*** leaning to one side, एक तरफ़ झुका हुआ, असंतुलित।

lord (लॉर्ड) ***n.*** 1. a ruler or sovereign, शासक, हाकिम, शाह। 2. a master, स्वामी, मालिक। 3. a nobleman, सामंत। 4. a respectful form of address, प्रभु! मालिक!

lordship (लॉर्डशिप) ***n.*** the position or authority of a lord, शासक का पद या अधिकार।

lorry (लॉरी) ***n.*** a large motor vehicle, लॉरी, मोटरगाड़ी।

lose (लूज़) ***v.*** (lost, losing) 1. to be unable to find or keep, खोना, गँवाना, खो या गँवा बैठना। 2. to be deprived of, to cause the loss of, वंचित रहना, पल्ले न पड़ना। 3. to fail to hear, see or obtain, सुन, समझ या पकड़ न पाना। 4. to fail to win, हार जाना। 5. to give all one's attention to, निमग्न होना।

loser (लूज़र) ***n.*** a person who loses, पराजित व्यक्ति, हारा आदमी।

loss (लॉस) ***n.*** 1. the act or fact of losing, नुक़सान, हानि। 2. one that is lost, वह जिसे खोया हो, क्षति। 3. amount lost in business transaction, घाटा।

lost (लॉस्ट) ***adj.*** 1. missing, खोया/गँवाया हुआ, ग़ायब, गुम। 2. absorbed in, निमग्न। 3. not won or not likely to be won, हारा हुआ। 4. strayed,

L

भटका हुआ। 5. bewildered, भौचक्का, हक्का-बक्का।

lot (लॉट) ***n.*** 1. one of a set of slips used in a draw, लॉटरी की पर्ची। 2. the choice resulting from it, निकलनेवाली पर्ची, जीती पर्ची। 3. allotted share, हिस्सा। 4. a great number, ढेर। 5. a set of articles for auction, नीलामी में रखी वस्तुएँ। 6. fate, भाग्य।

loth (लोथ) ***adj.*** = loath.

lotion (लोशन) ***n.*** a cosmetic liquid, लोशन।

lots (लॉट्स) ***n.*** (plu.) great numbers, ढेरों।

lottery (लॉटरी) ***n.*** 1. a game of chance in which winners are chosen by lots, लॉटरी। 2. gamble, जुआ।

lotus (लोटस) ***n.*** a kind of water lily, कमल, पंकज।

loud (लाउड) ***adj.*** 1. producing much noise, ऊँचा। 2. noisy, कोलाहलपूर्ण। 3. gaudy, भड़कीला, चटकीला (रंग)। ***adv.*** loudly, ज़ोर से, ऊँचे।

loudly (लाउडली) ***adv.*** in a loud manner, ज़ोर से।

loudspeaker (लाउडस्पीकर) ***n.*** a device for making the sound loud, लाउडस्पीकर, ध्वनि-विस्तारक।

lounge (लाउन्ज) ***v.*** to sit, lie or walk in a relaxed manner, आराम करना। ***n.*** a public room for sitting, लांज, बैठने का कमरा, विश्राम-कक्ष।

louse (लाउस) ***n.*** (plu. lice) 1. a small insect that lives on the skin, जूँ या चीलर। 2. a contemptible person, हेय व्यक्ति।

louver (लूवर) ***n.*** a frame with sloping bands of wood, metal etc., झिलमिली।

lovable (लवेबल) ***adj.*** 1. worthy of love, प्रिय, प्यारा। 2. attractive, आकर्षक।

love (लव) ***v.*** 1. to have a great affection (for, से) प्यार करना, मुहब्बत करना। 2. to feel love (for, से) प्यार हो जाना। ***n.*** 1. affection, प्यार, प्रेम, मुहब्बत। 2. sexual affection, रति। 3. strong liking for a thing, प्यार, प्रेम, मुहब्बत। 4. a loved person, प्रिय व्यक्ति, प्रेमी या प्रेयसी।

love affair (लव अफ़ेअर) ***n.*** romantic relationship between a man and woman, प्रेमसंबंध।

lovelorn (लवलॉर्न) ***n.*** deprived of love or one's lover, प्रेमी द्वारा ठुकराया हुआ।

lovely (लवली) ***adj.*** 1. beautiful, प्यारा, ख़ूबसूरत। 2. delightful, सुहावना। ***n.*** a beautiful woman, कामिनी, सुंदरी।

lovesick (लवसिक) ***adj.*** pining for love, प्रेमातुर।

loving (लविंग) ***adj.*** feeling or showing love, प्यार-भरा, प्रेममय, स्नेहमय।

low[1] (लो) ***v.*** to moo, रंभाना।

low[2] ***adj.*** 1. having little height, नीचा, कम ऊँचा। 2. of small extent upward, निचला, निम्न, नीचा। 3. involving relatively small amount, अल्प, कम। 4. not loud, मंद, मद्धिम। ***adv.*** 1. in a low position, नीचे, तले। 2. at a low pitch, मंद स्वर में। 3. cheaply, सस्ते में। ***n.*** low level, निम्न स्तर।

low caste (लो कास्ट) ***n.*** a caste of persons of low social status, छोटी जाति, निम्न जाति।

lower (लोअर) ***adj.*** below someone or something, निचला, अवर, निम्नतर।

L

v. 1. to make or become less, कम होना या करना। 2. to bring to lower level, निम्नस्तर पर लाना। 3. to bring down in rank or estimation, महत्त्व या मान गिराना।

low-key (लो-की) ***adj.*** restrained, संयत।

lowland (लोलैन्ड) ***n.*** low-lying land, नीची ज़मीन, निम्नभूमि।

low tide (लो टाइड) ***n.*** the tide when at its lowest level, भाटा।

loyal (लॉइअल) ***adj.*** faithful, वफ़ादार, निष्ठावान।

loyalty (लॉइअल्टी) ***n.*** the state or quality of being loyal, वफ़ादारी, निष्ठा।

lozenge (लॉज़िन्ज) ***n.*** 1. a rhombus, समचतुर्भुज। 2. a piece of medicated candy, टिकिया।

lubricant (लूब्रिकेन्ट) ***n.*** oil or grease serving to lubricate, लुब्रिकेन्ट, चिकनाई।

lubricate (लूब्रिकेट) ***v.*** to oil or grease, तेल या ग्रीस देना।

lubricious (लूब्रिशस) ***adj.*** 1. oily, चिकना। 2. slippery, फिसलवाँ। 3. lewd, लंपट।

lucid (ल्यूसिड) ***adj.*** 1. easy to understand, प्रांजल, सुबोध। 2. sane, स्वस्थचित्त।

lucidity (ल्यूसिडिटी) ***n.*** the state or quality of being lucid, प्रांजलता, सुबोधता; मानसिक स्वस्थता।

luck (लक) ***n.*** 1. fortune, भाग्य, क़िस्मत। 2. good fortune, सौभाग्य।

lucky (लकी) ***adj.*** 1. having good luck, भाग्यशाली। 2. bringing good luck, शुभ।

lucrative (ल्यूक्रेटिव) ***adj.*** profitable, लाभप्रद, लाभदायी।

lucre (लूकर) ***n.*** 1. money, धन। 2. profit, लाभ।

ludicrous (लूडिक्रस) ***adj.*** 1. laughable, हास्यास्पद। 2. absurd, भोंडा, बेतुका। 3. foolish, मूर्खतापूर्ण, बेवकूफ़ी-भरा।

ludo (लूडो) ***n.*** a game of dice, लूडो।

lug (लग) ***v.*** to drag, घसीटना।

luggage (लगिज) ***n.*** a traveller's baggage, सामान, असबाब।

lukewarm (ल्यूकवार्म) ***adj.*** 1. mildly warm, गुनगुना, कुनकुना। 2. expressing little enthusiasm, निरुत्साह, उदासीन।

lull (लल) ***v.*** 1. to cause to soothe, आराम पहुँचाना, राहत देना। 2. to calm, शांत करना। 3. to become quiet, शांत हो जाना। ***n.*** a period of quiet or inactivity, सन्नाटा।

lullaby (ललबाइ) ***n.*** a song with which to lull a child to sleep, लोरी।

lumbago (लम्बेगो) ***n.*** backache, कमर-दर्द।

lumbar (लम्बर) ***adj.*** in the lower back, कमर में होनेवाला, कमर का।

lumber (लम्बर) ***n.*** 1. timber, इमारती लकड़ी। 2. useless household articles, काठ-कबाड़। ***v.*** 1. to cut trees into timber, (पेड़ काटकर) इमारती लकड़ी तैयार करना। 2. to move in a clumsy way, भद्दे ढंग से चलना। 3. to overburden, लाद देना।

lumberman (लम्बरमैन) ***n.*** 1. a timber merchant, काष्ठ-व्यवसायी। 2. a dealer of discarded things, कबाड़ी।

luminary (लूमिनरी) ***n.*** 1. a light-giving celestial body, नक्षत्र। 2. a notable person, लब्धप्रतिष्ठ

L

व्यक्ति, जाना-माना व्यक्ति।

luminosity (ल्यूमिनॉसिटी) ***n.*** light, प्रकाश।

luminous (ल्यूमिनस) ***adj.*** 1. shining, चमकता हुआ, प्रकाशमान। 2. clear, स्पष्ट।

lump (लम्प) ***n.*** 1. a small solid mass or piece, डला, ढेला। 2. an abnormal swelling, सूजन, गाँठ, गूमड़। ***v.*** 1. to collect into a mass, डले या ढेले बनाना। 2. to grow into lumps, ढेले बनना। 3. to consider as a single group, एक ही मानना। 4. to move in a heavy manner, भद्दे ढंग से चलना।

lump sum (लम्प सम) ***n.*** a relatively large sum of money paid at one time, एकमुश्त दी जानेवाली मोटी रकम।

lumpy (लम्पी) ***adj.*** full of lumps, डलेदार, ढेलेदार।

lunacy (ल्यूनेसी) ***n.*** 1. insanity, पागलपन, उन्माद। 2. foolishness, मूर्खता।

lunar (ल्यूनर) ***adj.*** of the moon, चंद्रमा-संबंधी, चांद्र।

lunatic (ल्यूनेटिक) ***adj.*** insane, पागल। ***n.*** an insane person, पागल व्यक्ति।

lunatic asylum ***n.*** a mental hospital, मानसिक चिकित्सालय, पागलख़ाना।

lunch (लन्च) ***n.*** a meal taken at midday, दोपहर का भोजन, मध्याह्न-भोजन, लंच। ***v.*** to eat lunch, मध्याह्न-भोजन करना, लंच करना।

lung (लन्ग) ***n.*** an organ in the chest, फेफड़ा, फुप्फुस।

lurch (लर्च) ***v.*** to stagger, लड़खड़ाना। ***n.*** an awkward position, भोंड़ी या गड़बड़ स्थिति।

lure (ल्यूर) ***v.*** to entice, लुभाना, आकृष्ट करना। ***n.*** 1. attraction, आकर्षण। 2. temptation, प्रलोभन। 3. bait or decoy, चारा।

luscious (लशस) ***adj.*** 1. delicious, ज़ायकेदार, स्वादिष्ट, सरस। 2. attractive, appealing, लुभावना, कमनीय।

lush (लश) ***adj.*** 1. ripe and full of juice, पका तथा रसदार, सरस। 2. abounding in lavish growth, हरा-भरा। 3. luxurious, विलासी, ठाठदार।

lust (लस्ट) ***n.*** 1. intense sexual desire, कामाग्नि, कामुकता। 2. intense desire, प्रबल इच्छा।

lustre, luster (लस्टर) ***n.*** 1. shine, brightness, चमक, दीप्ति। 2. beauty, कांति, रौनक़। 3. polish, पालिश। ***v.*** to make or become lustrous, चमकदार बनना या बनाना।

lustrous (लस्ट्रस) ***adj.*** 1. shining, चमकता हुआ, प्रदीप्त। 2. bright, चमकीला, उजला।

lusty (लस्टी) ***adj.*** strong, robust, हृष्ट-पुष्ट।

lute (ल्यूट) ***n.*** a stringed instrument, वीणा।

luxuriate (लग्ज़ूरिएट) ***v.*** to take pleasure, मज़े लेना, मौज करना।

luxurious (लग्ज़ूरिअस) ***adj.*** given to luxury, विलासिताप्रिय, विलासी।

luxury (लग्ज़री) ***n.*** 1. something costly but not necessary that provides comfort or enjoyment, विलासिता की वस्तु। 2. the enjoyment of rich living, सुखभोग, विलासिता।

lymph (लिम्फ़) ***n.*** a colourless fluid containing white blood cells, लसीका।

lynch (लिन्च) ***v.*** to oppress, सताना, अत्याचार करना।

lynx (लिंक्स) ***n.*** a wild cat, बनबिलाव।

lyre (लाइर) ***n.*** a stringed musical instrument, वीणा।

lyric (लिरिक) ***adj.*** गेय। ***n.*** a short poem of songlike, गीत, प्रगीत।

lyrical (लिरिकल) ***adj.*** lyric, प्रगीतात्मक।

lyricist (लिरिसिस्ट) ***n.*** one who writes lyrics, प्रगीतकार।

M, m (एम) ***n.*** the thirteenth letter of the English alphabet, अंग्रेज़ी वर्णमाला का तेरहवाँ वर्ण।

macabre (मकाब्र) ***adj.*** ghastly, बीभत्स।

macaroni (मैकॉरोनी) ***n.*** a food made from flour paste, मैदे का एक व्यंजन, मैकरोनी।

macaw (मकॉ) ***n.*** a parrot with long tail, लंबी पूँछवाला तोता।

mace (मेस) ***n.*** 1. a rod as a sign of power, राजदंड। 2. a medieval weapon, गदा। 3. a spice, जावित्री।

machiavellian (मैकिअवेलिअन) ***adj.*** deceitful, धोखेबाज़, तिकड़मी।

machinations (मैकिनेशन्ज़) ***n.*** (plu.) clever scheming, कपट-योजना, षड्यंत्र।

machine (मशीन) ***n.*** an apparatus to perform work, मशीन, यंत्र, कल। ***v.*** to make or produce by machine, मशीन से बनाना, उत्पादन करना।

machine-gun (मशीन-गन) ***n.*** an automatic gun, मशीनगन।

machinery (मशीनरी) ***n.*** 1. a set of machines, यंत्रसमूह, यंत्रावली, मशीनरी। 2. the working parts of a machine, मशीन के चलनेवाले हिस्से। 3. system or organisation, पद्धति, संघटन या तंत्र।

mackintosh (मैकिन्टॉश) ***n.*** a raincoat, बरसाती।

macrame (मैक्रमे) ***n.*** a fringe, झालर, गोट।

mad (मैड) ***adj.*** 1. insane, पागल, बावला, उन्मत्त। 2. foolish, मूर्ख। 3. angry, क्रुद्ध। 4. excited, उत्तेजित, आवेशयुक्त।

madam (मैडम) ***n.*** a form of address to a woman, मालकिन, गृहिणी, देवीजी, महोदया।

madcap (मैडकैप) ***adj.*** crazy, सिरफ़िरा, सनकी।

madden (मैडन) ***v.*** 1. to make or become mad, पागल बनना या बनाना। 2. to make or become angry, क्रुद्ध होना या करना।

madhouse (मैडहाउस) ***n.*** a mental hospital, पागलख़ाना।

madness (मैडनिस) ***n.*** 1. the state of being mad, पागलपन, विक्षिप्तता। 2. a foolish act, folly, बेवकूफ़ी का काम, पागलपन।

maestro (माइस्ट्रो) ***n.*** 1. a distinguished musician, महान संगीतज्ञ। 2. a master of any art, महान कलाकार।

mafia (माफ़िआ) ***n.*** a secret terrorist or criminal group, माफ़िया।

magazine (मैगज़ीन) ***n.*** 1. a periodic publication, पत्रिका, रसाला, मैगज़ीन। 2. a building for storing weapons, शस्त्रागार। 3. a chamber in a gun for holding cartridges, पेटा, मैगज़ीन।

magenta (मजेन्टा) ***adj.*** bright purplish red, जामुनी, मैजेंटा। ***n.*** जामुनी रंग।

maggot (मैगट) ***n.*** a larva, इल्ली।

magic (मैजिक) ***n.*** the art of controlling and influencing events by supernatural power, जादू।

magical (मैजिकल) ***adj.*** जादुई, जादू-भरा।

magician (मजिशन) ***n.*** a person who

is skilled in magic, जादूगर।

magic lantern ***n.*** a slide projector, चित्रदर्शी।

magisterial (मैजिस्टिरिअल) ***adj.*** 1. of or relating to a magistrate, मजिस्ट्रेट-संबंधी। 2. authoritative, आधिकारिक।

magistrate (मैजिस्ट्रेट) ***n.*** a civil officer concerned with the administration of law, मजिस्ट्रेट, दंडाधिकारी।

magma (मैग्मा) ***n.*** the molten matter under the earth's crust, मैग्मा।

magnanimity (मैग्नेनिमिटी) ***n.*** the quality of being magnanimous, विशालहृदयता, उदारता।

magnanimous (मैग्नैनिमस) ***adj.*** generous and noble, विशालहृदय, उदार।

magnate (मैग्नेट) ***n.*** a wealthy and powerful person, गण्यमान्य तथा प्रभावी व्यक्ति।

magnesium (मैग्नीशियम) ***n.*** a metal, मैग्नेशियम।

magnet (मैग्निट) ***n.*** a body that attracts iron, चुंबक।

magnetism (मैग्निटिज़म) ***n.*** 1. the property of attraction of a magnet, चुंबक शक्ति, चुंबकत्व। 2. power of attraction, आकर्षण-शक्ति।

magnetize (मैग्नेटाइज़) ***v.*** to give magnetic properties to, चुंबक बना देना।

magnification (मैग्निफ़िकेशन) ***n.*** the act of magnifying, बड़ा करना, आवर्धन।

magnificent (मैग्निफ़िसन्ट) ***adj.*** imposing, splendid, भव्य, शानदार, महान।

magnify (मैग्निफ़ाइ) ***v.*** to increase in size, आवर्धन करना, बढ़ाना।

magnitude (मैग्निट्यूड) ***n.*** 1. size or extent, आकार-प्रकार या विस्तार। 2. importance, महत्त्व।

magpie (मैगपाई) ***n.*** 1. a noisy bird, मैना की जाति का पक्षी। 2. a chatterer, बातूनी।

mahogany (महॉगनि) ***n.*** a tree and its wood, महोगनी (वृक्ष और उसकी लकड़ी)।

mahout (महाउट) ***n.*** an elephant driver, महावत।

maid (मेड) ***n.*** a woman servant, नौकरानी, दाई, दासी।

maiden (मेडन) ***n.*** 1. a young unmarried woman, कन्या, कुमारी, अविवाहित स्त्री। 2. an over in which no runs are scored, मेडन ओवर, शून्य ओवर। ***adj.*** 1. unmarried, अविवाहित (स्त्री)। 2. first, पहली बार का, पहला, प्रथम। 3. untried, unused, अप्रयुक्त, अव्यवहृत।

maid servant (मेड सर्वेन्ट) a female servant, नौकरानी।

mail (मेल) ***n.*** 1. letters etc., sent or received by post, डाक। 2. the postal system, डाक-व्यवस्था। ***v.*** to post, डाक से भेजना।

mail train (मेल ट्रेन) ***n.*** a train that carries the mail, डाकगाड़ी।

maim (मेम) ***v.*** 1. to cripple, पंगु/अपंग बना देना, लंगड़ा-लूला कर देना। 2. to make defective, बिगाड़ देना।

main (मेन) ***adj.*** chief, मुख्य, प्रमुख, प्रधान। ***n.*** the main cable or pipe, मुख्य तार या नल।

mainland (मेनलैन्ड) ***n.*** the main part of the country, मुख्य भूभाग।

mainly (मेनली) ***adv.*** chiefly, मुख्यत:।

mains (मेन्स) ***n.*** (plu.) the main

cables, (बिजली के) मुख्य तार।

mainstay (मेनस्टे) ***n.*** the chief support, मुख्य सहारा, संबल।

maintain (मेन्टेन) ***v.*** 1. to carry on, बनाए रखना, चलाए रखना। 2. to retain or preserve, रखे रहना, सँभाले रहना। 3. to keep in good condition, अच्छी हालत में रखना। 4. to sustain, पालन या भरण-पोषण करना। 5. to defend, रक्षा करना, बचाना। 6. to assert, दावे से कहना, (सत्य) घोषित करना। 7. to support, समर्थन करना।

maintenance (मेन्टिनेन्स) ***n.*** 1. the act of maintaining or the state of being maintained, चलाए चलना, बनाए रखना, रखरखाव, अनुरक्षण, पालन-पोषण। 2. the provision made for a spouse after divorce, गुज़ारा, निर्वाह-भत्ता।

maize (मेज़) ***n.*** corn, मक्का, मक्की।

majestic (मजेस्टिक) ***adj.*** 1. stately, royal, राजसी, शाही। 2. grand, शानदार, भव्य।

majesty (मैजिस्टी) ***n.*** 1. sovereign power, kingliness, राजसत्ता, शाहीपन। 2. grandeur, impressiveness, शान, गौरव।

major (मेजर) ***adj.*** 1. larger in extent, number etc., अधिकांश, बड़ा, भारी। 2. chief, मुख्य, प्रधान। ***n.*** 1. a military officer, मेजर। 2. an adult, वयस्क, बालिग।

majority (मेजॉरिटी) ***n.*** 1. the greater part of the total number of a given group or class, the greater number, बहुमत। 2. the status of legal age, वयस्कता।

make (मेक) ***v.*** (made, making) 1. to create, बनाना, रचना, निर्मित करना। 2. to form or shape, रूपायित करना, बनाना। 3. to compel, मजबूर या विवश करना। 4. to do or perform, करना, निष्पादित करना। 5. to arrive at, पहुँचना। 6. to achieve, gain or acquire, प्राप्त करना। 7. to prepare, तैयार करना। 8. to develop into, बनना। □ **make do,** काम चलाना; **make for,** की ओर बढ़ना, में सहायक होना; **make fun of,** मज़ाक उड़ाना; **make good,** (i) सफल होना, समृद्ध होना, (ii) क्षतिपूर्ति करना; **make it**, सफलता प्राप्त करना; **make out,** समझ पाना; **make over,** सौंप देना; **make up,** बनाना, तैयार करना; समझौता करना; सजाना। ***n.*** 1. the act or process of making, बनाव, बनावट। 2. brand, छाप।

make-believe (मेक-बिलीव) ***n.*** a pretence, बहाना, स्वाँग।

maker (मेकर) ***n.*** one who makes something, बनानेवाला, रचयिता, निर्माता।

makeshift (मेकशिफ़्ट) ***adj. & n.*** serving as a temporary substitute, अस्थायी स्थानापन्न।

make-up (मेकप) ***n.*** 1. the way something is made up, बनावट, रचना। 2. cosmetics applied to the face, रूप-सज्जा के लिए प्रयुक्त सौंदर्य-प्रसाधन। 3. a person's character and temperament, चरित्र तथा स्वभाव।

mal-adjustment (मैलजस्टमेन्ट) ***n.*** poor adjustment, कुसमंजन, मेल न बैठना।

mal-administration (मैलडमिनि-स्ट्रेशन) ***n.*** bad or poor administration, कुशासन।

malady (मैलडी) ***n.*** illness, बीमारी, रोग।

malaise (मैलेज़) ***n.*** 1. feeling of uneasiness, बेचैनी, घबराहट, कष्ट,

तकलीफ़। 2. feeling of illness, अस्वस्थता।

malaria (मलेरिआ) ***n.*** a disease caused by mosquitoes, मलेरिया।

malcontent (मैलकन्टेन्ट) ***adj.*** discontented, असंतुष्ट, विक्षुब्ध।

male (मेल) ***adj.*** 1. pertaining to the male sex, नर-संबंधी, नर। 2. of a man, masculine, मर्दों-जैसा, मर्दाना, पुरुषोचित। ***n.*** the male person or animal, नर, पुरुष।

malefaction (मैलिफ़ैक्शन) ***n.*** a wrong act, दुष्कर्म, ग़लत काम।

malevolence (मलेवलेन्स) ***n.*** ill-will, द्वेष।

malevolent (मलेवलेन्ट) ***adj.*** wishing harm to others, द्वेषी।

malfunction (मैलफंक्शन) ***v.*** to fail to function properly, ठीक ढंग से काम न करना। ***n.*** failure to function properly, ठीक ढंग से काम न करने की अवस्था।

malice (मैलिस) ***n.*** ill-will, द्वेष, दुर्भाव।

malicious (मैलिशस) ***adj.*** feeling or expressing malice, द्वेषी या द्वेषपूर्ण।

malign (मलाइन) ***adj.*** harmful, अहितकर, अमांगलिक। ***v.*** to defame, बदनाम करना।

malignant (मलिग्नेन्ट) ***adj.*** 1. feeling or showing ill-will, द्वेषी या द्वेषपूर्ण। 2. highly injurious, fatal, संघातक, घातक।

malignity (मलिग्निटी) ***n.*** the condition of being malign, अमंगल, अहित।

malinger (मलिन्गर) ***v.*** to avoid work by pretending to be sick, काम से जी चुराना, काम से बचने के लिए बीमारी का बहाना बनाना।

mall (माल) ***n.*** 1. a shaded path, छायादार मार्ग, माल रोड। 2. a shopping centre, बाज़ार।

malleable (मैलिएबल) ***adj.*** 1. capable of being shaped by hammering, (धातु) जिसे पीटकर कोई रूप दिया जा सके, घन-वर्धनीय। 2. easily influenced, जिसे सरलता से प्रभावित किया जा सके, मान जानेवाला।

mallet (मैलिट) ***n.*** a wooden hammer, मूँगरा, मोगरा, हथौड़ी।

malnutrition (मैलन्युट्रिशन) ***n.*** poor nutrition, कुपोषण।

malodorous (मैलोडरस) ***adj.*** having a bad smell, बदबूदार, दुर्गंधित।

malpractice (मैलप्रैक्टिस) ***n.*** improper or negligent treatment, professional misconduct, कदाचार।

malt (मॉल्ट) ***n.*** 1. sprouted dried barley (used for brewing) भिगोकर सुखाए हुए जौ। 2. an alcoholic beverage brewed from malt, माल्ट ह्विस्की।

maltreat (मैलट्रीट) ***v.*** to treat badly or cruelly, दुर्व्यवहार करना।

mama (मामा) ***n.*** mother, माँ।

mammal (मैमल) ***n.*** any animal fed when young on milk from the mothers body, स्तनपायी।

mammalian (मैमेलिअन) ***adj.*** of mammals, स्तनपाइयों से संबद्ध।

mammoth (मैमथ) ***n.*** an extinct elephant, मैमथ। ***adj.*** of gigantic size, विशाल, विशालकाय, भारी-भरकम।

man (मैन) ***n.*** (plu. men) 1. a human being, आदमी, मनुष्य, मानव, इनसान। 2. a person, आदमी, व्यक्ति। 3. an adult male person, a manly person, नर, पुरुष, वयस्क। 4. a male servant, नौकर, कामगार, कर्मी। 5. a soldier, सैनिक। 6. a piece in the game of chess, गोटी, मोहरा, प्यादा। ***v.***

M

to provide with men for operation, आदमी देना या लगाना।

manacle (मैनेकल) ***n.*** a handcuff, हथकड़ी। ***v.*** to put manacles on, हथकड़ी पहनाना।

manage (मैनिज) ***v.*** 1. to control, नियंत्रित करना। 2. to handle, चलाना। 3. to be able to cope, काम निकालना, सँभालना। 4. to administer, शासित करना, प्रबंध करना।

manageable (मैनिजेबल) ***adj.*** that can be managed, जिसे नियंत्रण में रखा जा सके, जिसे सँभाला जा सके, प्रबंधनीय।

management (मैनिजमेन्ट) ***n.*** 1. the act of managing, प्रबंध, प्रबंधन, व्यवस्था, संचालन। 2. managers or employers collectively, प्रबंधकगण, व्यवस्थापकगण।

manager (मैनिजर) ***n.*** 1. one who manages, प्रबंधक, व्यवस्थापक, मैनेजर। 2. a person who is in charge of a team, मैनेजर। [Fem. manageress, व्यवस्थापिका]

mandamus (मैन्डेमस) ***n.*** a writ issued to perform a specified duty, परमादेश।

mandate (मैन्डेट) ***n.*** 1. a command, अधिदेश। 2. the support given to the government policy through an electoral victory, जनसमर्थन, जनादेश। ***v.*** to give by a mandate, अधिदेश देना, जनादेश देना।

mandatory (मैन्डेटरी) ***adj.*** a compulsory, अनिवार्य, ज़रूरी।

mandible (मैन्डिबल) ***n.*** a jaw or jaw-like part, जबड़ा, चोंच।

mane (मेन) ***n.*** the long hair on a horse's or lion's neck, घोड़े या शेर की गरदन पर के लंबे बाल, अयाल।

man-eater (मैन-ईटर) ***n.*** any animal that eats human flesh, नरभक्षी।

maneuver (मनूवर) ***n.*** = manoeuvre.

manganese (मैन्गानीज़) ***n.*** a metal, मैंगनीज।

manger (मेन्जर) ***n.*** a box or trough from which cattle feed, नाँद।

mangle (मैन्गल) ***v.*** to spoil, नष्ट करना, ख़राब करना।

mango (मैन्गो) ***n.*** a tree and its fruit, आम।

manhandle (मैनहैन्डल) ***v.*** to handle roughly using force, दुर्व्यवहार करना, धींगामुश्ती करना, हाथापाई करना।

manhour (मैनऑवर) ***n.*** the unit of work one person can do in one hour, श्रम-घंटा।

mania (मेनिआ) ***n.*** 1. a mental disorder, उन्माद, पागलपन। 2. extreme enthusiasm, सनक, झक।

maniac (मेनिऐक) ***n.*** 1. suffering from mania, insane person, उन्मत्त व्यक्ति, पागल। 2. one with excessive enthusiasm, झक्की।

manicure (मैनिक्यूर) ***n.*** care for the fingernails, नख-प्रसाधन।

manifest (मैनिफ़ेस्ट) ***adj.*** clearly visible, स्पष्ट, प्रकट। ***v.*** 1. to show clearly, स्पष्ट रूप से दिखलाना, प्रकट करना। 2. to appear in visible form, प्रकट होना। 3. to express, अभिव्यक्त करना। ***n.*** a list of cargo/passengers, माल-सूची, यात्री-सूची।

manifesto (मैनिफ़ेस्टो) ***n.*** a public declaration or statement of aims and policies of a political party, राजनीतिक दल का घोषणापत्र।

manifold (मैनिफ़ोल्ड) ***adj.*** of many kinds, तरह-तरह का, बहुविध, नानारूप।

manipulate (मैनिप्युलेट) ***v.*** 1. to operate or use skillfully, कौशल से काम चलाना। 2. to manage deceitfully, तिकड़म से काम करना, जोड़-तोड़ भिड़ाना।

manipulation (मैनिप्युलेशन) ***n.*** 1. the act of manipulating or something manipulated, जोड़-तोड़, तिकड़म।

mankind (मैनकाइन्ड) ***n.*** humanity, मनुष्य-जाति, मानव-जाति।

manliness (मैन्लिनिस) ***n.*** the quality of being manly, पौरुष, मर्दानापन।

manly (मैन्ली) ***adj.*** having qualities generally attributed to a man, पुरुषोचित, मर्दाना।

mannequin (मैनिकिन) ***n.*** 1. a woman displaying clothes in a fashion show, मॉडल। 2. a life-size dummy used to display clothes, डम्मी।

manner (मैनर) ***n.*** 1. a way of doing, ढंग, रीति। 2. a person's bearing and behaviour, रंग-ढंग, चाल-ढाल। 3. kind, प्रकार। 4. a style, शैली। 5. (plu.) etiquette, be-haviour, व्यवहार, शिष्टाचार। 6. (plu.) the prevailing customs, प्रचलित रीति-रिवाज।

mannerism (मैनरिज़म) ***n.*** a peculiarity of manner, बनावटी/विचित्र व्यवहार।

mannerly (मैनर्ली) ***adj.*** polite, शिष्ट, शिष्टतापूर्ण।

manoeuvre, maneuver (मनूवर) ***n.*** 1. a planned action or movement, युक्ति। 2. a deceptive action or move, चाल, तिकड़म। 3. a large-scale military exercise, युद्धाभ्यास। ***v.*** 1. to perform a military manoeuvre, युद्धाभ्यास करना। 2. to manipulate, जोड़-तोड़ करना, तिकड़म करना।

manpower (मैनपावर) ***n.*** the total number of people needed for a job, जनशक्ति।

mansion (मैन्शन) ***n.*** a large and imposing house, भवन, कोठी, हवेली।

mantelpiece (मैन्टलपीस) ***n.*** a shelf above a fire place, आतिशख़ाना।

manual (मैन्युअल) ***adj.*** 1. of the hands, हाथों का। 2. operated by hand, हस्तचालित। 3. physical, शारीरिक। ***n.*** 1. a handbook, पुस्तिका, गुटका। 2. a book of rules, नियमावली।

manually (मैन्युअली) ***adv.*** by hand or hands, हाथ या हाथों से।

manufacture (मैन्युफ़ैक्चर) ***v.*** 1. to make by machinery on a large scale, to produce, उत्पादन करना, निर्माण करना। 2. to make, बनाना। ***n.*** the process of manufacturing, उत्पादन-कार्य, निर्माण।

manufacturer (मैन्युफ़ैक्चरर) ***n.*** one who manufactures (goods), उत्पादक, निर्माता।

manure (मन्युअर) ***n.*** material used to fertilize soil, खाद। ***v.*** to apply manure to, खाद देना या डालना।

manuscript (मैन्युस्क्रिप्ट) ***n.*** a handwritten or typewritten version of a book, पांडुलिपि।

many (मैनी) ***adj.*** a large number of, numerous, अनेक, बहुत से, बहुतेरे। ***n.*** 1. a large number, बहुत बड़ी संख्या। 2. **the many** (plu.) most people, अधिकतर लोग। ***pron.*** a large number of persons or things, बहुत अधिक व्यक्ति या वस्तुएँ।

M

map (मैप) ***n.*** a diagrammatic representation of earth's surface or part of it, नक़्शा, मानचित्र। ***v.*** to make a map of, मानचित्र बनाना, नक़्शा बनाना।

mar (मार) ***v.*** to spoil, बिगाड़ना, बिगाड़ देना।

marathon (मैरथन) ***n.*** 1. a long distance foot race, लंबी दौड़। 2. any long or arduous task, कोई लंबा या कठिन काम।

marble (मार्बल) ***n.*** 1. a kind of stone, संगमरमर, मार्बल। 2. a small ball of glass, कंचा।

marbled (मार्बल्ड) ***adj.*** variegated, चितकबरा।

March (मार्च) ***n.*** the third month of the year, मार्च (महीना)।

march (मार्च) ***v.*** 1. to walk with regular steps like a soldier, मार्च करना, प्रयाण करना। 2. to progress steadily, to proceed, अग्रसर होना, आगे बढ़ना। ***n.*** 1. the act of marching, मार्च, प्रयाण। 2. a long walk, लंबी पदयात्रा। 3. progress, प्रगति।

mare (मेअर) ***n.*** a female horse or donkey, घोड़ी या गधी।

margarine (मार्जरिन) ***n.*** a substitute for butter, कृत्रिम मक्खन, मारजरीन।

margin (मार्जिन) ***n.*** 1. an edge or border, किनारा, सीमा। 2. the blank space bordering the written or printed page, हाशिया, मार्जिन। 3. the vertical line on a page delineating this space, उपांत-रेखा, मार्जिन। 4. the amount by which one thing differs from another, अंतर। 5. the profit on a transaction, किसी सौदे में होनेवाला लाभ।

marginal (मार्जिनल) ***adj.*** 1. written in a margin, हाशिए में लिखा/छपा हुआ। 2. of or at an edge, किनारे का। 3. very slight in amount, बहुत थोड़ा, न्यूनतम, नाममात्र का। 4. close to a lower limit, सीमांत; marginal cost, सीमांत लागत।

marginalize (मार्जिनलाइज) ***v.*** to make less important, किनारे कर देना।

marigold (मैरिगोल्ड) ***n.*** a plant and its flower, गेंदा।

marijuana (मैरिजुआना) ***n.*** the dried leaves of hemp plant used as drug, गाँजा।

marinade (मैरिनेड) ***n.*** a seasoned flavoured liquid, सिरका।

marinate (मैरिनेट) ***v.*** to soak in marinade, सिरके में डुबाना या रखना।

marine (मरीन) ***adj.*** 1. of or relating to the sea, समुद्री। 2. of or relating to shipping, नौवहन-संबंधी। ***n.*** a soldier serving on the ship, नौसैनिक।

mariner (मैरिनर) ***n.*** a sailor, नाविक।

marital (मैरिटल) ***adj.*** of marriage, वैवाहिक।

maritime (मैरिटाइम) ***adj.*** 1. of sea, समुद्री। 2. of shore, तटीय। 3. of shipping, नौवहन-संबंधी।

mark (मार्क) ***n.*** 1. a visible trace as a spot or dent, चिह्न, निशान। 2. a written or printed symbol, मारका, चिह्न, निशान। 3. a distinguishing feature or characteristic, लक्षण, चिह्न। 4. a unit awarded for the merit, अंक। 5. a lasting impression, छाप। 6. a target, लक्ष्य। ***v.*** 1. to make a visible impression on, निशान लगाना। 2. to distinguish with a mark, मारका लगाना। 3. to give numbers, अंक देना। 4. to watch carefully, ध्यान देना।

marked (मार्क्ड) ***adj.*** 1. having a mark, चिह्नित, निशान लगा या दाग़ा हुआ। 2. clearly noticeable, स्पष्ट, दृश्य।

marker (मार्कर) ***n.*** 1. a person who marks, मार्का लगानेवाला। 2. an object which marks a place, किसी स्थान का सूचक चिह्न।

market (मार्किट) ***n.*** 1. a place where people meet to buy & sell goods, बाज़ार, मंडी, हाट। 2. trade or commerce, व्यापार या वाणिज्य। ***v.*** 1. to do shopping, बाज़ार करना। 2. to sell, बेचना।

marketing (मार्किटिंग) ***n.*** the art of selling, विपणन।

marksman (मार्क्समैन) ***n.*** one skilled at shooting, निशानेबाज़।

marmalade (मार्मलेड) ***n.*** a kind of jam, मुरब्बा।

maroon (मरून) ***adj.*** brownish red, करौंदे के रंग का, करौंदिया, मारून। ***n.*** brownish red colour, मारून, करौंदिया रंग।

marquetry (मार्किट्री) ***n.*** inlaid work in wood, brass, ivory etc., जड़ाऊ काम, जड़ाई।

marriage (मैरिज) ***n.*** 1. a wedding, wedlock, विवाह, शादी। 2. a close union, घनिष्ठता, गठबंधन।

marriageable (मैरिजेबल) ***adj.*** fit for marriage, विवाह के योग्य, विवाह-योग्य।

marrow (मैरो) ***n.*** 1. the fatty material inside the bones, मज्जा।

marry (मैरी) ***v.*** 1. to accept someone as one's husband or wife, विवाह करना, शादी करना। 2. to give in marriage, शादी कर देना। 3. unite closely, घनिष्ठतापूर्वक संबद्ध होना, जुड़ना।

Mars (मार्ज़) ***n.*** the fourth planet from the sun, मंगल ग्रह।

marsh (मार्श) ***n.*** low watery land, दलदल।

marshal (मार्शल) ***n.*** 1. an army officer, मार्शल। 2. a high administrative officer, मार्शल। ***v.*** 1. to arrange in order, क्रम से रखना या लगाना, क्रमबद्ध करना, व्यवस्थित करना। 2. to guide or lead, साथ ले जाना, मार्गप्रदर्शन करना।

marshy (मार्शी) ***adj.*** of or like a marsh, दलदल से भरा, दलदला।

mart (मार्ट) ***n.*** a market, मार्केट, बाज़ार।

martial (मार्शल) ***adj.*** 1. of or concerning war, युद्ध-संबंधी। 2. of or concerning soldiers, सैनिक-संबंधी, फ़ौजी।

martial law ***n.*** military rule, सैनिक-शासन।

martyr (मार्टर) ***n.*** 1. one who sacrifices oneself for a cause, आत्मबलिदानी, बलिदानी, शहीद। 2. one who endures great sufferings, कष्टभोगी। ***v.*** 1. to put to death, बलि चढ़ाना। 2. to give one's life for a cause, शहीद होना।

martyrdom (मार्टर्डम) ***n.*** 1. the state of being a martyr, बलिदान, शहादत। 2. the death or suffering of a martyr, आहुति, बलिदान।

marvel (मार्वल) ***n.*** a wonderful thing, अद्‌भुत वस्तु, चमत्कार। ***v.*** to be filled with wonder, आश्चर्यचकित हो जाना।

marvellous (मार्वलस) ***adj.*** 1. wonderful, चमत्कारिक, अद्‌भुत। 2. excellent, बहुत बढ़िया।

M

Marxism (मार्क्सिज़म) ***n.*** the doctrines of Karl Marx, मार्क्सवाद।

mascara (मैस्कारा) ***n.*** a cosmetic for darkening the eyelashes, बरौनियाँ रंगने का प्रसाधन।

mascot (मैस्कॉट) ***n.*** a person or thing thought to bring good luck, शुभंकर, शगुन।

masculine (मैस्क्यूलिन) ***adj.*** 1. related to class of words that refer to males, पुल्लिंग। 2. of or pertaining to the male sex, मर्दों जैसा, मर्दाना, पुरुषोचित।

masculinity (मैस्क्यूलिनिटी) ***n.*** the quality or state of being masculine, पुंसत्व, पौरुष, मर्दानगी।

mash (मैश) ***n.*** a soft pulpy mass, मलीदा। ***v.*** to crush into mash, मलीदा करना, मसलना।

mask (मास्क) ***n.*** 1. the covering worn over the face, नक़ाब। 2. a likeness of face or head, मुख़ौटा। ***v.*** 1. to put on a mask, नक़ाब पहनना, मुख़ौटा लगाना। 2. to conceal, छिपाना।

masked (मास्क्ड) ***adj.*** having put on a mask, नक़ाबपोश।

mason (मेसन) ***n.*** one who builds with bricks or stones, राजमिस्त्री या संगतराश।

masonry (मेसनरी) ***n.*** 1. bricklaying or stonelaying, राजगीरी या संगतराशी। 2. brick work or stone work, चिनाई, पत्थर की चिनाई।

masquerade (मास्करेड) ***n.*** false outward show, दिखावा। ***v.*** to pretend to be, स्वाँग रचना, बनना।

mass (मैस) ***n.*** 1. a unit of matter with no specific shape, पिंड, पुंज, ढेर। 2. a large number or amount, राशि। ***v.*** to gather together, to assemble, इकट्ठा होना, ढेर लगना, जमा होना। ***adj.*** 1. done or occurring on a large scale, बड़े परिमाण में होनेवाला। 2. consisting of a mass or large number (of people), जिसमें अधिक (लोग) सम्मिलित हों।

massacre (मैसेकर) ***n.*** merciless killing of large number of people, नरसंहार, जनसंहार। ***v.*** to kill in large number, नरसंहार करना।

massage (मैसाज) ***n.*** the act of rubbing and pressing the parts of body, मालिश, चंपी। ***v.*** to give a massage to, मालिश/चंपी करना।

masseur (मैसर) ***n.*** a person who gives massages, मालिश करनेवाला, मालिशी। [Fem. masseuse मैसिज़]

massive (मैसिव) ***adj.*** 1. heavy, bulky, भारी, भारी-भरकम। 2. imposing, भव्य, विशाल।

mass media ***n.*** the means of communication that reach large number of people, जनसंचार।

mass production ***n.*** production on a large scale, बड़े पैमाने पर होनेवाला उत्पादन।

mast (मास्ट) ***n.*** 1. a pole for carrying flags and sails on the ship, मस्तूल। 2. a flag pole, ध्वजदंड। 3. a pole, खंभा।

master (मास्टर) ***n.*** 1. the owner, मालिक, स्वामी। 2. one in authority, अधिपति, सरकार। 3. a head of the household, गृहस्वामी। 4. a male teacher, मास्टर, अध्यापक। ***adj.*** 1. most important, अत्यधिक महत्त्वपूर्ण। 2. chief, मुख्य, प्रमुख, प्रधान। ***v.*** 1. to become proficient in, मास्टर

हो जाना, कुशलता प्राप्त कर लेना। 2. to bring under control, नियंत्रित करना, क़ाबू में लाना।

master key ***n.*** a key that opens a number of locks, मास्टर कुंजी।

masterly (मास्टरली) ***adj.*** showing great skill, कौशलपूर्ण, उच्च कोटि का।

mastermind (मास्टरमाइन्ड) ***n.*** a person of great ability, सुयोग्य व्यक्ति, निपुण व्यक्ति, दिमाग़दार आदमी। ***v.*** to plan and direct, योजना बनाना तथा कार्यान्वित करना।

masterpiece, masterwork (मास्टरपीस, मास्टरवर्क) ***n.*** a best piece of work, सर्वोत्तम कृति या रचना।

mastery (मास्टरी) ***n.*** 1. full understanding of a subject, विषयगत पूर्ण निपुणता। 2. outstanding skill, कौशल।

masthead (मास्टहेड) ***n.*** the top of mast, मस्तूल की चोटी या सिरा।

masticate (मैस्टिकेट) ***v.*** to chew, चबाना।

mastication (मैस्टिकेशन) ***n.*** the act of masticating, चबाना, चर्वण।

masturbate (मैस्टर्बेट) ***v.*** to stimulate sex organ by hand, हस्तमैथुन करना।

masturbation (मैस्टर्बेशन) ***n.*** the act of masturbating, हस्तमैथुन।

mat (मैट) ***n.*** a floor-covering of straw etc., चटाई, मैट। ***v.*** to make or become entangled, उलझना या उलझाना।

matador (मैटडॉर) ***n.*** one who kills a bull in bullfight, द्वंद्व में साँड़ को मारनेवाला।

match[1] (मैच) ***n.*** 1. one equal to another, जोड़। 2. a person considered possible husband or wife, जोड़ीदार, मेल। 3. a marriage, विवाह, शादी। 4. a contest in a game, मैच। ***v.*** 1. to be similar to, समान होना। 2. to find something suitable for use with, मेल खाना। 3. to find a match for, जोड़ मिलना।

match[2] ***n.*** a stick of a matchbox, तीली, काँटी।

match-box (मैच-बॉक्स) ***n.*** a box for holding matches, दियासलाई की डिबिया।

matching (मैचिंग) ***adj.*** (of colours or clothes) which are the same or suited, एक-से, एक-जैसे, मेल के।

matchless (मैचलिस) ***adj.*** unequalled, बेजोड़, अद्वितीय।

mate[1] (मेट) ***n.*** 1. a close associate, सहयोगी, साथी, संगी। 2. a spouse, जीवन-संगी। 3. one of a pair of breeding animals, पशुओं का यौन-साथी। ***v.*** 1. to pair for reproduction, जोड़ा खाना। 2. to join as a pair, संगी या साथी बनना। 3. to marry, विवाह करना।

mate[2] ***n.*** checkmate, किश्त, शहमात।

material (मटीरिअल) ***n.*** 1. the substance from which something can be made, पदार्थ, चीज़, सामग्री। 2. information, facts, जानकारी, तथ्य। 3. cloth, कपड़ा, वस्त्र। ***adj.*** 1. consisting of matter, पदार्थ-संबंधी। 2. physical, भौतिक। 3. bodily, शारीरिक। 4. significant, महत्त्वपूर्ण, तात्त्विक।

materialism (मटीरिअलिज़्म) ***n.*** excessive regard for material well-being rather than spiritual values, भौतिकवाद।

materialize (मटीरिअलाइज़) ***v.*** to appear or happen, प्रकट होना, अस्तित्व ग्रहण करना।

M

maternal (मटर्नल) ***adj.*** 1. of a mother, माता-संबंधी, मातृ-। 2. related through one's mother, ममेरा। 3. motherly, मातृ-सुलभ।

maternity (मटर्निटी) ***n.*** motherhood, मातृत्व। ***adj.*** of pregnant woman or pregnancy, गर्भावस्था या गर्भवती स्त्री से संबद्ध।

mathematician (मैथिमटिशन) ***n.*** one who is skilled in mathematics, गणितज्ञ।

mathematics (मैथिमैटिक्स) ***n.*** the study or science of numbers, गणित, हिसाब।

matinee (मैटिने) ***n.*** an afternoon performance of a theatre, मैटिनी शो।

matriarch (मेट्रिआर्क) ***n.*** the female head of a tribe, कुलमाता।

matriarchy (मेट्रिआर्की) ***n.*** the social system in which the woman is the head of a family, मातृतंत्र।

matricide (मेट्रिसाइड) ***n.*** the act of killing one's own mother, मातृहत्या, मातृघात।

matriculate (मैट्रिक्युलेट) ***v.*** to become successful in a high school examination, हाई स्कूल परीक्षा में उत्तीर्ण होना, मैट्रिक में पास होना। ***adj.*** having passed high school examination, मैट्रिक पास, हाईस्कूल में उत्तीर्ण।

matrimonial (मैट्रिमोनियल) ***adj.*** of marriage, विवाह-संबंधी, वैवाहिक।

matrimony (मैट्रिमनी) ***n.*** marriage, विवाह, शादी।

matrix (मेट्रिक्स) ***n.*** (plu. matrixes, matrices) a mould, साँचा।

matron (मेट्रन) ***n.*** 1. a head nurse in a hospital, अस्पताल की प्रधान नर्स। 2. an elderly married woman, प्रौढ़ा।

matter (मैटर) ***n.*** 1. a substance or material, पदार्थ। 2. things of a specified kind, सामग्री, चीज़, वस्तु। 3. the substance of thought or expression, विषय-वस्तु, सामग्री। 4. a subject of concern or action, मामला, विषय, बात। 5. a difficulty, कठिनाई। 6. something written or printed, मैटर। 7. pus, पीब। ***v.*** to be of importance, महत्त्वपूर्ण होना।

matter-of-fact (मैटर-ऑफ़-फ़ैक्ट) ***adj.*** concerned with facts, तथ्यपरक।

matting (मैटिंग) ***n.*** a mat, चटाई।

mattress (मैट्रिस) ***n.*** a large pad used on or as a bed, गद्दा।

maturation (मैच्युरेशन) ***n.*** the process of maturing, पकना, परिपक्व होना, प्रौढ़ता।

mature (मैच्योर) ***adj.*** 1. fully grown, ripe or developed, परिपक्व। 2. grown-up, प्रौढ़। 3. due or payable, देय। ***v.*** 1. to become ripe or mature, परिपक्व होना, प्रौढ़ होना। 2. to become due for payment, देय होना।

maturity (मैच्योरिटी) ***n.*** 1. the state of being mature, परिपक्वता, प्रौढ़ता। 2. the time of being mature, भुगतान-तिथि।

maul (मॉल) ***v.*** to injure badly, घायल करना, क्षत-विक्षत करना।

mausoleum (मॉसोलीअम) ***n.*** a tomb of an important person, मक़बरा।

mauve (मोव) ***adj.*** purple, बैंगनी (रंग)।

mawkish (मॉकिश) ***adj.*** excessively sentimental, अत्यंत भावुक।

maxi (मैक्सी) ***n.*** a woman's garment reaching to the ankles, मैक्सी।

maxilla (मैक्सिला) ***n.*** the jawbone, जबड़े की हड्डी।

maxim (मैक्सिम) ***n.*** an expression of a general truth or a concise rule of conduct, सूक्ति।

maximize (मैक्सिमाइज़) ***v.*** to make as great as possible, अधिक से अधिक करना या बढ़ाना।

maximum (मैक्सिमम) ***adj.*** the greatest or highest possible, अधिक से अधिक, अधिकतम।

May[1] (मे) ***n.*** the fifth month of the year, मई।

may[2] (मे) ***aux v.*** used to express wish, permission or possibility, इच्छा, अनुमति या संभावना की सूचक सहायक क्रिया।

maybe (मेबी) ***adv.*** perhaps, शायद।

mayhem (मेहेम) ***n.*** 1. the crime of wilfully maiming a person, अंगभंग का अपराध। 2. a wilful violent destruction, ज़ोर-ज़बरदस्ती से किया हुआ ध्वंस, विध्वंस।

mayor (मेअर) ***n.*** the head of the city, नगरप्रमुख, महापौर। [Fem. mayoress]

maze (मेज़) ***n.*** a labyrinth, भूलभुलैया।

me (मी) ***pron.*** the objective case of I, मुझको, मुझे।

meadow (मेडो) ***n.*** a field of grass, घास का मैदान।

meagre (मीगर) ***adj.*** 1. thin, lean, दुबला-पतला। 2. deficient in quantity, बहुत थोड़ा।

meal (मील) ***n.*** 1. the food served and eaten in one sitting, भोजन। 2. coarsely ground grain, आटा।

mealy (मीली) ***adj.*** like or containing meal, आटे-जैसा।

mean[1] (मीन) ***v.*** (meant, meaning) 1. to denote or convey, अर्थ देना। 2. to indicate, सूचित करना। 3. to have as purpose, अभिप्राय होना। 4. to have the importance, महत्त्व होना।

mean[2] ***adj.*** 1. low in quality, घटिया, तुच्छ, नगण्य। 2. low in status, अधम, नीच। 3. ignoble, कमीना, नीच, तुच्छ। 4. miserly, कंजूस।

mean[3] ***n.*** the middle point, state or course between two limits, औसत, मध्य।

meander (मीऐन्डर) ***v.*** 1. to follow a winding course, टेढ़ा-मेढ़ा चलना। 2. to wander aimlessly, बेकार घूमना। ***n.*** a winding course, टेढ़ा-मेढ़ा रास्ता।

meaning (मीनिन्ग) ***n.*** 1. sense, import, अर्थ, आशय, तात्पर्य। 2. significance, महत्त्व।

meaningful (मीनिन्गफ़ुल) ***adj.*** 1. full of meaning, अर्थ-भरा, अर्थपूर्ण। 2. significant, सार्थक, महत्त्वपूर्ण।

meanness (मीननिस) ***n.*** the quality of being mean, अधमता, घटियापन, नीचता।

means (मीन्ज़) ***n.*** (singular) 1. a course of action by which some end is achieved, साधन। 2. wealth, धन।

meant (मेन्ट) ***v.*** p.t. & p.p. of mean.

meanwhile (मीनवाइल) ***adv.*** 1. in the meantime, इसी बीच, इतने में। 2. at the same time, उसी समय।

measles (मीज़ल्ज़) ***n.*** an infectious disease characterized by red spots on the skin, खसरा।

measure (मेज़र) ***n.*** 1. size, नाप, माप। 2. quantity, परिमाण, मात्रा। 3. a unit or standard used in measuring,

पैमाना, नपना, मानदंड। 4. a device for measuring, नापने का उपाय (फ़ीता, गज़ आदि)। 5. a criterion, कसौटी, मानदंड। ***v.*** 1. to determine the size, amount, degree of by measurement, नापना, मापना। 2. to appraise, आँकना, अनुमान लगाना। 3. to be as specified in extent, amount etc., नाप में होना, नपना। 4. to compare, तुलना करना।

measurement (मेज़रमेन्ट) ***n.*** 1. the act of measuring, मापन। 2. size, नाप।

meat (मीट) ***n.*** animal flesh as food, मांस, गोश्त, आमिष।

meaty (मीटी) ***adj.*** 1. fleshy, मांसल। 2. full of import, सारगर्भित।

mechanic (मकैनिक) ***n.*** a skilled workman, मिस्त्री, मकैनिक, कारीगर।

mechanical (मकैनिकल) ***adj.*** 1. of or pertaining to machines or tools, मशीनी, यांत्रिक। 2. as if done by habit, not will, बँधा-सधा, अविचारित।

mechanically (मकैनिकली) ***adv.*** in a mechanical way, यंत्रवत्।

mechanics (मकैनिक्स) ***n.*** 1. the science of making machines, यांत्रिकी। 2. process, प्रक्रिया, क्रियाविधि।

mechanism (मेकनिज़म) ***n.*** 1. the structure of a machine, यंत्र-विन्यास, रचना-तंत्र। 2. the parts of a machine, कल-पुर्ज़े। 3. the working of a machine, क्रिया-प्रणाली, क्रियाविधि। 4. the process or means, प्रक्रिया, साधन, तंत्र।

medal (मेडल) ***n.*** a piece of metal given as a reward in memory of some event, पदक, तमगा।

medallion (मडैल्यन) ***n.*** 1. a large medal, बड़ा पदक या तमगा। 2. a pattern like this, पदक-जैसा डिज़ाइन।

medallist (मेडलिस्ट) ***n.*** a recipient of a medal, पदक-विजेता, पदकधारी।

meddle (मेडल) ***v.*** to interfere, टाँग अड़ाना, दख़ल देना, हस्तक्षेप करना।

meddler (मेडलर) ***n.*** one who interferes, हस्तक्षेपकर्ता।

media (मीडिआ) ***n.*** (plu. of medium) **the media,** the means of communication that reach large number of people, समाचारपत्र, रेडियो तथा टेलीविजन, जनसंचार माध्यम।

mediaeval (मिडीवल) ***adj.*** = medieval.

median (मीडिअन) ***adj.*** medial, बिचला, मध्य। ***n.*** (maths.) a medial point or line, माध्यिका।

mediate (मीडिएट) ***v.*** to negotiate between two opposing sides, मध्यस्थता करना, बीच-बचाव करना।

mediation (मीडिएशन) ***n.*** the act of mediating, मध्यस्थता, बीच-बचाव।

mediator (मीडिएटर) ***n.*** one who mediates, मध्यस्थ।

medical (मेडिकल) ***adj.*** 1. of medicine, औषध-संबंधी। 2. of the treatment of disease, चिकित्सा-संबंधी, चिकित्सा-।

medicare (मेडिकेअर) ***n.*** a system of medical care, चिकित्सा-सुरक्षा।

medicinal (मेडिसिनल) ***adj.*** 1. of medicine, औषधीय। 2. having healing properties, रोगहर, स्वास्थ्यकर।

medicine (मेडिसिन) ***n.*** 1. a substance used to treat disease, औषध, दवा। 2. the science of treating diseases, चिकित्सा-विज्ञान, वैद्यक।

M

medicine man ***n.*** a witch doctor, झाड़-फूँक करनेवाला, ओझा।

medieval (मिडीवल) ***adj.*** of the middle ages, मध्ययुगीन।

mediocre (मीडिओकर) ***adj.*** of medium quality, औसत दर्जे का, साधारण।

mediocrity (मीडिऑक्रिटी) ***n.*** 1. the quality of being mediocre, औसत दर्जा। 2. an average person, साधारण व्यक्ति।

meditate (मेडिटेट) ***v.*** to contemplate, to reflect deeply, मनन करना, ध्यान लगाना।

meditation (मेडिटेशन) ***n.*** the act of meditating, मनन, ध्यान।

Mediterranean (मेडिटरेनिअन) ***adj.*** of the Mediterranean Sea, भूमध्यसागरीय। ***n.*** Mediterranean Sea, भूमध्य सागर।

medium (मीडिअम) ***n.*** (plu. media) 1. a method of giving information, माध्यम। 2. an agency or means by which something is done, माध्यम। 3. a middle position, मध्य। 4. one who communicates with the spirits, माध्यम। 5. (plu. the media) a means of mass communication, जनसंचार। ***adj.*** occurring midway, intermediate, बीच का, मध्यम, मँझोला।

medley (मेड्ली) ***n.*** 1. confused mixture, घाल-मेल। 2. a musical arrangement of several melodies, स्वर-संगम।

meek (मीक) ***adj.*** 1. humble, नम्र, विनम्र, विनीत। 2. submissive, दब्बू।

meekness (मीकनिस) ***n.*** 1. humility, विनम्रता। 2. submissiveness, दब्बूपन।

meet (मीट) ***v.*** (met, meeting) 1. to encounter, सामना होना। 2. to come into contact with, मुलाकात या भेंट होना। 3. to get to know or be introduced to first time, परिचय होना। 4. to gather in the company of, मिलना, साथ होना, एकत्र होना। 5. to find or experience, सामना होना, अनुभव करना, भोगना। 6. to deal with, हल करना। 7. to satisfy, पूरा करना। 8. to pay, भुगतान करना, चुकाना। ***n.*** a sports meeting, खेल, खिलाड़ियों का जमावड़ा।

meeting (मीटिंग) ***n.*** 1. the act of coming together, मिलन। 2. union, संगम। 3. an assembly or gathering, सभा, गोष्ठी या बैठक। 4. an encounter, सामना, मुठभेड़, भिड़ंत।

mega (मेगा) ***adj.*** one million, दस लाख।

megalith (मेगालिथ) ***n.*** a stone of great size, महापाषाण।

megaphone (मेगाफ़ोन) ***n.*** an instrument to amplify voice, ध्वनिवर्धक, भोंपू, मेगाफोन।

melancholy (मेलेन्कली) ***n.*** mental depression, अवसाद, विषाद, उदासी। ***adj.*** sad, gloomy, उदास, विषादयुक्त।

meld (मेल्ड) ***v.*** to mix or blend, मिलाना, मिश्रित करना।

melee (मेले) ***n.*** 1. a disorderly crowd, भीड़-भाड़, जमावड़ा। 2. a confused fight, मार-धाड़।

mellow (मेलो) ***adj.*** 1. ripe and sweet, रसीला, रस-भरा। 2. melodious, सुरीला। 3. kind-hearted, दयालु, सहृदय।

melodious (मलोडिअस) ***adj.*** full of melody, श्रुतिमधुर, सुरीला, लययुक्त।

melodrama (मेलोड्रामा) ***n.*** 1. an emotional or sensational drama, भावोत्तेजक या उत्तेजनायुक्त नाटक।

M

2. overdramatic behaviour, अतिनाटकीय व्यवहार।

melodramatic (मेलोड्रामैटिक) ***adj.*** of melodrama, भावोत्तेजक या अतिनाटकीय।

melody (मेलडी) ***n.*** 1. a pleasing arrangement of sounds, स्वर-संगम, स्वर-लहरी। 2. a song or tune, गान या धुन।

melon (मेलन) ***n.*** a plant and its fruit, ख़रबूज़ा और उसकी लता।

melt (मेल्ट) ***v.*** 1. to cause to become liquid, पिघलाना, गलाना। 2. to become liquid, पिघलना, गलना। 3. to become gentler, द्रवित होना, पसीजना। 4. to cause to become gentler, द्रवित करना। 5. to dwindle or fade away, छीजना, घुलना।

member (मेम्बर) ***n.*** 1. one who belongs to an organisation, committee or club, सदस्य, मेंबर। 2. a part of a whole, अंग, अवयव, घटक।

membership (मेम्बरशिप) ***n.*** 1. the state of being a member of an organisation, committee etc., सदस्यता, मेंबरी। 2. the total number of members, सदस्य-संख्या।

membrane (मेम्ब्रेन) ***n.*** soft thin skin in the body, झिल्ली।

memento (ममेन्टो) ***n.*** a souvenir, स्मारिका, स्मृति-चिह्न, यादगार।

memo (मेमो) ***n.*** a memorandum, पुर्ज़ा, रुक्का।

memoir (मेम्वार) ***n.*** 1. a biography, जीवन-वृत्तांत। 2. an essay, निबंध।

memoirs (मेम्वार्ज़) ***n.*** (plu.) a collection of reminiscences, संस्मरण।

memorable (मेमरेबल) ***adj.*** worth remembering, स्मरणीय, स्मरण रखने योग्य।

memorandum (मेमरैन्डम) ***n.*** (plu. memoranda) 1. a note, पुर्ज़ा, नोट, टिप्पण। 2. a written statement for submission, ज्ञापन।

memorial (ममोरिअल) ***n.*** something serving as a memory of someone or some event, स्मारक। ***adj.*** serving as a memorial, स्मारक।

memorize (मेमराइज) ***v.*** to learn and remember, स्मरण करना, याद कर लेना।

memory (मेमरी) ***n.*** 1. the ability to remember, स्मरणशक्ति, स्मृति, याददाश्त। 2. all that a person can remember, याद, स्मृति।

menace (मेनस) ***v.*** to threaten. धमकी देना। ***n.*** 1. a threat, धमकी। 2. a source of danger, nuisance, उपद्रव। 3. a troublesome person or thing, आफ़त, बला।

mend (मेन्ड) ***v.*** 1. to repair, मरम्मत करना। 2. to set right, सुधारना।

mendicant (मेन्डिकन्ट) ***n.*** a beggar, भिक्षु।

menfolk (मेनफ़ोक) ***n.*** (plu.) 1. men in general, लोग। 2. the men of a particular family, किसी परिवार के लोग।

menial (मीनिअल) ***n.*** a domestic servant, घरेलू नौकर। ***adj.*** pertaining to or appropriate for a servant, lowly, छोटा; menial work, छोटा काम।

meninges (मिनिन्जीज़) ***n.*** membrane that encloses the brain, मस्तिष्क की झिल्ली, तानिका।

meningitis (मेनिन्जाइटिस) ***n.*** inflammation of the meninges, मस्तिष्क की झिल्ली की सूजन, तानिका-शोथ।

menopause (मेनोपॉज़) ***n.*** cessation of menstruation, रजोनिवृत्ति।

menses (मैन्सीज़) ***n.*** (plu.) blood discharged in menstruation, मासिक धर्म।

menstruation (मेन्स्ट्रुएशन) ***n.*** menses, मासिक धर्म।

mensuration (मेन्शुरेशन) ***n.*** 1. the act of measuring, मापन। 2. technique of measuring, माप विज्ञान।

menswear (मेन्ज़विअर) ***n.*** clothes for men, पुरुषों के वस्त्र, पुरुष-परिधान।

mental (मेन्टल) ***adj.*** of the mind or affected by mental illness, मानसिक, दिमाग़ी।

mental hospital ***n.*** hospital for persons affected by mental illness, मनोचिकित्सालय।

menthol (मेन्थॉल) ***n.*** an organic compound found in pepperment oil, पुदीने का सत, मेन्थॉल।

mention (मेन्शन) ***v.*** to refer, उल्लेख, चर्चा या ज़िक्र करना। ***n.*** the act of mentioning or the state of being mentioned, उल्लेख, चर्चा, ज़िक्र।

mentor (मेन्टर) ***n.*** a trusted adviser, विश्वसनीय परामर्शदाता।

menu (मेन्यु) ***n.*** list of dishes for a meal, व्यंजन-सूची, मेनू।

mercantile (मर्कन्टाइल) ***adj.*** commercial, व्यापारिक, वाणिज्यिक।

mercenary (मर्सनरी) ***n.*** a man hired for service in a foreign army, भाड़े का सैनिक। ***adj.*** motivated by greed or gain, धनलोलुप।

merchandise (मर्चन्डाइज़) ***n.*** commercial goods, बिक्री की वस्तुएँ, पण्य माल। ***v.*** to promote sales, बिक्री बढ़ाना।

merchant (मर्चन्ट) ***n.*** a trader, व्यापारी, सौदागर, वणिक, बनिया।

merchant navy ***n.*** ships engaged in foreign trade, वणिक-बेड़ा।

merciful (मर्सिफ़ुल) ***adj.*** showing or giving mercy, क्षमाशील, दयावान।

merciless (मर्सिलिस) ***adj.*** showing no mercy, दयाहीन, निष्ठुर, निर्दय।

mercurial (मर्क्यूरिअल) ***adj.*** 1. of mercury, पारदीय, पारदमय। 2. active, lively, तेज़, जीवंत।

Mercury (मर्करी) ***n.*** the smallest planet, बुध ग्रह।

mercury ***n.*** a heavy silver-white liquid metal, पारा, पारद।

mercy (मर्सी) ***n.*** 1. clemency, क्षमा, दया, दयालुता। 2. a fortunate occurrence, सौभाग्य की बात।

mere (मिअर) ***adj.*** being nothing more than what is specified, बस इतना ही, सिर्फ़, निरा।

merge (मर्ज) ***v.*** 1. to join or combine into a whole, मिल जाना, विलीन हो जाना, विलय हो जाना। 2. to cause to join or combine, मिला देना, विलय करना।

merger (मर्जर) ***n.*** the act of merging or the state of being merged, विलय।

meridian (मरिडिअन) ***n.*** one of the imaginary lines joining the north and the south poles, याम्योत्तर रेखा।

merino (मरीनो) ***n.*** 1. a breed of sheep, भेड़ों की एक जाति। 2. the long fine wool of these sheep, उक्त भेड़ों की बढ़िया ऊन।

merit (मेरिट) ***n.*** a praiseworthy quality, गुण, विशेषता, ख़ूबी। ***v.*** to deserve, (के) योग्य होना, (का) पात्र होना।

meritorious (मेरिटोरिअस) ***adj.*** 1. having merit, गुणी, गुणवान। 2.

M

praiseworthy, प्रशंसनीय, सराहनीय।

mermaid (मर्मेड) ***n.*** an imaginary woman with fish's tail, मत्स्यकन्या।

merriment (मेरिमेन्ट) ***n.*** amusement, fun, मौज-मस्ती, आनंद-मंगल, आमोद-प्रमोद।

merry (मेरी) ***adj.*** 1. cheerful, प्रसन्नचित्त, उत्फुल्ल। 2. joyous, मज़ेदार, मौज-मस्ती-भरा।

merry-go-round (मेरी-गो-राउन्ड) ***n.*** a revolving machine on which children can ride round and round, round about, घुमौआ झूला, हिंडोला।

mesh (मेश) ***n.*** 1. a network, जाली। 2. an open space between the threads of a network, छेद। 3. a trap, जाल, फंदा। ***v.*** 1. to catch or ensnare, पकड़ना, जाल में फँसाना। 2. (of a toothed wheel) to engage with another, जुड़ना, बैठना।

mesmerism (मेज़मरिज़म) ***n.*** hypnotism, सम्मोहन।

mesmerize (मेज़मराइज़) ***v.*** to hypnotise, सम्मोहित करना, सम्मोहन करना।

mess (मेस) ***n.*** 1. a jumble, घाल-मेल, गड्ड-मड्ड। 2. a difficult or confused situation, झंझट। 3. the place where meals are taken, मेस, भोजनालय। ***v.*** 1. to jumble, गड्ड-मड्ड करना। 2. to spoil, चौपट करना। 3. to interfere, हस्तक्षेप करना। 4. to group together for eating, साथ-साथ भोजन करना।

message (मेसिज) ***n.*** 1. a spoken or written communication, संदेश, पैग़ाम। 2. the important or central idea, महत्त्वपूर्ण या प्रेरणादायक विचार।

messenger (मेसिन्जर) ***n.*** the bearer of a message, संदेशवाहक, दूत, हरकारा।

Messiah (मेसाइआ) ***n.*** 1. Christ, येशु, मसीहा। 2. a deliverer, मोक्षदाता, मसीहा।

Messrs (मेसर्ज़) ***n.*** plu. of Mr., सर्वश्री।

messy (मेसी) ***adj.*** 1. jumbled, गड्ड-मड्ड, अस्तव्यस्त। 2. dirty, गंदा।

metabolism (मेटैबॉलिज़म) ***n.*** the chemical process that living things carry on to maintain life, चयापचयन।

metal (मेटल) ***n.*** a mineral substance, धातु।

metalled (मेटल्ड) ***adj.*** made with broken stone, रोड़ीदार, पक्की (सड़क)।

metallic (मटैलिक) ***adj.*** of or like metal, धात्विक, धात्वीय।

metallurgy (मेटलर्जी) ***n.*** the science or technology of extracting metals from ores, धातु-विज्ञान, धातुकर्म।

metamorphosis (मेटामॉर्फ़सिस) ***n.*** the change of form or character, रूपांतरण, कायापलट।

metaphor (मेटाफ़र) ***n.*** a figure of speech to imply resemblance, रूपक (अलंकार)।

metaphorical (मेटाफ़ॉरिकल) ***adj.*** 1. of or like a metaphor, रूपक-संबंधी। 2. figurative, लाक्षणिक।

metaphysics (मेटाफ़िज़िक्स) ***n.*** the science which deals with reality and knowledge, तत्त्व-विज्ञान।

mete (मीट) ***v.*** to suffer, भोगना, बर्दाश्त करना।

meteor (मीटिअर) ***n.*** a bright moving body seen in the sky when entering the earth's atmosphere, उल्का।

meteorite (मीटिअराइट) ***n.*** a fallen meteor, उल्कापिंड, उल्काश्म।

meteorologist (मीटिअरॉलोजिस्ट)

n. an expert in meteorology, मौसमविज्ञानी।

meteorology (मीटिअरॉलोजी) ***n.*** the scientific study of atmospheric conditions, मौसमविज्ञान।

meter (मीटर) ***n.*** = metre.

method (मेथड) ***n.*** 1. a way of doing something, ढंग, तरीक़ा, पद्धति, विधि। 2. orderliness, क्रमिकता, क्रमबद्धता।

methodical (मिथॉडिकल) ***adj.*** systematic, व्यवस्थित, सिलसिलेवार, क्रमिक।

methodology (मेथडॉलोजी) ***n.*** procedure, क्रिया-पद्धति, कार्यविधि।

methylated spirit ***n.*** alcohol for burning, मेथिलित स्पिरिट, मद्यसार।

meticulous (मिटिक्युलस) ***adj.*** extremely careful and precise, अत्यंत सतर्क, तथा यथातथ्य।

metre[1] (मीटर) ***n.*** a unit of length equivalent to 39.37 inches, मीटर।

metre[2] ***n.*** a machine that indicates the quantity of substance consumed, the distance travelled or the like, मीटर।

metre[3] ***n.*** an arrangement of words in verses, छंद।

metric (मेट्रिक) ***adj.*** 1. of or relating to metre or meteric system, मीटरी। 2. of poetic metre, छंदोबद्ध, पद्यात्मक।

metric system ***n.*** a decimal system of weights and measures, मीटरी पद्धति।

metric ton ***n.*** 1000 kilograms, १००० किलोग्राम।

metro (मेट्रो) ***n.*** a subway train, भूगर्भ गाड़ी।

metropolis (मेट्रॉपलिस) ***n.*** the main city of a country, महानगर, राजधानी।

metropolitan (मेट्रपॉलिटन) ***adj.*** of a metropolis, महानगरीय।

mettle (मेटल) ***n.*** 1. courage, साहस, जीवट। 2. strength of character, चरित्रबल।

mew (म्यू) ***n.*** the cry of a cat, म्याऊँ। ***v.*** (of a cat) to make its typical cry, म्याऊँ म्याऊँ करना।

mezzanine (मेज़नीन) ***n.*** an intermediate storey, दुछत्ती, म्यानी।

mica (माइका) ***n.*** a mineral, अभ्रक।

mice (माइस) ***n.*** plu. of mouse, चूहे।

micro (माइक्रो) ***adj.*** very small, सूक्ष्म।

microbe (माइक्रोब) ***n.*** 1. any microscopic organism, सूक्ष्मजीव। 2. a bacterium, रोगाणु।

microbiology (माइक्रोबाइऑलोजी) ***n.*** the science of micro organisms, सूक्ष्मजीव-विज्ञान।

microchip (माइक्रोचिप) ***n.*** a small bit carrying a complex electronic circuit, माइक्रोचिप।

microcosm (माइक्रकॉज़्म) ***n.*** a small world, लघु ब्रह्मांड।

micro-organism (माइक्रोऑर्गनिज़्म) ***n.*** a minute organism, सूक्ष्मजीव।

microphone (माइक्रोफ़ोन) ***n.*** an instrument that changes sound waves into electric current, माइक्रोफ़ोन।

microscope (माइक्रोस्कोप) ***n.*** an instrument that produces magnified picture, सूक्ष्मदर्शी।

microscopic (माइक्रोस्कॉपिक) ***adj.*** extremely small, अतिसूक्ष्म।

microwave (माइक्रोवेव) ***n.*** an electro-magnetic wave, सूक्ष्म विद्युत् तरंग।

mid (मिड) ***adj.*** middle, मध्य।

M

mid-air (मिड-एअर) ***n.*** some point above ground level, बीच आसमान (में), बीच हवा (में)।

middle (मिडल) ***n.*** 1. an intermediate part, मध्य। 2. the waist, कमर। ***adj.*** in or nearly in centre, मध्यवर्ती।

middle-aged ***adj.*** of middle age, अधेड़।

Middle Ages ***n.*** the period between 1000 to 1400 A.D., मध्ययुग।

middle class ***n.*** the class of society between the lower and upper classes, मध्यवर्ग। ***adj.*** of the middle class, मध्यवर्गीय।

middle finger ***n.*** the longest finger, बीच की उँगली, मध्यमा।

middleman ***n.*** a trader who purchases goods from producers and sells to shopkeepers, दलाल, बिचौलिया।

midi (मिडी) ***n.*** a woman's garment of medium length, घुटने और टखने के बीच पहुँचनेवाला जनाना पहनावा, मिडी।

midland (मिडलैन्ड) ***n.*** the middle part of a country, मध्यदेश।

midnight (मिडनाइट) ***n.*** the middle of the night, आधी रात, मध्यरात्रि।

midpoint (मिडप्वाइन्ट) ***n.*** a point in the middle, मध्यबिंदु।

midst (मिड्स्ट) ***n.*** the middle part, मध्य भाग।

midstream (मिडस्ट्रीम) ***n.*** the middle of a stream, मध्य धारा, मँझधार।

midterm (मिडटर्म) ***n.*** the middle of a term, मध्यावधि।

midwife (मिडवाइफ़) ***n.*** a woman who assists women in childbirth, दाई।

might[1] (माइट) ***n.*** power, शक्ति, बल, पराक्रम।

might[2] ***aux. v.*** 1. used to express a weaker or more remote possibility, संभावना है कि। 2. to express higher degree of politeness, अनुमति है क्या, आज्ञा है क्या।

mighty (माइटी) ***adj.*** 1. strong, powerful, पराक्रमी, बली, शक्तिशाली। 2. important, महत्त्वपूर्ण।

migraine (माइग्रेन) ***n.*** a severe headache affecting only one side of the head, आधे सिर का दर्द, अधकपारी, आधासीसी।

migrant (माइग्रन्ट) ***n.*** one who migrates, प्रवासी।

migrate (माइग्रेट) ***v.*** to move from one country to settle in another, रहने के लिए विदेश जाना, प्रवास करना।

migration (माइग्रेशन) ***n.*** the act of migrating, प्रवास।

migratory (माइग्रेटरी) ***adj.*** migrating, प्रवासी, प्रवासशील।

mike (माइक) ***n.*** a microphone, माइक।

milch (मिल्च) ***adj.*** giving milk, दुधारू।

mild (माइल्ड) ***adj.*** 1. gentle, विनम्र, भला। 2. moderate, मध्यम कोटि का, सौम्य, सुहावना। 3. not strong in taste, हलका, नरम, मृदु।

mildew (मिल्ड्यू) ***n.*** a type of fungus, फफूँदी, भुकड़ी।

mildness (माइल्डनिस) ***n.*** the quality of being mild, सौम्यता, नरमी, हलकापन।

mile (माइल) ***n.*** a unit of length of 1760 yards, मील।

mileage, milage (माइलिज) ***n.*** distance measured in miles, मील-दूरी, माइलेज।

milestone (माइलस्टोन) ***n.*** 1. a roadside stone that shows the distance from one place to another,

मील का पत्थर। 2. a significant event in life or history, जीवन या इतिहास की कोई महत्त्वपूर्ण घटना, मोड़।

militancy (मिलिटेन्सी) ***n.*** aggressiveness, लड़ाकूपन, युयुत्सा, युद्धप्रियता।

militant (मिलिटेन्ट) ***adj.*** aggressive, लड़ाकू, युयुत्सु, युद्धप्रिय। ***n.*** लड़ाकू।

militarism (मिलिटरिज़्म) ***n.*** predominance of military ideals, सैन्यवाद।

military (मिलिटरी) ***n.*** the armed forces, सेना, फ़ौज। ***adj.*** 1. of soldiers, सैनिक। 2. of warlike matters, सामरिक।

militia (मिलिश्या) ***n.*** citizens trained as soldiers, नागरिक सेना।

milk (मिल्क) ***n.*** 1. a white fluid secreted by female mammals, दूध, दुग्ध। 2. a milklike liquid, दूध, दूधिया रस। ***v.*** 1. to draw milk (from), दूहना। 2. to exploit, दोहन करना।

milkmaid (मिल्कमेड) ***n.*** a woman who milks cows, दूध दूहनेवाली स्त्री, ग्वालिन।

milkman (मिल्कमैन) ***n.*** one who sells milk, दूधवाला, ग्वाला, दुग्ध-विक्रेता।

milkpowder ***n.*** a powder prepared from milk, दुग्धचूर्ण।

milk tooth (मिल्कटुथ) ***n.*** any of the first (temporary) teeth, दूध का दाँत।

milky (मिल्की) ***adj.*** 1. of or like milk, दुधिया, दूधिया। 2. not clear, धुँधला।

mill (मिल) ***n.*** 1. a machine to grind flour, चक्की। 2. a factory, फ़ैक्टरी, मिल। ***v.*** 1. to grind, पीसना। 2. to process in a mill, कारख़ाने में तैयार करना।

millennium (मिलेनिअम) ***n.*** a period of thousand years, सहस्राब्दी।

millepede, millipede (मिलिपीड) ***n.*** a crawling creature, गोजर, कनखजूरा।

millet (मिलिट) ***n.*** a cereal plant and its seeds, ज्वार, बाजरा आदि, मोटा अनाज।

milli (मिलि) ***prefix.*** one thousandth, हज़ारवाँ भाग, मिली।

million (मिल्यन) ***adj. & n.*** one thousand thousand, दस लाख।

millionaire (मिल्यनेअर) ***n.*** having million rupees, dollars etc., लखपति, करोड़पति।

millstone (मिलस्टोन) ***n.*** 1. one of a pair of stones used to grind grain, (चक्की का) पाट। 2. (fig.) mental burden, मानसिक बोझ।

milometer (माइलोमीटर) ***n.*** a device for counting mileage, मीलमापी।

mime (माइम) ***n.*** 1. expression of ideas by gestures, इशारों द्वारा विचारों की अभिव्यक्ति, स्वाँग। 2. an actor of this type, मूक अभिनय करनेवाला, स्वाँगिया, स्वाँगी। 3. a jester, clown, नकल उतारनेवाला, मसख़रा। ***v.*** to express by gestures, स्वाँग करना या रचना, मूक अभिनय करना, नक़ल उतारना।

mimic (मिमिक) ***v.*** (mimicked, mimicking) to imitate, नक़ल उतारना, अनुकरण करना। ***n.*** a person, animal or bird that copies, नक़ल उतारनेवाला, नक़लची।

mimosa (मिमोसा) ***n.*** a plant, लाजवंती या छुईमुई का पौधा।

minaret (मिनरेट) ***n.*** a tower of a mosque, मीनार।

mince (मिन्स) ***v.*** 1. to cut into very small pieces, क़ीमा करना, भुर्ता बनाना। 2. to walk or speak in an affected manner, बनना, ढोंग करना। ***n.*** minced meat, क़ीमा।

mind (माइन्ड) ***n.*** 1. brain, दिमाग़, मन। 2. memory, स्मरणशक्ति, स्मृति। 3. thought, विचार। 4. opinion, राय, मत। 5. intention, इरादा, मंशा। 6. a sound mental state, मानसिक स्वस्थता। ***v.*** 1. to take care of, ध्यान रखना। 2. to be opposed to, विरुद्ध होना। 3. to object to, आपत्ति करना। 4. to bear in mind, स्मरण रखना।

mind-blowing (माइन्ड-ब्लोइंग) ***adj.*** affecting the mind, विक्षिप्त कर देनेवाला।

minded (माइन्डिड) ***adj.*** having certain interests, inclined, प्रवृत्ति या रुचिवाला।

mindful (माइन्डफ़ुल) ***adj.*** aware, जागरूक।

mindless (माइन्डलिस) ***adj.*** 1. stupid, मूर्ख। 2. careless, असावधान।

mind's eye (माइन्ड्स आइ) ***n.*** the imagination, मानसिक चक्षु, कल्पना-शक्ति।

mine[1] (माइन) ***pron.*** something belonging to me, मेरा। ***adj.*** belonging to me, मेरा।

mine[2] ***n.*** 1. a deposit of ore or minerals, ख़ान। 2. an abundant source, विशाल स्रोत, भंडार। 3. an explosive device usu. buried in the ground, सुरंग। ***v.*** 1. to dig from a mine, खान से निकालना, खुदाई करना। 2. to make a hole by digging, खोदना। 3. to lay explosive mines, बारूदी सुरंगें बिछाना।

mine detector (माइन डिटेक्टर) ***n.*** an instrument to detect mines, सुरंगों का पता लगानेवाला यंत्र।

miner (माइनर) ***n.*** one who works in a mine, खान खोदनेवाला, खनिक।

mineral (मिनरल) ***adj.*** excavated from the earth, खनिज। ***n.*** something excavated from the earth, खनिज पदार्थ।

mineralogy (मिनरैलोजी) ***n.*** the scientific study of minerals, खनिज-विज्ञान।

mingle (मिन्गल) ***v.*** 1. to mix or blend, मिलाना। 2. to mix together in close as-sociation, मिलना-जुलना, घुल-मिल जाना।

mini (मिनी) ***adj.*** small, छोटा, मिनी। ***n.*** something distinctly smaller than others of its class, मिनी, लघु।

miniature (मिनिएचर) ***n.*** 1. a very small model, लघु प्रतिकृति। 2. a very small painting, लघुचित्र। ***adj.*** very small, लघु।

minimal (मिनिमल) ***adj.*** least in amount, नाममात्र का, थोड़ा, ज़रा-सा।

minimize (मिनिमाइज़) ***v.*** 1. to reduce to the least possible amount, घटाकर न्यूनतम करना। 2. to belittle, महत्त्व घटा देना।

minimum (मिनिमम) ***adj.*** being the least possible in amount, कम-से-कम, न्यूनतम। ***n.*** the least possible amount, न्यूनतम राशि।

minion (मिन्यन) ***n.*** 1. an employee of lowrank, अदना कर्मचारी। 2. a servile follower, ख़ुशामदी टट्टू, चाटुकार।

minister (मिनिस्टर) ***n.*** 1. the head of government department, मंत्री। 2. a clergyman, ईसाई पुरोहित। ***v.*** 1. to take care of, देखभाल करना। 2. to attend to the needs of others,

दूसरों का ख़्याल रखना, सेवा करना।

ministerial (मिनिस्टीरिअल) ***adj.*** 1. of a minister, मंत्री-संबंधी। 2. of ministry, मंत्रालय-संबंधी।

ministry (मिनिस्ट्री) ***n.*** 1. a government department headed by a minister, मंत्रालय। 2. ministers collectively, मंत्रिमंडल। 3. office and duty of a clergyman, ईसाई पुरोहित का पद तथा कार्य।

mink (मिन्क) ***n.*** 1. a weasel-like animal, ऊदबिलाव। 2. its fur, इसका फ़र।

minor (माइनर) ***adj.*** 1. lesser in amount or size, लघु, गौण। 2. not of legal age, अल्पवयस्क, अवयस्क, नाबालिग़। ***n.*** a person under legal age, अवयस्क, नाबालिग़।

minority (माइनॉरिटी) ***n.*** 1. the smaller of the two groups or factions, अल्पमत, अल्पसंख्यक। 2. the state of being minor, अवयस्कता।

minster (मिन्स्टर) ***n.*** a cathedral, बड़ा गिरजा।

mint[1] (मिन्ट) ***n.*** a place where money is coined, टकसाल। ***v.*** to make coins by stamping metal, सिक्के ढालना या बनाना।

mint[2] ***n.*** 1. a plant, पुदीना। 2. peppermint, पिपरमिंट।

minus (माइनस) ***prep.*** 1. reduced by, से घटाने को। 2. lacking, without, के बिना, से रहित। ***n.*** the minus sign, ऋण-चिह्न (–)। ***adj.*** 1. negative, ऋणात्मक। 2. less than zero, शून्य से कम।

minuscule (मिनस्क्यूल) ***adj.*** very small, minute, सूक्ष्म, बहुत छोटा।

minute[1] (मिनिट) ***n.*** 1. one-sixtieth of an hour, मिनट, क्षण। 2. (maths.) one-sixtieth of a degree used in measuring angles, कोण के नाप में एक अंश का साठवाँ भाग, मिनट। 3. (plu.) a record or a proceedings at a meeting, कार्य-विवरण, कार्यवृत्त।

minute[2] (माइन्यूट) ***adj.*** very small, बहुत छोटा, सूक्ष्म।

minutely (माइन्यूटली) ***adv.*** precisely, closely, सूक्ष्म रूप से, अत्यंत सावधानी से।

minx (मिंक्स) ***n.*** a cheeky or impudent girl, शरारती या ढीठ लड़की।

miracle (मिरकल) ***n.*** a marvellous event, wonder, चमत्कारपूर्ण घटना, चमत्कार।

miraculous (मिरैक्युलस) ***adj.*** 1. wonderful, चमत्कारपूर्ण, चमत्कारी। 2. surprising, अनोखा, आश्चर्यजनक।

mirage (मिराज) ***n.*** 1. an optical illusion of water that seems to appear in a desert, मृगमरीचिका, मरीचिका। 2. something illusory, भ्रांतिजनक वस्तु, मृगतृष्णा।

mire (माइर) ***n.*** mud, कीचड़। 2. a marshy area, दलदल।

mirror (मिरर) ***n.*** 1. a looking glass, दर्पण, शीशा। 2. a thing that reflects or depicts something else, दर्पण। ***v.*** to reflect, प्रतिबिंबित करना/होना।

mirth (मर्थ) ***n.*** 1. merriment, उल्लास, आमोद-प्रमोद। 2. laughter, हँसी-विनोद, ठहाका।

mirthful (मर्थफ़ुल) ***adj.*** full of mirth, उल्लसित, उल्लासपूर्ण।

mis (मिस) ***prefix.*** 1. bad, बुरा। 2. wrong, ग़लत। 3. lack of, अभाव।

misadventure (मिसैडवेन्चर) ***n.*** 1. misfortune, दुर्भाग्य। 2. a mishap, दुर्घटना।

M

misapprehension (मिसैप्रिहेन्शन) ***n.*** a misunderstanding, ग़लतफ़हमी।

misappropriation (मिसप्रोप्रिएशन) ***n.*** embezz-lement, गबन।

misbehave (मिस्बिहेव) ***v.*** to behave badly, दुर्व्यवहार करना, अभद्र व्यवहार करना।

misbehaviour (मिस्बिहेव्यर) ***n.*** bad behaviour, दुर्व्यवहार, अभद्र व्यवहार, अभद्रता।

misbelief (मिस्बिलीफ़) ***n.*** a wrong conviction, ग़लत धारणा।

miscalculation (मिस्कैल्क्युलेशन) ***n.*** wrong calculation, ग़लत तख़मीना/अंदाज़।

miscarriage (मिस्कैरिज) ***n.*** premature expulsion of a foetus, गर्भस्राव।

miscellaneous (मिसलेनिअस) ***adj.*** of various kinds, प्रकीर्ण, विविध, फुटकर।

mischief (मिस्चिफ़) ***n.*** naughtiness, शरारत, शैतानी, नटखटपन, पाजीपन।

mischievous (मिस्चीवस) ***adj.*** naughty, शैतान, नटखट, शरारती।

miscible (मिसिबल) ***adj.*** capable of being mixed, जो मिश्रित हो सके।

misconceive (मिस्कन्सीव) ***v.*** to have an erroneous conception of, ग़लत धारणा बना लेना।

misconception (मिस्कन्सेप्शन) ***n.*** misunderstanding, ग़लत धारणा।

misconduct (मिस्कॉन्डक्ट) ***n.*** 1. bad, improper or unlawful behaviour, बुरा व्यवहार या आचरण। 2. adultery, व्यभिचार। 3. mismanagement, कुप्रबंध।

misconstrue (मिस्कन्स्ट्रू) ***v.*** to interpret mistakenly, ग़लत अर्थ लगाना या करना।

miscreant (मिस्क्रीएन्ट) ***n.*** a villain or wrongdoer, गुंडा, बदमाश।

misdeed (मिस्डीड) ***n.*** a wrong act, बुरा काम, पाप, कुकर्म, दुष्कर्म।

misdemeanour,
misdemeanor (मिस्डीमीनर) ***n.*** a minor offence, छोटा-मोटा अपराध।

miser (माइज़र) ***n.*** a stingy person, कंजूस, कृपण।

miserable (मिज़रेबल) ***adj.*** 1. full of misery, दुःखी, त्रस्त। 2. causing misery, दुखप्रद, क्लेशकारी। 3. wretchedly poor, दयनीय, दरिद्र।

misery (मिज़री) ***n.*** 1. extreme suffering, घोर दुख। 2. something causing this, मुसीबत। 3. poverty-stricken conditions, दरिद्रता।

misfire (मिस्फ़ाइर) ***v.*** 1. to fail to fire or fire incorrectly, निशाना चूक जाना। 2. to fail to start, (इंजन का) चालू न होना। 3. to fail to achieve intended result, वांछित फल प्राप्त न कर पाना।

misfortune (मिस्फ़ॉर्चून) ***n.*** 1. bad luck, दुर्भाग्य, बदक़िस्मती। 2. an unfortunate event, कोई बड़ी दुर्घटना।

misgiving (मिसगिविंग) ***n.*** a feeling of doubt or suspicion, शंका, संदेह।

misguide (मिस्गाइड) ***v.*** to guide badly, गुमराह करना।

mishap (मिस्हैप) ***n.*** an unfortunate accident, दुर्घटना।

misinterpret (मिसिन्टर्प्रिट) ***v.*** to interpret wrongly, ग़लत अर्थ करना।

misjudge (मिस्जज) ***v.*** to judge incorrectly, (व्यक्ति को) ठीक से समझ न पाना, (किसी के बारे में) ग़लत धारणा बनाना।

mislay (मिस्ले) ***v.*** (mislaid, mislaying) to put at a wrong place, ग़लत जगह पर रख देना।

misleading (मिस्लीडिंग) ***adj.*** wrong, false, भ्रामक।

mismanagement (मिस्मैनेजमेंट) ***n.*** poor management, कुप्रबंध, दुर्व्यवस्था।

mismatch (मिस्मैच) ***n.*** a bad match, बेमेल जोड़ा। ***v.*** to match badly, मेल न खाना, बेमेल होना।

misnomer (मिस्नोमर) ***n.*** an incorrect name, ग़लत नाम।

misplace (मिस्प्लेस) ***v.*** 1. to put (something) at a wrong place, (कोई चीज़) ग़लत जगह रख देना। 2. to bestow on a wrong person, ग़लत व्यक्ति पर भरोसा करना।

misquote (मिस्कोट) ***v.*** to quote incorrectly, ग़लत उद्धरण देना।

misrepresent (मिस्रेप्रिजेन्ट) ***v.*** to represent misleadingly, ग़लत या मिथ्या विवरण देना, ग़लतबयानी करना।

misrule (मिसूरूल) ***n.*** bad government, बुरा शासन, कुशासन।

miss[1] (मिस) ***n.*** a title for an unmarried woman or girl, सुश्री, कुमारी।

miss[2] ***v.*** 1. to fail to reach or catch, न पहुँच पाना, न पकड़ पाना। 2. to fail to hear, see or understand, सुन, देख या समझ न पाना। 3. to fail to achieve or perform, विफल होना, चूक जाना। 4. to misfire, निशाना चूक जाना। 5. to feel the absence of, कमी महसूस करना। 6. to avoid or escape from, बच जाना या बच निकलना।

missile (मिसाइल) ***n.*** 1. a weapon that is projected at a target, क्षेप्यास्त्र। 2. an object suitable for throwing at a target, फेंककर मारने योग्य वस्तु।

missing (मिसिंग) ***adj.*** 1. lost, खोया हुआ, लुप्त। 2. not present, अनुपस्थित, नदारद। 3. one whose whereabouts are unknown, लापता।

mission (मिशन) ***n.*** 1. a body of envoys to a foreign country, मिशन, शिष्टमंडल। 2. the duty or purpose for which these people are sent, मिशन, प्रयोजन, उद्देश्य। 3. the establishment of these persons, संस्थान, मिशन। 4. a person's vocation, जीवन-लक्ष्य, ध्येय, मिशन।

missionary (मिशनरी) ***n.*** 1. one sent to spread Christian faith in a foreign country, ईसाई धर्मप्रचारक, मिशनरी। 2. a propagandist for a belief, मत-प्रचारक। ***adj.*** 1. of missions, मिशन-संबंधी। 2. of or like missionaries, ईसाई मिशनरियों के जैसा।

misspell (मिस्स्पेल) ***v.*** (misspelled/ misspelt, misspelling) to spell incorrectly, अशुद्ध वर्तनी लिखना या बताना।

mist (मिस्ट) ***n.*** mass of tiny drops of water suspended in the atmosphere, कोहरा, कुहासा, धुंध। ***v.*** to become covered with mist, कोहरा छा जाना।

mistake (मिस्टेक) ***n.*** 1. an error, भूल, ग़लती, अशुद्धि। 2. a misunderstanding, ग़लतफ़हमी। ***v.*** (mistook, mistaken, mistaking) 1. to misunderstand, ग़लतफ़हमी हो जाना। 2. to choose incorrectly, ग़लती करना, ग़लत चुनाव करना।

mister, Mr. (मिस्टर) ***n.*** a formal form of address to a man, श्री, श्रीमान, महोदय।

mistreat (मिस्ट्रीट) ***v.*** to treat badly or abusively, दुर्व्यवहार करना, भला-बुरा कहना।

mistress (मिस्ट्रिस) ***n.*** 1. a female master, मालकिन, स्वामिनी। 2. a person's illicit lover, रख़ैल। 3. a female teacher, अध्यापिका।

misty (मिस्टी) ***adj.*** 1. full of mist, कोहरे से भरा। 2. indistinct, धुँधला।

misunderstanding (मिसन्डर-स्टैन्डिंग) ***n.*** 1. a failure to understand correctly, भ्रांति, धोखा या ग़लतफ़हमी। 2. a disagreement, अनबन, झगड़ा।

misuse (मिस्यूज़) ***v.*** to use badly or wrongly, दुरुपयोग करना। ***n.*** wrong use, ग़लत प्रयोग।

mite (माइट) ***n.*** 1. an insect, कुटकी। 2. a small child, बच्चा। 3. a small contribution, अल्प अंशदान।

mitigate (मिटिगेट) ***v.*** to make or become less severe or intense, मंद होना या करना, शमित करना या होना, हलका होना या करना।

mix (मिक्स) ***v.*** 1. to combine, मिलाना, एक करना। 2. to be social, मिलना-जुलना। ***n.*** 1. a mixture, मिश्रण। 2. a group of different things, घाल-मेल।

mixed farming (मिक्स्ड फ़ार्मिंग) ***n.*** farming of both crops and live-stock, कृषि तथा पशुपालन।

mixed-up (मिक्स्ड-अप) ***adj.*** suffering from mental confusion, दुविधाग्रस्त, भ्रमित, चिंतित।

mixer (मिक्सर) ***n.*** 1. a device for mixing, मिक्सर, मिश्रक, मिक्सी। 2. a sociable person, मिलनसार व्यक्ति।

mixture (मिक्स्चर) ***n.*** something made by mixing, मिश्रण।

mix-up (मिक्स-अप) ***n.*** a confused state. of things, गड्ड-मड्ड अवस्था, गड़बड़ी।

moan (मोन) ***n.*** 1. sound of sorrow or pain, कराह, ओह, हाय-हाय। 2. complaint, grumble, शिकायत। ***v.*** to make a sound like moan, कराहना, हाय-हाय करना।

moat (मोट) ***n.*** a ditch round a castle, खाई, परिखा।

mob (मॉब) ***n.*** 1. a disorderly or riotous crowd, भीड़, भीड़-भाड़, उग्र भीड़। 2. the common people, जन-साधारण। ***v.*** 1. to crowd around, भीड़ लगाना। 2. to attack in a group, भीड़ का चढ़ आना।

mobile (मोबाइल) ***adj.*** capable of moving or of being moved, चल, गतिशील, चलता-फिरता।

mobility (मोबिलिटी) ***n.*** the state of being mobile, गतिशीलता।

mobilization (मोबिलाइज़ेशन) ***n.*** the act of mobilizing or the state of being mobilized, लामबंदी, सैन्यीकरण; mobilization of resources, साधन-संग्रह।

mock (मॉक) ***v.*** 1. to deride or jeer, उपहास करना, मज़ाक उड़ाना। 2. to mimic, नक़ल उतारना। 3. to spoil or destroy, चौपट कर देना। ***n.*** 1. the act of mocking, उपहास, खिल्ली। 2. imitation, नक़ल। ***adj.*** not real, sham, झूठा, नक़ली, बनावटी।

mockery (मॉकरी) ***n.*** derision, उपहास, हँसी।

modal (मोडल) ***adj.*** of or concerning the mood of a verb, क्रियार्थद्योतक।

mode (मोड) ***n.*** 1. way, manner, ढंग, रीति, पद्धति। 2. the current fashion, फ़ैशन, चाल, रिवाज। 3. (music) राग।

model (मॉडल) ***n.*** 1. the small copy of an object, नमूना, प्रतिमान, मॉडल। 2. exact copy, प्रतिकृति, प्रतिरूप।

3. an example or standard to be imitated, उदाहरण, आदर्श। 4. a person employed to pose for an artist, or to display or advertising, मॉडल। ***adj.*** exemplary, आदर्श। ***v.*** 1. to make or construct, बनाना, गढ़ना। 2. to design, डिज़ाइन बनाना। 3. to work as an artist's model, मॉडल के रूप में काम करना।

moderate (मॉडरिट) ***adj.*** 1. average, औसत दर्जे का। 2. within sensible limits, हलका, मर्यादित। 3. not holding extremist views, उदार, नरम दलीय। ***v.*** 1. to make or become moderate, औसत दर्जे का बनना या बनाना, मर्यादित करना या होना। 2. to reduce in force or degree, हलका करना, मर्यादित करना।

moderately ***adv.*** to a moderate degree, औसत दर्जे से अधिक नहीं।

moderation (मॉडरेशन) ***n.*** the act of moderating, मर्यादित करना या बनाना, परिमार्जन।

moderator (मॉडरेटर) ***n.*** 1. one who moderates, परिमार्जक। 2. an arbitrator, मध्यस्थ।

modern (मॉडर्न) ***adj.*** 1. of a recent time, आधुनिक। 2. of current fashion, नया।

modernist (मॉडर्निस्ट) ***n.*** one who favours modernism, आधुनिकतावादी।

modernization (मॉडर्नाइज़ेशन) ***n.*** the act of modernizing or the state of being modernized, आधुनिकीकरण।

modest (मॉडिस्ट) ***adj.*** 1. having or showing moderate estimation of oneself, humble, शालीन, विनयी। 2. shy, संकोची, लज्जालु।

modification (मॉडिफ़िकेशन) ***n.*** the act of modifying or the state of being modified, हलका परिवर्तन, संशोधन।

modify (मॉडिफ़ाई) ***v.*** 1. to make partial changes in, थोड़ा-बहुत परिवर्तन करना, संशोधन करना। 2. to make less severe, हलका करना, मंद करना।

modish (मोडिश) ***adj.*** in the current fashion, जो रिवाज या फैशन में हो, चलता हुआ।

modulate (मॉड्यूलेट) ***v.*** to change the tone, सुर में परिवर्तन लाना, आरोह-अवरोह करना।

module (मॉड्यूल) ***n.*** a standard of measurement, मापदंड, माप।

modus operandi (मोडस ऑपरैन्डी) ***n.*** particular way of doing something, विशेष पद्धति, कार्य-प्रणाली या कार्यविधि।

mohair (मोहेअर) ***n.*** long silky hair of angora goat, अंगोरा बकरी के लंबे रेशमी बाल।

moist (मॉइस्ट) ***adj.*** damp, गीला, नम, तर, आर्द्र।

moisten (मॉइसन) ***v.*** to become or make wet, भीग जाना या भिगो देना, नम होना या करना।

moisture (मॉइस्चर) ***n.*** dampness, नमी, आर्द्रता।

moisturize (मॉइस्चराइज़) ***v.*** to add moisture, नम करना, भिगोना।

molar (मोलर) ***n.*** any of the grinding teeth, दाढ़।

molasses (मोलैसिज़) ***n.*** unrefined sugar syrup, शीरा।

mole[1] (मोल) ***n.*** a small dark raised mark on the skin, तिल।

mole[2] ***n.*** a small burrowing animal, छछूँदर।

molecular (मॉलिक्यूलर) ***adj.*** of molecule, आणविक।

M

molecule (मॉलिक्यूल) ***n.*** the smallest unit of atoms, अणु।

molehill (मोलहिल) ***n.*** a small mound of loose earth thrown up by a mole, छछूँदर की बाँबी।

molest (मलेस्ट) ***v.*** 1. to trouble, परेशान करना, रौंदना। 2. to attack sexually, छेड़छाड़ करना।

molestation (मोलेस्टेशन) ***n.*** the act of molesting, छेड़छाड़, छेड़खानी।

mollification (मॉलिफ़िकेशन) ***n.*** the act of mollifying, प्रशमन।

mollify (मॉलिफ़ाइ) ***v.*** (mollified, mollifying) to calm, शांत करना, प्रशमित करना।

mollusc, mollusk (मॉलस्क) ***n.*** a class of animals usually covered with a shell, कवचधारी प्राणी, कवचित जीव।

molt (मोल्ट) ***v.*** = moult.

molten (मोल्टन) ***adj.*** melted, पिघला हुआ।

mom (मॉम) ***n.*** mother, माँ, माता।

moment (मोमन्ट) ***n.*** 1. a brief interval of time, पल, क्षण। 2. a specific point in time, समय, घड़ी। 3. importance, महत्त्व।

momentary (मोमन्टरी) ***adj.*** lasting for a moment, क्षणिक।

momentous (मोमेन्टस) ***adj.*** of great importance, महत्त्वपूर्ण।

momentum (मोमेन्टम) ***n.*** 1. impetus gained by movement, संवेग। 2. (fig.) driving power or strength, तेज़ी, बल, वेग।

monarch (मॉनर्क) ***n.*** a king, राजा, महाराजा।

monarchy (मॉनर्की) ***n.*** govt. by a monarch, राजतंत्र।

monastery (मॉनस्टरी) ***n.*** the dwelling place of monks, मठ, साधु-विहार, आश्रम।

Monday (मन्डे) ***n.*** the second day of the week, सोमवार।

monetary (मॉनिटरी) ***adj.*** of or pertaining to money, मुद्रा-संबंधी, मौद्रिक।

monetization (मॉनिटाइज़ेशन) ***n.*** the act of monetizing or the state of being monetized, मुद्रीकरण।

monetize (मॉनिटाइज़) ***v.*** to establish as legal tender, मुद्रा के रूप में स्थापित करना।

money (मनी) ***n.*** 1. coins and bank notes (as medium of exchange), रुपया-पैसा, मुद्रा। 2. amount of money, धन, रक़म। 3. currency, मुद्रा।

moneyed (मनीड) ***adj.*** rich, धनी, धनाढ्य।

moneylender (मनीलेन्डर) ***n.*** one who lends money at interest, महाजन, साहूकार।

money order ***n.*** a form to send money to someone through post office, धनादेश, मनीऑर्डर।

money-spinner (मनी-स्पिनर) ***n.*** a source of wealth, धन का अजस्र स्रोत।

mongoose (मॉन्गूस) ***n.*** a small mammal that kills snakes and rats, नेवला, न्योला।

mongrel (मन्ग्रल) ***n.*** a plant or animal of mixed breed, दोग़ली नस्ल का पशु या पौधा, संकर।

monism (मॉनिज़म) ***n.*** the doctrine that reality consists of only one substance, अद्वैतवाद, एकात्मवाद।

monitor (मॉनिटर) ***n.*** 1. a leader of a class, मॉनीटर, कक्षानायक। 2. an electronic device of observing,

checking or testing some process, मॉनीटर। ***v.*** to observe, check or test, पड़ताल करना, चेक करना, देखना।

monk (मन्क) ***n.*** a religious male person living in a monastery, विहार या आश्रम में रहनेवाला ईसाई साधु।

monkey (मंकी) ***n.*** a long-tailed tree-climbing animal, बंदर, वानर। ***v.*** 1. to imitate, नक़ल उतारना। 2. to play about mischievously, शरारत करना, उछल-कूद करना। 3. to deride, हँसी उड़ाना।

mono (मॉनो) ***prefix.*** single, one, एक।

monochromatic (मॉनोक्रोमैटिक) ***adj.*** black and white, श्वेत-श्याम, एकरंगा।

monogamy (मॉनोगमी) ***n.*** the custom or practice of having only one wife/husband at a time, एक पति और एक पत्नी का सिद्धांत, एक विवाह-प्रथा।

monogram (मॉनोग्रैम) ***n.*** a design of one or more letters, मोनोग्राम।

monograph (मॉनोग्राफ़) ***n.*** an essay on one particular subject, एकबंध।

monolith (मॉनोलिथ) ***n.*** a large pillar of single stone, एकाश्म, एक ही पत्थर का बना बहुत बड़ा खंभा।

monologue (मॉनोलॉग) ***n.*** 1. a long speech, लंबा भाषण। 2. a speech by an actor, esp. when alone, स्वगत भाषण, एकालाप।

monopolist (मनॉपलिस्ट) ***n.*** one who has a monopoly, एकाधिकारी।

monopoly (मनॉपली) ***n.*** a sole right of doing some business or dealing one commodity, एकाधिकार।

monorail (मॉनोरेल) ***n.*** 1. a railway with a single rail, एकल पटरी पर चलनेवाली गाड़ी। 2. the rail of such a railway, एकल पटरी।

monosyllable (मॉनोसिलेबल) ***n.*** a word of one syllable, एकाक्षर शब्द।

monotheism (मॉनोथीइज़्म) ***n.*** the theory of one god only, एकेश्वरवाद।

monotone (मॉनोटोन) ***n.*** the manner of singing in a single tone, एकतानता, एकस्वरता।

monotony (मनॉटनी) ***n.*** the state of being monotonous, एकरसता, नीरसता।

monotype (मॉनोटाइप) ***n.*** a machine for casting types, मॉनोटाइप।

monsoon (मॉनसून) ***n.*** 1. winds that bring rains, मानसून, पावस। 2. rainy season, बरसात, वर्षा ऋतु।

monster (मॉन्स्टर) ***n.*** 1. an imaginary person of abnormal size and power, दैत्य, राक्षस। 2. one who inspires horror and disgust, अत्याचारी या नृशंस व्यक्ति।

monstrous (मॉन्स्ट्रस) ***adj.*** 1. huge, भीमकाय, भीमाकार। 2. frightening, विकराल, विकट, डरावना।

month (मन्थ) ***n.*** one of the 12 named divisions of the year, महीना, मास, माह।

monthly (मन्थली) ***adj.*** occurring, published or payable once a month, मासिक, माहवारी। ***n.*** a monthly magazine, मासिक पत्रिका। ***adv.*** once a month, प्रतिमास।

monument (मॉन्युमेन्ट) ***n.*** 1. a historical structure, स्मारक। 2. a tombstone, समाधि-शिला।

moo (मू) ***n.*** the sound made by a cow, गाय के रंभाने का शब्द। ***v.*** to make the sound that a cow makes, रंभाना।

mood[1] (मूड) ***n.*** 1. a state of mind, मन:स्थिति, मनोदशा। 2. disposition,

स्वभाव, मिज़ाज, तबीयत। 3. a fit of bad temper, तुनुकमिज़ाजी।

mood² ***n.*** any of three groups of forms of a verb i.e. indicative, imperative or subjunctive, क्रिया के संकेतार्थ, विध्यर्थ और संभावनार्थ तीन प्रकारों में से कोई एक।

moody (मूडी) ***adj.*** temperamental, मनमौजी, तुनुकमिज़ाज।

moon (मून) ***n.*** 1. the natural satellite of the earth, चंद्रमा, चाँद। 2. any natural satellite, उपग्रह। ***v.*** to wander about in a dreamy or aimless manner, बिना मतलब घूमते रहना।

moonlight (मूनलाइट) ***n.*** the light of the moon, चाँदनी, ज्योत्स्ना।

moonshine (मूनशाइन) ***n.*** 1. foolish talk, मूर्खतापूर्ण बात। 2. illegally distilled whisky, अवैध शराब।

moor¹ (मूर) ***v.*** to fasten (a boat or ship) by ropes or anchor, (नाव या जहाज़ को) लंगर डालकर या रस्से से बाँधकर खड़ा करना।

moor² ***n.*** barren land, बंजर भूमि।

mooring (मूरिंग) ***n.*** 1. a place where boats are moored, नावें बाँधने का स्थान। 2. ropes or cables by which something is moored, नावें बाँधने के रस्से आदि।

moot point (मूट प्वाइंट) ***n.*** an undecided point, विवाद-विषय।

mop (मॉप) ***n.*** an implement for cleaning floor, फ़र्श पोंछने का उपकरण। ***v.*** to clean with a mop, साफ़ करना, पोंछना।

mope (मोप) ***v.*** to be dejected, उदास होना।

moped (मोपेड) ***n.*** a motorbike, मोपेड।

moraine (मॉरेन) ***n.*** a mass of debris carried down by glacier, हिमनद द्वारा लाया हुआ मलबा, हिमोढ़।

moral (मॉरल) ***adj.*** according to the established standard of good behaviour, सदाचारपूर्ण, नीतिपूर्ण, नैतिक। ***n.*** 1. the principle taught by a story or event, निष्कर्ष। 2. morals (plu.) rules of (sexual) conduct, सदाचार, नीति।

morale (मराल) ***n.*** 1. mental confidence, मनोबल। 2. moral confidence, नैतिक बल।

morality (मरैलिटी) ***n.*** 1. rightness of behaviour, नीति, सदाचार, नैतिकता। 2. moral principles, नैतिक सिद्धांत।

morally (मॉरली) ***adv.*** with regard to morals, नैतिक रूप/दृष्टि से।

moratorium (मॉरेटोरिअम) ***n.*** (plu. moratoria) an order of stopping or delaying an activity temporarily, अस्थायी निलंबन आदेश।

morbid (मॉर्बिड) ***adj.*** 1. unhealthy, रुग्ण, अस्वस्थ। 2. gruesome, भयावह, बीभत्स।

morbidity (मॉर्बिडिटी) ***n.*** 1. the state of being morbid, रुग्णता, रुग्णावस्था। 2. gruesomeness, बीभत्सता।

more (मोर) ***adj.*** 1. greater in number, और अधिक। 2. greater in size or degree, और बड़ा। 3. additional, अतिरिक्त। ***n.*** a greater quantity or number, अपेक्षया अधिक परिमाण या संख्या। ***adv.*** 1. in a greater degree, और अधिक। 2. again, दुबारा, पुनः, फिर।

moreover (मोरोवर) ***adv.*** besides, इसके अतिरिक्त/सिवा।

morgue (मॉर्ग) ***n.*** a building in which dead bodies of unknown persons are kept temporarily, मुरदाघर।

morning (मॉर्निन्ग) ***n.*** 1. the early part of the day, सुबह, सवेरा। 2. dawn, प्रातः, भोर।

moron (मोरॉन) ***n.*** 1. a person of weak mind, मंदबुद्धि, अल्पबुद्धि। 2. a stupid person, मूर्ख व्यक्ति।

morose (मरोस) ***adj.*** 1. ill-tempered, चिड़चिड़े स्वभाववाला। 2. sad, gloomy, उदास, खिन्न।

morpheme (मॉर्फ़ीम) ***n.*** the smallest meaningful grammatical unit, रूपिम, रूपग्राम।

morphology (मॉर्फ़ॉलोजी) ***n.*** 1. the study of word formation, रूपिम-विज्ञान। 2. the science dealing with the form and structure of organisms, रूप-विज्ञान।

morsel (मॉर्सल) ***n.*** 1. a mouthful of food, कौर, ग्रास, निवाला। 2. a bit, टुकड़ा।

mortal (मॉर्टल) ***adj.*** 1. liable to death, मरणशील, मर्त्य। 2. fatal, deadly, घातक, प्राणघातक। 3. fierce, violent, intense, प्रचंड, उग्र, विकट, घोर। ***n.*** a human being, आदमी, मानव, मनुष्य।

mortality (मॉर्टैलिटी) ***n.*** 1. the state of being a mortal, मरणशीलता। 2. great loss of life, बहुत अधिक लोगों का मरना। 3. the number of deaths from a certain cause, मृत्यु-संख्या।

mortar[1] (मॉर्टर) ***n.*** a mixture of lime, sand and water, गारा, मसाला।

mortar[2] ***n.*** 1. a vessel for pounding, ऊखल, खरल। 2. a small cannon, छोटी तोप।

mortgage (मॉर्गिज) ***v.*** to give someone something as security for payment of a loan, रेहन या गिरवी रखना, बंधक रखना। ***n.*** pledging of a property as security against loan, गिरवी रखी हुई वस्तु, बंधक, रेहन।

mortgagee (मॉर्गिजी) ***n.*** one who keeps property as security against loan, रेहनदार, गिरवीदार, बंधकी।

mortgagor (मॉर्गिजर) ***n.*** one who mortgages one's property, अपनी संपत्ति रेहन/गिरवी रखनेवाला, बंधकदाता।

mortification (मॉर्टिफ़िकेशन) ***n.*** the act of mortifying or the state of being mortified, नीचा दिखाना या देखना, शर्मिंदा करना या होना।

mortify (मॉर्टिफ़ाइ) ***v.*** (mortified, mortifying) to humiliate, शर्मिंदा करना, नीचा दिखाना, ज़लील करना।

mortise, mortice (मॉर्टिस) ***n.*** a hole cut in a piece of wood into which the end of another part is inserted, खाँचा, छेदा।

mortuary (मॉर्ट्युअरी) ***n.*** a morgue, लाशघर।

mosaic (मोज़ेइक) ***n.*** a design made up of small pieces of stone or glass, मोज़ैक।

mosque (मॉस्क) ***n.*** a Muslim place of worship, मसजिद।

mosquito (मॉस्कीटो) ***n.*** a blood-sucking winged insect, मच्छर।

mosquito net ***n.*** a net to keep mosquitoes out, मच्छरदानी, मसहरी।

moss (मॉस) ***n.*** a class of plants, काई, शैवाल।

most (मोस्ट) ***adj.*** greatest in number,

M

अधिकतर, अधिकांश। *n.* the greatest number, अधिकांश। *adv.* used as suffix, forming the superlative of greater number of adjectives and adverbs, बहुत अधिक, सबसे अधिक।

mostly (मोस्टली) *adv.* chiefly, ज़्यादातर, अधिकतर।

motel (मोटेल) *n.* a hotel built for travelling motorists, वह होटल जिसमें गाड़ियों को ठहराने की व्यवस्था हो, मोटल।

moth (मॉथ) *n.* a winged insect, कपड़े में लगनेवाला कीड़ा, कपड़कीड़ा।

mothball (मॉथबॉल) *n.* a ball for keeping away moths from clothes, फ़िनायल की गोली।

mother (मदर) *n.* 1. one's own female parent, माँ, माता, अम्मा, जननी। 2. a term of address for an old woman, माता (जी)। 3. a woman who is head of a religious order, माता। *v.* to look after in a motherly way, लालन-पालन करना, पालना पोसना।

motherhood (मदरहुड) *n.* the state of being a mother, मातृत्व।

mother-in-law (मदर-इन-लॉ) *n.* the mother of one's wife or husband, सास।

motherland (मदरलैन्ड) *n.* one's native country, मातृभूमि।

motherly (मदरली) *adj.* like a mother, माता के जैसा, माँ का-सा।

mother tongue *n.* one's native language, मातृभाषा।

motif (मोटीफ़) *n.* underlying idea in a piece of literature or art, मूल भाव।

motile (मोटिल) *adj.* capable of motion, गतिशील।

motility (मोटिलिटी) *n.* the state of being motile, गतिशीलता।

motion (मोशन) *n.* 1. the act or state of moving, गति, चाल। 2. a gesture, इंगित, संकेत। 3. a proposal, प्रस्ताव। 4. the evacuation of the bowels, excrement, टट्टी, पाख़ाना। *v.* to make a gesture, इंगित/इशारा करना।

motionless (मोशनलिस) *adj.* not moving, गतिहीन, निश्चल।

motion picture *n.* a film, चलचित्र।

motivate (मोटिवेट) *v.* to inspire, प्रेरणा देना, प्रेरित करना।

motive (मोटिव) *n.* the reason for certain course of action, हेतु, प्रयोजन, कारण या अभिप्रेरणा। *adj.* acting as a motive, कारण स्वरूप, अभिप्रेरक।

motley (मॉट्लि) *adj.* 1. varied, मिला-जुला, खिचड़ी। 2. multi-coloured, रंग-बिरंगा।

motor (मोटर) *n.* 1. something that produces motion, मोटर। 2. a vehicle driven by an engine, मोटर, मोटरगाड़ी। *v.* to travel in an automobile, मोटर से यात्रा करना। *adj.* 1. driven by a motor, इंजन-चालित। 2. producing motion, गतिकारक।

motorcade (मोटरकेड) *n.* a procession of motorcars, कारों का काफ़िला।

mottled (मॉटल्ड) *adj.* marked with different patches of colour, चित्तीदार।

motto (मॉटो) *n.* a word, phrase or sentence expresing a principle or goal, नीति वाक्य, आदर्श वाक्यांश, उद्देश्य।

mould[1] (मोल्ड) *n.* 1. a frame to give a definite form to fluid, साँचा। 2. something shaped in a mould, साँचे में ढली वस्तु। 3. specific nature or character, स्वभाव, चरित्र। *v.* 1. to make in a mould, साँचे

में ढालना। 2. to guide and control the development of, (चरित्र, आचार) निर्माण करना।

mould[2] ***n.*** a fungi, भुकड़ी, फफूँदी।

moulding (मोल्डिंग) ***n.*** 1. the act of shaping in a mould, ढलाई। 2. something moulded, ढली हुई वस्तु।

mouldy (मोल्डी) ***adj.*** 1. covered with mould or fungi, जिसपर भुकड़ी जमी हो, भुकड़ीदार, फफूँद लगा। 2. old, पुराना, दकियानूसी।

moult, molt (मोल्ट) ***v.*** to shed feathers or skin, पंख झाड़ना या केंचुली छोड़ना। ***n.*** the process of moulting, पंख झाड़ना या केंचुली छोड़ना।

mound (माउन्ड) ***n.*** any heap or pile, टीला, ढूह।

mount[1] (माउन्ट) ***v.*** 1. to go up or climb, ऊपर जाना या चढ़ना। 2. to ride, सवारी करना या सवार होना। 3. to increase, बढ़ना। 4. to fix, जड़ना या मढ़ना। ***n.*** 1. a horse or other animal on which to ride, घोड़े आदि की सवारी। 2. the act of mounting, चढ़ना, ऊपर जाना। 3. something on which a thing is mounted, आधार, चौखटा।

mount[2] ***n.*** a mountain, पहाड़।

mountain (माउन्टिन) ***n.*** 1. a natural upward projection of the earth's surface, पहाड़, पर्वत। 2. a huge mass or heap, ढेर। ***adj.*** mountainous, पहाड़ी।

mountaineer (माउन्टिनिअर) ***n.*** one who climbs mountains, पर्वतारोही।

mountainous (माउन्टिनस) ***adj.*** 1. full of mountains, पहाड़ी, पर्वतीय। 2. huge, विशाल, पर्वताकार, पर्वत-सदृश।

mountain range ***n.*** a group of mountains in a row, पर्वतमाला।

mourn (मोर्न) ***v.*** 1. to express sorrow for the death of someone, शोक प्रकट करना। 2. to observe the customs of mourning, मातम मनाना।

mournful (मोर्नफ़ुल) ***adj.*** showing grief, शोकपूर्ण, मातमी।

mouse (माउस) ***n.*** (pl. mice) 1. a rat, चूहा। 2. a small device, कंप्यूटर का एक छोटा उपकरण।

mousetrap (माउसट्रैप) ***n.*** a trap for catching mice, चूहेदानी।

mousseline (मूस्लिन) ***n.*** muslin, मलमल।

moustache (मस्टैश) ***n.*** hair growing on the upper lip, मूँछ, मूँछें।

mousy, mousey (माउसी) ***adj.*** 1. of mice, चूहों का। 2. brownish grey, चूहों के रंग का। 3. shy, दब्बू।

mouth (माउथ) ***n.*** 1. the opening through which animals take food into their bodies, मुँह, मुख। 2. any opening resembling a mouth, मुँह। 3. a place where a river enters the sea, मुहाना। ***v.*** 1. to take something into the mouth, मुँह में डालना। 2. to speak in a low tone, फुसफुसाना।

mouthful (माउथफ़ुल) ***n.*** as much as fills the mouth, कौर, ग्रास, निवाला।

mouth-organ (माउथ-ऑर्गन) ***n.*** a musical instrument, फूँककर बजाया जानेवाला एक बाजा, माउथऑर्गन।

mouthpiece (माउथपीस) ***n.*** 1. a part of some instrument held in or near the mouth, बाजे का वह अंश जिसे मुँह में रखकर बजाया जाता है। 2. a person who speaks on someone's behalf, दूसरे की तरफ़ से बोलनेवाला।

mouthwash (माउथवाश) ***n.*** a solution

M

for cleaning the mouth, कुल्ला करने का सुगंधित द्रव्य।

movable (मूवेबल) ***adj.*** able to be moved, not fixed, चल, जंगम।

move (मूव) ***v.*** 1. to change in position or place, हिलना, हिलना-डुलना। 2. to cause to change in position or place, हिलाना, हिलाना-डुलाना। 3. to transfer (a piece) in a board game, (प्यादे आदि को) चलाना, बढ़ाना-हटाना। 4. to settle in a new place, जगह बदलना, अन्यत्र जा रहना। 5. to motivate, अभिप्रेरित करना। 6. to provoke emotion in, द्रवित या अभिभूत करना। 7. to present a resolution, प्रस्ताव पेश करना। ***n.*** 1. the act of moving, हिलना-डुलना, आगे बढ़ना। 2. the change of residence, घर बदलना। 3. the act of moving a piece, मोहरे को चलाना। 4. player's turn to move a piece, मोहरा चलने की बारी, चाल।

moveable (मूवेबल) ***adj.*** = movable.

movement (मूवमेन्ट) ***n.*** 1. the act of moving or the state of being moved, हिलना-डुलना, गति, हरकत। 2. a series of combined activities of a group, आंदोलन। 3. activity, चेष्टा, हलचल। 4. (plu.) activities, क्रियाकलाप, गतिविधियाँ।

mover (मूवर) ***n.*** 1. one who moves a resolution, प्रस्तावक। 2. one whose occupation is transporting furnishings, वह जो गृहस्थी का सामान एक घर से उठाकर दूसरे घर तक ले जाता हो, परिवाहक।

movie (मूवी) ***n.*** a motion picture, चलचित्र।

moving (मूविंग) ***adj.*** 1. that moves, चल, गतिमान। 2. touching, हृदयस्पर्शी।

mow (मो) ***v.*** (mowed, mown, mowing) to cut down (grass, corn etc.,) with scythe or machine, (घास आदि) काटना।

mower (मोअर) ***n.*** 1. a person that mows, घास काटनेवाला, घसियारा, लुनेरा। 2. a machine for mowing, घास काटने की मशीन, लुनाई मशीन।

Mr. (मिस्टर) ***n.*** the title to a man's name, मिस्टर, श्री, श्रीमान, श्रीयुत, जनाब।

Mrs. (मिसिज़) ***n.*** the title to a married woman's name, श्रीमती।

Ms. (मिज़) ***n.*** the title to a married or unmarried woman's name, सुश्री।

much (मच) ***adj.*** (more, most) great in quantity, degree or extent, बहुत ज़्यादा, अधिक। ***n.*** a large quantity or amount, अधिक मात्रा या राशि। ***adv.*** 1. to a great degree, बहुत, अधिक। 2. almost, क़रीब-क़रीब।

mucilage (म्यूसिलिज) ***n.*** gum or glue, गोंद या लासा।

muck (मक) ***n.*** filth, कूड़ा-करकट। ***v.*** to make dirty, गंदा करना।

mucky (मकी) ***adj.*** dirty, filthy, गंदा।

mucus (म्यूकस) ***n.*** a sticky substance secreted by mucous membranes, गले, नाक, आँख आदि से निकलनेवाला मल; कफ़, बलगम, आदि।

mud (मड) ***n.*** wet, sticky, soft earth, कीचड़, पंक।

muddiness (मडिनिस) ***n.*** the quality or state of being muddy, गंदलापन, धुँधलापन।

muddle (मडल) ***v.*** 1. to mix up, घाल-मेल करना। 2. to confuse, भ्रम में डालना। ***n.*** 1. a muddled condition, घाल-मेल। 2. disorder, अव्यवस्था। 3. confusion, भ्रांति।

muddy (मडी) ***adj.*** 1. filled with mud, कीचड़-भरा, पंकिल, गंदला। 2. not bright or clear, धुँधला। ***v.*** to make muddy, गंदला कर देना।

mudguard (मडगार्ड) ***n.*** a cover over a vehicle's wheel, मडगार्ड।

muffin (मफ़िन) ***n.*** a round cake, चपाती, फुलका, कुलचा।

muffle (मफ़ल) ***v.*** 1. to wrap up (the head) for warmth or protection, (सिर को) लपेट लेना। 2. to cover, ढकना। 3. to deaden the sound, आवाज़ दबा देना। ***n.*** something that muffles, लपेटने का वस्त्र, स्कार्फ़ या गुलूबंद।

muffler (मफ़लर) ***n.*** a heavy scraf worn round the neck, गुलूबंद, मफ़लर।

mufti (मुफ़्टी) ***n.*** civilian dress, साधारण कपड़े।

mug[1] (मग) ***n.*** a large drinking cup, बड़ा प्याला, मग।

mug[2] ***n.*** a face, चेहरा। ***v.*** 1. to make faces, मुँह बनाना। 2. to rob with violence, लूट-मार करना।

mugging (मगिंग) ***n.*** a robbery with violence, लूट-मार।

muggy (मगी) ***adj.*** humid, उमस-भरा, घुटन-भरा।

Muhammadan (मुहमेडन) ***n.*** a Muslim, मुसलमान।

mulberry (मल्बेरी) ***n.*** a tree and its fruit, शहतूत (पेड़ और फल)।

mule (म्यूल) ***n.*** 1. an offspring of male donkey and female horse, खच्चर। 2. a stubborn person, ज़िद्दी या हठी आदमी।

mulish (म्यूलिश) ***adj.*** stubborn, हठी, अड़ियल।

mullah (मुला) ***n.*** a Muslim religious teacher, मुल्ला।

multi (मल्टि) ***prefix.*** many, अनेक, बहुत, बहु-।

multifarious (मल्टिफ़ेरिअस) ***adj.*** of many kinds, विविध या विविधतापूर्ण।

multiform (मल्टिफ़ॉर्म) ***adj.*** of many forms or kinds, नानारूप, नानाविध।

multiple (मल्टिपल) ***adj.*** consisting of more than one individual or part, अनेक, विविध, बहुत, बहु-; multiple party system, बहुदलीय पद्धति। ***n.*** a number which contains another number an exact number of times, अपवर्त्य, गुणज।

multiplex (मल्टिप्लेक्स) ***adj.*** having many forms or parts, बहुविध।

multiplicand (मल्टिप्लिकैन्ड) ***n.*** the number that is to be multiplied by another, गुण्य।

multiplication (मल्टिप्लिकेशन) ***n.*** 1. the act of multiplying, गुणन। 2. increase, बढ़ोतरी।

multiplicity (मल्टिप्लिसिटी) ***n.*** great variety, विविधता।

multiplier (मल्टिप्लाइअर) ***n.*** the number by which a quantity is multiplied, गुणक।

multiply (मल्टिप्लाइ) ***v.*** 1. to perform multiplication, गुणा करना। 2. become more numerous, बढ़ना, बढ़ाना।

multistage (मल्टिस्टेज) ***adj.*** having more than two sections, बहुस्तरीय।

multitude (मल्टिट्यूड) ***n.*** a great number of things or people, जमघट, भीड़।

mum (मम) ***adj.*** not talking, चुप, शांत।

mumble (मम्बल) ***v.*** to speak indistinctly, बुदबुदाना।

mummify (ममिफ़ाइ) ***v.*** to preserve a corpse, शव को सुरक्षित रखना।

mummy[1] (ममी) ***n.*** a preserved corpse, ममी, सुरक्षित शव।

mummy[2] ***n.*** mother, माँ।

mumps (मम्प्स) ***n.*** an acute painful

M

swelling of the salivary glands, कनपेड़ा, गलसुआ।

munch (मन्च) ***v.*** to chew with a noise, चबड़-चबड़ करना।

mundane (मन्डेन) ***adj.*** worldly, सांसारिक, संसार-विषयक।

municipal corporation (म्युनि-सिपल कॉर्पोरेशन) ***n.*** the governing body of a big city, नगर-निगम।

municipality (म्युनिसिपैलिटी) ***n.*** self-governing town and its governing body, नगरपालिका।

munificence (म्युनिफ़िसेन्स) ***n.*** the state of being munificent, दानशीलता, उदारता।

munificent (म्युनिफ़िसेन्ट) ***adj.*** very generous, अत्यंत उदार, दानी।

mural (म्यूरल) ***adj.*** of or on a wall, दीवार-संबंधी। ***n.*** a wall painting, दीवार पर बना चित्र, भित्तिचित्र।

murder (मर्डर) ***n.*** an unlawful killing of a person, हत्या, वध, ख़ून। ***v.*** to kill, हत्या करना, ख़ून करना, वध करना, मारना।

murderer (मर्डरर) ***n.*** one who murders someone, हत्यारा, ख़ूनी। [Fem. murderess, हत्यारिन]

murky (मर्की) ***adj.*** 1. dark, अँधेरा। 2. gloomy, विषादपूर्ण। 3. unclear, cloudy, धुँधला।

murmur (मर्मर) ***n.*** an indistinct utterance, बड़बड़ाहट। ***v.*** to make a murmur, बड़बड़ाना।

muscle (मसल) ***n.*** 1. a tissue composed of cells, मांसपेशी। 2. muscular power, शारीरिक बल, बाहुबल।

muscular (मस्क्युलर) ***adj.*** 1. of muscles, मांसपेशीय। 2. having well-developed muscles, गठीला, हृष्ट-पुष्ट, हट्टा-कट्टा।

muse (म्यूज़) ***v.*** to ponder, विचार करना, चिंतन करना।

museum (म्यूज़ीअम) ***n.*** a building in which objects of historical value are exhibited, संग्रहालय, अजायबघर, म्यूज़ियम।

mushroom (मशरूम) ***n.*** an umbrella-shaped fungus, कुकुरमुत्ता, छत्रक, खुंबी। ***v.*** to grow rapidly, तेज़ी से बढ़ना या फैलना।

mushy (मशी) ***adj.*** 1. pulpy, गूदेदार। 2. sentimental, भावुक।

music (म्यूज़िक) ***n.*** pleasing combination of voices or sounds, संगीत।

musical (म्यूज़िकल) ***adj.*** 1. of music, संगीत-संबंधी। 2. melodious, मधुर, संगीतात्मक, संगीतमय।

musical instrument ***n.*** an instrument that plays tunes, बाजा, वाद्य।

musician (म्यूज़िशन) ***n.*** one skilled in music, संगीतकार, संगीतज्ञ।

musk (मस्क) ***n.*** a substance secreted by male deer used in perfumery, कस्तूरी।

musket (मस्किट) ***n.*** a gun with a long barrel, पुरानी चाल की बंदूक, तुपक।

musketeer (मस्केटिअर) ***n.*** a soldier armed with a musket, बंदूकची।

Muslim (मुस्लिम) ***n.*** a follower of Islam, मुसलमान, मुस्लिम। ***adj.*** of Muslims, मुसलमानी।

muslin (मज़्लिन) ***n.*** a fine thin cotton fabric, मलमल।

must (मस्ट) ***aux. v.*** indicating necessity, obligation, inevitability, certainty, insistence etc., आवश्यकता, निश्चितता, आग्रह आदि की बोधक सहायक

क्रिया। ***n.*** an absolute requirement, परम आवश्यकता।

mustache (मुस्टैश) ***n.*** = moustache।

mustard (मस्टर्ड) ***n.*** a plant with yellow flowers and pungent seeds, सरसों।

muster (मस्टर) ***v.*** 1. to assemble, जमा होना या करना। 2. to gather up, जुटाना। ***n.*** gathering, जमावड़ा, सभा।

mutable (म्यूटेबल) ***adj.*** subject to change, fickle, परिवर्तनशील, विकारी।

mutate (म्यूटेट) ***v.*** 1. to undergo change, परिवर्तन होना, बदलना। 2. to cause to undergo change, परिवर्तन करना, बदलना।

mutation (म्यूटेशन) ***n.*** 1. a change, परिवर्तन। 2. change in name, नाम-परिवर्तन, दाखिल-ख़ारिज।

mute (म्यूट) ***adj.*** 1. not speaking, चुप। 2. not spoken, मूक (वर्ण)। 3. dumb, गूँगा (प्रायः बहरा और गूँगा)। ***n.*** 1. a deaf and mute person, गूँगा आदमी। 2. a device to deaden the sound of a musical instrument, वाद्यों के तारों की गूँज को कम करने की क्लिप।

mutilate (म्यूटिलेट) ***v.*** 1. to damage by cutting an important part, अंग भंग करना। 2. to disfigure, विकृत करना, रूप बिगाड़ देना।

mutiny (म्यूटिनी) ***n.*** rebellion against authority, विद्रोह, बग़ावत। ***v.*** to engage in mutiny, विद्रोह करना, बग़ावत करना।

mutter (मटर) ***v.*** 1.to speak indistinctly in low tone, बुड़बुड़ करना, बुड़बुड़ाना, बड़बड़ाना। 2. to grumble or complain, शिकायत करना। ***n.*** muttered words, बुड़बुड़ाहट।

mutton (मटन) ***n.*** the flesh of a sheep or goat, भेड़/बकरी का गोश्त।

mutual (म्यूचुअल) ***adj.*** 1. reciprocal, आपसी, पारस्परिक। 2. shared by both, साँझा।

muzzle (मज़ल) ***n.*** 1. the projecting jaw and nose of certain animals, थूथन। 2. a strap fitted over an animal's nose, मोहरा। 3. the front end of the barrel of a gun, नालमुख। ***v.*** 1. to put a muzzle on, मोहरा पहनाना। 2. to restrain from expressing opinion, विचार या मत प्रकट करने से रोकना, मुँह बंद करना।

my (माइ) ***pron.*** belonging to me, मेरा। ***interj.*** an exclamation of surprise, अरे!

myopia (माइओपिआ) ***n.*** short sightedness, क्षीण दृष्टि (विशेषतः दूर की चीज़ न देख पाना)।

myriad (मिरिअड) ***n.*** a vast number, बहुत बड़ी संख्या।

myself (माइसेल्फ़) ***pron.*** reflexive form of I, स्वयं, ख़ुद।

mysterious (मिस्टिरिअस) ***adj.*** 1. full of mystery, रहस्यपूर्ण, रहस्यमय। 2. obscure, गूढ़। 3. puzzling, भ्रामक।

mystery (मिस्टरी) ***n.*** 1. an inexplicable event, रहस्यपूर्ण घटना, रहस्य। 2. a puzzle, पहेली।

mysticism (मिस्टिसिज़म) ***n.*** union with God, रहस्यवाद।

myth (मिथ) ***n.*** 1. a traditional story, पौराणिक कथा, आख्यान। 2. a belief about natural phenomena or social customs, मिथ, काल्पनिक सत्य।

mythology (मिथॉलोजी) ***n.*** 1. a body of myths, पुराण। 2. the study of myths, पुराणों का अध्ययन।

N

N, n (एन) ***n.*** the fourteenth letter of the English alphabet, अंग्रेज़ी वर्णमाला का चौदहवाँ वर्ण।

nab (नैब) ***v.*** 1. to arrest (a criminal) in the act, (अपराधी को) रँगे हाथ पकड़ना। 2. to seize or grab, पकड़ना, धर लेना।

nadir (नेडिअर) ***n.*** the lowest point, अधोबिंदु।

nag (नैग) ***v.*** 1. to annoy by constant complaining or scolding, जान खाना, पीछे पड़ जाना। 2. to be a constant source of worry, आफ़त हो या बन जाना।

nail (नेल) ***n.*** 1. a small metal pin, कील, कँटिया। 2. a fingernail, नख, नाख़ून। ***v.*** to fasten with a nail, कील जड़ना।

naive (नेव) ***adj.*** devoid of worldy experience, भोला-भाला, सीधा, निश्छल।

naked (नेकिड) ***adj.*** 1. without clothes on, नंगा, नग्न। 2. without the usual covering, आवरण या खोल से रहित, खुला।

name (नेम) ***n.*** 1. the word or words that someone or something is called or known by, नाम। 2. reputation, ख्याति, नाम। ***v.*** 1. to give a name to, नामकरण करना, नाम रखना। 2. to mention by name, नाम लेना। 3. to nominate or appoint, नामित या नियुक्त करना।

namely (नेमली) ***adj.*** that is to say, अर्थात्, यानी।

namesake (नेमसेक) ***n.*** a person with the same name as that of the other, नामराशि।

nap¹ (नैप) ***n.*** a short sleep or doze, झपकी, उँघाई, ऊँघ। ***v.*** to have a nap, झपकी लेना।

nap² ***n.*** the raised fibres, (कपड़े में) निकले हुए रोएँ।

nape (नेप) ***n.*** the back part of the neck, गरदन।

naphthalene (नैफ़्थलीन) ***n.*** a moth repellent substance, नैफ़्थलीन।

napkin (नैप्किन) a square piece of cloth used at meals to protect one's clothes, नैपकिन।

nappy (नैपी) ***n.*** a piece of cloth worn between the legs and around the waist of a baby, पोतड़ा, लंगोट।

narcissism (नार्सिसिज़म) ***n.*** excessive admiration for oneself, अपना गुणगान, आत्मप्रशंसा।

narcotic (नार्कॉटिक) ***adj.*** 1. causing unconsciousness or drowsiness, बेहोशी लानेवाला, नशीला, स्वापक। ***n.*** a narcotic addict, स्वापक व्यसनी। 2. a drug, नशीली दवा, स्वापक ओषधि।

narrate (नैरेट) ***v.*** to describe or relate, वर्णन करना।

narrative (नैरेटिव) ***n.*** spoken or written account, वर्णन, वृत्तांत। ***adj.*** in the form of a narrative, वर्णनात्मक, आख्यानात्मक।

narrow (नैरो) ***adj.*** 1. of small width, तंग, सँकरा। 2. limited, सीमित, अत्यल्प। 3. narrow-minded, संकीर्ण, संकुचित। ***v.*** to make or become narrower, सँकरा करना या होना, संकीर्ण होना या बनाना।

narrow-minded ***adj.*** bigoted or prejudiced, संकीर्ण-हृदय या पूर्वग्रही।

nasal (नेज़ल) ***adj.*** 1. of or pertaining to the nose, नासिका-संबंधी। 2. uttered so that most of the air is exhaled through the nose, नासिक या अनुनासिक (वर्ण)।

nascent (नैसन्ट) ***adj.*** coming into existence, नवजात, प्रारंभिक।

nasty (नैस्टी) ***n.*** 1. filthy, foul, गंदा, बुरा। 2. malicious, द्वेषपूर्ण। 3. spiteful, घृणित।

natal (नेटल) ***adj.*** relating to birth, पैदाइशी, जन्म-संबंधी।

nation (नेशन) ***n.*** people of common descent, history, language or organised under one government, राष्ट्र, कौम।

national (नैशनल) ***adj.*** of a nation, राष्ट्रीय, क़ौमी, राष्ट्र-। ***n.*** a citizen of the country, राष्ट्रवासी।

nationalism (नैशनलिज़म) devotion to one's nation, राष्ट्रभावना, राष्ट्रवाद।

nationality (नैशनैलिटी) ***n.*** the status of belonging to a particular nation, राष्ट्रीयता।

nationalize (नैशनलाइज़) ***v.*** to put (industries, bank etc.) under government control, राष्ट्रीयकरण करना।

nationwide (नेशनवाइड) ***adj.*** extending throughout the whole nation, राष्ट्रव्यापी।

native (नेटिव) ***n.*** 1. an original inhabistant, मूल वासी। 2. belonging to the place of one's birth, स्थानीय, देशीय। 3. natural, प्रकृत। 4. inborn, जन्मजात।

nativity (नेटिविटी) ***n.*** 1. birth, जन्म। 2. origin, उत्पत्ति।

NATO (नैटो) ***n.*** North Atlantic Treaty Organisation, नैटो।

natural (नैचरल) ***adj.*** 1. of nature or produced by nature, प्राकृतिक, नैसर्गिक, प्रकृत। 2. normal, स्वाभाविक, सहज, अकृत्रिम। 3. inborn, जन्मजात। 4. to be expected, प्रत्याशित। ***n.*** 1. a person obviously suited or qualified, सही व्यक्ति। 2. pale fawn colour, हलका पीला रंग।

naturalism (नैचरलिज़म) ***n.*** a movement for realistic description, प्रकृतवाद, यथार्थवाद।

naturalize (नैचरलाइज़) ***v.*** 1. to grant full citizenship to, नागरिक बना लेना, नागरिकता प्रदान करना। 2. to adopt and acclimatize, अपना लेना, (अपने को) ढाल लेना।

naturally (नैचरली) ***adv.*** 1. of course, निस्संदेह। 2. according to the nature of someone or something, प्रकृतिशः, स्वभावतः। 3. in a manner to be expected, आशानुरूप।

nature (नेचर) ***n.*** 1. the physical world, भौतिक सृष्टि, प्रकृति, निसर्ग। 2. inherent character, मूलभूत चारित्रिक गुण, स्वभाव, प्रकृति। 3. intrinsic quality, गुण, स्वभाव। 4. kind or type, प्रकार, क़िस्म, रूप।

nature cure, naturopathy ***n.*** healing by natural objects, प्राकृतिक चिकित्सा।

naturism (नेचरिज़म) ***n.*** nudism, नग्नवाद।

naught (नॉट) ***n.*** 1. nothing, कुछ नहीं। 2. zero, शून्य, सिफ़र।

naughtiness (नॉटिनिस) ***adj.*** 1. the quality of being naughty, पाजीपन। 2. a mischievous act, शरारत।

naughty (नॉटी) ***adj.*** 1. behaving

badly, mischievous, शरारती, नटखट। 2. improper, अनुचित, अशिष्टतापूर्ण।

nausea (नॉसिआ) ***n.*** 1. a feeling of sickness accompanied by an involuntary impulse to vomit, मिचली, मतली, उबकाई। 2. a feeling of disgust, घिन, घृणा, जुगुप्सा।

nautical (नॉटिकल) ***adj.*** 1. of sailors, नाविक-संबंधी। 2. of navigation, नौचालन-संबंधी।

naval (नेवल) ***adj.*** 1. of navy, नौसैनिक। 2. of warships, युद्धपोत-संबंधी।

nave (नेव) ***n.*** the central place in a church, गिरजे का लंबा मध्य भाग।

navel (नेवल) ***n.*** the mark in the centre of the abdomen, नाभि।

navigable (नैविगेबल) ***adj.*** 1. deep and wide enough to be sailed through, नौगम्य। 2. to be sailed, जिसे खेकर चलाया जा सके।

navigate (नैविगेट) ***v.*** 1. to direct the path of a ship or aircraft, नौचालन करना, जहाज़ चलाना। 2. to voyage over water, संतरण करना, समुद्री यात्रा करना।

navigator (नैविगेटर) ***n.*** one who controls the course of a ship or aircraft, जलयान या विमान का पथनिदेशक।

navy (नेवी) ***n.*** 1. all of the nation's warships, राष्ट्र के युद्धपोतों का समूह। 2. the officers and soldiers of these, नौसेना, जलसेना।

navy blue ***adj.*** very dark blue, गहरा नीला।

near (निअर) ***adv.*** 1. close to, निकट, समीप, पास। 2. nearly, almost लगभग, प्राय:। ***adj.*** 1. close, नज़दीकी, समीपवर्ती। 2. closely related, नज़दीकी। ***v.*** to come to, निकट आना/पहुँचना।

nearly (निअर्ली) ***adv.*** 1. almost, लगभग, क़रीब-क़रीब, प्राय:। 2. closely, घनिष्ठ रूप से।

nearness (निअरनिस) ***n.*** the state of being near, निकटता, समीपता।

neat (नीट) ***adj.*** 1. orderly, सुव्यवस्थित। 2. clean, स्वच्छ, साफ़-सुथरा, परिष्कृत। 3. simple and exact, सरल और सही। 4. skillfully executed, चतुराई-भरा, दक्षतापूर्ण। 5. undiluted, अमिश्रित (शराब), शुद्ध।

neatness (नीटनिस) ***n.*** cleanliness, स्वच्छता, सफ़ाई।

nebula (नेब्यूला) ***n.*** 1. a mass of gas or dust among the stars, धुंध, नीहारिका।

nebulous (नेब्यूलस) ***adj.*** hazy, indistinct, धुंधला, अस्पष्ट।

necessaries (नेसिसरिज़) ***n.*** (plu.) the things needed, आवश्यक वस्तुएँ।

necessary (नेसिसरी) ***adj.*** 1. essential, आवश्यक, ज़रूरी। 2. inevitable, अपरिहार्य, अनिवार्य।

necessity (निसेसिटी) ***n.*** 1. the state of being necessary, आवश्यकता, ज़रूरत। 2. something that is necessary, आवश्यक वस्तु।

neck (नेक) ***n.*** 1. the part of the body joining head and trunk, गर्दन, ग्रीवा। 2. the part of a garment around the neck, गरेबान। 3. a narrow part of anything, गला, गर्दन। 4. the length of the head and neck of a horse, घोड़े की गर्दन की लंबाई।

necklace (नेकलिस) ***n.*** an ornament worn around the neck, कंठहार, कंठा।

necrosis (नेक्रोसिस) ***n.*** the death of bone or tissues, ऊतकक्षय, अस्थिक्षय।

nectar (नेक्टर) ***n.*** 1. the drink of the gods, अमृत। 2. a delicious drink, मधुरस, मधुर पेय।

N

nee (नी) ***n.*** (used to identify a married woman by her maiden family name, विवाहित स्त्री को उसके कुँआरेपन के नाम से पहचानने के लिए प्रयुक्त होता है) born with the name, पूर्वनाम, जन्मनाम।

need (नीड) ***n.*** 1. necessity, आवश्यकता, ज़रूरत। 2. something desired or wanted, चाह, ज़रूरत, इच्छित वस्तु। 3. poverty, ग़रीबी। ***v.*** 1. to require, आवश्यक होना। 2. to be under a necessity, बाध्य होना।

needful (नीड्फ़ुल) ***adj.*** necessary, आवश्यक, ज़रूरी।

needle (नीडल) ***n.*** 1. a thin piece of steel for sewing purposes, सुई। 2. something resembling this, use, सुई, सलाई। 3. a pointer of a compass, सुई, हाथ। ***v.*** to goad or tease, छेड़ना या तंग करना।

needless (नीडलिस) ***adj.*** unnecessary, अनावश्यक, निरर्थक।

needlework (नीडलवर्क) ***n.*** sewing and embroidery सिलाई, बुनाई या कढ़ाई।

needy (नीडी) ***adj.*** 1. being in need, ज़रूरतमंद। 2. poor, निर्धन।

nefarious (निफ़ेरिअस) ***adj.*** evil, wicked, दुष्ट या दुष्टतापूर्ण, बुरा, निंद्य।

negate (निगेट) ***vt.*** 1. to nullify, निराकरण करना, निष्प्रभावी करना। 2. to disprove, अमान्य करना, रद करना। 3. to deny, इन्कार करना, झुठला देना।

negation (निगेशन) ***n.*** the act of negating or the state of being negated, निराकरण, अमान्यकरण, इन्कार।

negative (नेगेटिव) ***adj.*** 1. expressing negation, refusal or denial, नकारात्मक, निषेधात्मक, निषेधक। 2. denoting a quantity less than zero, ऋणात्मक। ***n.*** 1. a negative word, statement or reply, इन्कार, नकार, निषेध, खंडन, नकारात्मक उत्तर। 2. negative quantity or quality, ऋणात्मक संख्या या गुणवत्ता। 3. a negative photograph, नेगेटिव।

neglect (निग्लेक्ट) ***v.*** 1. to ignore, उपेक्षा करना। 2. to fail to give proper attention to, लापरवाही कर जाना। ***n.*** 1. the act of neglecting or the state of being neglected, उपेक्षित अवस्था। 2. negligence, लापरवाही।

neglectful (निग्लेक्टफ़ुल) ***adj.*** paying no heed or attention, असावधान, लापरवाह।

negligence (नेग्लिजेन्स) ***n.*** 1. the condition of being negligent, प्रमाद, असावधानी, लापरवाही, बेख़बरी। 2. neglect, उपेक्षा।

negligent (नेग्लिजेन्ट) ***adj.*** habitually guilty of neglect, असावधान, लापरवाह, बेख़बर।

negligible (नेग्लिजिबल) ***n.*** 1. worthy of neglect, उपेक्ष्य। 2. नगण्य।

negotiable (निगोशिएबल) ***adj.*** that can be negotiated, जिसे वार्ता से सुलझाया जा सके, संलाप्य; जो दिया-लिया जा सके, जिसे पार किया जा सके।

negotiate (निगोशिएट) ***v.*** 1. to confer with a view to reach an agreement, समझौते के लिए बातचीत करना, समझौता-वार्ता करना। 2. to transfer a cheque, title etc., in return for value received, लेन-देन करना, सौदा करना। 3. to get through (an obstacle, कठिनाई से) पार पाना।

negotiation (निगोशिएशन) ***n.*** (usu. plu.) discussion aimed at reaching

N

an agreement, वार्ता, बातचीत, समझौता-वार्ता।

negress (नीग्रिस) ***n.*** a female negro, हब्शिन।

negro (नीग्रो) ***n.*** a person of dark-skinned race, हब्शी, नीग्रो।

neigh (ने) ***n.*** the sound made by a horse, हिनहिनाहट। ***v.*** to make a neigh, हिनहिनाना।

neighbour, neighbor (नेबर) ***n.*** one who lives near another, पड़ोसी, साथवाला, बग़लवाला, प्रतिवेशी। ***v.*** to live close to, पड़ोस में रहना या होना।

neighbourhood (नेबरहुड) ***n.*** 1. immediate environment, surroundings, पड़ोस, प्रतिवेश। 2. people living near by, पड़ोसी लोग, पास-पड़ोसवाले।

neither (नाइदर, नीदर) ***pron.*** not either, न यह न वह, कोई भी नहीं। ***conj.*** not either, न तो, Neither Ram nor Shyam went, न तो राम गया न श्याम। ***adj.*** not either, कोई भी नहीं। ***adv.*** also not, भी नहीं।

neo (नीओ) ***prefix.*** new, नव-, नव्य-।

neolithic (नीओलिथिक) ***adj.*** of the later stone age, नव-पाषाणकालीन।

nephew (नेफ़्यू) ***n.*** 1. one's brother's or sister's son, भतीजा या भानजा।

nepotism (नेपटिज़्म) ***n.*** act of favouring one's relatives and friends, भाई-भतीजावाद, कुनबा-परस्ती।

Neptune (नेप्ट्यून) ***n.*** 1. the Roman god of sea, जल-देवता। 2. a planet in the solar system, वरुण ग्रह।

nerve (नर्व) ***n.*** 1. any of the fibres of the body carrying feelings or messages to and from the brain, तंतु, स्नायु, तंत्रिका। 2. a vein in a leaf, नस, रेशा। 3. bravery, courage, वीरता, साहस, जीवट।

nervous (नर्वस) ***adj.*** 1. of or related to the nerves or nervous system, स्नायु-तंत्र-संबंधी। 2. easily excited, घबरा जानेवाला, उत्तेजित हो जानेवाला।

nervous system ***n.*** the system of nerves throughout the body, स्नायु-तंत्र।

ness (निस) ***n.*** a cape, अंतरीप, रास।

nest (नेस्ट) ***n.*** 1. a shelter made by a bird, घोंसला, नीड़। 2. a similar shelter for insects, fish etc. घरौंदा, बाँबी, घर, घोंसला। 3. a hut, झोंपड़ी, बसेरा। 4. a snug place or refuge, अड्डा, शरणस्थल। ***v.*** 1. to make a nest, घोंसला बनाना। 2. to inhabit a nest, घोंसला बनाकर रहना।

nestle (नेसल) ***v.*** 1. to lie snugly, सुखपूर्वक लेटना या लेटाना। 2. to settle snugly, शांति से रहना।

nestling (नेस्लिंग) ***n.*** a young bird not yet fledged, घोंसले में रहनेवाले पक्षी का छोटा बच्चा, पोया।

net[1] (नेट) ***n.*** 1. an open work meshed fabric, जाली, जालदार काम। 2. a device of capturing animals made of meshed fabric, जाल। 3. something that entraps, जाल, फंदा। ***v.*** to catch in a net, जाल में पकड़ना या फँसाना।

net[2] ***adj.*** 1. remaining after all deductions, निवल; शुद्ध। 2. final, अंतिम।

nether (नेदर) ***adj.*** below, beneath, निचला, निम्न, अधोलोक।

netting (नेटिंग) ***n.*** any netted fabric, जाली।

nettle (नेटल) ***v.*** to irritate, क्षुब्ध करना, चिढ़ाना। ***n.*** a plant, बिच्छू बूटी।

network (नेटवर्क) ***n.*** 1. an open fabric in which cords, wires etc., cross at regular intervals, जाल। 2. an interconnected group or system, तंत्र, जाल।

neural (न्यूरल) ***adj.*** of nerves, स्नायु-संबंधी, तंत्रिकीय, स्नायवीय।

neuritis (न्यूराइटिस) ***n.*** inflammation of nerves, तंत्रिका-शोथ, स्नायु-शोथ।

neurologist (न्यूरॉलोजिस्ट) ***n.*** an expert in neurology, स्नायु-विज्ञानी, तंत्रिका-विज्ञानी।

neurology (न्यूरॉलोजी) ***n.*** the study of nervous system, तंत्रिका-विज्ञान, स्नायु-विज्ञान।

neuron (न्यूरॉन) ***n.*** a nerve cell, स्नायु-कोशिका।

neurosis (न्यूरोसिस) ***n.*** a disorder of the mind, मनोविक्षेप।

neuter (न्यूटर) ***adj.*** 1. (of a noun) neither masculine nor feminine, नपुंसकलिंग। 2. without male or female parts, नपुंसक, क्लीव। ***n.*** 1. a neuter word, नपुंसकलिंग शब्द। 2. a neuter plant or animal, क्लीव पौधा/जंतु।

neutral (न्यूट्रल) ***adj.*** 1. not siding with any party, तटस्थ; neutral zone, तटस्थ क्षेत्र। 2. belonging to neither side, निष्पक्ष। 3. neither positive nor negative, न्यूट्रल, उदासीन।

neutrality (न्यूट्रैलिटी) ***n.*** the state of being neutral, तटस्थता, निष्पक्षता।

neutralization (न्यूट्रलाइज़ेशन) ***n.*** the act or process of neutralizing, तटस्थीकरण; निष्प्रभावीकरण।

neutralize (न्यूट्रलाइज़) ***v.*** 1. to make neutral, तटस्थ बनाना। 2. to make ineffective, निष्प्रभावी करना, न्यूट्रल करना।

neutron (न्यूट्रॉन) ***n.*** a neutral particle, न्यूट्रॉन।

never (नेवर) ***adv.*** 1. at no time, कभी नहीं। 2. in no case, बिल्कुल नहीं।

nevertheless (नेवरदिलेस) ***adv.*** in spite of this, तो भी, तिस पर भी, फिर भी।

new (न्यू) ***adj.*** 1. not old, recent, नया, नवीन, नव। 2. unfamiliar, unknown, अपरिचित, नया। 3. recently started or introduced, अभी-अभी आरंभ होनेवाला, नया। ***adv.*** recently, अभी हाल में।

newfangled (न्यूफ़ैन्गल्ड) ***adj.*** excessively modern, अति आधुनिक, विशेषत: अटपटा।

newly (न्यूली) ***adv.*** recently, हाल का।

new moon ***n.*** the bright thin edge of the moon, नवचंद्र, दूज का चाँद।

news (न्यूज़) ***n.*** 1. information about recent happenings, समाचार, ख़बर। 2. a broadcast report of this, समाचार, ख़बरें।

news-agent (न्यूज़-एजेन्ट) ***n.*** a shopkeeper selling newspapers, magazines etc., पत्र-पत्रिका विक्रेता।

newsletter (न्यूज़लेटर) ***n.*** a periodical bulletin of an institution, संवाद-पत्र, वृत्त-पत्र।

newspaper (न्यूज़पेपर) ***n.*** a daily publication giving news, समाचारपत्र, अख़बार।

newsprint (न्यूज़प्रिन्ट) ***n.*** the paper of the newspaper, अख़बारी काग़ज़।

newsworthy (न्यूज़वर्दी) ***adj.*** that can be printed in a newspaper, छपने योग्य।

New Year ***n.*** the year which has just begun, नववर्ष।

N

next (नेक्स्ट) ***adj.*** 1. immediately following, अगला, बादवाला, आगामी। 2. immediately adjoining, साथवाला, बाज़ूवाला। ***n.*** the next person or thing, अगला आदमी या अगली वस्तु। ***prep.*** in the next place to, के अनंतर, के बाद में, के आगे।

nexus (नेक्सस) ***n.*** 1. a link, कड़ी। 2. a connection between objects, ideas etc., अंतर्संबंध, गठजोड़।

nib (निब) ***n.*** the metal point of a pen, निब।

nibble (निबल) ***v.*** to take small repeated bites (of something, किसी चीज़ को) कुतरना, टूँगना, खाना। ***n.*** the act of nibbling, कुतरना, टूँगना, खाना।

nice (नाइस) ***adj.*** 1. pleasant, excellent, बढ़िया, बहुत अच्छा, सुंदर, चारु। 2. gentle, भला, सहृदय। 3. subtle, सूक्ष्म।

nicety (नाइसिटी) ***n.*** 1. precision, सूक्ष्मता, बारीक़ी। 2. dainty, चारुता। 3. a pleasant thing, बढ़िया चीज़।

niche (निच) ***n.*** 1. a hollow place in a wall, आला। 2. a suitable place or position, उपयुक्त स्थान।

nick (निक) ***n.*** a small cut, खरोंच।

nickel (निकल) ***n.*** a hard silvery metal, निकल। ***v.*** to put a thin layer of nickel, निकल चढ़ाना।

nickname (निकनेम) ***n.*** 1. a derisive name, छेड़ने या चिढ़ाने का नाम, छेड़, चिढ़। 2. a familiar name, प्रसिद्ध नाम। ***v.*** to give a nickname to, नाम धरना, छेड़ डालना, चिढ़ाना।

nicotine (निकोटीन) ***n.*** a toxic substance found in tobacco, तंबाकू में होनेवाला विषाक्त तत्त्व, निकोटीन।

niece (नीस) ***n.*** one's brother's or sister's daughter, भतीजी या भानजी।

niggard (निगर्ड) ***n.*** a very stingy person, कंजूस व्यक्ति, मक्खीचूस।

niggle (निगल) ***v.*** 1. to criticise or pay too much attention on small details, नुक्ताचीनी करना। 2. to annoy, चिढ़ाना, अप्रसन्न करना।

niggling (निगलिंग) ***adj.*** 1. showing too much attention to details, नुक्ताचीन। 2. annoying, अप्रसन्न करनेवाला, चिढ़ानेवाला।

nigh (नाइ) ***adv.*** near, नज़दीक।

night (नाइट) ***n.*** the dark part of the day, रात, रात्रि।

nightfall (नाइटफ़ॉल) ***n.*** the approach of darkness, रात पड़ना, अँधेरा होना, सांध्य-वेला।

nightgown (नाइटगाउन) ***n.*** a nightdress, गाउन।

nightingale (नाइटिन्गेल) ***n.*** a song-bird, बुलबुल।

nightlong (नाइटलॉन्ग) ***adv.*** & ***adj.*** throughout night, सारी रात (चलनेवाला), सारी रात (का), रात-भर (का)।

nightmare (नाइटमेअर) ***n.*** 1. a dreadful dream, भयानक सपना, दुःस्वप्न। 2. unpleasant experience, कटु अनुभव।

night shelter ***n.*** a place for taking shelter at night, रैनबसेरा, रात्रि-निवास।

nihilism (नाइहिलिज़्म) ***n.*** a doctrine that totally rejects all prevailing values and beliefs, शून्यवाद।

nihilist (नाइहिलिस्ट) ***n.*** a believer in nihilism, शून्यवादी।

nil (निल) ***n.*** nothing, शून्य।

nimble (निम्बल) ***adj.*** agile, फ़ुर्तीला।

nimbleness ***n.*** the quality of being nimble, फ़ुर्तीलापन, फ़ुर्ती।

N

nimbus (निम्बस) ***n.*** 1. a rain cloud, वर्षा करनेवाला मेघ, वर्षामेघ। 2. a halo, प्रभामंडल।

nine (नाइन) ***adj. & n.*** 1. one more than eight, नौ। 2. a card with nine spots, नहला।

nineteen (नाइन्टीन) ***adj. & n.*** one more than eighteen, उन्नीस।

ninety (नाइन्टी) ***n.*** nine times ten, नब्बे।

nip[1] (निप) ***v.*** 1. to squeeze between the finger and thumb, चिकोटी काटना, चुटकी काटना, चुटकी भरना, दबा देना। 2. to bite quickly with the front teeth, दाँतों से नोच लेना। ***n.*** 1. a sharp pinch, चिकोटी। 2. a bite, दाँत काटना। □ **nip in the bud,** जनमते ही मार देना, पनपने से पहले ही नष्ट कर देना।

nip[2] ***n.*** a cold wind, सर्द हवा।

nip[3] ***n.*** a small amount of drink, घूँट।

nippers (निपर्स) ***n.*** forceps, चिमटी।

nipple (निपल) ***n.*** 1. a small projection of breasts, चूची। 2. a rubber teat, निप्पल।

nippy (निपी) ***adj.*** 1. quick, फुर्तीला। 2. bitingly cold, बहुत ठंडा।

nit (निट) ***n.*** the egg or larva of a louse, लीख।

nitrogen (नाइट्रोजन) ***n.*** a colourless gas that forms 78% of the air, नाइट्रोजन।

nitwit (निटविट) ***n.*** a foolish person, मंदबुद्धि व्यक्ति।

no (नो) ***adv.*** 1. used to express denial, नहीं। 2. not at all, बिल्कुल नहीं। ***n.*** 1. a negative reply, नहीं, नकार। 2. a negative vote, विरुद्ध मत। ***adj.*** 1. not any, कोई/कुछ भी नहीं। 2. far from being, थोड़े ही, नहीं।

Noah (नोआ) ***n.*** the patriarch of jews, यहूदियों का आदि पुरुष, नूह।

Nobel Prize (नोबेल प्राइज़) ***n.*** one of a group of prizes awarded annually, नोबेल पुरस्कार।

nobility (नोबिलिटी) ***n.*** 1. nobleness, moral excellence, कुलीनता, सच्चरित्रता। 2. aristocratic people, अभिजात वर्ग।

noble (नोबल) ***adj.*** 1. of or belonging to nobility, अभिजात वर्ग का, कुलीन। 2. having or showing qualities of high moral character, नीतिवान, श्रेष्ठ, उदार। 3. exalted, ऊँचा, महान। ***n.*** a person of noble birth or rank, अभिजात पुरुष, कुलीन व्यक्ति, अमीर।

noble-minded (नोबल-माइन्डिड) ***adj.*** noble in mind, उदारचरित।

nobody (नोबडी) ***pron.*** no person, कोई नहीं। ***n.*** an insignificant person, नगण्य व्यक्ति।

no-confidence (नो-कॉन्फ़िडेन्स) ***n.*** want of confidence, अविश्वास।

nocturnal (नॉक्टर्नल) ***adj.*** of or in the night, रात्रिकालिक, रात्रिक।

nocturne (नॉक्टर्न) ***n.*** a lyrical piece of music associated with night, निशा गीत।

nod (नॉड) ***v.*** 1. to lower and raise the head quickly to indicate agreement, सिर हिलाना। 2. to bow, सिर झुकाना। 3. to be drowsy, (बैठे-बैठे) ऊँघने लगना। ***n.*** 1. a quick down and up movement of the head, सिर हिलाना, हामी भरना या अभिवादन करना। 2. a signal to proceed, आगे बढ़ने का संकेत।

node (नोड) ***n.*** 1. a knot or knob, गाँठ, ग्रंथि, गूमड़ा। 2. a joint, जोड़।

nodule (नॉड्यूल) ***n.*** a small knot

N

or nob, गाँठ, गूमड़ा, ग्रंथि।

noggin (नॉगिन) *n.* a small measure of alcohol, थोड़ी-सी मदिरा।

noise (नॉइज़) *n.* 1. sound, ध्वनि, आहट। 2. uproar, शोर, हल्ला।

nolseless (नॉइज़लिस) *adj.* quiet, शांत।

noisome (नॉइसम) *adj.* 1. objectionable, आपत्तिजनक, नागवार। 2. harmful, हानिकर। 3. foul, गंदा, बदबूदार, घृणित।

noisy (नॉइज़ी) *adj.* 1. making much noise, शोर करनेवाला/मचानेवाला, ऊधमी। 2. full of noise, शोर से भरा।

nomad (नोमैड) *n.* a member of a roaming tribe, ख़ानाबदोश, यायावर।

nomenclature (नोमन्क्लेचर) *n.* a set of names or ways of naming, नामावली, नामपद्धति।

nominal (नॉमिनल) *adj.* 1. existing in name only, नाममात्र (का), नाम को, सांकेतिक। 2. (of gram.) pertaining to nouns, संज्ञा-संबंधी। 3. insignificant, तुच्छ, नगण्य।

nominate (नॉमिनेट) *v.* 1. to propose as a candidate for election, नामांकित करना। 2. to appoint to an office, नामित/मनोनीत करना।

nomination (नॉमिनेशन) *n.* the act of nominating, नामांकन, मनोनयन, नामज़दगी।

nominative case (नॉमिनेटिव केस) *n.* the case indicating the subject of a verb, कर्ताकारक।

nominee (नॉमिनी) *n.* a person who has been nominated, नामांकित/मनोनीत व्यक्ति।

nonagenarian (नोनजिनेरिअन) *adj.* being between 90 and 100 years old, नब्बे और सौ वर्ष के बीच की अवस्थावाला।

non-aggression (नॉनग्रेशन) *n.* the act of not attacking, अनाक्रमण।

non-aligned (नॉनलाइन्ड) *adj.* not in alliance with any power block, निर्गुट, तटस्थ, गुटनिरपेक्ष।

non-alignment (नॉनलाइनमेन्ट) *n.* the state of being non-aligned, तटस्थता, गुट-निरपेक्षता।

non-bailable (नॉन्-बेलेबल) *adj.* not bailable, ग़ैरज़मानती।

nonchalant (नॉन्शेलेन्ट) *adj.* carefree, निश्चिंत, बेफ़िक्र।

non-conductor (नॉन्-कन्डक्टर) *n.* a substance that does not conduct electricity, अचालक।

nonconformist (नॉन्कन्फ़ॉर्मिस्ट) *n.* one who does not conform to accepted customs, beliefs etc., रूढ़ियों को न माननेवाला, परंपराविरोधी, रूढ़िभंजक, रूढ़िविरोधी।

non-cooperation (नॉन्-कोऑपरेशन) *n.* refusal to cooperate, असहयोग।

nondescript (नॉन्डिस्क्रिप्ट) *adj.* very ordinary looking, साधारण, मामूली।

none (नन) *pron.* 1. not any, no amount or part, कुछ नहीं, कुछ भी नहीं। 2. no one, nobody, कोई नहीं, कोई भी नहीं। *adv.* not at all, बिल्कुल नहीं, कुछ भी नहीं।

nonentity (नॉनेन्टिटी) *n.* a person or thing of no importance, नगण्य वस्तु या व्यक्ति, तुच्छ वस्तु या व्यक्ति।

none-the-less (नन-द-लेस) *adv.* however, फिर भी, तो भी।

non-payment (नॉन-पेमेन्ट) *n.* act of not paying, भुगतान न करना, ग़ैर-अदायगी।

nonplus (नॉन्प्लस) *v.* (nonplussed, nonplussing) to confuse or confound, किंकर्तव्यविमूढ़ कर देना।

non-recurring (नॉन्-रिकरिंग) *adj.* not recurring, अनावर्ती, अनावर्तक।

non-renewable (नॉन्-रिन्यूएबल) *adj.* not renewable, अनवीकरणीय।

non-resident (नॉन्-रेज़िडेन्ट) *adj.* not residing, अनिवासी।

non-resistant (नॉन्-रिज़िस्टेन्ट) *adj.* not resisting, अप्रतिरोधी।

nonsense (नॉनसेन्स) *n.* 1. foolish behaviour, बेवकूफ़ी का व्यवहार। 2. absurd language, बेतुकी बातें।

non-stop (नान्-स्टॉप) *adj.* 1. without stopping, बिना रुके, सीधे। 2. without an interruption, लगातार।

non-vegetarian (नॉन्-वेजिटेरिअन) *adj.* other than vegetarian, मांसाहारी।

non-violence (नान्-वाइअलेन्स) lack of violence, अहिंसा।

noodles (नूडल्स) *n.* (plu.) strips of dough, नूडल्स, सेवईं।

nook (नुक) *n.* 1. a corner, कोना। 2. a hidden or secluded place, गुप्त स्थान या एकांत।

noon (नून) *n.* midday, दोपहर, मध्याह्न।

noose (नूज़) *n.* a loop of rope, फंदा।

nor (नॉर) *conj.* and not, न (तो)।

norm (नॉर्म) *n.* 1. desired standard or pattern, मानदंड, प्रतिमान, मानक। 2. an average level, सामान्य स्तर।

normal (नॉर्मल) *adj.* 1. usual or standard, सामान्य या मानक। 2. free form physical or emotional disorder, सामान्य, प्रकृत। *n.* 1. a normal person, सामान्य व्यक्ति। 2. the usual state or level, सामान्य स्थिति या स्तर।

normalcy (नार्मल्सी) *n.* the state of being normal, सामान्य स्थिति।

normality (नॉर्मैलिटी) *n.* = normalcy.

normalize (नॉर्मलाइज़) *v.* to make normal, सामान्य बनाना।

north (नार्थ) *n.* 1. one of the four directions, उत्तर, उत्तर दिशा। 2. the northern part of some region, किसी प्रदेश का उत्तरी भाग।

north-east (नार्थ-ईस्ट) *n.* the direction between north and east, उत्तर-पूर्वी दिशा।

north-west (नॉर्थ-वेस्ट) *n.* the direction midway between north and west, उत्तर-पश्चिम दिशा। *adj.* उत्तर-पश्चिमी।

nose (नोज़) *n.* 1. the organ for breathing and smelling, नाक, नासिका, थूथन। 2. sense of smell, सूँघने की शक्ति, घ्राणशक्ति। 3. the front end of something, अग्रभाग। *v.* 1. to perceive by smell, सूँघकर पता लगाना। 2. to push with the nose, नाक से धकेलना। 3. to move or cause to move forward, आगे बढ़ना या बढ़ाना।

nosebag (नोज़बैग) *n.* a bag containing fodder, hung around a horse's head, तोबड़ा।

nosedive (नोज़डाइव) *v.* to dive straight down, आकाश में वायुयान का गोता लगाना, नाक के बल तेज़ी से नीचे आना।

nostalgia (नॉस्टैल्जिआ) *n.* 1. longing for home, घर की याद। 2. longing for the things of the past, पुरानी (बातों की) याद।

nostril (नॉस्ट्रिल) *n.* either of the holes of the nose, नासाद्वार, नथुना।

nosy, nosey (नोज़ी) *adj.* inquisitive, जिज्ञासु।

N

not (नॉट) ***adj.*** expressing denial, refusal or negation, नहीं, न।

notable (नोटेबल) ***adj.*** 1. remarkable, उल्लेखनीय। 2. important, महत्त्वपूर्ण।

notary (नोटरी) ***n.*** a person authorized to certify, नोटरी।

notation (नोटेशन) ***n.*** 1. accepted set of standard symbols, संकेत-समूह। 2. a system of such symbol, संकेत-पद्धति।

notch (नॉच) ***n.*** 1. a v-shaped cut, खाँचा। 2. a narrow pass, दर्रा। 3. one of the levels in graded system, स्तर। ***v.*** to make a notch, खाँचा बनाना।

note (नोट) ***n.*** 1. a brief written record, टिप्पणी। 2. an official communication, चिट्ठी, पत्र। 3. a commentary, टीका। 4. a piece of paper currency, नोट। 5. (in music) a tone of definite pitch, स्वर। 6. a bird's sound, चहक, कलरव। 7. eminence, उत्कृष्टता। 8. attention, ध्यान। ***v.*** 1. to pay attention, ध्यान देना। 2. to write down, नोट करना।

notebook (नोटबुक) ***n.*** a book of blank pages for notes, कापी, नोटबुक।

noted (नोटिड) ***adj.*** well-known, प्रसिद्ध।

noteworthy (नोटवर्दी) ***adj.*** 1. remarkable, उल्लेखनीय। 2. important, महत्त्वपूर्ण।

nothing (नथिंग) ***pron.*** 1. not anything, कुछ नहीं। 2. non-existence, अस्तित्व न होना। 3. unimportant thing or person, नगण्य वस्तु या व्यक्ति। 4. zero, शून्य।

nothingness (नथिंगनिस) ***n.*** 1. non-existence, कुछ न होने की अवस्था। 2. void, ख़ालीपन, सूनापन।

notice (नोटिस) ***n.*** 1. an information about something, सूचना, ख़बर। 2. a written or printed announcement, सूचना। 3. attention, observation, ध्यान। 4. review (of a book), समीक्षा। ***v.*** to pay attention, ध्यान देना।

noticeable (नोटिसेबल) ***adj.*** 1. worth noticing, ध्यान देने योग्य। 2. evident, स्पष्ट।

notice-board (नोटिस-बोर्ड) ***n.*** a board on which notices are fixed, सूचना-पट्ट।

notification (नोटिफ़िकेशन) ***n.*** a formal notice, अधिसूचना, सूचना।

notify (नोटिफ़ाइ) ***v.*** 1. to inform, सूचना देना। 2. to announce, घोषणा करना।

notion (नोशन) ***n.*** 1. a vague opinion, धारणा। 2. understanding, समझ।

notional (नोशनल) ***adj.*** abstract, imaginary, अमूर्त, काल्पनिक।

notoriety (नोटराइटी) ***n.*** the state or quality of being notorious, बदनामी, कुख्याति।

notorious (नोटोरिअस) ***adj.*** infamous, बदनाम, कुख्यात।

notwithstanding (नॉटविद्स्टैन्डिंग) ***prep.*** inspite of, के बावजूद (भी)। ***adv.*** nevertheless, तो भी, फिर भी।

nought (नॉट) ***n.*** naught, शून्य।

noun (नॉउन) ***n.*** a word or phrase that refers to a person, place or thing, नाम, संज्ञा, संज्ञापद।

nourish (नरिश) ***v.*** 1. to provide with substance necessary for life and growth, पोषण/पोषित करना। 2. to encourage or foster, बढ़ावा देना।

nourishing (नरिशिंग) ***adj.*** giving

nourishment, पोषक, पुष्टिकारक।

nourishment (नरिशमेन्ट) ***n.*** 1. an act of nourishing, पोषण। 2. a substance that nourishes, पोषक आहार।

novel (नॉवल) ***adj.*** of a new kind, नया, नूतन। ***n.*** a fiction, उपन्यास।

novelette (नॉवलेट) ***n.*** a short novel, उपन्यासिका।

novelist (नॉवलिस्ट) ***n.*** a writer of novels, उपन्यासकार, उपन्यास-लेखक।

novelty (नॉवल्टी) ***n.*** 1. the quality of being novel, नवीनता। 2. a novel thing, नवीन वस्तु।

November (नोवेम्बर) ***n.*** the eleventh month of the year, नवंबर (माह)।

novice (नॉविस) ***n.*** 1. a beginner, नौसिखिआ, नवशिक्षु। 2. a person who has joined some other religion, नवदीक्षित, नवधर्मी।

now (नाउ) ***adv.*** 1. at this time, अब, इस समय। 2. immediately, अभी, इसी समय।

now-a-days (नाउ-ए-डेज़) ***adv.*** in modern times, आजकल, इन दिनों।

nowhere (नोवेअर) ***adv.*** not anywhere, कहीं नहीं।

noxious (नॉक्शस) ***adj.*** harmful. दूषित, हानिप्रद।

nozzle (नॉज़ल) ***n.*** a projecting part with an opening from which fluid is discharged, टोंटी।

nuance (न्यूआन्स) ***n.*** a subtle difference in meaning, सूक्ष्म अर्थभेद, अर्थछटा, रंगत।

nubile (न्यूबाइल) ***adj.*** 1. marriageable, विवाह-योग्य (लड़की)। 2. attractive, आकर्षक।

nuclear (न्यूक्लिअर) ***adj.*** 1. of nucleus, नाभिकीय। 2. of or using nuclear energy, नाभिकीय।

nuclear energy ***n.*** energy released from an atomic nucleus, नाभिकीय ऊर्जा।

nuclear family ***n.*** father, mother and their children, एकक परिवार (जिसमें पति-पत्नी और उनके बच्चे हों), छोटा परिवार।

nuclear reactor ***n.*** a device in which a nuclear chain reaction is started, नाभिकीय रिऐक्टर।

nucleus (न्यूक्लिअस) ***n.*** (pl. nuclei) 1. central part, केंद्रीय भाग, केंद्रक। 2. the central part of an atom, नाभिक।

nude (न्यूड) ***adj.*** naked, नंगा, नग्न, निर्वस्त्र। ***n.*** a nude human figure, नग्न (मानव का) चित्र।

nudge (नज) ***v.*** (nudged, nudging) to push with the elbow, कोहनी मारना।

nudism (न्यूडिज़्म) ***n.*** the belief or practice of going nude, नग्नतावाद, नग्नवाद।

nudity (न्यूडिटी) ***n.*** the state of being nude, नग्नता, नंगापन।

nugget (नगिट) ***n.*** a lump of gold, सोने का डला।

nuisance (न्यूसेन्स) ***n.*** a person or thing that is inconvenient or annoying, परेशानी, खुराफ़ात, काँटा।

null (नल) ***adj.*** 1. having no legal force, अमान्य, अवैध, रद। 2. insignificant, तुच्छ। 3. amounting to nothing, बेकार।

nullify (नलिफ़ाइ) ***v.*** 1. to invalidate, अवैध ठहराना या रद करना। 2. to counteract. व्यर्थ कर देना।

numb (नम्ब) ***adj.*** 1. unable to feel anything, सुन्न, निस्पंद, जड़।

N

2. stunned, (भय से) सन्न, निश्चेष्ट। ***v.*** to make numb, सन्न कर देना।

number (नम्बर) ***n.*** 1. a member of the system used in counting and measuring, संख्या, नंबर। 2. the quantity or amount, राशि, संख्या। 3. crowd, भीड़। 4. one item in a series, नंबर। 5. a numeral assigned to an object, person etc., for identification, नंबर, बारी। ***v.*** 1. to reach as a total, संख्या में होना, गिनती में होना। 2. to count, गिनना। 3. to include in, शामिल करना। 4. to assign a number to, नंबर देना या डालना।

numberless (नम्बरलिस) ***adj.*** countless, असंख्य, अगणित, बेशुमार।

numeral (न्यूमरल) ***n.*** a figure, अंक, संख्या।

numerate (न्यूमरेट) ***v.*** to count, गिनना।

numerator (न्यूमरेटर) ***n.*** the number above the line in fraction, अंश।

numerical (न्यूमेरिकल) ***adj.*** of number, संख्यात्मक, संख्यावाचक।

numerous (न्यूमरस) ***adj.*** many, अनेक, बहुत।

numismatics (न्यूमिज़्मैटिक्स) ***n.*** the scientific study of coins, मुद्राशास्त्र।

nun (नन) ***n.*** a woman who belongs to a Christian religious order, भिक्षुणी, नन।

nuncio (नन्शिओ) ***n.*** Pope's representative, धर्मदूत।

nunnery (ननरी) ***n.*** a convent for nuns, ईसाई भिक्षुणी निवास, ननघर।

nuptial (नप्शल) ***adj.*** of marriage, वैवाहिक।

nuptials (नप्शल्ज़) ***n.*** (plu.) a wedding, विवाह, विवाहोत्सव।

nurse (नर्स) ***n.*** 1. a person trained to take care of the sick, नर्स। 2. a woman employed to take care of a young child, आया, धाय। ***v.*** 1. to suckle, दूध पिलाना, स्तनपान कराना। 2. to act as a professional nurse, नर्स होना, देख-रेख करना, सेवा-शुश्रूषा करना। 3. to treat, इलाज करना। 4. to foster, पालन-पोषण करना, पालना। 5. to hold a bad feeling in mind, मन में रखना।

nursery (नर्सरी) ***n.*** 1. a room or play-room for children, बालकक्ष, शिशुशाला। 2. a place where plants are grown for sale, पौधशाला, नर्सरी।

nursery school ***n.*** a school for young children, शिशुशाला, शिशु-पाठशाला।

nursing home (नर्सिंग होम) ***n.*** परिचर्या-गृह, नर्सिंग-होम।

nurture (नर्चर) ***n.*** the process of nurturing, पालन-पोषण। ***v.*** 1. to care for by providing nourishment, खिलाना-पिलाना, पालना-पोसना। 2. to help the development of, विकसित करना।

nut (नट) ***n.*** 1. a fruit with a hard shell, काष्ठफल। 2. its kernel, उक्त फल की गिरी, मेवा। 3. a foolish person, मूर्ख व्यक्ति। 4. a small block of a metal with a hole, ढिबरी, नट।

nutmeg (नटमेग) ***n.*** a seed of a tree, जायफल।

nutrient (न्यूट्रिएन्ट) ***adj.*** providing nourishment, पोषक, पुष्टिकर।

nutrition (न्यूट्रिशन) ***n.*** 1. nouri-shment, पोषण। 2. something that nourishes, पोषक पदार्थ।

nutritious (न्यूट्रिशस) ***adj.*** nourishig, पोषक, पौष्टिक।

nutshell (नटशैल) ***n.*** the shell of

a nut, अखरोट, बादाम आदि का मोटा कड़ा छिलका। □ **in a nutshell,** अति संक्षेप में।

nuzzle (नज़ल) ***v.*** to push or rub with a nose or snout, नाक से रगड़ना या धकेलना।

nylon (नाइलॉन) ***n.*** a synthetic fibre and the fabric made from it, नाइलॉन।

nymph (निम्फ़) ***n.*** a female spirit, परी।

nymphomania (निम्फ़मेनिआ) ***n.*** abnormal sexual appetite in woman, स्त्रियों का कामोन्माद, अदम्य कामेच्छा।

O, o (ओ) ***n.*** the fifteenth letter of the English alphabet, अंग्रेज़ी वर्णमाला का पंद्रहवाँ वर्ण, स्वर। ***interj.*** a natural exclamation for sudden emotion or feeling, ओह!

oaf (ओफ़) ***n.*** a clumsy person, बेढंगा आदमी।

oak (ओक) ***n.*** a tree and its wood, शाहबलूत और उसकी लकड़ी।

oar (ओर) ***n.*** a device to propel a boat, डाँड, चप्पू।

oarsman (ओर्ज़मैन) ***n.*** one who rows a boat, rower, मल्लाह, नाविक।

oasis (ओएसिस) ***n.*** a green spot in a desert, मरुद्वीप, नखलिस्तान।

oat (ओट) ***n.*** 1. a cereal plant and its grain, जई, जुंदरी।

oath (ओथ) ***n.*** a solemn promise to fulfil a pledge, सौगंध, क़सम, शपथ।

obduracy (ऑब्डुरेसी) ***n.*** stubbornness, ढिठाई, हठ।

obdurate (ऑब्डुरिट) ***adj.*** stubborn, ढीठ, हठी।

obedience (ओबीडिएन्स) ***n.*** the act of obeying, आज्ञाकारिता, आज्ञापालन।

obedient (ओबीडिएन्ट) ***adj.*** obeying or willing to obey, आज्ञाकारी, आज्ञापालक।

obeisance (ओबेसेन्स) ***n.*** a bow expressing respect, प्रणति, नमन।

obelisk (ऑबेलिस्क) ***n.*** a tall pointed stone pillar, पत्थर का स्तंभ।

obese (ओबीस) ***adj.*** very fat, बहुत मोटा।

obesity (ओबीसिटी) ***n.*** fatness, मुटापा।

obey (ओबे) ***v.*** 1. to carry out an order, आज्ञा का पालन करना, हुकुम बजा लाना। 2. to be obedient, किसी की आज्ञा के अनुसार चलना, आज्ञाकारी होना।

obit (ओबिट) ***n.*** = obituary.

obituary (ओबिचुअरी) ***n.*** a death notice, शोक-समाचार, निधन-संबंधी समाचार।

object[1] (ऑब्जिक्ट) ***n.*** 1. a thing, material thing, वस्तु, चीज़, पदार्थ। 2. a person or thing as a focus of attention, पात्र, भाजन। 3. aim, purpose, उद्देश्य, लक्ष्य। 4. a noun that is affected by the action of a verb, कर्म।

object[2] (ऑब्जेक्ट) ***v.*** to present an opposing or dissenting argument, आपत्ति करना, प्रतिवाद करना।

objection (ऑब्जेक्शन) ***n.*** a statement or feeling of opposing or disapproving, आपत्ति, एतराज़, प्रतिवाद।

objective (ऑब्जेक्टिव) ***adj.*** 1. having to do with a material object, not subjective, विषयगत, वस्तुनिष्ठ। 2. real, वास्तविक, यथार्थ। 3. (gram.) of the objective case, कर्मवाचक, कर्मवाची। ***n.*** 1. the object of one's effort, goal, लक्ष्य, ध्येय, उद्देश्य। 2. (gram.) the objective case, कर्मकारक।

objectively (ऑब्जेक्टिवली) ***adv.*** 1. really, यथार्थतः, वस्तुतः। 2. impartially, निष्पक्ष भाव से ।

objectivity (ऑब्जेक्टिविटी) ***n.*** 1. objectiveness, वस्तुनिष्ठा। 2. reality, वास्तविक़ता।

oblation (ऑब्लेशन) ***n.*** a religious offering to a deity, चढ़ावा, आहुति या अर्पण।

obligation (ऑब्लिगेशन) ***n.*** 1. a binding, बाध्यता, विवशता, बंधन। 2. duty, कर्तव्य, दायित्व। 3. the state of being obliged to do something, एहसान, आभार।

obligatory (ऑब्लिगेटरी) ***adj.*** compulsory, अनिवार्य।

oblige (ऑब्लाइज) ***v.*** 1. to compel, विवश करना, बाध्य करना।2. to make indebted, अनुगृहीत करना। 3. to do favour for, उपकृत करना।

obliged (ऑब्लाइज्ड) ***adj.*** grateful, उपकृत, एहसानमंद।

oblique (अब्लीक) ***adj.*** 1. slanting or sloping, आड़ा, तिरछा, ढालुआँ। 2. not straightforward, कुटिल, वक्र। 3. evasive, टालू, अनिश्चित, अस्पष्ट। 4. (gram.) inflectional, विकारी। ***n.*** a mark used to separate numbers, words etc. तिर्यक रेखा।

obliquely (अब्लीकली) ***adv.*** slantingly, टेढ़े/तिरछे बल।

obliterate (अब्लिटरेट) ***v.*** 1. to destroy नष्ट कर देना, मिटा देना।

obliteration (अब्लिटरेशन) ***n.*** the act of obliterating or the state of being obliterated, विनाश; उन्मूलन।

oblivion (अब्लिविअन) ***n.*** 1. forgetfulness, भुलक्कड़पन, विस्मरण, विस्मृति। 2. the state of being oblivious, बेख़बरी।

oblivious (अब्लिविअस) ***adj.*** 1. unaware, बेख़बर। 2. forgetful, भुलक्कड़।

oblong (ऑब्लॉन्ग) ***adj.*** rectangular, आयताकार। ***n.*** a rectangular figure, आयत।

obnoxious (अब्नॉक्शस) ***adj.*** 1. nasty, offensive, घृणित, घिनौना, बीभत्स। 2. objectionable, आपत्ति-जनक।

oboe (ओबो) ***n.*** a woodwind instrument, शहनाई, नफ़ीरी।

obscene (ऑब्सीन) ***adj.*** nasty, dirty, अश्लील, गंदा।

obscenity (ऑब्सीनिटी) ***n.*** the state of being obscene, अश्लीलता।

obscure (ऑब्स्क्युर) ***adj*** 1. dark, indistinct, अस्पष्ट, धुँधला, धूमिल। 2. not easily understood, गूढ़, दुर्बोध। 3. hidden, छिपा हुआ, प्रच्छन्न। 4. not famous, अप्रसिद्ध। ***v.*** 1. to canceal or hide, छिपाना, ढकना। 2. to make difficult to understand, दुर्बोध बना देना।

obscurity (ऑब्स्क्युरिटी) ***n.*** the state or quality of being obscure, धुँधलापन या अंधकार; गूढ़ता, दुर्बोधता, अस्पष्टता; प्रच्छन्नता।

obsequies (ऑब्सिक्वीज़) ***n.*** (plu.) the last rites, अंतिम संस्कार, अंत्येष्टि।

obsequious (ऑब्सिक्विअस) ***adj.*** fawning, चापलूस, ख़ुशामदी।

observable (ऑब्ज़र्वेबल) ***adj.*** 1. that can be observed, अनुपालनीय, पालनीय। 2. perceptible , दृष्टिगोचर।

observance (ऑब्ज़र्वेन्स) ***n.*** 1. the act of complying with a rule or law, अनुपालन, पालन। 2. the act of celebrating (a festival or holiday), मनाना।

observation (ऑब्ज़र्वेशन) ***n.*** an act of observing or noticing, अवलोकन, प्रेक्षण, निगरानी, देख-रेख, टिप्पणी, मंतव्य, निरीक्षण, अनुवीक्षण।

observatory (ऑब्ज़र्वेटरी) ***n.*** a place for scientific observation of stars or weather, वेधशाला।

O

observe (ऑब्जर्व) ***v.*** 1. to perceive or notice, देखना। 2. to watch attentively, ध्यानपूर्वक देखना, निरीक्षण करना, ग़ौर करना। 3. to make scientific observation of, अनुवीक्षण करना। 4. to comment, टिप्पणी करना। 5. to abide by, पालन करना, अनुपालन करना। 6. to celebrate, मनाना।

observer (ऑब्ज़र्वर) ***n.*** one who observes, प्रेक्षक, निरीक्षक; अनुवीक्षक; पालनकर्ता या पालक; मनानेवाला।

obsession (ऑब्सेशन) ***n.*** 1. abnormal preoccupation with an unwanted feeling or idea, मनोग्रंथि, ग्रस्तता। 2. such feeling or idea, वहम, भ्रम, सनक।

obsolescence (ऑब्सोलेसेन्स) ***n.*** obsoleteness, लोप, लोपोन्मुखता।

obsolescent (ऑब्सोलेसेन्ट) ***adj.*** obsolete, लुप्त, लोपोन्मुख।

obsolete (ऑब्सलीट) ***adj.*** 1. out of use, अप्रयुक्त, अप्रचलित। 2. out of date, दिनाप्त, पुराना।

obstacle (ऑब्स्टेकल) ***n.*** anything that obstructs or hinders something, बाधा, अड़चन, विघ्न; obstacle race अवरोध-दौड़।

obstetrician (ऑब्स्टिट्रिशन) ***n.*** a specialist in obstetrics, प्रसव-विज्ञानी।

obstetrics (ऑब्स्टेट्रिक्स) ***n.*** the science of medicine and surgery concerning with childbirth, प्रसव-विज्ञान।

obstinacy (ऑब्स्टिनेसी) ***n.*** stubbornness, हठ, जिद, दुराग्रह।

obstinate (ऑब्स्टिनिट) ***adj.*** 1. stubborn, हठी, ज़िद्दी, दुराग्रही। 2. not willing to obey, हठीला। 3. not easy to subdue or defeat, दुस्साध्य।

obstruct (ऑब्स्ट्रक्ट) ***v.*** 1. to block, prevent or hinder, अवरुद्ध कर देना, बंद कर देना। 2. to put difficulties in the way of, बाधाएँ खड़ी कर देना, रुकावटें डालना, रोड़े अटकाना।

obstruction (ऑब्स्ट्रक्शन) ***n.*** 1. the act of obstructing, अवरोध खड़ा करना, बाधक होना। 2. the person or thing that obstructs, बाधा, रुकावट, अड़चन।

obtain (ऑब्टेन) ***v.*** to get or acquire, प्राप्त करना, हस्तगत करना।

obtainable (ऑब्टेनेबल) ***adj.*** that can be obtained, प्राप्य, सुलभ।

obtuse (ऑब्ट्यूस) ***adj.*** 1. foolish, मूर्ख, मंदबुद्धि। 2. not sharp, not pointed, blunt, भोथरा, कुंद। 3. (maths.) ~ angle अधिक कोण।

obverse (ऑबवर्स) ***n.*** 1. the front side of a coin, (सिक्के का) सामने का पहलू। 2. serving the counterpart, प्रतिवस्तु, पूरक। 3. the logical opposition of something, विपर्याय। ***adj.*** facing the observer, सामने का।

obviate (ऑब्विएट) ***v.*** to do away with, परे करना, दूर हटाना, भगाना।

obvious (ऑब्विअस) ***adj.*** evident, clear, स्पष्ट, प्रकट, प्रत्यक्ष।

occasion (अकेज़न) ***n.*** an opportunity, उपयुक्त समय, अवसर, मौक़ा। ***v.*** to cause, उत्पन्न करना, (का) कारण होना।

occasional (अकेज़नल) ***adj.*** 1. occurring from time to time, समय-समय पर होनेवाला। 2. occurring on special occasion, प्रासंगिक।

occasionally (अकेज़नली) ***adv.*** not regularly, कभी-कभी।

occident (ऑक्सिडेन्ट) ***n.*** the countries of Europe and America, पश्चिमी देश।

occult (ऑकल्ट) ***adj.*** 1. secret,

गूढ़, रहस्यमय। 2. mystical or supernatural, जादू-टोना या तंत्र-मंत्र-संबंधी, तांत्रिक।

occupancy (ऑक्यूपेन्सी) ***n.*** the act of occupying or the state of being occupied, अधिकार, दख़ल, क़ब्ज़ा।

occupant (ऑक्यूपेन्ट) ***n.*** one who has possession over a house etc., tenant, दख़लकार, क़ाबिज़।

occupation (ऑक्यूपेशन) ***n.*** 1. the act of occupying or the state of being occupied, दख़ल, अधिकार। 2. taking possession by force, क़ब्ज़ा। 3. one's employment, धंधा, पेशा, रोज़गार, व्यवसाय।

occupational (ऑक्यूपेशनल) ***adj.*** of one's occupation, धंधे का, पेशे का, व्यावसायिक।

occupy (आक्यूपाइ) ***v.*** 1. to take and hold possession of, दख़ल कर लेना, अधिकार कर लेना। 2. to dwell in, रहना, बसना। 3. to hold (an office, किसी पद पर) आसीन होना। 4. to engage or busy (oneself, अपने को) व्यस्त रखना। 5. to fill (a space, जगह) घेरना। 6. to fill (a time, समय) लेना।

occur (अकर) ***v.*** 1. to take place, घटित होना, घटना, होना। 2. to be found, मिलना, पाया जाना। 3. to come into mind, सूझना, एकाएक मन में आना।

occurrence (अकरेन्स) ***n.*** an event, घटना।

ocean (ओशन) ***n.*** the great mass of salt water, समुद्र, महासागर।

oceanic (ओशीऐनिक) ***adj.*** of the ocean, समुद्री।

ochre (ओकर) ***n.*** a brownish clay, गेरू।

o'clock (ओक्लॉक) ***adv.*** according to the clock, बजे।

octagon (ऑक्टगन) ***n.*** a polygon having eight sides, अष्टभुज।

octave (ऑक्टेव) ***n.*** 1. a group of eight things, आठ का समूह, अष्टक। 2. a period of eight days, अठवाड़ा। 3. a group of eight lines of the poetry, अष्टपदी। 4. (music), सरगम, सप्तक।

octavo (ऑक्टेवो) ***n.*** the paper produced by folding a sheet of paper 3 times so as to give 8 leaves or 16 pages, अठपेजी।

octet (ऑक्टेट) ***n.*** a group of eight, आठ का समूह।

October (ऑक्टोबर) ***n.*** the tenth month of the year, अक्तूबर।

octogenarian (ऑक्टजिनेरिअन) ***n.*** a person who is in his (her) eighties, ८० से ९० वर्ष के वय का व्यक्ति।

octroi (ऑक्ट्रॉइ) ***n.*** a toll tax, चुंगी।

octroi post ***n.*** a place where octroi is charged, चुंगी चौकी, चुंगी नाका।

ocular (ऑक्युलर) ***adj.*** of eye, नेत्र-संबंधी।

oculist (ऑक्युलिस्ट) ***n.*** an eye-doctor, ophthalmologist, नेत्र-चिकित्सक।

odd (ऑड) ***adj.*** 1. strange, unusual, अजीब, विचित्र, विलक्षण। 2. not even, not divisible by two, विषम। 3. not part of a set, बेमेल। 4. not regular, अनियमित।

oddity (ऑडिटी) ***n.*** 1. strangeness, विचित्रता, विलक्षणता। 2. a strange person or thing, विचित्र वस्तु या व्यक्ति।

odds (ऑड्ज़) ***n.*** (plu.) liklihood, (spl. a ratio expressing the probability of an event), संभावना। □ **at odds with,** अनबन के चलते; **by all odds,**

O

निश्चय ही; **odds and ends,** विविध वस्तुएँ या विषय।

ode (ओड) ***n.*** a type of usually long poem, लंबी कविता, काव्य।

odometer (ओडॉमीटर) ***n.*** a metre that shows travelled distance by a vehicle, milometre, दूरीमापी।

odorous (ओडरस) ***adj.*** smelly, गंधमय, महकदार।

odour, odor (ओडर) ***n.*** smell, महक, गंध।

odyssey (ओडिसी) ***n.*** a long, adventurous journey, लंबी साहसिक यात्रा।

oesophagus (इसॉफ़िगस) ***n.*** a gullet, ग्रास-नली, भोजन की नली।

of (ऑव) ***prep.*** 1. indicating relationship, concerning or belonging to, का। 2. from, से। 3. about, के विषय में।

off (ऑफ़) ***adv.*** 1. away, दूर, परे। 2. so as to be unattached, अलग, पृथक। 3. so as to be fewer or smal-ler, थोड़ा, छोटा। 4. so as to be away from work or duty, बंद, खाली। 5. so as to get rid of, पीछा छुड़ाकर। 6. on a trip, यात्रा पर। 7. so as to be no longer taking place, ख़त्म, रद। ***prep.*** 1. so as to be removed or distant from, से दूर, से अलग, से हटकर। 2. situated near to or leading away from, के पास या से आगे। 3. from, से। 4. away or relieved from, से मुक्त। ***adj.*** 1. more distant or remote, दूरवर्ती। 2. detached, अलग, पृथक। 3. not continuing or functioning, बंद। 4. less, inferior or wrong, कम, घटिया या ग़लत। 5. absent, अनुपस्थित।

offbeat (ऑफ़बीट) ***adj.*** unconventional, रूढ़िमुक्त, रूढ़िविरोधी।

offcolour (ऑफ़कलर) ***adj.*** not in one's usual health, कुछ-कुछ अस्वस्थ, बुझा-सा।

offence, offense (ऑफ़ेन्स) ***n.*** 1. a breach of law, अपराध। 2. a bad deed, crime, पाप, अपकर्म।

offend (ऑफ़ेन्ड) ***v.*** 1. to cause displeasure to, नाराज़ करना, खिझाना। 2. to hurt the feelings of, ठेस या चोट पहुँचाना। 3. to break law, क़ानून तोड़ना।

offender (ऑफ़ेन्डर) ***adj.*** one who offends, अपराधी, पापी।

offensive (ऑफ़ेन्सिव) ***adj.*** 1. aggressive, आक्रामक। 2. repulsive, unpleasant, अरुचिकर, अप्रिय। 3. used in attacking, आक्रमण में काम आनेवाला। ***n.*** an aggressive action or campaign, चढ़ाई, आक्रमण।

offer (ऑफ़र) ***v.*** 1. to present (for acceptance), प्रस्ताव रखना, प्रस्तुत करना, पेश करना या देना। 2. to give in worship, अर्पित करना। 3. to show willingness (to do something), इच्छा जतलाना, इच्छा प्रकट करना। ***n.*** 1. a proposal, प्रस्ताव। 2. something offered to a deity, चढ़ावा, नैवेद्य, भोग। 3. the amount offered, अर्पित राशि।

offering (ऑफ़रिंग) ***n.*** 1. something offered, अर्पित वस्तु (दान, भोग, चढ़त आदि)। 2. a sacrifice, बलि।

offhand (ऑफ़हैन्ड) ***adv. & adj.*** without forethought, बिना विचारे (किया जानेवाला), आकस्मिक रूप से (होनेवाला)।

office (ऑफ़िस) 1. a room (or rooms) where work is carried out, दफ़्तर, कार्यालय, ऑफ़िस। 2. the holding of an official position, पद।

officer (ऑफ़िसर) ***n.*** a person who holds the position of authority in the office, अधिकारी, अफ़सर।
officer-in-charge ***n.*** प्रभारी अधिकारी।
official (ऑफ़िशल) ***n.*** one who holds an office or position, अधिकारी, पदाधिकारी। ***adj.*** 1. of or relating to the administration, शासकीय, राजकीय, सरकारी। 2. authoritative, आधिकारिक। 3. pertaining to an office, पद-संबंधी, पदीय। 4. formal, औपचारिक। 5. authorised, अधिकृत, प्राधिकृत।
officially (ऑफ़िशली) ***adv.*** 1. authoritatively, आधिकारिक रूप से। 2. in an official manner, सरकारी तौर पर।
officiate (ऑफ़िशिएट) ***v.*** 1. to perform the duties and functions of an official, आधिकारिक रूप से कार्य करना, कार्यवहन करना। 2. to serve as a substitute, स्थानापन्न होना। 3. to conduct a religious ceremony, अनुष्ठान संपन्न कराना।
officiating (ऑफ़िशिएटिंग) ***adj.*** working at someone's place, स्थानापन्न।
offset (ऑफ़सेट) ***n.*** 1. a process of printing, ऑफ़सेट छपाई। 2. a machine for such printing, ऑफ़सेट मशीन।
offshoot (ऑफ़शूट) ***n.*** a shoot from a stem. शाखा, प्रशाखा।
offshore ***adv. & adj.*** away from the shore, तट से दूर।
offspring (ऑफ़स्प्रिंग) ***n.*** 1. progeny, संतान, संतति। 2. something that results from something else, फल, नतीजा, परिणाम।
off-white (ऑफ़-वाइट) ***adj.*** a yellowish or greyish white, हलका सफ़ेद।
oft (ऑफ़्ट) ***adv.*** often, प्रायः।
often (ऑफ़न) ***adv.*** frequently, अक्सर, प्रायः, बहुधा।
ogre (ओगर) ***n.*** a man-eating giant, नरभक्षी दानव, राक्षस। [fem. ogress]
oh (ओह) ***interj.*** 1. an exclamation of surprise, fear etc., ओह! 2. an exclamation for emphasis, ज़ोर देने के लिए प्रयुक्त निपात; अच्छा!
ohm (ओम) ***n.*** a unit of electrical resistance, विद्युत् प्रतिरोध की इकाई, ओम।
oil (ऑइल) ***n.*** a fatty liquid, तेल, तैल। ***v.*** to apply oil to, तेल देना या मलना।
oilcake (ऑइलकेक) ***n.*** a cake of crushed oil seed's residue, खली।
oilcan (ऑइलकैन) ***n.*** a can for keeping oil, कुप्पी।
oilcloth (ऑइलक्लॉथ) ***n.*** a kind of waterproof cloth, मोमजामा, लिनोलियम।
oil colour ***n.*** colour prepared in oil, तैलरंग।
oil crusher (ऑइलक्रशर) ***n.*** a device for crushing oil seeds, कोल्हू।
oilfield (ऑइलफ़ील्ड) ***n.*** an area containing oil deposits, तैलक्षेत्र।
oil painting ***n.*** a picture painted in oil colours, तैलचित्र।
oilseed (ऑइलसीड) ***n.*** seeds from which oil is obtained, तिलहन।
oily (ऑइली) ***adj.*** of or like oil, तेल लगा, तेलहा, स्निग्ध, चुपड़ा।
ointment (ऑइन्टमेन्ट) ***n.*** an oily substance to be rubbed on the skin, मलहम।
okay (ओके) ***adj. & adv.*** all right, ठीक, सही।
old (ओल्ड) ***adj.*** 1. having lived or

O

existed for a relatively long time, लंबी उम्रवाला, पुराना या बूढ़ा। 2. worn with use or age, घिसा-पिटा या जर्जर। 3. skilled through long experience, कुशल, निपुण।

old age ***n.*** the period of a person's life when one is old, बुढ़ापा, वृद्धावस्था।

old-fashioned (ओल्ड-फ़ैशन्ड) ***adj.*** no longer common or in use, पुरानी तरह का, पुराना, दकियानूसी।

olfactory (ऑल्फ़ैक्टरी) ***adj.*** of the sense of smell, घ्राण-संबंधी।

oligarchic, oligarchical (ऑलिगार्किक, ऑलिगार्किकल) ***adj.*** of, relaiting to, or based on an oligarchy, अल्पतंत्रीय।

oligarchy (ऑलिगार्की) ***n.*** 1. a government by the few, अल्पतंत्र, गुटतंत्र। 2. a state governed by the few, वह देश जहाँ उनका शासन हो।

olive (ऑलिव) ***n.*** a tree, its flowers and fruits, जैतून।

Olympic (ओलिम्पिक) ***adj.*** of the Olympic Games, ओलंपिक।

ombudsman (ओम्बड्समैन) ***n.*** an investigation officer to whom applications about maladministration are lodged, लोकपाल, लोकायुक्त।

omen (ओमेन) ***n.*** a sign of future good or evil, सगुन, शकुन।

ominous (ऑमिनस) ***adj.*** pertaining to an evil omen, अशुभ, अनिष्टसूचक।

omission (ओमिशन) ***n.*** 1. the act of omitting or the state of being omitted, छूट, भूल, चूक, त्रुटि। 2. something that has been omitted, छूट, चूक।

omit (ओमिट) ***v.*** 1. to leave out, छोड़ देना। 2. to fail to do, न करना।

omnibus (ऑम्निबस) ***n.*** 1. a public bus, बस, ऑमनीबस। 2. a volume containing author's all or several works, रचनावली, समग्र।

omnipotent (ऑम्निपटेन्ट) ***adj.*** having unlimited powers, सर्वशक्तिमान।

omnipresent (ऑम्निप्रेज़ेन्ट) ***adj.*** present everywhere, सर्वव्यापक, सर्वव्यापी।

omniscient (ऑम्निशन्ट) ***adj.*** knowing everything, सर्वज्ञ।

omnivorous (ऑम्निवोरस) ***adj.*** eating both animal and vegetable substances, सर्वभक्षी, सर्वभक्षक।

on (ऑन) ***prep.*** 1. in contact with the surface, पर। 2. concerning or attached to, पर, से संबद्ध। 3. to, towards, को, की ओर। 4. at the time of, (समय) पर; The train came on time, गाड़ी समय पर आई। 5. about, के बारे में, के विषय में। 6. by means of, पर, के द्वारा। 7. because of, के कारण। 8. with the support of, के सहारे। 9. in a state of (as on strike or on journey, हड़ताल/यात्रा) पर। 10. after, के बाद। 11. in the possession of, with, के पास। ***adv.*** 1. continuously, निरंतर, बराबर। 2. further in space or time, आगे। 3. in a direction towards something, की तरफ़। 4. in or into operation, चालू रूप में। ☐ **on and off,** यदा-कदा, कभी-कभी, समय-समय पर।

once (वन्स) ***adv.*** 1. one time, एक बार। 2. on one occasion, एक ही अवसर पर।3. at some past time, पहले कभी। **at once,** अभी। **once**

upon a time, एक समय, प्राचीन काल में।

oncoming (ऑनकमिंग) ***adj.*** approaching, आता हुआ, पास आया हुआ।

one (वन) ***adj.*** 1. single, not two, एक। 2. being distinct from all others, एक ऐसा। ***n.*** 1. any indefinite on unspecified person, एक। 2. the smallest whole number, १, एक। 3. a person or thing, एक व्यक्ति या वस्तु।

one-act play ***n.*** a drama of one act, एकांकी।

one-fold (वनफ़ोल्ड) ***adj.*** folded once, इकहरा।

onerous (ऑनरस) ***adj.*** heavy, burdensome, भारी, मुश्किल, दुर्वह।

oneself (वनसेल्फ़) ***pron.*** used reflexively, ख़ुद, स्वयं।

one-sided (वन-साइडिड) ***adj.*** 1. biased, इकतरफ़ा, पक्षपातपूर्ण। 2. unequal, असमान।

one-time (वन-टाइम) ***adj.*** former, पुराना, भूतपूर्व।

ongoing (ऑनगोइंग) ***adj.*** continuing, जारी, चालू।

onion (अन्यन) ***n.*** a plant and its bulb, प्याज़।

onlooker (ऑनलुकर) ***n.*** a spectator, दर्शक, द्रष्टा, तमाशबीन।

only (ओनली) ***adj.*** 1. alone in its kind or class, अकेला, इकलौता। 2. having no siblings, अकेला, जिसका भाई या बहन न हो। ***adv.*** 1. without anyone or anything, एकमात्र, सिर्फ़, केवल, मात्र। 2. no more than, सिर्फ़, अधिक नहीं। ***conj.*** except that, के अलावा।

onset (ऑनसेट) ***n.*** 1. a beginning, शुरुआत। 2. an attack, आक्रमण, चढ़ाई, धावा।

onshore (ऑनशोर) ***adj.*** coming towards the shore, तटोन्मुख। ***adv.*** towards the land, तट की ओर।

onslaught (ऑनस्लॉट) ***n.*** a fierce attack, भीषण आक्रमण।

onus (ओनस) ***n.*** burden, भार, दायित्व।

onward (ऑनवर्ड) ***adv.*** in a direction that is ahead, आगे, आगे की ओर। ***adj.*** directing or moving forward, आगे की ओर बढ़ता हुआ।

onwards (ऑनवर्ड्ज़) ***adv.*** = onward.

onyx (ऑनिक्स) ***n.*** a gem stone. सुलेमानी (पत्थर)।

ooze[1] (ऊज़) ***v.*** to trickle or leak slowly, रिसना, चूना, टपकना।

ooze[2] ***n.*** a soft thin mudlike sediment found at the bottom of rivers and lakes, नदियों तथा झीलों के तल में जमनेवाली मिट्टी की परत।

opacity (ओपैसिटी) ***n.*** the state or quality of being opaque, अपारदर्शिता।

opal (ओपल) ***n.*** a white gem-stone used in jewellery, दूधिया पत्थर।

opaque (ओपेक) ***adj.*** 1. not emitting or reflecting light, अपारदर्शी। 2. hard to understand, गहन, गूढ़।

open (ओपन) ***adj.*** 1. not closed or sealed, खुला। 2. having no cover, खुला, अनावृत्त। 3. accessible to all, खुला। 4. frank, निष्कपट। 5. not finally decided, अनिर्णीत। ***n.*** 1. open space, खुला मैदान। 2. an open competition, खुली स्पर्धा। ***v.*** 1. to make or become open, खुलना या खोलना। 2. to begin or start, शुरू होना/करना, प्रवृत्त होना/करना। 3. to declare open, शुभारंभ करना।

open-ended (ओपन-एन्डिड) ***adj.*** without any fixed limit, निस्सीम।

opener (ओपनर) ***n.*** a device for

O

opening bottles, cans etc., बोतल आदि खोलने का उपकरण।

open-handed (ओपन-हैन्डिड) ***adj.*** generous, उदार, मुक्तहस्त।

opening (ओपनिंग) ***adj.*** coming first, प्रारंभिक, आरंभिक। ***n.*** 1. the act of making or becoming open, प्रारंभ, शुरुआत। 2. a hole, छेद। 3. a way, मार्ग, रास्ता।

openly (ओपनली) ***adv.*** publicly, प्रकट रूप से, खुले आम।

open-mouthed (ओपन-माउथ्ड) ***adj.*** 1. greedy, लोभी, लालची। 2. surprised, चकित, हक्का-बक्का।

openness (ओपननिस) ***n.*** 1. the state or quality of being open, खुलापन। 2. frankness, स्पष्टवादिता।

opera (ऑपरा) ***n.*** a musical play, संगीत-नाटक, संगीतिका।

operable (ऑपरेबल) ***adj.*** 1. that can be operated, ऑपरेशन-योग्य। 2. practicable, करणीय, व्यवहार्य।

opera house ***n.*** a theatre built for operas, संगीत-नाट्यशाला।

operate (ऑपरेट) ***v.*** 1. to perform a surgical operation, ऑपरेशन करना, शल्य-चिकित्सा करना। 2. to cause to function, to run, परिचालन या चालू करना, चलाना।

operatic (ऑपरेटिक) ***adj.*** relating to or suitable to opera, संगीत-नाटक-संबंधी।

operation (ऑपरेशन) ***n.*** 1. the act or method of operating, प्रचालन, चलाना। 2. the condition of being operative, चलने या लागू होने की अवस्था। 3. a process, संक्रिया। 4. a surgical procedure, आपरेशन, शल्य-चिकित्सा। 5. a military action or project, सैनिक कार्रवाई। 6. (maths) any process performed according to specific rules, संक्रिया।

operational (ऑपरेशनल) ***adj.*** 1. of or relating to an operation, प्रचालन-संबंधी; संक्रियात्मक। 2. in working order or ready to use, चालू, व्यवहार्य। 3. of surgical operation, ऑपरेशन-संबंधी, शल्यकर्म-संबंधी।

operator (ऑपरेटर) ***n.*** 1. one who operates a machine, परिचालक। 2. a linesman, लाइन्समैन।

operetta (ऑपरेटा) ***n.*** a short opera, छोटा संगीत-नाटक।

ophthalmologist (ऑफ़्थैल्मॉलो-जिस्ट) ***n.*** a specialist in opthalmology, नेत्र-चिकित्सक।

ophthalmology (ऑफ़्थैल्मॉलोजी) ***n.*** the science dealing with eyes and their diseases, नेत्र-चिकित्सा-विज्ञान।

opiate (ओपिएट) ***n.*** a narcotic containing opium, निद्राकारी ओषधि।

opine (ओपाइन) ***v.*** to hold or express an opinion, राय बनाना या व्यक्त करना।

opinion (अपिन्यन) ***n.*** a belief held often without proof, मत, राय।

opinionated (अपिन्यनेटिड) ***adj.*** holding stubbornly to one's opinion, अड़ियल।

opium (ओपिअम) ***n.*** a drug made from dried juice of poppies, अफ़ीम।

opponent (अपोनेन्ट) ***n.*** one who opposes another or others, विपक्षी, विरोधी।

opportune (ऑपर्चून) ***adj.*** occurring at an appropriate or favour-able time, अवसरोचित या समयोचित।

opportunism (ऑपर्चूनिज़म) ***n.*** the practice of taking advantage of an opportunity, अवसर से लाभ उठाने की प्रवृत्ति, अवसरवाद।

opportunity (ऑपर्चूनिटी) ***n.*** a favourable time for a certain purpose, अवसर, सुअवसर, मौका।

oppose (अपोज़) ***v.*** 1. to fight against or resist, विरोध करना। 2. to be in opposition to, विरोध में होना।

opposite (ऑपोज़िट) ***adj.*** 1. situated on the other side, उधरवाला, सामनेवाला। 2. of a contrary kind, प्रतिकूल, विपरीत। 3. diametrically opposed, उलटा। ***n.*** one who is opposite to the other, विरोधी। ***prep.*** facing, के सामने।

opposition (ऑपोज़िशन) ***n.*** 1. the act of opposing or the state of being opposed, विरोध। 2. the people who oppose, विरोध-पक्ष, विरोधी दल।

oppress (ऑप्रेस) ***v.*** 1. to treat with injustice and cruelty, दुखी करना, उत्पीड़ित करना, सताना, अत्याचार करना। 2. to burden unjustly, दबाना।

oppression (ऑप्रेशन) ***n.*** the act of oppressing or the state of being oppressed, उत्पीड़न, दमन, अत्याचार।

opprobrious (ऑप्रोब्रिअस) ***adj.*** 1. expressing scorn or contempt, अपमानसूचक, निंदासूचक। 2. shameful, लज्जाजनक।

opt (ऑप्ट) ***v.*** to make a choice, चुनना, चयन करना।

optic (ऑप्टिक) ***adj.*** of the eye or vision, आँख या दृष्टि-संबंधी।

optical (ऑप्टिकल) ***adj.*** 1. of or relating to the sight, दृष्टि-संबंधी, चाक्षुष, दृक्-। 2. of or relating to optics, प्रकाश-विज्ञान-संबंधी।

optician (ऑप्टिशन) ***n.*** a maker or seller of spectacles, चश्मा निर्माता/विक्रेता।

optics (ऑप्टिक्स) ***n.*** the scientific study of sight and its medium light, प्रकाश-विज्ञान।

optimism (ऑप्टिमिज़्म) ***n.*** hopefulness, आशावाद।

optimize (ऑप्टिमाइज़) ***v.*** to make (something) as good as possible, (किसी चीज़ को) अच्छे से अच्छा बनाना।

optimum (ऑप्टिमम) ***adj.*** most favourable or advantageous, best, इष्टतम, अनुकूलतम। ***n.*** (plu. optima) the most favourable conditions or amount, अनुकूलतम परिस्थिति या राशि।

option (ऑप्शन) ***n.*** 1. an alternative, विकल्प। 2. freedom to choose, चयन-स्वतंत्रता। 3. something chosen, चुनी या पसंद की हुई वस्तु।

optional (ऑप्शनल) ***adj.*** left to personal choice, not compulsory, वैकल्पिक, ऐच्छिक।

opulent (ऑप्युलेन्ट) ***adj.*** 1. abundant, प्रचुर, विपुल। 2. wealthy, prosperous, धनाढ्य, समृद्ध।

opus (ओपस) ***n.*** (pl. opera) a musical work, संगीतमय रचना।

or (ऑर) ***conj.*** used to denote an alternative or synonymous expression, या, अथवा।

oracle (ऑरेकल) ***n.*** 1. a message of divine truth revealing God's will, देववाणी। 2. an agency through which this message is transmitted, देववाणी का माध्यम। 3. a wise person, विवेकी व्यक्ति।

oral (ओरल) ***adj.*** 1. verbal, spoken, ज़बानी, मौखिक। 2. done or taken by the mouth, मुखीय।

O

orange (ऑरिन्ज) ***n.*** a tree and its round juicy citrus fruit, नारंगी, संतरा। ***adj.*** reddish yellow, नारंगी के रंग का, नारंगी।

oration (ओरेशन) ***n.*** 1. a public speech, सार्वजनिक भाषण। 2. a long speech, लंबा भाषण।

orator (ऑरेटर) ***n.*** a public speaker, भाषणकर्ता। [fem. oratress, भाषणकर्त्री]

orb (ऑर्ब) ***n.*** a sphere of globe, गोलाकार पिंड, मंडल।

orbit (ऑर्बिट) ***n.*** 1. the circular path of a celestial body, कक्षा। 2. a sphere of influence, प्रभाव-क्षेत्र। ***v.*** to move in an orbit, कक्षा में घूमना, चक्कर लगाना।

orchard (ऑर्चर्ड) ***n.*** a garden of fruit trees, फलों का बाग़, फलोद्यान।

orchestra (ऑर्किस्ट्रा) ***n.*** 1. a group of musicians who play together on various instruments, वादकदल, वादकवृंद। 2. a set of different musical instruments, वाद्ययंत्रों का समूह, वाद्यवृंद।

ordain (ऑर्डेन) ***v.*** 1. to make someone a priest, पुरोहित बनाना। 2. to order, आदेश देना।

ordeal (ऑर्डील) ***n.*** 1. a trying or painful experience, कटु या दुखद अनुभव। 2. a method of trial for determining someone's innocence, अग्नि-परीक्षा, कसौटी।

order (ऑर्डर) ***n.*** 1. a logical arrangement, sequence, तर्कसंगत क्रम, सिलसिला। 2. condition or state, स्थिति। 3. a peaceful condition of society, व्यवस्था। 4. (often plural) a class or rank in society, वर्ग, श्रेणी। 5. a system of rules, पद्धति। 6. a command, आदेश, हुकुम। 7. a request to supply goods, आदेश, माँग। 8. such goods, माँगी हुई वस्तुएँ। ***v.*** 1. to arrange, सुव्यवस्थित करना, क्रम से रखना। 2. to give a command to, आदेश करना। 3. to request to be supplied with, आदेश भेजना, माँग करना।

orderly (आर्डरली) ***adj.*** 1. well-arranged, सुव्यवस्थित। 2. peace-loving and well-behaved, शांतिप्रिय तथा सुशील। ***n.*** an attendant to an officer, अर्दली।

ordinance (ऑर्डिनेन्स) ***n.*** an order given by the head of a state, अध्यादेश।

ordinarily (ऑर्डिनेरिली) ***adj.*** in an ordinary way, साधारणतः, साधारणतया, सदा की भाँति।

ordinary (ऑर्डिनेरी) ***adj.*** common, usual, साधारण, मामूली।

ordnance (ऑर्डनेंस) ***n.*** 1. military supplies, especially weapons and ammunitions, युद्ध-सामग्री विशेषतः अस्त्र-शस्त्र और बारूद। 2. heavy guns, बड़ी तोपें।

ore (ओर) ***n.*** a mineral from which a metal can be extracted, कच्ची धातु, अयस्क।

organ (ऑर्गन) ***n.*** 1. a musical instrument, एक प्रकार का बाजा, ऑरगन। 2. a distinct part of a living thing, अवयव, अंग। 3. a periodical, पत्रिका, मुखपत्र।

organic (ऑर्गैनिक) ***adj.*** 1. of or pertaining to living plants and animals, जैव। 2. of or pertaining to an organ of a body, अंगीय, आंगिक।

organism (ऑर्गनिज़म) ***n.*** a living being, जीव।

organist (ऑर्गनिस्ट) ***n.*** one who plays the organ, ऑरगन (बाजा) बजानेवाला।

organisation, organization (ऑर्ग-नाइज़ेशन) ***n.*** 1. the act of organising, संगठन, संघटन। 2. an organised group of people for a particular end, संगठन, संस्थान। 3. management, व्यवस्था, प्रबंध।

organize, organise (ऑर्गनाइज़) ***v.*** 1. to arrange in a systematic way, संघटित करना। 2. to form an association or concern, संघटन बनाना। 3. to arrange, आयोजित करना।

orgasm (ऑर्गैज़्म) ***n.*** the most tense point during sexual excitement, संभोग का चरम क्षण, रति-सुख।

orgy (ऑर्जी) ***n.*** 1. a wild gathering marked by unrestrained sexual activity, excessive drinking etc., मदनोत्सव, हुल्लड़-बाजी। 2. an excessive amount of a particular activity, घोर कृत्य, घोरता, प्रचंडता।

Orient (ओरिएन्ट) ***n.*** **the Orient,** the countries of the East, पूर्वी देश, विशेषतः पूर्वी एशिया।

orient ***adj.*** eastern, पूर्वी, प्राच्य। ***v.*** 1. to acquaint with a new environment, नए वातावरण से परिचित कराना। 2. to direct, दिशानिर्देश करना।

oriental (ओरिएन्टल) ***adj.*** eastern, पूर्वी, प्राच्य। ***n.*** a native of the Orient, पूरब का निवासी।

orientate (ओरिअन्टेट) ***v.*** = orient.

orientation (ओरिअन्टेशन) ***n.*** the adjustment of oneself with the new situation or surroundings, नई स्थिति या परिस्थितियों के अनुकूल अपने को बनाना।

orifice (ऑरिफ़िस) ***n.*** an opening or vent, छेद, छिद्र, मुँह।

origin (ऑरिजिन) ***n.*** 1. the primary source (of something), मूल, उद्‌गम, स्रोत। 2. birth, जन्म। 3. ancestry, वंश, वंशक्रम।

original (ऑरिजिनल) ***adj.*** 1. of or pertaining to an origin or beginning, मूल, मौलिक, मूलभूत, प्रारंभिक। 2. novel, नवीन, नया। ***n.*** the first form of something, मूल रूप।

originality (ऑरिजिनैलिटी) ***n.*** the quality of being of a new type, मौलिकता।

originate (ऑरिजिनेट) ***v.*** 1. to begin, आरंभ होना या करना। 2. to cause to begin, आरंभ कराना।

ornament (ऑर्नमेन्ट) ***n.*** a decorative object, something that adorns, आभूषण, अलंकार, गहना, शोभा बढ़ानेवाली वस्तु। ***v.*** to adorn or decorate, आभूषित करना, सजाना।

ornamental (ऑर्नमेन्टल) ***adj.*** serving as an ornament, शोभा बढ़ानेवाला, आलंकारिक।

ornate (ऑर्नेट) ***adj.*** over-embellished, heavily ornamented, आभूषणों से लदा, अत्यधिक सजा-धजा।

ornithology (ऑर्निथॉलोजी) ***n.*** the scientific study of birds, पक्षी-विज्ञान।

orphan (ऑर्फ़न) ***n.*** a child whose parents are dead, अनाथ, यतीम। ***v.*** to deprive of parents, अनाथ बना देना।

orphanage (ऑर्फ़नेज) ***n.*** an institution for orphans, अनाथालय, यतीमख़ाना।

orthodontics (ऑर्थोडॉन्टिक्स) ***n.*** the science of correcting unaligned teeth, दंताकृति-विज्ञान।

O

orthodox (ऑर्थोडॉक्स) ***adj.*** adhering to established standard esp. in religion, behaviour or attitude, रूढ़िवादी।

orthopaedics (ऑर्थोपीडिक्स) ***n.*** the branch of medicine that deals with disorders of bones, muscles and joints, अस्थि सुधार विज्ञान।

oscillate (ऑसिलेट) ***v.*** 1. to move from side to side regularly, डोलना, दोलन करना। 2. to fluctuate, घटते-बढ़ते रहना। 3. to waver between opinions, बीच में झूलना, अनिश्चय की स्थिति में होना।

oscillation (ऑसिलेशन) ***n.*** 1. the act of oscillating, दोलन। 2. uncertainty, अनिश्चय।

osmosis (ऑज़्मोसिस) ***n.*** diffusion of fluid to another fluid through membrane, द्रव का छिद्रिल झिल्ली से निकलकर दूसरे द्रव में जा मिलना, परासरण।

ossify (ऑसिफ़ाइ) ***v.*** 1. to change into bone, अस्थिमय करना। 2. to become rigid, कठोर हो जाना।

ostensible (ऑस्टेन्सिबल) ***adj.*** seeming, professed, बाहरी, ऊपरी।

ostentation (ऑस्टेन्टेशन) ***n.*** 1. pretentious display, दिखावा। 2. showy display, तड़क-भड़क, आडंबर।

ostler (ऑस्लर) ***n.*** a stableman, तबेलची, साईस।

ostracize (ऑस्ट्रसाइज़) ***v.*** to banish from a group or society, जाति से बहिष्कृत करना, हुक्का-पानी बंद कर देना।

ostrich (ऑस्ट्रिच) ***n.*** an African bird, शुतुरमुर्ग।

other (अदर) ***adj.*** different, दूसरा, अन्य, भिन्न। ***n. & pron.*** other person or thing, अन्य व्यक्ति या वस्तु, वह।

otherwise (अदरवाइज़) ***adv.*** 1. in a different way, differently, अन्यथा। 2. in other respects, वैसे तो।

otter (ऑटर) ***n.*** a mammal with webbed feet, ऊदबिलाव।

ought (ऑट) ***aux. v.*** expressing desirability or probability, चाहिए।

ounce (आउन्स) ***n.*** a unit of weight, औंस (28.35 ग्राम)। ***adj.*** in a small quantity, थोड़ा सा।

our (आउर) ***possessive adj.*** belonging to us, हमारा।

ours (आउर्ज़) ***possessive pron.*** the things belonging to us, हमारा।

ourselves (आउरसेल्व्ज़) ***pron.*** reflexive, हम (खुद)।

oust (आउस्ट) ***v.*** to force out, निकाल बाहर करना, निकाल देना।

out (आउट) ***adv.*** 1. outside, बाहर। 2. away from home, घर से बाहर। 3. to extinction, समाप्ति पर। 4. into the open, खुले में, सामने, बाहर। 5. unconscious, बेसुध। 6. completely, पूर्णत:। ***prep.*** out through, में से। ***interj.*** an exclamation for dismissal, get out, बाहर निकलो! ***v.*** to be revealed, सर्वविदित होना, निकल आना, प्रकट होना, सामने आना।

outbid (आउटबिड) ***v.*** (outbid, outbidding) to bid higher than (someone, किसी से) बढ़कर बोली देना।

outboard (आउटबोर्ड) ***adj.*** placed outside of the stern of a boat, नाव पर लगा (इंजन)।

outbreak (आउटब्रेक) ***n.*** a sudden start of something, सहसा होनेवाला आरंभ, शुरुआत, प्रकोप।

outburst (आउटबर्स्ट) ***n.*** 1. a

sudden and violent expression of emotions, उद्गार, भड़ास। 2. explosion, धमाका, विस्फोट।

outcaste (आउटकास्ट) ***n.*** 1. a person who has been expelled from a caste, जाति-बहिष्कृत। 2. a person having no caste, वह व्यक्ति जिसकी कोई जाति न हो।

outcome (आउटकम) ***n.*** consequence, result, परिणाम, फल, नतीजा।

outcry (आउटक्राइ) ***n.*** 1. uproar, चिल्लपों, चीख-पुकार। 2. a strong protest, कड़ा विरोध।

outdated (आउटडेटिड) ***adj.*** out of date, दिनातीत, पुराना।

outdo (आउटडू) ***v.*** (outdid, outdone, outdoing) to surpass in performance, से आगे निकल जाना, हरा देना।

outdoor (आउटडोर) ***adj.*** out-of-door, घर से बाहर का।

outdoors (आउटडोर्ज़) ***adv.*** in the open air, खुले में, बाहर।

outer (आउटर) ***adj.*** external, बाहरी।

outermost (आउटरमोस्ट) ***adj.*** farthest out, सबसे बाहर का, बाह्यतम।

outfit (आउटफ़िट) ***n.*** 1. clothing/equipment for a special purpose, विशिष्ट प्रयोजन हेतु परिधान/उपकरण।

outflow (आउटफ़्लो) ***n.*** anything that flows out, बहिर्प्रवाह, बाहर बह जाना।

outgoing (आउटगोइंग) ***adj.*** 1. going out, बाहर जानेवाला, निर्गामी, जावक। 2. just retired, जो हाल में पदनिवृत्त हुआ हो। 3. sociable, मिलनसार। 4. (plu.) the amount of money one spends, खर्च, व्यय।

outgrow (आउटग्रो) ***v.*** (outgrew, outgrown, outgrowing) to grow larger and faster than, अपेक्षाकृत अधिक तेज़ी से बढ़ना।

outgrowth (आउटग्रोथ) ***n.*** 1. something that grows out of something else, ऐसी वस्तु जो किसी अन्य वस्तु से निकली हो, उद्वृद्धि। 2. development, विकास। 3. natural result, स्वाभाविक परिणाम।

outhouse (आउटहाउस) ***n.*** an outbuilding, उपभवन, उपगृह।

outing (आउटिंग) ***n.*** a pleasure trip, excursion, सैर-सपाटा।

outlaw (आउटलॉ) ***n.*** a person living as a fugitive, विधिबहिष्कृत, भगोड़ा। ***v.*** 1. to declare an outlaw, भगोड़ा घोषित करना। 2. to declare illegal, अवैध घोषित करना।

outlay (आउटले) ***n.*** an expenditure of money, व्यय, ख़र्च।

outlet (आउटलेट) ***n.*** 1. a passage for exit, बाहर निकलने का रास्ता, निकास। 2. a means of expression, अभिव्यक्ति का साधन। 3. a market for goods, बाज़ार।

outline (आउटलाइन) ***n.*** 1. a line showing the outer boundary of a figure or object, बहिर्रेखा। 2. a sketch or drawing without shading, ख़ाका, रूपरेखा। 3. a summary, सारांश, संक्षिप्त विवरण। ***v.*** to sketch, रूपरेखा बनाना, ख़ाका तैयार करना।

outlive (आउटलिव) ***v.*** to live longer than, अपेक्षया लंबी उम्र पाना।

outlook (आउटलुक) ***n.*** 1. the view from a place, दृश्य। 2. a mental attitude, दृष्टिकोण। 3. future prospects, आशा, संभावना।

outlying (आउटलाइंग) ***adj.*** remote, बहिर्वर्ती, दूरस्थ।

O

outmoded (आउटमोडिड) ***adj.*** not in fashion, फ़ैशन से उठा हुआ, फ़ैशन-बाहर, पुराना।

out-patient (आउट-पेशन्ट) ***n.*** a patient not staying at the hospital, बाहरी रोगी, बहिर्रोगी।

outpost (आउटपोस्ट) ***n.*** a distant place where soldiers are stationed, सीमा-चौकी।

output (आउटपुट) ***n.*** 1. the amount produced, उपज, उत्पादन। 2. the work done by a computer, कम्प्यूटर द्वारा किया हुआ काम, निकासी, आउटपुट।

outrage (आउटरेज) ***n.*** 1. a cruel act, नृशंसता। 2. violation of decency, अशिष्टता। 3. resentful anger, रोष। 4. insult, अपमान। 5. injury, आघात, चोट। ***v.*** 1. to offend, आघात पहुँचाना। 2. to rape, बलात्कार करना।

outrageous (आउटरेजस) ***adj.*** 1. grossly offensive, अत्यधिक आघात पहुँचानेवाला। 2. unrestrained in behaviour, अतिचारी, अतिचारपूर्ण।

outright (आउटराइट) ***adv.*** 1. entirely, पूरी तरह से, पूर्ण रूप से। 2. frankly, साफ़-साफ़। ***adj.*** without limitations, पूर्ण या पक्का।

outset (आउटसेट) ***n.*** the beginning, आरंभ, प्रारंभ।

outside (आउटसाइड) ***n.*** 1. the outer side, बाहरी तरफ़। 2. the space beyond a boundary, सीमा से परे का स्थान। 3. the utmost limit, अधिकतम सीमा। ***adj.*** 1. of outside, बाहरी। 2. remote, दूरस्थित। ***adv.*** on the outside, बाहर, खुले में। ***prep.*** 1. on the other side of, के उस तरफ़, के उधर। 2. beyond the limits of, सीमा से परे।

outskirts (आउटस्कर्ट्स) ***n.*** (plu.) bordering areas of a city, नगर या बस्ती के बाहर का भाग, बाह्यांचल।

outspoken (आउटस्पोकन) ***adj.*** bold in speech, very frank, स्पष्टवादी।

outstanding (आउटस्टैन्डिंग) ***adj.*** 1. unpaid, बकाया। 2. excellent, उत्कृष्ट, प्रमुख।

outstation (आउटस्टेशन) ***n.*** a station other than one's own, बाहर, दूसरा नगर या स्थान।

outward (आउटवर्ड) ***adj.*** 1. going toward the outside, बाहर जानेवाला। 2. external, बाहरी, बाह्य।

outweigh (आउटवे) ***v.*** to be greater in weight or importance, (अपेक्षया) भारी/महत्त्वपूर्ण हो जाना।

outwit (आउटविट) ***v.*** to get the better of by cunning, चतुराई में बीस निकलना।

ova (ओवा) ***n.*** plu. of ovum.

oval (ओवल) ***adj.*** egg-shaped, अंडाकार।

ovarian (ओवेरिअन) ***adj.*** of an ovary, अंडाशय-संबंधी।

ovary (ओवरी) ***n.*** 1. the female reproductive gland, अंडाशय। 2. the part of the pistil containing ovules, बीजाशय।

ovation (ओवेशन) ***n.*** 1. enthusiastic applause, करतलध्वनि। 2. enthusiastic public welcome, अभिनंदन, जयजयकार।

oven (अवन) ***n.*** a receptacle for heating, baking etc., ओवन; तंदूर।

over (ओवर) ***prep.*** 1. above, के ऊपर। 2. on upon, पर। 3. above in authority, से ऊपर। 4. across, के आर-पार, के ऊपर। 5. on the other side, के उधर, की उस ओर। 6. in excess of, besides, से अधिक। 7. during, के दौरान। 8. along the length of, के साथ-साथ। 9. on account of, के विषय में, के लिए। 10. at the end, अंत में। ***adv.*** 1. above, ऊपर। 2. across, पार। 3. on the other side, दूसरी तरफ़। 4. completely, पूर्ण रूप से, पूर्णतया। 5. excessively, अत्यधिक। 6. repeatedly, बार-बार। 7. thoroughly, अच्छी तरह। ***n.*** six balls delivered by a bowler at a time, ओवर। ***prefix.*** 1. above or outer, ऊपरी, बाहरी। 2. too much, अत्यधिक, अति-।

overactive (ओवरऐक्टिव) ***n.*** too active, अतिसक्रिय।

overall (ओवरॉल) ***adj.*** 1. including everything, कुल, पूरा। 2. on the whole, सभी दृष्टियों से होनेवाला। ***adv.*** 1. generally, सामान्यत:। 2. taken as a whole, कुल मिलाकर।

overalls (ओवरॉल्ज़) ***n.*** loose dress worn over other clothes, वस्त्रों के ऊपर पहना जानेवाला परिधान।

overawe (ओवरऑ) ***v.*** to subdue with awe, आतंकित करना, धमकाना।

overbalance (ओवरबैलेन्स) ***v.*** 1. to become unbalanced, असंतुलित होना, डगमगा जाना या गिर पड़ना। 2. to cause to become unbalanced, असंतुलित कर देना, डगमगा देना।

overbearing (ओवरबेअरिंग) ***adj.*** 1. domineering, दबंग, निरंकुश। 2. arrogant, हेकड़।

overbid (ओवरबिड) ***v.*** (overbid, overbidding) to outbid, बढ़कर बोली देना। ***n.*** a higher bid, ऊँची बोली।

overboard (ओवरबोर्ड) ***adv.*** from a boat or ship, नाव या जहाज़ पर से। ☐ **go overboard,** अत्यधिक उत्सुकता दिखलाना।

overcast (ओवरकास्ट) ***adj.*** covered with clouds, मेघाच्छादित।

overcautious (ओवरकॉशस) ***adj.*** too cautious, अति सावधान, बहुत अधिक चौकन्ना।

overcoat (ओवरकोट) ***n.*** a long heavy coat, ओवरकोट।

overcome (ओवरकम) ***v.*** (overcame, overcome, overcoming) 1. to succeed in subduing, अभिभूत या वशीभूत कर लेना। 2. to be victorious, विजयी होना।

overdo (ओवरडू) ***v.*** (overdid, overdoing) 1. to do excess, अति कर देना, ज़्यादती करना। 2. to exaggerate, अतिरंजित करना। 3. to work too hard, कठोर परिश्रम करना। 4. to cook too long, ज़्यादा पका या भून देना।

overdose (ओवरडोज़) ***n.*** excessive dose of a drug etc., बड़ी या भारी ख़ुराक, अतिमात्रा।

overdraft (ओवरड्राफ़्ट) ***n.*** 1. the act of overdrawing an account, खाते में जमा से अधिक रक़म निकालना। 2. the amount overdrawn, इस प्रकार निकाली हुई राशि, ओवरड्राफ़्ट।

overdraw (ओवरड्रॉ) ***v.*** (overdrew, overdrawn, overdrawing) to withdraw more than the amount credited, (बैंक खाते में) जमा से अधिक धन निकालना, ओवरड्राफ़्ट करना।

overdress (ओवरड्रेस) ***v.*** to dress too formally or finely, सजना-सँवरना, बनना-ठनना।

overdrive (ओवरड्राइव) ***n.*** a very high gear used at high speed, तेज़ गति में प्रयुक्त किया जानेवाला गियर।

overdue (ओवरड्यू) ***adj.*** being unpaid after becoming due, अवधि बीतने पर भी जो चुकाया न गया हो, विलंबित।

overflow (ओवरफ़्लो) ***v.*** to flow over, (किनारे से बाहर) बहने लगना।

overgrow (ओवरग्रो) ***v.*** (overgrew, overgrown, overgrowing) to grow beyond normal size, बहुत अधिक बढ़ जाना।

overgrowth (ओवरग्रोथ) ***n.*** abnormal growth, अतिवृद्धि।

overhang (ओवरहैंग) ***v.*** (overhung, overhanging) to extend beyond, आगे या बाहर निकलना, आगे या बाहर लटका होना।

overhaul (ओवरहॉल) ***v.*** to make all the necessary repairs, पूरी तरह से मरम्मत करना, ओवरहाल करना।

overhead (ओवरहेड) ***adj.*** above the level of one's head, सिर के ऊपर से होनेवाला। ***n.*** pl. the operating expenses (of a firm or office), ऊपरी ख़र्च।

overhear (ओवरहिअर) ***v.*** (overheard, overhearing) to hear without the knowledge of the speaker, छिपकर या चोरी से सुनना।

overland (ओवरलैन्ड) ***adv.*** by land, स्थल मार्ग से।

overlap (ओवरलैप) ***v.*** to extend over and partly cover it, ढक लेना, आच्छादित कर लेना।

overleaf (ओवरलीफ़) ***adv.*** on the other side of the page, पृष्ठ के उस तरफ़, पन्ने के दूसरी ओर।

overload (ओवरलोड) ***v.*** to load too much, अधिक लादना। ***n.*** a load that is too great, भारी बोझ।

overlook (ओवरलुक) ***v.*** 1. to have a look from above, ऊपर से देखना। 2. to ignore deliberately, अनदेखी करना।

overmatch (ओवरमैच) ***v.*** to be more than the match of, भारी पड़ना।

overnight (ओवरनाइट) ***adv.*** during the length of night, रात-भर, रात-भर में। ***adj.*** 1. staying for the night, रात-भर का। 2. occurring in the night, रात्रिकालीन।

overpopulated (ओवरपाप्यूलेटिड) ***adj.*** having over population, अधिक जनसंख्यावाला।

overpower (ओवरपाउअर) ***v.*** to subdue or overwhelm, (को) अभिभूत/पराजित करना।

overrate (ओवररेट) ***v.*** to assess too highly, अधिक मूल्यांकन करना।

override (ओवरराइड) ***v.*** (overrode, overridden, overriding) 1. to trample upon, कुचल देना। 2. to set aside, निरस्त कर देना।

overrule (ओररूल) ***v.*** to rule or decide against, निरस्त या रद कर देना।

overrun (ओवररन) ***v.*** (overran, overrun, overrunning) 1. to spread or swarm over, छा जाना, फैल जाना। 2. to exceed, आगे बढ़ जाना।

overseas (ओवरसीज़) ***adv.*** beyond the sea, समुद्र पार।

oversee (ओवरसी) ***v.*** (oversaw, overseen, overseeing) to inspect, निरीक्षण करना।

overseer (ओवरसिअर) ***n.*** one whose job is to oversee something, ओवरसियर।

oversensitive (ओवरसेन्सिटिव) ***adj.*** too much sensitive, अतिसंवेदनशील।

overshadow (ओवरशैडो) ***v.*** 1. to cast a shadow over, परछाईं से ढक देना, दबा

देना। 2. to surpass in importance, महत्त्व में बढ़-चढ़कर होना।

overshoot (ओवरशूट) ***v.*** (overshot, overshooting) to shoot over or beyond, निशाना चूक जाना।

oversight (ओवरसाइट) ***n.*** an unintentional omission, दृष्टिभ्रम, चूक, भूल-चूक।

overstatement (ओवरस्टेटमेन्ट) ***n.*** an exaggerated statement, अत्युक्तिपूर्ण कथन।

overstay (ओवरस्टे) ***v.*** to stay longer than, अपेक्षया अधिक समय ठहरना।

overstep (ओवरस्टेप) ***v.*** to go beyond, हद से परे जाना।

overt (ओवर्ट) ***adj.*** open, खुला, प्रकट, प्रत्यक्ष।

overtake (ओवरटेक) ***v.*** (overtook, overtaken, overtaking) 1. to get past, पीछे से तेज़ी से आकर किसी व्यक्ति, गाड़ी आदि से आगे निकल जाना। 2. to take by surprise, चकित कर देना।

overthrow (ओवरथ्रो) ***v.*** (overthrew, overthrown, overthrowing) 1. to overturn, (तख़्ता) उलट देना। 2. to throw past, दूर फेंकना।

overtime (ओवरटाइम) ***n.*** 1. working hours in addition to the regular schedule, ओवरटाइम, अतिरिक्त समय। 2. the payment for such work, ओवरटाइम (का भुगतान)। ***adv.*** beyond the regular time, समयोपरि, अतिकालिक, नियत समय के बांद।

overtone (ओवरटोन) ***n.*** 1. (music) higher tone, अधिस्वर। 2. an additional meaning or implication, छाया, रंगत, आभा; गूढ़ार्थ।

overture (ओवर्चर) ***n.*** a gesture initiating a relationship, संबंध बढ़ाने का इशारा।

overturn (ओवरटर्न) ***v.*** 1. to turn over, उलट जाना। 2. to overthrow, उलट देना, पलट देना।

overview (ओवरव्यू) ***n.*** a general survey, सिंहावलोकन।

overwhelm (ओवरव्हैल्म) ***v.*** 1. to overcome, अभिभूत कर लेना। 2. to overpower, पराभूत कर लेना, हावी हो जाना। 3. to bury, गाड़ या दबा देना।

overwhelming (ओवरव्हैल्मिंग) ***adj.*** very strong or excessive, ज़ोरदार, अत्यधिक, भारी।

ovoid (ओवाइड) ***adj.*** egg-shaped, अंडाकार।

ovulate (ओव्युलेट) ***v.*** to discharge ova, अंडाणु उत्पन्न करना।

ovum (ओवम) ***n.*** (plu. ova) a female reproductive egg cell, डिंब, अंडाणु।

owe (ओ) ***v.*** 1. to have to pay to an obligation due to be in debt to, देनदार होना। 2. to be morally obliged to, आभारी होना।

owing (ओइंग) ***adj.*** owed and not yet paid, देय। □ **owing to,** के कारण, के परिणामस्वरूप।

owl (आउल) ***n.*** a bird that flies in the night, उल्लू।

own (ओन) ***adj.*** of or belonging to oneself, अपना, निजी। ***v.*** 1. to have or possess, पास होना, धारणा करना, रखना। 2. to acknowledge or admit, स्वीकार करना।

owner (ओनर) ***n.*** one who owns something, स्वामी, मालिक।

ownership (ओनरशिप) ***n.*** the state of being an owner, स्वामित्व, स्वत्व।

ox (ऑक्स) ***n.*** (plu. oxen) a castrated bull, बैल।

O

oxidation (ऑक्सिडेशन) ***n.*** the act or process of oxidizing, ऑक्सीकरण।

oxidization, oxidisation (ऑक्सि-डाइज़ेशन) ***n.*** = oxidation.

oxygen (ऑक्सिजन) ***n.*** a gaseous element, ऑक्सीजन।

oyster (ऑइस्टर) ***n.*** a kind of shellfish, खाद्य शुक्ति, एक प्रकार की घोंघा मछली।

ozone (ओज़ोन्) ***n.*** a form of oxygen, ओज़ोन।

P, p (पी) ***n.*** the sixteenth letter of the English alphabet, अंग्रेज़ी वर्णमाला का सोलहवाँ वर्ण।

pace (पेस) ***n.*** 1. a single step, पग, क़दम, डग। 2. manner of walking, चाल, चलने का ढंग। 3. the rate of progress, प्रगति की दर। ***v.*** 1. to walk with regular pace, बँधी हुई चाल से चलना। 2. to set the pace for, क्रम चलाना या बाँधना, गति निर्धारित करना। 3. to measure by pacing, क़दमों से नापना।

pace-maker (पेस-मेकर) ***n.*** 1. one who sets the pace, क्रम-निर्धारक, गति-निर्धारक। 2. a device to control the heartbeat, हृदय की धड़कन को नियमित करनेवाला यंत्र, पेस-मेकर।

pachyderm (पैकिडर्म) ***n.*** a thick skinned mammal, मोटी चमड़ीवाला प्राणी (जैसे—हाथी)।

Pacific (पैसिफ़िक) ***n.*** the Pacific Ocean, प्रशांत महासागर।

pacific ***adj.*** peaceful, शांतिप्रिय, शांतिपूर्ण।

pacify (पैसिफ़ाइ) ***v.*** 1. to calm the anger, शांत/ठंडा करना। 2. to restore peace, शांति स्थापित करना।

pack (पैक) ***n.*** 1. a bundle, पुलिंदा, गठरी, पोटली, बंडल। 2. a complete set of playing cards, ताश की गड्डी। 3. a group of animals, झुंड, समूह। ***v.*** 1. to wrap or put into a container, (चीज़ों को) लपेटना, बाँधना या गठियाना, पैक करना। 2. to cram or press into, भरना, ठूँसना। 3. to carry something regularly, लादे फिरना।

package (पैकिज) ***n.*** 1. a bundle or parcel, बंडल, पार्सल, पैकेज। 2. a small container, पैकट, पेटी, बक्सा। 3. a sale offer of a few or more things, कई चीज़ों का इकट्ठा सौदा। ***v.*** to make into a package, पैक करना, बंडल बनाना।

package deal ***n.*** a number of things jointly offered for sale, एकमुश्त सौदा।

package tour ***n.*** an arranged tour, पैकेज टूर।

pack animal ***n.*** an animal used to transport goods, लद्दू घोड़ा, बैल आदि।

packed (पैक्ड) ***adj.*** 1. placed in a container, पैक किया हुआ। 2. filled or full, भरा हुआ, खचाखच, ठसाठस।

packer (पैकर) ***n.*** one who packs, बंडल, पैकेट आदि बाँधनेवाला कर्मचारी।

packet (पैकिट) ***n.*** a small package, पैकेट, डिबिया।

pact (पैक्ट) ***n.*** 1. an agreement, समझौता। 2. a treaty, संधि।

pad (पैड) ***n.*** 1. something soft that serves as a cushion, गद्दी, पैड। 2. number of sheets of paper glued together, पैड। 3. a flat surface, चौरस भूमि। ***v.*** 1. to fill with soft material, नरम चीज़ भरना। 2. to stuff, भरना। 3. to expand, विस्तार बढ़ाना। 4. to walk slowly on foot, धीरे-धीरे पैदल चलना।

padding (पैडिन्ग) ***n.*** soft material used to pad things, भराई, पैडिंग।

paddle (पैडल) ***n.*** 1. an oar, चप्पू, डाँड। 2. an oar like instrument, बेलचा। ***v.*** to row, नाव खेना।

P

paddy (पैडी) ***n.*** rice in the husk, धान।

padlock (पैडलॉक) ***n.*** a kind of lock, ताला। ***v.*** to fasten with a padlock, ताला लगाना।

paediatrician (पीडिऐट्रिशन) ***n.*** a specialist in paediatrics, बाल-रोग चिकित्सक।

paediatrics (पीडिऐट्रिक्स) ***n.*** the science concerned with the diseases of children, बाल-रोग चिकित्सा।

pagan (पेगन) ***n.*** a heathen, काफ़िर, विधर्मी। ***adj.*** heathen, दूसरे धर्म का, विधर्मी।

page[1] (पेज) ***n.*** one side of one of the leaves of a book etc., पृष्ठ, सफ़ा। ***v.*** to number the pages of a book etc., पृष्ठों पर नंबर लगाना, पृष्ठांकन करना।

page[2] ***n.*** one employed to run errands, लड़का, नौकर।

pageant, pageantry (पैजन्ट, पैजन्ट्री) ***n.*** a colourful procession of people, जुलूस, शोभायात्रा।

pager (पेजर) ***n.*** a device for receiving messages, संदेश प्राप्त करने का एक उपकरण, पेजर।

pagoda (पगोडा) ***n.*** a Buddhist tower with several stories, स्तूप, पगोड़ा।

paid (पेड) ***adj.*** p.t. & p.p. of pay. ***adj.*** receiving pay, hired, वेतनभोगी।

paid-up (पेड-अप) ***adj.*** given in payment, चुकता, प्रदत्त, अदा।

pail (पेल) ***n.*** a bucket, बालटी, डोल।

pailful (पेलफ़ुल)***n.*** as much as a pail will hold, बालटी-भर।

pain (पेन) ***n.*** 1. suffering, पीड़ा, दर्द। 2. mental suffering, व्यथा, वेदना। 3. trouble taken, कष्ट। 4. (plu.) great care or effort, सावधानी या प्रयत्न। ***v.*** to cause pain to, दुख देना।

painful (पेनफ़ुल) ***adj.*** 1. causing pain, कष्ट या दुख देनेवाला। 2. suffering pain, दर्द-भरा, दुखनेवाला, दुखता हुआ। 3. hardworking, परिश्रमी, लगकर काम करनेवाला।

painkiller (पेनकिलर) ***n.*** a pain relieving medicine, वेदनाहर या पीड़ानाशक ओषधि।

painless (पेनलिस) ***adj.*** not causing pain, जिससे पीड़ा न हो, पीड़ाशून्य।

painstaking (पेन्ज़टेकिंग) ***adj.*** 1. very careful, अति सावधान। 2. hard working, परिश्रमी।

paint (पेन्ट) ***n.*** a mixutre for colouring a surface, रोग़न, पेंट। ***v.*** 1. to coat with paint, रोग़न करना, पेंट करना, रँगाई करना। 2. to portray, चित्रांकन करना, पेंट करना।

painter[1] (पेन्टर) ***n.*** 1. one who paints, रंगसाज़ 2. one who paints pictures, चित्रकार।

painter[2] ***n.*** a rope attached with a boat, नाव में लगी रस्सी, गून।

painting (पेन्टिंग) ***n.*** 1. the art of applying paints, चित्रकला। 2. a painted picture, रंगीन चित्र।

pair (पेअर) ***n.*** 1. two similar or corresponding things, जोड़ा, जोड़ी। 2. a couple, युगल। ***v.*** 1. to arrange people in groups of twos, जोड़ियाँ बनाना। 2. to mate, जोड़ा खाना।

pal (पैल) ***n.*** a close friend, घनिष्ठ मित्र, पक्का यार।

palace (पैलिस) ***n.*** 1. the sovereign's residence, महल, राजमहल।

2. a large or splendid residence, कोठी, हवेली।

palanquin (पैलनकीन) ***n.*** a covered litter carried by four persons, पालकी।

palatable (पैलेटेबल) ***adj.*** 1. agreeable to the taste, स्वादिष्ट, ज़ायकेदार। 2. acceptable to mind, अनुकूल, रुचिकर।

palatal (पैलेटल) ***adj.*** of or relating to the palate, तालु-संबंधी, तालव्य।

palate (पैलिट) ***n.*** 1. the roof of the mouth, तालु। 2. taste, स्वाद।

palatial (पैलेशल) ***adj.*** 1. like a palace, महल जैसा। 2. spacious and splendid, विशाल और भव्य।

pale (पेल) ***adj.*** 1. yellowish in complexion, पीत, पीला, ज़र्द। 2. dim, faint, मंद, मुरझाया हुआ, विवर्ण। ***v.*** 1. to turn pale, पीला पड़ जाना। 2. to become dim or faint, मंद पड़ जाना, दब जाना।

paleolithic (पेलिओलिथिक) ***adj.*** of the early period of stone age, पूर्व-पाषाणयुगीन।

palette (पैलिट) ***n.*** 1. a thin board on which an artist mixes colours, रंग-पट्टिका। 2. colours used by a particular artist, किसी चित्रकार द्वारा प्रयुक्त रंग।

palindrome (पैलिन्ड्रोम) ***n.*** a word or phrase that reads the same backwards as it does forwards, वे शब्द या पद जो उलटे-सीधे एक समान हों। (e.g. rotator; उदाहरणार्थ—जहाज़)।

palish (पेलिश) ***adj.*** somewhat pale, पीला-सा, पीला, पीताभ।

pall (पॉल) ***n.*** 1. a cloth covering for a coffin or bier, ताबूत या अर्थी के ऊपर डाली जानेवाली चादर। 2. a cover, covering, आवरण, आच्छादन। ***v.*** to become boring, उबाऊ होना।

pallbearer (पॉलबेअरर) ***n.*** one who carries the coffin or bier, ताबूत या अर्थी उठानेवाला।

pallet[1] (पैलिट) ***n.*** 1. a mattress stuffed with straws, फूस/पयाल का गद्दा। 2. a makeshift bed, उठौआ चारपाई। 3. a large tray, बड़ी ट्रे।

pallet[2] ***n.*** a potter's instrument for shaping, थापी।

palliate (पैलिएट) ***v.*** to make less severe, हलका कर देना, उपशमन करना।

palliation (पैलिएशन) ***n.*** the act of palliating, उपशमन।

pallid (पैलिड) ***adj.*** pale, पीला, ज़र्द।

palm[1] (पाम) ***n.*** 1. the inner surface of the hand, हथेली, करतल। 2. the breadth or length of the hand, बालिश्त, बित्ता। ***v.*** to con-ceal in one's hand, हाथ में छिपा लेना।

palm[2] ***n.*** a tall tree with large leaves, खजूर या ताड़।

palmistry (पामिस्ट्री) ***n.*** the art of telling fortunes by examining the lines and bumps on the palm, हस्तरेखा-विज्ञान, सामुद्रिक विद्या।

palpable (पैल्पेबल) ***adj.*** 1. obvious, सुस्पष्ट, साफ़। 2. able to be touched or felt, इंद्रियगोचर।

palpitate (पैल्पिटेट) ***v.*** 1. to throb rapidly, धकधक करना, धड़कना। 2. to quiver, काँपना।

palsy (पॉल्ज़ी) ***n.*** paralysis, लकवा, पक्षाघात।

paltry (पॉल्ट्री) ***adj.*** insignificant, थोड़ा, अल्प, नगण्य।

pampas (पैम्पज़) ***n.*** (plu.) wide

P

treeless plains in South America, दक्षिण अमरीका के विशाल वृक्षहीन मैदान, पंपास।

pamper (पैम्पर) ***v.*** to cuddle, दुलार करना, दुलारना।

pamphlet (पैम्फ़्लट) ***n.*** a leaflet or folder containing information, पेंफ़लेट, छोटी पुस्तक, इश्तहार।

pan[1] (पैन) ***prefix.*** all, अखिल, सर्व—; pan-Africanism, सर्व-अफ़्रीकावाद।

pan[2] ***n.*** 1. a flat base container for cooking purposes, पैन, तवी। 2. the bowl of a pair of scales, पलड़ा। ***v.*** 1. to wash (gravel) in pan, पैन में रखकर धोना। 2. to criticize severely, कड़ी आलोचना करना।

panacea (पैनेसीआ) ***n.*** a remedy for all troubles, रामबाण।

panache (पनैश) ***n.*** 1. a plume, कलगी। 2. a stylish manner, ढंग, शैली।

pancake (पैनकेक) ***n.*** a thin flat cake, पुआ, चिल्लड़ा, चीला।

pancreas (पैन्क्रीअस) ***n.*** a gland that produces insulin, अग्न्याशय।

panda (पैन्डा) ***n.*** a bearlike mammal, पंडा।

pandemic (पैन्डेमिक) ***adj.*** occurring over a vast region, दूर-दूर तक फैला हुआ (रोग)।

pandemonium (पैन्डेमोनिअम) ***n.*** uproar, tumult, शोर, कोलाहल; घोर अव्यवस्था।

pane (पेन) ***n.*** a sheet of glass in a window or door, पल्ले या चौखट में जड़ा शीशा।

panel (पैनल) ***n.*** 1. a flat rectangular framed piece, दिलहा, फलक। 2. a list or group of persons selected to act as a team, नामसूची, पैनल, नामिका। 3. a group of persons participating in a discussion, विचार-विमर्श में सम्मिलित होनेवाले व्यक्तियों का समूह। ***v.*** to furnish with panels, (चौखट में) दिलहा लगाना, जड़ना या भरना।

panellist (पैनलिस्ट) ***n.*** a member of a panel, जिसका नाम नामसूची में हो, नामिक।

pang (पैंग) ***n.*** sudden sharp sensation, as of pain, टीस, कसक।

panic (पैनिक) ***n.*** 1. a sudden overwhelming feeling of terror, तहलका, आतंक। 2. a sudden overwhelming feeling of anxiety, खलबली। ***v.*** 1. to be affected with panic, तहलका या खलबली मचना। 2. to cause to feel panic, तहलका या खलबली मचाना।

panicky (पैनिकी) ***adj.*** filled with terror, आतंकित।

panorama (पैनोरामा) ***n.*** 1. a view of unlimited area, परिदृश्य। 2. a picture or photograph of this, परिदृश्य। 3. a view of a constantly changing scene of events, परिदृश्य।

pant (पैन्ट) ***v.*** 1. to breathe rapidly and heavily, हाँफना। 2. to utter breathlessly, हाँफते हुए (कुछ) कहना। ***n.*** 1. the act or instance of panting, हँफनी। 2. extreme eagerness, बेताबी, छटपटाहट।

pantaloons (पैन्टलून्ज़) ***n.*** (plu.) men's trousers, पैंट, पतलून।

pantheism (पैन्थीइज़्म) ***n.*** the belief that God is everywhere and everything is God, सर्वेश्वरवाद।

pantheist (पैन्थीइस्ट) ***n.*** a believer in pantheism, सर्वेश्वरवादी।

panther (पैन्थर) ***n.*** a large wild cat, तेंदुआ।

panties (पैन्टीज) ***n.*** (plu.) short underpants for women or children, जाँघिया।

pantile (पैन्टाइल) ***n.*** a curved roof tile, खपड़ा, खपरैल।

pantomime (पैन्टोमाइम) ***n.*** a type of theatrical entertainment, in which bodily movements in place of words, are the means of expression, मूक अभिनय।

pantry (पैन्ट्री) ***n.*** 1. a small room for storing food, dishes etc., रसोई-भंडार। 2. a large cupboard for keeping food etc., रसोई का सामान रखने की आलमारी।

pants (पैन्ट्स) ***n.*** (plu.) 1. trousers, पैंट। 2. underpants, जाँघिया, कच्छा।

papa (पापा) ***n.*** father, पापा, पिताजी।

papacy (पेपसी) ***n.*** office or term of office of Pope, पोप का पद या शासनकाल।

papal (पेपल) ***adj.*** of Pope or papacy, पोप-संबंधी, पोपीय।

papaya (पपाया) ***n.*** a plant and its fruit, पपीता।

paper (पेपर) ***n.*** 1. a material used for writing, काग़ज़। 2. a newspaper, समाचारपत्र, अख़बार। 3. an essay, निबंध। 4. a research paper, शोधपत्र। 5. a question paper, प्रश्नपत्र। 6. (plu.) documents, काग़ज़-पत्र, दस्तावेज। ***adj.*** made of paper, काग़ज़ी। ***v.*** to cover with wall paper, (दीवार पर) काग़ज़ लगाना, काग़ज़ मढ़ना।

paperback (पेपरबैक) ***n.*** a book with a flexible paper binding, ऐसी पुस्तक जिसकी जिल्द काग़ज़ या कार्डबोर्ड की हो, पेपरबैक।

paperweight (पेपरवेट) ***n.*** a small heavy object to keep papers in place, दाब।

papier-mache (पेप्यर-माशे) ***n.*** paper pulp, लुगदी।

papyrus (पपाइरस) ***n.*** 1. a reed like plant, एक प्रकार का सरकंडा। 2. paper made of it, उक्त से बना काग़ज़।

par (पार) ***n.*** 1. normal average, सामान्य औसत। 2. face value, अंकित मूल्य।

parable (पैरेबल) ***n.*** a moral story, नीति-कथा, शिक्षाप्रद कथा।

parabola (पैराबोला) ***n.*** (maths.) a curve like path, परवलय।

parachute (पैराशूट) ***n.*** an umbrella-shaped device used for descending from the aircraft, हवाई छतरी, पैराशूट। ***v.*** to descend or drop by parachute, पैराशूट की सहायता से उतरना या गिराना।

parade (परेड) ***n.*** 1. a ceremonial public procession, जुलूस। 2. a military display or march, क़वायद, परेड। ***v.*** 1. to march or walk as if in parade, परेड करना, जुलूस निकालना। 2. to exhibit ostentatiously, दिखावा करना, प्रदर्शन करना। □ **on parade,** प्रदर्शनार्थ।

paradigm (पैराडाइम) ***n.*** 1. a list of all the inflectional forms of a word, रूप-तालिका। 2. a pattern or example, प्रतिमान, उदाहरण।

paradise (पैराडाइज़) ***n.*** 1. heaven, स्वर्ग, बहिश्त, जन्नत। 2. a place of perfect happiness, अत्यंत सुखद स्थल, दिव्यभूमि।

paradox (पैराडॉक्स) ***n.*** a situation that seems contradictory or absurd but that may be true in fact, विरोधाभास।

P

paraffin (पैराफ़िन) *n.* a white waxy substance obtained from petroleum, मोम।

paragon (पैरागॉन) *n.* a model of excellence, आदर्श, प्रतिमान।

paragraph (पैराग्राफ़) *n.* a distinct subdivision of a chapter, dealing with a particular point, अनुच्छेद, पैरा। *v.* to arrange in paragraphs, पैरों में बाँटना।

parakeet (पैराकीट) *n.* a small parrot with a long tail, टुइयाँ।

parallel (पैरेलल) *adj.* 1. (of lines) separated by equal distance at every point, समानांतर, समांतर। 2. similar, corresponding, अनुरूप, तुल्य। *n.* 1. a set of parrallel lines, समांतर रेखाएँ। 2. similarity, अनुरूपता। 3. comparison, तुलना।4. any of the imaginary lines parallel to the equator, अक्षांश। *v.* 1. to be parallel to, समांतर होना। 2. to compare, तुलना करना।

parallelogram (पैरेलेलोग्रैम) *n.* a four-sided figure having the opposite sides parallel and equal, समांतर चतुर्भुज।

paralyse, paralyze (पैरालाइज़) *v.* 1. to be affected with paralysis, लकवा मार जाना। 2. to bring to a standstill, ठप कर देना।

paralysis (पैरालिसिस) *n.* 1. loss of ability to move a part of the body, लकवा, पक्षाघात। 2. cessation of activity, ठप हो जाना।

paramedical (पैरामेडिकल) *adj.* assisting medical professionals, चिकित्सक-सहायक।

parameter (पैरामिटर) *n.* (maths.) a constant factor, पैरामीटर, प्राचल।

paramilitary (पैरामिलिटरी) *adj.* assisting armed services, सेना-सहायक, अर्ध-सैनिक।

paramount (पैरामाउन्ट) *adj.* supreme, सर्वोपरि, परमोच्च।

paramour (पैरामुअर) *n.* a lover, प्रेमी या प्रेमिका, यार या रख़ैल।

paranoia (पैरानॉइआ) *n.* 1. a mental disorder characterised by delusions, भ्रांतिरोग, व्यामोह। 2. a tendency to mistrust others, दूसरों पर अविश्वास करने की प्रवृत्ति।

parapet (पैरापिट) *n.* a low wall along the edge of a roof, मुँडेर।

paraphernalia (पैरेफ़रनेल्या) *n.* 1. personal belongings, वैयक्तिक सामान, लवाज़मा। 2. the articles used in an activity, साज़-सामान, साज़, सज्जा।

paraphrase (पैराफ्रेज़) *v.* to express a passage in other words, पदच्छेद करना, भावानुवाद करना। *n.* rewording in this way, पदच्छेद।

paraplegia (पैराप्लीजिआ) *n.* paralysis of the lower half of the body, कमर से निचले हिस्से का लकवा।

parasite (पैरासाइट) *n.* 1. an organism that lives on another organism, परजीवी। 2. a person who lives at the expense of others, परजीवी।

paratroops (पैराट्रूप्स) *n.* (plu.) troops equipped to parachute, छतरी सेना।

parboil (पारबॉइल) *v.* to boil briefly, हलका उबाला देना।

parboiled rice *n.* a kind of rice, भुजिया चावल।

parcel (पार्सल) *n.* 1. a package, पार्सल। 2. a piece of land, भूखंड। *v.* (parceled/parcelled, parceling/

P

parcelling) 1. to make a parcel of, पार्सल बनाना। 2. to divide into portions, विभक्त करना, बाँटना।

parch (पार्च) ***v.*** 1. to dry up, सुखा देना या सूख जाना। 2. to roast, भूनना। 3. to make thirsty, प्यास लगाना, प्यासा बना देना।

parchment (पार्चमेन्ट) ***n.*** 1. the skin of a sheep used for manuscripts, चर्मपत्र, चमड़ा-काग़ज़। 2. a kind of paper, एक तरह का काग़ज़।

pardon (पार्डन) ***v.*** to forgive, क्षमा करना, माफ़ कर देना। ***n.*** forgiveness, क्षमा, माफ़ी।

pare (पेअर) ***v.*** 1. to peel, छिलका उतारना, छीलना। 2. to cut (nails, नाख़ून) कतरना, काटना। 3. to reduce little by little, धीरे-धीरे कम करना, घटाते चलना।

parent (पेअरेन्ट) ***n.*** 1. a father or mother, माता या पिता। 2. a source, origin, मूल, उद्गम। 3. (plu.) father and mother, माता-पिता, माँ-बाप।

parentage (पेअरेन्टिज) ***n.*** 1. parenthood, जनक या जननी होने का भाव, जनकता। 2. origin, बाप-दादा आदि पूर्वज। 3. lineage, वंश, वंशानुक्रम।

parental (परेन्टल) ***adj.*** of parents, माता-पिता-संबंधी, पैतृक।

parenthesis (परेन्थिसिस) ***n.*** either of a pair of characters ( ), कोष्ठक के दो चिह्नों में से कोई एक।

parenthood (पेअरेन्टहुड) ***n.*** the state of being a parent, जनकता।

par excellence ***adv.*** beyond comparison, सबसे बढ़कर।

pariah (पैरिआ) ***n.*** a social outcaste, अछूत, छोटी जाति का व्यक्ति।

paring (पेअरिंग) ***n.*** a piece or part pared off, छिलका, छीलन।

parity (पैरिटी) ***n.*** 1. equality, बराबरी, साम्य। 2. amount of foreign currency equal to a specific sum of domestic currency, तुल्यराशि।

park (पार्क) ***n.*** 1. a ground or garden for public recreation, सार्वजनिक उद्यान, पार्क। 2. a playing field, खेल का मैदान। ***v.*** to place and leave a car, scooter etc. temporarily, थोड़ी देर के लिए गाड़ी, स्कूटर आदि कहीं ठहराना और छोड़ देना।

parkinson's disease (पार्किन्सन्ज़ डिसीज़) ***n.*** a disease of the nervous system characterized by muscular tremor, काँपा, कँपनी, झूलन रोग।

parlance (पार्लेन्स) ***n.*** 1. a particular manner of speaking, बोल-चाल, बात-चीत का ढंग। 2. language, भाषा। □ **in common parlance,** बोल-चाल में।

parley (पार्ली) ***n.*** a discussion between opponents so as to make peace, संधिवार्ता। ***v.*** to hold a parley, संधिवार्ता करना।

parliament (पार्लमेन्ट) ***n.*** the national legislative assembly, संसद्, पार्लियामेंट।

parliamentary (पार्लमेन्टरी) ***adj.*** of or pertaining to a parliament, संसद्-संबंधी, संसदीय।

parlour, parlor (पार्लर) ***n.*** 1. a room in a house for entertaining visitors, बैठक, आगत-कक्ष। 2. an establishment for a particular business, पार्लर, कक्ष।

parochial (परोकिअल) ***adj.*** 1. of or pertaining to a parish, पल्ली-संबंधी। 2. local, स्थानीय। 3. narrow, limited, संकीर्ण।

parochialism (परोकिअलिज़म) ***n.*** narrow-mindedness, संकीर्णता।

P

parodist (पैरोडिस्ट) ***n.*** well-versed in making parodies, पैरोडीकार।

parody (पैरोडी) ***n.*** a satirical imitation of a well-known literary work, पैरोडी। ***v.*** to compose a parody of, पैरोडी करना।

parole (परोल) ***n.*** release of a prisoner from a prison on condition of good behaviour, जेल से क़ैदी की सशर्त रिहाई, पैरोल। ***v.*** to release on parole, पैरोल पर रिहा करना।

paroxysm (पैरॉक्सिज़म) ***n.*** 1. a sudden attack of a disease, दौरा। 2. a sudden outburst of emotion, भावावेश।

parricide (पैरिसाइड) ***n.*** 1. an act of killing one's parent, माता या पिता की हत्या। 2. one who kills his or her parent, माता या पिता का हत्यारा, मातृहंता या पितृहंता।

parrot (पैरट) ***n.*** a bird with a short hooked bill, तोता। ***v.*** to repeat mechanically, यंत्रवत् दोहराना, रटना।

parry (पैरी) ***v.*** 1. to ward off, (वार) बचा जाना। 2. to evade, टाल देना, किनारा कर जाना।

parse (पार्ज़) ***v.*** to give grammatical details of a word or phrase, शब्द या पद का परिचय देना।

parsing (पार्ज़िंग) ***n.*** grammatical details about a word or phrase, पद-परिचय।

part (पार्ट) ***n.*** 1. a piece, portion or division, भाग, हिस्सा। 2. a bit, टुकड़ा। 3. a component of a machine, पुर्ज़ा। 4. an actor's role, भूमिका, रोल। 5. duty, कर्तव्य, फ़र्ज़। 6. a side in an agreement or dispute, पक्ष। 7. (plu.) a territory, भूभाग। ***v.*** 1. to divide into separate parts, विभक्त करना। 2. to keep apart, अलग-अलग करना। 3. to break, टुकड़े करना। 4. to distribute, वितरण करना, बाँटना। 5. to do away, विदा या अलग होना, चले जाना। ***adj.*** partial, अंशतः। आंशिक।

partake (पार्टेक) ***v.*** (partook, partaken, partaking) to participate, सम्मिलित/शरीक होना, शिरकत करना।

partial (पार्शल) ***adj.*** 1. relating to only a part, आंशिक। 2. incomplete, अधूरा, अपूर्ण, -खंड; partial eclipse, खंडग्रास। 3. biased, पक्षपातपूर्ण।

partiality (पार्शिऐलिटी) ***n.*** bias, पक्षपात, तरफ़दारी।

participant (पार्टिसिपेन्ट) ***n.*** one who participates, सहभागी, भागीदार।

participate (पार्टिसिपेट) ***v.*** to take part in something, सम्मिलित या शामिल होना, शिरकत करना।

participation (पार्टिसिपेशन) ***n.*** the act of participating, or the state of being participated, शिरकत, भाग लेना, सहभागिता।

participle (पार्टिसिपल) ***n.*** a word formed from a verb, कृदंत।

particle (पार्टिकल) ***n.*** 1. a very small piece or part, कण, ज़र्रा। 2. the smallest possible amount, लवलेश। 3. (gram.) a short and undeclinable part of speech, निपात।

particular (पर्टिक्यूलर) ***adj.*** 1. separate and distinct from others, विशिष्ट, विशेष, ख़ास। 2. careful, सतर्क, सावधान, जागरूक। □ **in particular,** विशेष रूप से। ***n.*** (plu.) details, ब्योरा, विवरण, तफ़सील।

parting (पार्टिंग) ***n.*** 1. separation, अलगाव, विभाजन, पृथक्करण।

2. a departure or leave-taking, विदा, रुख़स्त।

partisan (पार्टिज़न) ***n.*** 1. a strong supporter, घोर या कट्टर समर्थक। 2. a guerilla, गुरिल्ला।

partition (पार्टिशन) ***n.*** 1. division into parts, विभाजन, बँटवारा। 2. a structure that divides (a room, कमरे को) बाँटनेवाला पर्दा, दीवार आदि। ***v.*** 1. to divide, विभाजन या बँटवारा करना। 2. to divide by a partition, आड़ या व्यवधान खड़ा करना।

partly (पार्टली) ***adv.*** in part, not fully or completely, कुछ अंशों में, अंशतः।

partner (पार्टनर) ***n.*** 1. a companion, खेल का साथी, गुइयाँ। 2. one of a pair of dancers, भागीदार, जोड़ीदार। 3. a member of a partnership, भागीदार, सहभागी, साझेदार।

partnership (पार्टनरशिप) ***n.*** the relationship of partners, साझा, साझेदारी, भागीदारी।

part of speech ***n.*** (gram.) शब्दभेद।

partridge (पार्ट्रिज) ***n.*** a bird of pheasant family, तीतर या चकोर।

part-time (पार्ट-टाइम) ***adj.*** for only a part of the working day, अंशकालिक।

party (पार्टी) ***n.*** 1. an organized political group, दल, पार्टी। 2. a group, जत्था, टोली। 3. a social gathering, सामाजिक गोष्ठी। 4. a person entering into a contract, पक्ष। 5. a person taking part in a legal proceedings, पक्ष, पार्टी। ***adj.*** of or relating to the party, दलीय, दलगत।

party line ***n.*** the policy of a party, दलनीति।

paschal (पैस्कल) ***n.*** of Easter, ईस्टर-संबंधी।

pasha (पाशा) ***n.*** a title of a high rank Turkish officer, पाशा।

pass (पास) ***v.*** 1. to move or cause to move, to go through, निकलना/निकालना, बीतना/बिताना, गुज़रना/गुज़ारना। 2. to proceed, to go forward or move over, to go beyond, आगे बढ़ना/बढ़ाना, आगे निकल जाना। 3. to go from one person to another, एक हाथ से दूसरे हाथ जाना, हस्तांतरित होना। 4. to run or extend, जाना, निकलना। 5. to happen, होना। 6. to transfer (the ball) to the teammate, (गेंद) अपने साथी की ओर बढ़ाना। 7. to utter or pronounce, कहना, बोलना। 8.to get through the examination, उत्तीर्ण या सफल होना। 9. to transfer, एक से दूसरे के हाथ या अधिकार में जाना, दिया या सौंपा जाना। 10. to examine and approve, जाँचकर पारित करना। 11. to elapse or allow to elapse, समाप्त होना या करना, बीतना या बिताना। 12. to undergo, भुगतना, बर्दाश्त करना। 13. to opt not to use one's right, अधिकार का प्रयोग न करना। ***n.*** 1. the act of passing, निकलना, गुज़रना, पार जाना। 2. a narrow passage between mountains, दर्रा। 3. a permit, प्रवेशपत्र, पारपत्र। 4. act of giving a ball to a teammate, साथी की ओर गेंद बढ़ाना। 5. to refuse to make a bid, (ताश के खेल में) बोली या हाथ न बोलना।

passable (पासेबल) ***adj.*** 1. capable of being passed or traversed, गम्य, जाने लायक। 2. fairly good, satisfactory, अच्छा-ख़ासा, संतोषजनक।

passage (पैसिज) ***n.*** 1. the act of passing, गमन, पारण। 2. a path, रास्ता,

P

मार्ग, पथ। 3. a corridor, गलियारा। 4. a journey यात्रा। 5. the right to travel, पारण-अधिकार, मार्गाधिकार। 6. a brief portion of a speech or written work, लेखांश, उद्धरण, अंश। 7. the enactment of law, विधायन।

passbook (पासबुक) ***n.*** a small book given to a customer by the bank in which account is maintained, पासबुक।

passenger (पैसन्जर) ***n.*** a person travelling in a vehicle, यात्री या सवारी।

passer-by (पासर-बाइ) ***n.*** a person who happens to pass by, राहचलता, बटोही।

passing (पासिंग) ***adj.*** 1. of brief duration, अल्पकालिक, क्षणिक। 2. casual, आकस्मिक।

passion (पैशन) ***n.*** 1. strong emotion, आवेश, भावावेश, भावावेग, राग। 2. sexual love, कामवासना, कामुकता। 3. great enthusiasm, उमंग, जोश।

passionate (पैशनिट) ***adj.*** 1. full of passion, कामोत्तेजित। 2. characterized by strong emotion, भावविह्वल।

passive (पैसिव) ***adj.*** 1. not active, अक्रिय, निष्क्रिय। 2. not resisting, प्रतिरोध-विहीन। ***n.*** the passive voice, कर्मवाच्य।

passivity (पैसिविटी) ***n.*** the state or quality of being passive, अक्रियता, निष्क्रियता।

passport (पासपोर्ट) ***n.*** a document granting permission to travel abroad, पासपोर्ट, पारपत्र।

password (पासवर्ड) ***n.*** a secret word (to distinguish friend from enemy), संकेत शब्द।

past (पास्ट) ***adj.*** 1. of a former time, भूतकालिक, बीते हुए समय से संबद्ध। 2. immediately preceding, गत, पिछला। 3. having served formerly, भूतपूर्व, निवर्तमान, निवृत। ***n.*** 1. the past tense, भूतकाल। (gram.) 2. the time before the present, विगत समय। ***prep.*** 1. beyond in time, के बाद। 2. beyond in place, से आगे। 3. above the reach, limit or scope of, के परे। ***adv.*** 1. ago, पहले। 2. on or onward, आगे।

paste (पेस्ट) ***n.*** 1. dough, गुँधा हुआ आटा, बेसन आदि। 2. dough like smooth-textured substance, लेई, पीठी आदि, पेस्ट। 3. moistened clay, (बर्तन बनाने की) गीली मिट्टी। ***v.*** to cause to adhere by applying paste, लेई से चिपकाना।

pastel (पैस्टल) ***n.*** a coloured pencil, रंगीन पेंसिल, पैस्टल।

pasteurization (पैस्चराइज़ेशन) ***n.*** a method of destroying bacteria by heating (milk) to a certain temperature and then cool it, (दूध आदि को) कीटाणु-विहीन करना, पास्तुरीकरण।

pastime (पासटाइम) ***n.*** an activity that occupies one's time pleasantly, खेल, क्रीड़ा, मनोरंजन।

pastmaster (पास्टमास्टर) ***n.*** an expert, विशेषज्ञ।

pastoral (पास्टोरल) ***adj.*** 1. of pasture, चरागाह-संबंधी, चरागाही। 2. of pastoralist, चरवाहे का, ग्वाल-संबंधी। 3. of rural life, ग्राम्य, ग्रामीण।

past perfect ***n.*** a tense expressing action completed before a given time, पूर्ण भूतकाल।

pastry (पेस्ट्री) ***n.*** a baked paste of flour, पेस्ट्री, मिष्टान्न।

P

pasturable (पास्चरेबल) ***adj.*** that can be used for pasture, चरने योग्य (भूमि)।

pasture (पास्चर) ***n.*** 1. a piece of land on which animals graze, चरागाह, गोचर-भूमि। 2. the grass growing on it, चरी, घास।

pasty (पेस्टी) ***n.*** a pie, गुझिया। ***adj.*** pale, yellow, पीला, ज़र्द।

pat (पैट) ***v.*** to stroke lightly with the palm of hand, थपथपाना, थपकी देना। ***n.*** a light stroke, थपकी। ***adj.*** exactly right, सही, उपयुक्त, अनुकूल। ***adv.*** 1. at once, तुरंत, तत्क्षण। 2. perfectly, पूर्णरूपेण।

patch (पैच) ***n.*** 1. a piece of cloth used to mend a garment, पैबंद, थिगली, चिकत्ती। 2. a piece of land, भूमि का टुकड़ा, भूखंड। 3. a period of time, समय-खंड, अवधि। ***v.*** to mend a garment with a patch, थिगली/पैबंद लगाना, चकती लगाकर सीना, मरम्मत करना। □ **patch up,** to settle, तय करना, निपटाना।

patchy (पैची) ***adj.*** 1. having or forming patches, पैबंदों से बना, पैबंदी। 2. not uniform, irregular, असमरूप, अनियमित।

patella (पटेला) ***n.*** the knee cap, चपनी।

patent (पेटन्ट) ***n.*** 1. the document granting a sole right to an inventor to make, use or sell his or her product, पेटेंट अधिकार। 2. something that is protected by a patent, पेटेंट। ***adj.*** 1. protected by a patent, पेटेंट द्वारा रक्षित। 2. obvious, स्पष्ट, प्रत्यक्ष। ***v.*** 1. to obtain a patent for, पेटेंट कराना। 2. to grant by patent, पेटेंट कर देना।

patentee (पेटन्टी) ***n.*** a person who has been granted a patent, पेटेंटधारी।

paternal (पैटर्नल) ***adj.*** 1. of a father, related to the father or inherited from the father, पैतृक, पित्रीय। 2. fatherly, पितृसुलभ।

paternity (पैटर्निटी) ***n.*** the state of being a father, पितृत्व।

path (पाथ) ***n.*** 1. a way, route or course, पथ, मार्ग, रास्ता। 2. a course of action, कार्य-प्रणाली, कार्यविधि।

pathetic (पथेटिक) ***adj.*** 1. arousing pity, moving, करुणाजनक, दयनीय। 2. inadequate, अपर्याप्त, कम, नाकाफ़ी।

pathogenic (पैथोजेनिक) ***adj.*** causing disease, रोगजनक, व्याधिकारक।

pathological (पैथोलॉजिकल) ***adj.*** of pathology, व्याधि-विज्ञान-संबंधी।

pathologist (पैथॉलोजिस्ट) ***n.*** an expert in pathology, रोग-विज्ञानी, व्याधि-विज्ञानी।

pathology (पैथॉलोजी) ***n.*** the scientific study of diseases, रोग-विज्ञान, व्याधि-विज्ञान।

pathos (पेथॉस) ***n.*** the quality or power of arousing feelings of pity, करुणभाव, करुण रस।

pathway (पाथवे) ***n.*** a path, पथ, मार्ग।

patience (पेशन्स) ***n.*** 1. tolerance, composure, धैर्य, सहनशीलता, सहिष्णुता। 2. a card game for one player, solitaire, ताश का ऐसा खेल जिसे एक ही व्यक्ति अकेला खेलता है।

patient (पेशन्ट) ***adj.*** tolerant, composed, धैर्यवान, सहनशील, सहिष्णु। ***n.*** one under medical treatment, मरीज़, रोगी।

P

patiently (पेशन्टली) ***adv.*** with patience, धैर्यपूर्वक।

patriarch (पेट्रिआर्क) ***n.*** 1. the male head of a family or tribe, कुलपिता, मुखिया या सरदार। 2. a bishop of high rank, ईसाई धर्माधिकारी, बिशप।

patriarchy (पेट्रिआर्की) ***n.*** a form of social system in which a male is the head of the family or tribe, पुरुष प्रधान परिवार का शासन, पितृतंत्र।

patricide (पैट्रिसाइड) ***n.*** 1. the act of killing one's own father, पितृहत्या, पितृघात। 2. one who kills one's own father, पिता का हत्यारा, पितृहंता।

patrimonial (पैट्रिमोनिअल) ***adj.*** hereditary, पैतृक, पुश्तैनी।

patrimony (पैट्रिमनी) ***n.*** property inherited from one's father, पैतृक संपत्ति।

patriot (पेट्रिअट) ***n.*** one who is loyal to one's country, देशभक्त।

patriotic (पेट्रिऑटिक) ***adj.*** inspired by partiotism, देशभक्तिपूर्ण।

patriotism (पेट्रिऑटिज़म) ***n.*** loyalty towards one's country, देशभक्ति।

patrol (पैट्रोल) ***v.*** to walk around and guard, गश्त लगाना। ***n.*** 1. the act of patrolling, गश्त। 2. one whose duty is to patrol, गश्त लगानेवाला।

patron (पेट्रन) ***n.*** 1. a protector, helper or benefactor, संरक्षक, आश्रयदाता। 2. a regular customer, नियमित ग्राहक।

patronage (पैट्रनिज) ***n.*** 1. support given by a patron, संरक्षण। 2. customers, ग्राहकों का समूह।

patroness (पेट्रनिस) ***n.*** a female patron, संरक्षिका।

patronize, patronise (पेट्रनाइज़) ***v.*** 1. to act as a patron toward, संरक्षक की तरह व्यवहार करना। 2. to be a regular customer, नियमित ग्राहक होना।

patronizing (पेट्रनाइज़िंग) ***adj.*** behaving patronizingly, कृपालु।

patronymic (पैट्रोनिमिक) ***n.*** a name received from a paternal ancestor, कुलनाम, गोत्र।

patter[1] (पैटर) ***n.*** a series of light, rapid taps, खटखट, पटपट। ***v.*** to make a patter, खटखट या पटपट करना।

patter[2] ***n.*** the glib, चटर-चटर। ***v.*** to glib, चटर चटर बोलना, जल्दी-जल्दी बोलना।

pattern (पैटर्न) ***n.*** 1. a model or design according to which something is made, नमूना, प्रतिमान। 2. an excellent example, उत्कृष्ट उदाहरण। 3. sample, बानगी, नमूना। ***v.*** to make something as per pattern, प्रतिमान के अनुरूप बनाना या रचना करना।

paucity (पॉसिटी) ***n.*** scarcity, कमी, अभाव।

paunch (पॉन्च) ***n.*** a protruding abdomen, तोंद।

pauper (पॉपर) ***n.*** a very poor person, कंगाल, अकिंचन।

pause (पाज़) ***v.*** 1. to suspend an action for a time, रुकना, ठहरना। 2. hesitate, हिचकना। ***n.*** 1. a temporary stop, विराम, यति। 2. hesitation, हिचक, झिझक।

pausingly (पॉज़िंगली) ***adv.*** intermittently, रुक-रुककर।

pave (पेव) ***v.*** to cover (a road) with concrete, asphalt, brick etc., (सड़क पर) मिट्टी, सीमेंट, अलकतरा आदि डालकर पक्का बनाना। ☐ **pave the way,** मार्ग प्रशस्त करना।

P

pavement (पेवमेन्ट) ***n.*** 1. a paved surface, पक्का फ़र्श। 2. a raised path at the side of a road for people to walk on, पटरी।

pavilion (पविलिअन) ***n.*** an open structure made for spectators, दर्शक-दीर्घा, दर्शक-मंडप।

paw (पॉ) ***n.*** 1. the clawed foot of an animal, पंजा, चंगुल। 2. a person's hand, हाथ। ***v.*** 1. to strike with a paw, पंजा मारना। 2. to handle rudely, मसलना, दुर्दशा कर देना।

pawn[1] (पॉन) ***n.*** anything given as a security, रेहन रखी हुई वस्तु। ***v.*** to deposit as a pawn, रेहन या गिरवी रखना, बंधक रखना।

pawn[2] ***n.*** 1. the chessman of the smallest size and least value, प्यादा। 2. a person manipulated by another, कठपुतली।

pawnbroker (पॉनब्रोकर) ***n.*** one who lends money on personal property left as security, गिरवी रखनेवाला, महाजन, साहूकार।

pawnee (पॉनी) ***n.*** one who deposits something as security against loan, रेहनदार, गिरवीदार।

pay (पे) ***v.*** (paid, paying) 1. to give money in return of goods or services, देना, चुकाना, भुगतान करना। 2. to give or bestow, देना, अर्पित करना। 3. to discharge a debt, ऋण चुकाना, शोधन करना। 4. to be profitable, लाभप्रद होना। 5. to suffer the consequences of, भोगना, बर्दाश्त करना। 6. to yield a return of, प्राप्ति कराना, देना। ***n.*** 1. salary or wages, वेतन, तनख्वाह। 2. payment, भुगतान।

payable (पेएबल) ***adj.*** that must be paid, देय, शोध्य।

payee (पेई) ***n.*** the person to whom the money or cheque should be delivered, पानेवाला, प्रापक, आदाता।

payment (पेमेन्ट) ***n.*** 1. act of paying, भुगतान। 2. the amount paid, प्रदत्त राशि, भुगतान।

payroll (पेरोल) ***n.*** a list of employees and wages due to each, वेतन-चिट्ठा, चिट्ठा।

pea (पी) ***n.*** a climbing plant and its round edible seeds, मटर।

peace (पीस) ***n.*** 1. freedom from clamour and confusion, शांति। 2. the state of law and order, शांति, अमन।

Peace Corps ***n.*** an organization of volunteers, शांति सेना।

peaceful (पीसफ़ुल) ***adj.*** characterized by peace, शांतिमय।

peacemaker (पीसमेकर) ***n.*** one who establishes peace, शांतिस्थापक।

peach (पीच) ***n.*** 1. a tree and its edible fruit, आड़ू। 2. a light yellowish pink colour, पीलापन लिये गुलाबी रंग। 3. an attractive young woman, सुंदर युवती, रूपसी।

peacock (पीकॉक) ***n.*** 1. a male crested bird having a fanlike tail, मोर, मयूर। 2. a proud person, घमंडी व्यक्ति।

peahen (पीहेन) ***n.*** a female peacock, मोरनी।

peak (पीक) ***n.*** 1. a pointed top of a mountain, चोटी, शिखर। 2. the point of highest value, development etc., चरम बिंदु, पराकाष्ठा, चोटी। ***v.*** 1. to reach a peak, चोटी पर पहुँचना।

P

2. to droop, दुर्बल हो जाना।

peaky (पीकी) ***adj.*** 1. lean and thin, क्षीणकाय। 2. sick, रुग्ण।

peal (पील) ***n.*** 1. the loud ringing of a bell or bells, घंटे या घंटियों की टनटन, टनटनाहट। 2. a set of bells, घंटे-घंटियाँ। ***v.*** to sound with peals, ज़ोर-ज़ोर से घंटे-घड़ियाल बजाना।

peanut (पीनट) ***n.*** 1. groundnut, मूँगफली। 2.(plu.) a very small amount of money, टुच्ची रक़म, अल्प राशि।

pear (पिअर) ***n.*** a tree and its fruit, नाशपाती।

pearl (पर्ल) ***n.*** 1. a rounded lustrous mass formed inside the shells, मोती; artificial pearl, नकली मोती। 2. yellowish white, खसखसी/मोतिया रंग।

pearly (पर्ली) ***adj.*** 1. decorated with pearls, मोतियों से सज्जित, मुक्ताजड़ित। 2. like pearls, मोती-सा, मोतिया।

peasant (पैज़न्ट) ***n.*** a farmer, किसान, खेतिहर।

peasantry (पैज़न्ट्री) ***n.*** peasants as class, किसानों का वर्ग, कृषक समुदाय।

peat (पीट) ***n.*** partially decomposed vegetable matter, (जलावन या खाद के काम आनेवाला) सड़ा-गला घास-पात।

pebble (पेबल) ***n.*** a small rounded stone, रोड़ी, बजरी।

peck (पेक) ***v.*** 1. to stroke or kick up with a beak, चोंच मारना, टोंचना। 2. to make a hole with a beak, चोंच से छेद करना। 3. to kiss, चुंबन लेना। ***n.*** 1. a stroke with the beak, चंचु-प्रहार। 2. a kiss, चुंबन।

pectin (पेक्टिन) ***n.*** a sugarlike substance found in ripe fruit, पेकटिन।

peculiar (पिक्यूलिअर) ***adj.*** 1. strange, unusual, विचित्र, अजीब। 2. distinct, विशेष, अनूठा। 3. belonging to a particular person or class, विशिष्ट।

peculiarity (पिक्यूलिऐरिटी) ***n.*** 1. strangeness, विचित्रता। 2. distinctness, अनूठापन। 3. a characteristic, विशिष्टता।

pecuniary (पिक्यूनिअरी) ***adj.*** of or relating to money, आर्थिक, धन-सबंधी।

pedagogy (पेडागॉजि) ***n.*** teaching the art of teaching, शिक्षाशास्त्र, अध्यापन-कला।

pedal (पेडल) ***n.*** a lever operated by the foot, पैडल। ***adj.*** of foot, पैर-संबंधी। ***v.*** (pedaled/pedalled, pedaling/pedalling) 1. to operate a pedal, पैडल चलाना। 2. to ride a cycle, साइकिल चलाना।

pedantic (पिडैन्टिक) ***adj.*** of a pedant or pedantry, पंडिताऊ।

pedantry (पेडन्ट्री) ***n.*** display of useless knowledge, पांडित्य-प्रदर्शन।

peddle (पेडल) ***v.*** to travel about selling goods, फेरी लगाना, घूम घूमकर सौदा बेचना।

peddler (पेडलर) ***n.*** one who sells door to door, फेरीवाला।

pedestal (पेडस्टल) ***n.*** a base for a column or statue, आधार, स्तंभाधार।

pedestrian (पिडेस्ट्रिअन) ***n.*** one travelling on foot, पैदल चलनेवाला, पदयात्री। ***adj.*** 1. going on boot, पैदल। 2. dull, नीरस।

pediatrician (पीडिऐट्रिशन) ***n.*** = paediatrician.

pediatrics (पीडिऐट्रिक्स) ***n.*** = paediatrics.

pedicure (पेडिक्युर) ***n.*** the act of

trimming and polishing of the toenails, पैरों के नाख़ून काटने तथा उनपर पालिश करने की क्रिया।

pedigree (पेडिग्री) ***n.*** 1. a family tree, वंशवृक्ष, वंशावली। 2. a recorded line of descent of an animal, किसी पशु का नस्ली विवरण।

pedlar (पेडलर) ***n.*** = peddler.

pedometer (पिडॉमिटर) ***n.*** a device measuring distance by registering the number of steps taken, पगों की गिनती करके दूरी बतानेवाला यंत्र।

pee (पी) ***v.*** to urinate, पेशाब करना।

peek (पीक) ***n.*** to peep, झाँकना।

peel (पील) ***n.*** the skin of vegetables and fruits, छिलका। ***v.*** 1. to remove the peel of, छिलका उतारना या छीलना। 2. to lose or shed skin, केंचुली आदि उतारना।

peeling (पीलिंग) ***n.*** anything peeled off, छिलका, खाल आदि।

peep[1] (पीप) ***v.*** to look furtively, लुक-छिपकर देखना, ताक-झाँक करना। ***n.*** a brief or furtive look, ताक-झाँक।

peep[2] ***v.*** to chirp like a baby bird, चींचीं करना। ***n.*** a chirp, चींचीं।

peephole (पीपहोल) ***n.*** a small hole to peep through, छेद, मोखा, झरोखा।

peer (पिअर) ***n.*** 1. one who is equal to another, समकक्ष व्यक्ति, समकक्षी। 2. a member of a peerage, अभिजात वर्ग का व्यक्ति। ***v.*** to look intently, गौर से देखना।

peerage (पिअरिज) ***n.*** the nobility, अभिजात वर्ग।

peerless (पिअरलिस) ***adj.*** without equal, unmatched, अद्वितीय, लाजवाब।

peevish (पीविश) ***adj.*** irritable, चिड़चिड़ा।

peg (पेग) ***n.*** 1. a wooden pin, खूँटा, खूँटी। 2. a wooden screw of a violin, खूँटी। 3. a measured drink, esp. of whisky or brandy with soda water in it, सोडावाटर मिश्रित ह्विस्की, ब्रांडी आदि की एक निश्चित मात्रा। ***v.*** 1. to put a peg into, खूँटा गाड़ना। 2. to fasten, बाँधना। 3. to keep prices at a fixed amount, क़ीमत स्थिर रखना।

pellet (पेलिट) ***n.*** 1. a small bullet or shot, गोली या छर्रा। 2. a small ball of a medicine, गोली, टिकिया। 3. a little ball of clay, खलेला, ढेला।

pellucid (पेल्यूसिड) ***adj.*** very clear, सुस्पष्ट, बिल्कुल साफ़।

pelmet (पेलमेट) ***n.*** a wooden structure over a door or window for hanging curtains, पेलमेट।

pelt (पेल्ट) ***v.*** 1. to throw missiles at, ढेले चलाना या मारना। 2. to beat heavily, पिटाई करना। 3. (of rain) come down fast, मूसलधार वर्षा होना।

pelvis (पेल्विस) ***n.*** the basin-shaped structure that supports the spinal column, श्रोणि।

pen[1] (पेन) ***n.*** an instrument for writing, क़लम, पेन। ***v.*** to write with a pen, क़लम से लिखना, क़लम चलाना।

pen[2] ***n.*** 1. an enclosure for cattle, बाड़ा। 2. an enclosure for birds, दड़बा। ***v.*** to shut in a pen, बाड़े या दड़बे में बंद करना।

pen[3] ***n.*** a female swan, मादा हंस, हंसनी।

penal (पीनल) ***adj.*** of or pertaining to punishment, दंड-संबंधी, दांडिक।

penalize (पीनआइज़) ***v.*** 1. to subject to a penalty, दंडित करना, दंड लगाना। 2. to put to a disadvantage, परेशानी उत्पन्न करना, परेशानी में डालना।

penalty (पेनल्टी) ***n.*** a punishment for breaking a law, दंड, सज़ा।

penance (पेनन्स) ***n.*** 1. the confession of a sin and submission to penalties imposed, प्रायश्चित्त। 2. any voluntary suffering as a religious act, तपस्या, तप।

penchant (पाँशाँ) ***n.*** strong inclination, पसंद, रुझान, झुकाव।

pencil (पेन्सिल) ***n.*** 1. an instrument for drawing and writing, पेंसिल। 2. a brush for painting, कूँची, तूलिका। ***v.*** to write or draw with a pencil, पेंसिल से लिखना या चित्रित करना।

pendant (पेन्डन्ट) ***n.*** a hanging object attached to a chain, लटकन।

pendency (पेन्डन्सी) ***n.*** the state of being pending, लंबन।

pending (पेन्डिन्ग) ***adj.*** not yet decided, अनिर्णीत तथा विचाराधीन, लंबित। ***prep.*** 1. during, इस दौरान। 2. until, जब तक।

pendulum (पेन्डुलम) ***n.*** a hanging object that swings freely, लोलक।

penetrate (पेनिट्रेट) ***v.*** 1. to enter into, घुसाना, घुसेड़ना। 2. to enter by piercing, वेधन या भेदन करना। 3. to grasp mentally, समझना। 4. to permeate, अंदर फैलना या फैलाना। 5. to affect deeply, अत्यधिक प्रभावित करना।

penetration (पेनिट्रेशन) ***n.*** 1. the act of penetrating, वेधन, भेदन, धँसाव। 2. the ability to penetrate, पैंठ। 3. keenness of mind, विचक्षणता।

penetrative (पेनिट्रेटिव) ***adj.*** 1. that penetrates, भेदक। 2. keen, विचक्षण।

pen-friend (पेन-फ़्रेन्ड) ***n.*** a friend with whom a person corresponds without meeting, लेखनी-मित्र, पत्र-मित्र।

penguin (पेन्ग्विन) ***n.*** a flightless bird, पेंग्विन।

peninsula (पनिन्सुला) ***n.*** a long projection of land into water, प्रायद्वीप।

peninsular (पनिन्सुलर) ***adj.*** of or pertaining to a peninsula, प्रायद्वीपीय।

penis (पीनिस) ***n.*** the male organ of urination, पुरुषेंद्रिय, लिंग, शिश्न।

penitence (पेनिटेन्स) ***n.*** remorse, पश्चात्ताप।

penitent (पेनिटेन्ट) ***adj.*** a repentant, पश्चात्ताप करनेवाला।

penitentiary (पेनिटेन्शरी) ***n.*** a prison, कारागृह।

pen-name ***n.*** an author's pseudonym, उपनाम।

pennant (पेनन्ट) ***n.*** a small triangular flag, झंडी।

penniless (पेनिलिस) ***adj.*** extremely poor, धनहीन, अकिंचन, कंगाल।

penpusher (पेनपुशर) ***n.*** a clerk, लिपिक।

pensile (पेन्सिल) ***adj.*** hanging, लटकता हुआ।

pension (पेन्शन) ***n.*** a periodic payment made to a retired employee, पेंशन।

pensionable (पेन्शनेबल) ***adj.*** having or giving right to a pension, पेंशन के योग्य।

pensioner (पेन्शनर) ***n.*** receiving a pension, पेंशनभोगी, पेंशनर।

pensive (पेन्सिव) ***adj.*** 1. thoughtful, ध्यानमग्न, विचारमग्न। 2. thoughtful and gloomy, उदास, विषादग्रस्त।

pentagon (पेन्टागॉन) ***n.*** a plane figure with five sides, पंचभुज।

pentagonal (पेन्टैगनल) ***adj.*** having five sides, पंचभुजीय।

penthouse (पेन्टहॉउस) ***n.*** a shed on the roof of a building, सायबान।

penultimate (पेनल्टिमिट) ***adj.*** next to last, अंतिम से ठीक पहला, उपांत्य, उपांतिम।

penumbra (पिनम्ब्रा) ***n.*** a partial shadow outside the full shadow, उपच्छाया।

penury (पेन्यूरी) ***n.*** extreme poverty, बेहद ग़रीबी, निर्धनता, दरिद्रता।

peon (पीअन) ***n.*** an attendant, चपरासी।

people (पीपल) ***n.*** (plu.) 1. human beings, लोग। 2. ordinary persons, साधारण लोग। 3. (singular) the persons comprising a tribe, race or nation, लोग, जाति।

pepper (पैपर) ***n.*** a vine; its fruit used as a condiment, काली मिर्च। ***v.*** 1. to season with pepper, मिर्च का तड़का लगाना। 2. to sprinkle around pepper, मिर्च छिड़कना।

peppermint (पैपरमिन्ट) ***n.*** a flavouring oil, पिपरमिंट।

pepsin (पेप्सिन) ***n.*** an enzyme in the stomach, पाचक रस, पेप्सिन।

peptic ulcer (पेप्टिक अल्सर) ***n.*** an ulcer in the stomach, पेट का फोड़ा।

per (पर) ***prep.*** 1. for each, प्रति, फ़ी। 2. according to, के अनुसार। 3. by, के द्वारा।

perambulation (परैम्ब्युलेशन) ***n.*** stroll, टहलना, चहलक़दमी।

perambulator (परैम्ब्युलेटर) ***n.*** a baby carriage, बच्चों को टहलाने की गाड़ी।

per capita ***adv, adj.*** per person, प्रतिव्यक्ति।

perceive (पर्सीव) ***v.*** 1. to observe or recognize, इंद्रियों द्वारा ग्रहण करना, देखना, दिखाई देना। 2. to become aware of, जानना, समझना, पता चलना, बोध होना।

percent (परसेन्ट) ***adv.*** out of each hundred, प्रतिशत।

percentage (परसेन्टिज) ***n.*** 1. the rate, amount or number in each hundred, प्रतिशत-दर, प्रतिशतता। 2. portion, अंश, भाग।

perceptible (पर्सेप्टिबल) ***adj.*** that can be perceived, बोधगम्य, दिखाई देने या प्रतीत होनेवाला।

perception (पर्सेप्शन) ***n.*** 1. the act of perceiving, इंद्रियों द्वारा ग्रहण, बोध। 2. the result of perceiving, प्रत्यक्ष ज्ञान, प्रत्यक्षण, बोध। 3. the ability to perceive, बोधक्षमता।

perceptive (पर्सेप्टिव) ***adj.*** having sensitive understanding, बोधक्षम, ग्रहणशील।

perch[1] (पर्च) ***n.*** a bird's resting place, अड्डा। ***v.*** to alight or rest on perch, (पक्षी का) अड्डे पर बैठना।

perch[2] ***n.*** a fresh water fish, कवई मछली।

percipient (पर्सिपिएन्ट) ***adj.*** perceptive, परिग्राहक, ग्रहणशील।

percolate (पर्कलेट) ***v.*** 1. to pass through a fine mesh, महीन छलनी या कपड़े से छनना या छानना। 2. to penetrate gradually, धीरे-धीरे रिसना, बहना या फैलना।

percolation (पर्कलेशन) ***n.*** the act of percolating, छनाई।

percolator (पर्कलेटर) ***n.*** an apparatus for preparing and

P

filtering coffee, कॉफ़ी-यंत्र।

percussion (परकशन) ***n.*** 1. the striking together of two bodies, समाघात। 2. the sound, shock or vibration caused by this, समाघात से उत्पन्न शब्द, आघात या कंपन। 3. a musical instrument in which sound is produced by striking, ढोलक, तबला आदि।

perdition (पर्डिशन) ***n.*** 1. hell, नरक। 2. utter destruction, पूर्ण विनाश।

peremptory (परेम्प्टरी) ***adj.*** 1. that cannot be changed, opposed or denied, अंतिम। 2. imperative, अनिवार्य, बाध्यकर। 3. dictatorial, तानाशाही।

perennial (परेनिअल) ***adj.*** 1. lasting or active throughout the year, बारहमासी। 2. lasting for ever, चिरस्थायी। 3. constantly recurring, निरंतर होता या बना रहनेवाला।

perestroika (पेरस्त्रॉइका) ***n.*** reconstruction, पुनर्निर्माण। (रूसी)

perfect (पर्फ़ेक्ट) ***adj.*** 1. complete, lacking nothing, पूर्ण, परिपूर्ण। 2. faultless, निर्दोष, त्रुटिहीन। 3. excellent, उत्तम, श्रेष्ठ। 4. exact, सही, सटीक, ठीक। ***v.*** to make perfect, पूर्ण बनाना, परिपूर्ण करना, त्रुटिरहित बनाना।

perfection (पर्फ़ेक्शन) ***n.*** 1. the quality of being perfect, परिपूर्णता। 2. the act of making perfect, परिपूर्ण बनाना। 3. an embodiment of perfection, पूर्णात्मा।

perfidious (पर्फ़िडिअस) ***adj.*** 1. treacherous, विश्वासघाती। 2. disloyal, बेवफ़ा।

perforate (पर्फ़रेट) ***v.*** to make a hole or holes by punching, छेद करना।

perforation (पर्फ़रेशन) ***n.*** 1. act of perforation, छेदन, छिद्रण। 2. a hole or holes punched, यंत्र द्वारा किया हुआ/किए हुए छेद, छिद्र।

perforce (परफ़ोर्स) ***adv.*** 1. by necessity, विवशतापूर्वक। 2. by force, बलात्, ज़बरदस्ती।

perform (परफ़ॉर्म) ***v.*** 1. to carry out, करना, पूरा करना, पालन करना। 2. to execute, निष्पादन करना। 3. to function, काम करना, ठीक चलना। 4. to act in a play, अभिनय करना।

performance (परफ़ॉर्मेन्स) ***n.*** 1. the act or manner of performing, पालन, निष्पादन। 2. accomplishment or deed, उपलब्धि, महत्त्वपूर्ण कार्य। 3. operation or functioning, काम करना, चलना। 4. acting, अभिनय, अदाकारी।

performer (परफ़ॉर्मर) ***n.*** 1. an actor, अदाकार, अभिनेता। 2. an executor, निष्पादक।

perfume (पर्फ़्यूम) ***n.*** 1. a sweet smell, सुगंध, सुवास। 2. fragrant liquid, scent, इतर। ***v.*** to apply perfume to, इतर लगाना, सुवासित करना।

perfumery (पर्फ़्यूमरी) ***n.*** a place where perfume is made or sold, गंधहाट, सुगंधशाला।

perfunctory (पर्फ़न्क्टरी) ***adj.*** done with little interest or care, बेपरवाही से किया हुआ।

perhaps (परहैप्स) ***adv.*** may be, possibly, शायद, कदाचित्।

peril (पेरिल) ***n.*** 1. serious danger, आपदा, ख़तरा, संकट। 2. something that endangers, जोख़िम। ***v.*** (periled/ perilled, periling/perilling) to risk, ख़तरा उठाना, जोख़िम उठाना।

perilous (पेरिलस) ***adj.*** exposed to danger, risky, ख़तरनाक, जोख़िम-भरा।

perimeter (पैरिमिटर) ***n.*** the outer boundary of a figure or closed area, घेरा।

period (पीरिअड) ***n.*** 1. a portion of time, अवधि, कालावधि, मियाद। 2. a division of time, युग। 3. a division of time of the academic day, घंटा। 4. a punctuation mark indicating full pause, पूर्णबिंदु, पूर्णविराम। 5. an instance of menstruation, रजोधर्म।

periodic (पीरिऑडिक) ***adj.*** occurring or happening at regular intervals, मियादी, आवधिक, आवर्ती।

periodical (पीरिऑडिकल) ***adj.*** periodic, आवधिक। ***n.*** a magazine, पत्रिका।

peripatetic (पेरिपटेटिक) ***adj.*** moving from place to place, भ्रमणशील।

peripheral (पेरिफ़रल) ***adj.*** 1. of periphery, परिरेखीय, परिधीय। 2. external, बाहरी।

periphery (पेरिफ़री) ***n.*** 1. the boundary of a figure or area, परिरेखा, परिधि। 2. the outside surface of something, बाह्यतल।

periscope (पेरिस्कोप) ***n.*** an optical instrument through which one can see the objects not in a direct line of sight, परिवीक्षण-यंत्र, पेरिस्कोप।

perish (पेरिश) ***v.*** (perished, perishing) to be utterly destroyed, नष्ट हो जाना।

perishable (पेरिशेबल) ***adj.*** likely or liable to dacay, शीघ्र सड़-गल जानेवाला, विनाशी, नश्वर।

perjury (पर्जरी) ***n.*** the wilful telling of lie while on oath, झूठी गवाही, शपथ-भंग।

perk[1] (पर्क) ***v.*** to raise the head, सिर ऊँचा करना।

perk[2] ***n.*** perquisite, परिलब्धि।

perky (पर्की) ***adj.*** gay, spirited, प्रफुल्ल, जीवंत।

permanence (पर्मनेन्स) ***n.*** the state or quality of being permanent, स्थायित्व।

permanent (पर्मनेन्ट) ***adj.*** lasting, स्थायी, चिरस्थायी, टिकाऊ।

permeable (पर्मीएबल) ***adj.*** that can be permeated, व्याप्त, पारगम्य।

permeate (पर्मीएट) ***v.*** to penetrate and spread through, व्याप्त हो जाना, पारगमन करना।

permissible (पर्मिसिबल) ***adj.*** allowable, अनुज्ञेय, स्वीकार्य।

permission (पर्मिशन) ***n.*** formal consent, अनुज्ञा, स्वीकृति, आज्ञा, अनुमति, छूट।

permissive (पर्मिसिव) ***adj.*** allowing great freedom, lenient or tolerant, खुला या सहिष्णु।

permit (पर्मिट) ***v.*** 1. to allow, अनुमति देना, अनुज्ञा देना। 2. to give opportunity, अवसर प्रदान करना। ***n.*** a written permission, अनुमति-पत्र, अनुज्ञा, परमिट।

permutation (पर्म्युटेशन) ***n.*** transformation made by reordering a given set of things in a group, क्रम-परिवर्तन।

pernicious (पर्निशस) ***adj.*** causing injury or destruction, हानिकर, विनाशकारी।

perorate (पेरोरेट) ***v.*** to sum up, उपसंहार करना।

P

perpendicular (पर्पन्डिक्यूलर) ***n.*** a straight line at right angles to another line, लंब। ***adj.*** exactly upright, सही-सही खड़ा, लंबवत्।

perpetrate (पर्पिट्रेट) ***v.*** to do something wrong, ग़लत काम करना, खुटाई करना।

perpetration (पर्पिट्रेशन) ***n.*** 1. the act of perpetrating, ग़लत काम करना। 2. something perpetrated, किया हुआ ग़लत काम।

perpetual (पर्पेचुअल) ***adj.*** 1. ever-lasting, seemingly ceaseless, शाश्वत, स्थायी। 2. often repeated, बार-बार का, नित्य का, रोज़-रोज़ का।

perpetuate (पर्पेचुएट) ***v.*** to make perpeptual, स्थायी/शाश्वत बना देना।

perpetuation (पर्पेचुएशन) ***n.*** 1. the act of perpetuating, स्थायीकरण। 2. the state of being perpetuated, स्थायित्व।

perplex (पर्प्लेक्स) ***v.*** to puzzle or confuse, हैरान कर देना, घबरा देना।

perplexity (पर्प्लेक्सिटी) ***n.*** the state of being perplexed, क्षोभ, घबराहट, परेशानी।

perquisite (पर्क्विज़िट) ***n.*** a benefit received in addition to one's pay or salary, परिलब्धि।

per se (पर से) ***adv.*** in or by itself, में, अपने में।

persecute (पर्सिक्यूट) ***v.*** 1. to trouble constantly, निरंतर तंग करना, सताना। 2. to harass or maltreat, उत्पीड़ित करना, अत्याचार करना।

persecution (पर्सिक्यूशन) ***n.*** the act of persecuting, उत्पीड़न, अत्याचार।

perseverance (पर्सिविअरेन्स) ***n.*** the act of persevering, अध्यवसाय, निरंतर परिश्रम करना।

perseverant (पर्सिविअरेन्ट) ***n.*** one who perseveres, अध्यवसायी, निरंतर परिश्रम करनेवाला।

persevere (पर्सिविअर) ***v.*** be resolved to do (something difficult, कोई कठिन काम) परिश्रमपूर्वक करना, जमकर करना, लगे रहना।

persist (पर्सिस्ट) ***v.*** 1. to continue steadfastly or obstinately, दृढ़ता या हठपूर्वक किसी काम को करते रहना, डटे या तुले रहना। 2. to continue in existence, अस्तित्व बनाए रखना या बने रहना।

persistence (पर्सिस्टेन्स) ***n.*** the act of persisting, ज़िद, हठ, दुराग्रह।

persistent (पर्सिस्टेन्ट) ***adj.*** 1. stubborn, refusing to relent, ज़िद्दी, हठी, दुराग्रही। 2. continue to exist or endure, अस्तित्व बनाए रखनेवाला।

person (पर्सन) ***n.*** 1. a human being, आदमी, व्यक्ति। 2. the living body of human being, शरीर। 3. (gram.) any of the three groups of pronouns, पुरुष।

personable (पर्सनेबल) ***adj.*** good looking, handsome, सुंदर, रूपवान।

personage (पर्सनिज) ***n.*** 1. a notable person, महत्त्वपूर्ण व्यक्ति। 2. a character of a play, novel etc., नाटक का चरित्र या पात्र।

personal (पर्सनल) ***adj.*** 1. private or relating to private life, वैयक्तिक, व्यक्तिगत, निजी। 2. belonging to a particular person, स्वकीय, निजी। 3. of grammatical person, पुरुषवाचक।

personality (पर्सनैलिटी) ***n.***

1. the quality of being a person, व्यक्तित्व। 2. a celebrity, विशिष्ट महानुभाव, महान व्यक्ति या व्यक्तित्व।

personalize (पर्सनलाइज़) ***v.*** to make personal, वैयक्तिक बनाना या रूप देना।

persona non grata (पर्सोना नॉन ग्राटा) ***n.*** a person not acceptable to, अग्राह्य व्यक्ति, अवांछित व्यक्ति।

personate (पर्सनेट) ***v.*** 1. to create a wrongful appearance of being someone other than oneself, छद्म रूप धारण करना, प्रतिरूपण करना।2. to act the part of, अभिनय करना।

personification (पर्सॉनिफ़िकेशन) ***n.*** the act of personifying or the state of being personified, मानवीकरण, मूर्तिकरण।

personify (पर्सॉनिफ़ाइ) ***v.*** to speak of a thing as a person, मानवीकरण करना, मूर्त रूप देना।

personnel (पर्सनेल) ***n.*** the people employed in any work or organisation, कार्यकर्तागण, कर्मचारीगण।

perspective (पर्स्पेक्टिव) ***n.*** 1. the way of representing three dimensional objects on a two dimensional surface, त्रि-आयामी चित्रण, परिप्रेक्ष्य। 2. the relationship of aspects of a subject to each other and to a whole, परिप्रेक्ष्य। 3. point of view, दृष्टिकोण।

perspiration (पर्स्पिरेशन) ***n.*** sweat, पसीना, स्वेद।

perspire (पर्स्पाइर) ***v.*** to sweat, पसीना आना।

persuade (पर्स्वेड) ***v.*** 1. to induce a person to believe or do something, समझाना-बुझाना। 2. to convince, राज़ी करना, मनाना।

persuasion (पर्स्वेज़न) ***n.*** 1. the act of persuading or the state of being persuaded, समझाव-बुझाव, मनावन। 2. religious belief or conviction, धारणा, मत, धार्मिक विश्वास।

pertain (पर्टेन) ***v.*** 1. to be a part of, अंग होना, लगा या जुड़ा होना। 2. to be relevant, संबद्ध होना।

pertinent (पर्टिनेन्ट) ***adj.*** to the point, relevant, प्रासंगिक, उपयुक्त।

perturb (पर्टर्ब) ***v.*** 1. to cause to upset, क्षुब्ध कर देना। 2. to make anxious, चिंतित कर देना।

perusal (पेरूज़ल) ***n.*** study, अध्ययन, परिशीलन।

peruse (पेरूज़) ***v.*** to study, अध्ययन करना, अनुशीलन करना।

pervade (पर्वेड) ***v.*** to pass and spread throughout, रच-बस जाना, व्याप्त होना, फैल जाना।

pervasion (पर्वेज़न) ***n.*** the act of pervading or the state of being pervaded, रचाव-बसाव, व्याप्ति, फैलाव।

perverse (पर्वर्स) ***adj.*** 1. directed away from what is normal, right or acceptable, पतित, भ्रष्ट, कुमार्गी, पथभ्रष्ट। 2. perverted, विकृत रुचिवाला। 3. wicked, दुष्ट।

perversion (पर्वर्ज़न) ***n.*** 1. the act of perverting or the state of being perverted, विकार, विकृति। 2. abnormal sex act, विकृत रति-क्रिया।

perversity (पर्वर्सिटी) ***n.*** = perversion.

pervert (पर्वर्ट) ***v.*** 1. to debase or corrupt, पतित या भ्रष्ट करना या होना। 2. to misuse, दुरुपयोग करना। 3. to interpret incorrectly, ग़लत निर्वचन करना। ***n.*** a person who practises

P

sexual perversion, विकृत रति-क्रियाओं में लिप्त व्यक्ति, विकृत-कामी।

pessary (पेसरी) ***n.*** a contraceptive device placed in a woman's vagina, एक गर्भ-निरोधक उपकरण, पेसरी।

pessimism (पेसिमिज़म) ***n.*** the tendency to take darker or gloomy view of things, निराशावाद।

pessimist (पेसिमिस्ट) ***n.*** one who takes darker or gloomy side of things, निराशावादी।

pest (पेस्ट) ***n.*** 1. any destructive insect, टिड्डी, दीमक आदि कीड़ा। 2. a troublesome person or thing, दुखदायी वस्तु/व्यक्ति।

pester (पेस्टर) ***v.*** to harass or bother continually, तंग/परेशान करना, पीछे पड़ जाना।

pesticide (पेस्टिसाइड) ***n.*** a substance used to kill pests, कीटनाशक पदार्थ।

pestilence (पेस्टिलेन्स) ***n.*** a fatal infectious disease, महामारी।

pestilent, pestilential (पेस्टिलेन्ट, पेस्टिलेन्शल) ***adj.*** 1. troublesome, दुखदायी, कष्टप्रद। 2. fatal, घातक। 3. harmful, हानिकर, नुकसानदेह।

pestle (पेसल) ***n.*** a tool used to pound substances, मूसल।

pet (पेट) ***n.*** 1. a domesticated animal kept for amusement, पालतू पक्षी या जानवर। 2. a darling, लाड़ला या दुलारा व्यक्ति। ***adj.*** 1. kept and treated as a pet, पालतू। 2. particularly cherished, दुलारा। ***v.*** 1. to fondle, प्यार-दुलार करना। 2. to pat gently, थपथपाना। 3. to keep as a pet, पालतू रूप में रखना।

petal (पेटल) ***n.*** any of the separate parts of a flower head, (फूल की) पंखुड़ी।

petite (पटीट) ***adj.*** (a woman) of small size and trim, ठिगनी और सजी-धजी (स्त्री)।

petition (पिटिशन) ***n.*** 1. a written application soliciting some favour, याचिका। 2. a request, आवेदन, प्रार्थना। ***v.*** 1. to make a petition, याचिका प्रस्तुत करना। 2. to request, प्रार्थना करना।

petrifaction (पेट्रिफ़ैक्शन) ***n.*** act of petrifying or the state of being petrified, पत्थरवत् कर देना या हो जाना, पथराना।

petrify (पेट्रिफ़ाइ) ***v.*** 1. to change into stony substance, पत्थर हो जाना। 2. to make rigid, कठोर बना देना।

petrol (पेट्रल) ***n.*** an oil obtained from petroleum, पेट्रोल।

petroleum (पट्रोलिअम) ***n.*** a mineral oil, खनिज तेल।

petticoat (पेटिकोट) ***n.*** a woman's undergarment, साया, लहँगा, घघरी, पेटीकोट।

pettish (पेटिश) ***adj.*** 1. ill-tempered, क्रोधी, बदमिज़ाज। 2. irritable, peevish, चिड़चिड़ा।

petty (पेटी) ***adj.*** 1. trivial, छोटा-मोटा, मामूली, साधारण। 2. small-minded, संकीर्ण विचारोंवाला।

petulant (पेचुलेन्ट) ***adj.*** 1. irritable, चिड़चिड़ा। 2. ill-tempered, बदमिज़ाज।

phallus (फ़ैलस) ***n.*** 1. penis, लिंग। 2. an image of the penis, लिंग-चिह्न।

phantom (फ़ैन्टम) ***n.*** 1. a ghost, प्रेतात्मा, प्रेत-छाया।

pharmaceutic, pharmaceutical (फ़ार्मस्यूटिक, फ़ार्मस्यूटिकल) ***adj.*** of medicinal drugs, औषधीय, भेषजीय।

pharmacology (फ़ार्मकॉलोजी) ***n.*** the

scientific study of medicinal drugs, भेषज-विज्ञान, औषध-विज्ञान।

pharmacy (फ़ार्मेसी) ***n.*** 1. the art of preparing and dispensing drugs, औषध-निर्माण। 2. a factory of drugs, औषधालय, औषधशाला। 3. a drugstore, दवाखाना।

pharynx (फ़ैरिन्क्स) ***n.*** the part of the alimentary canal at the back of nose and throat, ग्रसनी।

phase (फ़ेज़) ***n.*** 1. a distinct stage, विशेष अवस्था या स्थिति, प्रावस्था। 2. any of the shapes of the moon, कला। 3. a side or aspect, पहलू, पक्ष। 4. a part, भाग, हिस्सा। ***v.*** to carry out in stages, थोड़ा-थोड़ा करके कई बार में (काम को) पूरा करना।

pheasant (फ़ेज़न्ट) ***n.*** any longtailed chicken like bird, तीतर, चेड़ या चकोर।

phenomenal (फ़िनॉमिनल) ***adj.*** 1. of a phenomenon, दृश्यमान, दृष्टवान। 2. outstanding, असाधारण, उल्लेखनीय।

phenomenon (फ़िनॉमिनॉन) ***n.*** (plu. phenomena) 1. any event or fact that can be perceived by the senses, इंद्रिय-ग्राह्य विषय, दृग्विषय। 2. a remarkable event, person or thing, कोई असाधारण घटना, व्यक्ति, वस्तु आदि।

phenyl (फ़ीनाइल) ***n.*** फिनाइल।

phial (फ़ाइअल) ***n.*** a small bottle, शीशी।

philander (फ़िलैन्डर) ***v.*** to make love without serious intent, इश्क़ लड़ाना।

philanderer (फ़िलैन्डरर) ***n.*** one who philanders, इश्क़बाज़।

philanthropy (फ़िलैन्थ्रॉपी) ***n.*** benevolence, परोपकार।

philately (फ़िलैटली) ***n.*** the collection of stamps, टिकट-संग्रह।

philology (फ़िलॉलोजी) ***n.*** linguistics, भाषा-विज्ञान।

philosopher (फ़िलॉसफ़र) ***n.*** an expert in philosophy, दर्शनशास्त्री, दार्शनिक।

philosophy (फ़िलॉसफ़ी) ***n.*** 1. speculative inquiry concerning the source and nature of human knowledge, दर्शनशास्त्र। 2. a system of principles for the conduct of life, दर्शनशास्त्र।

phlegm (फ़्लैम) ***n.*** mucus ejected through mouth, कफ़, बलग़म, श्लेष्मा।

phlegmatic (फ़्लैग्मेटिक) ***adj.*** 1. of phlegm, श्लैष्मिक। 2. unemotional, शांत।

phobia (फ़ोबिआ) ***n.*** dread, भीति, भय।

phoenix (फ़ीनिक्स) ***n.*** a legendary bird, ऐसा कल्पित पक्षी जो स्वयं जलकर मर जाता है और उसी राख से पुनः पैदा हो जाता है, अमर-पक्षी।

phone (फ़ोन) ***n.*** a telephone, टेलीफ़ोन, दूरभाष। ***v.*** to telephone, टेलीफ़ोन करना।

phoneme (फ़ोनीम) ***n.*** one of the smallest units of speech that serves to distinguish one word from the other, स्वनिम, धवनिग्राम।

phonetic (फ़ोनेटिक) ***adj.*** 1. of phonetics, स्वनिक, ध्वनि-विज्ञान-संबंधी। 2. conforming to pronunciation, ध्वन्यात्मक।

phonetics (फ़ोनेटिक्स) ***n.*** the study of speech sounds, स्वन-विज्ञान, ध्वनि-विज्ञान।

phosphorescence (फ़ॉस्फ़रेसेन्स) ***n.*** the quality or state of being phosphorescent, टिमटिमाहट।

P

photo (फ़ोटो) ***n.*** a photograph, फ़ोटो।
photo finish ***n.*** a race finish so close that the winner can be decided by the photograph only, ऐसी दौड़ जिसमें जीतनेवाले का पता फ़ोटो से ही हो सके, कड़ी स्पर्धा।
photogenic (फ़ोटोजेनिक) ***adj.*** artistically suitable for being photographed, जिसका चित्र सुंदर उतरता हो, चित्रोचित।
photograph (फ़ोटोग्राफ) ***n.*** a picture made by photography, फ़ोटो, फ़ोटोग्राफ़, फ़ोटोचित्र। ***v.*** to take a photograph of, फ़ोटो खींचना।
photography (फ़ोटोग्रफ़ी) ***n.*** the art or profession of taking photographs, फ़ोटो-चित्रण, फ़ोटोग्राफ़ी।
photostat (फ़ोटोस्टैट) ***n.*** 1. a machine that makes photographic copies, फ़ोटोस्टैट। 2. a copy made by such machine, फ़ोटोस्टैट कापी।
photosynthesis (फ़ोटोसिन्थिसिस) ***n.*** प्रकाश-संश्लेषण।
phrase (फ्रेज़) ***n.*** a group of words forming a unit, पदबंध। ***v.*** to express in words, शब्दों में व्यक्त करना।
phraseology (फ्रेज़िऑलोजी) ***n.*** the way in which words and phrases are used, शब्दों के प्रयोग तथा विन्यास का ढंग, पदविन्यास।
phylum (फ़ाइलम) ***n.*** (plu. phyla) any of the basic divisions of plants, animals, etc., पौधों, पशुओं, आदि के मूल समूहों में से कोई एक, संघ।
physical (फ़िज़िकल) ***adj.*** 1. of the matter, भौतिक, वस्तुगत। 2. of or relating to the nature, प्राकृतिक। 3. of the body, शारीरिक।
physician (फ़िज़िशन) ***n.*** a medical practitioner, वैद्य, डॉक्टर या हकीम।
physicist (फ़िज़िसिस्ट) ***n.*** an expert in physics, भौतिक-विज्ञानी।
physics (फ़िजिक्स) ***n.*** the science of matter and energy and of the interactions between the two, भौतिक शास्त्र, भौतिकी।
physiological (फ़िज़िअलॉजिकल) ***adj.*** of or pertaining to physiology, शारीरिक, शरीरतंत्रीय।
physiology (फ़िज़िऑलोजी) ***n.*** the science concerned with the functioning of organisms, शरीर-विज्ञान, शारीरिकी, दैहिकी।
physiotherapy (फ़िजिओथेरपी) ***n.*** physical therapy, भौतिक चिकित्सा।
physique (फ़िज़ीक) ***n.*** the constitution of the body, शरीर की बनावट या गठन, अंगलेट।
pianist (पिऐनिस्ट) ***n.*** one who plays piano, पियानोवादक।
piano (पिऐनो) ***n.*** a musical instrument played by depressing keys, पियानो।
piazza (पिऐज़ा) ***n.*** 1. crossing, चौराहा। 2. a porch, पोर्च।
pick (पिक) ***v.*** 1. to select, छाँटना, चुनना। 2. to gather, इकट्ठा करना। 3. to pluck, (फूल) तोड़ना, चुनना। 4. to nibble, चुगना। 5. to dig, कुरेदना, खोदना। 6. to steal, चुराना। 7. to provoke, उकसाना। ***n.*** 1. selection, चयन। 2. a person preferred, चुनिंदा व्यक्ति। 3. the best part of the lot, चुनिंदा हिस्सा।
pickaxe, pickax (पिकैक्स) ***n.*** a tool for breaking up hard ground, गैंती।
picket (पिकिट) ***n.*** 1. a worker or group of workers stationed

before the entrance to a factory to persuade other workers from entering during strike, धरना। 2. a group of such workers, धरना देनेवाले लोग। ***v.*** to act as a picket, धरना देना।

pickings (पिकिंग्ज़) ***n.*** 1. leftovers, बचे-खुचे टुकड़े। 2. a share of spoil, लूट का हिस्सा।

pickle (पिकल) ***n.*** 1. vegetables preserved in mustard oil, vinegar, etc., अचार। 2. a difficult situation, कठिन स्थिति। ***v.*** to preserve in oil or vinegar, अचार डालना।

pickpocket (पिकपॉकिट) ***n.*** one who steals money from other people's pockets, जेबकतरा, गिरहकट।

pick-up (पिकप) ***n.*** 1. a small open truck, माल ढोने की खुली गाड़ी, पिकअप, पिकप। 2. ability to accelerate rapidly, सहसा गति बढ़ाने का गुण। 3. a casual acquaintance, आकस्मिक मुलाक़ाती।

picnic (पिक्निक) ***n.*** a meal eaten outdoor on excursion, सैर-सपाटा, पिकनिक। ***v.*** to go on a picnic, सैर-सपाटे पर जाना, पिकनिक पर जाना।

pictorial (पिक्टोरिअल) ***adj.*** illustrated by pictures, सचित्र, चित्रीय। ***n.*** an illustrated periodical, सचित्र पत्रिका।

picture (पिक्चर) ***n.*** 1. an image painted, drawn or photographed, चित्र, तस्वीर। 2. something that looks beautiful, चित्र-सी सुंदर वस्तु। 3. a painting, चित्र। 4. a film, motion picture, फ़िल्म। 5. an account or description, वर्णन। ***v.*** 1. to make a picture, तस्वीर बनाना, चित्रित करना। 2. to describe vividly, वर्णन करना, चित्रित करना।

picturesque (पिक्चरेस्क) ***adj.*** 1. like a picture, चित्रात्मक, चित्रवत्, चित्रोपम, सजीव। 2. very beautiful, अति सुंदर। 3. very expressive, अभिव्यंजक।

picturize (पिक्चराइज़) ***v.*** to make into a motion picture, फ़िल्म बनाना, फ़िल्मांकन करना।

pie (पाइ) ***n.*** 1. a pastry type baked dish, कचौड़ी। 2. a mixed disordered collection of types, पाई। 3. a disordered collection, घाल-मेल, खिचड़ी।

piebald (पाइबॉल्ड) ***adj.*** spotted, चितकबरा, विशेषत: सफ़ेद और काला।

piece (पीस) ***n.*** 1. a portion or slice, टुकड़ा, खंड। 2. a part, अंश, भाग, हिस्सा। 3. a chessman or other small object moved on a board, गोटी। 4. an artistic, musical or literary work, कलाकृति, रचना। 5. a fixed unit of work, छोटा-मोटा काम।

piecemeal (पीसमील) ***adv.*** one piece at a time, एक-एक करके। ***adj.*** made piece by piece, एक-एक कर बनाया हुआ।

piecework (पीसवर्क) ***n.*** work paid for according to the quantity produced, खुदरा काम, उजरती काम।

pied (पाइड) ***adj.*** having two or more colours, रंग-बिरंगा, चितकबरा।

pier (पिअर) ***n.*** 1. the structure built over the water used as a landing place, पोत-घाट। 2. a pillar of a bridge, पाया।

pierce (पिअर्स) ***v.*** 1. to pass through like a sharp-pointed instrument, घुसेड़ना, भोंकना, चुभोना। 2. to force one's way through, (भीड़ को चीरते हुए) रास्ता निकालना।

P

piercing (पिअर्सिंग) ***adj.*** 1. penetrating sharply, भेदक। 2. sharp, तेज़, प्रचंड।

piety (पाइटी) ***n.*** piousness, पवित्रता या सच्चरित्रता।

pig (पिग) ***n.*** 1. a domestic or wild mammal having a broad nose, सुअर। 2. a dirty and greedy person, गंदा और लोभी व्यक्ति।

pigeon (पिजन) ***n.*** a bird of the dove family, कबूतर, कपोत।

pigeonhole (पिजनहोल) ***n.*** 1. a compartment in a desk, ख़ाना। 2. a set of small boxes for pigeons to nest in, दरबा। ***v.*** to put in a pigeonhole, ख़ाने में रखना।

piggery (पिगरी) ***n.*** a place where pigs are kept, pigsty, सुअर-बाड़ा।

pig-headed (पिग-हेडिड) ***adj.*** stubborn, जिद्दी।

pig iron ***n.*** crude iron that is the direct product of the blast furnace, कच्चा/ढलवाँ लोहा।

piglet (पिगलिट) ***n.*** a young pig, सुअर का बच्चा।

pigment (पिगमेन्ट) ***n.*** colouring matter, रंगद्रव्य, वर्णक।

pigtail (पिगटेल) ***n.*** ponytail, स्त्रियों की कमर पर लटकती वेणी।

pike (पाइक) ***n.*** 1. a fish with a long narrow snout, एक तरह की मछली। 2. a spear, भाला, बरछा।

pile[1] (पाइल) ***n.*** 1. a heap, ढेर, अंबार, चट्टा। 2. a large accumulation, बड़ा भारी संग्रह, संचय, अंबार। ***v.*** 1. to heap up, ढेर लगाना। 2. to accumulate, संग्रह करना, इकट्ठा करना। 3. to crowd, भीड़-भाड़ करना।

pile[2] ***n.*** a heavy beam driven into the earth as a support for a structure, लकड़ी की चाँड़, बल्ली, खंभा।

piles (पाइल्ज़) ***n.*** (plu.) haemorrhoids, बवासीर।

pilfer (पिल्फ़र) ***v.*** to steal small items, छोटी-मोटी चीज़ें चुराना/उड़ा ले जाना, उठाईगीरी करना।

pilferage (पिल्फ़रिज) ***n.*** the act of pilfering, उठाईगीरी।

pilgrim (पिल्ग्रिम) ***n.*** a person who goes on a pilgrimage, तीर्थयात्री।

pilgrimage (पिल्ग्रिमिज) ***n.*** a journey to a sacred place, तीर्थयात्रा।

pill (पिल) ***n.*** a small ball of medicine, दवा की गोली, बटी।

pillage (पिलिज) ***v.*** 1. to plunder, लूट-पाट करना। 2. to take as a spoil, लूट का माल प्राप्त करना। ***n.*** 1. plunder, लूट-पाट। 2. booty, लूट का माल।

pillar (पिलर) ***n.*** 1. a column, खंभा, स्तंभ। 2. a chief supporter, प्रमुख या दृढ़ समर्थक।

pillion (पिलिअन) ***n.*** a seat behind the driver of a scooter, motorcycle etc., स्कूटर, मोटरसाइकिल आदि की पिछली सीट।

pillow (पिलो) ***n.*** a pillow used to support the head, तकिया। ***v.*** to rest one's head on the pillow, तकिया लेना/लगाना।

pilot (पाइलट) ***n.*** 1. an operator of an aircraft, विमानचालक। 2. a leader or guide, नेता या मार्गप्रदर्शक। ***v.*** (piloted, piloting) 1. to serve as the pilot of, विमान चलाना। 2. to lead or guide, मार्गप्रदर्शन करना। ***adj.*** experimental, प्रयोगात्मक।

pimp (पिम्प) ***n.*** one who procures customers for a prostitute, रंडी का

दलाल, कुटना। *v.* to serve as a pimp, दलाली करना।

pimple (पिम्पल) *n.* any small inflamed swelling of the skin, फुंसी, मुँहासा आदि।

pin (पिन) *n.* 1. a short, stiff and pointed piece of wire for fastening things together, पिन, आलपीन। 2. a nail, कील। 3. a peg, खूँटी। *v.* (pinned, pinning) 1. to fasten with a pin, पिन लगाकर नत्थी करना। 2. to attach, जोड़ना, लगाना।

pincers (पिन्सर्ज़) *n.* a tool for pulling nails, एक तरह की चिमटी या सँड़सी, पिंसर।

pinch (पिन्च) *v.* 1. to press lightly between finger and thumb, चिकोटी काटना, चुटकी भरना। 2. to press or tighten, दबाना, जकड़ना, कसना। 3. to steal or take without asking, चुरा लेना या उठा ले जाना। *n.* 1. a squeeze, चिकोटी, चुटकी। 2. a very small quantity, चुटकी-भर सामान। 3. painful stress, कष्टकारी दबाव, तकलीफ़।

pindrop silence (पिनड्रॉप साइलेंस) *n.* total silence, पूर्ण नीरवता, निस्तब्धता।

pine[1] (पाइन) *v.* 1. to become thin through worry, चिंता से सूख जाना। 2. to yearn, लालसा करना।

pine[2] *n.* 1. an evergreen tree, चीड़ या देवदार। 2. its wood, चीड़ या देवदार की लकड़ी।

pineapple (पाइनेपल) *n.* a plant and its fruit, अनानास, अनन्नास।

ping (पिन्ग) *n.* a sharp ringing sound, तड़तड़, तड़तड़ाहट। *v.* to make this sound, तड़तड़ाना।

pingpong (पिंग-पॉन्ग) *n.* = table tennis.

pinion (पिनिअन) *n.* 1. a bird's wing, डैना, पंख। 2. a fog-wheel, दाँतेदार चक्र, गरारी। *v.* 1. to clip the wings of a bird, पक्षी के पर या डैने बाँध या काट देना। 2. to fix in one place, जकड़ देना, बाँध देना।

pink (पिन्क) *adj.* pale red, गुलाबी। *n.* a pale reddish colour, गुलाबी रंग। *v.* to pierce or stab lightly, हथियार से छेदना।

pinnacle (पिनकल) *n.* 1. a peak, चोटी, शिखर। 2. a tower, बुर्ज, मीनार। 3. the highest point, चरमबिंदु, पराकाष्ठा।

pinpoint (पिनपॉइन्ट) *n.* the point of the pin, पिन की नोक। *v.* to show the exact location of, सही जगह बताना।

pint (पाइन्ट) *n.* a measure of liquid equal to 0.568 litre, पिंट।

pioneer (पाइनिअर) *n.* a person who initiates something new, अग्रगामी, पुरोगामी, पथप्रदर्शक। *v.* to initiate or lead, पहल करना या पथप्रदर्शन करना।

pious (पाइअस) *adj.* 1. devout, धर्मपरायण, धर्मशील। 2. holy, पवित्र, पावन, पाक।

pip (पिप) *n.* 1. a dot on a playing card or dice, बिंदी, बुँदकी। 2. a seed of an orange, apple etc., संतरे, सेब आदि का बीज। 3. a short high sound used as a time signal, टिक, पिप।

pipe (पाइप) *n.* 1. a tube used to convey a fluid or gas, पाइप, नली। 2. a flute, बाँसुरी। 3. boat's whistle, (नाविक की) सीटी। 4. a chirp, चींचीं। 5. a container (of whiskey, शराब का) पीपा। *v.* 1. to convey through pipes, पाइप/नल से ले जाना। 2. to play

P

on a flute, बाँसुरी/सीटी बजाना। 3. to chirp, (पक्षियों का) बोलना, चहकना। 4. to ornament with piping, गोट या झालर लगाना।

pipe dream ***n.*** a fanciful plan, काल्पनिक योजना।

pipeline (पाइपलाइन) ***n.*** 1. a pipe for conveying petroleum, gas etc., पाइपलाइन। 2. a channel of supply, पूर्ति का मार्ग। 3. a channal of information, सूचना का मार्ग।

piper (पाइपर) ***n.*** a person who plays on a pipe, बाँसुरीवादक।

pipette (पिपेट) ***n.*** a glass tube for measuring liquids, नलिका, पिपेट।

piquant (पीकन्ट) ***adj.*** 1. pleasantly pungent, चटपटा, मसालेदार। 2. stimulating, उद्दीपक, उत्तेजक। 3. interesting and exciting, मन में खलबली पैदा करनेवाला, रोचक।

pique (पीक) ***v.*** to cause to feel resentment, खिझाना, चिढ़ाना। ***n.*** the feeling of resentment, खीझ, चिढ़।

piracy (पाइरेसी) ***n.*** 1. robbery of ships, समुद्री डकैती, जलदस्युता। 2. unauthorised use of a patented or copyrighted work, पेटेंट या कापीराइट की चोरी, साहित्यिक चोरी।

pirate (पाइरेट) ***n.*** 1. a sea-robber, समुद्री डाकू, जलदस्यु। 2. one who infringes another's copyright, चोर, कापीराइट की चोरी करनेवाला, साहित्यिक चोर। ***v.*** to reproduce someone's work illicitly, साहित्यिक चोरी करना।

Pisces (पिसीज़) ***n.*** the twelfth sign of Zodiac, मीन राशि।

pisciculture (पिसिकल्चर) ***n.*** breeding and rearing of fish, मछलीपालन, मत्स्यपालन।

piss (पिस) ***v.*** to urinate, पेशाब करना, मूतना।

pistachio (पिस्टैशिओ) ***n.*** a tree and its nut, पिस्ता।

pistil (पिस्टिल) ***n.*** (Bot.) the female reproductive part of a flower, फूल का बीजोत्पादक मादा हिस्सा, स्त्रीकेसर, गर्भकेसर।

pistol (पिस्टल) ***n.*** a small firearm, पिस्तौल।

piston (पिस्टन) ***n.*** a cylinder or disc that slides in a hollow, पिस्टन।

pit[1] (पिट) ***n.*** 1. a hole in the ground, गड्ढा। 2. a pitfall, चोरगड्ढा। 3. a depression in the skin, गड्ढा। 4. a mine, खान। ***v.*** to make pits, गड्ढे बनाना।

pit[2] ***n.*** the stone of a fruit, गुठली।

pitch[1] (पिच) ***v.*** 1. to hurl or throw, फेंकना। 2. to erect (a tent, टेंट) खड़ा करना। 3. to encamp, पड़ाव डालना। 4. to establish, स्थापित करना। 5. to fall heavily, धड़ाम से गिरना। 6. to set a tune, सुर बाँधना। 7. to plunge, डुबकी लगाना। ***n.*** 1. an act or manner of throwing the ball, बाल फेंकने का ढंग। 2. the degree of elevation or depression, ऊँचाई या निचाई का मान। 3. slope, ढाल। 4. the area between the stumps, पिच, खेल-पट्टी। 5. the degree of highness or lowness of the voice or a musical note, स्वर की ऊँचाई या मंदी की मात्रा।

pitch[2] ***n.*** tar or asphalt, अलकतरा। ***v.*** to apply pitch to, अलकतरा डालना।

pitched battle ***n.*** 1. in former times, a battle on a chosen ground between complete forces, घमासान

युद्ध। 2. any fierce encounter, ज़ोरदार भिड़ंत।

pitcher (पिचर) ***n.*** an earthen vessel with a narrow neck, घड़ा, मटका, सुराही।

pitchfork (पिचफ़ोर्क) ***n.*** a fork for lifting hay, पाँचा।

pitfall (पिटफ़ॉल) ***n.*** 1. a covered pit used as a trap, चोर-गड्ढा। 2. a difficulty or danger, झमेला, ख़तरा।

pith (पिथ) ***n.*** 1. the spongy substance, गूदा, मज्जा। 2. the essential part, सार, सारांश। 3. force, strength, शक्ति, ज़ोर, दबाव।

pithy (पिथी) ***adj.*** 1. full of pith, गूदेदार। 2. (fig.) full of meaning, अर्थपूर्ण, सारगर्भित।

pitiable (पिटिएबल) ***adj.*** 1. arousing pity, दयनीय, करुणाजनक। 2. deserving contempt, घृणित।

pittance (पिटन्स) ***n.*** a meagre allowance or salary, नाम मात्र का भत्ता या वेतन।

pituitary (पिट्यूइटरी) ***n.*** a gland secreting mucus, श्लेष्मा ग्रंथि, पीयूषिका।

pity (पिटी) ***n.*** 1. compassion, दया, तरस, रहम। 2. cause of regret, खेद की बात, बुरी बात। ***v.*** to feel pity for, दया करना, तरस खाना।

pivot (पिवट) ***n.*** 1. the rod or shaft on which something rotates, धुरी, कीली। 2. a central point, केंद्र, केंद्रबिंदु। ***v.*** (pivoted, pivoting) to turn on a pivot, धुरी पर घूमना।

pivotal (पिवटल) ***adj.*** 1. of or being a pivot, धुरीवाला, अक्षीय। 2. of central importance, अत्यंत महत्त्वपूर्ण, प्रधान, केंद्रीय।

pizza (पिज़ा) ***n.*** an Italian dish, पिज़ा।

placard (प्लेकार्ड) ***n.*** a poster, पोस्टर, इश्तहार। ***v.*** to stick posters on the wall, पोस्टर लगाना, इश्तहार लगाना।

placate (प्लेकेट) ***v.*** to pacify, to calm and satisfy, समझाना-बुझाना, राज़ी करना।

place (प्लेस) ***n.*** 1. a portion of space, जगह, स्थान। 2. a definite location, स्थल। 3. a person's position, पद, स्थिति। 4. a relative position in a series, क्रमिक स्थान। ***v.*** 1. to put, रखना। 2. to appoint, नियुक्त करना। 3. to rank, पद या पदवी देना, किसी वर्ग में रखना। 4. to make, करना।

placement (प्लेसमेन्ट) ***n.*** 1. the act of placing or the state of being placed, स्थापन, स्थानन। 2. arrangement, विन्यास। 3. the process of finding employment, नौकरी की ढूँढ़-खोज।

placenta (प्लेसेन्टा) ***n.*** an organ formed in the womb of a mammal in pregnancy, गर्भनाल, खेड़ी।

placid (प्लैसिड) ***adj.*** calm and peaceful, सौम्य, शांत।

placing (प्लेसिंग) ***n.*** the position in a list or in an order, क्रमिक स्थान।

plagiarist (प्लेजिरिस्ट) ***n.*** one who plagiarizes, दूसरों के विचारों की चोरी करनेवाला।

plagiarize (प्लेजिराइज़) ***v.*** to steal and use the ideas of others, दूसरों के विचारों की चोरी करना।

plague (प्लेग) ***n.*** 1. a contagious epidemic, प्लेग, ताऊन। 2. a cause of annoyance, परेशानी का कारण। ***v.*** to pester, बराबर तंग करना, दुख देना।

plaid (प्लैड) ***n.*** a piece of woolen cloth worn over the shoulders, दुशाला।

P

plain (प्लेन) ***n.*** a large level area, विस्तृत तथा समतल भूभाग, सपाट मैदान। ***adj.*** 1. flat, level, समतल, सपाट। 2. unembellished, ordinary, अनलंकृत, साधारण। 3. clear, evident, स्पष्ट, सुस्पष्ट, बोधगम्य। 4. simple, सादा। 5. frank, स्पष्टवादी। 6. lacking beauty, असुंदर, अनाकर्षक।

plaintiff (प्लेन्टिफ़) ***n.*** a complainant, मुद्दई, वादी।

plaintive (प्लेन्टिव) ***adj.*** expressing sorrow, करुण, शोकपूर्ण, विषादमय।

plait (प्लेट) ***n.*** 1. a braid, चोटी, वेणी। 2. a pleat, (सिलाई में) प्लेट। ***v.*** 1. to make a plait, चोटी गूँथना। 2. to make by plaiting, (सिलाई में) प्लेट या प्लेटें डालना।

plan (प्लैन) ***n.*** 1. a detailed scheme, योजना। 2. programme, कार्यक्रम या कार्य-प्रणाली। 3. an outline, sketch, drawing, रेखाचित्र, नक़्शा, रूपरेखा। ***v.*** 1. to formulate a plan, योजना बनाना। 2. to draw a plan, नक़्शा बनाना। 3. to intend, इरादा करना।

plane[1] (प्लेन) ***adj.*** level, समतल, सपाट। ***n.*** 1. a level surface, समतल भूमि या सतह। 2. a level of thought, वैचारिक धरातल।

plane[2] ***n.*** a tool for smoothing the surface of wood etc., रंदा। ***v.*** to smooth with a plane, रंदे से समतल करना, चौरस करना।

planet (प्लैनिट) ***n.*** any celestial body revolving around the Sun, ग्रह।

planetarium (प्लैनिटेरिअम) ***n.*** a model representing the solar system, (कृत्रिम) तारागृह।

planetary (प्लैनिटरी) ***adj.*** 1. of a planet, ग्रह-संबंधी। 2. global, भूमंडलीय।

plank (प्लैन्क) ***n.*** a thick piece of lumber, तख़्ता, पटरा।

plankton (प्लैन्क्टन) ***n.*** the tiny form of plant or animal organism that floats in water, जल में तैरने वाला सूक्ष्म जीव।

planned (प्लैन्ड) ***adj.*** schemed, योजनाबद्ध, नियोजित; planned family, नियोजित परिवार।

plant (प्लान्ट) ***v.*** 1. to sow, बोना, रोपना, लगाना। 2. to place firmly, जमाना, लगाना, रोपना। 3. to establish, स्थापित करना। 4. to place for the purpose of spying or deception, किसी के यहाँ कोई चीज़ चोरी से रख या छिपा देना। ***n.*** 1. a living organism that is smaller than a shrub or tree, पौधा, पादप। 2. a factory or its machinery, संयंत्र, प्लांट। 3. a thing positioned secretly for discovery by another, चोरी से किसी के यहाँ छिपाई हुई वस्तु।

plantation (प्लैन्टेशन) ***n.*** 1. a group of cultivated plants or trees, उगाया हुआ पादप-समूह या वृक्ष-समूह। 2. the area of land on which they grow, बाग़ान।

planter (प्लैन्टर) ***n.*** 1. the owner of a plantation, बाग़ान-मालिक। 2. a machine for planting of seeds, बीज बोने का यंत्र। 3. a container for decorative plants, गमला।

plaque (प्लाक) ***n.*** 1. a commemorative inscribed plate, स्मृतिपट, स्मृतिफ़लक। 2. a film on teeth, दाँतों पर जमी हुई मैल या काई।

plasma (प्लैज़्मा) ***n.*** the yellowish fluid portion of blood, रक्त का पीला तरल भाग, प्लाविका।

plaster (प्लास्टर) ***n.*** a mixture of

cement, sand and water that is applied to walls, पलस्तर। ***v.*** to apply a plaster to, पलस्तर करना या प्लास्टर लगाना।

plastic (प्लैस्टिक) ***n.*** a synthetic compound that can be moulded in any shape when it is hot, प्लास्टिक। ***adj.*** 1. made of plastic, प्लास्टिक का बना हुआ। 2. able to be shaped or moulded, जिसे गढ़ा और सँवारा जा सके, सुनम्य।

plate (प्लेट) ***n.*** 1. a small flat utensil for serving a dish, प्लेट, तश्तरी, रकाबी। 2. anything served in the plate, प्लेट में रखी हुई वस्तु। 3. a sheet, शीशे, धातु आदि का पतला खंड। 4. a thin layer of a metal, पत्तर, चद्दर। ***v.*** 1. to cover with a thin layer of metal, पत्तर चढ़ाना, चद्दर मढ़ना। 2. to electroplate, मुलम्मा चढ़ाना।

plateau (प्लैटो) ***n.*** 1. a tableland, पठार। 2. a stable condition, स्थिर स्थिति।

platform (प्लैटफ़ार्म) ***n.*** 1. a raised area at a railway station, रेलवे प्लेटफ़ार्म। 2. a raised area from where a speaker gives a speech, मंच। 3. the programme of a political party, राजनीतिक दल का कार्यक्रम।

plating (प्लेटिंग) ***n.*** a coating of a thin layer of a metal, पत्तर की परत।

platinum (प्लैटिनम) ***n.*** an element, प्लेटिनम।

platitude (प्लैटिट्यूड) ***n.*** a hackneyed remark, घिसी-पिटी बात, निस्सार उक्ति।

platonic (प्लैटॉनिक) ***adj.*** 1. of or relating to Plato, प्लैटो-संबंधी, अफ़लातूनी। 2. spiritual, आत्मिक, आध्यात्मिक।

platoon (प्लैटून) ***n.*** a subdivision of military company, पलटन।

platter (प्लैटर) ***n.*** 1. a dish of wood, काठ की रकाबी। 2. a dish, तश्तरी।

plausible (प्लॉज़िबल) ***adj.*** apparently valid or truthful, ऊपर से देखने में सही या सच्चा लगनेवाला, सत्याभासी।

play (प्ले) ***v.*** 1. to occupy oneself in sport or amusement, खेलना, क्रीड़ा करना, विहार करना। 2. to put (a card, पत्ता) खेलना या चलना। 3. to act (a role, पात्र का) अभिनय करना। 4. to perform (on a musical instrument, बाजा) बजाना। 5. to cause (a record or tape recorder) to sound, बजाना। 6. to toy, खिलवाड़ करना। ***n.*** 1. a drama, नाटक। 2. an activity undertaken for pleasure, खेल, क्रीड़ा, मनोरंजन।

playback singer ***n.*** one who sings behind the scene, पार्श्वगायक।

player (प्लेअर) ***n.*** 1. one who participates in a game, खिलाड़ी। 2. an actor, अभिनेता। 3. a performer on a musical instrument, वादक।

playful (प्लेफ़ुल) ***adj.*** 1. full of fun, मज़ाकिया, चंचल, ख़ुशदिल। 2. not serious, किसी काम या बात को हलके ढंग से लेनेवाला, अगंभीर।

playground (प्लेग्राउन्ड) ***n.*** a field for outdoor games, खेल का मैदान, क्रीड़ाक्षेत्र।

playhouse (प्लेहाउस) ***n.*** a theatre, रंगशाला।

playing cards ***n.*** (plu.) cards used in playing various games, ताश।

playmate (प्लेमेट) ***n.*** a friend or partner in play, खेल का साथी, क्रीड़ा-मित्र।

P

playwright (प्लेराइट) ***n.*** a dramatist, नाटककार।

plaza (प्लाज़ा) ***n.*** 1. a public square, चौक, चौमुहानी। 2. a market place, बाज़ार।

plea (प्ली) ***n.*** 1. a statement in defence of justification, सफ़ाई, अभिवचन, दलील, तर्क। 2. an appeal or request, अपील, निवेदन। 3. an excuse, बहाना, युक्ति।

plead (प्लीड) ***v.*** 1. to argue for or against, सफ़ाई या दलील देना, अभिवचन करना। 2. to appeal or request, अपील या निवेदन करना।

pleader (प्लीडर) ***n.*** one who pleads, अभिवक्ता, वकील।

pleasant (प्लेज़न्ट) ***adj.*** 1. pleasing, delightful, सुहावना, रमणीय, रूचिर। 2. having an agreeable manner, प्यारा।

pleasantry (प्लेज़न्ट्री) ***n.*** a pleasant remark, चुटकुला, हँसी-मज़ाक की बात।

please (प्लीज़) ***v.*** 1. to make glad, प्रसन्न करना। 2. to think desirable, ठीक समझना, चाहना। ***interj.*** for request, कृपया!

pleasurable (प्लेज़रेबल) ***adj.*** giving or causing pleasure, सुखद, सुखदायक।

pleasure (प्लेज़र) ***n.*** 1. a feeling of joy or satisfaction, सुख, मज़ा, आनंद। 2. choice or desire, पसंद, इच्छा। 3. grace, प्रसाद, अनुग्रह।

pleat (प्लीट) ***n.*** a flat fold in cloth made by doubling the material upon itself, चुनट। ***v.*** to make pleats in, चुनट डालना।

plebeian (प्लिबीअन) ***adj.*** of the lower social class, निम्नवर्गीय।

plebiscite (प्लेबिसाइट) ***n.*** a referendum, जनमत-संग्रह।

pledge (प्लेज) ***n.*** 1. a solemn promise, प्रण, प्रतिज्ञा, वचन। 2. a thing given or held as security, धरोहर, अमानत। ***v.*** 1. to promise solemnly, वचन देना, प्रतिज्ञा करना। 2. to deposit as a pledge, धरोहर रखना।

pledgee (प्लेजी) ***n.*** a person with whom a pledge is deposited, महाजन, साहुकार।

pledger (प्लेजर) ***n.*** a person who pledges, रेहनकर्ता, गिरवीकर्ता।

plenary (प्लीनरी) ***adj.*** 1. complete, full, परिपूर्ण, पूर्ण। 2. attended by all members, जिसमें सभी सदस्य उपस्थित हों, पूर्ण, भरा, पूरा।

plenitude (प्लेनिट्यूड) ***n.*** abundance, plenty, बहुतायत, प्रचुरता।

plenty (प्लेन्टी) ***n.*** abundance, प्रचुरता, विपुलता। ***adv.*** in abundance, प्रचुर मात्रा में।

plethora (प्लेथोरा) ***n.*** an over abundance, अतिप्रचुरता।

pleurisy (प्लूरिसी) ***n.*** inflammation of the pleura, फेफड़े की झिल्ली की सूजन, प्लूरिसि।

pliability (प्लाइअबिलिटी) ***n.*** the state or quality of being pliable, लचीलापन, आनम्यता।

pliable (प्लाइएबल) ***adj.*** 1. flexible, लचीला, आनम्य। 2. easily influenced, जिसे प्रभावित किया जा सके, दब्बू, कमज़ोर।

pliancy (प्लाइअन्सी) ***n.*** = pliability.

pliant (प्लाइअन्ट) ***adj.*** = pliable.

pliers (प्लाइअर्ज़) ***n.*** (plu.) a tool for handling small objects, चिमटी।

plight[1] (प्लाइट) ***n.*** a condition of adversity, दुर्दशा।

plight[2] ***v.*** to promise, वचन देना।

plinth (प्लिन्थ) ***n.*** a base of a statue, column etc., कुर्सी।

plod (प्लॉड) ***v.*** 1. to walk heavily or laboriously, पाँव घसीटना, ज़ोर लगाकर धीरे-धीरे चलना। 2. to work slowly, मंद गति से काम करना।

plodder (प्लॉडर) ***n.*** a steady worker, परिश्रमी व्यक्ति, कोल्हू का बैल, अध्यवसायी।

plop (प्लॉप) ***n.*** the sound of something dropping into water, डुप, गड़प, छप।

plot (प्लॉट) ***n.*** 1. a piece of land, भूखंड।2. the story of a novel, film, drama etc., कथानक, कथावस्तु। 3. a secret plan, conspiracy, षड्यंत्र, कुचक्र। ***v.*** 1. to divide in plots, भूखंडों में बाँटना। 2. to make a map, नक़्शा बनाना। 3. to conspire, षड्यंत्र रचना, कुचक्र रचना।

plotter (प्लॉटर) ***n.*** one who conspires, conspirator, षड्यंत्रकारी, कुचक्री।

plough, plow (प्लाउ) ***n.*** a farm implement for turning the soil, हल। ***v.*** 1. to break and turn up earth with a plough, जोतना, हल चलाना। 2. to move or proceed forcefully, रास्ता निकालना।

ploy (प्लॉइ) ***n.*** a manoeuvre, चाल, तिकड़म।

pluck (प्लक) ***v.*** 1. to pick (फूल) चुनना, तोड़ना, बीनना। 2. to pull out or snatch, नोचना, तोड़ डालना। ***n.*** 1. a jerk, झटका। 2. animal's liver or heart used as food, कलेजी। 3. courage, हिम्मत, साहस।

plucky (प्लकी) ***adj.*** brave, courageous, हिम्मती, साहसी, दिलेर।

plug (प्लग) ***n.*** 1. a stopper for a hole, छेद या मुँह बंद करने की वस्तु, डाट। 2. an electrical device, (बिजली का) प्लग। ***v.*** to put a plug into, डाट या प्लग लगाना।

plum (प्लम) ***n.*** a fruit of the peach family, आलूबुख़ारा, आलूचा।

plumage (प्लूमिज) ***n.*** a bird's feathers, पंख, पर।

plumb (प्लम) ***n.*** a device to determine vertical direction or the depth of water, साहुल। ***adj.*** 1. vertical, सीधा, लंब। 2. exactly, ठीक, सही। ***v.*** 1. to determine the depth, गहराई नापना, थाहना, थाह लेना। 2. to test the alignment with a plumb, साहुल से नापना, सीधा करना। 3. to hang, लटकाना।

plumber (प्लमर) ***n.*** one who fits and repairs water pipes, नलकार, प्लंबर।

plume (प्लूम) ***n.*** 1. a feather, पंख, पर। 2. something resembling a feather, पंख के आकार की वस्तु।

plummet (प्लमिट) ***n.*** a plumb tied to a cord, साहुल-सूत्र।

plump (प्लम्प) ***adj.*** 1. fleshy, fat, स्थूल, मांसल, मोटा। 2. full and rounded in form, गोल-मटोल। ***v.*** to make or become plump, गोल-मटोल होना या बनाना।

plunder (प्लन्डर) ***v.*** to rob forcibly, लूटना, लूटपाट करना। ***n.*** 1. property robbed forcibly, लूट का माल। 2. the act of plundering, लूट, लूट-मार।

plunge (प्लन्ज) ***v.*** 1. to dive, डुबकी लगाना, गोता लगाना। 2. to thrust, ज़बरदस्ती डालना या घुसेड़ना। 3. to snatch, झपटना, लपकना।4. to be immersed, डूब जाना। ***n.*** 1. a dive, डुबकी, गोता। 2. the act of snatching, झपट्टा, लपक।

plunger (प्लन्जर) ***n.*** 1. a diver,

P

गोताख़ोर। 2. a device to unclog drains and pipes, बंद पाइपों को साफ़ करने का एक उपकरण, जिसके मुँह पर रबर का कप लगा रहता है।

plural (प्लूरल) ***n.*** the form of a noun or verb denoting more than one person or thing, बहुवचन। ***adj.*** of this form, बहुवचन का सूचक।

plurality (प्लूरैलिटी) ***n.*** the state of being plural, बहुवचनत्व, अनेकत्व, बहुलता।

plus (प्लस) ***prep.*** 1. with the addition of, में जमा करने से। 2. and more, और साथ ही। 3. above zero, शून्य से ऊपर। ***n.*** 1. the plus sign, धन चिह्न (+)। 2. an advantage, लाभ, अच्छी बात। ***adj.*** more than the quantity indicated, धनात्मक, धन, अतिरिक्त।

plush (प्लश) ***n.*** a kind of fabric, मखमल, प्लश। ***adj.*** luxurious, विलासितापूर्ण।

Pluto (प्लूटो) ***n.*** a planet in the solar system, प्लूटो।

plutocracy (प्लूटोक्रेसी) ***n.*** government. by the wealthy, धनिकतंत्र।

plutonium (प्लूटोनिअम) ***n.*** a metallic element, प्लूटोनियम (तत्त्व)।

ply[1] (प्लाइ) ***v.*** 1. to carry on, चलाए चलना। 2. to use, काम में लाना, प्रयुक्त करना।3. to keep offering or supplying, देते चलना, पूर्ति करते चलना, भरमार करना। 4. to travel regularly, नियमित रूप से यात्रा करते रहना, आते-जाते रहना।

ply[2] ***n.*** 1. a thickness of cloth or wood, कपड़े या लकड़ी की मोटाई। 2. a layer of cloth or wood, कपड़े या लकड़ी की परत। 3. a strand of yarn, लड़।

plywood (प्लाइवुड) ***n.*** a board consisting of thin layers, प्लाइवुड।

pneumatic (न्यूमैटिक) ***adj.*** of, filled with or operated by air or gas, वायवीय, वायु-चालित।

pneumonia (न्यूमोन्या) ***n.*** inflammation of a lung or lungs, फेफड़ों में सूजन तथा जकड़न, निमोनिया।

poach[1] (पोच) ***v.*** to simmer in a water, milk etc., सिझाना, उबलते पानी में पकाना।

poach[2] ***v.*** to hunt illegally, चोरी से शिकार करना।

poacher (पोचर) ***n.*** a person who poaches, चोर-शिकारी।

pocket (पॉकिट) ***n.*** 1. a pouch in a garment, जेब, पाकेट। 2. a pouchlike compartment, ख़ाना। 3. a cavity in earth, गड्ढा, गर्त। 4. a small isolated area, अलग-थलग छोटा क्षेत्र, लघुक्षेत्र। ***adj.*** small, लघु, जेबी। ***v.*** 1. to place in a pocket, जेब में डालना। 2. to earn unlawfully, अनुचित ढंग से कमाना।

pocket-book (पॉकिट-बुक) ***n.*** 1. a small bag for money or papers, बटुआ, बैग। 2. a small book for writing in, नोटबुक।

pod (पॉड) ***n.*** a seed case as of a pea, फली।

podgy (पॉजी) ***adj.*** chubby, गोल-मटोल।

podium (पोडिअम) ***n.*** 1. a dais, चबूतरा, मंच। 2. a pedestal, पीठिका।

poem (पोइम) ***n.*** a composition in verse, कविता, नज़्म।

poet (पोइट) ***n.*** a writer of poems, कवि, शायर। [fem. poetess, कवयित्री]

poetic (पोएटिक) ***adj.*** 1. of poetry, काव्यात्मक। 2. having the characteristics of poetry, कवित्वपूर्ण, काव्योचित। 3. in verse, छंदोबद्ध, पद्यात्मक।

poetry (पोइट्री) ***n.*** 1. the art of a poet, काव्यकला। 2. poems in general, काव्य। 3. verse, पद्य।

poignant (पॉइनन्ट) ***adj.*** 1. deeply moving, मर्मस्पर्शी, मार्मिक, हृदयविदारक। 2. pungent, कटु, तीक्ष्ण, चरपरा, तीखा।

point (पॉइन्ट) ***n.*** 1. a dot, बिंदु। 2. the sharp end, नोक। 3. a particular space or time, स्थान, समय आदि का अंश, स्थल या घड़ी। 4. aim, purpose or reason, लक्ष्य, उद्देश्य, प्रयोजन, अभिप्राय। 5. a distinctive feature, गुण, विशेषता। 6. a thing under discussion, विचाराधीन बात या विषय, मुद्दा, बिंदु। 7. an important or essential factor or idea, महत्त्वपूर्ण तथ्य या विचार। 8. a distinctive quality, विशिष्टता, गुण। 9. a single unit, इकाई। 10. an electrical contact, प्वाइंट। 11. in cricket, a field position in the off side near the batsman, प्वाइंट। 12. an individual mark or score, अंक। 13. a junction of railway tracks, काँटा। 14. a question, प्रश्न। ***v.*** 1. to bring to notice, to indicate the position or direction, संकेत करना, बतलाना। 2. to face or be turned in a particular direction, (किसी ओर) मुँह होना या करना, उन्मुख होना या करना। 3. to stress, ज़ोर देना।

point-blank (पॉइन्ट-ब्लैंक) ***adj.*** aimed or fired at very close range, बहुत नज़दीक से किया जानेवाला, सटाकर किया जानेवाला।

pointed (पॉइन्टिड) ***adj.*** 1. having a point, incisive, नुकीला, पैना। 2. obviously directed toward a particular person or thing, लक्षित किया हुआ, अभिहित, संकेतपूर्ण। 3. clearly evident, साफ़, सुस्पष्ट।

pointer (पॉइन्टर) ***n.*** 1. an indicator, संकेतक, सूचक। 2. a suggestion, सुझाव। 3. a hunting dog, एक शिकारी कुत्ता।

pointless (पॉइन्टलिस) ***adj.*** 1. meaningless, निरर्थक, बेमतलब। 2. irrelevant, अप्रासंगिक।

poise (पॉइज़) ***n.*** 1. balance, संतुलन। 2. stability, स्थिरता। 3. a composure, मनःसंतुलन, गंभीरता, धीरता। ***v.*** to balance or be balanced, संतुलित करना या होना।

poison (पॉइज़न) ***n.*** a substance that causes death, ज़हर, विष। ***v.*** 1. to give poison to, ज़हर देना। 2. to add poison to, ज़हर मिला देना। 3. to turn someone's mind (against someone, किसी के प्रति) किसी के मन में ज़हर भर देना।

poisonous (पॉइज़नस) ***adj.*** containing poison, ज़हरीला, विषैला, विषाक्त।

poke (पोक) ***v.*** 1. to push or thrust, ठेलना, घुसेड़ना। 2. to push sharply out of or through an opening, झाँकना। 3. to harass, परेशान करना। 4. to meddle, हस्तक्षेप करना। 5. to make a hasty search, ढूँढ़-खोज करना। ***n.*** a push, thrust, धक्का।

poker (पोकर) ***n.*** 1. a metal rod for stirring fire, कुरेदनी, सीख। 2. a game of cards, ताश का एक खेल।

poky (पोकी) ***adj.*** small and uncomfortable, छोटा और असुविधाजनक।

P

polar (पोलर) ***adj.*** 1. of the North Pole or South Pole, ध्रुव-संबंधी, ध्रुवीय। 2. directly opposite, ठीक उलटा, विपरीत।

polarization (पोलराइज़ेशन) ***n.*** the producing of polarity in something, दो ध्रुवों का बनना, दो ध्रुवों में बँटना, ध्रुवण, ध्रुवीकरण।

pole (पोल) ***n.*** 1. a long straight round post used as a support, खंभा। 2. a shaft, (ताँगे/बग्घी का) बम। 3. the North Pole or South Pole, उत्तरी ध्रुव या दक्षिणी ध्रुव। 4. the end or extremity, सिरा।

polemic (पलेमिक) ***n.*** a controversy, वाद-विवाद।

polemical (पलेमिकल) ***adj.*** controversial, विवादपूर्ण, विवादास्पद।

pole star ***n.*** a bright star near the North Pole, ध्रुवतारा।

police (पलीस) ***n.*** a govt. department for keeping public order, पुलिस। ***v.*** 1. to control by police, पुलिस द्वारा नियंत्रण करना। 2. to deploy policemen, पुलिस तैनात करना। 3. to keep a watch on, निगरानी रखना।

policeman (पलीसमैन) ***n.*** a member of the police force, सिपाही, पुलिसमैन।

police station ***n.*** the office of the police force, थाना, नाका, कोतवाली।

policy[1] (पॉलिसी) ***n.*** a general plan of action adopted by an individual, party or government, नीति, कार्य-योजना।

policy[2] ***n.*** a document containing a contract of insurance, पॉलिसी।

polio (पोलिओ) ***n.*** = poliomyelitis.

poliomyelitis (पोलिओमाइ अलाइटिस) ***n.*** an acute infectious viral disease producing temporary or permanent paralysis esp. affecting children, पोलियो।

polish (पॉलिश) ***v.*** 1. to make shiny by rubbing, रगड़कर चमकाना, पॉलिश करना। 2. to refine, परिष्कृत करना। ***n.*** 1. the act of polishing or the state of being polished, चमकाने की क्रिया या चमकने की अवस्था। 2. shine, चमक, पॉलिश। 3. a substance of polishing, पॉलिश, रोग़न। 4. refinement, परिष्कार।

polite (पोलाइट) ***adj.*** 1. courteous, mannerly, नम्र, शिष्ट। 2. refined, सुसंस्कृत।

politeness (पोलाइटनिस) ***n.*** the quality or state of being polite, नम्रता, शिष्टता, भद्रता।

politic (पॉलिटिक) ***adj.*** 1. prudent, wise, सयाना, नीतिकुशल।

political (पॉलिटिकल) ***adj.*** of or relating to politics, or to government policymaking, राजनीतिक।

politician (पॉलिटिशन) ***n.*** a person engaged in politics, राजनीतिज्ञ।

politics (पॉलिटिक्स) ***n.*** 1. the art or science of political government, राजनीति-शास्त्र। 2. the policies or affairs of a government, सरकारी नीतियाँ और कार्य। 3. manoeuvring for power etc., within group, कूटनीति, चालबाज़ी, राजनीति। 4. (plu.) political principles, राजनीतिक सिद्धांत।

polity (पॉलिटी) ***n.*** 1. a form of government, शासन-प्रणाली। 2. politicaly organized society, राजनीतिक दृष्टि से संघटित समाज, राज्य।

poll (पोल) ***n.*** 1. the casting of

votes in an election, मतदान। 2. the number of votes cast, पड़े हुए मत। 3. the survey of public opinion, जनमत-सर्वेक्षण। *v.* 1. to vote at an election, मतदान करना। 2. to receive as votes, (प्रत्याशी द्वारा) मत प्राप्त करना। 3. to clip or shear, काटना, छाँटना, कतरना।

pollen (पोलन) ***n.*** a powder-like substance produced by flowering plants, पराग।

pollinate (पॉलिनेट) ***v.*** to fertilize with pollen, परागण करना।

pollination (पॉलिनेशन) ***n.*** the act of pollinating, परागण।

polling (पोलिंग) ***n.*** the act of casting votes, मतदान।

pollutant (पल्यूटैन्ट) ***n.*** a substance that pollutes, प्रदूषक पदार्थ।

pollute (पल्यूट) ***v.*** 1. to make dirty, impure or unclean, प्रदूषण फैलाना, प्रदूषित करना, गंदा करना। 2. to corrupt, भ्रष्ट करना।

pollution (पल्यूशन) ***n.*** the act of polluting or the state of being polluted, प्रदूषण।

polo (पोलो) ***n.*** a game played by two teams on horseback, पोलो, चौगान।

poly-(पॉली) ***prefix.*** many-, बहु-।

polyandrous (पॉलिऐन्ड्रस) ***adj.*** married to more than one husband, जिसके कई पति हों, बहुपतिका।

polyclinic (पॉलिक्लिनिक) ***n.*** a hospital devoted to treatment of all diseases, वह अस्पताल जिसमें सभी रोगों का निदान होता हो।

polyester (पॉलिएस्टर) ***n.*** a synthetic fibre, पॉलिएस्टर, पॉलिस्टर।

polygamist (पॉलिगैमिस्ट) ***n.*** a person having more than one wife, वह जिसकी एक से अधिक पत्नियाँ हों, बहुपत्नीक।

polyglot (पॉलिग्लॉट) ***adj.*** 1. knowing many languages, बहुभाषी। 2. written in many languages, अनेक भाषाओं में लिखित।

polygon (पॉलिगॉन) ***n.*** a figure having five or more sides, पाँच या अधिक भुजाओं वाली आकृति, बहुभुज।

polyp (पॉलिप) ***n.*** a tube-shaped organism, पोलिप।

polyphony (पॉलिफ़ोनी) ***n.*** the combination of two or more melodies, स्वर-संगति।

polytechnic (पॉलिटेक्निक) ***n.*** a technical training institution, बहुशिल्प केंद्र। ***adj.*** relating to technical instruction, बहुशिल्पीय, बहुशिल्प-।

polytheism (पॉलिथीइज़म) ***n.*** the worship of more than one god or belief in more than one god, बहुदेववाद।

polytheistic (पॉलिथीइस्टिक) ***adj.*** of polytheism, बहुदेववादी।

polythene (पॉलिथीन) ***n.*** a synthetic material for making bags, पॉलिथीन।

pomegranate (पॉमिग्रैनिट) ***n.*** a tree and its round fruits, अनार।

pommel (पॉमेल) ***n.*** 1. a knob on the hilt of a sword, (तलवार की मुठिया की) गाँठ। 2. the upper front part of a saddle, काठी का आगे का भाग, हरना।

pomp (पॉम्प) ***n.*** 1. splendour, शान, ठाट-बाट। 2. ostentatious display, आडंबर, दिखावा।

P

pompom (पॉमपॉम) ***n.*** a tuft on a cap, फुँदना।

pompous (पॉम्पस) ***adj.*** 1. splendid, भव्य, शानदार। 2. ostentatious, तड़क-भड़कवाला, आडंबरपूर्ण। 3. ostentatiously self-important, आडंबरप्रिय।

poncho (पॉन्चो) ***n.*** a blanket-like cloak with a hole in the centre for the head, गर्म कपड़े का बिना सिला लबादा, पोंचू।

pond (पॉन्ड) ***n.*** a still body of water, पोखरा, ताल, तालाब, कुंड।

ponder (पॉन्डर) ***v.*** 1. to consider carefully, सोच-विचार करना, सोचना-विचारना। 2. to meditate, मनन करना।

ponderous (पॉन्डरस) ***adj.*** 1. heavy, huge, भारी, भारी-भरकम। 2. dull, भद्दा।

pontiff (पॉन्टिफ़) ***n.*** 1. a bishop, धर्माचार्य। 2. the Pope, पोप।

pontificate (पॉन्टिफ़िकेट) ***v.*** to speak or bahave like a pontiff, धर्माचार्य की तरह बोलना या व्यवहार करना।

pontoon-bridge (पॉन्टूनब्रिज) ***n.*** a temporary bridge of hollow metal cylinders, पीपे का पुल।

pony (पोनी) ***n.*** a horse of small breed, टट्टू।

pooh (पू) ***interj.*** an exclamation of disdain; contempt etc., छी, उँह।

pooh-pooh (पू-पू) ***v.*** to express disdain for, तिरस्कार करना, घिन करना।

pool[1] (पूल) ***n.*** 1. a small area of still water, पोखरा, ताल। 2. a shallow patch of water, blood etc., गिरा-पड़ा पानी, ख़ून आदि। 3. a swimming pool, तरणताल।

pool[2] ***n.*** 1. common fund for speculation, निधि, साझी निधि। 2. a combination of business firms, व्यापारिक गठजोड़। ***v.*** to contribute to the common fund, निधि स्थापित करना।

poop (पूप) ***n.*** the stern of a ship, जलयान का पिछला भाग, दुंबाल।

poor (पुअर) ***adj.*** 1. poverty-stricken, ग़रीब, निर्धन, अकिंचन। 2. unfortunate, अभागा, बेचारा, दीनहीन। 3. bad, ख़राब, बुरा। 4. deserving sympathy, दया का पात्र, दीनहीन।

poorly (पुअर्ली) ***adj.*** in a poor health, ill, अस्वस्थ। ***adv.*** badly, बहुत ख़राब (ढंग से)।

pop[1] (पॉप) ***n.*** a small sharp explosive sound, तड़, फट। ***v.*** 1. to make a pop, तड़ शब्द करना, फट शब्द करना। 2. to come or go rapidly, जल्दी से आना या जाना। 3. to protrude, बाहर निकला होना। 4. to put suddenly, जल्दी से डाल देना।

pop[2] ***n.*** music of general appeal, पॉप संगीत। ***adj.*** in a popular modern style, आधुनिक तथा लोकप्रिय।

popcorn (पॉपकॉर्न) ***n.*** the puffed kernels of maize, मक्की का लावा।

pope (पोप) ***n.*** the head of Roman Catholic Church, ईसाई धर्मगुरु, पोप।

poplar (पॉप्लर) ***n.*** a tree, पहाड़ी पीपल।

poplin (पॉप्लिन) ***n.*** a fine cotton fabric, पॉपलिन।

poppy (पॉपी) ***n.*** a plant, पोस्ते का पौधा।

poppy seed ***n.*** the seed of the poppy, पोस्ते का दाना, खसखस।

populace (पॉप्यूलेस) ***n.*** the common people, जनता।

popular (पॉप्यूलर) ***adj.*** 1. liked by the common people, लोकप्रिय, जनप्रिय। 2. common, public, जनता-संबंधी, लोक-।

popularity (पॉप्यूलैरिटी) ***n.*** the state or quality of being popular, लोकप्रियता।

popularize (पॉप्यूलराइज़) ***v.*** 1. to make popular, लोकप्रिय बनाना। 2. to make easily understandable, सुबोध या सुगम बनाना।

populate (पॉप्यूलेट) ***v.*** 1. to supply with inhabitants, (स्थान का) बसना/बसाना, आबाद होना/करना। 2. to live, रहना, बसना।

population (पॉप्युलेशन) ***n.*** the total inhabitants of a place or country, जनसंख्या, आबादी।

populous (पॉप्यूलस) ***adj.*** containing many inhabitants, घना बसा हुआ (स्थान)।

porcelain (पोर्सलिन) ***n.*** a hard white ceramic, चीनी मिट्टी।

porch (पोर्च) ***n.*** a roofed structure at an entrance to a house, ड्योढ़ी, द्वारमंडप, पोर्च।

porcupine (पॉर्क्यूपाइन) ***n.*** a rodent covered with long sharp spines, साही (जंतु)।

pore (पोर) ***n.*** 1. a tiny opening in the skin, रोमकूप। 2. a small hole, छिद्र।

pork (पोर्क) ***n.*** the flesh of a pig, सुअर का गोश्त, शूकर-मांस।

pornography (पोर्नॉग्रफ़ी) ***n.*** writings, pictures, films etc. to arouse sexual desire, अश्लील लेखन, अश्लील साहित्य।

porous (पोरस) ***adj.*** full of pores, छेदों से भरा, छिद्रिल।

porridge (पॉरिज) ***n.*** boiled cereal esp, oatmeal, दलिया।

port (पोर्ट) ***n.*** a harbour, बंदरगाह, पत्तन।

portable (पोर्टेबल) ***adj.*** able to be carried easily, सुवाह्य, पोर्टेबल।

portal (पोर्टल) ***n.*** a gateway, प्रवेशद्वार, मुख्यद्वार, सिंहद्वार।

portend (पोर्टेन्ड) ***v.*** to give warning of, पूर्वसूचना या चेतावनी देना।

portent (पोर्टेन्ट) ***n.*** 1. a warning, पूर्वसूचना या चेतावनी। 2. an omen, शकुन/अपशकुन।

porter (पोर्टर) ***n.*** a man employed to carry traveller's luggage, सामान ढोने-वाला मज़दूर, कुली, भारिक।

portfolio (पोर्टफ़ोलिओ) ***n.*** 1. a case for holding loose papers, काग़ज़-पत्र रखने का चमड़े का बैग, पोर्टफ़ोलियो। 2. the post of a cabinet member, मंत्री को दिया जानेवाला विभाग।

portico (पोर्टिको) ***n.*** a covered entrance to a building, द्वारमंडप, पोर्टिको।

portion (पोर्शन) ***n.*** a part of something, अंश, हिस्सा, भाग। ***v.*** to divide into portions, हिस्से लगाना, बाँटना।

portly (पोर्टली) ***adj.*** 1. stout, हट्टा-कट्टा। 2. impressive, प्रभावपूर्ण।

portrait (पोर्ट्रेट) ***n.*** 1. a painting or photograph, तस्वीर, चित्र, फोटो। 2. a description in words, शब्दचित्र।

portray (पोर्ट्रे) ***v.*** 1. to depict pictorially, चित्रित करना। 2. to describe in words, शब्दचित्र प्रस्तुत करना। 3. to play the role, भूमिका निभाना, अभिनय करना।

pose (पोज़) ***v.*** 1. to assume a desired position, कोई विशिष्ट मुद्रा धारण करना। 2. to pretend, बनना। 3. to present, प्रस्तुत करना। ***n.*** 1. a physical attitude, ठवन, भंगिमा, मुद्रा, पोज़। 2. an attitude, रुख़। 3. a pretence, ढोंग, आडंबर, बनावट।

P

posh (पॉश) ***adj.*** 1. of the upper class, उच्चवर्गीय। 2. fashionable, smart, फैशनेबुल।

posit (पॉज़िट) ***v.*** to assume as a fact, तथ्य मानकर चलना।

position (पोज़िशन) ***n.*** 1. place, situation or location, स्थिति। 2. a point of view, दृष्टिकोण। 3. rank or status, पदवी। ***v.*** to put in a particular place or position, स्थित करना, स्थापित करना, रखना।

positional (पोज़िशनल) ***adj.*** of or relating to position, स्थिति-संबंधी, स्थितिपरक।

positive (पॉज़िटिव) ***adj.*** 1. displaying affirmation, सकारात्मक, स्वीकारात्मक। 2. definite, सुस्पष्ट, सुनिश्चित। 3. real, वास्तविक। 4. (photo) having the lights and shades in the actual, पॉज़िटिव, सहिक। 4. (maths. & elect.) greater than zero, धनात्मक।

positively (पॉज़िटिवली) ***adv.*** certainly, निश्चित रूप से।

posse (पॉसी) ***n.*** a group or gong, दल, टुकड़ी।

possess (पज़ेस) ***v.*** 1. to own, होना, रखना, पास होना। 2. to be under the influence of, अभिभूत होना।

possessed (पज़ेस्ड) ***adj.*** controlled by an evil spirit, प्रेतग्रस्त, बाधाग्रस्त।

possession (पज़ेशन) ***n.*** 1. the act or fact of possessing, क़ब्ज़ा, स्वामित्व। 2. a right, अधिकार। 3. the state of being dominated by an evil spirit, भूतावेश, भूत-बाधा।

possessive (पज़ेसिव) ***adj.*** 1. of or pertaining to possession, स्वामित्व या स्वत्वबोधक। 2. (gram.) genitive, संबंध-वाचक।

possibility (पॉसिबिलिटी) ***n.*** the condition or fact of being possible, संभावना।

possible (पॉसिबल) ***adj.*** capable of being in existence, taking place, being done or used, संभव, संभावित।

post[1] (पोस्ट) ***n.*** a pillar, खंभा। ***v.*** to fasten a notice at public place, सूचना, पोस्टर आदि चिपकाना या लगाना।

post[2] ***n.*** 1. an assigned position of a sentry, पोस्ट, चौकी। 2. a position of employment, पद। ***v.*** 1. to assign to a specific position or station, स्थान विशेष पर तैनाती करना।

post[3] ***n.*** 1. the system of transporting and delivering mail, डाक-व्यवस्था। 2. a letter or package sent by post office, डाक। ***v.*** 1. to mail, डाक से पत्र आदि भेजना। 2. to enter an item in a ledger, खतियाना, खाते में चढ़ाना।

post[4] ***prefix.*** after, पश्च-, उत्तर-।

postage (पोस्टिज) ***n.*** the charge for mailing a letter, package etc., डाकव्यय।

postage stamp ***n.*** a ticket for attaching to mail, डाक-टिकट।

postal (पोस्टल) ***adj.*** of post office or mail, डाक या डाकघर-संबंधी।

postcard (पोस्टकार्ड) ***n.*** a card sent by post, पोस्टकार्ड।

postdated (पोस्टडेटिड) ***adj.*** having a future date, उत्तरदिनांकित, बाद की तारीख़वाला।

poster (पोस्टर) ***n.*** an advertisement posted in a public place, इश्तहार, पोस्टर।

posterior (पॉस्टिरिअर) ***adj.*** 1. rear, पश्च, पिछला। 2. subsequent, परवर्ती।

3. later, उत्तरकालीन। *n.* the buttocks, नितंब, चूतड़।

posterity (पॉस्टेरिटी) *n.* future generation, भावी पीढ़ी।

postgraduate (पोस्टग्रैजुएट) *adj.* involving or pursuing studies after taking a bachelor's degree, स्नातकोत्तर।

posthumous (पॉस्ट्यूमस) *adj.* 1. born after the death of the father, पिता की मृत्यु के बाद उत्पन्न होनेवाला। 2. given or happening after one's death, मरणोत्तर।

postman (पोस्टमैन) *n.* one who carries and delivers mail, डाकिया, पोस्टमैन।

postmark (पोस्टमार्क) *n.* a mark stamped on a mail, डाकघर द्वारा चिट्ठियों आदि पर लगाई जानेवाली मोहर।

postmaster (पोस्टमास्टर) *n.* a person in charge of a post office, डाकपाल, पोस्टमास्टर।

post meridiem (p.m.) (पोस्ट मरिडिअम) *n.* afternoon, अपराह्न।

post-mortem (पोस्ट-मॉर्टम) *n.* 1. a medical examination of the dead body, शव-परीक्षण, पोस्टमार्टम। 2. analysis of a recent event, किसी ताज़ा घटना की समीक्षा।

postnatal (पोस्टनेटल) *adj.* occurring after birth, जन्मोत्तर।

post office (पोस्ट ऑफिस) *n.* an office where postal business is conducted, डाकघर, पोस्ट ऑफ़िस।

post-operative (पोस्ट-ऑपरेटिव) *adj.* occurring or executed after surgery, ऑपरेशन के बाद का।

postpone (पोस्टपोन) *v.* to put off or delay until a future time, स्थगित करना, मुलतवी रखना।

postposition (पोस्टपोज़ीशन) *n.* a connective used after a noun or pronoun, परसर्ग।

postscript (पोस्टस्क्रिप्ट) *n.* a message added at the end of a letter, esp. after signature, पुनश्च।

postulate (पॉस्चलेट) *v.* to assume to be true, मान लेना।

posture (पॉस्चर) *n.* a position of the body, ठवन, मुद्रा।

pot (पॉट) *n.* a vessel, बर्तन, पात्र। *v.* 1. to put in a pot, बर्तन में रखना। 2. to plant, रोपना।

potable (पोटेबल) *adj.* fit to drink, पीने-योग्य, पेय।

potash (पोटैश) *n.* potassium carbonate, पोटाश (खाद आदि में प्रयुक्त)।

potato (पटेटो) *n.* a plant and its edible root, आलू।

potato chip *n.* a thin fried slice of potato, आलू की कचरी।

pot-belly (पॉट-बेली) *n.* a protruding belly, तोंद।

potency (पोटेन्सी) *n.* power, force, शक्ति, सामर्थ्य।

potent (पोटेन्ट) *adj.* 1. powerful, forceful, सशक्त, तेज़। 2. influential, प्रभावी।

potential (पोटेन्शल) *adj.* 1. having potency, सशक्त, समर्थ। 2. that can develop into something in future, संभाव्य, संभावी, संभावित। *n.* possibility, संभाव्यता, संभावना।

pot-hole (पॉट-होल) *n.* a deep hole, गहरा गड्ढा।

potted (पॉटिड) *adj.* 1. placed in a pot, बर्तन में रखा हुआ। 2. grown

P

in a pot, गमले में उगाया जानेवाला। 3. abridged, संक्षिप्त।

potter (पॉटर) ***n.*** a person who makes pottery, कुम्हार।

pottery (पॉटरी) ***n.*** 1. earthenware, मिट्टी के बर्तन। 2. the business of a potter, कुम्हार का व्यवसाय, कुम्हारी।

potty (पॉटी) ***n.*** a small pot used by children as a toilet, छोटे बच्चों के टट्टी-पेशाब करने का पात्र, शौच-पात्र। ***adj.*** 1. foolish, मूर्खतापूर्ण। 2. trivial, तुच्छ।

pouch (पाउच) ***n.*** 1. a small bag, थैली। 2. a pouch like cavity, थैलीनुमा अंग, थैली।

poulterer (पोल्टरर) ***n.*** one who rears domestic fowls, मुर्गीपालक।

poultice (पोल्टिस) ***n.*** a soft heated dressing applied to aching or inflamed part of the body, पुलटिस।

poultry (पोल्ट्री) ***n.*** domestic chickens, ducks etc., पालतू मुर्गियाँ, बतखें आदि।

poultry farm ***n.*** a place for rearing chickens, ducks etc., मुर्गी-फ़ार्म।

pounce (पाउन्स) ***v.*** to fall up on to snatch something, झपट्टा मारना। ***n.*** the act of pouncing, झपट्टा।

pound[1] (पाउन्ड) ***v.*** to strike heavily with repeated blows, कूटना या पीटना।

pound[2] ***n.*** 1. a unit of weight equal to 16 ounces, पौंड। 2. the standard monetary unit of England, पौंड।

pound[3] ***n.*** an enclosure for the confinement of stray animals, कांजी-हाउस।

pour (पोर) ***v.*** 1. to flow or cause to flow in a stream, उँड़ेलना। 2. to rain heavily, मूसलधार वर्षा होना।

pout (पाउट) ***v.*** to push out one's lips in displeasure, होंठ बिचकाना।

poverty (पॉवर्टी) ***n.*** 1. lack of money, ग़रीबी, निर्धनता। 2. lack, deficiency, अभाव, कमी।

powder (पाउडर) ***n.*** 1. a mass of fine solid particles, चूर्ण, चूरा, बुकनी, पाउडर। 2. face powder, मुँह पर लगाने का पाउडर। 3. gun powder, बारूद, मसाला। ***v.*** 1. to pulverize, पीसना। 2. to cover with powder, पाउडर लगाना।

power (पाउअर) ***n.*** 1. strength, force, बल, शक्ति, क्षमता। 2. authority, सत्ता। 3. a powerful nation, शक्तिशाली राष्ट्र। 4. (maths.) an exponent, घात। 5. a particular form of energy, शक्ति; nuclear power, नाभिकीय शक्ति।

powerful (पाउअरफ़ुल) ***adj.*** having great power, शक्तिशाली।

powerless (पाउअरलिस) ***adj.*** without power, शक्तिहीन, निर्बल, लाचार।

powerloom (पाउअरलूम) ***n.*** a loom operated by electricity, पावरलूम।

power of attorney ***n.*** the legal authority to act for another person, मुख़्तारनामा।

power station ***n.*** a building where electric power is generated, बिजली-घर।

practicable (प्रैक्टिकेबल) ***adj.*** capable of being done, that can be carried out, व्यवहार्य, साध्य।

practical (प्रैक्टिकल) ***adj.*** 1. feasible, workable, not theoretical, व्यावहारिक। 2. clever at doing or making things, व्यवहारशील, व्यवहारकुशल। 3. obtained through practice or action, प्रायोगिक, प्रयोगात्मक। 4. virtual, वास्तविक, यथार्थ। ***n.*** a practical examination, प्रायोगिक परीक्षा।

practice (प्रैक्टिस) ***n.*** 1. a custom, रिवाज, प्रथा, चलन, दस्तूर। 2. a habit, आदत। 3. repeated performance or exercise, बार-बार करना, अभ्यास। 4. business, profession, व्यवसाय, पेशा।

practise (प्रैक्टिस) ***v.*** 1. to do or perform repeatedly to become efficient, अभ्यास करना। 2. to work at or follow a profession, व्यवसाय करना।

practitioner (प्रैक्टिशनर) ***n.*** a person practices a profession, व्यवसायी।

pragmatic (प्रैग्मैटिक) ***adj.*** of practical point of view, व्यवहारशील।

pragmatism (प्रेग्मैटिज़्म) ***n.*** the act or method of solving problems by practical means, व्यवहारशीलता।

prairie (प्रेअरी) ***n.*** a treeless grassy plain, घास का मैदान, प्रेयरी।

praise (प्रेज़) ***v.*** 1. to express admiration (for, की) प्रशंसा करना। 2. to extol, स्तुति करना, गुणगान करना। ***n.*** admiration, प्रशंसा, स्तुति, गुणगान।

praiseworthy (प्रेज़वर्दी) ***adj.*** commendable, प्रशंसनीय, श्लाघ्य, स्तुत्य।

pram (प्रैम) ***n.*** (perambulator का संक्षिप्त रूप) बच्चागाड़ी, शिशुयान।

prance (प्रान्स) ***v.*** (pranced/pranst, prancing) 1. to rise upon hind legs, (घोड़े का) पिछले पैरों पर खड़ा होना। 2. to ride on a prancing horse, घोड़े को पिछले पैरों पर नचाना।

prank (प्रैन्क) ***n.*** a mischievous trick, शरारत, चुहल।

prankster (प्रैन्क्स्टर) ***n.*** a trickster, चुहलबाज़।

prattle (प्रैटल) ***v.*** to talk in a childish way, बच्चों की तरह बोलना, बड़बड़ करना।

prawn (प्रॉन) ***n.*** a small edible fish, झींगा (मछली)।

pray (प्रे) ***v.*** 1. to utter a prayer, प्रार्थना/अनुनय करना। 2. to entreat, चिरौरी करना।

prayer (प्रेअर) ***n.*** 1. a solemn request to God, प्रार्थना, विनती। 2. an earnest request, अनुनय, याचना।

pre- (प्रि) ***prefix.*** before in time, position etc., पूर्ववर्ती, पूर्व-।

preach (प्रीच) ***v.*** 1. to give a sermon on religious instructions, प्रवचन करना, उपदेश करना। 2. to give moral instructions, सीख/शिक्षा देना। 3. to advocate, प्रचार करना।

preacher (प्रीचर) ***n.*** one who delivers sermons, धर्मोपदेशक, उपदेशक।

preamble (प्रीऐम्बल) ***n.*** an introductory statement, आमुख, प्रस्तावना।

precarious (प्रीकेरिअस) ***adj.*** dangerous, unsafe, ख़तरनाक, असुरक्षित।

precaution (प्रिकॉशन) ***n.*** an action taken beforehand, एहतियात, पूर्वोपाय।

precede (प्रिसीड) ***v.*** to be before in time, place etc., से पहले होना; से पहले आना, पहुँचना या जाना।

precedence (प्रेसिडेन्स) ***n.*** priority, अग्रता।

precedent (प्रेसिडेन्ट) ***adj.*** a previous example, convention, पूर्वोदाहरण।

precept (प्रीसेप्ट) ***n.*** a rule or principle for action, नीतिवचन, उपदेश, सीख।

P

precinct (प्रीसिन्क्ट) ***n.*** 1. an area reserved for a particular activity, किसी विशेष कार्य के लिए आरक्षित क्षेत्र। 2. a boundary, सीमा। 3. (plu.) the area surrounding a place, आसपास का क्षेत्र, परिक्षेत्र।

precious (प्रेशस) ***adj.*** 1. of great value, very costly, मूल्यवान, बहुमूल्य। 2. beloved, प्रिय। 3. fastidious, affected, बनावट-भरा, कृत्रिम।

precipice (प्रेसिपिस) ***n.*** a very steep cliff, खड़ी चट्टान।

precipitate (प्रिसिपिटेट) ***v.*** 1. to throw down headlong, धकेलना, झोंकना। 2. to hasten, जल्दी करना, हड़बड़ी मचाना। 3. to condense and cause to fall as rain, snow etc., वाष्प का जमकर ओस, ओले या वर्षा के रूप में गिरना। 4. (chem.) to cause to deposit in solid form, घोल में से ठोस पदार्थ तैयार करना या निकालना। ***adj.*** done rashly, जल्दी में या हड़बड़ाकर किया हुआ। ***n.*** a substance separated out of a solution, किसी घोल से तैयार होनेवाला ठोस पदार्थ, अवक्षेप।

precipitation (प्रिसिपिटेशन) ***n.*** 1. hastiness, haste, हड़बड़ी, उतावली। 2. rain or snow, वृष्टि, वर्षण। 3. (chem.) the formation of a precipitate, अवक्षेपण।

precis (प्रेसी) ***n.*** a concise summary, abstract, संक्षेप, सार। ***v.*** to make a precis of, संक्षेप तैयार करना।

precise (प्रिसाइस) ***adj.*** 1. exact, correct, सही-सही। 2. stated clearly, स्पष्ट। 3. taking care to be exact, सही ढंग से काम करनेवाला।

precision (प्रिसिज़न) ***n.*** accuracy, परिशुद्धता, यथार्थता।

preclude (प्रीक्लूड) ***v.*** to make impossible, असंभव कर या बना देना, होने न देना।

precocious (प्रिकोशस) ***adj.*** developed earlier than usual, अकाल प्रौढ़, अकाल पक्व।

precognition (प्रिकॉग्निशन) ***n.*** the ability to see future events, पूर्वज्ञान, भविष्यदर्शन।

preconceive (प्रीकन्सीव) ***v.*** to form an idea beforehand, पहले से धारणा बना रखना।

preconception (प्रीकन्सेप्शन) ***n.*** the act of preconceiving, पूर्वधारण, पूर्वधारणा।

precondition (प्रीकन्डिशन) ***n.*** a condition to be fulfilled first, पूर्व शर्त।

precursor (प्रिकर्सर) ***n.*** one that precedes, पूर्वगामी।

predator (प्रेडेटर) ***n.*** a predatory animal, जीवभक्षी पशु।

predatory (प्रेडटरी) ***adj.*** living by seizing prey, जीवभक्षी (प्राणी)।

predecessor (प्रेडिसेसर) ***n.*** 1. one who precedes another in an office, पूर्ववर्ती अधिकारी, पूर्वाधिकारी। 2. an ancestor, पूर्वज।

predestination (प्रिडेस्टिनेशन) ***n.*** the doctrine that God has foreordained all that happens, नियतिवाद।

predetermine (प्रीडिटर्मिन) ***v.*** to decide in advance, पहले से निश्चय कर लेना, पूर्वनिश्चय करना।

predicament (प्रिडिकमेन्ट) ***n.*** a difficult or unpleasant situation, विकट या अप्रिय स्थिति।

predicate (प्रेडिकिट) ***n.*** (gram.) the part of a sentence that expresses what is said about the subject, विधेय।

predict (प्रिडिक्ट) ***v.*** to foretell, भविष्यवाणी करना।

prediction (प्रिडिक्शन) ***n.*** something predicted, भविष्यवाणी।

predilection (प्रीडिलेक्शन) ***n.*** liking, पसंद, अभिरुचि।

predisposition (प्रीडिस्पज़िशन) ***n.*** previous tendency, पूर्ववृत्ति।

predominant (प्रिडॉमिनेन्ट) ***adj.*** 1. superior in power or importance, जिसका आधिपत्य या प्राधान्य हो, प्रधान। 2. most common or numerous, अपेक्षया अधिक, सर्वाधिक।

predominate (प्रिडॉमिनेट) ***v.*** 1. to be of greater power or importance, अधिक शक्तिशाली या महत्त्वपूर्ण होना। 2. to have controlling influence, प्रभुत्व होना।

pre-eminence (प्री-एमिनेन्स) ***n.*** the state or quality of being eminent, प्रकृष्टता।

pre-emption (प्री-एम्प्शन) ***n.*** the right to purchase property before others, हक़शफ़ा।

preen (प्रीन) ***v.*** 1. to clean with the beak, (पक्षियों का अपने परों को) चोंच से साफ़ करना। 2. to dress up, सजना-सँवरना, बनना-ठनना।

prefabricate (प्रीफ़ैब्रिकेट) ***v.*** to fabricate beforehand, पहले से रचना कर लेना, पूर्व रचना करना।

prefabrication (प्रीफ़ैब्रिकेशन) ***n.*** the act of prefabricating or the state of being prefabricated, पूर्वरचना।

preface (प्रेफ़िस) ***n.*** a foreword, introduction, प्रस्तावना, आमुख, भूमिका। ***v.*** 1. to write an introduction, प्रस्तावना लिखना। 2. to begin, आरंभ करना।

prefect (प्रीफ़ेक्ट) ***n.*** an administative official, प्रशासक।

prefer (प्रिफ़र) ***v.*** 1. to like better, अधिक पसंद करना, वरीयता देना, तरजीह देना। 2. to promote, प्रोन्नत करना।

preference (प्रेफ़रेन्स) ***n.*** the liking for something over another, वरीयता, अधिमान।

preferential (प्रेफ़रेन्शल) ***adj.*** giving or receiving preference, वरीय।

prefix (प्रीफ़िक्स) ***n.*** the affix that precedes the stem, उपसर्ग। ***v.*** to fix or place before, पहले रखना या लगाना, पूर्वयोजन करना।

pregnancy (प्रेग्नेन्सी) ***n.*** the state of being pregnant, गर्भावस्था।

pregnant (प्रेग्नेन्ट) ***adj.*** 1. having a young developing in the womb, गर्भवती। 2. meaningful, सगर्भ, सारगर्भित। 3. full of, भरा हुआ, परिपूर्ण।

prehistoric, prehistorical (प्री-हिस्टॉरिक, प्रीहिस्टॉरिकल) ***adj.*** of the period before the recorded history, पूर्व-ऐतिहासिक, इतिहास-पूर्व।

prejudice (प्रेजुडिस) ***n.*** 1. bias, कुभाव, पूर्वग्रह। 2. dislike for a person, group, custom etc., कुभाव। 3. harm, injury, प्रतिकूल प्रभाव, क्षति, हानि। ***v.*** 1. to cause to have a prejudice, पूर्वग्रह उत्पन्न करना। 2. to harm, क्षति पहुँचाना।

prejudicial (प्रेजुडिशल) ***adj.*** causing prejudice, कुभाव या पूर्वग्रह उत्पन्न करनेवाला; क्षतिकारक।

preliminary (प्रिलिमिनरी) ***adj.*** introductory, प्रारंभिक, प्राथमिक। ***n.*** (plu.) preliminary procedure, प्रारंभिक तैयारी, उपोद्घात।

P

prelude (प्रेल्यूड) ***n.*** 1. an introduction, भूमिका, प्रस्तावना। 2. an introductory performance or event, पूर्वरंग, मंगलाचरण।

premarital (प्रीमैरिटल) ***adj.*** of the time before marriage, विवाह-पूर्व।

premature (प्रीमच्योर) ***adj.*** 1. too early, समय से पूर्व होनेवाला, अकालिक, समयपूर्व। 2. born before time, अधूरा, कच्चा।

premeditate (प्रिमेडिटेट) ***v.*** to consider beforehand, पूर्वमनन करना।

premeditation (प्रिमेडिटेशन) ***n.*** the act of premeditating, पूर्वमनन।

premier (प्रिमिअर) ***n.*** Prime Minister, प्रधानमंत्री। ***adj.*** 1. chief, प्रधान, मुख्य। 2. first, earliest, सर्वप्रथम।

premiere (प्रिमिअर) ***n.*** a first public presentation of a film or play, सर्वप्रथम प्रदर्शन।

premise (प्रेमिस) ***n.*** (log.) the basis of a proposition, आधार-वाक्य।

premises (प्रेमिसिज़) ***n.*** (plu.) the land and the buildings on it, कोई भूखंड तथा उसपर बनी इमारतें, परिसर।

premium (प्रीमिअम) ***n.*** 1. an instalment for an insurance policy, बीमे की क़िस्त, प्रीमियम। 2. a prize, reward, पुरस्कार। 3. the amount charged in addition to standard price, मानक मूल्य से ली जानेवाली अधिक रक़म, अधिशुल्क।

premonition (प्रीमनिशन) ***n.*** an intuition of a future, पूर्वबोध, अग्रबोध।

preoccupation (प्रीऑक्युपेशन) ***n.*** engrossment, तल्लीनता, निमग्नता।

preparation (प्रेपरेशन) ***n.*** the act of preparing, तैयारी, उपक्रम।

preparatory (प्रिपैरेटरी) ***adj.*** serving to prepare, प्रारंभिक।

prepare (प्रिपेअर) ***v.*** 1. to become or make ready, तैयार होना/करना। 2. to make ready for use, बनाना।

prepay (प्रिपे) ***v.*** (prepaid, prepaying) to pay beforehand, पूर्वभुगतान/अग्रभुगतान करना।

preponderance (प्रिपॉन्डरेन्स) ***n.*** the state of being preponderant, महत्ता; प्रचुरता।

preponderant (प्रिपॉन्डरेन्ट) ***adj.*** 1. that preponderates, अधिक शक्तिशाली, महत्त्वपूर्ण या वज़नी। 2. greater in amount, प्रचुर।

preposition (प्रेपज़िशन) ***n.*** (gram.) a word used before nouns to show its relation to another word, पूर्वसर्ग।

prepossess (प्रीपज़ेस) ***v.*** 1. to prejudice, पूर्वाग्रह उत्पन्न करना। 2. to impress, प्रभावित करना।

prepossessing (प्रीपज़ेसिंग) ***adj.*** impressive or attractive, प्रभावपूर्ण या आकर्षक।

preposterous (प्रिपॉस्टरस) ***adj.*** 1. ridiculous, हास्यास्पद। 2. absurd, भद्दा, बेतुका, असंगत।

prerequisite (प्रिरेक्विज़िट) ***n.*** something required as a prior condition, पूर्वापेक्षा।

prerogative (प्रिरोगेटिव) ***n.*** an exclusive right, परमाधिकार, विशिष्टाधिकार।

presage (प्रेसिज) ***n.*** 1. an omen, सगुन, लक्षण। 2. foreboding, पूर्वाभास। ***v.*** 1. to be a omen, शकुन होना। 2. to predict, भविष्यवाणी करना।

prescribe (प्रिस्क्राइब) ***v.*** 1. to set down as a rule, नियम के रूप में निर्धारित करना। 2. to recommend, सिफ़ारिश करना, आवश्यक बतलाना।

3. to advise the use of a medicine, नुस्ख़ा लिखना।

prescribed (प्रिस्क्राइब्ड) ***adj.*** that has to be followed, studied etc., निर्धारित।

prescription (प्रिस्क्रिप्शन) ***n.*** 1. the act of prescribing, निर्धारण। 2. a written instruction, लिखित आदेश या नुस्ख़ा।

presence (प्रेज़न्स) ***n.*** 1. the state of being present, उपस्थिति, मौजूदगी, विद्यमानता। 2. one that is present, attendance, हाज़िरी, उपस्थिति। 3. person's bearing, व्यक्तित्व।

present[1] (प्रेज़न्ट) ***adj.*** 1. in attendance, उपस्थित, हाज़िर। 2. existing, विद्यमान, वर्तमान। 3. now being discussed, जिसकी चर्चा हो रही हो। 4. (gram.) of present tense, वर्तमानकालिक। ***n.*** 1. the present time, वर्तमान। 2. (gram.) the present tense, वर्तमान काल।

present[2] (प्रिज़ेन्ट) ***v.*** 1. to offer formally, भेंट करना, प्रदान करना। 2. to show, दिखाना, प्रस्तुत करना। 3. to act, अभिनय करना। 4. to appear, उपस्थित होना।

presentable (प्रिज़ेन्टेबल) ***adj.*** 1. fit to be presented, भेंट करने के योग्य। 2. fit to be displayed, प्रस्तुत करने के योग्य, प्रस्तुति के योग्य, प्रस्तुत्य।

presentation (प्रेज़न्टेशन) ***n.*** 1. the act of presenting or the state of being presented, प्रदान। 2. a gift, उपहार, भेंट। 3. a preformance of a play, प्रस्तुति, प्रस्तुतीकरण। 4. the formal introduction, उपस्थापन।

presently (प्रेज़न्टली) ***adv.*** 1. in the present time, आजकल, इन दिनों, संप्रति। 2. in a short time, soon, थोड़ी ही देर में, जल्दी।

preservation (प्रेज़र्वेशन) ***n.*** the act of preserving, हिफ़ाज़त, सुरक्षा, परिरक्षण।

preservative (प्रिज़र्वेटिव) ***n.*** a chemical added to foods to preserve them, खाद्य पदार्थों को परिरक्षित रखनेवाला रासायनिक पदार्थ।

preserve (प्रिज़र्व) ***v.*** 1. to keep safe, to protect, हिफ़ाज़त से रखना, रक्षा करना, परिरक्षण करना। 2. to maintain, keep up, बनाए रखना। 3. to protect from decay or fermentation, (खाद्य वस्तु को) सड़ने-गलने या विकृत होने से बचाना, परिरक्षण करना। ***n.*** 1. preserved fruit, jam, मुरब्बा, जैम। 2. an area reserved for some activity, परिरक्षित क्षेत्र।

preside (प्रिज़ाइड) ***v.*** 1. to chair the meeting, अध्यक्षता करना। 2. to exercise authority, अधिकार का प्रयोग करना, नियंत्रित करना।

presidency (प्रेज़िडेन्सी) ***n.*** 1. the office of a president, राष्ट्रपति का पद। 2. the term of a president, राष्ट्रपति का कार्यकाल। 3. province, प्रांत।

president (प्रेज़िडेन्ट) ***n.*** 1. the head of a company or institution, अध्यक्ष, प्रधान। 2. the head of a republic, राष्ट्रपति।

presiding (प्रिज़ाइडिंग) ***adj.*** taking charge of a meeting, office etc, पीठासीन।

presidium (प्रिसिडिअम) ***n.*** a powerful committee as a governing body, प्रधान परिषद, प्रेसीडियम।

press (प्रेस) ***v.*** 1. to apply weight or force, दबाना, ज़ोर लगाना। 2. to squeeze, निचोड़ना। 3. to iron (the clothes, कपड़ों को) इस्त्री

P

करना। 4. to throng closely, भीड़ लगाना। 5. to carry on, चलाए चलना, लगे रहना। □ **be pressed for,** कमी अनुभूत होना। ***n.*** 1. a machine for applying pressure, कोल्हू। 2. a printing machine, छपाई मशीन। 3. a printing establishment, प्रेस-प्रतिष्ठान। 4. newspapers and magazines, समाचार-पत्र तथा पत्रिकाएँ। 5. the act of applying pressure, दबाव। 6. setting of proper crease in a garment, इस्त्री करना। □ **go to press,** छपने जाना।

press conference ***n.*** an interview held for newsmen, पत्रकार-सम्मेलन।

pressing (प्रेसिंग) ***adj.*** 1 urgent, अत्यावश्यक, निहायत ज़रूरी। 2. persisting, आग्रहपूर्ण।

press release ***n.*** information given to the press, प्रेस-विज्ञप्ति।

pressure (प्रेशर) ***n.*** 1. the exertion of force, दबाव, दाब। 2. influence, प्रभाव, दबाव।

pressure group ***n.*** a group that exerts pressure on the members of a legislature to advance its interests, प्रभावी दल।

pressurize (प्रेशराइज़) ***v.*** 1. to keep (a cabin) at a constant atmospheric pressure, वायु का एक सा दबाव बनाए रखना। 2. to increase or apply pressure to, दबाव डालना या बढ़ाना।

prestige (प्रेस्टीज) ***n.*** reputation, प्रतिष्ठा।

prestigious (प्रेस्टिजस) ***adj.*** renowned, प्रतिष्ठापूर्ण।

presto (प्रेस्टो) ***adv.*** (music) quickly, द्रुतगति से।

presumably (प्रिज़्यूमेबली) ***adv.*** in all likelihood or probability, संभाव्यतः, अनुमानतः।

presume (प्रिज़्यूम) ***v.*** 1. to take for granted, मान लेना, अनुमान कर लेना। 2. to dare, धृष्टता करना।

presumption (प्रिज़म्प्शन) ***n.*** the act of presuming or something presumed, अनुमान, प्रकल्पना।

presumptuous (प्रिज़म्प्चुअस) ***adj.*** bold, impudent, अक्खड़, ढीठ, धृष्ट।

presuppose (प्रिसपोज़) ***v.*** 1. to take for granted, पहले से मान लेना। 2. to require as a necessary prior condition, की अपेक्षा रखना।

pretence, pretense (प्रिटेन्स) ***n.*** 1. a pretext, बहाना, हीला। 2. a false action to deceive, ढोंग।

pretend (प्रिटेन्ड) ***v.*** 1. to create a false appearance of something, ढोंग रचना। 2. to make a claim, दावा करना।

pretension (प्रिटेन्शन) ***n.*** 1. a false claim, झूठा दावा। 2. an unfounded allegation, झूठा आरोप। 3. outward show, आडंबर, दिखावा।

pretext (प्रीटेक्स्ट) ***n.*** a pretence, बहाना।

prettify (प्रेटिफ़ाइ) ***v.*** to make pretty, आकर्षक बनाना।

pretty (प्रिटी) ***adj.*** 1. pleasing in a graceful way, कमनीय, मनोहर, रमणीय। 2. excellent, fine, उत्तम, बढ़िया। ***adv.*** fairly, बहुत कुछ, एक सीमा तक।

prevail (प्रिवेल) ***v.*** 1. to win out, to succeed, अभिभूत कर लेना, जीत जाना। 2. to be common or frequent, व्याप्त या प्रचलित होना। □ **prevail on or upon,** राजी कर लेना, मना लेना।

prevailing (प्रिवेलिंग) ***adj.*** prevalent, प्रचलित, व्याप्त।

prevalent (प्रेवेलेन्ट) ***adj.*** current, existing and widespread, प्रचलित, चालू, व्याप्त।

prevent (प्रिवेन्ट) ***v.*** 1. to keep from doing something, (कोई काम) न करने देना। 2. to keep from happening, रोक-थाम करना, निवारण करना।

prevention (प्रिवेन्शन) ***n.*** the act of preventing, रोक, रोक-थाम, निवारण, परहेज़।

preventive (प्रिवेन्टिव) ***adj.*** preventing something (sply. disease), रोकनेवाला, निरोधक, निवारक।

previous (प्रीविअस) ***adj.*** 1. coming before in time, पहले का, पहला। 2. coming before in order, पिछला, पूर्व, पूर्ववर्ती।

prey (प्रे) ***n.*** 1. an animal or bird hunted or caught, शिकार। 2. one who is injured, harmed or cheated, victim शिकार। ***v.*** 1. to take as a prey, शिकार करना। 2. to rob, लूटना।

price(प्राइस) ***n.*** the amount of money asked or given for something, क़ीमत, दाम, मूल्य।

priceless (प्राइसलिस) ***adj.*** invaluable, अनमोल, अमूल्य।

prick (प्रिक) ***v.*** 1. to pierce slightly, चुभाना, गोदना, वेधना। 2. to goad, कचोटना, सालना। 3. to feel pricking sensation, चुभन होना। ☐ **prick up one's ears,** कान खड़े होना, सहसा सावधान होना। ***n.*** 1. a hole, छेद, सुराख। 2. pricking sensation, चुभन। 3. a pain caused by being pricked, कचोट, टीस।

prickle (प्रिकल) ***v.*** 1. to prick, चुभाना। 2. to feel or give pricking sensation, चुभन होना, गोदना। ***n.*** a small thorns, काँटा।

prickly (प्रिक्ली) ***adj.*** 1. having thorns, कँटीला, काँटेदार। 2. pricking, itching, काँटे की तरह चुभनेवाला। 3. irritable, चिड़चिड़ा।

prickly heat ***n.*** an acute itching irruption of the skin, पित्ती, पित्त, गर्मी दाना, अम्होरी।

pride (प्राइड) ***n.*** 1. unduly high opinion of one's merits, घमंड, अहंकार, अभिमान। 2. self-respect, गर्व, गौरव, आत्मसम्मान।

priest (प्रीस्ट) ***n.*** a clergyman, पादरी, याजक, पुरोहित, पुजारी। [Fem. priestess]

prig (प्रिग) ***n.*** a smug, दंभी व्यक्ति।

prim (प्रिम) ***adj.*** fastidious, तुनुकमिज़ाज, दंभी।

primacy (प्राइमेसी) ***n.*** supremacy, श्रेष्ठता, प्रमुखता, प्रधानता।

prima facie (प्राइमा फेसी) ***adv.*** as it seems at first, ऊपर से देखने पर, प्रत्यक्षत:।

primal (प्राइमल) ***adj.*** 1. original, first, आदिम, आद्य। 2. most important, सबसे महत्त्वपूर्ण।

primary (प्राइमरी) ***adj.*** 1. initial, first in the series, प्राथमिक, प्रारंभिक। 2. basic, fundamental, मौलिक, मूलभूत।

prime (प्राइम) ***adj.*** 1. first, पहला, प्रथम। 2. main, chief, प्रधान, मुख्य, मूल। 3. (maths.) (number) that can be divided exactly only by itself, अभाज्य, रूढ़। ***n.*** 1. the state of greatest perfection, परिपूर्णता। 2. the best part, उत्तम भाग। ***v.*** 1. to prepare, to make ready, तैयारी करना,

तैयार करना। 2. to brief, अवगत कराना।

primer (प्राइमर) ***n.*** 1. an elementary or introductory text book, प्रवेशिका। 2. a paint applied to surface at base, पहला अस्तर।

primeval (प्राइमीवल) ***adj.*** of the earliest times, आद्य, आदिकालीन।

primitive (प्रिमिटिव) ***adj.*** 1. of earliest times, आदिम, आदिकालीन। 2. old, ancient, प्राचीन, पुरातन। 3. crude, अनगढ़, अपरिष्कृत।

primordial (प्राइमॉर्डिअल) ***adj.*** primitive, आदिकालीन।

prince (प्रिन्स) ***n.*** 1. a son of a sovereign, राजकुमार। 2. a ruler, छोटी-मोटी रियासत का राजा, नरेश।

princely (प्रिन्स्ली) ***adj.*** 1. royal, राजसी, शाही, शानदार, प्रतापपूर्ण। 2. generous, उदार।

princess (प्रिन्सेस) ***n.*** a female member of a royal family, राजकुमारी।

principal (प्रिन्सिपल) ***adj.*** chief, main, प्रधान, मुख्य। ***n.*** 1. the head of a college, प्रिंसिपल, प्रधानाचार्य। 2. capital, मूलधन। 3. a person who plays the leading role, (किसी नाटक का) मुख्य कलाकार।

principle (प्रिन्सिपल) ***n.*** 1. a rule, सिद्धांत, नियम। 2. a basic source, मूल तत्त्व, आधारभूत कारण। 3. a basic truth, मूल सत्य। 4. a policy, नीति।

print (प्रिन्ट) ***v.*** 1. to make a mark by pressing or stamping, ठप्पा लगाना। 2. to make marks by types or machine, छापना, मुद्रण करना। ***n.*** 1. a mark made by pressure or stamping, ठप्पा, छाप। 2. lettering produced in ink, छपाई, मुद्रण। 3. a design or picture reproduced by printing, छाप, छपाई। 4. a fabric with a stamped dyed pattern, छींट।

printer (प्रिन्टर) ***n.*** 1. one who prints, मुद्रक। 2. a machine that prints, छपाई मशीन, मुद्रण-यंत्र, प्रिंटर।

printout (प्रिन्टआउट) ***n.*** material produced in printed form from a printer, प्रिंटर से निकली छपी प्रति।

prior (प्राइअर) ***adj.*** 1. previous, पूर्व, पूर्ववर्ती। 2. taking precedence in order or importance, अग्र, वरीय।

priority (प्राइऑरिटी) ***n.*** the state of being prior, पूर्ववर्तिता; अग्रता, वरीयता।

priory (प्राइअरी) ***n.*** a monastery, ईसाई मठ।

prism (प्रिज़म) ***n.*** a triangular body of glass that breaks up light into a spectrum, समपार्श्व, प्रिज़्म।

prison (प्रिज़न) ***n.*** a building used to confine convicted criminals, बंदीगृह, कारागार, क़ैदखाना।

prisoner (प्रिज़नर) ***n.*** a person kept in a prison, बंदी, क़ैदी।

pristine (प्रिस्टीन) ***adj*** 1. primitive, आदिम, आद्य। 2. new, नया, नूतन।

privacy (प्राइवेसी) ***n.*** the condition of being secluded, एकांत, एकांतता, एकांतवास।

private (प्राइवेट) ***adj.*** 1. own, निजी, स्वकीय। 2. personal, वैयक्तिक, व्यक्तिगत। 3. not holding a public office, ग़ैर-सरकारी, अराजकीय। ***n.*** a soldier, सिपाही, सैनिक।

privation (प्राइवेशन) ***n.*** lack of the necessities of life, जीवन की आवश्यकताओं अथवा सुख-सुविधाओं का अभाव।

privatize (प्राइवेटाइज़) ***v.*** to transfer something from state centrol to private ownership, (उद्योगों का) निजीकरण करना।

privilege (प्रिवलिज) *n.* a special right, विशेषाधिकार।

privileged (प्रिवलिज्ड) *adj.* having a privilege, विशेषाधिकार-प्राप्त।

privy (प्रिवी) *adj.* (privier, priviest) secret, गुप्त, प्रच्छन्न। *n.* a latrine, शौचालय।

prize (प्राइज़) *n.* 1. something offered or won as an award, पुरस्कार, इनाम। 2. something striven for, अभीप्सित वस्तु, नेमत। *v.* to value highly, अत्यधिक महत्त्व देना।

pro[1] (प्रो) *n.* 1. supporter, समर्थक। 2. a favourable argument, अनुकूल तर्क। ☐ **the pros and cons,** किसी बात के पक्ष तथा विपक्ष में होनेवाले तर्क, तर्क-वितर्क। *adv.* in favour, पक्ष में।

pro[2] *pref.* in front of, सामने।

probability (प्रॉबेबिलिटी) *n.* 1. the condition of being probable, प्रायिकता, संभावना। 2. a probable event, संभावित घटना।

probable (प्रॉबेबल) *adj.* likely to happen, संभावित, प्रायिक, संभाव्य।

probate (प्रोबेट) *n.* a certificate stating a will to be genuine, वसीयतनामे का प्रमाणपत्र।

probation (प्रोबेशन) *n.* 1. a trial of person's character or ability, आचरण या योग्यता का परीक्षण, परिवीक्षा। 2. a trial period, परिवीक्षा-अवधि।

probationer (प्रोबेशनर) *n.* a person on probation, जिसकी परिवीक्षा चल रही हो, परिवीक्षार्थी, परिवीक्षाधीन।

probe (प्रोब) *n.* 1. a surgical instrument for exploring a wound, वह सलाई जिससे डॉक्टर घाव आदि देखते-परखते हैं, शलाका। 2. the act of probing or investigating, जाँच, परख, अनुसंधान। *v.* 1. to explore with a probe, शलाका से देखना-परखना। 2. to investigate, जाँच-पड़ताल करना।

probity (प्रोबिटी) *n.* integrity, honesty, सत्यनिष्ठा, ईमानदारी।

problem (प्रॉब्लम) *n.* 1. a question or situation that presents difficulty or uncertainty, समस्या। 2. a question put forward for solution, प्रश्न, सवाल।

problematic (प्रॉब्लमैटिक) *adj.* 1. having the nature of a problem, समस्यात्मक, समस्यापूर्ण, जटिल। 2. uncertain, संदिग्ध, अनिश्चित।

procedure (प्रसीजर) *n.* 1. a way or course of action, कार्यविधि, कार्य-पद्धति, क्रिया-प्रणाली। 2. a particular or established way of doing something, विशिष्ट विधि, बँधा व्यवहार।

proceed (प्रोसीड) *v.* 1. to advance or carry on, अग्रसर होना, आगे बढ़ना, जारी रखना। 2. to arise, उत्पन्न होना, खड़ा होना। ☐ **proceed against,** (किसी के विरुद्ध) मुक़दमा दायर करना।

proceeding (प्रसीडिंग) *n.* 1. a course of action, procedure, कार्रवाई, कार्यवाही, कार्यविवरण। 2. (plu.) transactions of an organization, अर्थागम। 3. legal action, क़ानूनी कार्रवाई।

proceeds (प्रोसीड्ज़) *n.* (plu.) 1. the amount of money derived from a commercial firm or fund raising venture, बिक्री या चंदे से प्राप्त धन, अर्थागम, आय, आमदनी। 2. profit, लाभ।

process (प्रोसेस) *n.* 1. a method of doing something, क्रिया-पद्धति,

P

प्रक्रिया, प्रक्रमण। 2. a series of natural changes, घटनाचक्र, समयचक्र। 3. a law suit, मुक़दमा। ***v.*** 1. to subject to a special process, अनेक प्रक्रियाओं द्वारा कोई वस्तु तैयार करना। 2. to serve a process on, (पर) कार्रवाई करना। 3. (computer) to perform operations to obtain required information, अपेक्षित सूचना प्राप्त करने के लिए विशिष्ट प्रक्रियाएँ करना, संसाधित करना।

procession (प्रसेशन) ***n.*** a group of persons or vehicles moving forward in a formal manner, जुलूस, शोभायात्रा।

proclaim (प्रोक्लेम) ***v.*** 1. to announce officially, एलान करना। 2. to announce publicly, सार्वजनिक घोषणा करना, उद्‌घोषणा करना।

proclamation (प्रॉक्लमेशन) ***n.*** an official announcement, ऐलान, उद्‌घोषणा।

procreate (प्रोक्रिएट) ***v.*** produce or beget, पैदा करना, प्रजनन करना।

procreation (प्रोक्रिएशन) ***n.*** the act of procreating, प्रजनन।

procure (प्रोक्योर) ***v.*** 1. to obtain, प्राप्त करना। 2. to obtain women to act as prostitutes, (औरतों की) दलाली करना।

procurement (प्रक्योरमेन्ट) ***n.*** act of procuring, प्रापण, प्राप्ति।

procurer (प्रक्योरर) ***n.*** 1. one who obtains, प्राप्त करने या करानेवाला, प्रापणकर्ता। 2. a pimp, (औरतों का) दलाल।

prod (प्रॉड) ***v.*** 1. to poke with a pointed instrument, कोंचना, तंग करना। 2. to stir, प्रेरित करना, उकसाना। ***n.*** a pointed instrument, अंकुश।

prodigal (प्रॉडिगल) ***adj.*** 1. extravagant, अपव्ययी, फ़िज़ूलख़र्च। 2. lavish, मुक्तहस्त, उदार।

prodigious (प्रडिजिअस) ***adj.*** amazing, आश्चर्यजनक।

prodigy (प्रॉडिजी) ***n.*** a young person with remarkable abilities, असाधारण प्रतिभाशाली युवक।

produce (प्रोड्यूस) ***v.*** 1. to yield, उत्पन्न करना। 2. to bear crops from the ground to manufacture (goods), उत्पादन करना। 3. to give birth to, बच्चे देना, पैदा करना। 4. to make, बनाना, रचना। 5. to present, प्रस्तुत/पेश करना। ***n.*** 1. yield, उपज, पैदावार। 2. production, product, उत्पादन, उत्पाद।

producer (प्रड्यूसर) ***n.*** one who produces, उत्पादक, (फ़िल्म आदि का) निर्माता, प्रस्तुतकर्ता।

product (प्रॉडक्ट) ***n.*** 1. something produced, उत्पाद, उपज, पैदावार। 2. (maths.) the result of the multiplication of two or more quantities, गुणनफल।

production (प्रडक्शन) ***n.*** 1. the act of producing, उत्पादन। 2. something produced, उपज, पैदावार। 3. the presentation of a play, नाटक की प्रस्तुति, प्रस्तुतीकरण।

productive (प्रडक्टिव) ***adj.*** producing abundantly, ख़ूब उत्पादन करनेवाला, उत्पादक।

profess (प्रोफ़ेस) ***v.*** 1. to acknowledge or admit, स्वीकार करना। 2. to declare, घोषणा करना, जतलाना। 3. to claim, दावा करना। 4. to affirm one's faith in a religion, धर्म में विश्वास प्रकट करना।

professed (प्रफ़ेस्ड) ***adj.*** 1. declared,

घोषित। 2. acknowledged, माना हुआ। 3. having taken the vow, प्रतिज्ञाबद्ध। 4. falsely claiming to be something, झूठा दावा करनेवाला।

profession (प्रफ़ेशन) ***n.*** 1. calling, business, पेशा, व्यवसाय, वृत्ति। 2. a declaration or avowal, अपनी धारणा, विश्वास या निष्ठा का प्रकटन।

professional (प्रफ़ेशनल) ***adj.*** of profession or engaged in a profession, जो किसी पेशे में लगा हो, व्यावसायिक, वृत्तिक, पेशेवर। ***n.*** a person following a profession, किसी पेशे में लगा हुआ व्यक्ति, पेशेवर व्यक्ति।

professor (प्रफ़ेसर) ***n.*** a university teacher, प्राध्यापक, आचार्य, प्रोफ़ेसर।

proffer (प्रॉफ़र) ***v.*** to offer, अर्पित करना, देना। ***n.*** an offer, अर्पण, नज़र, भेंट।

proficiency (प्रफ़िशन्सी) ***n.*** the state or quality of being proficient, dexterity, competence, प्रवीणता, निपुणता।

proficient (प्रफ़िशन्ट) ***adj.*** expert in an art, dexterous, प्रवीण, निपुण।

profile (प्रोफ़ाइल) ***adv.*** 1. a side view of a person or thing, पार्श्वचित्र, पार्श्वदृश्य। 2. outline, रेखाचित्र, रूपरेखा। 3. a short account of a person's character or career, संक्षिप्त चरित्र-चित्रण, संक्षिप्त जीवनी, चारित्रिक लेख, ख़ाका।

profit (प्रॉफ़िट) ***n.*** 1. gain, लाभ, मुनाफ़ा, फ़ायदा। 2. benefit, advantage, हित, क़ल्याण, भला, भलाई। ***v.*** to obtain or bring an advantage, लाभ प्राप्त करना, फ़ायदा होना, भलाई होना।

profitably (प्रॉफ़िटेबली) ***adv.*** in a profitable manner, लाभ प्राप्त करते हुए।

profiteer (प्रॉफ़िटिअर) ***n.*** one who makes excessive profits, मुनाफ़ाख़ोर।

profligate (प्रॉफ़्लिगेट) ***adj.*** 1. extravagant, अपव्ययी। 2. abandoned to vice, लंपट, अनाचारी।

profound (प्रफ़ाउन्ड) ***adj.*** 1. very deep, अत्यंत गहरा, गंभीर, अथाह। 2. deeply felt, अत्यंत गहरा, हार्दिक। 3. marked by intellectual depth, प्रभूत, प्रकांड।

profundity (प्रफ़न्डिटी) ***n.*** the state or quality of being profound, गंभीरता; हार्दिकता; प्रभुता।

profuse (प्रफ़्यूज़) ***adj.*** 1. plentiful, विपुल, प्रचुर, अत्यधिक। 2. generous, मुक्तहस्त।

profusion (प्रफ़्यूज़न) ***n.*** 1. abundance, प्रचुरता। 2. generosity, उदारता।

progenitor (प्रोजेनिटर) ***n.*** 1. a father or founder, प्रजननकर्ता, प्रजनक, प्रतिष्ठापक। 2. an ancestor, पूर्वपुरुष, पुरखा, पूर्वज।

progeny (प्रॉजनी) ***n.*** children, descendants, संतान, संतति।

programme, program (प्रोग्रैम) ***n.*** a list of procedures, कार्यक्रम, प्रोग्राम। ***v.*** to design as a programme, कार्यक्रम बनाना।

progress (प्रॉग्रेस) ***n.*** steady advance or improvement, प्रगति। ***v.*** to move toward perfection, प्रगति करना।

progression (प्रग्रेशन) ***n.*** 1. advance, progress, प्रगति। 2. sequence, प्रगति-क्रम, सिलसिला, अनुक्रम।

progressive (प्रग्रेसिव) ***adj.*** 1. pertaining to progress, प्रगामी। 2. successive, क्रमिक, उत्तरोत्तर। 3. favour-ing social or political reforms, प्रगतिशील। ***n.*** one who favours a progressive policy, प्रगतिवादी, सुधारवादी।

P

prohibit (प्रोहिबिट) ***n.*** 1. to forbid by authority, निषेध करना, निषिद्ध करना। 2. to prevent, रोकना।

prohibition (प्रोहिबिशन) ***n.*** 1. the act of prohibiting, निषेध, मनाही। 2. forbiding by law the cousumption of a alcoholic beverages, मद्यनिषेध।

prohibitory (प्रोहिबिटरी) ***adj.*** intending to prohibit, निषेधात्मक।

project[1] (प्रॉजेक्ट) ***n.*** a scheme or plan, परियोजना।

project[2] (प्रजेक्ट) ***v.*** 1. to cast or throw outward, प्रक्षिप्त करना, प्रक्षेपण करना, फेंकना। 2. to extend outward, बाहर निकालना या बढ़ाना। 3. to cause an image to appear, छायाचित्र बनाना। 4. to present, प्रस्तुत करना, चित्रित करना।

projectile (प्रजेक्टाइल) ***adj.*** that can be projected, प्रक्षेप्य। ***n.*** a missile, प्रक्षेप्यास्त्र।

projection (प्रजेक्शन) ***n.*** 1. a thing that is projected, झाँप। 2. act of projecting, प्रक्षेपण। 3. the process of showing film on a screen, पर्दे पर फ़िल्म का प्रदर्शन, छायाचित्रण।

projector (प्रजेक्टर) ***n.*** an instument that shows film on a screen, प्रोजेक्टर, प्रक्षेपित्र (यंत्र)।

prolapse (प्रोलैप्स) ***v.*** to slip out of place, (अंग का अपने स्थान से) खिसक जाना।

proletariat (प्रोलिटेरिअट) ***n.*** all wage-earners collectively, श्रम-जीवियों का वर्ग, सर्वहारा वर्ग।

proliferate (प्रोलिफ़रेट) ***v.*** to increase in numbers or reproduce rapidly, तेज़ी से संख्या में बढ़ना या संतान उत्पन्न करना।

proliferation (प्रोलिफ़रेशन) ***n.*** the act of proliferating, बहुप्रजनन।

prologue (प्रोलॉग) ***n.*** an introduction (to a play, नाटक की) भूमिका।

prolong (प्रलॉन्ग) ***v.*** to lengthen in extent, विस्तार देना, लंबा करना, दीर्घ बनाना, खींचना।

prolongation (प्रोलॉन्गेशन) ***n.*** the act of prolonging, दीर्घीकरण।

promenade (प्रॉमिनेड) ***n.*** 1. a leisurely walk, stroll, सैर, चहलक़दमी। 2. a place for strolling, सैरगाह विशेषत: तटपथ। ***v.*** to stroll, टहलना, घूमना, सैर करना।

prominence (प्रॉमिनेन्स) ***n.*** the state of being prominent, प्रमुखता, प्रधानता।

prominent (प्रॉमिनेन्ट) ***n.*** 1. eminent, प्रमुख, प्रधान। 2. well-known, लब्धप्रतिष्ठ, महत्त्वशाली। 3. projecting, बाहर निकला हुआ, प्रक्षिप्त। 4. conspicuous, स्पष्ट, सुव्यक्त।

promiscuity (प्रमिस्क्यूइटी) ***n.*** the quality or state of being promiscuous, लंपटपना, घाल-मेल।

promiscuous (प्रमिस्क्युअस) ***adj.*** 1. having sexual relations with many persons, लंपट, स्वच्छंदाचारी। 2. indiscriminate, अविवेकी। 3. jumbled, गड्ड-मड्ड।

promise (प्रॉमिस) ***n.*** 1. a commitment, an undertaking, वचन, वादा, प्रतिज्ञा। 2. an assurance, आश्वासन, आशा, प्रत्याशा। ***v.*** 1. to give an undertaking, वचन देना, वादा करना। 2. to assure, विश्वास दिलाना, आश्वासन देना। 3. to hold out a hope, आशा बँधाना।

promising (प्रॉमिसिंग) ***adj.*** 1. full of promise, आशाजनक। 2. up and coming होनहार, उदीयमान।

promote (प्रमोट) ***v.*** 1. to raise in position or rank, पदोन्नत करना, दर्जा चढ़ाना। 2. to further, आगे बढ़ाना। 3. to advocate or publicize, प्रचारित करना।

promoter (प्रमोटर) ***n.*** one who promotes, प्रोत्साहक, संवर्धक।

promotion (प्रमोशन) ***n.*** 1. the act of promoting or the state of being promoted, पदोन्नति, तरक़्क़ी, पदवृद्धि। 2. publicity, प्रचार, बढ़ावा, प्रोत्साहन।

prompt (प्रॉम्प्ट) ***adj.*** 1. swift, quick, त्वरित, सत्वर, तात्कालिक, अविलंब। 2. punctual, समयनिष्ठ। ***v.*** 1. to urge or encourage, प्रेरित/प्रोत्साहित करना। 2. to help or suggest, सहायता या सुझाव देना।

promptness (प्रॉम्प्टनिस) ***n.*** swiftness, quickness, तत्परता, शीघ्रता, सत्वरता।

promulgate (प्रॉमल्गेट) ***v.*** to put into effect by formal declaration, घोषणा द्वारा कोई नियम लागू करना, प्रख्यापन करना।

promulgation (प्रॉमल्गेशन) ***n.*** the act of promulgating, प्रख्यापन।

prone (प्रोन) ***adj.*** 1. having a tendency, inclined, उन्मुख, प्रवण, प्रवृत्त। 2. lying with the face downward, अधोमुख, औंधा।

prong (प्रॉन्ग) ***n.*** one of the sharply pointed end of fork, काँटे का कोई सिरा।

pronged (प्रॉन्ड) ***adj.*** having prongs, नुकीले सिरों वाला।

pronoun (प्रोनाउन) ***n.*** a substitute for a noun, सर्वनाम।

pronounce (प्रनाउन्स) ***v.*** 1. to utter, उच्चारण करना। 2. to declare officially, घोषणा करना।

pronounced (प्रनाउन्स्ड) ***adj.*** 1. uttered, उच्चारित। 2. definite, एकदम स्पष्ट।

pronunciation (प्रनन्सिएशन) ***n.*** the act or manner of pronouncing sounds, उच्चारण।

proof (प्रूफ़) ***n.*** 1. the evidence that helps to show the truth or validity of something, प्रमाण, सबूत। 2. a trial impression of printed matter, प्रूफ़। ***adj.*** able to resist, fully resistant, -सह; waterproof, जलसह।

prop (प्रॉप) ***n.*** a support used to keep something from falling, टेक, थूनी, आश्रय, सहारा। ***v.*** to support, सहारा देकर खड़ा करना, सहारा देना।

propaganda (प्रॉपेगैन्डा) ***n.*** publicity, प्रचार, प्रोपेगैंडा।

propagate (प्रॉपेगेट) ***v.*** 1. to publicize, प्रचार करना। 2. to broadcast, प्रसारित करना। 3. to reproduce or breed, उपजाना, उपजाकर बढ़ाना।

propagation (प्रॉपेगेशन) ***n.*** 1. the act of propagating, प्रसारण। 2. publicity, प्रचार, प्रचार। 3. procreation, प्रजनन।

propel (प्रपेल) ***v.*** 1. to cause to continue in motion, to drive, आगे बढ़ाना, चलाना, नोदन करना। 2. to impel, उकसाना, बढ़ावा देना, ठेलना।

propellant, propellent (प्रपेलेन्ट) ***n.*** that propels, नोदक।

propeller (प्रपेलर) ***n.*** a device that propels something, (पोत या वायुयान का) नोदक।

propensity (प्रपेन्सिटी) ***n.*** tendency or inclination, प्रवृत्ति या झुकाव।

proper (प्रॉपर) ***adj*** 1. appropriate, suitable, उचित, समुचित। 2. correct, right, सही। 3. in the strict sense of a word, सही अर्थवाला, ठीक; proper city, ठीक शहर।

proper noun ***n.*** the name of a

P

particular person, place etc., व्यक्तिवाचक संज्ञा।

property (प्रॉपर्टी) ***n.*** 1. a thing owned, holding, संपत्ति, जायदाद। 2. ownership, स्वामित्व। 3. characteristic quality, गुण, गुणधर्म।

prophecy (प्रॉफ़ेसी) ***n.*** a forecast or prediction, भविष्यवाणी।

prophesy (प्रॉफ़ेसाइ) ***v.*** to foretell, भविष्यवाणी करना।

prophet (प्रॉफ़िट) ***adj.*** 1. a divinely inspired teacher, पैग़ंबर। 2. one who foretells, भविष्यवक्ता।

prophylactic (प्रोफ़िलैक्टिक) ***adj.*** 1. preventing disease, रोग-निरोधी। 2. preventing misfortune, दुर्भाग्य-निवारक।

propitiate (प्रपिशिएट) ***v.*** to placate, शांत करना, राज़ी करना।

propitiation (प्रपिशिएशन) ***n.*** the act of propitiating, प्रशमन, शांत करना।

propitious (प्रपिशस) ***adj.*** 1. auspicious or favourable, शुभ या अनुकूल। 2. kind, generous, favourable, कृपालु, दयालु, उदार।

proponent (प्रपोनेन्ट) ***n.*** a supporter, समर्थक।

proportion (प्रपोर्शन) ***n.*** 1. a ratio or correct relationship, सही अनुपात या संबंध, समानुपात। 2. a part or share, अंश।

proportional (प्रपोर्शनल) ***adj.*** in correct proportion, समानुपातिक, समानुपाती।

proportionate (प्रपोर्शनेट) ***adj.*** proportional, सही अनुपात में होनेवाला, समानुपातिक।

proposal (प्रपोज़ल) ***n.*** 1. a plan or offer presented for acceptance or consideration, प्रस्ताव। 2. an offer of a marriage, विवाह-प्रस्ताव।

propose (प्रपोज़) ***v.*** 1. to put forward, प्रस्तुत या पेश करना। 2. to recommend or nominate, परामर्श देना, संस्तुति करना या नामांकित करना। 3. to make an offer (of marriage, विवाह का) प्रस्ताव करना।

proposer (प्रपोज़र) ***n.*** one who proposes, प्रस्तावक।

proposition (प्रॉपज़िशन) ***n.*** 1. a proposal, प्रस्ताव। 2. a subject for discussion, विचारार्थ विषय। ***v.*** to make a (sexual) proposal, (संभोग का) प्रस्ताव करना।

propound (प्रपाउन्ड) ***v.*** to put forward for consideration, विचारार्थ प्रस्तुत करना।

proprietary (प्रप्राइटरी) ***adj.*** belonging to a proprietor, मालिकाना, स्वामीय।

proprietor (प्रप्राइटर) ***n.*** an owner, मालिक, स्वामी।

propriety (प्रप्राइटी) ***n.*** appropriateness, fitness, औचित्य, मर्यादा, सही रंग-ढंग।

propulsion (प्रपल्शन) ***n.*** 1. the act of propelling, आगे बढ़ाने की क्रिया या भाव, नोदन। 2. the force of propelling, नोदन-शक्ति।

pro rata (प्रो राटा) ***adv.*** in proportion, यथानुपात। ***adj.*** proportional, आनुपातिक।

prorogation (प्रोरोगेशन) ***n.*** an act of proroguing, सत्रावसान।

prorogue (प्रोरोग) ***v.*** to discontinue or end the session (of the legislature), सत्रावसान करना।

prosaic (प्रोज़ेइक) ***adj.*** 1. dull, शुष्क। 2. lacking imagination or interest, कल्पनाविहीन या अरोचक।

proscribe (प्रोस्क्राइब) ***v.*** to prohibit or outlaw, निषिद्ध करना, ग़ैरकानूनी ठहराना।

prose (प्रोज़) ***n.*** written or spoken language different from poetry, गद्य। ***adj.*** 1. of prose or in prose, गद्यात्मक। 2. dull, नीरस।

prosecute (प्रॉसिक्यूट) ***v.*** 1. to bring a criminal charge or action against, मुक़दमा चलाना, अभियोजन करना। 2. to continue to do, जारी/चालू रखना।

prosecution (प्रॉसिक्यूशन) ***n.*** 1. the act of prosecuting or the state of being prosecuted, मुक़दमा, अभियोजन। 2. the prosecution, the party prosecuting another for the crime, अभियोजन-पक्ष।

prosecutor (प्रॉसिक्यूटर) ***n.*** one who prosecutes, अभियोक्ता।

prosody (प्रॉसडी) ***n.*** the study of metrical structures of verse छंदशास्त्र।

prospect (प्रॉस्पेक्ट) ***n.*** 1. a probability of future success, आसार, लक्षण। 2. (plu.) chances, सुयोग।

prospective (प्रस्पेक्टिव) ***adj.*** expected, probable, जिसके आसार हों, संभावित, प्रत्याशित।

prospectus (प्रस्पेक्टस) ***n.*** a printed document outlining the main features of a business venture or a forthcoming project, विवरण-पत्रिका, विवरणिका।

prosper (प्रॉस्पर) ***v.*** to thrive or flourish, फूलना-फलना, पनपना।

prosperity (प्रॉस्पेरिटी) ***n.*** the state of being prosperous, समृद्धि, सुख-समृद्धि।

prosperous (प्रॉस्परस) ***adj.*** flourishing or well-off, समृद्ध, संपन्न, ख़ुशहाल।

prostate gland (प्रॉस्टेट ग्लैन्ड) ***n.*** a gland in the male mammals, पुरस्थ ग्रंथि।

prostitute (प्रॉस्टिट्यूट) ***n.*** a woman who engages in sexual intercourse for money, वेश्या, रंडी। ***v.*** 1. to offer oneself for sexual acts in return of money, वेश्यावृत्ति करना। 2. to devote to unworthy cause, ग़लत कामों में लगना, फलतः अपनी शक्ति का दुरुपयोग करना।

prostitution (प्रॉस्टिट्यूशन) ***n.*** 1. the trade of a prostitute, वेश्यावृत्ति। 2. abuse, दुरुपयोग।

prostrate (प्रॉस्ट्रेट) ***adj.*** 1. lying face downward, साष्टांग दंडवत करता हुआ, प्रणत। 2. exhausted or defeated, थका हारा या पराजित। ***v.*** 1. to lay down flat, प्रणत होना। 2. to throw down flat, धराशायी करना।

protagonist (प्रटैगनिस्ट) ***n.*** 1. a main character, प्रमुख चरित्र या नायक। 2. a leader of a movement, आंदोलन का नेता, अगुआ।

protect (प्रटेक्ट) ***v.*** 1. to save from injury, harm or attack, बचाव करना, रक्षा करना, हिफ़ाज़त करना। 2. to assist, (domestic industries, घरेलू उद्योगों की) सहायता करना या संरक्षण देना।

protection (प्रटेक्शन) ***n.*** 1. act of protecting, बचाव, रक्षण, रक्षा, हिफ़ाज़त। 2. the system of protecting domestic products, संरक्षण।

protector (प्रटेक्टर) ***n.*** 1. one who protects, रक्षक। 2. the head of a state, राज्याध्यक्ष।

protectorate (प्रटेक्टरिट) ***n.*** the territory under a protector, संरक्षित राज्य।

P

protege (प्रोटेज़े) ***n.*** a person aided and guided by some influential person, चेला या पिट्ठू, चमचा, आश्रित। (लैटिन)

protein (प्रोटीन) ***n.*** an organic compounds in all living beings that is essential for growth, प्रोटीन।

protem (प्रोटेम) ***adv.*** for the time being, temporarily, थोड़े समय के लिए। (लैटिन)

protest (प्रोटेस्ट) ***v.*** 1. to express strong objections (to), एतराज़ करना, आपत्ति करना। 2. to express disapproval, विरोध/प्रतिवाद करना। ***n.*** 1. an objection, आपत्ति, एतराज़। 2. disapproval, विरोध, प्रतिवाद।

Protestant (प्रॉटिस्टन्ट) ***n.*** a Christian other than the Roman Catholic or the Eastern Church, प्रोटेस्टैन्ट।

proto (प्रोटो) ***prefix.*** first, original, आद्य-, आदि-, पूर्व- अग्र-, प्राक्-।

protocol (प्रोटोकॉल) ***n.*** the forms of ceremony and etiquette observed by diplomats, राजनयिक आचार-संहिता।

proton (प्रोटॉन) ***n.*** a particle with a positive electric charge, प्रोटॉन।

protoplasm (प्रोटप्लैज़म) ***n.*** a semi-fluid constituent of all animal and vegetable cells, जीवद्रव्य, प्रोटोप्लाज़्म।

protozoa (प्रोटज़ोआ) ***n.*** a single-celled microscopic organism, प्रजीवाणु।

protract (प्रोट्रैक्ट) ***v.*** to lengthen or prolong, लंबा करना, खींचना, बढ़ाना।

protractor (प्रोट्रैक्टर) ***n.*** an instrument for measuring angles, कोणमापक, चाँदा।

protrude (प्रोटूड) ***v.*** to project from a surface, उभरना या उभारना, बाहर निकला हुआ होना।

protrusion (प्रोटूज़न) ***n.*** the state of being protruded, उभार, बाहर निकला हुआ होना।

protuberance (प्रोट्यूबरेन्स) ***n.*** 1. a part or thing that protrudes, उभार, गुमटा। 2. projection, बाहर निकला हुआ भाग।

proud (प्राउड) ***adj.*** 1. conceited, haughty, अभिमानी, घमंडी। 2. self-respecting, स्वाभिमानी, गर्वीला। 3. highly respected, गौरवशाली, गौरवपूर्ण।

provable (प्रूवेबल) ***adj.*** that can be proved, साबित करने योग्य, साध्य, प्रमाण्य।

prove (प्रूव) ***v.*** 1. to establish (something) true, सिद्ध करना, प्रमाणित करना। 2. to test, जाँचना, परखना। 3. to be found by trial or experience, सिद्ध होना, निकलना।

provenance (प्रॉविनेन्स) ***n.*** a place of origin, उद्गम-स्थल।

proverb (प्रॉवर्ब) ***n.*** a short saying, a short popular saying, कहावत, लोकोक्ति।

proverbial (प्रवर्बिअल) ***adj.*** 1. of the nature of a proverb, कहावती, लोकोक्तीय। 2. well-known, जाना-माना, लोकप्रसिद्ध।

provide (प्रवाइड) ***v.*** 1. to supply or furnish, उपलब्ध कराना, मुहैया करना, अभिपूर्ति करना। 2. to prepare (for), तैयार होना, तैयारी करना। 3. to state as condition, शर्त लगाना।

provided (प्रवाइडिड) ***conj.*** on the condition, इस शर्त पर कि।

Providence (प्रॉविडेन्स) ***n.*** God, ईश्वर।

providence ***n.*** divine care, ईश्वरीय संरक्षण, ईश्वर की कृपा।

provident (प्रॉविडेन्ट) ***adj.*** providing

for future needs, भावी आवश्यकताओं की पूर्ति करनेवाला।

provident fund ***n.*** a fund for future needs, भविष्यनिधि।

providential (प्रॉविडेन्शल) ***adj.*** 1. resulting from divine providence, ईश्वर की कृपा से होनेवाला, दैवकृत। 2. happening very luckily, सौभाग्यपूर्ण।

province (प्रॉविन्स) ***n.*** 1. an administrative division of a country, region, प्रांत, प्रदेश। 2. an area of activity, learning etc., कार्यक्षेत्र।

provincial (प्रविन्शल) ***adj.*** of a region, प्रांतीय, प्रादेशिक।

provision (प्रविज़न) ***n.*** 1. the act of providing, अभिपूर्ति। 2. something that is provided, वह वस्तु जिसकी पूर्ति की गई हो, रसद। 3. a stock of food, भंडार। 4. a stipulation, शर्त, प्रावधान।

provisional (प्रविज़नल) ***adj.*** not final, temporary, अनंतिम, अस्थायी।

proviso (प्रवाइज़ो) ***n.*** a stipulation, शर्त, प्रावधान।

provocation (प्रॉवकेशन) ***n.*** the act of provoking, उत्तेजन, उत्तेजना, छेड़खानी।

provocative (प्रवॉकेटिव) ***adj.*** that provokes, उत्तेजनापूर्ण, उत्तेजक।

provoke (प्रवोक) ***v.*** 1. to excite, उत्तेजित करना। 2. to irritate, बौखला देना, छेड़खानी/छेड़खानी करना।

provost (प्रोवोस्ट) ***n.*** 1. the head of a college, प्रधानाचार्य। 2. the head of a church, धर्माध्यक्ष, धर्माचार्य।

prowess (प्राउइस) ***n.*** 1. bravery, शौर्य, वीरता। 2. unusual ability or skill, प्रवीणता।

prowl (प्राउल) ***v.*** to roam about furtively for a prey, शिकार के लिए दबे पाँव निकलना। ***n.*** the act of roaming for a prey, शिकार के लिए दबे पाँव निकलना।

proximal (प्रॉक्सिमल) ***adj.*** nearest, समीपस्थ, निकटस्थ।

proximity (प्रॉक्सिमिटी) ***n.*** nearness, आसन्नता, सन्निकटता।

proxy (प्रॉक्सी) ***n.*** a person empowered to act or vote for another, प्रतिनिधि, प्रतिपुरुष।

prudence (प्रूडेन्स) ***n.*** the quality of being prudent, सयानापन, विवेकशीलता, दूरदर्शिता।

prudent (प्रूडेन्ट) ***adj.*** sensible, discreet, सयाना, विवेकी, दूरदर्शी।

prudish (प्रूडिश) ***adj.*** too modest, अतिशालीन, पाखंडी।

prune[1] (प्रून) ***n.*** a dried plum, आड़ू या आलूबुख़ारा।

prune[2] ***v.*** to remove by cutting off, काटना-छाँटना।

prurient (प्रूरिएन्ट) ***adj.*** lustful, lewd, कामुक, लंपट।

pry (प्राइ) ***v.*** to inquire impertinently, खोद-खोदकर पूछना।

psalm (साम) ***n.*** a sacred song, भजन, स्तुतिगान, स्तोत्र।

pseudo (स्यूडो) ***adj.*** false, छद्म, कूट।

pseudonym (स्यूडोनिम) ***n.*** a fictitious name used by an author, छद्म नाम, कूटनाम।

psyche (साइकी) ***n.*** 1. the human soul, जीवात्मा, आत्मा। 2. the human mind, मानव मस्तिष्क।

psychiatrist (साइकिअट्रिस्ट) ***n.*** an expert in psychiatry, मनोचिकित्सक।

psychic (साइकिक) ***adj.*** 1. of the soul, आत्मा-संबंधी, आत्मिक। 2. of the

P

mind, मन-संबंधी, मानसिक। 3. beyond natural laws or physical world, अतींद्रिय।

psychoanalysis (साइकोअनैलिसिस) ***n.*** analysis of feeling and behavi-our to investigate mental disorder, मनोविश्लेषण।

psychological (साइकलॉजिकल) ***adj.*** of phychology, मनोवैज्ञानिक।

psychologist (साइकॉलोजिस्ट) ***n.*** an expert in psychology, मनोविज्ञानी।

psychology (साइकॉलोजी) ***n.*** 1. the study of mind and its working, मनोविज्ञान। 2. mental characteristics, मानसिक विशेषताएँ।

psychosis (साइकोसिस) ***n.*** serious mental disorder, मनोविकृति।

psychosomatic (साइकोसोमैटिक) ***adj.*** involving both the mind and the body, मनोदैहिक, मनोकायिक।

psychotherapy (साइकोथेरेपी) ***n.*** the psychological treatment of nervous disorder, मनश्चिकित्सा।

P.T.O. please turn over (a page, पृष्ठ) उलटें।

pub (पब) ***n.*** a bar, मदिरालय।

puberty (प्यूबर्टी) ***n.*** the state of maturation in which a person becomes capable of sexual reproduction, तरुणाई।

pubic (प्यूबिक) ***adj.*** of the lower part of the abdomen, पेड़ू के नीचे के भाग से संबद्ध; pubic hair, झाँट।

public (पब्लिक) ***adj.*** 1. of the people, for or used by the people, सार्वजनिक, लोक-, जन-। 2. widely known, सर्वविदित। ☐ **go public,** (किसी कंपनी के शेयर) जनता के लिए खोल देना। ***n.*** 1. the people as a whole, आमलोग, जनता, जन-साधारण। 2. a group of people sharing a common interest, जनवर्ग, जनसमूह।

publican (पब्लिकन) ***n.*** a keeper of a public house, मदिरालय का मालिक, सुरागृह का स्वामी।

publication (पब्लिकेशन) ***n.*** 1. the art of publishing, प्रकाशन। 2. something published, प्रकाशन (पुस्तक या समाचारपत्र)।

public convenience ***n.*** a public lavatory, सार्वजनिक शौचालय।

public house ***n.*** a bar, मदिरालय, मधुशाला।

publicity (पब्लिसिटी) ***n.*** the process of drawing public attention to a thing or person, प्रचार।

publicize (पब्लिसाइज़) ***v.*** to give publicity to, प्रचार करना।

publicly (पब्लिकली) ***adv.*** openly, in public, खुले आम, सार्वजनिक रूप से।

public prosecutor ***n.*** लोक अभियोजक।

public sector ***n.*** वे उद्योग जो राज्य के नियंत्रण में हों, सार्वजनिक क्षेत्र।

public spirited ***adj.*** devoted to public welfare, लोकहितैषी, जनहितैषी।

public trial ***n.*** खुला मुक़दमा।

public works department ***n.*** लोक निर्माण विभाग।

publish (पब्लिश) ***v.*** 1. to issue a book, newspaper, pamphlet etc. to the public, प्रकाशित करना। 2. to announce, घोषणा करना।

publisher (पब्लिशर) ***n.*** one who publishes books etc., प्रकाशक।

puce (प्यूस) ***adj.*** brownish purple, बैंगनी भूरा।

pucker (पकर) ***n.*** 1. a wrinkle, झुर्री।

2. a fold, सिकुड़न। *v.* 1. to gather into wrinkles, झुर्रियाँ पड़ना। 2. to gather into folds, सिकुड़न पड़ना।

pudding (पुडिन्ग) *n.* a sweet dessert, फिरनी की तरह जमाया हुआ व्यंजन, पुडिंग।

puddle (पडल) *n.* a small pool of water left after rain, बरसाती पोखरा।

puerile (प्युअरिल) *adj.* childish, बचकाना।

puff (पफ़) *n.* 1. a short sudden gust, झोंका। 2. a bit of smoke or air expelled at one time, फूँक, साँस, कश। 3. a powder puff, पाउडर लगाने की गद्दी। 4. a stuffed pastry, गुंजिया। 5. a piece of extravagant praise, अतिप्रशंसा। *v.* 1. to send out puffs, धुआँ, साँस आदि छोड़ना। 2. to pant, हाँफना। 3. to swell, फूलना।

puffed (पफ़्ड) *adj.* swollen, फूला हुआ।

pugnacious (पग्नेशस) *n.* aggressive, आक्रामक, लड़ाकू, झगड़ालू।

pull (पुल) *v.* 1. to draw, drag or attract, खींचना, घसीटना। 2. to propel (a boat) by pulling on its oars, (नाव को) खींचना, खेना। 3.to attract, आकर्षित करना।

pulley (पुली) *n.* a small wheel in which a rope runs, पुली, घिरनी, गड़ारी, चर्ख़ी।

pull-out (पुल-आउट) *n.* retreat, पीछे हटना।

pullover (पुलोवर) *n.* a sweater, जर्सी, स्वेटर।

pulmonary (पल्मनरी) *adj.* of or pertaining to lungs, फेफड़े का, फुप्फुस।

pulp (पल्प) *n.* 1. the soft part of a fruit, गूदा। 2. any soft moist ground-up mass, लुगदी। 3. beaten moist mass, कचूमर, भुरता। *v.* to reduce to pulp, गूदा कर देना।

pulpit (पुल्पिट) *n.* a stage, मंच।

pulsate (पल्सेट) *v.* to quiver or throb, काँपना, सिहरना, स्पंदित होना, फड़कना।

pulsation (पल्सेशन) *n.* vibration, throbbing, स्पंदन, सिहरन।

pulse[1] (पल्स) *n.* throbbing of an artery, नाड़ी का स्पंदन। *v.* to pulsate, स्पंदित, होना फड़कना या धड़कना।

pulse[2] *n.* the edible seeds of plants having pods, दाल।

pulverization (पल्वराइज़ेशन) *n.* an act of pulverizing, पिसाई, पेषण।

pulverize (पल्वराइज़) *v.* 1. to grind into powder, पीसना। 2. to crush, पीस डालना, कुचल डालना।

pumice (पमिस) *n.* a piece of porous lightweight volcanic rock, झाँवाँ।

pummel (पमल) *v.* to pound with the fists, मुक्के या घूँसे मारना।

pump (पम्प) *n.* 1. a device for filling in or drawing out water, air etc., पंप। 2. a kind of shoe, एक प्रकार का जूता। *v.* 1. to draw out, बाहर निकालना। 2. to fill in, भरना।

pumpkin (पम्पकिन) *n.* a gourd-like fruit, कद्दू, लौकी, घीया।

pun (पन) *n.* a humorous use of words having similar sound but different meanings, यमक (अलंकार)।

punch[1] (पन्च) *n.* a tool driven or pressed against a surface, छेदन यंत्र। *v.* to pierce with a punch, छेदना।

punch[2] *n.* a blow with a fist, मुक्के का प्रहार। *v.* to blow with a fist, मुक्का मारना।

punctual (पन्क्चुअल) *adj.* acting

P

or arriving at an appointed time, समयपालक, समयनिष्ठ, वक़्त का पाबंद।

punctuate (पन्क्चुएट) ***v.*** 1. to insert or divide punctuation marks, विराम-चिह्न लगाना। 2. to interrupt, बीच में रोकना।

punctuation mark ***n.*** any of the signs used in punctuation, विराम-चिह्न।

puncture (पन्क्चर) ***n.*** 1. a hole made by a sharp point in a tube, ट्यूब में होनेवाला छेद, पंचर। 2. the act of piercing with a sharp point, छेदना। ***v.*** to pierce or to be pierced with a sharp point, पंचर होना या करना।

pundit (पन्डित) ***n.*** a learned person, पंडित।

pungent (पन्जेन्ट) ***adj.*** 1. acrid, तीता, तिक्त। 2. sharp, तीक्ष्ण, कटु, तीखा।

punish (पनिश) ***v.*** to give punishment, दंडित करना, सज़ा देना।

punishment (पनिशमेन्ट) ***n.*** a penalty imposed for wrong-doing, दंड, सज़ा।

punitive (प्युनिटिव) ***adj.*** intended to inflict punishment, दंडात्मक।

punk (पन्क) ***n.*** a worthless person or thing, बेकार व्यक्ति या वस्तु। ***adj.*** worthless, useless, व्यर्थ का, बेकार।

punt (पन्ट) ***n.*** a flat-bottomed boat, डोंगी। ***v.*** to propel a boat, डोंगी खेना।

puny (प्युनी) ***adj.*** small and insignificant, कमज़ोर और ठिगना, पिद्दी-सा।

pupa (प्यूपा) ***n.*** an insect after larva stage, प्यूपा।

pupil (प्यूपिल) ***n.*** 1. one who is taught by another, शिष्य, चेला, शागिर्द। 2. a part of the eye, आँख की पुतली।

puppet (पपिट) ***n.*** 1. a small doll moved by strings, कठपुतली। 2. a person whose actions are controlled by another, कठपुतली।

puppy (पपी) ***n.*** a young dog, पिल्ला।

purchase (पर्चेज़) ***v.*** 1. to buy, ख़रीदना, क्रय करना। 2. to obtain by sacrifice or effort, अर्जित या प्राप्त करना। ***n.*** 1. act of buying, खरीदारी। 2. something bought, खरीदी हुई वस्तु, सौदा।

purdah (पर्दा) ***n.*** 1. a veil or curtain, पर्दा। 2. a system of keeping women from the sight of elders or strangers, पर्दा-प्रथा।

pure (प्योर) ***adj.*** 1. genuine, unmixed, शुद्ध, विशुद्ध, ख़ालिस, निर्मल। 2. free from evil or sin, निर्दोष, निष्पाप, पवित्र। 3. dealing with theory only, शुद्ध।

pure-bred (प्योर-ब्रेड) ***adj.*** of unmixed descent, ख़ालिस नस्लवाला, असंकर।

puree (प्यूरी) ***n.*** the thick liquid of tomatoes, प्यूरी।

purgative (पर्गटिव) ***adj.*** laxative, विरेचक। ***n.*** a drug for purging the bowels, जुलाब।

purge (पर्ज) ***v.*** 1. to empty the bowels by a purgative, जुलाब लेना/देना। 2. to clear (a person) of a charge, दोषमुक्त करना। ***n.*** 1. a purgative, जुलाब। 2. purification. शुद्धि, परिष्करण।

purification (प्युरिफ़िकेशन) ***n.*** the act of purifying or the state of being purified, शुद्धिकरण, शोधन।

purify (प्यूरिफ़ाइ) ***v.*** to make pure, शोधन करना, शुद्ध करना।

puritan (प्यूरिटन) ***n.*** one who

adheres to strict moral or religious principles, नियमनिष्ठ, धर्मनिष्ठ, शुद्धाचारवादी।

purity (प्यूरिटी) ***n.*** the state or quality of being pure, शुद्धता, विशुद्धता, शुचिता।

purl[1] (पर्ल) ***n.*** a backward stitch, उलटा फंदा।

purl[2] ***v.*** to move with a murmuring sound, कलकल करते हुए (नदी का) बहना। ***n.*** murmuring sound, कलकल।

purloin (पर्लॉइन) ***v.*** to steal, चुराना।

purple (पर्पल) ***adj.*** reddish blue, बैंगनी।

purport (पर्पर्ट) ***n.*** meaning, sense, अर्थ आशय। ***v.*** to mean, अर्थ देना।

purpose (पर्पस) ***n.*** 1. an aim, design, प्रयोजन, उद्देश्य, लक्ष्य। 2. will-power, इच्छाशक्ति, संकल्पशक्ति।

purposeful (पर्पसफ़ुल) ***adj.*** 1. having a purpose, उद्देश्यपूर्ण। 2. meaningful, अर्थगर्भित।

purr (पर) ***n.*** the sound made by a cat, घुरघुर।

purse (पर्स) ***n.*** 1. a small bag for carrying money, बटुआ, पर्स। 2. money, रुपया। 3. a sum of money as a prize or present, पुरस्कार, भेंट, नज़र। ***v.*** to contract lips, होंठ बंद करना।

pursue (पर्स्यू) ***v.*** 1. to chase, पीछा करना। 2. to follow closely or persistently, पीछे लगना, पीछे पड़ना। 3. to apply oneself to, रत होना, लगे रहना।

pursuer (पर्स्यूअर) ***n.*** one who pursues, पीछा करनेवाला।

pursuit (पर्स्यूट) ***n.*** 1. the act of pursuing, पीछा। 2. an activity, क्रियाकलाप, धंधा, पेशा आदि।

purulent (प्युअरुलेन्ट) ***adj.*** full of pus, मवाद-भरा, पीपदार।

purvey (पर्वे) ***v.*** to supply, पूर्ति करना।

purview (पर्व्यू) ***n.*** 1. scope of operation, कार्यक्षेत्र। 2. range of outlook, दृष्टि-क्षेत्र।

push (पुश) ***v.*** 1. to exert force against, धक्का देना, धकेलना, खिसकाना। 2. to put pressure, ज़ोर डालना, दबाव डालना। 3. to inspire, उकसाना, प्रेरित करना। ***n.*** 1. pressure, दबाव, दाब। 2. thrust, धक्का। 3. an attempt to advance, बढ़ाव, बढ़ावा।

pushing (पुशिंग) ***adj.*** ambitious, उच्चाकांक्षी, उद्यमी, उत्साही।

pussy (पुसी) ***n.*** a cat, बिल्ली।

pustule (पस्ट्यूल) ***n.*** a small elevation of the skin containing pus, फुंसी।

put (पुट) ***v.*** (put, putting) 1. to place or set, रखना। 2. to subject, डालना। 3. to attribute, लगाना। 4. to throw, फेंकना। 5. to express, व्यक्त करना। 6. to estimate, कूतना। 7. to impose, लगाना। 8. to bring up, उठाना, (प्रश्न) करना। ☐ **put across,** (i) समझाना, (ii) अच्छे ढंग से प्रस्तुत करना; **put by,** बचा रखना, रख छोड़ना; **put down,** (i) लिख या टाँक लेना, (ii) दमन करना, दबा देना, (iii) गाड़ी से उतार देना, (iv) अस्वीकृत कर देना, (v) सिर नीचा कर देना; **put forth,** लगाना, प्रयुक्त करना; **put in,** (i) के अंदर रख देना, सन्निविष्ट कर देना, (ii) सेवारत या कार्यरत रहना; **put off,** (i) उतारना, (ii) टालना, स्थगित कर देना; **put on,** (i) पहनना, धारण करना, (ii) मंचन करना; (iii) भ्रमित करना, (iv) बहाना करना; **put out,** (i) बुझाना, (ii) खिझलाना, क्रुद्ध करना; **put through,** (i) निष्पादन करना, (ii) टेलीफ़ोन (का नंबर) मिलाना; **put up with,** बर्दाश्त करना, सहना।

P

putative (प्यूटेटिव) ***adj.*** supposed, माना हुआ, प्रसिद्ध।

putrefaction (प्यूट्रिफ़ैक्शन) ***n.*** the process of putrefying, सड़न।

putrefy (प्यूट्रिफ़ाइ) ***v.*** to decay or rot, सड़ना।

putrescent (प्यूट्रेसेन्ट) ***adj.*** rotten, decaying, सड़ा हुआ, सड़ता हुआ।

putrid (प्यूट्रिड) ***adj.*** 1. rotten, decaying, सड़ा हुआ। 2. foul smelling, दुर्गंधपूर्ण।

putt (पुट) ***v.*** to strike a ball lightly, गेंद पर धीरे से प्रहार करना।

putty (पटी) ***n.*** a paste for filling up holes of window and door frames,पुटीन।

puzzle (पज़ल) ***n.*** 1. a problem to test one's knowledge, पहेली, प्रहेलिका। 2. a problem, उलझन, समस्या। ***v.*** 1. to perplex, हैरान कर देना, घबरा देना। 2. to be perplexed, हैरान हो जाना, घबरा जाना।

puzzled (पज़ल्ड) ***adj.*** perplexed, घबराया हुआ, उलझन में पड़ा हुआ, भ्रांत।

pygmy (पिग्मी) ***n.*** a dwarf, बौना। ***adj.*** very small, ठिगना, बौना।

pyjamas (पजामज़) ***n.*** pajamas, पायजामा।

pyorrhoea (पाइअरीआ) ***n.*** inflammation of the gums, पाइरिया।

pyramid (पिरमिड) ***n.*** a royal tomb built by the ancient Egyptians, पिरामिड।

pyre (पायर) ***n.*** a pile of wood on which a dead body is burned, चिता।

pyrogenic (पाइरोजेनिक) ***adj.*** 1. producing heat, तापोत्पादक। 2. produced by heat, तापोत्पन्न।

pyromania (पाइरोमेनिआ) ***n.*** an impulse to start destructive fire, आग लगाने का उन्माद।

pyrophobia (पाइरोफ़ोबिआ) ***n.*** fear of fire, अग्नि-भीति।

python (पाइथन) ***n.*** a large snake, अजगर।

Q, q (क्यू) ***n.*** the seventeenth letter of the English alphabet, अंग्रेज़ी वर्णमाला का सत्रहवाँ वर्ण।

qua (क्वे) ***prep.*** in the capacity, की हैसियत से, के नाते, के रूप में।

quack[1] (क्वैक) ***n.*** the cry of a duck, बतख की काँकाँ, क्वैंक्वैं। ***v.*** to utter this sound, काँकाँ या क्वैंक्वैं करना।

quack[2] ***n.*** an unqualified medical practitioner, नीमहकीम, कठवैद्य।

quad, quadrangle (क्वॉड, क्वॉड्रेन्गल) ***n.*** a figure with four corners, चतुष्कोण।

quadrant (क्वॉड्रन्ट) ***n.*** a quarter (of a circle, वृत्त का) चतुर्थांश, वृत्तपाद।

quadrilateral (क्वॉड्रिलैटरल) ***n.*** a figure with four sides, चतुर्भुज।

quadruped (क्वॉड्रुपेड) ***n.*** a four-footed animal, चौपाया।

quadruple (क्वॉड्रूपल) ***adj.*** 1. four times as much as, चौगुना। 2. fourfold, चौहरा। 3. consisting of four (persons or parts), चतुष्क।

quagmire (क्वैगमाइर) ***n.*** 1. an area of soft wet ground, bog, दलदल। 2. an awkward situation, बेढंगी स्थिति।

quail[1] (क्वेल) ***n.*** a chicken like short-tailed bird, बटेर।

quail[2] ***v.*** to shrink back in fear, सहम जाना, सिहर उठना।

quaint (क्वेन्ट) ***adj.*** unusual, विचित्र, अनोखा।

quake (क्वेक) ***n.*** shake or tremble, कँपकँपी, थरथराहट, कंपन। ***v.*** to shake or tremble, काँपना, सिहरना।

qualification (क्वॉलिफ़िकेशन) ***n.*** an ability, quality or attribute, योग्यता, अर्हता।

qualified (क्वॉलिफ़ाइड) ***adj.*** 1. having qualifications, योग्यता-प्राप्त, अर्हता-प्राप्त। 2. limited, सीमित।

qualifier (क्वॉलिफ़ायर) ***n.*** a word that qualifies, विशेषण, विशेषक।

qualify (क्वॉलिफ़ाइ) ***v.*** 1. to become eligible or competent, उपयुक्त/योग्य होना। 2. to attribute some quality to, विशेषित/मर्यादित करना। 3. to make less strong, सीमित/हलका कर देना।

qualitative (क्वॉलिटेटिव) ***adj.*** 1. concerned with quality, गुणात्मक। 2. (gram.) having some qualities, गुणवाचक।

quality (क्वॉलिटी) ***n.*** 1. a distinguishing characteristic, गुण, लक्षण। 2. degree of excellence, गुणवत्ता। 3. kind, प्रकार, क़िस्म।

qualm (क्वाम) ***n.*** 1. a sudden feeling of sickness or nausea, मिचली। 2. faintness, बेहोशी। 3 a pang of doubt, संदेह की टीस।

quandary (क्वॉन्डरी) ***n.*** 1. a state of perplexity, predicament, असमंजस, दुविधा। 2. uncertainty, अनिश्चितता। 3. a difficult situation, उलझन, परेशानी।

quantify (क्वॉन्टिफ़ाइ) ***v.*** to express the quantity of, परिमाण बताना।

quantitative (क्वॉन्टिटेटिव) ***adj.*** of or concerned with quantity, मात्रात्मक, परिमाणवाचक, परिमाणात्मक।

quantity (क्वॉन्टिटी) ***n.*** 1. a specified

Q

amount or number, उल्लिखित परिमाण या मात्रा। 2. a large amount or number, अत्यधिक मात्रा या परिमाण।

quantum (क्वॉन्टम) ***n.*** quantity or amount, मात्रा या राशि।

quarantine (क्वॉरन्टीन) ***n.*** a period of isolation or detention to prevent the spread of disease, संगरोधन। ***v.*** to put into quarantine, संगरोधन करना।

quarrel (क्वॉरल) ***n.*** 1. discord, angry disagreement, झगड़ा, लड़ाई-झगड़ा। 2. a cause of grievance, शिकायत का सबब। ***v.*** 1. to engage in quarrel, झगड़ा करना, झगड़ना। 2. to disagree, असहमत होना।

quarrelsome (क्वॉरलसम) ***adj.*** inclined to quarrel, झगड़ालू, लड़ाका।

quarry[1] (क्वॉरी) ***n.*** a mine, खदान, खान। ***v.*** to extract from a quarry, खुदाई करना, खनना।

quarry[2] ***n.*** 1. a prey, शिकार। 2. anything pursued, ऐसा विषय या बात जिसकी तलाश हो।

quart (क्वॉर्ट) ***n.*** a quarter of a gallon, चौथाई गैलन, क्वार्ट।

quarter (क्वॉर्टर) ***n.*** 1. one of four equal parts, चतुर्थांश। 2. a district, क्षेत्र, प्रदेश। 3. a source of help, सहायता का स्रोत। 4. (plu.) lodgings, क्वाटर। ***v.*** 1. to divide into four equal parts, बराबर-बराबर चार हिस्से करना/लगाना। 2. to put soldiers into lodgings, सेना ठहराना।

quarter-final (क्वार्टर-फ़ाइनल) ***n.*** one of the matches before semifinal, क्वार्टर-फाइनल।

quarterly (क्वार्टर्ली) ***adj.*** occurring once in three months, त्रैमासिक, तिमाही। ***n.*** a periodical issued every three months, त्रैमासिक पत्रिका।

quartermaster (क्वॉर्टरमास्टर) ***n.*** a military personnel in charge of stores, सेना का रसद-अधिकारी।

quartet (क्वॉर्टेट) ***n.*** a set of four, चार का समूह, चौका।

quartz (क्वार्ट्स) ***n.*** a kind of hard mineral, स्फटिक, बिल्लौर, क्वार्ट्ज़।

quash (क्वॉश) ***v.*** 1. to suppress, दबा या कुचल देना। 2. to reject, रद कर देना, निरस्त कर देना।

quasi- (क्वाज़ी) ***prefix.*** 1. seeming to be something but not really so, as if, प्रतिभासिक, मानो। 2. half, अर्ध।

quatrain (क्वॉट्रेन) ***n.*** a stanza of four lines, चार चरणों का पद्य, चतुष्पदी।

quaver (क्वेवर) ***v.*** 1. to quiver or tremble, काँपना/कँपाना। 2. to sing with a trembling voice, काँपती हुई आवाज़ में बोलना। ***n.*** a quavering sound, काँपती हुई आवाज़।

queasy (क्वीज़ी) ***adj.*** 1. feeling slightly sick, वमनकारी, वमनेच्छु। 2. causing a feeling of sickness, जिसे देखकर कै आती हो। 3. fastidious, तुनकमिज़ाज, नकचढ़ा। ☐ **queasy conscience,** पापभीरु अंतःकरण।

queen (क्वीन) ***n.*** 1. the wife of a king or the female sovereign, रानी, महारानी, बेगम। 2. a playing card bearing the picture of a queen, (ताश की) बेगम। 3. a most powerful piece in chess, (शतरंज की) रानी, वज़ीर। 4. the only fertile female in a colony of bees, ants etc., रानी-मक्खी या रानी-चींटी।

queenly (क्वीनली) ***adj.*** like a queen, रानी-जैसा।

queen mother ***n.*** the mother of a king or queen, राजमाता।

Q

queer (क्विअर) ***adj.*** 1. odd, strange, विचित्र, अजीब। 2. eccentric, सनकी, पागल। 3. of questionable character, संदिग्ध। ***n.*** a homosexual, समलिंगकामी।

quell (क्वेल) ***v.*** to suppress, कुचल या दबा देना, दमन या शमन करना।

quench (क्वेन्च) ***v.*** 1. to extinguish, (आग) बुझाना, शमन करना। 2. to satiate, (प्यास) बुझाना, तृप्त होना। 3. to cool, ठंडा करना।

querulous (क्वेरुलस) ***adj.*** peevish, झींखनेवाला, चिड़चिड़ा।

query (क्वेरी) ***n.*** 1. a question, प्रश्न, सवाल, शंका। 2. a question-mark, प्रश्न-चिह्न। ***v.*** 1. to question, प्रश्न/सवाल करना, पूछताछ करना। 2. to express doubt, संदेह प्रकट करना।

quest (क्वेस्ट) ***n.*** search, खोज, तलाश। ***v.*** to go in search (of, की) खोज करना।

question (क्वेस्चन) ***n.*** 1. a sentence requesting answer or information, प्रश्न, सवाल। 2. a problem, समस्या, विवाद। 3. an issue, विषय, बात। 4. doubt, संदेह, शंका। ***v.*** 1. to ask question, प्रश्न करना, सवाल पूछना। 2. to express doubt, शंका प्रकट करना।

questionable (क्वेस्चनेबल) ***adj.*** open to doubt, dubious, संदेहास्पद, शंकास्पद, संदिग्ध, संदेहात्मक।

question mark ***n.*** a mark placed after a question, ?, प्रश्नचिह्न।

questionnaire (क्वेस्चनेअर) ***n.*** a list of questions, प्रश्नावली, प्रश्नमाला।

queue (क्यू) ***n.*** a line, लाइन, पंक्ति, कतार, ताँता। ***v.*** (queued, queuing) to wait in a queue, लाइन लगाना, लाइन में खड़े हो जाना।

quibble (क्विबल) ***n.*** a trivial objection, झूठमूठ की आपत्ति, झिकझिक। ***v.*** to argue about small differences, झूठमूठ की आपत्ति करना, बाल की खाल निकालना।

quick (क्विक) ***adj.*** 1. fast, तेज़। 2. swift, prompt, फ़ुर्तीला, शीघ्र काम करनेवाला। 3. brief, संक्षिप्त। 4. deft, कुशल। 5. lively, जीवंत, जीवित। ***n.*** a sensitive area under a fingernail or toenail, नाखून के नीचे का कोमल मांस।

quicken (क्विकन) ***v.*** 1. to make or become quicker, तेज़ करना या होना। 2. to stimulate, उत्तेजित करना, अनुप्राणित करना।

quick-tempered (क्विक-टेम्पर्ड) ***adj.*** easily angered, तेज़ मिज़ाज, ग़ुस्सैल।

quick-witted (क्विक-विटिड) ***adj.*** nimble of mind, हाज़िर-जवाब, प्रत्युत्पन्नमति।

quid pro quo (क्विड्-प्रो-क्वो) ***n.*** something given in return for something, बदले में दी हुई वस्तु, प्रतिदान।

quiescent (क्विएसेन्ट) ***adj.*** 1. inactive, निष्क्रिय। 2. dormant, सुप्त।

quiet (क्वाइअट) ***adj.*** calm, चुप, मौन, शांत, स्थिर। ***n.*** quietness, नीरवता, शांति, चुप्पी। ***v.*** to make or become quiet, शांत होना या करना, चुप होना या करना।

quieten (क्वाइटन) ***v.*** to quiet, शांत होना या करना, चुप करना या कराना।

quill (क्विल) ***n.*** 1. a large feather, पंख। 2. the long hollow part of a feather, पंख की डंडी। 3. a feather made into a pen, पंख की क़लम। 4. any of the spines of a porcupine, साही का काँटा।

quilt (क्विल्ट) ***n.*** a thick bed cover, गद्दा, रजाई।

Q

quinine (क्विनीन) ***n.*** a drug to treat malaria, कुनैन।

quinquennial (क्विन्क्वेनिअल) ***adj.*** lasting for five years or happening every five years, पंचवर्षीय।

quintal (क्विन्टल) ***n.*** a unit of weight equal to 100 kilograms, क्विन्टल।

quintessence (क्विन्टेसेन्स) ***n.*** essence, सारतत्व, सार, निचोड़, सारांश।

quip (क्विप) ***n.*** 1. a sarcastic remark, ताना, व्यंग्य, बोली। 2. a witty saying, चुटकुला। ***v.*** to make a quip, ताना देना, व्यंग्य करना; चुटकुला छोड़ना।

quire (क्वाइर) ***n.*** a set of twenty-five sheets, (काग़ज़ का) दस्ता।

quirk (क्वर्क) ***n.*** 1. a trick of fate, भाग्य का खेल। 2. peculiar behaviour, विचित्र व्यवहार।

quit (क्विट) ***v.*** (quit/quitted, quitting) 1. to give up, छोड़ देना, छोड़ना, खाली कर देना। 2. to depart from, चल देना।

quite (क्वाइट) ***adv.*** 1. completely, बिल्कुल। 2. really, सचमुच। 3. to some extent, बहुत-कुछ।

quits (क्विट्स) ***adj.*** on even terms, बराबर।

quiver[1] (क्विवर) ***n.*** a case for holding arrows, तरकस।

quiver[2] ***v.*** to tremble, काँपना। ***n.*** an act or state of trembling, कंपन, कँपकँपी।

quiz (क्विज़) ***v.*** to examine by questioning, पूछताछ करना। ***n.*** a short test, पूछताछ या पहेली।

quorum (क्वॉरम) ***n.*** minimum number of members to be required to start a meeting, गणपूर्ति, कोरम।

quota (क्वोटा) ***n.*** fixed share, नियतांश, कोटा।

quotation (क्वोटेशन) ***n.*** 1. a passage quoted, उद्धरण। 2. the rated state for doing some work or for supplying some commodity, कोटेशन।

quotation mark ***n.*** marks to punctuate a quotation, उद्धरण चिह्न ("...")।

quote (क्वोट) ***v.*** 1. to produce or recite as a quotation, उद्धरण देना, उद्धृत करना। 2. to offer rate for doing a job or supplying a commodity, रेट देना।

quotient (क्वोशन्ट) ***n.*** the result of the division of one quantity by another, भागफल, लब्धि।

R

R, r (आर) ***n.*** the eighteenth letter of the English alphabet, अंग्रेज़ी वर्णमाला का अठारहवाँ वर्ण।

rabbit (रैबिट) ***n.*** a hare, ख़रगोश।

rabble (रैबल) ***n.*** 1. a mob, भीड़, भीड़-भाड़। 2. **the rabble,** निम्न वर्ग, जनसाधारण।

rabid (रैबिड) ***adj.*** 1. furious, घोर, उग्र। 2. fanatical, कट्टर। 3. relating to rabies, जलातंक-संबंधी।

rabies (रेबीज) ***n.*** a fatal disease of animals esp. dogs, transmitted to man by the bite, जलातंक।

race[1] (रेस) ***n.*** 1. a contest of speed, दौड़। 2. a strong fast current, तेज़ धारा। ***v.*** 1. to compete in race, दौड़ में हिस्सा लेना। 2. to operate with full speed, (मशीन) दौड़ा देना, दौड़ाना।

race[2] ***n.*** 1. a group of people having certain physical characteristics in common, प्रजाति। 2. a breed, नस्ल, जाति।

racecourse (रेसकोर्स) ***n.*** a track for race, रेसकोर्स।

racial (रेशल) ***adj.*** 1. of a race, प्रजाति-संबंधी, प्रजातीय। 2. occurring between races, जातिगत, जातीय।

racialism (रेशलिज़्म) ***n.*** = racism.

racism (रेसिज़्म) ***n.*** 1. a belief that a particular race is better than others, जातिवाद, प्रजातिवाद, प्रजातीयता। 2. racial discrimination, प्रजातिगत भेदभाव, रंग-भेद।

rack[1] (रैक) ***n.*** 1. a stand, सामान आदि रखने का लकड़ी/लोहे का टाँडदार ढाँचा, रैक। 2. a toothed bar, दंतुरदंड। 3. an instrument for torture, यातना देने का शिकंजा। ***v.*** 1. to torture on the rack, शिकंजे में कसना। 2. to cause great suffering to, घोर कष्ट देना, सताना। □ **rack up**, सफलता पाना।

rack[2] ***n.*** destruction, तबाही।

racket[1] (रैकिट) ***n.*** 1. clamour, din, शोरगुल, कोलाहल, होहल्ला, शोर-शराबा। 2. a fraudulent business, ठगी, धोखाधड़ी।

racket[2] ***n.*** a bat for playing tennis, रैकिट।

racketteer (रैकिटिअर) ***n.*** a dishonest businessman, धोखेबाज़ या दुष्ट व्यापारी।

racy (रेसी) ***adj.*** 1. lively, सजीव, जीवंत। 2. interesting, रोचक। 3. slightly indecent, कुछ-कुछ अश्लील, अश्लील-सा।

radar (रेडार) ***n.*** a device for detecting distant objects, राडार।

radial (रेडिअल) ***adj.*** 1. relating or pertaining to rays, किरणीय, रश्मिगत। 2. of a radius, त्रिज्य।

radian (रेडियन) ***n.*** the angle between two radii of a circle, त्रिज्या-कोण, रेडियन।

radiance (रेडिएन्स) ***n.*** glow, brightness, कांति, चमक।

radiant (रेडिएन्ट) ***adj.*** 1. sending out rays of light, विकिरणकारी, विकिरक। 2. showing pleasure or joy, उत्फुल्ल, प्रफुल्ल।

radiate (रेडिएट) ***v.*** to send out rays (of light or heat), विकिरण करना, फैलाना।

radiation (रेडिएशन) ***n.*** act of

R

sending out radioactive particles, विकिरणन, विकिरण।

radical (रैडिकल) *adj.* 1. basic, fundamental, मूलभूत, आधारभूत। 2. advocating extreme changes or reforms, अति-सुधारवादी, अतिवादी। 3. drastic, प्रचंड, आमूल। *n.* a person with radical, views, आमूल परिवर्तनवादी।

radically (रैडिकली) *adv.* 1. basically, मूलतः। 2. completely, आमूलतः।

radio (रेडिओ) *n.* 1. the process of sending and receiving messages without wires, विद्युत् लहरों के द्वारा ध्वनियाँ प्रेषण तथा ग्रहण करने की पद्धति, रेडियो। 2. an equipment for sending or receiving such messages, उक्त ध्वनियाँ प्रेषित करने या ग्रहण करनेवाला यंत्र, रेडियो।

radioactive (रेडिओऐक्टिव) *adj.* of or showing radioactivity, रेडियोधर्मी।

radioactivity (रेडिओऐक्टिविटी) *n.* the property of having atoms that radiate, रेडियोधर्मिता।

radiograph (रेडिओग्राफ़) *n.* an image produced by X-rays, एक्स-रे चित्र, रेडियोग्राफ़।

radiography (रेडिऑग्रफ़ी) *n.* production of radiographs, विकिरणी-चित्रण, रेडियोग्राफ़ी, एक्स-रे चित्रण।

radiotherapy (रेडिओथेरपी) *n.* the treatment of disease by X-rays, विकिरण-चिकित्सा।

radish (रैडिश) *n.* a plant and its edible root, मूली।

radium (रेडिअम) *n.* a radioactive metallic element, रेडियम नामक तत्त्व।

radius (रेडिअस) *n.* 1. a straight line joining the centre of a circle with any point on its surface, त्रिज्या, व्यासार्ध। 2. a bone of the forearm, कुहनी की हड्डी, बहिर्प्रकोष्ठिका।

raffle (रैफ़ल) *n.* a lottery that offers prizes, लॉटरी। *v.* to offer as a prize in a raffle, लॉटरी द्वारा पुरस्कार देना।

raft (रैफ़्ट) *n.* a floating platform, बेड़ा, तरापा। *v.* to travel on a raft, बेड़े पर यात्रा करना।

rafter (रैफ़्टर) *n.* a beam, शहतीर, धरन।

rag[1] (रैग) *n.* 1. a scrap of cloth, लत्ता, चिथड़ा। 2. a piece or shred, टुकड़ा।

rag[2] *v.* 1. to play rough jokes, घटिया मज़ाक करना। 2. to tease, तंग करना, छेड़छाड़ करना।

ragamuffin (रैगमफ़िन) *n.* a ragged person, वह जो चिथड़े लपेटे हो, गूदड़साईं।

rage (रेज) *n.* 1. fury, ग़ुस्सा, क्रोध, रोष। 2. a fad or craze, सनक, झक। *v.* 1. to feel or exhibit intense anger, क्रुद्ध होना, ग़ुस्सा खाना। 2. to be violent, प्रचंड रूप धारण करना।

raglan (रैग्लन) *n.* a coat or jumper with sleeves that continues to the neck, रैगलान।

raid (रेड) *n.* 1. a sudden surprise attack, धावा; air raid, हवाई धावा। 2. a surprise visit by authorities or police to arrest or seize, छापा। *v.* to make a raid, धावा बोलना; छापा मारना।

rail[1] (रेल) *n.* 1. a horizontal bar of wood or metal in a fence, डंडा, छड़। 2. a line of metal bar, पटरी, लाइन। 3. railing, जंगला, रेलिंग। 4. rail transport, रेल परिवहन। *v.* to provide with a rail, छड़ या डंडा लगाना।

rail[2] *v.* to complain bitterly, कोसना, निंदा करना, शिकायत करना।

railing (रेलिंग) *n.* a set of rails

supported by posts, जंगला, रेलिंग।
railway (रेलवे) ***n.*** 1. a track for trains, रेलपथ। 2. the organisation responsible for the operation of rail system, रेल-संघटन, रेल-तंत्र, रेलवे।
rain (रेन) ***n.*** 1. shower, वर्षा, बरसात। 2. a large quantity of anything, बौछार। ***v.*** to fall as or like rain, बरसना।
rainbow (रेनबो) ***n.*** a coloured arc in the sky, इंद्रधनुष।
raincoat (रेनकोट) ***n.*** a waterproof coat, बरसाती कोट, बरसाती।
rain gauge ***n.*** an instrument for measuring rainfall, वर्षामापी।
rainproof (रेनप्रूफ़) ***adj.*** not permitting rain to come through, वर्षासह।
rainy (रेनी) ***adj.*** characterized by heavy rains, वर्षा-संबंधी।
raise (रेज़) ***v.*** 1. to move to higher level, to elevate, ऊँचा करना, खड़ा करना, उठाना। 2. to build or construct, निर्मित करना, बनाना। 3. to increase, बढ़ाना। 4. to stir up, उद्वेलित करना, उकसाना। 5. to improve, सुधारना, ऊँचा उठाना। 6. to bring to end, उठाना, ख़त्म करना। 7. to gather or collect, एकत्र करना, जुटाना। 8. to bring up, (बच्चों आदि का) पालन-पोषण करना, पालना। ***n.*** an increase, बढ़ती, बढ़ोतरी।
raisin (रेज़िन) ***n.*** a sweet dried grape, किशमिश।
rake[1] (रेक) ***n.*** a long handle with prongs, पाँचा। ***v.*** to gather or collect with a rake, पाँचे से इकट्ठा करना।
rake[2] ***n.*** an immoral person, लंपट या दुराचारी व्यक्ति।
rakish (रेकिश) ***adj.*** given to immoral conduct, dissolute, लंपट, दुराचारी।
rally (रैली) ***v.*** 1. to come or bring together for a common purpose, एकजुट होना या करना। 2. to reassemble (after defeat, पराजय के बाद) पुनः एकजुट होना। 3. to rouse, उठ खड़े होना। 4. to recover one's strength after illness, स्वस्थ होना। ***n.*** 1. an act of rallying, जुटने की क्रिया या भाव, जमावड़ा। 2. a mass meeting to generate enthusiasm, विशाल जनसभा, रैली। 3. a notable rise in prices (after decline, उतार के बाद) क़ीमतों में चढ़ाव। 4. a long distance race of cars etc., over public roads, रैली।
ram (रैम) ***n.*** 1. a male sheep, मेढ़ा, भेड़ा। 2. Aries, मेष राशि। 3. a bar used to drive, batter or crush, थापी, दुरमुस आदि। ***v.*** 1. to strike with a ram, दुरमुस से पीटना। 2. to force into, धकेलना। 3. to collide, टकराना, भिड़ जाना।
ramble (रैम्बल) ***v.*** 1. to wander aimlessly, घूमना, भ्रमण/सैर करना। 2. to write or talk disconnectedly, ऊटपटाँग ढंग से लिखना या बोलना। ***n.*** a leisurely stroll, सैर, भ्रमण।
ramification (रैमिफ़िकेशन) ***n.*** 1. the act of ramifying or the state of being ramified, शाखा निकलने की प्रक्रिया, प्रशाखन। 2. a part of a complex structure, उपशाखा।
ramp (रैम्प) ***n.*** a sloping surface that joins two levels of floor, दो फ़र्शों को जोड़नेवाली ढाल।
rampage (रैम्पेज) ***v.*** to act or behave violently, ऊधम मचाना, तहस-नहस कर डालना। ***n.*** a violent frenzied action or behaviour, उत्पात, ऊधम, तहस-नहस।
rampant (रैम्पेन्ट) ***adj.*** 1. unrestrained, अनियंत्रित। 2. growing

R

or spreading unchecked, बेतहाशा बढ़ने या फैलनेवाला।

rampart (रैम्पार्ट) ***n.*** surrounding wall or embankment of a fort, परकोटा।

ramshackle (रैमशैकल) ***adj.*** dilapidated, crumbling, जर्जर, ख़स्ता।

ranch (रैन्च) ***n.*** a farm for rearing certain animals, पशुफ़ार्म। ***v.*** to manage a ranch, पशुफ़ार्म चलाना।

rancid (रैन्सिड) ***adj.*** smelling or tasting unpleasant, stale, बासी।

rancorous (रैंकरस) ***adj.*** malicious, विद्वेषपूर्ण।

rancour, rancor (रैंकर) ***n.*** deep-seated ill will, द्वेष, विद्वेष।

random (रैन्डम) ***adj.*** haphazard, बिना, संयोगजन्य, सांयोगिक, इत्तफ़ाक़िया। ☐ **at random,** यों ही, बेतरतीब।

randy (रैन्डी) ***adj.*** lustful, कामुक, कामातुर।

range (रेन्ज) ***n.*** 1. a series of mountains, पर्वतमाला, पर्वतश्रेणी। 2. a kind or class, श्रेणी, वर्ग, प्रकार। 3. the distance over which a bullet or missile can travel, (बंदूक की) मार, परास। 4. the area or sphere of activity, प्रभाव-क्षेत्र, क्रियाक्षेत्र, क्षेत्र। 5. a large open area on which livestock graze, चरागाह। 6. a place for shooting practice, चाँदमारी। ***v.*** 1. to arrange in specified way, क्रम से रखना या लगाना। 2. to vary between limits, घटना-बढ़ना। 3. to wander, घूमना-फिरना।

ranger (रेन्जर) ***n.*** a forest officer, वन-रक्षक, वनपाल।

rank (रैंक) ***n.*** 1. official position, पदवी। 2. eminent position, ऊँचा या महत्त्वपूर्ण पद। 3. a row or line, पंक्ति। 4. a series, माला, श्रेणी। ***v.*** 1. to arrange in rows, पंक्तिबद्ध करना। 2. to assign a rank to, पदवी देना। 3. to have a certain rank, पद प्राप्त होना।

ransack (रेनसैक) ***v.*** 1. to search thoroughly, तलाशी लेना, छान डालना। 2. to plunder or rob, लूटना-खसोटना।

ransom (रैन्सम) ***n.*** the price demanded for the release of a captive, फिरौती। ***v.*** to obtain the release of a captive in return for money, फिरौती देकर अपहृत व्यक्ति को छुड़ाना।

rant (रैन्ट) ***v.*** to speak loudly and at length, प्रलाप करना, गला फाड़ना।

rap (रैप) ***v.*** to strike sharply, to knock, ठकठक/खटखट करना। ☐ **rap out,** कह डालना; **rap over the knuckles,** कोसना, झाड़ना। ***n.*** 1. a quick sharp sound, knock, ठकठक, खटखट। 2. a blame, दोषारोपण, लांछन।

rapacious (रैपेशस) ***adj.*** greedy, लोभी।

rapacity (रपैसिटी) ***n.*** greed, लोभ।

rape (रेप) ***n.*** 1. a sexual act committed by force, बलात्कार। 2. the act of spoiling, चौपट करना, विनाश। ***v.*** 1. to commit rape upon, बलात्कार करना। 2. to destroy, नष्ट करना।

rapid (रैपिड) ***adj.*** quick, swift, तीव्रगामी, तेज़ द्रुत, द्रुतगामी। ***n.*** a swift current, तेज़ धारा।

rapids (रैपिड्स) ***n.*** (plu.) the part of a river where the current is very fast, नदी का वह स्थान जहाँ बहाव अत्यधिक तेज़ हो।

rapier (रेपिअर) ***n.*** a double-edged sword, कटार।

rapist (रेपिस्ट) ***n.*** one who rapes, बलात्कार करनेवाला, बलात्कारी।

R

rapport (रैपोर) ***n.*** sympathetic or close relationship, मेल-जोल, घनिष्ठता।

rapprochement (रैप्रोचमेन्ट) ***n.*** the establishment of cordial relations, मेल-मिलाप।

rapt (रैप्ट) ***adj.*** 1. engrossed, तन्मय, मग्न। 2. enthralled, मुग्धकारी, मनोहर।

rapture (रैप्चर) ***n.*** intense delight, आनंद, हर्ष, ख़ुशी।

rare (रेअर) ***adj.*** 1. seldom found, विरल, विरला, दुर्लभ। 2. unusually great or fine, असाधारण। ***adj.*** somewhat cooked, अधपका।

raring (रेअरिंग) ***adj.*** enthusiastic, उत्साही, उतावला।

rascal (रैस्कल) ***n.*** a mischievous person, धूर्त, दुष्ट, बदमाश।

rash[1] (रैश) ***adj.*** too hasty, जल्दबाज़ी-भरा, दुस्साहसपूर्ण।

rash[2] ***n.*** an eruption on the skin, चकत्ता, ददोरा।

rasp (रैस्प) ***n.*** a coarse file, रेती। ***v.*** 1. to rub with a rasp, रेती से रगड़ना, रेतना। 2. to utter gratingly, चिढ़कर बोलना, कर्कश ध्वनि करना।

raspberry (रैज़बेरी) ***n.*** a shrub and its fruit, मकोय, रसभरी।

rat (रैट) ***n.*** 1. a mouse, चूहा। 2. a scoundrel, दुष्ट व्यक्ति। ***v.*** to betray the trust, वचन तोड़ना, वचन-भंग करना।

ratchet (रेचिट) ***n.*** a toothed wheel, दाँतेदार पहिया जो एक दिशा में घूमता है, रैचट।

rate (रेट) ***n.***1. the amount of one thing in relation to units of something else, दर, भाव। 2. a fixed ratio, अनुपात। 3. price or value, मूल्य। 4. speed, गति, रफ़्तार। 5. a class or rank, कोटि; of first rate, उत्तम कोटि का। ***v.*** 1. to estimate the value of, दाम आँकना या लगाना। 2. to put into a particular class, किसी विशिष्ट श्रेणी में रखना। 3. to esteem, महत्त्व देना या मानना।

rather (रादर) ***adv.*** 1. slightly, कुछ-कुछ, कुछ, किंचित्। 2. more exactly, वस्तुतः, निश्चय ही। 3. by preference, ज़्यादा करके। 4. on the contrary, but, बल्कि, उलटे। □ **rather than,** (i) के बदले, के बजाय, (ii) पर, बल्कि।

ratification (रैटिफ़िकेशन) ***n.*** an act of ratifying, confirmation, अभिपुष्टि।

ratify (रैटिफ़ाइ) ***v.*** to give formal sanction to, अभिपुष्टि करना।

rating (रेटिंग) ***n.*** 1. rank or grade, श्रेणी, कोटि। 2. a placement in a certain rank, किसी श्रेणी या कोटि में रखा जाना, क्रम-निर्धारण। 3. an estimate of financial status, आर्थिक स्थिति का निर्धारण, मूल्य-निर्धारण। 4. an amount determined as a rate, दर के रूप में निश्चित की हुई राशि, निर्धारित मूल्य।

ratio (रेशो) ***n.*** proportion, अनुपात।

ration (रैशन) ***n.*** fixed quantity or allotment of food or provisions, नियत अंश, राशन। ***v.*** to restrict to limited allotments, राशनिंग करना, कंट्रोल लगाना, नियंत्रण लगाना।

rational (रैशनल) ***adj.*** 1. sane, intelligent, (व्यक्ति) बुद्धिशील, तर्कशील। 2. reasonable, बुद्धिसंगत, तर्कसंगत, तर्कमूलक।

rationale (रैशिअनालि) ***n.*** 1. logical basis, तर्कसंगत आधार। 2. explanation of principles, सिद्धांतों का स्पष्टीकरण।

rationalization (रैशनलाइज़ेशन) ***n.*** the act of rationalizing, तर्कसम्मतीकरण, सुव्यवस्थीकरण।

R

rationalize (रैशनलाइज़) ***v.*** 1. to make logical, तर्कसम्मत बनाना। 2. to cause to appear logical, देखने में तर्कसंगत बनाना।

rat race ***n.*** a continual or exhausting routine of competitive struggle to maintain one's position, अंधी दौड़।

rattle (रैटल) ***v.*** to make a series of short sharp sounds, खड़खड़ करना, खनखनाना। ***n.*** a rapid succession of sharp short sounds, खड़खड़, खड़खड़ाहट, खनखन।

rattling (रैटलिंग) ***adj.*** 1. vigorous, ज़ोरदार। 2. very much, अत्यधिक, बहुत; a rattling good story, बहुत बढ़िया कहानी।

ravage (रैविज) ***v.*** to devastate, तहस-नहस करना, नष्ट कर देना।

rave (रेव) ***v.*** 1. to talk wildly as if in fever or mad, (बेहोशी में) बड़बड़ाना। 2. to roar, गर्जन करना, गरजना। 3. to praise enthusiastically, ख़ूब प्रशंसा करना।

ravel (रैवल) ***v.*** to separate knitted fabric into threads, उधेड़ना। 2. to be tangled, उलझना।

raven (रेवन) ***n.*** a large black bird, काला कौआ, डोम कौआ। ***adj.*** glossy black, काला और चमकीला।

ravenous (रैवनस) ***adj.*** 1. starving, भुखमरा। 2. very hungry, बहुत भूखा। 3. greedy लोभी।

ravine (रैवीन) ***n.*** a deep narrow valley, गहरी संकरी घाटी।

raving (रेविंग) ***adj.*** 1. talking wildly, delirious, बड़बड़ाता हुआ, उन्मत्त। 2. notable, उल्लेखनीय, महत्त्वपूर्ण।

ravish (रैविश) ***v.*** 1. to rape, बलात्कार करना। 2. to enrapture, प्रफुल्लित होना।

ravishing (रैविशिंग) ***adj.*** 1. delightful, आनंददायक। 2. very beautiful, अतिसुंदर।

raw (रॉ) ***adj.*** 1. not cooked, कच्चा। 2. in a natural and unrefined state, not fully processed, कच्चा, अपरिष्कृत, अनगढ़। 3. unskilled, ignorant, अनाड़ी, अकुशल। 4. harshly cold or damp, बहुत ठंडा या सीलन-भरा। 5. unjust, अनुचित।

raw-boned (रॉ-बोन्ड) ***adj.*** gaunt, दुबला-पतला, मरियल।

ray (रे) ***n.*** a beam of light, किरण, रश्मि।

rayon (रेऑन) ***n.*** a synthetic fibre, रेयॉन।

raze (रेज़) ***v.*** to demolish, to destroy completely, पूरी तरह ध्वस्त करना, पूरी तरह ढाना।

razor (रेज़र) ***n.*** an instrument with a sharp blade for shaving, उस्तरा।

razzle-dazzle (रैज़ल-डैज़ल) ***n.*** 1. showy fuss, होहल्ला। 2. spree, रंगरली।

re (रि) ***prefix.*** again, पुनर्।

reach (रीच) ***v.*** 1. to stretch out or extend, पहुँच होना, हाथ ले जाना। 2. to arrive at, पहुँचना। 3. to touch, छूना। 4. to establish communication with, संपर्क करना। 5. to amount to, जा पहुँचना। ***n.*** 1. the act of reaching, पहुँच। 2. the extent covered by one's mental power or ability, उड़ान, पहुँच।

react (रीऐक्ट) ***v.*** to act in response to something in a contrary manner, प्रतिक्रिया करना।

reaction (रीऐक्शन) ***n.*** an opposing action, प्रतिक्रिया।

reactive (रीऐक्टिव) ***adj.*** tending to react, प्रतिक्रियक, प्रतिक्रियात्मक।

reactivity (रीऐक्टिविटी) ***n.*** ability to react, प्रतिक्रिया क्षमता।

reactor (रीऐक्टर) ***n.*** an apparatus for the controlled production of nuclear energy, नाभिक ऊर्जा उत्पन्न करने का यंत्र, रिएक्टर।

read (रीड) ***v.*** (read, reading) 1. to understand the meaning of something written or printed, पढ़ना, पढ़ लेना। 2. to speak aloud something written or printed, ज़ोर से पढ़ना या पढ़ कर सुनाना। 3. to determine the intent or mood of, to comprehend, समझना, भाँपना, ताड़ना। 4. to indicate, बताना, बतलाना। □ **read between the lines,** छिपा अर्थ ढूँढ़ निकालना।

readable (रीडेबल) ***adj.*** 1. able to be read, सुपाठ्य। 2. interesting, रोचक।

reader (रीडर) ***n.*** 1. one who reads, पढ़नेवाला, पाठक, वाचक। 2. a senior university lecturer, रीडर, उपाचार्य। 3. a text book, पाठ्य पुस्तक।

readership (रीडरशिप) ***n.*** 1. all the readers collectively, पाठक-संख्या। 2. the post of a reader, रीडर या उपाचार्य का पद।

readily (रेडिली) ***adv.*** 1. willingly, ख़ुशी-ख़ुशी। 2. easily, आसानी से, सुगमता से। 3. promptly, quickly, तत्परतापूर्वक, शीघ्रतापूर्वक।

readiness (रेडिनिस) ***n.*** the state or quality of being ready, तैयारी, तत्परता, उपलब्धता।

readjust (रीएडजस्ट) ***v.*** to adjust again, पुनःसमायोजित करना।

readmit (रीएडमिट) ***v.*** to admit again, पुनर्प्रवेश करना/कराना।

ready (रेडी) ***adj.*** 1. prepared, प्रस्तुत, तैयार। 2. willing or eager, इच्छुक या उत्सुक। 3. prompt, तत्पर, उद्यत। 4. quick in understanding, विचक्षण। 5. available for action or use, तैयार, उपलब्ध।

readymade (रेडीमेड) ***adj.*** already made, सिला-सिलाया, बना-बनाया, तैयार।

ready-reckoner (रेडीरेकनर) ***n.*** a table of number for simple calculations, गणन-फलक।

reagent (रीएजन्ट) ***n.*** (chem.) a substance used to produce chemical change, रीएजेंट।

real (रीअल) ***adj.*** 1. actual, असली, वास्तविक, यथार्थ। 2. genuine, विशुद्ध, असली।

real estate ***n.*** land including permanent building on it, ज़मीन-जायदाद, भूसंपत्ति।

realism (रीअलिज़म) ***n.*** the depiction of reality, यथार्थ चित्रण; यथार्थवाद।

reality (रीएलिटी) ***n.*** 1. the quality or state of being real, actuality, वास्तविकता, यथार्थता, असलियत। 2. truth, सच्चाई।

realizable (रीअलाइज़ेबल) ***adj.*** that can be realized, वसूलने योग्य।

realization (रीअलाइज़ेशन) ***n.*** the act of realizing or something realized, वसूली, उगाही, उपलब्धि, प्राप्ति, बोध, अनुभूति।

realize (रीअलाइज़) ***v.*** 1. to collect, वसूल करना, उगाहना। 2. to obtain, उपलब्ध/प्राप्त करना। 3. to bring to fruition, परिणत/चरितार्थ करना, पूरा करना। 4. to convert into money by selling, दाम खड़ा करना। 5. to

R

become aware of, अनुभूत या महसूस करना, बोध/भान होना, समझना।

realm (रेल्म) ***n.*** 1. a kingdom, राज्य। 2. a field, क्षेत्र।

realty (रीअल्टी) ***n.*** real estate, भूसंपत्ति, जमीन-जायदाद।

ream (रीम) ***n.*** five hundred sheets of paper, रीम।

reap (रीप) ***v.*** 1. to cut a crop, फ़सल काटना, कटनी करना, लुनना। 2. to get as a reward of some action, भरना, पाना, प्राप्त करना, किए का फल पाना या भोगना।

reaper (रीपर) ***n.*** 1. one who reaps, लुनेरा। 2. a machine for reaping, रीपर।

rear[1] (रिअर) ***n.*** the back part of something, पिछला भाग, पिछवाड़ा, पृष्ठभाग।

rear[2] ***v.*** 1. to bring up, पालना-पोसना। 2. to lift upright on the hind legs, (घोड़े आदि का) पिछले पैरों पर खड़े होना। 3. to lift up, ऊपर उठाना। 4. to build, निर्मित करना।

rearm (रीआर्म) ***v.*** to arm again, पुनरस्त्रीकरण करना।

rearmament (रीआर्ममेन्ट) ***n.*** the act of rearming or the state of being rearmed, पुनरस्त्रीकरण।

rearrange (रीअरेन्ज) ***v.*** to arrange again, दुबारा क्रम से लगाना, पुनर्विन्यास करना।

rearward (रिअरवर्ड) ***adv.*** toward the rear, पीछे की ओर।

reason (रीज़न) ***n.*** 1. a cause or justification for something, तर्क, दलील, कारण, हेतु। 2. sanity, sound mind, intelligence, बुद्धि, विवेक। ***v.*** 1. to think logically, सही ढंग से सोचना, तर्क करना। 2. to work out by reasoning, तर्क से काम निकालना। 3. to persuade (someone) by argument, समझाना-बुझाना।

reasonable (रीज़नेबल) ***adj.*** 1. sensible, समझदार, विवेकशील। 2. in accordance with reason, युक्तियुक्त, तर्कसंगत। 3. moderate, उचित, समीचीन।

reasoning (रीज़निंग) ***n.*** 1. the act of drawing conclusions from facts etc., तर्कणा, विचारण। 2. the use of one's reason, विवेकशक्ति। 3. an argument, तर्क।

reassure (रीअश्योर) ***v.*** to assure again, फिर से आश्वस्त करना।

rebate (रीबेट) ***n.*** discount, कमीशन, बट्टा।

rebel[1] (रिबेल) ***v.*** to resist by force an established government, ruling authority or convention, विद्रोह करना, बग़ावत करना।

rebel[2] (रेबल) ***n.*** one who rebels, विद्रोही, बग़ावत करनेवाला।

rebellion (रिबेल्यन) ***n.*** armed resistance to a government, बग़ावत, विद्रोह।

rebound[1] (रिबाउन्ड) ***v.*** to bounce back, फेंकी हुई वस्तु का किसी चीज़ से टकराकर फिर वापस आना, प्रतिक्षेप होना।

rebound[2] (रीबाउन्ड) ***n.*** 1. the act of springing back, प्रतिक्षेप। 2. reaction, प्रतिक्रिया।

rebuff (रिबफ़) ***n.*** blunt refusal or rejection, रूखा या कठोर जवाब। ***v.*** to snub, रुखाई से प्रत्युत्तर देना।

rebuke (रीब्यूक) ***v.*** to scold, डाँटना-फटकारना। ***n.*** a sharp reproof, डाँट-फटकार।

rebut (रिबट) ***v.*** to refute, मानने से इन्कार करना, खंडन करना।

recalcitrant (रिकैल्सिट्रेन्ट) ***adj.*** disobedient, अवज्ञाकारी, अड़ियल, उद्धत।

recall (रिकॉल) ***v.*** 1. to call back, वापस बुलाना। 2. to remember or recollect, याद करना, स्मरण करना। 3. to cancel, रद करना, वापस लेना। ***n.*** 1. the act of recalling, वापस बुलाना, वापसी की बुलाहट। 2. recollection, स्मरण, अनुस्मरण। 3. cancellation, रद करना, निरस्त करना, निरसन।

recant (रिकैन्ट) ***v.*** 1.to make a formal denial or repudiation of a previously held belief, अपना मतत्याग करना। 2. to retract, मुकर जाना।

recapitulate (रीकपिचुलेट) ***v.*** to repeat briefly, सार रूप में फिर से कहना, संक्षेप में दुहराना।

recapture (रीकैप्चर) ***v.*** 1. to capture again, पुनः क़ब्जा करना, पुनः अपने अधिकार में कर लेना। 2. to recollect, अनुस्मरण करना। ***n.*** 1. the act of recapturing, फिर से होनेवाला क़ब्जा। 2. recollection, अनुस्मरण।

recast (रीकास्ट) ***v.*** (recast, recasting) 1.to cast again, फिर से ढालना, नया रूप देना। 2.to reconstruct, फिर से बनाना, लिखना आदि। 3. to provide a new cast for a play, पात्र बदल देना।

recede (रिसीड) ***v.*** 1.to move back, पीछे हटना। 2. to diminish, घटना। 3. to slope backward, पीछे की ओर झुका होना।

receipt (रिसीट) ***n.*** 1. the act of receiving, प्राप्ति। 2. a written acknowledgment, पावती, रसीद। 3. (plu.) the amount of money received, आय, धनराशि। ***v.*** to write a receipt (for), रसीद लिखना या लिख देना।

receive (रिसीव) ***v.*** 1. to get, accept or acquire, प्राप्त करना, पाना, ग्रहण क़रना। 2. to greet on arrival, आनेवाले का स्वागत करना। 3. to experience, सहना, भोगना। 4. to take in or contain, धारण करना। ☐ **on the receiving end,** भुगतनेवाला।

receiver (रिसीवर) ***n.*** 1. one who receives, प्राप्तकर्ता, पानेवाला। 2. a person appointed by a court to administer the property of parties involved in a law suit, आदाता, रिसीवर। 3. a device for receiving electrical waves, रिसीवर।

recent (रीसन्ट) ***adj.*** new, modern, नूतन, अर्वाचीन, आधुनिक, हाल का।

receptacle (रिसेप्टेकल) ***n.*** a container, आधान, पात्र।

reception (रिसेप्शन) ***n.*** 1. a welcome, स्वागत, अगवानी। 2. a formal party for guests, स्वागत-समारोह। 3. an area in a hotel where visitors are received, स्वागत-कक्ष, स्वागत विभाग। 4. (tech.) receiving of electromagnetic signals, अभिग्रहण।

receptionist (रिसेप्शनिस्ट) ***n.*** a person who receives callers and answers the telephone, स्वागती, स्वागत अधिकारी।

receptive (रिसेप्टिव) ***adj.*** quick to receive new ideas or suggestions, ग्रहणशील।

receptor (रिसेप्टर) ***n.*** (tech.) a receptive, अभिग्राही।

recess (रिसेस) ***n.*** 1. a temporary cessation from business, अवकाश, विराम, मध्यावकाश। 2. a small cavity, छिद्र, छेद, गड्ढा। 3. a niche, ताक, आला।

recession (रिसेशन) ***n.*** a temporary

R

decline in economic activity, (व्यापारिक) मंदी।

recharge (रीचार्ज) ***v.*** to charge again, (बैटरी को) पुनः चार्ज करना, पुनःपूरण करना।

recidivism (रिसिडिविज़म) ***n.*** the tendency to return to criminal habits, अपराधवृत्ति, अपराधशीलता।

recipe (रेसिपी) ***n.*** 1. directions for preparing food, पाकविधि। 2. a way of achieving something, प्राप्त करने की विधि या ढंग।

recipient (रिसिपिएन्ट) ***n.*** one who receives, प्राप्तकर्ता।

reciprocal (रिसिप्रोकल) ***adj.*** mutual, पारस्परिक, आपसी, अन्योन्य।

reciprocate (रिसिप्रकेट) ***v.*** 1. to interchange, आदान-प्रदान करना, लेना-देना। 2. to move backwards and forwards, मशीन के पुर्ज़े का एक बार आगे और दूसरी बार पीछे जाना।

recital (रिसाइटल) ***n.*** 1. the act of reciting, कविता पाठ। 2. description, विवरण, वृत्तांत। 3. a programme given by a soloist, एकल वादक द्वारा प्रस्तुत कार्यक्रम।

recitation (रेसिटेशन) ***n.*** 1. a recital, पढ़ने की क्रिया या भाव, कविता-पाठ। 2. an account, विवरण। 3. something recited, उद्धरणी।

recite (रिसाइट) ***v.*** 1. to repeat from memory, पढ़ना, सुनाना, पाठ करना। 2. to state facts in order, तथ्यों को क्रम से कहना।

reckless (रेकलिस) ***adj.*** 1. heedless, careless, लापरवाह। 2. rash, जल्दबाज़, उतावला।

reckon (रेकन) ***v.*** 1. to count, गिनना, गिनती करना। 2. to consider as, मानना, समझना। 3. to estimate, अनुमान लगाना। 4. to rely or depend, भरोसा करना।

reckoning (रेकनिंग) ***n.*** 1. the act of counting, गिनती। 2. guess, अनुमान। ☐ **a day of reckoning,** क़यामत का दिन।

reclaim (रीक्लेम) ***v.*** 1. to regain possession (of something, किसी चीज़ को) पुनः प्राप्त करना। 2. to make (land) usable for growing crops, कृषियोग्य बनाना। 3. to reform, सुधारना, सन्मार्ग पर लाना।

reclamation (रेक्लमेशन) ***n.*** 1. the act of reclaiming, पुनः प्राप्त करने की क्रिया। 2. a reform, सुधार।

recline (रिक्लाइन) ***v.*** to rest in a leaning position, (सुस्ताने के लिए) लुढ़कना, ढलकना, टिकना।

recluse (रिक्लूस) ***n.*** one who lives in solitude, एकांतवासी साधु, संन्यासी।

recognition (रेकग्निशन) ***n.*** 1. the act of recognizing, पहचान, अभिज्ञान। 2. approval, मान्यता।

recognize (रेकग्नाइज़) ***v.*** 1. to identify, पहचान लेना। 2. to approve of, to acknowledge formally, मान्यता देना। 3. to accept, स्वीकार करना।

recognized (रेकनाइज़्ड) ***adj.*** 1. identified, पहचाना हुआ, अभिज्ञात। 2. given recognition, मान्यताप्राप्त, मान्य।

recoil (रिकॉइल) ***v.*** 1. to shrink back, पीछे हटना, दुबकना। 2. to jerk back, (बंदूक का) पीछे आघात करना, झटका देना। ***n.*** a jerk back, झटका, पश्चाघात।

recollect (रेकलेक्ट) ***v.*** to call back to mind, याद करना, स्मरण करना।

recommend (रेकमेन्ड) ***v.*** 1. to advise as the best choice, सिफ़ारिश

करना, अनुशंसा करना। 2. to advise, राय देना, सलाह देना।

recommendation (रेकमेन्डेशन) ***n.*** 1. an act of recommending, सिफ़ारिश करना। 2. a letter recommending a person or thing, सिफ़ारिशी पत्र। 3. advice, राय, परामर्श, सिफ़ारिश।

reconcile (रेकन्साइल) ***v.*** 1. to restore friendship between, आपस में समझौता या मेल करना। 2. to bring (oneself) to accept, राजी हो जाना। 3. to settle a dispute, झगड़ा निपटाना। 4. to make consistent, संगति बैठाना।

reconciliation (रेकन्सिलिएशन) ***n.*** the act of reconciling or the state of being reconciled, मेल, मेल-मिलाप, समझौता, संराधन।

recondition (रीकन्डिशन) ***v.*** to restore to good condition, मरम्मत करके नया बना देना।

reconnaissance (रिकॉनिसेन्स) ***n.*** a close survey of a region, गहन सर्वेक्षण।

record (रिकॉर्ड) ***v.*** 1. to set down in writing, दर्ज़ करना, लिख लेना, अभिलिखित करना। 2. to indicate, सूचित करना, बतलाना। 3. to serve as evidence of, साक्षी देना, प्रमाणित करना। ***n.*** 1. a written account, अभिलेख। 2. a recorded fact about anything, लिखित तथ्य, प्रमाण। 3. the best performance, कीर्तिमान, रिकार्ड। 4. a flat disc on which sound has been recorded, रिकार्ड, तवा।

recorded (रिकॉर्डिड) ***adj.*** on record, अभिलिखित, अभिलेखबद्ध।

recorder (रिकॉर्डर) ***n.*** 1. one who keeps records, अभिलेखपाल। 2. a machine that records, (यंत्र) अभिलेखी।

recount (रिकाउन्ट) ***v.*** 1. to count again, दुबारा या फिर से गिनना, पुनर्गणना करना। 2. to narrate or relate, विवरण देना। ***n.*** the act of recounting, पुनर्गणना।

recoup (रिकूप) ***v.*** 1. to recover what one has lost, पुनर्प्राप्त करना, दुबारा पाना। 2. to compensate, क्षति-पूर्ति करना।

recourse (रिकोर्स) ***n.*** a turning to someone for protection or help, शरण या सहायता की पेशकश।

recover (रिकवर) ***v.*** 1. to find again, पुनः प्राप्त करना। 2. to obtain the return of something lost, बदले में पाना। 3. to gain a normal condition, सामान्य अवस्था प्राप्त करना, चंगा हो जाना। 4. to collect, वसूल करना।

recoverable (रिकवरेबल) ***adj.*** that can be recovered, वसूलने योग्य।

recovery (रिकवरी) ***n.*** 1. the act of recovering or the state of being recovered, पुनर्प्राप्ति, वसूली। 2. a return to normal state of health, स्वास्थ्य-लाभ।

recreate (रेक्रिएट) ***v.*** to refresh mentally or physically, मनबहलाव करना।

recreation (रेक्रिएशन) ***n.*** enjoyment, मनबहलाव, मनोविनोद।

recriminate (रिक्रिमिनेट) ***v.*** to accuse in return, दोष लगानेवाले पर दोष लगाना, प्रत्यारोप करना।

recrimination (रिक्रिमिनेशन) ***n.*** the act of recriminating or an accusation made in retaliation, प्रत्यारोप।

recruit (रिक्रूट) ***n.*** a new and unexperienced member of the armed forces, रंगरूट। ***v.*** to enlist as a recruit, रंगरूट भर्ती करना।

rectangle (रेक्टैन्गल) ***n.*** (maths.) a four-sided figure with four right angles, आयत।

rectification (रेक्टिफ़िकेशन) ***n.*** the act of rectifying, परिशोधन।

rectify (रेक्टिफ़ाइ) ***v.*** to put right, सुधारना, परिशोधन करना।

rectilinear (रेक्टिलिनिअर) ***adj.*** consisting of or formed by a straight line or lines, ऋजुरेखीय।

rectitude (रेक्टिट्यूड) ***n.*** moral correctness, ईमानदारी, सदाचार।

rector (रेक्टर) ***n.*** 1. a clergyman in charge of a parish, पल्ली पुरोहित, रेक्टर। 2. a head of a college or university, अधिष्ठाता, रेक्टर।

rectum (रेक्टम) ***n.*** the lower end of the alimentary canal, मलाशय।

recuperate (रिक्यूपरेट) ***v.*** to recover, स्वास्थ्य-लाभ करना।

recur (रिकर) ***v.*** 1. to happen again, दुबारा घटित होना। 2. to come up again, दुबारा प्रकट होना।

recurrence (रिकरन्स) ***n.*** the act of recurring or the state of being recurred, दुबारा या बार-बार होना, पुनरावृत्ति।

recurring (रिकरिंग) ***adj.*** occurring again and again, आवर्तक, आवर्ती।

red (रेड) ***adj.*** 1. of the colour of blood, रक्तवर्ण, लाल, सुर्ख। 2. communist, कम्युनिस्ट, साम्यवादी, लाल। ***n.*** 1. a red colour, लाल रंग। 2. a communist, कम्युनिस्ट, वामपंथी, साम्यवादी। ☐ **in the red,** लाल स्याही से लिखा हुआ (ऋण या घाटे का सूचक); **see red,** आपे से बाहर हो जाना।

red alert (रेड अलर्ट) ***n.*** an order to make alert the police force for an emergency to occur, रेड अलर्ट।

Red Cross (रेडक्रॉस) ***n.*** an international organization, रेड क्रॉस।

redden (रेडन) ***v.*** to make or become red, लाल करना या होना।

redeem (रिडीम) ***v.*** 1. to set free, उद्धार करना, मुक्त करना या कराना। 2. to fulfil (a promise, वचन) निभाना, पूरा करना। 3. to buy back, पुनः ख़रीद लेना, पुनः प्राप्त करना। 4. to atone for, प्रायश्चित्त करना। 5. to compensate, क्षतिपूर्ति करना।

redeeming (रिडीमिंग) ***adj.*** that redeems, सुधार करनेवाला। ☐ **redeeming feature,** something good in a thoroughly bad person or thing, सराहनीय गुण, ख़ूबी, अच्छी बात।

redemption (रिडेम्पशन) ***n.*** 1. the act of redeeming or the state of being redeemed, उद्धार, छुटकारा, मुक्ति; शोधन। 2. atonement, प्रायश्चित्त। 3. compensation, क्षतिपूर्ति।

redeploy (रीडिप्लॉइ) ***v.*** to move (troops) from one front to another, एक स्थान से दूसरे स्थान पर (सेना) भेजना या लगाना।

red-handed (रेड-हैन्डिड) ***adv.*** in the act of doing something wrong, रँगे हाथ।

redhot (रेडहॉट) ***adj.*** 1. very hot, लाल, जलता हुआ। 2. new, recent, नवीन, नवीनतम।

redirect (रीडाइरेक्ट) ***v.*** to send to another address or place, दूसरे पते से भेजना, पुनर्प्रेषण करना।

red-letter (रेड-लेटर) ***adj.*** 1. memorable, स्मरणीय। 2. happy, सुखद।

redlight area ***n.*** an area of

prostitutes, वेश्याओं का मुहल्ला, चकला, शृंगारहाट।

redolence (रेडोलेन्स) ***n.*** odour, smell, गंध, महक।

redolent (रेडोलेन्ट) ***adj.*** 1. having the odour or smell, तेज गंधवाला, गंधयुक्त, महकदार। 2. suggestive, सूचक, संकेतक।

redoubtable (रिडाउटेबल) ***adj.*** formidable, प्रबल, दुर्जेय।

redress (रिड्रेस) ***v.*** 1. to set right, rectify, (ग़लती को) सुधारना। 2. to compensate, क्षतिपूर्ति करना। ***n.*** 1. correction, सुधार। 2. compensation, क्षतिपूर्ति।

red tape ***n.*** official time-consuming procedures, लालफ़ीताशाही।

reduce (रिड्यूस) ***v.*** 1. to diminish, कम करना या होना, घटाना या घटना। 2. to make lower in status, दर्जा घटना, पदावनत करना। 3. to bring to a certain condition, किसी विशिष्ट स्थिति में ला देना, परिवर्तित कर देना। 4. (maths.) to change an expression to its simple form, (किसी समीकरण को) सरल बनाना। 5. (chem.) to make thin, तनुकरण/अपचयन करना।

reduction (रिडक्शन) ***n.*** 1. the act of reducing or the state of being reduced, कमी, घटाव, घटती, ह्रास। 2. commission, छूट, बट्टा, कटौती। 3. anything made by reducing, लघु प्रति।

redundancy (रिडन्डेन्सी) ***n.*** 1. the state or quality of being redundant, फ़ालतूपन। 2. verbosity, शब्दाडंबर।

redundant (रिडन्डेन्ट) ***adj.*** 1. superfluous, excessive, अनावश्यक, फ़ालतू, बेकार। 2. verbose, शब्दाडंबरपूर्ण।

reed (रीड) ***n.*** 1. a tall, hollow-stemmed plant, सरकंडा, नरकट, नरकुल। 2. a thin piece of this plant used in a wind instrument to produce various sound, पत्ती। 3. a flute, बाँसुरी।

reedy (रीडी) ***adj.*** 1. full of reeds, सरकंडों से भरा। 2. melodious, सुरीला, मधुर।

reef (रीफ़) ***n.*** a line or ridge of rock or sand lying near the surface of water, समुद्र में स्थित चट्टान या बालू की श्रेणी, शैलभित्ति।

reef knot (रीफ़ नॉट) ***n.*** a common square knot, दुहरी गाँठ, पोल गाँठ।

reek (रीक) ***n.*** 1. a strong foul smell, बदबू, दुर्गंध। 2. smoke, steam etc., धुआँ, भाप आदि। ***v.*** 1. to emit strong smell, बदबू करना/देना। 2. to emit smoke, steam etc., धुआँ छोड़ना या देना।

reel (रील) ***n.*** a spool on which something is wound, रील। ***v.*** 1. to wind on a reel, रील पर लपेटना। 2. to say or write fluently, धड़ल्ले से बोलना या लिखना।

refectory (रिफ़ेक्टरी) ***n.*** a dining hall, भोजन-कक्ष।

refer (रेफ़र) ***v.*** 1. to direct to a source of help, अभिदेश करना, निर्दिष्ट करना। 2. to mention, उल्लेख/ज़िक्र करना। 3. to direct to (some authority, किसी अधिकारी) के पास भेजना, पेश करना। 4. to turn (to a thing) for information, (कोई चीज़) देखना। 5. to concern, से संबंध रखना, के बारे में होना।

referee (रेफ़री) ***n.*** a person to whom

R

anything is referred for decision, रेफ़री। *v.* to act as a referee, रेफ़री का काम करना।

reference (रेफ़रन्स) *n.* 1. the act of referring, अभिदेशन। 2. something that can be referred to, संदर्भ, हवाला। 3. mention, उल्लेख, ज़िक्र। 4. connection, संबंध। 5. a person to whom one refers for testimony, प्रमाणित करनेवाला व्यक्ति, प्रमाणपत्र देनेवाला व्यक्ति।

referendum (रेफ़रेन्डम) *n.* the referring of a question to a direct popular vote, जनमत-संग्रह।

refill (रीफ़िल) *v.* to fill again, फिर से भरना। *n.* a new filling, रिफ़िल।

refine (रिफ़ाइन) *v.* to purify, शोधन/परिष्कार करना।

refined (रिफ़ाइन्ड) *adj.* 1. purified, शोधित, परिष्कृत। 2. cultured, polished, शिष्टतापूर्ण, शिष्ट, सभ्य।

refinery (रिफ़ाइनरी) *n.* a plant for refining crude oil, तेलशोधक कारख़ाना, शोधनशाला।

reflect (रिफ़्लेक्ट) *v.* 1. to throw backward, परावर्तित करना। 2. to mirror, प्रतिबिंबित करना। 3. to ponder, विचार करना। 4. to express, व्यक्त करना।

reflection (रिफ़्लेक्शन) *n.* 1. the act of reflecting, परावर्तन। 2. a reflected image, प्रतिबिंब। 3. deep thought, चिंतन, मनन, सोच-विचार।

reflector (रिफ़्लेक्टर) *n.* a thing that reflects images, light, heat etc., परावर्तक।

reflex (रिफ़्लेक्स) *n.* reaction, प्रतिक्रिया। *adj.* reflected back, परावर्ती।

reflexive (रिफ़्लेक्सिव) *adj.* (gram.) referring back to the subject, निजवाचक।

reform (रिफ़ॉर्म) *v.* 1. to correct, सुधरना/सुधारना। 2. to make better, सुधार करना। *n.* improvement, सुधार।

reformatory (रिफ़ॉर्मेटरी) *n.* an institution to discipline young offenders, बाल-सुधारगृह।

refract (रिफ़्रैक्ट) *v.* to deflect, (की) दिशा बदलना या मोड़ना, अपवर्तन करना।

refractory (रिफ़्रैक्टरी) *adj.* 1. stubborn, हठी, अड़ियल। 2. not yielding to treatment, असाध्य (रोग)। 3. resistant to heat, ऊष्मासह।

refrain[1] (रिफ़्रेन) *v.* to hold oneself back from doing something, बाज़ आना।

refrain[2] *n.* a line repeated at intervals in a poem or song, टेक।

refresh (रिफ़्रेश) *v.* to make or become fresh, तरोताज़ा होना या करना।

refresher course (रिफ़्रेशर कोर्स) *n.* a course to keep abreast, पुनश्चर्या पाठ्यक्रम।

refreshment (रिफ़्रेशमेन्ट) *n.* 1. the act of refreshing or the state of being refreshed, ताज़गी। 2. food and drink, भोज्य तथा पेय पदार्थ।

refrigerate (रिफ़्रिजरेट) *v.* to cool or chill, प्रशीतन करना।

refrigerator (रिफ़्रिजरेटर) *n.* an apparatus for refrigerating, प्रशीतक, रिफ़्रिजिरेटर।

refuel (रिफ़्यूअल) *v.* 1. to supply again with fuel, पुनः ईंधन भरना। 2. to be filled again with fuel, पुनः ईंधन भरा जाना।

refuge (रेफ़्यूज) *n.* 1. a structure to give protection, shelter, शरण,

आश्रयस्थल। 2. one who gives shelter, शरणदाता।

refugee (रेफ़्यूजी) ***n.*** one who has been forced to leave his/her home or country and seeks refuge elsewhere, शरणार्थी।

refulgent (रिफ़ल्जेन्ट) ***adj.*** shining, देदीप्यमान, चमकदार।

refund (रिफ़न्ड) ***v.*** to give back, वापस करना, लौटाना। ***n.*** the act of refunding or something refunded, वापसी रक़म, लौटान।

refundable (रिफ़न्डेबल) ***adj.*** that can be refunded, जो लौटाया जा सके, प्रतिदेय।

refusal (रिफ़्यूज़ल) ***n.*** denial, इन्कार, अस्वीकृति।

refuse[1] (रिफ़्यूज़) ***v.*** to decline to accept or grant, इन्कार कर देना।

refuse[2] ***n.*** waste, rubbish, कूड़ा, क़तवार।

refutation (रेफ़्युटेशन) ***n.*** the act of refuting, खंडन।

refute (रिफ़्यूट) ***v.*** to prove wrong or false, खंडन करना, (तर्क) काटना।

regain (रिगेन) ***v.*** 1. to obtain again, to get back, पुनः प्राप्त कर लेना। 2. to reach again, पुनः पहुँच जाना।

regal (रीगल) ***adj.*** royal, राजसी, शाही, भव्य।

regale (रिगेल) ***v.*** to entertain thoroughly, भरपूर मनोरंजन करना, आह्लादित करना। 2. to feed sumptuously, अघा देना।

regalia (रिगेलिआ) ***n.*** the emblems or robes of royalty, राजसी वस्त्र, आभूषण, मुकुट आदि; राजचिह्न।

regard (रिगार्ड) ***n.*** 1. esteem, आदर, आदर-भाव। 2. a look, gaze, टकटकी। 3. attention, heed, ध्यान। 4. (plu.) greetings, अभिवादन। ***v.*** 1. to hold in respect, आदर करना, आदरभाव दिखलाना। 2. to look upon in a specified way, मानना। 3. to give attention, ध्यान/तवज्जह देना।

regarding (रिगार्डिंग) ***prep.*** in respect of, के विषय में।

regatta (रिगैटा) ***n.*** an organized series of races of boats, नौका-दौड़।

regency (रीजेन्सी) ***n.*** the office or duration of a regent, शासक या प्रशासक का पद या कार्यकाल।

regenerate (रिजेनरेट) ***v.*** 1. to reform, सुधार करना, सुधारना। 2. to form or create anew, नवीन रूप देना, नया बना देना।

regeneration (रिजेनरेशन) ***n.*** the act of regenerating or the state of being regenerated, सुधार, नवीन रूप, पुनरुत्थान।

regent (रीजन्ट) ***n.*** a ruler or administrator of a country, शासक या प्रशासक।

regime (रेजीम) ***n.*** 1. a system of government, शासन-पद्धति। 2. a social system, सामाजिक पद्धति। 3. = regimen.

regimen (रेजिमेन) ***n.*** a prescribed diet, exercise, behaviour etc., नियत आहार-विहार।

regiment (रेजिमेन्ट) ***n.*** 1. an army unit, सैन्य दल। 2. army, फ़ौज। ***v.*** to control strictly कठोर शासन में रखना।

region (रीजन) ***n.*** 1. an area considered as a unit, भूभाग। 2. a division of a country, प्रदेश, क्षेत्र। 3. a part of the body, हिस्सा, अंग।

regional (रीजनल) ***adv.*** of or

R

pertaining to some regions, प्रादेशिक, क्षेत्रीय।

register (रेजिस्टर) ***n.*** 1. an official list or record, आधिकारिक अभिलेख या सूची। 2. a book in which this is kept, रजिस्टर, पंजी। ***v.*** 1. to record officially, रजिस्टर में लिखना। 2. to express, अभिव्यक्त करना। 3. to send by registered post, रजिस्ट्री से भेजना।

registrar (रेजिस्ट्रार) ***n.*** an official who keeps records, रजिस्ट्रार, निबंधक, पंजीयक।

registry (रेजिस्ट्री) ***n.*** a place where records are kept, निबंधन-गृह, पंजीयन-कार्यालय।

regret (रिग्रेट) ***v.*** to feel sorry, खेद प्रकट करना। ***n.*** sorrow, grief, खेद।

regretful (रिग्रेट्फुल) ***adj.*** feeling regret, जिसे खेद हो, खिन्न, दुखी।

regular (रेग्यूलर) ***adj.*** 1. occurring at fixed time or in a uniform manner, usual, normal, नियमित। 2. permanent, स्थायी। 3. (maths.) equilateral and equiangular, सम। 4. (gram.) belonging to a standard mode of inflection, सामान्य। ***n.*** 1. a member of the permanent armed forces, नियमित सैनिक। 2. a regular customer, नियमित ग्राहक।

regulate (रेग्यूलेट) ***v.*** 1. to bring into conformity with a rule, विनियमित करना। 2. to adjust or control, ठीक करना, व्यवस्थित करना।

regulation (रेग्यूलेशन) ***n.*** 1. the act of regulating, विनियमन। 2. a principle, rule or law, विनियम।

regulator (रेग्यूलेटर) ***n.*** a device for controlling flow, pressure, temperature etc., विनियामक, रेगुलेटर।

rehabilitate (रीअबिलिटेट) ***v.*** 1. to restore (a building) to a good condition, (मकान की) मरम्मत कराना, रहने योग्य बनाना। 2. to give shelter to refugees, पुनर्वास करना, फिर से बसाना। 3. to restore to usual life, सामान्य जीवन व्यतीत करने योग्य बनाना। 4. to reinstate, बहाल करना।

rehearsal (रिहर्सल) ***n.*** the act of rehearsing, पूर्वाभ्यास, रिहर्सल।

rehearse (रिहर्स) ***v.*** to practise in preparation, पूर्वाभ्यास/रिहर्सल करना।

reign (रेन) ***n.*** 1. a sovereign's rule, शासन, राजकाल। 2. dominance, प्रभुत्व। ***v.*** 1. to exercise sovereignty, राज्याध्यक्ष होना, राज करना। 2. to be prevalent, प्रचलित होना, व्याप्त होना, छा जाना।

reimburse (रीइम्बर्स) ***v.*** to repay or refund, to pay back, वापस कर देना, चुकाना, अदा करना, प्रतिपूर्ति करना।

rein (रेन) ***n.*** a strap to control and guide the horse, लगाम, रास, बागडोर। ***v.*** to hold reins, लगाम खींचना/लगाना।

reincarnate (रीइन्कार्नेट) ***v.*** to be reborn in another body, पुनर्जन्म लेना।

reindeer (रेन्डिअर) ***n.*** a large deer with branched antlers, बारहसिंगा, रेनडियर।

reinforce (रीइन्फ़ोर्स) ***v.*** 1. to strengthen, प्रबलित करना, सहायता करना। 2. to strengthen with additional troops, अतिरिक्त कुमुक या सहायता भेजकर प्रबलित करना।

reinforced (रीइन्फ़ोर्स्ड) ***adj.*** strengthened, प्रबलित।

reinstate (रीइन्स्टेट) ***v.*** to restore to a prior position, बहाल करना, पुनर्स्थापन।

reiterate (रीइटरेट) ***v.*** to repeat, बार-बार दुहराना, आवृत्ति करना।

reject (रीजेक्ट) ***v.*** 1. to refuse to accept, to deny, अस्वीकार करना। 2. to throw out, to discard, ख़ारिज कर देना, ठुकरा देना।

rejection (रिजेक्शन) ***n.*** the act of rejecting or discarding, अस्वीकरण।

rejoice (रीजॉइस) ***v.*** to feel or express great joy, ख़ुशियाँ मनाना, रंगरलियाँ मनाना।

rejoicing (रिजॉइसिंग) ***n.*** merrymaking, jubilation, आनंद-मंगल, रंगरलियाँ।

rejoin (रीजॉइन) ***v.*** 1. to join again, फिर से शामिल हो जाना, फिर से मिल जाना। 2. to join together again, फिर से जोड़ या मिला देना।

rejoinder (रिजॉइन्डर) ***n.*** 1. a reply, जवाब। 2. a defendant's reply to a plaintiff, प्रतिवादी का उत्तर।

rejuvenate (रिजूविनेट) ***v.*** to restore the youthful vigour or appearance, युवा बना देना, जीवंत बना देना, कायाकल्प कर देना।

relapse (रिलैप्स) ***v.*** to lapse back to former condition after some recovery, फिर से पहलेवाली (ख़राब) स्थिति में आ जाना, पलटा खा जाना। ***n.*** the act of relapsing or the state of being relapsed, पलटा, पलटाव।

relate (रिलेट) ***v.*** 1. to tell, narrate or describe, सुनाना, बतलाना, वर्णन करना। 2. to bring into relation, संबंध जोड़ना। 3. to have connection with, संबद्ध होना।

relation (रिलेशन) ***n.*** 1. the state of being related, रिश्ता, नाता। 2. a relative, रिश्तेदार, नातेदार। 3. (plu.) dealings or associations with others, व्यवहार या संबंध।

relative (रेलटिव) ***n.*** a person who is related by blood or marriage, रिश्तेदार। ***adj.*** 1. connected, संबद्ध, संबंधित। 2. considered in relation to something else, सापेक्ष। 3. (gram.) referring to an antecedent, संबंधवाचक; relative pronoun, संबंधवाचक सर्वनाम।

relativity (रेलटिविटी) ***n.*** the condition or quality of being relative, सापेक्षता।

relax (रिलैक्स) ***v.*** 1. to take rest, विश्राम करना। 2. to make (muscles) less tense, ढीला छोड़ना, शिथिल करना। 3. to make (rules) less rigid, शिथिल करना या बनाना।

relay (रीले) ***n.*** a fresh set of people or animals to relieve others in work, पड़ाव-पड़ाव पर बदलने के लिए नए जानवर या आदमी। ***v.*** to receive and broadcast on, सह-प्रसारण करना।

release (रिलीस) ***v.*** 1.to set free or liberate, मुक्त करना, रिहा करना। 2. to issue for sale, circulation etc., जारी करना, विमोचन करना, निकालना, प्रकाशित करना। ***n.*** 1. the act of freeing, मुक्ति, छुटकारा। 2. the act of issuing, विमोचन, प्रकाशन।

relent (रिलेन्ट) ***v.*** to become less severe or soften, नरम पड़ जाना, पसीजना।

relentless (रिलेन्टलिस) ***adj.*** pitiless, निर्दय, निष्ठुर, निर्मम।

relevance (रेलिवेन्स) ***n.*** the state or quality of being relevant, प्रासंगिकता, संबद्धता।

relevant (रेलिवेन्ट) ***adj.*** related to the matter in hand, प्रासंगिक, संबद्ध।

R

reliable (रिलाइएबल) ***adj.*** dependable, trustworthy, विश्वसनीय, भरोसेमंद।

reliance (रिलाइएन्स) ***n.*** 1. trust, dependence, विश्वास, भरोसा। 2. someone or something relied on, वह जिसपर भरोसा किया जाए।

relic (रेलिक) ***n.*** 1. something that has historic interest, स्मृति-चिह्न। 2. (plu.) the body or the part of the body of a dead person, अवशेष, अस्थियाँ।

relief (रिलीफ़) ***n.*** 1. ease from discomfort, pain or anxiety, राहत, चैन, छुटकारा। 2. a diversion from monotony, चैन, आराम, छुटकारा। 3. assistance given to the needy, सहायता, मदद। 4. the projection of figures or forms from a flat background, उभारदार नक़्क़ाशी या चित्रण। 5. redress of a grievance, दुःखनिवारण, क्षतिपूर्ति। 6. reinforcement, कुमुक। 7. a person who replaces another at some task or duty, स्थानापन्न व्यक्ति।

relieve (रिलीव) ***v.*** 1. to lessen, to ease, राहत देना, चैन पहुँचाना, (पीड़ा) कम करना। 2. to free from fear, pain or anxiety, मुक्त करना। 3. to free from duty or burden, भारमुक्त करना। ☐ **relieve oneself,** टट्टी या पेशाब करके राहत पाना।

religion (रिलिजन) ***n.*** an organized system of beliefs and rituals usually expressed in worship, मत, धर्म।

religious (रिलिजस) ***adj.*** 1. of or relating to a religion, धार्मिक। 2. pious, godly, धर्मपरायण, धर्मनिष्ठ। 3. scrupulous, अतिसावधान।

relinquish (रिलिंक्विश) ***v.*** to give up, त्याग देना, परित्याग करना।

relish (रेलिश) ***n.*** 1. enjoyment of something eaten or experienced, स्वाद, लुत्फ़, मज़ा। 2. a spicy condiment served with other food, मसाला। ***v.*** to enjoy, स्वाद लेना, मज़ा लेना।

relocate (रीलोकेट) ***v.*** to move to a different place, नई जगह जाना।

reluctant (रिलक्टन्ट) ***adj.*** disinclined, unwilling, अनिच्छुक।

rely (रिलाइ) ***v.*** (relied, relying) to depend (on), निर्भर करना, भरोसा करना।

remain (रिमेन) ***v.*** 1. to stay behind, पीछे रहना। 2. to continue to be, बना रहना। 3. to be left, बाक़ी बचना, शेष रह जाना।

remainder (रिमेन्डर) ***n.*** the quantity left after subtraction, बाक़ी, शेष, शेषफल।

remains (रिमेन्ज़) ***n.*** 1. (plu.) ancient buildings or their parts that have survived, अवशेष। 2. a dead body, शव।

remand (रिमान्ड) ***v.*** to send back (to custody, जेल) वापस भेजना। ***n.*** the act of sending back, न्यायालय द्वारा अभियुक्त को फ़िलहाल हिरासत में रखने के लिए कहा जाना।

remark (रिमार्क) ***v.*** 1. to make a comment, टिप्पणी करना। 2. to notice, ध्यान से देखना। ***n.*** a comment, टिप्पणी।

remarkable (रिमार्केबल) ***adj.*** 1. worthy of notice, ध्यान देने योग्य, उल्लेखनीय। 2. extraordinary, विशिष्ट, उत्कृष्ट।

remedial (रिमीडिअल) ***adj.*** providing a remedy for a disease, उपचारात्मक।

remedy (रेमिडी) ***n.*** 1. a drug, दवा, ओषधि। 2. treatment, इलाज, उपचार, चिकित्सा। 3. something that corrects an error or evil, उपचार, उपाय। ***v.*** 1. to cure, उपचार करना। 2. to rectify, सुधारना।

remember (रिमेम्बर) ***v.*** 1. to keep in one's mind, याद रखना। 2. to racall to one's mind, याद करना, स्मरण करना।

remembrance (रिमेम्ब्रन्स) ***n.*** 1. the act of remembering or the state of being remembered, स्मरण। 2. a keepsake, स्मृति-चिह्न, चिह्नानी। 3. something remembered, याद रखी हुई बात।

remind (रिमाइन्ड) ***v.*** to cause to remember, याद दिलाना।

reminder (रिमाइन्डर) ***n.*** a letter sent to remind someone, स्मरण-पत्र।

reminiscence (रेमिनिसेन्स) ***n.*** a narration of past experiences, संस्मरण।

remiss (रिमिस) ***adj.*** negligent, लापरवाह, असावधान।

remission (रिमिशन) ***n.*** 1. forgiveness for sin, क्षमादान, माफ़ी। 2. release from obligation or penalty, छूट। 3. lessening of pain, पीड़ा में होनेवाली कमी।

remit (रिमिट) ***v.*** 1. to send (money, पैसा) भेजना। 2. to forgive, क्षमा करना।

remittal (रिमिटल) ***n.*** = remittance.

remittance (रिमिटेन्स) ***n.*** 1. the act of remitting, प्रेषण। 2. money sent to someone, भेजी हुई राशि।

remnant (रेम्नेन्ट) ***n.*** a part left over, शेषांश, शेष।

remonstrant (रिमॉन्स्ट्रेन्ट) ***n.*** one who remonstrates, आपत्तिकर्ता, विरोध करनेवाला।

remonstrate (रिमॉन्स्ट्रेट) ***v.*** to argue in protest, आपत्ति करना, विरोध करना।

remorse (रिमोर्स) ***n.*** a sense of guilt felt for one's wrong actions, ग्लानि, पश्चात्ताप।

remote (रिमोट) ***adj.*** 1. distant, दूरस्थ, सुदूर, दूर का। 2. slight or faint, हलका, मंद।

removal (रिमूवल) ***n.*** the act of taking away or being taken away, हटाने या हटाए जाने की क्रिया या भाव, निष्कासन या पदच्युति।

remove (रिमूव) ***v.*** 1. to take away, परे करना, हटा देना। 2. to take off, उतार देना। 3. to dismiss, निकाल या हटा देना, बर्ख़ास्त करना। ***n.*** a step, क़दम।

remuneration (रिम्यूनरेशन) ***n.*** pay or reward for a work, पारिश्रमिक, मेहनताना।

renaissance (रिनेसन्स) ***n.*** 1. a new birth, नया जन्म। 2. revival of art, culture or literature, कला, साहित्य या संस्कृति का पुनर्जन्म या नवजागरण, पुनर्जागरण।

renal (रीनल) ***adj.*** of or pertaining to kidneys, गुर्दे का, वृक्कीय।

rend (रेन्ड) ***v.*** (rent, rending) 1. to tear or rip, (कपड़ा) फाड़ या नोच डालना। 2. to remove forcibly, ज़बरदस्ती हटाना या उठा ले जाना।

render (रेन्डर) ***v.*** 1. to present or submit, प्रस्तुत या पेश करना। 2. to give or make available, देना, उपलब्ध कराना। 3. to cause to become, बना देना, कर देना। 4. to translate, अनुवाद करना। 5. to depict, वर्णन या चित्रण करना।

R

rendering (रेन्डरिंग) ***n.*** 1. the act of presenting, प्रस्तुतीकरण। 2. the act of translating, अनुवाद करना। 3. the act of making payment, भुगतान करना।

rendezvous (रान्डिवूज) ***n.*** 1. a pre-arranged meeting place, पहले से निश्चित मिलने की जगह, अभिसार-स्थल। 2. a popular gathering place, अड्डा। 3. a pre-arranged meeting, पहले से तय किया हुआ मिलन। ***v.*** to meet at certain time and place, निश्चित किए हुए समय तथा स्थान पर मिलना, अभिसार करना।

rendition (रेन्डिशन) ***n.*** the act of rendering, प्रस्तुतीकरण; प्रदान।

renegade (रेनिगेड) ***n.*** a rebel or traitor, विद्रोही, विश्वासघाती।

renege (रिनिग) ***v.*** to play a card of another suit deliberately, जानबूझकर ग़लत रंग का पत्ता चलना, बेईमानी करना।

renew (रिन्यू) ***v.*** 1. to recommence, फिर से शुरू करना। 2. to grant or obtain the extension of, नवीकरण करना।

renewable (रिन्यूएबल) ***adj.*** that can be renewed, नवीकरणीय।

renewal (रिन्यूअल) ***n.*** the act of renewing or the state of being renewed, नवीकरण।

renounce (रिनाउन्स) ***v.*** 1. to give up, छोड़ देना, त्याग देना। 2. to repudiate or disown, अस्वीकार करना, परित्याग करना, संबंध तोड़ लेना।

renovate (रेनोवेट) ***v.*** 1. to restore to good condition, अच्छी हालत में लाना, नया रूप देना, नया कर देना। 2. to repair, मरम्मत करना।

renowned (रिनाउन्ड) ***adj.*** famous, reputed, प्रसिद्ध, प्रतिष्ठित, विख्यात।

rent[1] (रेन्ट) ***n.*** periodic payment for the use of another's property, किराया, भाड़ा या लगान। ***v.*** 1. to let out on rent, किराए पर देना, भाड़े पर चढ़ाना। 2. to pay rent for the use of, किराए पर लेना।

rent[2] ***n.*** 1. a torn place in a garment, चीर, फटा अंश। 2. split, दरार।

rental (रेन्टल) ***n.*** the amount paid or received as rent, किराया, भाड़ा।

renunciation (रिनन्सिएशन) ***n.*** the act of renouncing, त्याग, परित्याग।

reorganize (रीऑर्गनाइज़) ***v.*** to organize again or anew, फिर से गठित करना, पुनर्गठन करना।

repair (रिपेअर) ***v.*** to restore to good condition, मरम्मत करना, ठीक करना। ***n.*** the act or process of repairing, मरम्मत, सुधार, जीर्णोद्धार।

repartee (रिपार्टी) ***n.*** a quick witty reply, सहसा दिया जानेवाला व्यंग्यपूर्ण उत्तर।

repatriation (रीपैट्रिएशन) ***n.*** the act of repatriating, स्वदेश-वापसी।

repay (रिपे) ***v.*** (repaid, repaying) 1. to pay back, लौटाना, चुकाना, शोधन करना। 2. to give in return, बदले में देना, बदला चुकाना।

repayment (रिपेमेन्ट) ***n.*** the act of repaying or something repaid, शोधन, वापसी, चुकौती, प्रतिदान।

repeal (रिपील) ***v.*** to annul officially, निरस्त करना, रद करना। ***n.*** the act of repealing, निरसन, रद्दगी।

repeat (रिपीट) ***v.*** to do, say or recur again once or several times, दुहराना, पुनरावृत्ति करना। ***n.*** the act of repeating, दुहराई, पुनरावृत्ति।

repeating (रिपीटिंग) ***adj.*** capable of discharging several shots, आवर्ती।

repel (रिपेल) ***v.*** 1. to force or drive back, पीछे धकेलना। 2. to produce a feeling of aversion, विकर्षण उत्पन्न करना।

repellent (रिपेलेन्ट) ***adj.*** tending to repel, repulsive, विकर्षक।

repent (रिपेन्ट) ***v.*** to feel regret or remorse for, पश्चात्ताप करना, पछताना।

repercussion (रीपर्कशन) ***n.*** 1. the recoil of something after impact, झटका, प्रतिघात। 2. an indirect effect of an event, फल, परिणाम या प्रतिक्रिया।

repetition (रेपिटिशन) ***n.*** the act of repeating, पुनरावृत्ति।

repine (रिपाइन) ***v.*** to be fretful, खीझना, कुढ़ना।

replace (रिप्लेस) ***v.*** to put in place of, प्रतिस्थापन करना।

replacement (रिप्लेसमेन्ट) ***n.*** the act of replacing, प्रतिस्थापन।

replenish (रिप्लेनिश) ***v.*** to fill again, to put fresh fuel on, फिर से भरना।

replete (रिप्लीट) ***adj.*** 1. full, भरा हुआ, ठसाठस। 2. satiated, तृप्त।

replica (रेप्लिका) ***n.*** an exact copy, प्रतिकृति।

replicate (रेप्लिकेट) ***v.*** 1. to make a replica of, प्रतिकृति बनाना। 2. to repeat, दुहराना।

reply (रिप्लाइ) ***v.*** to say or give as answer, उत्तर देना, जवाब देना। ***n.*** an answer, उत्तर, जवाब।

report (रिपोर्ट) ***n.*** 1. a formal written account of something, रिपोर्ट, रपट, विवरण। 2. a rumour, अफ़वाह। 3. an explosive noise, धमाका। ***v.*** 1. to tell or write about an event, to present an account of, किसी घटना के संबंध में बताना या लिखना, रिपोर्ट करना। 2. to serve as a reporter, संवाद भेजना। 3. to present oneself, उपस्थित होना, हाज़िरी देना।

reporter (रिपोर्टर) ***n.*** one who gathers news for a newspaper, संवाददाता।

repose (रिपोज़) ***v.*** 1. to lie at rest, आराम करना। 2. to place (trust etc. विश्वास आदि) रखना, धरना। ***n.*** 1. the act of resting, विश्राम, श्रांति। 2. peace, शांति।

repository (रिपॉज़िटरी) ***n.*** 1. a place where things are stored, संग्रह-स्थल, भंडार। 2. a place of burial, क़ब्रगाह। 3. a confidant, विश्वस्त व्यक्ति।

reprehend (रेप्रिहेन्ड) ***v.*** 1. to rebuke, झिड़कना, फटकारना, डाँटना-डपटना। 2. to criticize, आलोचना करना, भर्त्सना करना।

reprehension (रेप्रिहेन्शन) ***n.*** 1. the act of reprehending, झिड़कने की क्रिया या भाव। 2. a reproof, झिड़की।

represent (रेप्रिज़ेन्ट) ***v.*** 1. to symbolize, प्रतीक होना। 2. to depict, चित्रित करना, वर्णन करना। 3. to serve as an example of, उदाहरण होना। 4. to serve as a representative, प्रतिनिधि होना या प्रतिनिधित्व करना।

representation (रेप्रिजेन्टेशन) ***n.*** 1. the act of representing, प्रतिनिधित्व, प्रतिनिधायन। 2. a dramatic performance, अभिनय या प्रदर्शन।

repress (रिप्रेस) ***v.*** 1. to suppress, दमन करना। 2. to hold back, रोक रखना, दबाना।

repression (रिप्रेशन) ***n.*** the act of suppressing, दमन।

reprieve (रिप्रीव) ***v.*** 1. to postpone or remit the punishment, माफ़ी देना या सज़ा घटाना, जान बख़्शना। 2. to give

R

temporary relief, राहत देना। *n.* 1. the postponement or remitting of a punishment, माफ़ी या सज़ा की कमी। 2. temporary relief, राहत।

reprimand (रेप्रिमान्ड) *n.* a rebuke, डाँट, फटकार। *v.* to rebuke, डाँटना-फटकारना।

reprisal (रिप्राइज़ल) *n.* retaliatory action, बदले की कार्रवाई।

reproach (रिप्रोच) *v.* 1. to rebuke severely, कड़ी भर्त्सना करना। 2. to blame, दोषारोपण करना। *n.* 1. a severe rebuke, कड़ी फटकार। 2. a blame, दोषारोप। 3. disgrace, अपमान।

reprobate (रेप्रोबेट) *adj.* 1. immoral, अनैतिक, भ्रष्ट। 2. unprincipled, सिद्धांतहीन।

reproduce (रीप्रोड्यूस) *v.* 1. to produce again, दुबारा बनाना, दुबारा पैदा करना, पुनरुत्पादन करना। 2. to bear offspring, बच्चा देना, जनना।

reproduction (रीप्रोडक्शन) *n.* the act of reproducing, पुररुत्पादन; प्रजनन।

reprove (रिप्रूव) *v.* to reprehend, फटकारना, भर्त्सना करना।

reptile (रेप्टाइल) *n.* a class of animals that moves about on its belly or short legs, रेंगनेवाला जंतु, सरीसृप।

republic (रिपब्लिक) *n.* a country ruled by its elected representatives, गणतंत्र।

republican (रिपब्लिकन) *adj.* pertaining to a republic, गणतंत्रीय। *n.* an advocate of a republican form of government, गणतंत्रवादी।

repudiate (रिप्यूडिएट) *v.* 1. to refuse or reject, जवाब दे देना, इन्कार कर देना, खंडन करना। 2. to cast off or disown, छोड़ देना, परित्याग करना।

repudiation (रिप्यूडिएशन) *n.* the act of repudiating, जवाब, इन्कार; खंडन; परित्याग।

repugnant (रिपग्नेन्ट) *adj.* 1. contrary, inconsistent, असंगत, प्रतिकूल। 2. distasteful, अप्रिय, नापसंद।

repulse (रिपल्स) *v.* 1. to drive back, भगा देना, हटा देना, खदेड़ देना। 2. to reject with coldness, ठुकरा देना।

repulsion (रिपल्शन) *n.* 1. the act of repulsing, खदेड़ने की क्रिया या भाव। 2. the feeling of aversion, घृणा, नफ़रत।

reputation (रेप्युटेशन) *n.* renown, ख्याति, प्रसिद्धि, नेकनामी, कीर्ति।

repute (रिप्यूट) *n.* renown, ख्याति, प्रसिद्धि।

reputed (रिप्यूटिड) *adj.* said or thought to be such, कथित या माना हुआ, ख्यात।

request (रिक्वेस्ट) *v.* to ask for, निवेदन या प्रार्थना करना। *n.* the act of requesting, प्रार्थना, निवेदन।

require (रिक्वाइर) *v.* 1. to need, अपेक्षा होना। 2. to call upon or insist upon, कहना, अनुरोध करना, ज़ोर देना।

requirement (रिक्वाइरमेन्ट) *n.* a need, अपेक्षा, ज़रूरत, आवश्यकता।

requisite (रेक्विज़िट) *adj.* 1. required, अपेक्षित। 2. necessary, आवश्यक। *n.* a necessity, आवश्यकता, अपेक्षा।

requisition (रेक्विज़िशन) *n.* 1. a formal request or demand, अपेक्षा, माँग। 2. the official form on which such a demand is made, माँगपत्र। *v.* to demand by a requisition, माँग करना।

resale (रीसेल) ***n.*** sale of something one has bought, पुनर्विक्रय।

rescind (रिसिन्ड) ***v.*** to cancel, रद करना।

rescue (रेस्क्यू) ***v.*** to save, बचाना, उद्धार करना। ***n.*** the act of rescuing or the state of being rescued, उद्धार।

research (रीसर्च) ***n.*** a scholarly or scientific study of a subject, शोध, अनुसंधान। ***v.*** to do research, शोध करना, अनुसंधान करना।

resemble (रिज़ेम्बल) ***v.*** to be like, मिलता-जुलता होना।

resent (रिज़ेन्ट) ***v.*** to feel angry, अप्रसन्नता प्रकट करना, नाराज़ होना।

resentful (रिज़ेन्टफ़ुल) ***adj.*** angry, अप्रसन्न, रुष्ट, नाराज़।

reservation (रेज़र्वेशन) ***n.*** 1. the act of reserving, आरक्षण। 2. something reserved, आरक्षित स्थान, पद आदि। 3. an act of withholding, रोक रखना। 4. a condition, शर्त।

reserve (रिज़र्व) ***v.*** 1.to set apart for a particular person or use, आरक्षण करना, रिज़र्व करना। 2. to set aside for future use, सुरक्षित रखना। 3. to postpone, स्थगित करना। ***n.*** 1. assets kept for future or particular use, बचाकर रखा हुआ धन, निधि। 2. the condition of being reserved, रक्षित होना। 3. a reserved tract of land, रक्षित भूभाग। 4. a substitute, स्थानापन्न। 5. armed services not in active service, रिज़र्व सेना। 6. self-restraint, आत्मसंयम।

reserved (रिज़र्व्ड) ***adj.*** 1. held for a particular person, आरक्षित। 2. not showing his/her feelings openly, restrained, संयत। 3. quiet, चुप्पा।

reservoir (रेज़र्वाअर) ***n.*** 1. a body of water, जलाशय, तालाब। 2. a tank, टंकी। 3. a source, स्रोत, भंडार, ख़ज़ाना।

reshuffle (रीशफ़ल) ***v.*** 1. to shuffle again, (पत्ते) दुबारा फेंटना, फेंटाई करना। 2. to make changes, परिवर्तन करना। ***n.*** an act of reshuffling, फेंटाई, फेरबदल; रद्दोबदल।

reside (रिज़ाइड) ***v.*** 1. to dwell, वास करना, रहना। 2. to be inherently present, निहित होना।

residence (रेज़िडन्स) ***n.*** an abode, आवास, निवास, निवास-स्थान।

resident (रेज़िडन्ट) ***adj.*** residing, वासी, निवासी।

residential (रेज़िडेन्शल) ***adj.*** suitable for residence, रिहाइशी, आवासिक।

residual (रिज़िडुअल) ***adj.*** remaining, बचा हुआ, शेष, अवशिष्ट।

residue (रेज़िड्यू) ***n.*** remainder, अवशिष्ट अंश, अवशेष।

resign (रिज़ाइन) ***v.*** 1.to give up a job or office, पदत्याग करना, इस्तीफ़ा देना। 2. to relinquish, छोड़ देना। 3. to yield or submit, झुक जाना या अर्पित कर देना।

resignation (रेज़िग्नेशन) ***n.*** 1. the act of resigning, पदत्याग। 2. a letter of stating one's wish to resign, त्यागपत्र, इस्तीफ़ा। 3. passive acquiescence, मौन स्वीकृति। 4. submission, अर्पण।

resigned (रिज़ाइन्ड) ***adj.*** acquiescent, राज़ी, सहमत, संतुष्ट।

resilience (रिज़िलिएन्स) ***n.*** elasticity, लचीलापन, लोच, प्रतिस्कंदन।

resin (रेज़िन) ***n.*** a semisolid substance secreted by some trees, राल।

R

resist (रिज़िस्ट) ***v.*** to oppose, to counteract, प्रतिरोध करना।

resistance (रिज़िस्टेन्स) ***n.*** the act of resisting, प्रतिरोध।

resistant (रिज़िस्टेन्ट) ***adj.*** offering resistance, प्रतिरोधक, प्रतिरोधी।

resistivity (रिज़िस्टिविटी) ***n.*** the power of resisting, प्रतिरोधकता।

resistor (रिज़िस्टर) ***n.*** an electrical device having resistance to the passage of electric current, प्रतिरोधक।

resolute (रेज़ल्यूट) ***adj.*** showing great determination, bold, firm, दृढ़-निश्चयी, संकल्पशील, दृढ़।

resolution (रेज़ल्यूशन) ***n.*** 1. determination, दृढ़ निश्चय, संकल्प। 2. a proposal, प्रस्ताव। 3. decision, निश्चय। 4. verdict, निर्णय। 5. solution, समाधान।

resolve (रिज़ॉल्व) ***v.*** 1. to determine, निश्चय/संकल्प करना। 2. to solve or settle, समाधान करना, निपटाना।

resonance (रेज़ोनेन्स) ***n.*** echo, अनुनाद, गूँज।

resonate (रेज़ोनेट) ***v.*** to resound, गूँजना।

resort (रिज़ॉर्ट) ***n.*** 1. a place to which people generally go for a picnic or recreation, घूमने-फिरने या छुट्टी मनाने के लिए उपयुक्त स्थल, आनंद-स्थली, सैरगाह। 2. the use of something as a help or recourse, उपाय या सहारा। ***v.*** 1. to have recourse to, उपाय अपनाना, सहारा लेना। 2. to go often or habitually, (कहीं) प्रायः जाते रहना।

resound (रिज़ाउन्ड) ***v.*** 1. to reverberate, गूँजना, प्रतिध्वनित होना। 2. to be famed, प्रसिद्ध होना।

resource (रिसोर्स) ***n.*** 1. a source of support or help, साधन, स्रोत। 2. the ability to deal with a situation, क्षमता, योग्यता। 3. (plu.) means, उपाय, साधन।

resourceful (रिसोर्सफ़ुल) ***adj.*** capable and clever, सक्षम तथा चतुर, साधनसंपन्न, साधनशाली।

respect (रिस्पेक्ट) ***n.*** 1. esteem, regard, आदर, इज़्ज़त। 2. attention, consideration, ध्यान, विचार। 3. relation, reference, संबंध, विषय। 4. a particular detail or aspect, विशेष बात या पहलू। 5. (plu.) greetings, अभिवादन, नमस्कार। ***v.*** 1. to have respect, आदर-भाव रखना। 2. to show respect for, आदर करना, सम्मान करना। 3. to pay proper attention to, पूरा ध्यान रखना।

respectable (रिस्पेक्टेबल) ***adj.*** 1. worthy of respect, आदरणीय, सम्मानित। 2. having social standing, प्रतिष्ठित। 3. fairly good, ठीक-ठाक या अच्छा खासा।

respectful (रिस्पेक्टफुल) ***adj.*** showing respect or full of respect, श्रद्धालु, श्रद्धापूर्ण।

respective (रिस्पेक्टिव) ***adj.*** 1. relating to each person or thing mentioned, हर एक की दृष्टि से उसका, अपना-अपना। 2. particular, विशेष, विशिष्ट।

respectively (रिस्पेक्टिवली) ***adv.*** each in the order named, क्रमशः, क्रमानुसार।

respiration (रेस्पिरेशन) ***n.*** act of breathing, साँस लेना और छोड़ना, श्वसन।

respiratory (रेस्पिरेटरी) ***adj.*** of or pertaining to respiration, श्वसन या श्वास-संबंधी।

respire (रिस्पाइर) ***v.*** to inhale and exhale, साँस लेना और छोड़ना।

respite (रेस्पाइट) ***n.*** 1. a short interval of relief, थोड़े समय की राहत। 2. a short interval of rest, अल्पविश्राम, थोड़ी फ़ुर्सत। 3. postponement, स्थगन।

resplendent (रिस्पलेन्डेन्ट) ***adj.*** shining, चमाचम, झकाझक।

respond (रिस्पॉन्ड) ***v.*** 1. to reply, उत्तर देना, जवाब देना। 2. to act in response, अनुक्रिया करना।

respondent (रिस्पॉन्डेन्ट) ***n.*** a defendant, प्रतिवादी।

response (रिस्पॉन्स) ***n.*** 1. a reply or answer, उत्तर, जवाब। 2. a reaction to a particular stimulus, अनुक्रिया, प्रतिक्रिया।

responsibility (रिस्पॉन्सिबिलिटी) ***n.*** 1.the state or quality of being responsible, जवाबदेही, ज़िम्मेदारी, उत्तरदायित्व। 2. a thing or person that one is responsible for, वह जिसकी ज़िम्मेदारी ली गई हो, दायित्व।

responsible (रिस्पॉन्सिबल) ***adj.*** 1. liable to be called to account for something, जवाबदेह, ज़िम्मेदार, उत्तरदायी। 2. being the cause or source of something, जो किसी बात का कारण हो। 3. involving important duties, उत्तरदायित्वपूर्ण। 4. trustworthy, विश्वसनीय।

responsive (रिस्पॉन्सिव) ***adj.*** reacting favourably to a suggestion, अनुकूल क्रिया करनेवाला, अनुक्रियक।

rest[1] (रेस्ट) ***n.*** 1. a period of relaxation, आराम, विश्राम। 2. sleep, नींद। 3. any relief from worry, राहत। 4. calm, शांति, चैन। 5. cessation from motion, खड़ा रहना, बंद होना। 6. a shelter, आश्रय। 7. a support, टेक। 8. a base, आधार। ***v.*** 1. to take rest, आराम करना, सुस्ताना, विश्राम करना। 2. to give rest, आराम देना, राहत पहुँचाना। 3. to be at ease, be calm, शांति से बैठना, चैन से बैठना। 4. to cease to move, खड़ा हो जाना, स्थिर होना, बंद होना। 5. to place or be placed for support, सहारा लेना या देना, टेक लगाना या लगना।

rest[2] ***n.*** 1. remainder, शेष। 2. the others, अन्य लोग, अन्य सभी। ***v.*** to remain, रहना।

restaurant (रेस्टरेन्ट) ***n.*** a place where meals are served to the customers, रेस्टोरेंट, रेस्त्राँ।

restive (रेस्टिव) ***adj.*** 1. restless, बेचैन, अशांत। 2. difficult to restrain or control, जिसको नियंत्रित करना मुश्किल हो, अड़ियल।

restless (रेस्टलिस) ***adj.*** 1. unable to rest or sleep, जिसे विश्राम न मिलता हो, विश्रामहीन, निद्राहीन। 2. worried, चिंतित, बेचैन, व्यग्र।

restoration (रेस्टोरेशन) ***n.*** 1. the act of restoring to a former condition or place, पुनरुद्धार; पुनर्स्थापन। 2. an object restored to its original state, पुनर्स्थापित वस्तु।

restorative (रिस्टॉरेटिव) ***adj.*** tending to restore health or strength, स्वास्थ्यकारक या पौष्टिक।

restore (रिस्टोर) ***v.*** 1. to bring back to its original condition, पूर्व स्थिति में लाना, पुनरुद्धार करना, पुनर्स्थापन करना। 2.to bring back to good health, पुनः अच्छा स्वास्थ्य प्रदान करना। 3. to reinstate, बहाल करना।

R

restrain (रिस्ट्रेन) ***v.*** 1. to restrict or hold back, to keep (one's emotions) under control, बाँध रखना, रोक रखना, नियंत्रित रखना। 2. to limit, सीमित रखना।

restraint (रिस्ट्रेन्ट) ***n.*** 1. the act of restraining or the state of being restrained, संयमन, संयम। 2. the ability to control one's passions, मनोनिग्रह। 3. a curb, रोक, बंधन।

restrict (रिस्ट्रिक्ट) ***v.*** to keep within limits, रोक रखना, प्रतिबंध लगाना, सीमित करना।

restriction (रिस्ट्रिक्शन) ***n.*** 1. the act of restricting, प्रतिबंध लगाना, रोक लगाना। 2. something that restricts, प्रतिबंध, पाबंदी।

result (रिज़ल्ट) ***n.*** 1. consequence, outcome, परिणाम, नतीजा। 2. the final outcome of a match, परिणाम, नतीज़ा, फ़ैसला। 3. examination's outcome, परीक्षाफल। ***v.*** to be the consequence, परिणाम निकलना, नतीजा होना।

resultant (रिज़ल्टेन्ट) ***adj.*** that results, परिणाम के रूप में होनेवाला, परिणामी।

resume (रिज्यूम) ***v.*** 1. to begin again, फिर से आरंभ करना, पुनरारंभ करना। 2. to occupy or assume again, (स्थान) फिर ग्रहण करना।

resume (रेज़ुमे) ***n.*** a summary, सारांश।

resumption (रिज़म्प्शन) ***n.*** the act of resuming or the state of being resumed, पुनरारंभ।

resurgence (रिसर्जेन्स) ***n.*** the act of rising again, पुनरुत्थान, पुनर्जीवन।

resurrect (रेज़रेक्ट) ***v.*** to bring back to life again, नवजीवन पाना या देना, पुनर्जीवित करना या होना।

resuscitate (रिससिटेट) ***v.*** 1. to restore to consciousness, होश में लाना। 2. to breathe new life into, पुनर्जीवित करना, नया जीवन देना।

retail (रीटेल) ***n.*** the sale of commodities individually to customers, फुटकर बिक्री, परचून। ***v.*** 1. to sell in small quantities to customers, फुटकर बेचना। 2. to relate in detail विस्तार से कहना।

retain (रिटेन) ***v.*** 1. to keep possession of, अपने पास रखे रहना। 2. to be able to hold or contain, धारण किए रहना। 3. to be able to remember, स्मरण रखना।

retaliate (रिटैलिएट) ***v.*** 1. to give tit for tat, to strike back, ईंट का जवाब पत्थर से देना, मुँहतोड़ जवाब देना। 2. to take revenge, बदला लेना।

retaliation (रिटैलिएशन) ***n.*** revenge, बदला, प्रतिकार।

retard (रिटार्ड) ***v.*** 1.to slow down (the speed or progress, गति या प्रगति) धीमी कर देना। 2. to check or impede, रोक देना या अवरुद्ध कर देना।

retardation (रिटार्डेशन) ***n.*** mental deficiency, मानसिक दुर्बलता।

retention (रिटेन्शन) ***n.*** the act of retaining, धारण, अवधारण।

reticent (रेटिसेन्ट) ***adj.*** 1. disinclined to speak out, घुन्ना, चुप्पा। 2. reserved, कम बोलनेवाला, अल्पभाषी।

retina (रेटिना) ***n.*** a light sensitive membrane at the back of the eyeball, दृष्टिपटल।

retinue (रेटिन्यू) ***n.*** a group of aides and retainers that accompany a person of rank, किसी बड़े आदमी के

आगे-पीछे रहनेवाले लोग, अनुचरों तथा परिचरों का समूह।

retire (रिटाइर) ***v.*** 1. to give up one's regular work or public life, अवकाश ग्रहण करना, सेवानिवृत्त होना, रिटायर होना। 2. to go to bed, to rest, सोने जाना, विश्राम करने लगना।

retired (रिटाइर्ड) ***adj.*** 1. withdrawn from regular work or public life, सेवानिवृत्त। 2. secluded, निर्जन।

retirement (रिटाइरमेन्ट) ***n.*** the state of being retired, अवकाशग्रहण, सेवानिवृत्ति।

retort (रिटॉर्ट) ***v.*** to reply to in a quick and resentful manner, मुँहतोड़ जवाब देना। ***n.*** a quick and resentful remark, मुँहतोड़ जवाब।

retract (रिट्रैक्ट) ***v.*** 1. to draw in, खींच लेना, सिकोड़ लेना। 2. to withdraw, पीछे हटना।

retraction (रिट्रैक्शन) ***n.*** the act of retracting, आकुंचन।

retreat (रीट्रीट) ***v.*** to withdraw, पीछे हटना, वापस होना। ***n.*** 1. the act of retreating or withdrawing, पीछे हटना, वापसी। 2. withdrawal into seclusion, एकांतवास। 3. a place to which one may retire, आश्रय या एकांत।

retrench (रिट्रेन्च) ***v.*** 1. to cut down, कटौती करना। 2. to reduce, कम करना, छँटनी करना।

retrenchment (रिट्रेन्चमेन्ट) ***n.*** the act of retrenching or the state of being retrenched, कटौती, छँटनी।

retribution (रेट्रिब्यूशन) ***n.*** a deserved punishment, उचित दंड, सही सज़ा।

retrieval (रिट्रीवल) ***n.*** recovery, पुनः प्राप्ति; सुधार।

retrieve (रिट्रीव) ***v.*** 1. to recover, पुनः प्राप्त करना। 2. to make amends, ग़लती सुधारना। 3. to find and bring back (killed or wounded game, मृत या घायल शिकार को) खोज और उठा लाना। ***n.*** retrieval, पुनः प्राप्ति; सुधार।

retro (रेट्रो) ***prefix.*** back or backward, पश्च-, पूर्व-।

retroactive (रेट्रोऐक्टिव) ***adj.*** effective as from a past date, पश्चव्यापी, पूर्वव्यापी।

retrogress (रेट्रोग्रेस) ***v.*** to deteriorate, बिगड़ना, भ्रष्ट होना, अवनत होना।

retrogression (रेट्रोग्रेशन) ***n.*** degeneration, अवनति, भ्रष्टता।

retrospect (रेट्रोस्पेक्ट) ***n.*** a survey of past events or time, पश्चावलोकन। ☐ **in retrospect,** पुरानी बातों या तथ्यों के विचार से।

restropective (रेट्रोस्पेक्टिव) ***adj.*** applying to the past, पूर्वव्यापी, पूर्वप्रभावी।

return (रिटर्न) ***v.*** 1. to go back, वापस जाना। 2. to come back, वापस आना। 3. to send back, वापस भेजना, लौटाना। 4. to elect, चुनना, निर्वाचित करना। 5. to yield, (मुनाफ़ा) देना, पैदा कराना। ***n.*** 1. coming or going back, वापस आना या जाना। 2. sending or paying back, वापस करना या चुकाना। 3. the profits of a transaction, मुनाफ़ा। 4. a reply, उत्तर। 5. a formal report, औपचारिक रपट या निवेदन।

reunion (रीयून्यन) ***n.*** 1. an act of reuniting, पुनर्मिलन। 2. a social gathering of friends and relatives, मित्र-समागम।

reuse (रीयूस) ***n.*** the act of using again, पुनर्प्रयोग। ***v.*** to use again, दुबारा काम में लाना, फिर से इस्तेमाल करना।

R

revamp (रीवैम्प) ***v.*** 1. to repair, मरम्मत करना। 2. to renovate, पुनरुद्धार करना।

reveal (रिवील) ***v.*** to expose to view, to uncover, प्रकट करना, बतलाना या दिखलाना।

revel (रेवल) ***v.*** to take great pleasure, रंगरलियाँ मनाना, मौज-मस्ती करना।

revelation (रेवेलेशन) ***n.*** 1. the act of revealing (something secret, रहस्य का) प्रकटीकरण या उद्घाटन। 2. something revealed, प्रकट रहस्य।

revenge (रिवेन्ज) ***v.*** to avenge, बदला लेना, परास्त कर देना। ***n.*** the act of revenging, बदला, प्रतिकार, प्रतिशोध।

revenue (रेवेन्यू) ***n.*** a country's annual income, राजस्व; revenue stamp, रसीदी टिकट।

reverberate (रिवबॅरेट) ***v.*** 1. to echo, प्रतिध्वनित होना या करना, गूँजना या गुँजाना। 2. to reflect, परावर्तन करना।

revere (रिविअर) ***v.*** to regard with great respect, आदर करना, श्रद्धा प्रकट करना।

reverence (रेवरेन्स) ***n.*** a feeling of respect, आदर-सम्मान, श्रद्धा।

reverend (रेवरेन्ड) ***adj.*** worthy of reverence, श्रद्धेय।

reverie (रेवरी) ***n.*** a day-dream, दिवास्वप्न।

reversal (रिवर्सल) ***n.*** 1. the act of reversing or the state of being reversed, उलटाव, पलटाव। 2. a change from better to worse, पलटा, बदलाव। 3. (law) change or annulment, परिवर्तन या निरसन।

reverse (रिवर्स) ***adj.*** turned backward in order, direction, position etc., उलटा, प्रतिकूल, विपरीत। ***v.*** 1. to turn backward or inside out, उलटना या उलटाना। 2. to move or cause to move backward, पीछे मुड़ना या मोड़ना, पलटना या पलटा खाना। 3. to exchange, अदला-बदली करना। 4. to annul or revoke, रद करना या पलट देना। ***n.*** 1. the opposite or contrary of something, उलटी तरफ़। 2. the back or rear of something, पृष्ठभाग, पिछला हिस्सा। 3. a change from good fortune to bad, पलटा।

reversion (रिवर्ज़न) ***n.*** 1. reversal, पलटा, उलटाव। 2. a return, वापसी।

revert (रिवर्ट) ***v.*** 1. to return to a former position, belief etc., पलट जाना, फिर अपना लेना। 2. to go back to former owner, प्रत्यावर्तन होना।

review (रिव्यू) ***v.*** 1.to look over or study again, पुनरवलोकन करना। 2. to reexamine or reconsider, पुनरीक्षण या पुनर्विचार करना। 3. to give a critical report on, समीक्षा करना। ***n.*** 1. a viewing again or studying again, पुनरवलोकन। 2. re-examination or reconsideration, पुनरीक्षण या पुनर्विचार। 3. a critical discussion dealing with a book, समीक्षा।

reviewer (रिव्यूअर) ***n.*** a person who reviews, समीक्षक।

revile (रिवाइल) ***v.*** to criticize in abusive language, गाली देना।

revise (रिवाइज़) ***v.*** 1. to re-examine and improve, पुनरीक्षण करना, संशोधन करना, पुनरीक्षित/संशोधित करना। 2. to study again, दुहराना।

revision (रिविज़न) ***n.*** the act of revising, पुनरीक्षण, संशोधन; पुनरावृत्ति।

revitalize (रीवाइटलाइज़) ***v.*** to give new life to, नया जीवन देना, जान डाल देना।

R

revival (रिवाइवल) ***n.*** 1. the act of reviving or the state of being revived, पुनर्जीवन। 2. restoration to activity, सक्रियकरण।

revive (रिवाइव) ***v.*** 1. to live again after death, पुनर्जीवित होना। 2. to bring back into use, to make effective, सक्रिय करना, पुनर्जीवित करना, जान डाल देना।

revocation (रेवोकेशन) ***n.*** (law) withdrawal or cancellation, वापसी, निरसन, रद्दगी।

revoke (रिवोक) ***v.*** to withdraw or cancel, वापस लेना या रद करना।

revolt (रिवोल्ट) ***n.*** 1. a rebellion, बग़ावत, विद्रोह। 2. sense of disgust, घृणा। ***v.*** 1. to take part in a rebellion, बग़ावत करना, विद्रोह करना। 2. to feel strong disgust, घृणा करना।

revolution (रेवोल्यूशन) ***n.*** 1. a political overthrow, क्रांति। 2. any complete change, क्रांति, क्रांतिकारी परिवर्तन।

revolutionary (रेवोल्यूशनरी) ***adj.*** of a revolution, क्रांतिकारी। ***n.*** a revolutionary person, क्रांतिकारी।

revolutionize (रेवोल्यूशनाइज़) ***v.*** to alter radically, क्रांति लाना।

revolve (रिवॉल्व) ***v.*** 1.to turn around, परिक्रमा करना, चक्कर लगाना। 2. to move in a circular orbit, घूमना, चक्कर खाना।

revolver (रिवॉल्वर) ***n.*** a kind of a pistol, रिवॉल्वर।

revulsion (रिवल्शन) ***n.*** 1. a feeling of disgust, घृणा। 2. withdrawing from something, पीछे हट जाने की क्रिया या भाव। 3. a sudden violent change, आकस्मिक परिवर्तन।

reward (रिवार्ड) ***n.*** 1. something given for a special service, पारितोषिक, पुरस्कार, पारिश्रमिक। 2. profit, लाभ, प्रतिफल। ***v.*** to give as a reward, पुरस्कार देना, पुरस्कृत करना।

rewind (रिवाइन्ड) ***v.*** (rewound, rewinding) to wind again, फिर से लपेटना।

rhapsody (रैप्सोडी) ***n.*** any estatic utterance, यशगान, प्रशंसा।

rhetoric (रेटॉरिक) ***n.*** 1. a science of figures of speech, अलंकारशास्त्र। 2. eloquence, वक्तृता, वाक्पटुता, वाग्मिता।

rheumatism (रूमटिज़्म) ***n.*** a disease characterized by inflammation and pain of the joints, संधिवात, गठिया।

rhino (राइनो) ***n.*** (plu. rhino, rhinos) = rhinoceros.

rhinoceros (राइनॉसरस) ***n.*** a large thick-skinned animal with a horn on its nose, गैंडा।

rhombus (रॉम्बस) ***n.*** (geom.) a parallelogram with four equal sides and oblique angles, समचतुर्भुज।

rhyme (राइम) ***n.*** 1. correspondence of terminal sounds of words or lines of verse, तुक, अंत्यानुप्रास, क़ाफ़िया। 2. poetry in rhyme, तुकबंदी। ***v.*** to form a rhyme, तुक जोड़ना, मिलाना या लगाना।

ryhthm (रिदम) ***n.*** a pattern of flow or movement in music, poetry etc., लय।

rhythmic, rhythmical (रिद्मिक, रिद्मिकल) ***adj.*** having rhythm, लयात्मक, लयबद्ध।

rib (रिब) ***n.*** 1. one of the curved

R

bones around the chest, पसली। 2. the vein of a leaf, शिरा, नस। 3. any narrow rib-like piece, that supports a structure, तीली। 4. a raised ridge in knitted material, उठी हुई पट्टी। ***v.*** 1. to support with ribs, तीलियों से खड़ा करना। 2. to tease, तंग करना।

ribald (रिबल्ड) ***adj.*** vulgar, फूहड़।

riband (रिबन्ड) ***n.*** = ribbon.

ribbon (रिबन) ***n.*** 1. a narrow strip of fabric, फीता, रिबन। 2. (plu.) rags, चिथड़े।

rice (राइस) ***n.*** 1. a grass producing seeds, धान। 2. its seeds, चावल।

rich (रिच) ***adj.*** 1. having much wealth, अमीर, धनी, धनाढ्य, रईस। 2. abundant, प्रचुर, विपुल। 3. having great value, बहुमूल्य। 4. prosperous, समृद्ध। 5. fertile, उर्वर। 6. deep or strong, गहरा या तीव्र। 7. having great food value, पौष्टिक।

riches (रिचिज़) ***n.*** (plu.) valuable or precious possessions, दौलत, धन-दौलत।

richly (रिचली) ***adv.*** 1. fully, amply, पूर्ण रूप से। 2. in a good manner, अच्छी तरह, भली-भाँति।

rick (रिक) ***n.*** a built stack of hay or straw, घास आदि का अंबार/ढेर।

rickets (रिकिट्स) ***n.*** a children's disease resulting in softening and deformity of bones, सूखा, सुखंडी।

rickety (रिकिटी) ***adj.*** 1. affected with rickets, सुखंडी। 2. weak, feeble, कमज़ोर।

rickshaw (रिक्शॉ) ***n.*** a two or three-wheeled mandrawn carriage, रिक्शा।

rid (रिड) ***v.*** (rid/ridded, ridding) to make free, मुक्त करना, छुटकारा देना।

riddance (रिडेन्स) ***n.*** deliverance, छुटकारा।

riddle[1] (रिडल) ***n.*** a puzzle, पहेली, बुझौवल।

riddle[2] ***v.*** 1. to make holes in, छेद करना, छेद डालना। 2. to sift, छानना। ***n.*** a sieve, छलनी।

ride (राइड) ***v.*** (rode, ridden, riding) 1. to sit on (a horse etc.), सवार होना, सवारी करना, (पर) चढ़ना। 2. to be conveyed in a vehicle, सवारी से सफ़र करना। 3. to travel over a surface, (गाड़ी आदि का) चलना। 4. to go ahead, आगे बढ़ना। 5. to float, तैरना, तिरना। 6. to tease, परेशान करना, छेड़ना। ***n.*** 1. a journey in a vehicle, सवारी से की हुई यात्रा। 2. a path made for riding, सवारी-पथ। 3. an act of riding, सवारी करना।

rider (राइडर) ***n.*** 1. a person who rides, सवार। 2. (law) an addition to a document, अतिरिक्त धारा।

ridge (रिज) ***n.*** 1. the long narrow top of something, शिखर पर का ऊँचा लंबा किनारा, सिरा। 2. a range of hills, पर्वत-श्रेणी। 3. a narrow raised strip on fabric, पट्टी। 4. any raised strip, मेड़।

ridicule (रिडिक्यूल) ***v.*** to make fun of, उपहास करना, मखौल उड़ाना, हास्यास्पद बनाना। ***n.*** making fun of someone, उपहास, मख़ौल।

ridiculous (रिडिक्यूलस) ***adj.*** 1. deserving to be laughed at, हास्यास्पद। 2. absurd, foolish, बेतुका, मूर्खतापूर्ण।

rife (राइफ़) ***adj.*** 1. widespread, व्याप्त। 2. prevalent, प्रचलित। 3. full, भरा हुआ। 4. abounding, प्रचुर, अत्यधिक।

rifle[1] (राइफ़ल) ***n.*** 1. a gun with a long barrel containing spiral grooves, राइफ़ल। 2. (plu.) troops equipped with rifles, राइफ़लधारी सेना।

rifle[2] ***v.*** to steal or rob, चुराना या लूटना।

rift (रिफ़्ट) ***n.*** 1. a crack, दरार। 2. a break in friendly relation, अनबन, खींचातानी।

rig[1] (रिग) ***v.*** to fit or equip, (जलयान आदि को) पाल, मस्तूल आदि उपकरणों, से सज्जित करना, साज़-सामान जुटाना। ***n.*** 1. the way the ships masts and sails are arranged, पोत के मस्तूल तथा पाल लगाने का ढंग। 2. a machine or equipment for drilling a well, गहरा कुआँ खोदने का यंत्र या उपकरण।

rig[2] ***v.*** to manage fraudulently, बेईमानी या हेराफेरी करना, छल करना।

right (राइट) ***adj.*** 1. good, ठीक, सही। 2. straight, सरल और सीधा। 3. proper, correct, उचित, उपयुक्त, न्यायसंगत। 4. of the right hand side, दाहिना, दायाँ, दक्षिण। 5. sound, स्वस्थ। ***n.*** 1. something one is entitled to, अधिकार, हक। 2. justice, न्याय, इंसाफ़। 3. propriety, औचित्य। 4. the right-handed part of a person, thing etc., दाहिना अंग या भाग। 5. the right wing, दक्षिणपंथ। ***adv.*** 1. on the right hand side, दाहिने। 2. straight, सीधे। 3. rightly, उचित रीति से, अच्छी तरह, भली-भाँति। 4. completely, पूरी तरह। 5. exactly, ठीक-ठीक, ठीक। ***v.*** 1. to become right or straight, ठीक हो जाना, सुधरना। 2. to set right, ठीक कर देना, सुधारना। ***interj.*** to agree to a request or to get peoples attention, ठीक! अच्छा!

righteous (राइचस) ***adj.*** 1. upright, virtuous, नीतिपरायण, सदाचारी या धर्मपरायण (व्यक्ति)। 2. ethical, just, right, सदाचारपूर्ण या न्यायसंगत (व्यवहार)।

rightful (राइटफ़ुल) ***adj.*** 1. just, उचित। 2. legal, वैध, वैधानिक।

rightist (राइटिस्ट) ***n.*** a political reactionary, दक्षिणपंथी।

rigid (रिजिड) ***adj.*** 1. not bending, अनम्य, दृढ़। 2. not yielding, strict, harsh, कठोर, सख़्त।

rigidity (रिजिडिटी) ***n.*** 1. inflexibility, अनम्यता, दृढ़ता। 2. strictness, कठोरता, सख़्ती।

rigmarole (रिग्मरोल) ***n.*** nonsense, बकवास।

rigor mortis (रिगर मॉर्टिस) ***n.*** the stiffening of the body after death, मृत्यु के बाद होनेवाली अकड़न।

rigorous (रिगरस) ***adj.*** 1. severe, harsh, कठोर। 2. logically correct, तार्किक दृष्टि से सही।

rigour (रिगर) ***n.*** 1. strictness, सख़्ती। 2. severity, कठोरता।

rill (रिल) ***n.*** 1. a small stream, नाला, धारा। 2. a brook, सोता, चश्मा।

rim (रिम) ***n.*** 1. the outer edge of a wheel, रिम। 2. the border, किनारा।

rime (राइम) ***n.*** frost, पाला, तुषार।

rind (राइन्ड) ***n.*** 1. a tough outer covering of some fruit, कुछ फलों का ऊपरी मोटा कड़ा छिलका। 2. bark, पेड़ की छाल।

ring[1] (रिंग) ***n.*** 1. the outline of a circle, घेरा, चक्र, मंडल। 2. any object that is circular, चक्राकार वस्तु। 3. a circular band worn on a finger,

R

छल्ला, अँगूठी। 4. a group of persons so as to form a circle, घेरा। 5. an enclosed space, घेरा। 6. a raised platform for wrestling, अखाड़ा। ***v.*** 1. to form a ring, घेरा बनाना। 2. to encircle, घेरना। 3. to fit a ring, छल्ला बैठाना या लगाना।

ring[2] ***v.*** (rang, rung, ringing) 1. to give out a resonant sound, घंटी गुंजाना। 2. to cause a bell to do this, घंटी बजाना। 3. to be filled with sound, गूँज उठना।

ring leader ***n.*** one who leads others (in illegal acts, ग़लत कामों में) अगुवाई करनेवाला नेता, रिंगलीडर।

ringlet (रिंगलिट) ***n.*** 1. a small ring, छोटी अँगूठी। 2. a curly lock of hair, अलक, लट।

ringworm (रिंगवर्म) ***n.*** an itching circular patch on the skin, दाद।

rink (रिंक) ***n.*** a stretch of ice used for skating, हिमतल (जिसपर स्केटिंग करते हैं)।

rinse (रिन्स) ***v.*** to wash with water, to wash out soap from, धोना, खँगालना।

riot (राइअट) ***n.*** 1. public disturbance, दंगा, दंगा-फ़साद। 2. uproar or unrestrained merrymaking, गुलगपाड़ा। ***v.*** 1. to take part in a riot, उपद्रव मचाना, दंगा करना। 2. to behave without restraint, गुलगपाड़ा मचाना।

riotous (राइअटस) ***adj.*** 1. unruly, ऊधमी। 2. boisterous, शोरगुल-भरा, उत्तेजनापूर्ण, उत्तेजित। 3. unrestrained, अनियंत्रित।

rip (रिप) ***v.*** 1. to tear apart, फाड़ देना। 2. to be torn, फट जाना, चिर जाना। 3. to move violently, तेज़ी से या बेतहाशा भागना। ***n.*** a tear, चीर।

ripe (राइप) ***adj.*** 1. matured and ready to be used, पका हुआ (फल)। 2. ready to be gathered, पकी (फसल)। 3. suitable, उपयुक्त। 4. matured, प्रौढ़।

ripen (राइपन) ***v.*** to make or become ripe, पकाना या पकना।

ripple (रिपल) ***n.*** 1. a small wave, लहर। 2. a sound like rippling water, कलकल। ***v.*** to form ripples, लहरें उठना।

rise (राइज़) v. (rose, risen, rising) 1. to get up, उठना, जाग उठना। 2. to stand, खड़ा होना। 3. to ascend, चढ़ना, ऊपर उठना। 4. to grow, उगना। 5. to rebel, बग़ावत करना, विरोध में उठ खड़े होना। 6. to increase in amount, बढ़ना। 7. to achieve a higher position, उन्नति करना। 8. to begin to flow, निकलना। ***n.*** 1. an act of rising, ऊपर उठना, उदित होना, उन्नति करना। 2. a beginning, उद्गम, शुरुआत, आरंभ।

risible (रिज़िबल) ***adj.*** 1. funny, मज़ाकिया, हँसानेवाला। 2. ridiculous, हास्यास्पद।

rising (राइहज़िंग) ***n.*** a revolt, बग़ावत।

risk (रिस्क) ***n.*** the possibility of incurring loss, जोख़िम, ख़तरा, रिस्क। ***v.*** to take a risk, जोख़िम या ख़तरा उठाना, रिस्क लेना।

risky (रिस्की) ***adj.*** full of risk, जोख़िमी, ख़तरनाक।

rite (राइट) ***n.*** the formal procedure of conducting a religious ceremony or other solemn act, रीति, अनुष्ठान, विधि, ढंग।

ritual (रिचुअल) ***n.*** 1. a rite, रीति, विधि।

2. a customary procedure, रीति-रिवाज। ***adj.*** of rituals, रीतिक, रिवाजी।

ritualist (रिचुअलिस्ट) ***n.*** one who practices rituals, कर्मकांडी, अनुष्ठान-परायण।

rival (राइवल) ***n.*** a competitor, प्रतिद्वंद्वी, प्रतिस्पर्धी। ***v.*** to attempt to equal or surpass, प्रतिस्पर्धा करना, बराबरी करना।

rivalry (राइवलरी) ***n.*** competition, प्रतिद्वंद्विता, प्रतिस्पर्धा।

river (रिवर) ***n.*** a large natural stream of fresh water, नदी, दरिया।

rivet (रिविट) ***n.*** a short metal pin for fastening two pieces of metal together, रिवट। ***v.*** (riveted, riveting) 1. to fasten with a rivet, रिवट जड़ना/लगाना। 2. to attract, आकृष्ट करना।

rivulet (रिव्यूलिट) ***n.*** a little stream, छोटी नदी या झरना।

road (रोड) ***n.*** 1. an open way providing passage from one place to another, सड़क, रोड। 2. a path, रास्ता, मार्ग।

road metal ***n.*** the stone used for making road, रोड़ी, गिट्टी।

roadworthy (रोडवर्दी) ***adj.*** fit for use on the road, सड़क पर चलाने योग्य, सड़क-लायक।

roam (रोम) ***v.*** to move or travel purposelessly, बिना प्रयोजन घूमना, मटरगश्ती करना।

roar (रोर) ***v.*** 1. to utter a loud deep sound, चिल्लाना, दहाड़ना, गरजना। 2. to laugh loudly, ज़ोरे-ज़ोर से हँसना, ठहाके लगाना। ***n.*** 1. a loud deep sound, चिल्लाहट, दहाड़ या गरज। 2. noise, शोर, होहल्ला।

roaring (रोरिंग) ***n.*** a loud prolonged cry, चीख़, चिल्लाहट, दहाड़, गरज। ***adj.*** 1. noisy, कोलाहलपूर्ण। 2. brisk or profitable, तेज़ या लाभप्रद। ***adv.*** noisily, दहाड़ते या गरजते हुए।

roast (रोस्ट) ***v.*** 1. to cook or to be cooked over an open fire, भूनना/भुनना, लाल करना/होना। 2. to bake, सेंकना या सिकना।

rob (रॉब) ***v.*** to take something by force, छीन लेना, लूट लेना।

robber (रॉबर) ***n.*** a person who robs, लुटेरा, डाकू।

robbery (रॉबरी) ***n.*** an act or instance of robbing, लूट, लूटपाट।

robe (रोब) ***n.*** a long loose flowing garment, लबादा। ***v.*** to dress in a robe, लबादा पहनना।

robot (रोबॉट) ***n.*** a machine that resembles a human being and capable of performing simple manual tasks, यंत्रमानव, रोबोट।

robust (रोबस्ट) ***adj.*** sturdily built, healthy and strong, हट्टा-कट्टा, हृष्ट-पुष्ट।

rock[1] (रॉक) ***n.*** a large stone, चट्टान, शैल।

rock[2] ***v.*** 1. to move or swing to and fro in a rhythmic motion, झूलना या झुलाना। 2. to shake violently, झकझोर देना।

rock-bottom (रॉक-बॉटम) ***n.*** the lowest point or level, निम्नतम बिंदु या स्तर।

rocker (रॉकर) ***n.*** 1. a curved piece on which a cradle or chair rocks, दोलक, रॉकर। 2. a rocking chair, दोलन कुर्सी।

rocket (रॉकिट) ***n.*** 1. a firework containing explosives that rises into the air when ignited and then

R

explodes, गोला, रॉकेट। 2. a weapon of this kind, रॉकेट। ***v.*** (rocketed, rocketing) to move swiftly upward, तेज़ी से ऊपर उठाना या जाना।

rock-garden (रॉक-गार्डन) ***n.*** a garden of rocks, शैल उद्यान।

rocky (रॉकी) ***adj.*** 1. full of rocks, चट्टानों से भरा, चट्टानी। 2. shaky, कमज़ोर।

rod (रॉड) ***n.*** 1. a thin long straight bar, छड़, सरिया या सलाई। 2. a cane for flogging people, बेंत।

rodent (रोडेन्ट) ***n.*** a rat or squirrel, चूहा या गिलहरी।

rogue (रोग) ***n.*** 1. a mischievous or dishonest person, दुष्ट या बेईमान व्यक्ति। 2. a scoundrel, बदमाश। 3. a wild animal driven away from the herd, झुंड से अलग बिछड़ा हुआ पशु।

roister (रॉइस्टर) ***v.*** to engage in unrestrained merrymaking, मौज-मस्ती या रंगरलियाँ मनाना।

role (रोल) ***n.*** 1. an actor's part in a play or film, भूमिका। 2. usual function, सामान्य कृत्य या कार्यकलाप।

roll (रोल) ***v.*** 1. to move along by turning over and over, कलाबाज़ी खाना, लुढ़कना। 2. to cause to move along by turning over and over, लुढ़काना, कलाबाज़ी खिलाना। 3. to revolve, घूमना। 4. to cause to revolve, घुमाना। 5. to form into a cylindrical shape, लपेटना। 6. to curl, घुमाव डालना। 7. to roar, गरजना। 8. to walk with a swaying gate, लड़खड़ाते हुए चलना। 9. to begin to operate, (मशीन का) चलना। 10. to make progress, प्रगति करना। ***n.*** 1. anything rolled up, गोला, मुट्ठा, रोला। 2. a scroll, खर्रा। 3. a register, रजिस्टर, पंजी। 4. a list of names, नामावली, सूची।

roll call ***n.*** the reading aloud of a list of names to mark attendance, हाज़िरी।

roller (रोलर) ***n.*** 1. a cylinder for flattening things, रोलर, बेलन। 2. a long swelling wave, ऊँची लहर, हिलोर।

rollicking (रोलिकिंग) ***adj.*** full of boisterous high spirits, मौज़-मस्ती और कोलाहल-भरा।

rolling stone ***n.*** a wandering person, घुमंता।

roly-poly (रोली-पोली) ***adj.*** short and fat, गोल-मटोल। ***n.*** a sweet, एक तरह की मिठाई।

Roman (रोमन) ***adj.*** 1. of Rome, रोम-संबंधी, रोमन। ***n.*** 1. an inhabitant of Rome, रोमवासी। 2. a type, एक तरह का टाईप।

romance (रोमैन्स) ***n.*** 1. a love story, प्रेम-कथा, प्रेमाख्यान। 2. a love affair, प्यार का चक्कर, प्रेम-प्रपंच, प्रेम-लीला। 3. romantic love, स्वच्छंद प्रेम, रोमांस। ***v.*** to engage in romantic activites, प्रेमाचार करना।

romantic (रोमैन्टिक) ***adj.*** 1. involving a love affair, प्रेम-संबंधी, रोमानी, रूमानी। 2. imaginary, fictitious, काल्पनिक। 3. unpractical, अव्यावहारिक।

romp (रॉम्प) ***v.*** 1. to play or run joyfully and boisterously, उछल-कूद मचाना। 2. to win a race easily, सरलता से दौड़ जीत लेना।

roof (रूफ़) ***n.*** 1. the top covering of a building, a car etc., छत। ***v.*** to cover with a roof, छत डालना।

rook[1] (रूक) ***n.*** 1. a black crow, एक प्रजाति का डोम कौआ। 2. one who cheats, बेईमानी करनेवाला। ***v.*** to cheat, छल करना, धोखाधड़ी करना।

rook[2] ***n.*** a chess piece that moves horizontally or vertically, रुख़, हाथी।

room (रूम) ***n.*** 1. an area of building surrounded by walls, कमरा, कक्ष। 2. space, जगह। 3. scope or opportunity, गुंजाइश, जगह।

roomy (रूमी) ***adj.*** spacious, खुला, विस्तृत।

roost (रूस्ट) ***n.*** a place where birds rest or sleep, पक्षियों का अड्डा, बसेरा। ***v.*** to rest or sleep, विश्राम करना या सोना।

rooster (रूस्टर) ***n.*** a male domestic fowl, मुर्ग़ा।

root[1] (रूट) ***n.*** 1. the underground part of a plant that draws water and nourishment, जड़। 2. origin, source, मूल, उद्गम। 3. (maths.) a number that when used as a factor in multiplication a given number of times produces a specified product, मूल। 4. (gram.) a word or word element from which other words are formed, धातु; root sign, धातु चिह्न। ***v.*** 1. to take root, जड़ जमना। 2. to cause to take root, जड़ जमाना।

root[2] ***v.*** 1. to dig with the snout, थूथन से कुरेदना या खोदना। 2. to search thoroughly, छान-बीन करना।

rope (रोप) ***n.*** a thick cord, रस्सा। ☐ **give (someone) enough rope,** ढील देना। ***v.*** 1. to fasten with a rope, रस्से से बाँधना। 2. to fence with ropes, रस्सों से घेरा बनाना। ☐ **on the rope,** पराजय के द्वार पर।

rosary (रोज़री) ***n.*** a string of beads, माला, सुमिरनी।

rose (रोज़) ***n.*** 1. a bush and its flower, गुलाब (पौधा और फूल)। 2. deep pink colour, गुलाबी रंग।

rosette (रोज़ेट) ***n.*** 1. a rose-shaped badge, गुलाब की शक्ल का बिल्ला। 2. a rose-shaped carving, गुलाब के फूल की नक़्क़ाशी।

roster (रोस्टर) ***n.*** a list of names, नामावली, तालिका।

rostrum (रॉस्ट्रम) ***n.*** (plu. rostra, rostrums) a raised platform for public speaking, मंच।

rosy (रोज़ी) ***n.*** 1. having a rose colour, deep pink, गुलाबी। 2. promising, bright, आशापूर्ण, उज्ज्वल, शुभ।

rot (रॉट) ***v.*** to decay or decompose, सड़-गल जाना, क्षय हो जाना। ***n.*** 1. the process of rotting, सड़न-गलन, क्षय। 2. something rotten, सड़ी-गली चीज़। 3. something worthless, बेकार चीज़।

Rotarian (रोटेरिअन) ***n.*** a member of the Rotary International, रोटरी क्लब का सदस्य।

rotary (रोटरी) ***adj.*** 1. operating by rotation, घूमनेवाला, चक्रिल, घूर्णी। 2. having a part that rotates (मशीन) जिसका कोई हिस्सा घूमता हो।

rotate (रोटेट) ***v.*** (rotated, rotating) to revolve, घूर्णन करना, घूमना, चक्कर लगाना।

rotation (रोटेशन) ***n.*** the act or process of rotating, घूर्णन। ☐ **in rotation,** बारी-बारी से।

rote (रोट) ***n.*** a fixed way, routine, नियत क्रम। ☐ **by rote,** रटकर।

rotten (रॉटन) ***adj.*** 1. decayed, decomposed, गला-सड़ा। 2. corrupt, भ्रष्ट। 3. worthless, बेकार। 4. unpleasant, अप्रिय, बुरा।

rotund (रोटन्ड) ***adj.*** rounded, plump, गोल-मटोल।

rouble (रूबल) ***n.*** a monetary unit of Russia, रूबल, रूस की मुद्रा।

roue (रूए) ***n.*** a rake, व्यभिचारी, लंपट।

rouge (रूज़) ***n.*** a fine red powder for colouring the cheeks, गालों पर लगाने का गुलाबी पाउडर, रूज़। ***v.*** to colour with rouge, गालों पर रूज़ लगाना।

rough (रफ़) ***adj.*** 1. not smooth, coarse, खुरदरा। 2. uneven, ऊबड़-खाबड़। 3. rude, unmannerly, रूखा, रूक्ष, अशिष्ट। 4. harsh, कर्कश, बेसुरा।5. violent, stormy, उग्र, प्रचंड। 6. crude, अनगढ़ या अपरिष्कृत। 7. difficult, taxing, कठोर, विकट। 8. not complete or exact, approximate, अपूर्ण, अनुमानित, कच्चा। ***v.*** 1. to make rough, खुरदरा बनाना। 2. to sketch roughly, कच्चा मसौदा तैयार करना। □ **rough up,** मारना-पीटना।

roughage (रफ़िज) ***n.*** the coarse indigestible contents of food, फ़ुज़्ला, खुज्जा, फोक।

roughen (रफ़न) ***v.*** to make or become rough, खुरदरा बनाना या बनना।

roughness (रफ़निस) ***n.*** the state or quality of being rough, खुरदरापन; रूखापन, रूक्षता।

round (राउन्ड) ***adj.*** 1. shaped like a circle, गोल, वर्तुल। 2. plump, गोल-मटोल। 3. approximate, स्थूल। 4. full, पूर्ण, पूरा। ***n.*** 1. something round, गोल वस्तु, गोला। 2. a circular course, फेरा, फेरी। 3. series, शृंखला। 4. a stage of a competition, चक्र; in second round, द्वितीय चक्र में। 5. beat, गश्त। 6. tour of inspection, दौरा। ***v.*** 1. to make round, गोल बनाना। 2. to become round, गोल बनना। 3. to make into round figures, पूर्ण अंकों में बनाना। 4. to surround, घेरना। ***adv.*** around, चारों तरफ़। ***prep.*** around, के चारों तरफ़।

roundabout (राउन्डअबाउट) ***adj.*** circuitous, चक्करदार, घुमाव-फिरावदार।

roundly (राउन्डली) ***adv.*** 1. severely, सख़्ती से, अच्छी तरह। 2. in a round form, गोलाकार रूप में। 3. frankly, स्पष्ट रूप से।

roundness (राउन्डनिस) ***n.*** the state or quality of being round, गोलाई।

round-up (राउन्ड-अप) ***n.*** 1. the act of gathering animals, peoples, things etc., एकत्रीकरण। 2. summary, सारांश।

roundworm (राउन्डवर्म) ***n.*** a worm with a rounded body living in the intestines of men, केंचुआ।

rouse (राउज़) ***v.*** 1. to wake, जागना। 2. to cause to wake, जगाना, जाग्रत करना। 3. to excite, उत्तेजित करना।

rousing (राउज़िंग) ***adj.*** grand, भव्य, शानदार।

rout (राउट) ***v.*** 1. to defeat completely, पूरी तरह से पराजित करना। 2. to put to flight, खदेड़ देना। ***n.*** 1. utter defeat, पूर्ण पराजय। 2. retreat of defeated forces, सेना का पीठ दिखाकर भाग खड़े होना।

route (रूट) ***n.*** a customary course to travel, बँधा हुआ मार्ग, रास्ता, पथ।

routine (रूटीन) ***n.*** 1. regular or

habitual procedure, नेम, नित्यकर्म। 2. prescribed procedure, पद्धति-क्रम। *adj.* regular, नियमित।

rove (रोव) *v.* to roam, घूमना, भ्रमण करना।

row[1] (रो) *n.* 1. a straight line (of people or things), सीधी पंक्ति, कतार। 2. a line of seats across a theatre, किसी छविगृह में बैठने की पंक्ति। 3. a continuous line of buildings, इमारतों की कतार।

row[2] *v.* to propel a boat by using oars, नाव खेना या चलाना। *n.* a trip in a boat, नाव की सैर।

row[3] (राउ) *n.* 1. a loud noise, ज़ोर का शोर। 2. a quarrel, झगड़ा। *v.* 1. to quarrel, झगड़ा करना, कहासुनी करना। 2. to reprimand, डाँटना।

rowdy (राउडी) *adj.* noisy, हुल्लड़बाज़। rough and disorderly, क्षुब्ध और अव्यवस्थित।

royal (रॉइअल) *adj.* 1. of kings or queens, राजसी, शाही। 2. of a government, राजकीय, सरकारी। 3. stately, majestic, शानदार, भव्य, उत्कृष्ट। *n.* a large size of paper (20 by 25 inches), रायल।

royalty (रॉइअल्टी) *n.* 1. royal position, sovereignty, राजत्व, राजसत्ता। 2. royal persons collectively, राजघराने के लोग। 3. a share of proceeds paid to an author or to the owner of a right, स्वामित्व, रॉयल्टी।

rub (रब) *v.* 1. to apply pressure and friction to, रगड़ना, घिसना। 2. to spread with pressure, मलना, लगाना। 3. to remove by rubbing, रगड़कर साफ़ करना, दाग़ हटाना। 4. to polish by rubbing, रगड़कर चमकाना। *n.* the act or process of rubbing, रगड़, रगड़ाई।

rubber (रबर) *n.* a tough elastic substance, रबर।

rubbish (रबिश) *n.* 1. waste, कूड़ा-करकट; rubbish dump, घूरा। 2. worthless material, काठ-कबाड़।

rubble (रबल) *n.* broken pieces of bricks, रोड़े-पत्थर।

ruby (रूबी) *n.* 1. a red precious gem, लाल, माणिक, रूबी। 2. deep red colour, गहरा लाल रंग।

ruche (रूश) *n.* a lace, झालर।

rucksack (रकसैक) *n.* a bag carried on the back, पीठ पर का थैला।

rudder (रडर) *n.* a device to steer a boat, ship etc., पतवार।

ruddy (रडी) *adj.* red or reddish, लाल, गुलाबी।

rude (रूड) *adj.* 1. boorish, uncivilized, ill-mannered, बदतमीज़, अशिष्ट, अभद्र। 2. harsh, कर्कश, रूखा, अशिष्टतापूर्ण। 3. uneducated, अशिक्षित, गँवार। 4. startling, आकस्मिक तथा चौंकानेवाला। 5. violent, ज़ोर, तीव्र, प्रचंड। □ **in rude health,** हृष्ट-पुष्ट, तगड़ा।

rudiment (रूडिमेन्ट) *n.* 1. a fundamental principle, मूल सिद्धांत। 2. (plu.) partially developed form of something, अल्पविकसित रूप, आरंभिक रूप।

rue[1] (रू) *v.* to feel remorse for, पश्चात्ताप करना।

rue[2] *n.* an aromatic plant, ब्राह्मी (बूटी)।

ruff (रफ़) *n.* coloured hair around the neck of certain birds or animals, कंठी।

ruffian (रफ़िअन) *n.* a rowdy fellow, hoodlum, गुंडा, बदमाश।

R

ruffle[1] (रफ़ल) ***n.*** a strip of frilled fabric, पट्टी, झालर।

ruffle[2] ***v.*** 1. to disturb the smoothness, अस्त-व्यस्त कर देना। 2. to become irregular, अनियमित या अस्त-व्यस्त हो जाना। 3. to annoy, चिढ़ाना। 4. to decompose, विघटित करना।

rug (रग) ***n.*** 1. a carpet, गलीचा। 2. a blanket, कंबल।

rugged (रगिड) ***adj.*** 1. having a rough surface, ऊबड़-खाबड़, खुरदरा। 2. stern, harsh, कड़ा, कठोर।

ruin (रूइन) ***n.*** severe destruction, विनाश, तबाही। ***v.*** to bring into ruined condition, नष्ट या बरबाद कर देना, तबाह कर देना।

ruins (रूइन्स) ***n.*** (plu.) the remains of something decayed or destroyed, अवशेष, खंडहर।

rule (रूल) ***n.*** 1. an authoritative direction, नियम। 2. a customary form or procedure, प्रथा, रिवाज, दस्तूर। 3. reign, शासन, हुकूमत। 4. a strip of metal, wood etc., रूला, रूल, पट्टी। ***v.*** 1. to govern, reign or control, शासन/हुकूमत करना। 2. to decide authoritatively, व्यवस्था देना।

ruler (रूलर) ***n.*** 1. one who rules, शासक, हाकिम। 2. a thin strip of wood, metal etc., for measuring or drawing purposes, रूलर, पटरी, रेखक।

ruling (रूलिंग) ***n.*** the decision of the chair, व्यवस्था।

rum (रम) ***n.*** an alcoholic liquor, रम।

rumble (रम्बल) ***v.*** to make a deep, long rolling sound, गरजना, चिंघाड़ना। ***n.*** 1. rumbling sound, गड़गड़, गरज। 2. a murmur of discontent, असंतोष का मंद स्वर, बुड़बुड़ाहट।

ruminate (रूमिनेट) ***v.*** 1. to chew the cud, जुगाली करना। 2. to meditate, मनन या चिंतन करना।

ruminative (रूमिनेटिव) ***adj.*** meditating, मननशील।

rummy (रमी) ***n.*** a card game, (ताश का खेल) रमी।

rumour (रूमर) ***n.*** 1. a report of uncertain truthfulness, उड़ती ख़बर, अफ़वाह। 2. hearsay, किंवदंती।

rump (रम्प) ***n.*** 1. the hindquarters of an animal, पुट्ठा। 2. a person's buttocks, चूतड़।

rumple (रम्पल) ***v.*** to make or become crumpled, शिकन डालना या पड़ना, अव्यवस्थित होना या करना।

rumpus (रम्पस) ***n.*** a noisy disturbance, उपद्रव, हो-हल्ला, हुल्लड़।

run (रन) ***v.*** (ran, run, running) 1. to move on foot faster than walking, दौड़ना, भागना। 2. to take part in a race, दौड़ना। 3. to compete for elected office, (चुनाव में) खड़ा होना। 4. to be in operation, (मशीन का) चलना। 5. to flow, बहना। 6. to spread rapidly, तेज़ी से फैलना। 7. to be effective, प्रभावी होना। 8. to thrust, घुसेड़ना। 9. to drive or ply, चलाना। 10. to manage, व्यवस्था करना, चलाना। 11. to extend, विस्तृत होना, फैला होना। 12. to be stated or reported, कहा जाना। 13. to publish or print, छापना या प्रकाशित करना। 14. to get or pass through, निकलना, निकल जाना। 15. to be subjected to, ग्रस्त होना। 16. to incur, उठाना; to run a risk, जोखिम उठाना। ***n.*** 1. a pace faster than the walk, दौड़। 2. a score of one obtained by running between the wickets, दौड़, रन (क्रिकेट में)। 3. flow, rush, गति, प्रवाह। 4. route, मार्ग। 5. unrestricted freedom, स्वतंत्रता। 6. demand, ज़ोरदार माँग।

runaway (रनअवे) ***n.*** a fugitive, भगोड़ा। ***adj.*** having run away, जो भाग गया हो।

rundown (रनडाउन) ***adj.*** 1. tired, थका-माँदा। 2. dilapidated, जीर्ण-शीर्ण। ***n.*** a detailed analysis, विस्तृत विवरण।

rung (रंग) ***n.*** one of a cross pieces of a ladder, सीढ़ी का डंडा।

runner (रनर) ***n.*** 1. one who runs, दौड़नेवाला, दौड़ाक। 2. a messenger, दूत, पत्रवाहक।

runner-up (रनर-अप) ***n.*** a contestant finishing a competition in second place, उपविजेता।

running (रनिंग) ***n.*** the act of one that runs, दौड़ना, दौड़। ***adj.*** 1. continuous, लगातार होनेवाला, सतत। 2. prevalent, प्रचलित, विद्यमान।

runway (रनवे) ***n.*** a path over which aircrafts take off and land, धावन-पथ।

rupee (रूपी) ***n.*** a standard monetary unit of India, रुपया।

rupture (रप्चर) ***n.*** 1. the act of breaking or bursting, टूटना, फटना। 2. the breach of friendly relation, अनबन, बिगाड़। 3. hernia, हर्निया। ***v.*** 1. to become burst, फटना, टूटना। 2. to cause a relationship to end, संबंध तोड़ देना। 3. to affect with hernia, हर्निया से ग्रस्त होना।

rural (रूरल) ***adj.*** of or pertaining to the country or village, ग्राम्य, ग्रामीण।

rush (रश) ***n.*** 1. an eager movement of many persons to one place all at once, भीड़। 2. press of work, काम का दबाव या ज़ोर। 3. haste, जल्दी, हड़बड़ी। ***v.*** 1. to act hastily, जल्दी मचाना/करना। 2. to assault, धावा बोलना।

rusk (रस्क) ***n.*** a cake toasted in an oven, रस।

Russian (रशन) ***adj.*** of Russia, रूसी।

rust (रस्ट) ***n.*** 1. oxide formed on iron, ज़ंग, मोरचा। 2. any injurious habit, बुरी आदत। ***v.*** to be affected with rust, ज़ंग लगना, ज़ंग खा जाना।

rustic (रस्टिक) ***adj.*** 1. typical of country life, गँवारू। 2. simple, सीधा-सादा, भोला। ***n.*** a rural person, देहाती, गँवारू।

rustle (रसल) ***v.*** 1. to make a crisp or cracking sound, सरसर करना, फड़फड़ करना। 2. to steal, चुराना। ***n.*** rustling sound, सरसर, फड़फड़।

rusty (रस्टी) ***adj.*** 1. affected with rust, ज़ंग-लगा। 2. impaired, विकृत, क्षतिग्रस्त।

rut (रट) ***n.*** a groove made in the ground by the wheel of a vehicle, पहिए की लकीर, लीक।

ruthless (रूथलिस) ***adj.*** without ruth, निर्दय, निष्ठुर, नृशंस।

rye (राइ) ***n.*** a grass and its grain, एक पौधा और उसके बीज, राइ।

S

S, s (एस) ***n.*** The nineteenth letter of the English alphabet, अंग्रेज़ी वर्णमाला का उन्नीसवाँ वर्ण।

Sabbath (सैबथ) ***n.*** a rest day, विश्राम-दिवस।

sable (सेबल) ***n.*** 1. a weasel-like animal, नेवले की जाति का एक पशु। 2. its fur, इस पशु की फर। ***adj.*** black, काला।

sabotage (सैबटाज़) ***n.*** the deliberate destruction or disruption, तोड़-फ़ोड़, विध्वंस। ***v.*** to destruct or disrupt, तोड़ना-फोड़ना, विध्वस्त करना।

saboteur (सैबटर) ***n.*** one who commits sabotage, तोड़-फोड़ करनेवाला, विध्वंसक।

sabre, saber (सेबर) ***n.*** a sword with curved blade, कटार।

sac (सैक) ***n.*** a pouch-like part in an animal or plant, किसी पशु या पादप में होनेवाला थैलीनुमा अंग, थैली।

saccharin (सैकरिन) ***n.*** a substitute for sugar, सैक्रीन।

sachet (सैशे) ***n.*** a small pouch, थैली।

sack[1] (सैक) ***n.*** 1. a large bag used as a container, बोरा, बोरी, थैला। 2. dismissal, बर्ख़ास्तगी, पदच्युति। ***v.*** 1. to put into a sack or sacks, बोरा या बोरे भरना। 2. to dismiss from employment, नौकरी से निकाल देना।

sack[2] ***v.*** to loot or plunder, लूटना, लूट-पाट करना। ***n.*** the act of sacking, लूट-पाट, लूट-मार।

sackcloth (सैकक्लॉथ) ***n.*** a rough coarse cloth, टाट।

sacrament (सैक्रमेन्ट) ***n.*** any of the sacred religious rites, धार्मिक अनुष्ठान या संस्कार।

sacred (सेक्रिड) ***adj.*** 1. holy, पवित्र, पावन। 2. religious, धार्मिक। 3. worthy of reverence, पूज्य, आदरणीय।

sacrifice (सेक्रिफ़ाइस) ***n.*** 1. a ritual killing of a man or animal to please a deity, बलि, पशुबलि। 2. an offering to a deity, चढ़ावा। 3. giving up of anything valuable for a good cause, बलिदान, क़ुर्बानी, उत्सर्ग। ***n.*** 1. to kill to please a deity, बलि चढ़ाना। 2. to give up, क़ुर्बानी देना, बलिदान करना, उत्सर्ग करना।

sacrilege (सैक्रिलिज) ***n.*** the misuse or desecration of something regarded as sacred, अपवित्रीकरण।

sacrosanct (सैक्रोसैन्क्ट) ***adj.*** sacred, holy, पवित्र, पावन।

sad (सैड) ***adj.*** 1. feeling or showing sorrow, उदास, दुखी। 2. regrettable, दुखद, खेदजनक।

sadden (सैडन) ***v.*** 1. to become sad, उदास या दुखी होना। 2. to make sad, उदास या दुखी करना।

saddle (सैडल) ***n.*** 1. a seat placed on a horse's back, काठी। 2. a seat on a bicycle, सीट। ***v.*** 1. to put a saddle on, काठी लगाना। 2. to load or burden, भार या बोझा लादना, दायित्व सौंपना।

sadism (सैडिज़्म) ***n.*** the getting of pleasure from hurting others, यातना देकर प्राप्त होनेवाला सुख, परपीड़न-सुख।

sadly (सैडली) ***adj.*** 1. in a sad manner, मुँह लटकाए। 2. unfortunately, दुर्भाग्य से।

safari (सफ़ारी) ***n.*** a journey for

hunting expedition, शिकार-यात्रा, आखेट-यात्रा।

safe (सेफ़) ***adj.*** free from danger, सुरक्षित, सही-सलामत।

safe-deposit vault ***n.*** a room in a bank for storing valuables, तिजोरी-घर।

safeguard (सेफ़गार्ड) ***n.*** a precautionary measure, सुरक्षोपाय। ***v.*** to protect, बचाव करना, रक्षा करना।

safety (सेफ़्टी) ***n.*** freedom from danger, सुरक्षा, क्षेम, बचाव।

safety pin ***n.*** a spring wire clasp, (आलपिन से अलग) सेफ़्टी पिन।

saffron (सैफ़्रन) ***n.*** yellow dried stigmas of a particular plant used for colouring and flavouring food, केसर।

sag (सैग) ***v.*** to hang downward, झुक, झूल, धँस, ढलक या लटक जाना। ***n.***the act or instance of sagging, झुकाव, झूल, लटकाव; ढलकाव, धँसाव।

saga (सागा) ***n.*** a long heroic tale, लंबी वीरगाथा।

sagacious (सगेशस) ***adj.*** shrewd and wise, सयाना, बुद्धिमान, दूरदर्शी।

sage (सेज) ***n.*** a profoundly wise person, ऋषि, मनीषी, संत।

sago (सेगो) ***n.*** a type of hard white grain, साबूदाना।

said (सेड) ***v.*** pt. and pp. of say. ***adj.*** afore-mentioned, उक्त, उपरोक्त।

sail (सेल) ***n.*** 1. a piece of canvas that aids in propelling a ship, boat etc., पाल। 2. a journey by ship or boat, नौका-यात्रा। ***v.*** (sailed, sailing) 1. to travel in a ship or boat, जलयान या नाव में यात्रा करना। 2. to move fast, तेज़ी से चलना।

sailor (सेलर) ***n.*** any member of a ship's crew, नाविक।

saint (सेन्ट) ***n.*** 1. a person of exceptional holiness, संत, पवित्रात्मा, महात्मा। 2. a very good person, भला आदमी।

sake (सेक) ***n.*** ☐ **for the sake of,** के कारण, के लिए।

salable (सेलेबल) ***adj.*** fit for sale, saleable, बिक्री-योग्य, विक्रेय।

salacious (सलेशस) ***adj.*** 1. lewd, lustful, कामुक। 2. obscene, अश्लील।

salad (सैलड) ***n.*** a dish of chopped raw vegetables, सलाद।

salaried (सैलरीड) ***adj.*** receiving a salary, वेतनभोगी।

salary (सैलरी) ***n.*** regular payment for services, वेतन, तनख़्वाह, पगार।

sale (सेल) ***n.*** 1. the exchange of goods for money, बिक्री। 2. the amount sold, बिक्री। 3. a special sale of goods at reduced rates, सेल।

saleable (सेलेबल) ***adj.*** = salable.

salesman (सेल्ज़मैन) ***n.*** a man employed to sell goods, विक्रेता, सेल्समैन।

salient (सेलिएन्ट) ***adj.*** striking, most noticeable, मुख्य, प्रमुख, उल्लेखनीय।

saline (सेलाइन) ***adj.*** containing salt, नमकीन, खारा।

saliva (सलाइवा) ***n.*** a watery fluid discharged by salivary glands, लार।

salivary gland (सैलिवरी ग्लैन्ड) ***n.*** saliva producing gland, लार-ग्रंथि।

sallow (सैलो) ***adj.*** 1. of pale or yellowish colour, पीला। 2. unhealthy, अस्वस्थ।

S

sally (सैली) ***n.*** 1. a sudden assault, धावा। 2. excursion, सैर। 3. a witty remark, व्यंग्य। ***v.*** to attack, धावा बोल देना।

salon (सैलॉन) ***n.*** 1. a guest-room, अतिथि-कक्ष, दीवानख़ाना, बैठक। 2. a gathering in such a room, अतिथि-कक्ष में बैठे हुए लोग, अतिथिगण। 3. a beauty parlour, सौंदर्यकक्ष।

saloon (सलून) ***n.*** 1. a large public room on a ship, जलयान का बड़ा सार्वजनिक कक्ष। 2. a large room (for specific purpose), बड़ा कमरा, हाल। 3. a bar, मदिरालय। 4. a type of car, बोगी, कार।

salt (साल्ट) ***n.*** 1. sodium chloride, नमक, लवण। 2. liveliness, जीवंतता। 3. beauty, लावण्य। ***adj.*** salty, खारा, नमकीन। ***v.*** 1. to season with salt, नमकीन बनाना। 2. to preserve with salt, नमक लगाकर रखना।

saltpetre, saltpeter (साल्टपीटर) ***n.*** potassium nitrate, शोरा।

salty (साल्टी) ***adj.*** 1. containing salt, नमकीन। 2. sharp, तेज़।

salubrious (सलूब्रिअस) ***adj.*** favourable to health, स्वास्थ्यवर्धक, स्वास्थ्यकर।

salutary (सैल्युटरी) ***adj.*** beneficial, हितकर, लाभप्रद, अच्छा।

salutation (सैल्युटेशन) ***n.*** 1. an expression of respect and greeting, अभिवादन, नमस्कार, सलाम। 2. a word or words used as courtesy at the time of giving a speech, संबोधन (महाशय, मान्यवर, आदरणीय आदि)।

salute (सल्यूट) ***v.*** 1. to greet, नमस्कार करना, सलाम करना, अभिवादन करना। 2. to honour formally, सलामी देना।

salvage (सैल्विज) ***n.*** 1. rescue (of a ship, जलयान) का बचाव, निस्तारण, उद्धार। 2. rescued property, बचाई गई संपत्ति। ***v.*** to rescue from destruction, नष्ट होने से बचा लेना, उद्धार करना।

salvation (सैल्वेशन) ***n.*** 1. the state of being saved, उद्धार, निस्तार, बचाव। 2. final deliverance, मोक्ष, निर्वाण, मुक्ति।

salve (सैल्व) ***n.*** 1. a soothing ointment, मरहम। 2. solace, सांत्वना।

salvo (सैल्वो) ***n.*** 1. a simultaneous discharge of guns on a ceremonial occasion, तोपों की सलामी। 2. a volley of applause, तालियों की गड़गड़ाहट।

same (सेम) ***adj.*** 1. identical in kind, alike, समान, वैसा ही, सदृश। 2. being the very one, वही। 3. previously mentioned, पूर्वोक्त, वही। ***pron.*** the same thing or person, वही। ***adv.*** in an identical manner, वैसे ही, उसी प्रकार।

sample (सैम्पल) ***n.*** 1. a portion, piece or segment representative of whole, नमूना, बानगी। 2. an example, उदाहरण। ***v.*** to take a sample (of किसी चीज़ का) नमूना लेना।

sanatorium (सैनेटोरियम) ***n.*** an establishment for treating tuberculous patients, स्वास्थ्य-सुधारगृह, आरोग्याश्रम।

sanctification (सैन्क्टिफ़िकेशन) ***n.*** the act of sanctifying or the state of being sanctified, पवित्रीकरण।

sanctify (सैन्क्टिफ़ाइ) ***v.*** 1. to make holy, पवित्र करना। 2. to free from sins, पापों से छुड़ाना।

sanctimony (सैन्क्टिमोनी) ***n.*** hypocritical righteousness, पाखंड, ढोंग।

sanction (सैन्क्शन) ***n.*** 1. authoritative permission, स्वीकृति, मंजूरी, संस्वीकृति। 2. confirmation, पुष्टि। 3. a coercive measure, दंडित करने का उपाय, दंडोपाय। 4. a penalty, दंड। ***v.*** 1. to give sanction to, स्वीकृति देना, मंजूरी देना, पुष्टि करना। 2. to impose sanctions दंडोपाय लगाना।

sanctity (सैन्क्टिटी) ***n.*** sacredness, holiness, पवित्रता, पावनता।

sanctuary (सैन्क्चुअरी) ***n.*** 1. a place for protection or refuge, शरणस्थल, शरणालय। 2. a place where birds and wild animals live freely, जंतु-विहार, अभयारण्य।

sanctum (सैन्क्टम) ***n.*** 1. a holy place, पावन-स्थली, मंदिर आदि। ☐ **sanctum sanctorum,** पवित्रतम स्थान, मंदिर का गर्भगृह। 2. a place of total privacy, एकांत।

sand (सैन्ड) ***n.*** 1. very fine loose fragments of rocks, रेत, बालू। 2. (plu.) a sandy area, रेतीला मैदान, रेती। ***v.*** 1. to sprinkle or cover with sand, बालू छिड़कना या फैलाना। 2. to polish with sand, बालू से रगड़कर चमकाना।

sandal (सैन्डल) ***n.*** a light shoe, सैंडल।

sandalwood (सैन्डलवुड) ***n.*** a kind of scented wood, चंदन की लकड़ी।

sandpaper (सैन्डपेपर) ***n.*** a paper with a coating of sand, बालू-काग़ज़, रेगमाल। ***v.*** to smoothen with sandpaper, रेगमाल से रगड़ना।

sandwich (सैन्डविच) ***n.*** two slices of bread with filling placed between them, सैंडविच। ***v.*** to insert (a thing) between two things, बीच में भरना/डालना।

sandy (सैन्डी) ***adj.*** 1. covered with sand, रेतीला, बलुआ। 2. yellow, (बालों का रंग) पीला।

sane (सेन) ***adj.*** 1. of sound mind, स्वस्थचित्त। 2. showing reason, समझदार।

sanguinary (सैन्ग्विनरी) ***adj.*** 1. blood thirsty, रक्तपिपासु। 2. bloody, ख़ूनी, रक्तमय।

sanguine (सैन्ग्विन) ***adj.*** hopeful, optimistic, आशावादी।

sanitarium (सैनिटैरिअम) ***n.*** = sanatorium.

sanitary (सैनिटरी) ***adj.*** 1. hygienic, स्वास्थ्यपरक। 2. of sanitation, स्वच्छता-संबंधी, स्वच्छ।

sanitation (सैनिटेशन) ***n.*** 1. arrangements to protect public health, स्वास्थ्य-व्यवस्था, स्वास्थ्य-रक्षा। 2. cleanliness, स्वच्छता, सफ़ाई।

sanity (सैनिटी) ***n.*** 1. the state or quality of being sane, स्वस्थचित्तता। 2. good sense, समझदारी।

sans (सैन्ज़) ***prep.*** without, के बिना।

sap (सैप) ***n.*** 1. watery fluid that circulates through a plant, पौधे का दूध, रस। 2. energy, vitality, ओज, तेज, स्फूर्ति। 3. a foolish person, मूर्ख व्यक्ति। 4. a trench, सुरंग, खंदक। ***v.*** to lexhaust gradually, धीरे-धीरे क्षीण होना।

sapling (सैप्लिन्ग) ***n.*** 1. a young tree, बाल-वृक्ष, किशोरतरु। 2. a youth, युवा।

sapphire (सैफ़ाइर) ***n.*** a blue gemstone, नीलम।

sarcasm (सार्कैज़्म) ***n.*** an ironical

S

remark, taunt, कटाक्ष, व्यंग्य, ताना, बोली।

sarcastic (सार्कैस्टिक) ***adj.*** ironical, taunting, व्यंग्यपूर्ण, तीखा, कटु।

sardonic (सार्डॉनिक) ***adj.*** sarcastic, व्यंग्यपूर्ण।

sartorial (सार्टोरिअल) ***adj.*** of tailoring, सिलाई-संबंधी।

sash (सैश) ***n.*** 1. a long strip of cloth worn over one's shoulder, अंगवस्त्र। 2. the frame of a window, खिड़की का चौखट।

Satan (सेटन) ***n.*** the devil, शैतान।

satanic (सटैनिक) ***adj.*** of Satan, devilish, शैतान-जैसा।

satchel (सैचल) ***n.*** a bag for carrying school books, स्कूली बस्ता।

satellite (सैटलाइट) ***n.*** a heavenly or artificial body orbiting around a planet, उपग्रह।

satiate (सेशिएट) ***v.*** to satisfy fully, पूर्णतः तृप्त कर देना।

satiation (सेशिएशन) ***n.*** satiety, तृप्ति, संतुष्टि।

satin (सैटिन) ***n.*** a glossy silken cloth, साटिन (कपड़ा)।

satire (सैटाइअर) ***adj.*** 1. the use of ridicule or sarcasm to deride follies, उपहास, व्यंग्य। 2. a satirical novel, film, poem etc., व्यंग्यप्रधान उपन्यास, फ़िल्म या कविता।

satiric (सटिरिक) ***adj.*** = satirical.

satirical (सटिरिकल) ***adj.*** containing satire, ironical, व्यंग्यपूर्ण, उपहासपूर्ण।

satirist (सैटिरिस्ट) ***n.*** one who writes satires, व्यंग्य-लेखक।

satisfaction (सैटिस्फ़ैक्शन) ***n.*** 1. the act of satisfying or the state of being satisfied, संतोष, संतुष्टि, परितोष। 2. something that satisfies, संतोष देनेवाली वस्तु या बात। 3. compensation, क्षतिपूर्ति।

satisfactory (सैटिस्फ़ैक्टरी) ***adj.*** giving satisfaction, संतोषजनक, संतोषप्रद।

satisfy (सैटिस्फ़ाइ) ***v.*** 1. to make contented, संतुष्ट करना। 2. to comply with, (नियम, शर्त आदि) पूरा करना, पूर्ति करना। 3. to convince, क़ायल करना, प्रसन्न करना।

saturate (सैचुरेट) ***v.*** to make thoroughly wet, तर बतर कर देना।

saturation (सैचुरेशन) ***n.*** the act of saturating or being saturated, गीला होना या करना, संतृप्ति।

Saturday (सैटर्डे) ***n.*** the day after Friday, शनिवार, शनि।

Saturn (सैटर्न) ***n.*** a planet in the solar system, शनिग्रह।

saturnine (सैटर्नाइन) ***adj.*** 1. sad, उदास। 2. lazy, सुस्त, मंद।

satyr (सेटर) ***n.*** a deity in human form but having goat's ears, tail and legs, वनदेवता।

sauce (सॉस) ***n.*** 1. a liquid dressing served with food, चटनी, सॉस। 2. rude behaviour, रूखा बरताव। ***v.*** to flavour with sauce, सॉस मिलाना।

saucepan (सॉसपैन) ***n.*** a cooking pot with a long handle, हत्थेवाला पकाने का एक बर्तन।

saucer (सॉसर) ***n.*** a small shallow dish for holding a cup, तश्तरी।

saucy (सॉसी) ***adj.*** impudent, rude, ढीठ, धृष्ट।

saunter (सॉन्टर) ***v.*** to walk leisurely, धीरे-धीरे चलना। ***n.*** a leisurely stroll, चहलक़दमी।

sausage (सॉसिज) ***n.*** chopped seasoned meat, कबाब।

savage (सैविज) ***adj.*** 1. wild, untamed, जंगली, वहशी। 2. not civilized, असभ्य। 3. ferocious, ख़ूँखार, बर्बर। ***n.*** 1. a brutal person, बर्बर व्यक्ति। 2. a rude person, उद्धत व्यक्ति। ***v.*** to attack brutally, बर्बरतापूर्वक आक्रमण करना, झपट पड़ना।

savanna (सवैना) ***n.*** a grassy plain, घास का मैदान, सवाना।

save (सेव) ***v.*** 1. to rescue from danger, बचाना, बचाव करना, उद्धार करना। 2. to preserve, सुरक्षित रखना। 3. to set aside for future use, भविष्य के लिए बचाकर रखना। 4. to avoid wasting, बचाना। ***n.*** the act of saving, बचाव। ***prep.*** except, but, को छोड़कर, के अतिरिक्त।

savings (सेविंग्स) ***n.*** (plu.) money saved for future use, बचत।

saviour (सेव्यर) ***n.*** one who saves, रक्षक।

savour, savor (सेवर) ***n.*** 1. the taste of something, स्वाद, ज़ायक़ा। 2. the smell of something, सुगंध। ***v.*** 1. to taste or smell a thing, चखना, स्वाद देखना। 2. to have a certain taste or smell, (अपना) स्वाद या ज़ायक़ा होना।

savoury (सेवरी) ***adj.*** 1. delicious, tasty, स्वादिष्ट, मज़ेदार। 2. having good smell, सुगंधित।

saw[1] (सॉ) ***n.*** a tool for cutting wood, आरा। ***v.*** (sawed, sawn/sawed, sawing) to cut with a saw, आरे से चीरना या काटना।

saw[2] ***n.*** a proverb, कहावत।

sawdust (सॉडस्ट) ***n.*** particles of wood formed by sawing, बुरादा।

saxophone (सैक्सोफ़ोन) ***n.*** a wind instrument, एक तरह का बाजा, सैक्सोफ़ोन।

say (से) ***v.*** (said, saying) 1. to speak, कहना, बोलना। 2. to tell, बतलाना। 3. to suppose, मान लेना। ***adj.*** 1. approximately, लगभग। 2. for example, उदाहरण के लिए। ***n.*** 1. the power to decide, (निर्णय का) अधिकार। 2. the chance to speak, बोलने का अवसर।

saying (सेइंग) ***n.*** a proverb, कहावत, लोकोक्ति।

scab (स्कैब) ***n.*** a crust like surface formed on healing wound, खुरंड।

scabby (स्कैबी) ***adj.*** having scabies, खुजली से पीड़ित।

scabies (स्कैबीज़) ***n.*** a skin disease, खुजली।

scabrous (स्कैब्रस) ***adj.*** indecent, अश्लील।

scaffold (स्कैफ़ल्ड) ***n.*** 1. a temporary framework used by construction workers, ढाँचा, पाइट, पाड़, मचान। 2. a platform on which criminals are executed, फाँसी का तख़्ता।

scald (स्कॉल्ड) ***v.*** 1. to clean with boiling water, गर्म पानी से धोना या साफ़ करना। 2. to be injured with hot water or steam, गर्म पानी या भाप से जल या झुलस जाना। ***n.*** an injury caused by scalding, झुलसना।

scale (स्केल) ***n.*** 1. (often plu.) an instrument or machine for weighing, तुला, तराजू। 2. a measuring rod, पैमाना, मापनी। 3. a series of steps or degrees, मापक्रम, अनुमाप श्रेणी। 4. a series of tones arranged in a sequence, स्वरग्राम। ***v.*** 1. to weigh, तौलना। 2. to ascend, ऊपर चढ़ना, फाँदना, लाँघना।

scalene (स्केलीन) ***adj.*** having

S

unequal sides, विषम, विषमबाहु (त्रिभुज)।

scalp (स्कैल्प) ***n.*** the skin of the head, खोपड़ी की चमड़ी।

scalpel (स्कैल्पल) ***n.*** a surgeon's knife, सर्जन की छुरी।

scam (स्कैम) ***n.*** a fraudulent scheme for making money quickly, धोखेधड़ी की योजना, कपट-योजना, स्कैम, घोटाला।

scan (स्कैन) ***v.*** 1. to look intently, गौर से देखना। 2. to analyse, विश्लेषित करना। 3. to analyse the coloured picture, चित्रों को रंगों में विभक्त करना।

scandal (स्कैन्डल) ***n.*** 1. shameful or disgraceful act, ग़लत काम, अनैतिक कार्य, कुकर्म, कलंक। 2. shame, public disgrace, किसी कुकर्म से होनेवाली बदनामी। 3. malicious gossip, चुगली।

scandalize (स्कैन्डलाइज़) ***v.*** to offend by one's immoral behaviour, (अपने) कुकर्म से दूसरों को दुखी करना।

scant, scanty (स्कैन्ट, स्कैन्टी) ***adj.*** insufficient, बहुत थोड़ा, अपर्याप्त।

scapegoat (स्केपगोट) ***n.*** one bearing blame of others, बलि का बकरा।

scar (स्कार) ***n.*** a mark of an old injury, घाव का निशान, व्रणचिह्न। ***v.*** 1. to mark with a scar, निशान डालना। 2. to be marked with a scar, निशान पड़ना।

scarce (स्केअर्स) ***adj.*** 1. rare, विरल। 2. not plentiful, दुष्प्राप्य।

scarcely (स्केअर्सली) ***adv.*** 1. hardly at all, मुश्किल से। 2. almost not, शायद ही।

scarcity (स्केअर्सिटी) ***n.*** 1. shortage, कमी, अभाव, तंगी। 2. rarity, विरलता।

scare (स्केअर) ***v.*** 1. to frighten, डराना-धमकाना, भयभीत करना। 2. to be frightened, डरना, भयभीत होना। ***n.*** alarm, fright, डर, भय।

scarecrow (स्केअरक्रो) ***n.*** an object in the shape of a man to scare birds from crops, बिजूखा, धोखा।

scarf (स्कार्फ़) ***n.*** (plu. scarves, searfs) a long narrow piece of cloth worn around the neck, स्कार्फ़, रूमाल, दुपट्टा।

scarlet (स्कॉर्लिट) ***adj.*** deep orange red, गहरा तथा चमकीला लाल, सिंदूरी।

scary (स्केअरी) ***adj.*** frightening, भयावह।

scathing (स्केदिंग) ***adj.*** harsh, severe, कटु, तीखा।

scatter (स्कैटर) ***v.*** to spread loosely, छितराना, बिखेरना।

scatterbrain (स्कैटरब्रेन) ***n.*** one who is unable to concentrate, वह जिसका मन एकाग्रचित न हो।

scatty (स्कैटी) ***adj.*** empty-headed, खर-दिमाग़, मूर्ख।

scavenge (स्कैविन्ज) ***v.*** 1. to clean up filth (from streets etc. गलियों आदि की) सफ़ाई करना। 2. to search for decaying flesh as food, (पशुओं का) सड़े-गले मांस की तलाश करना।

scavenger (स्कैविन्जर) ***n.*** one who scavenges, सफ़ाई करनेवाला, सफ़ाई कर्मचारी, झाड़ूबरदार, भंगी।

scenario (सिनारिओ) ***n.*** 1. a script or outline of a film, फ़िल्म की पटकथा या रूपरेखा। 2. an outline of possible future events, भावी घटनाओं की संभावित रूपरेखा।

scene (सीन) ***n.*** 1. a subdivision of an act, a stage set, दृश्य। 2. an event, घटना। 3. a place of occurrence, घटनास्थल। 4. the scenery, दृश्यबंध, दृश्यावली।

S

scenery (सीनरी) ***n.*** 1. the general or picturesque features of a landscape, दृश्यबंध, दृश्यावली। 2. the painted backdrops, मंच के चित्रित पर्दे।

scenic (सीनिक) ***adj.*** 1. of or relating to the scenery, दृश्यावली-संबंधी। 2. having beautiful natural scenery, सुंदर दृश्यावलीवाला, दृश्योपम।

scent (सेन्ट) ***n.*** 1. a distinctive smell of something, गंध, महक। 2. an instinctive ability for detecting, (गंध से) पीछा करने की शक्ति। 3. perfume, इत्र। ***v.*** 1. to recognize by smell, गंध से जान लेना। 2. to have an inkling of, आभास होना। 3. to put scent on, सुगंधित/सुवासित करना।

sceptic, sceptical (स्केप्टिक, स्केप्टिकल) ***n.*** one who doubts the truth, संशयात्मा, संशयवादी। ***adj.*** doubtful, संशयपूर्ण।

scepticism (स्केप्टिसिज़म) ***n.*** 1. a doubt, संशय, अविश्वास। 2. doubt or disbelief of religious doctrines, संशयवाद।

sceptre (सेप्टर) ***n.*** a staff carried by a sovereign, राजदंड।

schedule (शेड्यूल) ***n.*** 1. a list of items, सूची। 2. a programme, कार्यक्रम। 3. a timetable, समयसारणी। 4. an appended list, अनुसूची। ***v.*** 1. to put in a schedule, सूची में डालना। 2. to make a schedule, सूची बनाना।

scheduled (शेड्यूल्ड) ***adj.*** 1. placed in the schedule, अनुसूचित। 2. fixed, नियत।

schematic (स्कीमैटिक) ***adj.*** 1. of a scheme, योजना-संबंधी। 2. planned, योजनाबद्ध।

scheme (स्कीम) ***n.*** 1. a systematic plan, योजना, स्कीम। 2. an underhand plan, तिकड़म, चाल, षड्यंत्र। ***v.*** 1. to plan, योजना बनाना। 2. to plan in a secret way, षड्यंत्र रचना, कुचक्र रचना।

scholar (स्कॉलर) ***n.*** 1. a learned person, विद्वान, पंडित, मर्मज्ञ। 2. one who studies, विद्याव्यसनी, अध्ययनकर्ता। 3. one who holds a scholarship, वृत्तिधारक छात्र।

scholarly (स्कॉलरली) ***adj.*** 1. pertaining to learning, विद्वत्तापूर्ण। 2. intellectual, बौद्धिक।

scholarship (स्कॉलरशिप) ***n.*** 1. learning, विद्वत्ता, पांडित्य, अध्ययनशीलता। 2. a grant awarded to a student, छात्रवृत्ति।

school[1] (स्कूल) ***n.*** 1. an institution for educating children etc., विद्यालय, पाठशाला, स्कूल। 2. its building or buildings, स्कूल का/ के भवन। 3. a particular group of artists, philosophers etc., शाखा, वर्ग। ***v.*** to train or discipline, प्रशिक्षित या अनुशासित करना।

school[2] ***n.*** a group of fish that swim together, मछलियों का गोल।

schooner (स्कूनर) ***n.*** 1. a ship with two or more masts, दो या अधिक मस्तूलोंवाला पोत। 2. a large glass, बड़ा गिलास।

sciatica (साइऐटिका) ***n.*** chronic neuralgic pain in the area of hip and thigh, जाँघ तथा नितंब में होनेवाली पीड़ा, गृध्रसी, साइटिका।

science (साइअन्स) ***n.*** a branch of knowledge dealing with natural laws, विज्ञान।

S

scientific (साइअन्टिफ़िक) ***adj.*** of science or conforming with the methods used in science, वैज्ञानिक।

scientist (साइअन्टिस्ट) ***n.*** an expert in any science, वैज्ञानिक, विज्ञानी, विज्ञानवेत्ता।

scimitar (सिमिटर) ***n.*** a short curved sword, ख़ंजर, कटार, शमशीर।

scintillant (सिन्टिलैन्ट) ***adj.*** sparkling, चमकता हुआ।

scintillate (सिन्टिलेट) ***v.*** 1. to sparkle, चिंगारियाँ छोड़ना। 2. to be brilliant, चमकना।

scion (साइअन) ***n.*** 1. a descendant, वंशज, संतति। 2. a shoot used as a graft, (पौधे की) क़लम।

scissors (सिज़र्ज़) ***n.*** (plu.) a cutting instrument made of two blades, कैंची।

scoff[1] (स्कॉफ़) ***v.*** to jeer, खिल्ली उड़ाना, हँसी उड़ाना।

scoff[2] ***v.*** to eat greedily, भकोसना, ठूँसना।

scold (स्कोल्ड) ***v.*** to reprimand harshly, डाँटना-डपटना, झिड़कना।

scolding (स्कोल्डिंग) ***n.*** rebuke, डाँट-डपट, झिड़की।

scoop (स्कूप) ***n.*** 1. a ladle, कलछी, पली। 2. a sensational news or story, सनसनी फैला देनवाला समाचार। ***v.*** 1. to lift with a scoop, कलछी आदि से (अन्न आदि) निकालना। 2. to print a sensational news or story (before others, औरों से पहले) कोई सनसनीखेज़ समाचार या कहानी छापना।

scooter (स्कूटर) ***n.*** a small or light-weight motorcycle, स्कूटर।

scope (स्कोप) ***n.*** 1. the range of something, क्षेत्र। 2. the range of some activities, कार्यक्षेत्र। 3. breadth, विस्तार, व्याप्ति, परिधि। 4. opportunity to function, गुंजाइश।

scorch (स्कॉर्च) ***v.*** to burn the surface of, झुलसना या झुलसाना।

scorching (स्कॉर्चिंग) ***adj.*** very hot, बहुत गर्म, झुलसानेवाला।

score (स्कोर) ***v.*** 1. to gain (a point, अंक) प्राप्त करना। 2. to make a total score of, अंकों का ब्योरा तैयार करना, हिसाब रखना। 3. to achieve, प्राप्त करना। 4. to compose music, स्वरलिपि तैयार करना। ***n.*** 1. the points scored, बनाए/जीते हुए अंक, गोल, रन आदि, प्राप्तांक। 2. a record of points scored, अंक-गणना, हिसाब। 3. a group of twenty items, कौड़ी, बीसी। 4. a reason, तर्क, दलील। 5. a line or mark cut into something, खाँचा, खरोंच। 6. the written form of a musical composition, स्वरलिपि। 7. reality, वास्तविकता।

scorer (स्कोरर) ***n.*** one who scores, अंक बनानेवाला।

scorn (स्कॉर्न) ***n.*** strong contempt, disdain, तिरस्कार, घृणा, अवमानना। ***v.*** 1. to feel or show strong contempt for, घृणा करना, तिरस्कार करना। 2. to reject with contempt, दुत्कार देना, ठुकरा देना।

scornful (स्कॉर्नफ़ुल) ***adj.*** feeling or showing scorn, तिरस्कार-भरा।

Scorpio (स्कॉर्पिओ) ***n.*** the sign of the scorpion, वृश्चिक (राशि)।

scorpion (स्कॉर्पिअन) ***n.*** an insect, having a venomous sting, बिच्छू, वृश्चिक।

scotch (स्कॉच) ***v.*** 1. to put an end to, ख़त्म कर देना। 2. to crush, कुचल देना।

Scotch (स्कॉच) ***n.*** a whisky from

Scotland, स्कॉच या स्कॉट ह्विस्की।

scot-free (स्कॉट-फ़्री) ***adv.*** without harm, loss or punishment, बेदाग़।

scoundrel (स्काउन्ड्रॅल) ***n.*** a villainous person, बदमाश, दुष्ट।

scour (स्काउर) ***v.*** 1. to clean by rubbing, रगड़कर साफ़ करना, माँजना। 2. to remove dust from, साफ़ करना, सफ़ा करना। 3. to search thoroughly, छान मारना, खोज-ढूँढ़ करना।

scourge (स्कर्ज) ***n.*** 1. an instrument for flogging, whip, कोड़ा। 2. a cause of great suffering, संकट, अनिष्ट, विपत्ति, बला। ***v.*** 1. to whip, कोड़े लगाना। 2. to punish severely, कठोर यातना या यंत्रणा देना।

scout (स्काउट) ***n.*** 1. the member of a world wide organization of young persons to serve humanity, स्काउट, बालचर। 2. one sent out to gather information, गुप्तचर, भेदिया। ***v.*** 1. to act as a scout भेद लेना। 2. to make a search, खोज में निकलना, खोजना-ढूँढ़ना।

scowl (स्काउल) ***v.*** to contract the brows in a threatening manner, त्योरी चढ़ाना, घूरना। ***n.*** a look of angry expression, त्योरी।

scrabble (स्क्रैबल) ***v.*** 1. to scratch, खुरचना, खरोंचना। 2. to grope, टटोलना।

scramble (स्क्रैम्बल) ***v.*** 1. to move or climb hastily, तेज़ी से चलना या चढ़ना। 2. to compete frantically, छीन-झपट करना। 3. to mix haphazardly, गड्ड-मड्ड करना। 4. to take off (an aircraft) hurriedly (वायुयान को) झटपट उड़ा ले जाना। 5. to cook while mixing and stirring, चलाते हुए तलना या भूनना। ***n.*** 1. an act of climbing, चढ़ाई। 2. struggle, संघर्ष। 3. race of motorcycles, मोटर-साइकिलों की दौड़।

scrap[1] (स्क्रैप) ***n.*** 1. a small bit or fragment, टुकड़ा, कतरन, छीलन। 2. waste material, रद्दी सामान विशेषतः धातु आदि के बचे टुकड़े, छीलन आदि। ***v.*** to discard as useless, रद्दी करना, व्यर्थ समझकर त्याग देना।

scrap[2] ***n.*** 1. a quarrel, झगड़ा। 2. a fight, लड़ाई। ***v.*** 1. to quarrel, झगड़ा करना। 2. to fight, लड़ाई करना।

scrape (स्क्रेप) ***v.*** 1. to make smooth (a surface), रगड़ना, खुरचना, कुरेदना। 2. to rub and clean, रगड़कर माँजना, साफ़ करना, चमकाना। 3. to be very economical, हाथ खींचकर खर्च करना। ***n.*** 1. the act of scrap-ing, रगड़, खरोंच। 2. an awkward predicament, मुसीबत, झंझट।

scrappy (स्क्रैपी) ***adj.*** fragmentary, छोटे-छोटे टुकड़ों से बना हुआ।

scratch (स्क्रैच) ***v.*** 1. to make a shallow cut (on the surface) with a sharp instrument, नोचना, बकोटना या खुजलाना। 2. to make a thin scraping sound, खड़खड़ाना। 3. to withdraw from a competition, (दौड़/प्रतियोगिता आदि से) हट जाना। 4. to write or draw awkwardly, लकीरें खींचना, क़लम घसीटना। ***n.*** a mark made by scratching, a slight injury, खरोंच।

scrawl (स्क्रॉल) ***n.*** bad or illegible handwriting, अस्पष्ट लिखावट, गिचपिच। ***v.*** to write hastily and illegibly, गिचपिच लिखना।

scream (स्क्रीम) ***v.*** 1. to make a piercing cry, चीखना, चिल्लाना। 2. to laugh in a wild manner, ठहाका लगाना। ***n.*** 1. a screaming cry, चीख़।

S

2. a thing or person that causes great amusement, हास्यास्पद वस्तु या व्यक्ति।

screech (स्क्रीच) ***v.*** to scream, चीखना, चिल्लाना। ***n.*** a sound that resembles the screech, फस, कर्कश ध्वनि।

screen (स्क्रीन) ***n.*** 1. a structure to divide or conceal, आड़, ओट। 2. a curtain to divide or conceal, पर्दा, पट। 3. the curtain or surface on which movies are projected, रजतपट, चित्रपट। ***v.*** 1. to conceal or protect, आड़ करना, आड़ में कर देना। 2. to show on a screen, पर्दे पर दिखाना। 3. to provide with a screen, पर्दा लगाना। 4. to examine care-fully, निरीक्षण करना, जाँच-पड़ताल करना।

screening (स्क्रीनिंग) ***n.*** 1. fine mesh for making screen, बढ़िया जाली। 2. the showing of a film, फ़िल्म का प्रदर्शन।

screenplay (स्क्रीनप्ले) ***n.*** the script of a film, फ़िल्म-कथा, पटकथा।

screw (स्क्रू) ***n.*** a metal pin with threads, पेच, स्क्रू, खूँटी। ***v.*** 1. to fasten with a screw, पेच से कसना। 2. to coerce, सताना। 3. to force, मजबूर करना।

scribe (स्क्राइब) ***n.*** a person who copies documents, copyist, लिपिक, मुंशी।

scrimmage (स्क्रिमिज) ***n.*** scuffle, rough struggle, हाथापाई, छीनाझपटी, गुत्थमगुत्था।

scrimp (स्क्रिम्प) ***v.*** to economize severely, हाथ खींचकर गुज़ारा करना।

script (स्क्रिप्ट) ***n.*** 1. handwriting, हाथ की लिखावट, हस्तलिपि। 2. alphabet, वर्णमाला, लिपि। 3. a manuscript, पांडुलिपि। 4. the text of a play or motion picture, पटकथा।

scripture (स्क्रिप्चर) ***n.*** any sacred religious writing, धर्मग्रंथ, शास्त्र।

scroll (स्क्रोल) ***n.*** 1. a roll of paper, खर्रा। 2. a list, सूची, नामावली। 3. a decorative carving, बेलबूटों की नक़्क़ाशी। ***v.*** 1. to roll up like a scroll, खर्रे की तरह लपेटना। 2. to carve, नक़्क़ाशी करना।

scrub (स्क्रब) ***v.*** 1. to clean by rubbing, माँजना-रगड़ना, चमकाना। 2. to remove by brushing, झाड़ू-पोंछा लगाना, झाड़ना-पोंछना। 3. to cancel or scrap, नामावली से नाम काटना। ***n.*** 1. a stunted shrub, बौनी झाड़ी। 2. useless or worthless fellow, बेकार या महत्त्वहीन व्यक्ति।

scrunch (स्क्रन्च) ***v.*** to crush, कुचलना। ***n.*** the act or sound of scrunching, कुचलने की क्रिया या कुचलने से होनेवाला शब्द।

scruple (स्क्रूपल) ***n.*** 1. a feeling of hesitancy, हिचक। 2. a dictate of conscience, आत्मा की पुकार। ***v.*** to hesitate, हिचकना।

scrupulous (स्क्रूपलस) ***adj.*** 1. very honest, सत्यनिष्ठ, सत्यवादी, ईमानदार। 2. principled, सिद्धांतवादी। 3. careful, सावधान।

scrutineer (स्क्रूटिनिअर) ***n.*** one who scrutinizes, समीक्षक, संवीक्षक।

scrutinize (स्क्रूटिनाइज़) ***v.*** to inspect minutely, संवीक्षा करना।

scrutiny (स्क्रूटिनी) ***n.*** minute inspection, संवीक्षा।

scud (स्कड) ***v.*** to move along swiftly

S

and smoothly, (मेघों, पोतों आदि का) तेज़ी से उड़ना, चलना, दौड़ना, बहना।

scuffle (स्कफ़ल) ***n.*** a disorderly struggle, हाथापाई। ***v.*** to fight in a disorderly manner, हाथापाई करना।

scull (स्कल) ***n.*** one of the pair of oars, (नाव खेने का) डाँड़। ***v.*** to propel with a scull or sculls, डाँड़ या डाँड़ों से नाव खेना।

sculptor (स्कल्पटर) ***n.*** one who makes sculptures, मूर्तिकार।

sculpture (स्कल्पचर) ***n.*** 1. the art of shaping, carving, chiselling or modelling figures, मूर्तिकला। 2. work made in this way, मूर्ति। ***v.*** to shape (stone, wood, clay) into sculpture, मूर्ति बनाना या गढ़ना।

scum (स्कम) ***n.*** 1. a filmy layer of impure matter, गंदी झिल्ली, मैल। 2. a waste matter, रद्दी, कूड़ा। 3. a worthless person or group, हेय व्यक्ति या हेय व्यक्तियों का समूह।

scupper (स्कपर) ***n.*** a drain to carry off water from the deck of a ship, (पोत का) परनाला। ***v.*** to destroy or ruin, चौपट या तहस-नहस कर देना।

scurf (स्कर्फ़) ***n.*** 1. flakes of dry skin, रूसी। 2. dry scaly matter on a surface, पपड़ी।

scurrility (स्करिलिटी) ***n.*** 1. indecency, coarseness, फ़ूहड़पन। 2. indecency of language, abusive language, फ़ूहड़/गंदी भाषा, फक्कड़पन।

scurry (स्करी) ***v.*** to run hurriedly, दौड़ना, भागना। ***n.*** the act of scurrying, जल्दबाज़ी, दौड़-भाग।

scurvy (स्कर्वी) ***n.*** a disease marked by swollen and bleeding gums, मसूढ़ों से रक्त बहने की बीमारी।

scut (स्कट) ***n.*** the short tail of animals, छोटी दुम या पूँछ।

scythe (साइद) ***n.*** a long-handled curved implement for mowing grass, हँसिया। ***v.*** to cut with a scythe, हँसिया से काटना।

sea (सी) ***n.*** the mass of salt water that covers the most part of the land, समुद्र, सागर, जलराशि।

seaboard (सीबोर्ड) ***n.*** the land bordering on the sea, समुद्रतटीय प्रदेश, समुद्रतट।

seafarer (सीफ़ेअरर) ***n.*** a sailor, नाविक।

seagod (सीगॉड) ***n.*** a god of the sea, वरुण देवता।

seahorse (सीहॉर्स) ***n.*** a fish having horselike head, एक तरह की छोटी समुद्री मछली, अश्वमीन।

seal (सील) ***n.*** 1. an aquatic mammal, सील मछली। 2. a die for stamping, मोहर, मुद्रा, सील। 3. a symbol, चिह्न; प्रतीक। ***v.*** 1. to affix a seal to, मोहर लगाना। 2. to close, बंद कर लेना या देना। 3. to settle or decide, पक्का करना, सुनिश्चित बनाना।

sealed (सील्ड) ***adj.*** affixed with a seal, मोहरबंद, मुद्रांकित; sealed tender, मोहरबंद निविदा।

sealing wax ***n.*** a hard material used for sealing letters, लाख।

seam (सीम) ***n.*** 1. the line along which two pieces of fabric are joined or sewn together, सीवन जोड़, मगज़ी जोड़। 2. a surface line, संधि-रेखा, जोड़। 3. a layer, परत। 4. a fissure, दरार। 5. a scar, क्षत-चिह्न। ***v.*** 1. to join, सीना, टाँके लगाना। 2. to make lines in knitting, धारियाँ

S

बनाना। 3. to crack, दरार पड़ना।

seaman (सीमैन) ***n.*** a sailor, नाविक।

seamstress (सीम्स्ट्रेस) ***n.*** a woman whose job is sewing clothes, दर्जिन, सिलाई करनेवाली।

seaplane (सीप्लेन) ***n.*** an aircraft designed to land on and take off from water, समुद्री विमान।

seaport (सीपोर्ट) ***n.*** a harbour, बंदरगाह।

sear (सिअर) ***v.*** 1. to get burned slightly, झुलसना। 2. to brand with hot iron, दाग़ना।

search (सर्च) ***v.*** 1. to examine thoroughly to find out something, खोजना, ढूँढ़ना, खोजबीन करना। 2. to examine the clothes and body of (a person) तलाशी लेना। ***n.*** the act of searching, खोज, ढूँढ़, तलाशी।

searching (सर्चिंग) ***adj.*** 1. keenly penetrating, भेदक। 2. seeking the truth, सत्यान्वेषी।

search-light (सर्चलाइट) ***n.*** a powerful light equipped with a reflector, खोज-बत्ती, बिजली की बड़ी तेज़ रोशनी का लैंप।

seascape (सीस्केप) ***n.*** a view of the sea, समुद्र का दृश्य।

seasickness (सीसिकनिस) ***n.*** dizziness resulting by the motion of a ship, जलयान के सफ़र के कारण होनेवाली मितली।

seaside (सीसाइड) ***n.*** the seashore, समुद्रतट।

season[1] (सीज़न) ***n.*** 1. one of the four (or six) parts of the year, ऋतु, मौसम। 2. a period of the year when something is common or plentiful, मौसम, अवधि, समय।

season[2] ***v.*** 1. to add spices to, छौंक लगाना, छौंकना, बघारना। 2. to dry (lumber) until usable, (लकड़ी को) सुखाना, सिझाना। 3. to make experienced, अनुभवी बनाना।

seasonal (सीज़नल) ***adj.*** of or relating to a particular season, मौसम-संबंधी, मौसमी।

seat (सीट) ***n.*** 1. a place for sitting, बैठने की जगह या स्थान। 2. a thing used for sitting on, सीट, आसन, पीढ़ा, काठी आदि। 3. a membership or the right to membership in a council, सीट, पद। 4. the buttocks, चूतड़। 5. the part of a trousers, skirt etc., covering the buttocks, कपड़े का वह भाग जो नितंबों पर पड़ता हो। 6. a capital, राजधानी। 7. the place where anything is located, पीठ; the seat of learning विद्यापीठ। ***v.*** 1. to place on a seat, बैठाना, आसीन करना। 2. to provide with seats, आसन/सीटें लगाना। 3. to set firmly in place, स्थापित करना।

seaward (सीवर्ड) ***adj.*** moving towards the sea, समुद्रगामी। ***adv.*** towards the sea, समुद्र की ओर।

seaworthy (सीवर्दी) ***n.*** in a fit condition for a sea voyage, समुद्रयात्रा के योग्य।

secateurs (सेकटर्ज़) ***n.*** a pair of shears for pruning, कैंचा।

secede (सिसीड) ***v.*** to withdraw from (any organisation किसी संस्था से) अलग हो जाना।

secession (सिसेशन) ***n.*** withdrawal (from confe-deration, संघ से) पृथकता, अलगाव।

seclude (सिक्लूड) ***v.*** to keep away or apart, दूर या अलग रहना।

secluded (सिक्लूडिड) ***adj.*** 1. kept apart from the company of others, अलग-थलग, एकांत।

seclusion (सिक्लूज़न) ***n.*** the act of secluding or the state of being secluded, एकांतता, पृथकता।

second (सेकन्ड) ***n.*** 1. a unit of time equal to 1/60 of a minute, सेकंड। 2. a short period of time, पल, क्षण। 3. one that is next from first, वह जो द्वितीय स्थान पर हो। 4. (plu.) articles of inferior quality, घटिया वस्तुएँ। ***adj.*** 1. next after the first, दूसरा, द्वितीय। 2. inferior or secondary, subordinate, दूसरे दर्जे का, मध्यम श्रेणी का या घटिया, गौण। 3. another, additional, अन्य, दूसरा। ***v.*** to endorse, समर्थन करना।

secondary (सेकन्डरी) ***adj.*** 1. one grade after the first, दोयम, द्वितीय श्रेणी का, दूसरे दर्जे का। 2. next in importance, गौण। 3. relating to the education of students of the age of eleven to eighteen, माध्यमिक।

second class ***adj.*** 1. of the class next to the first, द्वितीय श्रेणी का। 2. second-rate, घटिया। ***n.*** the class next to the first, द्वितीय श्रेणी।

secondhand (सेकन्डहैन्ड) ***adj.*** 1. previously owned or used, not new, बरता हुआ, पुराना। 2. obtained from others, इधर- उधर का, सुना-सुनाया।

second nature ***n.*** a habit, बनी हुई आदत, बान, टेक।

second person ***n.*** the form of a word that refers to the person (s) spoken to, मध्यम पुरुष।

second-rate (सेकन्ड-रेट) ***adj.*** second in quality, second-class, घटिया, साधारण।

second thought ***n.*** an idea that occurs afterward, बाद में सूझनेवाली बात।

secrecy (सीक्रिसी) ***n.*** 1. the condition of being secret, गोपनीयता। 2. ability to keep secrets, रहस्य-गोपन। 3. mystery, रहस्य।

secret (सीक्रिट) ***adj.*** kept from the knowledge of others, गुप्त, गोपनीय। ***n.*** 1. something kept hidden, भेद, गोपनीय बात। 2. something beyond understanding, mystery, रहस्य, मर्म।

secretariat (सेक्रिटेरिएट) ***n.*** the office of a secretary, सचिवालय।

secretary (सेक्रिटरी) ***n.*** an official incharge of an administrative department of the government, सचिव।

secretary general ***n.*** a chief administrative official, महासचिव।

secrete[1] (सिक्रीट) ***v.*** to generate and release (a secretion, स्राव) देना, निकालना या छोड़ना, रिसना।

secrete[2] ***v.*** to hide, छिपाना, लुकाना-छिपाना।

secretion (सिक्रीशन) ***n.*** the fluid secreted by a gland or organ, स्राव।

secretive (सिक्रीटिव) ***adj.*** close-mouthed, uncommunicative, चुप्पा, घुन्ना।

sect (सेक्ट) ***n.*** a subdivision of any religious group, पंथ, मत, संप्रदाय।

sectarian (सेक्टेरिअन) ***n.*** a member of a sect, संप्रदायवादी, पंथी। ***adj.*** 1. pertaining to a sect, संप्रदायवादी, मतावलंबी। 2. narrow in outlook, संकीर्ण, कट्टर।

section (सेक्शन) ***n.*** 1. a part of something, अंश, भाग, खंड। 2. a

S

subdivision of a book, परिच्छेद। 3. a distinct part of a country or population, वर्ग। 4. a sub-division of a department, अनुभाग। *v.* to cut into sections, विभाजन करना, बाँटना।

sectional (सेक्शनल) ***adj.*** 1. of or relating to a section, अनुभागीय। 2. of a group or community, सांप्रदायिक, वर्गीय। 3. partial, आंशिक।

sector (सेक्टर) ***n.*** 1. the part of the circle between two radii and the arc, वृत्त की दो त्रिज्याओं के बीच का क्षेत्र, वृत्तखंड। 2. a division of a city, अंचल, सेक्टर। 3. area, क्षेत्र।

secular (सेक्यूलर) ***adj.*** 1. not concerned with religious affairs or views, धर्मनिरपेक्ष। 2. worldly, लौकिक, सांसारिक।

secure (सिक्युअर) ***adj.*** 1. safe, free from danger, सुरक्षित, निरापद। 2. stable, सुदृढ़, मज़बूत, पक्का। 3. trustworthy, reliable, विश्वसनीय। 4. sure, निश्चित। ***v.*** 1. to obtain, प्राप्त कर लेना। 2. to make secure, सुरक्षित करना, निरापद बनाना। 3. to assure by giving security, सुनिश्चित करना। 4. to make firm, दृढ़ बनाना।

secured (सिक्युर्ड) ***adj.*** safe, सुरक्षित।

security (सिक्युरिटी) ***n.*** 1. safety, सुरक्षा। 2. a thing given as a guarantee or pledge, ज़मानत, प्रतिभूति। 3. (plu.) stocks or bonds, बंधपत्र।

sedate (सिडेट) ***adj.*** calm and composed, sober, धीर, गंभीर, शांत।

sedative (सेडटिव) ***adj.*** having a soothing or calming effect, राहत या आराम पहुँचानेवाला, शांतिदायक।

sedentary (सेडन्टरी) ***adj.*** 1. involving or requiring sitting, बैठे-बैठे किया जानेवाला। 2. moving about very little, बहुत कम चलने-फिरनेवाला।

sediment (सेडिमेन्ट) ***n.*** the matter that settles at the bottom of a liquid, तलछट, अवसाद।

sedition (सिडिशन) ***n.*** the conduct or language that makes people rebel against the authority of a state, राजद्रोह।

seduce (सिड्यूस) ***v.*** 1. to tempt, बहकाना-फुसलाना। 2. to persuade to do something wrong, ग़लत काम करने के लिए दबाव डालना, भ्रष्ट कर देना।

see[1] (सी) ***v.*** (saw, seen, seeing) 1. to perceive with the eyes, देखना, अवलोकन करना। 2. to examine, जाँचना, निरीक्षण करना। 3. to understand, समझना। 4. to experience, अनुभव प्राप्त करना। 5. to pay attention, गौर से देखना, ध्यान देना। 6. to consider, विचार करना। 7. to meet, मिलना, मुलाक़ात करना। 8. to make sure, आश्वस्त करना।

see[2] ***n.*** the position or authority of a Bishop, ईसाई धर्माध्यक्ष का पद या अधिकार।

seed (सीड) ***n.*** 1. a fertilized ovule of a plant, बीज, मूल। 2. seeds collectively, बीज। 3. semen, शुक्र। 4. a source, स्रोत, मूल। 5. a seeded player, मानांकित खिलाड़ी। ***v.*** 1. to plant seeds in, बीज बोना, बीज डालना। 2. to remove seeds from (fruit) बीज निकालना। 3. to give a player ranking, मानांकन करना।

seedling (सीडलिंग) ***n.*** a very young plant growing from a seed, बीज से निकला छोटा पौधा, पौध।

S

seedy (सीडी) ***adj.*** 1. full of seeds, containing too much seeds, बीजों से भरा, बिजैला। 2. shabby, फटीचर, फटेहाल।

seek (सीक) ***v.*** (sought, seeking) 1. to search of, खोजना, ढूँढ़ना। 2. to try, प्रयास करना। 3. to go to, जाना।

seem (सीम) ***v.*** 1. to be evident, to appear, जान पड़ना, प्रतीत होना, लगना। 2. to be apparently true, ऊपर से सही दिखना।

seemly (सीमली) ***adj.*** 1. proper, उचित। 2. of pleasing appearance, भला।

seen ***v.*** p.p. of see.

seep (सीप) ***v.*** to ooze or leak, रिसना, बहना।

seepage (सीपिज) ***n.*** 1. the act of seeping or the amount that seeped, रिसाव, रिसन। 2. a small spring, सोता।

seer (सीअर) ***n.*** a prophet, भविष्यद्रष्टा, ऋषि, पैगंबर।

see-saw (सी-सॉ) ***n.*** 1. a long plank balanced on a central support for riding up and down alternately, झुलानेवाला तख़्ता, झूला-पट्टी, झुलावा। 2. an up and down movement that is constantly repeated, बार-बार ऊपर-नीचे जाना, झुलावा, उतार-चढ़ाव, घटती-बढ़ती।

seethe (सीद) ***v.*** 1. to boil, उबाल आना, खौलना। 2. to be agitated, विकल हो जाना, व्यग्र हो जाना।

segment (सेग्मेन्ट) ***n.*** a part, portion, slice or wedge, टुकड़ा, खंड, परिच्छेद, फाँक। ***v.*** to divide into segments, खंड-खंड करना, विभाजन करना।

segregate (सेग्रिगेट) ***v.*** to separate from the main group, अलग-अलग करना, अलग-अलग बसाना।

seismic (साइज़्मिक) ***adj.*** of, caused by or relating to earthquakes, भूकंप-संबंधी, भूकंपीय।

seismograph (साइज़्मोग्राफ) ***n.*** an instrument for detecting and measuring earthquakes, भूकंपलेखी।

seismology (साइज़्मॉलोजी) ***n.*** the study of earthquakes, भूकंप-विज्ञान।

seize (सीज़) ***v.*** 1. to take hold of (a thing) forcibly, to confiscate, छीन लेना, ज़ब्त कर लेना, पकड़ लेना, क़ब्जे में लेना। 2. to arrest or take into custody, पकड़ लेना, गिरफ़्तार कर लेना। 3. to have a sudden effect upon, आक्रांत कर लेना, दबोच लेना, ग्रस्त कर लेना।

seizure (सीज़र) ***n.*** the act of seizing or the state of being seized, जब्ती, गिरफ़्तारी, बीमारी का झटका, दौरा।

seldom (सेल्डम) ***adv.*** not often, rarely, शायद ही कभी, कदाचित्, बिरले ही।

select (सिलेक्ट) ***v.*** to choose among several, चयन करना, चुनना।

selection (सिलेक्शन) ***n.*** 1. the act of selecting or the state of being selected, चयन, वरण। 2. the things or persons selected, संकलन, चयन, चयनिका।

self (सेल्फ़) ***n.*** 1. a person as an individual, स्वयं (व्यक्ति), अपना। 2. a person's own nature, स्वप्रकृति, आपा। 3. one's own interest, हित, लाभ। ***adj.*** 1. of the same material, वैसा ही। 2. pertaining to self, of oneself, अपने से संबद्ध, आत्म।

self-centred (सेल्फ़-सेन्टर्ड) ***adj.*** selfish, आत्मरत, आत्मकेंद्रित, स्वार्थी।

self-confident (सेल्फ़-कॉन्फ़िडेन्ट) ***n.***

S

having full confidence in oneself, आत्मविश्वासी।

self-conscious (सेल्फ़-कॉन्शस) ***adj.*** 1. conscious of oneself or one's ego, अस्मिताबोधी, आत्मचेतन। 2. shy, संकोची।

self-contained (सेल्फ़-कन्टेन्ड) ***adj.*** 1. complete in oneself, आत्मपूर्ण, स्वतःपूर्ण। 2. having all amenities, सभी सुविधाओं से युक्त।

self-control (सेल्फ़-कन्ट्रोल) ***n.*** control of one's desires, emotions, actions etc., आत्मनिग्रह, आत्मसंयम।

self-denial (सेल्फ़-डिनाइअल) ***n.*** sacrifice of one's own desires or pleasures, आत्मत्याग, अपनी इच्छाओं को मारना।

self-evident (सेल्फ़-एविडेन्ट) ***adj.*** evident without need of proof, स्वस्पष्ट।

self-interest (सेल्फ़-इन्ट्रेस्ट) ***n.*** selfish regard for one's personal interest, स्वार्थ।

selfish (सेल्फ़िश) ***adj.*** concerned only with one's personal interests, स्वार्थी।

selfless (सेल्फ़लिस) ***adj.*** without concern for oneself, unselfish, निस्स्वार्थ।

self-made (सेल्फ़-मेड) ***adj.*** made by one's own efforts, स्वनिर्मित।

self-possessed (सेल्फ़-पज़ेस्ड) ***adj.*** calm, composed, धीर, शांत।

self-respect (सेल्फ़-रिस्पेक्ट) ***n.*** proper respect for oneself, आत्मसम्मान।

self-seeker (सेल्फ़-सीकर) ***n.*** selfish, स्वार्थी।

self-service (सेल्फ़-सर्विस) ***n.*** the act of serving oneself in a store, restaurant etc., स्वयंसेवा।

self-sufficiency (सेल्फ़-सफ़िशन्सी) ***n.*** self-reliance, आत्मनिर्भरता।

self-willed (सेल्फ़-विल्ड) ***adj.*** willful, obstinate, हठी, ज़िद्दी।

sell (सेल) ***v.*** (sold, selling) 1. to dispose of something to a purchaser in exchange for money, बेचना, बिक्री करना। 2. to be disposed of in exchange for money, बिकना, बिक्री हो जाना। 3. to deal in, धंधा या रोजगार करना।

seller (सेलर) ***n.*** one who sells something, बेचनेवाला, विक्रेता।

sell-out (सेल-आउट) ***n.*** 1. the selling of all tickets of a show, किसी कार्यक्रम की सभी टिकटों का बिक जाना। 2. a betrayal, विश्वासघात।

selvage (सेल्विज) ***n.*** the edge of a cloth to prevent ravelling, (कपड़े का) किनारा, कन्नी, गोटा।

semantics (सिमैन्टिक्स) ***n.*** the science dealing with meanings, अर्थविज्ञान।

semblance (सेम्ब्लेंस) ***n.*** an outward form or appearance, बाह्य रूप या आकार।

semen (सीमन) ***n.*** the whitish sperm-bearing liquid produced by sex organ of males, वीर्य, शुक्र।

semester (सिमेस्टर) ***n.*** one of the two terms of an academic year, term, छह महीने का अध्ययनक्रम, सत्र।

semi- (सेमि) ***prefix.*** 1. exactly half, आधा, अर्ध-। 2. partly, अल्प।

semicircle (सेमिसर्कल) ***n.*** half of a circle, अर्धवृत्त।

semi-final (सेमि-फ़ाइनल) ***n.*** the match or round preceding the final, सेमीफ़ाइनल।

seminal (सेमिनल) ***adj.*** 1. of or pertaining to semen, वीर्य-संबंधी, शुक्रीय। 2. highly original, बिल्कुल नया, अत्यंत मौलिक।

seminar (सेमिनार) ***n.*** a meeting for holding discussions on an important subject, अध्ययन-गोष्ठी, परिसंवाद।

seminary (सेमिनरी) ***n.*** a school for training priests, रोमन कैथोलिक पुरोहितों का प्रशिक्षणालय, पुरोहित प्रशिक्षणालय।

semination (सेमिनेशन) ***n.*** the act of sowing seeds, बोआई, बुआई, वपन।

semi-precious (सेमि-प्रेशस) ***adj.*** of lower value, अल्पमूल्य।

semolina (सेमोलीना) ***n.*** hard grains of crushed wheat, सूजी, दलिया।

senate (सेनिट) ***n.*** 1. an upper house of the Parliament, सीनेट, राज्यसभा। 2. the governing body of a university, विश्वविद्यालय का शासन-निकाय, विद्वद् परिषद्।

senator (सेनटर) ***n.*** 1. a member of a senate, सीनेटर, विद्वद् परिषद् का सदस्य।

send (सेन्ड) ***v.*** (sent, sending) 1. to cause to be conveyed, भेजना। 2. to produce from itself, देना, निकालना, छोड़ना। 3. to transmit, प्रेषित करना।

senile (सीनाइल) ***adj.*** suffering from weakness because of old age, जराग्रस्त, जराजन्य।

senior (सीनिअर) ***adj.*** 1. older in age, ज्येष्ठ। 2. higher in rank, वरिष्ठ।

seniority (सीनिऑरिटी) ***n.*** the state of being senior, ज्येष्ठता, वरिष्ठता।

sensation (सेन्सेशन) ***n.*** 1. a feeling coming from the senses, संवेदन, संवेदना, अनुभूति। 2. a condition of intense interest and excitement, सनसनी, उत्तेजना।

sensational (सेन्सेशनल) ***adj.*** 1. causing sensation, producing excitement, सनसनीखेज़। 2. wonderful, आश्चर्यजनक।

sense (सेन्स) ***n.*** 1. any of the faculties of sight, hearing, smell, taste or touch, ज्ञानेंद्रिय। 2. feeling perceived through one of the senses, इंद्रियजन्य ज्ञान, अनुभूति। 3. mental perception, भावना, बोध। 4. moral discernment, विवेक, बुद्धि। 5. meaning or import, अर्थ या आशय। ***v.*** 1. to become aware of, पता चलना, अनुभूत होना, महसूस होना। 2. to understand, समझना, समझ में आना।

senseless (सेन्सलिस) ***adj.*** 1. unconscious, अचेत, बेसुध, बेहोश। 2. foolish, मूर्ख, मूर्खतापूर्ण।

sensible (सेन्सिबल) ***adj.*** 1. having or showing good sense, समझदार या समझदारी का। 2. aware, चौकन्ना, चौकस, सचेत। 3. reasonable, युक्तियुक्त या युक्तिशील। 4. sensitive, संवेदनशील।

sensitive (सेन्सिटिव) ***adj.*** 1. aware of and responsive to external conditions or the feeling of others, receptive, संवदेनशील, सुग्राही। 2. easily offended, भावुक, नाजुक-मिज़ाज। 3. delicate, नाजुक, सुकुमार।

sensitivity (सेन्सिटिविटी) ***n.*** 1. the quality or state of being sensitive, receptiveness, संवदेनशीलता, सुग्राहिता। 2. sentimentality, भावुकता।

sensitize (सेन्सिटाइज़) ***v.*** to make sensitive, संवेदनशील बनाना।

sensory (सेन्सरी) ***adj.*** pertaining to the senses, इंद्रिय-संबंधी, ऐंद्रिय।

S

sensual (सेन्शुअल) ***adj.*** 1. of or pertaining to the senses, ऐंद्रिय। 2. concerned with sexual pleasures, विषयासक्त, विषय-वासना-संबंधी, वैषयिक।

sensuality (सेन्शुऐलिटी) ***n.*** fondness for sensual pleasures, भोगविलास।

sensuous (सेन्शुअस) ***adj.*** appealing to the senses, pleasing to the senses, इंद्रियगत, इंद्रियगम्य।

sentence (सेन्टेन्स) ***n.*** 1. a group of words as an expression of thought, वाक्य। 2. a punishment awarded by a law court to a person found guilty, सज़ा, दंडादेश, दंडाज्ञा। ***v.*** to pass sentence on, दंडादेश देना।

sententious (सेन्टेन्शस) ***adj.*** 1. moralizing, नीतिविषयक, उपदेशात्मक। 2. pithy, अर्थगर्भित, सारगर्भित।

sentient (सेन्शिअन्ट) ***adj.*** aware, conscious, जागरूक, सावधान, सचेत।

sentiment (सेन्टिमेन्ट) ***n.*** 1. exaggerated emotion or feeling, भावुकता। 2. a thought, opinion or view coloured with emotion, विचार, भाव, भावना।

sentimental (सेन्टिमेन्टल) ***adj.*** 1. swayed by sentiment, influenced by tender feeling, भावुक। 2. concerning the emotion, emotional, भावपूर्ण, भावुकतापूर्ण।

sentimentality (सेन्टिमेन्टैलिटी) ***n.*** the state or quality of being sentimental, भावुकता, भावप्रवणता, भावावेश।

sentinel, sentry (सेन्टिनल, सेन्ट्री) ***n.*** a guard or watchman, संतरी, प्रहरी।

sepal (सेपल) ***n.*** any of the leaves forming a calyx, (फूल का) बाह्यदल।

separate (सेपरेट) ***v.*** 1. to put apart or divide, अलग-अलग करना, अलगाना। 2. to part, जुदा या अलग हो जाना, साथ छोड़ देना। ***adj.*** 1. not joined, united or connected, अलग, पृथक्, जुदा। 2. different, भिन्न। ***n.*** anything separate, अलग चीज़ या वस्तु।

separating (सेपरेटिंग) ***adj.*** that separates or disjoins, पृथक्कारी।

separation (सेपरेशन) ***n.*** 1. the act of separating or the state of being separated, अलगाव, पृथक्करण, वियुक्ति। 2. the formal agreement to live separately, पार्थक्य, विच्छेद। 3. division, विभाजन।

separatist (सेपरेटिस्ट) ***n.*** a person or party who favours separation from a larger unit, अलगाववादी, पृथकतावादी।

sepoy (सीपॉइ) ***n.*** a policeman, सिपाही।

sept (सेप्ट) ***n.*** a clan, वंश, कुल, घराना।

September (सेप्टेम्बर) ***n.*** the ninth month of the year, सितंबर।

septic (सेप्टिक) ***adj.*** of or caused by poisonous bacteria, पूतिक, सेप्टिक।

septic tank ***n.*** an underground tank for disposing of sewage, सेप्टिक टैंक।

septuagenarian (सेप्टुअजनेरिअन) ***n.*** a person in his (her) seventies, वह जिसकी अवस्था ७० और ८० वर्ष के बीच हो।

sepulchre, sepulcher (सेपल्चर) ***n.*** a tomb or grave, क़ब्र, मक़बरा, समाधि।

sequel (सीक्वल) ***n.*** 1. a consequence, परिणाम, फल। 2. a novel or play that continues the story of an earlier one, उत्तर कथा।

sequence (सीक्वन्स) ***n.*** a set of

things, events or actions following each other continuously or in a particular order, अनुक्रम, सिलसिला।

sequential (सिक्वेन्शल) ***adj.*** forming a sequence, सिलसिलेवार, आनुक्रमिक।

sequester (सिक्वेस्टर) ***v.*** 1. to seize or confiscate, ज़ब्त कर लेना, क़ब्ज़े में कर लेना। 2. to seclude, अलग करना।

seraph (सेरफ़) ***n.*** an angel of the highest rank, देवदूत।

serenade (सेरिनेड) ***n.*** a song sung or music played by a lover under the window of his beloved, प्रेमगीत या प्रेम-संगीत। ***v.*** to play or sing a serenade, प्रेमगीत गाना या प्रेम-संगीत बजाना।

serene (सरीन) ***adj.*** completely calm and peaceful, शांत, शांतचित्त, धीर।

serf (सर्फ़) ***n.*** a person in feudal servitude bound to the land, मध्यकालीन सामंतों का बंधुआ मज़दूर, भूदास।

serge (सर्ज) ***n.*** twilled woollen cloth, एक प्रकार का ऊनी कपड़ा, सर्ज।

sergeant (सार्जन्ट) ***n.*** an army officer, सेनाधिकारी।

serial (सिअरिअल) ***n.*** a story broadcast or published in a series of regular instalments, धारावाहिक, सीरियल। ***adj.*** 1.of or forming a serial, धारावाहिक रूप में होनेवाला, क्रमिक, सिलसिलेवार। 2. of or arranged in series, शृंखलाबद्ध।

serial number ***n.*** a number, usually one of series that identifies one item, क्रमांक।

sericulture (सेरिकल्चर) ***n.*** the business of raising silk worms, कोया उद्योग।

series (सिअरीज़) ***n.*** a group of things coming one after another, माला, शृंखला, श्रेणी, अवली।

serious (सिअरिअस) ***adj.*** 1. grave, sober, thoughtful, गंभीर, गंभीरतापूर्ण। 2. causing anxiety, चिंताजनक चिंतनीय, घोर। 3. not light hearted, sincere, जो हँसी-मज़ाक के रूप में न हो, सही, सच्चा। 4. difficult, कठिन, विकट।

sermon (सर्मन) ***n.*** a religious discourse, प्रवचन, उपदेश।

sermonizer (सर्मनाइज़र) ***n.*** one who delivers sermons, प्रवचनकर्ता, उपदेशक।

serpent (सर्पेन्ट) ***n.*** a large snake, बड़ा साँप, नाग।

serrated (सिरेटिड) ***adj.*** saw-like, दाँतेदार।

serum (सिअरम) ***n.*** the watery fluid separated from the blood, रक्त का जलीय अंश, सीरम।

servant (सर्वेन्ट) ***n.*** 1. one employed to do domestic work, नौकर, चाकर। 2. an employee, कर्मी, कार्यकर्ता, नौकर, सेवक।

serve (सर्व) ***v.*** 1. to work for, सेवा करना, ख़िदमत करना। 2. to spend (time, समय) काटना या भुगतना। 3. to attend to, हाज़िरी बजाना, सेवा में उपस्थित होना। 4. to meet a need, आवश्यकता पूरी करना, काम आना। 5. to be of assistance to, सहायक होना, मददगार होना। 6. to place (food) before, परसना, परोसना, देना या लगाना। 7. to put a ball in play, (टेनिस, बैडमिंटन आदि खेलों में) सर्विस करना। 8. (law) to deliver (a summons, समन) तामील करना।

service (सर्विस) ***n.*** 1. the act of serving, the act of help or assistance, सेवा। 2. the occupation of a servant, नौकरी, चाकरी, सेवा। 3. helpful or beneficial work, सेवा, टहल, जनहित कार्य। 4. public worship (in certain prescribed forms), अनुष्ठान, पूजा, अर्चना। 5. maintenance and repairs provided by a dealer, सर्विस। 6. the act or manner of serving food, (भोजन) परोसने का कार्य या ढंग। 7. the serving (of a summons, समन) तामील करना। 8. to serve in a game, सर्विस करना। ***v.*** 1. to repair or overhaul, मरम्मत या ओवरहॉलिंग करना। 2. to provide service to, सेवा अर्पित करना, सेवा करना। 3. to mate with (a female animal) जोड़ा खाना।

serviceable (सर्विसेबल) ***adj.*** 1. usable, काम में लाने योग्य। 2. durable, टिकाऊ, मज़बूत।

serviceman (सर्विसमैन) ***n.*** a male member of the army, फ़ौजी, सैनिक।

service station ***n.*** 1. a place where automobile repair is available, सेवा-केंद्र, सर्विस स्टेशन। 2. a filling station, पेट्रोल पंप।

servile (सर्वाइल) ***adj.*** 1. of a slave, दासोचित। 2. mean, हेय, नीच। 3. too submissive, जी-हज़ूर। 4. flattering, चापलूस।

servility (सर्विलिटी) ***n.*** the quality or state of being servile, जी-हज़ूरी; चापलूसी।

servitude (सर्विट्यूड) ***n.*** slavery, bondage, दासता, ग़ुलामी।

sesame (सेसमी) ***n.*** oil seeds of a plant, तिल।

session (सेशन) ***n.*** 1. a meeting of a legislature etc., अधिवेशन, सत्र, बैठक। 2. an academic term, सत्र।

set (सेट) ***v.*** 1. to put or place in a specified position, रखना, धरना। 2. to fix or adjust, जड़ना, बैठाना, लगाना। 3. to prescribe or determine, नियत करना, निश्चित करना। 4. to arrange or restore to proper state, व्यवस्थित करना, (खाने की मेज़) लगाना, (अक्षर) बैठाना। 5. to establish, स्थापित या प्रस्थापित करना। 6. to give (a piece of work) to do, काम देना। 7. to disappear below the horizon, अस्त होना, डूबना। 8. to become solid, जम जाना, पत्थर हो जाना। 9. to give a particular setting पृष्ठभूमि तैयार करना। ☐ **set about,** आरंभ करना; **set in,** (i) आरंभ होना, आना, चल पड़ना, (ii) जड़ना, लगाना; **set off,** (i) कार्य आरंभ करना, (ii) यात्रा आरंभ करना, (iii) विस्फोट करना; **set up,** खड़ा करना, लगाना, स्थापित करना; **set upon,** आक्रमण करना। ***adj.*** 1. fixed, predetermined, नियत, निश्चित, पूर्व-निर्धारित। 2. firm, स्थिर, अटल, दृढ़। 3. ready, प्रस्तुत, तैयार। ***n.*** 1. a group of certain connected things forming a unit, सेट। 2. a collection of things having a common property, कुलक, समुच्चय, सेट।

setback (सेटबैक) ***n.*** 1. a blow, आघात। 2. defeat, पराजय।

set square ***n.*** (maths) a triangular piece of wood, plastic etc., having one of its angles as right angle, कोनिया।

settee (सेटी) ***n.*** a seat for two or more people, a small sofa, बेंच, सेटी।

setter (सेटर) ***n.*** 1. one who sets something, स्थापित करनेवाला, रखनेवाला, बैठानेवाला। 2. a hunting dog, एक शिकारी कुत्ता।

setting (सेटिंग) ***n.*** 1. the surroundings in which something is set, पृष्ठभूमि, परिवेश। 2. a set of tableware at one place on a table, मेज़ पर एक जगह रखे जानेवाले बर्तन।

settle (सेटल) ***v.*** 1. to put into order, व्यवस्थित करना। 2. to put, plant or set in place, लगाना, जमाना या बैठाना। 3. to establish, स्थापित करना। 4. to establish residence in, बसना या रहना। 5. to end (a dispute, झगड़ा) निपटाना, तय करना। 6. to become composed, शांत होना।

settlement (सेटलमेन्ट) ***n.*** 1. a newly colonized region, बस्ती, उपनिवेश। 2. residence, आवास। 3. arrangement, व्यवस्था, बंदोबस्त। 4. agreement, क़रार, समझौता, निपटारा। 5. payment, भुगतान, देना।

seven (सेवन) ***adj & n.*** 1. the number equal to the sum of six plus one, सात। 2. the card with seven points, सत्ता।

seventeen (सेवन्टीन) ***n.*** the cardinal number between sixteen and eighteen, सत्रह (१७)।

seventy (सेवन्टी) ***n.*** the cardinal number between sixty-nine and seventy-one, सत्तर (७०)।

sever (सेवर) ***v.*** 1. to cut, break off or separate, कटना या काटना, अलग करना या होना। 2. to dissolve, विघटित करना या होना।

several (सेवरल) ***adj.*** 1. many, अनेक, कई। 2. different, separate, विभिन्न या पृथक्।

severally (सेवरली) ***adv.*** separately, respectively, अलग-अलग, पृथक्-पृथक्।

severe (सिविअर) ***adj.*** 1. stern, strict, कड़ा, कठोर। 2. violent, intense, घोर, प्रचंड, तीव्र। 3. sharp, rigorous, तेज़, तीक्ष्ण, तीखा।

severity (सिवेरिटी) ***n.*** 1. strictness, कड़ाई, कठोरता। 2. seriousness, गंभीरता।

sew (स्यू) ***v.*** (sewed, sewn/sewed, sewing) to fasten with a needle and thread, सीना, सिलाई करना।

sewage (स्यूइज) ***n.*** the water and waste matter carried off by sewers, मलजल।

sewer (स्यूअर) ***n.*** underground pipe or drains for carrying off water and waste matter, मलनाली, सीवर।

sex (सेक्स) ***n.*** 1. either of the two divisions of the organisms as male or female, प्राणियों के दो विभाग—नर और मादा, स्त्री और पुरुष; sex ratio, स्त्री-पुरुष अनुपात। 2. sexual urge, कामावेग, कामेच्छा। 3. sexual intercourse, मैथुन, संभोग, सहवास।

sexagenarian (सेक्सजिनेरिअन) ***n.*** a person between sixty and seventy years of age, साठ और सत्तर वर्ष के बीच का व्यक्ति।

sexism (सेक्सिज़म) ***n.*** discrimination by members of one sex against the other, लिंग-भेद की भावना, लैंगिक भेदभाव।

sex organ ***n.*** the organ of sex, कामेंद्रिय।

sexridden (सेक्सरिडन) ***adj.*** dominated by sexual desire, कामातुर, कामोन्मत्त।

sextant (सेक्सटेन्ट) ***n.*** an instrument for measuring altitudes of the celestial bodies, आकाशीय पिंडों की दूरी नापने का यंत्र।

S

sextet (सेक्सटेट) ***n.*** a group of six musicians, छह गायकों या वादकों का दल।

sexual (सेक्स्युअल) ***adj.*** of or pertaining to sex or sexes, यौन-संबंधी, काम-संबंधी।

sexuality (सेक्स्युऐलिटी) ***n.*** sexual desire, कामवासना, कामभाव, यौनभाव।

sexy (सेक्सी) ***adj.*** arousing sexual desire, कामोद्दीपक, कामोत्तेजक।

shabby (शैबी) ***adj.*** 1. worn-out, फटा-पुराना, चिथड़ा। 2. dirty, मैला-कुचैला। 3. showing neglect or improper care, फूहड़, भद्दा।

shabbily (शैबिली) ***adv.*** in a shabby manner, भद्दे ढंग से, फूहड़पन से।

shack (शैक) ***n.*** a small house or hut, साधारण छोटा मकान, झोंपड़ी, झुग्गी।

shackle (शैकल) ***n.*** a metal fastening for encircling the wrist or ankle of a prisoner, हथकड़ी या बेड़ी। ***v.*** to put shackles on, हथकड़ी या बेड़ी पहनाना।

shade (शेड) ***n.*** 1. comparative darkness or partial light, छाया। 2. representation of darkness in painting or drawing, छायांकन। 3. a small difference or shade, छाया, रंगत, बारीकी। 4. a touch or trace, पुट, थोड़ा-सा अंश। 5. a device to screen from light, छाया करनेवाला भाग, झाँप। 6. anything lacking reality, अवास्तविक वस्तु, छायाभास, छाया। 7. a spirit or ghost, प्रेतात्मा। ***v.*** 1. to protect or screen from light or heat, छाया करना। 2. to put a shade on, शेड लगाना। 3. to make dim, धुँधला करना। 4. to darken, छायांकन करना।

shadow (शैडो) ***n.*** 1. shade cast upon a surface, परछाईं, साया। 2. image, प्रतिबिंब। 3. gloom, depression, अवसाद, विषाद। 4. a slight trace, लेशमात्र। 5. something unreal, छायाभास, मरीचिका। ***v.*** 1. to cast shadow over, छाया डालना, परछाईं डालना। 2. to protect, रक्षा करना। 3. to make dark, धुँधला करना। 4. to make gloomy, उदास या खिन्न करना। 5. to foreshadow, आभास देना। 6. to follow, पीछा करना। ***adj.*** imaginary, काल्पनिक, नक़ली।

shady (शेडी) ***adj.*** 1. giving shade, छायादार। 2. of dubious character, निंद्य, कुत्सित, गर्हित।

shaft (शैफ़्ट) ***n.*** 1. long stem (of a spear, arrow, axe etc., भाले, तीर, कुल्हाड़े आदि का) दंड/डंडा। 2. the handle of a hammer etc., डंडा, बेट। 3. a revolving rod, axle, धुरा। 4. a beam, शहतीर, धरन, बल्ली। 5. a ray, प्रकाश-किरण।

shag (शैग) ***n.*** 1. a mass of matted hair, झबरे बाल या उलझे रेशों का गुच्छा। 2. a napped fabric, रोएँदार कपड़ा। 3. shredded coarse tobacco, कटा तंबाकू।

shake (शेक) ***v.*** (shook, shaken, shaking) 1. to cause to move with short, quick movements, ज़ोर से हिलाना, झकझोरना। 2. to tremble or quiver, हिल उठना, थर्राना, कँपाना। 3. to unsettle, विचलित होना/करना। 4. to stagger, लड़खड़ाना, डगमगाना। □ **shake down,** झकझोर देना; **shake out,** झकझोरकर गिराना; **shake up,** (i) हिला-डुलाकर मिलाना, (ii) तंग करना।

shake-up (शेक-अप) ***n.*** reorganisation of drastic nature, आमूल परिवर्तन, पुनर्संघटन।

shale (शेल) ***n.*** a fine grained rock, स्लेटी पत्थर।

shall (शैल) ***v.*** used as an auxiliary verb indicating future predictions, भविष्यत्काल की सूचक सहायक क्रिया।

shallow (शैलो) ***adj.*** 1. not deep, छिछला, उथला। 2. superficial, सतही।

sham (शैम) ***n.*** 1. a pretence, बहाना। 2. something not genuine, दिखावा, ढोंग या धोखा। ***adj.*** 1. not genuine, नक़ली। 2. pretended, ढोंग-भरा, पाखंड-भरा। ***v.*** 1. to pretend, बहाना करना। 2. to pretend to be, बनना।

shamble (शैम्बल) ***v.*** to move along in an awkward or unsteady way, पैर घसीटते हुए या भद्दे ढंग से चलना।

shambles (शैम्बल्ज़) ***n.*** 1. condition of great destruction, विनाश-लीला। 2. condition of great disorder, खड़मंडल, अस्त-व्यस्तता।

shame (शेम) ***n.*** 1. disgrace, ignominy, लज्जा, शर्म, शर्मिंदगी। 2. something that brings disgrace, लज्जा की बात या काम, बेशर्मी की बात। ***v.*** to make ashamed, शर्मिंदा करना।

shameful (शेमफ़ुल) ***adj.*** bringing or causing shame, लज्जाजनक, शर्मनाक।

shameless (शेमलिस) ***adj.*** 1. having no feeling of shame, निर्लज्ज, बेशर्म, बेहया। 2. obstinate, impudent, ढीठ, उद्धत।

shampoo (शैम्पू) ***v.*** to wash the hair, सिर धोना, केश धोना। ***n.*** 1. the washing of hair, केश-धुलाई, सिर-धुलाई। 2. a preparation of soap to wash hair, शैंपू।

shank (शैन्क) ***n.*** 1. the part of leg between the knee and ankle, पिंडली। 2. a long narrow middle part of something, डंडी।

shanty (शैन्टी) ***n.*** a small house or hut, shack, झुग्गी, झोंपड़ी।

shape (शेप) ***n.*** 1. a form with a definite outline, आकृति, शक्ल, रूप। 2. organized or definite form, शक्ल, सूरत। 3. mould, ढाँचा। 4. pattern, प्रतिमान, नमूना। 5. condition, स्थिति। ***v.*** 1. to give a particular form to, रूपायित करना। 2. to take a particular form, रूपायित होना। 3. to plan or devise, चरितार्थ करना, रूपायित करना। 4. to develop, विकास करना।

shapely (शेपली) ***adj.*** 1. having a pleasing shape, सुंदर आकृतिवाला, नयनाभिराम। 2. well-formed, सुडौल, सुगठित।

share (शेअर) ***n.*** 1. a part or portion belonging to someone, अंश, हिस्सा, भाग। 2. one of the equal parts forming a business company's capital, पत्ती, शेयर, हिस्सा। 3. the portions into which some property is divided, अंश, भाग, हिस्सा। ***v.*** 1. to distribute in shares, to divide in portion, हिस्से लगाना/बाँटना। 2. to participate, हिस्सा लेना, सम्मिलित होना।

sharecropper (शेअरक्रॉपर) ***n.*** a farmer who gives a share of crop to the landlord, बँटाईदार।

shareholder (शेअरहोल्डर) ***n.*** one who holds a share, अंशधारी, शेयर-होल्डर।

shark (शार्क) ***n.*** 1. a large sea fish, शार्क। 2. (fig.) a cheat, धोखेबाज़, ठग।

sharp (शार्प) ***adj.*** 1. having a fine edge for cutting, तेज़ धारवाला, पैना। 2. clear, distinct, पूर्णतः स्पष्ट, सुस्पष्ट, तीखा; sharp features, तीखे

S

नाक-नक़्श। 3. severe, प्रचंड, तीव्र। 4. intelligent, बुद्धिमान, कुशाग्रबुद्धि। 5. harsh, कटु, कठोर, तीखा। 6. pungent, चरपरा, तीता। 7. involving a sudden change in direction, अंधा; sharp turn, अंधा मोड़।

sharpen (शार्पन) *v.* 1. to make sharp, तेज़ करना, धार तेज़ करना, धार रखना या लगाना। 2. to become sharp, तेज़ होना।

sharpness (शार्पनिस) *n.* the quality or state of being sharp, तेज़ी, तीक्ष्णता, पैनापन।

shatter (शैटर) *v.* 1. to break violenty into pieces, चूर-चूर करना। 2. to destroy, नष्ट करना।

shave (शेव) *v.* (shaved, shaven/ shaved, shaving) 1. to cut the beard with a razor, दाढ़ी बनाना। 2. to cut the hair, बाल काटना या मूँड़ना। 3. to cut off in very thin pieces or slices, पतले-पतले टुकड़े करना। 4. to come close to in passing, बच जाना। *n.* an act, process or result of shaving, दाढ़ी बनाने का काम या बनी दाढ़ी।

shaver (शेवर) *n.* 1. a shaving device, दाढ़ी बनाने की मशीन। 2. a razor, उस्तरा। 3. a person who shaves, नाई, हज्जाम।

shavings (शेविंग्स) *n.* (plu.) thin strips of wood, छीलन।

shawl (शॉल) *n.* a piece of fabric used as covering, शाल।

she (शी) ***pron.*** used for female person or thing, वह (plu. they वे) । *n.* a female animal, मादा प्राणी; she-goat बकरी।

sheaf (शीफ़) *n.* a bunch or bundle of cut stalks of grain, पूला, पुलिंदा।

shear (शिअर) *v.* (sheared, shorn/ sheared, shearing) 1. to remove (wool) by cutting, (भेड़ आदि को) मूँड़ना, ऊन कतरना। 2. to deprive, छीन लेना, लूटना-खसोटना।

shears (शिअर्ज़) *n.* a large-sized scissors, बड़ी कैंची, कैंचा।

sheath (शीथ) *n.* 1. a case for the blade of a sword, म्यान, असिकोष। 2. any similar close fitting covering or case, आवरण, गिलाफ़। 3. a condom, निरोध।

sheathe (शीद) *v.* 1. to put into a sheath, म्यान में डालना या रखना।

shed[1] (शेड) *n.* a small structure for storage or shelter, सायबान, शेड।

shed[2] *v.* (shed, shedding) 1. to pour forth, बहना। 2. to cause to pour forth, बहाना। 3. to take off, उतारना। 4. to lose, झड़ना। 5. to repel, हटाना, दूर करना।

sheen (शीन) *n.* lustre, चमक, दीप्ति।

sheep (शीप) *n.* (sing. & plu.) a grass-eating animal, भेड़।

sheepfold (शीपफ़ोल्ड) *n.* an enclosure for sheep, भेड़ों का बाड़ा।

sheepish (शीपिश) ***adj.*** timid, meek or bashful, भीरु, डरपोक, शर्मीला।

sheer[1] (शिअर) ***adj.*** 1. pure, विशुद्ध। 2. absolute, नितांत, निरा, सिर्फ़। 3. very thin and transparent, पतला और पारदर्शक। 4. very steep, खड़ा।

sheer[2] *v.* to deviate from the course, सही रास्ते से भटक जाना।

sheet[1] (शीट) *n.* 1. a rectangular piece of cotton used as a bedsheet, चादर। 2. rectangular thin piece of metal, चद्दर। 3. a

rectangular piece of paper, ताव। 4. a wide expanse of snow or water, विस्तृत सतह या तल। *v.* 1. to spread a sheet, चादर बिछाना। 2. to cover or wrap with a sheet, चादर ओढ़ाना या चादर से लपेटना।

sheet[2] *n.* a chain or rope attached to a sail, पाल से लगा हुआ रस्सा या जंजीर।

sheikh (शेक) *n.* the leader of an Arab tribe, अरब जनजाति का मुखिया, शेख़।

shelf (शेल्फ़) *n.* a flat piece of wood, metal etc., fixed in a wall or almirah for supporting objects, टाँड़, शेल्फ़, ख़ाना।

shell (शेल) *n.* 1. the hard outer covering of snails, tortoises etc., बाहरी कड़ा आवरण, खोल (जैसे सीपी, शंख, आदि का)। 2. the hard outer layer of some fruits, मोटा कड़ा छिलका। 3. a cartridge designed to explode in the air, बारूद का गोला, तोप का गोला। *v.* 1. to remove the shell of, खोल या छिलका उतारना। 2. to fire explosive shells at, गोले/बम बरसाना। □ **shell out,** (धन) देना, चुकाना।

shellac (शलैक) *n.* the flakes of lac, चपड़ा, लाख की पपड़ी।

shellfire (शेलफ़ाइर) *n.* the firing of explosive shells, गोलाबारी।

shelter (शेल्टर) *n.* 1. something that provides protection, आश्रय। 2. the state of being sheltered, शरण। *v.* 1. to provide with shelter, आश्रय देना। 2. to find or take shelter, आश्रय पाना, शरण लेना।

shelve (शेल्व) *v.* 1. to put on a shelf, टाँड़ पर रखना। 2. to provide with shelves, टाँड़ लगाना। 3. to postpone, to put aside, उठा रखना, स्थगित करना। 4. to slope gently, थोड़ा-थोड़ा ढलवाँ होना।

shepherd (शेपर्ड) *n.* one who tends sheep, भेड़ें चरानेवाला, गड़रिया। [Fem. shepherdess, गड़ेरिन]। *v.* 1. to graze sheep, भेड़ें चराना। 2. to guide (people, लोगों को) राह दिखलाना, सँभालकर ले चलना।

sheriff (शेरिफ़) *n.* an executive officer, शासनाधिकारी।

sherpa (शेर्पा) *n.* a mountaineer-cum-labourer of Nepal, शेरपा।

shield (शील्ड) *n.* 1. an armour to protect the body, कवच, ढाल। 2. a trophy, ट्राफ़ी। *v.* 1. to protect, रक्षा करना। 2. to screen, छिपाना।

shift (शिफ़्ट) *v.* 1. to move for another place, जगह बदलना, स्थान परिवर्तित करना। 2. to change from one position to another, दूसरे पद पर जाना। 3. to remove, हटाना। 4. to change (gear, गियर) बदलना। *n.* 1. the act of shifting, स्थानांतरण, स्थान-परिवर्तन। 2. the group of workers who start work as another set finishes, पारी। 3. a change of direction or attitude, बदलाव, अंतरण।

shifty (शिफ़्टी) *adj.* 1. given to evasions, बहानेबाज़। 2. untrustworthy, अविश्वसनीय।

shimmer (शिमर) *v.* to shine with a flickering light, टिमटिमाना। *n.* flickering light, टिमटिमाहट।

shin (शिन) *n.* the front of the leg below the knee, घुटने के नीचे की नली। *v.* to climb, (पेड़, खंभे आदि पर) चढ़ना।

shindy (शिन्डी) *n.* 1. a boisterous festive gathering, उत्सव तथा हल्ला-

S

गुल्ला मचाते हुए लोगों का समूह। 2. a commotion, झगड़ा-फ़साद, हंगामा।

shine (शाइन) ***v.*** (shone, shining) 1. to emit light, to glow, चमकना। 2. to cause to shine, चमकाना। ***n.*** lustre, चमक।

shiny (शाइनी) ***adj.*** shining, चमकदार, चमकीला।

ship (शिप) ***n.*** a large floating vessel, जलयान, पोत। ***v.*** 1. to put or take on board a ship, जहाज़ पर लादना या सवार होना। 2. to send or transport by any carrier, किसी भी साधन से माल आदि भेजना।

shipment (शिपमेन्ट) ***n.*** 1. the act of sending goods by a ship, जलयान या पोत द्वारा माल भेजने का कार्य, पोत-प्रेषण। 2. a load of goods in a ship, पोत-लदान।

shipshape (शिपशेप) ***adj.*** trim, orderly, tidy, सुव्यवस्थित, साफ़-सुथरा, ठीक-ठाक।

shipwreck (शिपरेक) ***n.*** the destruction of a ship, पोत-ध्वंस। ***v.*** to cause to wreck ship, पोत को ध्वस्त कर देना।

shipyard (शिपयार्ड) ***n.*** a yard where ships are built or repaired, पोतशाला।

shirk (शर्क) ***v.*** to avoid work or duty, काम से भागना, जी चुराना।

shirt (शर्ट) ***n.*** a garment worn in the upper part of the body, कमीज़।

shit (शिट) ***n.*** faeces, excrement, गूह, मल।

shiver (शिवर) ***v.*** to tremble, काँपना, सिहर उठना।

shoal[1] (शोल) ***n.*** a group of fish, मछलियों का झुंड, गोल।

shoal[2] ***n.*** a shallow place, वह स्थान जहाँ पानी छिछला हो।

shock (शॉक) ***n.*** 1. a violent impact or blow, धक्का, आघात, सदमा। 2. the disturbance of mental equilibrium, दहशत। 3. tangled mass of hair, जटा-जूट, जटा। 4. an electric shock, बिजली का झटका। ***v.*** 1. to give a shock, धक्का देना या लगाना, सदमा पहुँचाना। 2. to make dumbfounded, चकित या स्तब्ध कर देना।

shocking (शॉकिंग) ***adj.*** highly offensive, घोर, भयावह या अपयशकर।

shoddy (शॉडी) ***adj.*** 1. inferior, घटिया। 2. dishonest, बेईमानी-भरा, अनुचित। ***n.*** 1. fibre made from old clothes, पुराने वस्त्रों से निकाला हुआ धागा। 2. cloth made from this, उक्त धागे से बुना हुआ कपड़ा।

shoe (शू) ***n.*** 1. a covering for the human foot, जूता। 2. a horse shoe, (घोड़े की) नाल।

shoehorn (शूहॉर्न) ***n.*** an appliance for putting on shoes, सीगड़ा (जिसकी सहायता से जूता पहना जाता है)।

shoestring (शूस्ट्रिंग) ***n.*** 1. a lace for fastening shoes, तस्मा। 2. a very small amount of money, थोड़ा-सा धन।

shoot (शूट) ***v.*** (shot, shooting) 1. to discharge a bullet or arrow, गोली या तीर चलाना, दाग़ना। 2. to grow or sprout, अंकुरित होना, कल्ला निकलना। 3. to record on films, (कैमरे से) फोटो लेना, चित्र लेना। ***n.*** a new growth of a plant, अंकुर, कल्ला।

shooting (शूटिंग) ***n.*** 1. the act of taking photographs, फ़िल्मांकन करना। 2. the discharging of bullets, गोलियाँ चलाना।

shooting pain ***n.*** a sudden severe pain, टीस, चमक।

shooting star ***n.*** a meteor, उल्का।

shop (शॉप) ***n.*** 1. a retail store, दुकान। 2. a workshop, कार्यशाला। ***v.*** to visit shops to buy things, दुकानों पर जाकर ख़रीदारी करना।

shop-lifter (शॉप-लिफ़्टर) ***n.*** one who steals goods from a shop, उचक्का, उठाईगीरा।

shopping (शॉपिंग) ***n.*** the act of buying goods, ख़रीदारी।

shore[1] (शोर) ***n.*** the land along the edge of a river, sea etc., समुद्रतट, तीर।

shore[2] ***n.*** a support, थूनी, टेक। ***v.*** to make safe with a prop, टेक या थूनी लगाना।

short (शॉर्ट) ***adj.*** 1. of little length, not long, small, छोटा, लघु, संक्षिप्त, ह्रस्व। 2. of limited duration, अल्पकालिक। 3. inadequate, deficient, कम, अल्प। 4. brief, छोटा, संक्षिप्त। 5. rude, रूखा, टुच्चा। 6. (vowel) not long, ह्रस्व। 7. without reaching a target, ओछा (निशाना)। ***n.*** 1. anything that is short, छोटे आकार-प्रकार की वस्तु। 2. a short drink, एक तरह की कड़वी शराब। 3. (plu.) men's undershorts, जाँघिया, कच्छा।

shortage (शॉर्टिज) ***n.*** insufficiency, deficiency, कमी, अभाव, अल्पता।

short-circuit (शार्ट-सर्किट) ***n.*** the flow of current by shorter route than the normal one, शॉर्ट सर्किट, लघु परिपथ।

shortcoming (शॉर्टकमिंग) ***n.*** 1. deficiency, कमी, कमज़ोरी। 2. a fault, दोष।

shortcut (शॉर्टकट) ***n.*** a shorter route, छोटा रास्ता।

shorten (शॉर्टन) ***v.*** 1. to make shorter, छोटा करना/बनाना। 2. to become shorter, छोटा हो जाना।

shortening (शॉर्टनिंग) ***n.*** butter or other fat used to make pastry, पेस्ट्री में मिलाया जानेवाला मक्खन या अन्य स्निग्ध पदार्थ।

shortfall (शॉर्टफ़ाल) ***n.*** shortage, deficit, कमी, न्यूनता।

shorthand (शॉर्टहैन्ड) ***n.*** a system of rapid handwriting using symbols, आशुलिपि।

shortly (शॉर्टली) ***adv.*** 1. in a short time, soon, जल्दी ही। 2. in brief, briefly, संक्षेप में। 3. in a rude manner, रुखाई से।

shortsighted (शॉर्टसाइटिड) ***adj.*** lacking foresight, अदूरदर्शी।

short-tempered (शॉर्ट-टेम्पर्ड) ***adj.*** easily angered, चिड़चिड़ा, बदमिज़ाज।

shot (शॉट) ***n.*** 1. the firing of a gun etc., प्रहार, प्रक्षेपण, (का) छोड़ा जाना। 2. a bullet of iron ball, गोली, छर्रा। 3. a person who shoots, निशानेबाज़। 4. a stroke with a bat, (गेंद पर किया जानेवाला) बल्ले से ज़ोरदार आघात। 5. a single photograph, फ़ोटो, चित्र। 6. guess, अनुमान, अंदाज़। 7. an injection, सुई। 8. an attempt, प्रयास, प्रयत्न। 9. a heavy metal ball, गोला। 10. a drink of liquor, शराब। ***v.*** p.t. & p.p. of shoot.

shotgun (शॉटगन) ***n.*** a gun for hunting small games, वह बंदूक जिससे छोटे जानवरों का शिकार करते हैं, छर्रेवाली बंदूक।

should (शुड) ***aux. v.*** used to express, (i) duty or obligation; You should have told us. आपको

S

हमें बताना चाहिए था। (ii) an expected future event; They should be here at this moment. इस समय उन्हें यहाँ पहुँच जाना चाहिए था। (iii) a possible event; If you should happen to see me.... यदि तुम फिर मुझसे मिले तो...। (iv) to form the subjunctive mood with I or we; I should like to see you, मैं तुमसे मिलना चाहता हूँ।

shoulder (शोल्डर) ***n.*** the part of the body at which the arm, foreleg or wing is attached, कंधा, स्कंध। ***v.*** 1. to push with one's shoulders, कंधे से मारना, कंधा मारना। 2. to carry on one's shoulders, कंधे पर रखना या लादना, कंधे पर ले जाना। 3. to take upon oneself, अपने ऊपर लेना, ओढ़ना।

shouldn't (शुडन्ट) ***v.*** = should not.

shout (शाउट) ***v.*** to utter loudly, चिल्लाना, चीखना। ***n.*** a loud cry, चिल्लाहट, चीख, शोर।

shove (शव्) ***n.*** a rude push, ज़ोर का धक्का। ***v.*** 1. to push roughly, धक्का देना, धकियाना। 2. to put, रखना।

shovel (शवल) ***n.*** a tool for picking up dirt, snow etc., बेलचा, खनित्र, खंती। ***v.*** 1. to move with a shovel, बेलचे से हटाना-बढ़ाना। 2. to thrust, ठूँसना।

show (शो) ***v.*** (showed, shown/ showed, showing) 1. to cause or allow to be seen, दिखलाना, दिखाना। 2. to display, exhibit or express, प्रदर्शित करना, प्रकट या व्यक्त करना। 3. to be able to be seen, दिखना, दिखाई पड़ना, दिखाई देना। 4. to prove (one's ability, अपनी योग्यता) सिद्ध करना। 5. to allege, आरोप लगाना। 6. to guide, राह दिखाना। ***n.*** 1. the act of showing, दिखाने की क्रिया या भाव, दिखावा। 2. the state of being shown, तमाशा, प्रदर्शन, दिखावा। 3. exhibition, प्रदर्शनी। 4. any public performance, शो; चित्र, खेल आदि का दिखाया जाना।

showbiz (शोबिज़) ***n.*** = show business.

show business ***n.*** the theatre, circus or motion pictures as a business, मनोरंजन व्यवसाय।

showdown (शोडाउन) ***n.*** an event that forces an issue to a conclusion, दो-दो हाथ, उठा-पटक, अंतिम परीक्षा/लड़ाई।

shower (शॉवर) ***n.*** 1. a brief fall of rain, फुहार, वर्षा। 2. a device in which water is sprayed on a person's body, फुहारा। 3. a brief fall of dust, stones, bullets etc., बौछार। ***v.*** 1. to pour down, बरसना या बरसाना। 2. to sprinkle or spray, फूल आदि बरसाना या गिराना। 3. to bathe in sprayed water, फुहार में नहाना।

showman (शोमैन) ***n.*** an organizer of a show business, प्रदर्शनकर्ता।

show-off (शो - ऑफ़) ***n.*** one who tries to impress others, दूसरों को प्रभावित करनेवाला व्यक्ति।

showroom (शोरूम) ***n.*** a room in which goods are exhibited for sale, प्रदर्शन-कक्ष।

showy (शोई) ***adj.*** 1. gaudy, भड़कीला। 2. ostentatious, आडंबरपूर्ण, दिखावटी।

shrank (श्रैन्क) ***v.*** p.t. of shrink.

shred (श्रेड) ***n.*** 1. a small piece torn from something, धज्जी। 2. a small amount, लेश, कण। ***v.*** to cut into shreds, धज्जियाँ, पट्टियाँ या लच्छे निकालना या बनाना।

shrewd (श्रूड) ***adj.*** 1. showing common sense, सयाना, समझदार। 2. well-reasoned, युक्तिशील, युक्तियुक्त।

shriek (श्रीक) ***n.*** a shrill and piercing cry, चीख़, कराह। ***v.*** to make a shriek, चीख़ेना, कराहना।

shrill (श्रिल) ***adj.*** high and sharp, तीक्ष्ण, कर्णकटु। ***v.*** to produce a shrill sound, चीखना, कराहना।

shrimp (श्रिम्प) ***n.*** 1. a small shellfish, शंखमीन। 2. a very small person, छुटभैया।

shrine (श्राइन) ***n.*** a temple, देवमंदिर, देवालय।

shrink (श्रिन्क) ***v.*** (shrank/shrunk, shrunk/shrunken, shrinking) 1. to contract or become smaller in size, सिकुड़ना। 2. to cause to contract, सिकोड़ना। 3. to withdraw, पीछे हट जाना। 4. to hesitate, हिचकना।

shrinkage (श्रिन्किज) ***n.*** 1. the act or fact of shinking, सिकुड़ना। 2. the amount by which something has shrunk, सिकुड़न।

shrivel (श्रिवल) ***v.*** 1. to become withered, कुम्हला, मुरझा या सूख जाना। 2. to make withered, कुम्हला देना, सुखा देना, मुरझा देना।

shroud (श्राउड) ***n.*** 1. a garment or piece of cloth in which a dead body is wrapped, कफ़न। 2. anything that envelops, आवरण। ***v.*** 1. to wrap in a shroud, कफ़न में लपेटना। 2. to cover or hide, छिपाना, ढकना।

shrub (श्रब) ***n.*** a low woody plant with several stems, झाड़ी।

shrubbery (श्रबरी) ***n.*** shrubs collectively, झाड़-झंखाड़।

shrug (श्रग) ***v.*** to raise and drop one' shoulders abruptly as a gesture of indifference or doubt, (उपेक्षा या संदेह प्रकट करने के लिए) कंधे उचकाना।

shudder (शडर) ***v.*** to tremble violently, काँप उठना, थरथरा जाना। ***n.*** a shuddering movement, कँपकँपी, थरथराहट।

shuffle (शफ़ल) ***v.*** 1. to drag (one's feet, पैर) घसीटते हुए चलना। 2. to mix (the playing cards, ताश के पत्तों को) फेंटना। 3. to get rid of, पीछा छुड़ाना, पिंड छुड़ाना। ***n.*** 1. the act of shuffling, घसीट चलाई। 2. mixing of cards, फेंटाई। 3. rearrangement, फेर-बदल, बदलाव, परिवर्तन।

shun (शन) ***v.*** to keep away from, दूर रहना, भागना, किनारा करना।

shunt (शन्ट) ***v.*** to move (a train) on to a side-track, शंटिंग करना।

shush (शश) = hush.

shut (शट) ***v.*** (shut, shutting) 1. to close, बंद करना। 2. to become closed, बंद होना।

shut-down (शट-डाउन) ***n.*** the closing of a business, कामबंदी।

shutter (शटर) ***n.*** a panel that can be closed over a door, कपाट, झिलमिली, शटर।

shuttle (शटल) ***n.*** 1. an instrument carrying the weft thread to and fro across the loom in weaving, ढरकी, भरनी। 2. a train that plies between two places, शटल गाड़ी।

shuttlecock (शटलकॉक) ***n.*** a cork with a ring of feathers used in badminton, कॉर्क की बनी बैडमिंटन की चिड़ी, चिड़िया।

S

shy[1] (शाइ) ***adv.*** 1. lacking confidence and timid, शर्मीला, झेंपू। 2. showing shyness, लजालु, लाज-भरा। 3. easily startled, चौंक या भड़क उठनेवाला। ***v.*** to jump or move suddenly in alarm, चौंक उठना, भड़क उठना।

shy[2] ***v.*** to throw or fling, फेंकना।

Siamese Twins (साइअमीज़ ट्विन्ज़) ***n.*** twin babies joined in some way at birth, जुड़वाँ बच्चे जो आपस में जुड़े भी हों, श्यामी जुड़वाँ बच्चे।

sibling (सिब्लिन्ग) ***n.*** a real brother or sister, सगा भाई या बहन।

sic (सिक) ***adv.*** so, thus, इस प्रकार।

sick (सिक) ***adj.*** 1. unwell, बीमार, रुग्ण। 2. disgusted, खिन्न, दुखी, ऊबा हुआ।

sickening (सिकनिंग) ***adj.*** disgusting, उबाऊ या घिनौना।

sickle (सिकल) ***n.*** a tool with curved blade for cutting grain, हँसिया।

sickly (सिकली) ***adj.*** 1. often ill, अकसर बीमार रहनेवाला। 2. causing ill health, बीमारी लानेवाला, रोग पैदा करनेवाला।

sickness (सिकनिस) ***n.*** 1. disease, बीमारी, रोग। 2. vomiting, मतली।

side (साइड) ***n.*** 1. a surface of an object, पहलू, पार्श्व। 2. either of the two surfaces of a flat object, तरफ़। 3. the space immediately next to someone or something, ओर, तरफ़। 4. an area separated from another by some intervening line, ओर, तरफ़। 5. one or two or more opposing groups or teams, दल, पक्ष, तरफ़, ओर। 6. an edge or border, किनारा। 7. an aspect, पहलू। 8. the line of descent, वंश-परंपरा। ***adj.*** 1. at or on the side, बग़ली। 2. additional, अतिरिक्त। ***v.*** to associate oneself with a faction, interest etc., पक्ष लेना।

sideboard (साइडबोर्ड) ***n.*** a piece of furniture in a dinning room for holding articles of table service, वह आलमारी जिसमें भोजन परोसने के बर्तन रखे रहते हैं।

sideburns (साइडबर्न्ज़) ***n.*** (plu.) long whiskers, गलमुच्छे।

side effect ***n.*** any secondary effect, गौण प्रभाव।

sideline (साइडलाइन) ***n.*** 1. a secondary job, उपजीविका। 2. a line marking the limit of a field, सीमा-रेखा। ***v.*** to remove from a game, (खिलाड़ी को) न खिलाना।

sidelong (साइडलॉन्ग) ***adj.*** oblique, directed to one side, तिरछा, आड़ा। ***adv.*** obliquely, तिरछे, आड़े।

sidereal (साइडिरिअल) ***adj.*** of the stars, नक्षत्र-संबंधी, नाक्षत्र।

side-show (साइड-शो) ***n.*** a minor show, (किसी बड़े खेल या प्रदर्शन के साथ होनेवाला) कोई छोटा-मोटा खेल या प्रदर्शन।

sidestep (साइडस्टेप) ***v.*** to evade, कतराना, कतरा जाना।

sidetrack (साइडट्रैक) ***v.*** to divert from the main issue, ध्यान बँटाना।

sideways (साइडवेज़) ***adv.*** towards or from one side, एक तरफ़।

siding (साइडिंग) ***n.*** a short stretch of a railroad track, पार्श्वपथ, बग़ली लाइन।

sidle (साइडल) ***v.*** to move in a furtive or stealthy manner, किनारे होकर या बचकर निकलना।

siege (सीज) ***n.*** the surrounding of a fortified place by the opposing forces, (क़िले की) घेरेबंदी, घेरा।

sierra (सिअरा) ***n.*** a row of sharply

pointed mountains, नुकीली चोटियोंवाली पर्वतमाला।

siesta (सिएस्टा) ***n.*** a short sleep after the midday meal, दुपहरी झपकी।

sieve (सीव) ***n.*** a device for separating, straining, sifting etc., चलनी, छलनी। ***v.*** to put through a sieve, (चलनी से) छानना।

sift (सिफ़्ट) ***v.*** 1. to pass through a sieve, छनना या छानना। 2. to examine closely, जाँच या छानबीन करना।

sigh (साइ) ***n.*** a long deep breath expressing sorrow or relief, आह, ठंडी साँस। ***v.*** 1. to exhale a long deep breath as in sorrow or relief, आह भरना, ठंडी साँस लेना। 2. to lament, विलाप करना।

sight (साइट) ***n.*** 1. something that is seen, दृश्य, नज़ारा। 2. the sense of seeing, दृष्टि, निगाह। 3. a place worth seeing, दर्शनीय स्थल।

sightless (साइटलिस) ***adj.*** blind, अंधा।

sightseeing (साइटसीइंग) ***n.*** visiting places of interest (in a town), दर्शनीय स्थानों की सैर, सैर-सपाटा।

sign (साइन) ***n.*** 1. a mark, चिह्न, निशान। 2. a gesture, संकेत, इशारा। 3. a board इश्तहार। 4. a portent, लक्षण। ***v.*** 1. to affix a signature, हस्ताक्षर करना, दस्तखत करना। 2. to make a sign, चिह्न बनाना। 3. to indicate by a sign, संकेत करना।

signal (सिग्नल) ***n.*** 1. an indication, संकेत। 2. an indicator, संकेतक। 3. a railway apparatus for communicating information to trains, सिग्नल। ***v.*** to express by a signal, संकेत करना, सिग्नल देना।

signatory (सिग्नेटरी) ***n.*** one who has signed an agreement, हस्ताक्षरी, हस्ताक्षरकर्ता।

signature (सिग्नेचर) ***n.*** the name of a person written by himself or herself, हस्ताक्षर, दस्तख़त।

signet (सिग्निट) ***n.*** an official seal, मुहर।

significance (सिग्निफ़िकेन्स) ***n.*** 1. importance, महत्त्व। 2. meaning, purport, अर्थ, अभिप्राय।

significant (सिग्निफ़िकेन्ट) ***adj.*** 1. important, notable, महत्त्वपूर्ण। 2. meaningful, suggestive, अर्थपूर्ण, अर्थगर्भित।

signify (सिग्निफ़ाइ) ***v.*** 1. to indicate or suggest, संकेत करना। 2. to stand as a symbol, प्रतीक होना। 3. to imply, आशय देना।

signpost (साइनपोस्ट) ***n.*** a post supporting a sign that gives information, संकेतपट।

silence (साइलन्स) ***n.*** 1. calm, noiselessness, शांति, नीरवता, सन्नाटा। 2. the absence or avoidance of speech, मौन, चुप्पी, ख़ामोशी। ***v.*** to bring to silence, शांत करना या चुप कराना। ***interj.*** quiet please, शांत रहें, शांति बनाए रखें।

silencer (साइलन्सर) ***n.*** a device for reducing noise, साइलेंसर।

silent (साइलन्ट) ***adj.*** 1. unspeaking, चुप, मौन। 2. calm, quiet, noiseless, शांत, नीरव, निःशब्द। 3. voiceless, अनुच्चरित (वर्ण/ध्वनि)।

silhouette (सिलुएट) ***n.*** a dark outline, छायाकृति, रेखाचित्र, रेखांकन। ***v.*** to represent in outline, रेखांकन करना, रेखाचित्र बनाना।

silica (सिलिका) ***n.*** a chemical

S

compound, सेलखड़ी, सिलिका।

silk (सिल्क) ***n.*** the fabric made from fibre produced by silkworms, रेशम, सिल्क।

silken (सिल्कन) ***adj.*** = silky.

silkworm (सिल्कवर्म) ***n.*** an insect that produces silk fibre, रेशम का कीड़ा।

silky (सिल्की) ***adj.*** 1. made of silk, रेशमी। 2. glossy, चमकीला। 3. soft, मुलायम, नरम।

sill (सिल) ***n.*** the flat piece of wood or stone below a window or door, दहलीज़, दासा।

silly (सिली) ***adj.*** 1. foolish, मूर्ख, बेवकूफ़। 2. ridiculous, उपहासास्पद, बेतुका।

silo (साइलो) ***n.*** an enclosure or pit in which fodder is stored, खत्ता, बखार।

silt (सिल्ट) ***n.*** a deposit of mud, sand etc. found at the bottom of rivers, गाद। ***v.*** to fill or become filled with silt, गाद से भरना या भरा जाना।

silty (सिल्टी) ***adj.*** full of silt, गाद से भरा।

silvan (सिल्वन) ***adj.*** = sylvan.

silver (सिल्वर) ***n.*** 1. a white metal used in jewellery, चाँदी, रजत। 2. a silver coin, चाँदी का सिक्का, रुपया। ***adj.*** 1. made of silver, चाँदी का, रुपहला। 2. like silver in colour, रुपहला, रजत।

silverfish (सिल्वरफ़िश) ***n.*** 1. a fish having a silvery colour, रजतमीन। 2. an insect of a silvery colour feeding on paper, cloth etc., रजतकीट, रुपहला कीड़ा।

silver-tongued (सिल्वर-टंग्ड) ***adj.*** eloquent, वाक्पटु।

silverware (सिल्वरवेअर) ***n.*** articles made of silver, चाँदी के बर्तन।

silvery (सिल्वरी) ***adj.*** 1. made of silver, चाँदी का, रुपहला। 2. like silver in colour, रुपहला, झलझल करता हुआ।

similar (सिमिलर) ***adj.*** alike, resembling, मिलता-जुलता, समान, समरूप।

similarly (सिमिलर्ली) ***adv.*** 1. in a similar way, so as to be similar, समान रूप से। 2. likewise, उसी प्रकार, उसी तरह।

simile (सिमिली) ***n.*** a figure of speech that makes comparison between two different things, उपमा अलंकार।

similitude (सिमिलिट्यूड) ***n.*** similarity, समानता, अनुरूपता।

simmer (सिमर) ***v.*** 1. to boil gently with a murmuring sound, खदबदाना। 2. to be filled with anger, उबलने लगना, खदबदाना।

simple (सिम्पल) ***adj.*** 1. ordinary, साधारण, मामूली। 2. easy, सरल, सहज। 3. plain, unadorned, सजावट से रहित, अनलंकृत, सादा। 4. unblended, अमिश्रित। 5. artless, निष्कपट, भोला-भाला।

simpleton (सिम्पल्टन) ***n.*** a stupid person, बुद्धू, भोंदू।

simplicity (सिम्प्लिसिटी) ***n.*** 1. the quality of being simple, सादगी, सरलता, भोलापन। 2. absence of showiness, अकृत्रिमता, सादगी। 3. foolishness, मूर्खता।

simplify (सिम्प्लिफ़ाइ) ***v.*** to make simple, सरल बनाना, सरलीकरण करना।

simplistic (सिम्प्लिस्टिक) ***adj.*** one-sided, एकांगी, एकपक्षीय।

simply (सिम्प्ली) ***adv.*** 1. in a simple manner, सादगी से। 2. easily, सरलता

से। 3. merely, just, सिर्फ़, बस। 4. absolutely, बिल्कुल।

simulate (सिमुलेट) ***v.*** to imitate, नक़ल करना, अनुकरण करना।

simulation (सिमुलेशन) ***n.*** 1. the act of imitating, अनुकरण, नक़ल। 2. a representation, अनुकृति।

simulator (सिमुलेटर) ***n.*** one who imitates, नक़लची, अनुकर्ता।

simultaneous (साइमल्टेनिअस) ***adj.*** occurring at the same time, contemporaneous, एक साथ होनेवाला, युगपत्, सहकालिक।

simultaneously (साइमल्टेनिअसली) ***adv.*** at the same time, एक ही समय में, साथ-साथ।

sin (सिन) ***n.*** any offence against a religious or moral law, पाप, गुनाह। ***v.*** to commit a sin, पाप करना।

since (सिन्स) ***adv.*** at a time between then and now, तब से अब तक। ***prep.*** from till now, उस समय से, तब से। ***conj.*** because, क्योंकि।

sincere (सिन्सिअर) ***adj.*** honest, true, ईमानदार, सच्चा, निष्ठावान।

sincerity (सिन्सेरिटी) ***n.*** honesty, good faith, ईमानदारी, सच्चाई, सद्भाव।

sine die (साइनी डाइ) ***adv.*** indefinitely, अनिश्चित काल के लिए।

sine qua non (साइनी क्वे नॉन) ***n.*** a necessary condition, अनिवार्य शर्त।

sinew (सिन्यू) ***n.*** 1. a tendon, नस, कंडरा। 2. physical strength, muscle power, शारीरिक बल। 3. (plu.) resources of power, शक्तिस्रोत, शक्ति-साधन।

sinewless (सिन्युलिस) ***adj.*** without strength, अशक्त, कमज़ोर, शक्तिहीन।

sinewy (सिन्युई) ***adj.*** 1. tough, चीमड़। 2. muscular, बलवान। 3. forceful, ज़ोरदार।

sinful (सिनफ़ुल) ***adj.*** full of sins, पापी या पापपूर्ण, अधर्मी।

sing (सिन्ग) ***v.*** (sang, sung, singing) 1. to produce musical sound with the voice, गाना। 2. to make a humming or buzzing sound, चहचहाना या भिनभिनाना।

singer (सिन्गर) ***n.*** one who sings, गायक।

single (सिन्गल) ***adj.*** 1. one only, सिर्फ़ एक, एक ही, अकेला। 2. for one person or user, एक व्यक्ति के लिए। 3. unmarried, अकेला, अविवाहित। 4. separate, अलग, भिन्न। ***n.*** 1. a separate person or thing, कोई एक व्यक्ति या चीज़। 2. an unmarried person, अविवाहित व्यक्ति। 3. a single run (scored), एक रन। 4. (plu.) a match between two players, एकल (मैच)।

single-handed (सिन्गल-हैन्डिड) ***adj.*** done by a single person, unaided, एक ही व्यक्ति द्वारा होनेवाला, अकेले ही किया हुआ, एकाकी।

single-minded (सिन्गल-माइन्डिड) ***adj.*** having but one purpose, undeviating, steadfast, एकनिष्ठ, एकाग्रचित्त, अनन्य।

singly (सिन्गली) ***adv.*** 1. alone, unaided, अकेले ही। 2. one by one, एक-एक करके।

singsong (सिन्गसॉन्ग) ***n.*** monotonous regularity of rhyme, एकसुरा या एकरस गाना। ***adj.*** monotonous, एकसुरा, एकरस, विरस।

singular (सिन्यूलर) ***adj.*** 1. being only one, अकेला। 2. (gram.) denoting

S

a single person or thing, एकवचन। 3. extraordinary, असाधारण। *n.* the singular number, एकवचन।

sinister (सिनिस्टर) ***adj.*** suggesting or threatening harm, हानिकारक, अमंगलकारी, बुरा, दूषित।

sink (सिन्क) ***v.*** (sank/sunk, sunk/sunken, sinking) 1. to go beneath the surface of water or liquid, डूबना। 2. to cause to descend beneath the surface of water or liquid, डुबोना, डुबाना। 3. to fall or descend gradually, धीरे-धीरे नीचे आना या गिरना, घटना। 4. to become lower in level, उतरना, स्तर नीचा होना। 5. to dig or drill, खोदना या धँसाना। 6. to invest money, धन का निवेश करना। 7. to lose money, धन गँवाना। 8. to put in a hole, डालना। ***n.*** 1. a basin fixed to a wall, सिंक। 2. a drain or sewer, मोरी या परनाला।

sinless (सिनलिस) ***adj.*** free from sin, without sin, निष्पाप, बेगुनाह।

sinner (सिनर) ***n.*** a person who sins, wrongdoer, पापी, गुनाहगार।

sinuous (सिन्युअस) ***adj.*** 1. serpentine, wavy, सर्पिल, लहरदार। 2. crooked, not honest, धूर्त, बेईमान।

sinus (साइनस) ***n.*** 1. a cavity in a bone, अस्थि-रंध्र। 2. a passage leading to a cavity containing pus, नासूर।

sip (सिप) ***v.*** to drink only a little at a time, चुस्की भरना या लेना। ***n.*** a small quantity sipped, चुस्की।

siphon (साइफ़न) ***n.*** a u-shaped apparatus for forcing liquid to flow to the other end, साइफ़न। ***v.*** to flow through a siphon, साइफ़न से निकलना, बहना।

sir (सर) ***n.*** a form of address to a man, सर, श्रीमान्, महोदय।

sire (साइअर) ***n.*** a male parent of an animal, पशु का जनक, प्रजनक। ***v.*** to beget, पैदा करना, जन्म देना।

siren (साइरन) ***n.*** 1. a device to make a loud prolonged sound as a signal, भोंपू। 2. a dangerously fascinating woman, मायाविनी, मोहिनी।

sister (सिस्टर) ***n.*** 1. a female having the same parents as another person, बहन, दीदी। 2. a fellow woman, धर्म-बहन, बहन, दीदी। 3. a nun, सिस्टर। 4. a nurse of a hospital, सिस्टर।

sister-in law (सिस्टर-इन-लॉ) ***n.*** (plu. sisters-in-law) 1. the sister of one's husband or wife, ननद या साली। 2. the wife of one's brother, भाभी या भौजी।

sit (सिट) ***v.*** (sat, sitting) 1. to take rest on one's buttocks, बैठना। 2. to cause to sit, बैठाना, आसन देना। 3. to be situated, स्थित होना। 4. to appear, (परीक्षा आदि में) सम्मिलित होना।

site (साइट) ***n.*** 1. a plot of land on which a town or building stood, stands or is to stand, स्थल, स्थान। 2. a place where some event took place, घटना-स्थल। ***v.*** 1. to locate, स्थित होना। 2. to install, स्थापित करना।

sitting (सिटिंग) ***n.*** 1. a continuous period of being seated, बैठक, बैठकी। 2. a term or session, बैठक, अधिवेशन। ***adj.*** 1. seated, बैठा हुआ। 2. present, वर्तमान।

sitting member ***n.*** a present member of a body, वर्तमान सदस्य।

sitting room ***n.*** a room used for sitting in, बैठक।

situate (सिचुएट) ***v.*** to place or put in a certain position, स्थित करना, स्थापित करना।

situation (सिचुएशन) ***n.*** 1. position, स्थिति, दशा। 2. location, स्थल, स्थान।

six (सिक्स) ***adj. & n.*** one more than five, छह। ☐ **at sixes and sevens,** अस्त-व्यस्त।

sixteen (सिक्सटीन) ***adj.*** one more than fifteen, सोलह।

sixty (सिक्सटी) ***adj. & n.*** one more than fifty-nine, साठ।

sizable, sizeable (साइज़ेबल) ***adj.*** quite large, of considerable size, अच्छे-ख़ासे आकारवाला, काफ़ी बड़ा।

size (साइज़) ***n.*** 1. extent of something, माप, साइज। 2. measurements, आकार-प्रकार। ***v.*** to arrange according to size, नाप-जोख के अनुसार बनाना।

sizzle (सिज़ल) ***v.*** to make a hissing sound of frying, छनछनाना, कड़कड़ाना। ***n.*** a hissing sound, छनछन, कड़कड़।

skate (स्केट) ***n.*** a shoe or plate for gliding over the ice, स्केट। ***v.*** to move on skates, स्केटिंग करना।

skein (स्केन) ***n.*** 1. loosely coiled bundle of thread or yarn, अंटी, लच्छी। 2. a flock of flying geese, उड़ते हंसों की टोली।

skeletal (स्केलिटल) ***adj.*** 1. of the skeleton, कंकाल-संबंधी। 2. very thin, like a skeleton, कंकाल-सा, ठठरीनुमा, मरियल।

skeleton (स्केलिटन) ***n.*** 1. the internal supporting framework of animal body, हड्डियों का ढाँचा, ठठरी, कंकाल। 2. a supporting structure or framework, ढाँचा, ढड्ढा। 3. an outline or sketch, रूपरेखा।

skeptic (स्केप्टिक) ***adj.*** = sceptic.

sketch (स्केच) ***n.*** 1. an outline, ख़ाका, रूपरेखा। 2. a brief account of something, रेखाचित्र। ***v.*** to make a sketch (of), रूपरेखा/रेखाचित्र तैयार करना।

sketchy (स्केची) ***adj.*** rough and not detailed, कच्चा और अधूरा, अपूर्ण, सतही।

skew (स्क्यू) ***adj.*** slanting, oblique, तिरछा, टेढ़ा, ढलवाँ। ***v.*** 1. to make slanting, तिरछा बनाना। 2. to bias, तरफ़दारी करना, पक्षपात करना। 3. to take an oblique course, तिरछे/टेढ़े चलना।

ski (स्की) ***n.*** one of a pair of long narrow strips of wood attached to a boot for gliding over snow, (बर्फ़ पर फिसलने के लिए) लकड़ी का पतला लंबा जूता, स्की। ***v.*** (skied, skiing) to travel on skis, स्की पहनकर बर्फ़ पर फिसलना, स्कीयन करना।

skid (स्किड) ***v.*** to slide uncontrollably on slippery grounds, फिसलना। ***n.*** the act of slipping, फिसलने की क्रिया।

skiff (स्किफ़) ***n.*** a small, flat-bottomed open boat, छोटी नाव, डोंगी।

skill (स्किल) ***n.*** the ability to do something well, कौशल, दक्षता।

skilled (स्किल्ड) ***adj.*** skilful, highly trained, दक्षताप्राप्त, कुशल, निपुण।

skim (स्किम) ***v.*** 1. to remove floating matter from milk or any other liquid, मलाई या झाग उतारना। 2. to glide smoothly, आसानी से फिसलना। 3. to read through quickly, सरसरी निगाह से देख या पढ़ जाना।

skimmed milk (स्किम्ड मिल्क) ***n.*** milk with cream removed, मखनिया दूध, सप्रेटा।

skimp (स्किम्प) ***v.*** 1.to be stingy,

S

कंजूस होना। 2. to keep expenses very low, कंजूसी करना।

skin (स्किन) ***n.*** 1. outer covering of an animal, त्वचा। 2. the outer covering of fruit, छिलका। 3. a container made of animal's skin, मशक। 4. film, झिल्ली, पपड़ी। ***v.*** to remove skin from, खाल उतारना।

skinflint (स्किनफ़्लिन्ट) ***n.*** a miser, कंजूस।

skinny (स्किनी) ***adj.*** very thin, दुबला-पतला, सींक-सलाई।

skip (स्किप) ***v.*** 1. to spring, फुदकना, उछलना-कूदना। 2. to leap, फाँदना। 3. to pass over, omit, छोड़ देना, लंघन कर जाना। 4. to leave hastily, खिसक जाना। ***n.*** a skipping movement, उछल-कूद, फुदकना।

skipper (स्किपर) ***n.*** a captain, कप्तान।

skirmish (स्कर्मिश) ***n.*** 1. a minor encounter in war, मुठभेड़, भिड़ंत। 2. any brisk conflict, झड़प।

skirt (स्कर्ट) ***n.*** 1. a female garment hanging from the waist, स्कर्ट। 2. the part of the dress below the waist, घेरा या पल्ला। 3. (plu.) an outlying area, बाह्यांचल। ***v.*** 1. to lie along the edge, किनारे पर होना। 2. to avoid, बचा जाना, छोड़ देना।

skit (स्किट) ***n.*** a short comic theatrical sketch, प्रहसन, व्यंगिका।

skittish (स्किटिश) ***adj.*** 1. playful, खिलवाड़ी। 2. nervous, घबराया हुआ। 3. whimsical, सनकी।

skulduggery (स्कलडगरी) ***n.*** deception, trickery, धोखाधड़ी, चालबाज़ी।

skulk (स्कल्क) ***v.*** 1. to move about stealthily, दुबककर चलना। 2. to shirk, (काम या उत्तरदायित्व से) भागना।

skull (स्कल) ***n.*** the bony framework of the head, खोपड़ी।

sky (स्काइ) ***n.*** the upper atmosphere, आसमान, आकाश।

skydiving (स्काइडाइविंग) ***n.*** the sport of jumping from the airplane and performing acrobatics in the air, हवाई जहाज़ से कूदकर दिखाई जानेवाली कलाबाज़ी, हवाबाज़ी।

skylark (स्काइलार्क) ***n.*** a bird noted for its singing while in flight, भरल। ***v.*** to frolic, खिलवाड़ या क्रीड़ा करना।

skylight (स्काइलाइट) ***n.*** a window in a roof or ceiling, रोशनदान, झरोखा।

skyscraper (स्काइस्क्रेपर) ***n.*** a very tall building, गगनचुंबी अट्टालिका।

slab (स्लैब) ***n.*** a broad thick piece of something solid, पटिया, स्लैब।

slack (स्लैक) ***adj.*** 1. loose, ढीला, शिथिल। 2. characterized by little trade or business, मंदा। 3. sluggish, सुस्त। 4. careless, असावधान। ***v.*** 1. to loosen, ढीला करना या होना। 2. to neglect (one's duty, कर्तव्य की) उपेक्षा करना। ***n.*** 1. the state of being hanging loose, ढील, शिथिलता। 2. the period of decreased activity, मंदी।

slacken (स्लैकन) ***v.*** 1. to make slack, ढीला करना। 2. to become slack, ढीला होना।

slag (स्लैग) ***n.*** the dross left after smelting ore, धातुमल।

slain (स्लेन) ***v.*** p.p. of slay.

slake (स्लेक) ***v.*** 1. to quench, (प्यास) बुझाना। 2. to combine water (with lime, चूना) बुझाना।

slam (स्लैम) ***v.*** 1. to shut with force

and loud noise, (दरवाज़ा) ज़ोर से भिड़काना या बंद करना। 2. to strike, आघात करना, प्रहार करना। 3. to criticize harshly, कटु आलोचना करना।

slander (स्लैन्डर) ***n.*** a false or malicious statement that damages the reputation of someone, निंदा, बुराई, मानहानि। ***v.*** to utter slander (about, किसी की) निंदा करना, बुराई करना।

slanderous (स्लैन्डरस) ***adj.*** defamatory, निंदापूर्ण, निंदात्मक।

slang (स्लैन्ग) ***n.*** non-standard colloquial usage, बोलचाल के ऐसे प्रयोग जिनका इस्तेमाल औपचारिक प्रसंगों में न किया जाता हो, अपप्रयोग या अपभाषा।

slant (स्लैन्ट) ***v.*** 1. to slope, ढालू होना या ढालू करना, तिरछा होना या तिरछा करना। 2. to be biased, पूर्वग्रह से युक्त होना। 3. to present (news) with a biased attitude, (समाचार को) विशेष दृष्टिकोण से प्रस्तुत करना। ***n.*** 1. slope, ढाल। 2. bend, झुकाव। 3. biased attitude, पूर्वग्रहयुक्त दृष्टिकोण, तरफ़दारी।

slap (स्लैप) ***n.*** a blow with the open hand, चपत, थप्पड़, चाँटा। ***v.*** to strike with a slap, चपत मारना, तमाचा जड़ना।

slapdash (स्लैपडैश) ***adj.*** 1. hasty, जल्दबाज़। 2. careless, लापरवाह।

slap-happy (स्लैप-हैपी) ***adj.*** cheerful, प्रसन्न, हर्षित।

slap-up (स्लैप-अप) ***adj.*** excellent, उम्दा, बढ़िया।

slash (स्लैश) ***v.*** 1. to cut with a violent sweeping stroke, झटके से चीर या काट डालना। 2.to reduce drastically, एकदम कम कर देना, भारी कमी करना। ***n.*** 1. a cut or gash, चीरा। 2. a deep wound, गहरा घाव।

slat (स्लैट) ***n.*** a narrow strip of wood or metal, लकड़ी या धातु की पट्टी।

slate (स्लेट) ***n.*** 1. a smooth fine-grained rock that splits into thin layers, स्लेटी पत्थर। 2. a writing tablet of slate, स्लेट। ***v.*** to cover with slates, पटिया से छाना।

slaughter (स्लॉटर) ***n.*** 1. the killing of animals for food, पशुओं का काटा जाना, पशुवध। 2. a massacre, संहार, नरसंहार या पशुसंहार। ***v.*** 1. to kill animals for food, पशुओं का काटा जाना, वध। 2. to kill in great numbers, संहार करना।

slaughter-house (स्लॉटर-हाउस) ***n.*** a place where animals are killed for food, बूचड़ख़ाना, कसाईख़ाना।

slave (स्लेव) ***n.*** a person who is held in bondage by another, ग़ुलाम, दास। ***v.*** to work like a slave, ग़ुलाम की तरह काम करना, कठोर परिश्रम करना।

slavery (स्लेवरी) ***n.*** 1. the state or condition of being a slave, दासता, ग़ुलामी। 2. the owning or keeping of slaves, दास-प्रथा। 3. hard work, कठोर परिश्रम।

slavish (स्लेविश) ***adj.*** 1. like slaves, दासों का-सा, दासीय। 2. imitative, नक़ली, अनुकृत।

slay (स्ले) ***v.*** (slew, slain, slaying) to kill, मार डालना, क़त्ल करना।

sleazy (स्लीज़ी) ***adj.*** cheap and dirty, दो कौड़ी का, गया-गुज़रा, फूहड़।

sledge (स्लेज) ***n.*** a vehicle mounted on runners for carrying loads across snow, हिमगाड़ी। ***v.*** to travel by sledge, हिमगाड़ी से यात्रा करना।

sledge-hammer (स्लेज-हेमर) ***n.*** a long heavy hammer, बड़ा हथौड़ा, घन।

sleek (स्लीक) ***adj.*** 1. smooth,

S

glossy, चिकना-चुपड़ा। 2. trim, graceful, बना-ठना।

sleep (स्लीप) ***n.*** a state of rest during which consciousness is suspended, नींद। ***v.*** (slept, sleeping) to be in a state of sleep, सोना, नींद लेना।

sleeper (स्लीपर) ***n.*** 1. सोनेवाला व्यक्ति। 2. a sleeping car, शयनयान। 3. a heavy timber beam, शहतीर, स्लीपर।

sleeping bag ***n.*** a bag in which a person may sleep, शयन-थैला।

sleepwalker (स्लीपवाकर) ***n.*** a person who walks while asleep, नींद में चलनेवाला, निद्राचर।

sleepy (स्लीपी) ***adj.*** 1. ready to sleep, drowsy, जिसे नींद आ रही हो, उनींदा, तंद्रिल। 2. inactive, अक्रिय, निष्क्रिय। 3. quiet, शांत।

sleet (स्लीट) ***n.*** falling of hail-stones, उपलवृष्टि। ***v.*** to shower in the form of sleet, उपलवृष्टि होना।

sleeve (स्लीव) ***n.*** the part of a garment that covers the arm, आस्तीन।

sleigh (स्ले) ***n.*** a light vehicle for use on snow, हिमगाड़ी, स्लेज।

sleight of hand (स्लाइट ऑफ़ हैन्ड) ***n.*** great skill in performing a trick, हाथ की सफ़ाई, हस्तकौशल।

slender (स्लेन्डर) ***adj.*** 1. of small width relative to height, छरहरा, पतला-दुबला। 2. inadequate, अयथेष्ट।

slept (स्लेप्ट) ***v.*** p.t. & p.p. of sleep.

sleuth (स्लूथ) ***n.*** a detective, जासूस, भेदिया।

slew[1] (स्लू) ***v.*** p.t. of slay.

slew[2] ***n.*** a large number or amount, बहुत बड़ी संख्या या राशि।

slew[3] ***n.*** to turn or swing around, घुमाना, मोड़ना।

slice (स्लाइस) ***n.*** 1. a thin flat piece cut from a larger object, कतला, फाँक। 2. a portion or share, अंश, भाग। 3. the flight of a ball that travels obliquely, गेंद की तिरछी उड़ान। ***v.*** 1. to cut with a knife, छुरी से काटना। 2. to divide with a knife, फाँकें निकालना, काटना। 3. to hit a ball with a slice, गेंद को तिरछे उड़ाना।

slicer (स्लाइसर) ***n.*** a tool for slicing, छुरी।

slick (स्लिक) ***adj.*** 1. smooth, चिकना। 2. flattering and glib, वाक्चपल। 3. deftly executed, दक्षतापूर्वक किया हुआ। 4. shrewd, सयाना, चालाक। ***n.*** smooth surface, चिकना तल। ***v.*** to make smooth, चिकना बनाना।

slide (स्लाइड) ***v.*** (slid, sliding) 1. to move or cause to move over smooth surface in continual contact with it, फिसलना या फिसलाना, सरकना या सरकाना। 2. to slip, खिसक जाना। ***n.*** 1. a sliding movement or action, फिसलाव, सरकन, सर्पण। 2. a landslide, भूस्खलन।

sliding (स्लाइडिंग) ***n.*** the act of a person or thing that slides, सर्पण।

slight (स्लाइट) ***adj.*** 1. slender, not stout, दुर्बल, कमज़ोर। 2. small in amount or extent, अल्प, थोड़ा। ***n.*** disrespectful treatment, insult, तिरस्कार, अनादर, उपेक्षा। ***v.*** to treat with disrespect, अनादर या उपेक्षा करना।

slightly (स्लाइटली) ***adv.*** in a slight degree, थोड़ी मात्रा में, कुछ-कुछ।

slightness (स्लाइटनिस) ***n.*** 1. disrespectful treatment, तिरस्कार,

अनादर, अवमानना। 2. weakness, कमज़ोरी, दुर्बलता।

slim (स्लिम) ***adj.*** 1. thin, पतला-दुबला (परंतु आकर्षक)। 2. meagre, scanty, तुच्छ, अल्प। ***v.*** to make or become slim, पतला-दुबला बनाना या बनना।

slime (स्लाइम) ***n.*** slippery substance, लिसलिसा पदार्थ।

slimy (स्लाइमी) ***adj.*** 1. full of slime, लिसलिसा, चिपचिपा। 2. filthy, गंदा।

sling (स्लिंग) ***v.*** (slung, slinging) to hurl or throw, फेंकना, उछालना। ***n.*** a device for shooting small stones, गुलेल।

slink (स्लिंक) ***v.*** (slunk, slinking) to move in a shamefaced way, मुँह छिपाकर, शरमा कर या लजाते हुए जाना।

slip[1] (स्लिप) ***v.*** 1. to move quitely and stealthily, चुपके से खिसक जाना। 2. to miss or lose one's footing, फिसल जाना। 3. to slide, फिसलना, सरकना। 4. to detach, छोड़ देना या छूट जाना। 5. to make a careless mistake, चूक करना। ***n.*** 1. the act of slipping, फिसलना, सरकना। 2. a blunder, चूक, ग़लती। 3. a petticoat, पेटीकोट। 4. a pil-lowcase, तकिए की खोली।

slip[2] ***n.*** 1. a small piece of paper bearing some information, चिट, पुर्ज़ा, पट्टी, धज्जी आदि। 2. a part of a plant cut off for planting or grafting, क़लम। 3. (in cricket) the position of a fielder to catch a snicked ball, स्लिप।

slipper (स्लिपर) ***n.*** a light shoe, घर में पहनने की चप्पल, स्लीपर।

slippery (स्लिपरी) ***adj.*** 1. liable to cause slipping, फिसलन-भरा, फिसलना; 2. difficult to understand, दुरूह, दुर्बोध।

slipshod (स्लिपशॉड) ***adj.*** 1. careless, असावधान या असावधानी-भरा। 2. poorly made or done, slovenly, फूहड़, बेढंगा।

slipway (स्लिपवे) ***n.*** the sloping area on which a vessel is launched, समुद्रतट का वह घाट जहाँ से जहाज़ पानी में उतारे तथा बाहर निकाले जाते हैं, जलावतरण-मंच।

slit (स्लिट) ***n.*** a long narrow cut, चीर। ***v.*** (slit, slitting) to make a long cut, चीरा देना, चीरना, फाड़ना।

slither (स्लिदर) ***v.*** to slip and slide, फिसलते हुए आगे बढ़ना।

slob (स्लॉब) ***n.*** a clumsy fellow, फूहड़ व्यक्ति।

slobber (स्लॉबर) ***v.*** to dribble saliva or food from the mouth, मुँह से लार आदि टपकना या टपकाना।

slogan (स्लोगन) ***n.*** a phrase adopted as a motto, नारा।

slope (स्लोप) ***n.*** an inclined surface, ढाल। ***v.*** to incline down-ward, ढालुआँ होना, ढाल होना। □ **slope off,** चुपचाप खिसक जाना।

sloping (स्लोपिंग) ***adj.*** that slopes or slants, ढालुआँ।

sloppy (स्लॉपी) ***adj.*** 1. (of food) watery, पानियल, पतला। 2. wet, गीला। 3. untidy, मैला-कुचैला, गंदा या फूहड़। 4. careless, लापरवाह। 5. loose, ढीला-ढाला (पाजामा)।

slot (स्लॉट) ***n.*** 1. a narrow opening, झिरी, छेद। 2. a groove or slit, खाँचा। ***v.*** to make a slot, झिरी डालना; खाँचा बनाना।

S

sloth (स्लॉथ) ***n.*** laziness, सुस्ती, आलस्य।

slouch (स्लाउच) ***n.*** an awkward drooping posture or gait, झुककर बैठने, खड़े होने या चलने की क्रिया या भाव। ***v.*** to stand, sit or move droopingly, झुककर बैठना, खड़े होना या चलना।

slough[1] (स्लाउ) ***n.*** 1. a swamp or marshy place, दलदल। 2. despair, निराशा। 3. depression, विषाद।

slough[2] (स्लफ़) ***n.*** 1. a snake's cast skin, केंचुली। 2. an outer layer of a wound, खुरंड। ***v.*** to cast dead skin, केंचुली छोड़ना।

slovenly (स्लवनली) ***adj.*** 1. untidy, फूहड़, बेढंगा। 2. careless, लापरवाह।

slow (स्लो) ***adj.*** 1. not quick or fast, sluggish, धीमा, मंद। 2. mentally dull, मंद, मंदबुद्धि। 3. (of a clock) indicating a time earlier than the correct time, धीमी गति से चलनेवाली। ***v.*** to decrease or cause to decrease in speed, धीमा करना या होना।

slow-witted (स्लो-विटिड) ***adj.*** dull, मंद-बुद्धि।

sludge (स्लज) ***n.*** 1. mud, mire, कीचड़। 2. sediment, तलछट, गंदगी।

sluggard (स्लगर्ड) ***n.*** a lazy person, आलसी आदमी।

sluggish (स्लगिश) ***adj.*** lazy, slow, सुस्त।

sluggishness (स्लगिशनिस) ***n.*** the quality of being sluggish, सुस्ती, आलस्य।

sluice (स्लूस) ***n.*** 1. a man-made channel, नहर। 2. a gate that controls the channel, जल-कपाट। ***v.*** 1. to let out water, (नहर में) पानी छोड़ना। 2. to wash in a sluice, नहर में धोना।

slum (स्लम) ***n.*** an urban area inhabited by poor people, गंदी बस्ती, मलिन बस्ती।

slumber (स्लम्बर) ***v.*** 1. to sleep, सोना। 2. to doze, झपकी लेना। ***n.*** 1. sleep, नींद। 2. doze, झपकी।

slump (स्लम्प) ***n.*** 1. a great fall in the demand of goods, मंदी। 2. a great fall in prices, क़ीमतों में भारी गिरावट, मूल्यह्रास। ***v.*** 1. to decline, गिरना, कम हो जाना। 2. to deteriorate, गिर जाना।

slung (स्लंग) ***v.*** p.t. and p.p. of sling.

slunk (स्लंक) ***v.*** p.t. and p.p. of slink.

slur (स्लर) ***v.*** 1. to pronounce indistinctly, अस्पष्ट उच्चारण करना। 2. to speak slightingly or disparagingly, लांछन लगाना। ***n.*** indistinct pronunciation, अस्पष्ट उच्चारण।

slurp (स्लर्प) ***v.*** to eat or drink noisily, इस प्रकार खाना या पीना कि मुँह से आवाज़ हो।

slurry (स्लरी) ***n.*** a thin mixture of water and cement, पतला मसाला।

slush (स्लश) ***n.*** 1. partially melted snow or ice, अधघुली बर्फ़। 2. mud, कीचड़। 3. silly senseless talk, बकबक।

sly (स्लाइ) ***adj.*** 1. cunning, कपटी या कपटपूर्ण। 2. mischievous, दुष्ट या दुष्टतापूर्ण।

slyness (स्लाइनिस) ***n.*** cunning-ness, कपट, धूर्तता।

smack[1] (स्मैक) ***v.*** 1. to kiss noisily, ज़ोर से चुम्मा लेना। 2. to slap noisily, ज़ोर से थप्पड़ लगाना। 3. a hard hit, ज़ोरदार प्रहार। ***n.*** 1. a noisy kiss, चुम्मा। 2. a loud slap, थप्पड़। ***adv.*** directly, सीधे, सीधे-सीधे।

S

smack[2] ***n.*** flavour, गंध, पुट, स्वाद। ***v.*** to have the flavour of, (किसी चीज़ की) गंध आना।

smack[3] ***n.*** heroin, हेरोइन, नशीली ओषधि।

small (स्मॉल) ***adj.*** 1. little in size, छोटा, नन्हा, लघु। 2. little in quantity, थोड़ा, अल्प। 3. of little importance, साधारण, नगण्य। 4. not fully grown, अवयस्क, छोटा। ***adv.*** 1. in small size, छोटे आकार में। 2. in small pieces, छोटे-छोटे टुकड़ों या दानों में। ***n.*** 1. a small slender part of something, किसी वस्तु का छोटा पतला अंश। 2. (plu.) small articles collectively, छोटी-छोटी चीज़ों का समूह।

small hours ***n.*** the first few hours following midnight, आधी रात के ठीक बाद का समय।

smallish (स्मॉलिश) ***adj.*** rather small, छोटा-सा।

small-minded (स्मॉल-माइन्डिड) ***adj.*** 1. mean, कमीना। 2. selfish, स्वार्थी।

smallpox (स्मॉलपॉक्स) ***n.*** an acute infectious disease that causes skin eruptions, चेचक, माता।

small talk ***n.*** light conversation, साधारण बातचीत, गपशप।

smarmy (स्मार्मी) ***adj.*** flattering, चापलूस।

smart (स्मार्ट) ***adj.*** 1. intelligent, होशियार। 2. shrewd, सयाना। 3. quick and witty, चुस्त और हाज़िरजवाब। 4. neat and elegant, बना-ठना, सजीला। 5. sharp, तेज़, तीव्र। ***n.*** 1. stinging pain, चमक, टीस। 2. a stinging feeling, चुभन, टीस, व्यथा। ***v.*** 1. to feel a stinging pain, टीस उठना, चुभन होना। 2. to suffer a penalty, दंड भरना।

smarten (स्मार्टन) ***v.*** to make or become smart, चुस्त-दुरुस्त बनना या बनाना, सजना-सँवरना या सजाना-सँवारना।

smartness (स्मार्टनिस) ***n.*** the state of being smart, चुस्ती, दुरुस्ती; होशियारी, सयानापन।

smash (स्मैश) ***v.*** 1. to break into with noise or violence, चकनाचूर हो जाना या कर देना। 2. to collide with crushing force, तेज़ी से भिड़ या टकरा जाना, भिड़ंत होना। 3. to ruin completely, नष्ट या ध्वस्त कर देना। ***n.*** 1. the sound of smashing, चकनाचूर होने का शब्द। 2. a collision, टक्कर, भिड़ंत। 3. a disaster, बरबादी, विनाश।

smashing (स्मैशिंग) ***adj.*** excellent, superb, अति उत्तम, उत्कृष्ट।

smattering (स्मैटरिंग) ***n.*** 1. slight knowledge, हलकी-फुलकी जानकारी, थोथा ज्ञान। 2. a small amount, अल्पराशि।

smear (स्मिअर) ***v.*** 1. to cover with oil, grease etc., लेप करना, लीपना-पोतना, लगाना। 2. to become smeared, लिप-पुत जाना, लग जाना। 3. to defame, बदनाम करना। ***n.*** 1. something smeared on the surface, लेप। 2. a smug or blot, धब्बा। 3. defamation, बदनामी।

smell (स्मेल) ***v.*** (smelled/smelt, smelling) 1. to perceive the smell of, सूँघना। 2. to emit an odour, महकना। 3. to give off an unpleasant smell, गंधाना, बू देना। ***n.*** 1. the sense by which odours are perceived, सूँघने की शक्ति, घ्राणशक्ति। 2. the odour of something, गंध, महक। 3. the act of smelling something, सूँघना।

S

smelt[1] (स्मेल्ट) ***v.*** to melt ore in order to get metal, अयस्क को गलाकर धातु निकालना।

smelt[2] ***v.*** p.t. & p.p. of smell.

smile (स्माइल) ***n.*** a facial expression showing pleasure or derision, मुस्कान, मुस्कराहट। ***v.*** 1. to have a smile, मुस्काना, मुस्कराना। 2. to look bright or favourable, अनुकूल होना।

smirk (स्मर्क) ***v.*** to smile in an obnoxious or offensive manner, आपत्तिजनक ढंग से मुस्कराना। ***n.*** obnoxious smile, आपत्तिजनक मुस्कान।

smith (स्मिथ) ***n.*** a metalworker, धातुकर्मी; blacksmith, लुहार; goldsmith, सुनार।

smitten (स्मिटन) ***adj.***; ☐ **smitten with,** deeply affected by, से प्रभावित, से ग्रस्त।

smock (स्मॉक) ***n.*** a loose outer garment, ऊपरी लबादा या ढीला-ढाला कुरता।

smog (स्मॉग) ***n.*** a mixture of smoke and fog, धुएँ और कोहरे का मिला-जुला रूप; धुंधुआँ (धुंध+धुआँ)।

smoke (स्मोक) ***n.*** 1. the vaporous matter arising from burning coal, wood etc., धुआँ, धूम्र। 2. the act of smoking tobacco etc., धूम्रपान। ***v.*** 1. to emit smoke, धुआँ छोड़ना। 2. to draw the smoke of tobacco, (तंबाकू या सिगरेट) पीना। 3. to subject to smoke, धुआँ दिखाना।

smoker (स्मोकर) ***n.*** one who habitually smokes tobacco, तंबाकू पीनेवाला, धूम्रपान करनेवाला।

smoke screen ***n.*** a mass of dense smoke to screen the military operations, धूम्रपट।

smoking (स्मोकिंग) ***n.*** act of smoking tobacco, तंबाकू पीना, धूम्रपान, धूमन।

smoky (स्मोकी) ***adj.*** 1. full of smoke, filled with smoke, धुएँ से भरा। 2. giving much smoke, बहुत अधिक धुआँ देनेवाला। 3. having the colour of a smoke, धुएँ के रंग का, काला।

smolder (स्मोल्डर) ***v.*** see 'smoulder'.

smooth (स्मूद) ***adj.*** 1. free from roughness, चिकना। 2. even, बराबर, समतल। 3. having fine texture, मुलायम, नरम। 4. pleasantly polite, मृदु। 5. having no obstructions or difficulties, सहज, सरल। ***v.*** to make smooth, चिकना या चौरस करना, बाधाएँ दूर करना, सहज कर या बना देना।

smooth-tongued (स्मूद-टंग्ड) ***adj.*** speaking in a polite and flattering manner, मृदुभाषी, ख़ुशामदी।

smother (स्मदर) ***v.*** 1. to suffocate or be suffocated, दम घोटना या दम घुटना। 2. to suppress or be suppressed, दबाना या दबना। ***n.*** a cloud of smoke that stifles, दमघोंटू धुएँ का गुबार।

smoulder (स्मोल्डर) ***v.*** 1. to burn slowly without flame, सुलगना। 2. to have or show violent feelings that are kept from being expressed, अंदर ही अंदर जलना, सुलगना, जलना-भुनना।

smudge (स्मज) ***v.*** 1. to smear or blur, गंदा करना, मलिन करना। 2. to blot, धब्बे डालना। ***n.*** stain, धब्बा।

smug (स्मग) ***adj.*** self-satisfied, आत्मतुष्ट।

smuggle (स्मगल) ***v.*** to bring or import dutiable goods illicitly, तस्करी करना।

smuggler (स्मगलर) ***n.*** a person

engaged in smuggling, तस्कर।

smut (स्मट) ***n.*** 1. a particle of dirt or soot, धूल या कालिख का कण। 2. a stain, धब्बा।

smutty (स्मटी) ***adj.*** 1. dirty, गंदा, मलिन। 2. obscene, अश्लील।

snack (स्नैक) ***n.*** a light meal, हलका नाश्ता, स्नैक।

snag (स्नैग) ***n.*** 1. a jagged or sharp projecting part, नुकीला सिरा, कोना या खूँट। 2. a tear in fabric caused by a snag or sharp object, खरोंच। 3. an unforeseen or hidden obstacle, कोई अदृश्य या गुप्त बाधा। ***v.*** 1. to tear or damage on a snag, खरोंच लगना। 2. to halt or impede, अटकना या फँसना।

snail (स्नेल) ***n.*** any of the slow moving molluscs with a shell, घोंघा।

snake (स्नेक) ***n.*** 1. a reptile with a long narrow body and no legs, साँप, नाग। 2. a worthless or treacherous fellow, निकम्मा या कपटी साथी। ***v.*** to move like a snake, साँप की तरह चलना, सर्पण करना।

snakes and ladders ***n.*** a game, साँप-सीढ़ी का खेल।

snakily (स्नेकिली) ***adj.*** in a snaky manner, छलपूर्वक, कपटपूर्वक।

snaky (स्नेकी) ***adj.*** 1. of or like a snake, साँप-जैसा, सर्पिल। 2. treacherous, छली, कपटी। 3. infested with snakes, साँपों से भरा, सर्पग्रस्त।

snap (स्नैप) ***v.*** 1. to make or cause to make a sharp cracking sound, चिटकना या चिटकाना। 2. to break or cause to break suddenly, तड़कना या तड़काना, चटकना या चटकाना, टूटना या तोड़ना। 3. to bite, काटना। 4. to seize with a snatching motion, झपट पड़ना, छीन-झपट करना। 5. to speak sharply, गुर्राना। 6. to take a snapshot, छोटे कैमरे से फ़ोटो लेना। 7. to take or accept eagerly, ले लेना। 8. to move or act suddenly, सहसा सक्रिय हो उठना। ***n.*** 1. a sharp cracking sound, चिटक, चटक, तड़क। 2. a sudden grab, पकड़, जकड़। 3. a sudden bite, सहसा काट खाना। 4. a photo, फ़ोटो। ***adj.*** happening unexpectedly, आकस्मिक।

snappish (स्नैपिश) ***adj.*** bad-tempered, चिड़चिड़ा, खटकना।

snapshot (स्नैपशॉट) ***n.*** an informal photograph taken with a small camera, स्नैपशॉट।

snarl (स्नार्ल) ***n.*** 1. a tangled mass of thread, hair etc., उलझट्टा, उलझाव। 2. a complication or tangle, उलझन। 3. a growl, दाँत निपोरने की क्रिया या भाव, गुर्राहट। ***v.*** 1. to make entangled, उलझा देना। 2. to become entangled, उलझ जाना। 3. to growl while baring the teeth, गुर्राना।

snatch (स्नैच) ***v.*** 1. to grab suddenly, छीन या झपट लेना। 2. to avail (a chance, मौके का) उपयोग करना। ***n.*** 1. the act of snatching, झपट्टा। 2. a bit or fragment, अंश, भाग। 3. a brief period, अल्पकाल, दौर।

snazzy (स्नैज़ी) ***adj.*** smart, चुस्त-दुरुस्त।

sneak (स्नीक) ***v.*** 1. to move in a stealthy way, चुपके-चुपके चलना। 2. to give or take in a quite stealthy way, चुपके-चुपके लेन-देन करना। 3. to steal, चुराना, उड़ा लेना। 4. to leave quietly, खिसक जाना, चुपके से चल देना। ***n.*** 1. a stealthy or underhand person, चोरी-छिपे काम करनेवाला व्यक्ति, धूर्त व्यक्ति। 2. an informer, मुख़बिर।

sneaking (स्नीकिंग) ***adj.*** 1. underhand, धूर्ततापूर्ण, चोरी-छिपे किया जानेवाला। 2. secret, गुप्त।

sneer (स्निअर) ***v.*** to smile scornfully, खिल्ली उड़ाना, उपहास करना। ***n.*** an act of sneering, खिल्ली, उपहास।

sneeze (स्नीज़) ***v.*** to make a sudden violent audible expiration of breath, छींक मारना, छींकना। ***n.*** an act of sneezing, छींक।

snicker (स्निकर) ***n.*** & ***v.*** see 'snigger'.

snide (स्नाइड) ***adj.*** malicious, दुर्भावनापूर्ण।

sniff (स्निफ़) ***v.*** 1. to inhale audibly through the nose, नाक से इस प्रकार साँस लेना कि सूँ सूँ शब्द हो। 2. to smell by inhalation through nose, सूँघना। 3. to show disdain, तिरस्कार करना। ***n.*** the act of sniffing, नाक से (सूँ सूँ करते हुए) साँस लेना।

sniffy (स्निफ़ी) ***adj.*** 1. disdainful, scornful, नकचढ़ा। 2. smelly, गँधैला, महकदार।

snigger (स्निगर) ***n.*** a sly laugh, खिल्ली। ***v.*** to utter such a laugh, खिल्ली उड़ाना।

snip (स्निप) ***v.*** to cut with short quick strokes, कतरना, कुतरना। ***n.*** 1. a cut made with scissors, चीर, टुक। 2. a small piece clipped, कतरन, टुकड़ा।

snippet (स्निपिट) ***n.*** a fragment, टुकड़ा।

snob (स्नॉब) ***n.*** one who has offensive air of superiority, अकड़ू, दंभी, गुमानी, घमंडी।

snobbery (स्नॉबरी) ***n.*** snobbish behaviour or character, अकड़, दंभ, गुमान।

snoop (स्नूप) ***v.*** to pry, ताक-झाँक करना।

snooze (स्नूज़) ***v.*** to take a nap, झपकी लेना। ***n.*** a nap, झपकी।

snore (स्नोर) ***v.*** to breathe during sleep with a hoarse noise, खर्राटे भरना। ***n.*** the act or noise of snoring, खर्राटा।

snort (स्नॉर्ट) ***v.*** to force breath suddenly and violently through the nose, फुफकारना। ***n.*** the act or sound of snorting, फुफकार।

snout (स्नाउट) ***n.*** the projecting nose and jaws of an animal, थूथन, नथुना।

snow (स्नो) ***n.*** ice, बर्फ़, हिम। ***v.*** 1. (of snow) to fall, बर्फ़ गिरना या पड़ना। 2. to cover with snow, बर्फ़ से ढकना या आच्छादित होना।

snowball (स्नोबॉल) ***n.*** snow pressed into a small ball for playing, बर्फ़ का गोला। ***v.*** 1. to throw snowballs (at), बर्फ़ के गोले (किसी पर) फेंकना। 2. to grow rapidly in size, importance etc., तेज़ी से बढ़ना, ज़ोर पकड़ना।

snowcapped (स्नोकैप्ड) ***adj.*** covered at the top with snow, हिममंडित।

snowfall (स्नोफ़ॉल) ***n.*** a fall of snow, हिमपात।

snowline (स्नोलाइन) ***n.*** the lower boundary of a perennial snowfield, हिमरेखा।

snowman (स्नोमैन) ***n.*** a figure of a man made in snow, हिममानव।

snowy (स्नोई) ***adj.*** (snowier, snowiest) 1. marked by or covered with snow, बर्फ़ीला। 2. snow-white, हिमश्वेत।

snub (स्नब) ***v.*** 1. to rebuke, झिड़की देना, झिड़कना। 2. to suppress, दमन करना। ***n.*** a rebuke, झिड़की।

snuff (स्नफ़) ***n.*** powdered tobacco for sniffing up the nostrils, सुँघनी, नसवार। ***v.*** to put out (the candle), (मोमबत्ती) बुझाना।

snug (स्नग) ***adj.*** 1. cosy, सुखद, आरामदेह। 2. fitting closely, चुस्त।

snuggle (स्नगल) ***v.*** to draw close, (किसी के साथ) जुड़कर बैठना।

so (सो) ***adv.*** 1. thus, इस प्रकार, इसी प्रकार। 2. in a way that is suggested, उक्त ढंग से, उसी तरह। 3. to such an extent, इतना। 4. too, भी। 5. to the same extent as, वैसे ही। 6. to a great extent, very, अत्यधिक। 7. for the reason, इसलिए। ***conj.*** 1. with the result that, परिणामस्वरूप, फलतः, इसलिए। 2. in order that, जिससे।

soak (सोक) ***v.*** 1. to absorb, जज़्ब करना, सोख या चूस लेना। 2. to be immersed, to become thoroughly wet, भिगोया जाना, तर होना। 3. to drink excessively, बहुत शराब पी लेना। ***n.*** 1. the act of soaking, सोखने की क्रिया। 2. a heavy drinker, भारी पियक्कड़।

so-and-so ***n.*** a person or thing that need not be named, अमुक, फ़लाँ।

soap (सोप) ***n.*** 1. a cleaning agent or substance, साबुन। 2. a serial dealing with the daily life of some characters, ऐसा धारावाहिक जिसमें उसके किसी एक पात्र या कुछ पात्रों के जीवन की झाँकी हो। ***v.*** to apply soap to, साबुन लगाना।

soapstone (सोपस्टोन) ***n.*** a soft stone, सेलखड़ी।

soapsuds (सोपसड्स) ***n.*** (plu.) foam or lather made from soap, साबुन की झाग।

soapy (सोपी) ***adj.*** 1. of or like soap, साबुन-जैसा, झाग-भरा, साबुनी। 2. oily, चिकना।

soar (सोर) ***v.*** 1. to rise high, ऊँचा उठना। 2. to fly high, ऊँचाई पर उड़ना, ऊँचे उड़ना।

sob (सॉब) ***v.*** 1. to weep with convulsive gasps, सिसकियाँ भरना, सिसकना। 2. to utter with sobs, सिसकियाँ भरते हुए कहना। ***n.*** the act or sound of sobbing, सिसकी।

sober (सोबर) ***adj.*** 1. temperate, संयमी, मर्यादित। 2. not intoxicated, जो नशे में न हो, सौम्य। 3. without exaggeration, अत्युक्ति-रहित, अतिशयोक्तिविहीन।

sobriety (सोब्राइटी) ***n.*** the state or quality of being sober, संयम; सौम्यता; अत्युक्तिविहीनता।

so-called (सो-कॉल्ड) ***adj.*** so named or designated, तथाकथित।

soccer (सॉकर) ***n.*** football, फ़ुटबॉल का खेल।

sociable (सोशेबल) ***adj.*** friendly and companionable, समाजशील, मिलनसार, मैत्रीपूर्ण।

social (सोशल) ***adj.*** living in a community or group, सामाजिक। ***n.*** an informal gathering, अनौपचारिक गोष्ठी, मेला।

socialism (सोशलिज़्म) ***n.*** a political and economic theory advocating ownership of society of the means of production, distribution etc., समाजवाद।

socialist (सोशलिस्ट) ***adj.*** socialistic, समाजवादी। ***n.*** one who advocates

S

or practices socialism, समाजवादी।

socialite (सोशलाइट) ***n.*** a person who is prominent in fashionable society, फ़ैशनपरस्त समाज में अग्रगण्य।

socialize (सोशलाइज़) ***v.*** to take part in social activities, सामाजिक क्रियाकलापों में सम्मिलित होना।

society (सोसाइटी) ***n.*** 1. a group of people having common culture or way of life, समाज। 2. a group of persons who unite to share common interest, संस्था। 3. the rich and fashionable social class, उच्चवर्ग। 4. companionship, company, साहचर्य, संगत। 5. a community, समुदाय।

socio-economic (सोशिओ-इकनॉमिक) ***adj.*** of or relating to a combination of social and economic factors, सामाजिक-आर्थिक।

sociologist (सोशिऑलोजिस्ट) ***n.*** a specialist in sociology, समाजविज्ञानी।

sociology (सोशिऑलोजी) ***n.*** the science of society, social institutions and social relationships, समाजविज्ञान।

sociopolitical (सोशिओपोलिटिकल) ***adj.*** of or relating to a combination of social and political factors, सामाजिक-राजनीतिक।

sock[1] (सॉक) ***n.*** a short stocking, मोज़ा, जुर्राब।

sock[2] ***v.*** to hit forcefully, ज़ोरदार आघात करना।

socket (सॉकिट) ***n.*** an opening or hollow place that forms a hollow space for something, गड्ढा, कोटर, घर।

sod[1] (सॉड) ***n.*** 1. an obnoxious person, घिनौना व्यक्ति। 2. a thing that causes problems, समस्याकारक वस्तु या व्यक्ति।

sod[2] ***n.*** a piece of grass-covered surface, घास का मैदान।

soda (सोडा) ***n.*** any compound of sodium, सोडा।

soda water ***n.*** a beverage charged with carbonic acid gas, सोडावाटर।

sodden (सॉडन) ***adj.*** heavy with moisture or water, तर, तर-बतर, भीगा हुआ, गीला।

sodium (सोडियम) ***n.*** a soft silver-white metal, सोडियम।

sodomy (सॉडमी) ***n.*** unnatural copulation between male persons or between a male person and an animal, लौंडेबाज़ी, गुदामैथुन।

sofa (सोफ़ा) ***n.*** a long seat with a back and arms, सोफ़ा।

soft (सॉफ़्ट) ***adj.*** 1. not hard or firm, मुलायम, नरम, कोमल, मृदु। 2. smooth, चिकना। 3. light, weak, हलका, दुर्बल। 4. comfortable, gentle, soothing, सुखद, प्रिय। 5. easy, सरल। 6. nonalcoholic, मद्यरहित। 7. (of water) free from mineral salts, सादा (पानी)। 8. (of colour) not bright or dazzling, सादा, हलका। 9. tenderhearted, भावुक।

soften (सॉफ़न) ***v.*** to make or become soft, नरम होना या बनाना।

softly (सॉफ़्टली) ***adv.*** in a soft manner, नरमी से, कोमलतापूर्वक।

softness (सॉफ़्टनिस) ***n.*** the quality or state of being soft, मृदुता, कोमलता।

softspot (सॉफ़्टस्पॉट) ***n.*** a sentimental fondness, कोमल भाव, स्नेह।

software (सॉफ़्टवेअर) ***n.*** computer programmes, कंप्यूटर-कार्यक्रम, प्रक्रिया-सामग्री, सॉफ़्टवेअर।

S

soggy (सॉगी) ***adj.*** 1. wet, गीला, तर-बतर। 2. marshy, दलदल-भरा, दलदला।

soil[1] (सॉइल) ***n.*** the upper layer of the earth, भूमि, धरती, ज़मीन।

soil[2] ***v.*** to make or become dirty, गंदा होना या करना। ***n.*** refuse, manure or excrement, कूड़ा, खाद या मल।

sojourn (सोजर्न) ***v.*** to stay at a place temporarily, अस्थायी रूप से कहीं ठहरना या टिकना, प्रवास करना। ***n.*** a temporary stay, अस्थायी निवास, प्रवास।

solace (सोलेस) ***n.*** comfort in misery or disappointment, तसल्ली, ढारस, सांत्वना। ***v.*** to console, तसल्ली देना, सांत्वना देना, ढारस बँधाना।

solar (सोलर) ***adj.*** of or relating to the sun, सूर्य-संबंधी, सौर।

sold (सोल्ड) ***v.*** p.t. & p.p. of sell.

solder (सोल्डर) ***n.*** a metal alloy for cementing metal parts, राँगा। ***v.*** to join with solder, राँगे से टाँका लगाना, झालना।

soldier (सोल्जर) ***n.*** one engaged in military service, सैनिक, फ़ौजी। ***v.*** to work as soldier, सैनिक की तरह काम करना।

sole[1] (सोल) ***n.*** 1. the under surface of a foot, (पैर का) तलवा। 2. the part of a footwear on which the sole rests, (जूते का) तल्ला। ***v.*** to furnish with a sole, तल्ला लगाना।

sole[2] ***adj.*** 1. being only one, इकलौता, अकेला, एकल। 2. belonging exclusively to one, एकमात्र।

solemn (सॉलम) ***adj.*** 1. performed with full ceremony, रीतिपूर्वक या विधिवत् किया जानेवाला, रीतिपूर्ण, विधिपूर्ण। 2. having a sense of religious like importance, सत्यनिष्ठ। 3. grave, गंभीर।

solemnity (सलेम्निटी) ***n.*** 1. the quality of being solemn, सत्यनिष्ठा। 2. a solemn event, पर्व, उत्सव, समारोह। 3. formality, औपचारिकता। 4. a formal religious act, अनुष्ठान। 5. seriousness, गंभीरता।

solemnize (सॉलम्नाइज़) ***v.*** 1. to perform with ceremony, रीतिपूर्वक या विधिवत् करना, अनुष्ठान करना। 2. to celebrate, मनाना, धूमधाम से मनाना, रचाना।

solicit (सलिसिट) ***v.*** 1. to entreat, याचना करना, चिरौरी करना। 2. to accost (a man) for immoral purposes, (वेश्या द्वारा पुरुष को) बुलाना।

solicitor (सलिसिटर) ***n.*** a lawyer who advises his clients and prepares cases for barristers etc., सॉलिसिटर।

solicitous (सलिसिटस) ***adj.*** 1. eager, उत्सुक, इच्छुक। 2. showing concern (for someone), चिंतित।

solicitude (सलिसिट्यूड) ***n.*** 1. eagerness, उत्सुकता। 2. concern, ध्यान, चिंता।

solid (सॉलिड) ***adj.*** 1. having a definite shape, not liquid or gaseous, ठोस। 2. not hollowed out, ठोस। 3. of good quality and substance, ठोस, मज़बूत। 4. sound, पक्का, मज़बूत। ***n.*** a solid figure, पिंड, घनाकृति।

solidarity (सॉलिडैरिटी) ***n.*** 1. unity of interest, purposes, sympathies among group or class, एकजुटता, एकता। 2. fellow-feeling, भाईचारा, बंधुभाव।

solidify (सलिडिफ़ाइ) ***v.*** to make or become solid, ठोस होना या बनाना।

soliloquy (सलिलक्वी) ***n.*** the act of

S

speaking to oneself, स्वगत कथन।

solitary (सॉलिटरी) ***adj.*** 1. alone, एकाकी, अकेला। 2. sole, एकमात्र। 3. lonely, unfrequented, तन्हा, निस्संग, एकांत में होनेवाला।

solitude (सॉलिट्यूड) ***n.*** 1. the condition of being alone, एकाकीपन, अकेलापन। 2. a lonely place, एकांत।

solo (सोलो) ***n.*** 1. a musical composition for a single voice or instrument, एक व्यक्ति के लिए गाने या बजाने के लिए तैयार की गई रचना। 2. a flight in which a pilot is unaccompanied, अकेले भरी जानेवाली उड़ान। 3. a performance carried out by a single person, एकल प्रदर्शन। ***adj.*** sole, alone, अकेला, एकल।

soloist (सोलोइस्ट) ***n.*** a person who plays on a solo, एकल वादक या गायक।

solstice (सॉल्स्टिस) ***n.*** either of the times in the year when the sun is farthest from the equator, एक अयन की समाप्ति और दूसरे का आरंभ, अयनांत; summer solstice, कर्क संक्रांति; winter solstice, मकर संक्रांति।

solubility (सॉल्युबिलिटी) ***n.*** the quality or state of being soluble, घुलनशीलता, विलेयता।

soluble (सॉल्युबल) ***adj.*** 1. capable of being dissolved, घुलनशील, विलेय। 2. solvable, समाधेय।

solution (सल्यूशन) ***n.*** 1. a liquid in which something is dissolved, सलूशन, घोल। 2. the act of solving a problem, समाधान, हल। 3. an answer to a problem, हल, समाधान।

solve (सॉल्व) ***v.*** to find a solution to, हल करना, समाधान करना।

solvent (सॉल्वन्ट) ***adj.*** 1. having enough money to pay one's debts, ऋण चुकाने में सक्षम। 2. capable of dissolving another substance, विलायक। ***n.*** a liquid capable of dissolving another substance, विलायक।

sombre, somber (सॉम्बर) ***adj.*** 1. sad, melancholy, खिन्न, दुखी। 2. grave, गंभीर। 3. gloomy, निराशाजनक। 4. dark, काला।

some (सम) ***adj. & pron.*** 1. being an unknown or unspecified one, कोई। 2. an unspecified number, quantity or extent, an amount that is less than the whole, कुछ। ***adv.*** 1. approximately, लगभग। 2. somewhat, कुछ-कुछ, कुछ।

somebody (सम्बॉडी) ***n. & pron.*** 1. an unspecified person, कोई। 2. a person of importance, विशिष्ट व्यक्ति।

somehow (समहाउ) ***adv.*** by some (unknown) means, किसी तरह, किसी न किसी तरह।

someone (समवन) ***n. & pron.*** somebody, कोई।

somersault (समरसॉल्ट) ***n.*** a leap or roll in which a person turns his heels over his head, कलैया, कलाबाज़ी। ***v.*** to perform a somersault, कलैया लगाना/मारना, कलाबाज़ी खाना।

something (समथिन्ग) ***n. & pron.*** some unspecified thing, कुछ, कोई चीज़।

sometime (समटाइम) ***adv.*** at sometime (in future), किसी समय (भविष्य में), कभी। ***adj.*** former, late, पुराना, भूतपूर्व।

sometimes (समटाइम्ज़) ***adv.***

sometimes but not always, occasionally, कभी-कभी।

somewhat (समवॉट) ***adv.*** to some extent, कुछ, कुछ-कुछ।

somewhere (समवेअर) ***adv.*** to a place unspecified or unknown, कहीं।

somnambulist (सॉमनैम्ब्यूलिस्ट) ***adj.*** a sleepwalker, नींद में चलनेवाला, निद्राचर।

son (सन) ***n.*** a male offspring of human beings, बेटा, पुत्र, लड़का।

sonata (सनाटा) ***n.*** a musical composition for one instrument or two, वाद्य-रचना, सोनाटा।

song (सॉन्ग) ***n.*** 1. a brief musical composition written for singing, गाना, गान। 2. an act or art of singing, गायन।

sonic (सॉनिक) ***adj.*** of or relating to sound waves, ध्वनि तरंगों से संबद्ध, ध्वनिक।

son-in-law (सन-इन-लॉ) ***n.*** (plu. sons-in-law) the husband of one's daughter, दामाद।

sonnet (सॉनिट) ***n.*** a poem of fourteen lines, चतुर्दशपदी।

sonorous (सॉनरस) ***adj.*** resonant, गूँजता हुआ, निनादी। 2. melodious, सुरीला। 3. impressive, प्रभावपूर्ण।

soon (सून) ***adv.*** 1. immediately, जल्दी ही। 2. at once, promptly, फ़ौरन, तुरंत।

soot (सूट) ***n.*** a black substance formed by combustion, कालिख़।

soothe (सूद) ***v.*** 1. to calm, शांत करना। 2. to ease, राहत पहुँचाना।

soothsayer (सूथसेअर) ***n.*** a person who foretells the future, भविष्यवक्ता, ज्योतिषी।

sooty (सूटी) ***adj.*** 1. covered with soot, कालिख़-लगा। 2. like soot, काला।

sop (सॉप) ***v.*** 1. to dip (in a liquid, तरल पदार्थ में) भिगोना, तर करना। 2. to take up by absorption, सोख लेना। ***n.*** 1. a piece of bread dipped in a liquid, तरल पदार्थ में भिगोया हुआ रोटी का टुकड़ा या कौर। 2. something given as appeasement, मुँह-भराई, रिश्वत, घूस।

sophisticated (सफ़िस्टिकेटिड) ***adj.*** 1. worldly-wise, दुनियादार, सयाना। 2. appealing to the taste of sophisticates, शिष्ट, शिष्टतापूर्ण। 3. complicated, जटिल। 4. refined, परिष्कृत।

sophistication (सफ़िस्टिकेशन) ***n.*** 1. the state or quality of being sophisticated, दुनियादारी, सयानापन। 2. refinement, परिष्करण, सुसंस्करण नफ़ासत।

sophistry (सॉफ़िस्ट्री) ***n.*** misleading argumentation, कुतर्क।

soppy (सॉपी) ***adj.*** 1. drenched, very wet, तर-ब-तर। 2. sentimental, भावुक।

sorcerer (सॉर्सरर) ***n.*** a person who practises sorcery, झाड़-फूँक करनेवाला, ओझा।

sordid (सॉर्डिड) ***adj.*** 1. foul, filthy, मलिन, गंदा, मैला-कुचैला। 2. wretched, हेय, घिनौना।

sore (सोर) ***adj.*** 1. causing annoyance, कष्टदायक। 2. distressed, दुखी। ***n.*** a sore place, दुखता अंग।

sorrel (सॉरल) ***n.*** reddish brown colour, लाली लिये भूरा रंग।

sorrow (सॉरो) ***n.*** 1. sadness or grief, due to disappointment or loss, दुख, व्यथा, शोक। 2. a cause of sadness or grief, दुख का कारण। *v.* 1. to feel sorrow, दुखी होना। 2. to express sorrow, व्यथा व्यक्त करना।

sorry (सॉरी) ***adj.*** feeling regret or sympathy, दुखी। ***interj.*** used to express mild regret or for apologizing, खेद या क्षमा द्योतित करने के लिए प्रयुक्त।

sort (सॉर्ट) ***n.*** a particular kind or variety, प्रकार, क़िस्म, तरह। ***v.*** to arrange according to class, size, address etc., छाँटना, छँटनी करना। □ **sort out,** (i) छाँटना, (ii) हल खोजना।

sortie (सॉर्टी) ***n.*** 1. a flight of a combat war-plane, बमबारी के लिए वायुयान द्वारा भरी गई उड़ान। 2. an armed attack, चढ़ाई, धावा।

SOS ***n.*** a call for help, सहायता के लिए पुकार, गुहार।

so-so (सो-सो) ***adj.*** mediocre, सामान्य-सा।

sot (सॉट) ***n.*** a habitual drunkard, पियक्कड़।

sought after (सॉट आफ़्टर) ***adj.*** much sought for purchase or use, (वस्तु) जिसके लिए हाय-तौबा मची हो।

soul (सोल) ***n.*** 1. the immortal element in a person, आत्मा। 2. a human being, person, जीवात्मा, जीव। 3. the central or vital part of something, प्राण, जान। 4. a person's feeling or moral nature, अंतरात्मा, अंत:करण।

sound (साउन्ड) ***n.*** 1. a distinctive noise, anything that can be heard, आवाज़, ध्वनि। 2. an articulation made by the vocal apparatus, मुँह से निकलनेवाली ध्वनि, शब्द। ***v.*** 1. to make a sound, आवाज़ करना, ध्वनित करना। 2. to utter, (वर्ण) बोलना। 3. to seem to be, प्रतीत होना। ***adj.*** 1. healthy, स्वस्थ। 2. free from damage, सुरक्षित। 3. based on valid reasoning, तर्कसंगत। 4. deep, गहरा।

soundly (साउन्डली) ***adv.*** 1. in a sound manner, अच्छी तरह। 2. completely, पूर्ण रूप से।

soup (सूप) ***n.*** a liquid food made by boiling vegetables, meat, fish etc., सूप, रसा, शोरबा।

soupy (सूपी) ***adj.*** 1. like soup, रसेदार। 2. over-sentimental, अति-भावुक।

sour (साउअर) ***adj.*** 1. having a sharp taste, खट्टा, अम्ल। 2. spoiled, ख़राब। 3. unpleasant, अप्रिय। 4. bad-tempered, क्रोधी, चिड़चिड़ा। ***v.*** to become sour, खट्टा या ख़राब हो जाना।

source (सोर्स) ***n.*** 1. a place of origin of a river, उद्‌गम, मूल। 2. the place from which something comes or is obtained, स्रोत। 3. a person or book that supplies information, सूचना-स्रोत।

south (साउथ) ***n.*** the direction opposite to north, दक्षिण, जनूब। ***adj.*** of or toward south, दक्षिणी, जनूबी।

southerner (सदर्नर) ***n.*** a native of the south, दक्षिणवासी।

souvenir (सुविनिअर) ***n.*** 1. something serving as a reminder of a person, place or occasion, स्मृतिचिह्न, सौग़ात, निशानी। 2. a magazine serving as a reminder, स्मारिका।

sovereign (सॉवरिन) ***n.*** 1. a supreme ruler, राजा, महाराजा या प्रधान शासक, संप्रभु। 2. British gold coin, एक पौंड का सिक्का, अशरफ़ी, गिन्नी। ***adj.***

possessing sovereign power, संप्रभु, प्रभुसत्तासंपन्न, प्रभुत्वसंपन्न।

sovereignty (सॉवरिनिटी) ***n.*** 1. sovereign power, प्रभुसत्ता। 2. complete independence, पूर्ण स्वराज्य।

sow (सो) ***v.*** (sowed, sowed/sown, sowing) 1. to plant seed in, बोना, बुआई करना। 2. to implant, introduce or spread, बीजारोपित करना, रोपना या छितराना। ***n.*** fully grown female pig, मोटी-ताज़ी सुअरनी।

soya bean (सॉइअबीन) ***n.*** a kind of bean used as food, सोयाबीन।

spa (स्पा) ***n.*** a mineral spring, खनिज जलवाला सोता, खनिज-सोता।

space (स्पेस) ***n.*** 1. the expanse in which solar system exists, आकाश; अंतरिक्ष। 2. distance, अंतराल, दूरी, फ़ासला। 3. a blank or empty area, ख़ाली जगह। 4. an area as an accommodation, जगह, ख़ाली जगह। 5. a period or interval of time, अंतराल, बीच का समय। ***v.*** to arrange with spaces between, बीच-बीच में जगह रखना, अंतर देना।

spacecraft, spaceship (स्पेसक्राफ़्ट, स्पेसशिप) ***n.*** a vehicle for travelling in outer space, अंतरिक्ष-यान।

spacious (स्पेशॅस) ***adj.*** having a large capacity or space, खुला, विस्तृत।

spade (स्पेड) ***n.*** 1. a tool for digging ground, कुदाल, फावड़ा। 2. any of a suit of playing cards with an inverted heart-shaped leaf, हुकुम (का पत्ता)। ***v.*** to dig with a spade, फावड़ा चलाना।

spadework (स्पेडवर्क) ***n.*** preparatory work, प्रारंभिक कार्य या तैयारी।

span (स्पैन) ***n.*** 1. space or interval (between two points, बीच का) फैलाव या विस्तार। 2. a period of time, अवधि; span of life, जीवन-काल। 3. the distance or part between the one support of the bridge to another, पुल के दो खंभों के बीच की दूरी या भाग। ***v.*** 1. to measure with a hand, बित्ते से नापना। 2. to bridge, पारना।

spangle (स्पैन्गल) ***n.*** a small thin piece of glittering material, चमकी, सितारा। ***v.*** to cover with spangles, चमकी लगाना, सितारे लगाना।

spank (स्पैन्क) ***v.*** to slap on the buttocks, चूतड़ पर प्रहार करना।

spanner (स्पैनर) ***n.*** a type of wrench, पाना, रैंच, स्पैनर।

spar[1] (स्पार) ***n.*** a mast, मस्तूल।

spar[2] ***v.*** 1. to box, मुक्केबाज़ी करना। 2. to wrangle, झगड़ा करना।

spare (स्पेअर) ***v.*** 1. to refrain from killing, छोड़ देना, बख़्श देना। 2. to refrain from destroying, छोड़ देना। 3. to exempt, जाने देना, छोड़ देना। 4. to use with great restraint, बचा रखना, सँभाले रहना। 5. to part with, छोड़ना। 6. to save, बचा रखना, पीछे रखना। ***adj.*** 1. extra, free, अतिरिक्त, फ़ालतू, ख़ाली। 2. kept in reserve, बचाकर रखा हुआ। 3. simple and plain, सादा, साधारण। ***n.*** a thing kept as a replacement in case of damage or loss, कोई अतिरिक्त पुर्ज़ा/वस्तु।

sparing (स्पेअरिंग) ***adj.*** thrifty, frugal, किफ़ायत करनेवाला, मितव्ययी।

spark (स्पार्क) ***n.*** 1. a glowing particle, as one thrown off by a burning substance, चिनगारी, स्फुलिंग। 2. a brief flash of light, प्रकाशकण।

S

3. a particle (of something, किसी चीज़ का) कण, लेश। *v.* to give off sparks, चिनगारियाँ छोड़ना।

sparkle (स्पार्कल) *v.* to glitter, चमचम करना, चमकना-दमकना। *n.* 1. a spark, चिनगारी। 2. gleam, चमक, दीप्ति।

sparkling (स्पार्कलिंग) *adj.* 1. glittering, चमचमाता हुआ, जगमग। 2. lively, ज़िंदादिल, रसिक, सहृदय।

sparrow (स्पैरो) *n.* a small bird, the house sparrow, चिड़िया, गौरैया।

sparse (स्पार्स) *adj.* 1. not dense, झिल्लड़। 2. scattered, छितराया हुआ।

Spartan (स्पार्टन) *adj.* 1. of or pertaining to the ancient Greek city of Sparta, स्पार्टा-संबंधी। 2. very strict, कठोर, अनुशासनप्रिय। *n.* a citizen of Sparta, स्पार्टा का निवासी।

spasm (स्पैज़्म) *n.* 1. muscular contraction, मांसपेशियों में होनेवाली सिकुड़न, ऐंठन या तनाव। 2. a sudden brief spell of activity or emotion, दौरा, प्रकोप।

spasmodic (स्पैज़्मॉडिक) *adj.* 1. of or like spasm, सिकुड़न या ऐंठन-संबंधी, 2. irregular, अनियमित।

spastic (स्पैस्टिक) *adj.* suffering from cerebral palsy, दिमाग़ी लकवे से पीड़ित।

spat *v.* p.t. & p.p. of spit.

spate (स्पेट) *n.* a sudden flood, अचानक आनेवाली बाढ़।

spatial (स्पेशल) *adj.* of space, आकाश-संबंधी, अंतरिक्ष-संबंधी।

spatter (स्पैटर) *v.* 1. to sprinkle, छिड़कना, छिड़काव करना। 2. to scatter, बिखेरना। 3. to splash, छींटे डालना, छपछपाना। *n.* a splash, छींटा।

spatula (स्पैचुला) *n.* a utensil with a broad flexible blade for lifting or stirring food, उथला चम्मच, चमची।

spawn (स्पॉन) *n.* the mass of eggs of fish, frogs etc., मछली, मेढक आदि के अंडों की ढेरी। *v.* 1. to produce eggs, अंडे देना। 2. to produce offspring, बच्चे देना।

speak (स्पीक) *v.* (spoke, spoken, speaking) 1. to utter, बोलना, बोलना-चालना। 2. to say, express, कहना, बतलाना, अभिव्यक्त करना। 3. to hold a conversation, बातचीत करना। 4. to make a speech, भाषण देना। 5. to be indicative or suggestive, सांकेतिक होना।

speaker (स्पीकर) *n.* 1. one who speaks, वक्ता। 2. the chairperson of a legislature, अध्यक्ष, प्रमुख। 3. a loudspeaker, लाउडस्पीकर।

spear (स्पिअर) *n.* a long shaft with a sharp blade, बरछा, भाला, नेज़ा।

spearhead (स्पिअरहेड) *n.* 1. the sharp head of the blade of a spear, बरछे की नोक, शूलाग्र। 2. one who leads the attack, सेना की अगुआई करनेवाला, अग्रणी। *v.* to be the spearhead of, अगुआ होना, अगुवाई करना।

special (स्पेशल) *adj.* distinct or exceptional, not general, विशेष, विशिष्ट, ख़ास। *n.* a special thing or person, विशिष्ट वस्तु या व्यक्ति।

specialist (स्पेशलिस्ट) *n.* one who has specialized in a special branch of learning or activity, विशेषज्ञ।

speciality (स्पेशैलिटी) *n.* a special quality, विशेष गुण, विशेषता, विशिष्टता।

specialize (स्पेशलाइज़) *v.* to devote oneself to special activity or study,

S

विशेष ज्ञान प्राप्त करना, (विषय का) विशेषज्ञ बनना।

species (स्पीसीज़) ***n.*** a kind, sort or variety, प्रजाति, जाति, वर्ग।

specific (स्पिसिफ़िक) ***adj.*** 1. particular, विशेष, ख़ास। 2. definite, निश्चित।

specify (स्पेसिफ़ाइ) ***v.*** to state in detail, ब्योरा देना, विस्तारपूर्वक वर्णन करना, विनिर्देश करना।

specimen (स्पेसिमन) ***n.*** an example of a whole or class, sample, नमूना, बानगी।

specious (स्पीशस) ***adj.*** 1. seeming true or correct but actually false or wrong, सत्याभासी। 2. useless, निरर्थक।

speck (स्पेक) ***n.*** a very small spot or particle, बिंदु, कण। ☐ **not a speck of,** कण-भर भी नहीं, तिल-भर भी नहीं, ज़रा भी नहीं।

spectacle (स्पेक्टकल) ***n.*** an interesting or impressive sight, तमाशा, नज़ारा।

spectacles (स्पेक्टकल्ज़) ***n.*** (plu.) eye-glasses, चश्मा, ऐनक।

spectacular (स्पेक्टैक्यूलर) ***adj.*** 1. grand, चमत्कारपूर्ण, शानदार। 2. dramatic, नाटकीय।

spectator (स्पेक्टेटर) ***n.*** an onlooker, viewer, दर्शक, तमाशबीन।

spectral (स्पेक्ट्रल) ***adj.*** 1. of or like a spectre, प्रेत-संबंधी। 2. of or pertaining to a spectrum, वर्णपट-संबंधी।

spectre (स्पेक्टर) ***n.*** 1. a ghost, प्रेत, भूत; spectre of war, युद्ध का भूत। 2. phantom, (काली) छाया।

spectrum (स्पेक्ट्रम) ***n.*** (plu. spectra) 1. the distribution of colours produced when white light is dispersed by a prism, वर्णक्रम, स्पेक्ट्रम। 2. reflection, प्रतिबिंब, परछाई।

speculate (स्पेक्युलेट) ***v.*** 1. to reflect, मनन करना, चिंतन करना। 2. to assume a business risk in the hope of gain, सट्टा खेलना, सट्टेबाज़ी करना। 3. to guess, अनुमान लगाना।

speculation (स्पेक्युलेशन) ***n.*** the act of speculating, चिंतन, अनुमान; सट्टा, सट्टेबाज़ी।

speculator (स्पेक्युलेटर) ***n.*** one who speculates, सट्टेबाज़, सटोरिया।

speech (स्पीच) ***n.*** 1. the act of speaking, भाषण। 2. the power of speaking, वाक्शक्ति। 3. that which is spoken, उक्ति, कथन।

speechless (स्पीचलिस) ***adj.*** unable to speak, मूक।

speed (स्पीड) ***n.*** 1. rate of motion, गति, रफ़्तार, चाल। 2. rapidity, तेज़ी। ***v.*** (sped/speeded, speeding) 1. to move rapidly, तेज़ी से चलना, जल्दी करना। 2. to drive at excessive or illegal speed, बहुत तेज़ गाड़ी चलाना, गति-सीमा का उल्लंघन करना।

speedometre (स्पीडॉमिटर) ***n.*** an instrument for measuring the speed of a vehicle, गतिसूचक यंत्र, गतियंत्र।

speedy (स्पीडी) ***adj.*** (speedier, speediest) moving speedily, तीव्रगामी, तेज़।

spell[1] (स्पेल) ***v.*** 1. to name or write in correct order the letters (of a word, किसी शब्द के) क्रमिक वर्णों को लिखना या बोलना, वर्णोच्चारण करना। 2. to mean, सूचित या व्यक्त करना।

spell[2] ***n.*** 1. a word or formula

S

believed to have magic power, जादू, सम्मोहन, वशीकरण, सम्मोहिनी। 2. a strong attraction, तीव्र आकर्षण।

spell[3] ***n.*** 1. a short period, अल्पावधि, दौर। 2. a period of rest from work, विश्रांति। 3. a period of illness or distress, दुख या बीमारी की घड़ी।

spellbound (स्पेलबाउन्ड) ***adj.*** fascinated, मंत्रमुग्ध।

spelt (स्पेल्ट) ***v.*** p.t. & p.p. of spell.

spelling (स्पेलिंग) ***n.*** the letters composing the words, वर्तनी, हिज्जे।

spend (स्पेन्ड) ***v.*** (spent, spending) 1. to pay out money in buying something, ख़र्च करना, व्यय करना। 2. to use up, उपयोग करना। 3. to pass, बीतना, गुज़ारना, व्यतीत करना। 4. to waste, ज़ाया करना, व्यर्थ गँवाना।

spendthrift (स्पेन्डथ्रिफ़्ट) ***n.*** one who spends money in an extravagant manner, फ़िज़ूलख़र्च, अपव्ययी, उड़ाऊ-खाऊ।

sperm (स्पर्म) ***n.*** 1. a male reproductive cell, शुक्राणु। 2. semen, वीर्य, शुक्र।

sphere (स्फ़िअर) ***n.*** 1. a round solid figure, गोल पिंड, गोला। 2. an area of influence, control or significance, अधिक्षेत्र, क्षेत्र।

spherical (स्फ़ेरिकल) ***adj.*** having the form of a sphere, गोलाकार, गोलीय।

sphinx (स्फ़िन्क्स) ***n.*** any of the ancient stone statues in Egypt having the body of a lion and the head of a man, ram or hawk, मिस्र की प्राचीन ऐसी प्रस्तर मूर्ति जिसका धड़ शेर का और सिर आदमी, भेड़े या बाज़ का हो, स्फिंक्स।

spice (स्पाइस) ***n.*** 1. any of various vegetable substances used as flavouring, मसाला। 2. any interesting or stimulating thing, कोई मनोरंजक या उद्दीपक बात। ***v.*** to flavour with spice, मसाला डालना, स्वादिष्ट बनाना, मज़ेदार बनाना।

spick-and-span ***adj.*** neat and clean, चमाचम, नया-जैसा, बना-ठना।

spider (स्पाइडर) ***n.*** an insect that spins webs, मकड़ी, लूता।

spike[1] (स्पाइक) ***n.*** 1. a sharp point, नोक। 2. a large nail, बड़ा कील, काँटा। 3. (plu.) shoes used by athletes, खिलाड़ियों के जूते। ***v.*** 1. to secure with a spike, कील जड़कर मज़बूत बनाना। 2. to pierce with a spike, कील से छेदना।

spike[2] ***n.*** an ear of a corn, बाली।

spiky (स्पाइकी) ***adj.*** long and pointed, लंबा और नुकीला।

spill (स्पिल) ***v.*** (spilled/spilt, spilling) 1. to cause to run, flow or fall out from a container, छलक उठना या छलका देना, गिर जाना, छितरा जाना। 2. to throw off, गिरा देना, फेंक देना। 3. to shed (blood, रक्त) बहाना। □ **spill the beans,** रहस्य प्रकट कर देना। ***n.*** 1. an act of spilling or the state of being spilled, छलकना या छलकाना। 2. the amount spilled, छलकी हुई राशि। 3. a fall from a horse, घोड़े से गिरना।

spin (स्पिन) ***v.*** (spun, spinning) 1. to rotate on an axis, धुरी पर घूमना, चक्कर लगाना। 2. to cause to rotate, घुमाना। 3. to draw out and twist into threads, कातना, कताई करना। 4. (in cricket) to cause to turn a ball, स्पिन कराना, प्रचक्रण करना। ***n.*** spinning movement, स्पिन, प्रचक्रण।

spinach (स्पिनिच) ***n.*** a vegetable with dark green leaves, पालक।

spinal (स्पाइनल) ***adj.*** of the spine, मेरुदंडीय; spinal column, मेरुदंड; spinal cord, मेरुरज्जु।

spindle (स्पिन्डल) ***n.*** 1. a slender rounded rod on which fibres are twisted, तकला, तकुआ। 2. a pin axis that revolves, धुरी।

spine (स्पाइन) ***n.*** 1. the backbone, रीढ़, मेरुदंड। 2. a bound edge of a book, (किताब का) पुट्ठा। 3. needle-like projection of certain vegetables or animals, (पशु/पक्षी का) काँटा, खाँग।

spineless (स्पाइनलिस) ***adj.*** 1. having no backbone, बिना रीढ़ का, मेरुदंडविहीन। 2. lacking courage or strength of character, साहसविहीन, दब्बू या ढुलमुल।

spinner (स्पिनर) ***n.*** 1. a person who spins, कातनेवाला व्यक्ति। 2. a machine that spins, कताई मशीन। 3. a bowler who bowls ball with a spinning motion, स्पिनर, चक्री गेंदबाज़।

spinning wheel ***n.*** a wheel-like machine for spinning, चरखा।

spinster (स्पिन्स्टर) ***n.*** a woman who has not married, अविवाहित स्त्री।

spiny (स्पाइनी) ***adj.*** (spinier, spiniest) full of spines, काँटों से भरा, कँटीदार।

spiral (स्पाइरल) ***adj.*** circling continuously around a point or centre in curves that constantly increase or decrease in size, सर्पिल, चक्करदार, पेंचदार। ***n.*** 1. a spiral line, सर्पिल रेखा। 2. a thing of spiral form, कुंडली, पेचक आदि। 3. a continuous upward or downward movement, निरंतर बढ़ोतरी या कमी। ***v.*** to assume spiral shape or course, सर्पिल रूप या चक्राकार रास्ता अपनाना।

spire (स्पाइर) ***n.*** a pointed structure in the form of a tall cone, नुकीला शिखर, मीनार, लाट।

spirit (स्पिरिट) ***n.*** 1. the animating force of living things, जीवनी शक्ति। 2. soul, आत्मा। 3. life, प्राण, जान। 4. a ghost, प्रेतात्मा, भूत। 5. a person's nature, मनुष्य की प्रकृति। 6. a person with certain qualities, मनीषी, महापुरुष। 7. the charac-teristic quality or mood of something, मुख्य गुण, मनोदशा या प्रकृति। 8. courage, साहस। 9. an alcoholic solution or beverage, मद्यसार, मद्य।

spirited (स्पिरिटिड) ***adj.*** 1. lively, vigorous, जीवंत, ज़ोरदार, साहसपूर्ण। 2. having spirits of certain kind, भावनावाला।

spiritless (स्पिरिटलिस) ***adj.*** 1. not spirited, निर्जीव, निस्तेज। 2. sad, उदास, खिन्न।

spiritual (स्पिरिचुअल) ***adj.*** 1. of the human spirit, आत्मा-संबंधी, आत्मिक। 2. not temporal, अध्यात्म-संबंधी, आध्यात्मिक।

spiritualism (स्पिरिचुअलिज़म) ***n.*** 1. the philosophical doctrine that reality is immaterial and therefore spiritual, अध्यात्मवाद। 2. the belief that the spirit of the dead communicates with the living, प्रेतात्मवाद, प्रेतविद्या।

spirt (स्पर्ट) ***v.*** = spurt.

spit (स्पिट) ***v.*** (spat/spit, spitting) 1. to expel saliva from the

S

mouth, थूकना, लार टपकाना। 2. to utter violenty, क्रोधपूर्वक बोलना। *n.* 1. spittle, थूक। 2. saliva, लार। 3. the act of spitting, थूकना।

spite (स्पाइट) *n.* an evil feeling against, malice, द्वेष, विद्वेष। *v.* 1. to treat maliciously, द्वेष करना, ईर्ष्या करना। 2. to vex, परेशान करना।

spitfire (स्पिटफ़ाइर) *n.* a quick-tempered person, अत्यंत क्रोधी, दुर्वासा।

spittle (स्पिटल) *n.* spit or saliva, थूक या लार।

spittoon (स्पिटून) *n.* a vessel for spitting into, थूकदान, पीकदान, उगालदान।

splash (स्प्लैश) *v.* 1. to cause (a liquid) to fly or scatter, (जल आदि) छींटना, उछालना, छपछप करना। 2. to dash (a liquid) upon, डालना, फेंकना। 3. to be splashed, फेंका जाना, (छींटें) पड़ना। 4. to display in large prints, (अख़बार आदि में) मोटे अक्षरों में छापना या महत्त्वपूर्ण स्थान पर छापना, उछालना। *n.* 1. the act or sound of splashing, छपछप, छपाक। 2. a quantity of liquid splashed, छींटा। 3. a patch, धब्बा।

spleen (स्प्लीन) *n.* an organ at the left of stomach functioning as a blood filter, तिल्ली।

splendid (स्प्लेन्डिड) *adj.* 1. magnificent, शानदार, भव्य, वैभवपूर्ण। 2. excellent, उत्कृष्ट।

splendour (स्प्लेन्डर) *n.* 1. great light or lustre, चमक-दमक। 2. magnificence, grandeur, शान, वैभव, गौरव।

splice (स्प्लाइस) *v.* to join the ends (of a rope) by weaving together, (रस्से के) दो सिरों को जोड़ना, गूँथना, गाँठना, सटाना।

splint (स्प्लिन्ट) *n.* a thin flexible wooden strip, खपची।

splinter (स्प्लिन्टर) *n.* a thin sharp piece of a glass, stone, wood etc., किरच।

split (स्प्लिट) *v.* (split, splitting) 1. to cut or divide into two or more parts, टुकड़े करना, काटना, चीरना या विभक्त करना। 2. to become broken into parts, टुकड़े-टुकड़े होना, फूटना, चिरना, विभक्त होना। 3. to part company, साथ छोड़ना, अलग होना। 4. to divide and share, बाँटना। 5. to separate or be separated into factions, गुटों में विभक्त करना या होना। *n.* 1. the act or process of splitting, टूट-फूट, विभाजन, विच्छेद। 2. something split or divided, टूटी, फूटी या विभक्त वस्तु।

split-up (स्प्लिट-अप) *n.* separation, अलगाव, विच्छेद, पार्थक्य।

splodge (स्प्लॉज) *n.* a stain, धब्बा, दाग़ या चित्ती। *v.* to mark with splodges, दाग़ लगाना, धब्बे या चित्तियाँ डालना।

splotch (स्प्लॉच) *n. & v.* = splodge.

splutter (स्प्लटर) *v.* 1. to make a rapid series of spitting sounds, थू-थू करना। 2. to speak rapidly and indistinctly, बड़बड़ाना। *n.* 1. an act or noise of spluttering, थू-थू। 2. incoherent speech, बड़बड़, बड़बड़ाहट।

spoil (स्पॉइल) *v.* (spoiled/spoilt, spoiling) 1. to damage, ख़राब कर देना, विकृत कर देना। 2. to become rotten, सड़-गल जाना, विकृत या ख़राब हो जाना। *n.* (plu.) plunder, लूट का माल।

S

spoke (स्पोक) ***n.*** 1. one of the rods connecting the hub and rim of a wheel, तीली। 2. a rung of a ladder, (सीढ़ी का) डंडा।

spokesman (स्पोक्समैन) ***n.*** one who speaks for another or others, प्रवक्ता।

sponge (स्पन्ज) ***n.*** a springy substance with a porous structure used for cleaning, washing etc., स्पंज। ***v.*** 1. to clean with a sponge, स्पंज से साफ़ करना। 2. to moisten with a sponge, स्पंज से पुचारा देना।

spongy (स्पन्जी) ***adj.*** springy and porous, स्पंजी।

sponsor (स्पॉन्सर) ***n.*** 1. a person or group who assumes responsibility for another for a television programme, प्रायोजक। 2. a supporter, समर्थक। 3. a godfather, धर्मपिता। ***v.*** 1. to act as a sponsor for, प्रायोजक बनना, प्रायोजित करना। 2. to be a supporter for, समर्थक बनना, समर्थन करना।

spontaneity (स्पॉन्टनीअटी) ***n.*** the quality or state of being spontaneous, सहजता, स्वाभाविकता।

spontaneous (स्पॉन्टेनिअस) ***adj.*** 1. resulting from natural impulse, अनायास होनेवाला, सहज, स्वाभाविक। 2. natural, नैसर्गिक, प्राकृतिक।

spoof (स्पूफ़) ***n.*** 1. a parody, पैरोडी। 2. a hoax, चकमा, झाँसा।

spool (स्पूल) ***n.*** a reel on which thread, wire, film, tape etc. is wound, चरखी, फिरकी।

spoon (स्पून) ***n.*** a utensil used in eating or serving food, चम्मच, चमचा। ***v.*** to take with a spoon, चम्मच से लेना।

sporadic (स्पोरैडिक) ***adj.*** occurring here and there, छिट-पुट, कहीं-कहीं होनेवाला।

spore (स्पोर) ***n.*** a tiny reproductive cell of plants, बीजाणु।

sport (स्पोर्ट) ***n.*** 1. an active pastime, game, खेल, क्रीड़ा। 2. playful or good-humoured joking, हँसी-खेल। 3. (plu.) games collectively, खेल-कूद। ***v.*** 1. to play, खेलना। 2. to amuse oneself, मन-बहलाव करना। 3. to wear or display, पहनना या दिखावा करना।

sporting (स्पोर्टिंग) ***adj.*** 1. interested in sport, खेलों का शौक़ीन। 2. concerned with sport, खेल-संबंधी। 3. courageous, साहसिक; sporting chance, साहसिक अवसर।

sportsman (स्पोर्ट्समैन) ***n.*** one who takes part in sports, खिलाड़ी।

sportsmanship (स्पोर्ट्समैनशिप) ***n.*** sportsman-like behaviour, खेल-भावना।

spot (स्पॉट) ***n.*** 1. a mark or stain, दाग़, धब्बा, चित्ती। 2. a position, location, स्थान, जगह। 3. a blemish, दोष, कलंक। ***v.*** 1. to mark with spots, निशान लगाना, चित्तियाँ बनाना। 2. to discern, देख या पहचान लेना।

spotless (स्पॉटलिस) ***adj.*** 1. without blemish, निष्कलंक, निर्दोष। 2. perfectly clean, साफ़-सुथरा, बेदाग़।

spotlight (स्पॉटलाइट) ***n.*** 1. a beam of light, प्रकाशरेखा। 2. fame, प्रसिद्धि।

spotty (स्पॉटी) ***n.*** 1. spotted, चित्तीदार, धब्बेदार।

spouse (स्पॉउज़) ***n.*** a person's husband or wife, पति या पत्नी।

spout (स्पाउट) ***v.*** 1. to eject (liquid)

in a stream, (किसी तरल पदार्थ का) धार के रूप में निकलना या बहना। 2. to utter or speak at length, विस्तारपूर्वक बोलना। ***n.*** 1. a projecting tube for pouring liquid, टोंटी। 2. a continuous stream or jet of liquid, धार, फुहार।

sprain (स्प्रेन) ***n.*** a painful injury of a joint, मोच। ***v.*** to subject to sprain, मुड़क जाना, मोच खा जाना।

sprang (स्प्रैन्ग) ***v.*** p.t. of spring.

sprawl (स्प्रॉल) ***v.*** 1. to sit or lie with arms and legs spread out, फैलकर बैठना या लेटना, पसरकर बैठना या लेटना। 2. to spread out awkwardly or haphazardly, बेतरतीब फैलना या फैलाना। ***n.*** 1. a sprawling posture, फैलकर बैठने या लेटने की अवस्था या भाव। 2. haphazard expansion, बेतरतीब या ऊलजलूल फैलाव।

spray[1] (स्प्रे) ***n.*** 1. water flying in small drops, फुहार। 2. any liquid dispersed in very small drops, फुहार के काम आनेवाला द्रव। 3. a liquid preparation for spraying, स्प्रे। 4. a device for spraying, स्प्रेअर, फुहारा। ***v.*** to disperse as a spray, फुहारा देना या लगाना, छिड़कना।

spray[2] ***n.*** a branch bearing buds, flowers, leaves or berries, कलियों, फूलों, पत्तों या फलों से युक्त टहनी।

spread (स्प्रेड) ***v.*** (spread, spreading) 1. to unroll, unfold or expand over, फैलाना, बिछाना, खोलना। 2. to apply on a surface, लगाना, पोतना, फैलाना। 3. to become longer or wider, फैल जाना, बढ़ जाना, व्याप्त हो जाना। 4. to scatter, बिखेरना या बिखरना। ***n.*** 1. the act or process of spreading, फैलाव, विस्तार। 2. extent of spreading, विस्तार। 3. something spread on, फैली हुई या फैलाई हुई चीज़। 4. a lavish meal, दावत, दिव्य भोजन।

spree (स्प्री) ***n.*** an unrestrained indulgence in drinking, flirting, buying etc., मद्यपान, इश्क़बाज़ी, खरीदारी आदि की ख़ब्त या सवार होनेवाली धुन।

sprig (स्प्रिग) ***n.*** a shoot or twig, टहनी, डाली।

sprightly (स्प्राइटली) ***adj.*** 1. lively, हँसमुख, प्रसन्नचित्त। 2. full of energy, सजीव, जीवंत।

spring (स्प्रिन्ग) ***v.*** (sprang/sprung, sprung, springing) 1. to move upward or forward suddenly, उछलना, उछलकर आगे बढ़ना। 2. to grow, or emerge suddenly, सहसा उत्पन्न होना या उगना। 3. to appear suddenly, सहसा प्रकट होना या सामने आना। ***n.*** 1. the act of springing, उछाल। 2. a jump, छलाँग। 3. a coil or strip of steel, स्प्रिंग, कमानी। 4. a natural outflow of ground water, झरना, सोता, चश्मा। 5. the season of the year between winter and summer, बसंत ऋतु, बहार का मौसम। 6. a source or origin, उद्‌गम, स्रोत।

spring board ***n.*** a flexible board for diving, वह तख़्ता जिसपर से गोताख़ोर कूदता है।

springy (स्प्रिन्गी) ***adj.*** 1. having an elastic quality, लचीला। 2. full of springs, कमानियों से भरा, कमानीदार।

sprinkle (स्प्रिन्कल) ***v.*** 1. to scatter in drops or tiny particles, छिड़कना, छिड़काव करना। 2. to drizzle, झींसी पड़ना।

sprint (स्प्रिन्ट) ***v.*** to run at a full speed, बहुत तेज़ी से दौड़ लगाना।

S

n. a short race run at a full speed, बहुत तेज़ छोटी दौड़।

sprite (स्प्राइट) *n.* 1. an elf, परी। 2. a goblin, बेताल।

sprout (स्प्राउट) *v.* 1. to grow, उगना, अंकुरित होना, उत्पन्न होना। 2. to develop, बढ़ाना। *n.* the shoot of a plant, अंकुर, अँखुआ, कल्ला।

spruce[1] (स्प्रूस) *adj.* smart, बना-ठना, सजीला। *v.* to smarten, सजाना, सँवारना, सजीला बनाना।

spruce[2] *n.* 1. a cone-bearing tree, एक प्रकार का देवदार (वृक्ष)। 2. its wood, इस पेड़ की लकड़ी।

sprung (स्प्रन्ग) *v.* p.t. & p.p. of spring.

spud (स्पड) *n.* a small spade for digging up weeds, खुरपा, खुरपी।

spun (स्पन) *v.* p.t. of spin.

spur (स्पर) *n.* 1. the pointed device attached to a rider's heel and used to urge the horse, एड़। 2. stimulus, प्रेरणा, प्रेरक शक्ति। 3. a spine, खाँग, काँटा, ख़ार। *v.* 1. to urge on with spurs, एड़ लगाना। 2. to encourage, प्रेरित/प्रोत्साहित करना। □ **on the spur of the moment,** एकाएक।

spurious (स्पूरिअस) *adj.* not genuine or authentic, अप्रामाणिक, नक़ली।

spurn (स्पर्न) *v.* 1. to kick, ठुकरा देना। 2. to reject disdainfully, तिरस्कारपूर्वक अस्वीकार कर देना।

spurt (स्पर्ट) *v.* 1. to gush forth in a sudden stream, धार या फुहारा छूटना, बह निकलना। 2. to increase one's speed suddenly, सहसा गति या रफ़्तार बढ़ा देना। *n.* 1. a sudden stream, धार, फुहार। 2. a sudden increase in a speed, सहसा होनेवाली गति में वृद्धि। 3. a short burst of activity, काम की झोंक या लहर।

sputter (स्पटर) = splutter.

sputum (स्प्यूटम) *n.* matter discharged from the respiratory passages, थूक, बलगम आदि।

spy (स्पाइ) *n.* a secret agent, जासूस, गुप्तचर, भेदिया। *v.* to keep watch secretly, भेद लेना, जासूसी करना।

squabble (स्क्वॉबल) *v.* to quarrel over a small matter, छोटी-मोटी बात पर झगड़ पड़ना। *n.* a quarrel of this kind, छोटी-मोटी बात का झगड़ा।

squad (स्क्वॉड) *n.* 1. the smallest unit of military personnel, सैनिक टुकड़ी, दस्ता। 2. a small group of persons organized for a specific purpose, जत्था।

squadron (स्क्वॉड्रन) *n.* an air force unit, वायुसेना का दल।

squall (स्क्वॉल) *n.* 1. a loud harsh out-cry, चीख़, पुकार। 2. a sudden strong wind, आँधी, अंधड़। *v.* to utter a squall, चीख़ना, पुकारना, चीत्कार करना।

squander (स्क्वॉन्डर) *v.* to spend extravagantly, (धन) फ़िज़ूल ख़र्च करना, बरबाद करना। *n.* an act of squandering, विनाश, बरबादी।

square (स्क्वेअर) *n.* 1. a rectangle with all four sides equal, वर्ग। 2. an area or object shaped like this, वर्ग की शक्ल की कोई वस्तु, चौकोर टुकड़ा। 3. a foursided area surrounded by buildings, खुला चौकोर क्षेत्र, चौक। 4. the product of a number multiplied by itself, वर्गफल। 5. L-shaped or T-shaped instrument for obtaining or testing

S

right angles, कोनिया, गुनिया। *adj.* 1. of square shape, वर्गाकार, चौकोर। 2. right-angled, आयताकार। 3. converted into square unit, वर्ग-। 4. honest, सच्चा, ईमानदार। 5. just, उचित, न्यायपूर्ण। 6. conventional, प्रथागत, रूढ़। *adv.* 1. honestly, ईमानदारी से। 2. firmly, दृढ़तापूर्वक। *v.* 1. to make square or rectangular, वर्गाकार या आयताकार बनाना। 2. to bring to a right angle, सीधा करना, ठीक बैठाना। 3. to multiply (a number) by itself, वर्गफल निकालना। 4. to bring into balance, to settle, हिसाब चुकता करना। 5. to even the score of, बराबर करना।

square deal *n.* a fair transaction, खरा सौदा।

square root *n.* a number when multiplied by itself gives a given number, वर्गमूल।

squash (स्क्वॉश) *v.* 1. to crush, कुचल देना। 2. to squeeze into pulp, कचूमर निकाल देना, भुरता कर देना। 3. to suppress, दबा देना, कुचल देना। 4. to silence with crushing reply, मुँह बंद कर देना। *n.* 1. the sound of squashing, दबने, कुचलने आदि से होनेवाला शब्द। 2. something squashed, कुचली या निचोड़ी हुई वस्तु। 3. pulp, गूदा, लुगदी, भुरता। 4. a kind of drink, एक पेय।

squat (स्क्वॉट) *v.* 1. to sit on one's feet, उकड़ू बैठना। 2. to crouch down, सिमट कर बैठना। 3. to grab (land, ज़मीन पर) ज़बरदस्ती क़ब्ज़ा जमा लेना। *adj.* short and thick, गोल-मटोल, फूहड़।

squatter (स्क्वॉटर) *n.* one who settles on land without right, अनधिकार ज़मीन पर क़ब्ज़ा जमा लेनेवाला।

squawk (स्क्वॉक) *n.* a loud harsh cry, चीख़, चिल्लाहट। *v.* to utter a squawk, चीख़ मारना।

squeak (स्क्वीक) *n.* a sharp shrill cry, चीं-चीं, चूँ-चूँ, चरमर। *v.* to utter or make a squeak, चीं-चीं करना, चूँ-चूँ करना, चरमराना। □ **to have a narrow squeak,** बाल-बाल बचना।

squeal (स्क्वील) *n.* a long shrill cry, चीख़। *v.* 1. to utter a squeal, चीख़ना, चीख़ मारना। 2. to turn informer, मुख़बिर बन जाना।

squeamish (स्क्वीमिश) *adj.* 1. easily nauseated, जल्दी-जल्दी बीमार पड़ जानेवाला, सुकुमार। 2. excessively fastidious, नकचढ़ा।

squeeze (स्क्वीज़) *v.* 1. to compress, दबाना। 2. to extract by applying pressure, निचोड़ना। 3. to push in a confined place, ठूँसना, भरना। 4. to hug closely, कसकर आलिंगन करना। 5. to get by extortion, (पैसा आदि) ऐंठना। *n.* 1. an act of squeezing, दबाने, या निचोड़ने की क्रिया। 2. an amount squeezed, निचोड़ा हुआ पदार्थ।

squib (स्क्विब) *n.* a small firework that makes a hissing sound, अनार, फुलझड़ी।

squint (स्क्विन्ट) *v.* 1. to look or glance sideways, कनखियाना, कनखी मारना। 2. to be cross-eyed, भेंगा होना। *n.* 1. a stealthy or sideways glance, कनखी, तिरछी नज़र। 2. cross-eye, भेंगापन।

squirm (स्क्वर्म) *v.* to writhe, छटपटाना, तड़पना, ऐंठना।

squirrel (स्क्विरल) *n.* 1. a small tree-climbing animal with a bushy tail, गिलहरी। 2. its fur, गिलहरी की खाल या फर।

S

stab (स्टैब) ***v.*** to injure with a sharp pointed knife etc., छुरा भोंकना या घुसेड़ना। ***n.*** 1. a thrust made with a sharp pointed knife, छुरा भोंकने से होनेवाला घाव। 2. a sensation of being stabbed, छुरा भोंके जाने का-सा कष्ट, टीस। 3. an attempt, प्रयत्न, प्रयास।

stability (स्टेबिलिटी) ***n.*** the state or quality of being stable, स्थिरता, स्थायित्व।

stabilize (स्टेबिलाइज़) ***v.*** स्थिर करना, स्थायी बनाना, दृढ़ करना।

stabilizer (स्टेबिलाइज़र) ***n.*** a device for maintaining something in a stable state, स्टेबिलाइज़र, स्थिरक।

stable[1] (स्टेबल) ***adj.*** 1. steady, firm, स्थिर, स्थायी, सुस्थिर। 2. lasting, टिकाऊ।

stable[2] ***n.*** 1. a building in which horses are kept, अस्तबल, घुड़साल। 2. the horses lodged in such a building, अस्तबल में रखे हुए घोड़े। 3. a training centre, प्रशिक्षण केंद्र। ***v.*** to keep in a stable, अस्तबल में रखना।

stack (स्टैक) ***n.*** 1. a pile or heap, ढेर, गड्डी या चट्टा। 2. a large quantity, अत्यधिक परिमाण या मात्रा। 3. a smokestack, चिमनी। 4. a rack, टाँड। ***v.*** to pile, ढेरी लगाना, चट्टा लगाना।

stadium (स्टेडिअम) ***n.*** an enclosed playground with tiers of seats, क्रीड़ांगन, खेल का मैदान, स्टेडियम।

staff (स्टाफ़) ***n.*** 1. a stick, pole or rod, डंडा, लाठी, लट्ठ। 2. a stick as a symbol of authority, दंड। 3. a group of assistants, कार्यकर्तागण या कर्मचारी। 4. (mus.) the set of horizontal lines on which musical notes are written, पाँच समांतर रेखाओं की संगीत-सारणी। ***v.*** to provide with a staff of employees, कर्मचारी नियुक्त करना या मुहैया करना।

stag (स्टैग) ***n.*** an adult male deer, हिरन, मृग।

stage (स्टेज) ***n.*** 1. a raised platform, मंच। 2. a platform on which plays are performed, रंगमंच, मंच, स्टेज। 3. a step, चरण। 4. a point or period of development, अवस्था। ***v.*** to perform on a stage, मंचित करना, अभिनीत करना।

stage-fright (स्टेज-फ़्राइट) ***n.*** nervousness felt while speaking or acting on the stage, मंच-भीति।

stagger (स्टैगर) ***v.*** 1. to move or go unsteadily, लड़खड़ाना, डगमगाते हुए चलना। 2. to shock deeply, चौंका देना, स्तंभित कर देना। 3. to waver or hesitate, विचलित होना या हिचकना। 4. to arrange in alternating or overlapping time periods or positions, भिन्न-भिन्न समयों या स्थितियों के अनुरूप निश्चित करना।

staggering (स्टैगरिंग) ***adj.*** astonishing, विस्मयकारी, आश्चर्यचकित करनेवाला। ***n.*** staggering motion, लड़खड़ाहट।

staging (स्टेजिंग) ***n.*** 1. a temporary platform, अस्थायी मंच। 2. the presentation of a play, मंचन, नाट्य-प्रदर्शन।

stagnant (स्टैग्नेन्ट) ***adj.*** 1. (of water) not flowing, रुका हुआ, रुद्ध। 2. motionless, गतिहीन। 3. sluggish, मंद।

stagnate (स्टैग्नेट) ***v.*** 1. to be stagnant, रुका होना, अवरुद्ध होना। 2. to become sluggish, मंद पड़ जाना।

staid (स्टेड) ***adj.*** sober, calm, गंभीर, शांत।

S

stain (स्टेन) ***v.*** 1. to discolour or become discoloured, बदरंग करना या होना, रंग बिगाड़ देना या बिगड़ जाना। 2. to blemish, कलंकित करना। ***n.*** 1. a spot, धब्बा, दाग़। 2. a blemish, दोष, कलंक।

stainless (स्टेनलिस) ***adj.*** free from stains or blemishes, बेदाग़, निर्दोष, निष्कलंक।

stair (स्टेअर) ***n.*** 1. one of the flight of steps, सीढ़ी का (कोई) डंडा। 2. stairs, सीढ़ी, सोपान।

staircase, stairway (स्टेअरकेस, स्टेअरवे) ***n.*** a flight of stairs and its supporting structure, सीढ़ी और उसका ढाँचा, ज़ीना, सोपान-मार्ग।

stake (स्टेक) ***n.*** 1. a pointed wooden post driven into the ground as a marker or support, खूँटी, खूँटा, थूनी। 2. the prize in a contest, प्रतियोगिता का पुरस्कार। 3. something that is staked for gain or loss, दाँव, बाज़ी, पण। ***v.*** 1. to fasten with a stake, खूँटी से बाँधना। 2. to mark with stakes, खूँटियाँ गाड़कर निशान लगाना। 3. to wager, दाँव लगाना, बाज़ी लगाना।

stale (स्टेल) ***adj.*** 1. having lost freshness, बासी। 2. uninteresting, नीरस, उबाऊ। ***v.*** 1. to become stale, बासी पड़ जाना, पुराना पड़ जाना। 2. to make stale, बासी कर देना।

stalemate (स्टेलमेट) ***n.*** deadlock, जिच, गतिरोध। ***v.*** to bring into a stalemate, जिच/गतिरोध उत्पन्न करना।

stalk[1] (स्टॉक) ***n.*** 1. a stem that supports a plant, डंठल, डंडी। 2. a similar support of an organ in animals, दंड।

stalk[2] ***v.*** 1. to follow (a prey) quietly, (शिकार) का पीछा दबे पाँव या छिपे-छिपे करना। 2. to walk in a haughty way, ताव से या अकड़कर चलना।

stall (स्टॉल) ***n.*** 1. a compartment in a stable for a domestic animal, चन्नी, थान, बरदवान। 2. a small compartment for selling goods, स्टॉल। 3. stalling of an engine, इंजन का बंद या ठप हो जाना। ***v.*** 1. to confine an animal in a stall, चन्नी में पशु को बाँधना। 2. to bring or come to a standstill accidentally, (इंजन का) एकाएक बंद हो जाना या बंद कर दिया जाना। 3. to employ delaying tactics, टाल-मटोल करना।

stallion (स्टैल्यन) ***n.*** an uncastrated male horse kept primarily for breeding, आँड़ू घोड़ा।

stalwart (स्टॉलवर्ट) ***adj.*** strong and sturdy, तगड़ा, हट्टा-कट्टा, हृष्ट-पुष्ट। ***n.*** a strong supporter, पक्का पक्षधर या समर्थक।

stamen (स्टेमन) ***n.*** the male reproductive organ of a flower, पुंकेसर।

stamina (स्टैमिना) ***n.*** enduring physical or mental power, staying power, दम-ख़म।

stammer (स्टैमर) ***v.*** to speak with involuntary pauses or rapid repetition of the same sound or syllable, हकलाना। ***n.*** the act or instance of stammering, हकलाहट।

stamp (स्टैम्प) ***v.*** 1. to bring (the foot) down heavily, (पैर) ज़ोर से पटकना। 2. to imprint or impress with a mark, (ठप्पा) लगाना, छापना। 3. to affix a stamp to, टिकट चिपकाना। 4. to form or cut out with a mould or die, बनाना, ढालना, काटना या निकालना। *n.* 1. an act of stamping, मुद्रांकन। 2. impression, छाप। 3. an instrument of stamping, ठप्पा, मोहर। 4. a postal ticket, टिकट।

stamp-duty (स्टैम्प-ड्यूटी) *n.* stamps to show that duty has been paid, स्टैम्प शुल्क।

stampede (स्टैम्पीड) *n.* a wild headlong rush, भगदड़।

stamping ground *n.* a habitual gathering place, अड्डा, मिलन-स्थल।

stance (स्टैन्स) *n.* position of the body, मुद्रा, ठवन।

stand (स्टैन्ड) *v.* (stood, standing) 1. to take or cause to take a stationary upright position, खड़ा होना या खड़ा करना। 2. to remain standstill, खड़ा होना, रुका या ठहरा होना। 3. to run as a candidate, (चुनाव में) प्रत्याशी के रूप में खड़े होना, उम्मीदवार होना। 4. to remain unchanged, अपरिवर्तित रहना। 5. to be situated, स्थित रहना। 6. to place, स्थापित होना। 7. to be valid, लागू रहना, मान्य होना। 8. to erect, खड़ा करना। 9. to remain firm, स्थिर या दृढ़ रहना। 10. to bear, endure, सहना, बर्दाश्त करना। *n.* 1. a position or base, स्थिति या आधार। 2. a ceasing of work or activity, काम या क्रिया का ठप होना, विराम। 3. a position or opinion one is prepared to defend, वह स्थिति या बात जिसका बचाव तथा समर्थन कोई करता हो। 4. a witness stand, कटघरा। 5. a stall or booth, दुकान, स्टॉल। 6. a parking place reserved for vehicles, गाड़ियों का अड्डा, स्टैंड।

standard (स्टैन्डर्ड) *n.* 1. a flag or banner, झंडा, ध्वज, पताका। 2. a thing, quality or specification for comparing or measuring, मानदंड, प्रतिमान। 3. a degree or level or requirement, excellence or attainment, मानक। *adj.* 1. conforming to a standard, मानक, प्रामाणिक। 2. well established by usage, मानक, परिनिष्ठित।

standardization (स्टैन्डर्डाइज़ेशन) *n.* the act or result of standardizing, मानकीकरण।

standardize (स्टैन्डर्डाइज़) *v.* to bring into conformity with a standard, मानकीकरण करना।

standard time *n.* the official time of a country or region, मानक समय।

standby (स्टैन्डबाइ) *n.* a person or thing that is ready and available as a substitute, स्थानापन्न।

standing (स्टैन्डिंग) *adj.* 1. permanent, स्थायी; standing committee, स्थायी समिति। 2. ready, तैयार। *n.* 1. status, हैसियत, प्रतिष्ठा। 2. past duration, गत काल; of long standing, पुराना।

stand-offish (स्टैन्ड-ऑफ़िश) *adj.* aloof, अलग-थलग।

standpoint (स्टैन्डपॉइन्ट) *n.* a point of view, दृष्टिबिंदु, दृष्टिकोण।

standstill (स्टैन्डस्टिल) *n.* 1. stalemate, ज़िच, गतिरोध। 2. a stoppage, विराम, ठहराव।

stanza (स्टैन्ज़ा) *n.* one of the divisions of a poem, बंद, पद।

staple[1] (स्टेपल) *adj.* principal, मुख्य। *n.* a major product, मुख्य उत्पाद।

staple[2] *n.* a u-shaped metal loop to bind or hold something, स्टेपल। *v.* to secure (papers) with staples, स्टेपल लगाना।

stapler (स्टेप्लर) *n.* an instrument

S

for stapling papers, स्टेपलर।

star (स्टार) ***n.*** 1. any of the celestial bodies appearing as points and emitting light in the night sky, तारा, सितारा, नक्षत्र। 2. an asterisk, तारिका चिह्न (*)। 3. a film actor or actress, अभिनेता या अभिनेत्री। ***v.*** 1. to ornament with stars, तारों से सजाना। 2. to put an asterisk, तारांकित करना। 3. to present as an actor or actress, अभिनेता या अभिनेत्री के रूप में प्रस्तुत करना। 4. to perform as an actor, अभिनय करना।

starboard (स्टारबोर्ड) ***n.*** the right hand side (of a ship, जहाज़ का) दायाँ पक्ष।

starch (स्टार्च) ***n.*** 1. a substance found in corn, wheat etc., used for stiffening fabrics, माँड़, कलफ़। 2. stiffness of man-ner, शुष्कता, रूखापन। ***v.*** to stiffen with starch, कलफ़ करना या लगाना।

stare (स्टेअर) ***v.*** to gaze fixedly with eyes wide open, आँखें फाड़-फाड़कर देखना, घूरना। ***n.*** a staring gaze, घूरने की क्रिया।

starfish (स्टार्फ़िश) ***n.*** a star-shaped fish, तारे की शक्ल की मछली, तारा मीन।

stark (स्टार्क) ***adj.*** 1. sharply evident, पूर्णत: स्पष्ट। 2. desolate, सूना।

starlight (स्टार्लाइट) ***n.*** light from the stars, तारों की रोशनी, नक्षत्र-प्रकाश।

starlit (स्टार्लिट) ***adj.*** lit by starlight, तारों से भरा, तारों से जगमग।

starry (स्टारी) ***adj.*** 1. lighted by or filled with stars, तारों से भरा, तारांकित। 2. shining like stars, तारों की तरह चमकता हुआ।

starry-eyed (स्टारी-आइड) ***adj.*** enthusiastic but impractical, उत्साही परंतु अव्यवहारशील।

start (स्टार्ट) ***v.*** 1. begin or commence, आरंभ करना, शुरू करना। 2. to set in motion, चलाना। 3. to be set in motion, चलना, चलने लगना। 4. to spring or jump suddenly, सहसा उछल या कूद पड़ना, चिहुँक उठना। ***n.*** 1. a beginning, commencement, शुरुआत, आरंभ। 2. a place or time of beginning, प्रारंभ करने का स्थान या समय। 3. a sudden involuntary movement, सहसा होनेवाली अनभिप्रेत क्रिया, चिहुँक। 4. a signal to proceed, कुछ करने का संकेत।

starter (स्टार्टर) ***n.*** 1. a device for starting an engine, motor etc., स्टार्टर। 2. one who starts (something, कोई काम) शुरू करनेवाला व्यक्ति। 3. one who gives signal for a race, दौड़ शुरू करने का संकेत देनेवाला। 4. a competitor who starts in a race, दौड़ में भाग लेनेवाला प्रतियोगी।

startle (स्टार्टल) ***v.*** 1. to be surprised or frightened, चौंक पड़ना। 2. to cause to be surprised or frightened, चौंका देना।

starvation (स्टार्वेशन) ***n.*** the act of starving or the state of being starved, भुखमरी।

starve (स्टार्व) ***v.*** 1. to die from prolonged lack of food, भूखों मरना। 2. to cause to die from prolonged lack of food, भूखों मारना। 3. to be badly hungry, भूख से विकल होना।

state (स्टेट) ***n.*** 1. a condition of being, अवस्था, दशा, स्थिति। 2. a country or nation, राज्य। 3. a government, सरकार, शासन। 4. a subdivision of a federation, state, राज्य। 5. position in life or society, हैसियत। □ **lie in state,** (शव का) दर्शनार्थ रखा जाना। ***adj.*** 1. of or relating to the state, राज्य-संबंधी, सरकारी, राजकीय। 2. used or done on ceremonial occasions, समारोही। ***v.*** 1. to set forth in words, अभिव्यक्त करना, कहना। 2. to declare, घोषित करना।

stated (स्टेटिड) ***adj.*** 1. put forth in words, अभिव्यक्त। 2. declared, घोषित। 3. fixed, नियत, निश्चित।

stately (स्टेटली) ***adj.*** 1. graceful, dignified, गौरवपूर्ण, शानदार। 2. imposing, प्रभावशाली।

statement (स्टेटमेन्ट) ***n.*** 1. something stated, कथन, वक्तव्य, बयान। 2. the act of stating, कथन। 3. a written summary of financial account, लेन-देन का ब्योरा, लेने-देने का विवरण।

statesman (स्टेट्समैन) ***n.*** a national leader, राजनेता।

statesmanship (स्टेट्समैनशिप) ***n.*** the quality of being a statesman, राजनेतृत्व।

static (स्टैटिक) ***adj.*** 1. not moving, not in motion, स्थिर, निश्चल। 2. not changing, अपरिवर्तनशील।

statics (स्टैटिक्स) ***n.*** the science dealing with bodies at rest, स्थिति-विज्ञान, स्थैतिकी।

station (स्टेशन) ***n.*** 1. a stopping place in a transportation route, स्टेशन, स्थल, केंद्र। 2. a transmission centre, रेडियो स्टेशन। 3. a place established to provide public service, सेवा-केंद्र, चौकी, स्टेशन। ***v.*** to post, to put at a certain place, नियुक्त करना, रखना, बैठाना।

stationary (स्टेशनरी) ***adj.*** not movable, स्थिर, अचल, स्थावर।

stationery (स्टेशनरी) ***n.*** paper, ink pens, pencils etc. writing materials, काग़ज़, कलम, स्याही आदि लेखन-सामग्री।

statistical (स्टैटिस्टिकल) ***adj.*** of or pertaining to statistics, सांख्यिकीय।

statistics (स्टैटिस्टिक्स) ***n.*** 1. the science of collecting and classifying numerical data, सांख्यिकी। 2. an item of information expressed in numbers, आँकड़ा।

statue (स्टैचू) ***n.*** a moulded or sculptured figure, मूर्ति, प्रतिमा।

stature (स्टैचर) ***n.*** 1. natural height of a person in an upright position, क़द, लंबाई। 2. level of achievment, status, पद, हैसियत, महिमा।

status (स्टेटस) ***n.*** 1. the legal character or condition of a person or thing, वैधानिक स्थिति। 2. a relative position in a social system, हैसियत, प्रतिष्ठा।

status quo (स्टेटस क्वो) ***n.*** the state of affairs as it was before (a recent change), यथापूर्व स्थिति।

statute (स्टैट्यूट) ***n.*** a law enacted by a legislative body, विधि, क़ानून।

statutory (स्टैट्युटरी) ***adj.*** of or relating to a statute, विधिक, क़ानूनी।

staunch (स्टॉन्च) ***adj.*** 1. firm, loyal, पक्का, निष्ठावान। 2. trustworthy, विश्वस्त।

stay[1] (स्टे) ***v.*** 1. to remain in a given place or position, रहना। 2. to reside temporarily, ठहरना, टिकना। 3. to stop, रुकना, ठहरना। 4. to postpone or discontinue, स्थगित करना, जारी न रखना। 5. to prop up, सहारा देना, टेक

S

लगाना। ***n.*** 1. a period of temporary dwelling or visiting, ठहराव, प्रवास। 2. a postponement, स्थगन। 3. a support, सहारा, टेक।

stay[2] ***n.*** a heavy rope or cable, मोटा रस्सा, तार आदि।

stead (स्टेड) ***n.*** a place or position, स्थान या स्थिति। □ **stand (someone) in good stead,** (किसी के लिए) उपयोगी होना।

steadfast (स्टेडफ़ास्ट) ***adj.*** 1. fixed, steady, स्थिर, निश्चल। 2. determined, निश्चयबद्ध, अटल।

steadily (स्टेडिली) ***adv.*** in a steady manner, अनवरत, निरंतर।

steady (स्टेडी) ***adj.*** 1. stable, स्थिर, अचल। 2. free form fluctuations, अपरिवर्तनशील। 3. not easily excited, जो जल्दी उत्तेजित न हो, धीर-गंभीर। 4. regular, नियमित। ***v.*** to make or become steady, स्थिर करना या हो जाना। ***adv.*** in a steady manner, सुस्थिर रूप से, नियमित रूप से या निरंतर।

steak (स्टीक) ***n.*** a thick slice of meat, fish etc., (तला या भूना हुआ) मांस आदि का टुकड़ा, टिक्का।

steal (स्टील) ***v.*** (stole, stolen, stealing) 1. to take away another's property without permission or unlawfully, चुराना, चोरी करना। 2. to move secretly, दबे पाँव चलना।

stealthily (स्टेल्थिली) ***adv.*** secretly, चुपके से, चोरी-छिपे।

steam (स्टीम) ***n.*** 1. the vapour into which water is changed by boiling, भाप, वाष्प। 2. the vapour used as motive power, वाष्प-शक्ति। ***v.*** 1. to emit steam, भाप छोड़ना। 2. to be emitted as steam, भाप छूटना। 3. to move by steam power, भाप से चलना। 4. to proceed quickly, तेज़ी से बढ़ना।

steamer (स्टीमर) ***n.*** 1. a boat or ship driven by steam engine, वाष्पचालित जहाज़। 2. a container in which things are cooked by steam, वह पात्र जिसमें भाप से चीज़ें पकाई जाती हैं, स्टीमर।

steamroller (स्टीमरोलर) ***n.*** a machine with heavy roller used for smoothing road surfaces, सड़कें बनानेवाला इंजन।

steamy (स्टीमी) ***adj.*** 1. full of steam, भाप से भरा। 2. like steam, भाप-जैसा।

steed (स्टीड) ***n.*** a horse, घोड़ा।

steel (स्टील) ***n.*** 1. a very hard alloy of iron and carbon, इस्पात, फ़ौलाद। 2. a quality suggestive of steel, फ़ौलाद जैसी शक्ति या दृढ़ता।

steelworks (स्टीलवर्क्स) ***n.*** a factory for making steel, इस्पात का कारखाना।

steep[1] (स्टीप) ***adj.*** 1. sloping sharply, बहुत ढालवाँ, खड़ा। 2. unreasonably high, बहुत ऊँचा।

steep[2] ***v.*** 1. to soak (in liquid, तरल पदार्थ में) भिगोना। 2. to imbue, ओत-प्रोत करना या होना, डूबना या डुबोना।

steeple (स्टीपल) ***n.*** a tower of a church, चर्च की मीनार।

steeplechase (स्टीपलचेस) ***n.*** a horse race with obstacles to be jumped, घोड़ों की बाधा-दौड़।

steer[1] (स्टिअर) ***n.*** a castrated male ox, बधिया किया हुआ बैल।

steer[2] ***v.*** 1. to direct the course of, to guide, चलाना, परिचालन करना। 2. to be able to be steered, (गाड़ी, नाव आदि को) खे, निकाल या आगे बढ़ा ले जाना।

stellar (स्टेलर) ***adj.*** of a star or stars, तारे या तारों से संबद्ध।

stem (स्टेम) ***n.*** 1. the main supporting part of a tree or plant, तना। 2. a slender part supporting a leave, flower or fruit, डंडी या डंठल। 3. the main part of a verb or noun, धातु। ***v.*** 1. to stop (the flow, प्रवाह) रोकना, बंद करना। 2. to remove the stem from, डंठल निकलना।

stench (स्टेन्च) ***n.*** a foul smell, बदबू, दुर्गंध।

stencil (स्टेन्सिल) ***n.*** a sheet of metal or card with design cut out, used for painting, धातु/दफ़्ती आदि का पत्तर जिसमें अक्षर/चित्र आदि कटे रहते हैं, स्टेंसिल। ***v.*** to mark a surface with stencil, स्टेंसिल से छापना।

stenographer (स्टेनॉग्रफ़र) ***n.*** a person employed to write shorthand, आशुलिपिक, स्टेनोग्राफ़र।

stenography (स्टेनॉग्रफ़ी) ***n.*** shorthand, आशुलिपि, स्टेनोग्राफ़ी।

step[1] (स्टेप) ***n.*** 1. the act of raising the foot and bringing it down as in walking, पग, क़दम, डग। 2. the space covered by such an act, पग, क़दम, डग। 3. a short distance, थोड़ा फ़ासला। 4. a rhythm in marching, चलने में दाएँ-बाएँ पैरों का होनेवाला मेल। 5. one of the series of actions, क़दम, पग। 6. a support for a foot while ascending or descending, पायदान, पौड़ी, डंडा। 7. one of the stages of process, अवस्था, चरण। 8. (plu.) stairs, सीढ़ी, ज़ीना। ***v.*** 1. to go on foot, चलना, आगे बढ़ना। 2. to measure by pacing क़दमों से नापना।

step[2] ***adj.*** related not by blood but by parent who has remarried, सौतेला, कठ।

steppe (स्टेप) ***n.*** a level grassy plain, घास का समतल मैदान।

stepping stone (स्टेपिन्गस्टोन) ***n.*** 1. a stone providing a foot-rest for crossing a stream, वह पत्थर जिसपर पैर रखकर नाला, झरना आदि पार करते हैं। 2. a thing that allows someone to make progress, प्रगति में सहायक वस्तु या बात।

stereo, stereophonic (स्टेरिओ, स्टेरिओफ़ोनिक) ***adj.*** (sound) reproduced by two channels, स्टीरिओफ़ोनिक।

stereotype (स्टेरिओटाइप) ***n.*** 1. a plate for printing cast from a mould of type, मुद्रणफलक। 2. a conventional idea, character or mould, रूढ़ धारणा, रूढ़ चरित्र या घिसा-पिटा साँचा। ***v.*** to give a conventional form to, रूढ़ या घिसा-पिटा रूप देना, पुराने साँचे में ढाल देना।

stereotyped (स्टेरिओटाइप्ड) ***adj.*** conventional, रूढ़, रूढ़िबद्ध, घिसा-पिटा; stereotyped personality, रूढ़ व्यक्तित्व।

sterile (स्टेराइल) ***adj.*** 1. barren, बंध्या, बाँझ। 2. unproductive, बंजर, अनुर्वर। 3. free from microbes, रोगाणुरहित।

sterilization (स्टेरलाइज़ेशन) ***n.*** the act of sterilizing or the state of being sterilized, बंध्याकरण, रोगाणुरहित करना।

sterilize (स्टेरलाइज़) ***v.*** to make sterile, बाँझ या बंध्या बनाना, अनुर्वर करना, रोगाणुरहित करना।

sterling (स्टर्लिन्ग) ***n.*** British money, ब्रितानवी मुद्रा। ***adj.*** 1. genuine, खरा,

S

शुद्ध। 2. excellent, उत्तम, उत्कृष्ट।

stern (स्टर्न) ***adj.*** 1. strict, सख़्त, कड़ा। 2. harsh, hard-hearted, कठोर, निर्दय। ***n.*** the rear end of a ship, जहाज़ का पिछला भाग।

sternum (स्टर्नम) ***n.*** the breast bone, उरोस्थि।

stethoscope (स्टेथस्कोप) ***n.*** an instrument for listening to the sounds within the body, स्टेथॅस्कोप।

stew (स्ट्यू) ***v.*** to cook food by simmering or boiling slowly, सिझाना, हलकी आँच में पकाना। ***n.*** 1. a dish cooked by stewing, सिझाकर तैयार किया हुआ व्यंजन। 2. a state of uneasiness, बेचैनी।

steward (स्ट्यूअर्ड) ***n.*** 1. one employed to manage one's property, finances or other affairs, प्रबंधक, कारिंदा। 2. one who manages the provisions and dining arrangements of a ship, aircraft, hotel etc., भंडारी। 3. an attendant, परिचारक।

stewardess (स्ट्यूअर्डिस) ***n.*** a female steward, परिचारिका।

stick[1] (स्टिक) ***n.*** 1. a long slender piece of wood, लकड़ी का पल्ला, डंडा। 2. a walking stick, छड़ी।

stick[2] ***v.*** (stuck, sticking) 1. to pierce with something pointed, छेदना, चुभोना, भोंकना या घुसेड़ना। 2. to fasten or hold fast, लगाना, कसना, नत्थी करना या चिपकाना। 3. to cause to become sticky, चिपकाना। 4. to remain for a long time, बना रहना, जमा रहना, स्थित रहना। 5. to tolerate, बर्दाश्त करना। 6. to be obstructed, रोका जाना, अवरुद्ध किया जाना।

sticker (स्टिकर) ***n.*** a gummed label, स्टिकर, चिपकौआ लेबल।

stickler (स्टिकलर) ***n.*** one who insists on something, किसी बात का आग्रही।

sticky (स्टिकी) ***adj.*** 1. tending to stick, चिपकनेवाला, चिपचिपा, लेसदार। 2. warm or humid, चिपचिपा, उमसदार। 3. painful, कष्टप्रद।

stiff (स्टिफ़) ***adj.*** 1. inflexible, rigid, अनम्य, कड़ा। 2. not moving or operating easily, कड़ा, सख़्त। 3. difficult, कठिन, मुश्किल। 4. formal, औपचारिक। 5. brisk, तेज़। ***n.*** a corpse, शव, लाश।

stiffen (स्टिफ़न) ***v.*** 1. to make stiff, कड़ा कर या बना देना। 2. to become stiff, कड़ा बन या हो जाना, कठोरता अपनाना।

stifle (स्टाइफ़ल) ***v.*** 1. to suffocate, गला घुटना या घोंटना। 2. to suppress, दबाना, दमन करना।

stigma (स्टिग्मा) ***n.*** 1. a mark of social disgrace, लांछन, कलंक। 2. a stain, spot, दाग़, चिह्न।

stigmatize (स्टिग्मेटाइज़) ***v.*** to mark with a stigma, लांछन लगाना, दाग़ लगाना।

still[1] (स्टिल) ***adj.*** 1. motionless, अचल, निश्चल, स्थिर। 2. silent, ख़ामोश, चुप। ***n.*** 1. silence, ख़ामोशी, नीरवता। 2. a still photograph, स्थिर चित्र। ***adv.*** 1. continuing even now, अब भी। 2. up to this time, अभी तक। 3. always, सदा। ***conj.*** nevertheless, तो भी।

still[2] ***n.*** an apparatus for distilling, भभका।

still birth (स्टिल बर्थ) ***n.*** birth of

a dead child, मरे हुए बच्चे का जन्म, मृतप्रसव।

still life ***n.*** a painting of inani-mate objects, पदार्थों का चित्र, पदार्थ-चित्र।

stilt (स्टिल्ट) ***n.*** either of a pair of two long poles for walking elevated above the ground, पैरबाँसा, गेड़ी।

stilted (स्टिलटिड) ***adj.*** 1. unnatural, अस्वाभाविक। 2. pompous, आडंबरपूर्ण।

stimulant (स्टिम्युलेन्ट) ***n.*** a drug that stimulates bodily functions, स्फूर्तिदायक औषध, स्फूर्तिदायक पदार्थ।

stimulate (स्टिम्युलेट) ***v.*** 1. to make more vigorous or active, अधिक स्फूर्त तथा सक्रिय करना। 2. to excite, उत्तेजित करना। 3. to inspire, प्रेरित करना, प्रेरणा देना।

stimulus (स्टिम्युलस) ***n.*** 1. something that stimulates, स्फूर्ति देने या उत्तेजना प्रदान करनेवाली चीज़ या बात। 2. inspiration, प्रेरणा, प्रोत्साहन।

sting (स्टिन्ग) ***n.*** 1. a sharp pointed part or organ of certain insects, डंक, दंश। 2. a sharp pointed part of certain plants, काँटा। 3. the wound or pain caused by stinging, डंक के लगने से होनेवाला घाव या पीड़ा, डंक, दंश। ***v.*** (stung, stinging) 1. to wound with a sting, डंक मारना, काटना। 2. to feel or cause to feel sharp pain, तेज़ दर्द होना या करना। 3. to cause to suffer, सताना, दुखी करना।

stingy (स्टिन्जी) ***adj.*** sparing in giving or spending, कंजूस, कृपण।

stink (स्टिन्क) ***n.*** 1. an offensive smell, बदबू, दुर्गंध। 2. a public outcry against something offensive, चिल्लपों, आक्रोश। ***v.*** (stunk/stank, stunk, stinking) 1. to give off an offensive smell, बदबू देना। 2. to be highly abhorrent, अत्यंत घृणित होना।

stint (स्टिन्ट) ***v.*** 1. to limit or restrict, सीमित करना। 2. to fix or allot, नियत करना, निर्धारित करना। ***n.*** amount of work to be performed within a given period, निर्धारित काम।

stipend (स्टाइपेन्ड) ***n.*** a fixed sum of money paid periodically, वज़ीफ़ा, वृत्ति।

stipendiary (स्टाइपेन्डिअरी) ***n.*** one who receives a stipend, वज़ीफ़ा पानेवाला, वृत्तिधारी या वैतनिक।

stipulate (स्टिप्युलेट) ***v.*** to specify as a condition of an agreement, अनुबंध में शर्त रखना।

stipulation (स्टिप्युलेशन) ***n.*** a condition of an agreement, शर्त, अनुबंध।

stir (स्टर) ***v.*** 1. to move, हिलना, डोलना। 2. to cause to move, हिलाना, हिलाना-डुलाना। 3. to mix with a spoon or stick, हिलाना, चलाना। 4. to excite or arouse, उत्तेजित या उद्दीप्त करना। ***n.*** 1. the act of stirring, हिलाना-मिलाना, चलाना। 2. a slight movement, हरकत। 3. agitation, disturbance or commotion, क्षोभ, हलचल, कोलाहल।

stirrup (स्टरप) ***n.*** a metal or leather loop to support the rider's foot, रकाब।

stitch (स्टिच) ***n.*** 1. a single movement of threaded needle in sewing, तोपा, टाँका। 2. a single complete movement of a needle or hook in knitting or crocheting, फंदा। 3. a sudden sharp pain, टीस, चमक। ***v.*** to sew, सिलाई करना।

stock (स्टॉक) ***n.*** 1. a store or

S

supply accumulated for sale, बिक्री का माल, भंडार, संग्रह। 2. an amount of something stored for future use, जुटाकर रखा हुआ माल। 3. raw material, कच्चा माल। 4. domestic animals, livestock, पशुधन। 5. the capital that a firm raises through the sale of shares, शेयर बेचकर इकट्ठी की हुई पूँजी, शेयर-पूँजी। 6. the capital of a business company, व्यापारिक संस्था का मूलधन। 7. the original progenitor of a family, कुल-पुरुष। 8. lineage, वंशक्रम। 9. broth, शोरबा, रसा। 10. a plant in which a graft is inserted, वह पौधा जिसमें क़लम लगाई गई हो। 11. a supporting structure, ढाँचा। 12. the wooden part of a gun, कुंदा। ***adj.*** 1. kept in stock, भंडार में रखा हुआ, उपलब्ध। 2. commonly used, प्रचलित, चलता हुआ। ***v.*** 1. to keep for sale, भंडार में रखना। 2. to supply, पूर्ति करना।

stockade (स्टॉकेड) ***n.*** a fence of stakes, घेरा।

stockbreeder (स्टॉकब्रीडर) ***n.*** one who raises livestock, पशुपालक।

stockbroker (स्टॉकब्रोकर) ***n.*** one who buys and sells securities on behalf of others, शेयर दलाल।

stock exchange/market ***n.*** a place where securities are purchased and sold, शेयर बाज़ार।

stocking (स्टॉकिन्ग) ***n.*** a close fitting covering for the foot, मोज़ा, जुराब।

stock-still (स्टॉक-स्टिल) ***adj.*** motionless, गतिहीन, खड़ा।

stock-taking (स्टॉक-टेकिंग) ***n.*** 1. making the inventory of stock in a shop, स्टॉक की सूची बनाना। 2. a review of one's position or resources, स्थिति-सर्वेक्षण।

stocky (स्टॉकी) ***adj.*** relatively thick in build, नाटा और गठीला।

stoic (स्टोइक) ***adj.*** not affected by passion or feeling, शांत, धीर, गंभीर।

stoicism (स्टोइसिज़म) ***n.*** indifference to pleasure and pain, उदासीनता, विरक्ति, संयम।

stoke (स्टोक) ***v.*** to put fuel in a furnace, भट्ठी में कोयला झोंकना, आग भड़काना।

stole[1] (स्टोल) ***v.*** p.t. of steal.

stole[2] ***n.*** a covering worn by women across the shoulders, दुपट्टा।

stomach (स्टमक) ***n.*** 1. a large saclike organ in the belly, आमाशय। 2. the belly or abdomen, उदर, पेट। 3. appetite, भूख। ***v.*** to endure, सहन करना।

stone[1] (स्टोन) ***n.*** 1. a piece of rock, पत्थर, पाषाण। 2. a piece of stone shaped for a particular purpose, सिल, पटिया। 3. a precious stone, रत्न, मणि। 4. the woody central part of some fruits, गुठली, गिटक। 5. a stonelike substance formed in the gallbladder or kidney, पथरी। 6. (plu. usually stone) a unit of weight equal to 14 pounds, १४ पौंड की तौल। ***v.*** to pelt with stones, पत्थरों से मारना। ***adj.*** made of stone, पत्थर का बना, पथरीला।

Stone Age ***n.*** the very early period of civilization characterized by the use of stone tools, पाषाण युग, प्रस्तर युग।

stonily (स्टोनिली) ***adv.*** in a stony manner, कठोरता से।

S

stony (स्टोनी) ***adj.*** 1. made of or full of stones, पत्थर का बना या पथरीला। 2. hard as stone, कठोर। 3. insensitive to pity or human feeling, निर्मम। 4. expressionless, भावशून्य।

stood (स्टुड) ***v.*** p.t. & p.p. of stand.

stooge (स्टूज) ***n.*** 1. a puppet, कठपुतली। 2. an entertainer or joker, विदूषक, मसखरा।

stool (स्टूल) ***n.*** 1. a backless and armless seat supported by three or four legs, स्टूल, चौकी। 2. waste matter evacuated from the bowels, मल, पाखाना, गूह।

stoop (स्टूप) ***v.*** 1. to bend forward and downward, आगे की ओर झुकना या झुकाना। 2. to debase (oneself, अपने को) गिरा देना, नीचे उतर आना। ***n.*** the act of stooping, झुकाव, नति।

stop (स्टॉप) ***v.*** 1. to cause to halt, रोकना, रोक देना। 2. to come to halt, रुक जाना, रुकना। 3. to close, बंद कर देना। 4. to prevent, मना कर देना, नहीं होने देना। 5. to desist from, छोड़ देना, बाज़ आना। ***n.*** 1. the act of stopping or the state of being stopped, रुकना, रोक, विराम। 2. a place where bus or train stops regularly, स्टॉप, ठहराव, अड्डा, स्टेशन। 3. something that stops or obstructs, बाधा।

stop-cock (स्टॉप-कॉक) ***n.*** a tap, टोंटी।

stopgap (स्टॉपगैप) ***n.*** temporary substitute, स्थानापन्न।

stopover (स्टॉपओवर) ***n.*** stopping place, पड़ाव, ठहरने की जगह, स्टेशन।

stopper (स्टॉपर) ***n.*** a device to close an opening, plug, डाट, काग।

stop press ***n.*** 1. the news inserted into a newspaper after the printing has been started, छपते-छपते। 2. the space left blank for this, उक्त के लिए छोड़ी हुई खाली जगह।

stopwatch (स्टॉपवाच) ***n.*** a type of watch with mechanism for starting and stopping instantly, विराम घड़ी।

storage (स्टोरिज) ***n.*** 1. the act of storing goods, वस्तु-संचय, संग्रह, संचयन, भंडारण। 2. space reserved for storing, भंडार, गोदाम। 3. the charges for it, गोदाम-भाड़ा।

store (स्टोर) ***v.*** to stock or accumulate, इकट्ठा कर रखना, जमा करना, संचित करना। ***n.*** 1. a stock or supply of something, संचय, संग्रह, भंडार। 2. a shop, दुकान। 3. a storehouse, गोदाम।

storehouse (स्टोरहाउस) ***n.*** a building for storing goods, भंडारगृह, गोदाम।

storey (स्टोरी) ***n.*** a set of rooms on one floor level of a building, इमारत की मंज़िल, खंड, तल्ला।

stork (स्टॉर्क) ***n.*** a large wading bird having long legs and long pointed bill, सारस।

storm (स्टॉर्म) ***n.*** 1. a violent weather condition with strong winds and heavy rain, तूफ़ान। 2. a violent commotion, हंगामा, होहल्ला, तूफ़ान। ***v.*** 1. to rain or snow violently, तूफ़ान आना। 2. to try to capture by sudden attack, सहसा धावा बोलकर क़ब्ज़ा करने का प्रयास करना।

stormy (स्टॉर्मी) ***adj.*** 1. full of storms, तूफ़ानी। 2. affected by storms, तूफ़ान से पीड़ित, तूफ़ानग्रस्त। 3. violent, उग्र, प्रचंड।

story (स्टोरी) ***n.*** 1. a short fictional

S

composition, कहानी। 2. an account of an event, वृत्तांत।

stout (स्टाउट) ***adj.*** 1. physically strong, तगड़ा, मज़बूत, हृष्ट-पुष्ट। 2. bold, निर्भीक, साहसी।

stove (स्टोव) ***n.*** an apparatus for cooking, स्टोव।

stow (स्टो) ***v.*** to store, संचित करना।

straddle (स्ट्रैडल) ***v.*** 1. to place oneself with a leg on either side, (किसी चीज़ पर) दोनों ओर टाँगें फैलाकर बैठना। 2. to stand with the legs wide apart, टाँगें फैलाकर खड़े होना।

straggle (स्ट्रैगल) ***v.*** 1. to stray from the path or fall behind, रास्ते से भटक जाना या पीछे रह जाना। 2. to scatter, बिखर जाना।

straight (स्ट्रेट) ***adj.*** 1. extending continuously in one direction without curving, direct, सीधा, ऋजु। 2. having no waves or bends, समतल। 3. in proper order, सुव्यवस्थित, व्यवस्थित। 4. honest, ईमानदार, सच्चा, निष्कपट, सीधा। 5. upright, erect, खड़ा। ***adv.*** 1. in a straight line, सीधे, नाक की सीध में, बिना मुड़े या घूमे। 2. without delay, सीधे, बिना विलंब के। 3. erectly, सीधे।

straightaway (स्ट्रेटअवे) ***adv.*** at once, तुरंत।

straighten (स्ट्रेटन) ***v.*** to make or become straight, सीधा करना या होना।

straightforward (स्ट्रेटफॉर्वर्ड) ***adj.*** 1. honest, ईमानदार, निष्कपट। 2. frank, स्पष्टवादी।

strain[1] (स्ट्रेन) ***v.*** 1. to stretch tightly, कसकर फैलाना, तानना। 2. to exert to the utmost, घोर परिश्रम करना, बहुत ज़ोर लगाना। 3. to injure or become injured by overexertion, अधिक परिश्रम से क्षति उठाना या अपनी क्षति करना। 4. to filter, छानना। ***n.*** 1. the act of straining or the state of being strained, तनाव, खिंचाव। 2. the force exerted, परिश्रम, दबाव। 3. an injury or distortion caused by straining, अधिक परिश्रम से होनेवाली क्षति या विकृति। 4. mental tension, दिमाग़ी तनाव।

strain[2] ***n.*** 1. the collective descendants of a common ancestor, वंश, कुल। 2. an inherited tendency, पुश्तैनी प्रवृत्ति।

strainer (स्ट्रेनर) ***n.*** 1. a sieve, छलनी, चलनी। 2. a filter, छन्ना।

strait (स्ट्रेट) ***n.*** 1. a narrow passage of water joining two seas, जलडमरूमध्य। 2. (often plu.) a difficult position, संकट।

straitented (स्ट्रेटन्ड) ***adj.*** 1. narrow, संकीर्ण, संकुचित। 2. difficult, कठिन।

straitlaced (स्ट्रेटलेस्ड) ***adj.*** excessively strict in morality, शुद्धाचारी, अतिसंयमी।

strand[1] (स्ट्रैन्ड) ***n.*** the edge of the body of water, किनारा, तट। ***v.*** 1. to drive (a ship) to the strand, किनारे या रेती पर जहाज़ को ले आना। 2. to put or come into a difficult position, मुसीबत में फँसना या फँसाना।

strand[2] ***n.*** 1. one of the threads or wires twisted together, लड़। 2. a ropelike string, डोरी। 3. a single hair, बाल।

stranded (स्ट्रैन्डिड) ***adj.*** left in difficulties, मुसीबत में पड़ा या फँसा, संकटग्रस्त।

strange (स्ट्रेन्ज) ***adj.*** 1. unfamiliar, अपरिचित, असामान्य, विचित्र। 2. unaccustomed, अनभ्यस्त।

S

stranger (स्ट्रेन्जर) ***n.*** an outsider or foreigner, अजनबी, परदेसी, विदेशी।

strangle (स्ट्रैन्गल) ***v.*** 1. to throttle, गला घोंट देना, मार डालना। 2. to restrict or suppress, रोक या दबा देना।

stranglehold (स्ट्रैंन्गलहोल्ड) ***n.*** complete control or grip, पूर्ण नियंत्रण, पूरी पकड़, कड़ी जकड़।

strangulate (स्ट्रैंग्युलेट) ***v.*** to compress (a vein, नस) दबा देना।

strangulation (स्ट्रैंग्युलेशन) 1. the act of strangulating or the state of being strangulated, नस का दबना या दबाया जाना। 2. the act of strangling or the state of being strangled, गला घोंटना या घोंटा जाना।

strap (स्ट्रैप) ***n.*** a band often with a buckle for holding, binding etc., फ़ीता, पट्टी, पेटी, तस्मा। ***v.*** 1. to bind with a strap, फ़ीते से बाँधना। 2. to beat with a strap, पेटी से मारना।

stratagem (स्ट्रैटिजम) ***n.*** a trick or scheme for gaining an end, गहरी चाल या युक्ति, तिकड़म।

strategic, strategical (स्ट्रटीजिक, स्ट्रटीजिकल) ***adj.*** 1. of strategy, युक्तिपूर्ण। 2. essential to effective military strategy, सामरिक दृष्टि से महत्त्वपूर्ण।

strategist (स्ट्रैटिजिस्ट) ***n.*** one who is skilled in planning things, नीतिकुशल, योजना कुशल।

strategy (स्ट्रैटिजी) ***n.*** the plan or policy adopted in a war, युद्ध-योजना, युद्धनीति।

stratify (स्ट्रैटिफ़ाइ) ***v.*** to form or arrange in layers or strata, परतें लगाना या बैठाना, स्तरित करना।

stratosphere (स्ट्रैटस्फ़िअर) ***n.*** a layer of earth's atmosphere between about ten to sixty kilometres above the earth's surface, दस से साठ किलोमीटर के बीच ऊँचा पृथ्वी का वायुमंडल, समतापमंडल।

stratum (स्ट्रेटम) ***n.*** (pl. strata) 1. a layer of rock, चट्टानी परत। 2. a social level, सामाजिक स्तर।

straw (स्ट्रॉ) ***n.*** 1. dry cut stalks of grain plants, पुआल, पयाल। 2. a dry coarse stem, तिनका, तृण। 3. a narrow tube for sucking up liquid, पाइप, सींक।

strawberry (स्ट्रॉबेरी) ***n.*** a plant and its fruit, स्ट्रॉबरी (फल)।

straw-board (स्ट्रॉ-बोर्ड) ***n.*** the board made of straw pulp, गत्ता।

stray (स्ट्रे) ***v.*** 1. to deviate from a direct course, भटक जाना, पथभ्रष्ट होना। 2. to deviate from a subject, विषय से भटक जाना, विषयांतर करना। ***adj.*** 1. having strayed, भटका या भटकता हुआ। 2. wandering, आवारा, छुट्टा। 3. occurring here and there, छिट-फुट।

streak (स्ट्रीक) ***n.*** 1. a line of different colour, धारी। 2. a narrow band of light, प्रकाश-किरण, प्रकाश-रेखा, वर्ण-रेखा। 3. a brief run, दौड़। 4. a consecutive series, सतत शृंखला। 5. a trace or element of something, पुट, चाशनी। ***v.*** 1. to mark with streaks, धारियाँ बनाना या डालना। 2. to rush, तेज़ी से भागना। 3. to run naked through a public place, नंगे होकर दौड़ना।

stream (स्ट्रीम) ***n.*** 1. a brook or river, चश्मा, नदी आदि। 2. any steady flow of water or other fluid, बहता पानी,

S

बहती धारा। 3. an unbroken flow, सतत धारा या प्रवाह। 4. a steady succession, ताँता, चलता क्रम। 5. a moving procession, चलता या बढ़ता हुआ जुलूस। ***v.*** 1. to flow, बहना। 2. to emit a stream of, धार फूटना। 3. to wave, लहराना।

streamline (स्ट्रीमलाइन) ***v.*** 1. to organize, संगठित करना। 2. to make simpler, सरल करना या बनाना। 3. to make more efficient, उपयोगी बनाना।

street (स्ट्रीट) ***n.*** a thoroughfare in a city or town, गली, मार्ग, सड़क।

strength (स्ट्रेन्थ) ***n.*** 1. physical power, शक्ति, बल। 2. moral courage, नैतिक बल। 3. capability, क्षमता। 4. the number of people available or present, उपलब्ध या उपस्थित लोग।

strengthen (स्ट्रेन्थन) ***v.*** to make or become strong, बलशाली बनना या बनाना, शक्ति बढ़ना या बढ़ाना।

strenuous (स्ट्रेन्युअस) ***adj.*** 1. making great effort, अध्यवसायी, कर्मठ, मेहनती। 2. requiring great effort, श्रमसाध्य, विकट।

stress (स्ट्रेस) ***n.*** 1. special emphasis or significance, ज़ोर, बल, महत्त्व। 2. extra force used in speaking a particular syllable, बलाघात। 3. pressure, ज़ोर, दबाव। 4. strain, stress, ज़ोर, दबाव। ***v.*** to lay stress on, (किसी अक्षर, शब्द, बात आदि पर) ज़ोर देना।

stretch (स्ट्रेच) ***v.*** 1. to extend, फैलाना। 2. to lengthen or widen by pulling, खींचना, तानना। 3. to become lengthened or widened, फैलना, तनना। 4. to be pulled, खींचा जाना, खिंचना। 5. to extend the limit, scope or meaning of, विस्तृत या व्यापक बनाना। 6. to prolong, बढ़ाना। ***n.*** 1. the act of stretching or the state of being stretched, खिंचाई, खिंचाव, फैलाव, तनाव। 2. the extent to which something can be stretched, फैलाव, लचीलापन। 3. a continuous period of time, अवधि, कालांश।

stretcher (स्ट्रेचर) ***n.*** a framework for carrying a sick or disabled person, स्ट्रेचर।

strew (स्ट्रू) ***v.*** (strewed, strewn/ strewed, strewing) to scatter, बिखेरना, छितराना।

stricken (स्ट्रिकन) ***adj.*** afflicted, ग्रस्त, आक्रांत, पीड़ित।

strict (स्ट्रिक्ट) ***adj.*** 1. severe in discipline, नियमबद्ध, अनुशासनप्रिय, कड़ा, सख़्त, कठोर। 2. precise, exact, सुनिश्चित। 3. complete, पूर्ण।

strictness (स्ट्रिक्टनिस) ***n.*** a strict action, कड़ाई, सख़्ती, कठोरता।

stricture (स्ट्रिक्चर) ***n.*** an adverse criticism, कटु आलोचना, निंदा, आक्षेप।

stride (स्ट्राइड) ***v.*** (strode, striden, striding) to walk with long steps, लंबे-लंबे डग भरना। ***n.*** 1. the act or manner of striding, लंबे-लंबे डग भरना। 2. a single long step, लंबा डग। 3. progress, प्रगति।

strident (स्ट्राइडेन्ट) ***adj.*** loud and harsh, तीव्र और कटु, रूक्ष।

strife (स्ट्राइफ़) ***n.*** 1. bitter or violent conflict, तकरार, झगड़ा, मार-पीट। 2. struggle, संघर्ष।

strike (स्ट्राइक) ***v.*** (struck, stricken/ struck, striking) 1. to hit sharply,

मारना, आघात करना। 2. to collide with, भिड़ंत होना, टक्कर होना या लगना। 3. to cancel or delete, रद करना या (काटकर) निकाल देना। 4. to chime or bell, घंटी बजना या बजाना। 5. to pierce, छेदना। 6. to make an attack, आक्रमण करना। 7. to become ignited, जलना। 8. to shoot, दाग़ना। 9. to make an impression, छाप छोड़ना। 10. to occur to the mind, सूझना, दिमाग़ में कौंधना। 11. to stop work in protest, to engage in a strike, हड़ताल करना। 12. to discover, पता लगना या लगाना। 13. to produce, उत्पन्न करना। 14. to reach (something) by digging or drilling, खुदाई करने पर (किसी चीज़ का) मिलना। 15. to lower (a flag, झंडा) झुकाना। 16. to take down (a tent, तंबू) उतारना। 17. to fill with fear, भयभीत करना। 18. to proceed (in a certain direction, किसी दिशा में) बढ़ना। 19. to make or conclude a bargain, सौदा तय करना। 20. to achieve (a balance, संतुलन) प्राप्त करना। ***n.*** 1. the act of striking, आघात करने की क्रिया या भाव। 2. an attack, आक्रमण। 3. a work stoppage by employees, हड़ताल। 4. a sudden achievement or dicovery, उपलब्धि, सफलता।

striker (स्ट्राइकर) ***n.*** 1. a worker who is on strike, हड़ताली। 2. one who strikes or hits, आघातक, प्रहारक।

striking (स्ट्राइकिंग) ***adj.*** remarkable, impressive, उल्लेखनीय, प्रभावशाली, आकर्षक।

string (स्ट्रिन्ग) ***n.*** 1. a cord for binding, डोरी, तनी, रस्सी, तस्मा, नाड़ा आदि। 2. the wire cord of a musical instrument, bow etc., (बाजे का) तार, तंत्री, (धनुष की) डोरी, प्रत्यंचा। 3. a set of objects threaded together, माला, लड़ी। 4. a sequence or series, माला, शृंखला, पंक्ति, सिलसिला। 5. (plu.) stringed instruments, तंतुवाद्य। 6. (plu.) conditions, शर्तें। ***v.*** 1. to fit with a string or strings, डोरी या तार लगाना। 2. to tighten, कसना। 3. to thread on a string, डोरी में पिरोना। 4. to hang with a string, डोरी से लटकाना।

stringent (स्ट्रिन्जेन्ट) ***adj.*** 1. strict, कड़ा, कठोर। 2. tight, तंग, कसा हुआ।

stringy (स्ट्रिन्गी) ***adj.*** 1. like string, डोरी जैसा। 2. fibrous, रेशेदार।

strip (स्ट्रिप) ***v.*** 1. to take off clothes, कपड़े उतारना, नंगा कर देना, नंगा हो जाना। 2. to tear the thread (of a bolt, पेच आदि की) चूड़ी ख़राब कर देना। 3. to remove furniture, equipments etc. from, फर्नीचर, उपकरण आदि हटा लेना। 4. to deprive, वंचित कर देना। ***n.*** 1. a long narrow area, (भूमि का) टुकड़ा या पट्टी। 2. a long narrow piece of cloth, धज्जी।

stripe (स्ट्राइप) ***n.*** a line of different colour, धारी। ***v.*** to make stripes on, धारियाँ बनाना या डालना।

striped (स्ट्राइप्ड) ***adj.*** having stripes, धारीदार।

strip-show, strip-tease (स्ट्रिप-शो, स्ट्रिप-टीज़) ***n.*** a show in which a woman strips her clothes before the audience, नंगा नाच, नग्न नृत्य।

strive (स्ट्राइव) ***v.*** (strove/strived, striven/strived, striving) 1. to struggle, संघर्ष करना। 2. to make great efforts, घोर प्रयास करना।

S

strode (स्ट्रोड) ***v.*** p.t. & p.p. of stride.

stroke (स्ट्रोक) ***n.*** 1. an act or instance of striking, blow, चोट, प्रहार, आघात। 2. an effort, प्रयास। 3. a single movement made by a pen, brush etc., स्पर्श। 4. a single mark made by a pen or brush, चिह्न, निशान। 5. a single movement of a piston, एकाकी क्रिया। 6. the sound made by a clock, घड़ी के बजने का शब्द, टन-टन। 7. an attack (of paralysis, apoplexy etc.), आघात। ***v.*** to rub lightly, हाथ फेरना, सहलाना।

stroll (स्ट्रोल) ***v.*** to walk in a leisurely manner, टहलना, चहलक़दमी करना। ***n.*** a leisurely walk, चहलक़दमी, टहलना।

strong (स्ट्रॉन्ग) ***adj.*** 1. having strength, सशक्त, हट्टा-कट्टा, तगड़ा। 2. powerful, effective, forceful, sound, शक्तिशाली, प्रभावशाली। 3. intense, ज़ोरदार, प्रचंड। 4. containing much alcohol, कड़ा, तेज़। 5. having an unpleasantly powerful smell or taste, तीखा, तेज़। 6. (of verb) changing the vowel in the past tense, अनियमित (क्रिया)। 7. having a specified number of units, निर्दिष्ट संख्यावाला; an army of ten thousand soldiers, दस हजार सैनिक।

stronghold (स्ट्रॉन्गहोल्ड) ***n.*** a fortress, दुर्ग, गढ़, क़िला।

strong language ***n.*** insulting or coarse language, अपशब्द, गाली, दुर्वचन।

strong-minded (स्ट्रॉन्ग-माइन्डिड) ***adj.*** determined, resolute, दृढ़-निश्चयी।

strop (स्ट्रॉप) ***n.*** a strip of leather on which a razor is sharpened, चमोटा।

strove (स्ट्रोव) ***v.*** p.t. & p.p. of strive.

struck (स्ट्रक) ***v.*** p.t. & p.p. of strike.

structural (स्ट्रक्चरल) ***adj.*** 1. relating to or having structure, संरचनात्मक। 2. used in building structures, इमारती।

structure (स्ट्रक्चर) ***n.*** 1. the manner of construction or organization, बनावट, संरचना। 2. arrangement of the parts of the construction, ढाँचा। 3. something constructed, रचना (जैसे भवन, पुल आदि)।

struggle (स्ट्रगल) ***v.*** 1. to strive, प्रयत्न करना, प्रयास करना। 2. to fight, लड़ना, संघर्ष करना। 3. to progress with great difficulty, जूझना, संघर्ष करना। ***n.*** 1. the act of struggling, संघर्ष। 2. a battle, लड़ाई।

strut (स्ट्रट) ***v.*** to walk in a stiff pompous manner, अकड़ या ऐंठकर चलना। ***n.*** the act of strutting, अकड़-भरी चाल।

stub (स्टब) ***n.*** 1. a short remaining piece, पेंसिल, सिगरेट आदि का बचा हुआ टुकड़ा, टोटा। 2. the stump of a tree, ठूँठ। ***v.*** 1. to dig up (the roots, जड़ें) खोदना। 2. to strike (with one's foot, पैर से) प्रहार करना, ठोकर लगाना।

stubble (स्टबल) ***n.*** 1. the short stiff stalks remaining after harvest, खूँटी। 2. a short growth of beard, खूँटीदार दाढ़ी।

stubborn (स्टबर्न) ***adj.*** obstinate, हठी।

stuck (स्टक) ***v.*** p.t. of stick. ***adj.*** 1. non-plussed, व्याकुल। 2. infatuated, मुग्ध।

stuck-up (स्टक-अप) ***adj.*** conceited, घमंडी।

S

stud[1] (स्टड) ***n.*** 1. a large headed nail, रिवट, गुलमेख, फूलदार कील। 2. a button like device used to fasten cuffs, स्टड, बटन। ***v.*** to decorate with studs, रिवटों या गुलमेखों से सजाना।

stud[2] ***n.*** a male horse for breeding, साँड़ घोड़ा।

student (स्टूडेन्ट) ***n.*** one who studies in a school, college, etc., विद्यार्थी/विद्यार्थिनी, छात्र/छात्रा।

studied (स्टडीड) ***adj.*** carefully calculated or premeditated, सुविचारित।

studio (स्टूडिओ) ***n.*** 1. the working room of an artist, स्टूडियो। 2. a room or building where motion pictures are made, स्टूडियो। 3. a room used to record radio or television programmes, स्टूडियो।

studious (स्टूडिअस) ***adj.*** given to study, devoted to study, अध्ययनशील, अध्यवसायी।

study (स्टडी) ***v.*** 1. to apply one's mind to learn and gain knowledge, अध्ययन करना, अनुशीलन करना। 2. to take (a course) in a school or college, पढ़ना, अध्ययन करना। 3. to examine closely, जाँच-पड़ताल करना। ***n.*** 1. the act of studying, अध्ययन, अनुशीलन, पढ़ाई। 2. a detailed examination, जाँच-पड़ताल। 3. a branch of knowledge, ज्ञान की शाखा। 4. a room for study, अध्ययन-कक्ष।

stuff (स्टफ़) ***n.*** 1. raw material, कच्चा माल। 2. belongings, सामान, असबाब। 3. worthless objects, बेकार चीज़ें, रद्दी चीज़ें। ***v.*** 1. to fill tightly, कसकर भरना, ठूँसना। 2. to fill the empty carcass, खाल में (भूसा आदि) भरना।

stuffed (स्टफ़्ड) ***adj.*** filled, भरा हुआ, भरवाँ।

stuffy (स्टफ़ी) ***adj.*** 1. lacking fresh air, घुटन-भरा, दमघोंटू। 2. narrow-minded, संकीर्ण विचारोंवाला, अनुदार।

stumble (स्टम्बल) ***v.*** 1. to trip or almost fall in walking or running, डगमगाना, लड़खड़ाना। 2. to lose one's balance, संतुलन खो बैठना। 3. to make mistakes, ग़लतियाँ करना। ***n.*** an act of stumbling, डगमगाहट, लड़खड़ाहट।

stumbling block (स्टम्ब्लिंग ब्लॉक) ***n.*** an obstacle, अड़ंगा, बाधा, रुकावट।

stump (स्टम्प) ***n.*** 1. the base of the tree that remains on the ground when the rest has fallen or has been felled, खूँट, जड़, मूल। 2. any of three upright wooden sticks, (क्रिकेट में) लगाए जानेवाले तीन में से कोई डंडा, यष्टि, स्टंप। ***v.*** 1. to walk in a stiff heavy manner, धमधम करते हुए चलना। 2. to baffle, चकरा देना। 3. to dismiss a batsman by knocking the stumps, गिल्लियाँ बिखेरकर आउट कर देना।

stumpy (स्टम्पी) ***adj.*** short and thick, गोल-मटोल।

stun (स्टन) ***v.*** 1. to render senseless by a blow, आघात करके अचेत कर देना। 2. to astound, चकित, चमत्कृत या विस्मित कर देना, भौंचक्का कर देना।

stunning (स्टनिंग) ***adj.*** 1. very attractive, अत्यंत आकर्षक, मुग्धकारी। 2. astonishing, विस्मयकारी।

stunt[1] (स्टन्ट) ***v.*** to hinder the development of, विकास या वृद्धि रोक देना, पनपने न देना।

stunt[2] ***n.*** 1. a feat of daring skill,

S

कमाल का काम, कौतुक। 2. anything unusual done for attention, लोगों का ध्यान आकृष्ट करने के लिए किया हुआ काम, कौतुक। *v.* to perform stunts, कौतुक करना।

stupefaction (स्टूपिफ़ैक्शन) *n.* astonishment, विस्मय; जड़ता।

stupefy (स्टूपिफ़ाइ) *v.* 1. to stun, भौंचक्का, चमत्कृत या विस्मित कर देना, हक्का-बक्का कर देना। 2. to dull the sense of, जड़ बना देना।

stupendous (स्टूपेन्डस) *adj.* astounding, विस्मयकारी, चमत्कृत करनेवाला।

stupid (स्टूपिड) *adj.* 1. slow of mind, मंद-बुद्धि। 2. foolish, मूर्ख।

stupidity (स्टूपिडिटी) *n.* 1. the quality of being stupid, मूर्खता। 2. a stupid act, मूर्खतापूर्ण कार्य।

stupor (स्टूपर) *n.* 1. the state of unconsciousness, बेहोशी, मूर्च्छा। 2. mental dullness, मानसिक शिथिलता।

sturdy (स्टर्डी) *adj.* 1. strongly built, हृष्ट-पुष्ट, तगड़ा। 2. hard, vigorous, कड़ा, ज़ोरदार।

stutter (स्टटर) *v.* to stammer, हकलाना।

sty (स्टाइ) *n.* 1. an enclosure for pigs, सुअरबाड़ा। 2. an inflamed swelling on the edge of the eyelid, बिलनी, गुहेरी।

style (स्टाइल) *n.* 1. the manner of writing, doing or performing, ढंग, शैली। 2. elegance, सौंदर्य, लालित्य। *v.*1. to name or call, नाम धरना या बुलाना। 2. to shape or design, सँवारना, बनाना, रचाना।

stylish (स्टाइलिश) *adj.* 1. conforming to current fashion, फ़ैशनेबुल। 2. elegant, सजीला, बना-ठना।

stylus (स्टाइलस) *n.* a pointed tool for engraving, सुई, शलाका।

suave (स्वाव) *adj.* civilized, भद्र, सभ्य।

sub- (सब) *pref.* 1. under, अधो, नीचे, निम्न। 2. subordinate, उप-, नायब, छोटा; sub-section, उपधारा।

subconscious (सबकॉन्शस) *n.* the part of the mind partly within one's conscious awareness, अवचेतन मन।

subcontract (सबकॉन्ट्रैक्ट) *n.* a contract between a party to an original contract and a third party, उपसंविदा।

subcutaneous (सबक्यूटेनिअस) *adj.* under the skin, खाल के नीचे का, अधस्त्वचीय।

subdue (सबड्यू) *v.* 1. to bring under control, वश में करना, वशीभूत करना। 2. to make less intense or quieter, मंद या धीमा करना।

subhuman (सबह्यूमन) *adj.* less than human, अवमानुषीय, अवमानवीय।

subject (सब्जेक्ट) *adj.* 1. not independent, under someone's authority, परतंत्र, पराधीन। 2. prone (to, की ओर) उन्मुख, प्रवृत्त। *n.* 1. a person under the rule of another person, प्रजा का कोई सदस्य। 2. a citizen, नागरिक। 3. a topic or theme, विषय। 4. a course of study, अध्ययन का विषय। 5. (gram.) the doer of the action, उद्देश्य, कर्ता। *v.* 1. to bring under one's control, अधीन कर लेना। 2. to cause to undergo or experience, अनुभूत कराना, विषय बनाना। □ **subject to,** के अधीन।

subjective (सब्जेक्टिव) *adj.* 1. existing in the mind of the

S

thinking subject, not objective, व्यक्तिनिष्ठ, आत्मनिष्ठ, स्वनिष्ठ। 2. (gram.) of or relating to a subject, कर्तृ, कर्तृपदीय।

subject-matter ***n.*** something written or printed, विषय-वस्तु।

subjects (सब्जेक्ट्स) ***n.*** (plu.) people governed by someone, प्रजा, प्रजाजन।

sub judice (सब्जुडिसी) ***adj.*** now being considered in law, न्यायाधीन।

subjugate (सब्जुगेट) ***v.*** 1. to subdue, दबाना, दमन करना। 2. to bring into subjection, वश में लाना, वशीभूत करना, अधीन करना।

subjunctive (सब्जंक्टिव) ***adj.*** (gram.) expressing an uncertainty, wish or unlikely condition, संभावनार्थक, संभाव्य; subjunctive mood, संभाव्य क्रियार्थ।

sublimate (सब्लिमेट) ***v.*** to improve or refine, परिष्कृत करना, उदात्त बनाना।

sublime (सब्लाइम) ***adj.*** of high spiritual, moral or intellectual worth, उदात्त, श्रेष्ठ।

subliminal (सब्लिमिनल) ***adj.*** subconscious, अवचेतन।

submarine (सबमरीन) ***n.*** a ship that can operate under the surface of the sea, पनडुब्बी। ***adj.*** under the surface of the sea, अंतःसमुद्री।

submerge (सबमर्ज) ***v.*** 1. to put under water, डुबोना, जलमग्न करना। 2. to go under water, डूबना, जलमग्न होना।

submersible (सबमर्सिबल) ***adj.*** capable of soperating while submerged, पानी के अंदर चल सकनेवाला।

submission (सबमिशन) ***n.*** 1. an act of submitting to an authority or the will of another, अधीनता स्वीकार करना, समर्पण। 2. an act of obeying, आज्ञापालन। 3. an act of submitting something for con-sideration, पेशी, प्रस्तुतीकरण; निवेदन।

submissive (सबमिसिव) ***adj.*** yielding, झुकनेवाला, नम्र, विनीत, आज्ञाकारी।

submit (सबमिट) ***v.*** 1. to yield to authority, झुकना, समर्पण करना। 2. to offer, पेश करना या सामने रखना, निवेदन करना। 3. to obey, आज्ञापालन करना।

subordinate (सबॉर्डिनेट) ***adj.*** 1. subject to the authority of another, अधीन, मातहत। 2. of lesser importance or rank, गौण। ***n.*** one who is subordinate, अधीनस्थ व्यक्ति या कर्मचारी। ***v.*** to make subordinate, अधीनस्थ बनाना।

subscribe (सबस्क्राइब) ***v.*** 1. to contribute, अंशदान करना। 2. to contract to pay for a periodical, (पत्रिका आदि का) चंदा देना। 3. to sign (one's name), हस्ताक्षर करना।

subscriber (सबस्क्राइबर) ***n.*** one who subscribes, अंशदान करनेवाला, चंदा देनेवाला।

subscription (सबस्क्रिप्शन) ***n.*** 1. the sum demanded or paid for some issues of a magazine, चंदा। 2. money paid or promised to some institution, अंशदान।

subsequent (सब्सिक्वेन्ट) ***adj.*** succeeding, following, बादवाला, अगला, उत्तरवर्ती।

subservient (सब्सर्विअन्ट) ***adj.*** 1. subordinate, अधीनस्थ, मातहत। 2. servile, चापलूस, जीहुजूरिया।

S

subside (सब्साइड) ***v.*** 1. to come to lower level, घटना, कम हो जाना, उतरना। 2. (of land) to sink, धँस या बैठ जाना। 3. to become tranquil, शांत होना, प्रशमित होना।

subsidiary (सब्सिडिअरी) ***adj.*** subordinate, auxiliary, सहायक, गौण। ***n.*** a subsidiary thing, सहायक या गौण वस्तु।

subsidize (सब्सिडाइज़) ***v.*** to give financial assistance, आर्थिक सहायता देना।

subsidy (सब्सिडी) ***n.*** financial assistance, आर्थिक सहायता, इमदाद।

subsist (सब्सिस्ट) ***v.*** to exist, विद्यमान रहना, जीवित रहना, बना रहना।

subsistence (सब्सिस्टन्स) ***n.*** the act of subsisting, जीवन-निर्वाह, गुज़ारा।

subsoil (सबसॉइल) ***n.*** the layer of soil beneath the earth's surface, अधोमृदा।

substance (सब्स्टैन्स) ***n.*** 1. the material from which something is made, पदार्थ, द्रव्य। 2. meaning, अर्थ, तात्पर्य। 3. essence, सत्त्व, सार। 4. reality, वास्तविकता।

substantial (सब्स्टैन्शल) ***adj.*** 1. worthwhile, सार्थक, सारभूत, उपयोगी। 2. of a considerable amount or size, अच्छी मात्रा या परिमाण का, अच्छा-खासा। 3. wealthy, धनी, संपन्न। 4. important, महत्त्वपूर्ण, सारभूत, सारवान। 5. real, true, वास्तविक, तात्त्विक।

substantiate (सब्स्टैन्शिएट) ***v.*** 1. to put into concrete form, मूर्त रूप देना। 2. to establish by proof, प्रमाण से सिद्ध करना, प्रमाणित करना।

substantive (सब्स्टैंटिव) ***n.*** a noun, संज्ञा। ***adj.*** 1. having existence as a separate being, स्वतंत्र सत्तावाला। 2. real, वास्तविक।

substitute (सब्स्टिट्यूट) ***n.*** a person or thing that serves in place of another person or thing, स्थानापन्न व्यक्ति या वस्तु। ***v.*** 1. to use as a substitute, स्थानापन्न वस्तु या व्यक्ति को प्रयुक्त करना, दूसरे से बदल देना। 2. to serve as a substitute, स्थानापन्न वस्तु या व्यक्ति की तरह प्रयुक्त होना।

substitution (सब्स्टिट्यूशन) ***n.*** 1. the act of substituting, एक की जगह दूसरे व्यक्ति या वस्तु से काम लेना; प्रतिस्थापन। 2. a substitute, स्थानापन्न वस्तु या व्यक्ति।

subtenant (सबटेनन्ट) ***n.*** one who rents property from a tenant, किराएदार का किराएदार, दर-किराएदार।

subterfuge (सब्टर्फ़्यूज) ***n.*** a trickery or excuse, तिकड़म या छलछंद।

subterranean (सब्टेरेनिअन) ***adj.*** underground, भूमिगत।

subtle (सटल) ***adj.*** 1. so slight as to be difficult to detect, सूक्ष्म, बारीक। 2. abstruse, गूढ़, दुर्बोध। 3. able to make fine distinctions, कुशाग्र। 4. clever, चपल, होशियार।

subtract (सब्ट्रैक्ट) ***v.*** to deduct, घटाना।

subtraction (सब्ट्रैक्शन) ***n.*** the act of subtracting, घटाने की क्रिया या भाव, घटाव।

subtropical (सब्ट्रॉपिकल) ***adj.*** of regions bordering on the tropics, उपोष्ण।

suburb (सबर्ब) ***n.*** residential area situated on the outskirts of a city, उपनगर।

suburban (सबर्बन) ***adj.*** of suburbs, उपनगरीय।

subversion (सबवर्ज़न) ***n.*** the act of subverting, उलट देने की क्रिया या भाव, तख़्ता-पलटाव, तोड़-फोड़, विनाश, विध्वंस।

subversive (सबवर्सिव) ***adj.*** tending to subvert, ध्वंसात्मक, विध्वंसक।

subvert (सबवर्ट) ***v.*** 1. to overthrow, उलट देना। 2. to ruin, विनष्ट कर देना।

subway (सबवे) ***n.*** an underground railway, तलमार्ग, सुरंग-पथ, सबवे।

succeed (सक्सीड) ***v.*** 1. to be successful, सफल होना, सफलता प्राप्त करना। 2. to come next in order, किसी की जगह आना, किसी का स्थान ग्रहण करना। 3. to inherit, विरासत में प्राप्त करना, वारिस या उत्तराधिकारी होना।

succeeding (सक्सीडिंग) ***adj.*** following, बादवाला, अनुवर्ती, उत्तरवर्ती।

success (सक्सेस) ***n.*** 1. the achievement of something attempted, सफलता, कामयाबी। 2. the gaining of fame or prosperity, धन या यश का लाभ।

succeessful (सक्सेसफ़ुल) ***adj.*** having success, सफल, कामयाब।

succession (सक्सेशन) ***n.*** 1. the act of following in order, सिलसिला, अनुक्रमण। 2. the act of taking the place of another, पदग्रहण। 3. inheritance, उत्तराधिकार, विरासत।

successive (सक्सेसिव) ***adj.*** following one after another, एक के बाद एक-एक करके आनेवाले, आनुक्रमिक, अनुक्रमी।

successor (सक्सेसर) ***n.*** one who succeeds, उत्तराधिकारी, वारिस।

succour (सकर) ***n.*** 1. help, aid, सहायता। 2. relief, राहत। ***v.*** to give aid to, सहायता करना।

succulent (सक्युलेन्ट) ***adj.*** 1. juicy, रसीला, रसदार। 2. having thick fleshy leaves, जिसके पत्ते गूदेदार हों।

succumb (सकम) ***v.*** 1. to yield to someone overpowering, झुक जाना, घुटने टेक देना। 2. to yield to overpowering desire, डिगना, वशीभूत हो जाना। 3. to die, मर जाना।

such (सच) ***adj.*** 1. of this kind, ऐसा। 2. similar, समान। ***adv.*** to such a degree, इतना, उतना। ☐ **as such,** अतः; **such as,** उदाहरणार्थ। ***n.*** such a person or thing, वह, ऐसा।

such-and-such ***adj.*** particular but not specified, अमुक।

suck (सक) ***v.*** 1. to draw (liquid) into the mouth by inhaling, चूसना। 2. to suckle, पीना, चूसना। 3. to draw in, खींचना, चूसना। ☐ **suck up to,** चापलूसी करना। ***n.*** the act of sucking, चूसने की क्रिया या भाव, चूषण।

suckle (सकल) ***v.*** to give suck to, छाती पिलाना, स्तनपान कराना।

suckling (सक्लिन्ग) ***n.*** an infant or young animal that is not yet weaned, दुधमुँहा बच्चा।

suction (सक्शन) ***n.*** 1. the act of sucking, चूसने की क्रिया या भाव, चूषण। 2. the force produced by a pressure difference that causes something to draw upward, चूषण।

sudden (सडन) ***adj.*** happening quickly or without warning, आकस्मिक, अप्रत्याशित।

suds (सड्ज़) ***n.*** foam of a soapy water, साबुन का फेन, झाग।

sue (स्यू) ***v.*** to bring suit against (someone, किसी के विरुद्ध) मुक़दमा चलाना।

suede (स्वेड) ***n.*** leather with raised fibres, रेशेदार चमड़ा।

S

suffer (सफ़र) ***v.*** 1. to undergo (pain or loss), झेलना, भोगना। 2. to tolerate, सहना, बर्दाश्त करना। 3. to beset at a disadvantage, नुकसान उठाना या परेशान होना।

sufferance (सफ़रन्स) ***n.*** 1. tolerance, बर्दाश्त करने का मादा, सहिष्णुता। 2. sanction or permission because there is no positive objection, मौन स्वीकृति, मौन सहमति।

suffice (सफ़ाइस) ***v.*** to be adequate, पर्याप्त होना।

sufficient (सफ़िशन्ट) ***adj.*** adequate, enough, पर्याप्त, यथेष्ट।

suffix (सफ़िक्स) ***n.*** an affix added at the end of a word, प्रत्यय। ***v.*** to add suffix to, प्रत्यय लगाना।

suffocate (सफ़केट) ***v.*** 1. to kill by stopping the breathing, दम घोंट देना, गला दबा देना। 2. to be killed by deprivation of oxygen, दम घुट जाना। 3. to feel discomfort from lack of fresh air, साँस रुकना, दम घुटना।

suffocation (सफ़केशन) ***n.*** 1. the act of suffocating or the state of being suffocated, गला घोंटने की क्रिया या गला घुटने की अवस्था या भाव। 2. feeling of discomfort from lack of fresh air, घुटन।

suffrage (सफ़्रिज) ***n.*** the right to vote in general election, मताधिकार।

suffuse (सफ़्यूज) ***v.*** to overspread, (किसी तल पर) फैलाना या बिखेरना।

sufi (सूफ़ी) ***n.*** a member of Muslim mystic sect, सूफ़ी।

sugar (शूगर) ***n.*** a sweet substance, चीनी, शक्कर। ***v.*** to sweeten with sugar, चीनी मिलाकर मीठा करना।

sugarcane (शूगरकेन) ***n.*** a plant that yields sugar, गन्ना, ईख।

suggest (सजेस्ट) ***v.*** 1. to propose as a possibility, सुझाव देना, सुझाना, प्रस्ताव करना। 2. to hint, संकेत करना।

suggestion (सजेस्चन) ***n.*** 1. the act of suggesting or something suggested, सुझाव, प्रस्ताव। 2. a hint, संकेत।

suggestive (सजेस्टिव) ***adj.*** 1. suggesting, सुझाव के रूप में होनेवाला। 2. indecent, अश्लील।

suicidal (सूइसाइडल) ***adj.*** 1. involving suicide, आत्महत्या-संबंधी। 2. tending to suicide, आत्मघातक, आत्मघाती।

suicide (सूइसाइड) ***n.*** 1. the intentional killing of oneself, आत्महत्या, ख़ुदकुशी। 2. one who commits suicide, आत्महंता। 3. ruin of one's own interest, आत्मघात।

suit (सूट) ***n.*** 1. a set of clothes to be worn together, जोड़, जोड़ा, सूट। 2. any of the four series of playing cards, ताश के किसी रंग के पत्तों का समूह। 3. a lawsuit, मुक़दमा, वाद, दावा। ***v.*** 1. to be fit or appropriate for, फबना, सजना, भला लगना, जँचना। 2. to be agreeable, अनुकूल होना, अच्छा लगना।

suitable (सूटेबल) ***adj.*** appropriate, befitting, उपयुक्त, अनुकूल, उचित।

suitcase (सूटकेस) ***n.*** a case for carrying clothes, सूटकेस।

suite (स्वीट) ***n.*** 1. a number of attendants or followers, अनुचरवर्ग, अनुचरवृंद। 2. a set, जोड़, सेट; suite of rooms, (दो-तीन) कमरों का सेट। 3. (music.) a set of musical pieces, वाद्यसंगीत रचना (जिसमें कई पद हों)।

suiting (सूटिंग) ***n.*** the fabric for making suits, सूट का कपड़ा।

sulk (सल्क) ***v.*** to be sulky, रूठ जाना, मान करना।

sulky (सल्की) ***adj.*** aloof because of resentment, रूठा हुआ, रुष्ट।

sullen (सलन) ***adj.*** 1. sulky, रुष्ट, रूठा हुआ, नाराज़। 2. gloomy, उदास, उचाट।

sully (सली) ***v.*** 1. to spoil, मैला या कलुषित करना। 2. to tarnish, कलंक लगाना, कलंकित करना।

sulphur (सल्फ़र) ***n.*** a pale yellow substance used in medicine, explosives etc., गंधक।

sultan (सल्टन) ***n.*** the sovereign of a Muslim country, सुलतान।

sultanate (सल्टनेट) ***n.*** the territory ruled by a sultan, सल्तनत, राज्य।

sultry (सल्ट्री) ***adj.*** 1. oppressively hot and humid, उमसदार। 2. hot, गरम। 3. sensual, कामुक।

sum (सम) ***n.*** 1. a total, जोड़, योग, योगफल। 2. a problem in arithmetic, गणित का प्रश्न। 3. an indefinite or specified amount of money, धनराशि, रक़म। ☐ **lump sum,** एकमुश्त रक़म; **sum up,** निचोड़ निकालना।

summarize (समराइज़) ***v.*** 1. to make a summary of, सारांश निकालना। 2. to express briefly, थोड़े में कहना।

summary (समरी) ***n.*** a brief account, condensed statement, संक्षेप, सार, सारांश। ***adj.*** 1. brief, संक्षिप्त। 2. performed quickly and without formality, सरसरी रूप से होनेवाला।

summation (समेशन) ***n.*** 1. a summary, संक्षेप, सार, सारांश। 2. a total number or amount, कुल जोड़, कुल योग।

summer (समर) ***n.*** the warmest season of the year, गरमी का मौसम, ग्रीष्म ऋतु, गरमी।

summit (समिट) ***n.*** 1. a top, शिखर, चोटी। 2. a meeting of heads of governments, शिखर-सम्मेलन।

summon (समन) ***v.*** 1. to order or request to come, बुलाना, आह्वान करना। 2. to order to appear in court, समन भेजना।

summons (समन्ज़) ***n.*** a written order to appear in the court of law, समन, आह्वान-पत्र।

sumptuous (सम्प्चुअस) ***adj.*** 1. splendid, राजसी, भव्य। 2. expensive, महँगा, बहुमूल्य।

sun (सन) ***n.*** 1. the star that gives light in the daytime, सूरज, सूर्य। 2. its heat and visible light, धूप, घाम। ***v.*** to expose to the sunshine, धूप में रखना, धूप दिखाना।

sunbath (सनबाथ) ***n.*** exposure of one's body to the sun, धूपस्नान।

sunburn (सनबर्न) ***n.*** an inflammation of the skin caused by prolonged exposure to the sun, धूप में होनेवाली झुलसन। ***v.*** (sunburned/sunburnt, sunburning) to be afflicted with sunburn, धूप से झुलसना।

Sunday (सनडे) ***n.*** the day following Saturday, रविवार, इतवार।

sunder (सन्डर) ***v.*** to break into pieces, टुकड़े-टुकड़े करना, छिन्न-भिन्न करना।

sundial (सनडाइअल) ***n.*** a device showing time during the daytime, धूप-घड़ी।

sundries (सन्ड्रीज़) ***n.*** various small items not named individually, फुटकर वस्तुएँ।

sundry (सन्ड्री) ***adj.*** various, विविध, फुटकर। ☐ **all and sundry,** हर कोई, सभी तरह के लोग।

S

sunflower (सनफ़्लाउअर) ***n.*** a plant and its flower, सूर्यमुखी।

sunken (सन्कन) ***adj.*** 1. submerged, डूबा हुआ। 2. depressed or hollow, दबा हुआ, खोखला।

sunlight (सनलाइट) ***n.*** the light from the sun, धूप।

sunny (सनी) ***adj.*** 1. full of sunshine, धूपयुक्त, धूपदार। 2. cheerful, प्रसन्न, प्रफुल्ल।

sunrise (सनराइज़) ***n.*** the rising of the sun above the horizon, सूर्योदय।

sunset (सनसेट) ***n.*** the setting of the sun below the horizon, सूर्यास्त।

sunshine (सनशाइन) ***n.*** the direct rays from the sun, धूप।

sunstroke (सनस्ट्रोक) ***n.*** a stroke caused by prolonged exposure, लू लगना।

super (सूपर) ***adj.*** excellent, उच्चकोटि का, बढ़िया, उत्कृष्ट।

super- (सूपर) ***pref.*** 1. above, over, ऊपर, से अधिक या बढ़कर, अधि-। 2. of greater size or quality, महा।

superannuation (सूपरैन्यूएशन) ***n.*** 1. retirement, सेवानिवृत्ति, अवकाश-प्राप्ति। 2. pension, पेंशन।

superb (सूपर्ब) ***adj.*** 1. excellent, उत्कृष्ट, बढ़िया। 2. imposing, majestic, भव्य, शानदार।

superficial (सूपर्फ़िशल) ***adj.*** 1. of or on the surface, ऊपरी, सतही। 2. shallow, छिछला, उथला।

superfine (सूपफ़ाइन) ***adj.*** 1. of extra high quality, ऊँची गुणवत्तावाला। 2. of extra fine texture, अत्यंत उत्कृष्ट बुनावटवाला।

superfluous (सूपफ़्लूअस) ***adj.*** excessive, अत्यधिक, अनावश्यक।

superhuman (सूपर्ह्यूमन) ***adj.*** 1. beyond human ability, अतिमानवीय। 2. supernatural, अलौकिक, दिव्य।

superimpose (सूपरिम्पोज़) ***v.*** to lay on or place over something else, ऊपर रखना, अध्यारोपण करना।

superintendent (सूपरिन्टेन्डन्ट) ***n.*** one who superintends, अधीक्षक।

superior (सूपीरिअर) ***adj.*** 1. higher in rank or status, ऊँचा, वरिष्ठ, श्रेष्ठ। 2. of higher quality, उच्चकोटि का, बढ़िया, उत्कृष्ट। 3. conceited, घमंडी। ***n.*** a person of greater rank or status, उच्चाधिकारी।

superiority (सूपीरिऑरिटी) ***n.*** 1. the quality or state of being superior, वरिष्ठता, श्रेष्ठता। 2. excellence, उत्कृष्टता।

superlative (सूपर्लेटिव) ***adj.*** 1. of highest degree, उत्तम, सर्वोत्कृष्ट, सर्वोत्तम। 2. (gram.) expressing the highest degree, उत्तमतासूचक, उत्तमावस्था का सूचक।

superman (सूपर्मैन) ***n.*** a man with more than human powers, अतिमानव।

supermarket (सूपर्मार्किट) ***n.*** a large self-service retail store, सुपर बाज़ार।

supernatural (सूपर्नैचुरल) ***adj.*** divine, अलौकिक, लोकोत्तर, दिव्य।

supernumerary (सूपर्न्यूमेरी) exceeding a regular or fixed number, नियमित या नियत संख्या से अधिक, अधिसंख्य।

superpower (सूपर्पाउअर) ***n.*** one of the powerful nations of the world, महाशक्ति।

supersede (सूपर्सीड) ***v.*** 1. to take the place of, दूसरे का स्थान ग्रहण करना,

दूसरे की जगह लेना। 2. to cause to be set aside, हटा देना, भंग करना।

supersonic (सूपर्सॉनिक) ***adj.*** moving at a speed greater than that of sound, पराध्वनिक, ध्वनि की गति से तेज़।

superstar (सूपर्स्टार) ***n.*** a great star, बहुत बड़ा अभिनेता, महाभिनेता।

superstition (सूपर्स्टिशन) ***n.*** an unreasoningly upheld belief, अंधविश्वास।

supervise (सूपर्वाइज़) ***v.*** to inspect the work of, काम की देख-रेख करना, पर्यवेक्षण करना।

supervision (सूपर्विज़न) ***n.*** the act of supervising, देख-रेख, पर्यवेक्षण।

supervisor (सूपर्वाइज़र) ***n.*** one who supervises, पर्यवेक्षक, सुपरवाइज़र।

supine (सुपाइन) ***adj.*** 1. lying with face upward, चित (लेटा हुआ)। 2. lacking in action, lazy, सुस्त, आलसी।

supper (सपर) ***n.*** an evening meal, रात का भोजन, रात्रिभोज।

supplant (सप्लान्ट) ***v.*** 1. to uproot, उखाड़ देना। 2. to supersede, दूसरे का स्थान (छल या बल से) ग्रहण करना।

supplement (सप्लिमेन्ट) ***n.*** 1. something that completes or makes an addition, पूरक, अनुपूरक। 2. a part added to a book, newspaper etc., to give extra information, परिशिष्ट। ***v.*** 1. to add or complete, जोड़ना, पूरा करना। 2. to add supplement to, परिशिष्ट जोड़ना या लगाना।

supplementary (सप्लिमेन्टरी) ***adj.*** 1. additional, अतिरिक्त। 2. added as a supplement, अनुपूरक।

supplicant (सप्लिकन्ट) ***adj. & n.*** a suppliant, चिरौरी करनेवाला।

supplicate (सप्लिकेट) ***v.*** to make a humble entreaty, चिरौरी करना, विनय करना।

supplier (सप्लाइअर) ***n.*** one who supplies, पूर्तिकर्ता, सप्लायर।

supply (सप्लाइ) ***v.*** 1. to provide, देना, प्रदान करना। 2. to make available for use or sale, पूर्ति करना, आपूर्ति करना। ***n.*** something supplied for sale or use, पूर्ति, आपूर्ति।

support (सपोर्ट) ***v.*** 1. to hold or maintain in position, सहारा देना, टेक देना, सँभालना। 2. to promote the interest or cause of, समर्थन करना। 3. to assist or help, सहायता करना। 4. to endure, बर्दाश्त करना। ***n.*** 1. the act of supporting or the state of being supported, समर्थन। 2. aid, help, सहायता। 3. a prop, टेक, सहारा।

supporter (सपोर्टर) ***n.*** one who supports, समर्थन करनेवाला, समर्थक।

suppose (सपोज़) ***v.*** 1. to assume, मान लेना, कल्पना करना। 2. to guess, अटकल लगाना।

supposition (सपज़िशन) ***n.*** something supposed, कल्पना; मान्यता।

suppress (सप्रेस) ***v.*** 1. to crush, कुचल डालना। 2. to quell, शांत कर देना। 3. to conceal, छिपा देना। 4. to prevent, रोक देना।

suppression (सप्रेशन) ***n.*** the act of suppressing or the state of being suppressed, दमन, निग्रह।

suppressive (सप्रेसिव) ***adj.*** that suppresses, दमनकारी, दमनात्मक।

supra (सूप्रा) ***adv.*** above or before, ऊपर या पहले।

S

supremacy (सूप्रेमेसी) ***n.*** the state or quality of being supreme, श्रेष्ठता, सर्वोच्चता।

supreme (सूप्रीम) ***adj.*** highest in rank or authority, उच्चतम, सर्वोच्च।

supremely (सूप्रीमली) ***adv.*** very, अत्यंत, अत्यधिक।

surcharge (सर्चार्ज) ***n.*** extra charge, अतिरिक्त देय, अधिप्रभार। ***v.*** to make a surcharge on, अधिभार लगाना।

sure (श्योर) ***adj.*** 1. that can be relied upon, विश्वसनीय। 2. confident, विश्वस्त। 3. certain, निश्चित। 4. true, सत्य, सच्चा। 5. certain to do something, अमोघ, अचूक।

surely (श्योर्ली) ***adv.*** certainly, निश्चित रूप से, निस्संदेह, निश्चय ही।

surety (श्योर्टी) ***n.*** 1. the state of being sure, certainty, निश्चय, असंदिग्धता। 2. a guarantee, गारंटी। 3. one who makes oneself responsible for another, ज़मानतदार, जामिन, प्रतिभू।

surf (सर्फ़) ***n.*** the white foam of breaking waves, समुद्री फेन। ***v.*** 1. to go surfing, सर्फबोर्ड पर यात्रा करना। 2. to move between sites on the internet, इन्टरनेट पर जानकारी लेना।

surface (सर्फ़िस) ***n.*** 1. the outside of an object, ऊपरी सतह, ऊपरी तल, धरातल। 2. the outward appearance, बाह्य रूप। ***adj.*** 1. of or on the surface, ऊपरी, सतही। 2. superficial, ऊपरी, साधारण, सामान्य। ***v.*** 1. to form the surface of, चौरस बनाना। 2. to come to the surface, सतह या तल पर आना।

surfeit (सर्फ़िट) ***v.*** to satiate, छककर खाना या खिलाना, अघा जाना या अघा देना। ***n.*** 1. the act of surfeiting or the state of being surfeited, अघाव। 2. an excessive amount, अत्यधिक मात्रा।

surge (सर्ज) ***v.*** to move like waves, लहरों की तरह बढ़ना, उफनना। ***n.*** a motion like that of great waves, उफान।

surgeon (सर्जन) ***n.*** a specialist in surgery, शल्यकार, जर्राह, सर्जन।

surgery (सर्जरी) ***n.*** 1. an act of operating, शल्यकर्म, शल्यचिकित्सा, जर्राही, सर्जरी। 2. an operating room, शल्यचिकित्सा कक्ष, शल्यकक्ष।

surly (सर्ली) ***adj.*** bad tempered, चिड़चिड़ा।

surmise (सर्माइज़) ***v.*** to guess or conjecture, अनुमान लगाना, अटकल लगाना। ***n.*** guess, conjecture, अटकल, अनुमान।

surmount (सर्माउन्ट) ***v.*** 1. to overcome or conquer, पार पाना, जीत लेना। 2. to climb, चढ़ना।

surname (सर्नेम) ***n.*** 1. a family name, कुलनाम, वंशनाम। 2. a given name, उपनाम।

surpass (सर्पास) ***v.*** 1. to excel, आगे निकल या बढ़ जाना, (दूसरों पर अपनी) श्रेष्ठता सिद्ध कर देना। 2. to outdo, मात कर देना।

surpassing (सर्पासिंग) ***adj.*** of a very high degree, असाधारण, बढ़ा-चढ़ा, श्रेष्ठ।

surplus (सर्प्लस) ***n.*** 1. an amount or quantity in excess of what is required, बेशी, बचा हुआ अंश, फ़ालतू चीज़। 2. an excess of receipts over disbursements, बचत, लाभ। ***adj.*** being a surplus, बचा हुआ, बचत के रूप में होनेवाला।

surprise (सर्प्राइज़) ***n.*** 1. the feeling caused by something happening unexpectedly or suddenly, आश्चर्य, विस्मय। 2. unexpected occurrence, आकस्मिक घटना। ***v.*** 1. to astonish, चकित कर देना, आश्चर्य में डाल देना, चौंका देना। 2. to attack or capture suddenly, सहसा टूट पड़ना या आक्रमण कर देना।

surprising (सर्प्राइज़िंग) ***adj.*** causing surprise, विस्मयकारी, आश्चर्यजनक।

surrealism (सरीअलिज़म) a movement in art and literature that seeks to express or portray the objects seen in the dreams, अतियथार्थवाद।

surrender (सरेन्डर) ***v.*** 1. to give up oneself to the authorities or a conqueror, आत्मसमर्पण करना, अभ्यर्पण करना। 2. to give up possessions, अर्पित कर देना। ***n.*** the act of surrendering or the state of being surrendered, आत्मसमर्पण, समर्पण।

surreptitious (सरेप्टिशस) ***adj.*** done or made stealthily, चोरी-छिपे किया जाने या बनाया जानेवाला, चोरी का।

surrogate (सरगेट) ***n.*** 1. a deputy, सहायक। 2. a substitute, स्थानापन्न।

surround (सराउन्ड) ***v.*** 1. to encircle, चारों ओर घेरा डालना, घेर लेना। 2. to enclose from all sides, चारों ओर से बंद कर देना।

surroundings (सराउन्डिंग्स) ***n.*** 1. the external circumstances, परिवेश, वातावरण। 2. the things around, आस-पास की चीज़ें, पास-पड़ोस।

surveillance (सर्वेलन्स) ***n.*** close observation, निगरानी, चौकसी, देख-रेख।

survey (सर्वे) ***v.*** 1. to look at and take general view of, सर्वेक्षण करना। 2. to determine and map out the location, boundaries etc., of a plot or building, नक़्शा बनाना। ***n.*** the act of surveying or the state of being surveyed, सर्वेक्षण।

surveyor (सर्वेअर) ***n.*** one who surveys, सर्वेक्षक।

survival (सर्वाइवल) ***n.*** the act of surviving or the state of being survived, बचे रहना, उत्तरजीविता।

survive (सर्वाइव) ***v.*** 1. to continue to be alive, जीवित रहना, बना रहना, चला चलना। 2. to live or exist longer (than others, दूसरों की अपेक्षा) लंबी उम्र पाना, उत्तरजीवी होना।

susceptible (ससेप्टिबल) ***adj.*** having a sensitive nature or feelings, जल्दी प्रभावित हो जानेवाला, संवेदी, ग्रहणशील।

suspect (सस्पेक्ट) ***v.*** 1. to suppose to be, संभावित लगना या प्रतीत होना। 2. to believe that (someone) is guilty, (किसी को) दोषी समझना, (किसी पर) संदेह करना। ***n.*** a person who is suspected of a crime, संदिग्ध व्यक्ति।

suspend (सस्पेन्ड) ***v.*** 1. to debar temporarily (from any office, किसी पद से) निलंबित करना। 2. to cause to stop temporarily, (कोई कार्य या सेवा) स्थगित करना। 3. to defer, or put off, टाल देना, आस्थगित करना, रोके रखना। 4. to hold without attachment, टँग जाना, अटक जाना, लटकना।

suspense (सस्पेन्स) ***n.*** 1. the condition or quality of being undecided, अनिश्चय की स्थिति, दुविधा, असमंजस। 2. the state of being uncertain as in awaiting a decision, अनिश्चयजन्य उत्सुकता।

S

suspension (सस्पेन्शन) ***n.*** 1. the act of suspending or the state of being suspended, निलंबन, मुअतली। 2. the act of hanging or the state of being hung, टँगने, अटकने या लटकने की क्रिया, अवस्था या भाव।

suspicion (सस्पिशन) ***n.*** 1. belief without sure proof, doubt, संशय, संदेह, शंका। 2. a hint, संकेत।

suspicious (सस्पिशस) ***adj.*** 1. causing suspicion, संदिग्ध, संशयजनक। 2. feeling suspicion, शंकालु, सशंक।

sustain (सस्टेन) ***v.*** 1. to keep alive, जीवित (बनाए) रखना। 2. to maintain, भरण-पोषण करना। 3. to bear, सहना, झेलना। 4. to support, समर्थन करना।

sustainable (सस्टेनेबल) ***adj.*** that can be sustained, जिसे जीवित रखा जा सके; जिसका भार उठाया जा सके, धारणीय।

sustained (सस्टेन्ड) supported, maintained, संपोषित; समर्थित; धारित।

sustenance (सस्टिनन्स) ***n.*** 1. livelihood, जीविका। 2. nourishment, पोषण।

swab (स्वॉब) ***n.*** 1. a piece of cotton attached to the end of a stick for cleansing or applying medicine, फाहा। 2. a mop, झाड़न या पुचारा। ***v.*** to cleanse with a swab, झाड़न या पुचारे से साफ़ करना।

swallow[1] (स्वॉलो) ***v.*** 1. to devour, निगल जाना, लीलना। 2. to grab, हड़प जाना/लेना। 3. to bear humbly, चुपचाप सहन करना, पी जाना। 4. to take back, वापस लेना। 5. to repress, दबा देना। ***n.*** 1. the act of swallowing, निगलने की क्रिया या भाव। 2. the amount swallowed at a time, एक बार में निगली जानेवाली मात्रा, घूँट या ग्रास।

swallow[2] ***n.*** a small bird with short legs and long pointed wings, अबाबील।

swam (स्वैम) ***v.*** p.t. of swim.

swami (स्वामी) ***n.*** a lord, स्वामी।

swamp (स्वॉम्प) ***n.*** a marsh, कीचड़, दलदल। ***v.*** 1. to submerge in water, जलमग्न कर देना या हो जाना। 2. to overburden or be overburdened, लाद देना या लादा जाना।

swan (स्वॉन) ***n.*** a large water bird having a long neck, a long slender beak and a white plumage, हंस, मराल।

swap (स्वॉप) ***v.*** to exchange, अदला-बदली करना, विनिमय करना। ***n.*** an exchange, अदला-बदली, विनिमय।

swarm (स्वॉर्म) ***n.*** a large group of bees, insects or animals, झुंड, दल, गिरोह।

swat (स्वॉट) ***v.*** to strike or hit sharply, (मक्खी आदि को) पंखी आदि किसी चपटी चीज से झटके से मारना।

sway (स्वे) ***v.*** 1. to swing or cause to swing, झूमना, झूलना या झुलाना। 2. to lean to one side, एक तरफ़ झुकना, उलरना। 3. to influence (the opinions or actions of others, दूसरों की राय या कार्य) बदल देना, प्रभावित करना। ***n.*** 1. a swinging movement, पेंग। 2. an act of swaying, झूलने की क्रिया या भाव, झुलाव। 3. influence, प्रभाव, ज़ोर।

swear (स्वेअर) ***v.*** (swore, sworn, swearing) 1. to state or declare on oath, शपथ लेना, शपथपूर्वक कहना। 2. to assert with great emphasis, ज़ोर देकर कहना।

swear-word (स्वेअर-वर्ड) ***n.*** an

obscene word, गाली, अपशब्द।

sweat (स्वेट) ***n.*** 1. perspiration, पसीना, स्वेद। 2. a laborious task, मेहनत का काम। 3. drops of moisture, जलकण। ***v.*** (sweat/sweated, sweating) 1. to perspire, पसीना होना, पसीने से तर-ब-तर होना। 2. to cause to perspire, पसीना लाना। 3. to work long and hard, देर तक कड़ी मेहनत करना, पसीना बहाना।

sweater (स्वेटर) ***n.*** a knitted jacket, स्वेटर।

sweep (स्वीप) ***v.*** (swept, sweeping) 1. to clean (with a broom, brush etc.) झाड़ू देना, बुहारना। 2. to move or remove by pushing, बहा ले जाना। 3. to win overwhelmingly, अच्छी ख़ासी जीत होना। 4. to extend gracefully, अच्छी तरह फैला होना। 5. to move proudly, शान से चलना, अकड़कर चलना। ***n.*** 1. the act of sweeping, सफ़ाई। 2. expanse, फैलाव, विस्तार।

sweeper (स्वीपर) ***n.*** 1. a person who sweeps, झाड़ू लगानेवाला, झाड़ूकश, मेहतर। 2. a machine for sweeping, सफ़ाई मशीन।

sweet (स्वीट) ***adj.*** 1. having a sugary taste, मीठा, मधुर। 2. melodious, मधुर, कर्णप्रिय। 3. fresh, जो बासी न हो, ताज़ा। 4. pleasant, अच्छा, प्रिय, ख़ुशगवार। 5. fragrant, ख़ुशबूदार, सुगंधित। ***n.*** 1. a sweetmeat, मिठाई, मिष्ठान्न। 2. any sweet dish, मधुर व्यंजन।

sweet corn ***n.*** a variety of maze, एक तरह की मक्की।

sweeten (स्वीटन) ***v.*** to make or become sweet, मीठा बनाना या बनना।

sweetheart (स्वीटहार्ट) ***n.*** a lover, प्रियतम या प्रियतमा, प्रेमी या प्रेयसी।

sweetmeat (स्वीटमीट) ***n.*** any sweet delicacy prepared with sugar, मिठाई।

sweet potato ***n.*** a plant and its root used as a vegetable, शकरकंद।

sweet tooth ***n.*** a strong liking for sweets, मिष्ठान्न-प्रेम।

swell (स्वेल) ***v.*** (swelled, swollen/ swelled, swelling) 1. to make or become larger in size due to internal pressure, फुलाना या फूलना, सुजाना या सूजना। 2. to make or become larger in numbers, amount, intensity etc., बढ़ाना या बढ़ना। ***n.*** 1. a swelling, सूजन, शोथ। 2. an increase in size, amount, intensity etc., बढ़ती, बढ़ोतरी, वृद्धि। 3. a person very fashionably dressed, छैला, बना-ठना व्यक्ति। ***adj.*** very good, बहुत बढ़िया।

swelling (स्वेलिंग) ***n.*** inflammation, सूजन।

swelter (स्वेल्टर) ***v.*** to perspire, पसीने-पसीने होना।

swerve (स्वर्व) ***v.*** to turn suddenly, एकाएक मुड़ना।

swift (स्विफ़्ट) ***adj.*** 1. fast, speedy, rapid, तेज़, तीव्रगामी। 2. prompt, उद्यत, तत्पर। ***n.*** a swift-flying bird resembling the swallow, अबाबील जाति का एक पक्षी, बतासी।

swim (स्विम) ***v.*** (swam, swum, swimming) 1. to move through water by movements of arms, legs, fins etc., तैरना। 2. to cause to swim, तैराना। 3. to reel, घूमना, चक्कर खाना। ***n.*** 1. the act of swimming, तैरने की क्रिया, संतरण। 2. a period of swimming, तैरने की अवधि।

S

swimming (स्विमिंग) ***n.*** the act of a person who swims, तैरने की क्रिया, संतरण। ***adj.*** affected with a dizzy, जिसका सिर घूम रहा हो।

swimmingly (स्विमिंगली) ***adv.*** 1. successfully, सफलतापूर्वक। 2. effortlessly, अनायास, आराम से।

swimming pool ***n.*** an indoor tank for swimming, तरणताल।

swindle (स्विन्डल) ***v.*** to cheat, धोखा देना, ठगना। ***n.*** an act of swindling, ठगी, धोखेबाज़ी।

swindler (स्विन्डलर) ***n.*** one who swindles, ठग, धोखेबाज़।

swine (स्वाइन) ***n.*** 1. a pig, सुअर। 2. a contemptible person, घिनौना व्यक्ति।

swing (स्विन्ग) ***v.*** (swung, swinging) 1. to hang freely, लटकना, झूलना। 2. to move backward and forward with regular movements, झूलना। 3. to cause to move backward and forward with regular movements, झुलाना। 4. to move or wave, (हथियार आदि) घुमाना, चमकाना। 5. to turn, घूमना या घुमाना। 6. to influence, प्रभावित करना। ***n.***1. the act of swinging, झूलने की क्रिया या भाव। 2. a hanging seat, झूला। 3. rhythm, लय, गति। 4. ch-anging of opinion, मत-परिवर्तन। □**in full swing,** ज़ोरों पर, बहार पर।

swinging (स्विन्गिंग) ***adj.*** lively, जीवंत।

swipe (स्वाइप) ***v.*** 1. to hit hard, ज़ोर से आघात करना। 2. to steal or snatch, चुराना या झपटना। ***n.*** a hard blow, जोर का आघात।

swirl (स्वर्ल) ***v.*** to move with a whirling movement, चक्कर खाते हुए चलना, भँवर की तरह चलना।

swish (स्विश) ***v.*** to move with a hissing sound, सरसराना। ***n.*** a hissing or rustling sound, सरसराहट।

Swiss (स्विस) ***adj.*** of Switzerland, स्विट्ज़रलैंड का। ***n.*** a native of Switzerland, स्विट्ज़रलैंड का वासी।

switch (स्विच) ***n.*** 1. a device used to open and close an electric circuit, (बिजली का) खटका, बटन, स्विच। 2. a device for diverting trains from one track to another, रेल की पटरियों की कैंची। 3. a shift (in opinion, policy etc., राय, नीति आदि में होनेवाला) परिवर्तन। 4. a stick or rod used for whipping, (मारने की) छड़ी या डंडा। ***v.*** 1. to turn a switch, खटका दबाना या उठाना। 2. to change or shift, बदलना। 3. to exchange, अदल-बदल करना। 4. to beat with a stick, छड़ी, बेंत आदि से मारना, पीटना।

switch board ***n.*** a board for controlling electric circuits, विद्युत्फलक, स्विचबोर्ड।

swivel (स्विवल) ***n.*** a coupling device that enables an attached part to rotate freely, अँकुड़ा, चूल, फिरकी, चूलछल्ला। ***v.*** to rotate freely, घूमना।

swollen (स्वोलन) ***adj.*** enlarged by swelling, सूजा हुआ, उभरा हुआ।

swoop (स्वूप) ***n.*** a pounce, झपट्टा, छीना-झपटी। ***v.*** to pounce, झपट्टा मारना, टूट पड़ना, छीन-झपट करना।

swop (स्वॉप) ***n.*** exchange, अदला-बदली। ***v.*** to exchange, अदला-बदली करना।

sword (सोर्ड) ***n.*** a cutting weapon with a long blade, तलवार।

swore (स्वोर) ***v.*** p.t. of swear.

sworn (स्वोर्न) ***adj.*** bound by an oath, शपथ से बँधा, सशपथ।

S

sycophant (सिकफ़ैन्ट) ***n.*** a person who uses flattery to win big people, खुशामदी, चापलूस, चाटुकार।

syllabic (सिलैबिक) ***adj.*** of or pertaining to the syllables, अक्षर-संबंधी, आक्षरिक।

syllable (सिलेबल) ***n.*** a unit of spoken language consisting of a single uninterrupted sound, अक्षर।

syllabus (सिलेबस) ***n.*** brief statement or main points of a course of study, पाठ्यचर्या, पाठ्य-विवरण।

sylvan (सिल्वन) ***adj.*** 1. of forest regions, वन्य, वन-संबंधी। 2. abounding in trees, वृक्ष-बहुल।

symbiosis (सिम्बिओसिस) ***n.*** the relationship of two or more different organisms, in a close association, जीवाणु-साहचर्य।

symbol (सिम्बल) ***n.*** something that suggests something else by association, resemblance or convention, प्रतीक।

symbolism (सिम्बलिज़्म) ***n.*** use of symbols to express things, प्रतीकवाद।

symbolize (सिम्बलाइज़) ***v.*** 1. to serve as a symbol, प्रतीक होना। 2. to express by symbols, प्रतीकों द्वारा व्यक्त करना।

symmetry (सिमिट्री) ***n.*** exact correspondence between the parts, सममिति, समरूपता।

sympathetic (सिम्पथेटिक) ***adj.*** 1. showing sympathy, सहानुभूति-परक, सहानुभूतिपूर्ण। 2. agreeable, अनुकूल।

sympathizer (सिम्पथाइज़र) ***n.*** 1. one who sympathizes, सहानुभूति रखनेवाला, ख़ैरख़ाह, हमदर्द। 2. a supporter, समर्थक।

sympathy (सिम्पथी) ***n.*** 1. a feeling of pity for the person in distress, दया, करुणा। 2. mutual affection or understanding, सहानुभूति, हमदर्दी। 3. sharing the feelings or interests of others, ख़ैरख़ाही, हितकारिता।

symphony (सिम्फ़नी) ***n.*** 1. a long orchestral composition, लंबी वाद्यवृंदीय रचना, सिम्फनी। 2. harmony of sounds, समस्वरता।

symposium (सिम्पोज़िअम) ***n.*** a meeting for discussion of a particular subject, परिचर्चा, विचार-गोष्ठी।

symptom (सिम्प्टम) ***n.*** 1. a sign of disease or physical disturbance, बीमारी का लक्षण। 2. an indication or sign, चिह्न, निशान।

symptomatic (सिम्प्टोमैटिक) ***adj.*** being a symptom of a disease, लक्षणात्मक, लाक्षणिक, रोगसूचक।

synagogue (सिनागॉग) ***n.*** a place for public Jewish worship, यहूदियों का सार्वजनिक पूजास्थल।

synchronic (सिन्क्रॉनिक) ***adj.*** happening at the same time, समकालिक।

synchronize (सिन्क्रनाइज़) ***v.*** to happen at the same time, साथ-साथ होना या घटना, समकालिक होना, समकालीन होना।

syndicate (सिन्डिकिट) ***n.*** an association of firms, व्यवसायी-संघ, अभिषद्, सिंडीकेट।

syndrome (सिन्ड्रोम) ***n.*** a group of symptoms of a particular disease, संलक्षण, लक्षण-समूह।

synonym (सिनॉनिम) ***n.*** a word with a meaning very similar to that of another, पर्याय, समानार्थी।

S

synonymous (सिनॉनिमस) ***adj.*** similar in meaning, पर्यायवाचक, समानार्थक।

synopsis (सिनॉप्सिस) ***n.*** an outline of a thesis or treatise, रूपरेखा, सारांश।

syntax (सिन्टैक्स) ***n.*** 1. grammatical arrangement of words in sentences, वाक्य-रचना। 2. the part of grammar dealing with this, वाक्य-विचार, वाक्य-विज्ञान।

synthesis (सिन्थसिस) ***n.*** the combining of separate parts to form a whole, संश्लेषण, संयोजन, संयोग।

synthetic (सिन्थेटिक) ***adj.*** 1. relating to synthesis, संश्लेषण-संबंधी, संश्लिष्ट, संश्लेषी। 2. manmade, मानव-निर्मित।

syphilis (सिफ़िलिस) ***n.*** a venereal disease, गरमी, आतशक।

syphon (साइफ़न) ***n.*** = siphon.

syringe (सिरिन्ज) ***n.*** an instrument for injecting medicine into the body, पिचकारी, सिरिंज। ***v.*** to inject with a syringe, पिचकारी द्वारा द्रव भीतर डालना या चढ़ाना।

syrup (सिरप) ***n.*** a thick sweet liquid, शर्बत, चाशनी, शीरा।

system (सिस्टम) ***n.*** 1. a particular method, पद्धति, प्रणाली। 2. orderliness, क्रमिकता, क्रमबद्धता। 3. a network, जाल।

systematic (सिस्टमैटिक) ***adj.*** methodical or orderly, व्यवस्थित, क्रमबद्ध।

systematize (सिस्टमटाइज़) ***v.*** to make systematic, व्यवस्थित या क्रमबद्ध करना।

systemic (सिस्टेमिक) ***adj.*** 1. of or affecting the body as a whole, पूरे शरीर को प्रभावित करनेवाला। 2. pervading, व्याप्त होनेवाला, व्यापी।

systole (सिस्टली) ***n.*** the contraction of the heart, हृदयसंकोच, प्रकुंचन।

T

T, t (टी) ***n.*** the twentieth letter of the English alphabet, अंग्रेज़ी वर्णमाला का बीसवाँ वर्ण।

tab (टैब) ***n.*** 1. a loop to hang up garments, घुंडी। 2. a projection attached to an object to aid in opening, handling etc., घुंडी। 3. a flap or label, लेबल। 4. close surveillance, निगरानी।

tabby (टैबी) ***adj.*** 1. having a striped design, धारीदार। 2. wavy, लहरिएदार। ***n.*** a tabby cat, धारीदार बिल्ली।

table (टेबल) ***n.*** 1. an article of furniture consisting of flat slab fixed on legs, मेज़। 2. a data arranged in rows and columns, सारणी, तालिका। 3. a multiplication table, पहाड़ा। ***v.*** 1. to put on the table, मेज़ पर रखना। 2. to submit for discussion, विचारार्थ प्रस्तुत करना, रखना।

tableau (टैब्लो) ***n.*** (plu. tableaux) 1. a silent scene, मूक दृश्य। 2. a dramatic scene, नाटकीय दृश्य।

tableland (टेबललैन्ड) ***n.*** a plateau, पठार।

tablespoon (टेबलस्पून) ***n.*** 1. a large spoon for serving food at the table, भोजन परोसने का बड़ा चम्मच। 2. the amount held by a tablespoon, बड़ा चम्मच-भर सामान।

tablet (टैब्लिट) ***n.*** 1. a pill, गोली, टिकिया। 2. a slab of stone or wood, तख़्ती, पट्टी।

table tennis ***n.*** a table game played with rackets and ball, टेबल टेनिस।

tabloid (टैब्लॉइड) ***n.*** a newspaper of small format, छोटे आकार का समाचारपत्र, लघुपत्र।

taboo, tabu (टैबू) ***n.*** any ban or prohibition resulting from social customs, वर्जन, निषेध। ***adj.*** prohibited by taboo, वर्जित, निषिद्ध। ***v.*** to avoid as taboo, निषिद्ध समझकर छोड़ देना।

tabular (टैबुलर) ***adj.*** 1. arranged in rows and columns, सारणीबद्ध। 2. flat, सपाट।

tabulate (टैबुलेट) ***v.*** to put into tabular form, सारणीबद्ध करना।

tacit (टैसिट) ***adj.*** implied or understood without being expressed, विवक्षित, ध्वनित या सांकेतिक, मौन।

taciturn (टैसिटर्न) ***adj.*** reserved, uncommunicative, चुप्पा, अल्प-भाषी।

tack (टैक) ***n.*** 1. a small nail, कटिया, छोटी कील। 2. a long loose stitch, कच्चा टाँका, तोपा। 3. stickiness, चिपचिपाहट। 4. a course of action, कार्यनीति, कार्यपद्धति। 5. a zigzag course, टेढ़ा-मेढ़ा रास्ता। 6. a course of a vessel, जलयान-पथ, पोत-मार्ग। ***v.*** 1. to fasten with tacks, कटिया जड़ना। 2. stitch loosely, तोपे या टाँके लगाना। 3. to add or append, जोड़ना, नत्थी करना। 4. to sail a zig-zag course, जहाज़ को टेढ़े-मेढ़े ले चलना।

tackle (टैकल) ***n.*** 1. a set of equipment used in lifting heavy weights, रस्सा-पुल्ली। 2. the equipment required for a

T

particular activity, औज़ार, साज़-सामान, साज़-सामग्री। 3. a physical challenge to an opponent, भिड़ंत। *v.* 1. to undertake (a task, काम) लेना या उठाना। 2. to come to grapple with, भिड़ना, जूझना। 3. to settle, निपटाना। 4. to try to overcome, अभिभूत करनें की चेष्टा करना।

tacky[1] (टैकी) ***adj.*** 1. sitcky, चिपचिपा। 2. not quite dry, जो ठीक से सूखा न हो, गीला।

tacky[2] ***adj.*** 1. shabby, फटेहाल। 2. vulgar, फूहड़।

tact (टैक्ट) ***n.*** skill in handling difficult persons or situations, व्यवहारकौशल, शऊर।

tactful (टैक्टफुल) ***adj.*** having or showing tact, व्यवहारकुशल।

tactic (टैक्टिक) ***n.*** 1. a tactical move, दाँवपेंच, युक्ति, चाल। 2. (plu.) plans to achieve a certain aim, योजना, योजना-कौशल, रणनीति।

tactile (टैक्टाइल) ***adj.*** 1. perceptible by touch, स्पृश्य, स्पर्शग्राह्य। 2. of or relating to the sense of touch, स्पर्शेंद्रिय-संबंधी।

tactless (टैक्टलिस) ***adj.*** without tact, कौशलहीन, बेशऊर।

tadpole (टैडपोल) ***n.*** larva of frogs, toads, etc., इल्ली।

taffeta (टैफ़िटा) ***n.*** a silk fabric, ताफ़्ता।

tag (टैग) ***n.*** 1. a metal point at the end of a shoelace, फ़ीते की घुंडी। 2. a strip of paper, metal or plastic etc., attached to something to show its price, लेबल, टिक्का, चिप्पी। 3. a loop or knot of a garment, घुंडी। 4. a much used phrase or quotation, hackneyed saying, घिसा-पिटा पदबंध या उद्धरण, घिसी-पिटी उक्ति। 5. a cardboard marker for identification, निशानी। *v.* 1. to fasten a tag, चिप्पी चिपकाना, लेबल लगाना। 2. to follow closely, पीछा करना।

tail (टेल) ***n.*** 1. a flexible appendage of the vertebrates, पूँछ, दुम। 2. the last or rear portion, अंतिम भाग। 3. a person following or shadowing another, जो किसी का पीछा करे या उसके पीछे लगा रहे। 4. (plu.) reverse of a coin, सिक्के का पट। *v.* 1. to follow or shadow closely, पीछा करना या पीछे लगे रहना। 2. to remove the tail of an animal, दुम काटना। □ **tail off,** निरंतर घटते जाना, निरंतर कम होना।

tailboard, tailgate (टेलबोर्ड, टेलगेट) ***n.*** a board or gate hinged downward at the rear of trucks, ट्रक का पिछला तख़्ता।

tail light (टेललाइट) ***n.*** the light at the rear of a vehicle, वाहन की पिछली बत्ती।

tailor (टेलर) ***n.*** one whose occupation is to make garments, दरज़ी। *v.* 1. to make garments, कपड़े काटना, सीना या बनाना। 2. to make or adapt for a special purpose, विशेष उपयोग के लिए बनाना, ढालना आदि।

tailoring (टेलरिंग) ***n.*** the occupation of a tailor, दरज़ी का धंधा, दरज़ीगीरी।

tailspin (टेलस्पिन) ***n.*** the dive of an aircraft in a nose down spiralling motion, चक्कर खाते हुए हवाई जहाज़ का सिर के बल नीचे उतरना।

taint (टेन्ट) ***n.*** 1. a defect or flaw, दोष, दूषण। 2. a contaminated influence, विकार, संदूषण। 3. a stain, धब्बा। ***v.*** 1. to make rotten, गला-सड़ा देना,

विकृत कर देना। 2. to tarnish, कलंकित कर देना।

take (टेक) ***v.*** (took, taken, taking) 1. to get into one's hand, लेना, पकड़ना, थामना। 2. to get possession of, अधिकार में लेना, क़ब्ज़ा करना। 3. to seize, छीनना, पकड़ना। 4. to catch, पकड़ना, लोकना। 5. to win, जीतना। 6. to carry with one to another place, एक स्थान से दूसरे स्थान पर ले जाना। 7. to charm or captivate, अभिभूत या मोहित कर लेना। 8. to assume, कल्पना करना, मान लेना। 9. to deduct, घटाना। 10. to assume (the seat, office, obligation etc.), ग्रहण करना। 11. to write down, लिखना, अंकित करना। 12. to accept, स्वीकार करना, ठीक मानना या समझना। 13. to purchase, खरीदना। 14. to start growing, उगना। 15. to have sexual intercourse with, सहवास करना, मैथुन करना। 16. to convey or transport, ले जाना या लाना। 17. to happen, हो जाना। ☐ **take after,** अनुरूप होना; **take at one's word,** किसी बात को सत्य मान लेना; **take down,** (i) लिख लेना, टाँक लेना, (ii) ध्वस्त कर देना, (iii) घटा या कम कर देना; **take for granted,** निश्चित मान बैठना; **take off,** (i) (कपड़े) उतारना, (ii) जहाज़ का उड़ान भरना, उड़ना, (iii) रवाना होना, (iv) जान लेना, मारना, (v) नकल उतारना; **take on,** (i) नौकर रखना, नौकरी पर रखना, (ii) किराए पर लेना, (iii) धारण करना, (iv) प्रस्तुत हो जाना, (v) लड़ना, भिड़ना, मुकाबला करना; **take over,** धारण या ग्रहण करना, भार या दायित्व ग्रहण करना; **take upon,** भार उठाना, दायित्व लेना। ***n.*** 1. the number of animals killed or captured, शिकार किए हुए नग। 2. the amount of anything taken, ली हुई रक़म या लिया हुआ दाम। 3. an instance of photographing a scene for a motion picture, चलचित्र के लिए लिया हुआ दृश्य।

take-off (टेक्‌-ऑफ़) ***n.*** 1. the act of taking off in flying, वायुयान का ज़मीन से उड़ान भरना। 2. an act of mimicry, नक़ल।

takeover (टेकओवर) ***n.*** 1. the act of seizing control, सत्ता हथियाने की क्रिया या भाव। 2. the act of seizing management, प्रबंधत्व ग्रहण करने की क्रिया या भाव।

talc (टैल्क) ***n.*** a fine-grained mineral used in making talcum powder, सेलखड़ी।

talcum powder ***n.*** a powder used for perfuming the body, पाउडर।

tale (टेल) ***n.*** 1. a story or report of happenings or events, क़िस्सा, वृत्तांत। 2. a short story, कहानी।

talent (टैलन्ट) ***n.*** natural or acquired ability of a superior quality, प्रतिभा, गुण।

talented (टैलन्टिड) ***adj.*** having talent, प्रतिभाशाली, प्रतिभावान, गुणी।

talisman (टैलिस्मन) ***n.*** an object supposed to bring good luck, an amulet or charm, तावीज़, जंतर।

talk (टॉक) ***v.*** 1. to articulate words, बोलना। 2. to converse by means of spoken language, बातचीत करना। ***n.*** 1. a speech, भाषण, व्याख्यान। 2. conversation, बातचीत, विचार-विमर्श। 3. rumour, अफ़वाह। 4. (plu.) negotiations, वार्ता, वार्तालाप।

talkative (टॉकेटिव) ***adj.*** talking too much, बड़बोला, गपोड़संख, बातूनी।

T

talkie (टॉकी) ***n.*** a talking picture, बोलपट, टाकी।

talking-to (टॉकिंग-टू) ***n.*** a reproof, डाँट, डाँट-फटकार।

tall (टॉल) ***adj.*** 1. of more than average height, लंबा। 2. having a specified height, निश्चित लंबाईवाला।

tall order ***n.*** a difficult task, मुश्किल काम, कठिन कार्य।

tallow (टैलो) ***n.*** animal fat used in soap, lubricants etc., चरबी, पशुवसा।

tally (टैली) ***v.*** 1. to count, गिनना, गिनती करना। 2. to correspond one with another, मिलान करना। 3. to agree, मेल खाना। ***n.*** 1. an account, विवरण (अंकों के रूप में होनेवाला)। 2. a counterpart or duplicate of something, मुसन्ना या प्रतिलिपि। 3. correspondence, मिलान। 4. agreement, मेल, अनुरूपता।

talon (टैलन) ***n.*** 1. a claw, चंगुल, पंजा। 2. (plu.) human fingers like a claw, पंजा।

tamable (टेमेबल) ***adj.*** that can be tamed, जिसे पालतू बनाया या सधाया जा सके।

tamarind (टैमरिन्ड) ***n.*** a tree with acid-flavoured pods, इमली।

tambourine (टैम्बरीन) ***n.*** a small drum-like musical instrument, डफली, खंजरी।

tame (टेम) ***adj.*** 1. changed from wild to a domesticated state, पालतू, सधाया हुआ (जानवर)। 2. meek and submissive, दब्बू, विनम्र, भला। 3. not interesting, uninspi-ring, अरुचिकर, नीरस। ***v.*** 1. to make tame, पालतू बनाना, सधाना। 2. to subdue or curb, वश में करना। 3. to make useful, उपयोगी बनाना।

tameable (टेमेबल) ***adj.*** = tamable.

tamp (टैम्प) ***v.*** 1. to fill up (a hole, सुराख को) भरना। 2. to drive down by a succession of blows, ठोंक-ठोंककर धँसाना।

tamper (टैम्पर) ***v.*** to interfere so as to weaken or change for the worse, छेड़खानी करना, छेड़-छाड़ करना, ख़राब कर देना या बिगाड़ देना।

tampon (टैम्पॉन) ***n.*** a plug of cotton etc., inserted into a bodily cavity or wound, फाहा, टैम्पन।

tan (टैन) ***v.*** 1. to convert hide into leather by treatment, चमड़ा बनाना, चमड़ा कमाना। 2. to make or become brown by exposure to the sun, ताँबियाना या ताँबिया जाना। 3. to beat or thrash, पिटाई करना, मारना-पीटना। ***n.*** 1. tree bark used in tanning hides, चमड़ा सिझाने के काम आनेवाली छाल। 2. yellowish brown colour, ताँबे का रंग, ताम्रवर्ण। ***adj.*** 1. yellowish brown, पीलापन लिये भूरा, ताम्रवर्ण। 2. having a suntan, धूप से झुलसा हुआ।

tandem (टैन्डम) ***adv.*** one behind the other, आगे-पीछे। ***n.*** a cycle built for two, बाइसिकल।

tang (टैन्ग) ***n.*** 1. a sharp odour, तेज गंध, महक। 2. a sharp taste, चरपराहट, झाल।

tangent (टैन्जन्ट) ***n.*** a straight line touching the circle, स्पर्शज्या।

tangible (टैन्जिबल) ***adj.*** 1. capable of being touched, जिसे छुआ जा सके, स्पृश्य, मूर्त। 2. material, भौतिक। 3. real, वास्तविक।

tangle (टैन्गल) ***v.*** 1. to intertwine in a confused mass, उलझना। 2. to ensnare, जाल में फँसाना। ***n.***

1. confused mass of fibres, hair, lines etc., उलझाव। 2. a complicated problem, उलझन, गुत्थी।

tangy (टैन्गी) ***adj.*** having a strong smell, महकदार।

tank (टैन्क) ***n.*** 1. a pond, तालाब। 2. a large container for water, gas etc., हौज़, टंकी। 3. an enclosed heavily armoured fighting vehicle, टैंक।

tanker (टैन्कर) ***n.*** a truck, ship or aircraft for carrying oil or other liquid in bulk, तेल-वाहक, टैंकर।

tanner (टैनर) ***n.*** one who tans hides, चर्मशोधक।

tannery (टैनरी) ***n.*** a place where hides are tanned, चर्मशोधक कारख़ाना।

tantalize (टैन्टलाइज़) ***v.*** to keep (someone) hanging on, (किसी को) झुलाए रखना, ललचाना, तरसाना।

tantamount (टैन्टमाउन्ट) ***adj.*** having equal force, value or effect, बराबर, समान।

tantrum (टैन्ट्रम) ***n.*** a fit of bad temper, झल्लाहट, बौखलाहट, क्रोधावेश।

tap[1] (टैप) ***n.*** 1. a plug or cork, डॉट, कॉर्क। 2. a device to control the flow of a liquid, gas etc., टोंटी। 3. a device for cutting an internal screw threads, किसी पाइप के अंदर चूड़ी काटने का उपकरण, सुंबा, टेप। 4. a connection for tapping a telephone, चोरी-छिपे किसी का टेलीफ़ोन सुनने के लिए लगाया हुआ कनेक्शन। ***v.*** 1. to fit or furnish with a tap, टोंटी लगाना। 2. to draw off liquid through a hole or tap, छेद या टोंटी से तरल पदार्थ निकालना। 3. to cut a screw thread inside, पाइप के अंदर सुंबे से चूड़ी करना। 4. to make a connection for overhearing someone's telephone, चोरी-छिपे किसी का टेलीफ़ोन सुनने के लिए कनेक्शन जोड़ना।

tap[2] ***v.*** to strike gently and lightly with the flat of the hand, थपकी देना, थपथपाना। ***n.*** 1. a quick light blow, खट, ठक। 2. the sound of this, खट, ठक।

tape (टेप) ***n.*** 1. a narrow strip of woven fabric, पट्टी, फ़ीता। 2. a narrow band of paper or other flexible material, टेप। ***v.*** 1. to bind or fasten with tape, फ़ीते से बाँधना या कसना। 2. to record on magnetic tape, टेप करना।

taper (टेपर) ***n.*** a waxed wick used to light candles, मोमबत्तियाँ जलाने की बत्ती। ***v.*** to make or become gradually narrower, बराबर सँकरा या पतला करते चलना या होते जाना, गावदुम होना या करना।

taperecorder (टेपरिकॉर्डर) ***n.*** an apparatus for recording sounds and playing back the recording, ध्वनि टेप करने तथा टेप की हुई उस ध्वनि को बजाने का उपकरण, टेपरिकॉर्डर।

tapestry (टैपिस्ट्री) ***n.*** a heavy woven textile for curtains, wall hangings etc., परदों आदि का मोटा कपड़ा।

tapeworm (टेपवर्म) ***n.*** a ribbon like flat worm, फ़ीता-कृमि।

tapioca (टैपिओका) ***n.*** a starchy substance obtained from cassava root, एक प्रकार का माड़ीदार पदार्थ, टैपियोका।

taproom (टैपरूम) ***n.*** bar-room, (होटल का) मदिरा-कक्ष।

tar (टार) ***n.*** coaltar, अलकतरा, तारकोल, डामर। ***v.*** to coat with tar, अलकतरा

T

डालना, डामर (की परत) बिछाना।

tardy (टार्डी) ***adj.*** 1. sluggish, सुस्त, शिथिल, धीमा। 2. occurring later than expected, देर से होनेवाला।

tare[1] (टेअर) ***n.*** 1. the weight of empty container/vehicle, खाली पेटी/वाहन का वज़न।

tare[2] ***n.*** a plant used as fodder, चरी।

target (टार्गिट) ***n.*** 1. a mark to shoot at, निशाना, लक्ष्य। 2. an object of attack, ridicule or criticism, निशाना, लक्ष्य। ***v.*** to make a target of, निशाना बनाना।

tariff (टैरिफ़) ***n.*** 1. a list of duties imposed on imports or exports. आयात या निर्यात शुल्क की सूची। 2. duty to be paid on imports or exports, प्रशुल्क, टैरिफ़। 3. a schedule for rates or fees, दर-सूची, मूल्य-सूची। ***v.*** to subject to a tariff, (पर) शुल्क लगाना।

tarmac (टार्मैक) ***n.*** 1. material for surfacing roads, तारकोली रोड़ी। 2. the road made with this, पक्की सड़क

tarnish (टार्निश) ***v.*** 1. to become or make discoloured, बदरंग हो जाना या कर देना, भद्दा हो जाना या कर देना। 2. to stain or become stained, धब्बे पड़ना या डालना, कलंकित होना या करना। ***n.*** 1. loss of lustre, रंग या चमक का उड़ना। 2. a stain, धब्बा।

taro (टारो) ***n.*** a plant with a tuberous root, अरबी या कचालू नामक कंद।

tarpaulin (टारपॉलिन) ***n.*** a heavy water-proof fabric coated with tar, तिरपाल।

tarsal (टार्सल) ***adj.*** of tarsus, टखने का।

tarsus (टार्सस) ***n.*** the bones of the heel collectively, टखना।

tart[1] (टार्ट) ***adj.*** 1. sharp in taste, तीखा, चरपरा। 2. biting, तीखा, उग्र।

tart[2] ***n.*** 1. a small pie containing jelly etc., गुजिया। 2. a prostitute, वेश्या।

tartar (टार्टर) ***n.*** a hard yellowish deposit on teeth, दाँतों पर जमी मैल।

Tartar (टार्टर) ***n.*** 1. a Mongol or Turk, मंगोल या तुर्क, तातार। 2. a ferocious person, ख़ूँखार व्यक्ति।

task (टास्क) ***n.*** an assigned piece of work to be done, काम।

task force ***n.*** a temporary grouping of forces and resources for the purpose of accomplishing a definite objective, किसी विशिष्ट उद्देश्य के लिए संगठित दल, कार्यबल।

taskmaster ***n.*** a person who assigns task to others, दूसरों को काम देने या सौंपनेवाला, दूसरों से काम करानेवाला सक्षम व्यक्ति।

tassel (टैसल) ***n.*** an ornamental bunch of loose threads or strips fastened at one end, फुँदना, झब्बा। ***v.*** to decorate with tassels, फुँदनों से सजाना, फुँदने लगाना।

taste (टेस्ट) ***v.*** 1. to test or ascertain the flavour of something by taking into mouth, स्वाद लेना या बताना। 2. to eat or drink small quantity (of), चखना। 3. to have the experience or enjoyment for the first time, पहली बार अनुभव होना, मज़ा आना या मिलना। ***n.*** 1. the sensation produced by something placed in the mouth, स्वाद। 2. one of the five senses which distinguishes the flavour of something, रसेंद्रिय। 3. a small quantity eaten to taste, चखी जानेवाली वस्तु। 4. a liking, सुरुचि, पसंद।

5. a limited or first experience, पहला अनुभव, सीमित अनुभूति। 6. the ability to perceive and enjoy what is beautiful, रसानुभूति, सौंदर्यानुभूति।

tasteful (टेस्टफ़ुल) ***adj.*** 1. having or showing good taste, सुरुचिसंपन्न। 2. conforming to a good taste, सुरुचिपूर्ण।

tasteless (टेस्टलिस) ***adj.*** 1. having no taste, स्वादहीन, बेस्वाद। 2. not exhibiting good taste, कुरुचिपूर्ण।

tasty (टेस्टी) ***adj.*** pleasing to the taste, स्वाद में बढ़िया, स्वादिष्ट, जायक़ेदार।

tata (टाटा) ***interj.*** good-bye, अलविदा! टा-टा!

tatter (टैटर) ***n.*** 1. a shred. धज्जी। 2. (plu.) torn and ragged clothing, फटे वस्त्र, चिथड़े। ***v.*** 1. to tear to tatters, चिथड़े कर देना। 2. to make or become ragged, फटीचर बनना या बनाना।

tattered (टैटर्ड) ***adj.*** ragged, फटेहाल।

tattle (टैटल) ***v.*** 1. to reveal the secrets of another, दूसरे के रहस्य खोलना। 2. to prate, बकबक करना। 3. to gossip, गप लड़ाना। ***n.*** a gossip, गप।

tattoo[1] (टैटू) ***n.*** 1. a military display, सैनिकों का प्रदर्शन। 2. a rhythmic drum beating, ढोल का ताल से बजना, थपथपाना।

tattoo[2] ***n.*** a mark or design made on the skin by pricking it, गोदना। ***v.*** (tattooed, tattooing) to mark with a tattoo, गोदना गोदना।

taught (टॉट) ***v.*** p.t. & p.p. of teach.

taunt (टॉन्ट) ***v.*** to deride jeeringly, ताना मारना, कटाक्ष करना। ***n.*** a sarcastic remark, कटाक्ष, ताना।

tauntingly (टॉन्टिन्गली) ***adv.*** in a taunting manner, कटाक्षपूर्वक, ताने के स्वर में।

Taurus (टॉरस) ***n.*** the second sign of Zodiac, वृष राशि।

taut (टॉट) ***adj.*** 1. tight, कसा हुआ। 2. tense, तनावग्रस्त। 3. firm, दृढ़। 4. trim, साफ़-सुथरा।

tauten (टॉटन) ***v.*** to make or become taut, कसना या कसा जाना, तानना या तनना।

tautology (टॉटॉलोजी) ***n.*** needless repetition of a word or idea, द्विरुक्ति, पुनरावृत्ति।

tavern (टैवर्न) ***n.*** 1. a bar, मधुशाला। 2. an inn, सराय।

tawdriness (टॉड्रिनिस) ***n.*** the state or quality of being tawdry, भड़कीलापन, दिखावट, दिखावा।

tawdry (टॉड्री) ***adj.*** cheap and gaudy, भड़कीला, दिखावटी।

tawny (टॉनी) ***adj.*** light golden brown, नारंगी के रंग का।

tax (टैक्स) ***n.*** 1. a charge levied by authority, कर, टैक्स। 2. an excessive demand, दबाव, भार, बोझ। ***v.*** 1. to levy a tax on, कर लगाना, टैक्स लगाना। 2. to make heavy demands upon, दबाव डालना।

taxable (टैक्सेबल) ***adj.*** that can be taxed, कर-योग्य।

taxation (टैक्शेसन) ***n.*** the act of levying taxes, करारोपण।

taxi (टैक्सी) ***n.*** a car that carries passengers for a fare, टैक्सी। ***v.*** (taxied, taxiing) 1. to ride in a taxi, टैक्सी करना, टैक्सी पर जाना। 2. to transport by taxi, टैक्सी से भेजना।

taxidermist (टैक्सिडर्मिस्ट) ***n.*** one who practices taxidermy, चर्म-प्रसाधक।

taxidermy (टैक्सिडर्मी) ***n.*** the art of

preparing, stuffing and mounting the skins of animals in lifelike forms, पशुओं की खाल में भूसा आदि भरकर उन्हें सजीव-सा बनाने का काम, चर्म-प्रसाधन।

taxing (टैक्सिंग) ***adj.*** onerous, burdensome, दूभर, विकट।

taxonomy (टैक्सॉनोमी) ***n.*** the science of classification of organisms on common characteristics, जीव-वर्गीकरण।

tea (टी) ***n.*** 1. a shrub, चाय। 2. leaves of this shrub, चाय की पत्ती। 3. a beverage prepared from the tea leaves, चाय का पानी। 4. an afternoon tea, शाम की चाय।

teach (टीच) ***v.*** (taught, teaching) 1. to impart knowledge or skill to, सिखाना, सिखलाना। 2. to cause to know a subject, पढ़ाना।

teacher (टीचर) ***n.*** a person who teaches, शिक्षक, अध्यापक।

teaching (टीचिंग) ***n.*** 1. the art or work of a teacher, अध्यापन, शिक्षण। 2. a doctrine or precept, सिद्धांत, उपदेश, नसीहत, सीख।

tea garden ***n.*** a tea plantation, चाय-बाग़ान।

teak (टीक) ***n.*** 1. a large tree, सागवान, सागौन। 2. its wood, सागवान या सागौन की लकड़ी।

team (टीम) ***n.*** 1. a number of persons associated together in work or activity, टीम, टोली। 2. a group of players in a game, दल, टीम। ***v.*** 1. to form a team, टीम बनाना। 2. to harness together to form a team, पशुओं की जोड़ी को गाड़ी, हल आदि में जोतना।

team spirit (टीम स्पिरिट) ***n.*** willingness to co-operate as part of a team, दल-भावना, समूह-भावना, टीम-भावना।

teamwork (टीमवर्क) ***n.*** 1. cooperative work, सहकार, सहयोग। 2. the ability to work efficiently as a team, सामूहिक कार्य।

teapot (टीपॉट) ***n.*** a vessel with a handle and a spout from which tea is served, चायदानी।

teapoy (टीपॉइ) ***n.*** a small three-legged stand, तिपाई।

tear[1] (टिअर) ***n.*** a drop of salty water falling from the eye, आँसू, अश्रु।

tear[2] (टेअर) ***v.*** (tore, torn, tearing) 1. to pull apart or to pieces by force, फाड़ना। 2. to make an opening by ripping, काटना, कतरना, चीरना। 3. to hurry, जल्दी करना, जल्दी में होना।

tearful (टिअरफ़ुल) ***adj.*** 1. shedding tears, रोता हुआ। 2. ready to shed tears, रुआँसा।

tease (टीज़) ***v.*** 1. to annoy, चिढ़ाना, तंग करना। 2. to vex playfully, छेड़ना, छेड़खानी करना। 3. to disentangle and lay parallel (cotton or wool) by carding, धुनना। 4. to brush up the nap (on cloth, कपड़े के) ब्रुश से रोएँ खड़े करना। ***n.*** one who teases, तंग करनेवाला।

teaset (टीसेट) ***n.*** a China set consisting of tea pot, sugar bowl, creamer, cups and plates, चाय परसने के बर्तन, टी-सेट।

teaspoon (टीस्पून) ***n.*** a small spoon for stirring and sipping tea, चाय का चम्मच।

teat (टीट) ***n.*** a nipple, चूची, चुचुक।

technic (टेक्निक) ***n.*** = technique.

technical (टेक्निकल) ***adj.*** 1. of or relating to a technique or applied arts, प्राविधिक, तकनीकी। 2. mechanical or scientific, यांत्रिक या वैज्ञानिक। 3. technological, पारिभाषिक। 4. existing due to a strict application of law, क़ानूनी दृष्टि से होनेवाला, विधिक।

technician (टेक्निशन) ***n.*** one who is expert in the techniques of a particular subject or craft, तकनीशियन, प्रविधिज्ञ, मिस्त्री।

technicolour (टेक्निकलर) ***n.*** a process of making colour motion pictures, टेकनिकलर।

technique (टेक्नीक) ***n.*** the systematic and scientific method of doing some mechanical or practical work, तकनीक, प्रविधि, ढंग।

technocracy (टेक्नॉक्रेसी) ***n.*** government by scientists and engineers, शिल्पी-तंत्र।

technocrat (टेक्नोक्रेट) ***n.*** a member of a technocracy, शिल्पी-तंत्र का सदस्य।

technological (टेक्नॉलॉजिकल) ***adj.*** of or pertaining to technology, शिल्पविज्ञान-संबंधी, प्रौद्योगिकी-संबंधी, प्रौद्योगिकीय।

technologist (टेक्नॉलोजिस्ट) ***n.*** an expert in technology, शिल्प-विज्ञानी, प्रौद्योगिकीवेत्ता।

technology (टेक्नॉलोजी) ***n.*** the application of scientific and mechanical knowledge to industry, प्रौद्योगिकी, शिल्पविज्ञान।

tedious (टीडिअस) ***adj.*** 1. boring, uninteresting, उबाऊ, नीरस। 2. tiresome, थकाऊ।

tedium (टीडिअम) ***n.*** tediousness, boredom, उबाऊपन, नीरसता।

teem (टीम) ***v.*** to abound, प्रचुर मात्रा में होना।

teenage (टीनेज) ***adj.*** of teenagers, किशोरों का या किशोरों-जैसा।

teenager (टीनेजर) ***n.*** a person in his/her teens, किशोर या किशोरी।

teens (टीन्ज़) ***n.*** (plu.) the years 13 to 19 in a lifetime, जीवन के १३ से १९ वर्ष तक का समय, किशोरावस्था।

teeny (टीनी) ***adj.*** tiny, छोटा, नन्हा।

teeter (टीटर) ***v.*** to move unsteadily, लड़खड़ाते हुए चलना, लड़खड़ाना।

teeth (टीथ) ***n.*** plu. of tooth, दाँत।

teethe (टीद) ***v.*** to grow teeth, (बच्चे के) दाँत निकलना।

teething (टीदिंग) ***adj.*** cutting one's teeth, जिसके दाँत निकल रहे हों। ☐ **teething troubles,** आरंभिक कठिनाइयाँ।

teetotaller (टीटोटलर) ***n.*** one who does not drink alcoholic beverages, वह जो शराब न पीता हो, मद्यत्यागी, संयमी व्यक्ति।

telecast (टेलिकास्ट) ***v.*** (telecasted/ telecast, telecasting) to broadcast by television, टेलीविज़न से प्रसारित करना।

telecommunications (टेलिकम्यु-निकेशन्ज़) ***n.*** (plu.) the technology of sending messages by electronic or electrical means, दूरसंचार प्रणाली।

telegram (टेलिग्रैम) ***n.*** a communication sent by telegraph, टेलीग्राम, तार।

telegraph (टेलिग्रैफ़) ***n.*** an apparatus

T

for communication at a distance by electric transmission over wire, तार-प्रेषण यंत्र। ***v.*** to send a telegram to, तार भेजना।

telegraphic (टेलिग्रैफ़िक) ***adj.*** of or pertaining to the telegraph, तार-संबंधी; telegraphic address, तार का पता।

telepathic (टेलिपैथिक) ***adj.*** of or pertaining to telepathy, दूरबोधी।

telepathy (टेलिपेथी) ***n.*** communication from one mind to another through means other than the senses, अतींद्रिय बोध, दूरबोध, टेलीपैथी।

telephone (टेलिफोन) ***n.*** a system and apparatus of transmitting sound over a distance, टेलीफ़ोन, दूरभाष। ***v.*** to communicate by telephone, टेलीफ़ोन करना।

telephonic (टेलिफ़ॉनिक) ***adj.*** of or pertaining to the telephone, दूरभाषिक।

telephotography (टेलिफ़टॉग्रफ़ी) ***n.*** the photography of distant objects, दूर-छायाचित्रण।

teleprinter (टेलिप्रिन्टर) ***n.*** a telegraphic machine that records messages like a typewriter, दूरमुद्रक, तारलेखी, टेलीप्रिंटर।

telescope (टेलिस्कोप) ***n.*** an optical instrument for viewing distant objects, दूरबीन, टेलीस्कोप। ***v.*** to force a way into, धँस जाना।

televise (टेलिवाइज़) ***v.*** to transmit by television, दूरदर्शन से प्रसारित करना, दूरदर्शन पर दिखाना।

television (टेलीविज़न) ***n.*** 1. a system of transmission and reception of images with accompanying sound, दूरदर्शन-प्रणाली। 2. an apparatus for receiving images transmitted by above system, दूरदर्शन, टेलीविज़न, टी.वी.।

telex (टेलेक्स) ***n.*** 1. a telegraph service for sending and receiving messages on a teleprinter, टेलेक्स। 2. a message received or sent by this, टेलेक्स। ***v.*** to send a message by telex, टेलेक्स भेजना।

tell (टेल) ***v.*** (told, telling) 1. to relate in detail, विस्तार से कहना, बतलाना, बताना। 2. to reveal, प्रकट करना। 3. to give information to, सूचना देना। 4. to assure emphatically, विश्वास दिलाना। 5. to say forcefully, आदेश देना, दृढ़तापूर्वक कहना। 6. to discern or identify, समझना या पहचानना। ☐ **tell apart,** विभेद करना; **tell on,** बुरा प्रभाव डालना।

teller (टेलर) ***n.*** 1. one who relates or narrates, वर्णन करनेवाला व्यक्ति। 2. one who counts votes, मतगणक। 3. a bank cashier, बैंक का ख़ज़ांची।

telling (टेलिंग) ***adj.*** having force, striking, ज़ोरदार, प्रभावपूर्ण, कारगर।

telltale (टैलटेल) ***n.*** 1. one who tells tales, चुग़लख़ोर। 2. an indicator, सूचक यंत्र। ***adj.*** revealing, सूचक, परिचायक।

temper (टेम्पर) ***n.*** 1. mood, मनोदशा, मन:स्थिति, तबीयत, मिज़ाज। 2. calmness, composure, शांति, धैर्य। 3. anger, rage, क्रोध, गुस्सा। 4. the degree of hardness of a metal, धातु का कड़ापन, टेंपर। ***v.*** 1. to harden a metal as by alternate heating and cooling, धातु को पहले गरम और

फिर ठंडा करके कड़ा बनाना, टेंपर देना, पानी चढ़ाना। 2. to soften, moderate or soothe, नरम करना, मृदु बनाना।

temperament (टेम्परामेन्ट) ***n.*** the characteristic way of behaving, स्वभाव, प्रकृति।

temperamental (टेम्परामेन्टल) ***adj.*** 1. of or caused by temperament, नैसर्गिक, स्वभावगत। 2. easily upset or irritated, चिड़चिड़े स्वभाववाला, तुनुकमिज़ाज।

temperance (टेम्परेन्स) 1. self-restraint, आत्मसंयम, मिताचार। 2. total abstinence from alcoholic drinks, मद्य का त्याग।

temperate (टेम्परिट) ***adj.*** 1. exercising self-restraint, आत्मसंयमी, मिताचारी, मद्यत्यागी। 2. having a mild temperature, neither hot nor very cold, मातदिल, शीतोष्ण।

temperature (टेम्परेचर) ***n.*** the degree of heat or cold in a body or environment, तापमान, टेंपरेचर।

tempest (टेम्पिस्ट) ***n.*** a violent storm, तूफ़ान, झंझा।

template (टेम्प्लिट) ***n.*** a pattern cut out in wood or metal, साँचा।

temple[1] (टेम्पल) ***n.*** a building for the worship of a god or deity, मंदिर, देवालय।

temple[2] ***n.*** the flat region at each side of the head between forehead and ear, कनपटी।

tempo (टेम्पो) ***n.*** 1. the time, speed or rhythm of a piece of music, लय, ताल। 2. the pace of any movement or activity, गति, रफ़्तार, तेज़ी।

temporal[1] (टेम्परल) ***adj.*** 1. of worldly affairs, लौकिक, सांसारिक, ऐहिक। 2. of or denoting time, कालवाचक।

temporal[2] ***adj.*** of or near the temples of the skull, कनपटी-संबंधी।

temporary (टेम्परेरी) ***adj.*** 1. lasting for a limited time only, अल्पकालिक। 2. not permanent, अस्थायी।

tempt (टेम्प्ट) ***v.*** to allure or induce, प्रलोभन देना, ललचाना, उकसाना।

temptation (टेम्प्टेशन) ***n.*** 1. the act of tempting or the state of being tempted, लालच, लोभ, प्रलोभन। 2. a thing or person that tempts, लुभानेवाली वस्तु या व्यक्ति।

tempting (टेम्प्टिंग) ***adj.*** attractive, alluring, लुभावना, मोहक।

ten (टेन) ***adj. & n.*** 1. one more than nine, दस। 2. a playing card with ten spots, दहला (ताश का)।

tenable (टेनेबल) ***adj.*** 1. defensible, रक्षणीय। 2. logical, तर्कसंगत। 3. that can be maintained, समर्थनीय, पोषणीय।

tenacious (टनेशस) ***adj.*** 1. holding firmly, दृढ़। 2. obstinate, हठी, दुराग्रही। 3. (of memory) retentive, धारण-सक्षम, तीक्ष्ण।

tenancy (टेनन्सी) ***n.*** 1. the temporary possession of land or property by a tenant, काश्तकारी, किराएदारी। 2. the period of this, किराएदारी या काश्तकारी की अवधि।

tenant (टेनन्ट) ***n.*** 1. a person who rents land or building from a landlord, काश्तकार, किराएदार। 2. the occupant or inhabitant, दख़लदार, क़ाबिज़, रहनेवाला।

tend[1] (टेन्ड) ***v.*** to take care of, देख-

T

रेख करना, ध्यान रखना, निगरानी करना।

tend[2] ***v.*** 1. to be inclined, झुकाव होना, उन्मुख या प्रवृत्त होना। 2. to be directed, (की ओर) जाना, बढ़ना, अग्रसर होना।

tendency (टेन्डन्सी) ***n.*** 1. an inclination to move in a particular direction, प्रवृत्ति। 2. the general course, रुझान, झुकाव।

tender[1] (टेन्डर) ***adj.*** 1. not hard, delicate, कोमल, सुकुमार, नाजुक, मृदु। 2. sensitive, संवेदनशील, कोमल।

tender[2] ***v.*** 1. to offer formally, प्रस्तुत करना, पेश करना, रखना, देना। 2. to make a tender, टेंडर देना, निविदा देना। ***n.*** 1. a formal proposal to carry out work or to supply goods, टेंडर, निविदा। 2. money, रुपया-पैसा, मुद्रा; legal tender, वैध मुद्रा।

tender[3] ***n.*** 1. a small boat towed or carried by a ship, जलयान पर माल लाने-ले जाने की छोटी नौका। 2. a car attached to a steam engine carrying fuel and water, इंजन के साथ का वह डिब्बा जिसमें कोयला तथा पानी रहता है, ईंधनगाड़ी।

tenderer (टेन्डरर) ***n.*** one who presents a tender, निविदाकार, टेंडरदाता।

tenderness (टेन्डरनिस) ***n.*** the state or quality of being tender, कोमलता, सुकुमारता।

tendon (टेन्डन) ***n.*** a cord or band of tough tissue that connects a muscle to some other part, कंडरा।

tendril (टेन्ड्रिल) ***n.*** a thread-like part of climbing plant, तंतु, प्रतान।

tenement (टेनिमेन्ट) ***n.*** 1. a dwelling place or residence, घर, मकान। 2. a large building divided into rooms or flats, बड़ा मकान जिसमें कई कमरे या फ्लैट हों।

tenet (टेनिट) ***n.*** a belief, opinion or doctrine, नियम, मत या सिद्धांत।

tenfold (टेनफ़ोल्ड) ***adj.*** ten times as much or as many, दस गुना।

tennis (टेनिस) ***n.*** a game played with rackets and ball, टेनिस।

tenon (टेनन) ***n.*** a projection on a piece of wood shaped to fit into a mortise, चूल, डबचूल।

tense[1] (टेन्स) ***n.*** any of the forms of a verb that indicates the time and completion of the action, काल।

tense[2] ***adj.*** 1. tightly stretched, तना, कसा। 2. under mental or emotional strain, तनाव-भरा, तनावग्रस्त। 3. producing or causing strain, तनाव उत्पन्न करनेवाला।

tensile (टेन्साइल) ***adj.*** 1. capable of being stretched, तन्य। 2. of tension, तनाव-पूर्ण, तनाव-भरा, तनावग्रस्त।

tension (टेन्शन) ***n.*** 1. the act of stretching or the state of being stretched, तन्यता, वितान। 2. the condition when feelings are tense, tenseness, मानसिक तनाव। 3. the strained relations between persons or groups, तनातनी, अनबन, तनाव। 4. stress, दबाव।

tent (टेन्ट) ***n.*** a portable shelter of canvas supported on poles, ropes and pegs, टेन्ट, तंबू, शामियाना।

tentacle (टेन्टकल) ***n.*** a slender flexible part extending from the body of certain creatures used for moving, feeling etc., स्पर्शिका।

tentative (टेन्टटिव) ***adj.*** 1.

provisional, अस्थायी। 2. uncertain, अनिश्चित।

tenterhook (टेन्टरहुक) ***n.*** ☐ **on tenterhooks,** in a state of anxiety, असमंजस में।

tenuous (टेन्युअस) ***adj.*** 1. thin, पतला, बारीक। 2. very slight, ज़रा-सा, सूक्ष्म।

tenure (टेन्यर) ***n.*** 1. the holding of an office, पदधारण, पदसेवन। 2. a period of holding an office or position lasts, पदावधि, कार्यकाल, सेवाकाल। 3. the legal right of holding a property esp. land, काश्तकारी।

tepid (टेपिड) ***adj.*** 1. slightly warm, luke warm, कुनकुना, गुनगुना, अल्पोष्ण। 2. unenthusiastic, उत्साहविहीन।

term (टर्म) ***n.*** 1. a limited period of time, अवधि, मियाद। 2. any of the divisions of the academic year, सत्र। 3. a word or phrase having a particular meaning, पद, शब्द; technical term, पारिभाषिक शब्द। 4. each of the quantities in a mathematical series, पद। 5. (plu.) conditions, शर्तें। ***v.*** to call by a certain term or expression, अभिहित करना, कहना।

terminal (टर्मिनल) ***adj.*** 1. of or relating to end or boundary, अंतिम, आख़िरी, अंत्य। 2. relating to or occurring in each term, आवधिक, सत्रीय, सात्रिक। 3. fatal, घातक। ***n.*** 1. a terminal point or part, अंतिम बिंदु या भाग, सीमा। 2. a terminus, अंतिम स्टेशन (रेल या बस का)।

terminate (टर्मिनेट) ***v.*** to bring or come to an end, अंत करना या होना, समाप्त करना या होना।

termination (टर्मिनेशन) ***n.*** 1. end in time or existence, अंत, समाप्ति। 2. conclusion, उपसंहार। 3. the last part of a word, suffix, प्रत्यय, अंत्य-प्रत्यय। 4. an abortion, गर्भपात।

terminology (टर्मिनॉलोजी) ***n.*** the special or technical terms used in a business, art or science, शब्दावली, पदावली।

terminus (टर्मिनस) ***n.*** last station, अंतिम स्टेशन, अंतिम स्थल।

termite (टर्माइट) ***n.*** white ant, दीमक।

ternary (टर्नरी) ***adj.*** of, relating to or produced by threes, त्रिक।

terrace (टेरस) ***n.*** 1. an open platform, चबूतरा। 2. a flat roof, छत। 3. balcony, छज्जा, बारजा। 4. a paved or planted area adjoining a building, मैदान।

terracotta (टेराकॉटा) ***n.*** 1. a hard brownishred clay, पक्व मृत्तिका, पकी मिट्टी। 2. something made of terracotta, उक्त मिट्टी से बनी वस्तु।

terrain (टैरेन) ***n.*** a piece of land with regard to its natural features, भूभाग।

terrapin (टेरपिन) ***n.*** a water tortoise, जल में रहनेवाला कछुआ।

terrestrial (टेरेस्ट्रिअल) ***adj.*** 1. of the earth, भू-संबंधी। 2. of or living on land, स्थलीय। 3. worldly, सांसारिक। ***n.*** an inhabitant of the earth, धरतीवासी, भूवासी।

terrible (टेरिबल) ***adj.*** 1. terrifying, डरावना, भयानक, भीषण। 2. very serious or extreme, घोर, प्रचंड, विकराल। 3. very bad, बहुत ख़राब। 4. very great, बहुत अधिक।

terrific (टेरिफ़िक) ***adj.*** 1. of great

T

size or intensity, भीषण, प्रचंड। 2. very frightening, भयानक, भयावह। 3. very good, excellent, बहुत अच्छा, बढ़िया, उत्कृष्ट।

terrify (टेरिफ़ाइ) ***v.*** to frighten greatly, दहला देना, भयभीत या संत्रस्त कर देना।

territorial (टेरिटोरिअल) ***adj.*** 1. local or regional, क्षेत्रीय या प्रादेशिक। 2. of land or territory, भूभागीय।

territory (टेरिटरी) ***n.*** 1. a geographical area under the control of a sovereign state, राज यक्षेत्र। 2. a particular area, क्षेत्र, इलाका, भूभाग।

terror (टेरर) ***n.*** 1. extreme fear, दहशत, संत्रास, आतंक। 2. a terrifying person, भयावह व्यक्ति, आतंकी। 3. a troublesome person, दुखदायी व्यक्ति, त्रासदायक व्यक्ति।

terrorism (टेररिज़म) ***n.*** political use of violence and intimidation (for achieving some goal), आतंकवाद।

terrorist (टेररिस्ट) ***n.*** one who uses terror, आतंकी, आतंकवादी।

terse (टर्स) ***adj.*** 1. brief and to the point, संक्षिप्त, संहत। 2. curt, रूखा।

tertiary (टर्शरी) ***adj.*** third in order, तृतीय, तीसरा, तृतीयक।

test (टेस्ट) ***n.*** 1. an act of examining, जाँच, परीक्षण, परख; test paper, परीक्षण-पत्र। 2. an examination, परीक्षा, इम्तहान। 3. criterion, कसौटी, मापदंड। ***v.*** to examine, जाँच करना, परखना।

testament (टेस्टमेन्ट) ***n.*** 1. a will, वसीयत, इच्छापत्र, वसीयतनामा। 2. a written statement of one's beliefs, आस्था-पत्रक।

testate (टेस्टेट) ***adj. & n.*** having left a will at death, वसीयत छोड़ जानेवाला।

testator (टेस्टेटर) ***n.*** one who has made a will, वसीयतकर्ता। [Fem. testatrix, वसीयतकर्त्री]

testes (टेस्टीज़) ***n.*** plu. of testis, अंडकोश।

testicle (टेस्टिकल) ***n.*** either of the two male reproductive glands, अंडग्रंथि, अंडकोश।

testification (टेस्टिफ़िकेशन) ***n.*** an act of testifying, साक्ष्यांकन, प्रमाणन।

testify (टेस्टिफ़ाइ) ***v.*** 1. to give evidence, साक्ष्य देना, गवाही देना। 2. to certify, प्रमाणित करना।

testimonial (टेस्टिमोनिअल) ***n.*** 1. a letter or statement testifying to a person's character or abilities, प्रमाणपत्र। 2. a tribute given for services or achievements, शंसापत्र।

testimony (टेस्टिमनी) 1. a statement made under oath, शपथ-पत्र। 2. evidence in support of something, साक्ष्य।

testis (टेस्टिस) ***n.*** a testicle, अंडकोश।

test tube ***n.*** a glass tube open at one end, टेस्ट ट्यूब, परखनली।

testy (टेस्टी) ***adj.*** irritable, touchy, चिड़चिड़ा, तुनुकमिज़ाज।

tetanus (टेटनस) ***n.*** an acute infectious disease in which the muscles contract and stiffen, धनुषटंकार, धनुकबाई।

tete-a-tete (टेट-अ-टेट) ***n.*** a private conversation, निजी बातचीत। ***adv.*** together in private, एक साथ एकांत में।

tether (टेदर) ***n.*** a rope or chain by which an animal is tied to a peg, वह रस्सी या चेन जिससे पशु को खूँटे से बाँधते हैं, पगहा। ***v.*** to fasten with a tether, खूँटे से बाँधना।

tetrahedron (टेट्राहीड्रन) ***n.*** a solid

with four sides, चतुष्फलक।

text (टेक्स्ट) ***n.*** 1. the original written or printed words of something, मूल पाठ। 2. a short passage from the scripture used as a starting point for a sermon, उद्धरण।

textbook ***n.*** a book used in the study of a subject, पाठ्य पुस्तक।

textile (टेक्स्टाइल) ***n.*** a woven cloth, बुना हुआ कपड़ा, वस्त्र। ***adj.*** of or relating to fabrics, वस्त्र-संबंधी, कपड़े का।

textual (टेक्स्चुअल) ***adj.*** of or relating to a text, मूल पाठ-संबंधी, मूल पाठ-विषयक।

texture (टेक्स्चर) ***n.*** 1. the structure formed by the threads of a fabric, बुनावट। 2. the general structure of the constituent parts of something, बनावट, गठन; texture of rock, शैल-गठन। 3. the distinctive character or quality of something, प्रकृति, स्वभाव, विशिष्टता।

than (दैन) ***conj.*** used to introduce the second element of comparison, से, की अपेक्षा, की बनिस्बत।

thank (थैंक) ***v.*** to express gratitude to, धन्यवाद देना, शुक्रिया अदा करना।

thankful (थैन्कफ़ुल) ***adj.*** feeling or expressing gratitude, grateful, कृतज्ञ।

thankless (थैन्कलिस) ***adj.*** 1. not likely to win or obtain thanks, बेकार का, फालतू। 2. not feeling or expressing gratitude, अकृतज्ञ, कृतघ्न।

thanks (थैन्क्स) ***n.*** (plu.) an expression of gratitude, धन्यवाद।

thanksgiving (थैन्क्सगिविंग) ***n.*** an act of giving thanks, धन्यवाद-ज्ञापन, कृतज्ञता-प्रकाश।

thankyou (थैन्क्यू) ***n.*** an expression of gratitude, धन्यवाद।

that (दैट) ***adj.*** (plu. those) being the one indicated or referred to, वह। ***pron.*** 1. the one indicated or referred to, वह। 2. who, whom or which, जो। ***conj.*** introducing a dependent clause, (आश्रित उपवाक्य के आरंभ में) कि।

thatch (थैच) ***n.*** 1. a roof covering made of straw, छप्पर। 2. a roofing material that consists of straw, reed etc., घास-फूस, सरकंडा। ***v.*** to cover with thatch, छप्पर छाना।

thaw (थॉ) ***v.*** 1. to go from frozen to liquid state, द्रवित होना, पिघलना, गलना। 2. to become active, सक्रिय होना। ***n.*** the spell of warm weather, गरम मौसम।

the (दि, द) ***article.*** 1. used to precede a noun that has been previously specified, पूर्वोल्लिखित संज्ञा से पहले प्रयुक्त होनेवाला प्रविशेषण। 2. used to emphasize excellence or importance, उत्कृष्टता या महत्त्व पर ज़ोर देने के लिए प्रयुक्त होनेवाला प्रविशेषण। ***adv.*** in that degree, by that amount, उस मात्रा में, उतना ही; The more the merrier. एक से दो भले।

theatre, theater (थीएटर) ***n.*** a building for theatrical performances, नाट्यशाला, रंगशाला, थियेटर।

theaterical (थिऐटरिकल) ***adj.*** 1. of or relating to the theater, नाट्यशाला-संबंधी। 2. exaggerated and showy, बनावटी, आडंबरपूर्ण, कृत्रिम।

thee (दी) ***pron.*** the objective case

T

of thou, तुझे, तुझको।

theft (थेफ़्ट) ***n.*** an act of steeling, चोरी।

their (देअर) ***adj.*** of or belonging to them, उनका, इनका।

theirs (देअर्स) ***pron.*** their own, उनका, इनका।

theism (थीइज़्म) ***n.*** belief in the existence of a god or gods, आस्तिकता, ईश्वरवाद।

theist (थीइस्ट) ***n.*** one who believes in a god or gods, आस्तिक, ईश्वरवादी।

them (देम) ***pron.*** the objective case of they, उन्हें या उनको, इन्हें या इनको।

thematic (थीमेटिक) ***adj.*** of or relating to a theme, विषय-संबंधी, कथ्यपरक।

theme (थीम) ***n.*** 1. an idea or topic of discourse, वर्ण्य विषय, कथ्य। 2. a melody, धुन।

themselves (देमसेल्व्ज़) ***pron.*** (plu.) the reflexive form of they or them, स्वयं, अपने-आप।

then (देन) ***adv.*** 1. at that time, उस समय, तब। 2. in that case, तो। 3. soon after that, उसके बाद, तत्पश्चात्, तदनंतर, फिर। ***adj.*** of that time, तत्कालीन। ***n.*** that time, वह समय।

thence (देन्स) ***adv.*** from that place, उस स्थान से, वहाँ से।

theocracy (थिऑक्रेसी) ***n.*** government by priesthood, पुरोहिततंत्र, धर्मतंत्र।

theologian (थीअलोजिअन) ***n.*** an expert in theology, धर्मतत्त्वज्ञ, धर्मवेत्ता, धर्मशास्त्री।

theology (थिऑलोजी) ***n.*** 1. a system of religion, धर्मतंत्र। 2. a particular body of opinion about religion, धर्मशास्त्र।

theorem (थीअरम) ***n.*** a mathematical statement that can be proved from previously proved propositions, प्रमेय।

theoretical (थीऔरैटिकल) ***adj.*** 1. based on theory or existing only in theory, सैद्धांतिक। 2. not practical, impractical, अव्यावहारिक।

theorist (थीअरिस्ट) ***n.*** one who theorizes, सिद्धांतवादी, सिद्धांतवेत्ता, सिद्धांतकार।

theorize (थीअराइज़) ***v.*** to form a theory or theories, सिद्धांत बनाना या स्थापित करना।

theory (थीअरी) ***n.*** 1. a set of statements or rules to explain a phenomenon, सिद्धांत, मत। 2. speculation, परिकल्पना।

theosophical (थिऑसफ़िकल) ***adj.*** of theosophy, देवविद्या-संबंधी, ब्रह्मविद्या-विषयक।

theosophy (थिऑसफ़ी) ***n.*** a philosophical system based on mystical insight, देवविद्या, ब्रह्मविद्या, थियॉसफ़ी।

therapeutic (थेरप्यूटिक) ***adj.*** having healing or curative powers, रोगोपचारक।

therapist (थेरपिस्ट) ***n.*** a specialist in a certain kind of therapy, चिकित्सक।

therapy (थेरपी) ***n.*** the treatment of illness or disability, चिकित्सा।

there (देअर) ***adv.*** 1. in or at that place, वहाँ, उस जगह। 2. in that matter or point, उस बात में। 3. to or toward that place, उधर। ***interj.*** used to express satisfaction, dismay etc., देखा!

thereabouts (देअरबाउट्स) ***adv.***

1. somewhere near here, के आसपास, के क़रीब। 2. somewhere near that number, time, etc., के लगभग, के आसपास।

thereafter (देअराफ़्टर) ***adv.*** after that, तत्पश्चात्, उसके बाद, फिर।

thereby (देअरबाइ) ***adv.*** by that means, उसके द्वारा, के फलस्वरूप।

therefore (देअरफ़ोर) ***adv.*** for that reason, इसलिए, उस कारण से।

therefrom (देअरफ़्राम) ***adv.*** from there, वहाँ से।

therein (देअरिन) ***adv.*** in that place, वहाँ।

thereof (देअरॉफ़) ***adv.*** of that, उसका।

thereto (देअरटू) ***adv.*** to that, उस तक।

thereupon (देअरपॉन) ***adv.*** immediately after that, उसके ठीक बाद, तदनंतर।

thermal (थर्मल) ***adj.*** of, relating to or caused by heat, तापीय, उष्मीय। ***n.*** a rising current of hot air, गरम हवा का झोंका।

thermometer (थर्मॉमिटर) ***n.*** an instrument for measuring temperature, तापमापी, थर्मामीटर।

thermonuclear (थर्मोन्यूक्लिअर) ***adj.*** of nuclear reactions that occur at very high temperature, तापनाभिकीय।

thermos (थर्मस) ***n.*** a kind of vaccum bottle, थर्मस।

thermostat (थर्मोस्टेट) ***n.*** an automatic device for regulating temperature, ताप-नियंत्रक।

thesaurus (थिसॉरस) ***n.*** a dictionary of synonyms, पर्याय शब्दकोश, पर्यायकोश।

these (दीज़) ***adj.*** plu. of this, ये।

thesis (थीसिस) ***n.*** 1. an essay or treatise resulting from original academic research, शोध-प्रबंध। 2. an idea or statement put forward for discussion, चर्चा का विषय।

they (दे) ***pron.*** 1. those ones (plu. of he, she, it.) , वे, वे लोग, वे चीज़ें। 2. people, लोग, जन-साधारण।

thick (थिक) ***adj.*** 1. having relatively great depth, गहरा, मोटा। 2. having relatively large diametre in relation to length, मोटा। 3. great in number, गिनती में अधिक। 4. of great consistency, गाढ़ा। 5. not clear, muddy or foggy, अस्पष्ट, गंदला या धुंधला। 6. dull, stupid, मंदबुद्धि, मूर्ख। 7. intimate, घनिष्ठ। ***n.*** the thickest part, मोटा हिस्सा, स्थूल भाग।

thicken (थिकन) ***v.*** 1. to make thick, गाढ़ा करना, सघन करना। 2. to become thick, गाढ़ा होना, सघन होना।

thicket (थिकिट) ***n.*** a dense growth of shrubs, झाड़-झंखाड़, झाड़ियों का झुरमुट।

thickness (थिकनिस) ***n.*** the quality or state of being thick, मोटाई, स्थूलता; गाढ़ापन, सघनता।

thickskinned (थिकस्किन्ड) ***adj.*** insensitive to criticism, insult etc., चिकना घड़ा।

thief (थीफ़) ***n.*** one who steals, चोरी करनेवाला, चोर।

thieve (थीव) ***v.*** to steal, चोरी करना, चुराना।

thievish (थीविश) ***adj.*** addicted to stealing, जिसे चोरी करने की लत हो, चोट्टा।

thigh (थाइ) ***n.*** the part of human

T

leg between hip and knee, जाँघ, रान, जंघा।

thimble (थिम्बल) ***n.*** a metal cap worn on the finger while sewing, अंगुश्ताना, दर्ज़ी का छल्ला।

thin (थिन) ***adj.*** 1. of little depth, बारीक, महीन, पतला। 2. having small diameter in relation to length, पतला, बारीक। 3. not dense or compact, झीना। 4. of little consistency, flowing easily, पतला। 5. lean, slender, दुबला-पतला। 6. not plentiful, कम, स्वल्प। ***adv.*** thinly, पतले रूप में, पतला-पतला। ***v.*** 1. to make thinner, पतला, बारीक या झीना करना। 2. to become thinner, पतला, बारीक या झीना हो जाना।

thine (दाइन) ***pron.*** of or belonging to thee, तेरा।

thing (थिन्ग) ***n.*** 1. any matter or object of perception, knowledge or thought, चीज़, वस्तु, पदार्थ। 2. an act, deed or event, कार्य या घटना। 3. a topic, विषय। 4. (plu.) circumstances, हालात, परिस्थितियाँ।

think (थिन्क) ***v.*** (thought, thinking) 1. to ponder, सोचना, विचारना, चिंतन करना। 2. to imagine, to formulate in the mind, कल्पना करना।

thinker (थिन्कर) ***n.*** one who thinks deeply, विचारक।

thinner (थिनर) ***n.*** a substance (usu. liquid) for reducing viscosity, थिनर।

third (थर्ड) ***adj.*** 1. preceded by two others in a series, तीसरा, तृतीय। 2. designating any of the three equal parts of something, एक-तिहाई। ***n.*** any of the three equal parts, तीसरा भाग।

third class (थर्ड क्लास) ***adj.*** 1. of the class next below the second, तीसरी श्रेणी या तृतीय श्रेणी का। 2. of poor quality, घटिया।

third degree ***n.*** torture by police to force a confession or information, सत्य या कोई सूचना उगलवाने के लिए पुलिस द्वारा अपराधी को दी जानेवाली यातना।

third party ***n.*** another person or party besides the two principal ones involved, अन्य पक्ष, तृतीय पक्ष।

third person ***n.*** the form of a noun or verb which refers to the person or thing spoken of, अन्य पुरुष।

third-rate (थर्ड-रेट) ***adj.*** third class, घटिया।

thirst (थर्स्ट) ***n.*** 1. the desire to drink, प्यास, पिपासा। 2. a craving, लालसा, उत्कंठा, पिपासा। ***v.*** (thirst, thirsting) to have a strong desire, उत्कंठा होना, तीव्र लालसा होना।

thirsty (थर्स्टी) ***adj.*** 1. feeling thirst, प्यासा। 2. dry, सूखा।

thirteen (थर्टीन) ***adj. & n.*** one more than twelve, तेरह।

thirties (थर्टीज़) ***n.*** (plu.) the numbers, years or degrees of temperature from 30 to 39, ३० से ३९ के बीच की अवस्था या संख्या।

thirty (थर्टी) ***adj. & n.*** the cardinal number between twenty-nine and thirty-one, तीस।

this (दिस) ***pron.*** (plu. these) 1. the person or thing present, nearby or just mentioned, यह। 2. the person or thing that is more nearer, यह। ***adj.*** 1. designating the person or thing mentioned or understood, यह। 2. being nearer than another or compared with another, यह।

thither (दिदर) ***adv.*** to or toward that place, उधर। ***adj.*** on that (more distant) side, उधर का, वहाँ का।

thong (थॉन्ग) ***n.*** 1. a whip, कोड़ा। 2. a strip or strap, पट्टी।

thorax (थौरैक्स) ***n.*** the chest, छाती, वक्ष, सीना।

thoracic (थरैसिक) ***adj.*** of or pertaining to the thorax, वक्षीय।

thorn (थॉर्न) ***n.*** 1. a sharp pointed protuberance on a plant, काँटा। 2. a shrub or tree bearing such thorns, कँटीली झाड़ी या पेड़।

thorny (थॉर्नी) ***adj.*** 1. having thorns, कँटीला। 2. like a thorn, काँटे जैसा। 3. full of obstacles, काँटों-भरा, कठिनाई-भरा।

thorough (थरो) ***adj.*** 1. complete in all respects, सभी दृष्टियों से पूर्ण, परिपूर्ण। 2. exhaustive, विस्तृत, व्यापक, ब्योरेवार। 3. having full mastery, दक्षताप्राप्त, कुशल। 4. laborious, अध्यवसायी। 5. arduous, श्रमसाध्य।

thoroughfare (थरोफ़ेअर) ***n.*** a main road, मुख्य मार्ग, आम रास्ता, सार्वजनिक मार्ग।

those (दोज़) ***adj. & pron.*** plural form of that, वे, उन।

thou (दाउ) ***pron.*** old form of you, तू।

though (दो) ***conj.*** despite the fact that, यद्यपि, भले ही। ***adv.*** however, तो भी, तथापि, फिर भी।

thought[1] (थॉट) ***v.*** p.t. & p.p. form of think.

thought[2] ***n.*** 1. the act or process of thinking, चिंतन, ख़्याल, चिंतन-प्रक्रिया। 2. an idea, opinion or concept, विचार, मत, धारणा। 3. expectation, प्रत्याशा, उम्मीद। 4. regard, care, ध्यान, ख़्याल।

thoughtful (थॉट्फुल) ***adj.*** 1. contemplative, विचारमग्न। 2. well thoughtout, सुविचारित। 3. considerate, विचारवान।

thought-provoking (थॉट-प्रवोकिंग) ***adj.*** giving rise to serious thought, विचारोत्तेजक।

thousand (थाउज़न्ड) ***adj. & n.*** ten hundred, (एक) हजार, सहस्र।

thrash (थ्रैश) ***v.*** 1. to beat with a whip, कोड़े लगाना। 2. to beat with a stick, बेंत लगाना, डंडे से पीटना। 3. to defeat utterly, पछाड़ देना, परास्त कर देना। 4. to move wildly, बेतहाशा आगे बढ़ना। □ **thrash out,** (i) गहन विमर्श करना, (ii) विचार-विमर्श द्वारा समस्या को हल करना।

thrashing (थ्रैशिंग) ***n.*** 1. flogging, कोड़े की मार। 2. beating, पिटाई। 3. a severe defeat, घोर पराजय।

thread (थ्रेड) ***n.*** 1. a thin length of twisted fibres of cotton, silk etc., धागा, तागा, सूत; sacred thread, जनेऊ। 2. something compared to this, a continuous element, link, सूत्र, तार, सिलसिला, कड़ी। 3. the helical ridge on a bolt, nut, screw etc., चूड़ी। ***v.*** 1. to pass thread through (something, किसी चीज़ में) धागा डालना। 2. to string on a thread, धागे में पिरोना। 3. to produce a screw thread, चूड़ी बनाना या काटना। 4. to make one's way through, बीच से रास्ता निकालना।

threadbare (थ्रेडबेअर) ***adj.*** 1. having the nap so worn off that the threads show through, फटा हुआ, जीर्ण-शीर्ण। 2. wearing old clothing,

T

फटे-पुराने कपड़े पहने हुआ।

threat (थ्रेट) ***n.*** 1. an intimidatory remark, धमकी। 2. a possible danger, apprehension, संभावित ख़तरा, डर, आशंका।

threaten (थ्रेटन) ***v.*** 1. to intimidate, धमकी देना, धमकाना। 2. to be a threat to, धमकी के रूप में होना, (किसी बात की) आशंका होना।

three (थ्री) ***adj. & n.*** one plus two, तीन।

three-dimensional (थ्री-डाइ-मेन्शनल) ***adj.*** having three dimensions, तीन विमाओं वाला, त्रिविम।

thresh (थ्रेश) ***v.*** 1. to separate seeds from the plants by beating, or mechanically, दाँवना, गाहना। 2. to thrash, पिटाई करना।

threshold (थ्रेशोल्ड) ***n.*** 1. a doorsill, दहलीज। 2. any doorway or entrance, द्वार, प्रवेशद्वार। 3. the (lowest) limit, (निम्न) सीमा।

threw (थ्रू) ***v.*** p.t. of 'throw'.

thrice (थ्राइस) ***adv.*** three times, तीन बार।

thrift (थ्रिफ़्ट) ***n.*** frugality, किफ़ायत, मितव्ययिता।

thrifty (थ्रिफ़्टी) ***adj.*** frugal, मितव्ययी, किफ़ायती, किफ़ायतशिआर।

thrill (थ्रिल) ***v.*** 1. to feel or experience a sudden sharp feeling of excitement, रोमांचित होना, पुलकित होना। 2. to cause such a feeling, पुलकित या रोमांचित करना। 3. to quiver or cause to quiver, काँपना या कँपाना। ***n.*** 1. emotional tremor, रोमांच। 2. a wave of feeling, कँपकँपी।

thriller (थ्रिलर) ***n.*** a thrilling or exciting story, रोमांचक कहानी।

thrive (थ्राइव) ***v.*** (thrived/throve, thrived/thriven, thriving) 1. to develop, विकसित होना, पनपना। 2. to prosper, समृद्ध होना।

throat (थ्रोट) ***n.*** 1. the front part of the neck, गला, कंठ, हलक। 2. the interior part of the neck esp. respiratory track, श्वासनली।

throb (थ्रॉब) ***v.*** to pulsate rapidly, धड़कना, धुकधुक करना। ***n.*** the act or sound of throbbing, धड़कन।

throes (थ्रोज़) ***n.*** (plu.) a condition of violent pangs, घोर पीड़ा, वेदना।

throne (थ्रोन) ***n.*** 1. the seat of a king or queen, सिंहासन, गद्दी, राजसिंहासन। 2. the royal power, राजसत्ता।

throng (थ्रॉन्ग) ***n.*** multitude, भीड़, भीड़-भाड़, जमावड़ा। ***v.*** to crowd together in large number, भीड़ लगना या लगाना।

throttle (थ्रॉटल) ***v.*** to compress the throat (of someone, किसी का) गला दबाना, गला नापना। ***n.*** valve controlling the flow of an engine's steam, भाप के प्रवाह को रोकने का वाल्व।

through (थ्रू) ***prep.*** 1. in at one side or point and out at the other, के आर-पार, में से होकर। 2. by way of, के रास्ते, से होकर। 3. be the means of, के द्वारा। 4. during the entire period of, up to and including, से लेकर·· तक; Monday through Saturday, सोमवार से लेकर शनिवार तक। 5. from the beginning to the end, के शुरू से अंत तक। ***adv.*** 1. from one end or side to the another, आर-पार। 2. from beginning to the end, आरंभ से अंत तक, आद्योपांत। ***adj.*** 1. admitting continuous passage,

सीधा; a through road, सीधी सड़क। 2. passing one end to another, (बिना बीच में रुके) सीधा जानेवाला; through train, सीधी गाड़ी।

throughout (थ्रूआउट) ***adv.*** 1. everywhere, सब जगह, हर जगह। 2. during the entire duration, पूरी अवधि में, सदा। ***prep.*** 1. all the way through, के प्रत्येक भाग में। 2. in or during the very period, के पूरे समय में।

throve (थ्रोव) ***v.*** p.t. of thrive.

throw (थ्रो) ***v.*** (threw, thrown, throwing) 1. to cast through the air (something) with a swift motion of the arm, to fling or hurl, फेंकना, क्षेपण करना। 2. to cause to fall, गिराना, पटकना। 3. to put off hastily, उतार फेंकना। 4. to abandon, छोड़ देना, त्याग देना। 5. to shape on a potter's wheel, (कुम्हार का) चाक पर (कोई चीज़) बनाना या गढ़ना। 6. to move (a switch or lever), चलाना। □ **throw a party,** पार्टी देना; **throw down the gauntlet,** चुनौती देना, ललकारना; आँखों में धूल झोंकना; **throw oneself at, throw over,** छोड़ देना; **throw up,** (i) कै करना, (ii) सहसा ऊँचा करना; (iii) छोड़ देना। ***n.*** 1. the act of throwing, क्षेपण, फेंकना। 2. the distance something is thrown, दूरी, परास।

thrush (थ्रश) ***n.*** 1. a singing bird, एक गानेवाली चिड़िया। 2. a disease of mouth, मुखपाक।

thrust (थ्रस्ट) ***v.*** (thrust, thrusting) 1. to push forcibly, धक्का देना, धकेलना, धकियाना। 2. to pierce or stab, भोंकना, घुसेड़ना। 3. to impose, थोपना, गले मढ़ना, ज़बरदस्ती लाद देना। ***n.*** 1. the act of thrusting, धकेलने की क्रिया या भाव। 2. a sudden forceful push, धक्का। 3. the general tendency, सामान्य रुझान।

thud (थड) ***n.*** a dull heavy sound, धम, धड़ाम। ***v.*** 1. to make a thud, धम शब्द करना। 2. to fall wih a thud, धड़ाम से गिरना।

thug (थग) ***n.*** a cheat or robber, ठग।

thumb (थम्ब) ***n.*** the short first digit of the hand, अँगूठा। ***v.*** to turn (pages) with the thumb, अँगूठे से (पन्ने) उलटना।

thumbnail sketch ***n.*** a brief description (of something, किसी चीज़ का) संक्षिप्त विवरण।

thump (थम्प) ***v.*** 1. to strike or beat so as to cause a dull sound, थपथप करना, थपथपाना। 2. to pound, पीटना। ***n.*** the sound made by a blow, थपथप, थपथपाहट।

thunder (थन्डर) ***n.*** 1. the sound that follows a flash of lightning, गरज, गड़गड़ाहट, मेघनाद। 2. any similar noise, गड़गड़ाहट। ***v.*** 1. to produce or make a noise like thunder, गरजना, गर्जन करना। 2. to utter loudly, गरजना।

thunderbolt (थन्डरबोल्ट) ***n.*** 1. a stone like mass hurled on earth in the lightning flash, गाज, वज्र। 2. something very startling as well as destructive, वज्रपात।

thunderclap (थन्डरक्लैप) ***n.*** a clap of thunder, बिजली की कड़क।

thundering (थन्डरिंग) ***adj.*** very great or excessive, बहुत बड़ा या बहुत अधिक।

thunderous (थन्डरस) ***adj.*** producing thunder, गरजनेवाला, गड़गड़ाहट-भरा।

thunderstorm (थन्डरस्टॉर्म) ***n.*** a

T

storm accompanied by lightning and thunder, तूफ़ान, तड़ित-झंझा।

Thursday (थर्ज़डे) ***n.*** the day of the week following Wednesday, गुरुवार, बृहस्पतिवार।

thus (दस) ***adv.*** 1. in this way, इस प्रकार, इस तरह। 2. therefore, इसलिए, अत:। 3. to this extent, इस सीमा तक।

thwart (थ्वार्ट) ***v.*** 1. to prevent, रोकना, रोक देना। 2. to oppose successfully, निष्फल कर देना। ***n.*** an oarsman seat lying across a boat, नाव में मल्लाह के बैठकर चप्पू चलाने की जगह।

thy (दाइ) ***adj.*** of or belonging to thee, तेरा।

thyme (थाइम) ***n.*** a plant and its fragrant seeds, अजवायन।

thyroid (थाइरॉइड) ***n.*** a gland at the front of the neck, टेंटुआ, अवटुग्रंथि।

tiara (टिऐरा) ***n.*** a woman's bejewelled crownlike headdress, स्त्रियों के पहनने की शृंगार-पट्टी या जड़ाऊ मुकुट।

tibia (टिबिआ) ***n.*** the shinbone, टाँग की मोटी नली, अंतर्जंघिका, टिबिया।

tic (टिक) ***n.*** twitching of the muscles, मांसपेशियों का संकुचन।

tick[1] (टिक) ***n.*** a small blood sucking insect, किलनी, चिचड़ा।

tick[2] ***n.*** 1. a regularly repeated clicking sound of a watch, घड़ी की टिकटिक। 2. a mark used to check an item on a list, सही का सूचक चिह्न (✓)। ***v.*** 1. to make a series of ticks, टिकटिक करना। 2. to mark with a tick, सही का निशान लगाना।

tick[3] ***n.*** credit, ऋण। □ **on tick,** ऋण पर, उधार।

ticket (टिकिट) ***n.*** 1. a paper slip or card that entitles the holder to a certain right, टिकट। 2. a label, लेबल। 3. the list of candidates nominated by a particular party at an election, टिकट।

tickle (टिकल) ***v.*** 1. to touch or stroke lightly so as to produce laughter, गुदगुदी करना, गुदगुदाना। 2. to delight, ख़ुश करना, बहलाना। ***n.*** tickling sensation, गुदगुदी।

ticklish (टिक्लिश) ***adj.*** 1. sensitive to tickling, जिसे बहुत गुदगुदी होती हो। 2. delicate or difficult, नाज़ुक या कठिन।

tidal (टाइडल) ***adj.*** of or relating to tides, ज्वार-संबंधी, ज्वारीय।

tidbit (टिडबिट) ***n.*** = titbit.

tide (टाइड) ***n.*** 1. the alternate rise and fall in the level of the sea, ज्वार-भाटा; high tide, ज्वार; low tide, भाटा। 2. a wide spread trend or tendency, व्यापक रुझान, व्यापक मनोदशा।

tidiness (टाइडिनिस) ***n.*** the quality or state of being tidy. साफ़-सुथरापन, स्वच्छता।

tidings (टाइडिंग्स) ***n.*** (plu.) news, समाचार।

tidy (टाइडी) ***adj.*** 1. neat, साफ़-सुथरा, स्वच्छ। 2. orderly, व्यवस्थित। ***v.*** 1. to make tidy, स्वच्छ बनाना। 2. to put in order, व्यवस्थित बनाना।

tie (टाइ) ***v.*** (tied, tying) 1. to fasten with a cord, rope etc., डोरी, रस्सी, फ़ीते आदि से कसना या बाँधना। 2. to form a knot or bow, गाँठ लगाना, कमान बाँधना। 3. to bring together, संयुक्त करना, जोड़ना। 4. to equal (an opponent or his score) in a contest, (खेल, प्रतियोगिता में) बराबर-बराबर होना। 5. to restrict, रोकना।

n. 1. a cord, rope etc. used for fastening, बाँधने की डोरी, रस्सी, फ़ीता आदि। 2. a necktie, नकटाई। 3. something that unites, link, बाँधनेवाली चीज़, कड़ी। 4. a restriction, बंधन। 5. relation, संबंध। 6. equality of score, खेल में बराबरी, टाई।

tie-breaker (टाइ-ब्रेकर) ***n.*** a game to decide a winner when teams have tied, टाइब्रेकर, निर्णायक खेल या बाज़ी।

tier (टिअर) ***n.*** one of the series of rows or layers placed one above another, ऊपर-नीचे की सीटों या कतारों में से कोई एक।

tie-up (टाइ-अप) ***n.*** collaboration of two or more groups, companies etc., गठबँधन, गठजोड़।

tiff (टिफ़) ***n.*** a petty quarrel, छोटा-मोटा झगड़ा, अनबन।

tiffin (टिफ़िन) ***n.*** a light midday meal, दोपहर का जलपान, टिफ़िन।

tiger (टाइगर) ***n.*** a large carnivorous wild animal of the cat family, बाघ।

tight (टाइट) ***adj.*** 1. fixed or fastened very firmly in place, कसा हुआ, कसावट-भरा, कड़ा। 2. fitting closely, चुस्त, तंग। 3. of close and compact construction, पक्का, दृढ़, रोधी; airtight, वायुरोधी। 4. difficult, कठिन। 5. strict, दृढ़, सख़्त। 6. packed to limit, filled, खचाखच, ठसाठस। 7. drunk, नशे में धुत। 8. difficult to obtain, जिसे प्राप्त करना कठिन हो।

tighten (टाइटन) ***v.*** to make or become tight, कसना या कसा जाना, कसकर बाँधना या बाँधा जाना।

tightfisted (टाइटफ़िस्टिड) ***adj.*** stingy, कंजूस, कृपण।

tightness (टाइटनिस) ***n.*** the quality or state of being tight, कसावट, कसाव; तनाव; तंगी।

tigress (टाइग्रिस) ***n.*** a she-tiger, बाघिन।

tile (टाइल) ***n.*** a thin slab of baked clay or other material used in rows for covering roofs, floors etc., खपड़ा, टाइल। ***v.*** to cover with tiles, टाइलें लगाना या बिछाना।

till[1] (टिल) ***v.*** to prepare the land for raising of crops by ploughing, (खेत) जोतना, हल चलाना।

till[2] ***conj. & prep.*** = until.

till[3] ***n*** . a cash box, गोलक, गल्ला, संदूकची।

tiller[1] (टिलर) ***n.*** one who tills land, जुताई करनेवाला, किसान, खेतिहर।

tiller[2] ***n.*** a lever used to turn a boat's rudder, गुटका, कर्णदंड।

tilt (टिल्ट) ***v.*** to slant, एक ओर झुकाना या झुकना। ***n.*** 1. a slope or slant, झुकाव, नति। 2. the act of tilting, झुकाने की क्रिया या भाव।

timber (टिम्बर) ***n.*** 1. wood as a building material, इमारती लकड़ी। 2. trees collectively suitable for timber, इमारती लकड़ी के पेड़। 3. a wooden beam, शहतीर, बल्ली, धरन।

timbre (टैम्बर) ***n.*** the distinct quality of the sound produced by a particular voice or instrument, ध्वनि-गुण।

time (टाइम) ***n.*** 1. the continued passage which is divided into past, present and future or stated in hours or minutes, समय, काल, वक़्त। 2. duration, अवधि। 3. an occasion or instance, अवसर, बार; first time, पहली बार। 4. (plu.) an age or era, युग। ***v.*** 1. to set or

T

arrange the time of, समय निश्चित करना। 2. to measure the time taken by, समय मापना।

time-barred (टाइम-बार्ड) ***adj.*** barred by time, कालातीत।

time-honoured (टाइम-ऑनर्ड) ***adj.*** honoured because of long tradition, चिरसम्मानित, अतिप्राचीन।

timelag (टाइमलैग) ***n.*** interval of time, अंतराल, बीच का (ख़ाली) समय।

timeless (टाइमलिस) ***adj.*** unaffected by time, कालातीत,, कालजयी।

timely (टाइमली) ***adj.*** occurring just at the right time, ठीक समय पर होनेवाला।

timepiece (टाइमपीस) ***n.*** a watch, घड़ी।

times (टाइम्ज़) ***n.*** multiplied by, को गुना करने पर; two times six is equal to twelve. छह को दो से गुना करने पर बारह होता है।

timetable (टाइमटेबल) ***n.*** a list showing the times of arrival and departure of trains, buses etc., the subjects to be taught in a class room or the events to take place, टाइमटेबल, समय-सारणी।

timid (टिमिड) ***adj.*** easily frigthe-ned, भीरु, डरपोक, दब्बू।

timidity (टिमिडिटी) ***n.*** the state or quality of being timid, भीरुता, दब्बूपन।

timing (टाइमिंग) ***n.*** the way something is timed, समय-निर्धारण।

timorous (टिमरस) ***adj.*** timid, डरपोक, भीरु।

timpani (टिम्पनी) ***n.*** (plu.) a set of kettledrums, नक़्क़ारों की जोड़ी, ताशों की जोड़ी।

tin (टिन) ***n.*** 1. a silvery-white metal, राँगा, टिन। 2. a container of tin, टीन। ***v.*** 1. to cover with tin, राँगा चढ़ाना, कलई करना। 2. to pack in tins, टीनों में भरना।

tincture (टिन्क्चर) ***n.*** 1. a medicinal solution, टिंचर। 2. a tint or tinge, आभा, झलक या पुट। ***v.*** to give a tint or tinge to, हलकी आभा देना, हलका रंग करना।

tinge (टिन्ज) ***v.*** 1. to colour or tint faintly, हलका रंग करना, हलकी रंगत देना। 2. to give a slight trace to, पुट देना। ***n.*** 1. a slight tint or colouring, हलकी रंगत। 2. any slight addition, पुट।

tingle (टिन्गल) ***v.*** 1. to have an itching or prickling sensation in the flesh, झुनझुनी होना, चुभन होना। 2. to cause such sensation, झुनझुनी या चुभन पैदा करना। ***n.*** itching or prickling sensation, झुनझुनी, चुभन।

tinker (टिन्कर) ***n.*** a travelling mender of metal household utensils, घूम-फिरकर बरतनों की मरम्मत करनेवाला, झलाईगर। ***v.*** 1. to work as a tinker, झलाईगीरी करना, बरतनों की मरम्मत करना। 2. to meddle with machine parts, मशीनी पुर्ज़ों से छेड़छाड़ करना, खिलवाड़ करना।

tinkle (टिन्कल) ***v.*** to make a series of small jingling sounds, टनटन करना, टनटनाना। ***n.*** a series of jingling sounds, टनटन।

tinned (टिन्ड) ***adj.*** 1. packed in a container, डिब्बाबंद, टीनबंद। 2. plated with tin, कलईदार।

tinplated (टिनप्लेटिड) ***adj.*** coated with tin, कलई किया हुआ।

tinsel (टिन्सल) ***n.*** a thread, sheet or strip of metal foil, पन्नी, सिलमा, सितारा आदि।

tint (टिन्ट) ***n.*** 1. a shade of a particular colour, किसी रंग का शेड। 2. a tinge, हलका रंग, रंगत, आभा, झलक। ***v.*** to colour or tinge, रंग करना, हलका रंग करना, टिंट करना।

tiny (टाइनी) ***adj.*** very small, बहुत छोटा, अत्यल्प, नन्हा।

tip[1] (टिप) ***n.*** 1. a narrow or pointed end of something, extremity, नोक, सिरा, छोर। 2. the top or summit, चोटी। ***v.*** 1. to provide with a tip, सिरा लगाना या बनाना। 2. to remove the tip of, सिरा या नोक हटाना।

tip[2] ***v.*** to tilt or cause to tilt, झुकना या झुकाना, तिरछा होना या करना। ***n.*** a slight tilt, झुकाव, तिरछापन।

tip[3] ***v.*** to strike gently, हलका आघात करना। ***n.*** a light blow, हलका आघात।

tip[4] ***n.*** 1. a small gift of money, बख़्शीश, टिप। 2. a piece of inside or secret information, सुराग़, पते की बात या गुप्त सूचना। ***v.*** to make a small gift of money, बख़्शीश देना।

tip-off (टिप-ऑफ़) ***n.*** 1. a hint, संकेत। 2. a warning, चेतावनी।

tipple (टिपल) ***v.*** to drink wine or whiskey habitually, आदतन मद्यपान करना।

tipsy (टिप्सी) ***adj.*** slightly drunk, जिसे हलका नशा हो, जो सरूर में हो।

tiptoe (टिपटो) ***v.*** (tiptoed, tiptoeing) to walk stealthily on the tips of one toes, चोरी-छिपे पंजों के बल चलना।

tiptop (टिपटॉप) ***n.*** the highest point, चोटी, पराकाष्ठा। ***adj.*** excellent, बढ़िया, उत्कृष्ट।

tirade (टाइरेड) ***n.*** abusive outburst, फटकार, डाँट-फटकार।

tire[1] (टाइअर) ***v.*** 1. to make or become tired, थकाना या थकना। 2. to become bored, ऊब जाना।

tire[2] ***n.*** a covering of wheel's rim, टायर।

tired (टाइअर्ड) ***adj.*** fatigued, थका हुआ, थका-माँदा, पस्त।

tiresome (टाइरसम) ***adj.*** 1. wearisome, थकाऊ। 2. tedious, ऊबाऊ।

tissue (टिशू) ***n.*** a group of cell of animal or plant body that are similar in form or function, ऊतक।

tissue paper ***n.*** very thin paper, अत्यंत पतला कागज़, टिशू पेपर।

tit[1] (टिट) ***n.*** a small bird, चिड़िया। ☐ **tit for tat,** जैसे को तैसा।

tit[2] ***n.*** a teat, चूची।

titanic (टाइटैनिक) ***adj.*** gigantic, भीमकाय, विशाल।

titbit (टिटबिट) ***n.*** 1. a tasty morsel, मज़ेदार कौर या निवाला। 2. a bit of interesting gossip, चुटकुला।

titilate (टिटिलेट) ***v.*** to excite pleasantly, to tickle, गुदगुदाना या सहलाना।

titilation (टिटिलेशन) ***n.*** the act of titilating, गुदगुदाहट।

title (टाइटल) ***n.*** 1. a descriptive name given to a book, poem, picture etc., शीर्षक, नाम। 2. an appellation, उपाधि। 3. designation, पदवी, पद। 4. a legal right to ownership, स्वत्वाधिकार।

titled (टाइटल्ड) ***adj.*** having a title, उपाधि या पदवीधारी, उपाधिप्राप्त, पदवीप्राप्त।

title deed ***n.*** a legal document proving a person's title to a

T

property, अधिकार-पत्र।

titter (टिटर) ***v.*** to utter a restrained laugh, ठींठीं करना, हींहीं करना। ***n.*** a restrained laugh, ठींठीं, हींहीं।

titular (टिट्युलर) ***adj.*** 1. bearing a title, उपाधिधारी। 2. in name only, नाममात्र का।

to (टु) ***prep.*** 1. in a direction toward, की तरफ़, दिशा में, को। 2. till, until, तक। 3. used to mark the indirect object of the verb, को; He told a story to the children. उसने बच्चों को कहानी सुनाई। 4. used to mark the infinitive of a verb; He wanted to go. 5. as compared with, की तुलना में, के मुक़ाबले; They won by four goals to one. वे एक के मुक़ाबले चार गोल से जीते। 6. for the purpose of, से; to that end, उस उद्‌देश्य से। 7. regarding or concerning, के लिए; He is deaf to her pleas. उसकी अनुनय-विनय सुनने के लिए वह तैयार नहीं है। 8. in accord with, के अनुसार; not to my liking, मेरी पसंद के अनुसार नहीं। 9. before the hour of, घंटे (घंटा बजने) से पहले; five to four, चार बजने को पाँच मिनट। 10. as against, के बदले; Five mangoes to the rupee, एक रुपया के पाँच आम। ***adv.*** in a certain direction or position, में; to the North of Delhi, दिल्ली के उत्तर में। □ **to and fro,** इधर-उधर, आगे-पीछे।

toad (टोड) ***n.*** a froglike animal, मेंढक की जाति का एक जंतु, भेक, टोड।

toady (टोडी) ***n.*** a flatterer, ख़ुशामदी व्यक्ति, चाटुकार, चापलूस। ***v.*** to flatter, खुशामद करना, चाटुकारी करना।

toast[1] (टोस्ट) ***n.*** 1. a slice of toasted bread, डबल रोटी का सेंका हुआ टुकड़ा, टोस्ट। 2. the act of drinking in someone's honour, किसी की मंगलकामना के लिए होनेवाला मद्यपान।

toast[2] ***v.*** 1. to make something brown and crisp by heating, सेंकना। 2. to wish happiness or success to someone by raising one's glass of wine, किसी की मंगलकामना के लिए जाम ऊँचा उठाना।

toaster (टोस्टर) ***n.*** an electrical device for toasting bread, डबल रोटी सेंकने का बिजली का उपकरण, टोस्टर।

tobacco (टबैको) ***n.*** 1. a plant grown for its leaves used chiefly for smoking, तंबाकू। 2. its leaves dried and prepared for chewing, snuff etc., तंबाकू, खैनी या सुरती।

today (टुडे) ***adv.*** 1. on the present day, आज। 2. nowadays, इन दिनों। ***n.*** 1. this day, आज का दिन। 2. the present age, वर्तमान युग।

toddle (टॉडल) ***v.*** to walk with short, unsteady steps (as a small child does, नन्हे-मुन्ने की तरह) ठुमक-ठुमककर चलना।

toddler (टॉडलर) ***n.*** a young child who toddles, ठुमक-ठुमककर चलनेवाला बच्चा।

toddy (टॉडी) ***n.*** a drink consisting of liquor with hot water, एक पेय जो शराब में गरम पानी मिलाकर तैयार करते हैं।

toe (टो) ***n.*** 1. any one of the digits of the foot, पैर की कोई उँगली या अँगूठा। 2. the forward part of a shoe or stocking covering the toe, जूते या मोज़े का पंजा। ***v.*** (toed, toeing) to touch with the toe, पैर के पंजे से छूना। □ **toe the line,** नियमों का सख़्ती से पालन करना।

toffee (टॉफ़ी) ***n.*** a sweet candy, टॉफ़ी।

together (टुगेदर) ***adv.*** 1. in company, unitedly, साथ मिलकर, एक साथ। 2. jointly, संयुक्त रूप से। 3. at one time, simultaneously, एक ही साथ, एक ही समय।

toggle (टॉगल) ***n.*** a pin for securing something in place, खूँटी।

toil[1] (टॉइल) ***v.*** to work hard and long, मेहनत करना, घोर परिश्रम करना। ***n.*** laborious effort, कड़ी मेहनत, घोर परिश्रम।

toil[2] ***n.*** a net, जाल।

toilet (टॉइलिट) ***n.*** 1. a place or room for urination and defecation, शौचालय। 2. the process of dressing and grooming oneself, प्रसाधन, शृंगार।

toiletries (टॉइलिट्रीज़) ***n.*** (plu.) articles used as cosmetics, शृंगार-सामग्री, प्रसाधन-सामग्री।

token (टोकन) ***n.*** 1. an indication, sign or representation of something, प्रतीक, संकेत, चिह्न। 2. a keepsake, निशानी, स्मृति-चिह्न। 3. a piece of stamped metal as a substitute for currency, टोकन। ***adj.*** 1. done as an indication, सांकेतिक; token strike, सांकेतिक हड़ताल। 2. done as a pledge, वचन या प्रतिज्ञा के रूप में किया जानेवाला; token payment, भुगतान का बयाना।

told (टोल्ड) ***v.*** p.t. & p.p. of tell. □ **all told,** कुल मिलाकर।

tolerable (टॉलरेबल) ***adj.*** 1. that can be tolerated, सहने योग्य, सह्य। 2. fairly good, संतोषजनक, कामचलाऊ।

tolerance (टॉलरेन्स) ***n.*** the state or quality of being tolerant, सहनशक्ति, सहिष्णुता।

tolerate (टॉलरेट) ***v.*** to be able to bear or suffer, सहना, बर्दाश्त करना।

toll[1] (टोल) ***n.*** 1. a tax or charge for the use of certain roads, bridges etc., मार्ग-कर, मार्ग-शुल्क, चुंगी, राहदारी। 2. the loss or damage caused by a disaster, किसी विपदा से होनेवाली हानि।

toll[2] ***v.*** to ring (a bell) slowly and recurrently for announcing a death, किसी की मृत्यु की सूचना देने के लिए बार-बार धीरे-धीरे घंटी बजाना।

tom (टॉम) ***n.*** a male cat, बिल्ला।

tomahawk (टॉमहॉक) ***n.*** a light axe, छोटी कुल्हाड़ी।

tomato (टमाटो) ***n.*** plant and its fruit, टमाटर।

tomb (टूम) ***n.*** 1. a grave for the dead, क़ब्र। 2. a burial monument, मक़बरा।

tombola (टॉम्बोला) ***n.*** a lottery at a fete, फ़ेट की लॉटरी, मेले की लॉटरी।

tomboy (टॉमबॉइ) ***n.*** a girl of boyish behaviour, मर्दाना लड़की, चुलबुली लड़की।

tombstone (टूमस्टोन) ***n.*** a stone with an engraved inscription about the tomb, क़ब्र पर लगा पत्थर, समाधि-शिला।

tomfoolery (टॉमफ़ूलरी) ***n.*** a foolish act, मूर्खतापूर्ण आचरण।

tommyrot (टॉमीरॉट) ***n.*** nonsense, utter nonsense, बेवक़ूफ़ी की बात, बकवास।

tomorrow (टमॉरो) ***n.*** 1. the day after today, कल। 2. the near future, निकट भविष्य। ***adv.*** on the day after today, कल।

T

tomtom (टॉमटॉम) ***n.*** a kind of drum, एक तरह का ढोल।

ton (टन) ***n.*** 1. a unit of weight equal to 1016.06 kilograms, टन। 2. a great quantity, बहुत बड़ी राशि।

tonal (टोनल) ***adj.*** of or relating to tone, स्वर-संबंधी, स्वरपरक, स्वरिक।

tone (टोन) ***n.*** 1. vocal or musical sound, स्वर, सुर, तान। 2. the manner of expression, अभिव्यक्ति का ढंग, लहज़ा। 3. the firmness of a living body, स्वास्थ्य, शारीरिक शक्ति। ***v.*** 1. to give a particular tone to, सुर देना या निकालना। 2. to make firm, दृढ़ बनाना।

toneless (टोनलिस) ***adj.*** 1. lacking in tone, स्वरहीन। 2. lacking in expression, अभिव्यक्ति से रहित।

tongs (टॉन्ग्ज़) ***n.*** (plu.) a grasping device of two arms, चिमटी, चिमटा या सड़सी।

tongue (टन्ग) ***n.*** 1. a flesh organ in the mouth, जीभ, ज़बान, जिह्वा। 2. a language, भाषा। 3. the quality of utterance, बोलने का ढंग।

tongue-tied (टन्ग-टाइड) ***adj.*** speechless, जिसकी बोलती बंद (हो गई) हो, मौन, चुप।

tonic (टॉनिक) ***adj.*** stimulating physical or mental vigour, शक्तिवर्धक, पुष्टिकारक, स्फूर्तिवर्धक। ***n.*** 1. a drug that stimulates vigour, शक्तिवर्धक या स्फूर्तिवर्धक ओषधि, टॉनिक। 2. a keynote in music, मूल स्वर।

tonight (टुनाइट) ***adv.*** on this present night or the night following this present day, आज रात। ***n.*** the present or the coming night, आज की रात।

tonnage (टनिज) ***n.*** 1. total weight in tons, टन भार, टन मान। 2. a charge per ton on cargo, प्रति टन भाड़ा। 3. the carrying capacity of a ship in tons, टनों में पोत की धारिताशक्ति, टन-भार।

tonsil (टॉन्सिल) ***n.*** one of the two glands near the root of the tongue, गदूद, गलतुंडिका, टॉन्सिल।

tonsillitis (टॉन्सिलाइटिस) ***n.*** inflammation of the tonsils, गदूद-शोथ।

tonsure (टॉन्शर) ***n.*** the act of shaving the head, मुंडन। ***v.*** to shave the head of, मुंडन करना, मूँड़ना।

tonsured (टॉन्शर्ड) ***adj.*** having the shaven crown, मुंडित, मूँड़ा हुआ।

too (टू) ***adv.*** 1. also, भी। 2. very, अत्यधिक, बहुत ही।

tool (टूल) ***n.*** 1. an instrument necessary in the practice of a profession or vocation, औज़ार, उपकरण। 2. a means to an end, साधन। 3. one who is manipulated by another, कठपुतली। ***v.*** 1. to shape, form or finish with a tool, औज़ार से बनाना या गढ़ना। 2. to equip with tools, औज़ारों से सज्जित करना।

toolbox (टूलबॉक्स) ***n.*** a chest for tools, औज़ार रखने की पेटी या बक्सा।

toot (टूट) ***v.*** to sound (a whistle or horn, सीटी या भोंपू) बजाना। ***n.*** 1. the act of tooting, सीटी/भोंपू बजाना। 2. the sound of a whistle or horn, सीटी या भोंपू की आवाज़।

tooth (टूथ) ***n.*** 1. one of a set of the hard white bony structures rooted in the gums, दाँत, दंत। 2. a toothlike part or projection, दाँता।

toothache (टूथेक) ***n.*** pain in a tooth, दाँत का दर्द, दंतशूल।

toothbrush (टूथब्रश) ***n.*** a brush for cleaning the teeth, दाँत साफ़ करने का ब्रुश।

toothed (टूथ्ड) ***adj.*** 1. having teeth, दाँतोंवाला। 2. having toothlike parts, दाँतेदार, दंतुर।

toothpaste (टूथपेस्ट) ***n.*** a paste for cleaning the teeth, दंतपेस्ट, टूथपेस्ट।

toothpick (टूथपिक) ***n.*** a small stick for removing bits of food from between the teeth, दंतखोदनी।

toothy (टूथी) ***adj.*** having large teeth, बड़े-बड़े दाँतोंवाला, दंतुल।

top[1] (टॉप) ***n.*** 1. the highest point or uppermost part of something, चोटी, शिखर, सिरा, ऊपरी तल। 2. a thing serving as an upper piece, lid or covering, ढक्कन या काग। 3. the garment covering upper part of the body, वक्षीय वस्त्र। 4. (plu.) **the tops,** very best, अत्यंत श्रेष्ठ। ***adj.*** situated on, relating to or serving as the top of something, ऊपरी, अत्यंत ऊँचा। ***v.*** 1. to reach the top of, सबसे ऊपर पहुँचना, शिखर पर पहुँचना। 2. to furnish with top, सिरा बैठाना, ढक्कन लगाना। 3. to exceed, बढ़ जाना। 4. to surpass, सबसे आगे निकल जाना।

top[2] ***n.*** a spinning toy, लट्टू।

topaz (टोपैज़) ***n.*** 1. a yellow sapphire, पुखराज। 2. the yellow colour, पीला रंग।

topcoat (टॉपकोट) ***n.*** a lightweight overcoat, हलका ओवरकोट।

top-heavy (टॉप-हेवी) ***adj.*** having the top part relatively much heavier than the lower one, ऊपरी हिस्सा भारी होने के कारण जिसके गिर पड़ने का अंदेशा हो।

topic (टॉपिक) ***n.*** a subject treated in a conversation, essay etc., theme, विषय, प्रकरण, प्रसंग।

topical (टॉपिकल) ***adj.*** 1. of or pertaining to the current topics, प्राकरणिक, सामयिक। 2. local, स्थानीय, स्थानिक।

topknot (टॉपनॉट) ***n.*** a tuft of hair on the top of head, जूड़ा।

toplevel (टॉपलेवल) ***adj.*** of the highest level, उच्चस्तरीय।

topmost (टॉपमोस्ट) ***adj.*** highest, उच्चतम।

topnotch (टॉपनॉच) ***adj.*** of highest quality, श्रेष्ठ, सर्वश्रेष्ठ।

topographical (टॉपग्रैफ़िकल) ***adj.*** of topography, स्थलाकृतिक।

topography (टपॉग्रफ़ी) ***n.*** detailed description of the physical features of a region, किसी क्षेत्र की भौगोलिक विशेषताओं का विस्तृत विवरण, स्थलाकृति।

topology (टपॉलोजी) ***n.*** topological study of a particular region, किसी क्षेत्र का भौगोलिक अध्ययन, संस्थिति-विज्ञान।

topper (टॉपर) ***n.*** one who is at the top of the list, सूची में सबसे ऊपर, सर्वप्रथम।

topple (टॉपल) ***v.*** 1. to fall (as if top-heavy, ऊपरी भाग भारी होने के कारण) गिर पड़ना। 2. to cause to fall, गिराना।

topsoil (टॉपसॉइल) ***n.*** the upper layer of the soil, मिट्टी की ऊपरी परत, उपरि मृदा।

topsy-turvy (टॉप्सी-टर्वी) ***adv.*** in utter confusion or disorder, घपले में,

T

अस्त-व्यस्त रूप में। ***adj.*** in a disorder condition, अस्त-व्यस्त, उलटा-पुलटा।

tor (टॉर) ***n.*** a high hill, ऊँची पहाड़ी।

torch (टॉर्च) ***n.*** 1. a burning stick used to give light, मशाल। 2. a portable device for emitting light, टॉर्च, बैटरी।

tore (टोर) ***v.*** p.t. of tear.

torment (टॉर्मेन्ट) ***n.*** 1. agony, यंत्रणा, यातना। 2. something causing this, यातना देनेवाला व्यक्ति, उत्पीड़ित करनेवाली वस्तु या बात। ***v.*** 1. to afflict pain, यातना देना, उत्पीड़ित करना। 2. to harass, परेशान करना, तंग करना।

tormentor (टॉर्मेन्टर) ***n.*** a tyrant, अत्याचारी, उत्पीड़क।

torn (टोर्न) ***v.*** p.p. of tear.

tornado (टॉर्नेडो) ***n.*** a violent and destructive whirling wind, चक्रवात, घूर्णवायु।

torpedo (टॉर्पीडो) ***n.*** an underwater missile, तारपीडो। ***v.*** to destroy with a torpedo, तारपीडो से ध्वस्त करना।

torpid (टॉर्पिड) ***adj.*** 1. inactive, अक्रिय, अचेष्ट, निश्चेष्ट। 2. sluggish, मंद, सुस्त।

torpor (टॉर्पर) ***n.*** 1. torpidity, निष्क्रियता। 2. sluggishness, सुस्ती।

torque (टॉर्क) ***n.*** a force that causes rotation, घूर्णन-बल।

torrent (टॉरन्ट) ***n.*** 1. a turbulent swift flowing stream, तेज़ धारा या प्रवाह। 2. a downpour of rain, मूसलाधार बारिश।

torrential (टरेन्शल) ***adj.*** relating to or resembling a torrent, प्रवाहपूर्ण, वेगपूर्ण।

torrid (टॉरिड) ***adj.*** 1. very dry and hot, शुष्क और गरम, उष्ण। 2. intense, घोर, उत्कट।

torsion (टार्शन) ***n.*** the act of twisting one end of an object while the other end is held motionless, ऐंठन, विमोटन।

torso (टॉर्सो) ***n.*** the trunk of a human body, धड़।

tort (टॉर्ट) ***n.*** a wrongful act, दुष्कर्म, दुष्कृति, अपकृत्य।

tortoise (टॉर्टस) ***n.*** a turtle, कछुआ, कच्छप।

tortuous (टॉर्चुअस) ***adj.*** 1. full of twists and turns, घुमावदार, चक्करदार, टेढ़ा-मेढ़ा। 2. not straightforward, कपटपूर्ण, धूर्ततापूर्ण।

torture (टॉर्चर) ***v.*** 1. to punish or coerce by inflicting severe pain, यंत्रणा देना, यातना देना, उत्पीड़ित करना। 2. to give mental anguish to, सताना। ***n.*** physical or mental anguish, यंत्रणा, यातना।

torturer (टॉर्चरर) ***n.*** one who tortures, उत्पीड़क, यंत्रणा देनेवाला।

Tory (टोरी) ***adj.*** of the British Conservative Party, ब्रिटेन के अनुदार दल से संबद्ध, टोरी। ***n.*** a member of the British Conservative Party, टोरी।

toss (टॉस) ***v.*** 1. to throw (a coin) in the air, (सिक्का) उछालना, फेंकना। 2. to decide an issue in this way, सिक्का उछालकर (किसी बात का) निर्णय करना। 3. to throw lightly or carelessly, झटकना, हिलाना। 4. to roll about from side to side, हिलना-डुलना, हिचकोले खाना। ***n.*** an act of tossing, फेंकना, उछालना।

tot[1] (टॉट) ***n.*** 1. a small child, छोटा बच्चा। 2. a small quantity of alcoholic drink, शराब की थोड़ी मात्रा।

tot[2] ***v.*** to add, जमा करना, जोड़ना।

total (टोटल) ***n.*** the number or quantity obtained by addition, योग, जोड़, टोटल। ***adj.*** complete, entire, सकल, कुल, समग्र, पूर्ण। ***v.*** to add up, जोड़ करना या लगाना, टोटल करना।

totalitarian (टोटैलिटेरिअन) ***adj.*** of a form of government in which only one party exercises full control, सर्वाधिकारी, सर्वसत्ताक।

totality (टोटैलिटी) ***n.*** 1. the state or quality of being total, सकलता, समग्रता, समष्टि। 2. total amount, कुल रक़म।

totem (टोटम) ***n.*** a symbol of a clan, क़बीले का प्रतीक चिह्न, कुलचिह्न।

totter (टॉटर) ***v.*** to move unsteadily, डगमगाना, लड़खड़ाना। ***n.*** an unsteady walk, लड़खड़ाहट।

touch (टच) ***v.*** 1. to press or push lightly, छूना, स्पर्श करना। 2. to take into the hand or mouth, छूना। 3. to paint or draw with light strikes, हलके हाथ से रँगना या चित्रित करना, छूना। 4. to meddle with, हाथ लगाना, छेड़छाड़ करना, हटाना-बढ़ाना। 5. to move emotionally, द्रवित होना, पसीजना, प्रभावित होना। 6. to persuade, दबाव डालना। ***n.*** 1. the act of touching, स्पर्श, संस्पर्श। 2. the sensation from a specific contact, स्पर्शानुभूति। 3. contact or communication, संपर्क या बातचीत। 4. a manner or style of doing something, काम करने का ढंग। 5. a slight trace, पुट, अल्पमात्रा।

touching (टचिन्ग) ***adj.*** capable of stirring emotionally, मार्मिक, हृदयस्पर्शी, करुणाजनक।

touchstone (टचस्टोन) ***n.*** 1. a fine-grained stone used to test the purity of gold or silver, कसौटी। 2. a criterion, कसौटी, निकष।

touchy (टची) ***adj.*** 1. easily offended, तुनुकमिज़ाज, चिड़चिड़ा। 2. very emotional, अतिभावुक। 3. sensitive to touch, अतिकोमल, सुकुमार, नाज़ुक।

tough (टफ़) ***adj.*** 1. strong, hard, कठोर, सख़्त, कड़ा। 2. having a determined will, टस-से-मस न होनेवाला, हठी। 3. difficult, कठिन, विकट, दुष्कर। 4. capable of enduring strain or hardship, सहिष्णु। ***n.*** a rough and violent person, गुंडा, बदमाश।

toughen (टफ़न) ***v.*** to make or become tough, कड़ा बनाना या हो जाना।

toughness (टफ़निस) ***n.*** the state or quality of being tough, चीमड़पन; कठोरता।

toupee (टूपीं) ***n.*** a wig, कृत्रिम केश, नक़ली बाल।

tour (टूर) ***n.*** 1. a journey for paying visits or giving performances at many places, टूर, दौरा। 2. a trip, यात्रा। ***v.*** to make a tour of, दौरे पर जाना।

tourism (टूरिज़म) ***n.*** the practice of travelling for recreation, पर्यटन।

tourist (टूरिस्ट) ***n.*** a person who visits places for pleasure or culture, पर्यटक।

tournament (टूर्नमेन्ट) ***n.*** a competition of skill among a number of players or teams, टूर्नामेंट, खेल-कूद प्रतियोगिता।

tourniquet (टर्निकिट) ***n.*** any device for compressing blood vessel to

T

stop bleeding, धमनी से रक्तस्राव रोकने की पट्टी।

tout (टाउट) ***v.*** 1. to solicit customers, ग्राहक को खरीदने के लिए कहना। 2. to give tips (about horse-racing, घुड़दौड़ के बारे में) संकेत देना। ***n.*** 1. one who solicits customers, दलाल। 2. one who gives tips, संकेत देनेवाला।

tow[1] (टो) ***v.*** to pull along behind by a chain or rope, रस्सी या चेन के सहारे खींचना या घसीटना। ***n.*** the act of towing, खींचने या घसीटने की क्रिया या भाव, अनुकर्षण।

tow[2] ***n.*** short hemp fibers, सन के छोटे रेशे।

toward (ट्वॉर्ड) ***prep.*** = towards.

towards (ट्वॉर्ड्ज़) ***prep.*** 1. in the direction of, की ओर, की दिशा में, को। 2. with relation to, के प्रति। 3. as a contribution to, के अंश के रूप में।

towel (टाउअल) ***n.*** a piece of absorbent cloth for drying oneself or wiping things dry, तौलिया, अंगोछा। ***v.*** to dry or wipe with a towel, तौलिए से पोंछना, तौलिए से रगड़कर साफ़ करना।

towelling (टाउअलिंग) ***n.*** a fabric used for making towels, तौलिए का कपड़ा।

tower (टाउअर) ***n.*** a tall circular structure, मीनार। ***v.*** to be of great height, बहुत ऊँचा होना।

towering (टाउअरिंग) ***adj.*** 1. of imposing height, lofty, बुलंद, उन्नत, ऊँचा। 2. outstanding, प्रमुख, प्रभावशाली। 3. intense, उग्र, प्रचंड।

town (टाउन) ***n.*** 1. a population centre larger than village but smaller than city, छोटा नगर, कस्बा, पुर। 2. its inhabitants, नगरवासी, शहरी, पुरवासी। 3. a commercial centre of an area, किसी क्षेत्र का व्यावसायिक केंद्र।

town hall ***n.*** a hall in a town for public events, टाउन हॉल, नगर-भवन।

township (टाउनशिप) ***n.*** a small town, नगरी, बस्ती।

toxaemia (टॉक्सीमिआ) ***n.*** blood-poisoning, रक्त का विषाक्त हो जाना, विषरक्तता।

toxic (टॉक्सिक) ***adj.*** 1. poisonous, विषैला, विषाक्त। 2. caused by poison, विषजन्य।

toxicity (टॉक्सिसिटी) ***n.*** the state or quality of being toxic, विषैलापन, विषाक्तता।

toxicologist (टॉक्सिकॉलोजिस्ट) ***n.*** a specialist in toxicology, विषविज्ञानी।

toxicology (टॉक्सिकॉलोजी) ***n.*** the scientific study of poisons, विषविज्ञान।

toxin (टॉक्सिन) ***n.*** a poisonous substance produced by microorganisms, जीवविष।

toy (टॉइ) ***n.*** 1. an object for children to play with, खिलौना। 2. something diminutive, छोटे आकार-प्रकार की वस्तु। 3. someone or something to be toyed with, खिलवाड़ की वस्तु। ***v.*** to amuse oneself as if with a toy, खिलवाड़ करना।

trace[1] (ट्रेस) ***n.*** 1. a mark or line left by something or someone that has passed by, लीक, पदचिह्न, निशान। 2.a very small quantity, लेश, अल्पमात्रा, पुट। 3. something traced or drawn, ख़ाका, रूपरेखा। ***v.*** 1. to sketch, ख़ाका उतारना, रूपरेखा तैयार करना। 2. to copy on transparent paper placed over it or by using carbon paper below, ट्रेस करना, अनुरेखित करना। 3. to follow the footprints, लीक पकड़ना, पदचिह्नों पर चलना। 4. to track down and find, खोज निकालना, पता लगा लेना।

trace[2] ***n.*** each of the two side straps by which a horse draws a carriage, जोत, जोतने की रस्सी या पट्टा।

traceable (ट्रेसेबल) ***adj.*** that can be traced, (i) जिसकी खोज की जा सके, (ii) जिसे ट्रेस या अनुरेखित किया जा सके।

trachea (ट्रेकिआ) ***n.*** the windpipe, श्वासनली।

tracing (ट्रेसिंग) ***n.*** the work of a person who traces, (i) खोज, (ii) अनुरेखन; tracing paper, अनुरेखन-काग़ज़।

track (ट्रैक) ***n.*** 1. a mark or trail left by something that has passed by, लीक, पदचिह्न, निशान। 2. any course or road, पथ, मार्ग। 3. a footpath, पटरी, पगडंडी। 4. the parallel rails of a railroad, रेल की पटरी, रेलपथ। 5. a magnetic tape on which something is recorded, टेप।

tracker (ट्रैकर) ***n.*** a person who tracks, खोजी।

tract[1] (ट्रैक्ट) ***n.*** 1. an extended area, भूभाग, इलाका, क्षेत्र। 2. a system of organs along which something passes, अंग-प्रणाली।

tract[2] ***n.*** a pamphlet of religious or political propaganda, पत्रक, पुस्तिका, निबंधिका।

tractable (ट्रैक्टेबल) ***adj.*** controllable, easily handled or managed, सँभाला जा सकने योग्य, वश्य, नियंत्रणीय।

traction (ट्रैक्शन) ***n.*** 1. the act of pulling, खींचने की क्रिया, अवस्था या भाव, कर्षण। 2. grip, पकड़। 3. a steady pull on a limb, अंग-कर्षण, ट्रैक्शन।

tractor (ट्रैक्टर) ***n.*** a motor vehicle used to pull farm machinery, ट्रैक्टर।

trade (ट्रेड) ***n.*** the business for buying and selling or bartering commodities, व्यापार, व्यवसाय। □ **the trade,** the people engaged in a particular trade, किसी व्यवसाय में लगे हुए लोग। ***v.*** 1. to buy and sell, व्यापार करना, व्यवसाय करना। 2. to enage in trade, व्यापार में लगना।

trade mark (ट्रेड मार्क) ***n.*** a registered mark used by a trader to identify his goods, व्यापार-चिह्न, ट्रेडमार्क, मार्का।

trader (ट्रेडर) ***n.*** a person whose business is buying and selling, व्यापारी, व्यवसायी।

trade union ***n.*** the union of workers, श्रमिक संघ।

tradition (ट्रैडिशन) ***n.*** a custom or belief handed down from generation to generation, परंपरा, प्रथा।

traditional (ट्रैडिशनल) ***adj.*** of or relating to a tradltlon on, परंपरागत, पारंपरिक।

traffic (ट्रैफ़िक) ***n.*** 1. the pedestrians and vehicles moving along a route, यातायात। 2. illegal or immoral trade, नियमविरुद्ध या अनैतिक व्यापार। ***v.*** (trafficked, trafficking) to carry on traffic, अवैध या अनैतिक व्यापार चलाए चलना।

tragedian (ट्रैजीडिअन) ***n.*** 1. a writer of tragedies, त्रासदी का लेखक। 2. an actor of tragedy, त्रासदी का अभिनेता।

tragedy (ट्रैजिडी) ***n.*** 1. a play with

T

sorrowful ending, दुखांत नाटक, त्रासदी। 2. a calamity, बहुत बड़ी दुर्घटना, त्रासदी।

tragic (ट्रैजिक) ***adj.*** 1. of or having the character of tragedy, त्रासदिक, त्रासद। 2. having a sad end, दुखांतक। 3. disastrous, अनर्थकारी, घातक।

tragically (ट्रैजिकली) ***adv.*** in a tragical manner, कारुणिक रूप में।

tragicomedy (ट्रैजिकॉमिडी) ***n.*** a play that combines with both tragic and comic elements, दुखसुखांतक।

trail (ट्रेल) ***v.*** 1. to drag or be dragged, घसीटना या घसीटा जाना। 2. to walk or proceed draggingly, घसीटते हुए चलना। 3. to track (game, शिकार का) पीछा करना। 4. to lag behind, (प्रतियोगी का) पीछे रह जाना। 5. to hang or float loosely, लटकना या झूलना। ***n.*** 1. something that trails esp. something that hangs loose and long, लटकती या झूलती हुई वस्तु। 2. a line of people or things following behind something, a chain of something, लाइन, कतार, लड़ी। 3. a trace or mark left by a moving body, पदचिह्न, गंध, सुराग़ आदि। 4. a track, पथ, पगडंडी आदि।

trailer (ट्रेलर) ***n.*** 1. one that trails, वह जो पीछे-पीछे घसीटता हुआ चले। 2. a vehicle designed to be hauled by a truck or tractor, ट्रेलर, अनुयान। 3. a short abridged form of a picture shown in advance, ट्रेलर, झलक।

train (ट्रेन) ***n.*** 1. a string of railway compartments, गाड़ी, रेल, ट्रेन। 2. a sequence of things, लड़ी, सिलसिला, ताँता। 3. a part of a dress that trails on the ground behind the wearer, छोर, पुछल्ला। 4. a body of followers, अनुचर-वृंद, मुसाहिबों की टोली। ***v.*** 1. to teach so as to be qualified and disciplined, प्रशिक्षित करना, प्रशिक्षण देना, सधाना। 2. to become qualified and disciplined by training, प्रशिक्षित होना, प्रशिक्षण प्राप्त करना। 3. to aim at an object, निशाना साधना।

trained (ट्रेन्ड) ***adj.*** having got training, प्रशिक्षित।

trainee (ट्रेनी) ***n.*** one who is undergoing training, प्रशिक्षणार्थी।

trainer (ट्रेनर) ***n.*** a person who trains, प्रशिक्षक।

training (ट्रेनिंग) ***n.*** the work of a person who trains, प्रशिक्षण।

trait (ट्रेट) ***n.*** a distinctive feature, विशेष गुण, विशेषता, लक्षण।

traitor (ट्रेटर) ***n.*** one who commits treason, देशद्रोही, गद्दार।

trajectory (ट्रजेक्टरी) ***n.*** the path of moving body spl. a bullet of rocket, प्रक्षेप-पथ, ट्रेजेक्टरी।

tram (ट्रैम) ***n.*** a street car that runs on tracks, ट्राम, ट्रामगाड़ी।

tramp (ट्रैम्प) ***v.*** 1. to walk with heavy steps, धपधप करते हुए चलना। 2. to traverse on foot, पैदल पार करना। 3. to trample, रौंदना, कुचलना। ***n.*** 1. one who travels on foot, पैदल चलनेवाला। 2. a sound of tramping, धपधप शब्द। 3. a long walk, पैदल यात्रा। 4. an immoral woman, कुलटा, पुंश्चली। 5. a freighter with no regular schedule, मालवाहक जहाज़ जिसके चलने का कोई बँधा समय न हो।

trample (ट्रैम्पल) ***v.*** 1. to tread under foot, कुचलना, रौंदना। 2. to kick, ठोकर मारना।

T

trance (ट्रान्स) ***n.*** 1. stupor, मूर्च्छा। 2. a state of profound absorption in contemplation, समाधि, ध्यान, आत्मविस्मृति।

tranquil (ट्रैन्क्विल) ***adj.*** calm, quiet, प्रशांत, शांतिपूर्ण।

tranquillize (ट्रैन्क्विलाइज़) ***v.*** to make calm or tranquil, प्रशांत करना, उपशमित करना।

tranquillizer (ट्रैन्क्विलाइज़र) ***n.*** a tranquillizing drug, प्रशांतकारी ओषधि।

trans (ट्रैन्स) ***prep.*** across, के पार, के उस पार; trans-yamuna, यमुना (के) पार।

transact (ट्रैन्ज़ैक्ट) ***v.*** 1. to carry out, कारोबार या लेन-देन करना, व्यवहार करना, चलाना। 2. to perform, निष्पन्न करना।

transaction (ट्रैन्ज़ैक्शन) ***n.*** 1. the act of transacting, लेन-देन, व्यवहार, संव्यवहार। 2. something transacted, ली-दी जानेवाली वस्तु, सौदा। 3. (plu.) a record of proceedings of a transaction, लेन-देन की कार्रवाई।

transcend (ट्रैन्सेन्ड) ***v.*** 1. to go beyond, (से) परे जाना, और आगे जाना, (की) सीमा पार करना। 2. to surpass, (से) बढ़कर या श्रेष्ठ होना।

transcendence (ट्रैन्सेन्डेन्स) ***n.*** the state or quality of being transcendent, अनुभवातीतत्व, अतींद्रियता, प्रागनुभव।

transcendental (ट्रैन्सेन्डेन्टल) ***adj.*** 1. going beyond the limits of ordinary experience, अनुभवातीत, प्रागनुभविक, इंद्रियातीत। 2. surpassing, उत्कृष्ट।

transcribe (ट्रैन्स्क्राइब) ***v.*** 1. to write or type a copy of, नक़ल उतारना, प्रतिलिपि करना, प्रतिलेखन करना। 2. to transliterate, लिप्यंतरण करना। 3. to make a recording of, रिकॉर्ड करना, रिकॉर्डिंग करना। 4. to adapt or arrange (a musical, composition, स्वरलिपि) तैयार करना।

transcript (ट्रैन्स्क्रिप्ट) ***n.*** a written copy, नक़ल, प्रतिलिपि, प्रतिलेख।

transcription (ट्रैन्स्क्रिप्शन) ***n.*** 1. the act of transcribing, प्रतिलिपिकरण, प्रतिलेखन, लिप्यंतरण। 2. a copy, प्रतिलिपि, नक़ल।

transducer (टैन्स्ड्यूसर) ***n.*** a device that converts one form of energy into another, ऊर्जा-परिवर्तक।

transfer (ट्रैन्स्फ़र) ***v.*** 1. to change or shift from one person or place to another, तबादला करना, स्थानांतरण करना, अंतरित करना। 2. to make over the possession or title of something to another, अंतरित करना, हस्तांतरित करना। ***n.*** 1. the act of transferring, तबादला, बदली, अंतरण। 2. a document pertaining to the transfer of some property, अंतरण-विलेख। 3. the design that is transferred or can be transferred from one surface to another, अनुचित्र।

transferable (ट्रैन्स्फ़रेबल) ***adj.*** that can be transferred, अंतरणीय, हस्तांतरणीय।

transfiguration (ट्रैन्स्फ़िगुरेशन) ***n.*** the act of transfiguring, स्वरूप-परिवर्तन।

transfigure (ट्रैन्स्फ़िगर) ***v.*** to change the form or shape of, स्वरूप बदल देना, रूप या आकार-प्रकार बदल देना।

transform (ट्रैन्स्फ़ॉर्म) ***v.*** 1. to change the form or appearance of, रूपांतरित करना। 2. to change the voltage (of electric current, बिजली की धारा का)

T

वोल्टेज बदल देना।

transformation (ट्रैन्स्फ़र्मेशन) ***n.*** the act of transforming or the state of being transformed, रूपांतरण।

transformer (ट्रैन्स्फ़ॉर्मर) ***n.*** an apparatus that transfers electric energy from one circuit to another, ट्रांस्फार्मर।

transfuse (ट्रैन्स्फ़्यूज) ***v.*** to inject (blood) in blood vessel, रक्तवाहिनी में सुई से (रक्त) देना, रक्ताधान करना।

transfusion (ट्रैन्स्फ़्यूज़न) ***n.*** the act of transfusing, रक्ताधान।

transgress (ट्रैन्स्ग्रेस) ***v.*** to pass beyond or go over the limit, to violate, अतिक्रमण करना, उल्लंघन करना।

transgression (ट्रैन्स्ग्रेशन) ***n.*** the act of transgressing or the state of being transgressed, violation, अतिक्रमण, उल्लंघन।

transgressor (टैन्स्ग्रेसर) ***n.*** one who transgresses, अतिक्रामक, उल्लंघनकर्ता।

tranship (ट्रैन्शिप) ***v.*** to transfer from one ship to another, एक जलयान से दूसरे जलयान पर (माल) भेजना, यानांतरण करना।

transhipment (ट्रैन्शिपमेन्ट) ***n.*** the act of transhipping, यानांतरण।

transience (ट्रैन्ज़िअन्स) ***n.*** the quality or state of being transient, अनित्यता, नश्वरता।

transient (ट्रैन्ज़िअन्ट) ***adj.*** transitory, not lasting or permanent, अनित्य, अस्थायी, क्षणिक।

transistor (ट्रैन्ज़िस्टर) ***n.*** an electronic device functioning as an electron tube, ट्रांज़िस्टर।

transit (ट्रैन्ज़िट) ***n.*** 1. the act of passing over, across or through, संक्रमण। 2. the conveyance of persons or goods from one place to another, पारगमन, पारवहन। □ **in transit,** रास्ते में, मार्ग में।

transition (ट्रैन्ज़िशन) ***n.*** the process of changing from one state, form, subject or place to another, संक्रमण, संक्रांति।

transitional (ट्रैन्ज़िशनल) ***adj.*** of or pertaining to transition, संक्रमणकालीन, संक्रामी।

transitive (ट्रैन्ज़िटिव) ***adj.*** (of a verb) having or requiring a direct object, सकर्मक।

transitory (ट्रैन्ज़िटरी) ***adj.*** of short or brief duration, अल्पकालिक, अनित्य, क्षणिक।

translate (ट्रैन्स्लेट) ***v.*** 1. to express in another language, अनुवाद करना, उल्था करना। 2. to express in simpler words, सरल शब्दों में अभिव्यक्त करना। 3. to convert, बदल देना, परिणत करना। 4. to move from one place to another, एक स्थान से दूसरे स्थान पर ले जाना।

translation (ट्रैन्स्लेशन) ***n.*** the act of translating or the state of being translated, अनुवाद, भाषांतर।

translator (ट्रैन्स्लेटर) ***n.*** one who translates, अनुवादक, अनुवादकर्ता।

transliterate (ट्रैन्स्लिटरेट) ***v.*** to represent in the characters of another language, लिप्यंतरण करना।

translucence (ट्रैन्स्ल्यूसेन्स) ***n.*** the quality or state of being translucent, पारभासकता।

translucent (ट्रैन्स्ल्यूसेन्ट) ***adj.*** semi-transparent, पारभासक, पारभासी।

transmigrate (ट्रैन्स्माइग्रेट) ***v.*** to pass

from one body to another after death, पुनर्जन्म होना, आवागमन होना।

transmigration (ट्रैन्स्माइग्रेशन) ***n.*** the state of being transmigrated, पुनर्जन्म, आवागमन।

transmission (ट्रैन्स्मिशन) ***n.*** 1. the act of transmitting, प्रेषण, पारेषण, प्रसारण, संचारण, अंतरण। 2. something transmitted, प्रेषित, पारेषित, प्रसारित या अंतरित की हुई वस्तु।

transmit (ट्रैन्स्मिट) ***v.*** 1. to send from one person, thing or place to another, प्रेषित करना। 2. to send out (signals as by radio, रेडियो द्वारा संकेत) पारेषित करना।

transmitter (ट्रैन्स्मिटर) ***n.*** 1. a device for transmitting signals, ट्रांस्मीटर, प्रेषित्र। 2. a person who transmits, प्रेषी।

transmutation (ट्रैन्स्म्यूटेशन) ***n.*** the act of transmuting or the state of being transmuted, परिवर्तन।

transmute (ट्रैन्स्म्यूट) ***v.*** to alter, बदल देना, परिवर्तित कर देना।

transparency (ट्रैन्स्पैरन्सी) ***n.*** 1. the quality of being transparent, पारदर्शिता। 2. a positive photograph, पारदर्शी चित्र,. पारदर्शिका।

transparent (ट्रैन्स्पैरन्ट) ***adj.*** 1. permitting light to pass through, clear, पारदर्शक, पारदर्शी। 2. easy to understand, स्पष्ट, सुबोध।

transpiration (ट्रैन्स्पिरेशन) ***n.*** the act of transpiring, प्रस्वेदन।

transpire (ट्रैन्स्पाइर) ***v.*** 1. to become known, जानकारी में आना, प्रकट होना। 2. (of plants) to give off vapours through pores, प्रस्वेदन करना।

transplant (ट्रैन्स्प्लैन्ट) ***v.*** 1. to remove and reset (a plant, पौधे को) प्रतिरोपित करना। 2. to transfer (an organ of a body, अंग) प्रत्यारोपित करना। ***n.*** the act of transplanting or the thing transplanted, प्रतिरोपण, प्रत्यारोपण; प्रत्यारोपित ऊतक या अंग।

transplantation (ट्रैन्स्प्लैन्टेशन) ***n.*** the act of transplanting or the state of being transplanted, प्रतिरोपण, प्रत्यारोपण।

transport (ट्रैन्स्पोर्ट) ***v.*** 1. to carry from one place to another, (माल या व्यक्तियों को) ढोना, वहन करना, परिवहन करना। 2. to exile, देश-निकाला देना। ***n.*** 1. the act of transporting, वहन, परिवहन। 2. means of conveyance, vehicle, यातायात का साधन, वाहन, सवारी। 3. the condition of being carried away for strong emotion, भावावेग।

transportation (ट्रैन्स्पोर्टेशन) ***n.*** 1. means of transporting, वाहन। 2. system of transporting, वाहन-व्यवस्था, परिवहन। 3. exile, देश-निकाला, निर्वासन।

transporter (ट्रैन्स्पोर्टर) ***n.*** one who is engaged in transport business, ट्रांस्पोर्टर, परिवहन-संचालक।

transpose (ट्रैन्स्पोज़) ***v.*** 1. to alter the positions of, विपर्यय करना, स्थान की अदला-बदली करना। 2. to change the order of, क्रम-परिवर्तन करना। 3. to change the key, सुर-लय बदल देना, स्वरांतरण करना।

transposition (ट्रैन्स्पज़िशन) ***n.*** the act of transposing, विपर्यय, क्रम-परिवर्तन; स्वरांतरण।

transverse (ट्रैन्स्वर्स) ***adj.*** lying in a crosswise direction, आड़ा, तिरछा।

transversely (ट्रैन्स्वर्सली) ***adv.***

T

crosswise, आड़े बल।

trap (ट्रैप्) ***n.*** 1. a device to catch animals, net, जंतुओं तथा पशुओं को पकड़ने का जाल, फंदा या पाश। 2. any plan by which someone is caught or stopped unawares, जाल, फाँसा, छलछंद। 3. a trapfall, चोरगड्ढा। 4. a U-shaped pipe, U की शक्ल का पाइप। 5. a light two-wheeled carriage, दुपहिया घोड़ा-गाड़ी। 6. a mouth, मुँह। ***v.*** to trap in or ensnare, जाल में पकड़ना या फँसाना।

trapdoor (ट्रैपडोर) ***n.*** a door in a floor or roof, चोर दरवाज़ा।

trapeze (ट्रैपीज़) ***n.*** a short horizontal bar suspended by two parallel ropes for acrobatics, सर्कस का आकाशी झूला।

trapezium (ट्रैपीज़िअम) ***n.*** a quadrilateral having two parallel sides of unequal length, समलंब चतुर्भुज।

trapper (ट्रैपर) ***n.*** one who traps animals, बहेलिया, शिकारी।

trash (ट्रैश) ***n.*** 1. rubbish, refuse, कूड़ा-कर्कट, कूड़ा। 2. junk, रद्दी सामान।

trauma (ट्रॉमा) ***n.*** (plu. traumata, traumas) 1. a wound or injury, घाव, जख़्म। 2. a powerful mental shock, मानसिक आघात, सदमा।

traumatic (ट्रॉमेटिक) ***adj.*** causing injury, आघात पहुँचानेवाला।

travel (ट्रैवल) ***v.*** (travelled/treveled, travelling/traveling) 1. to make a journey, यात्रा करना, सफ़र करना, यात्रा पर निकलना। 2. to go through an area, किसी क्षेत्र में से होकर जाना, भ्रमण करना। ***n.*** 1. a journey, यात्रा, सफ़र। 2. a voyage, विदेश-यात्रा। 3. (plu.) a series of journeys, यात्रा-शृंखलाएँ।

traveller, traveler (ट्रैवलर) ***n.*** one who travels or is travelling, यात्री, मुसाफ़िर।

travelogue (ट्रैवलॉग) ***n.*** a film or description on travel, यात्रा-फ़िल्म; यात्रा-वृत्तांत, सफ़रनामा।

traversal (ट्रैवर्सल) ***n.*** the act of traversing, पारगमन।

traverse (ट्रैवर्स) ***v.*** 1. to travel across, पार जाना, पार करना। 2. to lie or extend across, आड़ा या तिर्यक होना। ***n.*** 1. a thing that lies across another, आड़े बल में रखी हुई वस्तु। 2. the act of traversing, पारगमन। ***adj.*** lying or extending across, तिरछा, टेढ़े बल में रखा हुआ, तिर्यक।

travesty (ट्रैविस्टी) ***n.*** mockery, absurd imitation, उपहास, मज़ाक, विडंबना। ***v.*** to make a travesty or mockery of, उपहास करना, मज़ाक बना देना।

trawl (ट्रॉल) ***n.*** a large fishing net, मछलियाँ पकड़ने का बड़ा जाल, ट्राल। ***v.*** to fish with a trawl, ट्राल से मछलियाँ पकड़ना।

tray (ट्रे) ***n.*** 1. a flat utensil for carrying articles of food, ट्रे। 2. a shallow receptacle for papers, ट्रे।

treacherous (ट्रेचरस) ***adj.*** 1. betraying a trust, विश्वासघाती। 2. deceitful, कपटी, छलछंदी।

treachery (ट्रेचरी) ***n.*** 1. violation of allegiance or faith, disloyalty, विश्वासघात, निष्ठाहीनता, बेवफ़ाई। 2. an act of betrayal, दग़ा।

tread (ट्रेड) ***v.*** (trod, trodden/trod, treading) 1. to walk in, on or over (something, किसी चीज़) पर चलना।

T

2. to crush with feet, पैरों से कुचल देना, रौंद देना। *n.* 1. a manner or style of walking, चलने का ढंग, चाल। 2. the top surface of a step in a staircase, सीढ़ी के डंडे का ऊपरी तल। 3. the sound of footsteps, पदचाप, पैरों की आहट।

treadle (ट्रेडल) *n.* a machine operated by pressing a lever with a foot, पैर से लीवर को दबाकर चलाई जानेवाली मशीन।

treadmill (ट्रेडमिल) *n.* 1. an old type of mill operated by the weight of men, पाँव चक्की। 2. a tiring work, थकाऊ काम।

treason (ट्रीज़न) *n.* betrayal of one's country or its ruler, देशद्रोह या राजद्रोह।

treasure (ट्रेज़र) *n.* 1. a collection of precious things, बहुमूल्य निधि। 2. something of great worth or value, अमूल्य वस्तु, अतिमूल्यवान वस्तु। 3. a beloved or highly valued person, प्रिय या महत्त्वपूर्ण व्यक्ति। *v.* 1. to collect and store up, जमा करना, संचय करना। 2. to value highly, बहुमूल्य समझकर समादर देना।

treasurer (ट्रेज़रर) *n.* one who looks after the funds of a company, society etc., ख़ज़ांची, कोषपाल।

treasury (ट्रेज़री) *n.* a place where treasure is kept and stored, कोष, कोषागार, ख़ज़ाना।

treat (ट्रीट) *v.* 1. to deal with in a specified manner, बरताव करना, व्यवहार करना। 2. to give medical treatment to, उपचार या चिकित्सा करना। 3. to entertain, ख़ातिर करना, सत्कार या आवभगत करना। 4. to act upon with some chemical agent, उपचारित करना; treated timber, उपचारित इमारती लकड़ी। *n.* 1. an entertainment given to invitees, ख़ातिर या दावत। 2. anything that gives extreme pleasrue or joy, अत्यंत हर्ष या ख़ुशी की कोई बात। □ **stand treat,** दावत का ख़र्च वहन करना।

treatise (ट्रीटिस) *n.* an essay or dissertation, निबंध, प्रबंध।

treatment (ट्रीटमेन्ट) *n.* 1. the act of treating someone or something, व्यवहार, बरताव, प्रतिपादन, निरूपण। 2. cure or medication, उपचार, इलाज, दवा-दारू।

treaty (ट्रीटी) *n.* the agreement made by negotiations between two or more countries, संधि, सुलह, समझौता।

treble (ट्रेबल) *adj.* 1. three-times as much or as many, तिगुना। 2. high-pitched, उच्च, बहुत ऊँचा। *n.* 1. a treble quantity, तिगुनी मात्रा या परिमाण। 2. a high sound or voice, उच्च स्वर।

tree (ट्री) *n.* a woody perennial plant with a single trunk, पेड़, वृक्ष, दरख़्त।

trek (ट्रेक) *n.* a long difficult journey, लंबी दुर्गम यात्रा। *v.* to make a trek, लंबी दुर्गम यात्रा पर निकलना।

trellis (ट्रेलिस) *n.* a frame of crossing wooden or metal bars, जाफ़री, जाली।

tremble (ट्रेम्बल) *v.* 1. to shiver or vibrate, काँपने या हिलने लगना। 2. to be affected with fear, भय से काँप या सिहर उठना, भयभीत या चिंतित होना। *n.* the act of trembling, कंपन, कँपकँपी।

tremendous (ट्रिमेन्डस) *adj.* 1. huge, mammoth, बहुत बड़ा, विशाल, भारी। 2. immense, अत्यधिक।

T

tremor (ट्रेमर) ***n.*** 1. a quivering or vibratory motion, कंप। 2. horripilation, रोमांच, सिहरन।

tremulous (ट्रेम्युलस) ***adj.*** 1. trembling, vibrating, काँपता या हिलता हुआ। 2. timid, भीरु, डरपोक।

trench (ट्रेन्च) ***n.*** a deep ditch, खाई, खंदक।

trenchant (ट्रेन्चन्ट) ***adj.*** strong and effective, प्रबल तथा प्रभावपूर्ण, दृढ़, ज़ोरदार।

trend (ट्रेन्ड) ***n.*** 1. a general tendency, सामान्य प्रवृत्ति, रुझान, झुकाव। 2. fashion or drift, चाल, रिवाज।

trendsetter (ट्रेन्डसेटर) ***n.*** one who creates a new fashion, नया फ़ैशन चलानेवाला।

trespass (ट्रेस्पस) ***v.*** to enter unlawfully upon the land of someone, अतिचार करना, अतिक्रमण करना। ***n.*** an unlawful entry upon another's land, अतिचार, अतिक्रमण।

trespasser (ट्रेस्पसर) ***n.*** one who trespasses, अतिचारी, अतिक्रामक।

tress (ट्रेस) ***n.*** a lock of hair, लट।

triad (ट्राइऐड) ***n.*** a set of three, त्रयी, त्रय।

trial (ट्राइअल) ***n.*** 1. the act or process of trying or testing, परीक्षण, जाँच, परख। 2. the formal hearing and judging of the facts by a court of law, विचारण। 3. an attempt, प्रयत्न, प्रयास। 4. a test of endurance, faith etc., धैर्य, निष्ठा आदि की परीक्षा।

triangle (ट्राइऐन्गल) ***n.*** 1. a figure having three sides and three angles, त्रिकोण, त्रिभुज। 2. something having a shape of triangle, त्रिकोण।

triangular (ट्राइऐन्युलर) ***adj.*** 1. relating to a triangle, त्रिकोण-संबंधी। 2. involving three sides, त्रिकोणीय।

tribal (ट्राइबल) ***adj.*** of a tribe or tribes, जनजातीय, आदिवासीय, क़बायली।

tribe (ट्राइब) ***n.*** 1. a racial group of backward people having common descent and culture, क़बीला, जनजाति। 2. a group having common characteristics, वर्ग, समुदाय या गिरोह।

tribulation (ट्रिब्युलेशन) ***n.*** great affliction or distress, घोर विपत्ति या संकट।

tribunal (ट्राइब्यूनल) ***n.*** a board of judicial officials appointed by government to inquire or make a judgment on a special matter or issue, अधिकरण।

tributary (ट्रिब्युटरी) ***n.*** a river or stream that feeds another larger one, सहायक नदी, उपनदी।

tribute (ट्रिब्यूट) ***n.*** 1. a payment by a ruler or state given to another as an acknowledgment of submission, कर, ख़िराज। 2. something said as a mark of respect, सम्मान, स्तुति, प्रशंसा या श्रद्धांजलि।

trice (ट्राइस) ***n.*** □ **in a trice,** क्षण-भर में।

tricentenary (ट्राइसेन्टिनरी) ***n.*** a 300th anniversary, त्रिशताब्दी।

trick (ट्रिक) ***n.*** 1. a crafty or deceptive act, छल, छक्का-पंजा। 2. a dexterous or clever act, चाल। 3. a particular way of doing something easily, युक्ति, तरकीब, ढंग। 4. a feat of skill, हाथ की सफ़ाई, बाज़ीगरी। ***v.*** to cheat or deceive,

धोखा देना, छलना। □ **trick up,** अलंकृत करना, सजाना।

trickery (ट्रिकरी) ***n.*** deception, छल, धोखा, धोखाधड़ी।

trickle (ट्रिकल) ***v.*** 1. to fall in drops, बूँद-बूँद करके टपकना। 2. to flow in a thin gentle stream, पतली धार के रूप में बहना। 3. to come or go slowly, धीरे-धीरे आना या जाना। ***n.*** 1. the act of trickling, टपटप, टपकन। 2. slow flow of something, धीमी धारा।

trickster (ट्रिक्स्टर) ***n.*** one who cheats, धोख़ेबाज़, तिकड़मी।

tricky (ट्रिकी) ***adj.*** 1. sly, धूर्त, चालाक। 2. requiring caution or skill, नाज़ुक या पेचीदा।

tricolour (ट्राइकलर) ***adj.*** having three colours, तिरंगा। ***n.*** a tricolour flag, तिरंगा झंडा।

tricycle (ट्राइसिकल) ***n.*** a three-wheeled cycle, तिपहिया साइकिल।

trident (ट्राइडेन्ट) ***n.*** a three-pronged spear, त्रिशूलनुमा बरछा, त्रिशूल।

triennial (ट्राइएनिअल) ***adj.*** happening or being done every three years, त्रिवार्षिक, त्रिवर्षीय।

trifle (ट्राइफ़ल) ***n.*** 1. something of little value or no importance, तुच्छ या महत्त्वहीन चीज़ या बात, छोटी चीज़ या बात। 2. an insignificant amount, अल्पमात्रा, अल्पराशि। ***v.*** to dally or toy with, से खिलवाड़ करना, से छेड़छाड़ करना।

trifling (ट्राइफ़्लिंग) ***adj.*** trivial, insignificant, तुच्छ, नगण्य, महत्त्वहीन।

trigger (ट्रिगर) ***n.*** a lever pressed by the finger so as to fire a gun, बंदूक का घोड़ा, लिबलिबी। ***v.*** to set off, चलाना, प्रवर्तित करना, खड़ा करना।

trigger-happy (ट्रिगर-हैपी) ***adj.*** inclined to shoot on slight provocation, बात-बात पर गोली चला देनेवाला।

trigonometry (ट्रिगनॉमिट्री) ***n.*** the branch of mathematics dealing with the relationship between the sides and angles of triangles, त्रिकोणमिति।

trilateral (ट्राइलैटरल) ***adj.*** having three sides, त्रिपक्षीय।

trilingual (ट्राइलिन्ग्वल) ***adj.*** speaking or using three languages, त्रिभाषी।

trill (ट्रिल) ***n.*** a vibrating sound made by the voice, गिटकिरी, स्वरकंपन। ***v.*** to sing with a trill, गिटकिरी भरना, स्वर में कंपन उत्पन्न करना।

trillion (ट्रिल्यन) ***n.*** 1. (in England) the number represented as one followed by eighteen zeros, एक करोड़ खरब, दस शंख। 2. (in the U.S.A.) the number represented as one followed by twelve zeros, एक लाख करोड़, दस खरब।

trim (ट्रिम) ***adj.*** 1. neat and spruce, बना-ठना, साफ़-सुथरा, सजा-सँवरा। 2. well-ordered, orderly, व्यवस्थित, सुव्यवस्थित। ***v.*** 1. to make (a tree) neat or tidy by cutting or clipping, काटना-छाँटना। 2. to decorate or adorn, सजाना-सँवारना। 3. to balance, संतुलित करना। ***n.*** 1. an act of trimming, काट-छाँट, कटाई-छँटाई, समकर्तन। 2. the state or quality of being neat and spruce, साफ़-सुथरे या बने-ठने होने की अवस्था या भाव। 3. decoration, सजावट, शृंगार।

trimly (ट्रिमली) ***adv.*** 1. neatly, सफ़ाई से। 2. orderly, अच्छे ढंग से, व्यवस्थित

T

रूप में।

trimming (ट्रिमिंग) ***n.*** 1. something trimmed, काट-छाँटकर तैयार किया हुआ पदार्थ। 2. something added as decoration, सजावट के लिए रखी या लगाई हुई वस्तु। 3. accessories, उपसाधन।

trinity (ट्रिनिटी) ***n.*** a group of three, त्रयी, त्रिमूर्ति।

trinket (ट्रिन्किट) ***n.*** a small ornament, छोटा-मोटा गहना।

trio (ट्रीओ) ***n.*** 1. a group of three, त्रयी। 2. a musical composition for three persons, तिगाना।

trip (ट्रिप) ***n.*** 1. a journey for pleasure or any specific purpose, यात्रा, भ्रमण। 2. an outward and return journey, फेरा। 3. an exciting or hallucinatory experience, कोई उत्तेजनात्मक या भ्रांतिजनक अनुभव। 4. a mistake, भूल, ग़लती। 5. a device for tripping a mechanism, छटकने या थिरकनेवाला यंत्र। 6. a false step, लड़खड़ाहट। ***v.*** 1. to walk or dance with light quick steps, फुदकना। 2. to stumble or cause to stumble, लड़खड़ा जाना या देना। 3. to release (a mechanism, पुर्ज़े का) छटक या थिरक जाना।

tripartite (ट्राइपार्टाइट) ***adj.*** having three parts or sides, त्रिपक्षीय।

triple (ट्रिपल) ***adj.*** 1. consisting of three parts, त्रिपक्षीय। 2. being three times as great or as many, तिगुना। ***v.*** 1. to make three times as great or as many, तिगुना करना। 2. to become three times as great or as many, तिगुना होना।

triplet (ट्रिप्लिट) ***n.*** 1. one of the three children or offsprings born at one birth, एक साथ उत्पन्न तीन बच्चों में से कोई एक, त्रिज। 2. a set of three things, त्रयी, त्रिक।

triplex (ट्रिप्लेक्स) ***adj.*** having three layers, तिपरती।

triplicate (ट्रिप्लिकेट) ***n.* in triplicate,** तीन प्रतियों में। ***adj.*** being a triplicate, तीन प्रतियों में होनेवाला। ***v.*** to make or be three identical copies of, एक जैसी तीन प्रतियाँ बनाना या बनना।

tripod (ट्राइपॉड) ***n.*** a three-legged stand, तिपाई, त्रिपाद।

tripping (ट्रिपिंग) ***adj.*** that trips, छटकने, थिरकने या फुदकनेवाला।

trisect (ट्राइसेक्ट) ***v.*** to divide into three (equal) parts, तीन (समान) हिस्सों में बाँटना, त्रिभाजित या समत्रिभाजित करना।

trite (ट्राइट) ***adj.*** commonplace, अतिसामान्य, घिसा-पिटा।

triumph (ट्राइअम्फ़) ***v.*** 1. to be victorious, विजयी होना। 2. to rejoice over a victory, जीत मनाना, विजयोत्सव मनाना। ***n.*** 1. victory, विजय, जीत। 2. the joy of victory, जीत की ख़ुशी, विजयानंद।

triumphant (ट्राइअम्फ़ेन्ट) ***adj.*** 1. victorious, विजयी। 2. successful, सफल। 3. exultant through triumph, विजय से उत्फुल्ल।

trivia (ट्रिविआ) ***n.*** (plu.) trivialities, छोटी-मोटी बातें या चीजें।

trivial (ट्रिविअल) ***adj.*** 1. ordinary, साधारण, मामूली। 2. of little worth, नगण्य, तुच्छ।

triviality (ट्रिविऐलिटी) ***n.*** 1. the quality or state of being trivial, तुच्छता, नगण्यता। 2. something trivial, तुच्छ वस्तु या बात।

trod (ट्रॉड) ***v.*** p.t. of tread.

trodden (ट्रॉडन) ***v.*** p.p. of tread.

troika (ट्राइका) ***n.*** a council of three persons, तीन व्यक्तियों की परिषद्, त्रिपरिषद्।

troll (ट्रॉल) ***v.*** to fish with a hook and line, बंसी से मछलियाँ पकड़ना।

trolley (ट्रॉली) ***n.*** 1. a wheeled vehicle for conveying food or transporting luggage, ट्रॉली, ठेला। 2. a basket type carriage suspended from an overhead track, ट्रॉली।

troop (ट्रूप) ***n.*** 1. a group or company of armed soldiers, सशस्त्र सेना की टुकड़ी, जत्था। 2. a unit of Scouts, बालचरों की टोली। 3. a flock of birds or animals, झुंड, गोल। ***v.*** 1. to assemble, इकट्ठा होना, एकत्र होना। 2. to move in large number, दल बनाकर चलना, दल बाँधकर चलना।

trooper (ट्रूपर) ***n.*** 1. a cavalry man, घुड़सवार सैनिक, अश्वारोही सैनिक। 2. a police officer on horseback, घुड़सवार पुलिस अधिकारी।

trophy (ट्रॉफ़ी) ***n.*** 1. a cup or shield given to a winner or winners in a contest, प्रतियोगिता में जीतनेवाले को दिया जानेवाला उपहार, ट्रॉफ़ी, वैजयंती। 2. something taken in war or hunting, युद्ध, आखेट में मिलनेवाली या हाथ लगनेवाली चीज़, पुरस्कार।

tropic (ट्रॉपिक) ***n.*** 1. either of two parallels of latitude, कर्क या मकर रेखा। 2. ***The tropics***, (plu.) the region of the earth's surface bounded by these latitudes, उष्ण कटिबंध।

tropical (ट्रॉपिकल) ***adj.*** 1. of tropics, उष्ण कटिबंधीय। 2. very hot, अत्यंत गरम।

troposphere (ट्रॉपस्फ़िअर) ***n.*** the lowest atmospheric layer which extends outward from seven to ten miles from earth's surface, क्षोभमंडल।

trot (ट्रॉट) ***n.*** 1. the moderately fast running action of a horse, घोड़े की दुलकी चाल। 2. a steady brisk pace, तेज़ चाल। ***v.*** to move or cause to move at a trot, दुलकी चलना या चलाना। ☐ **trot out,** प्रस्तुत करना, पेश करना।

trouble (ट्रबल) ***n.*** 1. difficulty or inconvenience, असुविधा, कष्ट, कठिनाई। 2. mental distress, परेशानी, व्यथा, वेदना। 3. a cause of distress, मुसीबत या कष्ट का कारण, विपत्ति। 4. faulty functioning of mechanism, body etc., ख़राबी, गड़बड़ी। ***v.*** 1. to stir up or agitate, विक्षुब्ध करना, अशांत बनाना। 2. to bother or perturb, तंग करना, परेशान करना। 3. to become agitated, विक्षुब्ध हो उठना। 4. to make an effort or take pains, प्रयास करना, कष्ट उठाना।

troublefree (ट्रबलफ़्री) ***adj.*** causing no trouble, निरापद।

troubleshooter (ट्रबलशूटर) ***n.*** one who traces the cause of trouble and removes it, दोष को पकड़ने तथा उसे ठीक करनेवाला।

troublesome (ट्रबलसम) ***adj.*** causing trouble, दुख देने या गड़बड़ी उत्पन्न करनेवाला, उपद्रवी, उत्पाती।

trough (ट्रॉफ़) ***n.*** 1. a long shallow receptacle for holding water or feed for animals, नाँद, कुंड। 2. a depression between two waves or ridges, गर्त। 3. the lowest point of the trade cycle, मंदी, अवसाद-काल।

T

trounce (ट्राउन्स) ***v.*** to defeat decisively, पछाड़ देना, हरा देना।

troupe (ट्रूप) ***n.*** a group of actors, a theatrical group, अभिनेताओं या कलाकारों की मंडली।

trouper (ट्रूपर) ***n.*** a member of a troupe, मंडली का सदस्य, अभिनेता या कलाकार।

trousers (ट्राउज़र्ज़) ***n.*** (plu.) a two-legged outer garment extending from the waist to the ankles, पाजामा या पतलून।

trowel (ट्राउअल) ***n.*** 1. a flat hand tool for spreading plaster, करनी, कन्नी। 2. a hand tool for lifting plants, खुरपी।

truant (ट्रूअन्ट) ***n.*** a boy who is absent without leave from school, पलायनशील बालक।

truce (ट्रूस) ***n.*** a temporary cessation of hostilities by agreement, अस्थायी शांति-संधि, अस्थायी युद्धविराम-संधि।

truck (ट्रक) ***n.*** 1. a vehicle for moving heavy loads, ट्रक। 2. a handcart, ठेला। ***v.*** 1. to load on a truck, ट्रक पर लादना। 2. to transport goods on a truck, ट्रक से ढुलाई करना।

truculent (ट्रक्युलेन्ट) ***adj.*** 1. fierce, उग्र। 2. aggressive, आक्रामक।

trudge (ट्रज) ***v.*** to walk laboriously, (थकावट के कारण) भारी पैरों से चलना, पैर घसीटते हुए चलना।

true (ट्रू) ***adj.*** 1. consistent with reality, सत्य, सच्चा, वास्तविक। 2. loyal, निष्ठावान। 3. exact, परिशुद्ध, सही, यथार्थ। ***adv.*** 1. truly, सचमुच, सच्चाई से। 2. accurately, सही-सही।

truly (ट्रूली) ***adv.*** 1. truthfully, indeed, सचमुच, सत्यतापूर्वक। 2. accurately, सही-सही, ठीक-ठीक। □ **Yours truly,** भवदीय, आपका ही।

trump (ट्रम्प) ***n.*** 1. any card from the suit chosen as trumps, रंग का पत्ता, तुरुप। 2. this suit itself, रंग (ताश में)। 3. a decisive move, निर्णायक चाल, अकाट्य युक्ति। ***v.*** to play a trump card, रंग का पत्ता चलना, तुरुप चलना, रंग के पत्ते से काट देना। □ **trump up,** (बहाना) बनाना।

trumps (ट्रम्प्स) ***n.*** (sing.) a suit whose cards are trumps for the duration of the hand, रंग के पत्ते, तुरुप।

trumpery (ट्रम्परी) ***adj.*** showy but worthless, झूठा, नक़ली।

trumpet (ट्रम्पिट) ***n.*** a wind instrument, तुरही। ***v.*** 1. to blow a trumpet, तुरही बजाना। 2. to make a loud resounding sound, गरजना, चिंघाड़ना।

truncate (ट्रन्केट) ***v.*** to shorten by cutting off the end, सिरा काटकर छोटा कर देना, रुंडित करना।

trundle (ट्रन्डल) ***v.*** to roll, लुढ़कना।

trunk (ट्रन्क) ***n.*** 1. the main stem of a tree, पेड़ का तना। 2. the human or animal body apart from head and limbs, धड़। 3. the long nasal part of an elephant, सूँड़। 4. a large packing case with a hinged lid, संदूक, ट्रंक। 5. (plu.) men's shorts for athletics, जाँघिया या घुटन्ना। ***adj.*** of a main railway or telephone line, मुख्य, ट्रंक; trunk line, मुख्य मार्ग।

trunk call ***n.*** a long-distance telephone call, ट्रंक कॉल।

truss (ट्रस) ***n.*** 1. a structural framework of beams or bars supporting a roof, bridge etc.,

कैंची। 2. a belt for supporting hernia in place, हर्निया की पेटी। 3. a cluster of flowers or fruit cluster, फूलों या फलों का गुच्छा। *v.* to tie or bind securely, कसकर बाँधना।

trust (ट्रस्ट) *n.* 1. the firm belief in the ability, strength or character of someone or something, विश्वास, भरोसा, यक़ीन। 2. responsibility, उत्तरदायित्व। 3. property legally entrusted to a person or board to be used or cared for in the interest of another, न्यास, ट्रस्ट। 4. something accepted as a responsibility, धरोहर, थाती। 5. a combination of firms, व्यावसायिक गुट या संघटन। *v.* 1. to have trust in, (किसी पर) विश्वास करना या रखना। 2. to entrust, सौंपना, जिम्मे करना, सुपुर्द करना। 3. to hope confidently, पूरी आशा करना या रखना।

trustee (ट्रस्टी) *n.* a person to whom some property is entrusted for specific purpose, न्यासी, ट्रस्टी।

trustworthy (ट्रस्टवर्दी) *adj.* reliable, विश्वसनीय, भरोसे का।

truth (ट्रूथ) *n.* 1. the quality of being true, सत्यता, सच्चाई। 2. a true statement, सच्ची बात, सत्य कथन।

truthful (ट्रूथफुल) *adj.* 1. corresponding to reality, सत्य, सच्चा, वास्तविक। 2. telling the truth, सत्यवादी, सत्यशील।

try (ट्राइ) *v.* 1. to make an attempt, प्रयास करना, चेष्टा करना, कोशिश करना। 2. to put to test in order to see whether it is satisfactory, परखना, आज़माइश करना। 3. to investigate, जाँच करना, जाँचना। 4. to hold a trial of, न्यायिक जाँच करना। 5. to make an attempt at, प्रयोग कर देखना, कोशिश कर देखना। *n.* 1. an attempt, प्रयास, चेष्टा। 2. a test, परीक्षण।

trying (ट्राइंग) *adj.* severely straining the powers of endurance, कष्टसाध्य।

tryst (ट्राइस्ट) *n.* 1. an appointment to meet, मिलने का निश्चय। 2. the place of such meeting, मिलन-स्थल।

tsar (ज़ार) *n.* the emperor of Russia (before 1917, १९१७ से पहले का) रूसी सम्राट, ज़ार।

tsetse (ट्सेट्सी) *n.* an African fly, अफ़्रीकी मक्खी।

T-shirt (टी-शर्ट) *n.* a short-sleeved cotton shirt, टीशर्ट।

T-square (टी-स्क्वेअर) *n.* a T-shaped ruler, T की शक्ल की पटरी या रूला।

tub (टब) *n.* a large open flat-bottomed metal container used for holding water or other liquid, टब।

tubby (टबी) *adj.* (tubbier, tubbiest) short and fat, गोल-मटोल।

tube (ट्यूब) *n.* 1. a long slender hollow container of glass for holding liquids, ट्यूब, नलिका, नली। 2. a collapsible cylindrical container for holding paste etc., ट्यूब। 3. a rubber tube of a cycle, car, truck etc., ट्यूब। 4. the tunnels through which the railway runs, तलमार्ग।

tuber (ट्यूबर) *n.* a fleshy underground root, कंद।

tubercle (ट्यूबर्कल) *n.* a small rounded swelling, गुमटा।

tubercular (ट्यूबर्क्युलर) *adj.* 1. of or pertaining to tuberculosis, क्षय-संबंधी। 2. affected by tuberculosis, क्षयग्रस्त, क्षय से पीड़ित।

tuberculosis (ट्यूबर्क्युलोसिस) *n.* a wasting disease, क्षय, तपेदिक, टीबी।

T

tube-well (ट्यूब-वेल) ***n.*** a device for lifting underground water through a long pipe, नलकूप, ट्यूबवेल।

tubular (ट्यूब्युलर) ***adj.*** having the shape of tube, नलिकाकार, नली के आकार का।

tuck (टक) ***n.*** a pleat in a part of garment, प्लेट, चुनट। ***v.*** 1. to make tucks or pleats in, प्लेटें या चुनट डालना। 2. to put away compactly, अच्छी तरह सँभालकर अलग या छिपाकर रखना। □**tuck in,** जी भरकर खाना।

tuck shop ***n.*** a shop where cakes and sweets are sold, मिठाई की दुकान।

Tuesday (ट्यूज़डे) ***n.*** the day of the week following Monday, मंगलवार।

tuft (टफ़्ट) ***n.*** 1. a short cluster of small fibres stitched at one side, फुँदना, झब्बा। 2. a cluster of grass, flowers etc., गुच्छा; tuft of hair, बालों का गुच्छा, केशगुच्छ।

tug (टग) ***v.*** 1. to pull hard, ज़ोर से खींचना या घसीटना। 2. to tow, (नाव) खींचकर ले जाना। ***n.*** 1. the act of pulling, खींचने की क्रिया या भाव, कर्षण। 2. a tugboat, कर्षण-नौका। □ **tug of war,** (i) रस्साकशी, (ii) खींच-तान।

tuition (ट्यूशन) ***n.*** the act or profession of teaching or instructing individually or in small groups, ट्यूशन, अनुशिक्षण।

tulip (ट्यूलिप) ***n.*** a garden plant and its flower, ट्यूलिप नामक पौधा और उसका फूल।

tumble (टम्बल) ***v.*** 1. to fall suddenly and helplessly, एकाएक (लड़खड़ाकर) गिर पड़ना, ढह जाना। 2. to cause to fall, गिरा देना। ***n.*** 1. the act of tumbling, गिरने या लड़खड़ाने की क्रिया या भाव, गिर पड़ना। 2. a disorderly state, अव्यवस्था, गड़बड़ी।

tumbler (टम्ब्लर) ***n.*** 1. a drinking glass, गिलास। 2. an acrobat, बाज़ीगर, कलाबाज़। 3. a lever in a lock, ताले का खटका।

tummy (टमी) ***n.*** the stomach, पेट, तोंद।

tumour (ट्यूमर) ***n.*** any abnormal swelling on or in the body, ट्यूमर, गाँठ, अर्बुद।

tumult (ट्यूमल्ट) ***n.*** 1. uproar, कोलाहल, हुल्लड़, शोरगुल। 2. agitation, क्षोभ, घबराहट। 3. confusion, भ्रांति।

tumultuous (ट्यूमल्चुअस) ***adj.*** uproarious, कोलाहलपूर्ण, हुल्लड़-भरा।

tun (टन) ***n.*** a large cask, बड़ा पीपा।

tundra (टुन्ड्रा) ***n.*** a vast treeless icy region of North Pole, उत्तरी ध्रुव का वृक्ष-विहीन बर्फ़ीला प्रदेश, टुंड्रा।

tune (ट्यून) ***n.*** 1. a melody, धुन, राग। 2. correct musical pitch, लय। ***v.*** 1. to put in tune, सुर मिलाना, समस्वरित करना। 2. to adjust to run smoothly, ठीक करना, समंजित करना, सुधारना।

tuneful (ट्यूनफ़ुल) ***adj.*** having a pleasing tune, सुमधुर, सुरीला।

tunic (ट्यूनिक) ***n.*** a knee-length simple garment without sleeves, बिना बाँह का कुरता या जाकेट।

tuning (ट्यूनिंग) ***n.*** the act of one who tunes, समस्वरण।

tunnel (टनल) ***n.*** a passage through or under something, सुरंग। ***v.*** (tunneled/tunnelled, tunneling/tunnelling) to dig or make a tunnel, सुरंग खोदना या बनाना।

turban (टर्बन) ***n.*** a head dress consisting of a long cloth wound

T

round the head, पगड़ी, साफ़ा।

turbid (टर्बिड) ***adj.*** 1. muddy, गँदला। 2. not clear, अस्पष्ट। 3. cloudy, मेघाच्छादित। 4. dense, घना। 5. confused, विभ्रमित।

turbine (टर्बाइन) ***n.*** a machine or motor that operates by the pressure of water, steam, gas or air, टरबाइन।

turbulence (टर्ब्युलेन्स) ***n.*** the state of agitation or confusion, विक्षोभ, कोलाहल, अशांति।

turbulent (टर्ब्युलेन्ट) ***adj.*** 1. causing disturbance, unrest or violence, unruly, उपद्रवी, उत्पाती, दंगाई। 2. characterized by agitation, विक्षुब्ध, आंदोलित, अशांत।

turf (टर्फ़) ***n.*** 1. the grassy ground as a thick mat, टर्फ़, घासी मैदान। 2. the race course, घुड़दौड़ का मैदान। 3. horse racing, घुड़दौड़। ***v.*** to cover with pieces of turfs, टर्फ़ बिछाना। ☐ **turf out,** फेंक देना, बाहर कर देना।

turgid (टर्जिड) ***adj.*** 1. swollen, सूजा हुआ, फूला हुआ। 2. bombastic, शब्दाडंबरपूर्ण।

Turk (टर्क) ***n.*** an inhabitant of Turkey, तुर्की का नागरिक, तुर्क।

turkey (टर्की) ***n.*** a large bird reared for its flesh in America, अमेरिका का एक पक्षी, पीरू।

turmeric (टर्मरिक) ***n.*** a bright yellow spice, हल्दी।

turmoil (टर्मॉइल) ***n.*** 1. great confusion, विक्षोभ। 2. disturbance, खलबली, अशांति।

turn (टर्न) ***v.*** 1. to cause to move around an axis, point or centre, घुमाना। 2. to move around an axis, point or centre, घूमना। 3. to make a course around, चक्कर लगाना। 4. to cause to change position by moving, मोड़ना या घुमाना। 5. to take a new direction, मुड़ना, घूम जाना। 6. to change or be changed, बदलना या बदल जाना, रूपांतरित करना या हो जाना। 7. to invert or reverse, उलटा कर देना या हो जाना, पलट देना या पलटा जाना। 8. to shape in a lathe, खरादना, गढ़ना। 9. to pass (a certain hour or age), हो जाना। ☐ **turn down,** अस्वीकार कर देना; **turn in,** (सोने के लिए) बिस्तर पर चले जाना; **turn off,** बंद कर देना; **turn on,** खोल देना, चालू कर देना; **turn out,** (i) निकलना, सिद्ध होना; (ii) निकाल देना; **turn the scales,** संशय की स्थिति समाप्त कर देना; **turn the tables,** स्थिति उलट या बदल देना, पासा पलट देना; **turn upon,** विरुद्ध हो जाना। ***n.*** 1. the act of turning or being turned, घुमाव, परिवर्तन; a good turn, उपकार; a bad turn, अपकार। 2. a change of direction, दिशा-परिवर्तन, मोड़। 3. a revolution, फेरा, चक्कर। 4. an angle, bend or corner, मोड़। 5. a deviation from a tendency, change in nature or condition, बदलाव। 6. the right or opportunity to do something in agreed order, बारी, पारी। 7. a short walk, चहलक़दमी, टहलान, सैर। 8. an attack of illness or fit of anger, दौरा। 9. tendency, झुकाव, प्रवृत्ति। ☐ **in turn,** बारी-बारी से; **out of turn,** बारी से पहले या पीछे।

turner (टर्नर) ***n.*** one who works with a lathe, ख़रादी, टर्नर।

turning (टर्निंग) ***n.*** 1. a bend, मोड़। 2. (plu.) scrab, ख़राद की छीलन।

T

turnip (टर्निप) ***n.*** a plant and its root, शलजम, शलगम।

turnout (टर्नाउट) ***n.*** 1. the quantity or amount produced, उत्पाद। 2. the number of people appearing together at a gathering, (लोगों की कुल) उपस्थिति, जमावड़ा।

turnover (टर्नोवर) ***n.*** 1. the amount of business transacted in a given period, कुल बिक्री। 2. the rate at which goods are sold, बिक्री-दर। 3. a filled pastry, गुझिया या किचौड़ी।

turnstile (टर्नस्टाइल) ***n.*** a revolving barrier that admits in one person at a time, चक्रद्वार।

turntable (टर्नटेबल) ***n.*** a revolving platform, परिभ्रामक मंच, घूमता मंच।

turpentine (टर्पन्टाइन) ***n.*** an oil for thinning paint, तारपीन का तेल।

turpitude (टर्पिच्यूड) ***n.*** depravity, अधमता, नीचता, कमीनापन।

turquoise (टर्क्वाइज़) ***n.*** 1. a sky-blue gemstone, फ़ीरोज़ा। 2. sky-blue colour, फ़ीरोज़ी रंग।

turret (टरिट) ***n.*** a small towerlike ornamental structure, बुर्ज, कंगूरा।

turtle (टर्टल) ***n.*** 1. a sea tortoise, समुद्री कछुआ। 2. its flesh, कछुए का मांस। □ **turn turtle,** उलट जाना, औंधा हो जाना।

tusk (टस्क) ***n.*** one of the pair of a long protruding tooth of a male elephant, हाथी का दाँत, गजदंत।

tusker (टस्कर) ***n.*** a male elephant with developed tusks, बड़े दाँतोंवाला हाथी।

tussle (टसल) ***v.*** 1. to fight roughly, हाथापाई करना। 2. to struggle, संघर्ष करना। ***n.*** 1. a rough fight, हाथापाई। 2. a struggle, संघर्ष।

tussore (टसर) ***n.*** a kind of silk, टसर।

tutor (ट्यूटर) ***n.*** a teacher who instructs pupils individually, व्यक्तिगत रूप से पढ़ानेवाला अध्यापक, अनुशिक्षक। ***v.*** to teach, पढ़ाना, सिखाना।

tutorial (ट्यूटोरिअल) ***adj.*** of or relating to a tutor, अनुशिक्षक-संबंधी।

twaddle (ट्वैडल) ***n.*** foolish talk, nonsense, बकवाद, बकबक। ***v.*** to talk nonsense, बकवाद करना, बकबक करना।

twang (ट्वैन्ग) ***n.*** 1. a sharp ringing sound of a plucked bowstring, धनुष की टंकार, धनुषटंकार। 2. nasal resonance in a person's speech, नासिक्य ध्वनि का पुट, नासिक्यरंजन। ***v.*** 1. to pluck the strings of a musical instrument, तार झंकृत करना, बजाना। 2. to speak with a nasal twang, नाक से बोलना, नकियाना।

tweak (ट्वीक) ***v.*** to twist, ऐंठना, मरोड़ना। ***n.*** a tweaking, ऐंठन, मरोड़।

tweed (ट्वीड) ***n.*** a woollen fabric of several colours, रंग-बिरंगा ऊनी कपड़ा, ट्वीड।

tweet (ट्वीट) ***n.*** a high chirping sound of a bird, चेंचें। ***v.*** to make a tweet, चेंचें करना।

twelve (ट्वेल्व) ***adj. & n.*** one more than eleven, बारह।

twenties (ट्वेन्टीज़) ***n.*** (plu.) the numbers of years or degrees of temperature from 20 to 29, बीस से उनतीस वर्ष का काल या बीस से उनतीस डिग्री तक का तापमान।

twenty (ट्वेन्टी) ***adj. & n.*** next after nineteen, बीस।

twice (ट्वाइस) ***adv.*** 1. two times, दो बार। 2. in double amount, दुगना, दूना।

twiddle (ट्विडल) ***v.*** 1. to turn over or around lightly, यों ही घुमाना-फिराना। 2. to trifle (with, से) खिलवाड़ करना।

twig[1] (ट्विग) ***n.*** a small slender branch, टहनी।

twig[2] ***v.*** to comprehend, समझना, समझ में आना।

twilight (ट्वाइलाइट) ***n.*** the light from the sky just after sunset, झुटपुटा, धुंधुलका।

twin (ट्विन) ***n.*** one of two children (animals) born at one birth, जुड़वाँ बच्चा। ***adj.*** being a twin, जुड़वाँ, युग्म।

twine (ट्वाइन) ***n.*** a cord or string made of two or more threads twisted together, बटा हुआ धागा, सुतली या रस्सी। ***v.*** to twist together, बटना, गूँथना।

twinkle (ट्विन्कल) ***v.*** to shine brightly and intermittently, टिमटिमाना। ***n.*** a twinkling light, टिमटिमाहट।

twirl (ट्वर्ल) ***v.*** to rotate briskly, तेज़ी से घूमना, चक्कर लगाना या खाना। ***n.*** 1. the act of twirling, घूर्णन, बटाई। 2. a round, चक्कर, फेरा।

twist (ट्विस्ट) ***v.*** 1. to wind two or more threads, wires etc., together, बटना, गूँथना। 2. to coil, घुमाना या लपेटना। 3. to give spiral shape to, घुमावदार या कुंडलीदार बनाना। 4. to turn or bend, मोड़ना या मरोड़ना, बल डालना। 5. to distort, बिगाड़ देना, विकृत कर देना। 6. to wrench or sprain, मुड़क जाना। 7. to take winding course, चक्करदार या टेढ़ा-मेढ़ा रास्ता अपनाना। ***n.*** 1. the act of twisting or the state of being twisted, बटाई, गुँथाई। 2. a turn or twirl, मरोड़, ऐंठन, बल। 3. a spiral curve, घुमाव या चक्कर। 4. a sprain or wrench, मुड़न, बल, मोच। 5. an unexpected turn of events, मोड़, परिवर्तन। 6. a dance performed with strenuous gyrations esp, of hips, अंगों को टेढ़ा-मेढ़ा करके किया जानेवाला नृत्य, ट्विस्ट। 7. distortion of meaning, अर्थ की खींच-तान या तोड़-मरोड़।

twister (ट्विस्टर) ***n.*** 1. a dishonest person, बेईमान व्यक्ति। 2. a whirlwind, चक्रवात।

twit (ट्विट) ***v.*** to make fun of, to ridicule, मज़ाक उड़ाना, फब्ती कसना। ***n.*** a foolish person, मूर्ख व्यक्ति।

twitch (ट्विच) ***v.*** 1. to pull with a jerk, झटका देना, झटकना। 2. to snatch, छीन लेना, झटक लेना। ***n.*** a pull or jerk, झटका।

twitter (ट्विटर) ***v.*** 1. to chirp, चहचहाना, चहकना। 2. to giggle, ही-ही करना। ***n.*** 1. chirping, चहचह, चींचीं। 2. giggle, ही ही।

two (टू) ***adj. & n.*** 1. one more than one, दो। 2. a playing card with two tips, दुक्की।

two-dimensional (टू-डाइमेन्शनल) ***adj.*** having two dimensions, द्विविम।

two-faced (टू-फ़ेस्ड) ***adj.*** 1. deceitful, धोखेबाज। 2. insincere, बेईमान।

two-fold (टू-फ़ोल्ड) ***adj.*** 1. having twice as much or as many, दुगना। 2. having two parts, दोहरा।

twosome (टूसम) ***n.*** two people together, जोड़ा, जोड़ी।

tycoon (टाइकून) ***n.*** a wealthy and powerful businessman or industrialist, धनी तथा शक्तिशाली व्यापारी या उद्योगपति, धनी-मानी।

type (टाइप) ***n.*** 1. a group or class of persons or things having

T

common characteristics, वर्ग, जाति, क़िस्म, प्रकार। 2. a typical example or model, नमूना, निदर्श। 3. a small block with raised letter or figure for printing, टाइप, मुद्री। *v.* 1. to classify according to a type or class, वर्गीकरण करना। 2. to typewrite, टाइप करना, टंकन करना।

typecast (टाइपकास्ट) *v.* (typecast, typecasting) to cast in the same role, (अभिनेता का) एक ही तरह की भूमिका करना।

typescript (टाइपस्क्रिप्ट) *n.* a typewritten copy, टंकित प्रति।

typesetter (टाइपसेटर) *n.* 1. one who sets types, टाइप बैठानेवाला, कंपोज़िटर। 2. a machine that sets types, टाइप बैठानेवाला यंत्र।

typewriter (टाइपराइटर) *n.* a machine that is used in typing, टाइपराइटर, टाइप मशीन।

typhoid (टाइफ़ॉइड) *n.* a disease caused by bacteria and characterized by high fever, टाइफ़ायड, मोतीझिरा, आंत्रज्वर।

typhoon (टाइफ़ून) *n.* a severe hurricane, तूफ़ान।

typhus (टाइफ़स) *n.* a disease caused by microorganisms, टाइफ़स।

typical (टिपिकल) *adj.* 1. having the nature of a type, ठेठ, प्रारूपिक, प्ररूपी। 2. characteristic, विशिष्ट, ख़ास।

typify (टिपिफ़ाइ) *v.* to serve as a typical example of, प्रारूप होना।

typist (टाइपिस्ट) *n.* one who types, टाइप-कर्ता, टाइपिस्ट।

typographical (टाइपग्रैफ़िकल) *adj.* of typography, मुद्रण-संबंधी, छपाई-संबंधी।

typography (टाइपॉग्रफ़ी) *n.* the art or practice of printing, मुद्रण-कला।

tyrannical (टिरैनिकल) *adj.* 1. of a tyrant or tyranny, अत्याचारी, अत्याचारपूर्ण। 2. despotic, निरंकुश, नृशंस।

tyranny (टिरैनि) *n.* 1. government of a tyrant, निरंकुश शासन, तानाशाही। 2. a tyrannical act, अत्याचार, जुल्म।

tyrant (टाइरन्ट) *n.* an oppressive or cruel ruler, निरंकुश शासक।

tyre (टाइअर) *n.* a covering fitted around the rim of a vehicle, टायर।

tyro (टाइरो) *n.* a novice, नौसिखुआ।

U, u (यू) the twenty-first letter of the English alphabet, अंग्रेज़ी वर्णमाला का इक्कीसवाँ वर्ण।

ubiquitous (यूबिक्विटस) ***adj.*** being everywhere at the same time, सर्वव्यापक, सर्वव्यापी।

udder (अडर) ***n.*** a bag-like milk secreting organ (of a cow, goat, sheep etc., गाय, बकरी, भेड़ आदि का) थन।

ugly (अग्ली) ***adj.*** 1. having unpleasant appearance, भद्दा, कुरूप, भोंडा। 2. frightful, shocking, भयावह, ख़तरनाक।

ulcer (अल्सर) ***n.*** an open sore that heals very slowly, नासूर।

ulema (ऊलिमा) ***n.*** (plu.) learned persons, विद्वान लोग।

ulterior (अल्टीरिअर) ***adj.*** 1. hidden or unexpressed, अप्रत्यक्ष, अव्यक्त।

ultimate (अल्टिमिट) ***adj.*** 1. final, अंतिम। 2. the highest, चरम, परम। 3. fundamental, मूलभूत, मौलिक।

ultimately (अल्टिमिटली) ***adv.*** finally, अंत में, अंततः, अंततोगत्वा, आख़िरकार।

ultimatum अल्टिमेटम) ***n.*** (plu. ultimata, ultimatums) a final condition, demand or proposal, rejection of which leads to force or other direct action, अंतिम चेतावनी, अंतिमेत्थम, अल्टिमेटम।

ultimo (अल्टिमो) ***adj.*** of or occurring in the last month, गत मास का, पिछले महीने का।

ultra (अल्ट्रा) ***prefix.*** 1. excessively, extremely, अति। 2. beyond, के परे, के पार। ***n.*** an extremist, अतिवादी।

ultramarine (अल्ट्रामरीन) ***adj.*** bright deep blue, गहरे नीले रंग का, लाजवर्दी। ***n.*** bright deep blue colour, गहरा नीला रंग।

ultrasonic (अल्ट्रासॉनिक) ***adj.*** supersonic, पराध्वनिक।

ultraviolet (अल्ट्रावाइलिट) ***adj.*** situated beyond the visible spectrum at its violet end, पराबैंगनी।

ultravires (अल्ट्रावाइरीज़) ***adj.*** beyond one's legal power, विधिक अधिकारों से परे का, अधिकारातीत।

umbilical (अम्बिलिकल) ***adj.*** of the navel, नाभि-संबंधी।

umbra (अम्ब्रा) ***n.*** the shadow cast by the moon on to the earth during a solar eclipse, ग्रहण के समय पृथ्वी पर चंद्रमा की पड़नेवाली छाया, प्रच्छाया।

umbrage (अम्ब्रिज) ***n.*** a feeling of being offended, रोष, नाराज़गी।

umbrella (अम्ब्रेला) ***n.*** 1. a small portable canopy for protection against rain or sun, छतरी, छाता। 2. protection, patronage, संरक्षण, छत्रछाया।

umpire (अम्पाइअर) ***n.*** a person having authority to decide and settle disputes in a game of cricket, baseball etc., अंपायर, निर्णायक। ***v.*** to act as umpire, अंपायर होना या बनना, अंपायरी करना।

umpteen (अम्प्टीन) ***adj.*** very many, बहुतेरे, बहुत से; umpteen times, बहुत बार।

unaccountable (अनकाउन्टेबल) ***adj.***

1. not accountable or responsible, जो ज़िम्मेदार न हो, अनुत्तरदायी। 2. inexplicable, अव्याख्येय।

unadvised (अनेडवाइज़्ड) ***adj.*** 1. rash, अविवेकपूर्ण। 2. not prudent, अविवेकशील।

unanimity (यूननिमिटी) ***n.*** the quality or state of being unanimous, मतैक्य, सर्वसम्मति, एकमत।

unanimous (यूनैनिमस) ***adj.*** having the consent of all, सर्वसम्मत।

unassuming (अनस्यूमिंग) ***adj.*** modest, विनम्र, निरभिमान।

unattended (अनटेन्डिड) ***adj.*** 1. not attended, जिसकी देख-भाल कोई न कर रहा हो, उपेक्षित। 2. unaccompanied, जिसके साथ कोई न हो, अकेला।

unavoidable (अनवॉइडेबल) ***adj.*** unable to be avoided, अपरिहार्य, अनिवार्य।

unawares (अनवेअर्ज़) ***adv.*** 1. without noticing, अनजाने में। 2. unexpectedly, अचानक, अकस्मात्।

unbalanced (अन्बैलन्स्ड) ***adj.*** 1. lacking balance, असंतुलित। 2. mentally unsound, विक्षिप्त।

unbeaten (अन्बीटन) ***adj.*** not defeated, अपराजित। 2. not surpassed, अलंघित।

unbeknown (अन्बिनोन) ***adj.*** unknown, अज्ञात।

unbending (अन्बेन्डिंग) ***adj.*** 1. inflexible, अनम्य। 2. refusing to yield, न झुकनेवाला।

unbiased (अन्बाइअस्ड) ***adj.*** not biased, पूर्वग्रह से मुक्त, पक्षपातरहित।

unbind (अन्बाइन्ड) ***v.*** (unbound, unbinding) to set free, मुक्त करना।

unblock (अन्ब्लॉक) ***v.*** to remove an obstacle or obstacles, बाधा या बाधाएँ हटाना, (रास्ता) साफ़ कर देना या खोल देना।

unbounded (अन्बाउन्डिड) ***adj.*** not bounded, अबद्ध, अनाबद्ध, मुक्त।

unbridled (अन्ब्राइडल्ड) ***adj.*** unrestrained, बेलगाम, अनियंत्रित।

unburden (अन्बर्डन) ***v.*** to relieve of a burden, भार-मुक्त करना।

uncalled-for (अन्कॉल्ड-फ़ॉर) ***adj.*** unnecessary, अनावश्यक।

uncanny (अन्कैनी) ***adj.*** 1. strange, विलक्षण। 2. mysterious, रहस्यमय।

unceasing (अन्सीज़िंग) ***adj.*** continuous, अविच्छिन्न, सतत।

unceremonious (अन्सेरिमोनिअस) ***adj.*** 1. not formal, अनौपचारिक। 2. undignified, अमर्यादित, मर्यादाहीन।

uncertain (अन्सर्टन) ***adj.*** 1. not certain or decided, अनिश्चित। 2. not confident, अविश्वस्त। 3. changeable, परिवर्तनशील, ढुलमुल।

unchaste (अन्चेस्ट) ***adj.*** not chaste, जो सच्चरित्र न हो, चरित्रविहीन या कुलटा।

unclaimed (अन्क्लेम्ड) ***adj.*** not claimed, लावारिस, अदावी, बेदावा।

uncle (अंकल) ***n.*** 1. the brother of one's father or mother, चाचा (ताऊ) या मामा। 2. husband of the sister of one's father or mother, फूफा या मौसा।

unclean (अन्क्लीन) ***adj.*** not clean, मैला, गंदा, अशुचि; of unclean morals, पातकी, व्यभिचारी।

uncomely (अन्कमली) ***adj.*** 1. not pleasant in appearance, भद्दा, भोंडा। 2. improper, अनुचित।

uncommon (अन्कॉमन) ***adj.*** 1. not common, असामान्य, असाधारण। 2. wonderful, अद्भुत।

U

uncommunicative (अन्कम्यूनिकेटिव) ***adj.*** not willing to talk, reserved, चुप्पा, अमिलनसार।

uncompromising (अन्कॉम्प्रमाइज़िंग) ***adj.*** not making concession, अपनी बात पर दृढ़ रहनेवाला, अटल, अनम्य या जिद्दी।

unconcerned (अन्कन्सर्न्ड) ***adj.*** 1. indifferent, उदासीन। 2. free from anxiety, निश्चिंत।

unconditional (अन्कन्डिशनल) ***adj.*** without conditions, बिना शर्त।

unconscionable (अन्कॉन्शनेबल) ***adj.*** unreasonable, unjust or unfair, अयुक्तियुक्त, अनैतिक, अनुचित।

unconscious (अन्कॉन्शस) ***adj.*** 1. not conscious, अचेतन। 2. unaware, अनभिज्ञ, अनजान।

unconsciousness (अन्कॉन्शसनिस) ***n.*** lack of consciousness, अचेतना, मूर्छा, बेहोशी।

uncountable (अन्काउन्टेबल) ***adj.*** not countable जो गिना न सके, अगणनीय, अगण्य।

uncouple (अन्कपल) ***v.*** to disconnect, वियुक्त करना, अलग कर देना।

uncouth (अन्कूथ) ***adj.*** 1. crude, अपरिष्कृत। 2. awkward, भद्दा

unction (अन्कशन) ***n.*** 1. anointing with oil, तेल का लेपन। 2. excessive politeness, अत्यधिक विनम्रता।

undecided (अन्डिसाइडिड) ***adj.*** 1. not decided, अनिर्णीत। 2. not having made up one's mind, अनिश्चयी।

undeniable (अन्डिनाइएबल) ***adj.*** 1. that cannot be denied, जिसे नकारा न जा सके, अकाट्य। 2. undoubtedly true, एकदम सत्य।

under (अन्डर) ***prep.*** 1. in a lower position than, के नीचे। 2. beneath the surface of, के नीचे, के तले। 3. governed or controlled by, के अधीन। 4. less than, से कम। 5. in the process of, की प्रक्रिया में, के अधीन। 6. in accordance with, के अनुसार। ***adv.*** 1. in a lower position, नीचे। 2. beneath, नीचे, तले। 3. below, घटकर, कम। ***adj.*** 1. lying or placed below, नीचेवाला, निचला। 2. subordinate, अवर, सहायक। 3. lower in amount or degree, कम, न्यून। ***prefix*** 1. below, अधः, अंतर्, निम्न-। 2. subordinate, अवर, सह-। 3. incomplete, अपूर्ण।

underage (अन्डरेज) ***adj.*** not yet adult, below the required age, निम्नायु, कमउम्र।

underarm (अन्डरार्म) ***adj.*** 1. under the armpit, काँख में दबाया हुआ। 2. executed with the hand kept below the level of the shoulder, बिना कंधे से ऊपर हाथ उठाकर फेंका जानेवाला (गेंद)।

underbred (अन्डर्ब्रेड) ***adj.*** 1. ill-bred, अल्पपोषित, कुपोषित। 2. not of pure breeding, जो सही नस्ल का न हो।

undercarriage (अन्डर्कैरिज) ***n.*** the supporting framework of an automobile, यान का निचला ढाँचा।

underclothes (अन्डर्क्लोद्ज़) ***n.*** (plu.) underwear, अंदर पहनने के कपड़े, अंतर्वस्त्र।

undercoat (अन्डर्कोट) ***n.*** a layer of paint under a finishing coat, रंग या पेंट का अस्तर, अवलेप।

undercover (अन्डर्कवर) ***adj.*** executed in secret, चोरी-छिपे किया जानेवाला, गुप्त।

U

undercurrent (अन्डर्करन्ट) ***n.*** 1. a current below another current, अंतर्धारा। 2. an underlying feeling or tendency, अंतर्भावना।

undercut (अन्डर्कट) ***v.*** (undercut, undercutting) 1. to cut under or below, नीचे से काटना। 2. to sell at a lower price, कम दाम में बेचना।

underdeveloped (अन्डर्डिवेलप्ड) ***adj.*** not fully developed, अपूर्णविकसित, अल्पविकसित।

underdone (अन्डर्डन) ***adj.*** 1. not sufficiently cooked, जो ठीक से न पका हो, अधपका। 2. not throughly done, जो अच्छी तरह से न किया गया हो, कच्चा, अधकचरा।

underemployed (अन्डरेम्प्लॉइड) ***adj.*** not fully employed, अपूर्ण नियोजित।

underestimate (अन्डरेस्टिमेट) ***v.*** to underrate, कम मूल्य या महत्त्व आँकना।

underfoot (अन्डर्फ़ुट) ***adv.*** under one's feet, पैरों के नीचे, पाँव तले।

undergo (अन्डर्गो) ***v.*** (underwent, undergone, undergoing) 1. to experience, अनुभूत करना, महसूस करना, भोगना। 2. to endure, सहना, भुगतना, झेलना। 3. to undertake, भार या बीड़ा उठाना, हाथ में लेना।

undergraduate (अन्डर्ग्रैजुएट) ***n.*** the student who has not yet received a degree, वह विद्यार्थी जो अभी स्नातक न हुआ हो, पूर्वस्नातक।

underground (अन्डर्ग्राउन्ड) ***adj.*** 1. under or below the surface of the ground, भूमि के नीचे का, भूगत, भूमिगत। 2. secret, गुप्त, गोपनीय। ***adv.*** 1. below the surface of the ground, ज़मीन के नीचे, भूमि के नीचे। 2. secretly, गुप्त रूप से। ***n.*** subway, ज़मीन के नीचे चलनेवाली रेल, अंतर्भौम रेल, सुरंग-रेल।

undergrowth (अन्डर्ग्रोथ) ***n.*** shrubs or bushes, झाड़-झंखाड़।

underhand (अन्डर्हैन्ड) ***adv.*** in a clandestine manner, चोरी-छिपे, चोरी-चोरी। ***adj.*** done slyly so as to evade notice, चालाकी या गुप्त रूप से किया जानेवाला, कपटपूर्ण।

underlay (अन्डर्ले) ***v.*** (underlaid, underlaying) to lay something under (a thing, किसी चीज़ के) नीचे कोई चीज़ रखना।

underlie (अन्डर्लाइ) ***v.*** (underlay, underlain, underlying) 1. to be located below, नीचे होना या रहना। 2. to be the support or basis for, आधार होना।

underline (अन्डर्लाइन) ***v.*** 1. to draw a line under, (शब्द या पद के) नीचे रेखा खींचना, अधोरेखांकित करना। 2. to emphasize, ज़ोर देना।

undermanned (अन्डर्मैन्ड) ***adj.*** having too few persons to operate, अल्पकर्मी; The hotel is undermanned. इस होटल में कर्मियों की कमी है।

undermentioned (अन्डर्मेन्शन्ड) ***adj.*** mentioned below, निम्नलिखित, अधोलिखित।

undermine (अन्डर्माइन) ***v.*** 1. to dig a mine beneath, सुरंग खोदना या बनाना। 2. to subvert, उलट देना। 3. to weaken, कमज़ोर हो जाना या कर देना।

undermost (अन्डर्मोस्ट) ***adj.*** lowest in relative position, सबसे नीचेवाला, निचला। ***adv.*** below in position, नीचे।

underpaid (अन्डर्पेड) ***adj.*** paid too

little, जिसे बहुत कम वेतन मिलता हो, अववैतनिक।

underpart (अन्डर्पार्ट) ***n.*** 1. the part underneath, निचला भाग। 2. a subordinate role, सहायक भूमिका।

underpin (अन्डर्पिन) ***v.*** 1. to support from beneath, टेक या चाँड़ लगाना। 2. to support, सहायता या समर्थन करना।

underpopulated (अन्डर्पाप्युलेटिड) ***adj.*** less populated, कम या थोड़ी आबादीवाला, कम जनसंख्यावाला।

underprivileged (अन्डर्प्रिविलिज्ड) ***adj.*** economically or socially deprived, अल्पाधिकारप्राप्त, अल्प-सुविधाप्राप्त।

underrate (अन्डर्रेट) ***v.*** to rate too below, कम मूल्य या महत्त्व आँकना।

underscore (अन्डर्स्कोर) ***v.*** to draw a line underneath, अधोरेखांकित करना।

under secretary (अन्डर सेक्रेटरी) ***n.*** a secretary immediately subordinate to a principal secretary, अवर सचिव।

undersell (अन्डर्सेल) ***v.*** (undersold, underselling) to sell at a lower price than others, दाम गिराकर बेचना, कम क़ीमत पर बेचना।

undershoot (अन्डर्शूट) ***v.*** (undershot, undershooting) to shoot short of a target, लक्ष्य तक निशाना न पहुँचा पाना।

undersigned (अन्डर्साइन्ड) ***n.*** one who has signed at the end of a document, अधोहस्ताक्षरी।

understand (अन्डर्स्टैन्ड) ***v.*** (understood, understanding) 1. to grasp the meaning of, समझना। 2. to know thoroughly, जानना, जान लेना। 3. to assume, मान लेना।

understanding (अन्डर्स्टैन्डिंग) ***n.*** 1. the power of comprehending, ग्रहणशक्ति, समझ, बुद्धि। 2. common view or mutual agreement, मतैक्य या समझौता। 3. the ability to feel sympathy, सहानुभूति की भावना, सद्भाव। ***adj.*** 1. having or showing good judgment, समझदारी-भरा। 2. sympathetic, kind, सहानुभूति-भरा।

understatement (अन्डर्स्टेटमेन्ट) ***n.*** a restrained statement, न्यूनोक्ति।

undertake (अन्डर्टेक) ***v.*** (undertook, undertaken, undertaking) 1. to take in hand, हाथ में लेना, ज़िम्मा लेना। 2. to commit, promise or guarantee, आश्वासन, वचन या गारंटी देना।

undertaker (अन्डर्टेकर) ***n.*** a person whose business is to prepare the dead for burial, अंत्येष्टि-प्रबंधक।

undertaking (अन्डर्टेकिंग) ***n.*** 1. a task, business or enterprise, काम, धंधा, उपक्रम। 2. a promise, commitment or guarantee, वचन, आश्वासन, गारंटी।

undertone (अन्डर्टोन) ***n.*** 1. a tone of low pitch or volume, मंद स्वर, हलकी आवाज़। 2. an underlying suggestion or implication, प्रच्छन्न भाव। 3. subdued colour, दबा हुआ रंग, हलका रंग।

undervaluation (अन्डर्वैल्युएशन) ***n.*** the act of undervaluing, अल्पमूल्यांकन, अवमूल्यन।

underway (अन्डर्वे) ***adv.*** in progress or action, जारी, चालू, सक्रिय।

underwear (अन्डर्विअर) ***n.*** a garment worn under the outer

U

clothes, अंदर का कपड़ा, बनियान या जाँघिया।

underworld (अन्डर्वर्ल्ड) ***n.*** 1. the abode of the dead under the earth, पृथ्वी के नीचे का लोक, पाताल। 2. the part of society engaged in crime, अपराध-जगत्, अधोलोक, अपराधशील वर्ग।

underwrite (अन्डर्राइट) ***v.*** (underwrote, underwritten, underwriting) 1. to endorse, पृष्ठांकन करना। 2. to assume financial responsibility for, आर्थिक उत्तरदायित्व लेना, माली ज़िम्मेदारी ओढ़ना।

undeserving (अन्डिज़र्विंग) ***adj.*** not worthy of, अयोग्य, अनधिकारी, अपात्र।

undesirable (अन्डिज़ाइरेबल) ***adj.*** 1. not desirable, अवांछनीय। 2. objectionable, आपत्तिजनक।

undeveloped (अन्डिवेलप्ड) ***adj.*** not developed, अविकसित।

undo (अन्डू) ***v.*** (undid, undone, undoing) 1. to cancel, रद करना। 2. to untie or unfasten, खोलना, ढीला करना। 3. to cause the ruin of, बर्बाद या तबाह कर देना।

undone (अन्डन) ***adj.*** 1. not done, जो किया न गया हो, अकृत। 2. unfastened, जो बंद न हो, खुला।

undoubted (अन्डाउटिड) ***adj.*** 1. not doubted, definite, असंदिग्ध, निश्चित। 2. undisputed, अविवाद्य।

undress (अन्ड्रेस) ***v.*** to remove the clothes of, कपड़े उतारना।

undue (अन्ड्यू) ***adj.*** 1. exceeding what is normal or appropriate, अनुचित या असंगत। 2. excessive, अत्यधिक।

undulate (अन्ड्युलेट) ***v.*** to move in a wavelike motion, तरंगित होना, लहराना।

unduly (अन्ड्यूली) ***adv.*** 1. excessively, अत्यधिक। 2. unjustly, अनुचित रूप से।

undying (अन्डाइंग) ***adj.*** everlasting, अमर, शाश्वत।

unearned (अनर्न्ड) ***adj.*** not earned by labour, skill or service, अनर्जित।

unearth (अनर्थ) ***v.*** 1. to dig up, खोदकर निकालना। 2. to bring to light, सामने लाना, खोजकर निकालना।

unearthly (अर्थली) ***adj.*** 1. not earthly, अपार्थिव, अलौकिक। 2. supernatural or mysterious, लोकोत्तर या रहस्यमय। 3. odd, बेतुका, ऊटपटाँग।

uneasy (अनीज़ी) ***adj.*** 1. restless, worried, आकुल, चिंतित, बेचैन। 2. not comfortable, असुविधाजनक।

uneconomic (अनीकनॉमिक) ***adj.*** not profitable, अलाभकर, अलाभप्रद।

unemployed (अनेम्प्लॉइड) ***adj.*** 1. not employed, jobless or out of job, बेरोज़गार, बेकार। 2. not in use, अप्रयुक्त।

unemployment (अनेम्प्लॉइमेन्ट) ***n.*** the state of being unemployed, बेरोज़गारी, बेकारी।

unending (अनेन्डिंग) ***adj.*** without an end, endless, असीम, अंतहीन।

unequal (अनीक्वल) ***adj.*** 1. not equal, जो बराबर न हो, असमान, असम। 2. dissimilar, different, भिन्न, विभिन्न।

unequalled (अनीक्वल्ड) ***adj.*** beyond compare, अद्वितीय, बेजोड़।

unequivocal (अनिक्विवोकल) ***adj.*** leaving no doubt, असंदिग्ध, सुस्पष्ट।

unerring (अन्अरिंग) ***adj.*** committing no error, accurate, अचूक।

UNESCO (यूनेस्को) ***n.*** United

Nations Educational Scientific and Cultural Organization, यूनेस्को।

uneven (अनीवन) ***adj.*** 1. not even, असमतल, असम। 2. not smooth, ऊबड़-खाबड़ या ख़ुरदरा। 3. odd, विषम।

unexampled (अनिग्ज़ेम्पल्ड) ***adj.*** without example, दृष्टांतविहीन, बेमिसाल।

unexceptionable (अनिक्सेप्शनेबल) ***adj.*** without flaw or fault, निर्दोष, त्रुटिहीन।

unexceptional (अनिक्सेप्शनल) ***adj.*** not exceptional, अपवादविहीन, साधारण।

unfailing (अन्फ़ेलिंग) ***adj.*** 1. not failing, न चूकनेवाला, अचूक, अमोघ। 2. constant, सतत।

unfair (अन्फ़ेअर) ***adj.*** 1. not just, अन्यायपूर्ण, अनुचित। 2. not impartial, पक्षपातपूर्ण।

unfaithful (अन्फ़ेथफ़ुल्) ***adj.*** 1. not faithful, disloyal, बेवफ़ा, निष्ठाहीन। 2. having committed adultery, बदचलन, व्यभिचारी।

unfeeling (अन्फ़ीलिंग) ***adj.*** incapable of feeling or sensation, असंवेदनशील, सहानुभूतिविहीन।

unfit (अन्फ़िट) ***adj.*** 1. not capable, incompetent, अयोग्य। 2. inappropriate, अनुपयुक्त।

unflappable (अन्फ़्लैपेबल) ***adj.*** remaining calm in a crisis, धीर, शांत, अनुद्विग्न।

unfold (अन्फ़ोल्ड) ***v.*** 1. to open and spread out, खोल देना, फैला देना। 2. to reveal, प्रकट कर देना।

unforeseen (अन्फ़ोर्सीन) ***adj.*** unexpected, अप्रत्याशित, अनपेक्षित।

unfortunate (अन्फ़ॉर्चुनेट) ***adj.*** having bad luck, अभागा, भाग्य का मारा, बदक़िस्मत।

unfounded (अन्फ़ाउन्डिड) ***adj.*** groundless, निराधार, बेबुनियाद।

unfrequented (अन्फ़्रीक्वेन्टिड) ***adj.*** not often visited by people, निर्जन-प्राय।

unfurl (अन्फ़र्ल) ***v.*** to open out or unroll, खोलना या फहराना।

ungainly (अन्गेनली) ***adj.*** awkward, clumsy, भोंडा, भद्दा, बेडौल।

ungodly (अन्गॉडली) ***adj.*** 1. irreligious, अधर्मी, नास्तिक। 2. wicked, sinful, दुष्ट, पापी। 3. awkward, बेतुका।

ungovernable (अन्गवर्नेबल) ***adj.*** uncontrollable, अनियंत्रणीय, बेक़ाबू।

ungracious (अन्ग्रेशस) ***adj.*** rude, रूखा, अभद्र।

unguarded (अन्गार्डिड) ***adj.*** 1. not guarded, अरक्षित। 2. incautious, असावधान।

unhappy (अन्हैपी) ***adj.*** 1. not happy, sad or depressed, अप्रसन्न, उदास। 2. unfortunate, दुर्भाग्यपूर्ण।

unhealthy (अन्हेल्दी) ***adj.*** 1. not in good health, अस्वस्थ। 2. not likely to give good health, अस्वास्थ्यकर।

unheard-of (अन्हर्ड-ऑव) ***adj.*** never heard of, अनुसना।

unhinge (अन्हिन्ज) ***v.*** 1. to remove from hinges, दरवाज़े का पल्ला या पल्ले खोलना। 2. to disrupt or upset. विखंडित या विचलित कर देना।

UNICEF (यूनिसेफ़) ***n.*** United Nations International Children's Emergency Fund. यूनिसेफ़।

unicorn (यूनिकॉर्न) ***n.*** a mythical horse, सफेद रंग का एक कल्पित घोड़ा

U

जिसके माथे के बीच में एक सींग है।

uniform (यूनिफ़ॉर्म) ***adj.*** 1. alike, समान। 2. unchanging in form, एकरूप, समरूप। ***n.*** a certain type of clothing worn by members of a particular group, वर्दी।

uniformity (यूनिफ़ॉर्मिटी) ***n.*** the quality or state of being uniform, एकरूपता।

unify (यूनिफ़ाइ) ***v.*** to make or become one, एक करना या होना।

unilateral (यूनिलैटरल) ***adj.*** done by only one side, एकपक्षीय, इकतरफ़ा।

unimpeachable (अनिम्पीचेबल) ***adj.*** beyond doubt or question, निर्दोष, बेदाग़।

uninhibited (अनिन्हिबिटिड) ***adj.*** not inhibited, जो रुद्ध या बाधित न हो, अनवरुद्ध।

uninterested (अनिन्टरिस्टिड) ***adj.*** not interested, रुचि या दिलचस्पी न लेनेवाला, उदासीन, विमुख।

union (यून्यन) ***n.*** 1. the condition of being united, मिलन, संयोग, एकता। 2. a combination of political entities, संघ। 3. a labour association, श्रमिक संघ।

unique (यूनीक) ***adj.*** 1. being the only one of its kind, अकेला, एकल। 2. unusual or remarkable, अद्वितीय, अनुपम, बेजोड़।

unisexual (यूनिसेक्शुअल) ***adj.*** of or for only one sex, एकलिंगी।

unison (यूनिसन) ***n.*** 1. identity of musical pitch, एकस्वरता, स्वर मेल। 2. agreement or union, मेल। □ **in unison,** एकबद्ध होकर, साथ-साथ।

unit (यूनिट) ***n.*** 1. a single quantity regarded as a whole, इकाई, एकक। 2. a part or group with a specified function, एकांश। 3. a subdivision of a larger military formation, टुकड़ी, दस्ता।

unitary (यूनिटरी) ***adj.*** of a unit or units, एकात्मक, ऐकिक; unitary government, एकात्मक शासन।

unite (यूनाइट) ***v.*** 1. to make or become one, एक हो जाना या कर देना, जुड़ जाना या जोड़ देना। 2. to work together, मिलकर काम करना।

unitedly (युनाइटिडली) ***adv.*** with united effort, संयुक्त रूप से, एकबद्ध होकर।

United Nations Organisation *n.* an international organization to promote peace and cooperation among the countries of the world, संयुक्त राष्ट्र संघ।

unity (यूनिटी) ***n.*** 1. the state of being one, एकता, एका, एकत्व। 2. agreement, मेल, सामंजस्य।

universal (यूनिवर्सल) ***adj.*** 1. of the universe, सार्वभौम। 2. worldwide, सार्वदेशिक, विश्वव्यापी, सर्वव्यापी, सार्वत्रिक। 3. of the whole of mankind, सर्वजनीन।

universe (यूनिवर्स) ***n.*** the aggregate of all existing things, energy and space, सृष्टि, ब्रह्मांड।

university (यूनिवर्सिटी) ***n.*** an institution of higher learning that awards degrees, विश्वविद्यालय, यूनिवर्सिटी।

unkempt (अन्केम्प्ट) ***adj.*** 1. not neat or tidy, मैला-कुचैला। 2. looking neglected, देखने में उपेक्षित, फूहड़ या अस्त-व्यस्त।

unkind (अन्काइन्ड) ***adj.*** 1. not kind,

अनुदार। 2. harsh, कठोर। 3. cruel, निर्दय, बेरहम।

unknown (अन्नोन) ***adj.*** not known, अपरिचित, अज्ञात।

unleash (अन्लीश) ***v.*** to set free, मुक्त कर देना।

unleavened (अन्लेवन्ड) ***adj.*** not leavened, जो ख़मीर उठाकर न बनाया गया हो।

unless (अन्लिस) ***conj.*** except on the condition that, यदि···नहीं, जब तक···नहीं।

unlettered (अन्लैटर्ड) ***adj.*** illiterate, अनपढ़, अशिक्षित।

unlike (अन्लाइक) ***adj.*** not like, different, असमान, असदृश, भिन्न। ***prep.*** not like, के विपरीत।

unlikely (अन्लाइकली) ***adj.*** 1. improbable, असंभव-सा। 2. likely to fail, संभावनाविहीन।

unload (अन्लोड) ***v.*** 1. to remove the load (from, पर से) बोझ उतारना। 2. to get rid of, पीछा छुड़ाना। 3. to remove the charge, (भरी हुई बंदूक आदि) खाली करना।

unmake (अन्मेक) ***v.*** (unmade, unmaking) to undo or destroy, चौपट या नष्ट करना।

unmanly (अन्मैनली) ***adj.*** not manly, जो पुरुषोचित न हो, अपुरुषोचित।

unmanned (अन्मैन्ड) ***adj.*** operated without a crew, बिना कर्मीदल का।

unmask (अन्मास्क) ***v.*** 1. to remove a mask from, नकाब उतारना। 2. to expose, पोल या कलई खोल देना।

unmentionable (अन्मेन्शनेबल) ***adj.*** not mentionable, unspeakable, अकथनीय (बुरा या अश्लील)।

unmistakable (अन्मिस्टेकेबल) ***adj.*** clear and unambiguous, सुस्पष्ट तथा असंदिग्ध, त्रुटिहीन, भ्रमरहित।

unmitigated (अन्मिटिगेटिड) ***adj.*** not diminished, घोर।

unmoved (अन्मूव्ड) ***adj.*** not moved, जो हिले नहीं, अचल, दृढ़।

unnerve (अन्नर्व) ***v.*** to cause to lose courage, हतोत्साह कर देना, हिम्मत तोड़ देना।

unnumbered (अन्नम्बर्ड) ***adj.*** 1. without number, संख्यारहित। 2. numberless, असंख्य।

unobtrusive (अनब्ट्रूसिव) ***adj.*** not obtrusive, जो स्पष्ट दिखाई न दे, अप्रत्यक्ष, परोक्ष।

unpack (अन्पैक) ***v.*** to remove from packing, खोलना, आवरण हटाना।

unpaid (अन्पेड) ***adj.*** not paid, अदत्त।

unparalleled (अन्पैरलल्ड) ***adj.*** having no parallel, अपूर्व, अद्वितीय, अप्रतिम।

unparliamentary (अन्पार्लमेन्टरी) ***adj.*** contrary to parliamantry customs or procedures, असंसदीय।

unpleasant (अन्प्लेज़न्ट) ***adj.*** not pleasing, not agreeable, अप्रिय, अरुचिकर, असुखकर।

unpleasantness (अन्प्लेज़न्टनिस) ***n.*** 1. the state of being unpleasant, अप्रियता। 2. an unpleasant situation, कटुता, मनोमालिन्य।

unprecedented (अन्प्रेसिडेन्टिड) ***adj.*** having no precedent, बेमिसाल, अभूतपूर्व।

unprepared (अन्प्रिपेअर्ड) ***adj.*** not ready or prepared, जो पहले से तैयार न हो या न किया गया हो, बिना तैयारी का।

U

unprepossessing (अनॅप्रीपज़ेसिंग) ***adj.*** not attractive, अनाकर्षक, अप्रभावी।

unprofessional (अन्प्रफ़ेशनल) ***adj.*** not professional, contrary to professional standards, जो व्यावसायिक मानकों के उपयुक्त न हो, अव्यावसायिक।

unqualified (अन्क्वॉलिफ़ाइड) ***adj.*** 1. not having proper qualifications, अयोग्य, अनर्ह। 2. not restricted, अबाधित, अप्रतिबंध।

unquestionable (अन्क्वेस्चनेबल) ***adj.*** 1. not questionable, beyond doubt, असंदिग्ध। 2. indisputable, निर्विवाद।

unquote (अन्कोट) ***v.*** to insert the closing quotation marks, उद्धरण चिह्न से बंद करना।

unravel (अन्रेवल) ***v.*** 1. to disentangle, सुलझाना। 2. to clear up, स्पष्ट करना, सुलझाना। 3. to be disentangled, सुलझना।

unrealised (अन्रीअलाइज़्ड) ***adj.*** not realised, अप्राप्त।

unreasonable (अन्रीज़नेबल) ***adj.*** 1. not acting according to reason, अयुक्तिशील, अतर्कशील। 2. not conformable to reason, अयुक्तियुक्त, अतर्कपूर्ण। 3. going beyond the limits or reason, अत्यधिक, घोर।

unrecognized (अन्रीकॉग्नाइज़्ड) ***adj.*** not recognized, मान्यतारहित।

unrelenting (अन्रिलेन्टिंग) ***adj.*** not yielding or softening, cruel, कठोर, टस से मस न होनेवाला।

unremitting (अन्रिमिटिंग) ***adj.*** not remitting, constant, निरंतर या लगातार होने या चलनेवाला।

unremunerative (अन्रिम्यूनरेटिव) ***adj.*** not remunerative, अलाभकर, अलाभकारी।

unreserved (अन्रिज़र्व्ड) ***adj.*** 1. not reserved, अनारक्षित। 2. without reserve or restriction, अबाध। 3. complete, पूर्ण। 4. frank, खरा, स्पष्टभाषी, स्पष्टवादी।

unrest (अन्रेस्ट) ***n.*** 1. disturbance, उपद्रव, अशांति। 2. restlessness, बेचैनी, घबराहट। 3. anxiety, चिंता।

unrighteous (अन्राइचस) ***adj.*** 1. unjust, अन्यायी, अनीतिपरायण। 2. wicked, दुष्ट।

unrivalled (अन्राइवल्ड) ***adj.*** incomparable, अनुपम, बेजोड़, अद्वितीय।

unroll (अन्रोल) ***v.*** to open out or become opened out, खोलना या खोला जाना।

unruffled (अन्रफ़ल्ड) ***adj.*** not upset or agitated, अक्षुब्ध, शांत।

unruly (अन्रूली) ***adj.*** not readily ruled or disciplined, उच्छृंखल, बेलगाम, अनुशासनहीन।

unsatiated (अन्सैटिएटिड) ***adj.*** not satiated, अतुष्ट, अपरितुष्ट।

unscathed (अन्स्केद्ड) ***adj.*** without any harm, totally unharmed, सही-सलामत, जिसे खरोंच तक न आई हो।

unscramble (अन्स्क्रैम्बल) ***v.*** 1. to disentangle, सुलझाना। 2. to restore to intelligible form, बोधगम्य बनाना।

unscrew (अन्स्क्रू) ***v.*** to draw the screw from, पेंच खोलना या निकालना।

unscrupulous (अन्स्क्रूप्युलस) ***adj.*** 1. not scrupulous, अविवेकी, सिद्धांतहीन, बेईमान। 2. immoral, अनैतिक, चरित्रहीन।

unseat (अन्सीट) ***v.*** 1. to remove

from a seat, अपदस्थ करना। 2. to remove from office or position, पदच्युत करना, हरा देना।

unseemly (अन्सीमली) ***adj.*** not in good taste, improper, अशोभनीय, अनुचित। ***adv.*** in an unseemly manner, अशोभनीय ढंग से, अनुचित रीति से।

unseen (अन्सीन) ***adj.*** not seen, अनदेखा।

unserviceable (अन्सर्विसेबल) ***adj.*** not serviceable, बेकार, बेकाम, अनुपयोगी।

unsettled (अनसेटल्ड) ***adj.*** 1. not settled, अस्थिर या अस्थापित। 2. not calm, अशांत। 3. undecided, अनिश्चित।

unshakable (अन्शेकेबल) ***adj.*** not shakable, स्थिर।

unsightly (अन्साइटली) ***adj.*** unattractive, अनाकर्षक, कुरूप, असुंदर।

unskilled (अन्स्किल्ड) ***adj.*** 1. not skilled, अकुशल, अदक्ष। 2. untrained, अप्रशिक्षित।

unsociable (अन्सोशेबल) ***adj.*** not sociable, अमिलनसार।

unsocial (अन्सोशल) ***adj.*** 1. unsociable, असामाजिक, असमाजशील। 2. not suitable for society, असामाजिक, समाज-विरोधी।

unsolicited (अन्सॉलिसिटिड) ***adj.*** not asked for, unrequested, अप्रार्थित।

unsophisticated (अन्सॉफ़िस्टिकेटिड) ***adj.*** 1. not refined, अपरिष्कृत। 2. not complicated, अजटिल।

unsound (अन्साउन्ड) ***adj.*** 1. not sound or healthy, अस्वस्थ। 2. not mentally normal, विक्षिप्त। 3. defective, दोषपूर्ण, त्रुटिपूर्ण।

unsparing (अन्स्पेअरिंग) ***adj.*** giving freely and lavishly, उदार, मुक्तहस्त।

unspotted (अन्स्पॉटिड) ***adj.*** 1. spotless, बेदाग़। 2. morally pure, शुद्ध आचरणवाला।

unstable (अन्स्टेबल) ***adj.*** 1. not firm, अस्थिर। 2. of fickle temperament, ढुलमुल।

unstinted (अन्स्टिन्टिड) ***adj.*** given freely or lavishly, उदारतापूर्वक दिया हुआ।

unstuck (अन्स्टक) ***adj.*** detached, असंलग्न, अलग, उखड़ा हुआ।

unsung (अन्सन्ग) ***adj.*** not sung, जिसका गुणगान न हुआ हो, अप्रशंसित।

unsuspecting (अन्सस्पेक्टिंग) ***adj.*** feeling no suspicion, जिसे संदेह न हो, संदेहविहीन।

unswerving (अन्स्वर्विंग) ***adj.*** unchanging, अविचल, अटल, दृढ़।

untenable (अन्टेनेबल) ***adj.*** not able to be defended, जिसका समर्थन न किया जा सके, असमर्थनीय।

unthinkable (अन्थिन्केबल) ***adj.*** 1. out of question, जिसके संबंध में सोचा भी न जा सके, असंभव, असोचनीय। 2. unimaginable, कल्पनातीत।

untie (अन्टाइ) ***v.*** (untied, untying) to unfasten, खोलना।

until (अन्टिल) ***prep.*** in or throughout the period before, ...तक।

untimely (अन्टाइमली) ***adj.*** 1. happening at an inopportune time, बेमौक़े होनेवाला, असामयिक। 2. happening sooner than is normal, समय से पहले होनेवाला, समयपूर्व।

untiring (अन्टाइरिंग) ***adj.*** not tiring, न थकनेवाला, अथक।

U

untold (अन्टोल्ड) ***adj.*** 1. not told or revealed, अकथित। 2. too numerous, अत्यधिक।

untouchability (अन्टचेबिलिटी) ***n.*** the state or quality of being untouchable, अस्पृश्यता।

untouchable (अन्टचेबल) ***adj.*** 1. forbidden to be touched, अस्पृश्य। ***n.*** one that is untouchable, अछूत, अस्पृश्य व्यक्ति।

untoward (अन्टवार्ड) ***adj.*** 1. unfavourable, अशुभ या बुरा। 2. difficult to manage, अवश्य, दुर्दम्य।

untraceable (अन्ट्रेसेबल) ***adj.*** that cannot be traced, जिसका पता न लगाया जा सके।

untruth (अन्ट्रूथ) ***n.*** 1. a lie, झूठी बात। 2. lack of truth, असत्य, झूठ।

unusual (अन्यूज़ुअल) ***adj.*** 1. not usual, अप्रायिक, अनियत या असामान्य। 2. remarkable, उल्लेखनीय।

unutterable (अनटरेबल) ***adj.*** incapable of being expressed in words, अकथनीय, वर्णनातीत।

unveil (अन्वेल) ***v.*** 1. to remove a veil or covering, अनावरण करना, पट या पर्दा हटाना। 2. to remove one's veil, घूँघट हटाना। 3. to make known, प्रकट करना, पर्दा हटाना।

unvoiced (अन्वॉइस्ड) ***adj.*** not voiced, अघोष (वर्ण)।

unwarranted (अन्वारन्टिड) ***adj.*** 1. unjustified, अन्यायपूर्ण, अन्याय-संगत। 2. unauthorized, अनधिकृत।

unwary (अन्वेअरी) ***adj.*** 1. not cautious, असतर्क, असावधान।

unwell (अन्वेल) ***adj.*** not well, अस्वस्थ।

unwieldy (अन्वील्डी) ***adj.*** difficult to carry or handle because of shape and size, दुर्वह, भारी-भरकम।

unwind (अन्वाइन्ड) ***v.*** (unwound, unwinding) 1. to uncoil, (कमानी आदि) खोलना। 2. to relax, आराम करना, सुस्ताना।

unworldly (अन्वर्ल्डली) ***adj.*** 1. not of this world, अलौकिक। 2. spiritual, आध्यात्मिक। 3. not worldly minded, जो दुनियादार न हो।

unworthy (अन्वर्दी) ***adj.*** not worthy, अयोग्य, निकम्मा।

unyielding (अन्यीलि्डंग) ***adj.*** not yielding, न झुकनेवाला, हठी।

up (अप) ***adv.*** 1. to an erect position, खड़ा। 2. at a higher place, ऊपर, ऊँचे। 3. in view or consideration, देखने या विचार के लिए; You never brought this up before. तुम पहले कभी इसे सामने नहीं लाए। 4. toward or up to a place, की ओर या तक। 5. into a condition of activity, सक्रिय रूप में। 6. apiece, हर एक के। 7. happening, घटित, होनेवाला। 8. to be finished, समाप्त। □ **up against,** सामना करना; **up to,** (i) निर्भर होना, (ii) समर्थ या पात्र होना। ***prep.*** 1. from a lower to higher point, नीचे से ऊपर, ऊँचे। 2. upward, ऊपर की ओर। ***adj.*** 1. moving or directed upward, ऊपर की ओर जाता हुआ या जानेवाला। 2. happy, प्रसन्न। ***v.*** 1. to raise or lift, ऊँचा करना, उठाना, बढ़ाना। 2. to begin to do something abruptly or surprisingly, एकाएक या अप्रत्याशित रूप से कोई काम करने लगना। ***n.*** the high point, ऊँचा बिंदु। □ **ups and downs,** उतार-चढ़ाव।

upbeat (अपबीट) ***adj.*** 1. cheerful,

U

प्रसन्न, प्रफुल्ल। 2. optimistic, आशावादी। ***n.*** the unaccented beat, अप्रघात (संगीत में)।

upbraid (अपब्रेड) ***v.*** to reprove angrily or sharply, झिड़कना, बिगड़ना।

upbringing (अपब्रिन्गिंग) ***n.*** the rearing and education of a person during childhood, (माता-पिता द्वारा बालक का) लालन-पालन तथा पढ़ाई-लिखाई।

update (अपडेट) ***v.*** to bring up-to-date, अद्यतन करना या बनाना।

upgrade (अपग्रेड) ***v.*** 1. to raise to a higher rank, पदोन्नत करना, ऊँची कोटि में भेजना। 2. to raise in value or importance, मूल्य या महत्त्व बढ़ाना। ***n.*** an upward slope, चढ़ाई।

upgrowth (अपग्रोथ) ***n.*** the process of growing upward, उठान, बढ़ाव।

upheaval (अपहीवल) ***n.*** 1. violent agitation, उग्र आंदोलन, उथल-पुथल। 2. violent change, कायापलट, महापरिवर्तन।

uphill (अपहिल) ***adj.*** 1. going up a hill, leading upward, चढ़नेवाला, चढ़ाऊ। 2. difficult, दुष्कर, कठिन।

uphold (अपहोल्ड) ***v.*** (upheld, upholding) 1. to defend against opposition, विरोध के बावजूद रक्षा करना, बनाए रखना। 2. to support, समर्थन करना।

upholstery (अपहोल्स्टरी) ***n.*** maintenance of furniture, फ़र्नीचर आदि की साज-सज्जा।

upkeep (अपकीप) ***n.*** the act of keeping something in good condition, रख-रखाव, सँभाल।

upland (अपलैन्ड) ***n.*** the highland, ऊँची भूमि या प्रदेश।

uplift (अपलिफ़्ट) ***v.*** 1. to lift up, ऊँचा उठाना। 2. to raise (the standard, स्तर) ऊँचा करना, उन्नत करना, उद्धार या उन्नयन करना। ***n.*** the act of lifting or the state of being uplifted, उद्धार, उन्नयन।

upon (अपॉन) ***prep.*** on, के ऊपर, पर। ☐ **once upon a time,** एक समय की बात है कि।

upper (अपर) ***adj.*** 1. higher in place, ऊपरी, ऊपरवाला। 2. higher in position or rank, उच्च, ऊँचा।

uppermost (अपरमोस्ट) ***adj.*** highest, उच्चतम।

uppish (अपिश) ***adj.*** 1. snobbish, दंभी या दंभ-भरा। 2. arrogant, उद्धत।

upraise (अपरेज़) ***v.*** to raise up, (ऊपर) उठाना।

upright (अपराइट) ***adj.*** 1. in a vertical position, उदग्र, उर्ध्वाधर। 2. erect, खड़ा, सीधा। 3. honest, ईमानदार, सच्चा।

uprising (अपराइज़िंग) ***n.*** a revolt or rebellion, विप्लव, विद्रोह, बग़ावत।

uproar (अपरोर) ***n.*** commotion, शोर, हंगामा, हो-हल्ला, गुलगपाड़ा।

uproot (अपरूट) ***v.*** 1. to remove by pulling up the roots, जड़ से उखाड़ना, उन्मूलन करना। 2. to displace, विस्थापित कर देना, खदेड़ना, उजाड़ना।

upset (अपसेट) ***v.*** (upset, upsetting) 1. to overturn, उलट देना। 2. to disrupt or disturb, छिन्न-भिन्न या अस्त-व्यस्त कर देना, गड़बड़ा देना। ***n.*** 1. reversal, उलट-पुलट, उलटाव। 2. disorder or disruption, गड़बड़ी। ***adj.*** 1. unhappy, दुखी। 2. worried, चिंतित। 3. disturbed, गड़बड़।

U

upshot (अपशॉट) *n.* conclusion, निष्कर्ष, परिणाम।

upstairs (अपस्टेअर्ज़) *adv.* to or on a higher floor, ऊपर, ऊपरी मंज़िल पर।

upstanding (अपस्टैन्डिंग) *adj.* 1. erect, खड़ा, सीधा। 2. honest, सच्चा, ईमानदार।

upstream (अपस्ट्रीम) *adv.* against the current, बहाव के विरुद्ध।

upsurge (अपसर्ज) *n.* 1. a sudden appearance of something, किसी चीज़ का एकाएक आ धमकना। 2. a sudden increase in something, एकाएक होनेवाली वृद्धि।

up-to-date (अप-टु-डेट) *adj.* 1. extending up to present time, अद्यतन। 2. modern, आधुनिक।

upturn (अपटर्न) *v.* to turn upward, उलट देना या औंधा कर देना। *n.* an improvement, सुधार।

upward (अपवर्ड) *adv.* in a direction from lower to higher, नीचे से ऊपर की ओर। *adj.* ascending, ऊर्ध्वमुख, ऊर्ध्वमुखी।

Uranus (युरेनस) *n.* a planet in a solar system, युरेनस ग्रह।

urban (अर्बन) *adj.* of or pertaining to the city, नगरीय, शहरी।

urbane (अर्बेन) *adj.* having refined manners, नगरीय सभ्यतापरक, शिष्ट, सुसंस्कृत।

urbanization (अर्बनाइज़ेशन) *n.* the act of urbanizing, नगरीकरण।

urchin (अर्चिन) *n.* a mischievous boy, नटखट बालक।

urethra (युरीथ्रा) *n.* the canal that carries the urine from the bladder, मूत्रमार्ग।

urge (अर्ज) *v.* 1. to plead and press to do something, अनुरोध करना। 2. to recommend earnestly, प्रेरित करना। 3. to drive onward, हाँकना। *n.* a strong impulse, अंत:प्रेरणा, आवेग।

urgency (अर्जेन्सी) *n.* the quality or state of being urgent, अत्यावश्यकता, तात्कालिकता।

urgent (अर्जन्ट) *adj.* 1. requiring speedy action, अत्यावश्यक, बहुत ज़रूरी। 2. immediate, तात्कालिक, तुरंत, अविलंब।

urinary (यूरिनरी) *adj.* of or relating to urine, मूत्रीय, मूत्र-संबंधी।

urinate (यूरिनेट) *v.* (urinated, urinating) to discharge urine, पेशाब करना, मूतना।

urine (यूरिन) *n.* the fluid excreted by the kidneys, पेशाब, मूत्र।

urn (अर्न) *n.* a vaselike vessel, कलश।

us (अस) *pron.* objective case of we, हमें।

usable (यूज़ेबल) *adj.* that can be used, जिसे प्रयोग में लाया जा सके, प्रयोज्य, व्यवहार्य।

usage (यूसिज) *n.* 1. the manner of using, प्रयोग, इस्तेमाल। 2. a custom, रूढ़ि, चलन, रीति।

use (यूज़) *v.* 1. to put into action or service, प्रयोग या इस्तेमाल करना। 2. to bahave, व्यवहार करना। 3. to consume, ख़र्च करना, उपयोग करना। □ **used to,** अभ्यस्त। *n.* 1. the act of using or the state of being used, प्रयोग, इस्तेमाल, व्यवहार। 2. purpose, प्रयोजन। 3. utility or usefulness, उपयोगिता।

used (यूज़्ड) *adj.* second hand, उपयोग में लाया हुआ, पुराना।

useful (यूसफ़ुल) ***adj.*** 1. having utility, उपयोगी। 2. serviceable, काम में आने योग्य।

useless (यूसलिस) ***adj.*** being of no use, बेकार, अनुपयोगी, निकम्मा।

user (यूज़र) ***n.*** one who uses, उपयोगकर्ता, प्रयोक्ता, उपभोक्ता।

usher (अशर) ***n.*** a person who escorts people to their seats in public halls, theatres etc., प्रवेशक, स्वागतक। ***v.*** to escort persons to their seats, प्रवेशक का काम करना, अपनी-अपनी सीटों पर लोगों को बैठाना।

usual (युज़ुअल) ***adj.*** 1. commonly or ordinarily used, सामान्य, साधारण, मामूली। 2. found in ordinary practice, customary, प्रारंभिक, आम।

usurp (यूज़र्प) ***v.*** to seize something by force, हड़पना, हड़प लेना।

usurper (यूज़र्पर) ***n.*** one who usurps, हड़पनेवाला।

usury (यूज़री) ***n.*** the practice of lending money at exorbitant rate, सूदख़ोरी।

utensil (यूटेन्सिल) ***n.*** a vessel or tool used in a household, बर्तन, भाँड़ा।

uterus (यूटरस) ***n.*** the womb, गर्भाशय।

utilitarian (यूटिलिटेरिअन) ***adj.*** associated with utility, उपयोगिता-संबंधी, उपयोगी।

utilitarianism (यूटिलिटेरिअनिज़म) ***n.*** a doctrine that considers utility as the criterion, उपयोगितावाद।

utility (यूटिलिटी) ***n.*** 1. the condition or quality of being useful, उपयोगिता। 2. a useful thing, उपयोगी वस्तु।

utilization (यूटिलाइज़ेशन) ***n.*** the act of utilizing or the state of being utilized, उपयोग।

utilize (यूटिलाइज़) ***v.*** to use, काम में लाना, उपयोग करना।

utmost (अटमोस्ट) ***adj.*** 1. extreme, चरम, परम। 2. of the greatest or highest amount or degree, उच्चतम, अधिकतम।

Utopia, utopia (यूटोपिआ) ***n.*** a place of imaginary perfection, कल्पनालोक, रामराज्य, आदर्शलोक।

utter[1] (अटर) ***adj.*** complete, absolute, पूर्ण, कुल, परम।

utter[2] ***v.*** 1. pronounce, उच्चारण करना। 2. to say, कहना।

utterance (अटरेन्स) ***n.*** 1. the act of uttering, उच्चारण करना या कथन करना। 2. something uttered, कही हुई बात।

uvula (यूव्युला) ***n.*** (plu. uvulae, uvulas) the small flesh mass hanging from the roof of the mouth, कौआ, अलिजिह्वा, घंटी।

V, v (वी) ***n.*** the twenty-second letter of the English alphabet, अंग्रेज़ी वर्णमाला का बाईसवाँ वर्ण।

vacancy (वेकन्सी) ***n.*** 1. the state or condition of being vacant, ख़ालीपन, रिक्तता। 2. an unoccupied post, office or accommodation, ख़ाली जगह, रिक्ति।

vacant (वेकन्ट) ***adj.*** 1. not filled or occupied, ख़ाली, रिक्त। 2. not busy, अव्यस्त, ख़ाली। 3. having a blank expression, भावशून्य।

vacate (वेकेट) ***v.*** 1. to make vacant, ख़ाली कर देना। 2. to make void, रद कर देना।

vacation (वेकेशन) ***n.*** 1. the period of rest and recreation when the colleges, courts etc. are closed, अवकाश। 2. a holiday, छुट्टी, अवकाश। 3. the act of vacating, खाली करना, रिक्तीकरण।

vaccinate (वैक्सिनेट) ***v.*** to inoculate with vaccine, टीका लगाना।

vaccination (वैक्सिनेशन) ***n.*** the act of vaccinating, टीका लगाने की क्रिया, टीकाकरण।

vaccine (वैक्सीन) ***n.*** a preparation used in vaccination esp. against smallpox, वैक्सीन, टीके की दवा।

vacuous (वैक्युअस) ***adj.*** 1. empty, ख़ाली। 2. showing lack of intelligence or experience, बुद्धिहीन, अनुभवशून्य।

vacuum (वैक्युअम) ***n.*** (plu. vacuums, vacua) 1. a space empty of contents or matter, ख़ाली जगह, शून्य। 2. a space out of which air has been taken, वह पात्र जिसमें से हवा निकाल ली गई हो, निर्वात।

vagabond (वैगबॉन्ड) ***n.*** a wanderer, घुमक्कड़ व्यक्ति।

vagary (वैगरी) ***n.*** a whim, सनक, ख़ब्त।

vagina (वेजाइना) ***n.*** the passage leading from vulva to the uterus in female animals, योनि, भग।

vagrancy (वेग्रन्सी) ***n.*** vagabondage, आवारागर्दी।

vagrant (वेग्रन्ट) ***n.*** an idle wanderer, घुमक्कड़, बनजारा।

vague (वेग) ***adj.*** not clear, indistinct, अस्पष्ट, अनिश्चित।

vain (वेन) ***adj.*** 1. useless, not successful, व्यर्थ, निष्फल, बेकार। 2. conceited, शेख़ीख़ोर, मिथ्या-भिमानी, दंभी।

vainglorious (वेनग्लोरिअस) ***adj.*** having extreme vanity, अत्यंत दंभी।

vainly (वेनली) ***adv.*** 1. without success, बेकार, व्यर्थ। 2. too proudly, दंभपूर्वक।

vale (वेल) ***n.*** a valley, घाटी, उपत्यका।

valediction (वैलिडिक्शन) ***n.*** an act or expression of leave-taking, विदाई, विदा।

valedictory (वैलिडिक्टरी) ***adj.*** said or done at parting, विदाई-संबंधी; valedictory address, विदाई भाषण।

valence (वेलन्स) ***n.*** the capacity of an atom to combine in specific proportions with other atoms, संयोजन-क्षमता।

valency (वेलन्सी) ***n.*** = valence.

valentine (वैलन्टाइन) ***n.*** 1. one's sweetheart, प्रेमी या प्रेयसी। 2. a greeting card or gift sent to one's sweetheart on St. Valentine's Day. वैलनटाइन दिवस पर अपने प्रेमी या प्रेयसी को भेजा जानेवाला शुभकामना-कार्ड या उपहार।

Valentine Day ***n.*** Saint Valentine's Day, संत वैलनटाइन दिवस १४ फरवरी।

valet (वैलिट) ***n.*** a personal servant, सेवक।

valiant (वैलिअन्ट) ***adj.*** brave or courageous, बहादुर या साहसी।

valid (वैलिड) ***adj.*** 1. legally acceptable, विधिमान्य, वैध। 2. logical, तर्कसंगत, मान्य।

validate (वैलिडेट) ***v.*** 1. to make legally valid, विधिमान्य बनाना। 2. to verify, सत्यापित करना।

validity (वलिडिटी) ***n.*** the fact of being valid, विधिमान्यता।

valley (वैली) ***n.*** a long low area between the hills, घाटी, उपत्यका।

valour, valor (वैलर) ***n.*** bravery, वीरता, बहादुरी, शौर्य।

valuable (वैल्युएबल) ***adj.*** precious, of great value, बहुमूल्य, मूल्यवान, क़ीमती।

valuables (वैल्युएबल्ज़) ***n.*** (plu.) valuable things, क़ीमती वस्तुएँ।

valuation (वैल्युएशन) ***n.*** estimation of the value or price of something, मूल्यांकन, मूल्य-निर्धारण, मूल्यन।

value (वैल्यू) ***n.*** 1. the equivalent of something in money, मूल्य, क़ीमत, दाम। 2. usefulness, उपयोगिता। 3. importance, महत्त्व। 4. (plu.) ideals or principles, आदर्श, सिद्धांत। ***v.*** 1. to estimate the value of, मूल्य आँकना, लगाना या निर्धारित करना। 2. to consider or regard highly, अत्यंत मूल्यवान समझना, अत्यधिक आदर करना।

valued (वैल्यूड) ***adj.*** 1. estimated, मूल्य-निर्धारित, मूल्यांकित। 2. esteemed, आदरणीय।

valuer (वैल्यूअर) ***n.*** one who estimates the value of something, मूल्य-निर्धारक, मूल्यांकनकर्ता।

valve (वैल्व) ***n.*** a device for controlling the flow of liquid, gas etc., कपाट, वाल्व।

vampire (वैम्पाइर) ***n.*** a ghost that sucks the blood of sleeping people, रक्तपिपासू प्रेत, रक्तचूषक पिशाच।

van (वैन) ***n.*** a covered vehicle, बंद गाड़ी, वैन।

vandal (वैन्डल) ***n.*** a person who wilfully destroys private or public property or artistic things, संपत्ति-विध्वंसक, कला-विध्वंसक।

vandalize (वैन्डलाइज़) ***v.*** to destroy property wilfully, जानबूझकर संपत्ति का विध्वंस करना।

vanguard (वैनगार्ड) ***n.*** the foremost position of the army, हरावल, सेनाग्र, सेनामुख।

vanish (वैनिश) ***v.*** to become invisible, to disappear, ग़ायब हो जाना, अंतर्धान हो जाना, ख़त्म हो जाना।

vanity (वैनिटी) ***n.*** 1. worthlessness, निरर्थकता। 2. conceit, अहंमन्यता, मिथ्याभिमान।

vanquish (वैन्क्विश) ***v.*** to defeat or overcome, हराना, परास्त करना।

vantage (वैन्टिज) ***n.*** a superior position, बढ़िया स्थिति।

vapour (वेपर) ***n.*** particles of moisture suspended in air, वाष्प, भाप।

V

variable (वेरिएबल) ***adj.*** liable to change, परिवर्तनीय, परिवर्तनशील, परिवर्ती।

variance (वेरिअन्स) ***n.*** 1. difference, भिन्नता, विभिन्नता। 2. difference of opinions, मतभेद। ☐ **at variance** संघर्षरत।

variation (वेरिएशन) ***n.*** 1. the condition or result of varying, परिवर्तन, विचरण या भिन्नता। 2. घट-बढ़।

varied (वेरीड) ***adj.*** 1. of different sorts, विविध। 2. full of variety, विविधतापूर्ण।

variegated (वेरिगेटिड) ***adj.*** of different colours or having patches of different colours, रंग-बिरंगा, चितकबरा।

variety (वराइटी) ***n.*** 1. the quality or condition of being various, विविधता, अनेकरूपता। 2. a collection of different things, विविध वस्तुओं का संग्रह। 3. a different kind, प्रकार, भेद, प्रभेद; variety show रंगारंग मनोरंजन, विविधतापूर्ण कार्यक्रम।

various (वेरिअस) ***adj.*** 1. of several kinds, विविध, नानारूप। 2. more than one, अनेक।

varnish (वार्निश) ***n.*** an oil-based preparation for coating, वार्निश। ***v.*** to coat with varnish, वार्निश करना।

vary (वेअरी) ***v.*** 1. to cause or undergo change, परिवर्तन होना या करना, बदल जाना या बदल देना। 2. to be of different kind, भिन्न होना। 3. to cause to be different, भिन्न बना देना, कुछ और बना देना।

vascular (वैस्क्युलर) ***adj.*** of or having vessels or ducts, वाहिका-संबंधी।

vase (वेस) ***n.*** a vessel used for holding cut flowers, पुष्पपात्र, फूलदान।

vasectomy (वसेक्टोमी) ***n.*** surgical removal of a duct through which semen passes from the testicles, नसबंदी।

vaseline (वैसलीन) ***n.*** a petroleum substance used as an ointment, वैसलीन।

vassal (वैसल) ***n.*** a humble servant, चाकर, टहलुआ।

vast (वास्ट) ***adj.*** 1. very great in size or extent, विशाल, विस्तृत। 2. very great in intensity or number, विपुल, प्रचुर।

vault[1] (वॉल्ट) ***n.*** 1. an arched roof, मेहराबदार छत, गुंबद। 2. an underground room or storage, तहख़ाना। 3. a burial chamber, मुर्दा गाड़ने का स्थान, शवकोष्ठ।

vault[2] ***v.*** to leap over, फलाँगना, फाँदना, छलाँग लगाना। ***n.*** an act of vaulting, फलाँग, कूद, छलाँग।

vector (वेक्टर) ***n.*** (math) a quantity that has both magnitude and direction, सदिश।

veer (विअर) ***v.*** to change direction, दिशा बदल लेना।

veg (वेज) ***n.*** a vegetable, सब्ज़ी, साग।

vegetable (वेजिटेबल) ***n.*** 1. a plant of which some part is edible, तरकारी, साग, सब्ज़ी। 2. an edible part of a plant, सब्ज़ी के रूप में प्रयुक्त वनस्पति।

vegetarian (वेजिटेरिअन) ***n.*** a person who eats no meat, शाकाहारी, निरामिषभोजी। ***adj.*** (food) consisting of only vegetables, शाकाहारी।

vegetation (वेजिटेशन) ***n.*** plants collectively, पेड़-पौधे, वनस्पति।

vegetative (वेजिटेटिव) ***adj.*** of

vegetation or plants, पेड़-पौधों-संबंधी, वानस्पतिक।

vehemence (वीहिमेन्स) ***n.*** 1. great force, प्रचंडता, प्रबलता। 2. intense feeling, उत्कट भावना।

vehement (वीहिमेन्ट) ***adj.*** 1. acting or moving with great force, प्रचंड, प्रबल। 2. violent, आवेशपूर्ण, हिंसापूर्ण।

vehicle (वीहिकल) ***n.*** 1. any device on wheels for conveying or transporting, यान, वाहन, सवारी। 2. a means by which ideas are expressed, साधन, माध्यम।

vehicular (वीहिक्युलर) ***adj.*** of or for vehicles, यान-संबंधी, वाहन-संबंधी।

veil (वेल) ***n.*** 1. a piece of fine fabric as part of head-dress to conceal the face, घूँघट, नक़ाब, परदा। 2. a screen, आड़, आवरण। ***v.*** 1. to cover the face with a veil, घूँघट निकालना। 2. to conceal, छिपाना, ढकना।

vein (वेन) ***n.*** 1. a blood vessel, रग, नस। 2. a streak or narrow strip, धारी। 3. a mood or manner, मनोदशा या ढंग।

velocity (विलॉसिटी) ***n.*** speed, वेग।

velvet (वेल्विट) ***n.*** a rich fabric of silk, मख़मल।

venal (वीनल) ***adj.*** that can be bribed or corrupted, भ्रष्ट, घूसख़ोर।

vendetta (वेन्डेटा) ***n.*** a feud, कुलवैर, प्रतिशोध, बदला।

vendor (वेन्डर) ***n.*** one who sells something, विक्रेता, बेचनेवाला।

veneer (विनिअर) ***n.*** 1. a thin layer of wood, plastic etc., that is bonded to wooden surface, काष्ठपरत, सज्जापरत। 2. a superficial appearance or show, दिखावा, आडंबर। ***v.*** to cover with a veneer, काष्ठपरत या सज्जापरत लगाना या मढ़ना।

venerable (वेनरेबल) ***adj.*** worthy of reverence, श्रद्धास्पद, श्रद्धेय, पूज्य, पूजनीय।

veneration (वेनरेशन) ***n.*** a feeling of reverence, श्रद्धाभाव, पूज्यभाव, सम्मान।

venereal (विनीरिअल) ***adj.*** caused by sexual intercourse, रति या मैथुन से उत्पन्न, रतिज, मैथुनिक।

vengeance (वेन्जन्स) ***n.*** the act of or desire for taking revenge, बदला या बदले की भावना, प्रतिशोध।

vengeful (वेन्जफ़ुल) ***adj.*** 1. seeking to avenge, प्रतिशोधी। 2. serving to gain vengeance, प्रतिशोधपूर्ण।

venom (वेनम) ***n.*** 1. poison secreted by a snake, सर्पविष, विष, ज़हर। 2. strong bitter feeling, वैमनस्य, वैर, विद्वेष, द्वेष।

venous (वीनस) ***adj.*** of or related to a vein, शिरा-, नस का।

vent (वेन्ट) ***n.*** a small opening for the escape of a liquid, gas etc., छेद, सुराख़। ***v.*** to make a vent in, छेद करना।

ventilate (वेन्टिलेट) ***v.*** 1. to cause air to enter and pass freely in a room, हवादार बनाना, संवातित करना। 2. to express (one's feelings, अपनी भावनाएँ) अभिव्यक्त करना, प्रकट करना।

ventilator (वेन्टिलेटर) ***n.*** an opening for ventilating a room, रोशनदान, वातायन।

ventricle (वेन्ट्रिकल) ***n.*** a cavity in a bodily part or organ, छेद, छिद्र, निलय।

venture (वेन्चर) ***n.*** an undertaking that involves risk, जोख़िम-भरा काम। ***v.*** to undertake the risk, जोख़िम उठाना।

V

venturesome (वेन्चरसम) ***adj.*** 1. daring, जोख़िम उठानेवाला, जोख़िमी। 2. involving great risk, जोख़िम-भरा।

venue (वेन्यू) ***n.*** 1. a meeting place, मिलन-स्थल, सभा-स्थल, अधिवेशन-स्थल। 2. the scene of an action, घटना-स्थल, आयोजन-स्थल।

Venus (वीनस) ***n.*** 1. a planet in the solar system, शुक्र ग्रह। 2. a goddess of love, प्रेम की देवी।

veracious (विरेशस) ***adj.*** 1. truthful, सच्चा, सत्यभाषी। 2. true, सत्य, सही।

veracity (विरैसिटी) ***n.*** truth, सच्चाई।

verandah, veranda (वरैन्डा) ***n.*** a roofed open gallery, बरामदा।

verb (वर्ब) ***n.*** a class of words that serve to indicate action, क्रिया, क्रियापद।

verbal (वर्बल) ***adj.*** 1. of a verb, क्रियार्थक। 2. of or relating to words, शाब्दिक, भाषाई। 3. not written, spoken, अलिखित, मौखिक।

verbal noun ***n.*** a noun derived from a verb, क्रियार्थक संज्ञा।

verbally (वर्बली) ***adv.*** orally, मौखिक रूप से, ज़बानी।

verbatim (वर्बेटिम) ***adv.*** in the same words, उन्हीं शब्दों में, अक्षरशः, शब्दशः।

verbose (वर्बोस) ***adj.*** containing much more words than are needed, शब्दाडंबरपूर्ण, शब्दबहुल।

verbosity (वर्बॉसिटी) ***n.*** the state or quality of being verbose, शब्दाडंबर, शब्दबहुलता।

verdant (वर्डेन्ट) ***adj.*** green, हरा।

verdict (वर्डिक्ट) ***n.*** 1. the findings of a jury, अधिमत (अधिकार+मत)। 2. any decision, निर्णय।

verdure (वर्जर) ***n.*** green vegetation, हरे-भरे पेड़-पौधे, हरियाली।

verge (वर्ज) ***n.*** an edge or brink, किनारा, छोर, कगार।

verification (वेरिफ़िकेशन) ***n.*** the act of verifying, सत्यापन।

verify (वेरिफ़ाइ) ***v.*** to establish the truth of, सत्यापित करना।

veritable (वेरिटेबल) ***adj.*** 1. true, सत्य, सच्चा। 2. actual, वास्तविक, सही।

vermilion (वर्मिल्यन) ***n.*** a bright red pigment, सिंदूर। ***adj.*** bright red, सिंदूरी।

vermin (वर्मिन) ***n.*** (plu.) small harmful and disgusting insects or animals, परेशान तथा नुक़सान करनेवाले छोटे-मोटे जीव-जंतु (जैसे चूहे, तिलचट्टे, जूँ आदि)।

vernacular (वर्नैक्युलर) ***n.*** 1. the dialect of a particular region, स्थानिक भाषा, जनभाषा, देसी बोली। 2. everyday speech, रोज़मर्रा की ज़बान, बोलचाल की भाषा।

vernal (वर्नल) ***adj.*** of or occurring in spring, वसंत ऋतु में होनेवाला, वासंतिक।

versatility (वर्सेटिलिटी) ***n.*** the state or quality of being versatile, बहुमुखी प्रतिभा, बहुविज्ञता।

versatile (वर्सेटाइल) ***adj.*** 1. able to do many different things well, बहुमुखी। 2. variable, विविधतापूर्ण।

verse (वर्स) ***n.*** 1. a line of metrical writing, पद्य का चरण। 2. poetry, पद्य, कविता। 3. a group of lines forming a unit in a poem, पद, छंद।

versed (वर्स्ड) ***adj.*** skilled, कुशल।

versification (वर्सिफ़िकेशन) ***n.*** 1. the act of versifying, पद्य रचना। 2. the metrical composition of a prose text, पद्यीकरण।

version (वर्ज़न) ***n.*** 1. translation from another language, अनुवाद, भाषांतर। 2. an account of a matter from a particular point of view, विशिष्ट पाठ, वृत्तांत या संस्करण। 3. a variant form of a thing, अन्य या विविध रूप।

versus (वर्सस) ***prep.*** against, बनाम, के विरुद्ध, और···के बीच।

vertebra (वर्टिब्रा) ***n.*** (plu. vertebrae, vertebras) one of the bony segments that form the backbone, कशेरुका।

vertical (वर्टिकल) ***adj.*** 1. upright, ऊर्ध्वाधर, सीधा, खड़ा, उर्ध्व। 2. extending in a perpendicular direction, लंबमान, लंबवत्। ***n.*** a vertical line or post, खड़ी रेखा, सीधा खंभा।

vertiginous (वर्टिजिनस) ***adj.*** causing dizziness, चक्कर लानेवाला।

vertigo (वर्टिगो) ***n.*** a sensation of dizziness, चक्कर आना, चक्कर।

very (वेरी) ***adv.*** 1. extremely, बहुत, अत्यधिक। 2. in the fullest sense, बिल्कुल, पूर्णतया। ***adj.*** 1. same, ठीक वही, ठीक उसी। 2. extreme, अति, अत्यधिक, बहुत।

vessel (वेसल) ***n.*** 1. a hollow or concave utensil, बर्तन, पात्र। 2. a boat or ship, नाव या जलयान।

vest (वेस्ट) ***n.*** 1. a short tight-fitting waist-length garment worn under a shirt by men, बनियान, गंजी। 2. a waistcoat, बंडी, फतूही, वास्कट। ***v.*** to place (power or authority) in the control of a person or group, व्यक्ति या समूह को (अधिकार या प्राधिकार से) निहित या युक्त करना, अधियुक्त करना।

vested (वेस्टिड) ***adj.*** bestowed with a right, निहित; vested interest, निहित स्वार्थ।

vestibule (वेस्टिब्यूल) ***n.*** a small entrance hall or lobby, बड़ी ड्योढ़ी, हॉल।

vestige (वेस्टिज) ***n.*** a mark or sign of something which has disappeared, अवशेष।

vestment (वेस्टमेन्ट) ***n.*** an official robe, रस्मी कपड़े, औपचारिक परिधान।

vet[1] (वेट) ***n.*** a veterinarian, पशु-चिकित्सक।

vet[2] ***n.*** a veteran, अनुभवी व्यक्ति।

vet[3] ***v.*** to examine carefully, सावधानी से निरीक्षण करना, परीक्षण करना।

veteran (वेटरन) ***n.*** a person of long experience in some service or position, पुराना आदमी, अनुभवी व्यक्ति, जानकार।

veterinarian (वेटरिनेरिअन) ***n.*** a veterinary physician or surgeon, पशु-चिकित्सक।

veto (वीटो) ***n.*** the right to reject something proposed by others, निषेधाधिकार, वीटो। ***v.*** to reject authoritatively, निषेध करना।

vex (वेक्स) ***v.*** to annoy, to irritate, तंग करना, परेशान करना, खिजाना।

vexation (वेक्सेशन) ***n.*** the act of annoying or the state of being annoyed, खीज, परेशानी।

via (वाइआ) ***prep.*** 1. by way of, के रास्ते, के मार्ग से। 2. through, के द्वारा।

viability (वाइअबिलिटी) ***n.*** the quality or state of being viable, जीवनक्षमता; व्यवहार्यता।

viable (वाइएबल) ***adj.*** 1. able to live, जीवनक्षम। 2. practicable, व्यवहार्य।

viaduct (वाइअडक्ट) ***n.*** a bridge to

V

carry a road or railway across a valley etc., घाटी पर बना पुल, सेतु।

vial (वाइअल) ***n.*** a small bottle for liquid medicine, शीशी, बोतल।

via media ***n.*** a middle way, मध्यमार्ग, समझौते का मार्ग।

vibrant (वाइब्रन्ट) ***adj.*** 1. vibrating, कंपायमान। 2. reso-nant, गूँजता हुआ, अनुनादी। 3. energetic, जीवंत, सक्रिय।

vibrate (वाइब्रेट) ***v.*** 1. to swing back and forth, डोलना, झूमना, कंपित होना, स्पंदित होना। 2. to resound, गूँजना।

vibration (वाइब्रेशन) ***n.*** 1. vibrating motion, कंपन, स्पंदन। 2. quiver, thrill, कँपकँपी।

vibrator (वाइब्रेटर) ***n.*** a device that causes vibration, कंपित्र।

vibratory (वाइब्रेटरी) ***adj.*** causing vibration, कंपनकारी।

vicarious (विकेरिअस) ***adj.*** 1. undergone or done as the substitute for another, प्रतिस्थानिक, परार्थकृत। 2. delegated, प्रत्यायोजित।

vice (वाइस) ***n.*** 1. a moral failing, दुर्गुण, दोष, व्यसन। 2. an immoral act, पापाचार, दुराचार। ***prep.*** in the place of, के स्थान पर। ***prefix.*** deputy, subordinate, उप।

vice chancellor (वाइस चान्सलर) ***n.*** an official next in rank below chancellor, उपकुलपति।

viceroy (वाइसरॉइ) ***n.*** a person ruling a country as the deputy of a sovereign, वाइसराय।

vice versa (वाइसि वर्सा) ***adv.*** the other way around, विपरीत क्रम से, इससे उलटे।

vicinity (विसिनिटी) ***n.*** 1. nearness, समीपता, निकटता। 2. a surrounding region, पड़ोस, प्रतिवेश।

vicious (विशस) ***adj.*** 1. depraved, immoral, mean, पतित, नीच, बुरा। 2. wicked, दुष्ट।

vicious circle ***n.*** a situation in which one problem gives rise to another, दुश्चक्र।

vicissitude (विसिसिट्यूड) ***n.*** (usu. plu.) ups and downs of fortune, भाग्य के फेर, जीवन के उतार-चढ़ाव।

victim (विक्टिम) ***n.*** 1. one who is harmed or injured by another or by accident or disease, पीड़ित, उत्पीड़ित। 2. one who is tricked or swindled, शिकार।

victimize (विक्टिमाइज़) ***v.*** to make a victim of, उत्पीड़ित करना, सताना।

victor (विक्टर) ***n.*** the winner in a battle, विजेता, विजयी।

victorious (विक्टोरिअस) ***adj.*** having won a victory, विजयी।

victory (विक्टरी) ***n.*** success in a battle or game, विजय, जीत।

video (विडिओ) ***n.*** 1. television, टेलीविज़न, दूरदर्शन। 2. television picture, दूरदर्शन में का चित्र। 3. a video cassette recorder, वीडियो। ***adj.*** of television, टेलीविज़न-संबंधी, दूरदर्शन-संबंधी।

vie (वाइ) ***v.*** (vied, vying) to compete, स्पर्धा करना।

view (व्यू) ***n.*** 1. seeing or looking, अवलोकन, दर्शन। 2. sight or scene, दृश्य। 3. critical contemplation, विचार, दृष्टि। 4. an opinion, राय, मत। ***v.*** 1. to see, देखना। 2. to inspect or survey, निरीक्षण या सर्वेक्षण करना। 3. to regard or consider, महत्त्व देना या मानना।

viewpoint (व्यूपॉइन्ट) ***n.*** a point of view, दृष्टिकोण।

vigil (विजिल) ***n.*** a purposeful watch, निगरानी, चौकसी।

vigilance (विजिलन्स) ***n.*** watchfulness, सतर्कता, चौकसी।

vigilant (विजिलन्ट) ***adj.*** watchful, alert, सचेत, चौकस, सावधान।

vigorous (विगरस) ***adj.*** 1. full of vigour, ओजपूर्ण, ओजस्वी। 2. powerful, ज़ोरदार, प्रबल।

vigour (विगर) ***n.*** 1. physical or mental energy, ओज, बल। 2. enthusiasm, जोश, उमंग। 3. effectiveness, प्रबलता, ज़ोर।

vile (वाइल) ***adj.*** (viler, vilest) 1. morally low, कमीना, नीच। 2. despicable, hateful, घृणित। 3. bad, बुरा।

vilification (विलिफ़िकेशन) ***n.*** abusive language, गाली-गलौज।

villa (विला) ***n.*** a large house, विशाल भवन, हवेली।

village (विलिज) ***n.*** a group of houses in the country, गाँव, ग्राम।

villager (विलिजर) ***n.*** an inhabitant of a village, गाँव का रहनेवाला, ग्रामीण, देहाती।

villain (विलेन) ***n.*** 1. a wicked person or wrongdoer, दुष्ट व्यक्ति, खल। 2. a wicked character in a play or story, खलनायक।

villainous (विलेनस) ***adj.*** 1. wicked, दुष्ट, खल। 2. bad, बुरा।

vim (विम) ***n.*** energy, ऊर्जा, शक्ति।

vincible (विन्सिबल) ***adj.*** that can be overcome, जिसे परास्त किया जा सके।

vindicate (विन्डिकेट) ***v.*** 1. to clear of suspicion, संदेहमुक्त करना। 2. to prove to be valid, वैध ठहराना।

vindication (विन्डिकेशन) ***n.*** the act of vindicating, संदेह या दोष से मुक्त करने की क्रिया, दोषमोचन।

vindictive (विन्डिक्टिव) ***adj.*** having or showing a desire for revenge, बदले की भावनावाला, प्रतिशोधी।

vine (वाइन) ***n.*** 1. a plant with a long thin stem that grows along the ground or climbs a tree, wall etc., लता, बेल। 2. a grapevine, अंगूर की लता।

vinegar (विनिगर) ***n.*** a kind of sour liquid, सिरका।

vineyard (विन्यार्ड) ***n.*** a plantation of grapevines, अंगूर बाग़ान।

vintage (विन्टिज) ***n.*** 1. the gathering of grapes for wine, शराब बनाने के लिए किया जानेवाला अंगूरों का एकत्रीकरण। 2. wine made from a particular season's grapes, किसी विशिष्ट ऋतु के अंगूरों की शराब। 3. a type or model, प्रकार, क़िस्म, मॉडल। ***adj.*** of high quality, ऊँची क़िस्म का, बढ़िया।

vinyl (वाइनिल) ***n.*** a kind of plastic, एक तरह का प्लास्टिक, वीनिल।

violate (वाइअलेट) ***v.*** 1. to break (a law, क़ानून का) उल्लंघन करना, अतिक्रमण करना। 2. to rape, बलात्कार करना। 3. to treat disrespectfully, अनादर करना।

violation (वाइअलेशन) ***n.*** the act of violating or the state of being violated, उल्लंघन, अतिक्रमण।

violence (वाइअलेन्स) ***n.*** 1. the use of physical force, ज़ोर-ज़बरदस्ती। 2. the use of physical force so as to injure or damage, हिंसा। 3. great force or intensity, प्रचंडता, प्रबलता, उग्रता।

V

violent (वाइअलेन्ट) ***adj.*** 1. caused by violence, हिंसात्मक। 2. furious, उग्र, प्रचंड।

violet (वाइअलिट) ***n.*** a bluish-purple colour, बैंगनी रंग। ***adj.*** of a violet colour, बैंगनी।

violin (वाइअलिन) ***n.*** a stringed instrument played with a bow, वायलिन, बेला।

violinist (वाइअलिनिस्ट) ***n.*** one who plays a violin, वायलिनवादक, बेलावादक।

viper (वाइपर) ***n.*** a poisonous snake, ज़हरीला साँप।

virgin (वर्जिन) ***n.*** 1. a young girl or woman who has not had sexual intercourse, कुमारी कन्या, अक्षतयोनि। 2. the mother of Christ, मरियम, मेरी। ***adj.*** 1. being a virgin, कुमारी, कुँआरी, अक्षता। 2. chaste or pure, पवित्र, विशुद्ध। 3. unused or untouched, अप्रयुक्त, अछूता।

virginity (वर्जिनिटी) ***n.*** 1. the quality or state of being virgin, कुआँरापन, कौमार्य। 2. chastity, पवित्रता। 3. purity, विशुद्धता।

Virgo (वर्गो) ***n.*** the sixth sign of the Zodiac, कन्या राशि।

virile (विराइल) ***adj.*** 1. manly, पुरुषोचित, पौरुषेय। 2. capable of procreation, वीर्यवान, जननक्षम।

virility (वरिलिटी) ***n.*** virile power, पौरुष, पुंसत्त्व।

virology (विरॉलोजी) ***n.*** the scientific study of viruses, विषाणु-विज्ञान।

virtual (वर्चुअल) ***adj.*** real (in fact though not in name), वास्तविक, यथार्थ।

virtue (वर्चू) ***n.*** 1. a good quality, goodness, सद्गुण। 2. chastity of a woman, पवित्रता, सतीत्व। ☐ **by virtue of,** के कारण से, के आधार पर।

virtuous (वर्चुअस) ***adj.*** morally good, सद्गुणी, सच्चरित्र, नेक।

virulent (विरुलेन्ट) ***adj.*** 1. poisonous, ज़हरीला, विषाक्त। 2. deadly, भयंकर, घातक, संघातिक। 3. bitter, कड़वा।

virus (वाइरस) ***n.*** an organism smaller than bacteria but capable of causing disease, रोगजनक सूक्ष्म विषाक्त जीवाणु, वाइरस, विषाणु।

visa (वीज़ा) ***n.*** an endorsement in a passport by officials of a foreign country permitting the bearer to enter their country, प्रवेशानुमति, वीज़ा।

vis-a-vis (वीज़े-वी) ***adv.*** face to face, आमने-सामने, के सामने। ***prep.*** in relation to, के संबंध में, की तुलना में। ***n.*** one opposite to another, आमना-सामना।

viscera (विसरा) ***n.*** (plu.) 1. the internal organs of the body, शरीर के भीतरी अंग (जैसे हृदय, गुर्दे, फेफड़े आदि), आंतरांग (आंतर + अंग)। 2. intestines, आँतें।

visceral (विसरल) ***adj.*** of or pertaining to viscera, आंतरांगी।

viscosity (विस्कॉसिटी) ***n.*** the state or quality of being viscous, चिपचिपापन।

viscount (वाइकाउन्ट) ***n.*** a nobleman ranking below an earl and above a baron, ब्रिटिश सामंत, विस्काउन्ट।

viscous (विस्कस) ***adj.*** gluey, चिपचिपा।

visibility (विज़िबिलिटी) ***n.*** the quality or state of being visible, दृश्यता।

visible (विज़िबल) ***adj.*** 1. that can be seen, दृश्य, दृष्टिगोचर। 2. evident or manifest, प्रकट, प्रत्यक्ष।

visibly (विज़िब्ली) ***adv.*** clearly, स्पष्ट रूप से, स्पष्टत:।

vision (विज़न) ***n.*** 1. the power or faculty of seeing, दृष्टि। 2. the ability of great perception, imaginative insight, अंतर्दृष्टि, दिव्यदृष्टि, दूरदर्शिता। 3. a mental image, मानसिक प्रतिबिंब या आकृति, मनोरूप। 4. something seen in a dream or trance, स्वप्न-चित्र। 5. a person or thing of unusual beauty, अति सुंदर व्यक्ति या वस्तु, दिव्य दर्शन।

visionary (विज़नरी) ***adj.*** 1. of the nature of a fantasy or dream, काल्पनिक, अवास्तविक। 2. given to impractical ideas, स्वप्नदर्शी। ***n.*** a person with visionary ideas, a visionary person, स्वप्नद्रष्टा, अंतर्द्रष्टा।

visit (विज़िट) ***v.*** 1. to go or come to meet or see, मिलने के लिए जाना या आना। 2. to stay with (someone, किसी के पास) ठहरना या रुकना। 3. to go or come to in a business or professional capacity, भेंट करना। 4. to inflict punishment, दंड देना, दंडित करना। ***n.*** 1. the act of seeing, अवलोकन। 2. the act of calling upon, meeting, भेंट, मुलाक़ात। 3. inspection, निरीक्षण।

visitor (विज़िटर) ***n.*** 1. one who pays a visit, आगंतुक, मुलाक़ाती, अतिथि। 2. one who comes to see, दर्शक।

visor (वाइज़र) ***n.*** a piece of armour that protects the face, मुखावरण।

vista (विस्टा) ***n.*** 1. a view, दृश्य। 2. a mental view, मानसदर्शन, सिंहावलोकन।

visual (विज़ुअल) ***adj.*** 1. of or used in seeing, दृश्य, चाक्षुष। 2. that can be seen, दृश्य; visual effect, दृश्य प्रभाव।

visualization (विज़ुअलाइज़ेशन) ***n.*** the act of visualizing, मन में चित्र बनाने की क्रिया, मानसदर्शन।

visualize (विज़ुअलाइज़) ***v.*** to form a mental image, मन में चित्र बनाना, मानसदर्शन करना।

vital (वाइटल) ***adj.*** 1. of or pertaining to life, जीवन-संबंधी। 2. essential to maintain life, जीवनाधार। 3. of greatest importance, अत्यंत महत्त्वपूर्ण।

vitality (वाइटैलिटी) ***n.*** 1. the power or ability to continue into existence, जीवंतता, प्राण-शक्ति। 2. energy or force, ऊर्जा या शक्ति।

vitals (वाइटल्ज़) ***n.*** (plu.) the vital parts of the body, मर्मस्थल।

vitamin (विटेमिन) ***n.*** any of the organic substances essential for health and found in food, विटामिन।

vitiate (विशिएट) ***v.*** 1. to spoil, बिगाड़ देना। 2. to weaken the force of, अशक्त कर देना। 3. to invalidate, अवैध कर देना।

viticulture (विटिकल्चर) ***n.*** the cultivation of grapevine, अंगूरों की खेती।

vitreous (विट्रिअस) ***adj.*** like glass, काँच जैसा, काचाभ।

vitrify (विट्रिफ़ाइ) ***v.*** to convert into glass, काँच बनाना।

vitriol (विट्रिअल) ***n.*** 1. sulphuric acid, गंधक का तेज़ाब। 2. harsh criticism, कटु आलोचना।

vituperate (वाइटूपरेट) ***v.*** 1. to speak abusively to or about, गाली देना,

V

गाली-गलौज करना। 2. to scold, बुरा-भला कहना, कोसना।

viva[1] (वीवा) ***interj.*** long live! अमर रहे!

viva[2] (वाइवा) ***n.*** an oral examination, मौखिक परीक्षा।

vivacious (विवेशस) ***adj.*** lively, जीवंत, सजीव, स्फूर्त, जानदार, प्राणवंत।

vivaciousness (विवेशसनिस) ***n.*** the state or quality of being vivacious, जीवंतता, सजीवता, ज़िंदादिली।

vivarium (वाइवेरिअम) ***n.*** an enclosed place for raising plants and animals under natural conditions, प्रकृतशाला, जीवशाला।

viva voce (वाइवा वोसी) ***n.*** the full form of viva.

vivid (विविड) ***adj.*** 1. full of life, lively, lifelike, जीवंत, सजीव, जीता-जागता। 2. bright or brilliant, चटक, शोख़। 3. strong, powerful, तीव्र, सशक्त। 4. very clear, सुस्पष्ट।

vivify (विविफ़ाइ) ***v.*** (vivified, vivifying) to make vivid, सजीव बनाना, जीवंत बनाना।

viviparous (विविपरस) ***adj.*** bearing or bringing forth living young, (प्राणी) जो बच्चों को (सीधे) जन्म दे (अंडों आदि से पैदा न करे), जरायुज।

vivisection (विविसेक्शन) ***n.*** an act of performing surgical experiments on living animals, जीवों पर किया जानेवाला (अध्ययनार्थ) शल्य-प्रयोग, जीवोच्छेदन।

vixen (विक्सन) ***n.*** 1. a female fox, लोमड़ी। 2. a quarrelsome woman, झगड़ालू स्त्री।

viz (विज़) ***adv.*** namely, अर्थात्।

vocabulary (वोकैबुलरी) ***n.*** 1. all the words of a language, शब्दभंडार, शब्द-समूह, शब्द-संपदा। 2. words used in a particular book, शब्दावली। 3. all the words used by a person or class, शब्दावली।

vocal (वोकल) ***adj.*** 1. uttered or produced by the voice, उच्चरित, वाचिक, वाक्; vocal cords, स्वरतंत्री। 2. outspoken, मुखर।

vocalist (वोकलिस्ट) ***n.*** a singer, गायक।

vocally (वोकली) ***adv.*** orally, मौखिक रूप से, ज़बानी।

vocation (वोकेशन) ***n.*** 1. any trade or profession, व्यवसाय, पेशा, वृत्ति। 2. a special urge to a religious work, किसी धार्मिक कार्य के प्रति होनेवाली अंत:प्रेरणा, बुलाहट।

vocational (वोकेशनल) ***adj.*** of a vocation, व्यावसायिक।

vocative (वॉकटिव) ***adj.*** of the case of noun, pronoun or an adjective used in direct address, संबोधनात्मक; vocative case, संबोधनकारक।

vociferous (वोसिफ़रस) ***adj.*** 1. making an outcry, चिल्लानेवाला। 2. noisy, कोलाहलपूर्ण।

vodka (वोड्का) ***n.*** a Russian alcoholic liquor, रूसी शराब, वोडका।

vogue (वोग) ***n.*** the current fashion or style, प्रचलित शैली, फ़ैशन, चालू रिवाज। □ **in vogue**, जो फ़ैशन में हो।

voice (वॉइस) ***n.*** 1. the sound made by the vocal cords, कंठध्वनि, घोष, आवाज़। 2. a specified quality or tone in speaking of a particular person, आवाज़, सुर। 3. an utterance, कथन। 4. opinion, विचार, मत। 5. expression, अभिव्यक्ति। 6. the right to express one's thought, बोलने का अधिकार।

7. one of the forms of the verb that shows the relation of the subject to the verb, वाच्य; active voice, कर्तृवाच्य, passive voice, कर्मवाच्य। ***v.*** 1. to utter, बोलना। 2. to express, व्यक्त करना, अभिव्यक्त करना।

voiced (वॉइस्ड) ***adj.*** 1. articulated with vibration of vocal cords, घोष (वर्ण)। 2. expressed by the voice, अभिव्यक्त, व्यक्त।

voiceless (वॉइसलिस) ***adj.*** not voiced, अघोष (वर्ण)।

void (वॉइड) ***adj.*** 1. vacant, empty, खाली, रिक्त। 2. invalid, अवैध, अमान्य, शून्य। ***n.*** 1. empty space, शून्य। 2. emptiness, खालीपन, रिक्ति।

voile (वॉइल) ***n.*** a thin fabric of cotton, वायल।

volatile (वॉलटाइल) ***adj.*** 1. quickly evaporating, वाष्पशील। 2. fickle-minded, अस्थिर चित्त, चंचल, चपल। 3. changeable, परिवर्तनशील।

volatility (वॉलटिलिटी) ***n.*** the quality or state of being volatile, वाष्पशीलता; चंचलता; परिवर्तनशीलता।

volcanic (वॉल्कैनिक) ***adj.*** of, thrown from, caused by or characteristic of a valcano, ज्वालामुखीय, ज्वालामुखी।

volcano (वॉल्केनो) ***n.*** an opening in the earth's crust through which lava, ash etc., are ejected, ज्वालामुखी।

volition (वोलिशन) ***n.*** determination, संकल्प, इच्छाशक्ति।

volley (वॉली) ***n.*** 1. the simultaneous discharge of a number of missiles, क्षेप्यास्त्रों की बौछार या वर्षा। 2. (the number of questions) put forward in quick succession, (प्रश्नों की) बौछार, झड़ी। 3. in tennis, return of the ball before it touches the ground, वाल्ली, वॉली। ***v.*** 1. to discharge in a volley, बौछार कर देना, झड़ी लगा देना। 2. to strike a ball before it touches the ground, वाल्ली लगाना।

volleyball (वॉलीबॉल) ***n.*** 1. a game played with two teams with a ball over a net, वॉलीबाल का खेल। 2. the ball used in this game, वॉलीबाल खेलने का बॉल।

volt (वोल्ट) ***n.*** the unit of electromotive force, वोल्ट।

volte-face (वोल्ट-फ़ास) ***n.*** a complete reversal of opinion, अपनी बात से फिर जाना, फेर, बदलाव, मत-परिवर्तन।

voluble (वॉल्युबल) ***adj.*** talking too much, बातूनी, वाचाल।

volume (वॉल्यूम) ***n.*** 1. a collection of written or printed sheets bound together, पुस्तक, किताब। 2. one of the books of a set, खंड, जिल्द। 3. the size or amount (of something, किसी चीज़ की) मात्रा या परिमाण; the volume of traffic, यातायात का परिमाण। 4. the quantity of loudness of sound, ध्वनि की प्रबलता, तारता। 5. the amount of space that a three dimensional thing occupies, आयतन।

voluminous (वल्यूमिनस) ***adj.*** having great size or number, bulky, बड़ा, भारी, भारी-भरकम।

voluntarily (वॉलन्टेरिली) ***adv.*** in a voluntary manner, स्वेच्छापूर्वक, अपने आप।

voluntary (वॉलन्टरी) ***adj.*** 1. serving or acting of one's own accord, स्वैच्छिक। 2. supported or aided by state or voluntary contributions, सहायताप्राप्त, दानाश्रित।

volunteer (वॉलन्टिअर) ***n.*** one who offers to do something of his own free will, स्वयंसेवक। ***v.*** to offer one's services, अपनी सेवाएँ अर्पित करना।

voluptuous (वलप्चुअस) ***adj.*** 1. fond of pleasures of the senses, विलासी, कामुक, इंद्रियपरायण, विषयरत। 2. (of a woman) having an appealing figure, हसीन, कमनीय या सुंदर (स्त्री)।

vomit (वॉमिट) ***v.*** to eject through the mouth, कै करना, उलटी करना। ***n.*** the matter ejected in vomiting, कै, उलटी।

voodoo (वूडू) ***n.*** a religious cult involving witchcraft, जादू-टोने पर आधारित एक (अफ़्रीकी) संप्रदाय।

voracious (वोरेशस) ***adj.*** 1. devouring large quantities of food, भुक्खड़, भकोसू। 2. exceedingly eager, लालायित।

voracity (वोरैसिटी) ***n.*** 1. voraciousness, भुक्खड़पन। 2. greediness, लालच, लोभ।

vortex (वॉर्टेक्स) ***n.*** 1. a whirling mass of water, भँवर, जलावर्त। 2. a whirlwind, चक्रवात, बवंडर।

vote (वोट) ***n.*** 1. a formal expression of one's opinion or choice, मत, वोट। 2. the right to express one's opinion in an election, मताधिकार। 3. the total number of vote cast, डाले हुए कुल मत। 4. a proposal, प्रस्ताव; vote of thanks, धन्यवाद-प्रस्ताव। ***v.*** 1. to cast a vote, मत देना, वोट देना। 2. to elect, चुनना।

voter (वोटर) ***n.*** one who has a right to vote, मतदाता।

votive (वोटिव) ***adj.*** given or undertaken in fulfilment of a vow, मन्नत माना हुआ।

vouch (वॉउच) ***v.*** 1. to attest, सत्यापित करना। 2. to give evidence for, के पक्ष में साक्ष्य देना। 3. to guarantee, गारंटी देना। 4. to say forcefully, दृढ़तापूर्वक कहना।

voucher (वॉउचर) ***n.*** a document serving as a receipt, वाउचर।

vouchsafe (वॉउचसेफ़) ***v.*** to grant or give as a favour, अनुग्रहपूर्वक देना।

vow (वॉउ) ***n.*** a solemn promise or pledge, संकल्प, प्रतिज्ञा, वचन। ***v.*** to promise or pledge, संकल्प करना, वचन देना।

vowel (वाउअल) ***n.*** 1. a voiced speech sound made without stopping of the breath, स्वर। 2. a letter representing such a sound, स्वर वर्ण।

vox populi (वॉक्स पॉपुली) ***n.*** public opinion, जनमत। (लैटिन)

voyage (वॉयेज) ***n.*** a journey by sea, समुद्री यात्रा, समुद्रयात्रा।

voyager (वॉयेजर) ***n.*** one who makes a voyage, समुद्रयात्रा करनेवाला, समुद्रयात्री।

vulcanize (वल्कनाइज़) ***v.*** to give (rubber) greater strength, वल्कनित करना।

vulgar (वल्गर) ***adj.*** 1. lacking good taste, गँवार, उजड्ड, फूहड़। 2. lacking manners, अशिष्ट, असभ्य।

vulgarity (वल्गैरिटी) ***n.*** 1. the state or quality of being vulgar, अभद्रता, अशिष्टता। 2. a vulgar act, अशिष्टतापूर्ण कार्य।

vulnerability (वल्नरेबिलिटी) ***n.*** the state or quality of being vulnerable, असुरक्षित स्थिति, सुभेद्यता; संवेदनशीलता।

vulnerable (वल्नरेबल) ***adj.*** 1. susceptible to danger or attack, जो ख़तरे में पड़ सकता हो, जिसपर आक्रमण संभव हो, भेद्य, सुभेद्य। 2. open to criticism, आलोचनीय। 3. weak or sensitive, कमज़ोर या नाजुक, संवेदनशील।

vulture (वल्चर) ***n.*** a large bird of prey, गीध।

vulva (वल्वा) ***n.*** the external genital organs of the female, भग, चूत।

vying (वाइंग) ***adj.*** that vies, स्पर्धा करनेवाला, होड़ करनेवाला। ***n.*** competition, स्पर्धा, होड़।

W, w (डबल्यू) the twenty-third letter of the English alphabet, अंग्रेज़ी वर्णमाला का तेइसवाँ वर्ण।

wacky (वैकी) ***adj.*** crazy, सनकी, ख़ब्ती।

wad (वॉड) ***n.*** 1. a soft small mass of cotton, (for padding), रुई का फाहा या गद्दी। 2. a bunch of currency notes, रुपयों की गड्डी। ***v.*** 1. to compress into a wad, गड्डी बनाना। 2. to hold in place by a wad, गद्दी लगाना; रुई से बंद करना। 3. to plug with a pad, मुँह बंद करना, डाट या गद्दी लगाना।

waddle (वॉडल) ***v.*** to walk like a duck, बतख की तरह चलना। ***n.*** a waddling gait, बतख जैसी चाल।

wade (वेड) ***v.*** 1. to walk through water, mud, sand or tall grass, पानी, कीचड़, बालू या लंबी घास को चीरते हुए आगे बढ़ना, हलना। 2. to go forward with much labour, बड़ी मुश्किल से आगे बढ़ पाना। ☐ **wade in,** हस्तक्षेप करना।

waders (वेडर्ज़) ***n.*** (plu) long waterproof boots, वाटरप्रूफ़ बड़े जूते।

wafer (वेफ़र) ***n.*** a kind of thin, crisp biscuit, एक प्रकार का बिस्कुट, वेफ़र।

waft (वाफ़्ट) ***v.*** 1. to float or swim, तैरना, तिरना। 2. to carry through air, हवा में उड़ना, तिरना। ***n.*** 1. the act of floating, तैराई। 2. an odour or sound carried through the air, तिरती हुई महक या ध्वनि।

wag[1] (वैग) ***v.*** 1. to cause to move rapidly to and fro, हिलाना-डुलाना, लहराना। 2. to move rapidly to and fro, हिलना-डुलना, झूमना। ***n.*** the act of wagging हिलाने-डुलाने की क्रिया।

wag[2] ***n.*** a joker, जोकर, मसख़रा।

wage (वेज) ***n.*** 1. payment in return for work or services, मज़दूरी। 2. (plu) regular payment given to an employee for his or her services, वेतन, तनख्वाह। ***v.*** to engage in, (काम में) लग जाना या व्यस्त होना।

wager (वेजर) ***n.*** a bet, शर्त, बाज़ी। ***v.*** to bet, शर्त लगाना।

waggle (वैगल) ***v.*** to wag, हिलना-डुलना या हिलाना-डुलाना।

wagon, waggon (वैगन) ***n.*** a four-wheeled vehicle for handling heavy loads, वैगन। ☐ **on the wagons,** जिसने मद्यपान छोड़ रखा हो, मद्यपान त्यागे हुआ।

waif (वेफ़) ***n.*** 1. an unowned or abandoned child, लावारिस बच्चा, अनाथ बालक। 2. anything found by chance that is without an owner, लावारिस वस्तु। ☐ **waifs and strays,** अनाथ बच्चे।

wail (वेल) ***v.*** 1. to cry in grief, रोना, चीखना-चिल्लाना। 2. to lament, विलाप करना। ***n.*** a mournful cry, चीख, विलाप।

wailful (वेलफ़ुल) ***adj.*** sorrowful, mournful, शोकपूर्ण, मातमी।

waist (वेस्ट) ***n.*** 1. the middle part of the human body between the ribs and hips, कमर, कटि। 2. the middle part of anything, किसी प्राणी या वस्तु का मध्य भाग।

waistcoat (वेस्टकोट) ***n.*** a man's sleeveless waist length garment, वास्कट।

wait (वेट) ***v.*** 1. to stay in one place

for a specified time or until some expected event occurs, प्रतीक्षा करना। 2. to serve food at a meal, भोजन परोसना। ***n.*** 1. an act of waiting, प्रतीक्षा, इंतज़ार। 2. a period of waiting, प्रतीक्षा की घड़ियाँ, प्रतीक्षाकाल।

waiter (वेटर) ***n.*** one who serves at tables in a hotel or restaurant, बैरा, परिचारक, वेटर।

waiting (वेटिंग) ***n.*** the act of one who waits, प्रतीक्षा, इंतज़ार।

waiting room ***n.*** a room in which passengers, customers etc., wait, प्रतीक्षालय।

waitress (वेटरिस) ***n.*** a female waiter, महिला बैरा, परिचारिका।

waive (वेव) ***v.*** 1. to give up voluntarily (one's right or claim, अपना अधिकार या दावा) स्वेच्छापूर्वक छोड़ देना, अधित्याग करना। 2. to refrain from insisting upon, (किसी बात के लिए) आग्रह न करना।

waiver (वेवर) ***n.*** a written document to waive a right or claim, अधित्याग-पत्र।

wake[1] (वेक) ***v.*** (woke/waked, woken/waked, waking) 1. to awaken, जाग उठना, आँख खुलना। 2. to cause to cease to sleep, जगाना। 3. to become active, जाग पड़ना, सक्रिय हो उठना, सचेत हो जाना। 4. to cause to become active, सक्रिय करना। ***n.*** 1. the state of being awake, जागरण। 2. the watch near the corpse, शव की निगरानी।

wake[2] ***n.*** the track left by a moving boat or ship through water, जल में नाव या पोत के आगे बढ़ने से पीछे बननेवाली लीक या रेखा, पनरेख। ☐ **in the wake of,** पीछे।

wakeful (वेकफ़ुल) ***adj.*** 1. unable to sleep, जिसे नींद न आती हो, जागनेवाला, जाग्रत। 2. sleepless, निद्राविहीन। 3. alert, जागरूक, सचेत।

walk (वॉक) ***v.*** 1. to move along on foot, पैदल चलना, पैरों चलना। 2. to cause to move along on foot, पैदल चलाना। 3. to go about on foot for exercise or pleasure, टहलना, सैर करना। ***n.*** 1. the act of walking, चलने की क्रिया या भाव। 2. a manner of walking, चाल। 3. a journey on foot, पदयात्रा, भ्रमण। 4. stroll, टहलान, सैर। 5. a place for walking, सैरगाह, भ्रमण-स्थल, घूमने की जगह।

walkie-talkie (वॉकी-टॉकी) ***n.*** a small radio set that can be carried by one person, एक प्रकार का छोटा रेडियो, वाकी-टाकी।

walkout (वॉकआउट) ***n.*** the act of leaving a meeting in protest, सदन-त्याग, वाक-आउट।

walkover (वॉकओवर) ***n.*** unopposed victory, (खिलाड़ी या दल को) बिना भिड़े ही मिलनेवाली जीत।

wall (वॉल) ***n.*** 1. a vertical construction of bricks, stones etc., दीवार, भित्ति। 2. anything like a wall that encloses, protects, separates or supports, दीवार। ***v.*** to surround or enclose with a wall, दीवार से घेरना।

walled (वॉल्ड) ***adj.*** enclosed with a wall, दीवार से घिरा हुआ।

wallet (वॉलिट) ***n.*** a money bag, बटुआ।

wallow (वॉलो) ***v.*** 1. to roll about in mud, sand etc., (पशुओं का) मिट्टी, बालू आदि में लोटनी लेना, लोट-पोट होना। 2. to revel, गुलछर्रे उड़ाना, भोगविलास

करना, मौजमस्ती करना। *n.* the act of wallowing, लोट-पोट; भोगविलास।

wallpaper (वॉलपेपर) *n.* the paper for covering the walls, वालपेपर।

walnut (वॉलनट) *n.* a tree, its wood and fruit, अख़रोट का पेड़ तथा इस पेड़ का फल और लकड़ी।

walrus (वॉलरस) *n.* a sea mammal of seal family, दरियाई घोड़ा।

wan (वॉन) *adj.* pale from sickness, बीमारी के कारण जिसका रंग पीला पड़ गया हो, पीला।

wand (वॉन्ड) *n.* 1. a stick for carrying in hand, छड़ी। 2. a magic rod, जादूगर का डंडा।

wander (वॉन्डर) *v.* 1. to ramble, इधर-उधर घूमना, मटरगश्ती करना। 2. to stray, भटक जाना। 3. to digress (from a subject, विषय से) बहक जाना।

wane (वेन) *v.* 1. to decrease in size or extent, कम होना, क्षीण होना। 2. to decrease in vigour or strength, दुर्बल होना, कमज़ोर होना। 3. to decline, घटना, ह्रास होना। *n.* 1. the act of waning or the state of being waned, क्षीणता, दुर्बलता, ह्रास। 2. downfall, अवनति।

wangle (वैन्गल) *v.* to manipulate for personal or fraudulent ends, तिकड़म रचना, जोड़-तोड़ करना या मार लेना।

want (वॉन्ट) *v.* 1. to desire for, to long for, इच्छा करना, चाहना। 2. to feel the need of, आवश्यकता होना। 3. to lack, अभाव होना, कमी होना। *n.* 1. the condition or quality of lacking, shortage, अभाव, कमी। 2. pressing need, आवश्यकता, अपेक्षा। 3. poverty, ग़रीबी, दरिद्रता, तंगी।

wanted (वॉन्टिड) *adj.* being sought by the police, जिसकी तलाश में पुलिस हो, वांछित।

wanting (वॉन्टिंग) *adj.* 1. lacking, विहीन, रहित। 2. deficient, कम।

wanton (वॉन्टन) *adj.* 1. unmanageable, undisci-plined, बेलगाम या अनुशासनहीन। 2. malicious, विद्वेषपूर्ण। 3. excessive, अत्यधिक। *n.* an immoral person sply. woman, लंपट, व्यभिचारी, विशेषत: छिनाल स्त्री।

war (वॉर) *n.* 1. a declared armed conflict between states or nations, युद्ध, लड़ाई, संग्राम। 2. a struggle between opposing forces, संघर्ष, युद्ध। *v.* 1. to wage a war, लड़ाई लड़ना।

warble (वॉर्बल) *v.* to chirp, पक्षियों का चहचहाना। *n.* the act of warbling, चह-चह, चहचहाहट।

war cry (वॉर क्राइ) *n.* a slogan or phrase shouted in a war, युद्ध में लगाया हुआ नारा, युद्धघोष।

ward (वॉर्ड) *n.* 1. a division of a city for administrative or electoral purposes, हल्का, वार्ड। 2. a division in a hospital with beds for patients, कक्ष, वार्ड। 3. a child or person not capable of handling his or her own affairs, प्रतिपाल्य, वार्ड। *v.* to keep watch over, निगरानी करना। □ **ward off,** परे करना, (से) बचाना।

warden (वॉर्डन) *n.* 1. one who has charge of something, custodian, अभिरक्षक। 2. a person in charge of a ward, हल्का-अधिकारी, वार्डन।

warder (वॉर्डर) *n.* the officer of a prison, कारापाल। [Fem. wardress]

wardrobe (वार्डरोब) *n.* 1. a closet for keeping or hanging clothes, कपड़े टाँगने की अलमारी। 2. a collection of clothes, वस्त्रसंग्रह, कपड़े।

ware *n.* (वेअर) 1. manufactured articles, goods, निर्मित वस्तुएँ, माल। 2. an article of merchandise, जिंस, सौदा।

warehouse (वेअरहाउस) *n.* a building for storing goods, गोदाम, भंडार। *v.* to store in a warehouse, (माल को) माल गोदाम में रखना।

warfare (वॉरफ़ेअर) *n.* 1. armed conflict, सशस्त्र संघर्ष। 2. struggle, संघर्ष।

warlike (वॉरलाइक) *adj.* 1. belligerent, युद्धप्रिय, लड़ाकू, जंगजू। 2. threatening war, युद्ध की धमकी देनेवाला।

warm (वॉर्म) *adj.* 1. moderately hot, गरम, गुनगुना, कुनकुना। 2. sending or giving out heat, गरम, ऊष्ण। 3. hearty, affectionate, हार्दिक, स्नेहिल। 4. marked by excitement, जोशीला, उत्तेजनापूर्ण। *v.* 1. to become warm, गरम होना, गरमाना। 2. to make warm, गरम करना, गरमाना, तपाना।

warm-blooded (वॉर्म-ब्लडिड) *adj.* having warm blood, नियततापी।

warmly (वॉर्मली) *adv.* in a warm manner, जोश-ख़रोश से, उत्साहपूर्वक या स्नेहभाव से।

warmonger (वॉरमन्गर) *n.* a person who advocates war, jingo, युद्धलोलुप, जंगख़ोर।

warmth (वार्म्थ) *n.* 1. warmness, गरमाहट। 2. the natural heat of a living body, शरीर की गरमी या तापमान। 3. enthusiasm, उत्साह, जोश। 4. love, anger or excitement, प्यार, आक्रोश या आवेश।

warn (वॉर्न) *v.* 1. to make aware of coming danger, आगाह करना, सावधान करना। 2. to advise or admonish, सलाह या चेतावनी देना।

warning (वॉर्निंग) *n.* the act of one who warns, चेतावनी।

warp (वॉर्प) *v.* 1. to become or cause to become out of shape, (आकार-प्रकार) बिगड़ जाना या बिगाड़ देना, टेढ़ा-मेढ़ा हो जाना या करना। 2. to bend, मुड़ जाना या मोड़ देना, टेढ़ा हो जाना या कर देना। 3. to move (a ship) by hauling on a rope, रस्से से पोत को खींचना। 4. to form a warp, (खड्डी में) ताना लगाना। *n.* 1. the state or condition of being twisted, distortion, विकृति, टेढ़, ऐंठन, ख़राबी। 2. threads that run lengthwise in a loom, ताना। 3. a rope for hauling a ship, पोत खींचने का रस्सा।

warrant (वॉरन्ट) *n.* 1. a written order to do something, वारन्ट, अधिपत्र। 2. authorization or justification to do something, कोई काम करने का अधिकार या औचित्य। *v.* 1. to authorize (someone) to do something, कुछ करने के लिए (किसी को) अधिकृत करना। 2. to attest, प्रमाणित करना। 3. to guarantee, गारंटी देना।

warranty (वॉरन्टी) *n.* 1. the written guarantee given by the seller to the purchaser for the integrity of a product on manufacturer's behalf, लिखित गारंटी, वारंटी। 2. authority for doing something, प्राधिकार। 3. justification for doing something, कोई काम करने का औचित्य या आधार।

warren (वॉरन) *n.* a place or colony where rabbits breed, खरगोशों का बाड़ा।

warrior (वॉरिअर) *n.* 1. a fighting man, योद्धा। 2. a brave person, शूरवीर, वीर।

W

wart (वॉर्ट) ***n.*** 1. a small hard roundish growth on the outer skin, मस्सा, मुँहासा। 2. a small protuberance on the plant, गूमड़।

warty (वॉर्टी) ***adj.*** full of warts, मस्सों से भरा।

wary (वेअरी) ***adj.*** cautious, सतर्क।

was (वॉज़) ***v.*** the first and third person singular past tense of be, था।

wash (वॉश) ***v.*** 1. to cleanse with water, soap etc., धोना, साफ़ करना, पखारना, प्रक्षालन करना। 2. to cleanse oneself, नहाना, स्नान करना। 3. to purify, शुद्ध करना, पवित्र करना। 4. to make wet or moist, तर करना, गीला करना, भिगोना। 5. to flow over, प्रक्षालित करना। 6. to cut into or erode, (सड़क आदि को) काट लेना, क्षय कर देना। 7. to cover with a thin layer of paint, रोग़न की पतली परत चढ़ाना। ☐ **wash dirty linen in public,** दूसरों के सामने अपने कुकृत्यों का बखान करना; **wash one's hands off,** (i) हाथ खींच लेना, (ii) ज़िम्मेदारी छोड़ देना; **wash out,** (खेल का) भारी वर्षा के कारण न हो पाना। ***n.*** 1. the act of washing, प्रक्षालन, धुलाई। 2. the state or quality of being washed, धोए जाने की अवस्था या भाव, धुलाई।

washable (वॉशेबल) ***adj.*** capable of being washed without damage, जो धोने पर ख़राब न हो।

washbasin (वॉशबेसिन) ***n.*** a basin for washing the face, hands etc., वाशबेसिन।

washer (वॉशर) ***n.*** 1. one who or that washes, धोनेवाला व्यक्ति या यंत्र। 2. a flat ring or disk placed under a nut to prevent friction, leakage etc., वाशर, छल्ला।

washerman (वॉशरमैन) ***n.*** a person whose work is washing clothes, धोबी।

washing (वॉशिंग) ***n.*** the clothes that have been washed or to be washed together on a single occasion, एक बार की धुलाई के कपड़े, धोव।

washout (वॉशआउट) ***n.*** complete failure, पूर्ण विफलता।

washy (वॉशी) ***adj.*** 1. diluted, watery, पतला, पानी के जैसा। 2. lacking strength, कमज़ोर, दुर्बल।

wasn't (वॉज़न्ट) ***v.*** = was not.

wasp (वॉस्प) ***n.*** a small winged insect with a vicious sting, ततैया, भिड़, बर्रे।

waspish (वॉस्पिश) ***adj.*** irritable, चिड़चिड़ा।

wast (वॉस्ट) ***v.*** the past tense of be used with thou, था।

wastage (वेस्टिज) ***n.*** loss by waste, wear or deterioration, छीजन, बर्बादी या अपव्यय।

waste (वेस्ट) ***v.*** 1. to use carelessly or expend extravagantly, बर्बाद करना या अपव्यय करना, व्यर्थ बना देना। 2. to use thoughtlessly or without an adequate result, दुरुपयोग करना। 3. to fail to take advantage of, चूक जाना, गँवाना; to waste an opportunity, अवसर गँवाना। 4. to make or become weaker, कमज़ोर हो जाना या कर देना, घुलना या घुलाना। ***n.*** 1. the act of wasting or the state of being wasted, बर्बादी, अपव्यय। 2. waste material or food, बेकार सामान,

रद्दी। 3. refuse, कूड़ा-कर्कट। 4. a stretch of barren land, बंजर भूभाग। ***adj.*** 1. rejected as useless, बेकार, रद्दी, फालतू, व्यर्थ। 2. unproductive, अनुत्पादक। 3. uncultivated, अकृष्ट। 4. uninhabited, निर्जन। 5. devastated, बर्बाद।

wasteful (वेस्टफ़ुल) ***adj.*** thriftless, extravagant, अपव्ययी, फ़ज़ूलख़र्च, ख़र्चीला, उजाड़ू।

wasteland (वेस्टलैन्ड) ***n.*** an empty area of barren land, बंजर ज़मीन।

watch (वॉच) ***v.*** 1. to look attentively, ध्यान से देखना, अवलोकन करना। 2. to keep under observation, निगाह रखना, देख-भाल करना, निगरानी करना। 3. to guard carefully, पहरा देना, रखवाली करना। ***n.*** 1. the act of watching, अवलोकन, निगरानी। 2. a small portable timepiece, घड़ी। 3. a period of vigil, पहरा।

watchdog (वॉचडॉग) ***n.*** 1. a dog kept to guard property, रखवाला कुत्ता, प्रहरी कुत्ता। 2. one who guards, प्रहरी।

watchful (वॉचफ़ुल) ***adj.*** alert or vigilant, सावधान या जागरूक।

watchmaker (वॉचमेकर) ***n.*** one who makes or repairs watches, घड़ीसाज़।

watchman (वॉचमैन) ***n.*** one who is employed to guard buildings and property, पहरेदार, चौकीदार, प्रहरी।

watchtower (वॉचटाउअर) ***n.*** a tower on which a watchman keeps watch, वह बुर्ज जहाँ से पहरेदार निगरानी रखता हो।

watchword (वॉचवर्ड) ***n.*** 1. a password, संकेत शब्द, पारण-संकेत। 2. a slogan, नारा।

water (वॉटर) ***n.*** 1. the liquid that descends from the clouds and found in rivers, oceans, lakes etc., पानी, जल। 2. a body of water, नदी, झील या समुद्र। 3. any fluid secreted from the body, पसीना, आँसू या पेशाब। 4. lustre or brilliance in a diamond, पानी, चमक। ***v.*** 1. to sprinkle with water, जल छिड़कना। 2. to irrigate, सींचना। 3. to secrete tears, आँसू बहाना। 4. to secrete saliva, मुँह से लार टपकाना। 5. to provide water, पानी देना।

water bird ***n.*** a bird that swims in water, जलपक्षी।

waterborne (वॉटरबोर्न) ***adj.*** carried or conveyed by water, जलमार्ग से ले जाया जानेवाला, जलवाहित।

water chestnut ***n.*** an aquatic plant bearing nutlike fruit, सिंघाड़ा।

water closet ***n.*** a toilet flushed by water, जल-शौचालय।

watercolour (वॉटरकलर) ***n.*** 1. water-soluble pigment, पानी में घुलनेवाला रंग, जलरंग। 2. a painting executed in water colours, जलरंगों से बना चित्र, जलरंगा चित्र।

watercourse (वॉटरकोर्स) ***n.*** a stream or river, नदी, धारा।

water cure ***n.*** hydropathy, जल-चिकित्सा।

waterfall (वॉटरफ़ॉल) ***n.*** a steep descent of water from height, जलप्रपात।

water lily ***n.*** an acquatic plant having flowers that float on the surface of water, कमल।

water line ***n.*** the line along which the surface of water touches a ship's side, जल-रेखा।

W

waterlogged (वॉटरलॉग्ड) ***adj.*** filled with water, जिसमें जल भरा हो, जलाक्रांत।

watermark (वाटरमार्क) ***n.*** a mark impressed on paper (visible when the paper is held up to light), वाटरमार्क, जलचिह्न।

watermelon (वॉटरमेलन) ***n.*** a large edible fruit with a sweet pulp, तरबूज।

watermill ***n.*** a mill driven by water power, पनचक्की।

waterproof (वॉटरप्रूफ़) ***adj.*** not penet-rable by water, जलसह, वाटरप्रूफ़।

watershed (वॉटरशेड) ***n.*** 1. a ridge that divides two rivers, जल-विभाजक। 2. a turning point, मोड़।

watertight (वॉटरटाइट) ***adj.*** not permitting water to come in or out, जलरोधी।

waterworks (वॉटरवर्क्स) ***n.*** (plu.) an establishment for supplying water to the community, जल-कल।

watery (वॉटरी) ***adj.*** 1. containing or relating to water, जलीय, पनीला। 2. (of colours) pale, पीला। 3. lifeless, निर्जीव।

watt (वॉट) ***n.*** unit of electric power, विद्युत शक्ति की इकाई, वाट।

wattle (वॉटल) ***n.*** 1. a framework of bamboos, twigs, branches etc., for use in construction, ठट्ठर। 2. a loose fleshy fold of skin hanging from the neck of certain birds, ललटी।

wave (वेव) ***n.*** 1. a ridge moving along the surface of water, लहर, तरंग। 2. a curve or succession of curves in or on a surface, लहरिया, तरंगावली। 3. a curve in the hair, बालों का घुमाव, घूँघर। 4. a wavelike motion, (ताप, प्रकाश, ध्वनि आदि की) तरंग। 5. a sudden rise, बढ़ाव, बाढ़। 6. a spell, दौर। ***v.*** 1. to move like waves, तरंगित होना। 2. to move to and fro, लहराना, फहरना या फहराना। 3. to move (one's hand, हाथ) हिलाना या (इस प्रकार) संकेत करना। 4. to set waves in, to make wavy, लहरिएदार बनाना।

waveband (वेवबैन्ड) ***n.*** a range of radio frequencies, तरंग-पट्टी, वेवबैंड।

wavelength (वेवलेन्थ) ***n.*** the distance between corresponding points in a sound wave, तरंगदैर्घ्य, वेवलेंग्थ।

wavelet (वेवलिट) ***n.*** a small wave, छोटी लहर, लहरी, उर्मि।

waver (वेवर) ***v.*** 1. to be unable to decide, अनिश्चय की स्थिति में होना, विचलित होना। 2. to quiver or lurch, काँपना या डगमगाना।

wavy (वेवी) ***adj.*** 1. full of waves, लहराता हुआ, तरंगित। 2. set in waves, घुँघराला। 3. of wavelike curves, लहरिएदार।

wax[1] (वैक्स) ***n.*** 1. a substance secreted by bees and used by them for constructing a honeycomb, beewax, मोम। 2. a waxlike susbstance obtained from petroleum, मोम। ***v.*** 1. to rub or polish with wax, मोम से रगड़ना, मोम से पालिश करना। 2. to coat with wax, मोम की परत चढ़ाना, मोम करना, या लगाना।

wax[2] ***v.*** to increase gradually in size, numbers, quantity, prosperity etc., बढ़ना, बढ़ोतरी होना।

waxwork (वैक्सवर्क) ***n.*** a figure or effigy made of wax, मोमी प्रतिमा, मोम का पुतला।

waxy (वैक्सी) ***adj.*** 1. made of wax, मोम का बना। 2. covered with wax, मोमी।

way (वे) ***n.*** 1. a thoroughfare for travel or transportation, path, road, पथ, रास्ता, मार्ग। 2. a manner or method of doing something, ढंग, पद्धति, तरीक़ा। 3. room enough to pass or proceed, जगह, रास्ता। 4. distance, दूरी, फ़ासला। 5. a specific direction, कोई या विशिष्ट दिशा। 6. a custom, रिवाज, प्रथा। 7. a state, condition, अवस्था, स्थिति। 8. a particular aspect of something, पहलू, पक्ष, दृष्टि। ☐ **be in a family way**, गर्भवती होना; **be in the way**, बाधक होना, रास्ते का काँटा होना; **by the way,** ऐसे ही, वैसे ही, यों ही; **go out of one's way**, सही या उचित रास्ते से हटकर काम करना, सामान्य से भिन्न आचरण करना; **in the way**, बाधक होनेवाला, रोड़ा; **make way**, रास्ता या जगह बनाना, रास्ता या जगह निकालना।

waybill (वेबिल) ***n.*** a paper giving a list of the goods carried by a transport vehicle, मार्ग-पत्रक।

wayfarer (वेफ़ेअरर) ***n.*** a traveller especially on foot, यात्री, पर्यटक, बटोही।

waylay (वेले) ***v.*** (waylaid, waylaying) to lie in wait for and attack, घात में बैठना, रास्ते में रोककर लूट लेना।

wayside (वेसाइड) ***n.*** the side of a road, सड़क का किनारा।

wayward (वेवर्ड) ***adj.*** fickle or erratic, ढुलमुल, चंचल, अस्थिर।

we (वी) ***pron.*** 1. used to refer to the speaker or writer and another or others, हम, हम लोग। 2. used instead of I, 'मैं' के लिए प्रयुक्त।

weak (वीक) ***adj.*** 1. lacking physical or mental strength or vigour, कमज़ोर, निर्बल, अशक्त। 2. not forceful, निस्तेज, दुर्बल, लचर 3. faint or feeble, हलका, मंद, क्षीण। 4. dilute, पतला, पनीला। 5. (of verbs) forming the past tense and past participle forms by means of ed, d or t suffixes, निर्बल।

weaken (वीकन) ***v.*** 1. to become weak, कमज़ोर हो जाना। 2. to make weak, कमज़ोर कर देना।

weakness (वीकनिस) ***n.*** 1. the quality or state of being weak, कमज़ोरी, दुर्बलता। 2. a weak point, failing, कमज़ोरी, कमी, अवगुण। 3. a special fondness or liking, चाहत, कमज़ोरी।

weal (वील) ***n.*** a raised mark on the skin produced by a blow, साँट, नील।

wealth (वेल्थ) ***n.*** 1. a great quantity of money and valuable possessions, धन-संपत्ति, धन-दौलत। 2. a great quantity, प्रचुरता, प्राचुर्य, बहुतायत।

wealthy (वेल्थी) ***adj.*** rich, अमीर, धनी।

wean (वीन) ***v.*** 1. to cause (a young mammal) to give up sucking, दूध छुड़ाना, स्तनपान छुड़ाना। 2. to cause to give up (a former habit, पुरानी आदत) छुड़ाना।

weapon (वेपन) ***n.*** 1. an instrument or object used to attack or to defend oneself from attack, अस्त्र-

W

शस्त्र, हथियार। 2. a means of getting the better of someone, अस्त्र।

wear[1] (विअर) *v.* (wore; worn, wearing) 1. to put on (a garment, कोट, कमीज़, वस्त्र, टोप आदि) पहनना, धारण करना। 2. to endure continued use, चलना, ख़ूब चलना। 3. (to cause) to deteriorate by long hard use, घिसना, घिस डालना। 4. to pass gradually, धीरे-धीरे बीतना, व्यतीत होना। ☐ **wear down,** पराभूत कर देना, प्रतिरोध या दबाव से शिथिल कर देना; **wear off,** लुप्त होना या करना, उड़ जाना या उड़ा देना; **wear out,** (i) घिस जाना या घिस डालना, (ii) थककर चूर हो जाना।

wear[2] *n.* 1. the act of wearing or the state of being worn, पहनने की क्रिया या पहने होने की अवस्था, पहनाव। 2. clothing, पोशाक, परिधान। 3. gradual deterioration or damage resulting from use or attrition, घिसाव, छीज। 4. the capacity to resist the effects of constant use, टिकाऊपन।

wear and tear *n.* damage or depreciation sustained as a result of ordinary use, टूट-फूट, कट-फट, क्षय, छीजन।

weariness (विअरिनिस) *n.* tiredness, थकावट, थकान।

wearisome (विअरिसम) *adj.* 1. causing fatigue, थकानेवाला, थकाऊ। 2. boring, उबाऊ।

weary (विअरी) *adj.* 1. tired, थका हुआ, श्रांत। 2. tiring, थकानेवाला। 3. tired of something, ऊबा हुआ। 4. dispirited, उदासीन। *v.* 1. to make weary, थका या ऊबा देना। 2. to become weary, थक या ऊब जाना।

weather (वेदर) *n.* the condition of the atmosphere of a particular place and time, मौसम, ऋतु। ☐ **under the weather,** अस्वस्थ। *v.* 1. to undergo changes due to the action of the weather, वातावरण या मौसम से प्रभावित होना। 2. to pass safely through, सकुशल पार होना, झेलना और बचकर निकल आना।

weather-beaten (वेदर-बीटन) *adj.* damaged by exposure to weather, धूप, बरसात, ठंड आदि से जो ख़राब हो गया हो।

weather-cock (वेदर-कॉक) *n.* a blade or plate in the shape of a cock that indicates wind direction, वायुदिशासूचक।

weave (वीव) *v.* (wove/weaved, woven, weaving) 1. to form (a fabric) by interlacing woof and warp threads on a loom, बुनना, बुनाई करना। 2. to spin or form (a cobweb, जाला) बुनना। 3. to contrive, गढ़ना, रचना। 4. to move in a zigzag course, टेढ़े-मेढ़े चलना। *n.* the act, process or pattern of weaving, बुनाई, बुनावट।

weaver (वीवर) *n.* one whose occupation is weaving, बुनकर, जुलाहा।

weaverbird (वीवरबर्ड) *n.* a bird that builds a nest of interlaced vegetation, बया पक्षी।

web (वेब) *n.* 1. a mesh of fine strands made by a spider, मकड़ी का जाला। 2. a membrane connecting the toes of duck, frogs etc., झिल्ली। 3. any intricate structure, जटिल या पेचीदी रचना।

webbed (वेब्ड) ***adj.*** having the digits (of the feet) connected by a membrane, जालपाद।

wed (वेड) ***v.*** (wed/ wedded, wedding) 1. to marry, विवाह करना। 2. to bind or unite, संयुक्त करना, जोड़ना।

wedding (वेडिंग) ***n.*** the marriage ceremony, विवाह की रस्म, विवाहोत्सव।

wedge (वेज) ***n.*** a piece of wood or metal that can be driven between the tightening, splitting etc., पच्चर, फन्नी। ***v.*** 1. to tighten by using a wedge, फन्नी लगाना, पच्चर जड़ना। 2. to split with a wedge, पच्चर लगाकर अलग-अलग करना।

wedlock (वेडलॉक) ***n.*** the state of being married, विवाहित अवस्था, वैवाहिक बंधन।

Wednesday (वेन्ज़डे) ***n.*** the day of the week following Tuesday, बुधवार।

wee[1] (वी) ***adj.*** very small, अत्यंत छोटा, लघु।

wee[2] ***v.*** = wee-wee.

weed (वीड) ***n.*** 1. a wild and useless plant that grows among cultivated plants, घास-पात, खर-पतवार। 2. a thin unattractive person, सींक-सलाई। ***v.*** to remove weed from, निराई करना, निराना। □ **weed out,** निकाल बाहर करना।

week (वीक) ***n.*** a period of seven successive days, सप्ताह, हफ़्ता।

weekday (वीकडे) ***n.*** a day other than Sunday, सोम से शनि तक का कोई दिन।

weekend (वीकएन्ड) ***n.*** the period from Friday night or Saturday night to Monday morning, शुक्र या शनि की रात से सोम की सुबह तक की अवधि, सप्ताहांत।

weekly (वीकली) ***adj.*** occurring, happening or payable once a week, साप्ताहिक। ***adv.*** once a week, every week, हर सप्ताह, प्रति सप्ताह। ***n.*** a weekly newspaper or magazine, साप्ताहिक।

weeny (वीनी) ***adj.*** very small, अत्यंत लघु, बहुत छोटा, नन्हा।

weep (वीप) ***v.*** (wept, weeping) 1. to shed tears, आँसू बहाना, रोना। 2. to exude a watery fluid, (फोड़े में से) मवाद निकलना। ***n.*** a spell of weeping, रुदन, रुलाई।

weevil (वीविल) ***n.*** a small beetle feeding on plants and plant products, घुन।

wee-wee (वी-वी) ***v.*** to urinate, मूतना, पेशाब करना। (बच्चों के लिए प्रयुक्त)

weft (वेफ़्ट) ***n.*** crosswise threads of the fabric, बाना।

weigh (वे) ***v.*** 1. to measure the heaviness of an object by means of scales or a balance, तौलना, वज़न करना। 2. to have weight, वज़न होना, भार होना। 3. to ponder or consider carefully, विचार करना, महत्त्व आँकना। 4. to be influential, प्रभावी होना। 5. to be burdensome, भार होना।

weighbridge (वेब्रिज) ***n.*** a platform for weighing vehicles, काँटा, तुला-चौकी।

weighing machine ***n.*** a machine for weighing, तुला, काँटा।

weight (वेट) 1. the amount that something weighs, वज़न, भार, गुरुत्व। 2. a unit or system of units by

W

which weight is measured, बाट-माप, बाट-माप प्रणाली। 3. a piece of metal, stone etc., used in weighing, बाट, बटखरा। 4. a burden, बोझ, भार। 5. importance, महत्त्व। 6. great force or influence, प्रभाव। ***v.*** 1. to add weight to, भार डालना या वज़न बढ़ाना। 2. to overburden or oppress, बहुत अधिक लाद देना, दबा देना। 3. to weigh, तौलना।

weighty (वेटी) ***adj.*** 1. heavy, भारी, वज़नदार, वज़नी। 2. burdensome, बोझिल, भारी। 3. important, महत्त्वपूर्ण, वज़नी।

weir (विअर) ***n.*** a small dam, छोटा बाँध।

weird (विअर्ड) ***adj.*** 1. strange, odd, विचित्र, अजीब। 2. mysterious, supernatural, रहस्यपूर्ण, लोकोत्तर।

welcome (वेल्कम) ***v.*** 1. to greet the arrival (of a guest, अतिथि का) स्वागत करना, अगवानी करना। 2. to greet hospitably and with courtesy, आदर-सत्कार करना, आवभगत करना। ***n.*** 1. the act of greeting (a guest, अतिथि का) स्वागत, अभिनंदन। 2. the act of receiving a guest hospitably, स्वागत, आदर-सत्कार, आवभगत। ***adj.*** 1. gladly accepted or received, ख़ुशी-ख़ुशी अपनाया या ग्रहण किया हुआ। 2. bringing pleasure, सुखद, सुखदायक। ***interj.*** used to express a greeting to a guest upon his arrival, आपका स्वागत।

weld (वेल्ड) ***v.*** 1. to join metal pieces by heating, hammering or pressure, झलाई करना, वेल्ड करना। 2. to unite, जोड़ना, एक करना। ***n.*** a joint made by welding, जोड़।

welder (वेल्डर) ***n.*** one who welds, झलाईगर, वेल्डर।

welfare (वेल्फ़ेअर) ***n.*** well being, भलाई, कल्याण, हित।

welfare state ***n.*** कल्याणकारी राज्य।

well[1] (वेल) ***n.*** 1. a pit below the earth surface to obtain water, oil, gas etc., कुआँ, कूप। 2. a spring or fountain, सोता, झरना। 3. a deep enclosed space for a staircase or elavator, कूपक। ***v.*** to rise up or gush, ऊपर उठना, उमड़ पड़ना, बह निकलना।

well[2] ***adj.*** (better, best) 1. in good health, स्वस्थ। 2. in a good condition, ठीक-ठाक, ठीक। ***adv.*** 1. in a good or proper manner, thoroughly, अच्छी तरह से, सही ढंग से, भली-भाँति। 2. skillfully, कुशलता से। 3. satisfactorily, संतोषजनक ढंग से। 4. carefully, सावधानी से। 5. kindly, favourably, उदारतापूर्वक, कृपापूर्वक, दयाभाव से। 6. perfectly, पूरी तरह से। 7. sufficiently, पर्याप्त मात्रा में। 8. too much, बहुत अधिक। ***interj.*** an exclamation used to express surprise, relief or resignation, अच्छा! ओह! भला!

well-appointed (वेल-अपॉइन्टिड) ***adj.*** excellently equipped, सुसज्जित।

well-being (वेल-बींग) ***n.*** the state of being healthy, happy or prosperous, स्वस्थ, सुखी या समृद्ध होने की अवस्था, संपन्नता, सुख-समृद्धि।

well-disposed (वेल-डिस्पोज़्ड) ***adj.*** favourable, अनुकूल।

well done (वेल डन) ***interj.*** an exclamation of approval of another's action, बहुत अच्छा! शाबाश!

W

well-founded (वेल-फ़ाउन्डिड) ***adj.*** based on facts, तथ्यों पर आधारित, सु-आधारित।

well-heeled (वेल-हील्ड) ***adj.*** rich, धनी।

well-intentioned (वेल-इन्टेन्शन्ड) ***adj.*** having good intentions, नेकनीयत।

well-knit (वेलनिट) ***adj.*** having a compact body, सुगठित।

well-meaning (वेल-मीनिंग) ***adj.*** done with good intentions, नेकनीयती से किया जानेवाला, सदाशयपूर्ण।

well-nigh (वेल-नाइ) ***adv.*** almost, क़रीब-क़रीब।

well-ordered (वेल-आर्डर्ड) ***adj.*** carefully arranged, सुव्यवस्थित।

well-preserved (वेल-प्रीज़र्व्ड) ***adj.*** of good condition inspite of age, सुस्थित, स्वस्थ।

well-reasoned (वेल-रीज़न्ड) ***adj.*** based on clear reasoning, सुविचारित।

well-spoken (वेल-स्पोकन) ***adj.*** 1. properly spoken, सुकथित। 2. speaking in a polite way, मृदुभाषी।

well-to-do (वेल-टु-डू) ***adj.*** well-off, समृद्ध, संपन्न, धनी।

well-wisher (वेल-विशर) ***n.*** one who wishes well to another, शुभचिंतक, हितैषी।

welsh ***v.*** (वेल्श) 1. to cheat, ठगना, धोखा देना। 2. to fail to fulfil (one's obligation, अपना दायित्व) न निभाना, नटना।

welter (वेल्टर) ***v.*** 1. to roll about, (मिट्टी, दलदल आदि में) लोटना, लोट-पोट होना। 2. to be soaked, भीगा या तर होना, लथ-पथ होना, नहाया होना। ***n.*** 1. turbulence, विक्षुब्ध अवस्था, विक्षोभ। 2. turmoil, होहल्ला, उपद्रव, हंगामा, अशांति। 3. medley, घालमेल।

wend (वेन्ड) ***v.*** 1. to go or proceed, जाना। 2. to travel, यात्रा करना।

went (वेन्ट) ***v.*** p.t. of go.

wept (वेप्ट) ***v.*** p.t. & p.p. of weep.

were (वर) ***v.*** past tense of are, थे।

west (वेस्ट) ***n.*** 1. the direction in which the sun sets, पश्चिम, मग़रब। 2. the western part of something, किसी चीज़ का पश्चिमी भाग। ***adj.*** of the west, western, पश्चिमी। ***adv.*** toward the west, पश्चिम की ओर।

westerly (वेस्टर्ली) ***adj.*** 1. toward the west, पश्चिम की ओर जानेवाला। 2. coming from the west, पश्चिम की ओर से आनेवाला, पश्चिमी, पछुआँ। ***n.*** a westerly wind, पछुआँ हवा।

western (वेस्टर्न) ***adj.*** 1. of the west, पश्चिमी। 2. in the west, पश्चिमी, पाश्चात्य।

westerner (वेस्टर्नर) ***n.*** a native of the west, यूरोपवासी या अमेरिकावासी।

westernize (वेस्टर्नाइज़) ***v.*** to make western in ideas, habits, character etc., पश्चिमी रंग में रँग देना, पाश्चात्यीकरण करना।

westward (वेस्टवर्ड) ***adj.*** in or toward the west, पश्चिमी। ***adv.*** toward the west, पश्चिम की ओर।

wet (वेट) ***adj.*** 1. drenched, गीला, तर, तर-बतर। 2. moistened, नम, आर्द्र। 3. rainy, बरसाती। 4. (a region) permitting the free sale of alcohol, (प्रदेश) जिसमें शराब की खुली बिक्री होती हो। ***n.*** 1. a liquid, तरल पदार्थ, जल। 2. moisture, नमी। ***v.*** 1. to make wet, गीला या तर करना, भिगोना। 2. to become

W

wet, गीला होना, तर होना, भीगना। 3. to urinate, पेशाब करना।

wetland (वेटलैन्ड) ***n.*** a marsh, दलदल।

wet-nurse (वेट-नर्स) ***n.*** a woman who suckles another's child, दूसरे के बच्चे को स्तनपान करानेवाली सेविका, धाय।

we've (वीव) = we have.

whack (वैक) ***v.*** to hit or strike with a sharp resounding blow, तड़ाक से मारना या प्रहार करना। ***n.*** 1. such a blow, तड़ाक से किया हुआ प्रहार। 2. sound made by a whack, तड़ाक।

whacked (वैक्ड) ***adj.*** tired, थका-माँदा।

whale (वेल) ***n.*** a large sea-animal, ह्वेल मछली। □ **a whale of,** बहुत बड़ा तथा प्रभावपूर्ण, विशाल; a whale of a time, बहुत अधिक समय।

wham (वैम) ***n.*** a forceful blow, ज़ोरदार आघात या प्रहार।

wharf (वार्फ़) ***n.*** a place where ships load and unload, घाट, जहाज़-घाट।

wharfage (वार्फ़िज) ***n.*** the charge for this, घाट के उपयोग का किराया, घाट-किराया।

what (वॉट) ***pron.*** 1. which thing, कौन सी चीज़ या बात, क्या? 2. a request for repeating something not heard properly, क्या? 3. that which or the thing that, जो। 4. whatever thing that, कुछ भी। ***adj.*** 1. used to ask for further information, which, which one, क़िस, कौन-सा?; 2. how great or how strange? कितना?, कैसा? 3. the thing or things that, जितना। ***adv.*** to what respect, extent or degree? कैसे? ***interj.*** an exclamation of surprise, अरे! ओह!

whatever (वॉटिवर) ***adj.*** 1. of any kind, हर प्रकार का। 2. of any number, चाहे जितना। ***pron.*** anything, कुछ भी।

whatsoever (वॉटसोएवर) ***adj.*** whatever, चाहे जिस प्रकार का या जितना।

wheat (वीट) ***n.*** a plant and its grain, गेहूँ का पौधा और दाने।

wheedle (वीडल) ***v.*** 1. to coax, फुसलाना, बहका लेना, राजी कर लेना। 2. to obtain by wheedling, ऐंठना, झाँसा देना।

wheel (वील) ***n.*** 1. a circular frame that revolves on axis, पहिया, चक्का। 2. anything resembling this, चक्कर, चाक आदि। 3. motion like that of a wheel, चक्रगति। 4. a turn, घुमाव। ***v.*** 1. to turn on axis, घूमना। 2. to roll on wheels, (पहियों का) चलना, आगे बढ़ना। 3. to whirl around, वृत्ताकार या चक्राकार घूमना। □ **wheel and deal,** अपना हित देखकर काम करना।

wheelbarrow (वीलबैरो) ***n.*** a small vehicle with a single wheel for carrying small loads, एक पहिएवाला ठेला।

wheel-chair (वील-चेअर) ***n.*** a chair mounted on wheels for invalids, पहिएदार कुर्सी।

wheeze (वीज़) ***v.*** to breathe with a whistling sound, इस प्रकार साँस लेना कि 'घर्र-घर्र' की ध्वनि हो। ***n.*** 1. wheezing sound, घर्र-घर्र, घरघराहट। 2. a hackneyed idea or joke, घिसा-पिटा विचार या मज़ाक।

whelk (वेल्क) ***n.*** a shell-fish, शंखमीन।

when (वेन) ***adv.*** 1. at what time? कब? किस समय? किस वक़्त? 2. at the time that, जब। ***n.*** the time, समय, वक़्त।

whence (वेन्स) ***adv.*** from where, कहाँ से।

whenever (वेनेवर) ***adv. & conj.*** at whatever time or occasion, जब, जब-जब।

where (वेअर) ***adv.*** 1. in what palace? कहाँ? 2. toward what place? किधर? 3. to the place in which, जहाँ, जिस जगह। ***pron.*** what place? कौन जगह? कौन-सा स्थान?

whereabouts (वेअरअबाउट्स) ***adv.*** about where? at what location? कहाँ? किस जगह? ***n.*** the location of something or something, पता-ठिकाना, अता-पता।

whereas (वेअरैज़) ***conj.*** 1. it being the fact that, चूँकि, क्योंकि। 2. but on the other hand, जबकि।

whereby (वेअरबाइ) ***adv.*** by which, जिससे, जिसके द्वारा।

whereupon (वेअरअपॉन) ***adv. & conj.*** upon which, जिसपर, किस पर।

wherever (वेअरेवर) ***adv. & conj.*** at whatever place, कहीं भी, जहाँ भी।

wherewithal (वेअरविदॉल) ***n.*** necessary means, आवश्यक साधन, पूँजी, माल।

whet (वेट) ***v.*** (whetted, whetting) 1. to make sharp by rubbing or grinding, (छुरी आदि) तेज़ करना, सान चढ़ाना। 2. to stimulate, उद्दीप्त करना, तेज़ करना, बढ़ाना।

whether (वेदर) ***conj.*** 1. used to introduce an alternative possibility, कि। 2. either, चाहे, या। ☐ **whether or not,**...... या नहीं।

whetstone (वेटस्टोन) ***n.*** a stone used for sharpening cutting tools, सान।

whey (वे) ***n.*** the watery part of the milk which separates from the cheese or curd after coagulation, छेने या दही द्वारा छोड़ा हुआ पानी।

which (विच) ***adj. & pron.*** 1. what particular one or ones of? कौन-सा? कौन? 2. the particular one or ones of, जो। 3. a person or thing previously named or referred to, जो।

whichever (विचेवर) ***adj. & pron.*** any (one or more), कोई या जो, चाहे कोई या जो, कोई भी या जो भी।

whiff (विफ़) ***n.*** 1. a breath or puff, साँस या कश। 2. a blowing, फूँक। 3. a brief passing odour carried in the air, गंध का झोंका।

while (वाइल) ***n.*** time or period, समय, अवधि। ***conj.*** 1. during the time that, जब तक, तब तक। 2. although, यद्यपि। 3. on the other hand, जबकि। ***v.*** to pass (time, समय) गुज़ारना या बिताना।

whim (विम) ***n.*** a sudden fanciful idea, सनक, झक, मौज।

whimper (विम्पर) ***v.*** to make a low whining plaintive sound, रिरियाना, पिनपिनाना, ठिनकना। ***n.*** a whimpering cry, पिनपिनाहट।

whimsical (विम्ज़िकल) ***adj.*** 1. full of whims, सनकी, मौज़ी, तरंगी, ख़ब्ती। 2. fanciful, सनक-भरा। 3. quaint, विचित्र, बेतुका।

whine (वाइन) ***v.*** 1. to express a plaintive high-pitched sound, चीख़ना, चिल्लाना। 2. to utter complainingly, चीख़-चीख़ कर बातें करना, चिल्लपों मचाना। ***n.*** a prolonged high-pitched cry, चीख़, चिल्लाहट, चिल्लपों।

whinny (विनी) ***v.*** (whinnied, whinnying) to neigh, (घोड़े का)

W

हिनहिनाना, हींसना। *n.* a neigh, हिनहिनाहट, हींस।

whip (विप) *n.* 1. a device with a cord and lash used for driving animals or for punishing persons, चाबुक, कोड़ा, हंटर। 2. a stroke with the whip, चाबुक की मार, कशाघात। 3. an official of a political party in the legislature who enforces and maintains party discipline, सचेतक। 4. a kind of dessert, एक प्रकार का मधुर व्यंजन। □ **have the whip hand**, किसी पर पूरा क़ाबू होना। *v.* 1. to strike with a whip, चाबुक मारना, हंटर लगाना। 2. to beat, (क्रीम, अंडे आदि) फेंटना। 3. to defeat, पराजित करना।

whipcord (विपकॉर्ड) *n.* a cord with twisted strands used in whip, कोड़े का बटा हुआ डोरा या पट्टी।

whiplash (विपलैश) *n.* the lash of a whip, चाबुक या कोड़े की साँट।

whirl (वर्ल) *v.* 1. to rotate or revolve, घूमना या घुमाना, चक्कर खाना या खिलाना। 2. to move or be moved at high speed, तेज़ रफ़्तार से चलना या चलाना। *n.* 1. whirling motion, rotation, चक्राकार गति, चक्र, चक्कर, फेरी। 2. a bustling activity, भाग-दौड़, गहमागहमी। 3. a state of confusion, विभ्रम।

whirlpool (वर्लपूल) *n.* a powerful current of water whirling in a circle, भँवर, जलावर्त।

whirlwind (वर्लविन्ड) *n.* a column of air whirling violently, चक्रवात, बवंडर, बगूला।

whirr (वर्र) *v.* 1. to flutter, (पंख) फड़फड़ाना। 2. to buzz, भनभन करना।

whisk (विस्क) *v.* 1. to brush or sweep, झाड़ू देना, सफ़ाई करना। 2. to go rapidly, तेज़ी से जाना। 3. to convey rapidly, तेज़ी से ले जाना। 4. to whip, (अंडे) फेंटना। *n.* 1. a broom, झाड़ू। 2. a rapid movement or speed, तेज़ गति। 3. a bundle made of peacock feathers, मोरछल। 4. an instrument for beating eggs, अंडे फेंटने का उपकरण।

whisker (विस्कर) *n.* one of the long stiff hair that grows near the mouth of rats, cats, lions etc., चूहे, बिल्ली, शेर आदि के मुँह पर का कड़ा लंबा बाल।

whiskered (विस्कर्ड) ***adj.*** having whiskers, जिसके गलमुच्छे हों।

whiskers (विस्कर्स) *n.* (plu.) the beard on the cheeks, गलमुच्छे।

whiskey, whisky (विस्की) *n.* a strong alcoholic liquor made by distilling fermented cereals, ह्विस्की, विस्की।

whisper (विस्पर) *v.* 1. to speak in a very low tone, खुसुर-फुसुर करना, फुसफुसाना। 2. to tell secretly and privately, कानाफूसी करना। *n.* 1. the act of whispering or something whispered, फ़ुसफुसाहट, कानाफूसी। 2. a hint, संकेत। 3. a rumour, अफ़वाह, किंवदंती।

whistle (विसल) *v.* 1. to produce a shrill sound by forcing air through an aperture formed by the lips, सीटी बजाना। 2. to produce a shrill sound by blowing a pipe or instrument, सीटी बजाना। *n.* 1. an instrument for making a shrill sound, सीटी। 2. a whistling sound, सीटी।

whit (विट) ***n.*** a smallest bit, लवलेश, ज़रा-सा टुकड़ा।

white (वाइट) ***adj.*** 1. having the colour of snow, common salt or lime, सफ़ेद, श्वेत। 2. having white skin, गोरा, सफ़ेद चमड़ीवाला। 3. light-coloured, pale, पीला, विवर्ण। 4. pure, शुद्ध। 5. honest, ईमानदार, सच्चा। ***n.*** 1. a white colour, सफ़ेद रंग। 2. white fluid of a bird's egg, अंडे की सफ़ेदी। ***v.*** to make or become white, सफ़ेद बनाना या बन जाना।

white ant ***n.*** a termite, दीमक।

white-collar (वाइट-कॉलर) ***n.*** an office worker, दफ़्तर का बाबू, सफ़ेदपोश बाबू।

white elephant ***n.*** a useless possession, the upkeep of which is very expensive, सफ़ेद हाथी।

white lie ***n.*** a harmless lie, ऐसा झूठ जो हानिकर न हो, सफ़ेद झूठ।

whiten (वाइटन) ***v.*** to make or become white, सफ़ेद बनना या बनाना।

white paper ***n.*** an official government report, आधिकारिक सरकारी रिपोर्ट, श्वेत-पत्र।

whitewash (वाइटवाश) ***n.*** 1. a substance used for whitening walls and ceilings, चूना, खड़िया आदि। 2. an act of concealing of flaws or defects, लीपापोती। ***v.*** 1. to cover with whitewash, सफ़ेदी करना, चूना करना, कलई करना। 2. to conceal, (दोष आदि) ढकना या छिपाना।

whitewashing (वाइटवाशिंग) ***n.*** the act of one who whitewashes, पुताई, कलई।

whither (विदर) ***adv. & conj.*** to what place? कहाँ? किधर?

whittle (विटल) ***v.*** 1. to cut strips from the wood with a knife, छुरी से लकड़ी में से पट्टियाँ या खपचियाँ निकालना। 2. to make or shape by paring or shaving, छीलना या तराशना, छील या तराशकर बनाना। 3. to wear away gradually, छीजना, धीरे-धीरे क्षय होना।

whiz (विज़) ***v.*** 1. to make a hissing or buzzing sound, सनसन या भनभन ध्वनि करना। 2. to move with a hissing sound, सनसन या भनभन करते हुए निकल जाना। ***n.*** a hissing or buzzing sound, सनसन, भनभन।

whiz kid ***n.*** very brilliant and pushing person, अत्यंत प्रतिभावान तथा ऊर्जस्वी व्यक्ति।

who (हू) ***pron.*** 1. What person? Which person? कौन? 2. the particular person, जो।

who'd (हूड) = who had or who would.

whoever (हूएवर) ***pron.*** whatever person, जो कोई, जो भी।

whole (होल) ***adj.*** 1. complete, entire, पूर्ण, समूचा, सारा, पूरा। 2. intact, unbroken, अखंड, अविभाजित, समूचा। ***n.*** a thing complete in itself, a complete entity, समष्टि, संपूर्णता। ☐ **on the whole,** (i) सब मिलाकर, (ii) सामान्यत:।

wholehearted (होलहार्टिड) ***adj.*** done with total sincerity, हार्दिक।

whole number ***n.*** a number containing no fraction, पूर्णांक।

wholesale (होलसेल) ***n.*** the business of selling goods in large quantities, थोक व्यापार। ***adj.*** 1. of such business, थोक व्यापार-संबंधी। 2. on a large scale, बड़े पैमाने

W

पर होनेवाला, थोक में होनेवाला। ***adv.*** 1. in large quantities, बड़े पैमाने पर, थोक में। 2. without discrimination, अंधाधुंध।

wholesaler (होलसेलर) ***n.*** a person engaged in wholesale trade, थोक व्यापारी।

wholesome (होलसम) ***adj.*** 1. good for health, स्वास्थ्य के लिए अच्छा, पुष्टिकर, पौष्टिक। 2. good for mental or moral well-being, हितकर।

wholly (होली) ***adv.*** entirely, पूर्ण रूप से।

whom (हूम) ***pron.*** the objective case of who, किसको, जिसको।

whooping cough ***n.*** (हूपिन्ग कफ़) a disease with repeated attack of coughing, काली खाँसी।

whopping (हॉपिन्ग) ***adj.*** large, बहुत बड़ा, दीर्घाकार।

whore (होर) ***n.*** a prostitute, वेश्या, रंडी।

whorl (वॉर्ल) ***n.*** 1. a ring of leaves around a stem, भ्रमि। 2. a ring of petals around a central point, भ्रमि।

whose (हूज़) ***pron. & adj.*** of whom, किसका, जिसका।

whosoever (हूसोएवर) ***pron.*** any person, जो कोई भी, जो भी।

why (वाइ) ***adv. & conj.*** 1. for what reason? क्यों? किसलिए? किस कारण से? 2. for the particular reason, जिस कारण से। ***interj.*** an expression for surprise, क्यों!

wick (विक) ***n.*** a cord or tape in the oil lamp, candle etc., बत्ती।

wicked (विकिड) ***adj.*** 1. bad, mischievous or corrupt, दुष्ट, भ्रष्ट। 2. immoral or unjust, अनैतिक या अन्यायपूर्ण। 3. mischievous, शरारती, नटखट।

wicker (विकर) ***n.*** 1. a thin flexible twig, पतली टहनी। 2. a splint, खपची।

wickerwork (विकरवर्क) ***n.*** a thing made of flexible twigs, पतली टहनियों या खपचियों की बनी टोकरी, कुर्सी आदि।

wicket (विकिट) ***n.*** 1. a small door within a larger one, बड़े फाटक में का छोटा दरवाज़ा। 2. in cricket, a set of three stumps struck in the ground, विकेट, यष्टित्रयी। 3. the strip of ground between the two sets of stumps, pitch, विकेट, खेल-पट्टी।

wide (वाइड) ***adj.*** 1. measuring much from side to side, चौड़ा। 2. of a specified extent from side to side, चौड़ा, विस्तृत। 3. far, apart, दूर का, दूरस्थ। ***n.*** in cricket, a delivered ball that is outside the batsman's reach, वाइड बॉल।

wide-awake ***adj.*** fully awake, पूर्ण रूप से जाग्रत, चौकन्ना, चौकस।

widen (वाइडन) ***v.*** to make or become wide, विस्तृत होना या करना, व्यापक होना या बनाना।

widespread (वाइडस्प्रेड) ***adj.*** found or extending over a wide area or region, दूर तक फैला हुआ, दूर-दूर तक प्राप्त, व्याप्त।

widow (विडो) ***n.*** a woman whose husband has died and who has not remarried, विधवा, बेवा, राँड।

widower (विडोअर) ***n.*** a man whose wife has died and who has not remarried, विधुर, रँडुआ।

width (विड्थ) ***n.*** 1. wideness, चौड़ाई, विस्तार। 2. a fabric that has a specified width, अर्ज़।

wield (वील्ड) ***v.*** 1. to use or handle skilfully, कुशलतापूर्वक प्रयोग करना या काम में लाना। 2. to show one's skill (in handling a weapon, शस्त्र को) चमकाना।

wife (वाइफ़) ***n.*** a woman to whom a man is married, पत्नी, धर्मपत्नी।

wig (विग) ***n.*** a covering of artificial or human hair for adornment, विग, केशिका, नक़ली बाल। ***v.*** to cover with a wig, विग लगाना।

wiggle (विगल) ***v.*** to move or cause to move from side to side, डोलना या डुलाना, हिलना-डुलना या हिलाना-डुलाना। ***n.*** a wiggling movement, हिलना-डुलना या हिलाना-डुलाना।

wild (वाइल्ड) ***adj.*** 1. living in natural state, not tamed or domesticated, जंगली, वन्य, बनैला। 2. occurring or growing without cultivation, not cultivated, जंगली। 3. unruly, uncivilized, savage, उद्धत, असभ्य या बर्बर, जंगली, वहशी। 4. lacking restraint or control, जंगली, नियंत्रणविहीन, उच्छृंखल। 5. very eager, excited or enthusiastic, उद्विग्न या बावला। 6. random, अनुमानित। ***adv.*** in a wild manner, असभ्यतापूर्वक; बर्बरता से। ***n.*** a desolate or uninhabited region, उजाड़, निर्जन प्रदेश।

wildcat strike (वाइल्डकैट स्ट्राइक) ***n.*** an unauthorised strike, अनधिकृत हड़ताल।

wilderness (विल्डरनिस) ***n.*** a desolate or uninhabited area, उजाड़ या निर्जन स्थान।

wildfire (वाइल्डफ़ाइर) ***n.*** a fire that spreads rapidly, जंगल की आग, दावानल।

wildgoose chase ***n.*** a hopeless pursuit or search, व्यर्थ की खोज-बीन, बेकार का पीछा।

wildlife (वाइल्डलाइफ़) ***n.*** 1. wild animals collectively, वन्य पशु। 2. wild plants collectively, जंगली पेड़-पौधे।

wile (वाइल) ***n.*** 1. a trick, चाल, छल, दाँव-पेंच। 2. a seductive trick, अठखेली, चोंचला या नख़रा। ***v.*** 1. to seduce, बहकाना, फुसलाना। 2. to entice, लुभाना।

wilful (विलफ़ुल) ***adj.*** 1. self-willed, मनमाना आचरण करनेवाला, हठी। 2. intentional, जान-बूझकर किया जानेवाला।

will[1] (विल) ***n.*** 1. a wish, desire, इच्छा, चाह। 2. a request or command, प्रार्थना या आदेश। 3. determination, दृढ़ता, इच्छा-शक्ति। 4. disposition or attitude toward others, दूसरों के प्रति होनेवाली भावना। 5. a document in which person's wishes are expressed about disposal of his property after his death, वसीयत, वसीयतनामा। ***v.*** 1. to wish or intend, चाहना, इरादा करना। 2. to bequeath by will, वसीयत करना।

will[2] auxiliary verb. (p.t. would) used to express future tense, willingness, resolution, obligation, command, ability, probability, expectation, etc., होगा।

willing (विलिंग) ***adj.*** 1. favourably inclined, राज़ी, इच्छुक, तैयार। 2. given or performed willingly, सहर्ष दिया या किया जानेवाला, इच्छित।

willingness (विलिंगनिस) ***n.*** 1. wish, इच्छा। 2. consent, सहमति। 3. curiosity, उत्सुकता।

W

will-o-the-wisp (विलोदविस्प) *n.* 1. a phosphorescent light, अगिया बेताल। 2. a hope that can never be realized, झूठी आशा, दुराशा।

willow (विलो) *n.* a tree or shrub with very flexible branches, बेंत, सरपत।

will-power (विल-पाउअर) *n.* firmness of will, संकल्प-शक्ति, इच्छा-शक्ति।

willy-nilly (विली-निली) *adv.* willingly or unwillingly, चाहे-अनचाहे।

wilt (विल्ट) *v.* 1. to become drooping, (पौधों का) सूख जाना, मुरझा जाना। 2. to cause to become drooping, सुखा या मुरझा देना। 3. to lose strength or courage, शिथिल हो या पड़ जाना, निस्तेज हो जाना।

wily (वाइली) *adj.* (wilier, wiliest) cunning, चालाक, धूर्त, चंट।

win (विन) *v.* (won, winning) 1. to gain victory, जीतना, विजय प्राप्त करना। 2. to be successful (in a competition, प्रतियोगिता में) सफलता प्राप्त करना, सफल होना। 3. to obtain (by luck or perseverance, भाग्य या परिश्रम से) प्राप्त करना। *n.* 1. victory, विजय। 2. success, सफलता।

wince (विन्स) *v.* 1. to draw back, पीछे हटना। 2. to shrink, सिकुड़ जाना। 3. to start, चौंक उठना, दहशत खाना।

winch (विन्च) *n.* a machine which lifts or pull heavy loads by means of cable, विंच मशीन।

wind[1] (विन्ड) *n.* 1. a current of air, हवा, पवन। 2. gas forming in the stomach, वायु, बाई, वात। 3. breath, श्वास। 4. a wind instrument, फूँककर बजाया जानेवाला बाजा। □ **get wind of,** भनक लगना; **in the wind,** जो भासित या घटित होनेवाला हो; **take the wind out of one's sails,** हवा निकाल देना, मायूस कर देना। *v.* 1. to blow, (बाजा) बजाना। 2. to detect by the scent, गंध के द्वारा पता लगाना।

wind[2] (वाइन्ड) *v.* (wound, winding) 1. to turn or be turned, घुमाना या घुमाया जाना। 2. to encircle or coil around some object, लपेटना। 3. to be coiled, लपेटा जाना। 4. to move in a spiral or circular course, टेढ़े-मेढ़े चलना। 5. to tighten the spring (of a clock, घड़ी में) चाबी भरना। 6. to lift by windlass, चरखी से उठाना। □ **wind up,** समापन करना। *n.* 1. the act of winding, घुमाने, लपेटने आदि की क्रिया या भाव। 2. a turn, घुमाव या लपेट।

windfall (विन्डफ़ॉल) *n.* an unexpected piece of good fortune, सौभाग्य से मिली कोई अप्रत्याशित वस्तु या अप्रत्याशित लाभ।

winding (वाइन्डिंग) *adj.* 1. turning, घूमा या लपेटा हुआ। 2. spiral, कुंडलाकार, सर्पिल। *n.* material wound into a coil, लपेटी हुई वस्तु (तार आदि)।

wind instrument *n.* a musical instrument sounded by the breath, फूँककर बजाया जानेवाला बाजा, सुषिर वाद्य।

windmill (विन्डमिल) *n.* a machine driven by the force of wind, पवन-चक्की।

window (विन्डो) *n.* an opening in a building, ship, vehicle etc., for admitting air and light, खिड़की, झरोखा।

window-pane (विन्डो-पेन) *n.* a sheet of glass in a window, खिड़की के पल्ले में लगा शीशा।

windowshop (विन्डो-शॉप) *v.* to look at goods displayed in shop window, दुकान की खिड़की में प्रदर्शित वस्तुओं को देखना।

windpipe (विन्डपाइप) ***n.*** the passage by which air reaches the lungs, श्वासनली।

windscreen (विन्डस्क्रीन) ***n.*** the sheet of glass at the window at the front of a car, truck etc., विंडस्क्रीन, कार आदि का सामने का शीशा।

windward (विन्डवर्ड) ***adj.*** of, situated in or moving toward the quarter from which the wind blows, जिधर से आँधी आ रही हो उस ओर स्थित या बढ़ता हुआ, पवनाभिमुख। ***adv.*** toward the wind, हवा के रुख के उलटे, हवा के विरुद्ध।

wine (वाइन) ***n.*** 1. the fermented juice of grapes or other fruits, मद्य, शराब, मदिरा। 2. dark purplish red colour, गहरा लाल रंग। ***v.*** to provide with wine, मदिरा परोसना या पिलाना।

wing (विन्ग) ***n.*** 1. one of the organs of an insect, bird etc., by which it flies, पर, पंख, डैना। 2. a part of a building attached to the main building, पार्श्व। 3. the side of a playground, पहलू, पार्श्व। 4. a forward player posted in a right or left wing, विंगर, पार्श्व खिलाड़ी। 5. a faction of a political party, पक्ष, गुट। ***v.*** 1. to make one's way swiftly, उड़ते हुए जाना, तेज़ी से जाना। 2. to cause to move swiftly, उड़ाना, तेज़ी से चलाना। 3. to provide wings, पंख लगाना।

wing-footed (विन्ग-फ़ुटिड) ***adj.*** swift, तीव्रगामी, तेज़।

wink (विन्क) ***v.*** 1. to close and open one eye as a hint or signal, कनखी मारना, आँख से इशारा करना। 2. to twinkle, टिमटिमाना।

winner (विनर) ***n.*** 1. one who wins, विजेता। 2. something successful, सफलता प्राप्त करनेवाली बात या चीज़।

winnings (विनिन्ग्स) ***n.*** money won in gambling, जुए में मिली जीत, जीत का माल।

winnow (विनो) ***v.*** to separate grain from chaff by means of wind or current of air, ओसाना।

winsome (विनसम) ***adj.*** charming, सुंदर, आकर्षक, लुभावना।

winter (विन्टर) ***n.*** the coldest season of the year, जाड़े का मौसम, शीत ऋतु। ***v.*** to spend the winter, जाड़ा बिताना या गुज़ारना। ***adj.*** of winter, जाड़े का, शीतकालीन।

wintry (विन्ट्री) ***adj.*** 1. of winter, जाड़े का, शीतकालीन। 2. lacking warmth, फीका, उत्साहविहीन।

wipe (वाइप) ***v.*** 1. to clean by rubbing, साफ़ करना, पोंछना। 2. to remove by wiping, रगड़कर मिटाना, पोंछ डालना। 3. to eradicate, उन्मूलन करना। □ **wipe out,** नष्ट करना, हत्या कर देना। ***n.*** the act of wiping, सफ़ाई, पोंछने की क्रिया या भाव।

wiper (वाइपर) ***n.*** 1. a piece of cloth used for wiping, पोंछा। 2. a device for wiping windspan, मोटर का शीशा साफ़ करने का उपकरण, वाइपर।

wire (वाइर) ***n.*** 1. a flexible strand of metal, तार। 2. a cable, टेलीफ़ोन आदि का तार। 3. a telegram, तार। 4. a piece of wire used to carry electric current, बिजली का तार। ***v.*** 1. to install wiring, तार लगाना, तार की फ़िटिंग करना। 2. to send a telegram, तार भेजना।

W

wire-gauze (वाइर-गॉज़) ***n.*** a material woven of wire, तार-जाली।

wireless (वाइरलिस) ***adj.*** without wires, बेतार। ***n.*** a radio, रेडियो।

wiring (वाइरिन्ग) ***n.*** a system of wires for conducting electricity in a building, वाइरिंग, तार की फ़िटिंग।

wisdom (विज़्डम) ***n.*** 1. understanding of what is true or lasting, ज्ञान। 2. good judgement, common sense, समझदारी।

wisdom tooth ***n.*** the back tooth on each side of each jaw in human beings, अक़्लदाढ़।

wise (वाइज़) ***adj.*** 1. having or showing wisdom, sensible, समझदार, बुद्धिमान, अक़्लमंद। 2. having knowledge, ज्ञानवान, ज्ञानी। 3. rational, युक्तिसंगत।

wisecrack (वाइज़क्रैक) ***n.*** a witty remark, चुटकुला। ***v.*** to make a wisecrack, चुटकुला छोड़ना।

wish (विश) ***n.*** 1. a desire, इच्छा, अभिलाषा। 2. something desired, इच्छित वस्तु। 3. expressed desire for someone's health or welfare, शुभकामना, कामना। ***v.*** 1. to desire, चाहना। 2. to hope or express hope for someone's health or welfare, शुभकामना प्रकट करना, कामना करना।

wishful thinking (विशफ़ुल थिन्किन्ग) ***n.*** a desire not based on facts, कोरी आशा, न पूरी होनेवाली आशा।

wishy-washy (विशी-वाशी) ***adj.*** 1. watery, पतला। 2. indecisive, निश्चयहीन, ढुलमुल। 3. weak, दुर्बल।

wisp (विस्प) ***n.*** 1. small bundle, पूला। 2. anything slender or delicate, नाज़ुक या नरम वस्तु। 3. a flock, झुंड।

wistful (विस्टफ़ुल) ***adj.*** longing sadly or pensively, चिंतातुर, उद्विग्न।

wit (विट) ***n.*** 1. the ability to make clever humourous effect by ironic remarks, विनोद, चोज़, वाग्वैदग्ध्य, वाक्‌चातुर्य। 2. a person possessing such an ability, वाग्विदग्ध, वाक्‌चतुर, हाज़िरजवाब। 3. (plu.) power of thinking and reasoning, युक्ति-कौशल। □ **at one's wit's end,** किंकर्तव्यविमूढ़।

witch (विच) ***n.*** 1. a woman who practices sorcery, टोनहाई, जादूगरनी, डाइन। 2. a fascinatingly attractive woman, मोहिनी।

witchcraft (विचक्राफ़्ट) ***n.*** sorcery, black magic, जादू-टोना।

witch-hunt (विच-हन्ट) ***n.*** a rigorous campaign to uncover subversive political activities, विनाशक राजनीतिक कार्यकलापों का भंडा फोड़ करने का अभियान।

with (विद) ***prep.*** 1. by means of, के द्वारा, से। 2. as a companion of, के साथ। 3. possessing or having, से। 4. on the side of, की तरफ़ से, के साथ। 5. because of, के कारण। 6. in the charge of, के पास। 7. in regard to, से, के प्रति, के विषय में। 8. in opposition to, से, के साथ। 9. in spite of, के बावजूद। 10. into, में। 11. in a manner, से।

withdraw (विदड्रॉ) ***v.*** (withdrew, withdrawn, withdrawing) 1. to draw back, पीछे (की ओर) खींचना। 2. to retreat, पीछे हटना या हटाना। 3. to remove (money from the bank, बैंक से रुपए) निकालना, आहरण करना। 4. to depart from, अलग हो जाना। 5. to recall, वापस लेना। 6. to

detach (oneself, अपने को) अलग कर लेना।

withdrawal (विदड्रॉअल) ***n.*** 1. the act of withdrawing, वापस लेना, वापसी। 2. the act of withdrawing (money, रुपए की) निकासी, आहरण।

withdrawn (विदड्रॉन) ***adj.*** 1. reserved or shy, ग़ैर-मिलनसार या शर्मीला, गुमसुम। 2. secluded or unresponsive, अलग-थलग या चुप्पा।

wither (विदर) ***v.*** 1. to fade or droop, कुम्हला या मुरझा जाना। 2. to disintegrate or decay, विघटित या नष्ट हो जाना। 3. to lose vitality, निस्तेज या शिथिल हो जाना।

withhold (विदहोल्ड) ***v.*** (withheld, withholding) 1. to keep back, रोक रखना। 2. to restrain, नियंत्रित करना।

within (विदिन) ***prep.*** 1. inside or indoors, के अंदर, के भीतर, में। 2. inside the limits of, के अंदर, से कम। ***adv.*** inside, inwardly, अंदर, भीतर।

without (विदाउट) ***prep.*** 1. not having, के बिना। 2. not accompanied by, के बिना। 3. not making use of, के बिना। 4. on the outside, के बाहर। ***adv.*** outside, बाहर।

withstand (विदस्टैन्ड) ***v.*** (withstood, withstanding) 1. to endure successfully, बर्दाश्त कर लेना, झेल लेना। 2. to remain firm, दृढ़ रहना, डटे रहना।

witness (विटनिस) ***n.*** 1. a person who saw or heard and can give a firsthand account of something, गवाह, साक्षी। 2. one who testifies, गवाह, साक्षी। 3. something that serves as evidence, गवाही। ***v.*** to be the witness of, गवाह होना।

witticism (विटिसिज़म) ***n.*** a witty or clever remark, ठिठोली, व्यंग्योक्ति, फब्ती।

witty (विटी) ***adj.*** 1. full of wits, व्यंग्यपूर्ण, मज़ेदार, विनोदपूर्ण। 2. intelligent, बुद्धिमान।

wizard (विज़र्ड) ***n.*** 1. a sorcerer, टोनहाया, ओझा। 2. a magician, जादूगर। 3. a very clever person, अत्यंत चतुर व्यक्ति।

wizened (विज़न्ड) ***adj.*** 1. full of wrinkles, झुर्रियों से भरा। 2. dried up, सूखा हुआ।

wobble (वॉबल) ***v.*** 1. to move unsteadily, लड़खड़ाना, डगमगाना। 2. to tremble or quiver, काँपना। 3. to waver in one's opinion, ढुलमुल होना। ***n.*** 1. a wobbling movement, लड़खड़ाहट। 2. a wobbling sound, कंपित स्वर।

wobbly (वॉब्ली) ***adj.*** shaky, काँपता हुआ, डाँवाँडोल, ढुलमुल।

woe (वो) ***n.*** 1. intense grief, घोर कष्ट, दुख, विषाद, शोक। 2. trouble causing this, विपत्ति। 3. misfortune, दुर्भाग्य।

woebegone (वोबिगॉन) ***adj.*** sad, उदास, ग़मगीन।

woeful (वोफ़ुल) ***adj.*** 1. full of woe, दुखमय। 2. causing sorrow, दुखद। 3. pitiful, दयनीय।

woke (वोक) ***v.*** p.t. of wake.

woken (वोकन) ***v.*** p.p. of wake.

wolf (वुल्फ़) ***n.*** (plu. wolves) 1. a wild animal of dog family, भेड़िया। 2. a greedy person, लोभी व्यक्ति। ***v.*** to eat greedily, भकोसना।

woman (वुमन) ***n.*** (plu. women) an adult female human being, औरत, स्त्री, नारी। ***adj.*** female, मादा, महिला।

womanhood (वुमनहुड) ***n.*** 1. the state of being a woman, स्त्रीत्व, नारीत्व। 2. womankind, स्त्री जाति।

womanize (वुमनाइज़) ***v.*** to seek the company of women, औरतों से यारी गाँठना।

womankind (वुमनकाइन्ड) ***n.*** female human beings collectively, स्त्री/नारी जाति।

womanly (वुमनली) ***adj.*** of or typical of a woman, स्त्रीसुलभ, स्त्रियोचित।

womb (वूम) ***n*** the uterus, गर्भाशय, कोख, बच्चेदानी।

women (विमिन) ***n.*** plu. of woman.

womenfolk (विमिनफ़ोक) ***n.*** (plu.) 1. women, स्त्री जाति। 2. the women of one family, एक परिवार की स्त्रियाँ।

won (वन) ***v.*** p.t & p.p. of win.

wonder (वन्डर) ***n.*** 1. a feeling of astonishment and admiration, अचंभा, आश्चर्य, ताज्जुब। 2. a person, thing or act that arouses such a feeling, चमत्कारिक व्यक्ति, वस्तु या कार्य, चमत्कार। ***v.*** 1. to be amazed, आश्चर्यचकित होना, आश्चर्य होना। 2. to have curiosity about, कुतूहल होना, जिज्ञासा होना।

wonderful (वन्डरफुल) ***adj.*** 1. amazing, अद्भुत, आश्चर्यजनक, चमत्कारपूर्ण। 2. excellent, fine, उत्कृष्ट।

wonderland (वन्डरलैन्ड) ***n.*** a wonderful imaginary realm, स्वप्नजगत्, कल्पनालोक।

wonderstruck (वन्डरस्ट्रक) ***adj.*** amazed, चकित, भौचक्का।

wont (वोन्ट) ***adj.*** accustomed, आदी, अभ्यस्त।

won't (वोन्ट) ***v.*** = will not.

woo (वू) ***v.*** 1. to seek the love (of a woman in order to marry, विवाह के उद्‌देश्य से किसी स्त्री को) राज़ी करना या फुसलाना। 2. to seek to achieve, कुछ प्राप्त करने के लिए सचेष्ट होना।

wood (वुड) ***n.*** 1. the hard fibrous substance of a tree, लकड़ी, काष्ठ, काठ। 2. this substance often cut and dried for use as a fuel or timber, जलाने या इमारत की लकड़ी।

woodblock (वुडब्लॉक) ***n.*** a woodcut, लकड़ी का ठप्पा।

woodcraft (वुडक्राफ़्ट) ***n.*** the art or skill of working with wood, काष्ठशिल्प।

wooded (वुडिड) ***adj.*** covered with trees, full of trees, पेड़ों से भरा।

wooden (वुडन) ***adj.*** 1. made of wood, लकड़ी का बना, लकड़ी का। 2. stiff, कड़ा, कठोर। 3. lifeless, निर्जीव।

woodland (वुडलैन्ड) ***n.*** a land covered with woods, वनस्थली।

woodpecker (वुडपेकर) ***n.*** a bird who taps trees with its bill for insects, कठफोड़वा।

woods (वुड्स) ***n.*** (plu.) an area of land smaller than a forest, छोटा जंगल।

woodwork (वुडवर्क) ***n.*** 1. the art or craft of making things in wood, लकड़ी का काम, काष्ठकर्म। 2. an object made of wood, लकड़ी की बनी वस्तु।

woodworm (वुडवर्म) ***n.*** an insect that bores into wooden objects, घुन।

woody (वुडी) ***adj.*** 1. made of wood, लकड़ी का बना। 2. full of trees, पेड़ों से भरा।

woof (वूफ़) ***n.*** weft, बाना, भरनी।

wool (वुल) ***n.*** 1. the soft hair of

sheep, goat etc., used to make yarn, ऊन। 2. yarn, cloth or clothing made of wool, ऊनी धागा या कपड़ा। ☐ **put the wool over someone's eyes,** दूसरों को अंधा बनाना, धोखा देना।

woollen (वुलन) ***adj.*** made of wool, ऊनी।

woollens (वुलन्ज़) ***v.*** (plu.) woollen cloth or clothing, ऊनी कपड़े।

woolly (वुली) ***adj.*** 1. consisting of wool, ऊनी। 2. resembling wool, ऊनी जैसा। 3. vague, अस्पष्ट। 4. (plu.) garments made of wool, ऊनी वस्त्र।

word (वर्ड) ***n.*** 1. a speech sound or series of speech sounds having meaning, शब्द, लफ़्ज़। 2. this represented by letters, शब्द। 3. an utterance, remark or comment, उक्ति, टिप्पणी। 4. a promise, वचन। 5. an order, आदेश। 6. information, सूचना। 7. news, समाचार।

wording (वर्डिन्ग) ***n.*** the way in which words are used, शब्दविन्यास।

wordy (वर्डी) ***adj.*** verbose, शब्दाडंबरपूर्ण, शब्दबहुल।

wore (वोर) ***v.*** p.t. of wear.

work (वर्क) ***n.*** 1. physical or mental effort directed in doing something, काम, कार्य। 2. employment, काम, नौकरी। 3. something made or done, काम। 4. any literary or musical composition, काम, रचना, कृति। 5. a task or duty, काम, कर्तव्य। 6. (plu.) a workshop, कर्मशाला, कार्यशाला। 7. (plu.) construction work, निर्माण-कार्य। 8. (plu.) mechanism, कल-पुर्ज़े। ***v.*** (worked/wrought, working) 1. to do, make or perform, करना, काम करना। 2. to labour, परिश्रम करना। 3. to be employed, काम पर लगे होना, नौकरी करना। 4. to operate or be in operation, चलाना या चलना, चालू करना या चालू होना। 5. to accomplish, पूरा करना, प्राप्त करना। 6. to make to work, काम करना। 7. to give a form, रूपायित करना।

workable (वर्केबल) ***adj.*** 1. practicable, व्यवहार्य। 2. feasible, साध्य। 3. able to be worked, जिसपर काम किया जा सके।

workbook (वर्कबुक) ***n.*** a manual or instruction book, कार्य-पुस्तक।

workday (वर्कडे) ***n.*** a day on which work is regularly done, कार्यदिवस, कार्यदिन।

worker (वर्कर) ***n.*** 1. a person who works for wages, मज़दूर, श्रमिक, कर्मी, कामगार। 2. an employee, कर्मचारी। 3. a sterile female bee, ant or wasp that performs specialized work, कर्मी मक्खी, चींटी या ततैया।

workhouse (वर्कहाउस) ***n.*** a house where poor jobless workers work in return for food and shelter, काम-घर, दरिद्रालय।

working (वर्किन्ग) ***adj.*** 1. engaged in work, काम में लगा हुआ, कार्यरत, कार्यकारी। 2. busy, व्यस्त। 3. of or for work, काम का, काम में आनेवाला। 4. adequate or satisfactory, उपयुक्त या संतोषजनक, काम-चलाऊ। ***n.*** 1. the act of one who works, कार्य-संचालन। 2. the way a thing works, काम करने का ढंग, कार्यप्रणाली, कार्यविधि।

working class ***n.*** people who earn wages, मज़दूर वर्ग, श्रमिक वर्ग।

working committee ***n.*** the committee of an institution which manages it, कार्य-समिति।

W

working day *n.* a workday, कार्यदिवस, कार्यदिन।

working order *n.* a condition in which a machine works adequately, चालू हालत।

workman (वर्कमैन) *n.* a person who performs labour for wages, कामगार, कारीगर।

workmanship (वर्कमैनशिप) *n.* the skill of a workman, कर्म-कौशल, कारीगरी।

workshop (वर्कशॉप) *n.* 1. a workroom, कार्यकक्ष। 2. a meeting of group of persons for exchange of ideas and mutual benefit, कार्यशाला।

world (वर्ल्ड) *n.* 1. everything in existence, universe, सृष्टि, ब्रह्मांड। 2. the earth as a complete environment, संसार, लोक, जगत्, दुनिया। 3. all the inhabitants of this world, संसार के लोग, मानवजाति। 4. worldly life, सांसारिक या लौकिक जीवन। 5. the state of existence, लोक, दुनिया, संसार। 6. material things and occupations, सांसारिक प्रपंच।

worldly (वर्ल्डली) *adj.* 1. of this world, लौकिक, सांसारिक। 2. not spiritual, material, भौतिक।

worldwide (वर्ल्डवाइड) *adj.* universal, विश्वव्यापक, विश्वव्यापी।

worm (वर्म) *n.* 1. a long slender creeping insect, कीड़ा, कृमि; earthworm, केंचुआ, glowworm, जुगनूँ। 2. a wretched person, नीच या अधम व्यक्ति। 3. a screw thread that resembles a worm, स्क्रूथ्रेड, पेच की चूड़ी। *v.* 1. to move like a worm, रेंगना। 2. to extract (secret information, गुप्त जानकारी) ऐंठना या प्राप्त करना। 3. to free from parasitic worms, कीड़े निकालना।

worn (वोर्न) *v.* p.p. of wear.

worn-out (वोर्न-आउट) *adj.* 1. used until no longer usable, घिसा-फटा, फटा-पुराना, बेकार। 2. exhausted, थका-हारा, थका-माँदा।

worried (वरीड) *adj.* feeling worry, चिंतित, परेशान।

worry (वरी) *v.* 1. to be anxious or uneasy, चिंतित होना, बेचैन होना। 2. to cause to be anxious or worry, चिंतित करना, व्याकुल करना। 3. to trouble or poke, तंग करना, परेशान करना। 4. to bite or tear with the teeth, दाँतों से काटना या फाड़ना। *n.* 1. anxiety, चिंता, परेशानी। 2. something that causes worry, चिंता की बात, परेशान करनेवाली चीज़। 3. troubled state of mind, विकलता, बेचैनी।

worse (वर्स) *adj.* (the comparative of bad) 1. very bad, बहुत बुरा, बदतर। (the comparative form of ill). 2. in bad health, दयनीय अवस्थावाला, दुर्दशाग्रस्त। *adv.* (comparative of badly and ill) in a worse way, बुरी तरह। *n.* something that is worse, और बुरी बात।

worsen (वर्सन) *v.* 1. to become worse, बदतर हो जाना, और बुरा हो जाना। 2. to make worse, बदतर कर देना, और बुरा कर देना।

worship (वर्शिप) *n.* 1. devotion and respect paid to a god or deity, भक्ति, श्रद्धा। 2. ceremonies or prayers displayed, पूजा, उपासना। *v.* 1. to pay worship to, पूजा करना, उपासना करना। 2. to love devotedly, to rever, श्रद्धा निवेदित करना, भक्ति करना।

worshipper (वर्शिपर) ***n.*** one who worships a god or deity, पुजारी, उपासक।

worst (वर्स्ट) ***adj.*** the superlative of bad, most bad, सबसे बुरा, बदतरीन। ***adv.*** in the most bad manner, बहुत ही बुरी तरह से। ***n.*** the worst part, state or thing, सबसे बुरी बात या अवस्था। ☐ **get the worst of,** हार मान लेना।

worsted (वर्स्टिड) ***n.*** a closely twisted thread made from long-staple fibres, ख़ूब बटा हुआ बढ़िया धागा।

worth (वर्थ) ***n.*** 1. value, price, मूल्य, क़ीमत। 2. importance, महत्त्व। 3. wealth, धन। ***prep.*** & ***adj.*** 1. having a value of, के मूल्य का। 2. deserving, के योग्य।

worthless (वर्थलिस) ***adj.*** 1. having no worth, valueless, किसी काम का नहीं, व्यर्थ, बेकार। 2. of no use, निकम्मा (व्यक्ति)। 3. without importance, महत्त्वहीन।

worthwhile (वर्थवाइल) ***adj.*** 1. sufficiently important, काफ़ी महत्त्वपूर्ण। 2. sufficiently valuable, काफ़ी क़ीमती। 3. doable, करने योग्य।

worthy (वर्दी) ***adj.*** 1. having sufficient worth, मूल्यवान। 2. deserving, योग्य, पात्र, अधिकारी। 3. hon-ourable, आदरणीय, श्रद्धेय।

would (वुड) ***v.*** p.t. of will.

would-be (वुड-बी) ***adj.*** 1. desiring or professing to be, इच्छुक या तथाकथित। 2. pertaining to future, भावी।

wouldn't (वुडन्ट) = would not.

wound[1] (वून्ड) ***n.*** 1. an injury to the body in which the skin is cut, torn or pierced, घाव, ज़ख़्म, क्षत। 2. an injury to person's feeling or reputation, चोट, ठेस। ***v.*** to inflict a wound on, चोट मारना, घायल करना, ज़ख़्मी करना।

wound[2] (वाउन्ड) ***v.*** p.t & p.p of wind.

wounded (वून्डिड) ***adj.*** having a wound or wounds, ज़ख़्मी, घायल।

woven (वोवन) ***v.*** p.p. of weave.

wow (वाउ) ***interj.*** an exclamation of wonder, enthusiasm etc., वाह!

wrangle (रैन्गल) ***v.*** 1. to quarrel angrily, झगड़ा करना, नोंक-झोंक करना। 2. to win by argument, दलील से जीतना। ***n.*** 1. noisy quarrel, झगड़ा, नोक-झोंक। 2. dispute, बहस, वाद-विवाद।

wrap (रैप) ***v.*** 1. to wind paper, cloth etc., around (a thing) so as to cover it, लपेटना। 2. to cover, ढकना, आच्छादित करना, आवरण डालना। ***n.*** 1. a covering, आवरण। 2. a shawl, scarf or blanket, शाल, गुलूबंद या कंबल।

wrapper (रैपर) ***n.*** a cover, आवरण।

wrath (रैथ) ***n.*** 1. violent anger, रोष, क्रोध। 2. divine vengeance, कोप।

wrathful (रैथफ़ुल) ***adj.*** full of anger, रोषपूर्ण, क्रुद्ध।

wreak (रीक) ***v.*** 1. to inflict (vengeance, ग़ुस्सा) उतारना। 2. to take vengeance for, बदला लेना।

wreath (रीथ) ***n.*** a ring made of flowers or leaves, पत्तियों या फूलों का चक्र, हार या माला, फूलचक्र, फूलमाला।

wreathe (रीद) ***v.*** 1. to form a wreath, पत्तियों, फूलों आदि का चक्र या हार बनाना, माला या हार गूँथना। 2. to coil or wind round, लपेट लेना। 3. to move in a curving line, टेढ़े-मेढ़े चलना।

W

wreck (रेक) ***v.*** 1. to destroy or damage badly, विनष्ट या नष्ट-भ्रष्ट कर देना, ध्वस्त कर देना। 2. to suffer destruction, विनष्ट या नष्ट-भ्रष्ट होना। ***n.*** 1. accidental destruction of a ship by storms, तूफ़ान से होनेवाला जलयान का विनाश। 2. the ship so wrecked, तूफ़ान से ध्वस्त या विनष्ट जलयान।

wreckage (रेकिज) ***n.*** 1. the act of wrecking or the state of being wrecked, विनाश। 2. the remains of something wrecked, विनष्ट वस्तु के अवशेष, मलबा।

wrench (रेन्च) ***v.*** 1. to pull with a jerk, झटका देना, झटके से हटा देना। 2. to twist or turn (so as to sprain a limb, अंग को) ऐंठना, मरोड़ना। ***n.*** 1. a tool for turning, (nuts, bolts etc., नट, बोल्ट को) घुमाने का उपकरण, रैंच। 2. a violent jerk or pull, तेज़ झटका।

wrest (रेस्ट) ***v.*** 1. to take by force, झटक लेना, छीन लेना। 2. to obtain with a great effort, अत्यधिक परिश्रम से प्राप्त करना।

wrestle (रेसल) ***v.*** 1. to grapple with, कुश्ती लड़ना। 2. to struggle hard, कड़ा संघर्ष करना, जूझना या भिड़ना।

wrestler (रेसलर) ***n.*** one who is skilled in wrestling, पहलवान।

wretch (रेच) ***n.*** an unfortunate person, अभागा व्यक्ति।

wretched (रेचिड) ***adj.*** 1. pitiable, दयनीय। 2. despicable, हेय, तुच्छ, नीच। 3. unfortunate, अभागा। 4. poor in quality, घटिया।

wriggle (रिगल) ***v.*** 1. to move with a twisting movement, टेढ़े-मेढ़े चलना। 2. to manoeuvre, तिकड़म करना, धोखा देना। ***n.*** wriggling movement, टेढ़ी-मेढ़ी चाल।

wring (रिन्ग) ***v.*** (wrung, wringing) 1. to twist and compress to squeeze, निचोड़ने के लिए मरोड़ना या दबाना। 2. to grip one's hand, (अभिवादन करते समय) कसकर हाथ पकड़ना। 3. to extort a confession, उगलवाना। ***n.*** an act of wringing, मरोड़ने, ऐंठने, दबाने, निचोड़ने आदि की क्रिया।

wrinkle[1] (रिन्कल) ***n.*** 1. a slight ridge or crease on a normally smooth surface, सिलवट, शिकन, झुर्री। 2. a slight problem, छोटी-मोटी समस्या। ***v.*** 1. to make or form wrinkles, सिलवटें डालना, झुर्रियाँ बनाना या डालना। 2. to become wrinkled, सिलवटें पड़ना, झुर्रियाँ पड़ना।

wrinkle[2] ***n.*** 1. a trick, चाल। 2. a hint, संकेत।

wrist (रिस्ट) ***n.*** the joint between the hand and forearm, कलाई, गट्टा, पहुँचा, मणिबंध।

writ (रिट) ***n.*** a formal court order directing a person to do or refrain from doing some specified act, रिट, आदेश।

write (राइट) ***v.*** (wrote, written, writing) 1. to form letters or symbols on a surface with a pen, pencil etc., लिखना। 2. to form words or message, लिखना। 3. to produce by writing, to compose, रचना करना; कहानी, लेख या पुस्तक लिखना। 4. to relate or communicate by writing, वर्णन करना, सूचित करना।

write-off (राइट-ऑफ़) ***n.*** the act of cancelling bad debt, डूबी रक़म को बट्टे खाते में डालने की क्रिया।

writer (राइटर) ***n.*** 1. a person who

writes books, articles, documents etc., लेखक। 2. a clerk, मुंशी, क्लर्क।

write-up (राइट-अप) ***n.*** a review, समीक्षा।

writhe (राइद) ***v.*** 1. to contort the body (as in pain, पीड़ा के कारण) शरीर का ऐंठना, छटपटाहट होना। 2. to suffer acutely from great shame, घड़ों पानी पड़ जना, शर्म से पानी-पानी हो जाना।

writing (राइटिन्ग) ***n.*** 1. the act or profession of one who writes, लेखन। 2. handwriting, हस्तलिपि, लिखावट। 3. a literary work, कृति, रचना।

writing material ***n.*** material used in writing, लेखन-सामग्री।

written (रिटन) ***v.*** p.p. of write.

wrong (रॉन्ग) ***adj.*** 1. not right or true, ग़लत, मिथ्या। 2. morally bad, बुरा, अनैतिक। 3. unfair or unjust, अनुचित या अन्यायपूर्ण। 4. not wanted or required, अनिच्छित या अनपेक्षित। ***adv.*** in a wrong manner, ग़लत ढंग से। ***n.*** 1. a sinful act, पाप, अधर्म। 2. injustice or harm, अन्याय या अहित। ***v.*** to treat unjustly, दुर्व्यवहार करना।

wrongheaded (रॉन्गहेडिड) ***adj.*** very obstinate, हठी।

wrote (रोट) ***v.*** p.t. of write.

wroth (रॉथ) ***adj.*** angry, अप्रसन्न, रुष्ट, नाराज़।

wrought (रॉट) ***v.*** p.t. and p.p of work. ***adj.*** shaped by beating or hammering, पीटकर बनाया हुआ।

wrought-up (रॉट-अप) ***adj.*** 1. very excited, अत्यधिक उत्तेजित, विक्षुब्ध।

wrung (रन्ग) ***v.*** p.t. & p.p. of wring.

wry (राइ) ***adj.*** (wrier/wryer, wriest/ wryest) 1. bent or crooked, टेढ़ा, टेढ़ा-मेढ़ा, वक्र, मोड़ा या मुड़ा हुआ। 2. ironical, व्यंग्यपूर्ण। 3. full of scorn, कटु, कटुतापूर्ण।

X, x (एक्स) ***n.*** the twenty-fourth letter of the English alphabet, अंग्रेज़ी वर्णमाला का चौबीसवाँ वर्ण।

xenophobia (ज़ेनोफ़ोबिआ) ***n.*** strong dislike of foreigners or strangers, विदेशियों या अज्ञात व्यक्तियों के प्रति होनेवाली घोर घृणा।

xerox (ज़िअरॉक्स) ***n.*** a copying machine, प्रतिलिपि तैयार करनेवाली मशीन, ज़ीरॉक्स।

X-max (क्रिस्मस) ***n.*** short form of Christmas.

x-rated (एक्स-रेटिड) ***adj.*** (of films) not be seen by persons under seventeen years old, (ऐसी फिल्में) जिन्हें सत्रह बरस से कम उम्र के लोगों के देखने पर प्रतिबंध हो।

X-ray (एक्स-रे) ***n.*** 1. a non-luminous ray, एक प्रकार की किरण, एक्स-रे। 2. a photograph made by X-rays, एक्स-रे।

xylography (ज़ाइलोग्राफ़ी) ***n.*** the art of graving on wood, लकड़ी पर की जानेवाली नक़्क़ाशी; काष्ठ-उत्कीर्णन।

xylophone (ज़ाइलोफ़ोन) ***n.*** a musical instrument with wooden bars which produce different notes when struck with a small hammer, काष्ठतरंग।

Y, y (वाइ) ***n.*** the twenty-fifth letter of the English alphabet, अंग्रेज़ी वर्णमाला का पच्चीसवाँ वर्ण।

yacht (यॉट) ***n.*** a small sailing motor driven vessel used for racing or pleasure trip, याट, केलिपोत।

yachting (यॉटिंग) ***n.*** racing or cruising in a yacht, याट में दौड़ लगाना या विहार करना।

Yahweh (यावे) ***n.*** The Hebrew name for god, Jehovah, ईश्वर का एक नाम, यहोवा।

yak (यैक) ***n.*** an ox of Tibbet, तिब्बती याक, सुरागाय, चमर।

yam (यैम) ***n.*** 1. a plant and its tuber, रतालू। 2. Indian yam, अरबी, अरुई, घुइयाँ।

yank (यैन्क) ***v.*** to pull with a jerk, झटका देना, झटकना। ***n.*** a sudden sharp jerk, झटका।

yap (यैप) ***v.*** to yelp, (कुत्ते का) भौंकना या चीख़ना। ***n.*** a bark, भौं-भौं।

yard[1] (यार्ड) ***n.*** 1. a measure of length equal to three feet or 0.9144 meters, गज़।

yard[2] ***n.*** 1. a piece of enclosed ground around a building, अहाता, प्रांगण, बाड़ा। 2. an area with so many railway tracks near the station, यार्ड, रेल-प्रांगण। 3. a place where ships rest, पोत-प्रांगण।

yardstick (यार्डस्टिक) ***n.*** a standard of comparison or judgment, मानदंड।

yarn (यार्न) ***n.*** 1. a continuous long twisted thread of cotton, wool etc., prepared for weaving, knitting etc., धागा, सूत। 2. a long invented or exaggerated tale, क़िस्सा।

yawn (यॉन) ***v.*** 1. to open mouth wide and taking in the air involuntarily as when sleeping or feeling bored, जँभाई लेना। 2. to open the mouth wide, मुँह खोलना या फैलाना। ***n.*** the act or instance of yawning, जँभाई।

year (यिअर) ***n.*** 1. the period of about 365 days, बरस, साल, वर्ष। 2. the period from 1st January to 31st December, बरस, साल, वर्ष।

yearbook (यिअरबुक) ***n.*** an annual book containing the information and events of the previous year, वार्षिकी, अब्दकोश।

yearling (यिअरलिन्ग) ***n.*** the young of an animal between one and two years old, एक और दो बरस के बीच का पशुशावक।

yearly (यिअरली) ***adj.*** occurring, appearing, done or payable once in a year, प्रतिवर्ष होनेवाला, वार्षिक, सालाना।

yearn (यर्न) ***v.*** to have a long strong desire, साध होना, लालसा होना।

yearning (यर्निंग) ***n.*** an act of a person who yearns, साध, लालसा।

yeast (यीस्ट) ***n.*** 1. a leavening agent, ख़मीर। 2. foam on beer, बियर की झाग।

yell (येल) ***v.*** to cry with a loud sound, चिल्लाना, चीख़ना। ***n.*** a cry (of pain, excitement or fear), चीख़, चीत्कार।

Y

yellow (येलो) ***adj.*** 1. of the colour of a lemon, पीला, पीत। 2. cowardly, डरपोक। ***n.*** 1. yellow colour, पीला रंग। 2. yellow of an egg, अंडे की ज़र्दी। ***v.*** to make or become yellow, पीला बना देना या हो जाना।

yellowish (येलोइश) ***adj.*** rather yellow, कुछ-कुछ पीला, पीला-सा।

yelp (येल्प) ***v.*** 1. to cry, चीखना। 2. to bark, भौंकना। ***n.*** 1. a scream, चीख़, चिल्लाहट। 2. a bark, भौं-भौं।

yen (येन) ***n.*** a standard unit of Japanese money, जापानी मुद्रा।

yeoman (योमैन) ***n.*** a farmer who owns land, वह किसान जो अपनी भूमि खुद जोतता-बोता हो।

yes (येस) ***interj.*** used to express, (i) agreement or affirmation, हाँ, ठीक है; (ii) consent to enter a room, आइए; (iii) emphasize a statement, हाँ, सचमुच। ***n.*** an affirmative reply, हाँ।

yes-man ***n.*** (येस-मैन) a person who always says yes to his superior's order, जी हुजूरिया, चमचा।

yesterday (येस्टर्डे) ***n.*** the day before the present day, बीता हुआ दिन, कल। ***adv.*** 1. in the day before today, कल। 2. a short while ago, कुछ समय पहले।

yet (येट) ***adv.*** 1. up to this time, or by this time, अब तक, अभी तक। 2. even still, अभी भी। 3. even, भी। ***conj.*** nevertheless, तो भी, फिर भी।

yeti (येटी) ***n.*** a snowman, हिममानव।

yield (यील्ड) ***v.*** 1. to produce, उत्पन्न करना, पैदा करना। 2. to grant or concede, दे देना, छोड़ देना। 3. to surrender, समर्पित करना। 4. to give way, रास्ता देना, पीछे हट जाना। ***n.*** 1. a crop, फ़सल, पैदावार। 2. the profit or return, लाभ, प्रतिफल।

yodel (योडल) ***v.*** to sing with rapid changing voice, आलाप करना, आलापना। ***n.*** the act of yodelling, आलाप।

yoga (योगा) ***n.*** 1. the system to be one with the god, योग। 2. physical exercises to gain control over body and mind, योग।

yoghurt, yogurt (योगर्ट) ***n.*** milk curdled by bacteria, दही।

yoke (योक) ***n.*** 1. a wooden frame used for joining two draught animals pulling a plough, cart etc., जुआ। 2. a frame fitting over a person's shoulders with baskets or buckets suspended from each end, बहँगी। 3. an oppressive force or burden, भार, बोझ। ***v.*** 1. to harness by means of a yoke, जोतना। 2. to unite, जोड़ना या जुड़ना। 3. to marry, विवाह करना।

yolk (योक) ***n.*** the yellow part of an egg, अंडे की ज़र्दी।

yonder (यॉन्डर) ***adj.*** being at that place, वहाँ का। ***adv.*** over there, वहाँ।

yore (योर) ***n.*** time long past, प्राचीन काल, पुराना ज़माना। □ **of yore**, पुराने ज़माने का। ***adv.*** long ago, बहुत पहले।

you (यू) ***pron.*** 1. the person or persons addressed, तुम। 2. people in general, सामान्य लोग।

young (यन्ग) ***adj.*** 1. in an early stage of life, छोटा, नन्हा, अल्पवयस्क। 2. of or relating to youth, youthful, युवा, जवान। ***n.*** the offspring of animals, बच्चे।

youngster (यन्ग्स्टर) ***n.*** a child, बच्चा।

your (युअर) ***pron & adj.*** of or belonging to you, तुम्हारा, आपका।

you're (यूर) ***phrase*** = you are.

yours (युअर्ज़) ***pron.*** 1. belonging to you, तुम्हारा। 2. (plu.) used at the end of a letter, भवदीय, आपका।

yourself (युअरसेल्फ़) ***pron.*** the reflexive form of you, तुम स्वयं, तुम ख़ुद।

youth (यूथ) ***n.*** 1. the quality or state of being young, जवानी, यौवन, तरुणाई। 2. a young man, जवान आदमी। 3. the period of early development, बचपन, आरंभिक काल। 4. young people collectively, नवयुवक समूह।

youthful (यूथफ़ुल) ***adj.*** 1. possessing youth, युवा, जवान। 2. active or vigorous, सक्रिय या स्फूर्त।

youth hostel ***n.*** a hostel providing cheap accommodation to young travellers, युवक-आवासगृह।

you've (यूव) = you have.

yowl (याउल) ***v.*** to howl or shout, हुआँना या चिल्लाना। ***n.*** a loud cry, हुआँ-हुआँ।

yule (यूल) ***n.*** the Christmas festival, बड़े दिन का त्योहार।

Z

Z, z (ज़ेड) the twenty-sixth letter of the English alphabet, अंग्रेज़ी वर्णमाला का छब्बीसवाँ वर्ण।

zany (ज़ेनी) ***n.*** 1. a clown, मसख़रा, विदूषक, भाँड़। 2. a foolish person, मूर्ख व्यक्ति। ***adj.*** comical, (बात) हास्यपूर्ण या हास्यजनक, (व्यक्ति) विनोदशील या मज़ाकिया।

zeal (ज़ील) ***n.*** enthusiasm, जोश, उत्साह, उमंग।

zealot (ज़ेलॉट) ***n.*** a fanatically zealous person, कट्टर या उन्मादी व्यक्ति।

zealous (ज़ेलस) ***adj.*** enthusiastic, उत्साही, जोशीला।

zebra (ज़ीब्रा) ***n.*** (plu. zebra, zebras) a horselike African animal with black and white stripes, ज़ेबरा।

zebra crossing ***n.*** the place marked with white and black stripes reserved for pedestrians to cross the road, ज़ेबरा-पट्टी।

zenith (जेनिथ) ***n.*** 1. the point of the sky that is directly above an observer, खमध्य, शिरोबिंदु। 2. the highest point or limit, चरम बिंदु या चरम सीमा, पराकाष्ठा।

zero (ज़ीरो) ***n.*** (plu. zeros, zeroes) ***n.*** 1. the symbol 0, शून्य, सिफ़र, सुन्ना। 2. nothing, कुछ नहीं, शून्य, अंडा। 3. the point between + and – on the scale, शून्य। ***adj.*** nothing at all, कुछ भी नहीं, ज़रा भी नहीं।

zero hour ***n.*** the hour or time at which some action is to begin, शून्यकाल, आरंभ काल।

zest (जेस्ट) ***n.*** 1. something that gives relish or flavour, सुस्वादु या ज़ायकेदार चीज़। 2. exciting flavour or relish, स्वाद, मज़ा। 3. keen enjoyment, मज़ा। 4. enthusiasm, उमंग, जोश।

zigzag (जिगज़ैग) ***adj.*** having curved short turns, टेढ़ा-मेढ़ा, सर्पिल, चक्करदार। ***n.*** 1. a zigzag line, टेढ़ी-मेढ़ी रेखा। 2. a zigzag course, टेढ़ा-मेढ़ा रास्ता। ***adv.*** in a zigzag manner, टेढ़े-मेढ़े। ***v.*** to move in a zigzag course, टेढ़े-मेढ़े रास्ते पर चलना।

zinc (ज़िन्क) ***n.*** a bluish white metallic element, जस्ता, ज़िंक। ***v.*** (zincked, zincking) to coat with zinc, जस्ता चढ़ाना।

zip (ज़िप) ***n.*** a fastening device, ज़िप। ***v.*** 1. to open or close with a zip, ज़िप खोलना या बंद करना। 2. to rush, तेज़ी से बढ़ना।

zipper (ज़िपर) ***n.*** a zip, ज़िप।

zircon (ज़र्कन) ***n.*** a hard mineral used as a gem, तुरसावा, ज़रकान।

zodiac (ज़ोडिऐक) ***n.*** 1. an imaginary area divided into 12 equal parts, in the heavens along which the heavenly bodies appear to travel, राशिचक्र; sign of a zodiac, राशि। 2. its diagram, राशिचक्र।

zombie (ज़ॉम्बी) ***n.*** a corpse brought to life by witchcraft, वह शव जो जादू-टोने या तंत्रमंत्र से जीवंत बना दिया गया हो, जीवित शव, जिन।

zonal (ज़ोनल) ***adj.*** of or pertaining to a zone, क्षेत्रीय, मंडलीय, आंचलिक।

zone (ज़ोन) ***n.*** 1. a particular area or region, क्षेत्र, मंडल, अंचल। 2. any of the five regions of the surface of the earth, कटिबंध। ***v.*** to divide into zones, क्षेत्रों में विभाजित करना।

zoo (ज़ू) ***n.*** a place where live animals are kept, bred and exhibited, चिड़ियाघर।

zoologist (ज़ोऑलजिस्ट) ***n.*** an expert in zoology, प्राणि-विज्ञानी।

zoology (ज़ोऑलोजी) ***n.*** the scientific study of animals, प्राणि-विज्ञान।

zoom (ज़ूम) ***v.*** to move with buzzing sound, सनसनाते हुए आगे बढ़ना। ***n.*** the act or sound of zooming, सनसनाहट।

zoophyte (ज़ोअफ़ाइट) ***n.*** any of the plantlike sea creatures, पादपप्राणी।

Classified Vocabularies
वर्गीकृत शब्दावलियाँ

Fruits फल

Almond बादाम
Apple सेब
Apricot खूबानी
Banana केला
Coconut नारियल
Custard apple शरीफा
Fig अंजीर
Grapes अंगूर
Gromia फालसा
Ground-nut मूँगफली
Guava अमरूद
Jujube बेर
Lime नीबू
Mango आम
Mozambique मौसमी
Mulberry शहतूत
Musk Melon खरबूजा
Orange संतरा
Papaya पपीता
Peach आड़ू
Pear नाशपाती
Pineapple अनन्नास
Pistachio-nut पिस्ता
Plum आलू बुखारा
Pomegranate अनार
Pompelmoose चकोतरा
Raisin किशमिश
Rose-apple जामुन
Walnut अखरोट
Water Melon तरबूज

Vegetables सब्जियाँ

Ash Pumpkin पेठा
Beans सेम
Beet Root चुकंदर
Bitter Gourd करेला
Brinjal बैंगन/भाटा
Cabbage बंदगोभी
Carrot गाजर
Cauliflower फूलगोभी, गोभी
Chillies मिर्च
Cluster Beans ग्वारफली
Colocasia अरबी
Coriander धनिया
Cucumber खीरा
Drumstick सहजन की फली
Fenugreek मेथी
Garlic लहसुन
Greens साग
Ivy Gourd कुंदरू
Jack fruit कटहल
Lady's Finger भिंडी

Long Cucumber ककड़ी
Mint पुदीना
Onion प्याज
Potato आलू
Potato Yam रतालू
Potherb, Spinach पालक
Pumpkin कद्दू, लौकी, घिया
Radish मूली
Ribbed Gourd तुरई
Round Gourd टिंडा
Snake Gourd चिंचिड़ा
Squash Gourd कोंहड़ा
Sweet Potato शकरकंद
Turnip शलजम
Yam सूरन

Flower फूल

Balsam गुलमेंहदी
Basel तुलसी
Coxcomb कलगा
Daisy मोगरा
Dehlia डेहलिया
Double Poppy हजारा
Gilly Flower गुल खैरा
Hollyhock हालीहक
Jasmine चमेली
Lily कमलिनी
Lotus कमल
Marigold गेंदा
Moon Flower गुल चाँदनी
Narcissus नरगिस
Pandanus केवड़ा
Peru Flower फूल दुपहरी
Poppy पोस्ता
Round Jasmine मोतिया
Small Chrysantheum गुल दाऊदी
Sun Flower सूरजमुखी
Sweet Jasmine जुही
Tulip गुल लाला
Yellow Jasmine चंपा

Grains and Pulse अनाज और दालें

Barley जौ
Black Gram उड़द
Cow Pea लोबिया
Finger Millet रागी
Gram चना
Green Gram मूँग
Horse Gram कुलथी
Maize मक्का
Millet बाजरा
Paddy धान
Pea मटर
Red Gram मोठ
Rice चावल
Wheat गेहूँ
White Gram काबुली चना
Yellow Gram अरहर

Miscellaneous Eatables विविध खाद्य पदार्थ

Betel Leaf पान
Betel Nut सुपारी
Biscuit बिस्कुट
Bread रोटी
Butter मक्खन
Butter Milk लस्सी
Cake केक
Cardamom इलायची
Cheese पनीर
Chocolate चॉकलेट
Clover लौंग
Cream मलाई
Curd दही
Egg अंडा
Ghee, Clarified butter घी
Ginger सोंठ
Jaggery गुड़
Jam मुरब्बा
Light Cheese छेना
Liquorice मुलैठी
Meat मांस
Milk दूध
Molasses राब
Mustard सरसों
Pastry पेस्ट्री
Pepper काली मिर्च
Porridge दलिया
Rice Milk खीर
Saffron केसर
Salt नमक
Salty Dish नमकीन
Sugar शक्कर/चीनी
Sweet Pudding हलवा
Sweetmeat मिठाई
Tamarind इमली
Toffee टॉफी
Turmeric हलदी

Clothes, etc. कपड़े-लत्ते

Apron अग्रवस्त्र
Bed Cover पलंगपोश
Bedding बिस्तरा
Belt पेटी, पट्टा
Blanket कंबल
Blouse अँगुलिया, ब्लाउज
Bolster मसनद
Boot बूट
Breeches बिरजस
Bushshirt बुशर्ट
Cap, Hat टोपी, टोप
Chemise शमीज
Cloak चोगा
Coat कोट
Collar कॉलर
Cover गिलाफ, गॉव तकिया
Curtain परदा
Cushion गद्दा, गद्दी
Dhoti धोती
Dress पोशाक
Frock फ्रॉक
Garment पहरावा

Gloves दस्ताने
Gown गाउन
Half Pant निकर
Handkerchief रूमाल
Hold-All होल्डाल
Jacket जैकिट
Kurta (Shirt) कुरता, कमीज
Mantle Veil बुरका
Muffler गुलूबंद, मफलर
Napkin नैपकिन
Neck Tie टाई
Overcoat ओवरकोट
Petticoat पेटीकोट
Pillow तकिया
Pyjama पाजामा
Quilt रजाई
Salwar, Trousers सलवार
Saree साड़ी
Shawl शॉल
Sheet चद्दर/चादर
Shoe जूता
Slipper स्लीपर, चप्पल
Socks मोजा, जुराब
Stockings बड़े मोजे
Sweater स्वेटर
Table Cloth मेजपोश
Towel तौलिया
Trousers पतलून
Turban पगड़ी
Underwear जाँघिया
Uniform वर्दी
Vest बनियान
Waistcoat वास्कट

Household Goods घरेलू सामान

Agarbatti अगरबत्ती
Almirah, Shelf अलमारी
Axe कुल्हाड़ी
Bangle चूड़ी
Bed पलंग
Bench बेंच
Books किताबें
Bottle बोतल
Bowl कटोरा
Broom झाड़ू
Bucket डोल, बाल्टी
Bulb बल्ब
Candle मोमबत्ती
Comb कंघी
Cot खाट, चारपाई
Cradle पालना
Cream क्रीम
Cup प्याला
Dewan दिवान
Earthen Lamp मिट्टी का दीया
Fire-Place, Stove चूल्हा
Frying Pan कढ़ाई
Glass गिलास
Glass Pane शीशा
Hubble हाँडी
Hubble Bubble हुक्का
Iron इस्तरी
Kettle केतली

Key चाबी
Lamp लैंप
Lantern लालटेन
Letter पत्र
Lock ताला
Milk Pot दूधदानी
Mirror आईना
Mortar ओखली
Oil तेल
Pan पतीला, तवा
Paper कागज
Pestle मूसल
Phial शीशी
Pitcher घड़ा
Plate प्लेट
Platter थाली
Powder पाउडर
Purse बटुआ
Radio रेडियो
Reed Stool मूढ़ा
Rolling Pin, Roller बेलन
Rope रस्सी
Saucer तश्तरी
Scale, Balance तराजू
Scythe हँसिया
Small Bowl कटोरी
Small Box डिबिया
Soap साबुन
Sofa सोफा
Spinning Wheel चरखा
Stool स्टूल
Stove स्टोव
Table मेज
Tea Pot चायदानी
Telephone टेलीफोन
Television टेलीविजन
Tongs चिमटा
Tub टब
Utensil, Pot बरतन
Watch, Clock घड़ी

Parts of the Body शरीर के अंग

Ankle टखना
Ankle Bone गट्टा
Anus गुदा
Arm बाँह
Armpit काँख, बगल
Back पीठ
Backbone रीढ़
Belly, Stomach पेट
Blood लहू, खून
Bone हड्डी
Brain दिमाग
Breast छाती, वक्षस्थल, सीना
Buttocks चूतड़
Calf of Leg पिंडली
Cheek गाल
Chest छाती
Chin ठुड्डी
Ear कान
Elbow कोहनी
Eye आँख

Eyelash पलक
Eyebrow भौंह
Face चेहरा
Finger उंगली
Fist मुट्ठी
Foot पाँव, पैर
Forehead माथा
Gland ग्रंथि
Grinder दाढ़
Gum मसूढ़ा
Hair बाल
Hand हाथ
Head सिर
Heart दिल/हृदय
Heel एड़ी
Intestine आँत/अँतड़ी
Jaw जबड़ा
Joint जोड़
Knee घुटना
Lap/Bosom गोद
Leg टाँग
Limb अंग
Lip ओंठ
Liver जिगर
Lung फेफड़ा
Mouth, Face मुँह/मुख
Muscle पेशी
Nail नाखून
Nape of Neck गुद्दी
Naval नाभि
Neck गरदन
Nose नाक
Nostrils नथुने
Palate तालु
Palm हथेली
Pulse नाड़ी
Pupil पुतली
Rib पसली
Shoulder कंधा
Skin चमड़ी, खाल
Skull खोपड़ी
Sole तलवा
Spleen तिल्ली
Teat/Breast चूचुक
Temple कनपटी
Thigh जाँघ
Thorax, Wind Pipe श्वासनली
Throat गला
Thumb अँगूठा
Tongue जीभ
Tooth दाँत
Trunk धड़
Vein नस
Waist, Loin कमर
Wrist कलाई

Designations पदनाम

Accountant लेखापाल
Additional अपर
Administrator प्रशासक
Adviser सलाहकार
Advocate अधिवक्ता
Ambassador राजदूत

Assistant सहायक
Attorney न्यायवादी
Auditor लेखा परीक्षक
Chairman सभापति
Chancellor कुलाधिपति
Chief मुख्य
Clerk लिपिक
Collector समाहर्ता
Commissioner आयुक्त
Consultant परामर्शदाता
Controller नियंत्रक
Deputy उप
Director निदेशक
Director General महानिदेशक
District Magistrate जिलाधीश
Governor राज्यपाल
Head अध्यक्ष
Inspector निरीक्षक
Judge जज, न्यायाधीश
Justice न्यायमूर्ति
Lawyer वकील
Lecturer व्याख्याता, प्राध्यापक, प्रवक्ता
Magistrate मजिस्ट्रेट
Mayor महापौर
Member सदस्य
Minister मंत्री
Observer प्रेक्षक
Officer अधिकारी
Officiating कार्यकारी, कार्यवाहक, स्थानापन्न
President राष्ट्रपति
Prime Minister प्रधानमंत्री
Principal प्राचार्य
Professor आचार्य
Record keeper अभिलेखपाल
Registrar (University) कुलसचिव
Registrar पंजीयक
Secretary सचिव
Station-in-Charge Police थानेदार
Stenographer आशुलिपिक
Sub-Inspector (Police) दरोगा
Superintendent अधीक्षक
Tehsildar तहसीलदार
Treasurer कोषाध्यक्ष
Vice-Chancellor कुलपति
Village Accountant, Patwari लेखपाल

Animals पशु

Alligator घड़ियाल
Antelope नीलगाय
Ass, Donkey गदहा
Baboon लंगूर
Buffalo भैंस
Bull साँड
Camel ऊँट
Cat बिल्ली
Ox, Bullock बैल
Chimpanzee बनमानुस
Colt, Calf बछेड़ा/बछड़ा
Cow गाय
Crocodile मगरमच्छ
Deer मृग, हिरन

Dog कुत्ता
Dromedary साँडनी
Elephant हाथी
Fox लोमड़ी
Giraffe जिराफ
Goat बकरी
Gorilla गोरिल्ला
Hare खरहा
He-Buffalo भैंसा
Hippopotamus दरियाई घोड़ा
Horse घोड़ा
Hound शिकारी कुत्ता
Hyena लकड़ बग्घा
Jackal सियार
Kangaroo कंगारू
Kid, Lamb मेमना
Leopard तेंदुआ
Lion सिंह
Mole, Musk Rat छछूंदर
Mongoose नेवला
Monkey बंदर
Mouse चूहा, मूस
Mule खच्चर
Musk Deer कस्तूरी मृग
Panther चीता
Pig सुअर
Pony टट्टू
Porcupine साही
Puppy पिल्ला
Rabbit खरगोश
Ram मेढ़ा, भेड़ा
Rhino गेंडा
Sheep भेड़
Squirrel गिलहरी
Stag बारहसिंहा
Tiger बाघ
Wolf भेड़िया
Yak याक
Zebra जेबरा

Insects/Reptiles कीड़े

Ant चींटी
Bee मधुमक्खी
Blank Ant चींटा
Boa अजगर
Bug खटमल
Butterfly तितली
Centipede गोजर
Chameleon गिरगिट
Cobra नाग
Cocoon कोया
Cricket झींगुर
Dung Beetle गुबरैला
Egg of Louse लीख
Flea पिस्सू
Fly मक्खी
Frog मेंढक
Glow Worm जुगनू
Grain Moth घुन
Grass hopper टिड्डा
Leech जोंक
Lizard छिपकली
Lobster घोंघा

Locust टिड्डी
Louse जूँ
Mosquito मच्छर
Moth पतंगा
Mother of Pearls सीप
Prawn झींगा
Scorpion बिच्छू
Shrimp झींगी
Snail केंचुआ
Snake साँप
Spider मकड़ी
Tick किलनी
Tortoise कछुआ
Wasp बर्रे
White Ant दीमक

Birds पक्षी

Bat चमगादड़
Blue-Necked Jay नीलकंठ
Brown-Becked Robin पिद्दा
Canary मैना, सारिका
Chicken चूजा
Cock मुर्गा
Cockatoo काकातुआ
Crane सारस
Crow कोआ
Cuckoo पपीहा
Duck बत्तख
Falcon, Hawk बहरी, बाज
Garud गरुड़
Goose, Swan हंस
Hen मुर्गी
Heron कूंज
Indian Cuckoo कोयल
Kite चील
Nightingale बुलबुल
Ostrich शुतुरमुर्ग
Owl उल्लू
Parrot तोता
Partridge तीतर
Peacock मोर
Pewit टिटहरी
Pigeon कबूतर
Quail बटेर
Red-Legged Partridge चकोर
Ruddy Goose चकवा
Sparrow गोरैया
Stork बगुला
Swallow अबाबील
Thrash मुनिया
Vulture गिद्ध, गीध
Wood Pecker हुदहुद, कठपोड़ा

Minerals खनिज पदार्थ

Antimony सुरमा
Arsenic सँखिया
Asphalt डामर
Base Silver रूपा
Borax सोहागा
Bronze पीतल

Cat's Eye लहसुनिया
Chalk खड़िया
Coal कोयला
Coal-tar तारकोल
Copper ताँबा
Diamond हीरा
Emerald पन्ना
Flint चकमक
Gem नग, मणि
Gold सोना
Iron लोहा
Lead सीसा
Marble संगमरमर
Mercury पारा
Mica अभरक
Ochre गेरू
Oil तेल
Philosopher's Stone पारस
Ruby माणिक्य
Sapphire नीलम
Silver चाँदी
Steel इस्पात
Sulphur गंधक
Tin राँगा
Topaz पुखराज
Turquoise फीरोजा
Vermilion सिंदूर
Vitriol तूतिया
Zinc जस्त

Name of Days दिनों के नाम

Monday सोमवार
Tuesday मंगलवार
Wednesday बुधवार
Thursday बृस्पतिवार/गुरुवार
Friday शुक्रवार
Saturday शनिवार
Sunday रविवार/इतवार

Name of Months महीनों के नाम

January जनवरी
February फरवरी
March मार्च
April अप्रैल
May मई
June जून
July जुलाई
August अगस्त
September सितंबर
October अक्तूबर
November नवंबर
December दिसंबर

Names of Indian Months महीनों के देशी नाम

वैसाख **[Starting from April 13]**
ज्येष्ठ (जेठ)
आषाढ़ (असाढ़)
श्रावण (सावन)
भाद्रपद (भादों)
आश्विन (क्वाँर)
कार्तिक (कातिक)
मार्गशीर्ष

पौष (पूस)

माघ

फाल्गुन (फागुन)

चैत्र (चैत)

Seasons ऋतुएँ

Spring वसंत

Summer ग्रीष्म

Rains वर्षा

Autumn पतझड़

Winter शीत

Weights and Measures माप-तौल

New नए

Old, Getting Obsolete पुराने

1 ग्राम= लगभग 15.48 ग्रेन*

माशा*16 औंस= 1 पौंड

1000 ग्राम= 1 किलोग्राम

14 पौंड= 1 स्टोन

100 किलोग्राम=1 क्विंटल

112 पौंड= 1 हंडरवेट

2240 पौंड= 1 टन

1 गेलन*=लगभग 4.5 लिटर

8 रत्ती=1 माशा

1 लिटर=1.75 पिंट*

12 माशे=1 तोला

1000 लिटर= 1 किलोलिटर

5 तोले=1 छटाँक

16 छटाँक=1 सेर

40 सेर=1 मन (Maund)

1 मीटर= लगभग 39.4 इंच*

12 इंच=1 फुट

100 सेंटीमीटर=1 मीटर

3 फुट=1 गज (Yard)

1000 मीटर=1 किलोमीटर

220 गज=1 फरलाँग

8 किलोमीटर= 5 मील*

8 फरलाँग=1 मील

1 हेक्टेयर= 2 एकड़ से कुछ अधिक*

100 हेक्टेयर= 1 वर्ग किलोमीटर

वर्ग इंच= 1441 वर्ग फुट, 9 वर्ग फुट= 1 वर्ग गज (Sq. Yd.), 4840 वर्ग गज=1 एकड़

* Old Weights and Measures for understanding समझाने के लिए पुराने तौल-माप।

□□□